Business
for
Higher Awards

Business
for
Higher Awards

Dave Needham
Rob Dransfield
Martin Coles
Rod Harris
Maureen Rawlinson

Heinemann Educational Publishers,
Halley Court, Jordan Hill, Oxford OX2 8EJ
A division of Reed Educational & Professional Publishing Ltd

Heinemann is a registered trademark of Reed Educational &
Professional Publishing Limited

OXFORD MELBOURNE AUCKLAND
JOHANNESBURG BLANTYRE GABORNE
IBADAN PORTSMOUTH NH (USA) CHICAGO

© Dave Needham, Rob Dransfield, Rod Harris, Martin Coles and
Maureen Rawlinson 1999

First published 1999
2003 2002 2001 2000 1999
11 10 9 8 7 6 5 4 3

A catalogue record for this book is available from the British Library
on request.

ISBN 0 435 453149

Designed by Red Giraffe

Cover designed by Sarah Garbett

Typeset by Tek-Art, Croydon, Surrey

Printed and bound by The Bath Press, Bath

CONTENTS

INTRODUCTION

Studying business enables us to make a more effective contribution to the organisations we are involved in. In particular it helps us to make more informed managerial decisions.

This text is designed to provide the student with a detailed understanding of the core areas of business which lie at the heart of modern Higher Awards qualifications including HNC, HND and other undergraduate qualifications. The book is based on all the latest research in the range of disciplines that make up business studies.

We have set out to make the book lively, interesting to read and challenging, with plenty of opportunities to read and discuss case studies based on very recent materials. We have included key references and further reading so that students can follow up topic areas in depth. We have also included an assignment at the end of each unit. Carrying out the assignments effectively will enable students to provide evidence of having acquired the knowledge and understanding required to meet national specifications for Higher Award qualifications in business.

Through carefully studying the text and responding to tasks, questions, and assignments, the student will acquire the necessary confidence and expertise to engage in organisational decision making from a position of strength based on sound practical knowledge.

This book follows up the highly successful first edition of *Business for Higher Awards*, but has been completely revised to take account of recent developments in business writing and research, and includes incisive new sections covering corporate strategy and law as well as giving more emphasis to quantitative techniques and psychological influences on motivation in the workplace.

Much of the work included in the text has stemmed from the business strand of the BSc Business and Technology course at The Nottingham Trent University, which has proved to be a highly popular course with outstanding results in terms of students going on to take up important and well-paid positions in the world of business and modern technology.

Acknowledgements
The authors would like to thank the lecturers on the BSc Business and Technology course at The Nottingham Trent University for their advice and support: Mick Baross, Wendy Davis, Steph Howkins, Barry Smith and Stevie Vanhegan. Also, for some interesting case study suggestions, Howard Bacon, Mark Simm, Simon Chapman, Sarah Pepper, Sarah Coatham, Alison Redwood, Andrea Carver, Rachel Lees, Darren Dovey, Sunny Blest, and Daniel Elsom. Special thanks go to Sarah Yeomans for help with the European section, and Joyce Steele for providing useful information on quantitative techniques. For the photograph of Bernard Ladet, special thanks to Elspeth Dransfield.
The authors and publishers would like to thank the following for permission to reproduce photographs:
Francesca Bondy/Trip
Radhika Chalasani/Rex Features
Adrian Dennis/Rex Features
Games Workshop Ltd
Hulton Getty Images
Christian Liewig; Temp Sport/Corbis
Rex Features
Tesco
Bob Thomas/Tony Stone
Bob Turner/Trip

Marketing

Marketing Process

This chapter introduces the marketing process and shows how the concept has developed in recent times. A number of key marketing concepts are discussed, which are looked at in more depth in subsequent chapters.

On completion of the chapter you should be able to explain the marketing process. To achieve this you must demonstrate the ability to:

- compare alternative definitions of marketing

- explain the various elements of the marketing concept

- identify and assess the benefits and costs of a marketing approach.

DEFINING MARKETING

Marketing does not simply focus on selling and advertising. It is an approach that seeks to uncover what the customer requires, and to convert this knowledge into products that are distributed and promoted in ways that will provide for the satisfaction of all concerned. Marketing provides a long-term understanding of customers' changing requirements, allowing adjustments to be made to a company's product, providing a platform for a customer-centred approach.

A marketing orientation involves all of the following actions.

1. Identify customer needs.
2. Design products and services that meet these needs.
3. Price the product to reflect costs, competition, and customers' ability to pay.
4. Communicate information about these products and services to prospective buyers.
5. Market the product or service at a time and place that meets customers' needs.
6. Provide for the necessary service and follow-up to ensure customer satisfaction.

The American Marketing Association (AMA) defines marketing as:

'the process of planning and executing the conception, pricing, promotion and distribution of ideas, goods or services to create exchanges that will satisfy individual and organisational objectives.'

This definition focuses attention on the behaviour of an organisation and how it generates value for customers. It affects all organisational functions, whether the business is concerned with fast-moving consumer goods or services, industrial or business-to-business marketing. As Lord Marshall, the chairman of British Airways says:

'Marketing starts from the very top of an organisation and has to involve everybody in the business. Whatever their responsibilities are, I believe they have a role to play which should add up to an overall and total marketing effort.'
(Chartered Institute of Marketing, Review of the Year 1997–98)

Here the emphasis is on involving everyone in an organisation with the marketing effort. Marketing thus becomes a generic skill needed by all employees.

Similarly, Tony Usley, in the Chartered Institute of Marketing Annual Lecture (1998), took the view that company culture is an important issue, as all must pull their weight internally as well as externally to maximise the potential of the organisation to fulfil its promise to its customer.

> *'To set yourself apart from your competitors, you must have a company of believers. To achieve that, you need a marketing programme that is as effective internally as it is externally.'*

Returning to the AMA's definition, certain points are worth noting:

- It focuses on the market variables of product price, place and promotion that are used to provide customer satisfaction.
- Consumer segments are selected and analysed prior to production, so that the customer, client or public determines the marketing programme.
- It recognises that the marketing concept also relates to non-profit organisations.

Other definitions, such as that used by the Chartered Institute of Marketing (CIM) in the UK, show a similar approach to marketing.

> *'Marketing is the management process responsible for identifying, anticipating and satisfying customer requirements profitably.'*

Another view of marketing takes contemporary issues into account, by identifying four types of marketing.

1 **Transaction marketing.** This involves the firm satisfying potential buyers by managing the elements of the **marketing mix**, which is made up of product, price, place, promotion (the 4 Ps, see Chapter 3). Separate buying transactions by the consumer, although repeated, are treated in isolation, and marketing is a formal and impersonal process. In this type of marketing, managers look to market a product or brand to an identified group of customers, often using market segmentation tactics. Marketing is seen as a function within the firm, and links are made to other functions to promote a co-ordinated effort to gain the customer's attention and interest.

2 **Database marketing.** This involves an information technology based tool, with the emphasis still on the market transaction. Marketers rely on IT to manage information on customers, and use it to form a relationship between the firm and the customer. Once current and potential customers are identified, differentiated messages can be delivered to each through a choice of media, focusing on the preferences of the customer. Over time, customers can be retained if there is sufficient flexibility to change the product to suit emerging needs.

3 **Interactive marketing.** Database marketing can be seen as a personalised approach to marketing, though still at a distance from the customer. Interactive marketing is based on personal contacts – bargaining and information exchanges are the norm, resulting in the establishment of individual relationships. The focus in this form of marketing moves from the products to the people and organisations that can promote on-going relationships.

Interactive marketing is not the preserve of the 'professional' marketer. Interaction involves many individuals who are not trying to sell, but are attempting to build a basis for joint action with the prospective purchaser.

This form of marketing is often used in the business-to-business area, but can now be seen in many consumer goods industries.

4 **Network marketing.** A network of firms who are involved in the production, distribution and use of goods can be the basis for a coordinated effort to maximise benefits. Marketers build the network, by developing personal and impersonal links that involve not just marketers but people from other functions and levels in the organisations involved.

For each of these four types of marketing, it is possible to identify the features of good practice, and the most appropriate approach for maximum effect. It is possible for an organisation to use transaction approaches based on the 4 Ps, but at the same time develop network-marketing initiatives to create new products and services, or even develop databases that can help drive the firm forward.

TASK

Why is it important to define marketing? Does it matter that the CIM in the UK and the AMA in the US have differing definitions?

MARKETING CONCEPT

Having established a working definition of marketing, it is important to look more closely at the core concepts or basic elements. The elements can be identified as:

1 needs and wants
2 products
3 value and satisfaction
4 exchange utility and transaction
5 markets.

Needs and wants

A **need** is a deprivation of some basic satisfaction, for example the need for food, shelter, clothing and belonging. **Wants**, on the other hand, are for specific items that can satisfy those needs, so that an individual may need to eat, but wants to consume either a certain type of food, or to eat at a certain restaurant. Unlike needs, which are a basic feature of all human society, wants are shaped by social forces and are influenced by such things as the peer group, the media and the business and political system.

Products

Products are anything offered to an individual to satisfy a need or want – including intangibles such as services. The importance of tangible goods lies in their use to satisfy a want, so a car is an item that delivers transportation. Services are provided by persons, places, activities, organisations or ideas, and can be delivered through physical objects such as an aircraft that provides transportation.

The term product can cover anything capable of delivering the satisfaction of a want or need, which is an important consideration as many firms may be tempted to concentrate on tangible products rather than the services or benefits those products provide. This is marketing myopia, a failure to recognise the scope of the business through focusing too narrowly on the product. For example, airlines can redefine their businesses as travel rather than just air transportation, offering complete travel services such as hotel accommodation, credit facilities and ground transportation in addition to air travel. Tobacco companies have used this approach to create a broader view of what they offer, for example Marlboro uses its 'lifestyle' concept to incorporate clothing.

Value and satisfaction

Marketers will have to face up to this issue if the successful sale of a product that satisfies a particular need or want is to be realised.

All consumers have a series of alternatives to choose from, but this is best understood by looking at the value derived from the use of a product that satisfies a set of goals. The complexity of consumer choice is looked at in more detail below, but it is sufficient here to note that it is vital for the marketer to understand the value placed by consumers on products and the satisfaction gained from their use, as the success of the marketing plan depends on this.

Exchange utility and transaction

For marketing to come into its own, an understanding of needs, wants and value is not enough. Exchange is the act of acquiring a product by offering something in return. Each party must, therefore, possess something of value that the other desires. The objective of marketing exchanges is to receive something that is desired more than that which is given up. This concept focuses attention on customer satisfaction.

Maintaining a good relationship with buyers is more than providing them with the opportunity to buy the product. It focuses attention on the activities of all the people who represent an organisation and come into contact with the consumer.

Markets

All those customers who share a common need and want, and who are in a position to engage in exchange to satisfy that need or want, constitute the market.

For markets to work efficiently, they will need to ensure four flows:

1 Goods and services from seller to buyer.
2 Communication from seller to buyer.
3 Money from buyer to seller.
4 Information from buyer to seller.

A failure in any one of these, or a reduced level of efficiency, could make it more difficult to achieve the exchange. This can be seen in the development of Internet business, often referred to as the 'marketspace'. For it to work efficiently it needs to ensure that all four flows are working well, but problems still remain. For example, money from buyer to seller can be transferred by on-line payment via credit or debit cards, but many people still regard this as insecure. This one problem holds up the use of the Internet for business purposes, putting off both businesses and consumers. The use of the Internet websites for gaining information is developing quickly, but until payment issues are sorted out it will not function fully as a marketplace.

Many of the ideas in marketing have been understood for a long time. However, the significance of marketing has varied over time, with its importance increasing as consumers become more sophisticated and industry more competitive. The following analysis provides an overview of the development and importance of the marketing concept.

The production era

Until the 1920s the prevailing attitude was that a good product (defined in terms of physical quality) needed little marketing. This production orientation stressed efficiency in producing a quality product, and the attitude towards marketing was that 'a good product will sell itself'. This attitude dominated business approaches for decades. Indeed, business success is still often defined in terms of production.

The sales era

During this period, which lasted until the 1950s, firms attempted to match their output to customers. Companies developed a sales orientation, a business philosophy which assumed that consumers would resist purchasing non-essential products and services, seeing marketing as being mainly concerned with the use of creative advertising and personal selling in order to overcome customers' resistance and convince them to buy – a view still held today by many producers and consumers. Although marketing departments began to emerge during the sales era, they tended to remain in a subordinate position to production, finance and engineering.

The marketing era

The emergence of the marketing concept followed the shift from a seller's market, characterised by a shortage of goods and services, to a buyer's market, where there is an abundance of goods and services. The advent of a strong buyer's market created a need for a switch to a consumer orientation, a way of meeting consumer needs and wants by designing a marketing package to suit them.

Marketing can no longer be regarded as supplementary activity performed after the production process has been completed. The marketer now plays a leading role in product planning, and all parts of the organisation are involved with the assessment and then the satisfaction of customers' needs and wants.

An organisation's ability to meet customer wants is subject to many restrictions, but none of these should be used as an excuse for failing to adopt the marketing-led approach. Good practice includes seeking marketing opportunities, selecting appropriate objectives, using effective strategic approaches, providing the right marketing mix, and the implementation of the marketing plan within effective control and review procedures. The following case studies show how marketing can be used to identify problems and come up with solutions.

Case Study

Horseracing

The British Horseracing Board spends £700 000 per year on marketing to raise the image of the sport and increase the revenue that comes to the horseracing industry. In addition to investors and prospective owners, the industry relies on individual racecourses to promote race meetings as entertainment, such as the popular family days organised by York and Ascot.

Public awareness of racing in the UK is high, mainly because of the betting industry's involvement and from the controversial point of view of animal welfare. The problem therefore is not one of awareness, but getting people interested in participating as owners or attending race meetings. Perceptions of the industry are that it is run by people who are old-fashioned and elitist, and that on-course betting is somewhat seedy. Consequently, there has been a crisis of confidence in the industry, with failing attendances, poor prize money and a lack of interest in owning race-horses. This has led some of the richer foreign owners to look to France and elsewhere for more exciting racing with higher prize money.

The Japanese Racing Association has an annual budget of £50 million to promote its products as stylish leisure pursuits. In the USA, the National Thoroughbred Racing Association has taken an aggressive approach, focusing on the excitement of the race itself and the risk and rewards of betting. Meanwhile, the French have promoted the romance of racing, and the way people can relax and enjoy themselves at the racecourse.

Trying to dent the sleazy, elitist images and address the animal welfare issues, the British Horseracing Board has recently launched a pack for school children aimed at 7–11 year olds, intended to help counter some of the bad press and to convince the audience that racing is fun.

Question

What are the issues that the British Horseracing Board faces in attracting a younger audience?

Case Study

Why worry about the customer?

Alfas Industries, a firm based in north-east England, is a manufacturer of sealants and construction materials. It can be judged a success on any number of factors. With a turnover of £5 million in 1998 and profits of £550 000, Alfas Industries has margins that are in the top quartile for the sector. However, after the company had been appraised in the UK Benchmarking Index, it was surprised to find that on customer satisfaction it was ranked as a poor performer. On other measures of performance, which included management, commitment to training, production process, business strategy and financial

management, Alfas was rated highly, so an outwardly successful company was seen as being less so by its own customers. Where did the problem lie?

Customers felt Alfas to be too aloof and rather an anonymous force in the marketplace. With 10 per cent of all customers being lost in any one year, this perception was clearly damaging to the company. Added to this, price competition and a slowdown in economic activity at the end of 1998 further threatened Alfas's position and it looked as though all the technical expertise of the company would be overriden by competitors who based their approach solely on price in an increasingly price-conscious market.

Following the results of benchmarking, Alfas's management undertook research with former customers and those who were significantly reducing their orders, to establish where the problems lay and to take appropriate action. Rather than enter into a price war with its competitors, the company wanted to emphasise its technical skill and superior products and to invest in what matters to customers, in this case getting the products to them on time, a vital issue in a sector where contracts must be completed on time and to a standard.

The company also began to explore export markets to see if a diversified approach would help to spread the risk of depending on the UK market alone, and again the need to understand customers' needs and requirements was considered paramount.

Question

Why might a successful company often overlook the needs of its customers?

Societal issues

To deal with broader issues that influence consumers, marketers have developed a societal marketing concept. This places an additional set of requirements on marketing managers. Its focus is on the process by which a company or organisation creates products for presentation to the marketplace, which may be seen to be counter to the long-term interests society and consumers have in preserving the environment and conserving resources. The societal marketing concept holds that the organisation's task is to determine the needs and wants of customers and to deliver the desired satisfaction efficiently and effectively, in a way that preserves or enhances the consumer's and society's well-being. This aim may appear in the company's mission statement, which often stresses the purpose of the organisation and its commitment to caring for the environment. Many, if not most, companies provide such a statement and they are judged on their ability to deliver on their promises. Ethical investment fund managers, for example, judge companies on their performances on welfare, environmental and personnel issues.

Green issues

Green marketing refers to the use of environmentally acceptable practices in the development, pricing, promotion and distribution of products. For example, car manufacturers such as BMW and Audi emphasise the recyclability of their cars, the use of lead-free petrol, and any feature that the environmentally aware consumer would wish to know about.

The UK government, through the Department of Trade and Industry, seeks to encourage organisations to undertake environmental audits that can identify, amongst other things, how to reduce excessive energy consumption. Many firms are now working towards a better understanding of the impact of their marketing approaches.

Customer and competitor orientation

Customer and competitor orientation are two facets of an overall marketing orientation. As has already been discussed, all personnel need to be aware of their role in customer care. Customers have more than one option when looking to spend their income, and their choices are not just between directly competing products – they may choose to spend their available resources on dissimilar products and services. If products are to be developed to meet customers' needs (marketing orientation), over time an organisation needs to develop competitor orientation, i.e. acquire an understanding of what the competition has to offer. If your competitors are in a better position to meet customer requirements, your customers' loyalty will be eroded, sales lost and profits hit.

Figure 1.1 shows that market relationships require an understanding of customers and competitors, but also depend on the need to work with suppliers and intermediaries. An effective marketing approach can successfully exploit this awareness for the benefit of the organisation and its customers.

The behaviour of competitors can be as complex as customer behaviour. It is necessary to understand competitors' objectives and strategies, how successful they have been, where their strengths and weaknesses lie and how they are likely to behave in the future. With this knowledge, marketers can seek to influence customers and even the conditions in the marketplace in order to maintain customer loyalty. Sustainable advantage is the goal, but in increasingly competitive markets it is hard to maintain, as new products, new processes and so on will be copied by competitors. Nevertheless, it should still be the goal of a company to maintain a unique position in the market, one that customers appreciate and competitors find difficult to emulate.

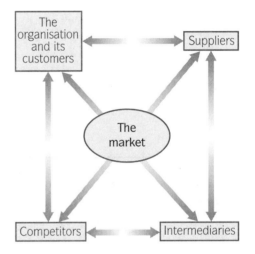

Figure 1.1 *Market relationships*

Customers buy benefits not products

Many UK industries compare less than favourably with their counterparts in other countries when it comes to efficiency. A drive to improve productivity has been one of the key aims of both Conservative and Labour governments in the 1980s and 1990s, particularly with the competitiveness White Papers. However, this is not the same as effectiveness. Making a certain type of product more efficiently may still mean that a company will go out of business. What counts is providing the right product to give customers the benefits they seek. The benefits sought in a car may be that it is safe, economical, comfortable and has a good radio/CD system. A car that doesn't provide these benefits will not sell to a customer seeking them. Likewise, a service such as banking that can't provide convenient opening hours, telephone banking, on-line banking, financial advice and approachable staff will not attract many new accounts.

To find out what a customer requires may not be easy, but to assume that the product will fulfil his or her needs can lead companies to make basic errors of judgement. Many product offerings promote the product itself rather than the benefits available to the consumer. Understanding the concept of benefits may mean changing the process rather than the product. For example, the customer may be perfectly satisfied with the spectacle frames offered by a high street optician, but not wish to wait three weeks for his or her choice to be available – getting the product more quickly to the customer is what will make the difference. In understanding benefits, organisations may have to restructure their operations radically in order to suit customer requirements.

Marketing principles

We are now in a position to summarise the basic principles of marketing. Corporate goals can be achieved via a marketing orientation. A marketing orientation meets customer needs more effectively than the competition, because all the activities of the company are focused on providing customer satisfaction, not in a piecemeal way but with an integrated approach, which is now made easier by the use of information technology. Marketing is therefore not just the preserve of the marketing department.

Some organisations try to carve out a route to high profit through anti-competitive behaviour, such as the formation of a monopoly or cartel. Suppliers may try to keep prices artificially high. However, customers can find out, via the Internet or through the work of various consumer groups, about these anti-competitive practices, so they may be successful only in the short term. High prices for cars and for food in the UK compared to other European and North American countries are often cited as possible examples.

Long-term success will best be achieved by adopting the marketing principles outlined above. The challenge lies in getting them to work effectively within the organisation.

TASK

What makes up the marketing concept? Should a company focus on its competitors rather than its customers?

MARKETING PROCESS OVERVIEW

Planning is the process of anticipating the future and determining courses of action for achieving organisational objectives. The planning process creates a blueprint that not only specifies the means for achieving organisational objectives, but provides checkpoints where performance can be compared with the plan to determine whether current activities are moving the organisation toward its objectives.

Steps in the marketing planning process

The marketing planning process involves the development of objectives and specifications for how they will be accomplished. There are five steps in the process.

1 Determination of organisational objectives

The basic objectives, or goals, of the organisation are the starting point for marketing planning. They serve as signposts from which marketing plans are established. These objectives provide direction for all phases of the organisation and serve as standards in evaluating performance. Goals vary among organisations; corporate objectives often emphasise profitability, market share and shareholder value – for example the Coca-Cola Company defines its goal as being to increase shareholder value.

Objectives should be specific and quantifiable (for example, 'Achieve a 12 per cent increase in profits over last year'; 'Attain a 20 per cent share of the market by 2003', '15 per cent increase in sales over last year'). In addition, they should be time-specific, with stated time periods within which they are to be accomplished.

2 and 3 Assessment of organisational resources and evaluation of environmental risks

The second and third steps of the marketing planning process occur at about the same time and involve the assessment of strengths, risks and available opportunities. Planning strategies are influenced by a number of factors both within and outside the organisation. Marketing opportunities are affected by organisational resources and environmental factors. Both are important considerations in the planning process.

Organisational resources include capabilities involving production, marketing, finance, technology and employees. By evaluating these resources, organisations can pinpoint their strengths and weaknesses. Strengths help organisations define their core competences, set objectives, develop plans for meeting objectives, and take advantage of marketing opportunities. For example, the Coca-Cola Company identifies its strengths as having the world's best-known trademark, financial soundness, an exceptional distribution system, marketing and advertising efficiency, new-product innovations, and a dedicated team of managers and employees. The firm's strategy involves capitalising on these resource strengths in addressing international marketing opportunities.

Resource weaknesses, on the other hand, may inhibit an organisation from taking advantage of marketing opportunities. When the US company General Mills decided to end its marketing efforts in toys and fashion clothing and instead concentrate on food marketing and restaurants, it concluded that toys and fashionwear did not offer immediate prospects of competitive advantage for the firm and that is marketing strengths could best be exploited in the areas where it clearly demonstrated superiority.

Planning needs appropriate and effective organisational structures to carry it out. In summary, we can say that the organisation's structure:

- determines who does what
- establishes rewards (understood in both monetary and non-monetary forms) that develop motivations
- allows/hinders integration between activities and functions, particularly with regard to the issue of centralisation and decentralisation.

This shows the degree of importance that is attached to getting both planning and organisation right. Organisations summarise their conclusions on environmental resources in a SWOT analysis (see page 12). This can be used to help formulate the corporate and marketing strategies.

4 Formulation of marketing strategy

Marketing planning efforts must be directed towards establishing marketing strategies that are efficient, flexible and adaptable. Marketing strategy is the overall company programme made up of the 7 Ps (price, promotion, place, product, people, process and physical evidence). It selects a particular target market and then satisfies consumers in that segment through careful use of the elements of the marketing mix. Examples of the likely constraints and opportunities in different types of markets are given below. In each case, firms would need fully to understand the market, customers and competitors in order to come to a sound decision on strategy.

- **Fragmented industries.** Where there are low barriers to market entry, for example when capital costs are low, new firms have easy access to the market and it is likely to become fragmented. In this situation there are no particular economies of scale to be achieved, so cost leadership is not possible. There could also be a rapid change in products, and a diverse product line. In these circumstances, what options are open to a firm? It may be in a position to stop the fragmentation if it can build up a position where others are squeezed out and it can achieve economies of scale. A firm may aim to improve market share either by growth or by merger. If, on the other hand, a firm is powerless to stop the process of fragmentation, it will have to plan its reaction – for example, it may need organisational changes such as decentralisation to cope with the fragmentation.
- **Growth industries.** When markets are growing they can be easier to enter, and in a growth industry a company can increase its turnover without necessarily increasing market share. However, such markets are not always easy – there can be great uncertainty as to how the market will develop, particularly with regard to changes in technology, customer behaviour and other factors that make it difficult to arrive at a suitable marketing mix. Further to this, the barriers to entry can be greater than expected, particularly if a rival firm has patented a new product or access is needed to distribution channels. To decide whether it is worth entering the market an estimate of its growth potential is required, along with forecasts of market share capabilities.

- **Mature markets.** A market or product that has reached maturity will experience low growth, but more significantly customers will tend to be brand loyal, having bought the product many times, so competition will be based on price and service. This would suggest that leadership will be harder to achieve, but cost leadership is an option, as is differentiated marketing (see below). A mature market can still be a very profitable place, but at a cost.
- **Declining markets.** Towards the end of the product life cycle, the firm will face strategic choices. Among those it may consider would be a repositioning strategy, involving moving the product to a new market segment and changing the marketing support expenditure.
- **Choice of products and markets.** A firm has to think how it can build on its perceived competitive advantages by looking at a mixture of market and product approaches. There are four options open to the firm in combining its products and markets.
  - **Market penetration.** A firm seeks to maintain or increase its share of the current market using the 7 Ps.
  - **Market development.** A firm could look at, say, the exporting of its products to justify its original investment.
  - **Product development.** A firm could seek to develop new products to replace its existing offerings, using the established distribution system.
  - **Diversification.** This can be of four types (horizontal, vertical, concentric or conglomerate), but will move the firm away from its existing market/product approach.

Once again the need to plan ahead and consider what the company is trying to achieve is of utmost importance in attaining objectives.

5 Marketing plans

Much of the planning effort is dedicated to the development of marketing plans that will best match product offerings to the needs of particular target markets. An appropriate match is vital to the firm's market success. Three basic alternative strategies for achieving consumer satisfaction are available:

- **undifferentiated marketing**
- **differentiated marketing**
- **concentrated marketing**.

Firms that produce only one product or one product line and market it to all customers with a single marketing mix practise **undifferentiated** or mass marketing.

Although marketing managers using an undifferentiated marketing strategy recognise the existence of numerous segments in the total market, they generally ignore minor differences and focus on the broad market. To reach the general market, they use mass advertising, mass distribution and broad themes.

However, there are dangers. A firm that attempts to satisfy everyone in the market faces the threat of competitors offering specialised products to smaller segments of the total market and better satisfying each segment. Indeed, firms that implement a strategy of differentiated marketing or concentrated marketing may enter the market and capture enough small segments to make the strategy of undifferentiated marketing unworkable for the competition.

Firms that produce numerous products with different marketing mixes designed to satisfy smaller segments practise **differentiated** marketing. This is aimed at satisfying a large part of the total market, but instead of marketing one product with a single marketing programme, the organisation markets a number of products designed to appeal to individual parts of the total market. For example, Reebok offers various walking shoes to satisfy the needs of different types of walkers. Its strategy is to segment the walking market, recognising that there is not just one type of walker, and therefore no one shoe will satisfy all walkers' needs.

By providing increased satisfaction for each of numerous target markets, the company with a differentiated approach can produce more sales than would be possible with undifferentiated marketing.

The costs of differentiated marketing are greater. Production costs usually rise because additional products mean shorter production runs and increased set-up time. Inventory costs rise because of the added space needed for the alternative products, and the increase in the amount of record-keeping that is necessary. Promotion costs also increase because unique promotional mixes are required for each market segment.

Although the costs of doing business are typically greater under a differentiated approach, consumers are usually better served because products are specifically designed to meet the needs of smaller segments. A firm that wants to employ a single marketing approach for an entire market may be forced to choose differentiated marketing instead, if competitors appeal to each segment within the total market.

Rather than attempting to market its product offerings to the entire market, a firm may choose to focus its efforts on profitably satisfying a smaller target market, i.e. **concentrated** marketing. The approach of concentrated marketing – directing all of a firm's marketing resources towards serving a small segment of the total market – is particularly appealing to new, small firms that lack the financial resources of their competitors.

Concentrated marketing, however, also poses dangers. Since the firms' growth is tied to a particular segment, changes in the size of that segment or in customer buying patterns may result in severe financial problems. Sales may also drop if new competitors appeal to the same market segment.

Environmental analysis

To reach their target markets successfully, organisations need to scan the environment in which they operate in order to understand the key factors that currently affect them, and anticipate future changes. Environmental scanning involves carrying out a systematic analysis – sometimes called a PEST analysis (political, economic, social and technological) – which includes all legal and environmental constraints. Teams of specialists build up a detailed picture of the key variables in the organisation's environment, including changes in government legislation, in the economy, in consumer buying habits, and in competitor activity.

A SWOT analysis is a useful approach to examining the relationship between an organisation and its marketing environment. The analysis focuses on the **S**trengths, **W**eaknesses, **O**pportunities and **T**hreats facing a business or its products. It includes an internal element and an external element. The internal element examines the organisation's own strengths and weaknesses, and the external looks at the opportunities and threats present in the environment in which it operates.

The analysis begins by identifying influences that have been significant in the past, then looks at those that are important today, and finally forecasts influences that are most likely to be prominent in the future. The results of this research are used to relate an organisation's strengths and weaknesses to external market forces, in order to develop policies that build on its strengths, minimise its weaknesses, and seize its opportunities, while taking measures to counter possible threats.

The target market

Figure 1.2 shows the stages that an organisation will move through when constructing its corporate and marketing plans. We have already seen that the organisation can set its objectives and then assess what it has to do to achieve them via an assessment of the environment and its own internal resources. This produces a SWOT analysis that creates the foundation for the development of the organisation's strategy, i.e. how it will achieve its objectives. Marketing will then be able to see its role as developing target markets to aim for, and from there to construct market plans with specific combinations of the 7 Ps to achieve a successful outcome.

There is a danger in taking Figure 1.2 literally. Although it shows good planning practice, it does not identify the importance of the customer. Good organisational and marketing practice must, as we have seen, always bear this in mind. The aim is always to retain the focus on customers and understand their needs and requirements. Therefore, another and more effective way of reading Figure 1.2 is to see that the target market takes priority, because understanding how it operates will determine the plans and approaches used by organisations.

The marketing mix variables are a way to see this in action, as the most effective combination will be that which works in the target market. Difficulties in the

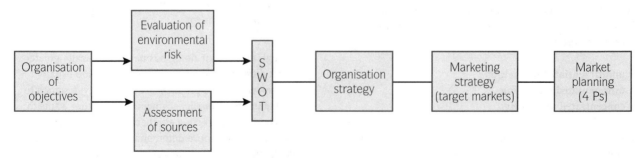

Figure 1.2 *External environment: political, economic, social, technological influences*

marketplace will mean that a change must be made either to the mix itself or to the marketing, or even corporate, strategies. Strategies and plans must be flexible enough to be changed as feedback is obtained from the marketplace. Organisations must always be willing to change their approach when evidence shows this to be necessary.

Introduction to the marketing mix variables

Product strategy

In marketing, as we have seen, the term product means more than a good or service, but instead is a concept that considers the satisfaction of all consumer needs in relation to the good or service. Product strategy is the part of marketing decision-making that involves developing the right good or service for the firm's customers. It includes not only deciding what products the firm should offer to a group of consumers but also the package design, brand names, trademarks, warranties, product life cycles, positioning, and new product development.

Pricing strategy

Pricing strategy is the element of marketing decision-making that deals with the setting of profitable and justifiable exchange values for goods and services. The pricing strategy is one of the most difficult areas of marketing decision-making – it can be regulated, as in the case of the UK telecommunications industry, or subject to considerable public scrutiny, as with the pricing of new cars in the UK compared with mainland Europe.

Place (distribution strategy)

Place strategy includes all the planning and activities involved in getting the right product to the firm's customers. Marketers develop distribution strategies to ensure that their products are available in the proper quantities at the right time and place. Distribution decisions involve modes of transportation, warehousing, inventory controls, order processing and selection of marketing channels, taking the product from the producer to the final customer.

Promotional strategy

Promotional strategy involves the appropriate blend of personal selling, advertising, public relations and sales promotion for use in communicating with and seeking to persuade potential customers. Organisations use many different means of sending messages about their products. The message may be communicated directly by salespeople, or indirectly through advertisements and sales promotion. In developing a promotional strategy, marketers blend the various kinds of promotion to produce a mix that will communicate most effectively with their target market.

MARKETING IN PRACTICE

A marketing approach has been shown to provide long-term advantages, as has the adoption of sound marketing management, in all types of businesses. We can examine various business sectors to see how each applies the basic marketing principles.

The service sector

The service sector accounts for a major part of any advanced country's economy, so marketing issues unique to this sector require careful consideration. (A detailed review of services and marketing is provided in Chapter 4.) Services are difficult to define, because it is hard to distinguish between certain kinds of goods and services. Personal services such as hairdressing and dry cleaning are easily recognisable as services rather than tangible goods, but they represent only a small part of the total industry. Many firms offer a combination of goods and services. One way of overcoming this problem of identification is to define services by the use of a product spectrum, which shows that most products have both a goods and services component. Figure 1.3 presents a goods–services continuum – a method for visualising the differences and similarities between goods and services.

Figure 1.3 *The goods–service continuum*

It is impossible to describe all the services available to the consumer and industrial purchaser, but a general definition can be offered: services are intangible tasks that satisfy consumer and industrial needs when efficiently developed and distributed to chosen market segments. Services are characterised by the following features, which have major marketing implications:

- They are intangible.
- They are inseparable from the service provider.
- They are perishable.
- They are not uniform between providers – they have heterogeneity.
- Their ownership remains with the seller.

This important sector has unique marketing problems, and may suffer because of a lack of understanding about what these mean for marketing management. From the first key feature mentioned above, intangibility, we can see that services do not have features that appeal to the consumer's sense of sight, hearing, smell, taste or touch. Therefore, they are difficult to demonstrate at trade shows, to display in retail stores, to illustrate in magazine advertisements and to sample. Consequently, personal selling and advertising must show the benefits of using the service. For example, an insurance agent can discuss the peace of mind provided by adequate home and car insurance; television commercials may show a car that has been repaired after a road accident.

Because of the differences between goods and services, the market has to adopt good practice and effective techniques – or develop new ones – to provide an effective approach. This is shown clearly in the example of retailing and the Internet.

Retailing revolution

Retailers in virtually every developed country are major employers, monopolise space in city centres and are considered to be an efficient way for people to purchase a variety of goods and services. From a marketing point of view, retailing adds value for customers by breaking bulk, allowing individual customers to purchase the quantities they require, providing choice, having enough stock to satisfy customer requirements, and providing other services such as advice, warranty protection, free delivery and so on.

Many retailers are now finding that growth prospects are diminishing, while at the same time new competitors are emerging. Some of these new developments are listed below.

1 **New-style retailers** operate with one or all of the following:
   a Information technology, particularly in their links with suppliers, so that as stock is sold the supplier can respond on a just-in-time basis (see page 412). Once stock is delivered, payment can be made directly to suppliers via electronic bank transfers. Any supplier who is averse to information technology would not become a partner to such retailers.
   b Fair-pricing strategies, creating a group of products that buyers require at the best possible price at the time, such as those found in the home improvement superstores B & Q and Homebase.
   c Reductions in the number of suppliers, where a few suppliers provide a variety of products, rather than maintaining a large number of suppliers to guarantee variety.
   Retailers need to be seen as customers by manufacturers, as without their support access to the marketplace would be more difficult. (This may change with the advent of electronic shopping – see below.)
2 **Partnerships.** Retailers and manufacturers can gain more by entering into partnerships, where they are part of a single and continuous process in getting goods to customers. For this to work, information on customers becomes of paramount importance. If information can be gathered and interpreted quickly and efficiently, then production and distribution can be re-engineered to provide Efficient Consumer Response (ECR), a system that can save on stock-holding costs and respond to need.
3 **Electronic shopping.** With many people working long hours, the opportunity to visit shops has become a major issue. Despite the relaxation of shopping-hour restrictions which has seen Sunday opening, all-night shopping and extended hours, a major alternative that is becoming available is shopping through the Internet, or via a catalogue. A recent study into electronic retailing suggests that these retailers can gain competitive advantage in distribution efficiency, the assessment of competitors' merchandise, the collection and use of customer information, the presentation of information through electronic formats, and the development of unique merchandise.
4 **Retailing and entertainment.** Retailing and entertainment are coming together, as can be seen in Disney stores, Warner Bros outlets and others. Traditional retailers are moving into entertainment to provide added value for shoppers. Increasingly, this is linked to education and training via Internet links, which can offer advice and support from trained advisers and tutors. Customers go to these outlets to buy, socialise and learn new skills.

The new developments provide a challenge to existing retailers, however successful. Marks & Spencer, one of the UK's leading retailers, is now looking to provide more fashionable clothes to women more quickly than it has done in the past, an indication that the media exposure of the latest fashion shows makes consumers unwilling to wait too long before they can buy mass-market versions at reasonable prices. Retailers will need to focus on improving services, and serving an ageing population, with new occupants appearing in shopping malls such as universities, entertainment companies and so on. A failure to react to these trends could limit growth options and bring a reduction in profitability.

Discussion point

Why are traditional retailers such as Marks & Spencer finding it difficult to deal with increased competition?

The non-profit sector

With the removal of many restrictions on advertising the services of professionals such as dentists, and the need for schools, colleges and universities to adopt marketing strategies, the public sector has had to come to terms with the problem of promoting a product – in its case usually a service. This is compounded by the need to learn quickly what marketing is all about. Many organisations, although not wishing to set themselves profit objectives, have developed good business practice.

Case Study

Arts marketing

The UK's Labour government announced in 1998 that all the major museums would be given extra funding over the following five years to guarantee free access for the public. This announcement appears to provide a guaranteed future for the museums. However, to justify the extra funding, these organisations will have to establish that they are providing a valuable service for the public, promoting accessibility and targeting those population groups that are underrepresented as users of their facilities. Marketing of museums will prove a challenge.

Museums and other arts venues, such as theatres, have to compete with a wide range of demands made on people's leisure time. There are other ways to access the information and performances that these venues provide. Digital TV and the Internet will provide strong challenges for these venues as they seek to break away from the eighteenth- and nineteenth-century traditions that served them well in the past.

Using marketing techniques for the arts risks creating misunderstandings between those who produce works of art, and who often head arts organisations, and those in marketing. Marketing has often been identified with the 'number of people through the door' approach, but it is more than that, involving issues such as who uses the facilities, which groups are excluded, and how accessible (in the fullest sense) museums and arts venues really are. The Centre for Audience Development Research (CADRE) was established in 1997 to develop a research database that can bring best practice to arts marketing and help marketers in the field to share knowledge and experience. There is now an Arts Marketing Association (AMA) to support their work.

In an age of competition for leisure time, public funding restrictions and an emphasis on strategic planning, marketing requires management to adopt sophisticated practices in order to understand audiences, how they spend their time, what attracts and motivates them to attend, and so on. Arts marketing practitioners are agreed that audience development must be sustainable and based on matching the product to its target market.

Questions

1. What barriers exist to making museums more accessible to underrepresented groups?

2. What are the pros and cons of marketing the arts?

Many other organisations have also experienced significant changes in the last decade. Trade union membership, for example, has shown dramatic decline, and a number of churches have experienced a fall in membership. These organisations are losing clients (members) and are finding it more difficult to raise money. As a consequence they turn to marketing, often with the notion that marketing concentrates on promotion and selling. After further acquaintance has shown this notion to be flawed, many have then adopted good marketing practice by appraising their environment, setting objectives and drawing up marketing plans.

An important distinction between non-profit and profit-making companies is that non-profit organisations often market to multiple publics, which complicates the decision about the correct market to target. Non-profit organisations normally have at least two major publics to work with – their clients and their funders.

Other distinguishing characteristics of non-profit marketing are as follows.

- A customer or service user may have less influence with a non-profit organisation than would be the case with a profit-seeking firm. For example, local government employees may be far more concerned with the influence of the Audit Commission than with the opinion of a service user.
- Many non-profit organisations possess some degree of monopoly power.
- Political influence may be brought to bear on a marketing programme.
- Non-profit organisations sometimes lack the discipline brought about by the measurement of performance against profitability. Such organisations may attempt to maximise their return from a specific service using a less exact approach, such as service level standards. It is often difficult to set marketing objectives that are aligned specifically with overall organisational goals.
- Non-profit organisations often have multiple organisational structures. For example, a hospital might have an administrative structure, a professional structure consisting of medical personnel, and a volunteer organisation. This can produce disagreements and a confusion over the goals of the organisation.

These difficulties should not detract from the main issue, which is that, whatever the sector, organisations should focus their attention on the satisfaction of the needs and wants of their consumers, however they are defined.

International sector

The international sector approaches the marketing problem somewhat differently, and this is one of the major challenges facing such firms.

Figures produced by the Organisation for Economic Cooperation and Development (OECD) show that the UK depends more than most on the success of its exports, with 31 per cent of its gross national product accounted for by exports, a figure well in excess of the Japanese at 7 per cent and Germany at 16 per cent.

The term international marketing is used to cover both export marketing, which conveys goods produced in one country to another, and the longer-term development of manufacturing bases and distribution and marketing systems in foreign countries. In both cases goods and services are marketed across political boundaries. This changes the scope of the marketing tasks, since the solutions to marketing problems and development of strategies for their implementation are influenced in ways not found in the national or home market.

The major decisions facing a firm that seeks to engage in international marketing are summarised in Figure 1.4. To look at this issue more carefully the following case study on small and medium-sized enterprises (SMEs) shows some of the challenges faced by firms that seek to market their goods abroad.

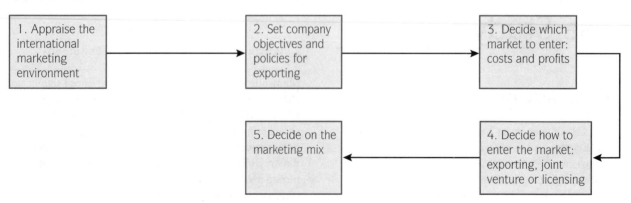

Figure 1.4 *International marketing management decision points*

Case Study

Exporting and small companies

Research carried out on 400 UK and Australian newly exporting SMEs produced the following results and analysis.

1 **Going abroad.** Many companies decide to enter a foreign market to try to build on their domestic success, or because they have found that the home market is too small for their product to be exploited profitably. A company may also be created with the aim of exploiting overseas markets. The spur to exporting may come from foreign travel or trade missions, or from an approach by an agent or distributor, wishing to seek out new products. The impetus to pursue exports can come from a combination of factors – ranging from a manager's personal interest, through to a realisation that profitable options exist for exploiting markets in other countries. Research suggests that there is usually little in the way of an analytical approach to the issue.

2 **Supporting the exporting effort.**

   a Potential exporters are provided with vast quantities of information, so much that they suffer from information overload, leading to a problem in knowing where to find help in interpreting the information. Using a consultant with previous experience has been found to help. A company's entry into a market depends on the commitment of the people in the organisation, commitment to its partners and the firm's long-term relationships.

   b Choosing a market involves, as the first stage, identifying one that a company feels comfortable with, often one that is at the least psychological distance. For example, UK companies often export to Ireland and Australia, rather than Russia and China. Once identified, research needs to focus on the consumers, how to reach them, how to support the distribution network and so on. These are surprisingly difficult matters to research, and need contacts and personal networks to be established. Experience suggests that this is more important than analysing competition, price levels and environmental factors. As long as the product is differentiated from other brands, it is likely that success will follow.

   c When moving into a foreign market for the first time, an SME will often use a distributor. Although over time the SME will build up expertise and perhaps look at setting up a local sales office and even production centre, the first stage will depend for its success on the relationship built up with the initial distributor.

The benefits of sharing knowledge between the exporter and the importer (distributor) will become clear as an active partnership is built. Research shows that the more successful exporters communicate more frequently with their distributors than less successful ones. This may all look like common sense, but many companies wish to control the relationship, rather than see it as one of equality and mutual interest.

   d The 'correct' approach to the marketing mix is to modify it in the light of research into the prevailing market conditions. Ambler and Styles (1998) argue that general practice favours trying the home product first in the foreign market and then making changes as experience is gained. The ability of a company to be flexible is, it seems, all-important. With this approach, the partnership of SME and distributor will be enhanced to the benefit of both.

SMEs looking at building understanding will be looking to the future, rather than a limited excursion into exporting. As new technology opens up many more markets, this will be a valuable lesson to learn and apply.

Questions

1. Why is exporting and marketing abroad going to be of increasing importance for SMEs?

2. What criteria do organisations use for choosing a market?

Over the next decade some problems for exporters will be reduced in importance or eradicated altogether, with the creation of a single currency for the European Union (EU), the convergence of tax rates and the free movement of capital, labour and goods across political borders within the EU. These changes are unpredictable in their timing and impact, and they will still leave a number of issues to be resolved concerning the movement of goods from the UK to mainland Europe. Apart from the EU, the potential of marketing to the USA, Japan and the economies of the Pacific basin also requires full appraisal if effective marketing management is to be achieved.

MARKETING COSTS AND MARKETING FUNCTIONS

Many attempts have been made to measure marketing costs as a percentage of overall product and service costs, and most estimates have ranged between 40 and 60 per cent. On average, one half of the costs involved in a product such as a bottle of Anaïs Anaïs perfume or a pair of Levi's jeans can be traced directly to marketing. These costs are not associated with fabrics, raw materials or ingredients or any of the other production functions. What, then, does the consumer receive in return for this 50 per cent of the cost? What functions are performed by marketing?

Marketing covers eight functions: buying; selling; transporting; storing; standardising and grading; financing; risk-taking and securing market information. These are summarised in Figure 1.5. Some functions are performed by manufacturers, others by retailers, and still others by marketing intermediaries such as wholesalers.

Marketing functions	Description
A Exchange functions	
1. Buying	Ensuring that product offerings are available in sufficient quantities to meet customer demand.
2. Selling	Use of advertising, personal selling and sales promotion to match product and service offerings to customer need.
B Physical distribution functions	
3. Transporting	Moving the product from its point of production to a location convenient for the purchaser.
4. Storing	Warehousing of products until needed for sale.
C Facilitating functions	
5. Standardisation and grading	Ensuring that product offerings meet established quality and quantity control standards in size, weight and other product variables.
6. Financing	Providing credit for channel members or consumers.
7. Risk-taking	Allowing for uncertainty about consumer purchases resulting from creation and marketing of products and services that consumers may purchase in the future.
8. Securing market information (market research)	Collection of information about consumers, competitors and channel members for use in making marketing decisions.

Figure 1.5 *The functions performed by marketing*

Buying and selling, the first two functions, represent exchange functions. Buying is important to marketing on several levels. Marketing must determine how and why consumers buy certain products or services, and intermediaries must seek out products that will appeal to customers. They must make decisions concerning likely consumer preferences that will be expressed several months after orders are placed. Selling is the second half of this exchange process, and involves advertising, personal selling and sales promotion in the attempt to match the firm's products and services to consumer needs.

Transporting and storing are physical distribution functions. Transporting involves the movement of the product from the seller to the purchaser. Storing involves the warehousing of goods until they are needed for sale. Both of these functions frequently involve manufacturers, wholesalers and retailers.

The final four marketing functions – standardising and grading, financing, risk-taking and securing market information – are often called facilitating functions because they assist the marketer in performing the exchange and physical distribution functions. **Standardising and grading** involves quality and quality control standards and grades, which are frequently set by the government or through European Union directives. These reduce the need for purchasers to inspect each item – standard tyre sizes, for example, allow car owners to request the size they need and know they will obtain a correct fit.

Financing is often required to fund inventories prior to sales. In many instances, manufacturers may provide financing for their wholesale and retail customers. In other cases, some types of wholesalers perform similar functions for their retail customers, and finally retailers frequently permit their customers to make purchases on credit.

Risk-taking is part of most ventures. Manufacturers create products and services based on research results that show a customer need for them. Wholesalers and retailers acquire inventory based on similar expectations of future consumer demand. Uncertainties about future consumer behaviour must be accepted by entrepreneurial risk-takers whenever they market products.

Securing market information involves gathering data about markets in order to make decisions about customers: who they are, what they buy, where they buy and how they buy. By collecting and analysing market information, marketers also seek to understand why consumers purchase some product offerings and reject others.

Constraints

When an organisation determines its corporate and marketing objectives it has to recognise the constraints under which it operates. Achieving profit objectives may seem to necessitate cutting the marketing budget, and achieving sales targets may appear to mean lowering price, which in turn reduces profitability. In addition to the trade-off between sales expansion and profitability, there are other constraints that may be overlooked. For example, if a firm wishes to enter a new market, how much does it understand of its market's dynamics? A new product may be launched, but is there the skill and knowledge to exploit its potential?

There are always limiting factors, which can range from a lack of money for financing new investment, a lack of spare capacity and high employee turnover, to lack of knowledge and understanding of a new marketplace. These have to be recognised and accounted for if the plan is to be operable.

COSTS AND BENEFITS

What are the benefits of providing customer satisfaction? Every business must try to assess this. In the case of hotels, guest questionnaires are often used. Hotels often seek to differentiate themselves by adding extras to hotel rooms, e.g. coffee-makers, but as such items become standard the need to maintain competitive advantage remains. Hotels have recognised the need to adopt the marketing concept only in the past fifteen to twenty years. They have needed new means of measuring results, and to find ways of getting closer to their customers.

The hotel chain Stakis launched an advertising campaign early in 1999, targeting specific UK regions, with the aim of creating an identity that suggested friendly informality. Research into the creation of a corporate identity had been supplemented by the use of database marketing targeted at the leisure part of the market, which accounts for 40 per cent of Stakis' market. The business travel market (60 per cent of the total) was supported by the Assured Meetings Initiative, bringing together dedicated teams, coordinators and standard packages for the small meetings market. This meant an investment in uniforms, furniture and décor.

The group recognised that there was a cost involved in getting the corporate concept and branding right. The practice of adding product features such as cable TV channels, used in previous years, had given way to an examination of the whole service that the business and leisure markets required. Customer satisfaction would be created by a constant delivery of service by all those involved in the hotel. Internal marketing, with all staff recognising the importance of their role, was just as important as external promotion.

Relationship marketing is important to many industries. It focuses on the building of a relationship over time, where the supplier and consumer build up an understanding that can last over a period and lead to repeat purchases. In each industry, however, the dynamics of this relationship will be different. In the hotel industry, the perceptions of the customer depend on his or her last experience of using the hotel, which varies much more than with an item purchased from a supermarket. To overcome this, the hotel group Inter-Continental (now owned by Bass) lays down service standards. Waiting time is kept to a minimum and staff approach guests rather than waiting for them to speak to staff. Loyalty and reward schemes have also been introduced to provide extras that appeal to guests, such as air miles.

What is true of the hotel chains is also true of individually-owned hotels, which have to find a niche market and build their marketing efforts around that market.

Pushing corporate identity too far, with a re-branding of a product, can mean that mistakes are made, however. Many hotel customers are loyal to a particular hotel, not to a chain, so any changes can lose customers rather than attract them. Likewise, a **narrow marketing focus**, such as on the business market for a hotel, would mean that at weekends and certain key holiday times the facilities would remain under-utilised. Focusing on both the leisure and business sectors means that Stakis and other hotel groups can balance their need to be efficient against the effective delivery of service to both markets.

Any industry, when seeking to understand customer benefits and create a customer care culture, will find that a relationship marketing approach costs time and money. The benefits come from increased use and repeat purchases. Failure can result from too narrow a focus on a market, forgetting that other groups in the market may wish to avail themselves of the benefits of the service and product, but with adjustments according to their individual needs. Hotels and other businesses require a professional approach to getting their strategy right and moving with the changing needs of the market.

TASK

Marketing costs money. In a recession, the temptation is to cut these costs. What arguments can be used to boost marketing expenditure in recession?

CHAPTER 2

Target Marketing

Target marketing helps to identify the important environmental factors that need to be examined and interpreted for the benefit of the organisation. This chapter discusses ways of appraising the macro and micro environments of a firm, along with buyer behaviour and segmentation approaches.

On completion of the chapter you should be able to explain and apply target marketing principles. To achieve this you must demonstrate the ability to:

- identify and explain macro and micro environmental factors which influence marketing decisions

- propose segmentation criteria to be used for two products in different markets

- explain how buyer behaviour affects marketing activities.

MACRO MARKETING ENVIRONMENT EXPLORED

A great deal of analysis can be undertaken in an attempt to understand the marketing (macro) environment. The example of the Ten Percenters reviewed in the case study below shows how many companies, in this case fast-growing small and medium-sized enterprises (SMEs), can exploit changes and opportunities in the environment to create and build successful businesses.

Case Study

The future prosperity of the economy rests on the ability of firms, small and large, to succeed in a competitive global economy. Creating new businesses to serve new markets is a vital aspect of this. So if new firms, which would mainly be small and medium-sized enterprises, fail to adopt best marketing and management practices, does this mean that they will fail, and what would this mean for the UK economy?

Research undertaken by Professor David Storey of Warwick Business School has focused on 7 000 companies who each have a turnover of between £5 million and £100 million per annum, selecting those that have achieved growth of at least 30 per cent per annum in the last four years. This comprises 10 per cent of the total, i.e. 700 firms, and explains the report's title 'The Ten Percenters', or the fastest growing SMEs in the UK. The report, which has been published annually since 1992, reveals that all the companies focus on niche markets that are showing rapid growth. Opportunities to explore niche markets come from changes in technology, along with social, economic and legislative changes.

The other noticeable feature is that these companies focus on customer service, depending on knowing their customers sufficiently well to be able to adapt to changing circumstances. However, the survey finds that the majority of the firms fail to apply textbook management practice, showing a range of internal organisation techniques. The companies find that flexible and adaptable approaches work well for them, allowing changes in jobs, financial control, etc., in order to move into a favourable position in the fast-expanding markets they served.

'The Ten Percenters' report reveals a high degree of volatility, with 18 per cent of companies dropping from the report listings each year. There can be various reasons for this. One reason is that a successful company may be purchased by a larger one;

some will cease to trade, and others will experience a falling away in their business. A high proportion fall by the wayside, and this suggests that many are overcome by events beyond their control. Likewise, some of the firms surveyed recognised that they were incapable of adapting to their success – as the business became larger, the informal, flexible ways no longer served them in managing a more complex organisation.

The dilemma for such companies is to maintain levels of customer service and flexibility, but at the same time provide more formal business structures that can take the firm through to the longer-term. For example, the travel company Bridge the World, founded in 1981 to provide long-haul travel, offers tailor-made holidays to customers who wish to specify particular requirements. Staff provide them with the services they request at the best possible price. With a turnover of £38 million the company is clearly successful, but it wishes to become a big player in its field. The company realises that it requires more formal management and marketing practices that will carry it through the transition into a bigger organisation. Unlike many of the companies in 'The Ten Percenters' report, Bridge the World conducts market research, obtains customer feedback on a systematic basis and appraises staff on their performance. These practices take time and effort, and cost the organisation money to implement, but the view of the senior management is that they will help to achieve long-term growth.

SMEs can apply their marketing knowledge successfully. The skill lies in helping to incorporate this into a more formal structure that works over the long term. It seems that larger firms could learn a lot from smaller firms' ability to exploit niche markets by focusing on customer satisfaction.

Questions

1. Explain why the future of the economy depends on SMEs.

2. Why do so many firms fail to exploit their early success?

The point to note from the case study is that in a dynamic and fast-changing environment a quick response is required, altering either the inputs to the organisations, such as personnel, materials and information, or the outputs, such as goods. The advantages gained by the fast-growing SMEs brought their own risks, with up to 25 per cent of companies falling off from high growth levels from one year to the next. However, the acceptance of risk brought the rewards of profitability to companies willing to seize opportunities.

All organisations have to face up to similar considerations. A failure to deal with a hostile or unfavourable environment puts companies at risk. Marketers have to assess how changes will affect them, and adjust their approach according to that assessment. In 1999 SMEs were faced with the challenge of preparing for the euro, despite the fact that the UK was not one of the original eleven countries to go ahead with the launch of the new currency. Oddly, given that Germany was one of the prime movers of the euro, UK SMEs were better prepared than their German counterparts (19 per cent well prepared compared to 8 per cent of the German firms), but it was mainly those UK firms involved in exporting and related services that had anticipated the changes. Even with the relatively better preparations of UK companies, there were 8 per cent with little or no idea how the introduction of the euro would affect them, either because they were providers only of local goods and services, or because they failed to understand what this change would mean for them. In other words, they were willing to react to changes, rather than anticipate them.

The competitive environment

Information on the competitive environment can be collected using secondary source material such as trade journals. It can also be gained by keeping an eye on competitors' changes in tactics and strategy. Two problems can arise. One is that too much information can overload the organisation; secondly, vital information on competitors' strengths and weaknesses can be difficult to find. However, despite these problems, the information available can provide a basis for analysis, leading to a thorough review of the threats and opportunities facing the organisation.

Environmental scanning and analysis focuses on the interactive process that occurs in the marketplace. Marketing decisions by one firm not only influence consumer responses, but also affect the marketing strategies of competitors through changes in products, channels, prices and promotional efforts.

Marketing efforts must be amended to suit changed circumstances. Marks & Spencers, for example, responded to a slowdown in UK sales in 1998 with an aggressive promotional and price-cutting campaign to woo back shoppers. In addition, new and more fashionable lines were adopted to make sure that stores could respond to an increased desire for fashionable products. This was a major initiative for the company, which for many years had eschewed advertising.

Companies may seem powerless to do anything other than take a passive approach to environmental changes, for example waiting for opportunities to present themselves and then taking action. But it is possible to take a more pro-active approach and seek to influence the environment. This can be done by lobbying the authorities to change a feature of the legislative and regulatory environment. In 1998, faced with increased smuggling of alcohol from France, where duty is a lot lower than in the UK, the resellers of alcohol lobbied the government to reduce excise duty to levels found in continental Europe. Another way of being pro-active is to invest in new processes that create a competitive advantage for the company.

Pro-active companies and organisations take many paths to the successful exploitation of opportunities and the countering of threats. For example, through a trade association, a company can lobby for changes that will benefit all and, at the same time, look to see if it can exploit new openings. A further example is the development of the Internet for business purposes, and the number of opportunities opened up by this change, for example the use of a website to promote a company, the development of on-line shopping, on-screen tracing of shipments and a whole range of other facilities to provide a tailored service for customers.

Analysing the environment

The marketing environment, due to its dynamic nature, requires management at every level continually to reevaluate marketing decisions in response to changing conditions. Even modest environmental shifts can affect marketing decisions. The environment can be analysed under four broad headings: economic, political/legal, technological and social/cultural. It is important to remember that although treated separately, each category can overlap with another. For example, an economic change in the shape of rising interest rates can delay investment in new equipment. Methods of reviewing the environment are best demonstrated by taking examples and collecting and analysing the date that are relevant. From here it is a short step to the recommendation of courses of action.

The economic environment

In a few instances, organisations enjoy a near or total monopoly position in the marketplace. Examples are utilities such as gas, electricity, water and cable television services, which have to accept considerable legislation from national governments of such marketing-related factors as prices, service levels and geographic coverage in exchange for exclusive rights to serve a particular group of consumers. However, such instances are rare. It is much more realistic to assume that companies will face some form of competition that will influence the decision-making process.

Broadly, markets can be classified as having:

* perfect competition
* monopoly
* oligopoly
* monopolistic competition

Perfect competition

A perfectly competitive market is never found in practice, but it acts as a yardstick against which markets may be measured. The conditions which would be found within such a market would include many sellers, none of whom could dictate price or restrict supply. Firms would not have the power to determine their prices independently because of the existence of rivals who would be willing to offer the same product at competitive prices. This would force all firms to set similar low prices, and require control over costs to ensure a profit.

Monopoly

At the other extreme to perfect competition is a monopoly, which exists when a firm has a product with no real competition or close substitutes, allowing high prices to be charged. Competitors and their products might seek entry to that market, but due to effective barriers they find this impossible. In practice, examples of monopolies are usually found in what are called natural monopoly markets, particularly utilities such as electricity and gas. Complete freedom from competition is rare, however, reducing the power to set high prices. For a monopoly to exist over a period of time, technical changes in the industry would have to be minimal. Technological advances can often change a monopoly position, for example in the telecommunications industry.

Oligopoly

An oligopoly exists where a few major sellers of a particular product dominate the market. Each understands the aims and actions of its competitors, and they often set prices at similar levels. Such companies are able to keep out competition because of the enormous capital costs of entering their industries – oligopolies are found among mass car producers, steel companies and oil producers. Price wars are avoided by oligopolies, who often use marketing tools, such as promotions and advertising, to replace price competition.

Monopolistic competition

The condition known as monopolistic competition can exist where barriers to entry are low and there are many sellers, but monopoly power can be gained for a short period of time by creating a competitive advantage. Many companies face this situation, forcing them to be aware that they need constantly to innovate to remain in touch with their customers.

Types of competition

For the marketer a knowledge of the four types of market is essential. The work of Porter on competitive forces (see page 29) provides a more managerial approach to this problem, with its emphasis on the competitive situation not only between members of the same industries, but also with reference to four other factors: the threat of new entrants, the threat of substitute products, the bargaining power of suppliers and the bargaining power of buyers.

It is important for the marketer also to understand competition as being of three types. The most direct form of competition occurs among marketers of similar products, such as among the companies that sell soap powder. A second type of competition involves products that can be substituted for one another. For example, in the transport industry, rail services compete with car rental services, airlines and bus services. In the building supply industry, cast-iron pipes compete with pipes made of synthetic materials such as polyvinyl chloride (PVC), and steel is losing ground to plastic in the production of cars. Some car manufacturers prefer plastic because it is lightweight, rustproof and is easier to modify than steel when making design changes, and this allows them to adapt quickly to market changes.

The third type of competition occurs among all organisations that compete for the consumer's attention. Traditional economic analysis views competition as a battle between companies in the same industry or between substitutable products and services. Marketers, however, accept the argument that all firms compete for a limited amount of discretionary buying power. Competition in this sense means that a car competes with a holiday and a CD competes with a film for the consumer's entertainment pound.

Because the competitive environment often determines the success or failure of a product, marketers must continually assess competitors' marketing strategies. New products offering technological advances, price reductions, special promotions or other competitive variations must be monitored and the firm's marketing mix may require adjustments to counter them. Among the first purchasers of any new products are that product's competitors. Careful analysis of its elements – physical components, performance attributes, packaging, retail price, service requirements and estimated production and marketing costs – allows marketers to forecast the product's likely competitive impact.

Other factors that make up the economic environment consist of those that influence consumer buying power and buying decisions, and impact on marketing strategies. These include the stages of the business cycle; inflation, unemployment rates, resource availability and changes in disposable income.

Business cycle

Traditionally, the economy followed a cyclical pattern consisting of four stages: boom, recession, depression (slump) and recovery (see Figure 2.1).

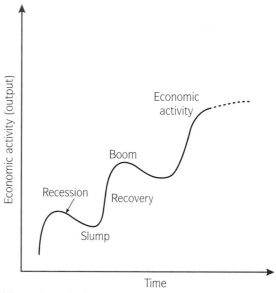

Figure 2.1 *The four phases of the trade cycle*

For marketers, an understanding of these stages will provide a general impression of the economic conditions facing the country. However, various industries, markets and even individual firms can defy the trend, either showing a decline in growth during a boom, or an expansion during a recession. Detailed research identifying marketing opportunities and good management practice are still needed, whatever the fortunes of the economy.

In each stage the typical symptoms can be identified – in times of prosperity consumer spending is brisk, often resulting from the feeling on the part of individuals that they are becoming better off, so they are willing to purchase goods from designer clothes to cars. Marketers often respond to this by expanding product lines, increasing promotional efforts, expanding distribution and raising prices, with consumers often willing to pay more for premium versions of well-known brands.

Consumer buying power declines during a recession, and may remain at a depressed level even when the economy enters the recovery period. The most recent slowdown in parts of the EU occurred during the late 1990s, with consumers shifting their buying patterns to basic, more functional products carrying a lower price, spending less on nonessential products and postponing decisions on the purchase of luxury items such as cars. During recessions, marketers consider lowering prices, reducing the scope of their product lines, and increasing promotional outlays to stimulate demand.

In the recovery stage, the economy emerges from a recession into prosperity and the consumer's purchasing power increases, but this stage is often characterised by caution. Remembering the tougher times of the recession, consumers may be more likely to save than to spend or buy on credit. As the recovery continues, consumers become more confident, buying convenience-type products and higher priced goods and services. The recovery stage is difficult for marketers, requiring them to assess how quickly consumers are making the transition from recession.

It is, of course, not only consumer behaviour that will be interest throughout the business cycle. The competitive conditions throughout the market will change, with power shifting from producers to buyers and back again, firms entering or leaving the market, and strategic alliances being created and dissolved, all of which need to be monitored and assessed.

Inflation

The rate of inflation and its trend upwards or downwards has a major impact on consumer spending. Rising price

levels result in reduced consumer buying power, although small amounts of inflation in the region of 2–3 per cent are not thought to be particularly harmful and may even be said to be beneficial. Inflation above this level tends to have a negative effect on economic prosperity. The UK has set itself the target of keeping annual inflation at 2.5 per cent or less. Consumer confidence can be dented by inflation, and it causes problems for the marketing manager as it not only introduces uncertainty into the market through its effects on production costs, marketing costs and sales forecasts, but also makes it difficult to decide the price to charge during the next budgeting period. An example of how inflation affects a society when it reaches very high levels can be seen in Russia, where inflation in the 1990s brought with it the need to take drastic action to rein back government expenditure.

Unemployment

Unemployment is defined as the situation where people who do not have jobs are actively looking for work, and this is a broader category than the numbers of people who are claiming benefit. Unemployment rises during recessions and declines in the recovery and prosperity stages of the business cycle. Like inflation, unemployment affects marketing by modifying consumer behaviour. The unemployed usually have less income to spend, and even if people are completely compensated for lost earnings by insurance or benefits, buying behaviour is likely to be affected. Instead of buying, they may choose to build up savings and, especially during periods of high inflation, become more price conscious in general.

When unemployment rates are high there are three possible outcomes, all of which are important to marketers. Consumers can elect to:

- buy now in the belief that prices will be higher later and/or that job security will go down
- alter purchasing patterns, or
- postpone certain purchases.

Another feature of the unemployment rate is that it generally lags behind changes in economic fortunes, going down even when the economy has moved into a recession and rising perhaps for eighteen months to two years into the recovery stage, thereby producing a complicated picture for the marketer.

Income

Income is another important factor in the economic environment because of its fundamental influence on consumer buying power. Studying income statistics and trends helps marketers estimate market potential and develop plans for targeting specific market segments. For example, average household incomes have grown in recent years and, coupled with a low rate of inflation during the middle to late 1990s, have resulted in increased purchasing power for millions of households. For marketers, a rise in income represents the potential for increasing overall sales. However, marketers are most interested in discretionary income, that is the amount of money people have to spend after they have paid for necessities such as food, clothing and housing.

Discretionary income varies greatly by age group and household type, with statistics showing that older couples, for example, have a significant amount of buying power compared to other groups which perhaps have higher incomes. Contributing to the buying power of the elderly are a smaller household size, the increased likelihood that spending on the education of children will be completed, and the fact that most older people no longer make mortgage payments. Based on this information, many firms are now aiming products and services at this once neglected market.

Case Study

Marketing to an affluent society

Britons' financial wealth is due to increase by £2 billion by 2005. Four million people, nearly 10 per cent of the adult population, had financial assets of more than £50 000, a figure that is set to rise to 5 million over the next decade. Forecasts predict that people will save more as the population as a whole becomes richer, helped by the inheritance of property, personal pensions and the change in behaviour that regards saving for retirement as an important activity.

As wealth increases, the problem facing the rising number of affluent people is choice – how to hold their wealth as a mixture of fixed assets with liquid or easily liquidised assets; which products and services to buy and at what price. The wide choice of financial products alone produces problems in setting prices. Pensions represent 35 per cent of the financial assets of the affluent group, and the purchase of equities (shares) or similar financial products will increase.

Increasing wealth and proliferating choices will spawn new advisory and consultancy services to provide help in finding a

way through the maze of financial products. It will not only be the affluent who wish to invest in these products – a much larger group will seek to boost their pensions. All groups will become more sophisticated consumers who wish to gain maximum advantage from what they buy.

Questions

1. What challenges will be faced in the future by companies wishing to sell to the more affluent consumer?

2. How would you characterise the profile of consumers wishing to increase their pensions?

Developing a competitive strategy

All marketers must develop an effective strategy for dealing with the competitive environment. Some compete in a broad range of markets in many areas of the world. Others specialise in particular market segments, such as those determined by geographical, age or income factors. Determining a competitive strategy involves answering three questions:

1. Should we compete?
2. If so, in what markets should we compete?
3. How should we compete?

The answer to the first question must be based on a firm's resources, objectives and expected profit potential. A firm may decide not to pursue a potentially successful venture because it doesn't match with its resources, objectives or profit expectations.

Answering the second question requires acknowledgement that the marketer has limited resources (sales personnel, advertising budgets, product development capability and the like) and that these resources must be allocated to the areas of greatest opportunity. Too many marketers have taken a 'shotgun' approach to market selection, working ineffectively in many markets rather than doing a good job in a selected few, as opposed to the 'rifle bullet' approach, which involves aiming at a chosen market segment.

To answer the third question the marketer needs to make the tactical decisions involved in setting up a comprehensive marketing strategy. Product, pricing, distribution and promotional decisions are the major elements.

The political/legal environment

Companies and organisations operate within a framework of laws and regulations. These will affect how an organisation carries on its business by regulating contracts, selling practices and product safety. Going further, the firm has to comply with laws that set a minimum wage, regulate its dealings with its employees and shareholders, and require it to control pollution. In short, laws and regulations (sometimes referred to disparagingly as red tape) affect every aspect of business.

Ignorance of or non-compliance with laws and regulations can result in fines, negative publicity and possibly expensive civil-damage suits. Considerable diligence is required in developing an understanding of the legal environment for marketing decisions. The legal framework has been constructed on a piecemeal basis, often in response to specific concerns, such as health and safety, advertising standards or environmental controls. Regulations affecting marketing have been enacted at all levels of government as well as by regulatory agencies, with an impact on all aspects of marketing decision-making – designing, labelling, packaging, distribution, advertising and promotion of products and services. To cope with the vastness, complexity and fluidity of the political/legal environment, many large firms regularly seek advice from solicitors. However, all marketers should be aware of the major regulations that affect their activities. The following are some of the major factors.

- **Regulatory forces**
  - UK government departments
  - local authorities such as district and county councils
  - self-regulatory bodies, such as the Advertising Standards Association, trade associations with codes of conduct
  - European Union: Commission, Parliament and Council of Ministers, and directives that change UK and other national laws

- **Legal forces**
  - competition legislation, affecting competition and unfair trading practices
  - Competition Commission and Office of Fair Trading
  - consumer protection legislation.

Controlling the legal/political environment

Marketers who operate within the laws and regulations as laid down by the national and local governments and regulatory bodies will be acting in a socially responsible and ethical way.

Firms can seek to influence the decision-making process through advertising and political lobbying. The regulatory and legislative authorities can be lobbied directly but are also subject to public opinion, so it pays to seek to influence opinion via promotional campaigns. Dairy farmers, for example, have formed a powerful lobby and have pooled their resources to support political parties that appear to represent the interests of their industry. However, lobbying in the interests of an industry may damage public perceptions if it aims to maintain practices that harm other groups or interests, such as poor environmental practices.

The technological environment

Technology develops mainly as a result of the knowledge derived from scientific research. This research, funded by governments and companies alike, affects the types of products made and sold. Advanced electronic appliances have moved into the home in the shape of CD players and cable and satellite TV, and into the industrial sector with the use of computer software and management information systems. Technology is changing the way we do things – at work, at home and in our leisure activities. In addition to the range and types of product on offer, technology affects the way products are made, with the use of labour-saving production equipment.

There is also a major impact on the way services are provided – high street banks use telephone banking, and shops encouraging the use of switchcards that transfer funds electronically from the customer's bank account into that of the firm, a trend that will continue with TV shopping channels and Internet shopping.

Technology has also spawned new industries: the development of lasers and of computers resulted in the creation of major industries in the past 30 years. Recent technological advances in superconductivity (the conducting of electricity with virtually no power loss) are expected to result in an annual £20 billion industry worldwide by 2003. Scientists and researchers around the globe are working to convert superconductor technology into commercial applications, as superconductors have the potential to make non-polluting electrical cars practical, to improve medical imaging systems, and to save the utilities millions of pounds, as well as enable computers to perform much more rapidly. Being aware of this scientific development is useful, but it is the ability to see the potential applications that is important.

Marketers must closely monitor the technological environment for a number of reasons. Adapting technology may be the means by which a firm remains competitive, as well as giving marketers the opportunity to improve customer service. Computer-aided design and computer-aided manufacturing speed up the process of bringing new products to market. Designing products by computer allows firms to test them thoroughly for potential problems, thus eliminating costly errors before they go into production. Computerised mapping systems give marketers instant geographical and customer information; for example the Geographical Information System (GIS) has been developed to help with decisions on the location of business. The car manufacturer General Motors creates colour-coded maps to help determine optimal dealership locations, 3M (the US company that brought us the Post-It note) uses computer-generated maps to analyse its sales territories, and the international courier company Federal Express uses digitised maps to dispatch its vans. Computer maps also help marketers in targeting markets, planning advertising, analysing competitors and distributing products.

Advances in communication technology have created computer networks that allow marketers to share information with dealers, salespeople and others in such areas as finance and research and development. Laptop computers and cellular phone technology have increased salesforce productivity, because salespeople do less paperwork and spend more time with customers and prospective clients. Technology should be viewed, therefore, as a way to help deliver the product, create new products, become more efficient and develop new services for the market. The real skill of the marketer is in turning an opportunity into a viable service that works from the customer's point of view.

The social/cultural environment

Social factors that can have an influence on companies can be grouped into three areas:

1. macro influences, such as population trends, or educational achievement standards in the workforce
2. employees – influences here involve changes in the composition of the labour market, attitudes to work, equal opportunities and so on
3. individuality – the way in which individuals spend their time and money, and how they interact with others.

A company needs to be aware of how its customers, employees, suppliers and other intermediaries may be affected by such changes.

Marketers, through a consideration of demography and culture, need to be sensitive to the current composition and structure of societies and the forces for change that will impact on many aspects of marketing.

Demography

Demographic studies look at population structure and the trends within it such as age distribution, family groupings, rate of growth/decline, and so on. In the UK the population has reached 60 million, but in recent years its composition has changed. The population is ageing, with the number of people living beyond 65 increasing. The numbers of young people becoming available for work declined in the 1980s and early 1990s, encouraging companies to take on older workers, such as women returners, who wish to re-enter the job market after they have raised a family. Numbers of people in dependent groups are set to rise, for example the number of pensioners is increasing, which will put an increased burden on long-term care provisions.

Taking these trends seriously, UK governments have started to encourage workers to prepare for their retirement by taking out private pensions, thereby reducing current discretionary income, but at the same time providing opportunities for the financial services industry. Demographic trends provide a useful background against which to plan for the introduction of new products and services.

Culture

Culture can be defined as the sum total of the beliefs, knowledge, attitudes of mind and customs to which people are exposed in their society. Individuals learn a language, acquire values and learn habits of behaviour and thought through contact with a culture. Cultural influences create the following:

- beliefs and values, which shape attitudes and create tendencies for individuals, groups and societies to behave in certain ways
- customs, which are accepted ways of behaving in given situations
- artefacts, the tools designed for the well-being of people and including products as well as art, buildings and technology
- rituals, including weddings, religious services, sporting events and legal procedures.

The need to understand this in an international context is important. If a firm is to market its goods abroad, then it must understand the different ways in which promotion, packaging and other forms of communication will be received. There are many examples of companies using images, colours or wording that has offended the target market, from ignorance of the cultural context. This also matters in the 'home' market. Ethnic groups with their varying cultures will often feel that they are excluded from participating in a market, as communication does not seem to be directed at them. Culture is composed of various characteristics, which are purposeful, learned, shared, cumulative and dynamic. These issues are reviewed in more detail later in the chapter when discussing consumer behaviour.

Identifying trends and understanding how culture will impact on company strategy is an important ingredient for success. All companies can buy copies of trends surveys, undertake desk research and keep an eye open for changes in society. The changing variables affect the way consumers react to different products and marketing practices. What may be unacceptable today may be most desirable in tomorrow's marketplace. Products that were once difficult to promote openly – such as condoms and feminine hygiene products – are now commonly advertised. A change in national attitudes towards the overt representation and discussion of sex has altered the way some firms advertise their products.

Ecological factors

Genetically modified foods (GM foods) have been praised as a scientific breakthrough that will increase yields, reduce the use of pesticides and provide valuable extra income for countries that, because of climatic conditions, struggle to produce enough food for their increasing populations. Marketers have attempted to persuade consumers of the benefits of the new products that have been developed, but at least in the UK this has not been successful. Strong

resistance from environmental campaigners and consumer groups has brought about a re-think as to whether there is enough scientific evidence that these new crops and food products are safe. Supermarkets who were selling products without adequate information being given to customers have had to improve labelling to draw their customers' attention to items containing GM ingredients, and even withdraw products.

Similarly, restaurants have started to look more carefully at the ingredients they are using, and in some cases have decided to inform customers which items on the menu have GM content.

Marketers are expected to provide customers with what they require, and in so doing help to increase profits for their organisation and prosperity for all. In many instances, however, they are accused of covering up the true nature of a product – in this case obscuring the fact that GM crops have not been proven safe – or ignoring the requirements of consumers to be properly informed about how a product is manufactured, how much pollution may have resulted, and so on. In all areas where marketers operate, from air transportation through to bank services, there are concerns that operations and business strategies may be unduly harming the resources of the planet and thereby damaging health and welfare. With air transportation, the burning of fossil fuels can add to the greenhouse effect; with banks, money can be lent to oppressive government regimes or to organisations that fell the rain forest or pollute the rivers.

Consumers care about these things as they favour a protected environment, clean air and sustainable forests. All aspects of marketing involve ecological concerns. The more obvious include the recyclability of products or the materials that package them. Can the plastics, boxes, paper, etc. be recycled? If they have to be buried or burnt, what will that do to the environment? Marketing, like other business operations, is required to consider where it might achieve reductions in its effect on the environment. This is, of course, a wise approach, as EU directives, changes in national law and international pressure all call for a response. But there is also a need to think in a more pro-active way, to see new products and markets emerging and respond appropriately. New needs constantly emerge for practices and products that protect the environment, and marketers can play their role in this.

A failure to monitor, understand and suggest new strategies is as dangerous for companies with regard to this aspect of the external environment as with any other. This is still an area where mistakes often occur, and where companies are caught out, as its impact is often overlooked, managers receive little training and new campaigns can build up very quickly.

TASK

Why is it important that a marketer understands the influence of the macro-environment of marketing decisions?

THE MICRO ENVIRONMENT

The micro environment includes all the factors that will have a direct impact on a firm and its operations. It includes internal aspects of the organisation such as corporate culture, all of which will have an impact on marketing strategy.

Assessing competitors' strategies

Reviewing an organisation's position has to be undertaken in relation to its competitors, either when looking at the market or in relation to the competition for resources. This

can be achieved through a focused review of the competitive environment, and the five-forces model developed by Porter provides a structure for this process (see Figure 2.2). Porter's forces are summarised below.

Figure 2.2 *Competitive forces*

Threat of entry

This depends on the effectiveness, or lack of effectiveness, of barriers to entry. The problem with the interpretation of this information is that it is often undertaken adopting an historical or static view of 'how things are now', rather than a dynamic view of how changes will influence business in the future.

Some of the main barriers to entry are associated with economies of scale, or the capital required to enter an industry. Others involve the regulatory regime or government policy, as can be seen in the telecommunication market in the USA and UK. Further barriers can be created by an effective strategy that has produced a clear preference for an organisation's goods and services. To compete against this established preference would take a great amount of investment, for which a new entrant may not have the financial resources or the nerve.

Power of buyers and suppliers

These two forces may be viewed as one issue, as both groups can have a major impact on strategy. A striking example is the power of supermarkets in the UK, which over the past two decades have had a significant impact on the prices paid to and the quality expected from suppliers, and for which many suppliers were unprepared. So great is the influence of supermarkets that they provide their own responses to major food problems such as the BSE crisis in the 1990s, when they were responsible for introducing quality schemes for beef throughout the industry.

The impact of supplier power can be particularly strong when there are few of them, when the brand which they supply is popular in the marketplace, and when switching from one supplier to another would be costly.

Likewise, buyer power can be high when there are only a few major purchasers in the market, when alternative sources of supply are available, or there is a threat of backward integration (acquiring control of suppliers) from the buyers.

It has been argued that the UK, unlike Japan, has a competitive situation in the field of supplier–buyer links. Some notable exceptions, such as Marks & Spencer's close relationship with its suppliers, tend to prove the rule that competition rather than cooperation can be most beneficial. Since foreign investment in the UK has increased, however, the move to create supplier networks, particularly in the automotive industry, has been significant.

Threat of substitutes

This threat can come form various sources, such as the substitution of one product for another (such as an electronic organiser for the paper-based personal organiser) or from the competition for alternative ways to spend household income, for example when the purchase of a car is balanced against a holiday or a major home improvement. The key issues here are how far the threat compromises the freedom of the company to set its prices or introduce a new product.

The ease of switching is also an important factor. At one time, for example, moving a mortgage from one financial institution to another was rare because switching costs were high and the advantages of doing so were small. With the deregulation of the finance industry, including retail banking, this is now less often the case, and switching costs have fallen.

Competitive rivalry

Rivalry is often greatest when an industry is mature, or when a protected and highly regulated industry is privatised and competition is first introduced. If entry barriers are low and substitutes increase, then rivalry will be intense. Equally, with mature markets, one firm may push to gain market leadership, and if excess capacity exists and exit costs are high, competition may ensue.

If each of the five forces detailed above is viewed as a separate issue, the overall picture may be lost. Sound judgement will have to be exercised in analysing the principal forces at work for the organisation. Competitors, assuming that they undertake a similar review of rivalry, are also attempting to deal with a competitive environment. It is vital to know about the objectives they have, the strengths they possess and their strategic approach.

Stakeholders

The concept of stakeholders is fully discussed in Chapter 14 (pages 341–349). As well as the obvious stakeholder groups such as employees, suppliers, customers, bankers and local residents, there are interest groups also known as 'publics' whose opinion will have an impact on a company or industry. Environmental groups such as Greenpeace campaign against actions by companies that they regard as harmful to wildlife and the natural environment. Many other groups have specific agendas. For example, the campaign to reduce third world debt has targeted banks; peace groups focus on arms sales to repressive regimes; while others seek the banning of genetically modified (GM) foods.

Interest groups often overlap with the trade unions who represent the employees of a particular company, and the local community where a factory or office is based. For example the inquiry into the Terminal 5 development at Heathrow had to take account of the views of local residents as well as environmentalists about the increase in noise pollution that would result from the 50 per cent increase in capacity proposed for the airport.

The interests of consumers play a vital role in company decision-making, and must be effectively addressed by the managers of a company if it is to avoid harmful consequences and bad publicity. It is obvious that other stakeholders, such as the organisation's owners (shareholders), and banks who have financed the company with loans, all have a fundamental influence on the freedom of an organisation to make decisions. Marketers need to be conscious of the implications of their decisions for all these groups, and to be aware that consulting with or providing information to all the various types of stakeholders is often vital for success. Oil companies such as Shell and BP now have dialogues with environmental groups and even employ their members as consultants.

MARKET SEGMENTATION

Having considered environmental variables it is important to look at market segmentation approaches.

Before a marketing strategy can be implemented, the marketer must identify, evaluate and select a target market. A market is made up of people and institutions, but they alone do not constitute a market. It requires not only people or institutions and the willingness to buy, but also purchasing power and the authority to buy.

Types of market

Products are often classified as either consumer goods or industrial goods. Consumer goods are products purchased by the ultimate consumer for personal use, whereas industrial goods are products purchased for use either directly or indirectly in the production of other goods or services or for resale. A similar distinction can be used for services. Most products purchased by individual consumers – books, CDs and clothes, for example – are consumer goods. Rubber and raw cotton, however, are generally purchased by manufacturers and are therefore classified as industrial goods. Rubber is used in many products, such as by Goodyear for tyres, while textile manufacturers convert raw cotton into cloth.

Sometimes the same product is destined for different uses. Spark plugs purchased for the family car constitute consumer goods, but spark plugs purchased by Rover for use on its assembly line are industrial goods, since they become part of another product destined for resale. Some marketers use the term commercial goods to refer to industrial products that are not used directly in producing other goods. The key to proper classification of goods is determining who is the initial purchaser and the reasons for the purchase.

The role of market segmentation

Selecting an appropriate target market depends on a careful review of just who the firm is trying to reach. For example, the car manufacturer that decides to produce and market a single model to satisfy everyone will encounter seemingly endless problems about such variables as the number of doors, the type of transmission, colour, styling and engine size. In its attempt to satisfy everyone, the firm may be forced to compromise in each of these areas and, as a result, may discover that it satisfies no one very well. On the other hand, firms that appeal to particular segments – the performance-oriented market, the prestige-conscious market, the larger family market, and so on – may capture most of the total market by satisfying the specific needs of each segment. This process of dividing the total market into several relatively homogeneous groups is called **market segmentation**, and it is used by both profit-oriented and non-profit organisations. Marketing mixes are adjusted to meet the needs of specified market segments.

Criteria for effective segmentation

Market segmentation cannot be used in all cases. To be effective, segmentation must meet the following basic requirements.

* The market segments must be measurable in terms of both purchasing power and size.
* Market segments must be sufficiently large to be potentially profitable.
* The number of segments must match the firm's marketing capabilities.

If one or more of the above requirements is missing, the marketer should reassess any proposed market segmentation strategy.

Segmenting consumer markets

Market segmentation results from the isolation of factors that distinguish a certain group of consumers from the overall market. These characteristics – age, sex, geographic location, income and expenditure patterns, and population size and mobility, among others – are vital factors in the success of the overall marketing strategy. For example, toy manufacturers study not only birth-rate trends but shifts in income and expenditure patterns. Colleges and universities are affected by such factors as the numbers of pupils finishing school, changing attitudes towards the value of further education, and the increasing enrolment of older adults.

The four commonly used bases for segmenting consumer markets are: **geographic segmentation**; **demographic segmentation**; **psychographic segmentation**; and **benefit segmentation**. These segmentation bases can be important to marketing strategies, provided they are significantly related to differences in buying behaviour.

Geographic segmentation

A logical starting point in market segmentation is to examine population characteristics. Geographic segmentation – the dividing of an overall market into homogeneous groups on the basis of population location – has been used for hundreds of years.

Consumers in different geographic locations are subject to varying conditions in terms of climate, terrain, natural resources and population density. Markets can be divided into regions because one or more of the geographical variables causes differences to appear from one region to another. A company that sells products throughout the EU will, for example, need to use different languages in the labelling of its goods.

City size can be an important segmentation variable. Some marketers want to focus their efforts on cities of a certain size. For example, major petroleum retailers such as Esso and Shell have traffic-density thresholds, below which they perceive a local market not to be viable. It is therefore quite common, particularly in villages and small towns in rural areas, to see local petroleum retailing dominated by independent garage owners and smaller petroleum companies.

Geographic segmentation is useful only when differences in preference and purchase patterns for a product emerge along regional lines. Moreover, geographic subdivisions of the overall market tend to be rather large and often too heterogeneous for effective segmentation without careful consideration of additional factors. In such cases, several segmentation variables may need to be used. An approach used by ACORN (A Classification of Residential Neighbourhood) uses information taken from the UK census, allowing individuals to be grouped together by the use of 40 variables including household size, cars per household, family size and so on. Customers can be profiled according to the area in which they live, and reached via the postcode for that area. This provides a very sophisticated marketing tool that can overcome some of the problems associated with broad geographic segmentation.

Demographic segmentation

The most common approach to market segmentation is demographic segmentation, the division of consumer groups according to demographic variables such as age, sex, income, occupation, education, household size, life style and stage in the family life cycle. Typically these are used to identify market segments and develop appropriate marketing mixes. Demographic variables are used in market segmentation for three reasons:

- they are easy to identify and measure
- they are associated with the sale of many products and services
- they are typically referred to in describing the audiences of advertising media, so that media buyers and others can easily pinpoint the desired market.

Vast quantities of data are available to assist marketers in segmenting potential markets on a demographic basis. The demographic variables most often used as bases for segmenting markets are described below.

Segmenting by sex. Sex is a traditional variable for segmenting certain markets because many products, notably magazines, toiletries and clothing, are sex specific. In recent years, however, more industries have discovered marketing opportunities for sex segmentation. Research by American Express revealed that women viewed credit cards as a male-specific product. In an effort to expand its cardholder base, American Express focused on women as the most promising target market, initiating an advertising campaign to attract new female cardholders. The approach succeeded. Now almost 50 per cent of new American Express cardholders are women, compared to 29 per cent when the campaign began.

Segmenting by age. Many firms identify market segments on the basis of age, and some market their products and services to specific age groups. Firms that market similar products for a wide variety of age groups often develop different marketing approaches for each group.

Age distribution and projected changes in age groups are important to marketers because consumer wants and needs differ among these groups. Markets for some products shrink when numbers decline in certain age groups. The young adult population aged 18–25 decreased during the 1980s, a trend that did not reverse itself until the mid-1990s. For colleges and universities, this decline resulted in a change from a seller's market to a buyer's market. It has forced most institutions to market their services in order to compete for a smaller number of students. Running counter to this, however, is an increase in the number of the under-25 age group who wish to enter higher education.

Segmenting by family life cycle stage. The family life cycle is the process of family formation and dissolution. Using this concept, the marketing planner combines the family characteristics of age, marital status and number and ages of children to develop a marketing strategy.

A five-stage family life cycle has been created with several subcategories. The major stages are young singles under 35 years, young marrieds under 35 years without children, other young people under 35 years including divorced people with and without children, young marrieds with children, middle-agers between 35 and 64 years, and older people aged 65 and over. The behavioural characteristics and buying patterns of people in each life cycle stage often vary considerably. Young singles have relatively few financial burdens, tend to be early purchasers of new fashion items, are recreation oriented and make frequent purchases of basic kitchen equipment, cars and holidays. In contrast, young marrieds with small children tend to be heavy purchasers of baby products, homes, television sets, toys, washing machines and tumble dryers. Their liquid assets tend to be relatively low, and they are more likely to watch television than are young singles or young marrieds without children. The empty-nest households in the middle age and older categories with no dependent children tend to have more disposable income, more time for recreation, self-education and travel, and have more than one member in the labour force more often than their full-nest counterparts with younger children. Similar differences in behavioural and buying patterns are evident in other stages of the family life-cycle.

Analysis of life cycle stages often gives better results than reliance on single variables such as age. The buying patterns of a 25-year-old bachelor are very different from those of a father of the same age. A family of five headed by parents in their forties is a more likely prospect for a set of encyclopaedias than a childless, 40-year-old divorced person.

Marketing planners can use published data such as census reports and divide their markets into more homogeneous segments than would be possible if they were analysing single variables. Such data are available for each classification of the family life cycle.

The Sagacity approach, developed in 1981, combines life cycle, income and socio-economic group information to enhance understanding of what happens to individuals as they pass through the various stages of their lives, noting how aspirations, behaviour and consumption of goods and services alter as they pass through these stages. This approach was welcomed by marketers, who found it to be of immense value in honing their family life cycle segmentation techniques.

Segmenting by household type. The size of the typical household of today is shrinking, and there are several reasons for this trend: lower fertility rates; the tendency of young people to postpone marriage or never marry; the increasing tendency among younger couples to limit the number of children or have no children; the ease and frequency of divorce; and the ability and desire of many young singles and the elderly to live alone.

The single-person household has emerged as an important market segment as it is the customer for single-serve food products, such as Campbell's Soup for One and Green Giant's single-serve casseroles and vegetables, as well as Sainsbury's and Marks & Spencer's offerings for the single person. There are also differences in spending patterns between men and women who live alone, with a larger share of women's budgets going on buying gifts, while men spend more on entertainment, food and alcohol. Because men eat meals away from home more often, they spend twice as much as women on food outside the home.

Historically, about 5 per cent of British people never marry, but that number is expected to increase. The proportion of never-married men and women in their late twenties and early thirties has more than doubled between 1970 and today. Specialised services, such as single travel agencies and dating services, cater for them. In some cases, the buying habits of singles are similar to those of married couples. For example, an increasing number of singles are buying homes and furnishing them with fine china, silver and crystal. To attract never-married customers, many major department stores have changed their traditional bridal services to 'gift' services.

Finally, one of the most highly sought after market segments is households of two adults with no children. With a high level of disposable income, such couples are big buyers of gourmet foods, luxury items and travel.

Segmenting by income and expenditure patterns. Earlier we defined markets as purchasing power. A common method of segmenting the consumer market is on the basis of income. Fashionable speciality shops stocking designer clothing make most of their sales to high-income shoppers. Other retailers aim to appeal to middle income groups. Still others focus almost exclusively on low-income shoppers.

Household expenditures can be divided into two categories: basic purchases of essential household needs, and other purchases made at the discretion of household members. About one-third of British households have substantial discretionary income.

Psychographic segmentation

Although geographic and demographic segmentation have been the primary bases for dividing consumer and industrial markets into homogeneous segments for use as target markets, marketers have long recognised the need for fuller, more lifelike portraits of consumers. While traditionally used variables such as age, sex, family life cycles, income, population size and location are important in segmentation, individual life styles of potential customers may prove equally significant.

Life style refers to the consumer's habits and mode of living. Consumers' life styles are regarded as composites of their individual psychological make-ups – their needs, motives, perceptions and attitudes. A life style also bears the mark of many other influences, such as that of a consumer's reference groups, culture, social class and family members.

In recent years, a new technique that promises to elicit more meaningful bases for segmentation has been developed and has become the main technique used to measure life style. **Psychographic segmentation** is generally defined as the development of psychological profiles of different consumers, derived from the responses of people asked to agree or disagree with certain statements. A collection of several hundred of these statements has been developed, dealing with the activities, interests and opinions of the respondents.

Behavioural segmentation

This type of segmentation looks at consumers' behaviour patterns with regard to products – they may be frequent or infrequent purchasers, show loyalty to a particular brand, or regularly switch brands.

Benefit segmentation

Benefit segmentation focuses on attributes such as product usage rates and the benefits derived from a product. In other words, it is the division of a market according to the benefits the consumer wants from the product. These factors may reveal important bases for pinpointing prospective target markets. One analysis of 34 segmentation studies indicated that benefit analysis provided the best predictor of brand use, consumption level and product type selected in 51 per cent of the cases. Many marketers now consider benefit segmentation the most useful approach to classifying markets.

Usage rates. Marketing managers may divide potential segments into two categories: users and non-users. Users may be divided into heavy, moderate and light. By identifying heavy users, marketers can target advertising and promotions at this group in an attempt to build customer loyalty. Several firms have adopted the airlines' frequent-flyer concept in rewarding heavy users with free trips, discounts on car hire and hotel accommodation, while book publishers divide their market into those who buy more than five books a year, those who buy six to fifteen, and so on. Sales analysis is a common method of identifying heavy users, and much of this information can be obtained from internal records. Marketers use databases to analyse patterns and then customise individual mailing lists for target groups.

Product benefits. Market segments may also be identified by the benefit buyers expect to derive from a product or brand. Where differences among competing brands are slight, a firm may introduce a brand with a new benefit that appeals to a certain market segment. According to one study, 55 per cent of consumers see few differences among washing powders, most of which are promoted as making clothes clean and bright, and smelling fresh and fragrant. In its search for a new benefit, Lever Brothers decided to target consumers concerned about body odour in clothes. Based on this benefit, Lever Brothers formulated Surf, a washing powder with odour-tackling properties, which quickly became one of the most popular washing powders in the UK.

Discussion point

1. How could the market for a household appliance such as a dishwasher be segmented?

2. How could the market for a financial product, such as the ISA, be segmented?

Segmenting industrial markets

The concept of segmentation is also used in industrial marketing.

Geographic segmentation is useful in industries whose customers are concentrated in specific geographic locations. It might also be useful where markets are limited to just a few locations.

Product segmentation is often used in the industrial market, because industrial users tend to have much more precise product specifications than do ultimate consumers. Thus industrial products often fit narrower market segments than consumer products. Designing industrial goods or services to meet buyer requirements is a form of market segmentation.

End-use application segmentation refers to examining the precise way in which the industrial purchaser will use the product.

Regardless of how it is carried out, market segmentation is as vital to industrial marketing as it is to consumer marketing.

Discussion point

How can market segmentation be applied to business applications of computer software?

Industrial classification

Marketers have access to large amounts of information concerning industrial markets, from which they can gain knowledge to assist them with the segmentation exercise. Much information is available from government and industrial sources, and can provide assistance with estimating the number of potential customers, locating them and estimating how much they are likely to spend.

The Standard Industrial Classification (SIC) system is a vital source of information that can assist with segmentation. The SIC groupings are devised by the Office for National Statistics, and each division is subdivided into classes, as shown in Figure 2.3. These classes are further divided into groups, and then into activities. The amount of information and market intelligence available from such a source is increasing, and it is becoming more freely accessible in government publications.

Information available for the SIC divisions will include the number of establishments, people working in each division, exports, growth rates, and the location of the main centres. On its own, however, the SIC data is not enough to form the basis of a subtle segmentation strategy. It needs to be refined to identify how customers can be reached and which ones are worth targeting.

Additional help with this can be drawn from input–output data, which identifies industries purchasing materials (inputs) from other industries in order to produce their output. Collating the SIC data with input–output information would show the business-to-business marketer where the potential buyers are, by town/city or county. From here, names and addresses of potential customers can be identified from business-to-business directories found in public libraries, which contain information on companies, their SIC classification, address, sales figures and so on.

Having undertaken this level of research, the potential of each customer can be gauged, and decisions have to be made about which specific firms to target. It is important at this stage to look closely at the benefits sought by potential customers, i.e. to understand the end use of the product.

Information on the size and value of an industry gleaned from SIC data will be a valuable tool for the marketer, not just as a one-off activity, but to identify trends over time that help the organisation gain a deeper understanding of the industry and its customers – a vital part of segmentation and targeting.

TASK

Why is segmentation an important part of marketing strategy?

DIVISION 0 – AGRICULTURE, FORESTRY AND FISHING

Farming and horticulture

Forestry

Commercial sea and inland fishing

DIVISION 1 – ENERGY AND WATER SUPPLY INDUSTRIES

Coal-mining and manufacture of solid fuels

Extraction of mineral oil and natural gas

Production and distribution of electricity, gas and other forms of energy

DIVISION 2 – EXTRACTION OF MINERALS AND ORES, MANUFACTURE OF METALS, MINERAL PRODUCTS AND CHEMICALS

Metal manufacture

Extraction of stone, clay, sand and gravel

Manufacture of non-metallic mineral products

Chemical industry (includes paints, varnishes and inks, pharmaceutical products, some perfumes, etc.)

DIVISION 3 – METAL GOODS, ENGINEERING AND VEHICLE INDUSTRIES

Foundries

Mechanical engineering

Electrical and electronic engineering

Manufacture of motor vehicles and parts

Instrument engineering

DIVISION 4 – OTHER MANUFACTURING INDUSTRIES

Food, drinks and tobacco manufacturing industries

Textile industry

Manufacture of leather and leather goods

Timber and wooden furniture industries

Manufacture of paper and paper products, printing and printing products

Processing of rubber and plastics

DIVISION 5 – CONSTRUCTION

Construction and repairs

Demolition work

Civil engineering

DIVISION 6 – DISTRIBUTION, HOTELS AND CATERING, REPAIRS

Wholesale distribution

Retail distribution

Hotel and catering (restaurants, cafés and other eating places, public houses and hotel trade)

Repair of consumer goods and vehicles

DIVISION 7 – TRANSPORT AND COMMUNICATION

Railways and other inland transport

Air and sea transport

Support services to transport

Postal services and telecommunications

DIVISION 8 – BANKING, FINANCE, INSURANCE, BUSINESS SERVICES AND LEASING

Banking and finance

Insurance

Business services

Renting of movables

Owning and dealing in real estate

DIVISION 9 – OTHER SERVICES

Public administration, national defence and social security

Sanitary services

Education

Medical and other health services, veterinary services

Other services provided to the general public

Recreational services and other cultural services

Personal services (laundries, hairdressing and beauty parlours)

Domestic services

Diplomatic representation, international organisations, allied armed forces

Figure 2.3 *Standard Industrial Classification groupings*

The market segmentation decision process

So far we have discussed the various segmentation bases used by consumer and industrial marketers. In both types of markets, marketing managers follow a systematic five-step decision process.

Stage 1: Select market segmentation bases

The process begins when a firm seeks bases on which to segment markets. Segmentation bases should be selected so that each segment contains customers who respond differently. In some cases, targeting this group is difficult to achieve. Consider the marketer seeking to reach the consumer segment that is over 50 years of age. Saturday evening television commercials can reach this group, but much of the expenditure may be wasted, since the other major viewing group at this time is teenagers.

Stage 2: Develop relevant profiles for each segment

Once segments have been identified, marketers should seek to understand the customers in each segment. Segmentation bases provide some insight into the nature of customers, but typically not enough on which to base the decisions that marketing managers must make in order to match more accurately customer needs with marketing offers. Characteristics that explain the similarities among customers within each segment, as well as account for differences between segments, must be identified. The task at this stage is therefore to develop profiles of the typical customer in each segment. Such profiles might include life style patterns, attitudes towards product attributes and brands, brand preferences, product-use habits, geographic locations and demographic characteristics.

Stage 3: Forecast market potential

In this stage, market segmentation and market opportunity analysis continue in order to produce a forecast of market potential within each segment. Market potential sets the upper limit on the demand that can be expected from a segment, and therefore determines maximum sales potential.

This step should constitute a preliminary decision point for management as to whether to proceed, since it must determine whether the total sales potential in each segment is sufficient to justify further analysis. Some segments will be screened out because they represent insufficient potential demand; others will be sufficiently attractive for the analysis to continue.

Stage 4: Forecast probable market share

Once full market potential has been estimated, the proportion of demand that the firm may capture must be determined. This step requires a forecast of probable market share. Market share forecasts depend on both an analysis of competitors' positions in target segments and the specific marketing strategy and tactics designed to serve these segments. Moreover, design of marketing strategy and tactics determines the expected level of costs involved in tapping the potential demand in each segment.

Stage 5: Select specific market segments

The information, analysis and forecasts accumulated through the entire market segmentation decision process allow management to assess the potential for achieving company goals and to justify the selection of one or more segments. For example, demand forecasts, when combined with cost projects, are used to determine the profit and return on investment that can be expected for each segment.

Analysis of marketing strategy and tactics will also determine whether they have been matched with the intended corporate image and reputation, as well as with the unique organisational capabilities that may exist for serving a segment. These assessments will, in turn, help management select specific segments as the target markets.

At this point in the analysis, the costs and benefits to be considered are not only financial, but include many organisational and environmental factors that are difficult to measure but may be critical. For example, the firm may not have enough experienced personnel to launch a successful attack in a new market, despite clear indications of potential financial success. Similarly, a firm with 80 per cent of the market may face legal problems with the regulatory authorities if it increases its market concentration. The assessment of both financial and non-financial factors is a difficult but vital final step in the decision process.

BUYER BEHAVIOUR

Before examining buyer behaviour, it is important in each case to establish who the buyer actually is. First, a distinction must be made between the **customers** for a product or service and the **consumers** of it – the person who buys is not always the person who uses a product or service. An example is the fact that most men's underwear is bought by women for their partners and sons. Here, the customer is the woman but the consumer is her partner or son.

Equally, we tend to think of a customer as an individual, but a purchase decision often involves two or more people. The group of people who have input into the decision is known as the **decision-making unit** or DMU. This is particularly relevant in organisational markets, but an example commonly found among ordinary consumers is the purchase of a family holiday or car – all members of the family, including young children, may influence the decision, as may friends and colleagues who are asked for information and advice.

Consumer behaviour

When a family is purchasing household furniture, or is planning a home improvement, who is the key decision-maker? When a DIY tool is being purchased to carry out the home improvement what factors will affect the purchase of this item? Women buy cars as much as men, but selling to women has been a problem for many in the car retail trade as the salesforce (mainly men) make certain assumptions about what interests buyers. Assumptions and bias can also cause problems when marketing to ethnic groups, who are often overlooked in the way a product is advertised and promoted.

Marketers need to understand the reasons for consumer purchase decisions, and the study of consumer behaviour is therefore a crucial issue. The main focus of research has been to try to understand the relationship between marketing stimuli and consumer responses.

Marketers need to determine what happens in the buyer's decision-making process or 'black box', so-called because marketers know very little of what goes on in the consumer's mind before, during and after making a purchase. Essentially, the marketer's aim is to understand how the various marketing stimuli are perceived in the black box and changed into buying responses.

A study of consumer behaviour involves looking at the role of motivation, personality, life style, social class, culture and subcultures, groups and reference groups, family and age and life cycles of consumers.

Cultural and social factors

There are broad forces which exert influence on buying behaviour. They may be grouped into the following categories:

- culture and subcultures
- role and status
- group influences and reference groups
- family influences
- social class.

Culture can be defined as the complex of values, ideas, attitudes, and other meaningful symbols that serve humans to communicate, interpret, and evaluate as members of society. It is the learned and handed-down way of life that gives each society its unique mix of values. The symbols of culture may be tangible (products, housing, tools,etc.) or intangible (values, attitudes, religion, laws, etc.), which means that culture has an influence on every aspect of our lives.

Cultures are not homogeneous entities giving universal values. Within each culture are numerous subcultures – subgroups with their own distinct modes of behaviour. Culture in countries such as the UK is composed of significant subcultures based on such factors as race, nationality, age, religion, rural versus urban location and geographical distribution. For example, nationality groups such as the West Indian, Irish, Chinese, Indian and Pakistani are found within the larger UK community, and they have distinct ethnic attitudes, values, tastes and interests. Marketers need to recognise these subcultural differences as they affect the type of products bought, and how the product can be successfully advertised and distributed. These groups constitute important market segments for marketers. Even geographic differences can constitute market segments – in the UK the geographical divide is normally between the north and south, and there are some distinct differences in purchase behaviour.

The earliest group experience for children is their membership in the family. From this group they seek total satisfaction of their psychological and social needs. As they grow older, they join other groups – play groups, school groups, athletic groups and friendship groups, etc. – from which they acquire both status and role.

Status is the relative position of any individual member in a group. **Roles** are what the other members of the group expect of individuals within it. Some groups (such as scouts and guides) are formal and others (such as friendship groups) are informal. Both types of groups supply each member with status and roles; in doing so, they influence that person's activities.

A **reference group** can be defined as a group that influences a person's values, attitudes and behaviour. Many individuals have several reference groups, such as close friends, church groups, football teams, family, religious and professional groups. The reference group serves as a source of information for an individual's buying patterns, with word of mouth often proving more effective than advertising in the mass media.

Consumers usually try to keep their purchase behaviour in line with what they perceive to be the values of their reference groups. The extent of reference group influence varies widely. In order for the influence to be great, two factors must be present.

- The item must be one that can be seen and identified by others.
- The item must be conspicuous – it must stand out, be unusual and be a brand or product that not everyone owns.

Reference group influence would be significant in the decision to buy a Rolex watch for example, but would have little or no impact on the decision to purchase a loaf of bread.

Of all the small groups, the **family** perhaps exerts the most significant and enduring influence on buyer behaviour. Most people are members of at least two families during their lifetimes – the family into which they are born (family of orientation) and the one they eventually form as they marry and have children (family of marriage or procreation).

Although an infinite variety of roles can be played in household decision-making, four role categories are often used:

- autonomic, in which an equal number of decisions is made by each partner
- husband dominant
- wife dominant
- syncratic, in which most decisions are jointly made by both partners

The role of children in purchasing decisions develops as they grow older. Children's early influence is generally centred around toys that are on the birthday or Christmas wish list, and the choice of cereal brands. Younger children are also important to marketers of fast-food restaurants.

As children grow older, they increasingly influence clothing purchases made on their behalf. Teenagers today buy more expensive items such as computers, bicycles, portable radio/cassette players and watches. Instead of spending their money going to the cinema, almost half now rent videotapes to watch at home.

A major determinant of consumer buying behaviour and perceptions is **social class**, and this is readily acknowledged by marketers. The division of society into social groups or social classes is known as social stratification. This is a process in which members of society are ranked into higher or lower positions of status. The criteria for establishing people into different groups or classes varies for different societies. In most European countries, including the UK, a number of criteria are considered in combination, ranging across income, education, occupation, wealth, tradition, family and other factors, and changes to these are regularly reviewed.

Case Study

1998 class classification system: Office for National Statistics

In 1998 the Office for National Statistics (ONS) changed the UK class classification system to reflect changes in the work that people undertake. The old system (A, B, C1, C2, D and E) described four out of the six classes as working class (C1–E). The new system has the population roughly split into 50 per cent middle class and 50 per cent working class. It has seven classes for those in work (see Figure 2.4) and one for the unemployed and those on benefits. In the top class are senior executives and others in a service relationship with their employer. These workers possess a salary, long-term contract, often a pension plan and a large degree of control over how they organise their jobs. At the bottom are workers who are in a labour contract with their employers. This is often a short-term contract, with pay related to time put in or piece rates, with no perks and no job security.

Questions

1. Why use a social classification system? What can it suggest about consumer behaviour?

2. What were the likely reasons for making these changes?

The role of social class in determining consumer behaviour continues to be a source of debate in the field of marketing. Some have argued against using social class as a market segmentation variable. Others doubt whether income and social class can be combined. One study revealed that social class was the best segmentation

1 **Higher managerial professional occupations:**
a Employers and managers in large organisations:
   Company directors
   Corporate managers
   Police inspectors
   Bank managers
   Senior civil servants
   Military officers
b Higher professionals:
   Doctors
   Barristers and solicitors
   Clergy
   Librarians
   Social workers
   Teachers

2 **Associated professionals:**
   Nurses and midwives
   Journalists
   Actors and musicians
   Prison officers
   Police
   Soldiers (NCO and below)

3 **Intermediate occupations:**
   Clerks
   Secretaries
   Driving instructors
   Computer operators
   Telephone fitters

4 **Small employers and own account workers:**
   Publicans
   Playgroup leaders
   Farmers
   Taxi drivers
   Bus inspectors
   Window cleaners
   Painter and decorators

5 **Lower supervisory, craft and related occupations:**
   Printers
   Plumbers
   Butchers
   TV engineers
   Train drivers

6 **Semi-routine occupations:**
   Shop assistants
   Traffic wardens
   Cooks
   Bus drivers
   Hairdressers
   Postal workers

7 **Routine occupations:**
   Waiters
   Road sweepers
   Cleaners
   Couriers
   Building labourers
   Refuse collectors

8 **Never worked/long-term unemployed/long-term sick.**

Source: ONS.

Figure 2.4 *Social Classification System*

variable for food and non-alcoholic beverage markets. Social class also influences shopping behaviour and evening television watching. Income is the superior segmentation variable for major appliances, soft drinks, mixes and alcoholic beverages. For other categories such as clothing, a combination of the two variables has been found to be the best approach.

Psychological factors affecting the consumer buying process

An individual's buying behaviour is influenced by a number of major psychological factors, such as:

- individual needs and motives
- perceptions
- attitudes and beliefs
- learning
- self-concept and personality.

The starting point in the purchase decision process is the recognition of a **need**. A need is simply the lack of something useful. It is an imbalance between the consumer's actual and desired condition. The consumer typically experiences numerous unsatisfied needs, but a need must be sufficiently aroused before it can serve as a motive to buy something.

Motives are inner states that direct a person towards a goal of satisfying a felt need. The individual is driven to take action to reduce a state of tension and to return to a condition of equilibrium – for example, by purchasing a desired item.

Individual behaviour resulting from motivation is affected by how stimuli are perceived. **Perception** is the meaning that a person attributes to incoming stimuli received through the five senses – sight, hearing, touch, smell and taste; it is the manner in which an individual selects, organises and interprets information. Different individuals can perceive the same phenomenon differently, and indeed an individual can perceive the same phenomenon in different ways at different times! This occurs because of the process of selectivity, which limits our perceptions. Psychologists once assumed that perception is an objective phenomenon, and that the individual perceives only what is there to be perceived. Researchers have recognised that what people perceive is as much a result of what they want to perceive as of what is actually there (selective exposure). Harrods, for example, is perceived differently from Woolworth's, and a Rolex watch differently from a Timex.

The perception of an object or event results from the interaction of two types of factors:

- stimulus factors – characteristics of the physical object, such as size, colour, weight or shape
- individual factors – characteristics of the individual, including not only sensory processes but experiences with similar items, and basic motivations and expectations.

People are continually bombarded with many stimuli, but most are ignored. In order to function, people must respond selectively. Determining which stimuli they will respond to is the problem of all marketers. How can marketers gain the consumer's attention so that he or she will read the advertisements, listen to the sales representative or react to the point-of-sale display? Increasingly, marketers are appealing to consumers' senses of smell and hearing. To gain the attention of shoppers, firms use point-of-sale displays that emit their products' fragrances or deliver pre-recorded advertising messages.

Although studies have shown that the average consumer is exposed to more than 500 advertisements daily, most of these never break through people's perceptual screens – the filters through which messages must pass. Sometimes breakthroughs are accomplished in the printed media through large advertisements. Doubling the size of an advert increases its attention value by about 50 per cent. Using colour in newspaper adverts, in contrast to the usual black and white, is another effective way to break through the reader's perceptual screen. Other contrast methods include using a large amount of white space (blank space)

around a printed area, or using white characters on a black background. In general, the marketer seeks to make the message stand out, to make it different from other messages so that it gains the prospective customer's attention.

The psychological concept of **closure** refers to people's tendency to produce a complete picture from fragments of the picture. Advertisements that encourage consumers to do this are successful in breaking through perceptual screens.

With such selective perception at work, it is easy to see the importance of the marketer's efforts to obtain brand loyalty. Satisfied customers are less likely to seek information about competing products, and even when it is forced on them, they are less apt than others to allow it to pass through their perceptual filters. They simply tune out information that does not accord with their existing beliefs and expectations. This process is known as selective distortion, whereby individuals may alter information that seems inconsistent with their beliefs or attitudes. For example, an individual may see or hear good points about the Honda Prelude, but may have a strong bias towards a BMW, so he or she is likely to distort the information received and conclude that the BMW is the better model. Information is being interpreted in ways that support preconceived ideas, and this distortion reduces the effectiveness of the Honda advertisement. This leads into the third aspect of selectivity, which is selective retention.

Selective retention is the process whereby a person remembers only information that supports his or her feelings, attitudes and beliefs, and will tend to forget information that does not support these views. Finally, individuals will act upon only part of what they retain – this is selective action.

Marketers are interested in consumers' **beliefs and attitudes** because they reflect feelings and value judgements towards products, brand images and services. To develop an effective marketing strategy, a marketer would need to know how attitudes are formed, measured and changed.

Attitudes about products and services are formed through individual experience and group contact (for example, in the family). Given that attitudes are important determinants of buyer behaviour, marketers need to measure consumer attitudes towards the product, packaging, quality, branding, promotional activities, etc. The most widely used techniques have been based on attitude ranking, whereby respondents are asked to rank products or other items in order of preference. Attitude measurement is not an easy process, and is complicated by the fact that attitudes consist of a number of components.

There are three related components of an attitude: cognitive, affective and behavioural. The **cognitive** component refers to the individual's information and knowledge about an item or concept. The **affective** component is the feelings or emotional reactions. The **behavioural** component involves personal tendencies to act in a certain manner. For example, in considering whether to shop at a warehouse-type food outlet, the individual would obtain information from advertising, trial visits and input from family, friends and associates (cognitive component). He or she would also receive input from others about their acceptance of shopping at this type of store, as well as information about the type of people who shop there (affective component). The consumer may ultimately decide to make some purchases of canned goods, cereals and bakery products there but continue to rely on a regular grocery store for major food purchases (behavioural component).

Consumer attitudes are difficult to change, and it is usually an expensive and arduous task to make them more positive towards the product or service. The marketer has two choices: to attempt to change consumer attitudes to make them consistent with the product offered, or to determine consumer attitudes first and then change the product to match them.

Learning theory has some important implications for marketing strategists. A desired outcome such as repeat purchase behaviour must be developed gradually. Shaping is the process of applying a series of rewards and reinforcements to encourage more complex behaviour to evolve over time. Both promotional strategy and the product itself play a role in the shaping process.

When marketers are attempting to motivate consumers to become regular buyers of a certain product, the first step could be to have an initial product trial with a free sample package as an inducement, perhaps including a substantial discount coupon for a subsequent purchase. This illustrates the use of a cue as a shaping procedure. The purchase response is reinforced by a satisfying product performance and a coupon for the next purchase. The second step is to entice the consumer to buy the product with little financial risk. The large discount coupon enclosed with the free sample prompts such an action. The package that is purchased may have a smaller discount coupon enclosed. Again the reinforcement is a satisfactory product performance and a second coupon. The third step is to motivate the person to buy the item again at a moderate cost. The discount coupon accomplishes this objective, but this time the only reinforcement is satisfactory product performance. The final test comes when the consumer is asked to buy the product at its full price. Repeat purchase

behaviour will have been shaped by effective application of learning theory within a marketing strategy context.

Research on consumer behaviour is a useful tool if applied carefully and with consideration. Although it can appear abstract, the study of motivation and social influences can reveal information that, if used properly, can make the difference between a successful campaign and a failed one.

Discussion point

How can the knowledge of consumer behaviour be applied to the following situations: (a) retailing, and (b) family holidays?

Organisational buyer behaviour

Organisational buyer behaviour tends to be more complex than the consumer decision process. There are several reasons for this.

- Many different people may exert an influence on organisational purchases, and considerable time may be spent in obtaining the input and approval of various organisation members.
- Organisational buying may be handled by committees, with more time required for approval.
- Many organisations attempt to use several sources of supply as a type of 'insurance' against shortages.
- Organisational buyers are influenced by both rational (cost, quality, delivery reliability) and emotional (status, fear, recognition) needs.

Most organisations have attempted to rationalise their purchases by employing a professional buyer – the purchasing manager or buyers or buying committee in the case of retailers and wholesalers. These employees are responsible for handling much of the organisation's purchases and securing needed products at the best possible prices. Unlike the ultimate consumer, who makes periodic purchase decisions, a firm's purchasing department devotes all of its time and effort to determining needs, locating and evaluating alternative sources of supply and making purchase decisions.

Two of the tools purchasers use are value analysis and vendor analysis. Value analysis is an examination of each component of a purchase in an attempt either to delete the item or replace it with a more cost-effective substitute.

Purchasing managers also use vendor analysis to evaluate potential suppliers. Vendor analysis is an on-going evaluation of a supplier's performance in categories such as price, ordering process, delivery time and attention to special requests. A checklist set up along these lines helps purchasers determine the most effective supply source for a particular item.

Buying centre

The buying centre is the group of people in an organisation who are involved in making purchase decisions. The concept helps in identifying the multiple buying influences in an organisation, as well as illuminating the industrial organisation buying process.

Individuals in a buying centre may play one or more of the following roles:

- **Users** are members of the organisation who actually use the product, for example a secretary for stationery or a cleaner for bleach, and who initiate the order with specifications and evaluate the product.
- **Influencers** are those who establish the specifications and evaluate competitors' products as well. These tend to be technical personnel with some form of expertise or those who have power within the organisation.
- **Deciders** are those who actually make the buying decision with respect to the product and supplier. In general, for a straightforward or repeat purchase, buyers are the deciders, but in situations requiring expensive outlays top management may be the deciders.
- **Buyers** are the people who select the suppliers and negotiate the terms of sale. This role is normally undertaken by the purchasing manager or purchasing agent. However, top management may decide where the item under consideration is expensive or complicated.
- **Gatekeepers** are those who control the flow of information to persons in the buying centre within the organisation. These people could be secretaries or technical personnel. The control of the flow of information can also be held by the purchasing department, especially information that flows from the supplier organisation to the user.

It is possible that the same person may play several roles, so that a secretary in any organisation may be an influencer, gatekeeper, user or even decider in the purchase of a personal computer. The size, structure and composition of a buying centre will vary according to:

- the size of organisation
- the type of product – in terms of complexity, expense, etc.
- the type of purchase, i.e. a repeat purchase compared to a new purchase
- the firm's culture regarding who should be involved in the purchase process.

The marketing priorities for a supplier firm are to establish who constitutes the buying centre, who influences the buying decision, who does the actual buying and who is most influential in the decision process. These are certainly challenges for the supplier firm's sales representative.

Model of organisational behaviour

In organisational markets, the purchase decisions are influenced by a number of interrelated factors, such as economic, legal, organisational, individual and behavioural influences. There are six steps a buyer will go through.

Stage 1 involves the recognition of a problem or need. This may arise in a number of ways – the firm may decide to introduce a new product line or a machine may break down.
Stage 2 involves examining the precise nature of purchase needs in terms of a repeat purchase, new buy or modified rebuy. At this stage, the quantity and characteristics of the product required are determined.
Stage 3 involves product specification, description and quantity of the required product. The role of users and influencers is quite strong at this stage, since they provide the necessary information and advice.
Stage 4 involves searching for products and possible sources of suppliers to solve the problem. Once the sources are located, the products and suppliers are evaluated for their suitability and whether they meet the product specifications.
Stage 5 is the selection of suppliers and the placing of an order, after the supplier's rates, proposals and terms have been evaluated and agreed upon.
Stage 6 involves a product evaluation in terms of whether it meets the product specification and whether its performance compares favourably with alternative products.

For repeat purchase or modified rebuy situations some of the above stages are omitted.

TASK

What are the main differences between consumer and organisational buying behaviour?

Marketing Mix

The marketing mix – product, place, price, promotion – is a major tool for the marketer, who must

be able to understand how to combine its various elements or components in an intelligent and effective way.

This chapter looks in more detail at the components themselves, as each one functions in unique ways,

requiring a careful consideration as to how they may interrelate and interact with each other.

On completion of the chapter you should be able to analyse the components of the marketing mix. To achieve this you must demonstrate the ability to:

- describe how products are chosen and developed to meet customers' and organisations' needs

- explain how products are chosen and developed to meet customer convenience

- explain how prices are set to reflect an organisation's objectives and market conditions

- illustrate how promotional activity is chosen to achieve its ams for the target market.

PRODUCT

What is a product? One answer to this question is to identify a product as a physical item. But is this the way potential customers see it? Do customers see a personal computer as a set of electronic components in a plastic container, with a screen and keyboard? Or do they see it as a means by which they can e-mail their friends and family across the world, keep up to date on their financial affairs via on-line banking, and see which hotels have accommodation available on a specific date?

A product should be seen as something that satisfies a consumer need or want. Customers may not, of course, realise that they have a need – for example the development of the personal stereo, the Sony Walkman, exploited a latent demand for such a product. It is all too easy to find companies and organisations who focus only on the physical attributes of a product rather than understand the benefits the customer receives from it.

Look at any product from a pair of Armani jeans to a dishwasher or car, and it can be seen that consumers are interested in what the product can provide for them. Likewise, industrial buyers (see Chapter 4) are also looking at how a piece of plant or machinery can help their organisation become more efficient. A product, therefore, is judged by its **benefits**.

Figure 3.1 shows how a product can be seen to operate on three levels. The core product, or core benefit, looks at the benefits that consumers gain when they purchase the product. For example, a washing machine washes clothes, but at the next level, the actual product, there are five characteristics to consider – features, brand, quality, design and packaging. Washing machine manufacturers therefore produce various models which can offer different features, such as more efficient use of water, to appeal to different customers. Lastly, the augmented product includes installation, warranty, after-sales support, delivery and credit. The customer may be tempted to purchase one washing machine in preference to another because that company offers installation at a preferred day and time. These last items are services attached to the physical product and its brand attributes, factors that can gain competitive advantages for those firms investing in their development.

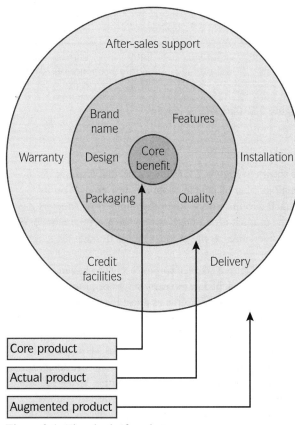

Figure 3.1 *Three levels of product*

A firm can take the augmented product concept and link it to its operations to gain advantages. Value-chain analysis identifies primary activities such as operations, together with support activities, such as human resource infrastructure, and focuses attention on the value added by activities and how they might be improved, for example to facilitate a speedier delivery service to consumers, or respond more quickly to a car manufacturer's request for component supplies (this would be based on a just-in-time (JIT) approach to introduce more flexibility and efficient operations).

Product life cycle

The product, once developed to cater for a particular need, will go through a life cycle. This needs careful research to see how long the life cycle is likely to be, and focuses attention on the challenges that the marketer faces as the product moves through each stage.

How long will the life cycle last? Can a product be relaunched (given a boost to its life)? Can new uses be found for an existing product that effectively move it to new customers? Analysis of the life cycle is a useful tool and can be used inventively. Figure 3.2 shows the four stages of the product life cycle.

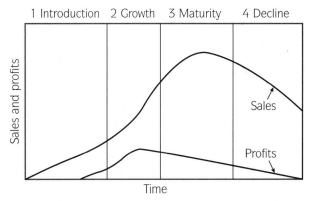

Figure 3.2 *The product life cycle*

1 Introduction

When a firm introduces a new product its objective is to stimulate demand, so the product is made known to the public through promotional campaigns. Promotion will require information on the product's unique features and attractiveness. Promotion efforts will also be directed to intermediaries in the distribution chain to encourage them to stock the product. Losses are common at this stage, because of the costs of promotion and a low take-up rate.

2 Growth

If a firm successfully moves through the introduction stage, which is where most products fail, then take-off occurs and word of mouth and advertising will help to consolidate this. As the firm gains profits from its investment, competitors enter the market and imitate the product.

3 Maturity

Sales for the whole market can continue to grow during this stage, but eventually they reach a plateau, when the market is saturated with competing products. The marketing tactic at this stage emphasises subtle differences, and brand competition intensifies. To increase market share at this stage will be at the expense of competitors, with price cuts often leading to falling revenues and the departure of some from the market.

4 Decline

In this stage there will be an absolute decline in industry sales as preferences shift and new products emerge.

Knowledge that profits will follow a life cycle helps future activity to be forecast. Likewise, promotional effort will shift from product information in the early stages to brand promotion in later ones, allowing the marketer to amend the elements of marketing mix. A firm's marketing efforts, for example, should stimulate demand at Stage 1, and the focus will shift to cultivating selective demand in the growth period, with market segmentation used at the maturity state. The life cycle can also be used in conjunction with the product portfolio, described in Chapter 4, to help decide where to invest money to promote high-growth products and when to cease production of a product that has little value to the company.

The life cycle can be extended by, for example, finding new uses for a product, increasing the frequency of use by current customers, adding new users, or by other changes in the marketing mix.

Consumer adoption

Consumers make decisions about whether to adopt a new product. In this process, consumers go through a series of stages from learning about a new product to trying it and deciding to purchase it. These stages are: awareness, interest, evaluation, trial and adoption/rejection. The marketer will wish to move the consumer through the adoption process and if the relationship progresses, then a purchase and repeat purchase stage will be reached.

Research into the adoption of new products has identified five categories of purchasers: innovators, early adopters, early majority, late majority and laggards, all of which are shown in Figure 3.3.

The diffusion process is the acceptance of new products and services by members of the community. The process,

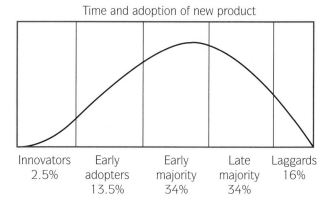

Time and adoption of new product

Innovators 2.5% | Early adopters 13.5% | Early majority 34% | Late majority 34% | Laggards 16%

Figure 3.3 *Categories of adopters*

as shown in Figure 3.3, follows a normal distribution. A small number of people adopt the new product on its launch into the market, then the numbers of adopters rise as the product is accepted, and so the potential number of consumers rises as the product moves through the market.

Locating first buyers of new products is a challenge. If they can be reached in the early stages of product development, this can serve as a test market. Early purchasers are often opinion leaders who can communicate positive attitudes to others. First adopters often tend to be young, have high social status, be well educated and have high incomes. However, working on these assumptions may still be misleading. When satellite TV was first introduced in the UK, it was thought that early adopters would be from the then social groups AB. However, it transpired that C1s and C2s were the first to adopt. It is possible to regard late adopters and laggards as having less importance than the rest, but they make up nearly 40 per cent of potential customers and can, therefore, be a very profitable group to target.

Product mix

The primary components of the product mix are the product line (a series of related products) and the individual offerings that make up the product line. For example a company such as Unilever would have hair shampoos comprising one of its product lines. Product mixes are measured in terms of width. Width refers to the number of products in the mix, and depth refers to the varieties of each product in terms or colours, sizes or models offered.

Several types of strategy can be used in the management of the product mix. An organisation may decide that it wishes to expand its present product mix by increasing the depth within a line or increasing the number of lines. Gaps in the assortment can be filled with new products or modified versions of existing ones. Quite clearly, a company would wish to avoid a new product that would adversely affect sales of one of its existing products – this would cannibalise the line, i.e. one product would be eating into the sales of another. Marketing research should be able to judge how great a danger this is, with forecasts of how much a new product would add to overall sales.

The following are further issues related to product mix strategies.

- **Line extensions.** The development of individual offerings that appeal to different market segments but are related to the existing product line is referred to as line extension. This would mean looking at existing products, as the audio equipment and TV manufacturer Sony did with the Walkman, and making a number of different models.
- **Growth.** Dependence on a single product would restrict the growth of a company; additional products will help the firm to grow.
- **Exploitation of company resources.** By increasing production, the firm can spread its costs of production, reducing unit costs and thereby helping it to become more competitive. Salespeople can sell additional products and the skills of employees can be better used.
- **Exploiting the product life cycle.** New products can replace ones that are nearing maturity. In addition, they can be promoted in the marketplace by associating them with the benefits that the older product has brought. For example, a successful older product would have shown the company and brand name to be dependable.
- **Product positioning.** This refers to the consumer's perception of a product's attributes, uses, quality and advantages relative to competing products. For example, a firm can position its product with a specific market segment – Lucozade was repositioned from a drink for convalescents to a drink that provides energy for those participating in sports.
- **Exploiting the brand.** Firms can introduce new products which exploit the brand name.

Case Study

Coke brand

Coca-Cola has launched a range of fashion and sports clothing which extends significantly the Coke brand. The company has signed up partners and franchisers worldwide to manufacture and market the Coca-Cola Wear label.

The range includes jeans, sports clothing and casual wear. The company believes that the clothes will connect back to the brand, thereby reflecting the company's values of 'authenticity, genuineness and being a part of people's lives'.

The company licenses the use of its logo, the design of the can and other symbols for more than 20 000 products, but the introduction of clothing will be the first time that it has used the brand name to provide substance to products that are not those simply intended to display its logo.

Other companies, such as Philip Morris (makers of Marlboro cigarettes) have also used their names to introduce a range of clothing.

Questions

1. What is a brand?

2. How could it be extended?

3. What are the dangers to a company in using its brand to introduce new products with which it has no previous experience or expertise?

New product planning and innovation

A company must carefully consider the introduction of a new product as it will be affected by the influences of the product life cycle and the strategies of competitors. The launch itself will need careful planning. In the food industry, thousands of new products are launched every year, but only one in ten will be a success. Although the need to develop and launch a new product is apparent, the risks are high.

In the UK textiles industry in 1998, thousands of redundancies were announced, blamed variously on the slowdown in the economy, the high pound, cheap imports and so on. Certain causes were often overlooked, however. What if the companies, or at least some of them, had chosen an inappropriate strategy, or suffered from corporate inertia, such as assuming that if they were a supplier to the high street retailer Marks & Spencer, then they were immune from constantly striving to improve their performance and introduce innovative products? The profit squeeze suffered by Marks & Spencer in 1998 produced a reduction in demand and factories were closed, leaving many companies suffering from the loss of their main customers.

All companies need to keep abreast of new trends, and to embrace innovation. There are various ways in which this can be undertaken, as detailed below.

- **Innovation.** If innovation is left simply to the marketing department, then all the other functions of the firm may fail to see their vital role in improving factors outside their contract, but which are important ingredients for offering customer satisfaction.
- **Acquisition.** This involves buying a company and acquiring new products that can be used to provide a stimulus in the marketplace. This approach fails to turn the purchasing organisation into an innovating one, however, and as research has shown, four out of six acquisitions fail to generate shareholder value.
- **Invention.** Science and technology companies are obvious examples of this process, but so too are service companies, such as the insurance company Direct Line with its development of a telephone service that provides discounts to customers. The advantage gained from invention is often difficult to maintain as copies and new entrants can soon steal sizeable chunks of the market.
- **Market-led approach.** This is a comprehensive approach that, because it relies on building relationships with customers, supply partners and staff in the organisation, has the potential to build a long-term commitment to innovation based on a critical understanding of the market and the customers (actual and potential) who comprise it.

Discussion point

How easy is it to encourage market-led innovation among people working in separate functions in an organisation?

New product development is time-consuming, risky and expensive, but it is also essential. It is vital for a company to plan as thoroughly as possible. Each firm's strategy for new product development will vary according to the existing product mix and the extent to which current market offerings match overall market objectives. Figure 3.4 identifies four development strategies: **product improvement, market development, product development** and **product diversification**.

	Existing product	New product
Existing market	Product improvement	Product development
New market	Market development	Product diversification

Figure 3.4 *Product development strategies*

1. Product improvement is a modification of the product offering, so that an improved or repackaged and repositioned product, for example, may be relaunched.
2. Market development concentrates on finding new markets for existing products, with these markets seeing the product as 'new'. For the marketer these are new challenges that require rethinking the market mix, as the consumers and the dynamics of the market are different. A danger here is that there could be an adverse effect within the existing market, as a price change to enter a new market may filter through to the established market.
3. Product development strategy is the introduction of new products into identifiable and established markets.
4. Product diversification strategy is the development of new products for new markets. In some cases the products complement existing markets, while in other circumstances they do not. Companies may try to achieve this by taking over other companies. Diversification is usually the riskiest of strategies.

Market and product positioning

Companies need to focus on the number and type (nature) of products to be aimed at the market segments chosen. Once a suitable market segment has been identified and the organisation feels that it is worth targeting, then price will play a vital role in signalling to the customer the value that the company is willing to supply.

In product positioning, therefore, the inputs are the tangible and intangible product attributes, and assessments of how the consumer will value these attributes in relation to the total product offering.

New product development

Having looked at the product life cycle, consumer adoption, the diffusion process and innovation, it is clear that new product development is a vital part of company activity. New products are regularly required, and this section considers how this process can be established.

Stages in new product development

This involves six stages, as detailed below.

1. **Idea generation.** The development of new products begins with an idea. The idea can come from a variety of sources, such as the salesforce, customers, research and development, retailers or wholesalers. Many companies now invite customers to phone a hotline to review or comment on their products.
2. **Screening.** This involves separating ideas with potential from those that do not meet corporate objectives. Organisations may use a checklist for this purpose, which can include such factors as product uniqueness, as well as compatibility with current product offerings. In other instances, the screen stage entails open discussion of new product ideas.
3. **Business analysis.** Product ideas that come through the screening process are subject to business analysis, which is the analysis of the new product's market potential, market-share possibilities and likely competitive strengths.
4. **Development.** Product ideas with profit potential can be converted into a physical product. This will involve many parts of the organisation; the marketing team can provide information on consumer feedback on product design, colour, features, pricing and any other issue related to the product. Tests, revisions and refinements should result in the introduction of a product that has a greater chance of success. Failure to determine how consumers feel about a product and how they will use it may lead to product failure.
5. **Testing.** Test marketing is the first stage at which the product has to perform in a realistic environment. It involves the selection of a specific city, or television coverage area that is considered typical of the total market. The product is launched with a complete marketing campaign in that area. Some firms omit test marketing and move directly from product development to full-scale production. There are four reasons for this:
   - test marketing is expensive
   - competitors can disrupt the test by changing their prices
   - test marketing of consumer durables, such as dishwashers, is seen to be unnecessary given the need to invest in a dealer network
   - test marketing can provide competitors with knowledge of a company's strategy.
6. **Commercialisation.** Products that successfully complete all stages in the development process proceed to full-scale marketing. Marketing programmes have to be set up, outlays for production facilities agreed and the salesforce, marketing intermediaries and potential customers must be made aware of the new product.

However, product failure is still a distinct possibility. The key factors that may contribute to this are detailed below.

- **Technical problems.** These include bad design, unsatisfactory performance and poor quality.
- **Market research.** The research that has been undertaken has overestimated the market, and sales are unable to recoup the investment made. There could also be insufficient knowledge of consumers' requirements or the motive for buying a product, or even how it will be used.
- **Timing.** The product was introduced to the market when a recession had taken hold of the economy, causing problems with sales, profits and cash flow.

Product strategy

The importance of product strategy for marketing is in the ability to select the right product for the right market, a task that requires a lot of thought, planning and the active participation of the marketing team. This is not a once-and-for-all activity; new products mature and the marketing mix changes. Some products need further investment, while the move of competitors into or out of the market needs to be monitored. One issue that can be overlooked is that the addition of services to products often provides further advantages in the marketplace. To support these and the product itself, the organisation must be able to assist customers with any aspect that affects their decision to purchase. Although this varies between consumer markets and industrial ones, the same point applies.

PLACE (DISTRIBUTION)

Having developed an effective product strategy, the issue of place – providing the product at a place convenient for consumers – needs to be considered. Research into this is just as important as any other feature of the marketing mix.

Channels of distribution

Channels of distribution are the link between producers and consumers or industrial users. A distribution channel consists of individuals and organisations who make products and services accessible to the ultimate consumer. Distribution is a vital part of making goods available to consumers when, where and in the form required. Sorting, storage and transportation of the goods are just some of the functions that give added value to the product.

Business units such as banks, market research firms, advertising agencies, warehousing firms, transport companies and insurance firms are not considered part of the distribution channel because they are not actively involved in the purchase or selling process, although they may help in the marketing process. These are referred to as facilitating agents.

The importance of distribution channels and market intermediaries can be explained in terms of the utilities they create and the functions they perform. These functions are described below.

- **Facilitating the exchange process.** Marketing intermediaries facilitate transactions by reducing the number of marketplace contracts, thereby being more efficient in making goods available to the consumer. For example, if originally there were four producers whose products were purchased by four buyers, a total of 16 transactions would be necessary. If one intermediary worked with the producer and the consumers, the transactions would be reduced to eight.

- **Sorting.** When products are combined to form a package of benefits for the consumer, this is known as an assortment with one of the functions of the distribution channel being to adjust the assortment to match the requirements of the consumer, i.e. sorting. The task is to collect together the products of various manufacturers divide these products into the desired properties required by the consumer, put various items together into the required assortment, and finally distribute this assortment to the consumer.

- **Standardising transactions.** Distribution channels standardise exchange transactions in terms of the product, such as the grading of apples, and in terms of the transfer process itself. Order point, prices, payment terms, delivery schedules and purchase lots tend to be standardised by distribution channel members.

- **Search process.** Channels accommodate the search process of both buyers and sellers, by which buyers search for specific products and services to fill their needs, while sellers attempt to find out what consumers want.

Strategy decisions

Several strategy decisions need to be taken, and the selection of a specific distribution channel is the most basic of these, while the level of distribution intensity also needs to be considered.

Selection of a distribution channel

Choice here is based on an analysis of market, product, producer and competitive factors. All factors are important, and often they are interrelated. The overriding consideration, however, is where, when and how consumers choose to buy their product or service.

Market factors

A major determinant of channel structure is whether the product is intended for the consumer or the industrial market. Industrial purchasers usually prefer to deal directly with the manufacturer, except for supplies of small items, but most consumers make their purchases from retail stores. Often, products for both industrial users and consumers are sold through more than one channel.

The needs and geographical location of the firm's market affect channel choice. Direct sales are possible where the firm's potential market is concentrated. A small number of potential buyers also increases the feasibility of using direct channels. Consumer goods are numerous and dispersed, and because consumers purchase a small volume at a given time, market intermediaries must be employed to supply products to them.

Order size also affects the channel decision. Producers like to use shorter, more direct channels in cases where retail customers or industrial buyers place relatively small numbers of large orders. Retailers often use buying offices to negotiate directly with manufacturers for large-scale purchases, while wholesalers may be used by small retailers.

Shifts in consumer buying patterns also influence channel decisions. The desire for credit and the growth of self-service outlets, along with the increasing use of direct marketing, all affect the channel decision.

Product factors

Perishable products such as fresh foods, or fashion items with short life cycles, typically move through relatively short channels directly to the retailer or consumer.

Complex products such as custom-made installations are sold by the producer directly to the buyer. Standardised goods usually are marketed by wholesalers. Products that require regular service or specialised repairs are not normally distributed through channels employing independent wholesalers, however. The lower the product's unit value, and the more standardised it is, the larger the channel will be. Convenience goods or industrial supplies with low unit values are marketed through relatively large channels.

Producer factors

Companies with good financial management and marketing resources are less compelled to use intermediaries in marketing their products. A firm with a broad product line, for example, may be able to market its products directly to retailers or individual users, since its salesforce can offer a variety of products. Larger total sales permit selling costs to be spread over a number of products and make direct sales feasible.

The manufacturer's need for control over the product can also influence channel selection. If aggressive promotion is desired at the retail level, the producer chooses the shortest available channel so that its influence can be felt. For new products, the producer may be required to develop an advertising campaign before independent wholesalers will agree to handle the items.

Competitive factors

Some firms are forced to develop unique distribution channels because of inadequate promotion of their product by independent intermediaries. A manufacturer may develop a direct salesforce or set up its own retail outlets, or consider the Internet as a way to overcome distribution problems.

How to determine distribution

The degree of distribution intensity is best seen as a continuum with three categories.

- **Intensive distribution.** Producers of convenience goods use intensive distribution, going for saturation coverage of the market, so that the purchaser can buy the product with ease. Goods using this approach include sweets, soft drinks and cigarettes.
- **Selective distribution.** This is a market coverage strategy in which a firm chooses a limited number of retailers in a market area to handle its product lines. By limiting the number of retailers, the firm can reduce its total marketing costs while establishing better working relationships within the channel. Where product service is important, the manufacturer usually provides dealer training and assistance. Price cutting is less likely, since fewer dealers are handling the firm's lines. Durable goods such as computers usually fall into this category.
- **Exclusive distribution.** When producers grant exclusive rights to a wholesaler or retailer to sell in a specific geographic location, they are practising exclusive distribution. Car dealerships are an example of this form of distribution. Some market coverage may be sacrificed under a policy of exclusive distribution, but the loss is offset by the development of an image of quality and prestige for the product, and by the reduced marketing costs associated with the small number of accounts. In exclusive distribution, producers and retailers cooperate closely in decisions concerning advertising and promoting the inventory to be carried by the retailer, and over prices.

Franchising

Franchising is a form of licensing in which the franchiser provides a total marketing programme, which involves the brand name, product, method of operation and management training and advice. Examples of franchisers include Prontaprint (printing) and Avis (car rental). Franchising accounts for 10 per cent of sales in the UK and in France, but is less popular in the rest of the European Union.

Many companies, including Body Shop and Benetton, have been very successful in exploiting this method of expansion. The advantages are that it is a means to expand rapidly into new markets, with a minimum of investment compared to alternative forms of market entry. The franchisee has an interest in making the venture work as he or she will have invested time and money and possess local market knowledge. When it works it is very profitable for the franchiser, who gains income from royalties and fees, while the franchisee retains maximum control over the product target.

Case Study

Internet marketing

Marketing via the Internet raises some interesting issues. Many companies in Europe are waiting to see how the Internet will develop before committing themselves to take advantage of it. A survey by the polling company NOP found that one in five small businesses in Europe rejects new technology and the possibilities that it offers. In contrast, companies in the most wired countries on earth, Finland and the USA use all the applications of the technologies.

Electronic commerce (e-commerce) is used by many organisations to improve efficiency and profitability, to gain new customers and to enter new markets. E-commerce involves the use of the Internet, Intranets (networks within organisations) and Extranets (networks between an organisation and its retailers and suppliers), to undertake business unhindered by geographic boundaries.

Because of its technical complexity, exploring the issues associated with the development of a simple Intranet would tend to confuse the average manager. E-commerce is a technical issue

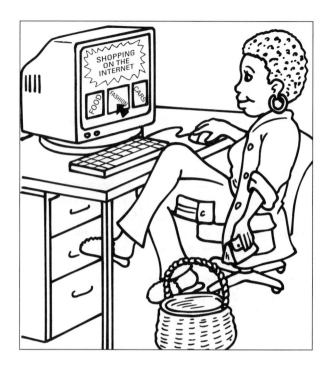

best handled by those with the technical expertise, but this means the issue is left to those whose interest can be one-dimensional. To address e-commerce in a positive way requires all the departments and functions of a company to understand what it means for them in the creation and delivery of a product to customers.

Developing an e-commerce site on the Internet requires a range of expertise. For example, the marketer has to show who to target and what the product is; a professional web designer must design the site; both software and hardware suppliers may be responsible for the secure system/server; the merchant service system must be sorted out with the banks; efficient fulfilment has to be in place to meet the new and unpredictable demand; and then how the web site is promoted and how to drive traffic to the site must be addressed. It is no wonder that small and medium-sized enterprises are put off, as they have limited resources. Even with groups of experts coming together to provide a unified service, it is still a daunting prospect.

With predictions of 50 million Europeans being on-line by 2002 and on-line trade of US$60 billion in that year, there are clearly going to be companies that gain substantial advantages from e-commerce. In addition, more business-to-business operations will be conducted on-line, a development that many experts believe will outweigh business-to-consumer applications of e-commerce.

The success of Amazon.Com, the US Internet book retailer, has shown the potential of the Internet for trade. Without any shops of its own, but offering discounts on a large selection of books, it quickly became the third biggest book retailer in the US. With

Amazon opening a UK operation, the bookseller Waterstones (now combined with Dillons) has introduced its own version of the service, while WH Smith has also responded. Publishers such as HarperCollins have launched a site that provides ordering facilities, the chance for users to discuss the books they have read, and the opportunity to contact authors.

Traditional book retailing will still account for 80–90 per cent of all sales in the UK over the next five years, so the use of e-commerce will be alongside the development of retailing in traditional stores. Marketing and business planning can combine the benefits of the Internet with the progressive development of traditional operations in order to appeal to as many target markets as possible.

Questions

1. What is e-commerce?

2. What changes might electronic commerce bring for the distribution of various products?

Physical distribution management

Distribution needs to be organised as efficiently as possible, and physical distribution management is a vital part of getting products to customers when they require them. This involves looking at transportation, materials handling, packaging, warehousing, inventory policy, stock control and order processing. Savings can be made by keeping inventory levels down, improving efficiency of transport methods and so on. Likewise, customer service levels can be improved by getting products to them as quickly as possible, processing orders efficiently and ensuring that goods are delivered undamaged. Physical distribution management has to balance the needs of the organisation to be efficient with the requirements of the customer for a wide choice of goods when they want them.

There are other factors to consider here. Low inventory costs may mean higher freight costs as stocks have to be replenished quickly when they run out. Reducing packaging to help reduce weight or become more environmentally friendly may lead to more breakages in transit. These considerations affect all aspects of distribution management. A system needs to be devised that maintains competitive advantage in the marketplace,

and the key parts of the system require certain questions to be answered.

- Transportation – how will the product be transported (air, rail, road, pipeline, sea) and what are the considerations of time and cost that need to be borne in mind?
- Materials handling – will the products be handled during transportation? Will containers be used? Can these easily be transferred from ship to rail to road? Will the wholesaler and retailer have the facilities to deal with the containers?
- Packaging – what requirements will there be to package goods for safe transportation and storage? What weight will be added by the material?
- Warehousing – where should inventory be stored, and how many warehouses should there be?
- Inventory policy, stock control and order processing – how much inventory should be held, and how quickly can it be turned over? How should orders be handled?

In a stable competitive environment answers to these questions can be provided by an effective managerial approach. However, when changes come about, such as those introduced by widespread use of the Internet, new challenges are created in physical distribution management. Whether the situation is stable or in flux, careful planning for physical distribution is vital for providing the goods at a place and time that meet customer needs.

TASK

Why is distribution becoming of increasing importance in marketing?

PRICE

Perceived value

What is it that customers value? When you are purchasing a newspaper, how much difference does it make if the price is reduced from say 40p to 20p? If a bank or credit card company awards points for the use of a card, is this of great benefit to the customer? When a new car is offered with a low interest rate deal and free insurance or servicing, how will this affect the purchase decision?

Each of the examples above shows that the judgement consumers must make as to what best suits their needs is a complex process. This is true even in an apparently straightforward situation, such as buying fruit from a market stall. If a full search of all the market stalls was undertaken, it may be found that fruit is being sold more cheaply elsewhere. Does the customer spend time and effort in the search for cheaper goods, or decide to settle for what he or she believes is the best (most convenient) deal? To the buyer, the price is the value placed on what is gained in exchange, i.e. money is exchanged for a product or service that provides satisfaction. The vital question is whether the benefit gained from the purchase of the item will be greater than the sacrifice of disposable income.

Role of price

Price therefore is the measure of value involved in exchange, but the calculation undertaken by the customer in deciding whether to purchase a given item at a certain price is affected by a range of financial and other considerations. When purchasing a new car, price is a consideration but so too are trade-in value, finance schemes, discount for cash and the availability of extras for a given price.

Obviously, price is also a consideration for the industrial buyer, and marketers have to be aware of what is likely to happen if prices are adjusted. Also, as price generates revenue, any adjustment will have implications for the overall profitability of the company. Price is the one element of the marketing mix that is capable of generating income, and achieving profits.

Price is heavily influenced by costs, which can lead to a rather inflexible approach to the setting of price in the marketplace. Cost elements do not tend to fluctuate so readily as market conditions, so the influence of costs can lead to rigidity in the setting of price if changed market circumstances are not taken into account.

If the marketing approach taken by the company has involved providing a variety of products to serve various market segments, the price may well not be varied enough to take account of the uniqueness of each segment. Marketing mix elements have to be supported by price, but this may not be the case if costs and short-term profit considerations overrule other considerations.

Many organisations set price objectives according to their own internal needs, such as profitability, but fail to give due credit to the importance of achieving profitability by manipulating price to attract customer interest and to convey a message that supports other elements of the mix. The following provides a guide to the general marketing issues that should be considered.

Generic pricing adjustments

Generic pricing strategies provide a firm with several options on the question of price and other factors.

Market skimming pricing

This technique or strategy is often seen with the introduction of a new product. The aim is to price the product in such a way that the price attracts the customer to the top end of the chosen market. At a later stage the price can be lowered to take the product through the diffusion process (see page 46). With a new product, the cost reduction that takes place as output is increased would warrant a price fall on its own. The whole technique assumes that the quality offered to the top of the market is the quality that the consumer demands.

Market penetration pricing

The firm adopting this approach would go for the opposite tactic to that reviewed above, with the price being set low to help achieve specific objectives. The main objective would be to achieve an increase in sales volume, but this can involve a major problem – if the existing competition is able to compete on price, a price war will develop.

This approach can, however, put off likely competitors from entering the market and will allow for the maximum take-up of a product in the last stages of its life.

Neutral pricing

Neutral pricing is where customers deem a price to be reasonable given the economic value they derive from the product.

Economic value is made up of two parts: reference value and differential value. **Reference value** is where the customer compares substitute products and the prices charged for them, whereas **differential value** is the customer's perception of the product's attributes as compared with the best substitute. The costs and benefits of competing products are therefore the two elements that determine economic value.

A neutral price approach is taken where price has a lower profile than it does with products suitable for either the skimming or penetration strategies. This will be an appropriate approach when penetration pricing may result in unacceptably low profit margins, or when there is too much market rivalry to allow a skimming approach.

Pricing and marketing objectives

Marketing objectives are achieved by pricing policy playing its part along with the rest of the mix. Price acts to help form perceptions among both channel (distribution) members and consumers, of the value or quality inherent in the product. If perceptual factors are accepted as a goal for pricing policy, the problem becomes one of determining the proper variables.

Further considerations include dissuading competitors from entering the market and using up spare capacity, as well as the longer-run objectives of helping to achieve market share.

Product life cycle pricing adjustments

The product life cycle is important in the determination of pricing strategy. The product life cycle involves the marketer in reconsidering the marketing mix throughout the product's life. At the introduction stage, price will give a clue as to the product's value, but as customers become aware of this, prices can be lowered to increase sales.

At the maturity stage a reduction in price is not likely to lead to many more sales, but there is a temptation to reduce price and go for increased market share. When the state of decline is reached, price can be used to defend market share, if elasticity of demand is researched – this should help the company arrive at a decision on price. If demand is inelastic, then the consumer is focusing on other attributes of the product, whereas if there is elastic

demand the customer will be sensitive to price changes. On its own, elasticity of demand does not provide the detailed analysis required, but it can give guidance on the pricing strategy appropriate to a given market.

Tactical issues

When the three generic pricing strategies and the product life cycle approaches have been considered, tactical issues should be reviewed to arrive at a final price. This is where the full understanding of the targeted consumer will be put to good use. The positioning of the product may have involved several market segments and price can be determined on the basis of the differences between the segments. This is the final adjustment that will help to achieve pricing objectives.

Demand elasticity

Changes in prices such as those referred to above for newspapers can play an important role. When *The Times* reduced its cover price in the early 1990s by 20p, demand increased rapidly, and this forced other papers to reduce their prices to protect their market. The influence of basic price over demand is known as price elasticity. If the price fall had not produced the increase in sales, *The Times* would not have benefited from this change. Where changes in price have a large effect on demand, demand is said to be elastic. Where they have little or no effect, demand is said to be inelastic.

The way of calculating this is as follows:

$$\text{Price elasticity of demand} = \frac{\% \text{ change in quantity demanded}}{\% \text{ change in price}}$$

When the answer is greater than 1, prices are elastic. Where it is less than 1, they are inelastic.

If a product has inelastic demand, then it would be possible to raise price and find that demand may fall by a small amount, but extra revenue will compensate for this.

Calculations of this sort can be made for a range of products, and the results can be of interest to governments (when setting indirect taxes) or companies (when setting prices). However, the change in elasticity over time also needs to be understood. A product that has an inelastic demand at one period may, due to changes in economic circumstances, become more elastic. Elasticity of demand is only one facet of a wider picture of competition and price.

Competition

Implied in the previous analysis of price is the fact that an awareness of competitors' pricing strategies is vital for an organisation. The example of newspaper pricing shows how a move caught out the competition. In many industries made up of oligopolies, such as the oil companies, price competition played a minor role right up until the end of the 1980s. Competition was based round non-price competition such as position. It was only in the late 1990s when supermarkets started to take a greater share of the petrol market that price competition came to play a major role.

Price wars can leave many casualties behind and may be of only temporary benefit to customers, as with fewer companies left after the war prices may start to climb. Taking price as the key factor may blind an organisation to the need to consider price as a key ingredient of the marketing mix. Firms seek to brand their products, aim them at different segments and then target these markets. Products can be perceived to be different from others, with additional features or levels of service creating a preference for that item. In other circumstances, products can be in the early stages of the diffusion process. High prices may start to come down as economies of scale appear and new segments are targeted. There may be a time lag in this process, however, leaving newer segments frustrated at the time it takes to see prices fall.

Branding, position, targeting, and location in the product life cycle are all factors affecting price and competition. Judging its price against that of competitors forces an organisation to look at its total product offering and consider how it can provide a unique offer that its customers are willing to pay for. Competitive pressures will force changes, but this can be dealt with in a thoughtful way that can maintain the loyalty of customers over time.

Price and costs

Many organisations still base their pricing decisions on costs alone. Costs must be an issue when setting price, so this can be used by marketers to set a floor below which the product cannot be priced. The following analysis looks at the influence of costs on price by looking at full-cost pricing and breakeven analysis.

Full-cost pricing

This is a simple method for setting prices, and also has the advantage of working towards a specified level of profit. Under this method the variable cost, the fixed cost and the profit per unit are added together to arrive at a selling price. The problem here is that although the system appears to be simple it suffers from some drawbacks.

- It is not so easy to calculate and attribute costs as may at first be imagined. For example, the allocation of fixed costs to individual products will depend on the level of product, but the level of production will be determined by the demand for the product and the demand will be affected by the price. If output falls during a recession, the amount of total cost will be spread over fewer units causing cost per unit to increase and prices to go up.
- This approach ignores price elasticity of demand, the impact that a price increase (or decrease) will have on demand. If price is increased and demand also increases, revenue will dramatically increase. A cost-plus pricing approach ignores the possibility of this.
- This approach generally disregards the competition.
- It does not suggest a realistic profit goal or a market share objective.
- It is inflexible in that it cannot take account of changes in circumstances, particularly with regard to the product's position in the market.

Breakeven analysis

The breakeven chart in Figure 3.5 draws attention to the importance of the two types of costs, variable and fixed. Fixed costs remain static as output rises, while variable costs are introduced when production and sales commence. As production rises, the amount and significance of variable costs will increase. On this level the two types of costs may be seen as:

- relatively easy to identify and measure
- the only types of cost that the organisation will face.

A simple addition of fixed and variable costs will produce total cost, and the total revenue will be the income enjoyed by the firm at any particular level of quantity and price. The breakeven point shown on the diagram is the level at which the firm makes neither profit nor loss. The breakeven graph is a series of static points showing the expected situation of the firm at each possible level of output.

This approach is of greater use to the marketer than the full-cost approach, particularly when the method is extended from the simplistic approach shown here.

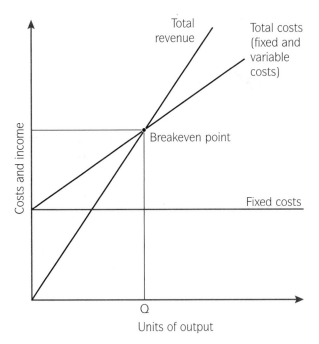

Figure 3.5 *A breakeven chart*

Psychological pricing

Marketers are aware that setting prices has to take account of the competition, costs and the ability to achieve the organisation's objectives. What is also important is the impact price can have on the buying decision. Psychological pricing uses the fact that a consumer can have an emotional, rather than a purely rational, response to a product and its price. One example of this is to price just below the full pound. Petrol prices are expressed as 69.9 pence per litre, not 70p. Many items are priced in this way, say £5.99 rather than £6. Pricing points like this are able to persuade many to buy, where a price rise over a psychological £6 barrier would deter many.

Discriminatory pricing

Price discrimination has long been recognised as a major issue for marketing. Eventually, price elasticity varies between two market segments, permitting the use of different prices to try and maximise profits. An example of this would be between peak and off-peak travel or electricity and gas consumption. The practice has to be consistent with the law, and should not upset customers in the segment that is being charged higher prices.

Many regulatory authorities seek to outlaw these practices where they feel it is a misuse of monopoly power. Companies point out that that discriminatory pricing is part of market segmentation, i.e. offering added value for higher prices. Judgement on the merits of this may take years to come about, but companies who use price discrimination need to be able to prove that it is not anti-competitive or harmful to consumers.

Product-line pricing

Most companies have a variety of products on offer to numerous markets. This does not affect the use of the techniques described above, provided there are no interrelationships between the products, so that they can be treated as separate entities in separate markets. However, many companies have a line of products that have interrelationships affecting pricing decisions.

There are two ways in which interrelationships can be identified. If a product is competitive with other products offered by the company, then a reduction in the price of one product may affect the sales of other products on offer. Complementary products are those where increased sales will have a beneficial effect on sales of other products in the line.

Market research will help to show how much of a danger this is that sales of one product will adversely affect sales of another. Pricing a line of products requires great skill so that price differences between products are realistic, not too close or too far apart so that there is either confusion on the part of the customer or the opportunity for a competitor to slot in a competing product.

In the product line offered to the market, the price of the least expensive item has a more than proportionate influence on sales of other products, particularly as it can draw in the marginally interested customer. Once enticed to purchase the product, a customer may eventually be encouraged to trade up to the next level.

Pricing for the channel of distribution

One major consideration that has a large impact on the chances of pushing products through the line of distribution is the margin that is sought by intermediaries.

The channel will have been chosen by the company to help it achieve its desired marketing mix, but the channel intermediaries receive their income and therefore their profits through payments for their services. Most of the payments to intermediaries take the form of discounts against a nominal price list. These may be trade discounts that compensate the intermediary for holding stock, distributing the product and so on. Quantity discounts can also be offered for those who buy in bulk. Promotional discounts encourage distributors to participate in the promotion of the product, and cash discounts are offered to encourage prompt payment.

The need to consider the discounts on offer reveals the power of the distributor to influence the final market price. The main problem is how far the price is to be set to encourage the distributor to take the product, or to appeal to the end-user. As ever the answer to this conundrum lies in the nature of the market. If the power rests with the distributors of the product, either because of their links with the end-user, or because they are major buyers in the market, for example supermarkets, then they will be aiming to increase their margins. In these circumstances the producers of goods can either seek to set up their own distribution channel, or try to ensure that both profit and price to the end-user can achieve corporate objectives.

Other considerations

Pricing cannot be divorced from wider considerations, which include the social, legal and political influences that impact on the pricing decision. Governments and pressure groups, and on occasions the media, will all seek to exert influence on the price of certain products for one reason or another.

TASK

What is unique about pricing from the marketer's point of view?

PROMOTION

Awareness and image

Consumers have to be made aware of the product and the company that is selling it. Promotion is the part of the marketing mix that provides information for all the parties, ranging from the wholesaler, retailer and customer to potential customers and pressure groups. Raising awareness will help to move a product not just from the shelves, but also through the life cycle and diffusion segments. Promotion is the key way to assist the product in the market. Firms will use controllable methods of promotion, such as advertising, sales promotion, personal selling and public relations, but there are also non-controllable forms of promotion such as word of mouth, personal recommendation and editorial comments from magazines and newspapers. A company needs to be conscious of these as they can damage the reputation of an organisation or product very quickly.

Companies wish to portray images of themselves to the outside world, perhaps as caring employers or protectors of the environment. Corporate image can be linked to products in a positive way, helping to achieve breakthroughs with new markets and products. Organisations place a lot of emphasis on getting their messages to the market to assist them in achieving corporate objectives. Promotional planning is therefore as important as corporate planning if all the benefits are to be realised. The following section looks at this more closely.

Branding

This is the way that a distinctive identity is created for a product or range of products, so that promotion leaves an identifiable presence in the marketplace. BT's logo and McDonald's name are all familiar examples. Companies spend millions on the design and regular redesign of their logos, attempting to achieve a modernisation of their image without losing their distinctive appearance in the eyes of the public.

The purpose of branding is to attract customers who will become brand loyal, resist switching to other brands and will undertake repeat purchases of the product. Brands can consist of an organisation itself, such as BP – this is known as an umbrella brand. An example of a branded product is the Big Mac for McDonald's. Brand names rather than logos are usually the way in which people come to be familiar with a company and its products – research shows that customers give preference to branded over non-branded goods. A brand name though must be easy to remember, distinctive and easy to pronounce.

Although it takes time to build a reputable brand, its value to the company can be immense, and it is now included as a balance sheet item. Companies may spend more money on buying a well-known brand than can be justified by the assets and sales of the organisation. In taking over Jaguar, Ford paid for the name more than the current product range.

A strong brand, either an umbrella brand or product brand, can be used to introduce new products that the public will tend to trust as they recognise the name and what it stands for. However, introducing a new product which does not match the quality and performance of other products in the range could work to the detriment of the company and damage the brand image.

A structured approach to communications

Communications and advertising models both provide marketing communicators with a framework that can help their decisions. One useful way of thinking about effective communications and the range of communications decisions that need to be made is to consider the 6Ms: market, mission, message, method, money and monitoring. These are shown in Figure 3.6.

A structured approach involving the following tasks will often be preferred.

1. Identify target audience (market).
2. Determine the communications objectives (mission).
3. Design the message (message).
4. Select the communications channels (method).
5. Develop the total promotional budget (money).
6. Decide on the promotion mix.
7. Measure the promotion results (monitoring).
8. Manage and coordinate the total marketing communications process.

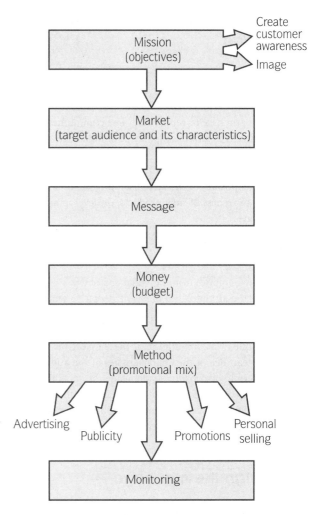

Figure 3.6 *The 6 Ms of effective communication*

This approach can be used to establish a framework for an effective communications input to the marketing mix.

1. Identify target-audience

Who is the audience and what message needs to be conveyed? Is the audience made up of potential buyers or current users? Are these people groups or individuals, and what role will they play? For example, are they the people who will be in a position to make a decision to buy, or simply have some influence upon the buying decision? Research would need to be carried out into audience needs, attitudes and preferences, and also competitors' promotional efforts and how they are likely to impact on the company.

2. Determine the communications objectives

It is vital to establish clear objectives – providing information, changing the consumer's attitude, or trying to persuade the customer to undertake a specific action, for example purchase or repurchase. The communication objectives linked to advertising may be summarised as follows:

- to ensure exposure for the advertised product or service
- to create awareness of new products, or developments of existing ones
- to improve customer attitudes towards the product and/or firm
- to increase sales and profits
- to generate enquiries from potential customers
- to change the attitudes and habits of people to whom the message is directed, for example to promote road safety.

To achieve one or a combination of these objectives requires a clear idea of the characteristics of the audience, and these should be considered alongside the capability of advertising (as opposed to other promotional methods) to achieve these purposes. For example, in business marketing, advertising may be less cost-effective than personal selling.

3. Design the message

This can be divided into four problems for the communicator to solve.

- What should the content of the message be in order to appeal directly to the target audience?
- How should the message be structured?
- What images should be used to appeal to the audience, for example pictures, colour, shape, etc.?
- What should the message source be – should it involve an expert or celebrity? To what extent should the message source be trustworthy and likeable, etc.?

These questions suggest the need for a knowledge of how involved the audience are with the product. This involvement has three levels?

Level 1. No involvement, where there is no interest in the product and no purchase behaviour takes place. It is quite possible for an advert to be liked and found amusing and informative, yet fail to persuade the market.
Level 2. Low involvement, where there is enough interest in the product to encourage use, but there is insufficient

interest in a particular brand to persuade customers of the benefits of brand loyalty – they will switch to another brand if the usual brand is not available.
Level 3. High involvement, where there is interest in the product and there is brand loyalty. Here the customer will prefer to wait until a brand becomes available if it is out of stock.

4. Select the communications channels

Communications channels can be divided into two main types – personal and non-personal.

Personal channels carry great weight, particularly where the product is expensive and purchased infrequently and/or when the product has a significant social character, for example clothing and cars. Companies can try to tap into personal influence channels by identifying influential individuals, by seeking to create opinion leaders or by working through prominent members of the community.

Unlike personal channels, non-personal channels do not entail personal contact or feedback and so it is more difficult to measure how messages have been received and decoded. These channels include the mass media and display media such as posters, as well as the more selective media such as magazines. In addition, the environment created in a retail outlet can create the right conditions for the purchase or consumption of the product.

The main point here is that, although personal channels are a very effective means of communicating with the target audience, non-personal channels are the only means of gaining access to mass consumer markets, such as in fast-moving consumer goods. The correct mix has to be tailored to the market or product that is being promoted, but in all cases a large element of non-personal communication is essential.

Examples of changing the promotional mix include?

- fast-moving consumer goods – equal proportions spent on personal selling, sales promotion and advertising, with no more than 2 per cent spent on publicity
- consumer durables – half the available budget spent on personal selling, one-third on advertising, with the remainder on publicity
- services – up to two-thirds spent on personal selling, with the remaining amount being spent mainly on sales promotion and advertising; publicity only receives a small proportion of this remaining money

- industrial goods – the highest spender on personal selling at over 80 per cent, with 10 per cent on advertising and the remainder split evenly between the other two areas
- capital goods – similar to the service sector in its promotional mix

5. Develop the total promotional budget

There are five main ways of establishing budgets, as follows.

- **Advertising to sales ratios.** In this situation a fixed percentage of sales revenue, based on past, current or forecast sales, is budgeted. This has the advantage of being relatively straightforward, but fails to take account of what is happening in the marketplace, the different stages of the product life cycle, or the position in the Boston matrix portfolio (see Chapter 4 page 87), which will be major influences.
- **Objective and task.** Here there is a need to define the advertising objectives, but it is difficult to be certain how well advertising has achieved its objectives. For example, what budget level is required to achieve the objective of increasing awareness of the company's products?
- **Matching the competition.** This is in fact a 'shout to be heard' approach, for which it is necessary to be able to calculate what the competition has spent and what it is likely to spend in the future. This assumes that the competition has got its budget right, which is by no means certain, and it may increase advertising spending. It ignores the differences that exist between organisations, such as their size and their ability to sustain a high advertising spend.
- **Matching market share to advertising share.** This approach takes the view that there is a relationship between increasing the advertising spend and increasing market share. Likewise, a falling advertising spend will lead to a fall in market share, usually after a time lag. This approach has to recognise the problem of the law of diminishing returns – at some point there would be a fall in the returns obtained from increasing the budget. Other factors also play a part in adjusting market share, such as the behaviour of the competition, the quality of the media available to serve that market, and the performance of the market given its growth potential.
- **'What we can afford'.** A popular approach is to base the budget on past experience and to make an estimate of the future affordability of advertisements the company wishes to use.

These five methods are by no means the only approaches available, but Figure 3.7 shows their popularity. Respondents may have chosen more than one method.

Method	
Objective and task	41%
What we can afford	34%
Percentage of expected sales	25%
Percentage of past sales	25%
Agencies' proposals	5%
Percentage related to current sales	5%
Target share of total industry	2%
Others	3%

Figure 3.7 *Methods used to determine advertising budgets*

6. Decide on the promotion mix

This has already been partly considered above, and is linked to the adoption and diffusion process (see page 46). The best promotional mix depends on the stage of consumer acceptance that has been reached, but the cycle is not necessarily a continuum and some products may appear only in the innovator and early adopter part of the cycle.

Another conclusion to be drawn from this is that different target audiences will require different promotional mixes. Other influences on the mix can be summarised as follows:

- the strengths and weaknesses of each promotional tool
- distribution and service requirements, for example whether it is appropriate to push products through the distribution chain – which involves aggressive promotion by the producer to the intermediaries – or pull products through the distribution chain through promotion to the consumer.

7. Measure the promotion results

At all stages in the process it is important to assess how effectively promotion has contributed to the communication process. In order to measure achievements, an organisation must have closely defined its communication objectives.

8. Manage and coordinate the total marketing communications process

These last two tasks can prove to be difficult, particularly when using non-personal means of communication. If the mix is to be effectively managed and reviewed, some means has to be found to measure effectiveness.

Advertising

Traditionally, promotion has been categorised as an above-the-line or below-the-line activity. These distinctions were based on UK tax regulations which were changed some time ago, but the definition can still be found in use. Advertising, which is directly paid for, is known as above-the-line activity, whereas publicity, which is not paid for directly, is below the line. Of more importance is the way in which advertising can be used to raise awareness and encourage purchase. The following provides an overview of the main issues.

An advertising campaign will be influenced by the following questions:

- is the aim of the campaign to increase awareness or to increase sales?
- what message will the organisation want to convey to its customers?
- what are the most appropriate media for the organisation to use?
- how frequently will a message need to be displayed?
- what style should the message adopt, e.g. factual, humorous?
- how large is the budget to support the aims of the campaign?
- what are the most appropriate evaluation methods to test reactions to the campaign?

Advertising objectives and message

These objectives cannot be separated from the other elements of the marketing mix – it is inappropriate to set an advertising objective without reference to the product's position in a specific market. Advertising is often classed under one of three headings, as shown below.

- **Informative advertising.** This is where advertising is concerned with conveying information and raising consumer awareness of the product or the organisation.
- **Persuasive advertising.** This type is more concerned with creating a desire for the product and stimulating purchase, so it tends to build brand preference, encourage brand switching and persuade the customer to purchase now.
- **Reminding advertising.** This is often used for well-established products and seeks to remind customers about the product or organisation, so it attempts to keep the product at the forefront of the customer's mind and suggest that it will be needed in the near future.

These approaches will be used in varying degrees over the product life cycle, but they will be less easy to apply to certain products. For example, in the financial services sector difficulties arise in advertising products because of the amount of information required prior to purchase. In addition, there are legal restrictions on the advertising of such products. Advertising is usually seen therefore merely as the first step in a promotion campaign, its main objective being to raise the consumer's awareness of the company and its product.

From the objectives to inform, persuade and remind, other objectives can be established – sales volume or revenue objectives are common. However, in most cases there is no direct link between the seller and the consumer, and the effect of advertising on sales is not easy to measure. Advertising is only one part of the marketing mix and many other influences have to be acknowledged as impinging upon the buying decision. Adverts may be aimed at increasing profitability, but the difficulties of tracing their impact here are the same as for sales volume.

Choosing the media

The choice of the most appropriate media for advertisements will depend upon the nature of the market to be reached and the complexity of the message. One of the more obvious considerations when choosing between media is the cost, e.g. the cost per number of consumers reached. On this basis, TV comes out high on total cost but low on cost per person, while direct mail shows the opposite result. Further considerations can be listed as follows.

- **Wastage** – the typical accuracy of any one media can be judged, with TV showing less accuracy than specialist magazines in a target market.
- **Reach of the media** – how many people may be exposed to an advert.
- **Regularity** – how often a medium can be used. Outdoor advertising scores poorly on this basis as adverts can be changed only at irregular intervals.
- **Performance** – magazine adverts score highly here as the number of exposures and the length of time the message remains with the customer are generally high.
- **Persuasive impact** – this is raised where a variety of images and sensations can be conveyed to the customer; obviously TV scores well here, as it can combine both audio and visual impact.

- **Clutter** – this is a problem, where one ad follows another closely, to the possible detriment of all.
- **Lead time** – the period between the placement of the advert to its display or transmission. Newspapers score well here compared to TV.

Media selection

The task of media selection is to find the most effective way to deliver the desired number of exposures to the target audience. This can be analysed by looking at the reach, which is the number of people in the audience who are exposed to the advertisement, and the frequency, which is the number of times within a specified period that individuals or groups will be exposed to it. The advertiser has to set objectives for the research and choice of media as well as look at the problems of reach, frequency and desired impact.

Media choice is also limited by budget constraints. Obviously, the higher-quality media will eat into the budget more quickly, thereby reducing the number of exposures (frequency), but usually increasing the reach into the specific market or segment required.

The advertiser needs to be well aware of the different media available that can deliver the required reach and achieve the desired frequency. If the media to be considered are newspapers, TV, direct mail, magazines, radio and outdoor media such as billboards it will be necessary to consider respective strengths and weaknesses. This will take into account audience characteristics, the cost, the type of product being promoted and the complexity of the message. It is here that advertising research provides an essential tool.

Campaign planning

Many companies select an advertising agency to help achieve promotional goals. The choice of an agency depends on issues such as the location of the agency and the ease of access to it – a London-based agency which seems to hold many attractions such as size and prestige may well be inaccessible on a regular basis.

The size of the agency is important – does it have the capacity to cope with a major promotional campaign, for example? In addition, companies may need to consider the suitability of the agency to deal with seasonal fluctuations in demand, i.e. will the agency be able to deal effectively with the company's account at all times?

Allied considerations include a possible conflict of interest if the agency is also working for competitors, how quickly it can respond to its clients' demands and to what extent the agency needs to have specialist knowledge of the product or market and the relevant media.

In selecting an agency companies are faced with a choice of types. A full-service agency offers the following services: creative campaign planning; media buying; advertising production; point-of-sale literature etc.; account management; research; marketing planning; public relations, and exhibitions organisation. Special-interest agencies offer the full range of services for clients in particular industries. Between these two are independent agencies, which buy in the services of a number of suppliers to implement the campaign. There is also the possibility of companies developing an in-house capability – this would be justified if the advertising spend is large enough to warrant setting up an internal advertising department.

Sales promotion

Sales promotion includes all those activities and events other than advertising or personal selling methods that companies use to encourage customers and distribution channel buyers to make purchasing decisions.

Sales promotion can be used to achieve a number of marketing objectives, as follows:

- to gain consumers and convert them into regular users, particularly of new or improved products
- to widen the distribution of a product
- to influence stock levels, which may be too high or too low
- to reduce sales peaks and troughs and maintain economic production levels
- to cushion the effect of a price increase
- to create new interest in an established product or improve results from in-store displays.

To achieve these objectives a variety of tools are available, including those detailed below.

- **Free sample.** This is one of the more successful promotional devices as it is the one most likely to entice consumers to try the product. However, the weakness of this approach lies in its cost to the producer, which can only be justified if the product is expected to sell in large quantities.

- **Off-price label.** This method features a reduction in price and is one of the more popular promotional methods, particularly as it does not carry the high cost of the free sample and can also be used by retailers in their promotions.
- **Branded offer.** This can take two forms, either using a well-known brand to carry a free sample of another non-competing product, or offering two for the price of one.
- **Premium offer.** This comes in three types – free gifts, free send-away premium (free gift in exchange for proof of purchase) and self-liquidating premiums (consumer has to send both money and proof of purchase).
- **Competition.** The main attraction to the consumer here is the possibility of winning a large prize. Competitions have long been used by newspapers and in direct mail literature to encourage consumption.
- **Personality promotion.** The method used here is to offer a prize if, for example, the person has the advertised product in the home when a 'personality' calls or if the respondent can recite a catchphrase. Examples of such 'personalities' include the fast food chain's Ronald McDonald, and they can be used with little inconvenience compared to some of the other promotional devices described. However, if the cost of in-store displays and leaflet distribution as well as the advertising of this promotion is included, then it can seem expensive.

Examples of sales promotions offered to the trade include direct money promotions such as financial incentives, or indirect money promotions such as extending credit. Likewise, free gifts and trial offers in coupons and vouchers are offered to the trade.

In some service industries such as banking, most of the standard sales promotion techniques described above will be of little use, as the intangibility of the product causes problems. Those that offer free gifts with the opening of a new account achieve some success, however as consumers perceived themselves to be getting something of greater value and interest, and this promotes a tangible link with the service. One solution adopted by banks and others in the financial services sector is to use a point-of-sale promotion. In-store displays and point-of-sale promotions can be used to influence the impulse buyer. Although the majority of point-of-sales promotion material is prepared centrally, it is possible to vary the display according to the characteristics of the customers. For example, a bank branch in an affluent retirement area will find it could profit from a display of leaflets on tax planning, trust services and other related financial products.

Setting objectives, undertaking research, setting budgets, implementation and control are all issues that should be addressed, but as many marketing writers have pointed out, these tend to be the least competently managed in the area of promotion. To solve this problem, the objectives of each promotion should be clearly stated, for example achieving repeat purchase, improving distribution, combating competition, and so on. Once set, objectives should be followed by selecting the appropriate technique, undertaking a pretest, mounting the promotion and then evaluating the result.

Packaging

Packaging is important in the promotion of a product. Good packaging obviously protects a product well, but it also makes it noticeable on the shelf, conveys a brand or corporate image, can give information, and so on. More and more products can be packaged to appeal directly to the customer.

Advertising can support the messages to be found on packaging, and likewise packaging can be used to advertise other products in the range. Packaging can bring together additional items in one offering, priced and promoted to suit the market. For example, textbooks are now packaged with a floppy disk or CD-Rom and student manual, to provide a full learning package.

Further development in the technology for packaging will give it increasing importance in bringing products to their market successfully.

Public relations

Public relations (PR) involves much more than simply relationships with the media – it is the way in which a business communicates with all who come into contact with it, as well as the way it relates to people who are important to it and maintains their goodwill. The Institute of Public Relations defines PR as the deliberate, planned and sustained effort to establish and maintain a mutual understanding between an organisation and its public, including stakeholders.

Public relations is an important part of the promotions mix and can help to fulfil many of the aims and objectives of the full marketing mix, particularly when looking to achieve understanding or to change opinions among the targeted public. These can be the customers, employees, shareholders, government agencies, or any specific group that the company thinks it is important to influence.

If the audience can be varied, then so too can the uses to which PR can be put. It may be used to promote brands, products, persons, places, ideas, activities and regions so there are many types of organisation which will wish to use PR methods.

The increasing importance of this type of promotion for organisations throughout the public, private and not-for-profit sectors means that careful thought needs to be given to its uses and its ability to meet objectives. The benefits of PR were revealed in market research that showed nearly 70 per cent of people in the UK think a company with a good reputation will have built this upon a foundation of good quality products. The research also showed that the better known a company is, the more highly it will be regarded.

PR includes the following activities:

- press releases
- product publicity
- corporate communications
- lobbying
- counselling – briefing managers about public issues, the company's position on these issues and company images.

Sponsorship

Products can be endorsed by personalities – an example is football boots endorsed by David Beckham. Companies can also sponsor events, from which they hope to gain credibility. Coca-Cola sponsors the Olympics, and Continental Tyres sponsors the Champions League in Europe. What benefit will be gained from paying for a personality to sponsor a product, or from the company sponsoring an event?

Apart from the direct payments involved, sponsorship requires additional spending on advertising to inform people of the link, and this further spending must be seen to have a tangible benefit. Nationwide Building Society's sponsorship of the Football League and the Royal Bank of Scotland's sponsorship of the Scottish Premiership must all be judged as ways of promoting their name to many more people than could be reached by traditional advertising. A rigorous review of the costs and benefits of sponsorship must be made, as with any other part of the promotional mix. Sponsors of the Millennium Dome in London, such as Marks & Spencer, would have adopted just such an

approach before agreeing to commit their money and names to the project. Setting objectives, defining strategy, managing implementation and review are all necessary features of sponsorship planning, as they would be for advertising or personal selling.

PR planning and management

As with all promotions work, PR must be properly established and managed. Figure 3.8 shows how a campaign may be set up.

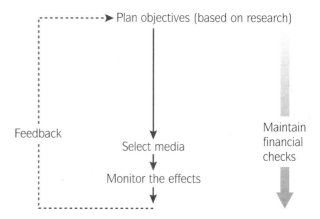

Figure 3.8 *Public relations planning*

Plan objectives and target audience

General objectives can be set, and these may be refined to produce clearly defined goals. For example, an objective could be to develop publicity aimed at various ethnic groups, or to encourage magazines and newspaper articles showing the environmental friendliness of a range of products. The target audience should be identified and the magazines and newspapers favoured by those groups could be supplied with press releases.

Carry out research

It is important to know how the company or organisation stands in the eyes of its public – does the company know what its weaknesses and shortcomings may be? If these are to be answered honestly, research will have to be undertaken to see whether the perceptions of the organisation are the same as those of the target audience.

A fundamental question to be addressed is who the groups are that are important for the company. One obvious group is 'our customers', but follow-up questions should induce further research – who are our present customers, should we include past customers, and who are our potential customers? The company should include suppliers, distributors and other stakeholders as it will have good reasons for promoting its interests with them.

Organise for PR

There are three main ways in which PR organisation can be done:

- internally, either as a function of the marketing department or as a separate section
- through the PR department of a full-service advertising agency
- through a specialist PR agency (often a subsidiary of an advertising agency).

The choice between the three depends on the importance of PR to the organisation, cost comparisons, and the ease with which this specialism could be incorporated into the organisation instead of given to an outside agency.

Select the media

An important consideration here is the nature of the information to be related about the product or the company. If there is no suitable medium to be found, the PR specialist may have to create it by means of benefit evenings, fairs and so on.

Once the right media have been chosen, the relationship between the PR specialist and contacts such as newspaper editors should be used to maintain links and achieve coverage. Press releases describing stories or events have to compete alongside many others in a busy newsroom, so care has to be taken over the design, layout and structure of the press release in order to attract the eye of journalists.

Monitor the effects

As with many other aspects of promotion, the effects of PR are difficult to monitor. However, three main methods of evaluation can be used to provide useful guidance.

- **Product awareness** can be measured on a before-and-after basis with the relevant public, taking into account other promotional influences.
- **Sales/profit impact** is a more satisfactory measure for the company wishing to judge the return it is obtaining on its PR investment. Here, however, some calculation has to be made as to how the impact of PR could produce a particular effect. It is worth remembering that PR can also be used to defend market share, or to maintain sales in a recessionary or declining market.
- **Exposure to the PR event** is the easiest measurement to make, and considers the numbers of people exposed to the event – for example, how many people have read a newspaper article about the company and its products. Many organisations prefer this method, particularly if they want to achieve a high exposure to raise the corporate profile. The difficulty with this method is knowing how effective the exposure is, particularly if the company wants to know how people have reacted to a story.

Discussion point

Advertising often fails to deliver its message to target groups. Should companies therefore invest more in the other parts of the promotion mix?

Personal selling and sales management

The range of sales activities under this heading are:

- deliverymen/women who also sell (for example milk deliverers, now often self-employed and acting as franchisees)
- sales staff within the premises of a sales organisation, for example the shop assistant
- travelling sales representatives who require little in the way of technical knowledge, for example in food
- salespeople who need technical expertise to sell the product
- salespeople who need to create a sale through their selling methods where an established market does not exist, for example for insurance policies.

A major issue is the cost of the salesforce, which in some companies will take the major share of the marketing budget. Personal selling is one of the most expensive forms of promotion in terms of cost per person contacted.

Because of the cost elements, personal selling is usually treated separately from the rest of the promotions mix. However, its importance lies in the creation of personal, face-to-face selling opportunities, which provide vital communications links that other items of the promotional mix lack. A personal relationship can be built up between the customer and the supplier, allowing the salesperson flexibility to test the selling proposal before closing a deal with the customer. In addition, it can allow for past mistakes and any customer dissatisfaction to be rectified during sales interviews.

The achievement of the organisation's goals will depend to a large extent on the professionalism of the salesforce, and the successful administration of this force will enhance the organisation's chances of reaching its goals.

Planning, control and design

Planning, control and design of personal selling will be influenced by various factors, among them the following.

- **Intensity of competition.** This will affect the choice of sales structure, for example when specialisation appears to give an advantage to a rival company.
- **Communications mix.** The company may have decided the most efficient way to sell will be by the use of a salesforce instead of advertising, and this will have an impact on the size and quality of that salesforce.
- **Specialisation.** This can be by function, product, type of customers, outlet or market. Whichever method is used, it should be justified.
- **Intermediaries.** The chain of distribution and the strategic issues associated with it will affect the size and importance of the salesforce, for example selling to the large supermarket chains will require a small workforce.

These factors give a broad approach only and it is necessary to decide on a detailed design such as the number of territories and specialisations.

Territorial design

The most common and often the simplest way of organising the salesforce is by territory. We would typically expect to see a pyramid organisation, with top management at head office, sales supervisors controlling the regional salesforce, and a salesperson for each territory. The company would then wish to look at further issues such as the span of control for each supervisor, which in turn would require a consideration of the amount of work involved in the supervisors' and salespersons' jobs and the physical conditions under which this work would be done.

The objective of territorial design is to reduce travelling time and costs, since research reveals that a high proportion of each salesperson's day is spent travelling. Additionally, the design should attempt to establish a sales area that will enable the individual salesperson to get to know customers, which will provide (as far as possible) an equitable workload and sales potential, and which will keep administration down to acceptable levels.

Specialisation by the nature of the product

This is a more sophisticated approach than design by territory, with the product (or group of products) being divided up to give special attention to each one. This could, for example, help to sell advanced technical goods to a knowledgeable customer. The salesforce will require training to achieve an indepth understanding of the product, and those recruited may need a high level of education, probably to degree level. This is countered by Stafford and Grant, however, who argue in their book *Effective Sales Management* (Heinemann, 1986) that the levels of education or product understanding should not be seen as prerequisites for all members of the salesforce. The best approach is to build a salesforce that can be trained in sales techniques and product knowledge, and by this means reduce the likelihood of high labour turnover.

Specialisation by range of market (market segments)

Specialisation could be by home and foreign markets, with the salesperson becoming familiar with the needs of a particular market. There are some drawbacks to this approach, however, particularly when the various market segments appear to require slightly different products and services, and when market boundaries become blurred (for example when the market is divided on an industrial/non-industrial basis, rather than into more straightforward home and foreign markets.)

Specialisation by range of customer

This is best explained by the example of industrial goods. These need specialised salespersons, each of whom deals with a small number of customers and gains an understanding of industrial buyer behaviour that can lead to large and valuable orders. Organising the salesforce in this way gives the potential to gain indepth knowledge of both present customer requirements and likely future needs of particular customers and the industry in general.

Planning and control

Planning and control strategies are needed to coordinate the sales effort with corporate and marketing objectives, i.e. to coordinate the work of the salesforce and sales management within the broader marketing and corporate objectives. This focuses attention on the sales organisation, which can adopt a four-stage approach.

1. **Identify clearly the objectives of the sales organisation.** These are likely to be based on sales volume and value, and probably on the complementary objectives of profit and expenses.
2. **Organise activities into major groups:**
   Group 1: marketing research and sales forecasting
   Group 2: advertising, promotion, sales contests, exhibiting
   Group 3: credit control, invoicing, etc.
3. **Organise groups into effective units.** This is similar to the approach mentioned previously, with the salesforce under the control of supervisors who report to regional managers.
4. **Allocate people to specific positions.** Planning is crucially dependent on the significance of personal selling in the communications mix, the need to achieve marketing and corporate objectives, the product to be sold and the external environment. This leads on to an assessment of competitors' positions, and how the company responds to them.

The performance of the sales team will need to be measured – its sales performance must be compared with the targets set out in the sales plan. Corrective action may be required, and in some circumstances this may necessitate changing the sales plan. Plans are not to be seen as inflexible but must reflect the current position of the company within its environment.

TASK

Outline the promotional mix and identify why this will change over the product life cycle.

Control is not exerted purely through a formal, quantified system. Both formal and informal systems are used, and together they produce a balanced approach.

Direct marketing

Direct marketing involves direct access to the customer. The major tools for this are telemarketing, direct mail, door-to-door selling, catalogues, electronic media (home shopping and cable television) and 'off-the-page' selling via cut-outs in magazines and newspapers.

This form of marketing has become an important method of selling over the past ten years, particularly in the UK, France, Belgium and Scandinavia. Several factors have contributed to this growth:

1. The costs of traditional forms of promotion such as advertising and sales promotion had risen steeply, forcing companies to look for alternatives.
2. Developments in information technology, in the use of databases and desktop publishing have facilitated the production of high quality direct marketing materials in-house.
3. Developments in mail technology have reduced the costs of distributing direct marketing materials.
4. The development and growth of the Internet has increased the availability of interactive facilities for customers to order directly.
5. The extensive use of direct marketing by companies has accelerated its acceptance and development.

The major benefit of direct marketing is that the organisation knows its customers: outcomes are measurable, names and addresses of consumers are stored in a database which can be used for future direct marketing and consumer profiles can be built from information contained in the company's sales files. Direct marketing is a convenient and effective marketing tool.

MARKETING MIX AND SERVICES: THE IMPORTANCE OF THE 7Ps

The original marketing mix – the 4Ps – has provided marketers with a useful tool with which to exploit their chosen markets. More recently, the augmented product concept, with its emphasis on services attached to the physical product (see page 44) has meant the 4Ps have required updating. People, process, physical evidence (ambience) have, therefore, been added to take account of the importance of services. This extended marketing mix – the 7Ps – is useful for services, but is also of fundamental importance to consumers who wish to avail themselves of high quality services to support the purchase and use of physical products.

People

Already referred to above, the important factor here is the contact that a potential consumer makes with the company, from pre-sales through the entire process to after-sales (and eventually repeat purchase). Interaction can occur at many levels throughout the organisation. A less-than-positive experience can dissuade the customer from seeking further contact with that organisation. This seems obvious, but what is not so clear is how a business organisation prepares itself and its staff to deal effectively with customers. The problem lies outside the marketing department and involves the selection, training and motivation of all personnel to provide the highest level of assistance to customers. In effect, all employees 'market' the organisation.

Process

Implied but not specifically stated above is that employees will only be able to provide an effective service if the process of delivery itself is well thought out and provides a flexible response to individual needs. Many customers expect to be kept informed of what is happening so that they can make plans based on this information. When travelling, say by plane, a business traveller would wish to be kept informed of any delays so that he or she could adapt plans accordingly. Likewise, a fog-bound airport might require large numbers of passengers to be accommodated overnight. Organising flows of information and transporting people to hotel accommodation would all require a 'fuss-free' service from the airline. Delays or failure in undertaking this will result in discontent. A further example is fast-food restaurants and other eating establishments, who have to provide prompt efficient service to match expectations.

Making payment an easy process, or providing a home-delivery service at a time and date convenient to the customer involves the organisation looking at its systems and procedures to facilitate this.

Physical evidence (ambience)

On entering a restaurant, leisure complex, pub, college or hospital, everybody has a first impression of how well designed it is, how welcoming, how easy to access, and the quality of the facilities. The noise and even the aroma count towards the atmosphere created. Many organisations in the public sector used to be characterised by spartan conditions, with very little in the way of customer facilities. Banking halls built in the 1930s or before created an imposing presence that many found intimidating; many potential customers preferred building societies as they offered a more intimate and welcoming environment. HSBC has spent millions of pounds changing the interior of its bank branches (formerly the Midland Bank) to make them more welcoming.

Arts facilities such as theatres are also places where the layout and terminology, such as stalls and grand circle, are not immediately understandable by the majority of the population who rarely attend them. Arts marketers have become aware that they can make their venues more understandable and less threatening. Once over this hurdle and with a positive experience of a theatre, art gallery or museum, many people will return to enjoy the facilities.

Shifting from the 4Ps to the 7Ps

The emphasis is still usually placed on the 4Ps because of the plethora of consumer products that exist. However, three-quarters of a developed economy's gross domestic product is comprised of services, and with this consideration the importance of incorporating the 7Ps becomes a little clearer. Allied to this is the number of physical products that are now sold with complementary services.

Further thought would also show that companies using best business practice focus carefully on the way the product is delivered to market. Many in both the public and private sectors now seek to gain competitive advantage through these means. Despite this, managers may still look on changes as opportunities to cut costs, raise margins and enhance shareholder value. The danger in this strategy is that it ignores the customer. But if by slimming down the organisation, layers of bureaucracy and red tape can be removed, decisions speeded up, information flows enhanced, and a better service offered to the customer, the organisation is more likely to thrive and prosper.

The burgeoning of e-commerce as a way of contacting new markets and market segments also requires a review of systems and procedures. For example, Amazon.Com, the US Internet bookshop is totally customer focused, providing a complete service to customers that allows ease of payment, tracing of shipments and even the ability to locate books that are out of print but stocked in second-hand bookshops. The 7Ps provide an enhanced understanding of what needs to be done in such an environment.

Discussion point

What extra insight do the items of people, process and physical evidence, added to the original 4Ps, offer to companies?

Market Segments

This chapter reviews in more depth the different types of markets that a firm may be engaged with. A firm may be involved in consumer markets, but also have an involvement in exporting. Likewise, a service firm may provide its product to a local charity and to a government agency. In each case, an organisation needs to be aware of the major issues it will have to address in order to be successful in its marketing. The chapter looks first at consumer and organisational markets, then offers an analysis of the provision of services, moving lastly to international and global markets.

On completion of the chapter you should be able to apply the marketing mix to different market segments. To achieve this you must demonstrate the ability to:

- recommend marketing mixes for two different segments in consumer markets

- explain the differences in marketing products and services to organisations rather than consumers

- explain how and why international marketing differs from domestic marketing.

CONSUMER MARKETS

Consumer markets consist of the individuals and households who purchase goods and services for consumption by themselves and their immediate family. In Chapter 2 the buyer behaviour of individuals and households was examined, and it was shown that an understanding of this process would enhance the ability of the organisation to supply a product that meets the needs of the target market.

Product classification

Figure 4.1 shows the ways in which consumer goods (products) can be classified, and the implications for

marketing of such an approach. The types of product in the table can be briefly summarised as follows.

Convenience goods

The consumer purchases convenience goods frequently – they include bread, milk and other everyday necessities. Often sold by brand name, these goods will be low priced. They can be further subdivided into staple, impulse and emergency items. Staple products, such as milk, need to be constantly available. Impulse goods are products purchased on the spur of the moment, with up to half of all supermarket products purchased being of this type. Emergency items, on the other hand, are necessary but infrequently purchased items such as a medical kit, or de-icer for the car.

Factors	Convenience goods	Shopping goods	Speciality goods
Consumer			
Planning time involved in purchase	Very little	Considerable	Extensive
Purchase frequency	Frequent	Less frequent	Infrequent
Importance of convenient location	Critical	Important	Unimportant
Comparison of price and quality	Very little	Considerable	Very little
Marketing mix			
Price	Low	Relatively high	High
Advertising	By manufacturer	Both manufacturer and retailer	Both manufacturer and retailer
Channel length	Long	Relatively short	Very short
Number of retail outlets	Many	Few	Very few – often one per market area
Store image	Unimportant	Very important	Important

Figure 4.1 *Consumer goods*

This has interesting implications for marketing. Doorstep milk deliveries, for example, have been declining in the UK as supermarkets and convenience stores have extended their opening hours, allowing this staple product to be purchased at almost any time. Until recent years, milk was not always available when required. Extended opening hours, coupled with the advent of freezers and larger fridges have changed the way milk is purchased and stored, providing a challenge to the marketers of a milk delivery business such as Express Dairies.

Shopping goods

These goods are purchased after the consumer has made comparisons of competing goods in various retail outlets on the basis of price, quality, style and so on. Shopping goods are typically more expensive than convenience goods, and include such items as clothing, furniture and white goods (fridges, cookers, etc).

Case Study

Consumers and information

A typical consumer in the USA has 150 national brands of breakfast cereal to choose from, with a typical supermarket carrying up to 90 of these items. To further confuse the consumer, each packet of cereal shows up to 100 separate items of information. The UK has fewer brands, but the consumer is still bombarded with a wide choice, leading possibly to confusion and reducing the chances that a purchase decision will lead to maximum satisfaction. This is true just for breakfast cereal, but the sheer volume of information received and processed on a vast range of goods is staggering.

Consumers, however, do not seem to be overwhelmed by the surfeit of information, usually focusing instead on a small amount of information which they use to make decisions. Research shows that experienced consumers are able to decide which attributes of a product can help to show its quality and performance. By contrast, when the markets of eastern Europe and Russia were first liberalised, consumers at first chose inferior goods, being unable to make effective choices.

Consumers do have difficulty using information, however, and consumer protection groups often highlight the problems such as what 'fat free' or 'only 5 per cent fat' really mean. Likewise, it is not always easy to recall or interpret information. What for example would be the consumer's interpretation of 'not expensive'? Does it mean the same as inexpensive?

It is possible for consumers to believe that a brand has certain characteristics, so a food brand may be considered to be of high quality, and from that consumers may assume that it is healthy and nutritious. This may not be true. Likewise, research has found that more people purchase minced beef described as 75 per cent lean, than when the same product is labelled 25 per cent fat.

So what do consumers do when shopping? The following points summarise the main points:

- Using **simplifying-choice rules**, the consumer saves time on a shopping trip. Consumers usually want to make a decision that meets minimum requirements. This involves considering items one at a time, and evaluating them first-hand relative to a minimum standard. if the product meets the stands, it is chosen. If it does not reach the standard, it is rejected and the next is reviewed.
- **Elimination by aspects** involves eliminating items if they perform poorly on a certain attribute, so cheapness may be a key attribute for the consumer, who will pick the option that is closest to this attribute.
- **Affect referral** is where consumers form an impression on first receiving information. This impression is kept in the memory and later used to assess the product. In this situation, not all information will be assessed.
- If a consumer repeatedly makes a decision to repurchase the same fast-moving consumer good (for example washing powder) research has shown that the consumer uses certain tactics to make these decisions. First, the consumer uses a simplified rule, such as finding the cheapest brand. If, when used, the product is seen to be satisfactory, it will be chosen again, so through trial and evaluation a **decision rule** will emerge that serves the consumer well. To test out this theory researchers observed 120 supermarket shoppers to watch the way they bought washing powders, a category that comprises a large number of brands and is seen to be a low-risk purchase. On average, consumers examined only 1.42 packages, and 72 per cent looked at only one.
- Consumers think of themselves as average. When they are unsure of their own preferences they infer that their taste will be consistent with the 'average' brand. This reduces the problem of choosing between a high quality, high price brand and a low price, lower quality one.

Questions

1. How do consumers use information to make decisions about preferred cereal brands?

2. How does branding influence consumers?

3. What use can be made of the above information by a company marketing cook-chill foods?

Important features of shopping goods are their physical attributes, price, styling and the place of purchase. As buyers expend some effort in making these purchases, marketers need to be aware of the most effective way to present information to them. Retailers and manufacturers work closely together in promoting shopping goods, and retailer purchases are often made directly from the manufacturer or its representative, rather than from a wholesaler. However, the challenge for producers is to ensure that consumers have the opportunity to view a product in favourable circumstances.

Case Study

Consumer choice – the producer's challenge

- High-speed, highly focused shopping is the norm. The average consumer inspects just 1.2 brands per purchase. If consumers make most of their decisions before entering the store, is the producer doing enough advertising outside the store? Is the brand prominent enough to capture attention inside?
- Consumers often use *ad hoc* product classification schemes, for example classifying drinks as cocktail ingredients. Producers need to consider whether there are any such schemes for which their product is an obvious candidate, and whether they can encourage retailers to run suitable themed promotions or displays.
- Are retailers displaying products by brand or product type? If a producer's line is extensive, brand displays will be likely to maximise sales; smaller lines are likely to benefit from product displays in which all brands are mingled.
- Brand extensions can boost a brand's strength, provided they do not overstretch it. New product categories must be suited to the associations of the brand, and the products that carry it must be at least as good as competitors' offerings.
- Co-branding is potentially a powerful strategy, provided that the brands reinforce rather than cancel one another out. The producer needs to ask: is it clear what benefit each brand can bring to the product? If not, customers will be confused.
- Competition between private label and national brands is increasing. National brands still predominate in many categories, because consumers perceive them as being of higher quality. The task for private label brands is to confront this perception by positioning themselves on quality at least as much as price.
- Consumers need to assimilate a vast amount of information in making purchase decisions. If a product performs well in areas that the public is concerned with (for example it contains relatively few artificial ingredients), the producer may want to inform the public of this or encourage retailers to do so.

Questions

1. Suggest how a food producer or a microwave oven manufacturer could meet the above challenges.

2. What, if any, is the downside of branding for
   a) consumers and b) producers?

Speciality goods

Purchasers of this type of product are well aware of what they require and are willing to go to great trouble to obtain it. Speciality goods possess some unique characteristics that cause the buyer to choose a particular brand. For these products, the buyer has complete information prior to the trip and is unwilling to accept substitutions. For example, the desire to buy a Rolex watch may not easily be met by the suggested purchase of a Cartier watch.

Speciality goods are typically high priced and frequently branded. Since consumers are willing to exert considerable effort to obtain them, fewer retail outlets are required.

Unsought goods

These are often goods that the consumer is unaware of, or maybe goods that the consumer is aware of but does not want at this particular moment. Products in the first category could, for some consumers, include notebook computers. The second category could include life assurance products. Immense marketing effort is required to sell unsought goods.

Advantages and disadvantages

The classification system provides additional information for marketers to use in developing strategy. Consumer behaviour patterns (see Chapter 2) differ for each type of good. But the classification system also poses problems. Although some products fit neatly into one category, others fall into the grey areas between categories. For example, how should a new car be classified? It is expensive, sold by brand and handled by a few exclusive dealers. But before classifying it as a speciality good, other factors must be considered, for example that most new car buyers shop around extensively among competing models and car dealers before deciding on the best deal. The classification system is at best a continuum representing degrees of effort expended by the consumer. At one end of the continuum are convenience goods, and at the other speciality goods.

On this continuum, the new car purchase can be located between the categories of shopping and speciality goods, but much closer to the speciality goods end.

A second problem within the classification system is that consumers differ in their buying patterns. One person may make a relatively unplanned purchase of a car, while another will shop extensively before making a more mundane purchase. One purchaser's impulse buying does not make a car a convenience good. Goods are, therefore, classified according to the purchase patterns of the majority of buyers.

Because of the investment levels necessary with luxury goods such as perfume, manufacturers will resist a move to make them available in more outlets and at lower prices. The move away from speciality to shopping goods may occur over time, however, as buyer behaviour changes. The classification of consumer goods is always in a state of flux, and marketers need to be aware of the ways in which any changes will affect their strategy. Figure 4.1 (see page 72) suggested some marketing mix combinations that are suitable for the different types of consumer goods. Using the knowledge built up from previous chapters, it is now possible to put together a marketing mix for such products, whether they are convenience goods, fast-moving consumer goods (FMCG) such items as branded groceries, confectionery, household wares, washing powders and so on, or shopping goods, such as an item of fashion clothing.

TYPES OF ORGANISATIONAL MARKET

For marketers to be effective they need to understand the market dynamics of both the consumer and organisational markets. The following sections examine industrial goods and their markets.

Industrial goods

Purchases by businesses are influenced by factors not found in the consumer marketplace. Industrial buyers are professional customers; their job is to make effective purchase decisions. The classification system for industrial goods is based on product use rather than on buying patterns, so they can be divided into five categories: installation; accessory equipment; component parts and materials; new materials; and industrial supplies.

Installation

Tools and machines used for production, such as cranes and paint spraying equipment, are sometimes standardised and perform similar tasks for many firms. Equipment of this type is expensive and purchases need to be authorised by senior managers. In many instances the decision-making is a lengthy process. For example, BMW's investment of £1.4 billion in the Rover plant at Longbridge, Birmingham in 1999, which required government support of some £200 million, was clearly dependent on many factors, such as the suitability of the site for new product models, the availability of other locations, and the feasibility of setting up new assembly lines on an existing site.

The company selling an installation will, in many cases, have to provide technical expertise. When custom-made equipment is ordered, representatives of the selling firm work closely with the buyer's engineers and production personnel to design the product to the buyer's specific requirements.

Price can often be a less important factor for such products, with the interest focused on the efficiency and performance likely to be obtained over the life of the equipment. While still a factor, price will have reduced importance in the overall negotiations.

Selling in this type of marketplace puts a greater emphasis on the use of trained salespeople with a technical background.

Accessory equipment

Accessory goods are capital items that are usually less expensive and have a shorter life span than installations. They include personal computers, lathes, hand tools and so on. Quality and service are important, but price plays a more important role in the purchase of such items. Here it is possible to use wholesalers to distribute the goods to customers, and therefore use third parties to assist with the marketing effort.

Component parts and materials

Component parts are used within a finished product, for example tyres are fitted to cars, batteries are placed in electrical appliances, and so on. Purchasers of these items need a regular supply of uniform goods produced to a high standard. Direct sale of these items is common, and if the purchaser is satisfied with quality and reliability a long-standing partnership may be established. This is particularly true of just-in-time production methods, when guarantees of supply at the right time to maintain production are essential.

Raw materials

Farm products, coal and timber are all new (raw) materials, which can become part of a final product. Since most raw materials are graded, the purchaser is assured of standardised products of uniform quality. Direct sale of raw materials is common, and this is often arranged on a centralised basis, for example a farmer may enter into a contract with a supermarket chain to supply vegetables. Purchasers buy raw materials from the firms they consider most capable of delivering to the required quality and quantity. Price is also an issue, but is not often the decisive factor.

Industrial supplies

Items that are regularly needed as part of a firm's daily operation, but not included in the final product, are known as industrial supplies. They include heating oil, cleaning fluids, office stationery and so on. The regular purchase of these supplies is a routine part of a purchasing agent's job. Wholesalers are often used as suppliers because the items have a low unit price, small volumes of sales and a large number of potential buyers. Since supplies are relatively standardised, price competition is often important. However, little time is spent making purchase decisions, with orders often placed over the phone or by fax.

Industrial markets

The industrial (producer) market is the largest part of the organisational market and consists of individuals and firms that acquire goods and services in order to produce other goods and services for resale, and to run their operations. Manufacturing firms, agriculture, mining and construction industries and a range of service industries such as transportation, public utilities, insurance and finance make up this market.

Reseller markets

The reseller market consists of organisations who buy finished goods to resell or rent. In general, the physical characteristics of the product are unchanged in the reseller markets. The market consists of wholesalers and retailers, the former purchasing products to resell to other wholesalers, to retailers and to governments. Retailers purchase products in order to sell them to the final consumer.

In most cases, resale products such as clothing, appliances, sports equipment and car parts are finished goods that are marketed to customers in the selling firm's market area. In other cases, some processing or repackaging may take place. For example, timber dealers and carpet retailers may purchase in bulk and then provide specific quantities and sizes to meet customers' specifications.

Government markets

The government market consists of national and local government. Billions of pounds are spent on goods and services to carry out government operations and provide services to the public such as schools, hospitals, roads and national defence. The government and its agencies buy items as diverse as furniture, cars, clothing and warships.

The government procurement process is quite different from the private sector, in that the government buys through the 'bidding' system. The purchaser advertises for bids and states the specifications for the product. In general, regulations oblige the government to accept the lowest bid. If the product concerned is complex or non-standard, the government department may negotiate a purchase contract with a supplier.

Many firms tend to avoid this market because of the effort necessary to sell to the government, with its complicated procedures and requirements, yet the government market can be very profitable for firms that pursue it.

Non-business (institutional) markets

The non-business or non-profit organisations include churches, trade unions, museums, universities, libraries and charitable institutions. These organisations purchase millions of pounds' worth of goods and services every year to run their operations.

They differ from profit-seeking business organisations in that they have different goals and usually have limited resources at their disposal. Marketing to these institutions will require a different kind of campaign, such as one stressing environmental advantages or opportunities for favourable publicity.

Primary characteristics of industrial market demand

Derived demand

The demand for an industrial good is derived from the demand for the consumer products in which it is to be used. For example, the demand for steel, an industrial good, will depend partially on the demand for cars which are consumer items.

Inelastic demand

The demand for many industrial products is relatively inelastic, i.e. it responds very little to an increase or decrease in price. A drop in the price of steel will not cause car manufacturers to purchase more steel. Industrial demand is often inelastic because most products contain many parts, so a rise in the price of a few components in a product will only marginally increase the cost per unit.

On the other hand, if the component represents a substantial proportion of production costs, it is likely that demand will be elastic because a price change will cause the price of the finished product to rise or fall sharply as the case may be, therefore affecting final demand. For example, if manufacturers of car engines significantly increase their prices, this may force car producers to increase the prices of their cars, thereby reducing demand.

Inelasticity of industrial demand may be evident in the short term, but over the long run demand is likely to be more elastic. For example, if the price of cotton for men's shirts increases, it is unlikely that the price of the final product will rise immediately. However, the change may be reflected in higher prices in the following year, and this will eventually influence the demand for shirts, and therefore the demand for cotton.

A final point to remember is that inelasticity of demand refers only to the overall demand of the industry, rather than that of an individual firm. For example, if one tyre manufacturer reduces its prices to vehicle producers it may achieve higher sales because more vehicle manufacturers may turn to it with their orders. This advantage may be short lived if competitors retaliate to regain their lost business. In the short term, therefore, the firm sees an elastic demand curve, but industry demand as a whole is inelastic for the particular product.

Joint demand

The demand for some industrial products is related to the demand for other industrial goods that are used jointly with it – this is joint demand. A shortage of one item will adversely affect the demand for the other. For example, coke and iron ore are both required for making pig iron. If the coke supply is reduced, there will be an immediate effect on the demand for iron ore.

Inventory adjustments

Changes in inventory policy can have an impact on industrial demand. A 60-day supply of raw materials may be considered the optimal inventory for firms in a particular industry to hold. If economic conditions or other factors dictate that this level be increased to a 90-day supply, the raw material supplier will be faced with a large increase in orders. Inventory adjustments can be a major determinant of industrial demand, and they often reflect changes in gross domestic product figures.

Demand variability

Because the industrial market largely consists of derived demand, there is immense variability in industrial demand. Suppose the demand for industrial product A is derived from the demand for consumer product B, an item whose sales have been growing at an annual rate of 10 per cent. If the demand for product B slows to a 5 per cent annual increase management may decide to delay further purchases of product A, relying on existing inventory until market conditions are clarified. Even modest shifts in the demand for product B could greatly affect product A's demand.

Knowledgeable market

In general, industrial buyers have the following characteristics compared to the final consumers:

• they are more knowledgeable about products
• they have alternative sources of supply
• they are aware of competitors' products.

The marketing implication for sellers of industrial products is that they need to select, train and remunerate their industrial salespeople well, concentrate more on personal selling and offer better after-sales services in order to capture a lucrative proportion of the industrial goods markets.

Other characteristics of organisational markets

There are marked differences between industrial and consumer buyer behaviour, which emanate from the nature of the markets, the products, the buyer–seller relationship and the motives of the buyers.

The make, buy or lease decision

Organisational buyers considering the acquisition of a new product have three basic options:

* to make the product themselves
* to purchase it from another organisation
* to lease it from another organisation.

If the company has the capability to manufacture the item itself, this may be the most desirable option. Considerable cost savings may be realised if the purchaser does not have to pay its manufacturing division all of the overhead or profit margin that would be charged to an outside buyer. Most organisational or industrial products cannot be made internally, however, and purchasing them from outside is the most common choice.

In industrial markets, organisational buyers often buy direct from the manufacturers. This is especially beneficial to a seller when the item concerned is expensive, complex and necessitates technical assistance. For example, British Airways can buy aircraft directly from Boeing or Airbus.

Leasing is a third possibility in many industrial situations, and is contingent upon the tax benefits to the company. Increasingly, organisations are leasing industrial products instead of buying them outright. These products range from construction equipment, off-shore drilling rigs and machine tools to photocopiers and company cars.

There are a number of advantages for the firm leasing out the equipment (the lessor), including the following

* total income after costs and expenses tends to be higher than if the equipment was sold outright
* there is an opportunity to do business with users who may not have been able to purchase the brand-new product
* it is an effective method to widen distribution.

There are also advantages for the firm leasing the equipment (the lessee), as follows:

* more capital remains available for other projects
* the seller's latest product is obtained
* there are advantages in those markets where rental payments are tax deductible
* leased equipment receives regular servicing, which removes the problem of maintenance and breakdowns
* leasing is appropriate for equipment required seasonally, such as construction equipment.

Complexity of organisational purchases

Where major purchases are involved, negotiations may take several weeks or even months, and the buying decision may rest with a number of persons in the organisation. The choice of a supplier for industrial drill presses, for example, may be made jointly by the purchasing agent and the managers of the company's production, engineering and maintenance departments. Each may have a different point of view to be taken into account in making a purchase. As a result, representatives of the selling firm must be well versed in technical aspects of the product or service and capable of interacting socially and professionally with managers of the various departments involved. In the chemicals industry, for example, it takes an average of seven face-to-face presentations to achieve a sale.

Frequency of purchase

In general, organisations tend to purchase infrequently. Large items of equipment are bought only once in many years, and smaller components and materials are usually ordered on a long-term contract, normally renewed once a year. Even office equipment is usually only bought every quarter or half year.

The marketing implications are that an emphasis on personal selling may be required. A potential customer may need to be contacted on a regular basis to ascertain when a purchase is imminent, and to be kept informed about new products.

Reciprocity

Reciprocity in industrial markets means the practice of organisational buyers choosing suppliers who also buy from them. This practice appears to be declining, partly as a result of the competitive aspects of organisational buying – the buyer needs to obtain a competitive price, service and quality from the supplier to justify the purchase.

TASK

Business-to-business marketing is an important activity for many companies. What are the differences between this and consumer markets?

Other factors of concern to organisational buyers

Organisational buyers are concerned with product servicing, quality and supply requirements.

Product servicing is crucial to many firms. Given that many industrial products are standardised, a seller may gain competitive advantage by providing a unique set of services both before and after the sale (see below). These may range from repair services and credit facilities to the training of staff and inventory maintenance.

In addition, the organisational purchaser will require quality products, as good quality materials save considerable trouble for a manufacturer. Normally, the seller is provided with a set of specifications, and if these are not met the purchaser will turn to other suppliers.

Another important factor for the organisational buyer is the adequacy of supplies. This is particularly true for agricultural products and extractive products such as timber, iron ore, etc., where environmental conditions can affect supply. A major development in recent times, partly as a result of the adoption of just-in-time manufacturing processes, is the desire for a reduction in stocks held. This reduces the cost to the user firm of carrying excess inventory, while delivery on time reduces the waiting period for supplies, spare parts or repairs, which costs the firm money.

Adding value through service

The services offered to organisational markets have always been a notable feature. However, this now goes to a much deeper level of commitment in seeking to understand the business dynamics of the customer. It has become increasingly necessary to understand the whole process of an industrial customer, in which a product fulfils a particular purpose. Being informed about the objectives and approaches of a customer organisation can help to set service levels that meet the organisation's need, for example, to have a piece of equipment serviced and repaired so that it can meet its just-in-time objectives. Selling the machine with an untailored service and support package would fail to meet that customer's expectations.

Working closely with the client could also mean that new service requirements could be identified over time, so that both seller and purchaser feel that they are gaining something of real value from the transaction. It might even be the case that service levels come to be regarded as being of equal importance with the product itself.

Classifying organisational buying situations

Organisational buying behaviour is affected by situational variables. Purchase decisions vary in terms of the degree of effort required and the involvement of different levels of management within the organisation. Three organisational buying situations are generally recognised: straight rebuy, modified rebuy and new-taste buying.

Straight rebuy

A straight rebuy is a recurring situation where an item that has performed satisfactorily is purchased again by the customer. When a purchaser is pleased with the goods or service and the terms of sale are acceptable, there is little reason to assess other options and therefore a routine buying format is adopted.

Low-cost products such as paper clips and pencils for the office are typical examples. If the purchaser is pleased with the products, prices and terms, future purchases will probably be treated as a straight rebuy from the current vendor. Even expensive items specially designed for a customer's needs can be treated as a straight rebuy in some cases. Marketers fortunate enough to be in a straight rebuy situation should concentrate on maintaining a good relationship with the buyer by providing good service and delivery. Competitors will then find it difficult to present unique sales proposals that would break down this relationship.

Modified rebuy

A modified rebuy is a situation in which purchasers are willing to reevaluate the options available. The decision-makers feel that it may be to their advantage to look at alternative product offerings, using established purchasing guidelines. This might occur if a seller has allowed a straight rebuy situation to deteriorate because of poor service or delivery. Perceived quality and cost differences can also create a modified rebuy situation.

Organisational marketers want to move purchasers into a straight rebuy position by responding to all of their products and service needs. Competitors, on the other hand, try to move buyers into a modified rebuy situation by correctly assessing the factors that would make purchasers reconsider their decisions.

New-task buy

New-task buying refers to first-time or unique purchase situations that require considerable effort from the decision-maker. After such a need has been identified, evaluative criteria can be established and an extensive search is launched. Alternative product or service offerings and vendors are considered. For example, a firm manufacturing a new product must seek suppliers of component parts that it did not purchase previously.

TASK

Why classify consumer and industrial markets?

How does this help the marketer?

Discussion point

Suggest a marketing mix for a firm selling photocopiers to businesses.

SERVICES

As discussed in Chapter 1, services make up a large part of an advanced economy, comprising more than 60 per cent of the gross domestic product. Services can either be 'pure' services, such as hairdressing, or services that support a product, for example after-sales service for a dishwasher. Many companies now see offering services as an important way to add value for the customer, and seek to gain competitive advantage by such additions to an existing product. Services are often provided alongside a tangible product, and they are varied and complex. The special nature of services derives from several distinctive characteristics that have a major impact on marketing strategies.

Characteristics of services

Intangibility

Services do not have tangible features – they cannot be tasted, heard, touched, seen or smelled before they are purchased. People going on holiday cannot sample the delights of the destination before purchasing travel services, just as people going to a dentist cannot see the results before they buy. Before making purchase decisions, consumers therefore tend to look for signs to indicate quality, such as the price, the promotional material, the place and the people involved. This characteristic of services means that promotional campaigns must concentrate on the benefits to be derived from the service and advertise the tangible features of its intangible offers. For example, an insurance company will need to promote such benefits as peace of mind and a quick and efficient claims service.

Inseparability

Services are normally sold, produced and consumed at the same time, unlike physical products which are manufactured, stored, sold later and consumed separately. Inseparability means that a service cannot be separated from the personality of the seller. Consequently, the seller's reputation is frequently a key factor in the buying decision. For example, if the band Blur had to withdraw from a concert and were replaced by another group, it would not be the same service.

It is, however, possible for a service to be provided by a person who represents a seller. Travel agents or insurance agents promote a service sold by other companies.

The marketing implications of inseparability are that the firm providing the service needs to establish high quality, reliable training programmes for staff.

Heterogeneity

The quality of a service may be variable, whether it is provided by a service industry or by an individual seller. It is impossible to maintain a standardised output as each unit of service will vary from other units of the same service. The quality of a particular provider's service will depend on the provider's mood, attitudes or other factors on the day, therefore it is difficult to assess quality in advance when buying a service. Service organisations need to establish and maintain a high level of quality control and aim for consistency of quality. This is why effective human resource policies on staff selection, training and motivation are so important in the hotel, banking, retailing and travel industries.

Perishability

In general, services are perishable as they cannot be produced and stored for periods of peak demand. Unsold cinema seats, unoccupied seats on airlines and empty hotel rooms all represent lost business that cannot be recovered. However, there are some types of service which can be said to be 'stored'. For example, life assurance services are held by the insurance company (the seller) until they are required by the beneficiary (the buyer) at a later date.

A major feature associated with service industries is fluctuating demand with variability ranging across the seasons or even across the hours of the day. For example, many summer holiday resorts are empty during the winter season, and public transport services such as London Underground trains experience fluctuating demands daily, with peak periods occurring during the morning and evening rush hours.

If demand was consistent, the perishability of services would not present such a problem, but the combined effect of perishability and fluctuating demand is that service firms have to maintain an operational capacity that can meet peak demands. Capacity may lie idle for some of the time and therefore the firm incurs extra costs. However, service firms can develop strategies to smooth out these fluctuations.

- Creative pricing strategies can be used to encourage off-peak demand. Examples include low fares on trains during non-peak times, low prices for afternoon cinema showings, low-cost weekend hotel packages, and low telephone tariffs during the evenings and weekends.
- Alternative uses can be introduced for equipment or capacities that are under-used during off-peak seasons. For example, some universities offer accommodation in their student halls of residence to tourists during the summer vacation months.

Ownership

A further characteristic of services is that ownership does not pass from seller to buyer, which has implications for marketing. Purchasing a service allows the buyer only to have access to or use of that facility, not the ownership and control that is involved with a physical product. Examples are hiring a suit as opposed to having your own or renting a television. This lack of ownership characteristic of services may make them less desirable than owning a physical product, and consumers' perception of the value of a service may be reduced. Service industries attempt to overcome this problem by informing those who lease televisions, photocopier machines and other industrial equipment of the advantages of non-ownership, emphasising that maintenance is provided, and that replacement with new and more up-to-date items is automatic.

Classification of services

Services can be classified in five ways:

1. market type
2. degree of labour involvement
3. degree of customer contact
4. skill levels of the provider
5. aims of the service provider.

The first method of classification may be subdivided into services intended for consumers and those for industrial buyers. The implications of this distinction are similar to those for products as discussed earlier in the chapter. When the same service (telephone, gas, water or electricity) is sold to both consumer and industrial buyers, the service provider sets up specialist teams for each customer segment. Consumer services may be described as convenience, shopping or speciality services. Dry cleaning, shoe repairs and similar personal services are normally purchased on a convenience basis, whereas car repairs and insurance are typically shopping services, because they involve some effort in comparing price and quality.

Speciality service are the professional ones such as financial, legal and medical services.

The second method of classification is based on whether the service relies extensively on human labour or on equipment. Services such as education, medicine and hairdressing are in the former category, while the latter category includes car repairs and public transport.

The third method is based on the level of customer contact, which can be divided into high- and low-contact services. With high-contact services the client's presence is necessary. The provider of services in a high-contact situation would need to be much more aware of the personal needs of the client, the facilities must display high levels of maintenance and hygiene, and the process undergone will be as important as the final outcome. Examples include dental checkups, meals in restaurants, hair treatments, etc. Low-contact services include repair shops and dry cleaners, where the services are directed towards physical objects and the buyers of the service are not normally required to be present.

The fourth method of classifying services is by the degree of skill necessary in the provider of the service. Professional services tend to be more complex, as in the case of solicitors, accountants and doctors. Non-professional services such as plumbers and catering are less complex and are usually self-regulated by trade associations.

The fifth way of classifying services is to examine the service provider's objectives, that is whether it is a profit-making or non-profit organisation and whether it operates in the private or public sector. For example, a state school will need a different marketing programme from an independent college.

Marketing mix for service firms

The development of the marketing mix for service organisations follows a similar approach to that used for goods, but with adaptations of emphasis where necessary to suit the particular characteristics of the services involved. As discussed in Chapter 3, service marketing has adopted the concept of 7Ps. It is useful here to review marketing mix issues for services in more depth.

Product

As in product planning, the service manager would need to make decisions about:

- the service to be offered
- the length and breadth of the service mix
- any augmentation to the service product such as guarantees, payment methods or branding.

Consumers need to understand the service offerings and to evaluate alternatives. Since services are intangible and cannot be defined in physical terms, many of the marketing strategies used with tangible goods are of little or no use. For example, packaging and labelling opportunities are limited – in fact, service marketers are rarely able to use packages as promotional tools. The use of sampling as a means of introducing a new service to the market is also limited. Marketers of services such as squash clubs and satellite television, however, frequently offer trial periods without charge or at greatly reduced rates to move potential customers through the stages of the adoption process and convert them to regular users.

Another aspect of the product offering is that the buyer invariably equates the service with the provider. For example, the flight attendant or the lawyer personifies the service an airline or solicitor's office provides. Services are perceived in terms of the service personnel because of the absence of any tangible product attributes. This means that customers' perceptions of the organisation and its product offering will be based on the performance of its personnel. For the service organisation this means that staff have a critical role in generating good value for customers.

Given the intangibility of services, it is quite difficult to define quality in an objective sense. Many consumers determine quality by comparing the perceived service with the service they expected. If the consumers' actual experience exceeds the expected service, it is likely that the service provider will receive repeat business. Managers of service industries therefore need to commit themselves to quality as an organisational objective, to monitor and control service performance, and to ensure good employee relations in the firm, as satisfied employees will help to create good customer relations.

Given the perishability of services and the fluctuating demand, service managers can alter their service mix by extending or contracting it to meet changing consumer demands or to reduce seasonal fluctuations. Some firms work jointly with companies in related services. A car rental company may have arrangements with hotels and airlines whereby customers arriving at a particular airport would have a hire car and perhaps a hotel reserved for them. Another example of service firms extending their product mix is the insurance company that offers a comprehensive package of investment and life policies.

Augmenting the service product is more difficult to achieve, however. For example, an attempt to brand a service would encounter difficulties because of the problems in maintaining a consistent quality, as mentioned earlier. But this does not prevent service firms from using physical evidence to associate with the service. For example, in-house credit cards or membership cards such as those of the AA could represent the service to consumer.

Price

Price determination strategies for services do not substantially differ from those for goods. In developing a pricing strategy the service marketer must consider the demand for the service, the production, marketing and administrative costs, and the influence of competition. Many of the pricing strategies already discussed can be applied. Variable pricing is used to overcome the problems associated with the perishable nature of services – for example, airlines offer discounted fares on many highly competitive routes, and car rental firms offer lower rates if their cars are rented for a week instead of a few days.

In general, the role of pricing in services tends to be more significant than in the case of tangible goods because customers perceive price as an indicator of quality in the absence of other indicators. Price setting in service industries plays a vital role in determining the firm's competitive edge.

There are several difficulties in setting prices for services, however. With tangible products the costs of production (fixed and variable costs) are clear-cut, but it can be quite difficult to determine accurate costs for service provision. Indeed, price negotiation is an important part of many professional service transactions (car repairs, medical insurance, etc.). Specialised business services such as equipment rental, market research and maintenance services are priced through direct negotiation. Price competition is prevalent in sectors such as banking, hotels and the travel industry, but may be limited in other services, especially the utilities (gas, water, etc.), where prices are closely monitored by government agencies.

Place (distribution)

Service channels in general are simpler and more direct than those for products – this is largely because of the intangibility of services. The service marketer is less concerned with storage, transportation and stock control and typically uses shorter channels for distribution (see Chapter 3). However, this is not to say that service providers escape physical distribution problems. For example, firms renting out equipment (videocassettes, cars, etc.) do have to deal with stock problems.

Most services are produced and consumed simultaneously and no intermediary is used, especially when the service cannot be separated from the provider, for example in medicine and entertainment. The advantage of direct contact with the consumer is that service providers can obtain immediate and detailed feedback, as well as having the opportunity to personalise their services to suit a particular target market. The drawback of direct contact is that since the service is not separated from the provider, the market is limited in that the seller cannot be in two places at the same time.

The marketing intermediaries used by service firms are usually agents or brokers. For example, in the travel industry retail agents often sell holiday packages developed by travel brokers, and these packages generally combine travel, hotel and restaurant services. Locating the service provider in a place convenient to the consumer is important and some service providers have extended their distribution system in a number of ingenious ways. The high street banks, for example, have installed automated cash dispensers outside their branches to enable consumers to withdraw funds, obtain bank statements, etc. at any time. Some banks have even installed these machines in supermarkets.

Promotion

The marketing strategy for services includes a promotional mix consisting of the most appropriate blends of personal and non-personal selling aimed at informing, persuading and reminding the individuals or businesses that represent the service provider's target market. Promotional strategies include the following.

- **Making the service 'tangible' by linking it to concrete images.** This frequently used strategy provides physical evidence associated with the service. For example, hotels stress physical features such as the elegance of their facilities and thereby provide clues to service quality. The insurance and banking industries use logos or symbols to help consumers identify their services – the insurance company Swinton emphasises ease of contact, while Legal and General's umbrella logo suggests it is protective of its customers' interests, and Barclays Bank's eagle logo symbolises power and dynamism. Other service marketers make their offerings seem more tangible by personalising them through advertising featuring well-known personalities and celebrities.

- **Creating a favourable image for the service or service provider.** The most commonly used themes for service organisations are efficiency, status and friendliness.
- **Showing the tangible benefits of purchasing an intangible service.** For example, a local bank may show a retired small-business owner relaxing in the sun thanks to a retirement fund established years ago. These and similar themes help buyers visualise the benefits of a particular service.
- **Personal selling.** The desire of many service buyers for a personal relationship with the service provider increases the importance of personal selling. Life assurance marketing provides a good illustration of the key role of the sales representative. Because insurance is a confusing and complex subject for the average buyer, the salesperson must be a professional financial adviser and must develop a personal relationship with the client. Insurance companies and other service firms need a well-trained highly motivated salesforce providing the high quality, personalised service that customers require.
- **Publicity campaigns.** Given that services are intangible, possibilities for sampling, demonstration and physical display are limited and service firms typically do not use premiums or contests. Publicity therefore becomes an important medium for many services, especially for entertainment and sports events. Television and radio reports, newspaper articles and magazine features inform the public about these events and stimulate interest. Contributions to charitable causes, services provided to non-profit organisations, sponsorship of public events and similar activities are also publicised to influence the public's opinion of the service firm. In general, service marketers rely more on publicity campaigns than those in the goods sector.
- **Internal marketing.** A service organisation must ensure that its service personnel who come into contact with customers, as well as other supporting staff, are effective and work as a team. This requires careful selection, training and development, good remuneration systems and a careful monitoring system. This will ensure an efficient delivery system as well as maintaining quality standards, and consumers tend to equate the efficiency and friendliness of employees with the quality of the service.

The Seven Ps

In Chapter 3, the 7 Ps as they apply to services were reviewed. Analysis of the marketing mix for services undertaken in this chapter can be enhanced by the consideration of the strategies reviewed there.

It is useful to remind ourselves of the increasing importance of services for all businesses. When looking at productivity or business effectiveness, government statistics concentrate on the time and cost involved in producing a product. This shows the UK, for example, as being a long way behind its main competitive rivals. This is obviously important, but it has been noted for some time that many UK exporters thrive in international markets with the total package of product and service that they offer. In other words, a total product offering is what counts to help build competitive advantage both at home and abroad.

In many service industries there is also the recognition that the intangible benefits they offer, such as a relaxing environment, can be enhanced by tangible benefits – for example, hotels may offer customers a memento of their stay. This item will act as a reminder of the hotel and hopefully encourage a return visit. Physical product markets are enhanced by services, just as service markets are enhanced by the addition of physical product offerings to the customer, often involving merchandising, free gifts and so on.

Services are now seen as a vital part of all provision, so the UK with its large service sector should be well placed to exploit this for the enhancement of manufacturing and other sectors of industry.

Discussion point

Suggest a marketing mix for a firm providing insurance services.

INTERNATIONAL MARKETS

Globalisation

Communications and travel have reduced the time and effort needed to transfer people and goods from one country to another. Changes have also been brought about by the reduction in trade barriers that have encouraged many companies to venture into foreign markets previously barred to them. Additionally, the creation of huge trade areas in Europe and North America have spurred many companies to adopt what they regard as a global strategy. This covers the purchase of materials (sourcing), and the production of a single range of products regardless of the countries for which they are destined.

Changes of the type mentioned here have a dramatic impact on all businesses, whether they are involved directly in international business or not. An obvious example is the use of the Internet for business purposes. As companies adopt this technology, orders outside the UK will be forthcoming, introducing them to foreign markets for the first time. Other UK companies who used to operate behind trade barriers no longer find such protection on offer. New competitors will be able to move in to compete directly with them. It has often been thought that local services are immune from this type of competition, but it has become more noticeable than ever that changes are being felt. For example, in 1999 fuel prices and excise duties for the UK haulage industries were raised above the level found in Europe. Within a few weeks, a Dutch company had won a contact with Nissan to transport cars in the UK. Although other factors would have played their part here, the change was seen as directly related to the fuel price increase. Whatever the case, an open market with Europe and the rest of the world has made inroads into what many believed were secure markets.

Strategic alliances have developed, such as those seen in the defence industries in Europe (e.g. Augusta of Italy and Westland of the UK), which are attempting to gain economies of scale to compete with their American counterparts and to survive the reduction in defence expenditure.

Globalisation is therefore made up of many elements, including developments in communication and travel, erosion of trade barriers and the development of global strategies. There are now, according to the IMF, over 100 trading groups. Certain political parties are against the introduction of competition in key industries in their countries, and it is still the case that foreign direct investment is no greater now than it was before the First World War – free trade was as advanced then as it is now, and many companies effectively were global in their outlook. The difference is the speed of communication. The globalisation advances that were made before the First World War were rolled back, and policy-makers are concerned that this can still happen even now. Despite this concern, the reality for most companies is that globalisation is new to them now and they have to deal with its implications.

Marketers have to be aware of the potential for the sourcing of product, new markets, new customers, investment opportunities, new competitors and therefore new threats. Although this is the last section in the marketing unit, it is in its way the most important as good marketing practice needs to be established and aided by an understanding of the international dimensions of marketing. Good marketing principles are transferable, the main difference being that they must be applied in a more complex environment. Likewise effective planning techniques are appropriate to all circumstances. The skill and understanding of workers and managers must be such, however, that they can exploit the new opportunities on offer.

Market attractiveness

Firms may consider moving into the international marketplace for a number of reasons, among them the following.

- The firm's managers may actively pursue entry into new export markets because they believe they can thereby boost profits and growth, use any spare capacity and become more efficient. These internal factors can be linked to external opportunities such as new opportunities that emerge, for example, as a result of a reduction in the protective barriers of a national market. British firms have in recent years looked to the European Union (EU) for their first opportunities to export, but they are encouraged by the government to look at global opportunities as markets become more integrated and easier to enter.
- Market saturation is a clear trigger for firms to look abroad. This situation occurs when growth rates in particular markets slow down and there is a restricted potential for further growth. Quite clearly, this means that the firm's resources are not being fully exploited and efficiency is reduced. Looking for new opportunities in

other markets, such as in the Asia–Pacific region, despite the current slowdown there, becomes an attractive option.

- In many industries, to obtain economies of scale a large market is essential. In car production, recent mergers such as that of Mercedes and Chrysler have been forged partly because of the need to gain scale economies. Gaining market share on an international scale obliges firms actively to seek expansion via foreign market penetration.
- The product life cycle shows that products can, after a period of time, experience a 'natural' reduction in sales. However, in other markets the life cycle for a product may be in its early stages, offering extended profitability.
- Market advantages may be exploited in markets abroad, i.e. the expertise and competitive advantage gained in the market can, with some adjustment, be transferred to new markets. It is not simply the product that provides advantages, but the expertise of staff that underpins the successful exploitation of the product.
- One of the criticisms levelled by countries outside the EU is that a 'Fortress Europe' mentality has been created that could exclude non-EU firms from competing successfully there. This has encouraged many US and Japanese firms (among others) to establish a presence in the EU in an attempt to overcome any barriers. Likewise, dozens of other nation-state trading groups exist in the world so UK firms may find themselves at a disadvantage if they fail to create a presence that can overcome trade barriers.

These reasons underpin the initial motives for entering a market. A successful first step will lead on to the next phase, common to the majority of firms, of expansion within the new markets. The reasons for pursuing expansion can be listed as follows.

- Expansion may see off local competitors.
- Having built networks and an infrastructure to support its marketing efforts, a firm will be able to use this to good effect in the expansion phase.
- Once established in a market, a firm can pursue a market penetration strategy.

In this phase the goal will be to develop local market potential, including looking at new products and/or new market segments. This is a move away from a domestic market approach to a multidomestic strategy.

A multidomestic approach aims to customise strategy to accommodate the differences between national markets. Each market will require its own strategy and this will not necessarily enable a coordinated approach to be developed in the early stages. At some point this multidomestic or country-by-country approach will become inefficient because of duplication of effort, for example in marketing.

The next phase of development is the true internationalisation of the company. The focus at this stage is on the synergies arising from operating on an international scale, and the company becomes able:

- to take advantage of the multinational character of its operations and exploit its products and brands across markets
- to eliminate the duplication of effort and cost inefficiencies inherent in the multidomestic approach
- to capture a share of the growing market of global consumers, i.e. those that share the same tastes, preferences and forms of behaviour
- to meet global competition by creating an efficient marketing approach.

Case Study

What makes a company strong?

In 1998 the *Financial Times* produced a survey of the world's most respected companies. Of the top 40 companies, 23 came from the USA, 13 came from Europe and four from Japan. The survey sought the views of chief executives from 53 countries, drawn from both the public and private sectors. For these chief executive officers (CEOs) the most important attribute of a company was its strategy.

The soft drinks giant Coca-Cola was perceived to be a company that could deliver a consistently good product anywhere in the world. Also rated highly was its expertise in marketing. The car company Toyota was praised for its total quality culture, combined with its customer focus.

Although many of the companies had little to gain from a globalisation strategy, those that did, such as General Electric of the USA, which was awarded first place, and car manufacturer Ford (equal ninth), were praised for their success in implementing a global strategy.

Questions

1. Why do you think CEOs felt that the most important attribute of a company was strategy?
2. Why would globalisation make a company stronger?

With the advent of global marketing, no longer are national markets regarded as possessing different characteristics. Similar structures and forms of buying behaviour can enable companies to adopt a global marketing approach, using similar marketing mix strategies right across the world.

It may be assumed that this would only apply to large firms, but because of technological changes and communications improvements, this is a strategy that small and medium-sized enterprises could adopt. Therefore, all firms might find themselves moving through the three general stages described above, with all that this implies for marketing strategy.

Selecting a market

Whatever the motivation or stage of development, a market must be selected on the basis of its attractiveness for the organisation. This selection should follow the good practice outlined in Chapters 1–3, and take account of the complex marketing environment. However, there is a need to be cautious when taking this line. First, the process of selecting a market can reveal as much about the threat to the home market as it can throw light on the targeted ones. Secondly, the very act of selecting a market and reviewing the marketing mix has implications for the whole organisation. Therefore, the process should be seen as an opportunity to review many aspects of the business.

One of the most commonly used approaches to the selection of markets is portfolio analysis, where the firm reviews current and potential portfolios of products and markets. Portfolio analysis identifies which business activity should be introduced, maintained, reduced or eliminated.

The Boston Consultancy Group (BCG) portfolio system looks at the role of each business unit or product of a company on the basis of its market growth rate and market share relative to competitors and cash flow potential. The Boston matrix (see Figure 4.2) highlights cash flow,

Market growth \ Relative market share	High	Low
High	Stars	Question marks
Low	Cash cows	Dogs

Figure 4.2 *Product portfolio mix*

investment and profitability characteristics of various businesses and the benefits of shifting financial resources between them to optimise the whole portfolio's performance. The characteristics of each type of product are as follows:

- 'Dogs' – these products have cost disadvantages as they fail to achieve economies of scale, have few opportunities for growth and no new business opportunities.
- 'Stars' – these products are market leaders, fast growing, and generate large profits, but they need investment to continue to grow.
- 'Cash Cows' – these products are profitable as they can generate more cash relative to the cost of maintaining their market share.
- 'Question marks' – these products enjoy rapid growth and low profit margins but need cash to defend or expand their market share.

Four strategies can be adopted. The most straightforward is for a firm to eliminate its 'dogs' and harvest cash from its 'cash cows' to assist with the growth of its 'stars' and to help the 'question marks'. However, there are environmental and competitive reasons why more subtle strategies may be required. For example, it may not be wise to get rid of a 'dog' as its presence in the market may deter potential competitors.

Portfolio analysis shows the importance of generating funds to promote the development of new products which can help the company grow. It also obliges the company to look at its relative market share, and the potential of the targeted market.

The matrix shown in Figure 4.3 assists the company in focusing on:

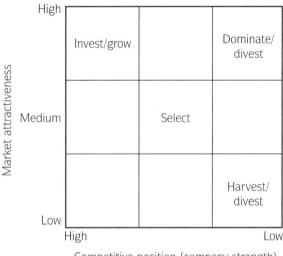

High

Market attractiveness

| Invest/grow | | Dominate/divest |

Medium — Select

Low

| | | Harvest/divest |

High ——— Low

Competitive position (company strength)

Figure 4.3 *Market attractiveness – competitive position matrix*

- resource requirements
- entry costs to foreign markets
- profitability levels.

The vertical axis on the matrix – market attractiveness – refers to the strengths and resources associated with the market, such as economies of scale, competitive interests, volume of sales, and the cost and feasibility of entering the market. The horizontal axis – competitive position – looks at relative market share, price competitiveness, product quality and market knowledge. Several possible strategies are available when using this approach.

1. **Invest/grow.** Markets in the upper left corner of the matrix are good candidates for additional investment.
2. **Harvest/divest.** Those in the lower right corner of the matrix call for strategies that harvest the profits or sell off the business. Markets in this area are not attractive and the firm lacks the competitive strategy to maintain its position. Any cash generated is required to maintain market share. The firm could still generate income without much investment by using a licensing strategy.
3. **Dominate/divest.** Markets in the upper right corner of the matrix are attractive, but the company lacks the competitive strengths necessary to exploit their potential. This could be because the firm does not have the right products or market expertise to enable it to dominate.
4. **Select.** For markets in the centre box of the matrix, where the situation is more complex the firm will need to assess each case carefully before making a decision. In some cases products will achieve good cash flows, but market share may be difficult to maintain.

Information used to determine market attractiveness, for example, does not on its own dictate the decision a company should make. Managers are required to use their expert knowledge of the market to assess the most appropriate way forward and act accordingly. A further example of the need to look at all aspects of the market is provided by Kellogg, the US breakfast cereal manufacturer.

Kellogg's great rival, General Mills, held 32.5 per cent of the US market for the first quarter of 1998 (calculated on dollars spent), compared to Kellogg's share of 31.6 per cent. First analysis of General Mills' improved position suggested that its success was due to its strategy of developing variations of its brand that could not easily be copied by rivals. Kellogg's well-known products, such as Cornflakes, Frosted Flakes and Rice Krispies, could more easily be duplicated, a fact borne out in UK supermarkets where there are own-label brands that mirror Kellogg's. In the USA the uniqueness of General Mills' products allows it to charge 30 cents more per item – its customers are willing to pay more for this uniqueness. All this is happening against a background of a shrinking market, as consumers turned to bagels and other foods for their breakfast snack.

In the UK and in other countries in the EU the dynamics are different. In France the market for breakfast cereals is expanding, as the traditional breakfast and visits to cafés are being replaced. In the UK the market is more mature than that in France, with competition coming from supermarket own-brands. Given that the majority of food is purchased from such stores, this provides stiff competition for Kellogg. Right from its entry into the breakfast cereal market – and many would credit it with the creation of such a market – Kellogg has spent money on advertising to create demand. As the company became successful and the market expanded, Kellogg moved into 100 countries, keeping prices high to cover its advertising campaigns. As market share has been lost and competition has increased, the company has started to reduce its prices and focus on faster selling lines, such as single portion packs.

Putting all this into perspective, Kellogg still sells US$1.8 billion worth of goods and still sells more by volume than General Mills.

In such circumstances how might Kellogg apply the portfolio and market attractiveness models introduced earlier? With sufficient technical and quantitative information some sense can be made of the two approaches, but ultimately it is a management decision as to where to focus effort and direct strategy. General Mills has explained its success by the fact that its cereals are complex to make, cannot be copied easily and therefore carry a premium with customers. Products such as Cheerios and Cinnamon Toast Crunch have been used to build the company's market share. Could this approach be applied successfully in the UK, where preferences are different? A review using the market attractiveness model could help to determine whether the UK is a market worthy of effort, what competitors would be likely to do in response, and whether customers would be likely to pay more for the product.

Does all this matter?

Product portfolio and market attractiveness matrices are ways to assist managers. The reduced market share of Kellogg in its home market, the fact that this market is shrinking, that its products can be copied and that consumers are not inclined to pay a premium price for them all mean that Kellogg is now seen as a take-over target, and is in the process of restructuring to save costs. Marketing managers and many others in the company need to be aware of the nature of the threat from rivals and how to compete successfully.

Company-specific issues

A factor that may be overlooked in moving into foreign markets is that within the firm there are certain influences that can turn the firm towards a new market. These range from the firm's objectives, through its experience of international ventures, to the control and risk issues that are part and parcel of a manager's job.

While it has been noted that many firms react to a downturn in their home market by looking elsewhere, or are approached to sell their products abroad, this is a reactive, rather than proactive, response to events. Many firms take a more practised line, which is seen within their mission statement and objectives, including a planned and measured approach to the consideration of new markets. Whether this becomes an effective reality depends on the willingness of managers and marketers to incorporate it into their thinking. Refocusing a company or organisation to take advantage of new opportunities requires perhaps a new or revised structure, new systems and procedures, new skills for employees, the ability of managers to assess risk, and knowledge of how to enter or even exit from a market. Entering a market can be done by franchising, licensing, setting up joint venture, organising local sales or local production. How will this change the marketing mix? What will be the best way to get the product to the consumer – via an agent, distributor or joint-venture partner? Will this mean that control is lost or reduced? How will this affect prices and promotion? Will the involvement of a third party, perhaps an agent, provide the way into a market, but only permit a short-term solution to the market-entry issue?

The number of questions to be asked and the uncertainty and risk associated with them should not put companies off. Research, as described below, shows that the successful companies both large and small are usually those that have expertise and interest in foreign markets at the core of what they do. Success in this instance means profitability through innovative and exciting products. The next section reviews some of the ways in which, having appraised the market, a firm can seek to enter it.

Strategic options

After making an assessment of its country portfolio, a firm must choose a competitive market strategy. Numerous strategies are available to a firm, range from the cooperative to the confrontational. Two of the better known are the generic strategies model and the product/market expansion strategy.

Porter's generic strategies approach

In developing a portfolio strategy, a firm can select from Porter's three generic strategies?

- overall cost leadership
- differentiation
- focus.

Operating in different markets, the firm can select different strategies or a combination of them for each market.

A **cost leadership strategy** is based on achieving low-cost production. This is normally associated with high-volume output, whereby economies of scale, experience and learning curve factors result in cost reductions. Experience curve economies result from the firm's increased experience in managing its functional activities. Learning curve economies are the result of workers becoming more efficient and effective as they learn from their mistakes over time, and hence increase their productivity.

A **differentiation strategy** involves differentiating the firm's products or services so that they will be perceived as being unique in quality, brand or some other feature. The firm is then in a position to market the products at a higher than average price. For example IBM holds a differentiated position in the computer market in terms of quality and research and development.

Focus strategy involves concentrating on a small market, product or geographic segment. The firm's efforts and resources are focused on serving a particular customer

group, and it does not compete on an industry-wide basis. For example, some computer software companies compete for certain customer segments such as the chemicals industry or banking sector only.

The generic strategies model is illustrated in Figure 4.4. Firms at the upper right of the curve are profitable and successful because they have a larger market share, due to lower prices and lower costs than their competitors or because they have differentiated their product offerings. Firms in the upper left of the curve are also successful because their focus strategy entails specialist products or markets which can command high prices. The firms that have difficulties are those situated in the middle portion of the curve, with fairly low market share and profits. Porter's model also illustrates the trade-off between profits and market share. For example, a focus strategy would give the firm higher profits but at a cost, as it would have a smaller market share.

Figure 4.4 *Generic strategies model*

Product/market expansion strategy

In developing its portfolio strategy, a firm can choose from a number of alternatives to generate growth. The four strategies available are as follows.

- **Product market penetration** involves the firm trying to increase the share for its product in the overseas markets it already serves. It can achieve this by several types of tactics such as the following.

- Product line stretching involves the firm adding new items to its existing product line in a market segment it has already penetrated. The aim is to attract more customers from rivals and among current non-users of the firm's products, i.e. to reach a broader market. For example, Coca-Cola has added new items to its basic product and now offers Diet Coke and Cherry Coke in some of its markets. Similarly, Japanese car manufacturers first penetrated the European car market with medium-sized cars. This product line was then stretched to include small cars, and now they have extended their product lines to target the luxury segments of the world car market.
- Product proliferation means offering many different product types, for example Seiko offers a variety of watches with different features, functions, etc.
- Product improvement is achieved by updating and augmenting the existing product. This could entail the application of the latest technology to improve the product's capabilities, improving customer services, etc.
- **Market development** involves developing new geographic markets for the firm's current product lines. This type of expansion is most suitable:
  - where minimal product modification is required
  - where profit margins are diminishing because of intense price competition in the firm's existing markets
  - if the life cycle of the product is similar in different markets.

  Many Pacific Basin economies such as Singapore and South Korea are adopting this type of expansion strategy.
- **Product market development** means the firm maintains its existing overseas markets but develops new product markets within them. For example, a firm selling software to the industrial segment in a market might go after the consumer segment in the same market.
- **Diversification** involves the firm entering new product markets outside its present business. The firm may wish to pursue this line of expansion when:
  - opportunities in the new product market are highly attractive
  - it wishes to reduce the impact of a negative environmental trend in its existing industry, for example to reduce the economic impact of a decline in cigarette smoking or the ageing of the UK population. Firms could engage in forward or backward integration, whereby the outlets or sources of supplies are joined with the firm. This practice is prevalent in the semiconductor industries, where manufacturers of microprocessors join forces with semiconductor producers to ensure a continuous supply. A conglomerate diversification strategy involves the firm expanding into businesses that have no relationship to the firm's current product, markets

or technology. For example, Coca-Cola purchased a movie company as a strategic move to counter the possible decline in the customer segment for its products, which is presently the youth group.

Entering foreign markets

The choice of method of entry into foreign markets is for many firms a fundamental and critical decision, since the entry technique will influence the rest of the marketing programme. For example, if the firm opts for a licensing agreement, its ability to influence product development, promotion or pricing will be severely curtailed. On the other hand, a decision is made to manufacture in the host country, the firm would be able to exert a high degree of control in terms of its marketing and production decisions, but this would entail higher costs and greater risks. Therefore, the market entry decision involves a trade-off between control, costs and risks. Furthermore, the choice of entry method will involve a long-term commitment from which it might be difficult for a firm to extricate itself without some cost.

Indirect exporting

This strategy involves the firm selling to an intermediary within the UK, who in turn resells the goods to a customer abroad. The manufacturing firm does not need to undertake the export operations such as documentation, freighting, etc. These are carried out by others, and in many instances take place without the knowledge of the manufacturer. Indirect exporting may occur through:

- export houses
- export management companies
- overseas buying offices
- international trading companies
- piggyback operations (joint-venture marketing operations).

Direct exporting

Here, the firm sells to a customer abroad, who may be the final user of the product/service or an intermediary such as a distributor or agent. In this case the firm has to undertake market research, transportation, documentation and the various other export procedures. In general, the move to direct exporting indicates a genuine commitment, with the resulting benefits of market feedback and greater control of the process, although it is a more expensive alternative. Direct exporting takes place through:

- sales by foreign distributors
- sales agents
- overseas sales subsidiaries.

Foreign manufacturing

In this case the firm is involved in production and distribution of the goods in the market concerned. This can take many forms, for example:

- assembly operations
- contract manufacturing
- licensing operations
- franchising
- joint ventures
- strategic alliances
- local production.

TASK

Discuss the differences between domestic marketing and international marketing.

Single currency, economic integration and marketing

To put international marketing in focus, it is worthwhile investigating the development of the single market in Europe and the euro. International influences through the activities of the EU and the World Trade Organisation (WTO) can come close to home for many companies, and they require a strategy to be developed for dealing with them effectively.

The aim of the EU is to forge political and economic links across the member states. This has required an acceptance that the differences between national markets had to be abolished by legislative and administrative changes agreed between all participating countries, by the global community via GATT (General Agreement on Tariffs and Trade) and latterly the WTO. A single currency will help

to create transparency in the prices of products sold across Europe, encouraging a more competitive environment within the Union.

There are many issues to consider from the marketer's point of view, and not all of these are to do with the final price of a product sold in the UK as well as Germany. The competitive environment is also changing, with new regulatory bodies determining interest rates, new euro markets in bonds, as well as the fact that economic and monetary policies of the member states are becoming more closely interrelated. For example, monetary policy is now determined by the European Central Bank (ECB) which will deal with the member countries as if they were part of a single market. No one country facing a particular problem, say rising inflation, will have the ability to change interest rates to resolve the situation. Only if all countries in the euro zone were having the same problem would the ECB act. Countries with an inflation problem will have to find other ways to deal with it, the most likely being the introduction of more flexible labour markets.

With the euro representing an economic group roughly similar in size to the USA, it is a currency that will rival the US dollar for trading purposes and may also be used by other countries outside the EU and NAFTA (North American Free Trade Agreement) when trading. UK companies will be affected by this as for settlement purposes both inside and outside the EU they will have to deal in euros.

The ECB has a legal obligation to maintain price stability in Europe, which means that inflation problems will be resolved by individual countries and the EU collectively introducing more flexible labour markets. This may lead to an easing of the legislative burden connected with the hiring and firing of labour, an approach similar to that adopted in the USA. Likewise, the differences in wage costs will be adjusted over time, bringing poorer countries' wage costs up while reducing the large costs of the richer countries in relative terms.

The euro, and the Economic and Monetary Union (EMU) agreement that preceded it, committed governments to strict budget guidelines, which effectively place a ceiling on government borrowing – 3% of gross domestic product – thereby preventing member governments faced with rising unemployment from spending their way out of the problem. Job creation approaches will have to incorporate a number of ways to boost the efficiency of labour markets, and/or reduce the cost of employing workers such as the high social costs paid by a company to help finance pensions.

Whether they are large or small, companies in the UK will encounter the euro in their everyday transactions as it takes its place as an equal partner with the US dollar. The UK traveller going to mainland Europe – the main holiday destination for most – will start to use the notes and coins from 2002, and before that will be able to undertake non-cash transactions such as writing a cheque in euros to pay a hotel bill. The banks in the UK provide euro accounts, euro loans and so on.

The marketer will find that the introduction of the euro will affect the organisation in many ways, including the following.

- Prices will be more transparent across Europe, with customers seeing the price in euros in each country. This could lead to more price sensitivity on the part of customers.
- Exchange costs will still exist between sterling and the euro so long as Britain does not adopt the currency, but these costs will not exist for the countries in the Euro-zone. UK exporters may have to recognise that price advantages will arise from this, for example for a German firm competing with a UK firm in the French market.
- Government policy, either the UK's or that of another EU country, will be less flexible than hitherto. Boosting economic activity will not be so easy for an individual government to achieve. This may lead to a focus on the marketplace, by introducing more competitors, for example to boost business activity.
- Stocks and bonds are already denominated in euros. Company shares will be quoted in euros on stock exchanges across Europe, making it easier to compare their performances.

Other changes and influences can be added to the above brief list, but more will continue to emerge – the implications of the euro for the marketplace will be shown over time. What marketers are required to do, as are all others who are involved in monitoring developments, is to decide which influences are most relevant for their organisation and take appropriate action. This can mean reconfiguring the market mix, or changing purchasing, employing or other practices in order to create competitive advantage.

Discussion point

Is it correct to say that all firms face a threat to their home market because of European integration?

Case Study

easyJet

The airline easyJet achieved profits of £2.3 million in 1998, having made a loss of £3.3 million in 1997, and this was the first profit the company had made since it was founded in 1995. Early in 1990 the airline had 12 Boeing 731s, rising to 20 by 2000.

As a low-cost, no frills airline which flies point-to-point, short-haul destinations, easyJet offers no in-flight meals and each aircraft is rapidly turned round to achieve high aircraft utilisation. The company is focused on the cost-conscious consumer who is willing to book directly with the company (15.7 per cent of the company's sales came from Internet bookings in early 1999, anticipated to rise to 30 per cent in 2000).

The company uses subcontractors to deliver its product, focusing itself on the provision of aircraft, pilots, cabin crew and markets. It depends on the performance of its subcontractors to run its check-in, 20-minute turnaround time, customer information and assistance, as well as safety.

Low-cost airline operators were first attracted to the market when the European Union deregulated the industry, with a view to increasing competition. No new airlines entered the market in 1995 and 1996, but of the 56 airlines who started operations in 1998, 17 went out of business after only one year. Competition is still limited, with fewer than 10 per cent of routes having more than two airlines. Low-cost airlines target the lucrative routes in Europe to destinations such as Nice, Barcelona and Geneva, flying from Luton and Liverpool.

Competition for easyJet comes from Debonair, Ryan Air and Virgin Express, all offering variations on the no-frills package. In 1998, British Airways established GO, its no-frills alternative, while other airlines such as KLM offered low-priced seats on their aircraft.

To remain in business easyJet had to emphasize brand recognition and its ability to offer a low-cost service and quick-turn-round time, particularly as it expanded to new links such as Amsterdam, where its ability to deliver the same approach could be threatened by the logistics of a busy airport. The existence of competitors such as GO would also mean that its price advantage would be lost, thereby proving the importance of the quality of service it can offer to customers.

New routes and links are being added to the airline's portfolio. The company decides whether to adopt a new route by estimating the route's expected profitability, basing this on information about airlines flying that route, but also looking at high-speed train services as well as load factors, demand and other relevant data on the destination.

The success of the company in making profits in 1998 persuaded the chairman and founder Stetio Haji-Uoannose to seek for a flotation of the company on the London stock exchange in 2000, while the family of the chairman would still keep majority control.

To achieve a successful flotation the company needed to satisfy the criteria that financial advisers had set, namely that the company could show it had a good profitability record, was able to continue to expand and grow, and could weather a recession.

To keep the company ahead of the competition easyJet has to use its marketing strategy to good effect, not only because of its move towards being a quoted company but as it expands and uses more subcontractors. These must maintain the standards of service set in the early years, as well as ensuring they offer the unique service that customers require. Equally, marketers must ensure there are enough customers to continue to expand the company as well as to maintain repeat business.

Questions

1. What are the chief environmental considerations facing easyJet?

2. What would be the most effective marketing mix for its targeted markets?

3. Outline the challenges that easyJet will face over the next few years.

4. Propose alternative approaches to the targeting of markets other than that pursued by the company.

FURTHER READING

Needham, D., Dransfield, R., Guy, P., Shaw, M. and Dooley, D., *Marketing for Higher Awards*, Heinemann Educational, 1999.

Johnson, G. and Scholes, K., *Exploring Corporate Strategy*, Prentice Hall, 1998.

Baker, M. (ed.), *The Marketing Book*, Heinemann/CIM, 1994.

Dibb, S., Simkin, L., Pride, W. and Ferrell, O., *Marketing*, Houghton Mifflin, 1997.

Mercer, D., *Marketing*, Blackwell, 1992.

Marketing Business, published quarterly by the Chartered Institute of Marketing.

Palmer, A. and Worthington, I. *The Business and Marketing Environment*, McGraw-Hill, 1992.

Foxall, G.R. and Goldsmith, R.E., *Consumer Psychology for Marketing*, Routledge, 1994.

Ford, D. *Understanding Business Markets*, Academic Press, 1990.

Dibb, S. and Simkin, L., *The Market Segmentation Workbook: Target Marketing for Marketing Managers*, International Thomson Business Publishing, 1996.

McDonald, M. and Dunbar, I., *Market Segmentation*, Macmillan, 1995.

Doyle, P., *Marketing Management and Strategy*, Prentice-Hall, 1994.

McGoldrick, P.J., *Retail Marketing*, 2nd edition, McGraw-Hill, 1997.

Burnett, J.J., *Promotion Management*, Houghton Mifflin, 1993.

De Mooij, M., *Advertising Worldwide*, Prentice Hall, 1994.

Smith, P.R., *Marketing Communications*, Kogan Page, 1993.

Bradley, F., *International Marketing Strategy*, 3rd edition, Prentice-Hall, 1996.

ASSIGNMENT

A small UK regional airline is seeking to expand its business into the low-cost market, in which the likes of easyJet, British Airways' GO and Debonair operate. You are part of a small marketing team brought in to help the company achieve its aim of gaining 5% of the expanding market within two years. The remit you have been given is to research and prepare a brief document for the team that looks at the dynamics of the market and identifies the main marketing challenges and possible strategies to deal with them.

Some information on easyJet has been provided by your line manager, but obtaining more background material will be a useful starting point for your research.

Task 1

Prepare a briefing document for the team that outlines the dynamics of the market, and the implications for the company in terms of the benefits and costs of a marketing approach.

Task 2

Prepare a report on the business environment in which your airline will be operating. Include a discussion of how current economic and political events might affect confidence in the market for low-cost travel, and influence strategy over the next twelve months.

Task 3

Suggest ways of segmenting the market for low-cost air travel. Explain how this would affect the marketing mix targeted at each segment. Produce a paper describing how a strategy of targeting market segments could help achieve the goal of 5% overall market share within two years.

Managing Financial Resources

Sources of Finance

This chapter introduces the major sources of finance that are available to new and existing businesses in the UK. The various types of finance are evaluated and illustrated with real-life case studies.

On completion of the chapter you should be able to identify the sources of finance available to businesses. To achieve this you must demonstrate the ability to:

- identify the major sources of finance for a business

- select appropriate sources of finance for a business project

- assess the implications of different sources of finance.

THE MARKET FOR FINANCE

The invention of money overcame the principal problem inherent in bartering. With an accepted currency it was no longer necessary for the provider of a good or service to have an immediate need for personal consumption of another good or service in return. It also meant that money could be conferred to others for a period of time, as a store of wealth and purchasing power. As the market for money has developed, the form of financial transactions has become more diverse and complex.

Small businesses rely heavily on the personal resources – money, as well as time and effort – of those participating directly in the firm, with a valuable top-up from banks. Larger businesses, which are too big for a few individuals to finance, make more use of the financial institutions that make up the **financial markets**.

Financial institutions in effect pool the funds made available by the general public by selling them financial products such as pension plans, savings schemes and unit trusts. These pooled funds are then invested in businesses under arrangements that provide the fund managers with appropriate levels of financial return, risk and liquidity.

Financial return is the price exacted for deferring consumption, such as the interest the funds could earn in a bank deposit account. **Risk** refers to the uncertainty of the recipient honouring the terms of the finance arrangement. **Liquidity** expresses how easily the investment can be turned back into cash. For example, the ability to sell shares in a company on a stock exchange suggests a highly liquid investment. Liquidity is important because it allows a fund manager to sell sufficient investments to meet the fund's obligations (e.g. to pensioners).

One function of the financial markets is to match the expectations of individual investors with the needs of business. Individuals often save on a short-term basis whereas businesses require long-term funds. Without banks and other financial institutions, individuals would have nowhere to save and invest for the future, and businesses would find it practically impossible to obtain the long-term

Individuals invest → FINANCIAL INSTITUTIONS: Banks, Finance houses, Pension funds, Insurance companies, Unit and investment trusts → Businesses receive funds

Figure 5.1 *The role of financial institutions*

finance they require. The financial markets therefore serve two main purposes:

- They pool the savings of individuals to enable the financing of business projects, large and small.
- They enable short-term savings to be invested over a longer period.

The legal status of a business can affect the range of funding arrangements available to it. Where investors require the funding they provide to be secured against the assets of a business, more satisfactory arrangements can be made for incorporated businesses (companies). For a sole trader or partnership, on the other hand, security is given by pledging the surrender of specific assets in the case of default. However, in the normal course of business, many such assets are either resold or consumed, so the availability of this security is often limited. This problem can be overcome when investing in a company, by arranging for a floating charge over the entire assets of the business. If the terms of the financing arrangement are breached, the assets in existence at that time are frozen and are used by an appointed administrator to pay the various creditors and investors their dues.

Another important concept is **financial security**. Imagine that person A provides a loan to a company, but before the loan matures (i.e. is due for repayment) wishes to regain the capital tied up. Person A can sell the loan to person B, if the loan is in the form of a financial security. The company then has to accept the new holder of the security, in this case person B, as the bone-fide creditor. A financial security is backed up by a certificate that entitles its holder to certain rights, such as the receipt of interest or dividends. The company, in issuing the security, is recognising its obligation to these regular payments and for the eventual repayment of the funds it has obtained. Examples of securities include shares in companies and certain types of loan stock. The financial security means that companies are generally more attractive to investors than are unincorporated businesses.

The ability of a business to tap into the various forms of finance available also depends crucially on its financial status. Clearly, the value of a security is enhanced if it is readily marketable, which it will be if the business that has issued the security is recognised by others as being a safe investment. Unfortunately this precludes most small firms from raising finance from outside the circle of business and professional contacts of the business owner.

The main sources of business finance are:

- individuals – founders, employees and private investors
- venture capitalists – individuals and organisations specialising in providing finance for companies that do not issue shares that are quoted on the stock exchange
- banks
- finance companies/funds, such as pension funds, insurance companies and unit trusts
- suppliers who provide products on credit
- profits retained in the business.

Many providers specialise in a particular type of finance for specific purposes. In this way they can gain competitive advantage in a particular niche of the market for business finance. For example, some financial institutions specialise in finance for plant and machinery; others provide finance for business premises, and others for working capital. By utilising specialist finance where appropriate, the business owners can use their personal financial resources to fund items that are less attractive to outside investors – for example, to provide start-up working capital to pay for salaries and expenses before receipts from sales are available.

MAIN SOURCES OF FINANCE

Owner's capital

The owners of a business are the ultimate risk-takers as they provide the business with capital and obtain a return only if the business proves to be profitable. Relative to other investors, providers of owners' capital benefit most when the firm is successful but stand to lose the most if it fails. The description of these funds and the precise terms attached depends on the legal form of the business.

Sole traders and partnerships

Unincorporated businesses comprise either individuals acting as sole traders or groups of individuals who set up in partnership. There are no legal procedures required to set up these businesses as they are not recognised in law as being separate from their owners. The assets and liabilities of the business belong directly to the owner or partners. This means that when a partner leaves or joins a partnership, the inconvenient situation arises of one partnership ceasing and another commencing. This also creates problems for ensuring a permanent capital base when ex-partners can withdraw their investment in the partnership irrespective of the needs of the business. Another disadvantage is that owners may be forced to transfer more of their personal wealth into the firm if the business cannot generate enough funds to pay its debts.

The obvious advantage of a partnership over a sole trader is the opportunity to raise funds from a number of individuals, although there are often problems of raising further funds from outside. Other investors cannot easily take their funds out of the business because their part of the partnership is not a financial security that can be freely traded.

Limited companies

Unlike sole traders and partnerships, **incorporated businesses** – known as limited companies – are legal identities separate from their owners. The capital contributed by the owners of the business is divided into 'shares' and hence an owner is called a **shareholder**. A share in a limited company is a tradable security which, subject to certain restrictions, can be bought and sold without directly affecting the business itself. Unless it is an issue of new shares, the sale proceeds pass between buyer and seller without cash implications for the business. This enables investors to obtain their money when required without affecting the company's ability to trade.

Shareholders enjoy a limited liability, as the maximum amount they can lose in the business is the amount they paid for the shares they hold. Shareholders receive benefits from profits earned, in the form of cash dividends and a potential increase in the value of their shares.

The distinction between a **private limited company** (Ltd) and a **public limited company** (Plc) is that the Plc can offer its shares to the general public, whereas the methods for issuing shares in a private company are restricted. Plcs that have obtained a listing on the **stock exchange** gain a number of additional advantages, including easier access to new funds and an enhanced reputation of the company. Also, employee share schemes give greater incentive where the shares are marketable and an up-to-date share price is readily available.

The disadvantages of a listing on the stock exchange include more onerous reporting requirements and a greater risk of the founders losing control if another organisation is able to buy large numbers of shares. The 'articles of association' of a private limited company restrict how shares can be sold, whereas a stock exchange listing

requires freely traded shares, including having at least 25 per cent of the shares held by the general public.

The stock exchange is primarily a market for the trading of previously issued shares. Hence an increased share price does not directly affect the company's finances unless new shares are being issued by the company. Importantly for its management, however, a higher share price gives reason for the existing shareholders to be satisfied with the company's performance.

The **Alternative Investment Market** (AIM) provides a market for shares in the smaller public limited companies and is supervised by the London stock exchange. It was launched in June 1995 as a stock market for companies that needed to raise more cash to grow. The AIM itself has grown from nothing to being a serious alternative to the finance provided by venture capitalists. By the end of 1998 there were over 300 companies quoted on the AIM, ranging in stock market value from £0.5 million to over £10 million.

The real attraction of the AIM is having marketable shares, which provides many of the advantages of a full listing. Unlike with a full stock exchange listing, however, there is no minimum capitalisation requirement, nor is there a need to have a three-year trading history. For existing shareholders who do not want a significant dilution in their holdings, AIM companies do not have to have a minimum of 25 per cent of their shares available to the general public. On the other hand, the procedures for obtaining an AIM listing do entail significant costs when compared with other sources of finance, such as the placing of shares with venture capitalists. A launch on the AIM may cost in excess of £100 000, together with the need to retain a nominated advisor and stockbroker. Other disadvantages include an on-going obligation to publish annual and interim accounts, to observe restrictions on share dealings, and to make announcements of events that affect the progress of the company.

Types of shares

Not all the shares issued carry the same rights to dividends and capital repayment. The types of shares issued and the rules governing them are initially decided by the company founders, but typically they fall into two main categories – ordinary shares and preference shares.

A holder of **ordinary shares** is entitled to the profits of the business after all other investors have been paid their dues. The shareholder is able to vote at general meetings of the company and is able to exert influence in direct proportion to the number of shares held. Items requiring shareholder authorisation include the appointment of the board of directors, the amount of profits distributed by way of a dividend to the shareholders, and the issuing or repurchasing of share capital.

Ordinary share capital is often called **equity capital** and can be likened to owner's equity in a private house. Equity for the householder is the difference between the current value of the house and the mortgage secured against it. In the case of a company, equity represents the difference between the value of assets owned by the business and the value of any outstanding loans and liabilities to other parties.

The amount of funds raised by the issuing of shares is limited only by the authorised share capital of the company and the availability of willing investors. However, the main consideration from the existing shareholders' point of view is that their ownership will be diluted if more shares are issued.

Preference shareholders are entitled to receive a dividend out of profits before distributions are made to ordinary shareholders. However, these dividends will be restricted if there are insufficient profits, and the right to receive payment will be rolled over to better years only in the case of 'cumulative' preference shares. In addition, these shareholders normally have no voting rights, which results in less influence on company policy. Because of the tax treatment of dividends compared with loan stock, UK companies do not issue significant numbers of preference shares.

Methods of issuing shares in a Plc

Issue by prospectus invites offers from the general public, with the prospectus giving information about the company and its future prospects. A disadvantage of this method is the risk that the share issue will not be successful, and the associated costs including newspaper advertisements can be high. Arranging for the issue to be 'underwritten' removes this uncertainty, as a finance house promises to take up any shares not subscribed for, in return for an underwriting fee. Alternatively, **offers for sale** involves the company selling its shares to an 'issuing house' which then publishes a prospectus. The success of the issue is more certain by this method, but the issuing house takes a proportion of the proceeds.

A **placing** involves blocks of shares being sold to a select number of investors. These are often financial intermediaries who then resell the shares to their clients. The placing could, however, be made direct to investors known by the company, such as personal investors, pension funds, unit trusts and investment trusts.

A **rights issue** gives existing shareholders the right to buy new shares in the company in proportion to their existing holding, usually at a favourable price. The risk of not all rights being taken up needs to be underwritten if the company is to be sure of getting the finance it needs.

A private limited company is unable to issue shares to the general public, so relies on placing shares and rights issues.

Share capital

The share capital of a business is classified into 'authorised' share capital and 'issued' share capital.

Authorised share capital is the value of the maximum number of shares the directors can issue according to the company's 'memorandum of association'. It can be increased only by the existing shareholders voting in a general meeting. In this way they can ensure that share issues are properly made with regard to company objectives and shareholder interests – such as protecting their proportionate ownership of the company. Approval to increase the authorised share capital is usually in accordance with specific plans to allow the funding of business growth, or to reduce the company's reliance on another form of finance, such as bank loans.

Issued share capital is the nominal value (see below) of the shares actually issued. On issuing shares the company will receive a consideration, either in cash or in the form of some other asset of value to the business. The share price on first issue will be the subject of negotiation, although where the company's shares are already listed on a stock exchange the market price will be an important factor for pricing new issues.

In the UK, shares have a **nominal value** which is the amount used to value 'share capital' in the accounts of the company. When new shares are issued, the difference between the market price and the nominal value is called a **share premium**. For example, a share with a nominal value of £0.50 and issued at £1.25 would result in an increase in share capital of £0.50 and an increase in share premium of £0.75.

The nominal value of a share may represent the price paid by the first shareholders in the company, but this is not necessarily the case. What is certain is that with the passage of time the pricing of new share issues will reflect the progress of the company, in terms of both its financial growth and the reduced risk of investing in an established business. As the nominal value of a share is fixed, the share premium will increase as the price of new shares increases.

TASK

J. Sainsbury Plc

The authorised share capital of J. Sainsbury at 7 March 1998 was made up of 2000 million shares of nominal value 25p each. The issued share capital was as follows:

	Number of shares (millions)	Nominal value (£m)	Share premium (£m)
At 9 March 1997	1840.0	460	1097
New shares issued	62.5	16	198
At 7 March 1998	1902.5	476	1295

1. What was the total consideration for the new shares?

2. What was the average price per share for the shares issued during the year?

3. For each new share, what was the nominal value and the average share premium?

Share buyback

A company may buy back its own shares if this increases the value for shareholders. Its management may perceive that, at the current price, shares in the company provide a better financial return than further investment in the activities of the business. By reducing the number of shares that have been issued, the company can benefit the remaining shareholders by saving on future dividends, and possibly by having a positive influence on the share price.

For a company to purchase its own shares there are a number of formalities that have to be addressed to protect the interests of creditors. The company has to seek the approval of its shareholders in a special resolution, and confirmation by a court that it may proceed. The court will want to be assured that creditors' interests are not being compromised by the withdrawal of capital from the business. This may take the form of insisting that creditors give formal approval, although for a company that is able to demonstrate that it clearly possesses funds in excess of its trading need, the court may forgo such a requirement.

Case Study

Frank Usher

The Frank Usher group designs and manufactures ladies' fashion clothing under its own labels such as 'Dusk', 'Coterie' and 'Oliver James'. Sales are split roughly equally between the UK and continental Europe. Having been in existence for 54 years, the company has a history of steady profits that have been used to develop the business and provide income for its shareholders. At 31 May 1997, the company had no debts outstanding apart from creditor balances arising in the normal course of trading. During the year to 31 May 1998, cash of £0.47 million was generated after dividends had been paid and £0.23 million invested in new capital equipment.

Despite satisfactory trading, the company's share price declined steadily during 1997/98. In the face of a rising value of the pound, the stock market became increasingly nervous about small manufacturing companies with exposure to overseas markets.

The directors decided to reduce the issued share capital and so the company purchased 325000 shares at an average net price of £1.43. By September 1998 the share price had fallen further to £1.12 despite the directors' confident view that financial results would improve in the long term. At the company's annual general meeting the directors proposed the purchase of a further 712000 shares which they believed would benefit shareholder value.

Questions

1. What evidence is there that Frank Usher does have funds in excess of its operating needs?

2. What is the logic behind increasing shareholder value with a further purchase of shares?

3. What conclusions may be drawn about the growth potential of a company that does purchase its own shares?

Retained profits

A major source of finance for many firms is the retention of its profits in the business. Instead of distributing all profits to owners, some of the wealth created each year is invested in further assets to increase earnings potential for the future.

The use of retained profit should not be considered a cheap form of finance. Although the business has not had to go to the market and offer an explicit return on the funds, there is an **opportunity cost** of using funds that otherwise would have been distributed to the owners. A payment out of profits earned can be reinvested elsewhere to provide the owners with additional income. Where management of a business is divorced from its ownership, as is often the case with public limited companies, the directors of the company are stewards of the shareholders' capital. As such they will be held accountable for ensuring that funds retained by the business earn at least as much as shareholders could have earned on alternative investments.

Case Study

Games Workshop

Games Workshop, according to its 1998 annual report, 'makes and sells the best model soldiers in the world'. Certainly an increasing number of enthusiasts agree, because sales turnover increased to £64.8 million in 1998 from £24.5 million in 1994.

The strategy is to establish and develop the Games Workshop hobby in each of the world's major economies. To this end, the retention of profits will continue to be a feature of the company's finances as it invests in capital infrastructure to enable the business to grow organically.

Total company assets amounted to £31.8 million at 31 May 1998 and retained profits had financed £16.7 million of this amount. In the year to 31 May 1998 alone, £4.7 million was retained out of a total profit after tax of £7.5 million. The remaining £2.8 million was distributed as a dividend to the holders of 31 080 934 shares – equating to 9 pence per share.

Questions

1. If the company had had no expansion plans and wished to distribute fully the profits earned, what would have been the dividend per share?

2. As shareholders have forgone this larger dividend, what obligation must the directors fulfil?

3. If the company directors fail shareholder expectations, what are the implications and when would they be evident?

Long-term loans

For unincorporated businesses the opportunity to arrange long-term loans is often limited to the purchase of land and buildings, when the property itself can provide security for the investor. Alternatively the proprietor will have to nominate personal assets – such as the family home – as security. Without adequate security, more emphasis will need to be placed on advancing the business proposition and the people committed to it.

For a company, on the other hand, long-term loans are usually in the form of **debentures**, a financial security made under the company's common seal. The terms 'debenture', 'company bond' and 'loan stock' are often used interchangeably.

Debentures can be described as being either 'secured' or 'unsecured', depending on whether a trust deed is in force to protect the debenture holder in the event of the company infringing the terms of the debt agreement. The rights of secured debenture holders are strengthened by a charge made in their favour over either specified assets of the company, or a floating charge over all of the assets. Where the security is a specified asset the loan stock is known as a 'mortgage debenture'. In the case of a floating charge the assets of the business will change over time, but at the point the company defaults on the debt the charge becomes fixed.

Secured loan stock can place restrictions on the use of an asset, particularly in the case of 'mortgage debentures' that are secured by specific assets. For example, changing the use of a property from offices to factory space may be prohibited because of a perceived adverse effect on the asset's value. Fixed charges will also preclude the selling of assets given as security without the permission from the relevant debenture holders.

The trust deed of a secured debenture will also describe such things as the rights of the debenture holders to hold meetings, to enforce contracts and to appoint a new manager (a receiver) to run the business until the obligations to them have been fulfilled. It will almost certainly preclude prior charges being made on the specified assets without the consent of debenture holders. An unsecured debenture has no trust deed, so the investor has to rely on the courts in the same way as other unsecured creditors.

In addition, debentures can either be 'redeemable' or 'irredeemable'. The company has to repurchase redeemable debentures on a fixed date or during a range of dates, whereas it has no obligation to do so for irredeemable debentures. For example, a 7 per cent irredeemable unsecured debenture of £10 000 will pay the debenture holder £700 per annum in perpetuity. There is no obligation on the company to pay back the capital sum

at any point, although of course it could negotiate a buyback if it had the cash available. If the debenture were traded on the stock exchange it could buy back at the prevailing market price.

'Convertible' debentures can be converted into shares in the company at some future date. For example, a 5 per cent convertible debenture '2003/2005' of £100 will pay annual interest of £5, and then in accordance with the terms of the debenture document will become convertible into ordinary shares at a predetermined price per share. In this example the debenture holder can exercise the option to convert during the period 2003 to 2005. The debenture holder will normally exercise the option only if the market price for an ordinary share is higher than the option price. The attraction for the debenture holder is the possibility of future capital growth but with the certainty of a fixed return in the meantime. For the company, the debenture yield should be less than on comparable non-convertible debentures and this will save on the interest bill in the short term. The other advantage is that the swap from debt to equity reduces financial gearing (discussed later) and will enable the company to borrow more in the future.

Company loan stocks are attractive to financial institutions such as pension funds, and to individual investors who require a reasonably certain fixed return.

Bank finance

The clearing banks, the biggest in the UK being NatWest, Barclays, HSBC and LloydsTSB, all provide financial products for business. However, the banks are adverse to risk and require detailed business plans before they lend. In general they will not lend more than the owners are putting into the business themselves, and are unlikely to agree finance for more than ten years.

Bank loans are taken out for a fixed period, with repayment being either in instalments or in full at the end of the agreed term. Security is usually required, and for a small business this is often in the form of a personal guarantee secured by the personal assets of the proprietor. Even in the case of companies where the major shareholders are also directors, the bank may insist on a charge over the family home or some other marketable asset.

The most flexible form of finance is a bank overdraft, because interest is charged only on the balance outstanding. The problem with a bank overdraft is that it is repayable on demand. In practice the bank usually provides some assurance that the facility will be available for a predetermined period (say six months or one year), after which it will be the subject of a review. Similar conditions to those for loans are required regarding security.

The bank will require a 'business plan' that shows how funds will be generated to repay the bank debt within the agreed timescale. Banks take the view that business ventures succeed or fail on the commitment and abilities of the management team, so the plan must sell the individuals involved as much as the business proposal.

One area in which the banks may be prepared to lend long term is for the purchase of land and buildings. A **mortgage** is a loan secured on land and buildings and can be used either to finance the purchase of the property, or in the case of property already owned, to provide security for a loan applied to some other purpose. It is a long-term financing arrangement of typically 10–30 years. In addition to the clearing banks, other financial institutions, such as insurance companies and pensions funds, are interested in this type of arrangement. The relatively high values for a single transaction can make a commercial mortgage an attractive component of a diversified investment portfolio.

Another form of finance for land and buildings involves the business selling its freehold property to an investment company, and then **leasing** it back over a predetermined period. This releases funds for other purposes in the business without incurring further debt. However, a major disadvantage is the loss of capital appreciation in times of rising property prices. For the financial institution, the attraction is an investment property with an immediate tenant.

Case Study

Tamaris

Tamaris plc is a fast-expanding nursing home operator that uses sale and leaseback as a strategy towards its objective of increasing shareholder value. The company buys nursing homes, sells the buildings to a finance house and then leases them back. Tamaris can in this way expand the number of beds it has under management without having to ask shareholders for more

funds. Return on capital is 35 per cent compared with 20 per cent if it were to use normal bank borrowing.

Questions

1. What is it about the nature of Tamaris' business that makes sale and leaseback such a viable source of finance?

2. What are the possible drawbacks of the company's strategy in the long run?

Hire purchase and leasing

Hire purchase (HP) allows a business to use an asset without having to find the money to pay for it immediately. A finance house buys the asset from the supplier and retains ownership of it during the period of the hire purchase agreement. The business pays a deposit and then further payments to the finance house as stipulated in the agreement. At the end of the HP agreement, ownership of the asset is passed to the business.

Leasing an asset provides similar benefits to hire purchase. A leasing agreement with a finance house (lessor) allows the business (lessee) to use an asset without having to buy it outright. The real distinction between the two forms of finance is that leasing does not confer an automatic right to eventual ownership of the asset. It is a very popular form of finance for company vehicles, office equipment and factory machinery. There are two types of lease – 'operating leases' and 'finance leases'.

An **operating lease** is a rental agreement for a short period of time relative to the asset's useful life. For example, two-year agreements for motor cars are fairly typical. The finance house realises a return on the arrangement by charging the business more than the anticipated reduction in the asset's value during the agreement.

A **finance lease** tends to run for a longer period. The agreement will cover most of the asset's useful life, and so the lessor typically requires payments under the agreement to total in excess of the cash price of the asset. Because the asset has relatively little value at the end of the lease term, the agreement often allows the lessee to continue leasing on a 'peppercorn' rent or to purchase the asset for a nominal sum.

The different nature of the two types of lease is reflected in other terms to the agreements. Under an operating lease the finance house is concerned that the asset retains a high resale value. So to ensure maintenance is carried out, its cost is often borne by the lessor (although of course this will have been considered when setting the lease terms). Under a finance lease, the risk of ownership is largely transferred to the lessee who usually has to maintain the asset.

One consequence of assets being acquired under HP or lease agreements will be restrictions on their modification and use, such as customisation of production line equipment or adaptations to motor vehicles. For operating leases, the lessor will wish to maintain high residual values. For the duration of HP and finance leases, the asset is security for the finance outstanding and its value could be impaired by anything that alters its standard specification.

For many businesses there is little difference in cost between leasing an asset and taking out a bank loan to make the purchase outright. One of the biggest advantages of leasing is the relative convenience because of the willingness of financial institutions to provide finance secured against specific assets. However, tax considerations may provide some cost advantages. If there are no taxable profits against which interest charges can be offset, then the relative cost of loan finance will be increased. This could be a consideration for start-up businesses.

Both HP and leasing are provided by finance houses that are often subsidiaries of the clearing banks or of equipment suppliers. Examples of these are Lombard Tricity Finance Ltd and Ford Motor Credit Co Ltd.

The finance house will want to be sure that company profits will be well in excess of the repayments due under the agreement, and that the company has a good payment record on existing finance arrangements. The agreement, under both types of finance, will place a charge over the asset being financed in case of default.

Factoring

A major problem for the cash flow of many businesses is the credit period taken by customers. The time between supplying goods or services and being paid for them is typically 30–60 days, and in some cases is considerably longer. However, despite the time taken to receive sales income the vast majority of it is collected eventually, and so this provides a valuable asset against which finance can be advanced. **Factors** provide finance against a business's

trade debt in two main formats – 'invoice factoring' and 'invoice discounting'.

With **invoice factoring**, the factor undertakes to collect amounts due from the business's debtors and immediately advances up to 80 per cent of the value of the invoices outstanding. The other advantage is that the task of debt collection is passed to the factor. As the monies are received from customers, the factor pays the business the balance of 20 per cent, less a charge. Many factors also provide cover for bad debts under 'non-recourse' agreements.

Invoice discounting also allows an advance of cash against trade debtors, but responsibility for debt collection remains with the business. Because the factor loses control over the receipt of monies direct from the business's customers, this arrangement is usually available only for larger and low-risk businesses.

An implication of placing trade debt with a factor is that it creates a break in personal contact with the customer. As recurring business from the same customers is a common feature for many businesses, this can be an important operational issue. Where this is the case the business should pursue the possibility of invoice discounting in preference to invoice factoring.

There was a time when factoring was seen as the last resort for struggling businesses. This was particularly unfortunate, bearing in mind that most such agreements are not confidential and customers are aware that their debt has been factored. However, in recent years factoring has experienced a facelift and is seen by many as a valuable component in building a financial strategy. It is a particularly appropriate source of finance for fast-growing businesses, as the amount of finance provided will grow automatically in line with the growth in sales. In 1997, invoice factoring amounted to £40 billion in the UK and was growing at 15–20 per cent annually.

The main providers are finance houses, such as Alex Lawrie Factors Ltd, RoyScot Factors Ltd and Lombard NatWest Commercial Services Ltd. In general the business requires a minimum annual turnover of £100 000 for factoring and around £1 million for discounting arrangements.

Asset-based finance

'Asset-based finance' is a term used to describe a form of finance that has only been generally available in recent years. It is basically a loan secured against certain assets in the business.

There has been a tradition of finance providers specialising in particular forms of finance, including sources for specific assets such as leases for plant and machinery and factors for debtor balances. However, influenced by finance companies coming from the USA, UK providers such as the factoring companies are taking a more holistic view of the business and its different types of assets. Asset-based finance may be arranged even for intangible assets such as intellectual property rights, especially if these are confirmed by registered patents.

Whilst debtors are the most liquid non-cash asset, and therefore tend to be the most attractive for finance houses, some are looking for other assets that may give the security they require for further advances. Stock tends to be the next most liquid asset but has been neglected until recently as security for finance. An advance against stock is an on-going arrangement reflecting the fact that, although the composition of stock changes on a daily basis, its existence as an asset is permanent for a going concern. The finance house will require periodic verification of stock levels.

Obviously, the less liquid the asset backing, the more diligent the finance company has to be to ensure the business is a viable going concern. However, with extra knowledge gained about the business, the more confident the finance provider is to make further advances. Companies that go down this route often find that they obtain more finance through one channel rather than go to different sources for different types of assets. Providers of finance for a wide range of assets include the UK's Burdale and NMB-Heller, but these have been joined by US companies such as Bank of America, Bank of New York and GE Capital.

Creditors

Suppliers are a valuable source of finance for many businesses. Just as a business may give credit to its own customers, it may be able to negotiate credit terms with its suppliers. Credit terms are typically 30 days from date of supply or 30 days from the end of the month of delivery. Trade credit has the advantage of being informal as it is considered part of normal terms of trade, and it is usually free.

However, a source of finance of this type for one business is a drain on resources for another. The situation has been aggravated by firms paying late, not because they cannot pay, but specifically to obtain free finance at the expense of their trading partners. This has become a particularly sensitive issue where big firms have exploited their smaller suppliers and forced them into accepting credit periods of 90 days or more. Although trading profitably, a firm may find itself with cash flow problems, as confirmed by one survey that found that a quarter of all business failures could be put down to late payment of sales income.

Aware of the hardship caused to smaller firms, the UK government has issued a statutory instrument requiring all trading companies to disclose in their annual reports the number of days credit taken from suppliers. In addition, from November 1998, new legislation came into force to give greater protection to businesses with fewer than 50 employees. Small firms can now charge large businesses interest on invoices paid outside agreed credit terms. However, small firms may only reluctantly enforce their legal rights because any action is bound to affect the business relationship. A change of attitude is required and this may be better encouraged by voluntary codes of practice. The Confederation of British Industry (CBI) has issued a *Code of Good Practice* on the prompt payment of suppliers, and this seems likely to be accompanied by similar campaigns to make larger firms aware of their responsibility to the wider business community.

In addition to credit obtained from trade suppliers, other creditors also arise in the normal course of business. In particular, the government is usually owed money at any point in time because taxes are payable retrospectively. Corporation tax is charged on company profits but it is not payable until nine months after the accounting period end; that is, some 21 months after the first profits have been earned. Income tax and National Insurance deducted from employees' pay is not payable to the Inland Revenue until 14 days after the end of the relevant fiscal period. Value-added tax is accounted for on either a monthly or quarterly basis and is not payable to Customs & Excise until the end of the month following the VAT period.

Other sources of creditor funding include shareholders, who do not receive dividends until after the relevant accounting period; pension scheme contributions (by both employee and employer); and interest on debt, paid at the end of the period to which it relates. One distinction between these 'other creditor' balances and other sources of finance is that they cannot be controlled, but they can be planned for.

At 2 May 1998, the independent brewer Greene King had total assets valued at £509.6 million. These were financed as follows:

	£m	Per cent
Shareholder funds (including retained profits)	285.7	56.1
Bank loans 2005 (unsecured)	131.0	25.7
Loan 2006 (secured)	32.5	6.4
Trade creditors	16.3	3.2
Corporation tax	12.1	
Other taxation and social security costs	10.3	8.6
Proposed dividend	7.9	
Accruals and deferred income	13.8	
	509.6	100.0

CHOOSING A SOURCE OF FINANCE

For any given business proposal there are likely to be a number of sources of finance that may be suitable. It is important to be aware of some basic principles and the relative advantages and disadvantages of each alternative. Financing strategy should take account of the following considerations and implications:

- the duration for which finance is required
- the available options for the particular purpose
- the cost of alternative sources of finance (considered in Chapter 6)
- gearing and interest cover – the financial implications of debt finance
- flexibility to adapt the amount of finance to changing needs
- the stage of development of the business
- security – asset backing demanded by the investor

- incentives from government agencies, such as grants and loan guarantee schemes.

It is usual to utilise a number of sources of finance to ensure that finance is appropriate to the business's needs.

Duration of finance

Just as an individual does not purchase a house using a bank overdraft, or a personal stereo with a 25-year mortgage, it is important for a business to consider the period for which finance is required. This makes sense:

- for the business – as it ensures that funds are guaranteed for as long as the need exists
- for the investor – where necessary it ensures that adequate security can be obtained for the duration of the loan (for example, a 20-year loan can be secured against property that will continue to have value in 20 years' time).

The purpose for which finance is being sought is therefore an important determinant in selecting an appropriate source of finance. Some items, such as property, will be required by the business into perpetuity, whereas temporary changes in working capital may require finance only for a matter of weeks or days. New plant and machinery may require finance for 5–10 years, motor vehicles for 2–3 years, and so on.

Some items of expenditure might seem quite short-term, such as cash for stock that tends to turn over perhaps every one to three weeks. However, it should be remembered that business is a continuous process, so working capital for such things as materials, wages and overheads will continue to be a long-term requirement. This may require external funding in the first year of trading, but subsequent retained profits could allow this to be repaid. A **business plan**, including a cash-flow forecast, is an important tool in identifying the required duration for finance.

As part of the planning process it is important to identify the *minimum* level of long-term finance required and ensure that this is properly funded. In Figure 5.2, the total finance required fluctuates over time because current assets are planned to vary. This might be because the business is seasonal and stocks and debtors rise and fall with the level of sales. The short-term fluctuations could be accommodated as they arise using appropriate sources of short-term finance, such as a bank overdraft. If permanent finance were arranged for the *total* need at all points in time, there would be occasions when funding would be in

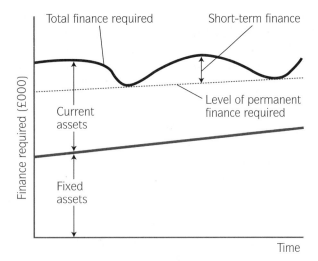

Figure 5.2 *Amount of finance required*

excess of requirements, at a cost to the business. This should be balanced against the risk of finance not being available when it is required. In general it is not good financial management to raise finance that results in a healthy bank balance, as the interest to be paid on excess funds is unlikely to offset the cost of raising the funds in the first place.

Source of finance	Type	Duration
Ordinary share capital	Long term	Indefinite
Preference share capital	Long term	Specified date of redemption, to indefinite
Retained profit	Long term	Indefinite
Debentures	Long term	Specified date of redemption, to indefinite
Commercial mortgage	Long term	Typically 10–30 years
Bank finance (lease, HP, loan)	Medium term	Typically 1–7 years
Bank overdraft	Short term	Up to one year on a rolling basis, although legally repayable on demand
Factoring	Short term	Typically 30–60 days, although depends on credit periods
Trade credit	Short term	Typically 30–60 days

Figure 5.3 *An analysis of the main sources of finance*

Figure 5.3 analyses the main sources of finance according to the period of funding they provide. There has traditionally been a shortage of medium-term finance in the UK, where banks have an arms-length relationship with their clients compared with the situation in continental Europe. This has been a major issue for UK industrial policy which successive governments have sought to rectify. The problem is seen as being particularly acute for small private businesses, which have difficulty in gaining the confidence of the financial institutions that prefer to invest in the medium-term debentures of larger firms.

Financial resources change on a daily basis in the normal course of business. However, long-term 'funds flow forecasts' (of which Figure 5.2 could be an example) will reflect changes in business assets, the maturity dates for existing sources of finance, and the accumulation of retained profits over a number of years. The evolving **capital structure** will point to appropriate new sources of finance, with the aim of maintaining appropriate levels of shareholder and debt finance.

Suitability of the source

Sources of finance can also be analysed according to whether they are general or are specific to the financing need. Specific sources available include:

- commercial mortgages and mortgage debentures for land and buildings
- hire purchase, leasing and bank loans for plant, machinery, office equipment and motor vehicles
- factoring for debtors.

General sources of finance include owner's equity, unsecured loan stock, bank overdrafts and creditors. When finance is hard to come by these sources should be reserved for financing items for which specific finance is not available – for example, stocks and running expenses.

Where the finance provider requires good asset backing for amounts advanced, then finance may be forthcoming only for goods with a standard specification. For example, a small business that is new to the provider is unlikely to be given finance for a bespoke computer system or machinery that is specific to that firm, because the value of these things would be very limited outside the business. In particular, operating leases tend to be available only for standard goods like motor vehicles that have a recognised second-hand market.

Flexibility: bank loan versus overdraft

Recognising the difficulty in planning cash flows accurately, the financial plan must have a contingency element. This may take the form of a permanent cash balance or other liquid asset, such as short-dated government bonds (which can be cashed in quite quickly). However, a less costly alternative is a bank overdraft facility (see Figure 5.4). Although interest rates for overdrafts are higher than bank base rates, the interest is paid on overdraft balances only on a daily basis. This contrasts with a bank loan which carries interest on the full amount outstanding whether it is used or merely sits in a current account. The situation is all the more stark because banks do not generally pay interest on current account credit balances, and many firms – especially smaller ones – fail to transfer daily credit balances to an interest-earning account.

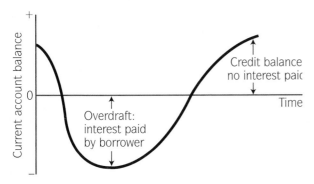

Figure 5.4 *A current account with overdraft facility*

Gearing: a financial implication of debt finance

Does the business enjoy stable demand for its goods or services, or does it suffer from volatile sales, perhaps in line with the economic cycles? This is important because loan stock and bank finance requires interest to be paid irrespective of the business's ability to pay. On the other hand, dividends to shareholders, even if somewhat reluctantly received, can be varied as profits rise and fall.

Gearing is the term used to describe the relationship between finance that enjoys a fixed rate of return, irrespective of the fortunes of the business, and equity that enjoys profit-related returns. So:

$$\text{Gearing ratio} = \frac{\text{Debt + Preference shares}}{\text{Ordinary share capital}}.$$

Figure 5.5 *The gearing effect*

There is no precise definition of the 'debt' figure used in the calculation. Debt may refer simply to long-term debt or alternatively to total debt including bank overdrafts. However, a cash balance can generate interest for the business to offset interest paid elsewhere, and it is also available to pay off debt if required. Hence many financial analysts use 'net debt' in the calculation; this includes debentures, obligations for the capital element of hire purchase and lease agreements, loans and bank overdrafts, *net* of cash balances and other liquid funds held in short-term deposit accounts. 'Ordinary share capital' includes share capital, share premium account, retained earnings and other reserves.

A question arises as to the inclusion of 'preference shares' in the calculation. Whilst here it is suggested that they be added to 'debt' because they too earn a fixed rate of return, there may be instances when they should be added to equity instead. If there are no profits, preference shareholders usually forgo their dividend in the same way as ordinary shareholders do – in contrast to debt providers who are due to receive interest irrespective of the fortunes of the business. As in other areas of 'ratio analysis', the circumstances and purpose of the gearing ratio should dictate the definition of terms used.

The importance of the gearing concept is demonstrated by the following illustration. Imagine that three companies each employ £100 000 of capital and in any one year can generate profits in the range £5000 to £20 000, before deducting interest payable on debt. Each company is financed by a different mixture of ordinary shares and 10 per cent debentures. *Company A* is financed by £10 000 of shares and £90 000 of debentures, so its gearing ratio is

$$\frac{£90\,000}{£10\,000} = 9.$$

Company B is financed by £50 000 of shares and £50 000 of debentures, so its gearing ratio is

$$\frac{£50\,000}{£50\,000} = 1.$$

Company C is financed by £90 000 of shares and £10 000 of debentures, so its gearing ratio is

$$\frac{£10\,000}{£90\,000} = 0.11.$$

Whatever the level of profits, debenture holders will always receive 10 per cent of the value of their debentures (e.g. £9000 when £90000 of debentures have been issued). However, the percentage return enjoyed by ordinary shareholders varies widely, being dependent on gearing in addition to the level of profits (see Figure 5.6). For example, when company A generates profits of £5000, shareholders actually suffer a loss of £4000. However, at the same profit level, company C's shareholders enjoy a return of £4000. That equates to 4.4 per cent of £90 000.

	A	B	C
Allocation of profits of £5000			
Shares	−4000	0	4000
Debentures 10%	9000	5000	1000
	5000	5000	5000
Allocation of profits of £10000			
Shares	1000	5000	9000
Debentures 10%	9000	5000	1000
	10000	10000	10000
Allocation of profits of £20000			
Shares	11000	15000	19000
Debentures 10%	9000	5000	1000
	20000	20000	20000

Figure 5.6 *Allocation of profits (see text)*

Taking the nine scenarios from Figure 5.6, it is possible to summarise the percentage returns to ordinary shareholders, as in Figure 5.7. It can be seen that the range of possible returns to ordinary shareholders increases as the gearing increases; that is, as gearing increases the shareholder returns become more volatile. For company A there is the possibility of earning a 110 per cent return on capital, but there is also a risk of incurring a loss.

	A	B	C
Gearing	9	1	0.11
On profits of £5000:	−40%	0%	4.4%
On profits of £10000:	10%	10%	10%
On profits of £20000:	110%	30%	21.1%
Range of returns (Percentage points)	150	30	16.7

Figure 5.7 *Returns on three profit levels (see text)*

Profits that are inadequate to meet legally due interest payments are eventually bad news for everybody, so the level of gearing is a concern to providers of all types of finance. However, it is difficult to generalise about the ideal value of the gearing ratio, as all businesses are different. In general, values under 0.25 indicate 'low gearing' and values in excess of one show 'high gearing'.

The main issue is the extent to which financial *risk* is affected by gearing. The more volatile the level of business profits, the more marked will be the effects of gearing. In the case of the companies illustrated in Figure 5.7, which do experience volatile profits, the lowly geared company C would appear to have the most appropriate capital structure. Businesses that are heavily influenced by economic cycles, such as capital goods suppliers, would not normally wish to be highly geared. On the other hand, stable industries such as food producers may be able to provide adequate interest cover at all stages of the economic cycle; they are unlikely to make losses for ordinary shareholders even if highly geared. Figure 5.8 illustrates this discussion diagrammatically.

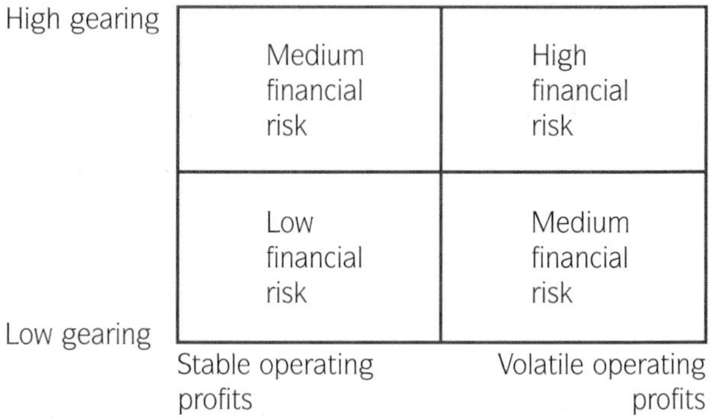

Figure 5.8 *Gearing and risk*

Interest cover

Another valuable measure of financial risk is the relationship between interest payments and the profits generated by the business. So:

$$\text{Interest cover} = \frac{\text{Profit before interest}}{\text{Interest paid}}.$$

A low interest cover ratio indicates that interest payments may become a problem if profits were to fall in the future. The larger the profits earned in relation to interest commitments, the less risk there is of interest payments pushing the business into a loss-making situation.

The stage of business development

The ability of a business to access the various sources of finance will depend on its **trading history**. Many providers of finance are looking for established profitable businesses with proven ability to develop new products/markets in the face of changing conditions. These offer relatively low-risk investments, and – in the case of debt finance in particular – give reasonable certainty for the payment of finance charges and debt repayments.

When a stable trading history cannot be demonstrated, many providers of finance will require substantial security in the form of personal assets or guarantees. Without this security, despite a good business idea, the clearing banks and leasing companies are loath to take on the financing of business start-ups. In these cases the provision of debt finance involves almost as much risk as equity finance but for little financial reward.

Businesses in the early stages of development or those undergoing fundamental change require investors who are not risk-adverse, and this precludes many of the financial institutions. As an alternative, a flotation on the stock exchange may not be successful, partly because the proposal is too risky and partly because the initial sums required may be too small to incur the costs of a listing.

This **equity gap** is being increasingly filled by 'venture capital' companies that wish to share in the success of businesses offering good growth potential. **Venture capital** is the term used to describe funds that are not fully secured, with the providers sharing in the risk of failure.

The business plan presented to the venture capital company must demonstrate not only a good business idea, but also realistic expectations with sound strategies to reduce risk. The assumptions in the plan will be the subject of rigorous testing and 'due diligence' work. This entails reviewing, amongst other things: the management organisation; the processes for production, quality and logistics; the assumptions underpinning financial forecasts; sales contracts and legal obligations; and the personal qualities and commitment of the management team. Providers of venture capital will assume a controlled measure of risk but often take up fewer than 10 per cent of the business proposals presented to them.

Venture capital providers in the UK are represented by the British Venture Capital Association (BVCA). The BVCA provides a means for businesses in need of finance to make contact with relevant venture capital organisations. Its members tend to specialise in certain industry sectors; this is another attraction for the business because, in addition to providing finance, they can help to ensure commercial success. In fact some individuals with capital to invest actively seek participation in the running of the business. These 'business angels' provide funding and management skills that give a firm foundation for business development.

Venture capital providers often concentrate on particular stages of business development:

- **Seed.** Developing the business idea may require further investment in research to evaluate its potential, or may require funding to produce a product prototype. This is a particularly risky stage as there is no certainty of a commercial launch or financial return. Fund providers will require a significant share of any future profits.
- **Start-up.** There are still considerable risks when a commercial venture is being planned, with a product and organisational structure ready to put in place. These risks are usually less than in a 'seed' situation.
- **Early stage.** Here the business idea has proved itself although it may not be generating profits. More funding is sought to develop its potential, perhaps by expanding manufacturing capacity or extending the distribution network.
- **Expansion.** An existing company may be trading profitably but further investment offers good growth prospects. Businesses that have had difficulties but can recover with a fresh strategy and a refinancing package also fall in this category.
- **Management buy-out.** Funds may be provided to enable the management of an existing company to purchase the business. The management will believe that the business offers good growth potential relative to the price to be paid to its current owners. The management team itself often has relatively little capital to invest but may be able to gain a majority shareholding if the venture capital provider is willing to invest mainly in debt finance; hence the term 'leveraged buy-out' as it implies a high level of gearing. The venture capital company may accept this position for the buy-out if the business promises exceptional capital growth on its share of the equity capital.

Over 80 per cent of venture capital goes to business proposals requiring at least £100000 each. The amount of work required to review a business goes against very small investments, although some providers will consider amounts down to £20000. Relatively little finance is provided for seed and business start-ups. During 1997, average amounts provided were £500000 for 'early stage', £1 million for expansions, and £5 million for management buy-outs. For amounts under £100000 it is often worth contacting a 'business angel' who is often motivated by reasons other than the purely financial.

The BVCA provides directories of venture capital companies and details of 'business angel' networks for those seeking finance. Thus, before approaching a provider the business is able to identify those interested in its stage of development, industry sector, location and amount of finance required.

The venture capital company usually provides a mix of equity and debt finance. The precise terms of the financing deal will depend on many factors, including the stage of business development, the nature of the business, its future potential, and the amount of funds provided relative to the total capital employed in the business. Despite often providing the majority of finance, it is in the interests of the venture capital provider that the business founders and management team are highly motivated to develop the business to its full potential. The management may therefore retain a majority stake in the ordinary share capital of the company. However, the finance provider, in requiring at least a 20 per cent return on investment, may insist on debt in the form of convertible loan stock to ensure it receives a good share of any future capital gain.

To minimise its risk, the venture capital company may provide stage finance in line with set milestones. It is then able to control future injections of cash and perhaps impose new conditions if there is any slippage against the business plan.

TASK

Using the figures above for companies A, B and C, the following interest cover ratios can be calculated when the profit before interest payments is £10000:

For A: £10000/9000 = 1.1
For B: £10000/5000 = 2.0
For C: £10000/1000 = 10.0

1. Calculate the interest cover for companies A, B and C when the profit before interest is £20000.

2. What do the ratios indicate?

TASK

Joyce and Gary Redfern wish to start up in business with £100000 of personal capital to be invested in ordinary shares. The business requires total finance of £500000 and this will be provided by a mixture of debt and equity finance. Debt finance is available in the form of 8 per cent loan stock for amounts of £100000 and £200000. However, if this were raised to £400000 the outside investors would require interest at 10 per cent to cover what they perceive as higher risk. The remaining finance required would be in the form of shares issued to the external parties. Annual business profits are forecast to be £120000, but with a chance they could be as low as £70000 and as high as £150000.

1. Calculate the gearing ratio for each level of debt.

2. Calculate the amount of interest payable and the residue available to the company's shareholders for each combination of profit level and gearing.

3. Calculate interest cover for each combination of profit level and gearing.

4. Calculate the percentage return on capital for ordinary shareholders for each combination of profit and gearing.

5. Produce a narrative addressed to Joyce and Gary to accompany your calculations, highlighting relevant points to help them decide on an appropriate financing mix.

TASK

For each of the following investment proposals, identify the most relevant sources of finance as requested, stating also when each would be most appropriate. Where the issue of share capital is recommended, also state the method of issue.

1. Roger Inman needs a new computer system costing £5000 for his business. Identify three ways of financing the purchase.

2. Harwood & Sons Ltd wants to expand its factory building. The cost will be £500 000. Identify three ways of financing the expansion.

3. Sinclair and Symons Ltd is having temporary problems with its cash flow. Identify two ways of financing its working capital shortfall.

4. Pantheon International Plc needs to raise £5 million for a new office complex. It currently has a gearing ratio of 2. Identify two ways of raising the finance.

5. EuroTunnel suffered trading losses in its first years of operation. If the company wanted to maintain its gearing ratio at the same level as in previous years, what type of finance would it have to raise?

6. Carlton Holdings Plc has a long-term strategy to increase the number of companies it owns. Identify three ways of financing this growth.

7. Connors and Moore Ltd has experienced poor sales in the last few years and this has resulted in substantial losses. The business needs to develop and launch a new product if it is to be saved. It could take up to four years for the new product to generate profits. The company's gearing ratio is currently just under 1. Identify two ways of financing this project.

Case Study

Yates Brothers Wine Lodges Plc

Yates Brothers' stated aim is 'to be a leading and profitable retailer of food and beverages'. To this end the company has been pursuing an aggressive expansion plan, opening 28 new pubs in 1997/98 alone.

At the end of March 1997 the company had shareholder funds of £71.4 million, a net bank overdraft of £3.4 million, and an unsecured bank loan of £17.5 million. During its financial year to March 1998, the company increased its investment in property, equipment and other business assets by £21.6 million. Although most of the existing property was freehold, £16.7 million of the spend on assets in 1997/98 was on short leaseholds.

The increase in assets was financed by increases in funding balances: £11.1 million in shareholder funds, £7.5 million in a bank loan, and £3.0 million in a bank overdraft. During the year profits before interest were £15.3 million (1997: £10.5 million) out of which interest of £1.7 million (1997: £1.8 million) was paid.

The company is confident about the future. For the year to March 1999, expenditure is anticipated on properties and kitchen and bar equipment, with the opening of a further 25 new outlets.

Questions

1. For the two years ending March 1997 and March 1998, calculate (a) interest cover, and (b) the gearing ratio.

2. Suggest alternative sources of finance to the increased bank finance during 1997/98.

3. Bearing in mind the ratios you have calculated and the nature of Yates Brothers' business, how could the on-going expansion of the company be financed?

Case Study

Filtronic Plc

Filtronic Plc, a company listed on the London stock exchange, specialises in electronics equipment for mobile phone base stations. The company operates in fast-growing markets where its sales demand is closely tied to the global growth in mobile phone usage. Industry product standards are still evolving, but the company's management has a global strategy to become a leading supplier to the telecommunication operators. At 31 May 1998, the company's shareholder funds and other funding comprised:

Called-up share capital	£4 903 000
Share premium account	£11 691 000
Revaluation reserve	£106 000
Profit and loss account	£12 531 000
	£29 231 000
Amount owed to financial institutions net of cash balances	£20 291 000

Of the authorised share capital of 60 million shares of 10p each, 49 031 600 had been issued during the lifetime of the company.

On 7 August 1998, Filtronic agreed to purchase the entire share capital of LK-Products, a subsidiary of Finnish company Nokia. As consideration, Filtronic agreed to pay £39.9 million in cash (which would increase indebtedness to financial institutions) and to issue 4 million Filtronic shares to Nokia.

On 20 August 1998, the company placed 4 903 979 new shares with institutional investors to raise £22.9 million after expenses, for working capital for the enlarged group. At the same time it issued a notice of an extraordinary general meeting at which approval would be sought to increase authorised share capital to 80 million shares.

Questions

1. Describe the meaning of the terms 'authorised share capital' and 'issued share capital'.

2. What was the total book value of shareholder funds at 31 May 1998?

3. Which of the various actions and proposals made during August 1998 would have resulted in actual transactions of cash?

4. How would the share placing amounting to £22.9 million be split between 'called-up share capital' and the 'share premium account'?

5. Assuming approval was given to increase the authorised share capital, how many shares would there then be that were authorised but not issued?

6. Why do you think Filtronic decided to fund its expansion plans with a mixture of equity and debt?

SUMMARY

The sources of finance used by a business should reflect the need for which the funds are required, having regard to duration, purpose and cost. In addition, consideration should be given to the nature of the business and its existing financial structure, in particular the level of gearing and interest cover.

It is also important to appreciate that finance for business is viewed from two perspectives – the business has its objectives, but so do external investors. External parties include insurance companies, pension funds and others, looking for opportunities to invest funds for periods from months to many years. Their willingness to do so will depend on the likely risk and financial return for their investment. They will be interested in how easy it is to liquidate their funds to discharge their own financial commitments.

Some investors may wish to participate in the profits of the business and so will join the business founders as partners or shareholders of the business. The ability to freely buy and sell shares in a listed company is likely to mean that these will prove more attractive to investors than will sole traders, partnerships and private limited companies.

Some providers of funds may require safe fixed returns but with the possibility of long-term capital growth. This could be met by offering preference shareholders and debenture holders fixed redemption dates and the option to convert loans into ordinary shares once the business has proved successful. Of course, options that reduce the risk and enhance the returns for one group of investors, correspondingly increase the risk and reduce the potential returns for other groups. As with many areas of business, a contingency approach should be used to the financing of new and on-going business operations.

Finance as a Resource

This chapter considers how finance is deployed in a business as a resource. The assets and liabilities that arise are examined in the context of the balance sheet.

On completion of the chapter you should be able to explain the use of finance as a resource within a business. To achieve this you must demonstrate the ability to:

- assess the cost of different types of finance for the business

- explain the importance of the flow of financial resources

- explain the importance and use of financial information for decision-making purposes

- define the different types of assets and liabilities owned by the business.

THE COST OF FINANCE

Just as there is a cost associated with the rental of an asset or the hiring of labour, finance also has a cost. The business is indebted to its investors for the finance provided and it is a responsibility of the management to provide a financial return on it. A financial return for the investor is a cost of capital for the business.

The cost of finance will depend upon the terms on which the funds were provided. Investors will expect a return that takes into account the priority for repayment of their money, the security offered, and the variability of the financial return. Some investors will receive an explicit rate of return (e.g. 7 per cent debenture stock). Others are prepared to accept uncertainty in the quest for higher returns (e.g. ordinary shareholders).

Ordinary share capital

The cost of using ordinary share capital, including retained profits, can be considered from the shareholders'

perspective. **Returns** to the shareholder come in two forms – the receipt of cash dividends, and the appreciation in value of the shares as the business grows. Total returns can be expressed as a percentage:

Return on investment in shares =
$$\frac{\text{Dividend per share} + \text{Share price movement}}{\text{Market price of share}} \times 100\%.$$

For public limited companies with a listing on the stock exchange, dividends are typically paid twice a year. First an interim dividend is paid some time after the publication of the half-year results, and then a final dividend is proposed at the company's annual general meeting after the directors have laid before the meeting the financial results for the year. Payment of dividend is then made to persons who were registered shareholders on a specified date.

Because shares in listed companies are continuously traded, it is important to ensure that both buyer and seller are certain as to who is entitled to the dividend. Clearly a share that has a forthcoming dividend payment attached to it is more valuable than a share immediately after the right to the dividend has passed. This can be observed by the movement in share prices before and after dividend rights have been frozen. Quoted share prices are expressed as

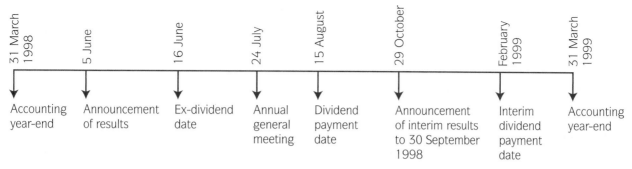

Figure 6.1 *The financial calendar of Pilkington Plc*

being either 'cum-dividend' or 'ex-dividend' depending on whether the share is being traded before or after the entitlement to dividend is set.

Check your understanding

Royston Ltd has come to the end of its first year of trading, having made a profit after tax of £200 000. The company's £1 million ordinary share capital had been provided by investors who could on average make 15 per cent per annum on alternative investments. The directors proposed a dividend for the year totalling £100 000.

The company's cost of capital is 15 per cent because this is the *opportunity cost* to investors. In its first year of trading the company has earned a return of 20 per cent (£200 000 as a percentage of £1 000 000) which, if paid out as dividends, would clearly meet investors' expectations. However, by paying out just 10 per cent, the shareholders' wealth will have increased by 20 per cent only if the shareholders perceive that their investment in the company has grown in value by £100 000. To achieve this there must be a 15 per cent return on the capital retained; i.e. profits must grow by a further £15 000 per annum.

In the case of Pilkington (see Figure 6.1), shares bought up to 15 June 1998 entitled the buyer to the dividend paid from profits earned up to 31 March 1998. For share trades after this date the share seller retained rights to receive the dividend even though it was not actually paid until 15 August 1998.

To sustain continuing growth in a company's share price it is necessary to make on-going investment in financial resources, at least some of which will be funded by retained profits. However, its management would be failing the shareholders if investment in business assets did not at least cover the opportunity cost of shareholders not receiving a full distribution of profits.

It should be evident that establishing the cost of shareholder funds is not a simple task. It requires forecasts of shareholders' expectations in respect of future dividends and share price appreciation. Especially problematic is putting a figure on a future share price, particularly when some shareholders hope merely for speculative gains.

Despite the widely held view that short-term share price changes are dictated by changes in sentiment for the economy as a whole, it is of more than academic interest that the company should be aware of its costs of finance. For investment in new projects, such as developing a new product, financial benefits must outweigh the cost of capital (Chapter 8 considers this in greater detail). If benefits do not exceed costs, then the business is not creating value for its owners or for the economy as a whole.

The share price for a company should reflect the growth potential of profits, but this can be the case only if it is based on timely and accurate information about the company's progress. For a company whose share price is quoted on the stock exchange, the management has a responsibility to inform the exchange if actual performance is not in line with market expectation; hence the periodic issue of 'profit warnings' by company's failing to meet those expectations.

All stock exchanges strive to be efficient markets for the securities traded there. This requires prompt communication when financial performance and share price levels are inconsistent. By ensuring that the current share price is a fair reflection of at least the short-term profit level, there can be informed discussions at investor briefings and annual general meetings that can attempt to resolve apparent differences between expectations and actual investment returns. In this way, and with other companies in the same industry sector as a benchmark, it should be possible to discern a long-term cost of equity finance.

In addition to the on-going costs of using shareholder funds, a quoted public limited company will also incur significant costs in the issuing of shares – up to a tenth of the sum raised. This is because there are onerous obligations laid down by the stock exchange to ensure that a fair and efficient market exists for a company's shares. It is necessary to publish a prospectus, and there will also be printing and postage costs when communicating with existing shareholders, underwriting premiums to insure against a failed flotation, and professional fees paid to legal and financial advisors.

Case Study

Cost of share issues

Roxspur Plc and Morland Plc, companies quoted on the London stock exchange, both issued shares during 1997/98.

Roxspur, an engineering company, acquired Clayhithe Plc for £30.9 million, an amount funded half by debt and half by additional share capital. Of the 201 763 872 new shares issued with a nominal value of 1p each, 70 522 316 were by way of an 'offer for sale' at 8.75p each. The 'offer for sale' incurred expenses of £603 000.

Morland, producers of the bitter 'Old Speckled Hen', continued the expansion of its managed pubs with the acquisition of Exchange Bar Diners, funded by a one-for-six rights issue (for every six shares held, existing shareholders could subscribe for one new share). The 4 607 367 new shares of 25p nominal value were issued at £5 each. The cost of the share issue was £758 000.

Questions

1. What is the distinction between a 'rights issue' and an 'offer for sale'?

2. Suggest why Roxspur funded its expansion with both new debt and new shares.

3. Calculate the gross amount raised from each share issue, split between nominal value and share premium.

4. What was the percentage cost of each share issue relative to the gross amount raised? Give two reasons for the disparity in the percentage costs.

Cost of fixed-return finance

The cost of using debt finance or preference shares is explicit with a stated interest rate or fixed dividend per share. *Preference shares* usually give a fixed rate of return; for example, 8 per cent £1 preference shares entitle the holder to 8p per year for each share held. Preference shares that are convertible into ordinary shares at some future date will potentially dilute future gains through an increase in ordinary shareholders, and this is an added cost which needs to be considered. As with ordinary shares, there may also be significant issuing costs for a listed company.

Debentures, too, carry a fixed rate of interest that must be paid irrespective of the level of profits earned. For example, 6 per cent unsecured loan stock issued in units of £100 would entail a cost of £6 a year for every unit of stock outstanding. For a public limited company there will be issuing costs for listed loan stock.

The cost of fixed-return finance will depend on the financial risk of the company and the prevailing interest rates in the marketplace for an investment with the same duration. For example, at a time when five-year government bonds are yielding 5 per cent, a debenture in a major company, with a five-year redemption date, might yield 6 per cent. The higher rate reflects a small risk premium compared with the government bond which is considered risk-free.

Changes in market interest rates will have a direct and proportional effect on the price of a debenture. For example, if a 7 per cent irredeemable debenture of £10 000 were issued when long-term interest rates were 8 per cent per annum for a similar investment, it is unlikely there would be a buyer at £10 000. The investor will require an 8 per cent return, so the 7 per cent debenture will be worth:

Value of debenture = £10 000 × 7%/8% = £8 750

i.e. the yield is $\frac{£700}{£8\ 750}$ × 100% = 8 per cent.

If long-term interest rates were to fall to 6 per cent, then the 7 per cent debenture would increase in market price.

Debenture value = £10 000 × 7%/6% = £11 667

i.e. the yield is $\frac{£700}{£11\ 667}$ × 100% = 6 per cent.

For redeemable loan stock – when the capital sum will be repaid on a specified date – the market price will reflect an appropriate yield for a loan of that duration. The full capital amount is eventually repaid, so the price of redeemable loan stock tends to be less sensitive to changes in interest rates.

Trade credit does not normally incur an explicit cost. However, in cases where a discount is offered for prompt payment, failure to take up the discount is usually expensive in annual terms. For example, if normal payment terms are within 60 days from the date of supply but a 2.5 per cent discount is offered for payment within 30 days, the opportunity cost incurred in continuing to 60 days is 2.5% to gain, in effect, just one month of extra credit. On an annual basis this equates to 2.5% × 12 months = 30%.

Bank loans, overdrafts and *commercial mortgages* are usually charged interest at an agreed premium over bank base rates. The premium may be as low as 0.5 per cent for a blue-chip company (one that is highly regarded) but will be substantially higher for small and risky businesses. A typical premium for a small business with little trading history but with a charge over the home of the entrepreneur could be around 3 per cent. In addition there may be arrangement fees and a security fee (if the loan is secured on personal or business assets) which for the smallest of loans could add several hundred pounds to costs.

Hire purchase and *finance lease* agreements include a charge that is made explicit in the terms of the contract. These arrangements are rarely cheap, but they are often convenient and costs are comparable with those of alternative sources of finance. Operating leases, particularly for motor vehicles, usually include the cost of maintenance and this should obviously be considered as part of the financial appraisal.

Debt factors charge interest typically at 1–3 per cent in excess of the bank base rate, so factoring is similar in cost to bank finance. For invoice factoring, a further charge of up to 3 per cent of the value of debtors is charged for sales ledger administration, but this needs to be considered in the light of saved internal costs for credit control.

Sale and leaseback releases funds which will either reduce the cost of borrowing or will provide a return on investment in the business. However, the cost of such an arrangement will be the on-going lease payments and potential loss of property value appreciation.

Weighted costs of finance

Although the capital structure of a business should reflect the nature of its operations, it is not always possible to

Check your understanding

A company has share capital of £100 000 and retained profits of £100 000 (i.e. £200 000 total), plus 10 per cent debentures of £50 000 and trade credit of £30 000. If the shareholders require a return of 15 per cent, what is the required return from the average business activity (ignoring tax considerations)? This will be equal to the average cost of capital, 'weighted' according to the various expectations:

Weighted average cost of capital

$$= \frac{\text{Total returns required}}{\text{Total finance employed}} \times 100\%$$

$$= \frac{\text{Return to shareholders} + \text{Return to debentures}}{\text{Shareholder funds} + \text{Debentures} + \text{Trade credit}}$$

$$= \frac{(£200\,000 \times 15\%) + (£50\,000 \times 10\%)}{(£200\,000 + £50\,000 + £30\,000)} \times 100\%$$

$$= 12.5 \text{ per cent.}$$

relate particular sources of finance to specific applications. It could be argued, on evaluating an individual project, that the *relevant* cost of capital relates to the *marginal increase* in financing. For example, the acquisition of a new factory machine on a financial lease could be appraised using just the finance charge included in the lease. In fact this approach is often used in practice. However, there may come a time, after continuing to finance expansion on an *ad hoc* basis, when the whole capital structure has to be reviewed. Then, either loan stock can be issued to consolidate debt finance, or further share capital will be sought.

Whilst individual finance agreements will each reflect short-term interest rates in the marketplace, the business must actually meet the expectations of many investors over the longer term. Despite marked variations in short-term interest rates, the returns expected by shareholders vary very little – an average annual rate of 5 per cent in addition to inflation is typical. Investors may expect greater returns when the economy and stock markets are booming, and less at times of recession; but in the long run the large shareholders, such as the pension funds and insurance companies, want to be sure of funding their own long-term financial obligations. It follows that a business should consider a long-term return that will meet investors' expectations and also reflects the long-term capital structure of the business. Therefore an individual project should earn sufficient to satisfy the business's long-term average cost of capital.

The rate required will vary over time, following movements in long-term market rates and changes in the perceived riskiness of the business.

Risk and rates of return

Risk is the uncertainty of predicting a particular outcome. Statistically it may be referred to in terms of the range of possible outcomes, or the deviation around some average value. Risk refers to the possibility of a result that can be better than, as well as worse than, expected. In general, certainty is something that most investors would make some sacrifice to achieve, in terms of potential financial returns. Risk can have two components:

- *The operational risk.* This depends on the technical and commercial viability of the business proposal, with special consideration given to the ability of the management and the inherent competitive advantage that the business has.

- *The financial risk.* This will depend on the financing terms and conditions (such as the duration of the investment), on the security provided in case the business defaults, and on the likely rate of return for the investor. The financial risk will also be affected by the terms given to other investors in the business; for example, because of the effects of gearing, a big new loan stock issue will increase the risk for shareholders.

The tradeoff between rate of return and risk is illustrated by the long-term returns on government bonds and on company shares. Government bonds give a modest rate of return but are considered risk free. In contrast, shares in a new business may promise high returns but are accompanied by a chance of failure, when the capital invested may also be lost. It follows that the cost of capital of a company cannot be stated without reference to the risk it poses for its investors.

However, when evaluating a single project, it may not be adequate to view the project in isolation from other aspects of the business. Portfolio theory suggests that, unless the returns on individual projects are perfectly and positively interrelated, the risk of one project may to some extent offset the risk of another. This means that the riskiness of a company may be less than the combined riskiness of its individual projects.

As an example, consider an engineering company that operates one factory supplying tooling to food manufacturers and another factory supplying components for construction equipment. Demand from construction plant customers will swing markedly with the economic cycle, whereas other factors, such as changing consumer tastes, will affect demand from food manufacturers. Thus, while the expected return from the company as a whole will be the weighted average of the returns from the two parts of the business, total risk will be less than the weighted average because the financial results of the two parts of the business are not perfectly and positively correlated.

Understanding how the risk of an individual project affects the cost of capital for the whole company is not easy. In practice, often the best that can be expected is at least some allowance, perhaps in the form of an **ABC risk classification** system, where **A** is low risk and **C** is high risk. Taking the risk-free rate as a benchmark, increasingly risky projects will be required to generate higher expected rates of return. So, for example, class C projects, perceived as high risk, will have a correspondingly large risk premium added to the risk-free rate (see Figure 6.2).

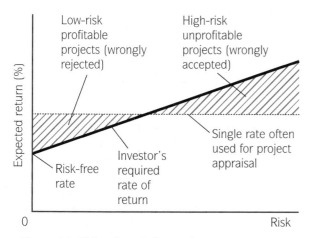

Figure 6.2 *Risk and required rates of return*

It is clear that businesses which choose a single return rate in project appraisal are in danger of selecting high-risk unprofitable projects at the expense of low-risk profitable ones. Investors will accept lower returns for low risk but will not want the business to enter into riskier projects without expecting a higher return.

Tax considerations

The British tax system affects the relative costs of different sources of finance, and has been instrumental in the growth of debt finance over preference shares. Put simply, interest charges are tax-deductible but dividends are not. This means that, in terms of net cost to the company, the percentage rates attached to preference shares and debentures are not directly comparable.

Imagine that two companies, X and Y, have both made annual profits of £500000 before finance charges and

	Company X (£000)	Company Y (£000)
Profit before interest	500	500
Interest @ 10%	50	0
Profit after interest	450	500
Corporation tax @ say 20%	90	100
Profit after tax	360	400
Preference dividends @ 10%	0	50
Profit attributable to ordinary shareholders	360	350

Figure 6.3 *Example (see text)*

taxation. Both companies have capital employed of £2 million and both have ordinary share capital of £1.5 million. But whereas company X is funded by £0.5 million of 10 per cent debentures, company Y is funded by £0.5 million of 10 per cent preference shares. For the providers of finance, preference shares and debentures both give a gross return of 10 per cent and are subject to the same rates of income tax. It is the ordinary shareholders who are affected by the different financing arrangements. As shown in Figure 6.3, the ordinary shareholders in company X have gained to the extent of the tax relief on the debenture interest; i.e. 20 per cent of £50000, or £10000.

It is because of the tax system that preference shares have fallen out of fashion. The attractiveness of debentures for investors is also enhanced because they give prior claims to payment of interest and capital. However, preference shares do have one important feature that should be considered – dividends are paid out of profit, so preference shareholders will not be paid when the business makes a loss. From the company's point of view, to this extent they improve gearing and interest cover when times are tough.

Our earlier calculation of the weighted average cost of capital (WACC) can now be refined, having regard to the tax position:

$$\text{WACC} = \frac{[\text{Debt finance} \times I \times (1 - T)] + \text{Return to all shareholders}}{\text{Debt finance} + \text{Share capital}}$$

in which I is the interest rate for the debt finance and T is the corporation tax rate.

Imagine that a company is funded by £1 million of ordinary share capital, £0.5 million of 8 per cent preference share capital and £0.5 million of 7 per cent loan stock (debt finance). Ordinary shareholders receive a dividend yield of 3 per cent and expect long-term capital growth of 7 per cent a year. Corporation tax is 40 per cent. The WACC can be calculated as follows:

$$\text{WACC} =$$
$$\frac{[£0.5m \times 7\% \times (1 - 0.4)] + (£0.5m \times 8\%) + (£1.0m \times 10\%)}{£0.5m + (£0.5m + £1.0m)}$$

$$= \frac{£21000 + £40000 + £100000}{£2000000} = 8.05 \text{ per cent.}$$

Note the relative costs after tax: for loan stock 4.2 per cent (i.e. 7×0.6) and for preference shares 8 per cent.

FLOW OF FINANCE

The flow (or cycle) of financial resources is similar to the water cycle in nature. Funds are transformed from a liquid (flexible) resource into other resources like property, equipment, stocks and labour. These resources generate income from customers, which is eventually received in the form of cash ready to continue the cycle. As with the life-giving qualities of water, the flow of cash is essential for a business to survive. The faster the flow the more financially efficient the business. It is vital, therefore, that the receipts

and payments of cash are properly understood, monitored and controlled.

Cash flow forecasts

The cash flow forecast is an invaluable tool in the financial management of a business. It is used to identify sources and applications of cash and to forecast the relevant timing and values of cash flows. As a planning tool, it identifies when extra finance may be required and when excess funds may be available for investment. As a control tool it provides a measure against which actual cash flows can be monitored. An example of a cash flow forecast is shown in Figure 6.4

The format of the cash flow forecast should convey a clear and accurate message to its user. The line descriptions should be relevant to the business and the division of time should be appropriate to the statement's purpose. The forecast may be for a number of days or could span several years.

Positive carried-forward balances indicate money in the bank; negative balances (usually indicated by placing the amount in parenthesis, as in Figure 6.4) indicate that finance is insufficient to pay for all the forecasted commitments. Arrangements have to be made to cover the deficit, perhaps by applying for an overdraft facility if it is seen as a temporary situation.

	Month 1	Month 2	Month 3	Month 4	Month 5	Month 6
RECEIPTS						
Share issue	5000					
Loan	3000					
Sales receipts		4000	5000	6000	7000	7000
Total receipts	8000	4000	5000	6000	7000	7000
PAYMENTS						
Salaries and wages	2000	2000	2000	2500	2500	3000
Rent and rates	1000			1000		
Power				500		
Purchase of materials	2000	1000	1250	1500	1750	2000
Equipment	3500	500				4000
Dividends						
Total payments	8500	3500	3250	5500	4250	9000
Receipts minus payments	(500)	500	1750	500	2750	(2000)
Balance brought forward	0	(500)	0	1750	2250	5000
Balance carried forward	(500)	0	1750	2250	5000	3000

Figure 6.4 *A cash flow forecast*

A forecast that indicates a continuing cash deficit should continue into future periods to identify the duration for which additional finance is required. It is not unusual for a new business venture to construct a cash flow statement for its first three years of operations, the first year analysed on a monthly basis, with the second and third years divided into quarters.

It is imperative to identify the point when cash is actually received or paid out. Hence if customers are allowed up to 30 days of credit before they need to pay for supplies, then the sales for month 1 will not be received until month 2. Likewise it may be possible to delay the payment of suppliers. Although it is important to be realistic, it is also wise to be prudent and not recognise receipts too early or payments too late.

The following is a simple example of the phasing of sales and purchases. Karen Cambra is in the process of preparing a three-month cash flow forecast to the end of June. Karen takes 30 days of credit from her suppliers, and experience shows that 60 per cent of her customers take 30 days to pay with the remainder paying within 60 days. Sales forecast: February £10 000, March £11 000, April £12 000, May £13 000 and June £14 000. Purchases

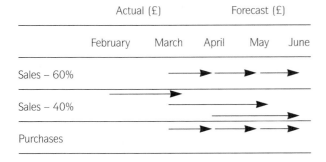

	Actual (£)		Forecast (£)		
	February	March	April	May	June
Sales – 60%					
Sales – 40%					
Purchases					

Figure 6.5 *Karen's forecast: phase sales and purchases to correspond with the periods when actual cash flows will arise*

	April (£)	May (£)	June (£)
Sales – 60%	6 600	7 200	7 800
Sales – 40%	4 000	4 400	4 800
Purchases	(6 500)	(7 000)	(7 000)
Net cash flow	4 100	4 600	5 100
Cash brought forward	5 000	9 100	13 700
Cash carried forward	9 100	13 700	18 800

Figure 6.6 *Karen's cash flow forecast to June*

forecast: February £5 000, March £6 500, April £7 000, May £7 000, and June £8 000. At the end of March her cash balance was £5 000. Figure 6.5 shows the situation diagrammatically, and Figure 6.6 is the more formal cash flow forecast.

Business activity and cash flow

Cash flows can be categorised as: operating, investment, returns on investment and servicing of finance, taxation, and financing. These are now examined in turn.

The operating cycle

The operating cycle describes the processes of everyday trading activity (see Figure 6.7). It starts with the procurement of resources, goes through the stages of producing and delivering goods or services to customers, and finishes with the receipt of cash from customers. Finance tied up in this operating cycle is called **working capital**.

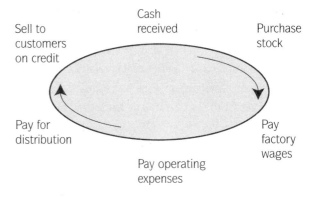

Figure 6.7 *The working capital cycle*

For any product going through this cycle, cash is being invested to increase its value until the customer finally pays. It is appropriate, therefore, to recognise that at different stages of the working capital cycle there are **assets** that can be measured in terms of their value to the business. Correspondingly, the business enters into transactions that create **liabilities**, such as the receipt of stock on credit where there remains an obligation to pay a third party at some time in the future.

TASK

Miles Thoroughgood is planning to set up in business from March as a renovator and retail outlet for antique pine furniture imported from eastern Europe. Before receiving sales income he requires property, a van and stock, which he will collect from the importer's premises. He has found a suitable building on a three-year let, £3 000 payable each quarter in advance. He has the opportunity of a second-hand van costing £3 700, which he intends to pay for out of the £7 000 capital he has paid into the business bank account.

He estimates that his first six months of stock purchases will be £5 000, £3 000, £2 000, £2 500, £3 000 and £3 000. Fortunately the importer is a former business acquaintance of Miles and so he has been able to negotiate payment in the month following purchase. Other items of expenditure are estimated to be: vehicle running costs, £500 in the first month and £200 per month thereafter; property-related running costs, £100 per month; occasional help in the shop, £300 per month; and consumable materials for renovation at 10 per cent of each month's stock purchases. Sales will be for cash only and are forecast to start from April, his second month in business. The first monthly sales are forecast to be £2 000, £3 000, £4 000, £5 000 and £5 000. Miles has decided to draw up to £700 out of the business each month, assuming there are adequate funds available at the bank.

1. Prepare a cash flow forecast for Miles for his first six months of trading.

2. What are the significant features of the cash flow?

3. If additional finance is required, suggest three suitable sources with a description of the relevant advantages and disadvantages.

An asset is defined by the Financial Reporting Board (FRB) as giving 'future economic benefits controlled by an entity as a result of past transactions or events'. For example, if goods priced at £100 are purchased with the intention of resale, it is clear that the future economic benefit is an eventual sale receipt, hopefully worth at least £100. It is therefore appropriate to recognise an asset called 'stock' valued at £100. In financial accounting terms, the assets that arise as a result of the working capital cycle are called **current assets**. These assets liquidate naturally into cash during the normal course of business.

Liabilities are defined by the FRB as 'obligations of an entity to transfer economic benefits as a result of past transactions or events'. An example is a contract to supply electricity where payment is required after the electricity has been consumed.

Stocks comprise the costs incurred in providing goods or services that will be sold to customers. There are three stock categories for manufactured goods: raw materials purchased from other businesses; work-in-progress, which includes the cost of used raw materials, labour and overheads relating to partly finished goods; and finished goods ready for sale. A company providing services that remain unfinished at a point in time will have incurred labour and expenses that will also be classified as work-in-progress.

The following is an illustration of stock valuation. Metal Pressings Ltd manufactures metal toolboxes which it sells to DIY stores and trade outlets. The production process requires machine operators for the guillotine and pressing machines used to cut and press sheet steel into the desired shapes. An average toolbox requires materials costing £3 and labour costing £2. The factory incurs overheads for rent, utilities, material storage, machine maintenance and supervision. These overheads equate to 200 per cent of actual wages paid. The business has a batch equivalent to 1 000 toolboxes in each category of stock: raw material, work-in-progress and finished goods. Figure 6.8 shows the situation. What is the total investment in stock?

	Raw materials	Work-in-progress (50% complete)	Finished goods ready for sale
	(£)	(£)	(£)
Materials	3 000	3 000	3 000
Labour		1 000	2 000
Overheads		2 000	4 000
Valuation of the stock – asset	3 000	6 000	9 000

Figure 6.8 *Metal Pressings Ltd: stock valuation*

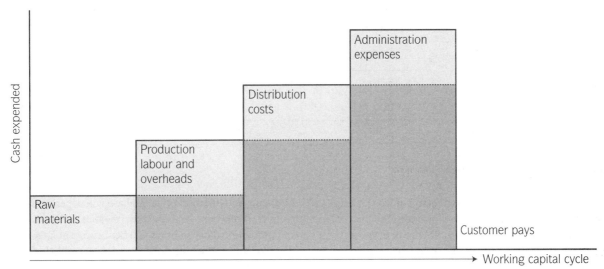

Figure 6.9 *Investment in the working capital cycle*

Once a stock item has been sold, it will be invoiced for payment. Cash will be received either immediately or, in the case of credit sales, at some future date. Balances owed to a business are called **debtors**, and amounts specifically in respect of unpaid sales invoices are called 'trade debtors'. As credit terms are typically in the 30–60 day range, debtors represent a monetary asset that will soon be converted into cash.

In addition to the cost of creating goods and services that are included in a stock valuation, the business will incur other operating expenses. These include distribution costs to customers and administration expenses for such things as accounting and general management (see Figure 6.9). These additional expenditures need to be financed out of working capital even though they do not give rise to further tangible assets.

Clearly, the greater the volume of business, the greater the investment in working capital. Taking the example of Metal Pressings Ltd above (Figure 6.8), if there were two batches at each stage of production, stock levels would double to £36 000. In the extreme, but not uncommon, situation of **overtrading**, financial resources are inadequate

to fund the current level of business activity. Then, sales growth means that the business is too successful for its own good! This occurs when business planning has failed accurately to forecast the level of finance required.

The following is a more detailed illustration of overtrading. Joanne Paterson commenced trading during January with a bank loan of £1 000 repayable nine months later. She knew that her suppliers had to be paid cash on delivery, despite the fact that her customers would demand one month's credit. Her first month's sales were £1 000, representing costs of £800 plus a 25 per cent mark-up. Joanne's business proved highly successful with sales increasing by roughly 50 per cent a month, as can be seen in the profit and loss account of Figure 6.10.

Joanne made a total six-month profit of £4 060, but her cash situation was not so good (Figure 6.11).

At the end of June, she owed a total of £2 340, which if unplanned would be a potential problem with her financial backers. Joanne was thus adding to her problems every month. At 50 per cent sales increase each month, her working capital requirement was growing faster than the

	January	February	March	April	May	June
Sales	1 000	1 500	2 200	3 300	4 900	7 400
Costs	800	1 200	1 760	2 640	3 920	5 920
Profit	200	300	440	660	980	1 480
Cumulative profit	200	500	940	1 600	2 580	4 060

Figure 6.10 *Joanne Paterson's profit and loss account*

	January	February	March	April	May	June
Sales receipts	0	1 000	1 500	2 200	3 300	4 900
Payments	(800)	(1 200)	(1 760)	(2 640)	(3 920)	(5 920)
Receipts less payments	(800)	(200)	(260)	(440)	(620)	(1 020)
Balance at the start of the month	1 000	200	0	(260)	(700)	(1 320)
Balance at the end of the month	200	0	(260)	(700)	(1 320)	(2 340)

Figure 6.11 *Joanne Paterson's cash flow statement*

business could generate money, even though it was making a profit. To ensure the survival of her business, Joanne needed to line up additional external finance or else control the pace of sales growth. The operating cycle does not always result in a consistent flow of cash. For certain types of business it is important to recognise that two phases affect the business operating cycle – the product life cycle and seasonal sales.

Product life cycle

The rate at which products use up or generate cash will depend on the point reached in the **product life cycle** (see Figure 6.12). During product development, cash will flow out of the business but none will flow in. Later in the cycle, cash receipts should exceed cash payments. For the financial well-being of a business that is subject to marked product life cycles, it is important that a balanced portfolio of products be maintained whereby sufficient funds are being generated for the development of new products.

The value and duration of each phase will depend on the product. It may also be found that on-going development and promotional expenditure will be incurred at later stages of the product life cycle to generate a period of further sales growth. But even as sales start to decline, there may be significant positive cash flows as little development and promotional expenditure is being incurred; hence the term 'cash cow' for products that are being 'milked' to generate funds for other uses.

Case Study

Chiroscience Plc

Chiroscience Plc is an emerging pharmaceutical company which uses its technological base to discover and develop unique medicines for a range of health conditions, including cancer and

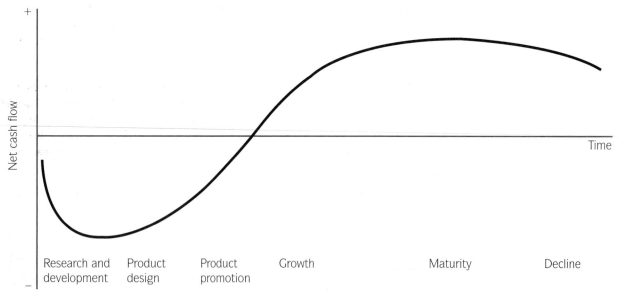

Figure 6.12 *Cash flows during the product life cycle*

autoimmune diseases. At 28 February 1998 the company had £4.9 million in the bank, having used up £25.8 million on operating activities during the previous year.

The basic steps for success are: develop a technology base, apply the technology to specific healthcare concerns, set up extensive clinical trials to satisfy the regulatory bodies, and then manufacture and distribute the product.

To find a partner that can market the drug on a worldwide basis is crucial to the commercial success of launching a new drug. The large drug companies, looking for another blockbuster like Zantac, can financially support firms like Chiroscience in a number of ways. They can contribute shareholder capital; they may sponsor R&D work, making payments at agreed milestones in the drugs development; and they pay royalties on the drugs they decide to license.

Chiroscience has a number of products which it has developed or is developing. Its flagship product, the long-acting local anaesthetic Chirocaine, was filed for regulatory approval in Europe in December 1997, and the US application followed soon after. In March 1998 it was announced than Zeneca, a world leading pharmaceutical company, had validated the product and would take up the licence rights to distribute the drug worldwide (excluding Japan). The deal would result in large royalties over the patent life of the drug. Partners have also been found to help fund the development of R&D into cancer and asthma drugs. These partners also had the marketing muscle to take the products to market when the time came.

Questions

1. At what stage of the product life cycle is the drug Chirocaine?

2. At 28 February 1998, Chiroscience had less than three months' worth of expenditure in the bank. What options were there to finance the business before royalties started to flow in?

3. Describe the advantages and disadvantages of each alternative.

Seasonal sales

Many businesses experience changing demand depending on the time of the year. Examples include travel and leisure industries, ice-cream, farming, and products bought for gifts. Extra cash will be tied up in the operating cycle when business activity increases because of the extra investment in working capital.

As seasonal businesses are in danger of utilising their various resources at only certain times of the year, it is important that they be operationally very flexible. They could close down during off-peak periods; for example, the hire of deck chairs at the seaside relies on casual labour. Alternatively, a complementary business could be developed that uses the same labour and plant; for example, a packing operation for building sand in the summer can be used to pack road salt in the winter months.

The investment cycle

Investment in 'fixed assets' is commonly known as **capital expenditure** and relates to assets actually used in the business to enable it to function. They have continuing value as a result of their ability to help generate future wealth over a number of years. There are three main categories of fixed asset – tangible, intangible and investments.

Tangible fixed assets are physical items such as land and buildings, machinery, computer equipment and motor vehicles. The relevant cost of a fixed asset includes the purchase price, modification costs to make it suitable for its intended purpose, and installation and professional fees associated with the purchase. In the case of land and buildings, the fixed-asset classification is not restricted to freehold properties; leases are included, whether they be short-term or long-term, as they represent the right to use the relevant resource for more than one year.

Intangible fixed assets do not have a physical form; examples are goodwill and research and development expenditure. *Goodwill* arises on the purchase of a business for more than the value of its tangible and net monetary assets. By way of illustration, the £120 000 purchase price of a grocery store comprising property of £80 000 and stock of £10 000 would imply a goodwill payment of £30 000. Goodwill in this illustration represents the value put on regular customers who help to provide an immediate economic return on capital employed. For other businesses, goodwill may arise because of established product brands or knowledge of business processes that provide competitive advantage.

Research and development (R&D) expenditure may, or may not, result in a valuable asset, depending on whether the knowledge gained gives rise to a commercially viable

TASK

Trevor Bentley is about to set up in business supplying bags of sand and gravel to garden centres and DIY stores. During summer there is heavy demand when the gardener and the DIY enthusiast are at their most active; demand is minimal during the depths of winter.

One aspect of the industry that makes it hard for a small business is the size of the major customers. They tend to be large national retail chains that use their purchasing power to dictate trading terms to their suppliers. One consequence of this is that Trevor will have to accept payment for his sales in the quarter following delivery. All purchases will have to be settled promptly.

	Spring (£)	Summer (£)	Autumn (£)	Winter (£)	Spring (£)	Summer (£)
Sales	45000	110000	50000	7000	45000	110000
Costs:						
Rent	5000	5000	5000	5000	5000	5000
Wages	12000	30000	15000	1500	13000	33000
Materials	25000	55000	20000	0	20000	45000
Other	5000	10000	5000	500	5000	10000

Trevor needs to purchase plant and machinery worth £100000, but he intends to rent premises, vehicles and other equipment as he requires them. He intends to set up a private limited company into which he will invest his personal capital of £60000. The remainder of the finance required will have to come from other sources. One possibility is his bank, but a number of friends and relatives have said they would like to invest in any venture he may have in mind.

1. Prepare a cash flow forecast for Trevor to show how much finance he will require to set up and run the business (excluding finance costs).

2. Describe the main factors that are affecting the pattern of cash flows.

3. Assuming that Trevor wishes to maintain control of his business, suggest how he could source finance from outside parties.

---

product or business process. There are fairly rigorous tests applied by the accountancy profession before expenditure is classified as an asset as opposed to being treated as an expense to be written off. The various tests seek to substantiate the business's ability to derive future benefits from R&D expenditure.

Investments are classified as fixed assets if they are strategic holdings in associated companies, as opposed to being purely speculative investments that would be more accurately classified as 'current assets'. They usually comprise shares and loan stock to be held for more than one year.

Unlike operating expenditure, spending on fixed assets is usually uneven; some periods may experience heavy expenditure, others none at all. However, for businesses that habitually retain profits it would be expected that the fixed asset base would see continual enhancement.

Case Study

J. Sainsbury Plc

A major objective for J. Sainsbury is to provide shareholders with good financial returns. This relies on the ability to invest for future growth, and £728 million was invested in the year to 7 March 1998 alone. The financial investment is seen in the following profile of retail outlets:

	1992	1994	1996	1998
Number of stores	459	514	781	823
Sales area (000 sq. ft)	13065	15241	25570	27299
Sales per sq. ft (£/week)	18.51	18.6	18.59	18.87
Share of market (%)	11.7	12.4	12.5	12.7

Questions

1. Describe the type of assets that would have made up the capital expenditure during 1997/8.
2. For planning and controlling capital expenditure, describe the significance of 'sales per square foot' and 'share of market'.
3. In an uncertain retail environment, what concerns should investors have about the dividend and capital investment policies of companies like J. Sainsbury?

Capital expenditure is clearly an outflow of cash, but the investment cycle will involve some receipts of cash when assets have reached the end of their economic lives in the business. Such proceeds are usually small in relation to capital expenditure, although businesses undergoing fundamental changes may decide to raise significant sums from the sale of fixed assets. This may be to:

- replenish cash balances after sustaining operating losses
- reduce overheads, as capital expenditure is accompanied by running costs, including depreciation of the assets concerned – a lower fixed asset base therefore tends to reduce overheads and allows the business to become 'fitter and leaner' for its new circumstances
- relinquish funds for more efficient use elsewhere – for example, selling under-used factory space to pay for a new production process.

Returns on investment and servicing of finance

Periodically the servicing of finance will be discharged with the payment of interest or dividends. These financing costs may be offset to some extent by the receipt of interest or dividends on investments that the business has made.

The simplest form of financial investment is a bank deposit. However, more sophisticated management will consider taking advantage of the money market and the trading of securities, such as company and government bonds. The overriding requirement is the security of funds invested, but other considerations will be the rate of return and the duration of the investment. It may also be important that the investment be flexible enough to be liquidated at short notice.

Taxation

Businesses pay tax on the profits that they earn and this can be a significant outflow of cash. Companies pay corporation tax, sole traders and partnerships pay income tax. Both taxes are calculated on a similar basis and are paid some months after the relevant year-end. For example, a company with an accounting year-end of 30 June would have to pay corporation tax for that year by 1 April of the following year.

Financing

The cash flow from financing commences with the business owners and other sources of finance injecting cash into the business. At a later date some of these providers may require repayment. More usually, repayments of capital relate to preference shares and loan stock that have fixed redemption dates.

The balance sheet

As the preceding sections have described, the flow of funds gives rise to various assets and liabilities that are continuously changing with business activity. To understand the financial position of the business, it is necessary to freeze the values of these financial resources at a point in time. These values, or balances, are then used to construct a **balance sheet**.

It is useful at this stage to understand the 'accounting equation' that provides the conceptual logic for the balance sheet. Business accounting is based on the 'separate entity' concept. This means that business finances are separated from the personal financial circumstances of the business owners, whether the firm is a limited company or an unincorporated firm. The fact that the business has assets to use is because (a) owners have invested capital in the business, and (b) liabilities have arisen through other parties providing either trade credit or debt finance. The accounting equation is therefore:

Assets = Capital + Liabilities.

Rearranged, this is:

Capital = Assets – Liabilities.

The balance sheet presents assets in the order of their liquidity (how easily they can be converted to cash), starting with the least liquid items. So, fixed assets come first, followed by current assets – recognising the operating cycle they have to go through to get to cash, starting with stocks, then debtors, then cash.

Balance sheet as at [year-end date]

	(£000)	(£000)	
Fixed assets			
Intangible		100	
Tangible		200	
Investments		50	
		350	
Current assets			Assets
Stocks	50		
Debtors	100		
Cash at bank and in hand	25		
	175		
Creditors due within one year	50		
Net current assets		125	
Total assets less current liabilities		475	Liabilities
Creditors due after more than one year		125	
Provisions		25	
Total net assets		325	Assets less liabilities
Shareholder funds:			
Share capital		50	Owners'
Share premium account		75	capital
Retained profits		200	
		325	

Figure 6.13 *Outline format of a balance sheet*

Liabilities are presented with those making demands on cash in the near future followed by those due at a later date. The usual order is thus:

- creditors payable within one year (alternatively called 'current liabilities')
- creditors payable after more than one year (alternatively called 'long-term liabilities')
- provision for liabilities and charges.

The last category includes items that have a measure of uncertainty but are likely to arise and for which a reasonable estimate can be made for the resulting financial outflow. Examples include 'deferred taxation' (arising from timing differences between accounting profits and taxable profits), and contingent liabilities, such as likely damages from legal proceedings against the company.

Figure 6.13 shows the outline format of a balance sheet. The conventional use of a two-column format as shown here is optional. Where it is used, the analysis of net current assets is inset to make it clear which balances have been included in each of the totals. The net current asset balance has traditionally been struck to indicate the funding tied up in the operating cycle, and for this reason

TASK

From the following balances prepare a balance sheet in the format of Figure 6.13 (where necessary consolidating figures to produce a total for each balance sheet heading). All the amounts are in thousands of pounds.

Bank overdraft, 7; Amounts owed by customers, 50; Plant and machinery, 125; Long term property lease, 75; Finished goods, 25; Nominal value of shares issued, 50; Raw material, 12; Share premium on shares issued, 50; Amounts owed to suppliers, 35; Capitalised research and development expenditure, 110; Debentures redeemable in five years, 100; Shares owned in an associated company 40; Work-in-progress, 5; Retained profits, 200.

has on occasion been labelled 'working capital'. However, interpretation of the net current asset balance must be done with care, as 'creditors due within one year' may include funding balances, such as bank overdrafts and short-dated loan stock. At a superficial level, the analysis of net current assets gives some indication of liquid assets available for paying off short-term liabilities.

The categories used in this format often comprise several individual balances that may be detailed in 'notes to the accounts'. For example, 'creditors due within one year' will include balances in respect of trade credit, short-term finance including bank overdrafts, and other creditors such as tax owed to government agencies. Where there are no relevant balances, the category is omitted from the statement.

FINANCIAL INFORMATION FOR DECISION-MAKING

Effective decision-making is about making informed choice. The decision-maker requires information in order to evaluate the implications of a particular alternative. For example, the decision about whether to buy a component from a supplier or to make it in-house should be based on a whole range of information, including the relative cost involved. Because business is about utilising financial resources in the quest for wealth creation, a substantial amount of information for decision-making is inevitably of a financial nature.

The use of financial information means that operational issues can be appreciated from a strategic perspective. Money is used to measure the relevant costs and benefits that would otherwise be difficult to compare. Examples of such issues include:

- is it worthwhile investing in a new machine to shorten production times?
- should quality control be strengthened to reduce product failure rates?
- should components be ordered in bigger batches to take advantage of quantity discounts?

Management decision-making requires information that is relevant to future conditions. This requires forecasts based on a set of assumptions, often with regard to historical information, from which valid conclusions can be drawn about future circumstances. For example, if customers are

habitually paying their debts late, the implication is that this will continue unless credit policies are changed.

Decisions requiring financial information can be categorised as relating to either planning or control.

Business planning aims to formulate appropriate strategies and policies to achieve the goals of the business. Their implementation gives leadership and motivation to employees and co-ordinates the various activities of the organisation towards a common objective. Planning decisions include:

- allocation of resources between alternative activities or projects, e.g. whether to proceed with product A or product B
- evaluation of alternative strategies/policies, e.g. whether to sell through agents or a dedicated sales team
- sources of finance for funding the business, e.g. to lease or buy from retained funds.

Control of activities is necessary to ensure that performance is acceptable and is in accordance with the plan. Criteria are formulated so that performance can be measured and compared against relevant benchmarks, which may include costs per unit and average selling prices achieved. Features of a financial control system include the following.

- Individuals are held accountable for specific areas, which may be locations such as branch offices, business processes such as credit control, or products.
- A process for performance measurement is established – recording data, collating data, and reporting information.
- Performance is compared against a benchmark, such as a planned amount or the value from a previous period.
- Appropriate feedback is given to the managers responsible.
- Deviations from acceptable performance should cause remedial action to be instigated.

Before the 1960s, the finance function was primarily charged with fulfilling regulatory requirements for financial reporting and taxation purposes, and as a by-product of this activity it was possible to prepare financial accounts on a monthly basis for internal use. In the past few decades these **management accounts** have been augmented with budgetary information and operational statistics primarily to facilitate the control of the business's activities. In addition to showing progress towards an annual target, they have provided benchmarks to facilitate 'management by exception'. For any particular item, for example travel costs, the current spend can be compared with a predetermined budget or a previous period's actual result. Exceptions, highlighted by the calculation of a variance to the benchmark, have been the trigger for management action.

In more recent years, with information technology speeding up basic book-keeping and report writing, the finance function has been able to turn to the specific demands of operational management. There has been a call for information to be more accessible and more relevant to the decision-making process. Whilst the finance team has always reported progress towards enhancing shareholder value, it is now required to contribute towards the goal itself. This has required finance managers to 'sit in' on the decision making process and to enhance the value of financial information provided.

Costs	Actual (£000)	Budget (£000)	Variance (£000)
Salaries	5,300	4,823	(477)
Property	4,950	4,970	20
Administration	1,205	1,210	5
Distribution	1,860	1,895	35

Salaries	Actual (£000)	Budget (£000)	Variance (£000)
Production	2,400	2,100	(300)
Engineering	950	940	(10)
Distribution	710	700	(10)
Administration	1,240	1,083	(157)

Admin salaries	Actual (£000)	Budget (£000)	Variance (£000)
Finance	600	460	(140)
Personnel	230	220	(10)
IT	305	300	(5)
Secretarial	105	103	(2)

Figure 6.14 *On-line analytical programming (drilling down)*

A primary requirement has been to relate the financial statements presented to senior management, like the profit and loss account and balance sheet, to the concerns further down the organisation structure. This requires financial variables to be expressed in terms understood by operational managers. For example, a wage budget represents so many weeks available to complete a specified task.

A top-level concern for any business, whether to grow or merely to survive, is the volume of business (throughput). It is not enough to know about conditions at a point in time, such as a bank balance. There must be information about business activity relating to a period of time, such as sales per week or units per hour.

Financial information must have the properties that distinguish information from mere data. It should be relevant, timely, accurate and give an appropriate level of detail.

Recent innovations in information technology have helped managers to access good quality financial information. When specific details are required, on-line reporting systems now allow users to investigate high-level summary figures, such as the running costs of the distribution network, by 'drilling down' to the level required, for example an analysis of freight costs (see Figure 6.14).

Check your understanding

A bus company employing salaried staff to operate its fleet of buses incurs annual costs of £1 million. Some costs, such as petrol and vehicle maintenance, will vary with the number of routes operated, but these will be relatively small compared with salaries, vehicle fixed costs, station costs and administration. With costs fixed, profitability will depend on ticket revenues. On average, weekly income must be at least £19 230 (£1 million/ 52) for the company to break even. This simple piece of financial information will be crucial for ensuring that management act when appropriate. In itself it provides no remedies, but will be a precursor to reviewing operational practices such as route planning, pricing and perhaps longer-term cost efficiencies. To be of value, the weekly income report should have the following minimum qualities:

- timeliness – reported early in the following week
- accuracy – no significant errors and reported in round pounds only
- appropriate detail – analysis for each route, analysed by day.

Access to information in various levels of detail and in different formats is important because managers tend to have specific needs depending on their function and level within the organisation.

Senior managers, with long-term planning horizons and wide areas of responsibility, require reports that underpin the primary financial performance indicator, often return on capital employed (see Chapter 7). From a strategic perspective, managers will want to know how financial resources are deployed in the business. This requires an analysis of fixed assets and working capital between the business's various divisions, whether these are factory sites, business functions or product groups. Together with information concerning income and costs, this information can identify how different areas of the business contribute towards financial goals. This information clearly has value for the control of existing activities, but also indicates areas for future expansion and contraction. A decision concerning a new investment or a change in business strategy requires an evaluation of its financial implications, and this is considered in Chapter 8.

Middle managers with functional responsibilities such as marketing, production, finance, etc., are concerned with medium-term planning and historical performance for a particular part of the business. Most of the financial information they receive is for control purposes and tends to involve the highlighting of variances against an approved budget. Factory management will be informed of production costs against production volumes. Sales management will be informed of sales costs and revenues for each sales team and individual. There will often be participation in forward planning, although perhaps restricted to annual budgets that relate to their area of responsibility.

The day-to-day management of financial resources is often the preserve of middle managers in the finance department. To fulfil their responsibilities, they rely heavily on financial information generated by accounting staff. Financial management is required to ensure the efficient deployment of financial resources and the raising of appropriate new finance when needed. Without active management, financial resources may be tied up unnecessarily in a form that generates more costs than benefits. For example, poor credit control is unlikely to improve customer relationships significantly, but the business will incur charges on the funds invested in trade debtors. Even more importantly, if cash flows cannot satisfy financial obligations to employees and suppliers, there is a threat to the business's very survival.

Stocks often represent a significant investment, and at each stage from raw materials to finished goods there is the potential for hold-ups, whether systematic or as a result of unplanned events. Good stock control minimises the risk of both too much and too little stock. Adequate stock needs to be held in order to satisfy customer demand in terms of range and delivery times. A stock-out situation may mean gross margin is irreversibly lost, and can even lead to lost future custom. On the other hand, storing materials also incurs significant costs: there is the financial cost of tying up funds that could have been deployed elsewhere, and there are the costs associated with storage, including handling, insurance and clerical costs. In addition, there is the risk of obsolescence, deterioiration or theft.

The general rule is to minimise stocks within the context of operational needs. A business should aim for high stock turnover with systematic ordering in line with economic batch quantities. In order to make appropriate decisions, it is important to have information concerning future demands, lead times, the costs for alternative batch sizes (set-up costs often discourage very small batches), the costs of reordering and the costs of storage. A significant amount of this information is financial.

Like stocks, debtors need to be minimised, with tight control maintained on the credit allowed to customers. Old debts become more difficult to collect, but in addition there is a danger of compounding bad debts with continuing supplies to a debtor.

It is necessary to develop a credit policy that addresses each stage, from sale through to final payment. The first step is to decide on the terms of trade, for example payment at the end of the month following delivery. Then the credit-worthiness of potential customers should be evaluated; this may require references from their bank and other businesses with which they trade. It may also be necessary to make enquiries with credit-rating agencies and obtain the customer's last set of accounts. The problem with many of these procedures is that they rely on information that can soon become dated, and in the case of references these may not be representative of how other creditors have been serviced. More information and confidence will be gained after trading with the customer for a period of time, so it may be appropriate to apply an initial credit limit that is reviewed at a later date.

Once a supply has been made, customers should be invoiced promptly and those customers who persistently extend the credit period afforded to them should be pursued. This requires information that is up to date and in sufficient detail for the credit controller to deal with customer queries. Information needs include an age analysis of each customer's debt, with a facility to 'drill down' to specific invoices and delivery details. A customer's payment record will also be an important consideration when deciding on whether to accept future sales orders.

Whilst investment in working capital causes most liquidity problems, funds can also be unnecessarily tied up in fixed assets. Any purchase of fixed assets must be the best use of funds available, and should be the subject of formal capital expenditure authorisation procedures. Unlike investment in working capital, fixed asset expenditure is often discretionary and its authorisation is usually the sole perogative of senior management.

The purpose of investment may be to:

- replace existing assets that are no longer economical to use, or are technologically obsolete
- comply with health and safety regulations
- expand capacity.

When cash is scarce, decisions have to be made either to defer certain items of expenditure, or consider alternatives, such as short-term hire in the case of assets used infrequently. If some assets are to be hired and some purchased, risk is reduced and flexibility maintained if business funds are tied up in general-purpose assets rather than specialist ones. A decision requires financial information about each alternative.

Once it has been decided what information individual managers require to carry out their decision-making responsibilities, this information must be delivered in a timely and appropriate way. In keeping with other business processes, reporting timetables are continually getting shorter. At one time it was acceptable for management accounts to be issued two weeks after the month end. Now, many firms are aiming for a lead time of just a few days for formal accounts, and immediate access to key performance indicators such as turnover and committed expenditure. This has been made possible by the advances in information technology. Many firms have replaced the traditional printed financial report with an electronic copy that can be accessed in the office or off-site, using business-wide intranets based on Internet technology. Financial reports are now either e-mailed directly to recipients, or made available in designated areas of the firm's computer network.

Internal financial reports typically display the following characteristics:

- *Reporting period* – prepared on a monthly basis (either calendar month or a discrete number of weeks) with figures for the month and year to date
- *Timeliness* – prepared to strict timetables, often within one week
- *Detail* – far greater analysis than accounts for publication, including a breakdown by department or cost-centre
- *Format* – an emphasis placed on clear presentation with a structure of accounts relevant to the activities of the business (unlike published accounts which comply with standard formats); different versions may be issued to different managers depending on their area and level of responsibility
- *Comparisons* – actual performance compared with budget and possibly with the same period of the previous year
- *Forecasts* – accounts may include a revised forecast of results up to the year-end
- *Performance measures* – financial and non-financial ratios may be included.

TASK

Downey Brothers is a department store, selling a range of products from clothing to kitchenware. Each department is a 'profit centre' and departmental managers are held directly responsible for the contribution they make towards general overheads and profit. General overheads comprise the running costs of the building, general management and central administration.

It is your job to ensure that managers receive financial information that is appropriate to their responsibilities and that monitors actual performance against budget.

1. Prepare a list of: (a) ten retail departments within Downey Bros.; (b) the type of costs incurred by each department; (c) the type of costs included in general overheads.

2. Prepare a monthly report for sales and costs using illustrative figures for: (a) a departmental manager; (b) the store's general manager.

3. Explain the main features of the reports and how the reports would aid decision-making.

SUMMARY

Financial resources have a cost, although the amount is not always explicit in the financing agreement. Cost of finance may be expressed as a fixed rate of return, but for risk capital its valuation will be more subjective, such as the returns expected by ordinary shareholders. The 'weighted average cost of capital' attempts to determine the business's overall cost of capital, having regard to the business taxation system that tends to favour debt finance over shareholder finance. When evaluating business investments, projects must promise a greater return than the cost of capital.

Financial resources are required to fund working capital and to acquire fixed assets. The flow of funds is demonstrated by the various categories of cashflow, such as the operating cashflow cycle. Good financial management aims to minimise hold-ups in the flow of funds by controlling the amounts invested in the various assets of the business. Efficient flow minimises risk and the amount of funds required, hence reducing finance costs. The assets and liabilities resulting from the flow of funds can be frozen at a point in time and presented in a balance sheet.

To make decisions that will benefit the financial position of the business, management must be properly informed. The needs of different managers are diverse, so financial information should be appropriately designed and delivered to management's requirements.

Financial Performance

This chapter discusses the need for financial information and introduces the main financial statements used to measure performance. Interpretation of the financial statements using accounting ratios is described.

On completion of the chapter you should be able to analyse the financial performance of a business. To achieve this you must demonstrate the ability to:

- explain the main financial statements, their purpose and use

- analyse financial performance using relevant accounting ratios

- make comparisons between two different businesses and compare their results to industry standards

INFORMATION NEEDS

The activities of business affect a wide range of individuals and organisations, each with their own particular areas of concern and each with their own demands for information. Management can ensure that it receives the information it requires by implementing an appropriate reporting system, but other parties, including employees, are at a disadvantage in obtaining information. To satisfy these needs, the government and other regulatory bodies impose reporting requirements on business.

It is widely recognised that the main responsibility of management is the stewardship of the financial resources entrusted to them by the business owners. This is evident for public limited companies, where the shareholders are divorced from the daily running of the business but have the right to appoint or sack the company directors. Hence most of the regulatory requirements for accounting information are from the perspective of safeguarding the interests of the shareholders.

However, the interests and priorities of business owners as a group are varied. For example, owners of unincorporated businesses are more likely to be involved in daily management, and so their interests may be more akin to those of an employee. It is also true that small business owners rely less on formal reporting systems to know how well the business is doing. However, the information needs of company shareholders detailed below are universal to all business owners, even if they do possess informal information channels:

- liquidity – to ensure survival and the ability to make dividend payments
- profit – to provide the desired financial return
- nature of the business's assets and liabilities
- financial risk stemming from the capital structure (e.g. the value of outstanding debt)
- future prospects – with an evaluation of market and financial conditions
- market risk – knowing what business the company is in allows owners and potential owners to judge the stability of the company's performance in the face of changing market conditions.

Creditors, whether providers of debt finance or of goods and services on credit, also have an interest in the financial position of a business. Of major concern is the ability to generate cash to discharge the firm's indebtedness, which largely depends on the firm's ability to continue as a going

concern. Where cash generation is difficult to forecast or is in some doubt, there is also interest in the value of marketable assets in relation to company debt, in case the business should cease trading.

Like suppliers, customers will be interested in the stability of their trading partners, and many businesses conduct a financial investigation into the affairs of new credit suppliers. The need for reliable and up-to-date information is particularly acute where the supply of goods or services is of strategic importance to the buying business. In the car industry there is significant investment in time and money to appraise the financial standing of potential component manufacturers. Production halted as a result of a bankrupt supplier could cost millions of pounds in lost production.

However, large profits earned by suppliers can also cause concern. Suspicion that they are being exploited is another reason customers demand financial information. Monopolies, especially those recently returned to the private sector, have their accounts appraised critically by consumer groups and industry watchdogs. For businesses with large market shares, it is a difficult task both to satisfy shareholders with high financial returns and to placate other parties who are intent on finding evidence of monopoly exploitation.

From a financial perspective, employees are concerned about job security and opportunities for personal gain. They want to be kept informed of:

• security of their markets and market share
• plans for organisational change and strategic direction
• financial solvency to pay their wages
• opportunities to negotiate a greater remuneration package.

Employers should set up proper channels of communication to keep employees informed, and some businesses do produce an employee report or newsletter. However, the financial information provided is often restricted in the case of listed companies because of stock exchange regulations. To ensure an efficient and equitable market in the trading of a company's shares, the exchange requires the communication of price-sensitive information to be made to the exchange in the first instance.

Government requires financial information about businesses and obtains this through appropriate forms and returns. The Inland Revenue is interested in payments to employees and subcontractors and the level of business profits. Customs & Excise collects value added tax (VAT) and therefore needs to monitor the value of taxable sales and purchases. The government uses the information obtained to compile statistics on business activity that can help it (and others) to plan economic and industrial policy.

These days there must be public access to information for others indirectly affected, especially by larger businesses. Public concerns are not necessarily financial in nature. Other issues include employment opportunities, and economic activity in the area – which in turn has a knock-on effect for other businesses for supplies and services demanded. People outside the business are concerned also about environmental impact, whether in terms of local conditions such as road noise or water pollution, or more generally the use of scarce natural resources.

REPORTING REGULATIONS

In recognition that businesses have external stakeholders (you can read more about stakeholders in Chapter 14), there are reporting regulations that vary significantly depending on the firm's legal framework. Individuals in business as sole traders or in partnership are generally required only to report financial information for tax purposes. For large partnerships, such as the professional practices, there may be reporting requirements specified in the partnership agreement; otherwise it falls on the individual partner or investor to ensure they receive the information they need.

The situation for companies is rather different. Companies are regulated by the Companies Act 1985 as amended by the Companies Act 1989, which ensure that shareholders receive financial information that meets prescribed rules in respect of content and accounting principles. With ownership and management of the business likely to be separated, a major issue is the stewardship of financial resources entrusted to the management of the company. As an example of this emphasis, financial statements must disclose the total salaries and other financial benefits that company directors enjoy.

The accountancy profession has added to the regulatory framework with *Financial Reporting Standards* (FRSs) issued by the Accounting Standards Board (ASB). These standards, together with the older *Statements of Standard Accounting Practice* (SSAPs) that remain in force, indicate current best accounting practice. They are to be applied to all financial statements intended to give a 'true and fair' view of the financial affairs of a business and of its performance for a particular accounting period. There is

an obligation on members of the main professional accounting bodies to comply with accounting standards in cases where they either prepare accounts or are required to audit them.

Some of the accounting standards are quite specialised and relate only to a certain type of business or to circumstances that occur infrequently; for example, FRS6 'Acquisitions and mergers'. However, others are more pervading; for example, all companies that use fixed assets should consider the requirements of SSAP12 'Depreciation'. It is the responsibility of the preparer of accounts to be aware of the accounting standards and to apply their requirements where appropriate.

For listed companies there are further regulations. The London stock exchange specifies the timing and form of company announcements, including interim reports, to ensure an efficient market for the buying and selling of company shares. These requirements are detailed in the exchange's *Yellow Book*. One requirement is to issue an interim financial report of performance, including details of turnover, profit and shareholder dividends. The provision of information on a more regular basis is important to ensure that buyers and sellers are properly informed of the progress of the companies they invest in.

The following documentation is required within ten months of the end of an accounting period for a private limited company and within seven months for a public limited company:

- balance sheet, profit and loss account and cash flow statement
- 'notes to the accounts' that describe the company's accounting policies and provide an analysis of certain items contained in the financial reports
- an auditor's report that confirms that the above information is consistent with the company's accounting records and that it provides a 'true and fair' view of the trading performance and state of financial affairs
- a directors' report that provides details of non-financial aspects of the business, such as principal activities and employee policies, in addition to certain explanations of the financial statements.

The directors' review of past performance and opinion concerning future developments can be particularly valuable for those not involved with the day-to-day running of the business. Where the management wishes to be more expansive regarding the operations of the business, there may be separate sections for the chairman's statement, review of operations and financial review.

This information is filed with the Registrar of Companies and is available for public inspection. Failure to conform to these reporting requirements leads to financial penalties for the company and the risk of criminal prosecution for the company's directors.

THE FINANCIAL STATEMENTS

The profit and loss account

The purpose of the profit and loss account is to show how value has been created by the firm over the reporting period. For published accounts this is usually one year, although interim accounts are produced after six months. It is a statement of the business's total revenues and costs and explains how any resulting profit has been applied.

Whereas the content of the profit and loss account for internal purposes will have been designed to meet the management's needs, published accounts are required to conform to standard formats. Of the four permitted formats for the profit and loss account, format 1 is the

most popular and is the one illustrated here (see Figure 7.1). The terminology is explained below.

- **Turnover** represents the value of goods and services provided to customers, excluding sales taxes (for example VAT).
- **Cost of sales** is the financial resource expended in creating the goods or services sold to customers. For example, for a manufacturer of engineering components, cost of sales comprises the wages paid to shopfloor workers, the cost of materials consumed and the factory overhead that has been apportioned over the total factory production. For a retail firm, cost of sales would comprise the purchase price of items sold.
- **Distribution costs** are incurred in delivering goods to the customer.
- **Administration expenses** include the cost of general management, accounting, legal fees and general insurances.
- **Interest** should be analysed according to whether it is payable or receivable, either on the profit and loss account or in a note to the accounts.
- **Taxation** relates to the tax on profits; in the case of companies this will be corporation tax.
- **Dividends** are the sum of interim and final dividends paid to preference and ordinary shareholders. The final dividend will be proposed at the annual general meeting to which the accounts will be presented and its payment requires the authorisation of the ordinary shareholders. An analysis between interim and final dividend, and dividend paid to ordinary shareholders and preference shareholders, should be provided either on the profit and loss account or in a note to the accounts.
- **Profit retained** is the amount of shareholder value not distributed by way of dividend and represents a further investment in the business by the shareholders.
- **Earnings per share** is the profit after tax divided by the average number of issued ordinary shares during the year. It is a quick measure of how much value has been created for one ordinary share.

The company Acts and accounting standards require further details for certain items and these are provided in the notes to the accounts. Notes related to the profit and loss account require:

- an explanation of accounting policies
- segmental reporting of turnover, operating profit and net assets (described in more detail below)
- the amount included within the operating profit calculation in respect of: depreciation of tangible fixed assets; amortisation of intangible fixed assets; hire of plant; wages and salaries, including an analysis of

Green Plc
Profit and loss account

For the year-ended [date]	Note	Year 2 (£000)	Year 1 (£000)	
Turnover	1	1 200	1 100	
Cost of sales		600	570	
Gross profit		600	530	How shareholder value has been created
Distribution costs		200	170	
Administration expenses		200	180	
Operating profit	2	200	180	
Net interest payable	3	40	50	
Profit before taxation		160	130	
Taxation	4	50	40	
Profit after tax		110	90	← Shareholder value
Dividends	5	60	55	How value has been applied
Profit retained		50	35	
Earnings per share	6	11p	9p	← Value created per share

Figure 7.1 *A profit and loss account in format 1*

directors' emoluments; auditor's remuneration; and an analysis of interest payable and interest receivable.

Difficulty can be experienced when attempting to interpret the accounts of companies involved in more than one type of business and/or operating in more than one geographical area. From the profit and loss account it is possible to determine the *average* profit margin on each £1 of sales, but this does not show how profitable each type of business is or the company's relative success in different areas of the world. Companies that engage in more than one **business segment** are required by SSAP25 to disclose separately for each class:

- turnover
- profit or loss before taxation (and usually before interest)
- net assets.

The geographical analysis should be on the basis of where the supply is made from (country of operation), but if materially different should also be analysed by area being supplied (country of destination).

Case Study

Pittards Plc

Pittards produces technically advanced leather for leading brands of gloves, luxury leathergoods and sports equipment. An extract from the notes to the accounts taken from the company's 1997 annual report showed:

Note 3 – Analysis of turnover, all of which is derived from the group's principal activities, analysed by geographical market:

	1997 (£000)	1996 (£000)
United Kingdom	39 781	42 720
Other EU	17 432	21 272
Other Europe	4 706	2 329
North America	4 053	3 206
Asia and other	35 601	39 536
	101 573	109 063

Question

How might this analysis of turnover be useful for analysts of Pittards' accounts?

Case Study

Yates Brothers Wine Lodges Plc

Yates Brothers saw 1998 as another good year for its distinctive 'concept' pub. It produced the following segmental information (all amounts are in thousands of pounds):

Questions

1. From this segmental analysis between 'retail' and 'wholesale', highlight the relevant trends that you believe should be explained in the annual report's review of operations.

2. How might this analysis be useful in comparisons with other companies in the pub sector?

	Turnover		Operating profit		Net operating asset	
	1998	1997	1998	1997	1998	1997
Retail	80 439	57 330	16 195	11 759	110 042	87 907
Wholesale	17 344	18 417	400	275	5 243	4 947
Central costs/ liabilities	–	–	(2 990)	(1 848)	(1 383)	(498)
Loans, overdrafts and cash	–	–	–	–	(31 434)	(20 935)
	97 783	75 747	13 605	10 186	82 468	71 421

The categories used to analyse the business activities are a matter of judgement for the company to decide. The overriding factor is to ensure that the user of the accounts is able to appreciate fully the implications of a number of major influences that affect (for each segment):

- rates of return on investments
- past growth and potential for future development
- the degree of risk.

With specific regard to the geographical analysis, the following considerations should help determine the relevant segments:

- the economic climate
- the stability and nature of the political regimes
- foreign exchange control regulations which might affect the company's ability to pay returns on investments
- foreign currency exchange rate fluctuations.

With regard to analysing by class of business, the following factors should be considered for each segment:

- the nature of the supply of goods or services
- the organisation of the company's activities
- the markets served and the channels of distribution used.

Reporting of financial performance

The accounting standard *Reporting of Financial Performance* (FRS3) was introduced to help the users of accounts understand a company's underlying performance. The progress of the company might not be so apparent if there have been significant changes to the nature of the company's business or if there has been a significant one-off event.

Before the issue of FRS3, it had become normal practice to distinguish between profits relating to normal trading activities and those of an extraordinary nature. Extraordinary items were excluded in important comparisons of profit and accounting ratios, but problems arose in the subjective judgement of what was extraordinary! It was widely accepted that companies would try to classify as extraordinary any large item that adversely affected the results. In addition, the existing reporting formats provided little information to help users of accounts understand the impact of restructuring consisting of the acquisition and disposal of parts of the business. In these cases it was difficult to make meaningful comparisons over time.

Since the issuing of FRS3, the profit and loss account must distinguish between operations that are continuing, analysed between existing and acquired businesses, and those that have been discontinued by the accounting year-end. An analysis is required of each profit and loss item, from turnover to operating profit (look back to Figure 7.1). Where this is not provided on the profit and loss account itself, the analysis must be included in the notes to the accounts.

Accounting for an item as being 'extraordinary' is now strongly discouraged because FRS3 makes it clear that all incidences, including those in the company's external environment, are part of the normal risk of carrying on in business. However, where items are considered abnormal in terms of their size or incidence, they should be highlighted as being exceptional items, either on the profit and loss account or in the notes to the accounts.

Case Study

Henlys Group Plc

Henlys underwent a major change in 1997, disposing of its motor dealership to concentrate on the manufacture of coach and bus bodies. Its profit and loss account for the year showed the following:

	Note	1997 (£000)	1996 (£000)
Turnover:	1		
Continuing operations		241 990	217 575
Discontinued operations (motor)		265 435	374 557
		507 425	592 132
Cost of sales	2	430 681	502 163
Gross profit		76 744	89 969
Other operating expenses	2	43 794	53 562
Operating profit:	1		
Continuing operations		27 317	28 636
Discontinued operations (motor)		5 633	7 771
		32 950	36 407
Exceptional item:			
Loss on disposal of discontinued motor operations	11	9 814	
Interest payable	3	1 621	3 073
Profit on ordinary activities before taxation		21 515	33 334

1. Comment on the relative profitability of the continuing and discontinued operations.

2. The final profit before tax fell by nearly £12 million during 1997, but what do the figures suggest for on-going financial performance?

The balance sheet

The balance sheet was introduced in Chapter 6. It shows the financial affairs of the business at a particular point in time. Its basic structure reflects the fact that the net financial resources invested in the business (assets less liabilities) have been provided by the business owners (for a company, the shareholder funds):

Owners capital = Assets – Liabilities.

Like the profit and loss account, the balance sheet is supported by notes to the accounts, which include the following information:

- *a fixed assets schedule* – providing, for each category of asset, an analysis of cost and depreciation and their movements during the year (illustrated in the Oasis Stores case study below)
- a description and basis of *valuation of investments*
- *analysis of stocks*, between raw materials, work-in-progress and finished goods
- *an analysis of debtors*, between trade debtors (amounts owed by customers), other receivable items, and 'prepayments' in respect of expenditure incurred for future periods (for example, rent paid in advance)
- notes on the *creditor balances*.

Notes on the creditor balances will detail amounts in respect of trade creditors (amounts owed to suppliers), other creditors (such as the tax authorities), and borrowings (such as bank overdrafts). This analysis is important to enable the identification of interest-bearing finance to be included as 'debt' in the calculation of capital employed and the capital gearing ratio.

Other notes concerning *share capital* and movements on *reserves* are of a technical nature, although they can be useful for reviewing amounts of capital raised during the period. The share premium account represents the amount received on share issues, in excess of the nominal value. The revaluation reserve, however, is merely a book-keeping entry which does not reflect an actual cash transaction. The property of the business has been revalued in the light of market trends and this requires a corresponding change in the revaluation account to show that equity in the business has been enhanced.

Case Study

Oasis Stores Plc

The following schedule has been extracted from the notes to the accounts of Oasis Stores Plc for year-ended 31 January 1998, relating to 'Tangible fixed assets'.

	Short leasehold property (£000)	Fixtures and fittings (£000)	Computer hardware/ software (£000)	Motor vehicles (£000)	Total (£000)
Cost					
At 26 January 1997	2 744	13 514	1 631	634	18 523
Additions	361	5 453	2 432	103	8 349
Disposals	(23)	(673)	0	(47)	(743)
At 31 January 1998	3 082	18 294	4 063	690	26 129
Depreciation					
At 26 January 1997	546	4 301	696	230	5 773
Charge for the period	211	2 876	740	116	3 943
Disposals	(7)	(367)	0	(31)	(405)
At 31 January 1998	750	6 810	1 436	315	9 311
Net book value					
At 31 January 1998	2 332	11 484	2 627	375	16 818
At 26 January 1997	2 198	9 213	935	404	12 750

Extract from the Chairman's statement: 'Most of our investment this year was due to the considerable growth of the company. Over the previous five years the number of outlets has grown from 26 to 108. ... Growth has brought with it challenges. Managing change, maintaining flexibility, meeting increased competition and further development of leading edge technology, whilst at the same time retaining the culture of the company, has imposed some strains.'

Questions

1. Which category of fixed asset appears to have received very little, if any, new capacity during the accounting year?

2. Which category of asset has been depreciated (a) the fastest, (b) the slowest? Explain why this should be the case.

3. What evidence is there that business expansion has continued during the year?

4. Which category of fixed asset has received considerable investment to help management retain control of an expanding business?

The cash flow statement

The cash flow statement, like the profit and loss account, is concerned with business activity during an accounting period. It shows the ability of the business to generate cash flows from its operating activities, and gives readers a fresh insight into the quality of profits earned and the ability of the business to remain solvent.

Not all businesses generate cash that can be distributed routinely to the shareholders as dividends. Even if the business is profitable there may have been further investments in working capital and fixed assets to fund current or future growth in the business. If businesses fail to generate positive cash flow and at the same time fail to deliver better prospects for the future, then the financial potential for the business must be limited.

The basic format of the cash flow statement reflects the various cash movements described in Chapter 6. The following headings should be covered (Figure 7.2 shows an example):

- **Net cash flow from operating activities** is sales receipts less payments to suppliers and employees.
- **Returns on investment and servicing of finance** is interest received (inflow) less interest paid (outflow).
- **Taxation** is an outflow (corporation tax).
- **Capital expenditure** is an outflow for fixed asset purchases and an inflow from proceeds of fixed asset sales.

- **Acquisitions** are an outflow for purchases of other businesses or an inflow of disposal proceeds from the sale of subsidiaries.
- **Equity dividends** are an outflow paid to ordinary shareholders.
- **Financing** is an inflow for share issues, loans and other financing agreements or an outflow for loan repayments.

For the year ended 30 April 1998	1998 (£000)	1997 (£000)
Net cash inflow from operating activities	989	5 522
Returns on investment and servicing of finance:		
Interest received	14	4
Interest paid	(422)	(258)
Net	(408)	(254)
Taxation	(1 145)	(935)
Capital expenditure:		
Payments to acquire tangible fixed assets	(593)	(1 303)
Receipts from sales of tangible fixed assets	80	38
Net	(513)	(1 265)
Acquisitions:		
Purchase of subsidiary undertakings	(726)	–
Net overdrafts acquired	(1 330)	–
Total	(2 056)	–
Equity dividends paid	(940)	(821)
Net cash (outflow)/inflow before financing	(4 073)	2 247
Financing:		
Issue of ordinary shares	388	–
Bank loans	3 251	–
Hire purchase repayments	(77)	(46)
Net cash inflow/(outflow) from financing	3 562	(46)
(Decrease)/increase in cash	(511)	2 201

Figure 7.2 *Precoat International Plc: consolidated cash flow statement*

The cash flow statement describes actual cash movements and figures will differ from similar items shown in the profit and loss account as the latter account complies with the 'matching concept'. For example, dividends in the cash flow statement will be those actually paid and will comprise the *previous* period's proposed dividend plus the current period's interim dividend. This contrasts with the profit and loss account which describes how a year's profit has been appropriated, not necessarily when it was eventually paid. Hence the profit and loss dividend will comprise the current year's interim plus the current year's final dividend, despite the fact that this is only proposed and will not be paid until after the current accounting period.

The cash flow statement starts with 'net cash inflow from operating activities', which can be derived from the operating profit on the profit and loss account. A note to the accounts reconciles operating profit to operating cash and provides a useful insight into the distinction between profit and cash flow (see Figure 7.3).

Reconciliation of operating profit to net cash inflow from operating activities	1998 (£000)	1997 (£000)
Operating profit	4 136	3 540
Depreciation charges	734	628
Profit on sales of tangible fixed assets	(33)	(26)
	4 837	4 142
Increase in stocks	(3 859)	(95)
Increase in debtors	(669)	(1 461)
Increase in creditors	650	3 116
Currency translation	30	(180)
Net cash inflow from operating activities	989	5 522

Figure 7.3 *Precoat International Plc: reconciliation note*

It is useful to consider why each of the adjustments has been made in respect of the Precoat example. The principle is to consider items in the profit and loss account that do *not* result in a corresponding transaction at the bank:

- *Depreciation* is a cost in the profit and loss account, but as it is not an outflow of money it should be added back to operating profit.
- *Profit on the sale of a fixed asset* is income in the profit and loss account as it represents the difference between sale proceeds of an asset and its net book value (original cost less accumulated depreciation). The cash flow resulting from this transaction is the sale proceeds, included elsewhere in the cash flow statement under 'investing activities'. Thus an accounting profit is merely another book-keeping item that needs to be deducted from profit in arriving at cash.
- An *increase in stocks* does not affect profit because it is merely a swap between one type of asset and another, but it has certainly decreased cash. It therefore needs to be deducted from profit to arrive at the cash position.

- An *increase in debtors* must mean that the cash received from debtors was less than the value of credit sales included in the profit and loss account. Therefore cash deteriorates if debtors increase so is a reduction in the reconciliation.
- An adjustment for a movement in *creditors* is necessary because, if creditors increase, as in the case of Precoat, then the cash paid out to creditors must have been less than the value of purchases charged to the profit and loss account.

Case Study

Precoat International Plc

Precoat International operates the leading pre-coated steel service centres in the UK and Canada. For the company's customers, pre-coated steel sheet removes the need to paint finished products, with advantages including reduced costs, enhanced quality, convenience and fewer environmental hazards. After a number of years of organic company growth, expansion has been boosted by the acquisition of another firm.

Attempt the following tasks having regard to the illustrations relating to Precoat's 'Cash flow statement' and 'Reconciliation of operating profit to net cash'.

Questions

1. Despite increased profits, net cash inflow from operating activities in 1998 was some £4.5 million lower than in 1997 (see the final line of Figure 7.3). What were the two main causes for this situation?

2. What other major item was a drain on cash resources during 1998 (see Figure 7.2)?

3. How were the items in (1) and (2) above largely financed?

4. Summarise the items that give cause for optimism or for concern with regard to future financial performance.

The interrelationships between financial reports

The three main financial reports come from the same basic data. The balance sheet is concerned with balances at a point in time. The profit and loss account and cash flow statements are concerned with describing how two of those balances change over the accounting period – profit and cash. Figure 7.4 demonstrates the relationships between the three types of report.

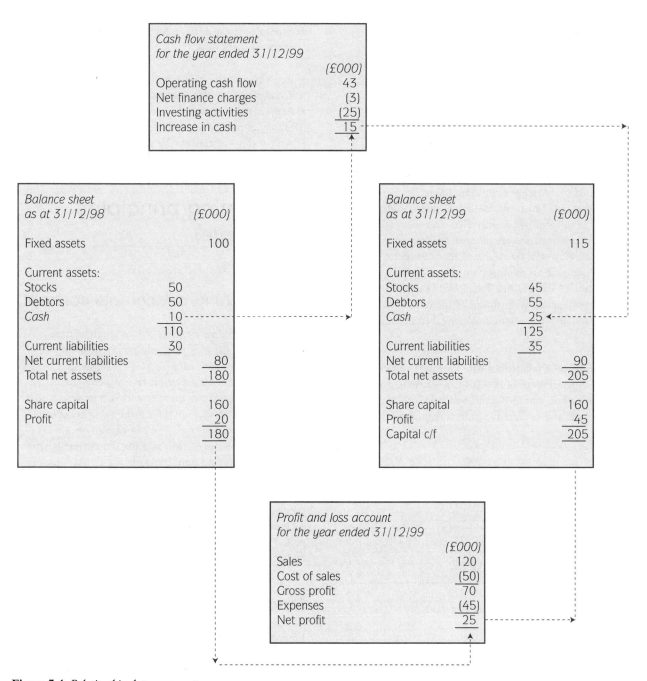

Figure 7.4 *Relationships between reports*

ACCOUNTING PRINCIPLES, BASES AND POLICIES

An overriding concern of many of the accounting regulations is **comparability**. Users of financial statements wish to compare the financial results of a business with its past results to establish trends, and with results of similar businesses to monitor performance. Without any guiding framework for the preparer of accounting information, there would be no consistency between financial statements and hence they would be of little value to the user.

Imagine that two identical businesses each generate operating income of £1 million, incur running costs of £0.7 million, and use fixed assets that cost £0.6 million. However, different depreciation policies are used. Company A depreciates fixed assets over two years and company B over three years. Assuming that the assets are indeed used over three years, the annual profits of the two businesses would be as calculated in Figure 7.5 (all amounts in millions of pounds). Note that the total profits for the three-year period are identical for the two companies. However, the timing of reported profits depends upon the accounting policy in respect of depreciation of fixed assets. Taking one year in isolation, the relative financial performance of the two companies can be evaluated only after considering their accounting policies.

However, because regulations have to relate to a whole range of organisations, of necessity, they tend to generalise about the appropriate accounting treatment of items. As demonstrated above, there is a general requirement to

Company A	Year 1	Year 2	Year 3	Total
Sales	1.0	1.0	1.0	3.0
Operating costs	0.7	0.7	0.7	2.1
Depreciation	0.3	0.3	0.0	0.6
Profit	0.0	0.0	0.3	0.3
Company B	Year 1	Year 2	Year 3	Total
Sales	1.0	1.0	1.0	3.0
Operating costs	0.7	0.7	0.7	2.1
Depreciation	0.2	0.2	0.2	0.6
Profit	0.1	0.1	0.1	0.3

Figure 7.5 *The effect of different depreciation periods*

depreciate fixed assets but there are many factors to be considered in applying a particular rate. For example, one firm may anticipate that computer hardware will be obsolete after 18 months whereas another may take a different view and consider a three-year life to be appropriate. As an element of discretion remains, it is inevitable that, even in identical situations, different businesses will apply different calculations or different criteria in the application of some of the rules.

In recognition of this situation, company law and accounting standards have developed a three-stage conceptual framework:

- Accounting **principles** (or concepts) underpin the accounts preparation process.
- Accounting **bases** are the accepted means by which the principles may be applied in practice.
- Accounting **policies** are the specific bases adopted by the business.

Accounting principles (concepts)

The matching or accruals concept

Financial statements are prepared for specified time periods; for example, a profit and loss account may be labelled 'for the year-ended 31 May 2000'. Despite the fact that work may be started before the year-end and cash received sometime after the year-end, it is important that the profit and loss account reflects the value being created *during the accounting period*. The 'matching' concept requires, irrespective of cash receipts and payments, that the profit and loss account measures the actual value of work supplied to customers and the value of resources consumed while making those supplies. For example, the purchase of stock for resale is a cost in the profit and loss account only if indeed it is sold during the reporting period; otherwise it is recognised as an asset at the year-end and included in the balance sheet.

Prudence

Financial statements should be prepared on a prudent basis. Gains should be recognised only when they are reasonably certain, and losses should be provided for as soon as there is a 50 per cent chance of them being incurred. The prudence concept prevails over the matching concept if the two conflict. An example of the prudence concept in practice is the valuation of stocks which are to be valued at the lower of cost and net realisable value. A possible loss is recognised immediately by 'writing down' the value of stocks and charging the loss to the profit and loss account. This contrasts with a profit, which is not recognised until a sale has been made.

The going-concern concept

When a business buys assets, whether for use in the business or for resale, it is on the basis that their recoverable amount will be in excess of cost. The recoverable amount is either the value that can be obtained by reselling the asset, as in the case of stocks, or is the future benefit that will accrue from using the asset in the business, such as a delivery van. The 'going-concern concept' assumes that the business will be in a position to realise the recoverable amount – that is, it will continue to trade in the foreseeable future. If the going-concern concept cannot be assumed, then the recoverable amount should be revised and if that is lower than cost it should be used as the valuation in the accounts. For a fixed asset in a distressed firm, this may require lowering its value to the amount realistically obtainable in an enforced sale.

Consistency

Items of a similar nature should be accounted for on a consistent basis from one period to the next. For example, if it has been accounting policy to depreciate motor vehicles over four years, then it would be inconsistent to depreciate over six years in the next accounting period. This is important so that the reported performance of one period can be properly compared with another.

Materiality

Strict observation of accounting convention need not be followed where items are not large in the context of understanding the business's performance and financial state of affairs. Take, for example, the classification of R&D expenditure. According to SSAP13, development expenditure can be deferred and treated as an intangible asset in the balance sheet only if certain rules are satisfied to demonstrate that the expenditure will give future benefits, such as a commercially viable new product. If a business with profits of £0.5 million incurs £50 000 development expenditure, then the treatment of the

expenditure is a material issue and so should be accounted for in strict accordance with the accounting standard. However, if Unilever, with operating profits in excess of £2 billion, were to incorrectly defer £1 million of development expenditure, then that would not be considered material to the understanding of the performance of the business. The materiality of an individual item will thus depend on the size of the business.

Basis for valuation

Accounts may be prepared according to two **valuation** conventions:

- **historical cost** – the value placed on an item or transaction at the time it arose
- **alternative cost** – a valuation based on current cost having made an adjustment for the changing value of money.

Most accounts are prepared on the historical-cost basis, although many companies do take the opportunity to revalue land and buildings to give better information concerning the assets of the business. This may be particularly relevant when sourcing more debt finance. The basis for valuation should be disclosed as an accounting policy of the business.

Accounting bases

Accounting bases are generally accepted methods of applying the accounting concepts to practical situations. Different bases have evolved in response to the needs of a diverse range of business activities.

Consider depreciation, for example. There are various accounting methods of spreading the cost of a fixed asset over the years that are to benefit from its use. One method simply spreads the cost evenly over the years involved; so, for a machine that costs £4000 and is to be used for four years before being scrapped (no value), the depreciation charge would be £1000 per annum. Another method is to estimate how many hours it will be used each year and spread the cost in direct proportion to this. Hence if the same machine's life is estimated to be 10 000 hours and it is used for 1 500 hours in its first year, the first year's depreciation charge is £4000 × 1500/10 000 = £600. Each method may be acceptable provided it is appropriate to the circumstances and is applied consistently.

Accounting policies

Accounting policies are the specific accounting bases adopted by a business. It is because the accounting policies directly affect the figures in the financial statements that

---

The accounts have been prepared in accordance with applicable accounting standards under the historical-cost convention. The principal accounting policies of the company are set out below.

(a) *Turnover*. Turnover represents the net value of goods sold, services provided or royalties received. Turnover excludes value-added tax.

(b) *Depreciation*. Tangible fixed assets are fully written off over their expected useful lives, as follows:

On a straight-line basis:
Short leasehold property – over the period of the lease
Fixtures and fittings – over 5–10 years
Computer hardware and software – over 3–4 years

On a reducing-balance basis:
Motor vehicles – at a rate of 25 per cent per annum

(c) *Deferred taxation*. Deferred taxation is provided only to the extent that it is probable that a liability or asset will crystallise.

(d) *Stocks and work in progress*. Stocks are valued at the lower of cost and net realisable value.

(e) *Operating leases*. On the acquisition of a number of leasehold properties, the company has negotiated rent-free periods of varying lengths. Where a rent-free period exceeds three months, the value of the additional benefit is treated as deferred income and written back to the profit and loss account over the period to the leasehold property's first rent review. Rental payments in respect of other operating leases are charged against operating profit as they are incurred.

(f) *Foreign exchange*. Transactions in foreign currencies are converted into sterling at applicable forward contract rates or the rates ruling on the date of the transaction where no forward cover exists. Assets and liabilities denominated in foreign currencies are translated at the rates ruling at the balance sheet date or at applicable forward contract rates. Exchange profits and losses arising are dealt with in the profit and loss account.

Figure 7.6 *Illustration of accounting policy note in the annual report*

they must be published to enable the analysis of a company's financial performance. It is not possible to compare financial results against a benchmark unless the impact of the company's accounting policies is properly understood. For published company accounts these are disclosed in a note to the accounts, as demonstrated in Figure 7.6.

To make comparisons between different companies, a review of their respective accounting policies should identify any material differences in accounting treatment of similar items. Where necessary, the reported figures should be restated on a common basis.

THE AUDITORS' REPORT

The accounts of a limited company are required by law to be audited by a firm of independent accountants who are registered auditors. The **audit report** is included in the annual report of the company.

The auditors are asked to verify the accuracy of the underpinning financial records and to ensure that the accounts are consistent with these records. The accounting treatment and disclosure of all material items should be confirmed as being in accordance with relevant legislation and complying with accounting standards where appropriate.

The overriding responsibility of the auditors is to confirm that the accounts provide a 'true and fair view' of the valuation of assets and liabilities as at the date of the accounts and of the profit or loss up to that date (usually one year). To fulfil this responsibility, the auditors may actually encourage or concur with a departure from an accounting standard if it facilitates a 'true and fair' view of the financial aspects of the company.

An important aspect will be to verify that it is appropriate to apply the 'going-concern' principle in the valuation of assets and liabilities. If assets have to be disposed of as a result of cessation of business, then appropriate (often lower) market values should be used in preparing the accounts. Hence some of the audit will be devoted to the company's future outlook.

Auditors may have difficulty confirming that the financial reports do give a true and fair view, in which case they may issue a 'qualified' audit report. Reasons for a qualified audit report fall into two main categories:

Obtain the latest annual report for a public limited company.

1. From the various narratives in the report, which may include a chairman's statement, a review of operations and a financial review, establish the following:

(a) the nature of the company's business

(b) a general impression of the company's progress over the past year

(c) the company's strategy to be competitive in its chosen markets

(d) in what assets the company is investing for the future

(e) the outlook for its future financial performance.

2. From the profit and loss account, is the latest year's turnover and profit better or worse than the year before?

3. Does the profit and loss account (or a supporting note to the accounts) give a segmental analysis of turnover? If so, what does the analysis tell you?

4. Does the profit and loss account show the financial effects of business restructuring, such as acquisitions and terminations? If so, what are the implications for the future?

5. From a relevant note to the accounts, calculate 'wages and salaries' as a percentage of turnover, for both years. Are employee costs increasing faster than sales income?

6. What percentage of profit after taxation is distributed as a dividend to the shareholders?

7. From the balance sheet, which assets have increased during the latest year?

8. From a balance sheet 'note', determine the value of the company's debt for each year.

9. Calculate the gearing ratio for each year.

10. Does the auditor's report confirm that the financial statements give a true and fair view of the company's financial performance? If not, why not?

11. What are your general impressions about the financial performance of the company?

- *Uncertainty.* The accounting records may be inadequate for them to carry out a full audit of financial transactions, or there may be uncertainty concerning the outcome of a known situation (e.g. a law suite) or the applicability of the going-concern concept.
- *Disagreement.* The accounting records may be deemed not to be factual or the financial reports not to be in accordance with the accounting records. The non-compliance with relevant legislation and accounting standards may also be cause for disagreement.

For interested parties, the reluctance of the auditors to state that the accounts provide a 'true and fair' view seriously undermines their value.

INTERPRETATION OF ACCOUNTS

When evaluating the financial performance of a business it is necessary to identify trends and be able to differentiate the significant from the unimportant. **Accounting ratios** are an important set of tools to aid the financial analyst with these objectives.

Accounting ratios compare one piece of financial data with another to aid the analysis of financial performance. Absolute money values are of little use unless they are set in the context in which they arose. For example, WHSmith incurs far greater cost than a local newsagent, but a comparison of costs in relation to sales revenue would almost certainly indicate the national chain enjoyed a cost advantage.

To give ratios meaning they are compared with **benchmarks**, which may be:

- the same ratio calculated over different time periods to detect favourable or adverse trends
- the same ratio calculated for comparable businesses, or against industry averages, to indicate whether the business is operating competitively and as efficiently as it should.

The ratios themselves are comparisons of figures, generally found in the main financial statements. Values taken from the profit and loss account are measures of activity (e.g. cost of sales for one year). Values taken from the balance sheet are measures of financial resources applied to a particular purpose (e.g. investment in stocks at a point in time). A ratio can be a comparison of two items from within the profit and loss account and this says something of the cost structure of the business; for example, labour cost divided by sales. A ratio comparing two items taken from the balance sheet is an expression of the capital structure of the business; for example, debt to equity or fixed assets as a percentage of total net assets.

A ratio based on one figure taken from the profit and loss account and one from the balance sheet is generally a

measure of financial efficiency; that is, how much financial resource is required to fund a particular level of business activity. For example, comparing annual 'cost of sales' to a 'stock' balance indicates how many times a year stock is 'turned over' (used and replaced). The ratio is therefore a measure of how well financial resources are working to support business activity.

No predetermined set of accounting ratios has been formally defined by the accounting profession. It is for the financial analyst to ensure that calculations give a fair appreciation of financial performance. Later in this chapter the limitations of accounting ratios are discussed.

Profitability ratios

Return on capital employed (ROCE) and equity (ROE)

Ratios that compare profit with capital invested are measures of financial return that allow comparison with other investment opportunities:

$$\text{Financial return} = \frac{\text{Profit}}{\text{Capital}} \times 100\%.$$

Arguably these ratios are of paramount significance because businesses that do not provide a return in excess of the cost of finance will fail. If owners' expectations are not met, and a change in management has not had the desired effect, ultimately the business will be liquidated or merged and restructured with another firm.

The total operating profit of the business, before the deduction of finance charges, is the amount available to meet the expectations of all investors in the business. It should be adequate to pay interest to the providers of debt finance, such as a bank overdraft and the debenture holders, and to allow dividends to be paid to shareholders, with a residue to be added to shareholder funds to enable further growth in the business. When calculating a ratio of return on capital employed, it is important that the profit figure extracted from the profit and loss account be matched with a relevant capital amount from the balance sheet.

As a measure of the effectiveness of management in *operating* the business, the chosen sources of finance are not relevant; therefore the operating profit should be compared with total capital employed. In the example in

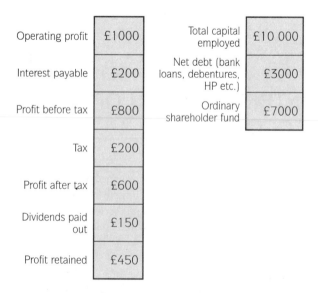

Operating profit	£1000		Total capital employed	£10 000	
Interest payable	£200		Net debt (bank loans, debentures, HP etc.)	£3000	
Profit before tax	£800		Ordinary shareholder fund	£7000	
Tax	£200				
Profit after tax	£600				
Dividends paid out	£150				
Profit retained	£450				

Figure 7.7 *Example (see text)*

Figure 7.7, this would result in a ratio of £1000 divided by £10 000, which is 0.10 or 10 per cent. This is commonly known as **return on capital employed** (ROCE) and is a measure of how effectively the financial resources invested in the business have been used. Formally, this ratio can be expressed as:

Return on capital employed (ROCE)

$$= \frac{\text{Operating profit}}{\text{Total capital employed}} \times 100\%,$$

in which the total capital employed is the total shareholder funds, plus debt, but minus cash. The deduction of cash (which gives 'net debt') is made on the grounds that this has provided an offsetting financial return not included in the operating profit.

In recognition that the balance sheet does indeed balance, the figure for capital employed can alternatively be calculated from the assets (excluding cash) less non-interest bearing liabilities.

Where an analyst is more interested in the returns for equity shareholders, then the profits available to shareholders (after the payment of interest) should be compared with the shareholder funds. This is known as the **return on equity** (ROE). In the example in Figure 7.7, this ratio would be either 11.4 or 8.6 per cent, depending on whether a gross or net-of-tax rate of return was used (i.e. £800 divided by £7000, or £600 divided by £7000).

Return on equity

$$= \frac{\text{Net profit (after preference dividend)}}{\text{Ordinary shares and equity reserves}} \times 100\%.$$

The ROE indicates how well the business has used the financial resources invested in it by the ordinary shareholders. It differs from ROCE because of the **gearing effect** caused by partially financing the business with fixed-return finance (see Chapter 5). Provided the business has been able to generate a higher return on capital employed than the interest paid to debt providers, the ROE will be higher than the ROCE.

With either ROCE or ROE, the profit figure used has arisen from trading during an accounting period, whereas the capital employed figure is a value at a particular point in time (i.e. the balance sheet date). Where the capital has changed significantly over the accounting period – for instance where there has been a new share issue – the ratios may give misleading results. A more accurate ratio would result from an average capital employed, even if this

were a simple average of two balance sheet figures. In fact this is true of most figures extracted from the balance sheet and it is beholden on the analyst to ensure the definition of terms is appropriate to the circumstances.

Another consideration is consistency. When presented with profit figures for years 1 and 2 and appropriate capital balances at the end of each year, it would be possible to calculate a simple average for capital employed during year 2 (i.e. capital year 1 plus capital year 2, divided by two) but not for year 1. Unless the capital balance for year 0 could be established, it may be better to use year-end balances and be aware of the inherent distortion when interpreting the ratios.

Extracting the relevant figures from published accounts will be demonstrated using the accounts for Yates Brothers Wine Lodges Plc, which start on this page.

Let us first calculate the ROCE for 1998. The figure for total capital employed for the bottom of the equation is made up of (in thousands of pounds): shareholder funds, £82 468; bank overdraft, £9740 and bank loan £25 000; less cash at bank and in hand (£3306). This gives total capital employed of £113 902. The operating profit before interest is £15 304. So:

ROCE

$$= \frac{\text{Profit on ordinary activities before interest} \times 100\%}{\text{Capital employed}}$$

$$= \frac{15\ 304 \times 100\%}{113\ 902} = 13.4 \text{ per cent}$$

Figure 7.8 *Extract from 1998 accounts of Yates Brothers Wine Lodges Plc*

Group profit and loss account	Note	1998 (£000)	1997 (£000)
Turnover	2	97 783	75 747
Net operating costs	3	(84 178)	(65 561)
Operating profit	4	13 605	10 186
Share of profits of associate		44	–
Exceptional items	5	1 655	1 118
Profit on ordinary activities before interest		15 304	11 304
Net interest payable	6	(1 719)	(796)
Profit on ordinary activities before tax		13 585	10 508
Taxation	7	(1 690)	(1 846)
Profit for the financial year		11 895	8 662
Dividends	8	(2 205)	(1 807)
Retained profit	19	9 690	6 855

Figure 7.8 *Continued*

Group balance sheet	Note	1998 (£000)	1997 (£000)
Fixed assets:			
Tangible	11	115789	92637
Investments	12	815	143
		116604	92780
Current assets:			
Stocks	13	5184	4817
Debtors	14	9068	8959
Cash at bank and in hand		3306	2641
		17558	16417
Creditors due within one year	15	(25582)	(19507)
Net current liabilities		(8024)	(3090)
Total assets less current liabilities		108580	89690
Creditors due after one year	16	(25388)	(17888)
Provisions for liabilities and charges	17	(724)	(381)
		82468	71421
Capital and reserves:			
Called-up share capital	18	15982	10491
Share premium account	19	13622	17687
Revaluation reserve	19	13367	16305
Profit and loss account	19	37710	26551
Deferred equity consideration	12	1787	387
Shareholders' funds		82468	71421

Note 3: Net operating costs	1998 (£000)	1997 (£000)
Cost of sales	37836	32024
Distribution costs	38246	27305
Administration costs	8377	6574
Other operating income: letting surplus space	(281)	(342)
	84178	65561

Note 5: Exceptional items	1998 (£000)	1997 (£000)
Realised profits on disposal of properties	2468	–
(Loss)/profit on other property transactions	(112)	1118
Loss on disposal of bottling business	(701)	–
	1655	1118

Note 5: Net interest payable	1998 (£000)	1997 (£000)
On bank overdraft	539	782
On bank loan repayable after five years	1722	328
Interest receivable	(24)	(15)
Interest capitalised	(518)	(299)
	1719	796

Note 8: Dividends	1998 (£000)	1997 (£000)
Interim: 1.15p (1997: 0.96p)	734	598
Final: 2.30p (1997: 1.92p)	1471	1209
	2205	1807

Note 10: Staff costs	1998 (£000)	1997 (£000)
Wages and salaries	19277	13976
Social security	1341	920
Pension costs	114	73
	20732	14969

Number of shares	1998 (£000)	1997 (£000)
Average for year	63303	60451
Year-end	63929	41963

Note 14: Debtors	1998 (£000)	1997 (£000)
Trade debtors	3159	3208
Debtor on sale of properties	2973	4152
Other debtors	742	309
Prepayments	2194	1167
Advance corporation tax recoverable	–	123
	9068	8959

Note 15: Creditors due within one year	1998 (£000)	1997 (£000)
Bank overdraft (unsecured)	9740	6076
Trade creditors	6838	6378
Social security and other taxes	620	692
Corporation tax payable	1247	1785
Other creditors	675	296
Accruals	4991	3071
Proposed dividend	1471	1209
	25582	19507

Note 16: Creditors due after one year	1998 (£000)	1997 (£000)
Bank loan: repayable after 5 years	25000	17500
Deferred cash consideration	388	388
	25388	17888

$$\text{ROE} = \frac{\text{Profit for the financial year}}{\text{Shareholder funds}} \times 100\%$$

$$= \frac{11\ 895}{82\ 468} \times 100\% = 14.4 \text{ per cent}$$

TASK

1. From the Yates Brothers accounts, calculate for 1997: (a) return on capital employed, (b) return on equity.

2. Is the company's financial performance improving or deteriorating?

A problem with the ROCE and ROE ratios calculated so far for Yates Brothers is that they have included exceptional items, which are not expected to recur in the future. The notes to the accounts indicate that these items relate to asset disposals. To gain a better understanding of the performance of the underlying business, then, the above ratios could be recalculated, excluding exceptional items. The ROCE recalculated gives 12.0 per cent for 1998 and 11.0 per cent for 1997 (try confirming this). These ratios still show an improving situation, but may be more relevant especially when comparing with ratios from other companies.

Profit ratios based on turnover

Ratios that compare items *within* the profit and loss account provide insight into the incidence of costs relative to sales turnover. They are a useful tool to management and to the external analyst in determining whether the business has a competitive cost structure. An improvement in the margin between revenues and expenditures is a sign of the business's ability to add value, indicating strong positions in the marketplace for the final product and in negotiations with suppliers.

The **profit margin** is a ratio that measures operating profit as a proportion of sales. The ratio is an indication of how profitable the business is without considering the cost of funds used in the business. As some expenses of businesses are fixed costs, the profit margin tends to increase as sales increase, provided sales prices have not been eroded to generate higher volumes. So:

$$\text{Profit margin} = \frac{\text{Operating profit}}{\text{Sales}} \times 100\%.$$

Further analysis of the profit margin can be achieved by considering the items that have been deducted from turnover to arrive at the operating profit. From a set of detailed management accounts, it will be possible to calculate ratios such as salaries to sales, warranty cost to sales, and materials cost to sales. The detail provided in published accounts will be restricted, although it will often be possible to calculate figures for 'cost of sales' to 'sales', 'administration expenses' to 'sales', and 'distribution costs' to 'sales'. So:

$$\begin{array}{l}\text{Expenses to sales} \\ \text{(in total and by expense type)}\end{array} = \frac{\text{Expenses}}{\text{Sales}} \times 100\%.$$

The ratio 'cost of sales' to 'sales', or its variant 'gross profit margin', can be particularly useful when comparing firms in defined market sectors, such as in the retail sector, as it shows the respective firms' mark-up strategies. Most businesses should aim to make a gross profit of 30–60 per cent in order to make a net profit after paying for other expenses. Figure 7.9 shows an example for Yates Brothers. Its gross profit to sales is 61.3% (sales less cost of sales).

	1998) (£000)	Ratio (%)
Sales	97 783	100.0
Cost of sales	37 836	38.7
Distribution costs	38 246	39.1
Administration expenses	8 377	8.6
Other operating income	(281)	(0.3)
	84 178	86.1
Profit margin	13 605	13.9

Figure 7.9 *Yates Brothers' profit margin*

TASK

1. For Yates Brothers (see Figure 7.8), calculate *for 1997* the following items *as a percentage of sales:* (a) cost of sales, (b) distribution costs, (c) administration expenses, (d) other operating income and (e) profit margin.

2. Highlight ratios that are improving and those that are deteriorating.

3. Suggest possible reasons for the changes in each ratio.

It is important to take care when making comparisons between companies. Different companies, even within the same sector, may categorise expenses differently. For example, Wetherspoon, another pub operator, includes all distribution costs within 'cost of sales'. Where there is sufficient information, it may be possible to recategorise expenses and costs before calculating the ratios, to ensure consistency across a number of firms.

Liquidity ratios

A business may be profitable, but it requires sufficient working capital to provide the *liquidity* to pay suppliers and employees on a day-to-day basis. Two ratios commonly used to measure financial liquidity are the **current ratio** and the more stringent **acid-test ratio**. Whereas the current ratio simply compares current assets to current liabilities, the acid-test ratio compares only cash and other monetary assets with short-term liabilities. Monetary assets are those with an obvious cash value, such as trade debtors which will be paid in the next month or so, and investments in the form of securities that can be readily traded. So:

$$\text{Current ratio (or working capital ratio)} = \frac{\text{Current assets}}{\text{Current liabilities}},$$

$$\text{Acid-test ratio} = \frac{\text{Current assets} - \text{Stock}}{\text{Current liabilities}}.$$

For Yates Brothers these are:

$$\text{Current ratio (1998)} = \frac{17\,558}{25\,582} = 0.69,$$

$$\text{Acid-test ratio (1998)} = \frac{17\,558 - 5\,184}{25\,582} = 0.48.$$

Obviously, the higher these ratios are, the more assets there are available to pay the firm's creditors. But high ratios may indicate that *excessive* funds are being tied up in working capital so that the business is incurring unnecessary finance charges. A current ratio of 2.0 and an acid-test ratio of 1.0 are much-quoted benchmarks, but it is difficult to generalise about the preferred value of either ratio. There are many examples, even within blue-chip companies, considerably below these values. The type of industry being analysed is an important factor. For example, retailers (including Yates) which have relatively few debtors and fast stock turnaround can survive on current ratios considerably less than 1. They are also helped by strong and stable cash flows from which they can pay their short-term creditors.

Probably more important than the actual value of the ratio itself is its comparison with previous periods and with other businesses in the same sector. A marked deterioration in the ratio over time might indicate possible cash flow problems ahead, or an improvement in the use of funds. Clearly, interpretation of the cause of a change in the ratios can be problematic and yet crucial if ratio analysis is to be meaningful. On their own, liquidity ratios are of limited value but what they can do is highlight trends that signal the need for further analysis. For example, if the current ratio is deteriorating, is it due to a decrease in assets, or to an increase in liabilities?

Working capital and efficiency ratios

The **working capital** and **efficiency** ratios are based on the principle that investment in assets should help to increase the level of business activity. Extra efficiency or different working capital policies, such as customer credit periods, should be demonstrated by differences in the relevant accounting ratio.

Ideally these ratios would be calculated using average balances over the relevant accounting period; but where information is limited, such as when using published accounts, it may be necessary to use period-end balances.

The measurement of **debtor days** is an indication of how long the average credit customer takes to pay for supplies received. For the external analyst, it is not always possible to determine the value of sales on credit, in which case a general measure of credit extended to customers could be calculated based on total sales. The calculation is based on 'trade debtors', which can be extracted from the analysis of total debtors in the notes to the accounts. So:

$$\text{Debtor days} = \frac{\text{Average trade debtors}}{\text{Credit sales}} \times 365 \text{ days}.$$

Although not important for trend analysis, the absolute figure for debtor days should be adjusted for the impact of VAT. If sales are taxable according to VAT regulations, then VAT is collected by adding 17.5 per cent (currently) to the amounts payable by the customer. As a receivable amount from the customer, VAT has to be included in debtor balances; but because the profit and loss account is concerned only with amounts earned by the business, VAT is excluded from credit sales. Hence debtor days should be adjusted by dividing by 1.175.

For Yates Brothers, the calculation is as follows:

$$\text{Debtor days (1988)} = \frac{\text{Trade debtors}}{\text{Total sales}} \times 365 \text{ days}$$

$$= \frac{3159}{97\,783} \times 365 = 11.8 \text{ days.}$$

Yates' sales are subject to VAT, so the figure for debtor days could be further refined as stated above. So, debtor days adjusted for VAT were 11.8/1.175 days, or 10 days.

The accounts for Yates Brothers demonstrate the difficulties in extracting relevant data from published accounts. Debtors should be related to credit sales, for which no separate figure is given. However, elsewhere in notes to the accounts there is an analysis of sales between wholesale and retail. Assuming that retail sales are for cash and wholesale are on credit, the average credit period taken by credit customers is in fact 56.2 days. Taken in isolation, it is not possible to determine whether Yates' debtor days figure is good or bad; it can be meaningful only in the context of ratios for previous periods or for other firms in the same industry.

The same principles used for measuring trade debtor levels can be applied to trade creditors. The period taken to pay for credit purchases (**creditor days**) indicates the extent to which the firm is using suppliers to finance its business. So:

$$\text{Creditor days} = \frac{\text{Average trade creditors}}{\text{Credit purchases}} \times 365 \text{ days.}$$

Creditor days should be maximised where possible because trade credit is free provided no settlement discounts are lost.

The trade creditors for Yates Brothers are to be found in note 15 (see Figure 7.8), but unfortunately no figures are given for purchases. For a retail business such as Yates where purchases are resold without further production costs, 'cost of sales' will be an adequate proxy measure of 'purchases'. So for Yates:

$$\text{Creditor days (1998)} = \frac{\text{Trade creditors}}{\text{Cost of sales}} \times 365 \text{ days}$$

$$= \frac{6838}{37\,836} \times 365 = 66.0 \text{ days.}$$

To ensure the efficient use of funds, the level of stocks should be kept to a minimum. Of course, the greater the level of business activity the greater the level of stocks needed to service customer demand. The efficiency of stock control can be measured by relating the stock balance to the level of stock usage to calculate **stock turnover**:

$$\text{Stock turnover} = \frac{\text{Annual cost of sales}}{\text{Average stock}}.$$

For Yates Brothers:

$$\text{Stock turnover (1988)} = \frac{\text{Cost of materials sold}}{\text{Stock balance}}$$

$$= \frac{37\,836}{5184} = 7.3.$$

This ratio indicates how many times a year stock is replenished. An alternative ratio, **stock days**, can be calculated in the same way as debtor and creditor days. For Yates Brothers, stock days is 365/7.3 = 50.0 days.

There will be difficulties in calculating stock turnover for businesses whose cost of sales includes elements of costs in addition to materials. For example, manufacturing businesses will incur factory labour and overheads, and in the published accounts format adopted may not disclose a separate materials figure. In instances where the composition of 'cost of sales' is not known, measuring stock levels against turnover may provide an adequate alternative. The principle is to determine a relationship between investment in stocks and business volumes.

A composite measure for reviewing the efficient use of working capital is the **cash operating cycle**, which sums the length of time that funds are tied up in working capital. So:

Cash operating cycle
= Stock turnover days + Debtor days – Creditor days.

For manufacturing businesses that have raw-material, work-in-progress and finished-goods stock, it is necessary to calculate stock turnover days for each category of stock. This requires each balance to be related to a relevant throughput value; i.e. raw materials used, cost of goods manufactured, and cost of sales, respectively.

The cash operating cycle is a rather crude measure. Stock and creditors relate only to materials purchased, whereas debtors also contain labour, overhead and profit elements. However, it is a consolidated measure of working capital efficiency that may be appropriate for a summary management report.

The same principle of relating balance sheet values to profit and loss activity can be applied to fixed assets and total working capital. The higher the level of business activity relative to investment in net assets, the greater will be the return on capital employed. So:

$$\text{Utilisation of capital employed} = \frac{\text{Sales}}{\text{Capital employed}},$$

$$\text{Utilisation of fixed assets} = \frac{\text{Sales}}{\text{Fixed assets}},$$

$$\text{Utilisation of current assets} = \frac{\text{Sales}}{\text{Current assets}},$$

$$\text{Utilisation of working capital} = \frac{\text{Sales}}{\text{Net current assets}}.$$

For Yates Brothers:

$$\text{Utilisation of capital employed (1998)} = \frac{97\ 783}{113\ 902} = 0.86,$$

$$\text{Utilisation of fixed assets (1998)} = \frac{97\ 783}{115\ 789} = 0.84.$$

Again, these ratios have little meaning in isolation. However, a utilisation ratio that shows an increasing trend means that more sales are being achieved for every £1 of financial resource. Provided that sales are profitable, that means return on capital employed should also increase.

TASK

1. From Figure 7.8, calculate the following ratios for Yates Brothers *for 1997*: (a) current ratio, (b) acid-test ratio, (c) debtor days, (d) creditor days, (e) stock turn, (f) utilisation of capital employed, (g) utilisation of fixed assets.

2. Provide a narrative explaining the changes in the ratios for Yates Brothers between 1997 and 1998, and the possible causes for these changes.

Investment ratios

Whereas the ratios discussed so far are tools to measure how various parts of a business are being managed, there is a further set of ratios concerned more with the investors' perspective of financial performance. In addition to wanting to know how management achieves a particular return on capital employed, the investor requires ratios that focus on the returns and risks of specific company securities that allow comparison with other companies across industrial sectors.

When investors buy shares in a company, they are not so much interested in the total profits of the business, but in the profits that are attributable to their personal shareholding. The **earnings per share** (EPS) is therefore a very significant statistic, and in published accounts it is usually expressed in pence at the foot of the profit and loss account. The basic calculation is: profit after tax and preference dividend, divided by the average number of shares in issue during the accounting period. Here, profit includes exceptional items, although many companies also provide a pre-exceptional EPS to indicate the company's notional underlying performance without the non-recurring items. So:

$$\text{Earnings per share} = \frac{\text{Net profit (after tax and preference dividend)}}{\text{Average number of ordinary shares in issue}}.$$

For Yates Brothers:

$$\text{Earnings per share (1998)} = \frac{£11\ 895\ 000}{63\ 303\ 000} = 18.8 \text{ pence.}$$

Without the exceptional items, the calculation could be:

$$\frac{(£11\ 895\ 000 - £1\ 655\ 000)}{63\ 303\ 000} = 16.2 \text{ pence.}$$

Once the profit attributable to an individual share has been established, it is possible to consider the price of a share. If two companies have the same growth prospects and the same level of risk, a share that provides a higher EPS should command a higher share price. It follows that the relationship between price and earnings, as measured by the **price/earnings** (PE) ratio, is a valuable indicator of value between shares of different companies. So:

$$\text{Price earnings ratio (PE)} = \frac{\text{Market price of share}}{\text{Earnings per share}}.$$

For Yates Brothers, based on the market share price on 11 December 1998:

$$PE = \frac{317p}{18.8p} = 16.9.$$

The price/earnings ratio is based on the most recent published accounts. Any variation in the ratio between companies is a statement of the market's perception concerning risk and growth prospects for each company. By way of comparison, if an individual placed £100 in a bank deposit account that paid 5 per cent interest, the price earnings ratio would be 20 (£100/£5). A bank deposit is relatively risk-free, and so for company shares to remain attractive with a PE ratio of 20, they must provide opportunity for earnings growth; for example the EPS shows potential to grow by 10 per cent per annum.

For companies listed on the stock exchange, the price/earnings ratio shows how many times its current earnings the stock market values the company. It is a measure of confidence in the growth potential of the company and its business sector.

An EPS includes amounts retained in the business, it is based on the total wealth created for the shareholders. It is not a measure of income actually to be received by the shareholders. It follows that the directors' policy regarding the proportion of earnings to be paid in dividends is often an important determinant for shareholders investing in a company. Perhaps because of their tax circumstances, shareholders will often have a preference as to whether they receive investment returns in the form of income or capital growth. For some shareholders, such as pension funds, an income stream is necessary to fund expenditures.

Dividend yield measures the financial return actually paid by the company to its shareholders. So:

$$Dividend\ yield = \frac{Dividend}{Market\ price\ of\ share} \times 100\%.$$

Because company directors are generally uncomfortable with declaring a reduced dividend, payouts tend to remain fairly stable from one year to the next. Dividends tend to increase at a slower rate than earnings, but when they do increase the directors are displaying confidence that they can maintain the new level in the long run. For Yates Brothers:

$$Dividend\ yield\ (1998) = \frac{3.45p}{317p} \times 100\%$$

$$= 1.1\ per\ cent.$$

Clearly Yates' dividend yield in 1998 was not high compared with bank deposits or many other shares. The company may thus be preferred by those investors looking for capital growth as opposed to regular income.

As has already been explained, the price of shares quoted on the stock exchange is largely determined by perceptions of future earnings potential, for which the PE ratio is often used. Investors, however, may at times be interested in the asset backing of a share (i.e. the balance sheet value of net assets divided by the number of shares). **Net asset value per share** may be particularly relevant where there is a practical possibility of realising the asset values of companies that are under-performing by other measures. So:

$$Net\ asset\ value\ per\ share = \frac{Shareholder\ funds}{Number\ of\ shares\ in\ issue}.$$

For Yates Brothers:

$$Net\ asset\ value\ per\ share = \frac{£82\ 468\ 000}{63\ 929\ 000} = £1.29.$$

With a share price of £3.17 at the end of 1998, the value of Yates Brothers has clearly been measured in terms of profit potential rather than the break-up value of the business. However, care must be taken in interpreting net asset values. Net assets in the business, and hence shareholder funds, are valued according to accounting conventions and not the amount that would be realised on the wind-up of the business. Accounting rules value the assets according to their value *to the business*, which usually assumes continued use for generating future earnings.

Other ratios of particular interest to the investor are the **gearing ratio** and the **interest cover ratio**. These were examined in Chapter 6.

Ratio framework

To be used in a systematic fashion, accounting ratios should be viewed within a logical framework (see Figure 7.10). Many of the ratios are interrelated, so if these relationships can be understood then ratio analysis is more likely to aid the correct interpretation of accounts.

For example, return on capital employed (profit/capital employed) is the product of profit margin (profit/sales) and utilisation of capital employed (sales/capital employed). So for Yates Brothers:

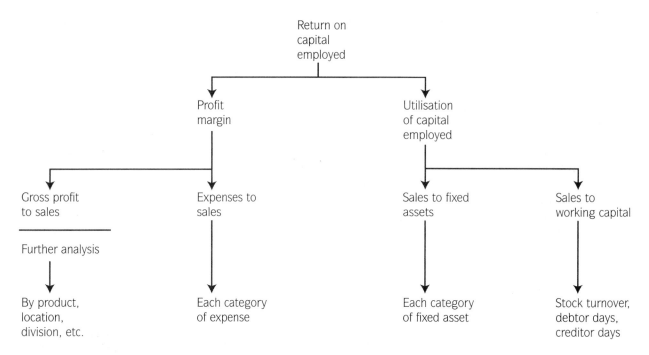

Figure 7.10 *Ratio framework*

Return on capital employed
= Profit margin (13.6%) × utilisation (0.86)
= 12 per cent

Note that this confirms the earlier calculation based on profit (before exceptionals) divided by capital employed. This approach to ratio analysis means that, for any change in ROCE between periods, it is possible to determine whether the change is due mainly to a change in profit margin or in utilisation. The next step would be to proceed down the ratio framework to fund the causes for a change to financial performance.

Case study

More about pubs

Regulatory pressure on the big brewers to sell off portions of their large estates of tied public houses has led to a proliferation of smaller pub chains. Whereas the pubs of the past were often run by tenants who were obliged to buy beers from their landlord, the new chains have been actively managed to promote distinctive brands. However, share prices in these growth-orientated companies were given a knock in 1998, after a profit warning by Regent and a general deterioration in consumer confidence. With a static market unlikely to increase sales per pub, growth is achieved only by opening more pubs.

- Yates Brothers Wine Lodges Plc intends to double its 93 pubs over the next five years.

- Regent Inns Plc has a number of branded formats, including its promising Walkabout Australian theme pubs. The company disappointed the stock market during 1998 with a statement that profits would be lower than expected partly as a result of accounting errors. Recent profits have benefited from sales of unwanted pub sites, although the number of Regent pubs increased from 67 to 70 during 1998.

- Slug & Lettuce sold off 19 non-core pubs during 1998 to concentrate on its 'Slug & Lettuce' format. Twelve new pubs were opened during 1998 to bring the total branded pubs to 26. Significant exceptional net losses have been incurred in reorganising the company, but another 11 pubs were expected to be opened during 1999.

- SFI has two main brands. The Litten Tree and Bar Med. The company focuses on the under-30 age group, with light and sound systems to appeal. The company is growth-orientated, to take the current 49 outlets up by another 12 during 1999.

- J.D. Wetherspoon opened 68 new pubs in 1998, bringing its total to 252. Like-for-like sales were depressed during the year; unlike many competitors, Wetherspoon decided against installing televisions for the football World Cup.

Figure 7.11 shows data extracted from company annual reports. This, together with the Yates Brothers data given earlier in the chapter, is relevant to the tasks that follow.

	Wetherspoon		Slug & Lettuce		SFI		Regent	
	1998 (£000)	1997 (£000)	1998 (£000)	1997 (£000)	1998 (£000)	1997 (£000)	1998 (£000)	1997 (£000)
Sales	188 515	139 444	22 660	23 803	29 791	16 398	50 782	43 981
Staff costs	39 996	29 642	5 668	5 676	6 782	4 002	14 315	9 705
Operating profit (before exceptionals)	28 367	22 939	2 582	2 885	6 345	2 926	12 810	12 573
Exceptional items	14 968	0	(833)	(1 197)	(39)	0	783	410
Interest paid	(8 202)	(5 373)	(1 007)	(824)	(979)	(635)	(1 285)	(819)
Profit after tax	34 407	16 796	615	526	4 635	2 153	11 634	11 008
Cash	12 750	7 196	1 989	554	1 057	427	0	0
Short term debt	5 785	1 000	900	4 590	3 552	2 104	5 322	7 943
Long term debt	137 881	94 833	10 460	5 822	16 451	9 350	12 498	12 234
Shareholder funds	159 192	124 663	14 182	14 451	30 534	25 561	70 754	57 366
Number of shares (000)	195 888	194 106	14 178	14 175	59 188	45 844	89 211	85 898
Share price (pence) (11/12/98)	200.5		162.5		135.0		102.5	

Figure 7.11 *Data for pub performance*

Questions

1. For each company, calculate for 1997 and 1998:
   (a) return on capital employed, including and excluding exceptional items; (b) profit margin, including and excluding exceptional items; (c) staff costs to sales; (d) sales to capital employed; (e) earnings per share, excluding exceptional items; (f) price/earnings ratio, excluding exceptional items (for 1998 only); (g) gearing ratio; (h) interest cover, excluding exceptional items.

2. Published accounts are required to state earnings per share including exceptional items. What is the relevance of calculating EPS excluding these items?

3. Bearing in mind that debt finance is generally cheaper than equity finance, highlight which companies if any may be restricted in using further debt to finance future growth.

4. Despite Wetherspoon having a better profit margin than Slug & Lettuce, the company has a lower ROCE (before exceptional items). Why is this the case?

5. For a pub manager wishing to improve his or her outlet's profitability, suggest which ratio from (1) above would be the most relevant to monitor? What additional ratios of the same type could be used for this purpose?

6. Which company has the lowest stock market rating? Why might this be the case?

7. From an investor's perspective, what are the opportunities and threats for the pub sector?

Case Study

Spot the industry

Figure 7.12 has been compiled from the accounts of companies listed on the London stock exchange, published during 1998.

Questions

1. Calculate the following ratios: (a) debtor days, (b) turnover to stocks.

2. Match the performance figures to the following companies: (i) Orange Plc (telecommunications); (ii) Somerfield Plc (food retailer); (iii) Independent Insurance Group Plc (insurer); (iv) Mayflower Corporation Plc (automotive engineer).

3. Explain how you came to your conclusions for (2) above, highlighting the key features of the published figures.

	A (£m)	B (£m)	C (£m)	D (£m)
Turnover	913.7	392.7	552.2	3 410.5
Operating profit/(loss)	(51.1)	37.2	20.0	2.8
Net interest receivable/ (payable)	(88)	(3.9)	45.1	(13.9)
Profit before taxation	(139.1)	33.3	65.1	(11.1)
Fixed assets	960.3	84.8	25.5	1 213.3
Investments	25.2	2.3	522.3	10.9
Stocks	17.2	40.9	0	355.6
Trade debtors	81.2	44.4	320.3	4.8
Other debtors	65.8	20.9	131.0	127.7
Cash	13.7	35.5	0.5	74.7
Total assets	1163.4	228.8	999.6	1 787.0
Borrowings	1 091.6	71.5	0	309.6
Other liabilities	332.5	96.4	775.7	924.8
Shareholder's funds	(260.7)	60.9	223.9	552.6

Figure 7.12 *Data for four companies*

SUMMARY

Limitations of accounting ratios

Financial performance indicators in the form of ratios place significant emphasis on short-term results. Shareholder ratios such as EPS and the ROCE are subject to accounting conventions that might deter businesses pursuing policies that are in their long-term interests. For example, most expenditure on research and development, and all staff welfare costs including training, are charged against the current year's profits, even though some or all of the benefits might accrue in subsequent years. Unfortunately, listed companies that are subject to the rigours of the stock market have to recognise that financial performance criteria are the main tools used by investors and so aim to produce good short-term results.

Other limitations

- Reported financial performance may not be representative because of distortions caused by non-recurring items. Whilst accounting regulations in recent years have required greater information concerning exceptional items and different classes of businesses, it is not likely that analysts will possess all the information necessary to come to full and accurate conclusions.
- The external analyst has to use information that is at least several months old.
- Comparison of results between companies is difficult as rarely are the business activities of one firm identical to those of another.
- Some values may have been affected more than others by changes in price levels. In particular, the value of property used in a business will very much depend on when it was purchased. Low property valuations will result in artificially high returns on capital employed.
- The valuations used on the balance sheet depend on the specific accounting policies adopted. Where different businesses are being compared, the accounts of each should be restated on a like basis before ratios are calculated. The policies relating to the depreciation of fixed assets, the capitalisation of research and development expenditure, and the valuation of stocks are all examples of areas that could make comparisons difficult.

Despite these problems, and the fact that they rarely provide immediate answers to business problems, financial performance indicators (ratios etc.) do have a valuable part to play in the management of a business. Accounting ratios provoke searching questions that should result in tighter control and a better understanding of the business.

Financial Decisions

This chapter examines the role of financial information in management decision-making processes. The chapter concludes with an assignment that draws on knowledge gained across the unit 'Managing Financial Resources'.

On completion of the chapter you should be able to make financial decisions based on the financial information available. To achieve this you must demonstrate the ability to:

- make decisions related to costs and budgeting

based on management information available

- make appropriate pricing decisions for the business

- use investment and project appraisal techniques to assess the viability of a project.

MANAGEMENT ACCOUNTING

Topics considered in earlier chapters in this unit have emphasised the reporting of financial performance to monitor the managers' stewardship of a business. However, financial measures such as profit and cash flow tend to give an holistic view of business operations with little direct reference to the performance of an individual product, process or department. In addition, financial reporting tends towards an historical perspective rather than being forward-looking.

Management requires information that is relevant to the decision-making process, such as cost projections for an individual product. Also, when global competition creates pressure for management to improve efficiency, the finance function of the business needs to take a more active role in advising and sharing in the responsibility for decisions. In particular, the provision and interpretation of cost information is required to evaluate proposed changes in product or process design.

To satisfy these needs, a branch of accountancy known as **management accounting** has developed. It concentrates on

the 'micro' aspects of a business, looking at costs in relation to business activity. The examination of historical cost information is not the passive 'we could have done better', but rather 'how does this affect what we do in future?'.

Comparing historical costs against a **benchmark** enables management to control adverse trends, and an understanding of how costs are incurred helps future planning and decision-making. The purpose of cost information is:

- to calculate the cost of providing the customer with a particular product or service
- to measure the cost of different parts of the business to monitor performance and control activities
- to satisfy financial reporting requirements in terms of the valuation of stocks
- to evaluate alternatives, for example in respect of further investment in plant and machinery.

The Chartered Institute of Management Accountants (CIMA) is the main UK professional body concerned with management accounting. Whereas financial accounting is required to conform with legal requirements, management accounting is adapted to meet the changing needs of individual businesses.

Analysis of costs

Costs can be analysed into three categories: **labour** costs are the payments to the business's employees; **materials** are the physical goods consumed in making a supply to a customer; and **expenses** are the costs of all the other resources consumed, such as rent and the services of other businesses.

Cost is measured in terms of the money used to acquire a particular resource. However, relating the actual costs to a particular part of the business or to a particular product is not always easy. Business operations often have a multitude of products and processes that share resources, such as a factory, and so the problem arises as to how to divide such common costs. Generally a cost can be identified as one of two **cost objects** (or concepts):

- **Cost units** are a measure of a firm's output. These cost units are defined by the CIMA as: 'a quantitative unit of product or service in relation to which costs are ascertained'. The unit of measure is decided by the nature of a firm's output. It may be an object like a computer, a specified service such as cleaning the windows of a building, or in standard units of measure such as the number of passenger-miles of an aircraft. If a business is aware of the total cost of one unit, this can be a basis for setting sales prices.
- A **cost centre** is part of an organisation's activities. Costs are then related to the department or section of the organisation that incurs them. The CIMA defines a cost centre as: 'a location, function or items of equipment in respect of which costs may be ascertained and related to cost units for control purposes'. How the business is analysed into cost centres usually follows the firm's organisational structure, so for example every department might be a cost centre. However, because of the nature of the business and the relative size of some of its resources, there may be further analysis. For example, a printing firm that uses printing presses costing £1 million each may decide that each machine is to be a cost centre. In this way the total cost of running each press can be ascertained, including costs for operating, maintenance and depreciation.

Costs that can be attributed to and recorded against a specific cost unit are known as **direct costs**. Thus, **direct labour** (or direct wages) is the term used to describe payments to workers who make products or provide services. An engineering firm will incur direct wages paid to machine operators, and an office cleaning firm will pay direct wages to its cleaners. In a similar vein, direct materials is the cost of materials used to make specific products or services. The engineering firm may require materials in the form of base metals and ready-made components, and the cleaning firm will require chemicals and materials for specific cleaning contracts. Finally, **direct expenses** are other costs incurred specifically for the final product or service. These include royalty payments that are based on output, and the cost of subcontractors directly working on cost units. The total of direct costs is called the **prime cost**.

Costs that are not direct costs are classified as **indirect costs**. They either cannot be attributed to specific cost units, such as property rent, or it is impractical to do so. For example, it may be decided to treat consumables such as rags and lubricating oils as a cost-centre expense (an indirect cost) because the values are not large.

Indirect labour relates to wages and salaries paid to employees while they are not making cost units. This category includes office staff for management, administration and distribution. It also includes factory workers not actually performing direct work, either because of the nature of their work (for example maintenance engineers and stores personnel), or because of enforced 'idle' time between direct jobs. **Indirect materials** are items that are too low in value to have recording systems to relate them to specific products. Again, examples are lubricating materials, rags for cleaning down machines and small nuts and bolts. **Indirect expenses** encompass a wide range of costs, including property rents, power, stationery and depreciation of fixed assets. Indirect costs are often called 'overheads' and are usually analysed into production, administration and distribution costs.

TASK

Consider the two organisations BT (telecommunications) and Marks & Spencer, the general retailer. For each firm:

1. Identify appropriate cost units and cost centres.

2. Describe the type of costs that will fall into each cost concept.

From a profitability perspective, the ultimate success of the business depends upon how total business costs relate to total business income, something the *profit and loss account* looks at for the whole business. However, understanding how individual products contribute towards business success is not easy for the multi-product firm because the two cost concepts – cost units and cost centres – are not easily reconcilable. This will be demonstrated by looking first at the cost build-up of a single-product (cost unit) business.

The Highland Sweater Co Ltd manufactures just one line of woollen sweater. Its annual production is 100 000 sweaters, and annual and unit costs are as shown in Figure 8.1. With a single product it is a simple matter to calculate the total unit cost (£12 in this case) and this provides a clear guide to the necessary selling price.

	Annual cost (£)	Per sweater (unit) (£)
Direct labour	500 000	5.00
Direct materials	400 000	4.00
Prime cost	900 000	9.00
Overheads	300 000	3.00
	1 200 000	12.00

Figure 8.1 *Highland Sweater Co Ltd*

A firm with two products has greater difficulty in product costing. Consider Metal Pressings Ltd which produces 10 000 tool boxes and 5 000 metal filing cabinets each year (Figure 8.2). The firm incurs £120 000 of overheads, but how should this be shared between the company's products? There is no 'correct' method, but there are a number of bases that can be considered.

	Boxes		Cabinets		Total
	Annual (£)	Unit (£)	Annual (£)	Unit (£)	(£)
Direct labour	20 000	2.00	50 000	10.00	70 000
Direct materials	20 000	2.00	75 000	15.00	95 000
Prime cost	40 000	4.00	125 000	25.00	165 000
Overheads:					
Building costs					40 000
Indirect wages					50 000
Machine costs					30 000
Total overheads					120 000
Total costs					285 000

Figure 8.2 *Metal Pressings Ltd*

Absorption costing

The inclusion of overheads in product costs is called **absorption costing** and is often a multi-stage process. For the valuation of stocks, it is a legal requirement in the UK to absorb overheads associated with bringing the product to its current condition and location. This relates particularly to manufacturing businesses that incur other unit costs in addition to the purchase of raw materials. Stocks should be valued with a fair proportion of business overheads related to the production function, to ensure that 'cost of sales' is accurately matched with revenues earned from customers (the **matching concept**). For financial reporting, distribution and administration expenses must be treated as period costs and charged to the profit and loss account as they are incurred, and so will not be absorbed into stock valuations.

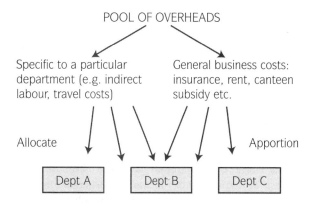

Figure 8.3 *The process of cost absorption*

Overhead costs need to be shared out to the various cost centres on a fair basis (see Figure 8.3). Where costs are known to have been incurred by a specific department (e.g. the wages of its indirect workers) then they should be *allocated* accordingly. If there are costs that cannot be allocated to individual cost centres (e.g. rent that is paid for the whole business), then they should be shared out as fairly as possible. This process is called **cost apportionment** and is based on some appropriate measure of how the cost is incurred, such as floor area or number of employees.

Some costs will relate to service departments that are not directly involved in the production process, although they may provide services to the production departments. Examples include departments for personnel management, stores, plant maintenance, canteen and production planning. Service department costs are then shared out to their internal 'customers' in proportion to the demands for services provided. This process is called **secondary apportionment**.

Having allocated or apportioned all production overheads to the production departments, these costs need to be included in the total costs of the products made. The process of including overhead in product costs is called **overhead absorption**. This is achieved by finding a measure that describes departmental activity, such as labour hours or machine hours. A cost per unit of activity can then be calculated, such as £10 per machine-hour. The amount of departmental activity demanded by a unit of product, say two hours, can then be attributed an overhead cost, in this example £20.

Referring back to the example of Metal Pressings Ltd (Figure 8.2), it has been established that the overheads relate to two production departments, the Press Shop and the Paint Shop. The following additional information is relevant:

	Press Shop	Paint Shop
Floor area (sq. ft)	2 000	3 000
Indirect salaries (£)	30 000	20 000
Machine value (£)	20 000	5 000
Direct hours required:		
Toolbox (hours)	0.5	0.125
Filing cabinet (hours)	3.0	0.25

The indirect salaries can be *allocated* to the respective cost centres, but the other overheads have to be *apportioned* on the basis of a suitable proxy measure of demand. From the information available, 'building' overheads will be apportioned on the basis of floor area and 'machine' overheads on machine value. It is now possible to construct an **overhead analysis schedule** (Figure 8.4).

Overheads are then absorbed into product costs on the basis of an **absorption rate**, based on some measure of departmental activity. Metal Pressings Ltd has decided to calculate a direct labour hour absorption rate (Figure 8.5). From this it can complete the production cost schedule (Figure 8.6).

	Basis	Press Shop (£)	Paint Shop (£)	Total (£)
Allocated				
Indirect wages	Allocation	30 000	20 000	50 000
Apportioned				
Building costs	Floor area	24 000	16 000	40 000
Machine costs	Value	24 000	6 000	30 000
Total overheads		78 000	42 000	120 000

Figure 8.4 *Metal Pressings: overhead analysis schedule*

	Press shop	Paint shop	Total
Total overheads (£)	78 000	42 000	120 000
Direct hours (h)	20 000	2 500	
Rate per hour (£)	3.90	16.80	
Overhead per unit			
Toolbox (£)	1.95	2.10	4.05
Filing cabinet (£)	11.70	4.20	15.90

Figure 8.5 *Metal Pressings: labour hour absorption*

	Boxes Annual (£)	Unit (£)	Cabinets Annual (£)	Unit (£)	Total (£)
Direct labour	20 000	2.00	50 000	10.00	70 000
Direct materials	20 000	2.00	75 000	15.00	95 000
Prime cost	40 000	4.00	125 000	25.00	165 000
Total overheads	40 500	4.05	79 500	15.90	120 000
Total costs	80 500	8.05	204 500	40.90	285 000

Figure 8.6 *Metal Pressings: production cost schedule*

In this example there were few alternatives on which to base the apportionment and absorption calculations. In reality there will be a myriad of possible proxy measures for apportionment, including number of employees, number of stores requisitions, and power demands for machinery.

There are six recognised bases for overhead absorption rate (OAR) calculations:

$$\text{Direct wage OAR} = \frac{\text{Overheads}}{\text{Direct wages}},$$

$$\text{Direct labour hours OAR} = \frac{\text{Overheads}}{\text{Direct labour hours}},$$

$$\text{Machine hours OAR} = \frac{\text{Overheads}}{\text{Machine hours}},$$

$$\text{Direct materials OAR} = \frac{\text{Overheads}}{\text{Direct materials of production}},$$

$$\text{Prime cost OAR} = \frac{\text{Overheads}}{\text{Prime cost of production}},$$

$$\text{Number of units OAR} = \frac{\text{Overheads}}{\text{Number of production units}}.$$

The direct labour hour OAR was the one demonstrated in the example of Metal Pressings. The basic principle in the selection of an absorption base is that it should be a fair measure of activity of the particular department, and it may be that different bases are used for different departments.

It follows, however, that some bases would seem more appropriate than others as a measure of activity. There must be very few instances in which the value of materials being processed has any bearing on the level of overheads, so this rules out the 'direct materials' and 'prime cost' bases for most businesses. Further, a problem with the 'number of units' basis is that units of different product may place different demands on a cost centre. Hence the number of units basis would seem appropriate only where the cost centre processes just one product.

It should be evident that overhead absorption is not an exact science. This might seem rather unsatisfactory because it implies that product costs, which are often perceived as fact, are the result of a rather subjective calculation. However, absorption costing is a realistic attempt at sharing production costs between products, and it is for this reason that the exercise is sometimes extended to consider total business costs. Distribution and administration costs are often absorbed as a percentage of factory cost or of sales value.

Cost behaviour

One failing of the absorption costing process is that it is concerned only with sharing costs between products, as opposed to explaining how costs change with different business scenarios. This is particularly pertinent for decision-making which requires some quantification of cost for alternative courses of action. Another area of cost accounting, often referred to as **marginal costing**, categorises costs according to how they change as business activity changes (see Figure 8.7).

- **Fixed costs** remain unchanged as business activity varies. Examples include property rents and interest payable on loans.
- **Variable costs** change in direct proportion to the level of business activity. Examples include materials used in the manufacture of products, and salesperson's commissions.
- **Semi-variable costs** contain fixed and variable elements. An example is vehicle maintenance costs; some costs such as the MOT certificate are fixed, others (including the replacement of tyres) vary with use.

TASK

A business has two production departments, Drill and Press, and two products, Alpha and Beta. It therefore has two cost centres and two cost units.

The factory budget for October is: rent, £3000; water, light, heat and other energy, £900; indirect labour, £11 500; depreciation of machinery, £4500; building maintenance, £600; salaries for factory management, £9000. Factory management salaries are apportioned according to the direct labour used. The following are the details of each cost centre:

	Drill	Press
Floor area (sq m)	2 000	4 000
Indirect workers (number)	2	5
Value of machinery (£)	50 000	40 000

To produce 50 units of product Alpha requires £15 000 of materials, £5000 of direct labour in the Drill shop, and £6000 of direct labour in the Press shop. To produce 300 units of product Beta requires £9000 of materials, £4000 of direct labour in the Drill shop and £10 000 of direct labour in Press shop.

1. Prepare an overhead analysis schedule for October.

2. Calculate the total production cost.

3. Calculate prime and total cost per unit, for Alpha and for Beta.

- **Stepped costs** are fixed for a range of business volume, but as volume increases there comes a point where the cost jumps to a new level. Supervision wages are an example. Supervisors become ineffective with wide spans of control and so the recruitment of one extra worker may result in the simultaneous need for a further

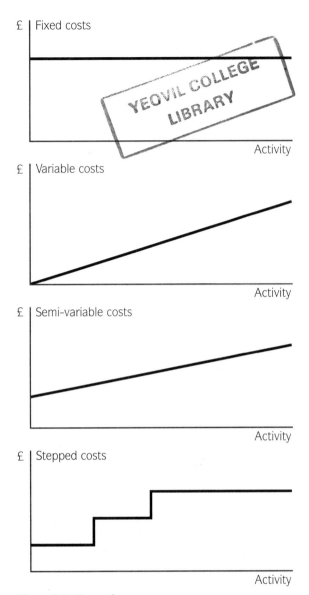

Figure 8.7 *Types of costs*

supervisor. Other examples include the use of assets, from equipment to whole factories. There comes a point where the current business structure is inadequate for greater capacities and investment in new resources becomes necessary.

Care must be taken when classifying costs as fixed or variable. In the long run all costs can be considered to be variable because there is always the possibility of closing down the whole business. However, in the short term, very few costs are actually variable because they become unavoidable, particularly where there is a contractual agreement to incur them. For example, direct labour is a variable cost in the short term only if workers are paid on a piecework basis. Where there is a contractual obligation to pay wages on a time period basis (e.g. an annual salary), wages are a fixed cost in the short term.

For many businesses, it is often impracticable and undesirable to change the size of the workforce in line with fluctuations in work load, even when considering periods running into several months. The need for contracts of employment, and the time taken to train new workers when activity increases again, means that most workforces have to be considered as fixed for at least a few months. Cost analysis will depend on the circumstances, but in the short run perhaps only material usage can be considered a variable cost.

Overheads, while fixed in the short term, are probably step costs in the longer term. As activity increases, the current business set-up becomes inadequate for greater capacities and investment in new business premises and operating plant becomes necessary. It is clear, then, that cost analysis depends upon the timescale being considered; for practical or contractual reasons, this determines how discretionary the costs really are.

Care also has to be exercised to ensure that the analysis between fixed and variable costs is relevant to the context of the business problem. Most analysis of cost behaviour is to understand how costs change as business volumes change. It is therefore important not to confuse variability of cost due to some other factor. For example, a transport business examining the viability of running a bus route should consider costs in relation to the number of passengers on board. The driver's wage is clearly fixed, as indeed are most of the other costs, including petrol. (The argument that petrol varies with the number of miles travelled is not relevant to this situation. The number of miles is fixed because a specific route is being considered.)

Total business costs can be calculated using the two classification methods:

Total cost = Direct costs + Indirect costs,

Total cost = Variable costs + Fixed costs.

Absorption and marginal costing compared

Absorption costing describes whether or not costs can be attributed to a particular product (direct and indirect costs), whereas marginal costing considers how costs vary with the level of production (fixed and variable costs). The two classifications are clearly closely related, because:

- direct costs are generally variable costs
- indirect costs will comprise fixed costs but may also include some variable costs.

However, do not lose sight of the differences between the two classifications. Variable costs (e.g. electricity charges) may not be easily attributed to specific products being produced. Even if each department were separately metered for electricity, numerous products might be worked on in an environment where electricity is being consumed in various ways, including machine power, heating and lighting. It would be difficult and time-consuming to relate expenditure on electricity directly to the specific products being produced.

TASK

For a computer assembly plant that is expecting to increase production during the coming month, the following costs are forecast to be incurred: the wages of piecework assembly workers, inspectors of goods received and items finished, the manager's secretary, a telephone switchboard operator, and a gardener; purchase of visual display units for stock; delivery vehicle running expenses; and advertising.

1. Explain the difference between direct costs and variable costs.

2. Classify each of the costs mentioned above into fixed, variable, semi-variable or stepped.

3. Classify each into direct or indirect.

4. Describe what possible events could change the value of fixed costs and stepped costs for this company.

Volume/profit analysis and the breakeven point

The profitability of a business is highly sensitive to the relationship of fixed costs to total costs. A business with a high proportion of fixed costs will experience relatively large changes in profits when sales revenue varies.

Check your understanding

For a certain firm, a 10 per cent increase in sales results in a 50 per cent increase in profits:

	Month 1		Month 2
Sales	10 000	+10%	11 000
Variable costs	5 000		5 500
Fixed costs	4 000		4 000
Profit	1 000	+50%	1 500

It is clear that an understanding of a business's cost structure is vital for achieving financial objectives. A major objective is usually the attainment of a particular level of profit; but as a minimum, the business will want to protect its survival by achieving the break-even point, where sales revenues equal total costs.

As a first step in breakeven analysis, a useful concept to grasp is that of **contribution**. This is the excess of sales value over variable costs:

Contribution per unit = Sales price – Variable cost.

Contribution is the amount generated to pay for fixed costs. It is now possible to calculate a breakeven point expressed in sales units:

Breakeven point in sales units

$$= \frac{\text{Fixed costs}}{\text{Contribution per unit}}$$

John Newell is preparing a business plan to present to his bank manager to raise finance for a new restaurant. He wants to show how many customers he needs to attract each week to breakeven. Fixed costs are estimated to be £480 a week and a typical meal priced at £12 will incur him in variable costs of £4. So:

Contribution per customer $= £12 - £4 = £8$,

Breakeven point $= \dfrac{£480}{£8}$,

equivalent to 60 customers per week.

Sales value at the breakeven point is the number of customers multiplied by the sales price: $60 \times £12 = £720$.

The level of sales needed to attain a target profit can be calculated using a similar approach. Hence:

Number of sales units $= \dfrac{\text{Fixed cost} + \text{Profit}}{\text{Contribution per unit}}$.

The breakeven point can alternatively be solved using a graphical approach. The first stage is to quantify costs and revenues at different volumes of sales, and then to plot revenue against cost. This has been done for John Newell's restaurant project in Figure 8.8 – fixed cost, total cost and sales revenue have been plotted against business activity, which in this case is numbers of customers. The lines for

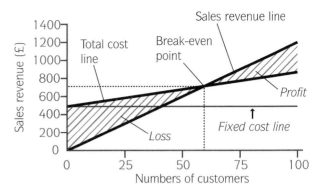

Figure 8.8 *Break-even chart for John Newell's project*

sales revenue and total cost intersect at the breakeven point. The breakeven level of activity can be ascertained from the horizontal axis and the breakeven sales revenue from the vertical axis. Any level of activity to the left of the breakeven point sees the total cost line above the sales revenue line, and the vertical gap between the two lines represents the *loss* made. Conversely, to the right of the breakeven point the gap between the two lines represents a *profit*.

The breakeven point is an operational statistic that non-financial managers can understand and relate to business circumstances. Once established it can be compared with expected volumes to test the viability of a business plan, or compared with actual activity to monitor business performance. The difference between planned or current volumes and the breakeven point represents the **margin of safety**, which can be expressed in percentage terms:

Margin of safety $=$

$\dfrac{\text{Actual volume} - \text{Breakeven volume}}{\text{Breakeven volume}} \times 100\%$.

If John Newell expected 90 customers a week, his margin of safety would be $(90 - 60)/60$, or 50 per cent.

Volume/profit analysis and decision-making

The cost behaviour model demonstrated above for breakeven analysis is to an extent a simplification of how revenues and costs actually change. As examples, costs per unit may vary because of volume discounts for materials, the effects of a learning curve on production times and material wastage, and the fact that some costs behave in a

The Rilton Chamber of Commerce is planning its annual dinner and the event organiser has requested your help in determining, from a financial perspective, the preferred location for the event. Past experience has suggested that £40 per delegate is an acceptable price and an average of 125 places will be taken up from the 200 members. You have been asked to consider the financial implications of between 75 and 175 delegates, in steps of 25. Two venues in Rilton are being considered, one in the north and one in the south of the town. The respective costings are as follows:

	North (£)	South (£)
Hire of room	1 000	1 536
Waiters/waitresses (cost each, with one being required for every 25 delegates)	25	20
Food and wine, per delegate	20	16
Main speaker	500	500
Chamber of Commerce receptionist	50	50
Printing invitations	300	300
Posting invitations (per member organisation)	0.25	0.25

1. Analyse the various items of expenditure into fixed and variable costs.

2. Prepare a breakeven *chart* for 'North', highlighting the breakeven point.

3. *Calculate* the breakeven point for 'South'.

4. Using the chart for 'North' and calculation for 'South', determine each location's profit if there were 175 delegates.

5. Calculate the margin of safety with 125 delegates attending each location.

6. Evaluate the financial implications of the alternative locations.

'stepped' fashion. In addition, the straight line of the revenue curve implies a constant selling price, when in fact lower prices may need to be offered to increase volumes.

However, these factors need to be incorporated if volume/profit analysis is to be relevant to the decision-making process. Volume/profit analysis draws upon marginal costing and on a similar approach to the analysis of sales revenues to consider all factors that affect a change in total sales value and total cost.

For example, if a business can sell 10 units at £100 each or 11 units at £95 each, then the **marginal revenue** for the eleventh unit is just £45 ((11 × £95) – (10 × £100)). If the marginal cost (i.e. the variable cost plus increase in stepped costs) is greater than £45, the business should not strive for the extra sale.

Volume/profit analysis is often applied in the following decision-making situations:

- *To make or to buy?* Should the company manufacture in-house or subcontract a supplier.
- *To terminate a business activity?* A part of the business or a particular product line may be reporting losses under the absorption costing system, but what would be the effect on total business profits of closing the activity? The focus should be on what costs will be saved and what revenues lost as a result of the closure.
- *What selling price is appropriate?*

Relevant costs

If, as a result of a decision, an item of cost will change, then it becomes 'relevant' to evaluating alternative courses of action. It follows that a cost already incurred is not a relevant cost in this sense; a 'sunk cost' is already determined and future decisions cannot change that fact. It is also the case that any 'unavoidable cost', incurred irrespective of the decision to be made, is not a relevant cost.

However, in addition to the change in costs that can be attributed directly to a particular course of action, a benefit that would arise if an alternative were taken is an **opportunity cost**. Because that benefit is forgone it becomes a relevant cost.

Imagine that Jill, an independent trader, has come to the end of another day selling fruit and vegetables at the local market. She purchased 100kg of bananas for £50 and has sold 90kg for a total of £90. The remainder will not keep until next week's market, but a local shop will take them for 25p/kg. She has already agreed to hire a hand trolley for £2 to move any unsold stock. In the final minutes of trading, what is the minimum price she should charge for the remaining 10kg of bananas?

An analysis of Jill's costs needs to identify which are relevant. The price she paid for the bananas is not relevant as it represents a sunk cost. The buying price offered by the local shop *is* relevant as it represents an opportunity cost if the bananas are sold to someone else. The trolley hire is an unavoidable cost (assuming the arrangement cannot be cancelled) and so is not relevant. There are no additional costs to be incurred, so the only cost is the opportunity cost of not selling to the local grocer. Hence the minimum price for customers should be 25p/kg.

The basic principle when using volume/profit analysis is to maximise the contribution from sales. Selling prices higher than the relevant cost provide a contribution towards fixed costs and profit. 'Fixed costs' are not relevant to decision-making, although an increase in 'step costs' may be.

The sales director of a furniture manufacturer is unhappy with their current selling price of £70 per chair. The director has forecast sales volume for a range of selling prices, as follows:

Selling price (£)	55	60	65	70
Volume (units)	5 750	5 250	4 500	3 500

For each chair the business incurs variable costs of £45. Fixed costs are £50 000 per month. On the basis of this information, at what price should the chairs be sold? The approach is to determine first the contribution at each selling price, as in Figure 8.9. This reveals that the sales price of £65 gives the highest contribution so is the desired price on this information (deducting fixed cost to calculate profit would lead to the same conclusion).

	(£)	(£)	(£)	(£)
Selling price	55	60	65	70
Total sales	316 250	315 000	292 500	245 000
Variable cost	258 700	236 250	202 500	157 500
Contribution	57 500	78 750	90 000	87 500

Figure 8.9 *Furniture manufacturer (see text)*

TASK

Jack Caroak forecasts increasing sales volume if he lowers sales price, but there will come a point where he would need to expand his premises if the volume increased above 18 000 units per month. The variable cost is £5 per unit, and projections of monthly activity are as follows:

Selling price	£12	£11	£10	£9
Volume (thousand units/month)	15	18	22	29
Factory expenses (£000)	30	30	35	35

1. What is the term used to describe the cost behaviour of Jack's 'factory expenses'?

2. What is Jack's contribution and net profit at each price level?

3. On the basis of this information, what monthly level of sales should Jack be planning for?

TASK

A factory extension has been started with £25 000 cost incurred to date. Further costs will amount to £100 000. Total future benefits from having the larger factory are now thought to be £100 000 less than the £200 000 originally forecasted. If work is terminated compensation of £20 000 will have to be paid to the builder. State, with reasons, your recommended course of action.

TASK

The SP Distribution Company, with four branches, supplies engineering firms with machine tools and consumable materials. The directors are reviewing the firm's financial results for the previous year.

	Richmond (£000)	Chester (£000)	Nottingham (£000)	Rugby (£000)
Sales	2 100	1 500	1 700	1 200
Cost of sales	1 100	800	950	700
Gross profit	1 000	700	750	500
Administration	500	500	400	300
Distribution	200	250	250	150
Apportionment of HO cost	210	150	170	120
Net profit	90	(200)	(70)	(70)

Head Office overheads are semi-variable, with 50% per cent of its expenses varying with the number of branches serviced. If any of the branches were discontinued, there would be no continuing costs or revenues from that location.

1. On the bases of these results, which of the branches should be closed down?

2. Assuming the branch(es) in (1) had been discontinued at the start of the previous year, what would have been the total company profit for the year?

The pricing decision: full cost pricing or marginal pricing?

The pricing of goods and services is obviously a major policy decision in the context of an overall marketing strategy. Whilst the product cost is clearly an important consideration if the firm is to be profitable, it should be evident from the discussion so far that it is not possible to calculate a definitive cost figure – certainly not one that would be relevant in all circumstances.

Economists draw upon the classical theory of the firm to state that profits will be maximised by producing up to the point where the cost of one additional unit matches the price that can be asked for it; i.e. **marginal cost equals marginal revenue**. The strength of this model is that it takes account of changes in both price and cost as volumes change, but there are problems in applying it in practice.

It assumes perfect knowledge about buyer behaviour and the extent to which this is influenced by price alone, in isolation from other factors such as sales promotion. It also assumes perfect knowledge about the behaviour of business costs, but in reality there are significant problems:

- Costs are either an estimate of amounts that will be incurred, or are based on historical data. They are rarely known on a 'real time' basis.
- The treatment of indirect costs has to be considered (the problems of absorption costing).
- Cost data appear to be 'hard' fact, but they have to be used in the context of an appropriate time frame. This often requires subjective forecast amounts, such as future demand. It is also common for events of one period to influence important variables in another (e.g. price discounts now to gain possible new customers in the future).

Accepting that there are limitations to the information available, the main approaches for determining selling prices from cost information are **full-cost pricing** and **marginal pricing**.

Full-cost pricing

Using the technique of absorption costing, indirect business costs are allocated or apportioned to cost centres and are then absorbed into the product cost. Non-production overheads such as administration and distribution costs are often absorbed as a percentage of the production cost. A selling price is derived by applying a mark-up on cost. For example:

Check your understanding

	(£)
Direct materials	100
Direct labour	50
Direct expenses	10
Prime cost	160
Production overhead absorbed	120
Total production cost	280
Administration and distribution (25% of cost)	70
Total cost	350
Profit (for 10% mark-up)	35
Selling price	385

The arbitrary nature of cost absorption has been described; remember that it is merely a method for sharing costs between products. There is a danger that through inappropriate apportionment and absorption bases, the firm will overstate the cost of some products and understate the cost of others. If this results in prices out of line with competitors', the products that are aggressively priced will sell well but will in reality be unprofitable. The firm could then find itself priced out of the market for its remaining products.

Another problem is the use of an accurate figure for production volumes. The apportionment and absorption calculations are routinely performed on *budgeted* performance; but if future performance is not in line with the budget, the cost per unit will also not be as budgeted. Even assuming no variance on overhead expenditure, the amount of overhead absorbed may be greater or less than actual expenditure.

This can be clarified with an example. XYZ Ltd manufacturers just one product for which it incurs direct costs of £20 per unit and £10 000 per month in respect of overheads. The firm budgets to sell 1000 units per month

with a 10 per cent mark-up. During the month of July the firm actually produced and sold only 800 units. The budget based on 1000 units is thus:

	Budget/unit (£)	Budget total (£)
Direct costs	20	20 000
Overheads	10	10 000
Total cost	30	30 000
Profit (for 10% mark-up)	3	3 000
Selling price	33	33 000

Based on this information the firm sets a selling price of £33 per unit. Then, for July:

July production of 800 units	Actual/unit (£)	Actual total (£)
Direct costs	20.0	16 000
Overheads:		
absorbed	10.0	8 000
under-recovered	2.5	2 000
Total cost	32.5	26 000
Profit	0.5	400
Selling price	33.0	26 400

Because XYZ did not achieve its budgeted output, each unit actually cost an additional £2.50 in overheads that were not planned for when setting the original £33 selling price.

The application of a **mark-up percentage** for profit also requires some care. A standard rate applied across the firm's product range will fail to recognise that individual products or markets may provide opportunities for **price differentiation**. However, recognising this with different product mark-ups seems to be a halfway house between full-cost and a marginal costing approach. It recognises the shortcomings of the full-cost method but fails to allow differentiation using the total contribution to fixed overheads and profit available under marginal pricing (see below).

While for some industries there may be widely accepted profit mark-ups, it is important that they be reviewed in the light of the firm's financial target. If that is expressed as a particular return on capital employed:

Return on capital employed (ROCE)
$$= \frac{\text{Profit}}{\text{Capital employed}} \times 100\%$$

$$= \frac{\text{Mark-up} \times \text{Annual costs}}{\text{Capital employed}} \times 100\%.$$

Therefore:

$$\text{Mark-up} = \frac{\text{Capital employed} \times \text{ROCE}}{\text{Annual costs}}.$$

Check your understanding

A firm utilising financial resources of £300 000 requires a return on capital employed of 15 per cent. To satisfy customer demand, total business costs are forecast to be £500 000. What profit mark-up should be applied to the product cost? The calculation is:

$$\text{Mark up} = \frac{£300\ 000 \times 15\%}{£500\ 000} = 9 \text{ per cent.}$$

Marginal pricing

Marginal pricing applies the principles of profit/volume analysis to the pricing problem. As previously discussed, this emphasises the maximisation of *contribution* to fixed overheads and profit.

Marginal pricing based on 'relevant' future costs allows for flexible pricing on a short-term basis. The technique is not hampered by standard cost rates or profit mark-ups. A sale will add to total profits if the price is in excess of the **marginal cost** (the change in total costs). So lower prices can be justified to fill under-utilised capacity in the short-term.

However, marginal pricing needs to be properly controlled. The technique provides no automatic safeguard when applied to long-run pricing decisions to ensure that the total contribution will be sufficient to cover fixed costs and produce a profit. For this very reason many firms do not encourage the use of marginal pricing even if this precludes its use at appropriate times.

Some businesses incorporate the features of both full-cost pricing and marginal pricing in a structured price list for the long term. Off-peak pricing for leisure and transport services draws on the principles of marginal pricing. The burden for generating a sufficiently high contribution for the firm to be profitable is then transferred to peak times.

Pricing and the product life cycle

Products using new technology can command higher prices. This is most clear in the consumer electronics industry, where premiums are charged for the latest digital video camera and televisions. Early consumers of these products accept that future prices will fall as market acceptance leads to higher sales volumes.

But that pattern is not evident in all industries. In the car industry, prices remain fairly stable over the life of the product, with relatively modest discounting prior to the launch of a replacement model. This is despite the fact that car firms have also incurred significant product development and sales promotion costs early in the product life cycle. Assuming that these different industries (electronics and car) are acting rationally from a commercial perspective, it is clear that if product cost information has a role in pricing, it is being used in a flexible manner.

In Chapter 6, the effect of the product life cycle on operating cash flows was discussed. Cash outflows sustained early in a product's life through high costs and low turnover should be exceeded in future periods by inflows on volume sales. But to what extent will businesses try to recoup high up-front costs with higher prices? Consider a product with a three-year life (Figure 8.10).

	Year 1	Year 2	Year 3	Total
Sales volume (number)	50	200	500	750
	(£000)	(£000)	(£000)	(£000)
Direct cost per unit	10	9	8	
Total direct costs	500	1 800	4 000	6 300
Overheads (incl. R&D and marketing)	1 200	1 000	1 500	3 700
Total cost	1 700	2 800	5 500	10 000
Profit mark-up (10%)	170	280	550	1 000
Total sales value	1 870	3 080	6 050	11 000
Price per unit	37.40	15.40	12.10	14.67

Figure 8.10 *Forecast sales and costs (see text)*

How should this cost schedule be used for pricing purposes? Should a price be charged for each year, ranging from £37.40 to £12.10? Or a standard price of £14.67 over the product's life. Or none of these? (putting aside the further problem of annual demand being directly related to price!).

It becomes a matter of judgement based on knowledge of the market. For the product to earn a 10 per cent mark-up overall, the average price achieved must equate to £14.67; but this cost information poses neither restriction nor gives guidance as to the minimum and maximum prices to be charged. Under normal circumstances, businesses would not normally charge less than variable cost, in this example something over the £8–£10 direct cost per unit. However, even this is not sacrosanct if there is a cohesive strategy to achieve a desired presence in the marketplace. An example is the widely practised policy of connecting households to cable communication networks at less than current cost to achieve a critical share of the home entertainment market.

The important issue is the achievement of some planned average price over the life of the product to give an adequate return on investment. If some customers are willing to pay more than the average, others can be attracted on lower prices.

TASK

Troy Engineering Ltd has incurred expenses of £4000 working to secure its first contract with British Aerospace. The contract will require 5000 hours of direct labour. The salaried shopfloor workers are paid £19 000 for a 1900 hour working year. The materials for the contract have erroneously already been purchased for £30 000. They can be returned to the suppliers for a 10 per cent handling charge. Owing to ferocious competition the managing director is concerned that the contract will not be won and an important opportunity lost to gain a large potential customer. The time has come to quote a price for the contract. Prepare a concise report advising the managing director of the relevant costs for the pricing decision.

Pricing summary

Despite its inherent problems, full-cost pricing is widely practised. For jobbing industries such as construction and car repairs, where each job is unique, the technique allows senior management to delegate the detailed pricing of individual jobs according to prescribed cost rates and profit mark-ups. It also forms a convenient basis for pricing late changes to product specifications, a common feature in the defence industry. However, a business that can augment long-term full-cost pricing with the flexibility offered by marginal pricing is likely to better achieve its marketing and financial objectives.

BUDGETS

A budget is a set of financial parameters against which actual performance will be compared. Budgets differ from forecasts in that they require regular management action to control, say departmental expenditure, within the budget constraint. The budgetary control system is therefore a management control mechanism for highlighting variations and a valuable tool for active management (see Figure 8.11).

The budgeting process results in separate 'budgets' for each area of business activity. The money values used in the budgets are often underpinned with quantities (units, weights and other measures) to ensure consistency across the various functions. They also provide some relevance to operational activity and so facilitate subsequent monitoring of a function's performance (see Figure 8.12). The exact nature of functional (subsidiary) budgets will depend on the organisation's structure and the operational processes of the business. It is, however, usual for each budget to be analysed by a time period, such as by week or by month.

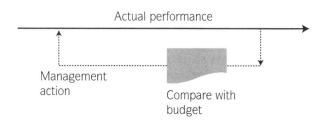

Figure 8.11 *The budget: a closed-loop control system*

Departmental budget (£000)

	Total	Jan	Feb	Mar	Apr	May	Jun	Jul	Aug	Sep	Oct	Nov	Dec
Salaries	127.0	10.0	10.0	10.0	10.0	10.0	10.0	11.0	11.0	11.0	11.0	11.0	12.0
Travel	37.0	1.5	1.5	2.0	2.0	3.0	5.0	4.0	4.0	6.0	4.0	2.5	1.5
Stationery	34.0	2.0	2.0	2.0	2.0	2.5	2.5	2.5	2.5	2.5	2.5	8.0	3.0

Monthly expenses report (£000)

	June			Year to date		
	Actual	Budget	Variance	Actual	Budget	Variance
Salaries	10.2	10.0	(0.2)	61.8	60.0	(1.8)
Travel	4.1	5.0	0.9	14.5	15.0	0.5
Stationery	1.9	2.5	0.6	12.9	13.0	0.1

Figure 8.12 *Budgetary control*

For control purposes, it is important that individual managers be held accountable for specific parts of the budget. However, it must be recognised that the ability to control financial transactions will depend on the amount of discretion delegated to various levels of the organisational structure. Can a particular manager, for example, affect the incidence of a specific cost such as wages paid to employees? This will depend partly on the manager's position in the organisational hierarchy. Some costs may be in the control of one manager but not his or her subordinate. For example, there may be a company policy for salary reviews that has been decided at board level. It is wrong and demotivating for individuals to be held accountable for costs over which they have no control. It is not unusual, when presenting reports monitoring past performance, to distinguish between costs that are controllable and those that are not.

Objectives of budgeting

Budgets provide numerous advantages, not least of which is the opportunity to examine and restate organisational objectives. Budget setting is a planning process that explains how the business is going to achieve a financial target. It is better to recognise that current strategies will fail to deliver target outcomes on paper, and before the budget period starts, rather than in actuality.

The examination of objectives and strategies requires a time horizon extending past the current financial year, and this helps management focus on issues beyond current day-to-day concerns. It also provides a framework on which short-term budgets can be formulated consistently. The objectives of departments and individuals are therefore consistent with those of the organisation as a whole. This provides greater coordination and allows managers to plan to achieve a common goal. For example, if the sales budget assumes an increase in volumes, the production department is made formally aware of the need to plan for higher production. It follows that senior management will have to authorise a production budget that allows for any necessary increase in financial resources.

The budget is also an important component of the communication system. Employees are made aware of company and departmental objectives and of their contribution towards them. It is also true that a budget integrated with the whole management process becomes of more value to external parties who require confidence in the on-going progress of the business. For example, it can become an important part of a business plan for seeking external funding, or it can provide an informed basis for making statements to shareholders, such as 'it is our intention to raise profits by 15 per cent per annum'.

As a tool for 'management by exception', the budget's role is not in doubt. Reporting on the comparison of actual and budgeted performance focuses management on the significant variances and acts as a catalyst for remedial action if necessary.

To attain its objectives, the budget exercise needs to be set in the context of long-term objectives and strategies that have been formulated by the highest level of management. Environmental factors need to be identified, including economic, social, technological and regulatory. Current and forecast market conditions concerning sales, supplies, labour and finance should be analysed for their implications on the business. It is important to recognise any limiting factor on business development, including sales demand and availability of factors of production.

To have the desired motivating effect on individuals in the organisation, it is necessary that as many people as possible are involved in the budgeting process to foster a sense of ownership. Departmental or team budgets need to be viewed as being attainable; to maximise actual performance they must be neither too difficult nor too easy. If the budget is merely a 'wish list' by senior management, at best the exercise becomes a waste of time, at worst the budget is misleading and fails to deliver its stated objectives.

Budget models are often constructed with specialist modelling programs or PC spreadsheets that provide decision-makers with valuable 'What-if?' tools. The effects of decisions are quickly simulated by a structure of functional interrelationships. For example, the effect on cash flow and profit of reducing the sales price by 5 per cent and increasing volumes by 10 per cent can be viewed in a matter of seconds, despite the need for perhaps thousands of recalculations in the business model. The logic expressed by budget models also helps managers understand the reasons for the incidence of cost and how different functions interact.

As already stated, one of the objectives of the budgeting exercise is to provide a formal framework on which the various functions of the business can coordinate their activities. During budget preparation it will be necessary to ensure that the budgets for each of the functions in the organisation are consistent with one another on a period-by-period basis. At this stage a 'limiting factor' or factors will be identified that will restrict business volume. This may be lack of skilled workers, machine capacity or the funding to finance working capital. For many businesses the limiting factor will be the level of sales. Where possible the effects of the limiting factor should be minimised by careful planning. For example, if a manufacturer of non-perishable goods identifies that production cannot keep up with sales during a particular month, it will be necessary to build up stocks during the preceding months.

Check your understanding

A manufacturer of souvenir mugs has a production capacity of 2000 mugs a month and aims to maintain a minimum stock of 500 mugs at any time. Sales of mugs are forecast to be 1000 in both March and April, 1500 in May, 2000 in June and 3000 in July. A production budget is needed to cover the five-month period.

The problem is that July will experience sales that are 1000 mugs in excess of production capacity. By working back from July it is possible to find the nearest months that will have sufficient excess production capacity to build up stocks in readiness for the July sales:

	March	April	May	June	July
Stock b/f	500	500	1 000	1 500	1 500
Production	1 000	1 500	2 000	2 000	2 000
Sales	1 000	1 000	1 500	2 000	3 000
Stock c/f	500	1 000	1 500	1 500	500

In June, maximum production is matched by sales, so April and May are the latest months available that can contribute towards a build-up in stocks before the July peak period. To increase stocks in March would increase unnecessarily the period of investment in higher stocks.

TASK

A manufacturer of T-shirts has a production capacity of 5000 a month and aims to maintain a minimum stock of 1000 at any time. Sales of T-shirts are forecast to be 2000 in both March and April, 4000 in May, 6000 in June and 8000 in July. Prepare the production budget to cover the five-month period from March to July.

Flexible budgeting

For control purposes, the original budget may need some adjustment in the light of actual business performance. If the sales force failed to achieve prices and volumes outlined in the budget, then the managers responsible would be required to provide senior management with satisfactory explanations. However, there could almost certainly be implications for other departments as well. A sales volume variance might result in other departments under- or over-spending on their budgets. For example, if the factory has to produce 20 per cent more to satisfy booming demand, other things being equal, production costs will increase. It would not be equitable to expect factory management to produce more without allowing them to use more resources. Therefore there is a need to 'flex' the budget.

Because not all costs rise in line with business activity, each cost item should be examined to discover its behaviour in relation to changed activity. Variable costs should be revised in line with activity; fixed cost should not vary; semi-variable costs will include features of both fixed and variable costs; and stepped costs may vary by more or less than the change in the level of activity.

For example, Figure 8.13 shows an extract from the annual budget for a bus company. Subsequent to setting the original budget, the company has increased the number of routes it operates, resulting in a 20 per cent increase in the number of miles being travelled. Variable costs such as diesel are changed in proportion to the number of miles travelled. Semi-variable costs have a fixed element of expenditure, so this part is not flexed. Depreciation is a book-keeping entry that will probably have been calculated on a time-based method, so the charge is fixed in the accounts irrespective of the number of miles travelled.

	Type of cost	Original budget (£)	Flexed budget (£)	Change %
Depreciation of vehicles	Fixed	50 000	50 000	0.0
Maintenance	Semi-variable (50/50)	25 000	27 500	10.0
Diesel	Variable	50 000	60 000	20.0
		125 000	137 500	10.0

Figure 8.13 *Bus company budget (see text)*

TASK

The following budget data for April 2002 relates to Brampton Tools Ltd, a manufacturer of machine tools.

	Budget (% of capacity)			Actual
	At 80% (£)	At 90% (£)	At 100% (£)	(£)
Direct materials	28 000	31 500	35 000	24 250
Direct labour	39 200	44 100	49 000	35 400
Rent	10 000	10 000	10 000	10 000
Electricity	3 400	3 650	3 900	3 450
Factory supervision	18 000	19 000	20 000	17 500
Administration	37 000	40 000	43 000	35 400
Selling/distribution	23 300	25 000	26 700	21 000
Total cost	158 900	173 250	187 600	147 000

The original budget was constructed on the assumption that business activity would be 90 per cent of factory capacity. This equated to 12 600 standard units of work and would produce a 20 per cent margin. An analysis of costs was undertaken at the time the budget was prepared and this was used to produce indicative amounts if output deviated by 10 per cent of total capacity. Actual production at 70 per cent capacity fell outside the expected range but budget selling price was achieved.

1. Produce a profit statement with columns for actual performance, original budget, flexed budget, and variance from flexed budget.

2. Comment on the results.

Contents of the budget

The 'budget pack' for most firms will be a set of schedules culminating in a 'master budget', comprising a budget profit and loss account, budget balance sheet and budget cash flow statement. The supporting schedules will provide analysis in volume and money terms of sales, production and stock levels. In addition there will be detailed statements of the make-up of debtor and creditor balances and of departmental expense budgets.

TASK

The cash flow forecast was introduced in Chapter 6 and here is an opportunity to practise its preparation.

Jack Stanton owns a small building firm, working mainly on house extensions and repairs. He employs four workers, each paid an average £6.00 an hour. They work for a basic 162.5 hour calendar month which equates to 7.5 hours a day. Where necessary he pays overtime at time and a half. Jack estimates that work measured in labour hours for the next 12 months together with related material costs will be:

Year 2000	Jul	Aug	Sep	Oct	Nov	Dec
Hours	900	850	900	800	600	300
Materials (£)	4000	4000	4000	3500	2500	1000

Year 2001	Jan	Feb	Mar	Apr	May	Jun
Hours	250	300	400	500	600	800
Materials (£)	1000	1500	2000	2500	2500	4000

He has agreed the following total number of holidays with his workers, including his own:

	Jul	Aug	Sep	Oct	Nov	Dec
Holidays	10	10	10	15	5	35

	Jan	Feb	Mar	Apr	May	Jun
	12	5	5	8	5	5

Jack takes £2000 out of the business each month and works a basic 37.5 hours a week on productive work. Running costs every month amount to £900 for his yard, and £500 for a van and various items of small plant. Hire of specialist equipment will incur him in about £1 of charges for every productive labour hour.

Building jobs are quoted at £15 per man-hour plus materials cost. There are no partly completed jobs at the end of each month and customers pay in the month following work completion. Jack believes in paying for all costs in the month in which they are incurred. On 30 June 2000 there was £250 in the business bank account and customers owed £16 000 for work completed in June 2000.

In February 2001 Jack plans to purchase a new van for £10 000 and a concrete mixer in May 2001 for £1800.

1. Prepare a 12-month cash flow budget for Stanton & Co from 1 July 2000 to 30 June 2001 (round all figures to whole pounds).

2. Comment on the pattern of cash flow for the firm and establish reasons for it.

3. Recommend ways in which the cash deficit could be financed, assuming similar trading activity in future years.

4. How could the firm's cash position be improved without resorting to additional finance?

INVESTMENT AND PROJECT APPRAISAL

Before investing in a new project, such as an item of capital expenditure or the development of a product, the project should be appraised to ensure it contributes towards the financial objectives of the business. This requires a quantification of the costs and benefits concerned. Benefits may include an increase in sales, improved labour productivity or reduced material wastage. Costs typically include investment in fixed assets and increased working capital.

Unfortunately many of the costs and benefits are qualitative by nature; for example, assessing the commercial benefit of a refurbished social clubhouse for employees. However, the process of appraisal is a valuable exercise and provides some rigour to an area that can easily be subject to the whim of individual managers.

Wherever possible the assumptions used in justifying a project should be measurable, so that as the project progresses it can be established whether the project has met initial expectations. This may seem academic for a completed project, but the discipline instilled by a post-investment monitoring system ensures that assumptions made by managers are reasonable, and the feedback from completed projects will help refine the appraisal process for new projects.

A feature of many investment programmes is the need to make an initial outlay, but with benefits received in a number of future years. In some cases there may even be significant costs at the end of the project, such as the decommissioning of a power station. The flow of cash over a number of years has implications for the cost of funding the project. The more complex appraisal techniques will consider the time value of money and allow a comparison of project returns against the finance charges likely to accrue.

Where funds are scarce and there are a number of projects that provide a return in excess of the cost of finance, the task of appraisal is to prioritise competing projects. The true cost of pursuing one project is the opportunity cost of not being able to fulfil the highest rated alternative. The comparison of competing projects against each other and against the business's cost of finance also requires consideration of financial risk; some projects will be required to return a risk premium.

Business X has the opportunity to invest in two projects, although owing to a shortage of funds it will be able to proceed with only one of them. Cost of finance is 10 per cent per annum, and at the end of the projects the investment in fixed assets will have no residual value.

Year	Project 1 cash flow (£)	Project 2 cash flow (£)
0 (Present) Investment in fixed assets	(30 000)	(30 000)
1	12 000	10 000
2	12 000	10 000
3	12 000	10 000
4		10 000

Figure 8.14 *Business X*

The main appraisal techniques will be illustrated using the project data given in Figure 8.14.

Accounting rate of return

Business performance is measured by its return on capital employed, so it is entirely consistent to appraise proposed projects on the same basis. The **accounting rate of return** (ARR) compares profits (calculated according to the accounting policies of the business) with the capital invested in the project. So:

Accounting rate of return

$$= \frac{\text{Average annual profits}}{\text{Average capital employed}} \times 100\%.$$

The project with the highest ARR is the preferred project. Project rates of return are compared with the business's cost of capital and the opportunity cost of having to forgo other investment opportunities.

Note that the ARR calculation requires a figure for average annual profits, whereas the data for Business X are presented in the form of cash flow. The fixed assets need to be depreciated over the lives of the projects to arrive at annual profit. So, for project 1:

Depreciation per annum $= £30\,000/3 = £10\,000$

Profit per annum $= £12\,000 - £10\,000 = £2\,000$.

Average capital employed is calculated by taking a simple average between the capital invested at the start of the project and the balance at the end of the project (nil residue value in this case). For project 1:

Average capital employed = £30 000/2 = £15 000,

Accounting rate of return

$$= \frac{£2000}{£15\,000} \times 100\% = 13.3 \text{ per cent.}$$

TASK

Calculate the ARR for project 2.

Payback period

The payback period is the time required for a project to repay the initial investment. The calculation is based on cash flows and not on profits. The annual cash flows are cumulated and the payback period is reached when the cumulative cash flow reaches zero.

For project 1 in Figure 8.14, the cumulative cash flow schedule is:

Year 1: − £18 000
Year 2: − £6000
Year 3: + £6000

So payback is reached between the end of year 2 and the end of year 3. The calculation is:

Payback period

= Years with negative cumulative cash flow

$$+ \frac{\text{Deficit remaining}}{\text{Cash flow in relevant year}} \times 12 \text{ months.}$$

The payback period for project 1 is 2 years + 12 months × £6000/£12 000, or 2 years and 6 months. The project with the shortest payback period is to be preferred as prolonged periods increase the risk of unforeseen circumstances arising.

TASK

Calculate the payback period for project 2.

Although the payback period gives some indication of the timing of cash flows, it does not consider the pattern within the payback period. Even more importantly, the calculation ignores completely the cash flows after the payback period and so provides no information on the profitability of a project. Despite these significant shortcomings, the technique is widely used because it is the simplest of the appraisal techniques to calculate and to evaluate. As part of a more sophisticated appraisal system, it is often used as a secondary measure to one of the other techniques.

Net present values

The main problem with the appraisal techniques described so far is that they fail to account fully for the timing of cash flows. Instinctively it is known that £1 in the hand today is worth more than being promised £1 on some future date. This is because there is a **time value of money** that allows for:

- the risk that unforeseen circumstances will prevent receipt of the amount expected
- inflation that will lower the real value of money
- an opportunity cost in forgoing a financial return on an alternative investment.

The time value of money is often represented by a composite annual percentage rate. For example, bank deposit rates include amounts to cover the elements described above.

The time value of money is considered by appraisal techniques that discount project cash flows. Consider a sum of £100 that is invested in a savings account that provides annual interest at 10 per cent. Assuming that the interest is left in the account at the end of each year, the savings account balance for the next four years will be:

Year	Interest (£)	Balance (£)
0		100.00
1	10.00	110.00
2	11.00	121.00
3	12.10	133.10
4	13.31	146.41

So, using an interest rate of 10 per cent, £100 is today worth the same as £110.00 will be in one years' time, £121.00 in two years, and so on. Conversely, £110.00 in one year's time will be worth £100.00 today, and £121.00 in two years' time will also be worth £100.00 today. It can also be said that £133.10 in three years' time will have the same value as £146.41 in four years' time. This can be demonstrated by restating the values in today's money; i.e. they are both worth £100 today invested at 10 per cent a year.

The technique of **discounting** future cash flows provides a valuable tool for valuing receipts and payments that occur at different times over the life of a project. By reducing all future cash flows to a common measure, comparisons can be made between projects. The total of all cash flows restated in today's money terms is called the **net present value** (NPV).

Unlike the accounting rate of return which is based on profits, NPV is based on actual cash flows. These will include:

Inflows:
- sales revenues phased for when they will actually be received
- sale proceeds from the disposal of fixed assets at the project's conclusion
- release at the end of the project of amounts invested in stocks
- government grants

Outflows
- investment in fixed assets
- creation of a working stock balance
- operating costs including material, labour and expenses
- tax payments.

The NPV of a future amount of cash is found by multiplying it by a **discount factor**. The size of the factor depends on the discount rate used and the number of years involved. The easiest way of finding a discount factor is to look it up in an NPV table (see Figure 8.15). For example, cash in four years time discounted at 10 per cent should be multiplied by a factor of 0.6830.

Years	Interest rate					
	5%	6%	7%	8%	9%	10%
1	0.9524	0.9434	0.9346	0.9259	0.9174	0.9091
2	0.9070	0.8900	0.8734	0.8573	0.8417	0.8264
3	0.8636	0.8396	0.8163	0.7938	0.7722	0.7513
4	0.8227	0.7921	0.7629	0.7350	0.7084	0.6830
5	0.7835	0.7473	0.7130	0.6806	0.6499	0.6209
6	0.7462	0.7050	0.6663	0.6302	0.5963	0.5645
7	0.7107	0.6651	0.6227	0.5835	0.5470	0.5132
8	0.6768	0.6274	0.5820	0.5403	0.5019	0.4665
9	0.6446	0.5919	0.5439	0.5002	0.4604	0.4241

Years	Interest rate					
	11%	12%	13%	14%	15%	20%
1	0.9009	0.8929	0.8850	0.8772	0.8696	0.8333
2	0.8116	0.7972	0.7831	0.7695	0.7561	0.6944
3	0.7312	0.7118	0.6931	0.6750	0.6575	0.5787
4	0.6587	0.6355	0.6133	0.5921	0.5718	0.4823
5	0.5935	0.5674	0.5428	0.5194	0.4972	0.4019
6	0.5346	0.5066	0.4803	0.4556	0.4323	0.3349
7	0.4817	0.4523	0.4251	0.3996	0.3759	0.2791
8	0.4339	0.4039	0.3762	0.3506	0.3269	0.2326
9	0.3909	0.3606	0.3329	0.3075	0.2843	0.1938

Figure 8.15 *Present value of 1.0000 at compound interest*

The discount factor can be calculated using a simple formula:

$$\text{NPV discount factor} = \frac{1}{(1 + r)n}$$

where *r* is the discount rate (a percentage must be converted to a decimal) and *n* is the number of years. For example, for cash received in four years' time to be discounted at 10 per cent (=0.1):

$$\text{NPV discount factor} = \frac{1}{(1 + 0.1)^4} = 0.6830.$$

Unfortunately, most cash flows do not occur precisely on the anniversary of the start of the project. For example, sales and operating costs arise continuously throughout the year. However, whilst there may be instances when precise timing is necessary, in practice the recognition of annual intervals is often adequate. Hence cash flows occurring during a particular year will be discounted assuming they arise at the end of the year.

Illustration using project 1 for Business X (Figure 8.14)

Year	Cash flow (£)	10% Discount factor	Net present value (£)
0 (Present)			
Investment in fixed assets	(30 000)	1.0000	(30 000)
1	12 000	0.9091	10 908
2	12 000	0.8264	9 917
3	12 000	0.7513	9 016
Total	6 000		(159)

The net present value is a negative £159, so the project fails to provide the 10 per cent return on funds invested despite making a total accounting profit of £6000.

TASK

Calculate the NPV for project 2.

Projects with positive net present values are providing financial returns in excess of the cost of capital. Negative net present values highlight projects that fail to provide adequate financial returns and should be discarded. Where a choice has to be made between projects competing for limited finance, the projects with the highest net present value should be given priority.

For project 1 and project 2, the following financial measures have been established:

	Project 1	Project 2
Accounting rate of return (%)	13.3	16.7
Payback (years)	2.5	3.0
Net present value (£)	(159)	1698

Although project 1 has the shortest payback period, it has the lower ARR and a negative NPV. Clearly project 2 is the preferred one.

Appraisal by net present values is the most comprehensive technique for project appraisal as it considers:

- all cash flows to the forecasting horizon
- the timing of cash flows
- the cost of capital.

In practice, however, the technique has its disadvantages. In addition to the difficulty of forecasting future cash flows, there is the difficulty of establishing an appropriate discounting rate. This is important because the net present value of a cash flow is highly sensitive to the discounting rate used.

Changes in the value of money (through inflation) have been a feature of most economies in recent years. Whilst the western world experienced relatively stable prices during the 1980s and 90s, the compound effect of even single-digit inflation can influence discounted cash flows significantly. There are two generally accepted methods for discounting cash flows during periods of changing prices:

- cash flows should be measured in money terms and discounted using the nominal cost of capital; or
- cash flows should be measured in real terms only and should be discounted at the real cost of capital.

Consider an example. MarCo is in the process of reviewing a project that requires an initial investment of £40 000 and, assuming no inflation, will generate stable net cash flows of £20 000 per annum for the next three years. However, annual inflation of 5 per cent is expected and this is reflected in the firm's cost of capital of 15 per cent. We can calculate the NPV of the project in real terms and in money terms. The firm's real cost of capital is:

$$\frac{1 + \text{Money cost of capital}}{1 + \text{inflation rate}} - 1$$

$$= \frac{1.15}{1.05} - 1 = 0.09524 \ (9.524 \text{ per cent}).$$

Considering the cash flow before inflation, we have:

Year	Cash flow before inflation (£)	Discount factor @ 9.524%	Present value (£)
0	(40 000)	1.0000	(40 000)
1	20 000	0.9131	18 262
2	20 000	0.8336	16 672
3	20 000	0.7612	15 224
NPV			10 158

After inflation of 5 per cent a year, this becomes:

Year	Cash flow before inflation (£)	Discount factor @ 15%	Present value (£)
0	(40 000)	1.0000	(40 000)
1	21 000	0.8696	18 262
2	22 050	0.7561	16 672
3	23 153	0.6575	15 224
NPV			10 158

Where cash flows experience the same rate of inflation, as here, the two approaches produce identical net present values. Otherwise, the 'money terms' approach will produce a more accurate outcome as the inflation rates of individual items can be properly accounted for.

Internal rate of return

The **internal rate of return** (IRR) is the discount rate required to give a *nil* net present value; that is, it expresses the true financial return on the capital invested. To obtain this rate, many financial analysts use spreadsheets which provide a built-in function to calculate the IRR from a range of annual cash flows. For example, in Excel the function is $=$IRR (range of values, discount rate).

Alternatively, an estimation of the IRR can be found by calculating the NPV of a project using two different discounting rates and by assuming that there is a straight-line relationship between the discounting rate and the NPV. Use one discounting rate that produces a small positive NPV and another giving a small negative NPV, and then extrapolate between them. Using project 2 data above, discounting rates of 10 and 15 per cent produce NPVs at the end of year 4 of £1698 and −£1450 respectively (check the calculations yourself), so clearly the IRR falls between 10 and 15 per cent. A gradient can be determined recognising there has been a £3,148 (£1,698 + £1,450) change in NPV with a change of 5 per cent in the discounting rate. So:

$$\text{IRR} = 10\% + \frac{1698}{3148} \times 5\%$$

$$= 12.7 \text{ per cent.}$$

Using a discounting rate of 12.7 per cent in fact produces an NPV of −£150. This results from the fact that the IRR line is a curve, not a straight line. The small error is unlikely to be vital in practice, although a more accurate IRR figure could be found by performing the exercise again with two discount rates closer to the IRR, say 12 and 13 per cent.

Rate of return measures, including IRR and ARR, need to be used with care. Their advantage of summarising complex cash flows with a single statistic is also the cause of a major weakness. Percentage returns are easily understood but they fail to recognise the absolute values being generated. For example, 12 per cent of £10 000 is greater than 20 per cent of £5000. This is particularly relevant to mutually exclusive projects that require substantially different amounts of capital to finance them.

TASK

TE Associates has £50 000 of excess funds which can be invested in one of two projects that have the following forecast cashflows:

Year	Project A (£)	Project B (£)
0	(20 000)	(50 000)
1	10 000	12 000
2	8 000	12 000
3	8 000	15 000
4	4 000	20 000
5	2 000	24 000

1. Calculate the payback period for each project.

2. Calculate net present values based on a 12 per cent discount rate.

3. Calculate an internal rate of return for each project.

4. Advise the firm on its best course of action, explaining any assumptions you have made.

TASK

Many businesses have the option to either *lease* or *purchase* plant and motor vehicles, and the situation provides a classic example of the application of the NPV technique. Consider the following figures concerning a motor car investment being appraised by a business with a 15 per cent cost of capital:

- *Purchasing*. The car can be purchased outright for £15 000. Annual maintenance costs over the following four years are estimated to be £300, £400, £500 and £800. After four years the car will have a resale value of £4000.
- *Leasing*. An operating lease for the same car incurs annual rentals of £5000, inclusive of maintenance costs.

1. Calculate the NPV for the purchasing and leasing options.

2. Advise, from a financial perspective, the preferred course of action.

TASK

XB Transmissions Plc designs and builds advanced gearshift assemblies for the automotive industry. It has a wealth of intellectual property rights concerning its unique technology, and undertakes customer projects to apply that technology to specific car models. The applied development for product and process design, partly funded by the car manufacturer, is an up-front cost to secure the eventual manufacturing contract.

The company has been approached by ToyCar, a leading manufacturer, for an automatic gearshift to fit its adapted manual gearbox. They require 20 000 gearshifts each year at a fixed price for two years of £200 per unit. Thereafter ToyCar expects the price to fall by 10 per cent a year.

The engineering manager estimates development will take one year and will cost: salaries £800 000 and prototype materials £700 000. XB's Feasibility Committee, which reviews all new projects, forecasts another year to develop and build the production line at a cost of £1 100 000. It estimates a unit production cost of £150 in the first year, with 5 per cent efficiency savings to accrue each subsequent year. With rapid technological changes with this new product, it is likely the company will incur a further £200 000 in engineering changes during the third year of production (fifth year of the project).

At the present time the company does have the engineering capacity to complete the project, but another manufacturer has made enquiries for engineering work it wishes to subcontract out. XB's salary cost of £800 000 would be charged out for £1 800 000. The company incurs a cost of capital of 12 per cent and routinely assumes a six-year product life cycle (eight years from start of design).

1. Calculate for the ToyCar project: (a) the payback period; (b) net present value.

2. Calculate the project's IRR.

3. Evaluate the financial performance of the project and advise XB's management on the course of action to take

SUMMARY

This chapter has examined the role of cost and management accounting in the decision-making process.

Absorption costing identifies two cost concepts – cost units and cost centres. Costs that can be related to specific cost units are called 'direct costs', while other costs are categorised as 'indirect costs' that are either allocated or apportioned to cost centres. Cost-centre costs are absorbed into unit costs using absorption rates based on some measure of cost-centre activity. Volume/profit analysis uses the concepts of marginal costing to understand the implications of cost behaviour for making decisions. The analysis between variable and fixed costs depends crucially on the timescales being considered.

Budgeting is a formal plan that facilitates a structured process to short- and medium-term decision-making. The monitoring of actual performance against budget is an instigator for management action where appropriate.

Investment appraisal uses one or more techniques to ensure that proposed projects meet the organisation's financial objectives. The more sophisticated techniques use discounted cash flows to consider the time value of money, whereas accounting rate of return and payback have the advantage of relative simplicity.

Unlike financial reporting which has to comply with regulations concerning format and timing, information for management decisions is designed to enable the business to achieve its objectives.

FURTHER READING

Davies, David, *The Art of Managing Finance*, McGraw-Hill, 1997.

Atrill, P., Harvey, D., and McLaney, E., *Accounting for Business*, Butterworth Heinemann, 1994.

Smith, Malcolm, *Strategic Management Accounting: Texts and Cases*, Butterworth Heinemann, 1997.

Drury, Colin, *Management Accounting Handbook*, Butterworth Heinemann, 1994.

Wilson, R., *Accounting for Marketing*, CIMA/Academic Press, 1999.

Northcott, D., *Capital Investment Decision-Making*, CIMA/Academic Press.

Watts, John, *Accounting in the Business Environment*, Pitman Publishing, 1996.

ASSIGNMENT

Quadstar Plc, a retailer of women's fashion clothing and accessories, employ you as a project accountant. The company floated on the stock exchange three years ago and promised investors steady growth as it pursued new markets abroad. Financial turmoil in the Far East and sluggish demand at home have hampered progress, although the firm's designers continue to produce distinctive and innovative styles that are regularly illustrated in the fashion media.

The company subcontracts the manufacture of its product to a number of firms, including Denham Fabrics Plc and Fosters Plc. Both companies are listed on the stock exchange and their shares have languished on a low rating along with the textiles sector in general. The current share prices are 12p for Denham and 40p for Fosters.

In view of the industry over-capacity, Denham has recently closed a factory in France and has withdrawn from supplying the French market altogether. The termination resulted in closure costs including redundancy payments, but fortunately the factory was sold to a property developer and the proceeds covered the net book value of the respective buildings and plant.

Study the extracts from the two companies' recently published financial results given in Figures A.1 and A.2.

		Denham (£m)		Fosters (£m)
Turnover:		80.5		75.4
Continuing operations	70.5		75.4	
Discontinued operations	10.0		0.0	
Operating profit:				
Continuing operations	7.3		6.5	
Discontinued operations	(1.8)	5.5	0.0	6.5
Exceptional items		(2.2)		0.0
Profit before interest		3.3		6.5
Interest payable		0.0		1.5
Profit before taxation		3.3		5.0
Taxation		1.1		1.3
Profit after taxation		2.2		3.7
Dividends		1.0		0.7
Retained profits		1.2		3.0

Figure A.1 *Operating results*

	Denham (£m)	Fosters (£m)
Fixed assets:		
Property	60.0	30.0
Machinery	45.5	25.0
Current assets	57.4	72.3
Creditors due within one year:		
Trade creditors	(25.8)	(23.3)
Bank overdrafts	0.0	(12.1)
Creditors due after one year:		
Loan stock	0.0	(20.0)
Net assets	137.1	71.9
Shareholders funds:		
Share capital	15.0	10.0
Share premium account	57.1	25.3
Revaluation reserve	30.0	0.0
Profit and loss account	35.0	36.6
	137.1	71.9
Number of shares issued (millions)	150	40

Figure A.2 *Balance sheet information*

The accounting principles of the two companies are similar except in respect of fixed assets. Denham has recently revalued its property in line with market prices and this has increased the depreciation charge to the profit and loss account by £2 million for the year. Fosters values its property at historical cost.

Task 1

1. Restate Denham's operating profit and capital employed using Fosters' accounting policy in respect of fixed assets.

2. Calculate the following ratios for the two companies (using the restated figures for Denham): (a) return on capital employed; (b) profit margin; (c) current ratio; (d) gearing ratio; (e) interest cover; (f) dividend yield; (g) earnings per share; (h) price earnings.

3. Describe the relative financial performance and capital structure of the two companies from the perspective of a potential investor.

Managing financial resources

The directors of Quadstar are interested in purchasing Denham to gain greater control over the supply side of the business. They have taken the view that the company has the potential to grow to meet Quadstar's long-term needs, although there may have to be continuing investment to increase capacity and efficiency. The company's financial advisors have suggested a cash bid price of 16p for each share in Denham Fabrics Plc.

The estimated cash flow savings which are currently paid to outside suppliers would be £85 million in the first year, increasing by 10 per cent a year in line with anticipated growth in retail sales. The enlarged group would incur additional operating costs of £78 million per annum which would increase by 5 per cent a year as output increased. The assumed efficiency savings would require expenditure on new fixed assets of £5 million every year.

Quadstar currently has shareholder funds of £210 million, on which the company is expected to earn 15% a year before tax. The only debt outstanding relates to a 9 per cent loan stock issue that raised £42 million. Any acquisition by the company would be funded in such a way as to maintain the same gearing and average cost of capital.

Task 2

1. Calculate Quadstar's weighted average cost of capital (before tax).

2. Calculate the net present value for the proposal to acquire Denham Fabrics Plc based on cash flows over the first five years.

3. From a purely financial perspective, advise Quadstar's directors regarding the purchase of Denham.

4. Assuming an offer were made and accepted, how much cash would need to be raised by: (a) a share issue, and (b) increased debt?

One of your first tasks after the successful acquisition of Denham is to review four new product lines from Quadstar, the production of which is about to be subcontracted to outside clothing manufacturers. The best quotes received for each product are as follows:

Product line: Charlotte Annabel Eloise Abigail
Best quote: £124 000 £188 000 £157 000 £105 000

You have asked the sales department at Denham to price up the jobs with their normal profit mark-up. The pricing schedule for each product is as shown in Figure A.3.

	Charlotte (£)	Annabel (£)	Eloise (£)	Abigail (£)
Direct materials	35 000	87 000	61 000	27 000
Direct labour	20 000	30 000	32 000	25 000
Factory overheads	40 000	50 000	64 000	50 000
Total production cost	95 000	167 000	157 000	102 000
Fixed administration and profit	9 500	16 700	15 700	10 200
Selling price	104 500	183 700	172 700	112 200

Figure A.3 *Pricing schedule*

You ascertain that direct labour is paid on a piecework basis and that overhead is recovered at 200 per cent of direct labour. Of total overheads, 60 per cent actually vary in line with direct wages and the remainder is fixed.

Denham currently has uncommitted capacity sufficient for all four jobs, but enquiries from traditional customers suggest that when the time comes it will eventually be filled. Every order accepted from Quadstar incurs an 'opportunity cost' in fulfilling one order less from other customers. An average order is priced as follows:

Product line:	(£)
Direct materials	50 000
Direct labour	25 000
Factory overheads	50 000
Total production cost	125 000
Fixed administration and profit	12 500
Selling price	137 500

Task 3

1. Explain the term 'opportunity cost'.

2. Based on the information given, advise which product lines should be taken 'in-house' for Denham to manufacture.

UNIT

Organisations and Behaviour

Approaches to Management

Over the course of the twentieth century, management thought moved on from a basic philosophy in which those who were paid to manage were expected to manage from above in top-down hierarchical organisations, to a new order in which responsibility has increasingly been vested in frontline employees interfacing directly with customers. This chapter examines various modern approaches to management.

On completion of the chapter you should be able to:

- describe the different approaches to management

- evaluate the different approaches to management and theories of organisation used by two organisations.

DEVELOPMENT OF MANAGEMENT THOUGHT

Rosabeth Moss Kanter, writing in 1995 in her book *The Change Masters* shows that in the new business environment, people at all levels of an organisation are affected by the power or the control or the interests others have in their area: 'And so the unquestioned authority of managers in the corporation of the past has been replaced by the need for negotiations and relationships outside the immediate managerial domain, by the need for managers to persuade rather than order, and by the need to acknowledge the expertise of those below.' In order to understand how we have come to this emphasis on participation we must first trace the history of management approaches in the 1900s.

Over the course of the twentieth century management thought moved on from a basic philosophy in which those who were paid to manage were expected to manage from above in top-down hierarchical organisations, to a new order in which responsibility has increasingly been vested in frontline employees interfacing directly with customers. **Empowerment** is the process of transferring power from *managers* (who are often remote from customers and front-

line business processes) to *operatives* so that they can use this power to further the interests of the organisation and increase customer satisfaction. Empowerment is about putting authority and responsibility in the hands of people who need these things in order to do their jobs. It involves answering the question: 'What is the nearest point to the customer at which this decision can effectively be made?' Empowering people at the operating level inevitably involves related changes in the roles of managers – managers become less concerned with taking decisions on issues passed up to them from below, and more with developing their subordinates' ability to take such decisions intelligently for themselves. Modern managers become coaches and mentors rather than commanders.

To trace the origins of these changes in approaches to management, we can begin with the 'scientific managers' who were in fashion at the start of the twentieth century.

SCIENTIFIC MANAGEMENT

Most early management theory was based on a mechanistic view of human behaviour. People were assumed to be alike and interchangeable and to be completely programmable. Their behaviour could and should be programmed by their managers. Scientific management is associated with developing 'scientific methods' of organising work. Its theory was closely associated with the work of **F.W. Taylor** (1856–1915), and with employers such as Henry Ford and Nelson D. Rockefeller. Taylor and others developed a systematic discipline of work study, piece-rate schemes and time and motion studies.

Taylor seems to have developed an obsession with order and routinised patterns early in his life. He counted his steps, calculated his time in carrying out various tasks, and studied his body's responses while doing basic domestic chores. Apparently, he had a regular nightmare about being pinned down by a large machine, and to prevent this happening he made sure that he slept in exactly the same position each night. After dropping out of law school Taylor took a job as a manual craft apprentice, before moving on to become a gang boss in a lathe department at the Midvale steel works, which was one of the most technologically advanced steel companies in the USA.

While working at Midvale, Taylor developed a determination to stamp out what was referred to as 'systematic soldiering' – organised attempts by groups of employees to work no harder than was absolutely necessary, for example by slowing down the work rate and extending breaks. Taylor sought to cut out 'systematic soldiering' by establishing working practices that made this impossible. He saw that the power of employees to restrict output rested in the fact that they usually had a greater understanding than their employers of the tools they worked with and working practices. They were able to disguise from their employers their real potential to produce more if they worked harder. Taylor wanted to give control back to employers by developing a science of work in which work would be controlled by the scientific manager. He carried out a series of systematic studies of shopfloor practice with the intention of redesigning jobs so that all knowledge expertise, and hence control of work, rested with management. Jobs were broken down and fragmented to their most basic components in an extreme division of labour.

Taylor also believed that monetary reward was an important motivating factor that would drive the system. Higher rates of pay could be offered as an inducement for increased rates of output. He used workers who were prepared to work hard to set a standard for others, 'rate busters' who would destroy any informal agreements about 'systematic soldiering' established by informal groups of workers.

Taylor sought to remove the knowledge advantage that craft workers had previously had about work processes by seeking to make sure that managers had a monopoly of this knowledge. In his book *On the Art of Cutting Metals* he created an entirely new set of standard tool sizes and shapes. These were given obscure titles and numbers. A horizontal miller no.7, for example, would become a 7MH; this meant that managers could hand over tools to employees to carry out particular jobs and then take them back. The employees would thus feel that they could carry out only routine operations as prescribed by management. The net effect was to disempower the workforce and give power and control to management.

Case Study

A high-priced man?

Speedy Taylor illustrated his methods in the following conversation which took place between him and a Pennsylvania Dutchman who worked at the Bethlehem Iron Company where Taylor had been employed to introduce efficient working methods.

'Schmidt, are you a high-priced man?'

'Vell, I don't know vat you mean.'

'Oh come now, you answer my question. What I want to find out is whether you are a high-priced man or one of these cheap fellows here. What I want to find out is whether you want to earn $1.85 a day or whether you are satisfied with $1.15 just the same as those cheap fellows are getting.'

'Did I vant $1.85 a day? Vas dot a high-priced man? Vell yes, I vas a high-priced man.'

'Now come over here. You see that pile of pig iron?'

'Yes.'

'You see that car.'

'Yes.'

'Well, if you are a high-priced man, you will load that pig-iron on that car tomorrow for $1.85. Now do wake up and answer my question. Tell me whether you are a high-priced man or not.'

'Vell – did I got $1.85 for loading dot pig iron on dot car tomorrow?'

'Certainly you do – certainly you do.'

'Vell den, I vas a high-priced man.'

'Now hold on, hold on. You know just as well as I do that a high-priced man has to do exactly as he's told from morning till night. You have seen this man before, haven't you?'

'No. I never saw him.'

'Well, if you are a high-priced man you will do exactly as this man tells you tomorrow, from morning till night. When he tells you to pick up a pig and walk, you pick it up and you walk, and when he tells you to sit down and rest, you sit down. You do that right straight through the day. And what's more no back-talk. Do you understand that? When this man tells you to walk, you walk, and when he tells you to sit down, you sit down, and you don't talk back at him. Now you come on to work here tomorrow and I'll know before night whether you are a high-priced man or not.'

(Source: Taylor, 1947)

Questions

1. What are the advantages of being a 'high-priced man'?

2. What are the drawbacks of being a 'high-priced man'?

3. Why were employees in the first decade of the twentieth century prepared, apparently, to accept Taylor's methods?

4. Why might employees be less prepared to become 'high-priced men' (and women) today?

5. To what extent does your personal experience tell you that the legacy of Taylorism is still with us?

Scientific management was typical of the organisation of many businesses in this country at least until the 1960s and can still be found in some organisations today. It is all about *control*. Power within an organisation is vested in those at the top of the organisation. Managers are then able to employ 'scientific management principles' to maintain their control of the organisation and its activities. Scientific management was concerned with finding the most efficient ways of organising activities in the workplace. Managers were solely responsible for setting work schedules and tasks, and the workers performed these tasks. Scientific management was widely adopted in factories as a way of increasing production and profits.

Scientific management has several defining characteristics:

- **Authority** is implemented through a hierarchical system of command and control.
- **Structure** is created through a highly formalised pattern of organisation. The major element of structure will be a top-down line organisation which will be supported by a servicing staff organisation structure.
- **Specialisation** – an organisation which uses extensive specialisation of labour, machinery, and offices.
- **Coordination** of activities is required by specialisation of activities so as to create an integrated and linked structure which is formulated and dictated by management with the purpose of maximising production.

The development of scientific management in the USA and the UK was based on the notion of **rationalism**, the belief that the human mind could develop systems and manage technology in such a way as to create the most efficient use of resources in society. The 'heroic' manager would then have a key role in managing and directing resources in order to achieve the best possible results.

Discussion point

Is scientific management dead, or is it still alive and kicking in British organisations? What do you think? Can you cite examples which support your point of view?

CLASSICAL ADMINISTRATION

This was a top-down view of how to run an organisation. Some of the key components of administrative theory were:

- A clear *chain of command* has to be established from the top to the bottom of a structure. Authority is then vested in those higher up the organisation. Each employee should have only one direct boss who passes down commands.
- Managers are responsible for *functional areas*, including responsibility for particular people.
- The organisation is based on the *division of labour*, and *functional specialisation*.
- *Orders* pass along and down the chain of command.
- Each official is responsible for about five or six *subordinates*.

- Jobs are designed to meet the *needs of the organisation*. Individuals are then recruited in order to fit the job requirements.

Bureaucracy

Max Weber (1846–1920) set out a model of how a bureaucratic organisation might operate, and this has served as a starting point for the study of organisational society ever since the widespread translation of Weber's work into English in the 1940s. Weber's model was developed at a time when large organisations were becoming increasingly important in industrial society. He argued that bureaucracies are the most functionally effective form of organisation, although at times they operate in an 'inhuman way'. The bureaucracy is based on the cold application of logic, and does not allow personalised relationships and non-rational, emotional considerations to get in its way.

Weber saw bureaucracies as representing the application of rational thought to practical problems in large industrial combines, in the civil service and in other important organisations such as schools, churches and government departments. His model of bureaucracy specified several typical characteristics.

- a set of official positions for the purpose of carrying out given organisational tasks, to be governed by a set of rules and procedures
- a hierarchical structure of official posts

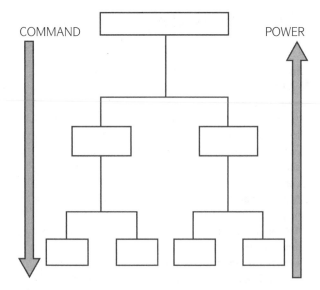

Figure 9.1 *A bureaucratic structure*

- management based on office procedures, files, documents and 'office staff'
- the appointment of trained officials to take on roles within the bureaucracy.

Today, various forms of bureaucracy are important ways of running political and economic systems in advanced industrial societies. Bureaucracy may be the most rational form of social organisation and it dominates the structure of many business organisations. Many managers lean towards bureaucracy because they prefer clear lines of communication, clear specifications of authority and responsibility, and clear knowledge of responsibilities within the organisation (see Figure 9.1).

Advantages of bureaucratic organisations

The bureaucratic division of labour, combined with new technologies, has made massive increases possible in the production of goods and services.

Secondly, a bureaucracy usually helps to create a predictable pattern for work cycles. People know what they are supposed to do, how they are supposed to do it and the extent of their responsibility. Production targets can be set, and plans established to meet them.

Thirdly, a bureaucracy is often seen as being a 'fair' way of doing things. Officials are appointed on the basis of their qualifications, and the organisation deals with individuals and groups with which it comes into contact on the basis of predetermined rules and procedures. Provided that officials stick to the rules, there should be no possibility of giving preferential treatment.

Criticisms of bureaucratic organisations

Bureaucracies are sometimes accused of being slow-moving, unimaginative organisations because of the way they stick to rules and procedures. Decisions may be arrived at slowly because they have to be processed through the 'right channels'.

Secondly, within a bureaucracy it is all too easy to lose sight of the principal objectives. Instead of bureaucracies focusing on the aims and purposes of the organisation, they can become wrapped up in procedures and paperwork. The end-result can be the loss of business and profits. In the extreme case, bureaucratic procedures confirm the old adage: 'The operation was a success, but the patient died.'

Thirdly, bureaucracies are sometimes seen to be inhuman structures which fail to account for the fact that many of their internal and external relationships are between people. This can have a depersonalising effect, concentrating on relationships that are remote and anonymous rather than on face-to-face contacts.

The human relations approach

By the 1930s evidence was beginning to accumulate that spectacular increases in productivity could be achieved by motivational methods that were not only different from those advocated by Taylor but in many respects fundamentally opposed. The human relations approach covers a broad group of writers whose ideas are very much in opposition to the scientific managers and bureaucrats. The approach draws on the work of humanistic psychologists, stressing the importance of developing human potential, giving individuals opportunities to influence their work environment, providing them with interest and challenges in their work, and recognising their unique and complex needs.

The scientific managers focused on the 'bottom line' and were concerned with 'structuring the structure' of the organisation so as to create profit and productivity. The

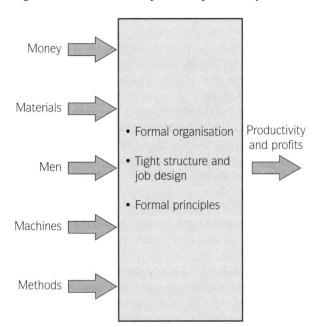

Figure 9.2 *An organisation based on scientific principles*

emphasis was very much on inputting the 'Five Ms' of money, materials, men, machines and methods into an organisation that was based on 'sound' scientific principles (see Figure 9.2).

In contrast, a human relations approach is concerned **both** with profitability and with social relations and outcomes in the organisation. Social organisation and business organisation are therefore seen as intertwining themes (see Figure 9.3).

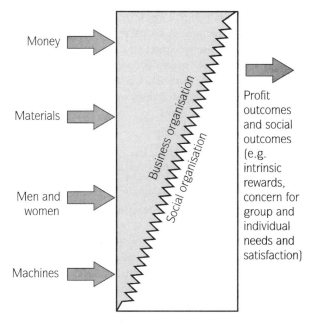

Figure 9.3 *An increased emphasis on the human side of organisation*

There is an increasing shift in many organisations **towards human resources**. No longer is human resources management seen as being solely the responsibility of the human resources (or personnel) department. Today this role is increasingly being seen as one for all managers across the organisation who are being given responsibilities for selecting, motivating, developing and evaluating employees. Perhaps more importantly, the emphasis has shifted from seeing employees as costs to seeing them as assets. There is an increasing recognition that employees are the most important resource in an organisation, particularly in creating a competitive edge.

The behavioural science writers like Blake, Mouton and Herzberg, who we will examine later in this chapter, emphasise that in organisations the proper study of mankind is 'man'. The human relations approach appeals directly to individual motivations, and to treating people as qualitatively different from the other resources that the organisation employs. The human relations approach places a strong emphasis on studying both the *formal* arrangements which influence organisational structures and the *informal* relationships which create the reality of day-to-day interactions between people within an organisation.

The systems approach

Systems theory is a helpful way of thinking about organisational structures. A system is a complex whole made from a set of interconnecting parts or things. A system processes input to produce outputs, and this can be illustrated by drawing three 'black boxes' (see Figure 9.4). In reality, organisational structures are made up of many inputs, processes and outputs.

Figure 9.4 *A black-box approach to systems*

In an *open system* the output does not affect the input. In contrast, in a *closed system* the output will directly affect the input. In the systems approach to organisations, they should be treated as open systems which are continually dependent upon and influenced by their environments.

According to Katz and Kahn (1964), 'systems theory is concerned basically with problems of relationship, of structure and of interdependence'. In the systems approach, therefore, there is a strong emphasis on the concept of transactions across boundaries – between the system and its environment and between different parts of this system. Systems theory helps to create an approach to organisational study which pushes the focus beyond simply looking at the organisation as a closed system, as was the case with scientific management and the human relations approaches.

In this way, systems theorists examine the relationships between the elements of the organisation, and the interactions with other systems in the environment. Human organisations are, on the whole, open systems which interact with elements in the wider environment. For example, a business interacts with customers, suppliers, the government, pressure groups etc. It is affected by social, economic and other changes.

Organisations are in a perpetual state of change so that there is a dynamic or moving equilibrium. People in an organisation seek to ensure that it survives, and often this involves moving the organisation 'on' to a new state of balance. Feedback of information is used to enable the organisation to adjust and modify.

Organisations are usually made up of several subsystems, and changes in one subsystem are extremely likely to have an impact on other subsystems. If one department changes the way it operates this may quickly affect the running of other departments. However, systems theory stresses the importance of looking at the organisation as a whole – the holistic approach. The synergy and interactions between the various subsystems are more important than the individual components on their own.

The contingency approach

The earliest management theorists such as **Henri Fayol** (writing in the 1930s) treated organisations almost as if they were devoid of people. The scientific management school then more or less discounted the human side of an organisation. In contrast, the human relations schools placed the emphasis on people. The systems approach was concerned with the way in which the system transforms inputs into outputs within its environment.

Each of the above approaches was based on the assumption that there was 'a single best way' to manage an organisation. In contrast, **contingency theorists** do not support the view that there is a single best way of designing an organisation or that simplistic approaches to classifying organisations are helpful. Contingency theorists based their views on studies of a range of organisations to show that structures and methods of operation depend on the circumstances and situation in which the organisation is operating. 'Classic' studies in the contingency framework include that by Burns and Stalker (1961) into a number of Scottish electronics firms, and Lawrence and Lorsch's (1976) study of six firms in the plastics industry.

Burns and Stalker set out their concept of mechanistic and organic organisations based on their research into the rate of change of the environment in which organisations operate.

- In a *stable environment*, a highly structured (mechanistic) organisation develops with specialised functions, clearly defined roles, strict administrative routines and a hierarchical system of exercising control – a top/down bureaucratic approach.

- In a *dynamic environment*, the structure will be more organic, individual responsibilities are less clear-cut, and organisational members must constantly relate what they are doing to the general situation of the organisation and specific problems. One of Burns and Stalker's most important conclusions was that there 'is no one optimum type of management system'.

Lawrence and Lorsch defined organisation as the process of coordinating different activities to carry out planned transactions with the environment. They saw the three aspects of environment upon which the design of the organisation is contingent as being the *market*, the *technology*, and *research and development*. These may be differentiated along such dimensions as *rate of change* and *uncertainty*. The process of reacting to complexity and change by differentiation creates a need for effective integration if the organisation as a whole is to adapt efficiently to the environment. The notions of **differentiation** and **integration** are Lawrence and Lorsch's key contributions to contingency theory.

Figure 9.5 *The best-fit approach*

The **modern contingency approach** argues that organisations consist of tasks which have to be performed and of people who perform those tasks. The tasks and the people exist within an organisational environment. The people with responsibility for designing organisations should try to create the best 'fit' between people, tasks and environment (see Figure 9.5). The best fit will depend on prevailing circumstances. Contingency theory therefore argues that there is no one best style of managing people – the most appropriate style is 'contingent' on existing conditions (the word *'contingent'* means 'dependent').

The implication is that even within the same organisation there will be scope for different organisational patterns and structures. For example, there may be scope for some activities to be carried out using a top-down hierarchical approach, while others are done in a far more democratic style.

Huczynski and Buchanan (1998), in their best-selling text *Organisational Behaviour*, distinguish four main classes of activities that are carried out within an organisation. These are:

- *steady-state activities* – the routine activities carried out in an organisation, comprising about 80 per cent of the tasks carried out by people
- *policy-making activities* – identifying goals, setting standards, allocating resources, and getting people to do things
- *innovation activities* – concerned with changing what a company does or how it does things (e.g. research and development, introducing new products)
- *breakdown activities* – concerned with dealing with emergencies and crises.

The way in which these activities are handled may be quite different, so a number of structures are likely to exist together. Within these structures there may be differences in:

- the type of people best suited for working within the structure
- the appropriate means of motivating people
- the management style.

Case Study

The dangerous folly called Theory Z

The following extracts are from an article by B. Bruce-Briggs that appeared in *Fortune* magazine in May 1982.

'America should learn from Japanese management, claims a recent spate of books and articles, including even some in Fortune. According to this outpouring of facile advice, Japan's economic success is founded on a superior concept of 'human resources' management that is directly needed here. One writer, William Ouchi, has called this approach **Theory Z** *and claims that it is already the practice in some highly successful US companies. As the Japanese might say in their understated way, the idea is not quite so good as it seems. In plain American, Theory Z is downright silly. It is also dangerous. ...*

'To the westerner, Japan may seem bizarre, even inhuman. But calling the Japanese 'robots' is unjust. The system was not adopted as policy by Japanese management nor willingly elected by Japanese workers. It has been imposed on them all ... Do you think they like to work hard? Do you think they enjoy singing company songs? Do you think the Kamikaze pilots wanted to splatter their guts on the decks of American ships? ...

'Learned commentaries on Japanese culture emphasise dominant values of on (obligation) and giri (duty) and so

forth – the values promoted from above. From below, however, the most relevant value is gaman – patience, endurance, putting up with it. ...

'In short, to imitate the Japanese we would need a labour force disciplined by a social hierarchy controlled by an oligarchy. The danger of Theory Z and allied nostrums is that they may strip us of what little competitive advantage we now have. Americans ... cannot match the Japanese at Corporatism. We can, however, innovate and invent. We can also move faster than the Japanese, unless hobbled up by pseudo-consensus. It is appalling to observe how much time and effort is expended by business cajoling people into doing what obviously must be done. We may have too much Theory Z already.... '

Questions

1. What do you understand by the term Theory Z?

2. Why might western companies be attracted to Theory Z?

3. Why does B. Bruce-Biggs feel that Theory Z cannot be transplanted to US corporations? Why is he opposed to it?

4. To what extent does this article support the view that there is no one best style of management?

5. What factors are likely to affect the best style of management in an organisation? Try to relate your answer to your own experiences of working in organisations.

MODERN APPROACHES TO MANAGEMENT

Since the 1970s a revolution has been occurring in parts of the scientific community. Instead of studying rigid scientific laws, some scientists began to study 'irregularities' or 'non-linearities' in nature, and once they began to look for these they turned out to be everywhere and important. Science had discovered what it came to call **chaos**.

One of the key concepts in chaos theory is that tiny changes in input can result in overwhelming differences in output, a phenomenon described as 'sensitive dependence

on initial conditions'. In the study of the weather this is known as 'the butterfly effect', because it is supposed that a butterfly flapping its wings over Beijing can, in theory, cause a storm over New York a week later. However, the notion has spread to many forms of interrelationships in the modern world, so that in the summer of 1998, for example, the *Independent* newspaper had a headline which read: 'A President unzipping his flies in the White House leads to Asian economic crisis the following week'.

In business theory there has been a similar shift in emphasis from order to potential chaos. We need to go no further than the titles of popular management books to appreciate this emphasis:

- 1947 – F. W. Taylor, *Scientific Management*
- 1979 – H. Mintzberg, *The Structuring of Organisations*
- 1988 – T. Peters, *Thriving on Chaos*
- 1992 – T. Peters, *Liberation Management – Necessary Disorganisation for the Nanosecond Nineties*
- 1995 – T. Peters, *The Pursuit of Wow! Every Person's Guide to Topsy-Turvy Times.*

Increasingly, the emphasis in business theory is on preparing for turbulence rather than for static conditions. As Brian Goodwin, professor of biology at the Open University, put it:

'The edge of chaos is a good place to be in a constantly changing world because from there you can always explore the patterns of order that are available ... What you do not want to do is get stuck in one particular state of order.'

Clearly the emphasis for the modern organisation should be on thriving on chaos. This requires forward-thinking and adaptive structures.

Tom Peters, who has been at the leading edge of applying chaos theory to organisational structure, made the following points in his 500th newspaper column in 1994:

- Organisations should not be overly frightened of failure. The blunders that sometimes accompany a leap into the unknown may be needed to thrive in these turbulent times.
- Developments such as continuous improvement, re-engineering, total quality, empowerment and customer service are only a prelude to the Age of Innovation based on perpetual revolution and re-invention.
- Organisations need to be wary of building core strengths and then staying with them regardless of changing market conditions. In turbulent times they may need to quickly get rid of core values and strengths in order to move on to the new areas.

- The existing structure of an organisation tends to determine its strategy, which may not be the best option.
- Design is important if new developments are going to be given a competitive edge. In the modern marketplace there are too many similar products. When Renault launched the Twingo it was doing so knowing that 40 per cent of potential consumers actively disliked it. However, 10 per cent were said to love it. The company went ahead and produced its distinctive product. It was a success.
- Too many organisations are dull and conservative. In chaotic times you need bubbling and challenging organisations.

Chaos theory is also concerned with how patterns change over time. Organisations exist in a turbulent world and so need to be able to live with chaos. Organisations and their environments are tightly coupled, so that changes within and without may have profound influences which are unpredictable.

An organisation will set up control systems which influence its own ongoing activities through a feedback loop. The influence of the feedback is often unpredictable because of the complexity of organisational activity. Business structures by their very nature can lead to disorder as well as order.

Business life today is therefore characterised by open-ended change resulting from internal systems as well as shocks and change in the external environment. Managers should understand that there are no simple sets of prescriptions and rules to help them cope with the open-ended changes. They need to develop new models for dealing with chaotic situations. They need to be aware that the traditional managerial model of setting objectives, planning and monitoring the feedback, may not be adequate in a dynamic field of operation – they may have to be planning and controlling as things unfold.

Flexible structures for flexible managers

Transformational change is the only approach likely to be successful for organisations operating in dynamic environments today. It is the approach that is concerned with thriving on chaos and introducing the Age of Innovation. New systems, techniques and designs will be required. Organisational structures need to be flexible and adaptive.

An **entrepreneurial organisation** does not simply analyse the past in order to predict the future; it looks for opportunities to use all resources more effectively. An organisation with an entrepreneurial culture will actively seek change and be quick to respond. It will be 'market-led' and prepared to take risks. For all this to be possible the organisation must have a flexible structure that can be adjusted rapidly to meet changing circumstances. Kenyon Greene has used the term **adaptive organisation**. He argues:

'The highest-level property of the adaptive organisation is the ability to change purposely the structure, function and behaviour of the organisation in keeping with experience and with the actual and dynamic demands imposed by the environment – that is, the highest-level property is the ability to learn. Top-level learning is itself a function of structure, including the degree to which learning ability is distributed throughout the various levels and parts of the organisation.'

Greene argues that the adaptive organisation should have a modular structure. At each level there should be functionally overlapping units, so that breakdown or malfunction of any one unit does not create a crisis. Each unit should be semi-autonomous and built on a culture of local problem-solving, decision-making and control. This decentralisation and empowerment creates both a flexible and a resilient organisation.

Clearly, these types of organisation – whether we call them flexible, adaptive or whatever – need employees who are highly motivated, capable of making decisions and solving problems, determined, and keen to accept new challenges. Is it realistic to expect that such individuals will be available to meet the needs of modern organisations?

Case Study

Lack of innovation

In her book, *The Change Makers*, Rosabeth Moss Kanter sets out her belief that there are two major types of US companies that produce little innovation.

- The first are the innovation avoiders which are generally capital-intensive, like oil or insurance, and see little economic leverage in their internal systems or operations. A few grand strokes of strategy occasionally are all these organisations think they need to survive and prosper.

- There is another type that are simply unschooled in how to innovate – naive rather than unconcerned, happier to learn. They are likely to be labour-intensive, like many consumer-goods manufacturers, or essentially service businesses like telephones, and they may even have progressive policies for the treatment of their people. But they grew out of earlier eras and have become encrusted with innovation-defeating traditions over time.

Questions

1. Can you identify examples of innovation-avoiders, and companies that are unschooled in how to innovate in the UK?

2. What difficulties do these organisations face?

3. How would you go about creating management structures and approaches that support innovation in these organisations?

Greiner's phases of organisational growth

In the 1970s, L. E. Greiner, in his book *Evolution and Revolution as Organisations Grow*, set out a typical growth pattern of organisations which is reflective of the types of changes that occurred in many large UK organisations during the twentieth century. Typically in the 1970s, organisations' response to problems associated with growth was to create more organised organisations in which the emphasis was on controls, procedures, lines of command, and a 'command and control' approach. Today, of course, the emphasis has changed to *re-engineering* the organisation so that it is more flexible, and gives greater powers to individuals in the organisation within an accountability framework.

Greiner set out five aspects of organisational growth:

- As the *size* of an organisation increases, problems of coordination and communication arise, particularly in a tall or dispersed organisation.
- The *older* an organisation is, the more deeply set will be the attitudes that exist within it, making it less flexible and more difficult to change.
- In *evolutionary periods* there is little change in the management of the organisation, and reorganisation is gradual.

- In *revolutionary periods*, there may be new management and new ideas. Substantial changes may need to be made because of the increase in size of the organisation or a radical alteration in its activities and environment.
- In a *rapidly growing industry*, a business organisation may be forced to make changes. However, if the organisation is profitable it may be able to continue with existing practices.

According to Greiner, each evolutionary period is characterised by a dominant management style, and each revolutionary period by a dominant management problem.

Phases of growth

There are five phases of growth (see Figure 9.6). Each has a calm evolutionary period leading to a management crisis in which there is considerable confusion and conflict within the organisation. The period of crisis is the 'revolution'. Understanding the nature of the revolution requires a clear knowledge of the organisation's history and development. The crises which occur during the growth of the organisation are as follows.

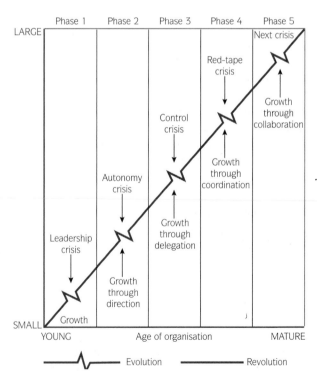

Figure 9.6 *Greiner's phases of growth*

Crisis of leadership

In the early days of a small organisation there are likely to be close relationships between the owners and employees. Informal communication channels can be successful and stakeholders in the organisation will be committed to its success. As the organisation grows, new members join who are perhaps not as committed, forcing the owners into playing more of a managerial role with which they may not be comfortable. A crisis of leadership leads to the appointment of a professional manager.

Crisis of autonomy

As the organisation continues to grow it spreads and becomes more complex. Ground-level supervisors will be more knowledgeable in specialist areas than managers. The supervisors will want to have more of a say in decision-making which lies within their competence. The crisis of autonomy will lead to a spreading of powers to those in junior management and supervisory posts.

Crisis of control

As the organisation devolves responsibilities lower down the hierarchy, senior managers begin to feel and to acknowledge that they are losing control of operations and over the interrelated functioning of the organisation. The crisis of control leads to the development of organisation-wide control systems.

Crisis of red tape

The organisation may start to become too large and bureaucratic, as a result of the complex coordination system. Confusion begins to develop between line and staff management and people are not clear about their responsibilities. There has to be collaboration involving more flexible management processes.

TASK

Identify an organisation that you are familiar with which is facing a particular crisis. How has the organisation arrived at this crisis position? How *should* the organisation be proceeding ?

When Greiner was writing in the 1970s this pattern of growth and crises was fairly typical. It may be less so today as many organisations are developed by entrepreneurs with management training who are able to avoid some of the crises by building forward-looking organisations. However, you have only to read the newspapers and to study organisations in your own locality to discover many falling into the trap of crisis after crisis.

Inverting the organisation

A popular approach to management in recent years has been to 'invert the organisation'. We can illustrate this process through a case example. The Equitable Life Assurance Society is a successful provider of financial and associated services consisting mainly of life assurance and pensions. It focuses on high-net-worth individuals and company pension schemes. In other words its customers (individuals and groups) are mainly people whose incomes and wealth are higher than average. In recent years, Equitable Life has set out its aim as that of 'Growing more contented customers'. This simple statement is very important: it sets out that the organisation will have a *marketing focus*. It will find out what its customers want and then set out to make sure that customers receive these benefits. The society has been restructured from top to bottom to achieve this.

In the 1960s and 70s many companies in the UK had a top-down approach, with senior managers appearing at the top of organisational charts with a flow of decisions passing down to lower-level employees. Today our thinking has completely changed. Now it is more typical

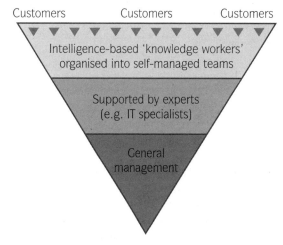

Figure 9.7 *The 'new-look' organisation*

to see *customers* placed at the top of an organisational chart, followed by the customer service employees who directly interface with customers (see Figure 9.7). In order for this to be successful, organisations like Equitable Life have focused on the recruitment and training of highly able customer service employees who are entrusted with taking responsibility for making decisions. These are the sort of people who will not wait to be given orders, but will be intelligent enough and innovative enough to make suitable decisions themselves. These employees will be comfortable using information technology to a high standard. They are what business writers term the 'knowledge workers'; and as many business writers have pointed out, intelligence is the greatest asset of the modern organisation.

FUNCTIONS OF MANAGEMENT

Management is usually defined as getting things done with or through other people. It involves deciding on objectives and ways of meeting those objectives. It is concerned with making decisions to ensure that objectives are met. Management involves planning, organising and coordinating activities. It is particularly concerned with bringing together sets of separate activities and tasks which contribute towards the completion of whole projects. It involves controlling – making sure that things are going to plan and that objectives are being met. This may involve setting up information systems to record progress.

Above all, management involves working with people. It is necessary, through effective communication, to make sure that people are committed to activities and to the organisation.

Peter Drucker in his important book, *The Practice of Management*, published in 1994, identifies five basic operations in the work of a manager. Together they result in the integration of resources into a living and growing organism. The five operations are:

1. *Setting objectives*. This is deciding what the objectives should be, and determining what the goals in each area of objectives should be. The manager decides what has to be done to reach these objectives, and makes the objectives effective by communicating them to the people whose performance is needed to attain them.

2. *Organising*. The manager analyses the activities, decisions and relations needed and classifies the work. He or she divides it into manageable activities and further divides the activities into manageable jobs. The manager groups these units and jobs into an organisation structure and selects people for the management of these units and for the jobs to be done.

3. *Motivation and communication*. The manager makes a team out of the people that are responsible for various jobs and does that through the practices with which he or she manages. The manager does it in his or her own relations to the employees managed, through incentives and rewards for successful work, and through a promotion policy. This involves constant communication, both from the manager to the subordinate, and from the subordinate to the manager.

4. *Measurement*. The manager establishes measuring yardsticks – and there are few factors as important to the performance of the organisation and of everyone in it. The manager sees to it that each employee in the organisation has measurements available to them which are focused on the performance of the whole organisation and which at the same time focus on the work of the individual and help him or her do it. The manager analyses performance, appraises it and interprets it.

5. *Developing people*. The manager directs people or misdirects them and brings out what is in them or stifles them. The manager strengthens the employees integrity or corrupts them.

Most people who work for an organisation will be concerned with 'management' in some aspects of their work. However, the range of managerial work varies considerably between one organisation and another, as do the ways in which individuals perform managerial roles. Perhaps what managers need to understand and recognise is the sheer diversity of managerial work.

Tony Watson, in his book *In Search of Management* published in 1994, argues that in the past managers were trained to identify the managerial role by remembering the mnemonic POSDCORB:

Planning
Organising
Staffing
Directing
Coordinating
Reporting
Budgeting.

He explains that more recent research gives a different picture of management and he quotes the summary Rosemary Stewart gives (in *Managing Today and Tomorrow*) of her research:

> *'The picture that emerges ... is of someone who lives in a whirl of activity, in which attention must be switched every few minutes from one subject, problem, and person, to another; of an uncertain world where relevant information includes gossip and speculation.'*

Management work varies widely from one manager to another depending on the type of organisation, the people he or she works with, the nature of the work, time constraints and many other factors. From Rosemary Stewart's perspective, management work becomes less clear-cut and perhaps more 'disorganised'. Tony Watson sets out to synthesise these disparate views based on his own experience of management work. He suggests that we:

> *'...recognise that management as a function does indeed have the various sub-functions of planning, co-ordinating, commanding and the rest. Yet we should equally recognise that the activities which bring about these functions do not fulfil them in as obvious or as direct a way as people once thought. Because of ... [factors such as widespread ambiguity, the existence within organisations of a variety of often conflicting interests and purposes, etc.] planning, co-ordinating, "commanding" and the rest can only be done in what amounts to "feeling the way in the dark". And this involves the incremental processes of incessant negotiating, guessing, manipulating, and speculating which researchers observe as central to managerial behaviour.'*

Watson, therefore, suggests using caution when making assumptions about the ease with which managers can manage. Management planning is often an imprecise art, struggling to achieve clarity and purpose in a changeable and sometimes hostile environment.

Planning

Management planning is concerned with developing a hierarchy of plans which can be translated into actions. It involves defining organisational objectives and setting out routes to meet these objectives. Planning also makes it possible to evaluate and control performance against clear performance standards. Without evaluation there is no control.

Figure 9.8 shows the relationship between activities and objectives. With a clear planning framework based on specific objectives, it becomes possible to direct many, if not all, operational activities towards meeting organisational objectives. However, in a dynamic business world characterised by turbulence, this is easier said than done. Nonetheless, developing a clear planning framework should be an important aim of any organisation.

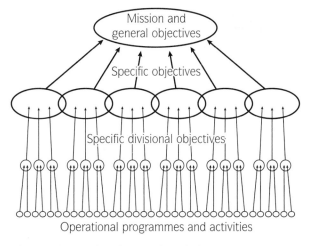

Figure 9.8 *Providing direction through planning*

Organisational planning takes place at a number of levels (see Figure 9.9). It is particularly important that managers be aware of these different levels and that top-level planning provides clear direction for lower-level planning.

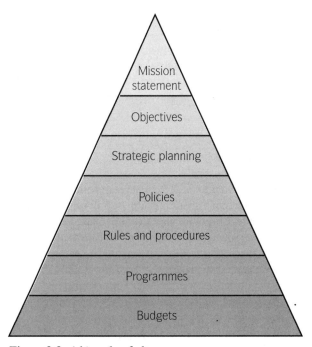

Figure 9.9 *A hierarchy of plans*

An important starting point is establishing the purpose or mission of the organisation. Objectives and goals can then be formulated which direct the organisation and its activities towards the achievement of its mission. Strategies can be formulated at a high level, setting out key aspects of direction and focus. Once strategies are in place, policies can be established to put into practice strategic decisions. At a lower level it is essential for the organisation to plan procedures and rules which outline day-to-day operations as well as programmes for putting activities into action. An important part of operating activity will be working towards budgetary plans.

From mission to ground-level operational activities

In this section we look at how the vision or mission of an organisation can be translated into a variety of individual activities which all pull towards the achievement of that mission. Imagine that a new manager of an English football team makes a public statement: 'Over the next five years we are going to become the team that all other teams want to emulate. We shall go on to head the premier league and win European honours, as well as playing the most attractive football in England.' This manager is building up a big vision (he certainly is optimistic about the period of his job tenure). However, the vision will not materialise unless it can be translated into all the activities the club engages in, including training, youth development, sponsorship projects, ticket sales, and supporter involvement. Effective planning, therefore, involves creating a framework of plans from top to bottom.

Objectives

Objectives should provide the reference point upon which all decisions about the future of an organisation can be made. Corporate objectives are made for the company as a whole and subsets of objectives are created for each subsection of the organisation. As part of the planning process managers will need to carefully construct objectives at each level. For example, a company might set itself the objective of becoming the market leader by the year 2005. This would translate down into specific sales and cost objectives for each of its products.

Strategic planning

Strategy is concerned with the basic directions, and broad intentions of business planning. Key strategic decisions are usually formulated at higher levels in organisations, but the planning of strategy should involve the input of managers throughout the organisation. For example, an organisation that up to now has been a leading ice-cream manufacturer may alter its strategy to diversify into soft drinks as well as ice-cream – strategic planning will identify the ways in which this change will happen.

Policies

Policies are general statements which guide thinking and action in decision-making. They define an area within which a decision is made and ensure that the decision contributes to the meeting of an objective. For example, a large organisation will have policies on equal opportunities, health and safety at work, dealing with customers, etc.

Increasingly, organisations set out their policies in writing. For example, all schools have written policies covering assessment, equal opportunities, discipline, sexual harassment at work and many other areas. Policies are forward-thinking – they clarify ways in which people should operate and act. People at work can then simply follow the guidelines of the policy rather than having to analyse a situation every time it appears. For example, if there is a clear equal opportunities policy, then the human resources department will be able to set up interviews as part of a selection procedure according to policy guidelines.

Rules and procedures

Rules and procedures set out a required method of handling particular activities. For example, the following is part of the customer care procedure at Body Shop:

'SMILE DAMMIT SMILE
Never treat customers as enemies,
approach them as potential friends.

Think of customers as guests,
make them laugh.

Acknowledge their presence within 30 seconds:
smile, make eye contact, say hello.

Talk to them within the first 3 minutes,

Offer product advice where appropriate,
Smile. Always thank customers and invite them back ...
TREAT CUSTOMERS AS YOU'D LIKE TO BE
TREATED.'

Rules must be followed and allow no discretion for interpretation; procedures set out more flexible guidelines.

Programmes

A programme is a set of policies, procedures, rules and tasks which make up a particular course of action, such as a road-building programme or a youth development programme. Programmes may involve planning on a very large scale (e.g. a school development programme) or on a small scale (e.g. a programme introduced by a single supervisor to increase the skills of a group of workers through training).

All programmes require the coordination and timing of a network of activities. They are usually part of a network of overlapping programmes. Planning programmes is important because it is concerned with an organisation's day-to-day activity.

Budgets

Resources need to be allocated to programmes. A budget will therefore need to be planned for each and every programme. Budgets will involve money in many cases, but budgets can also be made out for other resources, such as the use of labour, machinery, raw materials, components or time. The financial operating budget is often called the profit plan. It is expressed in numbers (e.g. units of money, units of product, labour hours, machine hours).

Organising

A key role of the manager will be to organise the organisation. This involves creating the structures, systems, procedures, programmes etc. which distinguish organisation from disorganisation. Organisation is fundamentally concerned with creating effective structures and in ensuring the systematic use of resources.

At an organisation-wide level, organising is concerned with creating the right kinds of structure and culture (see Chapter 10). At each level in the particular organisation it is then necessary to create appropriate and smooth-running structures.

Organising resources involves creating the systems and procedures which will best enable the organisation to make optimum use of its resources. For example, it involves prioritising activities – deciding what are the organisation's critical (most important) activities, its secondary activities, and its less important activities. Resources can then be channelled to where they are most required.

Commanding

Scientific management theory placed a lot of emphasis on the role of manager as commander:

- Decision-making was located at the top of the organisation and worked down.
- Commands and official information had to be transmitted through 'proper' channels of information, from the top to the bottom of the organisation.
- Authority derives from status in the organisation's hierarchy, etc.

A good manager was therefore an effective commander who played the rules 'by the book', and who was always aware of the correct channels of communication and appropriate procedures. The manager supported the official patterns and codes of conduct within the organisation.

Today, we have moved on from this 'old fashioned' approach. The modern manager should be able to give commands where appropriate, but is far more likely to work through relationships based on trust which empower fellow employees. The effective manager will create new structures and frameworks which encourage people to use their own talents and skills to meet the needs of the organisation while furthering their own personal development.

Coordinating

Coordination is another key aspect of management that involves bringing together resources to create a series of well-managed sequences. Essentially coordination is about bringing a range of often seemingly disparate activities into an integrated whole.

When plans, operations and activities are well coordinated then things fall into place, and order and efficiency characterises the organisation. To coordinate effectively, managers need to have a good understanding of the objectives that are being worked towards, and how the various components that can be drawn on to meet objectives can fit together smoothly.

Coordinating is different from commanding and requires different skills. The effective coordinator knows how to share out responsibility, while having a continual eye on the bigger picture, and being able to spot when things are not working as intended and take the appropriate rectifying actions.

Coordination often requires the use of a range of mathematical and statistical management tools such as decision-tree and critical-path analysis. Managers nowadays need to have the ability to use computers to help them in the decision-making process.

Controlling

Control is the measurement and correction of performance, and planning and controlling should go hand in glove. Indeed many writers on management theory argue that the two cannot be separated. Without objectives and a plan, control will not be possible because performance has to be compared with some agreed criteria. Responsibility for control rests with all managers and supervisors who are charged with putting plans into practice.

Control processes are broadly the same for a wide range of organisational activities. All involve, for example, ensuring product quality, the administration of financial activities, and so on. There are three main steps in the control process (see Figure 9.10).

Control processes can be established only in the context of the plans that have been drawn up. **Standards** should be established by clarifying performance criteria. These need to be set out in an understandable and precise way. Comparison of actual performance against the performance criteria will enable managers to ascertain how successful an operation is. For example, if a production manager's plan is to produce 100 units per hour with no breakages, and the plant produces only 90 units with a 50 per cent breakage rate, then something is clearly wrong and remedial action needs to be taken.

There are many different types of standard. For example, verifiable goals are a clear type. An example of a verifiable

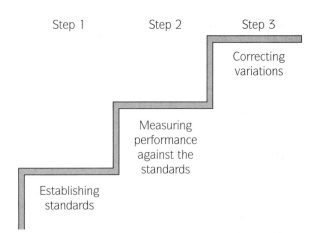

Figure 9.10 *Three steps in the control process*

goal would be for a group of workers to install a new machine by a given date, using a given number of hours of installation time; it could easily be verified whether this standard has been met. It becomes more difficult to measure the achievement of standards when goals are not so clear-cut – that is, where there are non-verifiable goals. Today the trend is increasingly to use performance indicators so that goals can be verified.

Ideally the **measurement of performance against standards** should be forward-looking. In other words, managers and supervisors should try to anticipate deviations from standards. However, if deviations cannot be anticipated then they should be identified as quickly as possible.

For some activities, especially routine tasks, it is relatively easy to measure performance against a standard. However, there are many activities where this is not easy – for example, when people are engaged in non-routine activities or are producing one-off work. How, for example, would you identify a standard for a unique task that has never been done before? When work is of an intellectual nature then it will be less easy to establish a standard – how would you establish a standard for a creative director in a film production team, or for a lecturer who has a riveting yet slightly off-beat style of working with students? The further removed a job is from the routine, the more difficult it will be to establish a standard of performance. Perhaps it is best, then, to resort to general performance indicators as a baseline and to recognise that some key aspects of performance may never be measurable.

A **deviation** occurs when performance does not meet the standard. If managers have accurately set out the performance expected of resources, then they will be able to see where under-performance occurs. They can then revise the plans, alter activities or change job descriptions as necessary. Deviations can be corrected by one or more of the following actions:

- redrawing the plans
- modifying the goals
- redesigning or clarifying duties
- instituting better leadership
- using additional staff and/or other resources
- improving training.

Managers need to be wary of an over-reliance on control as a means of running an organisation. Walton (1985) is critical of the traditional control model in which work is divided up into specialised tasks and performance expectations are defined as 'standards' that define the *minimum* acceptable performance. Both expectations and standards are the lowest common denominators. No attempt is made to establish maximum or potential performance. The control model seems to produce reliable but not outstanding performance, and since the 1970s it has been clear that this is not enough. *Competitive advantage* can be created out of high performance, which requires high levels of commitment. Managers therefore need to move on from seeing themselves as controllers to seeing themselves as creators of systems which encourage a genuine commitment to the organisation based on empowerment processes.

THE NATURE OF MANAGERIAL AUTHORITY

Power

To have power is to have the ability to influence people and events. Power is acquired by individuals and groups through their personalities, their activities and the situations in which they operate. Politics is concerned with the way in which leaders gain and use power and involves them in all sorts of activities such as bargaining, striking deals and forming coalitions with others.

The four major types of power that individuals develop or acquire are personal, legitimate, expert and/or political (see Figure 9.11).

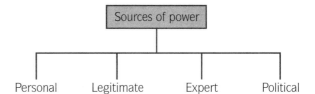

Figure 9.11 *Types of power*

Personal power

Personal power is possessed by certain individuals and is sometimes termed 'charismatic' or 'referent' power. Some individuals have tremendous charisma and are able to build up personality cults. Other people look to these individuals to make decisions for them – they can be very forceful and determined. Charismatic leaders (whether you like them or not) have a personal magnetism which draws other people to accept their right to lead. These leaders may sense the needs of their followers and provide a focus which meets those needs. Often leaders of new religious cults have this sort of personal magnetism and can persuade others to follow them down many uncharted paths.

Legitimate power

This is based on people having positions within a legitimate framework. In a particular culture, power will be delegated to various offices or positions and this will be accepted by members as being legitimate. Most people believe that it is desirable and necessary to run and maintain society in this way. For example, in Norman England people accepted that there was a king, with rich landholding barons, who would have their own stewards and officials who would control activities in a particular locality. In large bureaucratic organisations it is accepted that senior officials will make major decisions and pass down commands to junior officials. There is social pressure within the organisation to accept the legitimacy of this decision-making process.

Expert power

Expert power is based on specialised knowledge. It frequently arises where there is complex knowledge that can be gained only through education and training. For example, when there has been a road accident resulting in casualties, we recognise that doctors and other members of the emergency services are the best people to make decisions. If there are structural defects in your house you might turn to an architect to tell you what to do, and so on. There are many situations in which we turn to the expert and hand over the authority to make decisions.

Political power

Political power stems from being supported by a group, so to gain political power a leader will need to be able to work with people and social systems to gain support and allegiance from them. Gaining political power involves having an understanding of those factors most likely to encourage others to support you, as well as understanding how systems can be used in your favour. Politicians have to set out to appease different groups in order to maintain their power base. Political leadership also involves having access to sanctions and rewards. A number of tactics can be employed to obtain and retain political power (see Figure 9.12).

Political **power-broking** is an aspect of organisational life. Anyone working in an organisation quickly becomes aware of internal politics and power alliances. Gaining political power in an organisation can be an immensely subtle and time-consuming activity.

Tactic	Example
Alliance	A group of department heads join together to exert pressure for improved health and safety standards in the organisation
Association with those with more power	An individual has social contact with someone in a senior position in his or her organisation (e.g. membership of the same social club); the power then 'rubs off' on the junior, increasing the latter's power base.
Tradeoffs	One department head supports another in return for reciprocal favours
Control of information	The market research department has first insights into customer needs and preferences which determines new products
Power plays	One manager increases the size of his or her sphere of influence by creating new subdivisions, departments, etc.
Selective service	Favouritism is shown to certain individuals, groups and departments in an organisation (e.g. their work is processed more quickly by another department)
Networks	Individuals can develop formal and informal contacts within an organisation to enhance their power base

Figure 9.12 *Tactics when seeking political power*

Discussion point

Can you think of examples in an organisation you are familiar with, involving each of the above tactics to build political power?

Power in action

Research has highlighted major sources of power for groups or departments within an organisation. This gives us a good idea as to how individuals and groups can build up power.

Control over critical resources

Some groups or departments within an organisation have most control over the critical resources on which others depend. The most commonly quoted example is the hold of the financier over the purse-strings. Without money other individuals and departments are highly restricted. For example, a common complaint of football managers is that they cannot produce good results without buying 'match-winning players'. Control over critical resources is thus a key determinant of organisational power. Those with power are most able to determine culture, so the accountant may be able to impose in some measure a finance-driven, profit-oriented culture on an organisation.

Power through dependence

One group in a company holds power if other groups' actions are contingent on what the specific group does. For example, if we consider critical-path analysis, the departments performing activites that lie along the critical path have considerable power; the success of the whole operation depends on their meeting targets on time so they are well-placed to demand priority over resources.

A grouping within an organisation can increase its power (or reduce lack of power) by reducing its dependence on other groups. Clearly, departments controlling strategic contingencies have the ability to be most influential within the organisation and, therefore, to contribute to organisational culture in a major way. In different industries, strategic contingencies will be vested in different departments. For example, in food-processing, which involves the development of new products, they may lie in research and sales.

Power sharing

Nowadays, of course, it is apparent that managers can benefit from the sharing of power with others. The most successful style of management seems to be one in which the manager shares power with subordinates. This style is likely to increase both the satisfaction and the effectiveness of those who are led. The most effective managers are those who empower others, while at the same time establishing accountabilities for the use of power. We seem to have moved well beyond the days of Count Niccolo

Machiavelli, the sixteenth century statesman and author, who suggested that: 'It is better to be feared than loved if you cannot be both.'

Case Study

John D. Rockefeller

Today we might describe someone as being 'a real Rockefeller', but many people are unaware of the origin of the term. For many years John D. Rockefeller was associated with the capitalist dream. He was the man who created Standard Oil in the USA in 1880. The company went from strength to strength until it was broken up by the US Supreme Court in 1911.

At an early age Rockefeller stumbled upon a resource that was to revolutionise society – oil. Rockefeller quickly developed a knowledge of the oil industry which was to be the envy of many others in the field. Not only did he know the ins and outs of oil extraction and refining, but more importantly he had a detailed understanding of all of the business aspects of running a successful operation. He was a strong-willed character who was able to stamp his ideas on his associates and subordinates. Within a short period he was able to gain a stranglehold on the market for kerosene in the USA, with 90 per cent of the market.

John D. Rockefeller

He was able to win this share by a ruthless policy. He crushed almost all of his refining rivals by a combination of undercutting on price, industrial espionage, the secret ownership of companies that pretended to be rivals and, above all, the securing of hidden rebates from railway companies for every barrel they shipped, not just of his oil but of oil produced by his competitors too. A good example of this ruthlessness occurred when grocery stores offered kerosene from independent refiners; they found that, suddenly, a competing store would open across the street in which everything, not just kerosen, would be suspiciously cheap.

In 1872 he perpetrated the 'Cleveland Massacre', in one stroke buying out 22 of his 26 rivals in the city. The result of the Rockefeller strategy of buy-out or crush was the virtual monopoly that Standard Oil quickly became. Standard Oil was referred to as 'the octupus'.

On a personal level, Rockefeller believed that his achievements were all for the greater good of society. Indeed he managed to bring the price of refined oil down from 23 cents to 7 cents per gallon.

Rockefeller believed that it was in the public interest to have large firms controlling industries, rather than the chaotic conditions of free competition in which new enterprises would enter the industry and then collapse owing to unregulated competition. Rockefeller was a devout Baptist and he believed that the system he supported was based on cooperation between the big railway companies, steel companies, oil companies etc. He believed that everyone would benefit from the actions of powerful individuals like himself who could dominate the market in the general interest of mankind. He expected people to listen to what he said, and to have confidence in his wisdom and trust in his abilities. He once referred to Standard Oil as 'the Moses who delivered them [the refiners] from their folly which had wrought such havoc in their fortunes'. He went on: 'It was not a process of destruction and waste: it was a process of upbuilding and conservation of all the interests ... in our efforts most heroic, well meant – and I would say, reverently, Godlike – to pull this broken-down industry out of the Slough of Despond.'

Rockefeller stated that: 'I believe it is my duty to make money, and still more money. And to use the money I make for the good of my fellow man according to the dictates of my conscience.' He was one of the greatest philanthropists the world has ever seen.

Questions

1. What do you think were the major sources of Rockefeller's power – individual, legitimate, expert, or political? How would these sources of power be important in different situations?

2. Contrast Rockefeller's sources of power with a more recent prominent business leader.

3. List five other charismatic leaders, living or historical. What do these leaders have in common?

4. What tactics might a political leader employ to maintain his or her power base?

5. Why is (a) the use of power, and (b) an understanding of the nature of power, of importance to a manager?

Authority

So far we have seen that power in organisations stems from a number of sources. Having power is different from having **authority**.

Authority is a form of legitimate power – an individual in an organisation can be authorised to play a particular role or carry out particular actions. We know for example, that when a police officer waves down our car we must stop because the police officer has the authority to behave in such a way, supported by detailed rules and laws. In a classroom the teacher is authorised to demand that the class should be silent during a test; there is raft of school rules and sanctions to support the teacher's position. In a similar way managers will be authorised to carry out particular actions within an organisation, and their actions will be supported by a contract of employment and the support of superiors as well as company rules.

We use the term 'exercising authority' when an individual uses powers legitimately held in a particular position. We speak of individuals 'overstepping the bounds of their authority' when trying to exert power they are not authorised to use, or 'lacking authority' when they don't effectively play the role one would expect them to play, perhaps because of a weakness in character. Authority is therefore closely tied up with power.

Responsibility

Individuals who are given power and authority will also be *accountable* for the ways in which they use these things. Today it is fashionable to talk about having 'trust' in people in the organisation, but trust needs to be coupled with accountability. Modern organisations have moved on from the traditional control-orientated approach to a new workforce management approach based on a 'commitment'. Walton (1985) suggests that workers respond best – and most creatively – not when they are tightly controlled by management, placed in narrowly defined jobs, and treated like an unwelcome necessity, but, instead, when they are given broader responsibilities, encouraged to contribute and helped to achieve satisfaction in their work.

Managers need to be trained to take on their responsibilities, and have a clear picture of what these entail. They also need to be paid accordingly. And today, of course, managers have much broader responsibilities than ever before. In the past a manager might have seen himself or herself as having a responsibility to the line manager and to subordinates, but that is changing. For example, the Business Roundtable, the leading lobby for America's largest corporations, issued a statement on corporate responsibility which declared: 'More than ever, managers of corporations are expected to serve the public interest as well as private profit.' Four **constituencies** were identified – customers, employees, communities and society at large, and shareholders – and the needs of each were delineated (e.g. for employees, financial security, personal privacy, freedom of expression, and concern for the quality of life, as well as fair play).

Delegation

Delegation involves turning over work to someone else. Managers are often criticised for either failing to delegate, or for delegating too much. Delegation does not automatically rid a manager of work and responsibility. Indeed, you can create more work for yourself by delegating the wrong work to the wrong person.

The two chief reasons for delegating are:

- the manager needs someone else to act because he or she lacks the time, skill, or other resources to do the job as it should be done
- to enable a subordinate to develop by taking on more responsibility.

Reasons why managers may *avoid* delegating include:

- a lack of trust in others to do the work in the required way or to the required standard, while the manager retains the responsibility for the results
- the time needed to show someone how to do the work

- the frustration of delegating a job and then having it done badly
- complaints and frustrations coming from the person who has been delegated work.

Delegation can involve three major types of work: assignments, projects, and areas of work. An **assignment** is a clear, specific single task which is given just once, such as to write a report on a particular topic, or to meet an important visitor at the airport. Assignments will relieve the manager of a particular piece of work on a one-off basis. Before delegating an assignment it is essential to make sure that it is carefully mapped out with clear objectives. A **project** is a larger and more complex set of tasks which will require more skill and often be more time-consuming. It, too, will be given on a one-off basis.

Areas of work are the most common subject of delegation. Some areas of work (e.g. filing or other day-to-day tasks in an office) can be delegated because they comprise routine operations that do not need the interpersonal skills of a manager. Other areas of work may be delegated simply because a manager finds them inconvenient, difficult to handle or messy!

MANAGERIAL ROLES

Henry Mintzberg (1973) identified broad roles for the manager which can, in turn, be further subdivided:

- **interpersonal roles** (leading):
  Figurehead
  Leader
  Liaison
- **informational roles** (administrating):
  Monitor
  Disseminator
  Spokesman
- **decisional roles** (fixing):
  Entrepreneur
  Disturbance handler
  Resource allocator
  Negotiator

Handy (1993) believes that the mix of roles varies from job to job. Top jobs have a larger element of leading roles, first-line supervisory jobs more fixing, while middle-layer jobs are inevitably landed with the administering or informational roles – but every job has some of each. The size of the organisation must also have some effect. The top jobs of small organisations are more mixed and there are more largely informational jobs in the bigger concerns.

The interpersonal role

Perhaps the most important attribute of the modern manager is the ability to work with other people, particularly in a motivational and leadership capacity. Developing strong interpersonal relationships is at a premium.

Many modern organisations are in the service sector which places a strong emphasis on identifying and meeting customer requirements in face-to-face situations. Sadler (1988) argues that 'the personality, approach, manner and cheerfulness of the service provider are essential parts of the service. Whereas it does not matter if the workers on the product assembly line look as if they are not enjoying making the customer's car, it matters enormously that the service worker looks as if he or she is enjoying serving the customer's drink, selling the customer a pair of shoes, or cashing his cheque.'

As we move increasingly towards people-centred business activity, the manager needs to be able to provide a role model for interpersonal skills. Perhaps the most important employees are 'knowledge' and 'talent' workers who can readily switch to working for alternative organisations, so the modern manager needs to take a very strong interest in their personal development. Management should see themselves in a coaching rather than a 'telling' role. Employees nowadays look for personal fulfilment and satisfaction in their work.

The intelligent organisation therefore places a strong emphasis on the development of its people in order to make best possible use of them and to motivate them. A key part of this development process is that of **coaching**. Coaching is an ongoing process in which one person works closely with another (the coach) to develop skills and abilities. Coaching can be seen as someone with more expertise supporting and mentoring someone with less expertise. It is an essential ingredient of effective management and managers need to learn to be good coaches. It is by building one-to-one relationships with the people with whom you work that you are most likely to win their loyalty and support, as well as unleashing their full potential.

The informational role

Managers must be able to process information with confidence. According to Peter Drucker in *The Practice of Management*, published in 1994:

'The manager has a specific tool: information. He does not "handle" people; he motivates, guides, organises people to do their own work. His tool – his only tool – to do all this is the spoken or written word or the language of numbers. No matter whether the manager's job is engineering, accounting or selling, his effectiveness depends on his ability to listen and to read, on his ability to speak and to write. He needs skill in getting his thinking across to other people as well as skill in finding out what other people are after.'

In this role the manager is supported by information technology which has perhaps been the most significant factor in transforming the business world in recent years. IT changes so rapidly, however, that the manager needs to keep up to date. Sadler (1988) identifies five distinct types of IT application in businesses:

- Where the product of the business is information (e.g. publishing, advertising, entertainment) IT makes it possible to produce a better product at lower unit cost.
- IT makes it possible to add value in the production process (e.g. computer control and monitoring systems in cars, programmable control systems in washing machines and other domestic applicances, automatic cash dispensers in banks).
- Information processing activities may be involved in producing the organisation's output. These activities are usually referred to as process automation, factory automation or office automation.
- IT may be used as part of a management information system (MIS).
- IT can be used to generate new products or services (product innovation).

The decisional role

Managers have to make decisions, and this involves choosing a course of action from a set of alternatives. Decision-making lies at the heart of the planning process.

Most classifications of decision into types are based upon the predictability of those decisions. For example, Herbert Simon (1957), in *Models of Man*, made an important distinction between programmed and non-programmed decisions:

- **Programmed decisions** are straightforward, repetitive and routine, so that they can be dealt with by a formal pattern (e.g. the reordering of stock).
- **Non-programmed decisions** are novel, unstructured and consequential. There is no cut-and-dried method for handling situations that have not arisen before.

Simon thought that these two types of decision were the two ends of a continuum, with all shades of grey lying in between. In **Business Decision Making**, Gilligan, Neale and Murray extend this analysis to identify three types of decisions that managers might encounter, depending on the degree of certainty or uncertainty associated with the outcome, the time period involved, the frequency with which decisions have to be made, the extent to which the subject is routine or non-routine, and the implications of the decision for the organisation (see Figure 9.13). Thus:

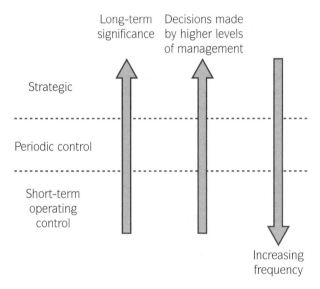

Figure 9.13 *Types of decisions*

- **Strategic decisions** are major decisions involving overall strategy. They often require a considerable exercise of judgement by the person responsible for making the decision, because, although such decisions require a considerable amount of analysis, important pieces of information will frequently be missing and so risk will be involved. Examples include the development of a new product, investment in new plant or the development of a new marketing strategy.
- **Periodic control decisions** are made less frequently than short-term decisions. They are concerned with monitoring how effectively an organisation is managing its resources. Such decisions might include the review of pricing strategies for certain products, the review of problems occurring in an on-going company budget, or the reappraisal of the way in which the sales force is being used. They are concerned with checking for and rectifying problems concerned with meeting company objectives.
- **Short-term operating control decisions** are those that have to be made frequently and involve predictable operations such as the ordering of new stock, the design

of a production schedule or the preparation of a transport route for deliveries.

THE DECISION-MAKING PROCESS

The structure of the decision-making process within an organisation should be based on the types of decision that need to be made. Routine decisions should, therefore, be dealt with by routine procedures, ensuring that time and money are not wasted unnecessarily. There would be no point, for example, in a senior manager spending large amounts of time on a routine task that could be done by someone with less experience. Similarly, decisions requiring in-depth analysis and thought will require careful consideration by someone with a breadth of experience. Organisations therefore need to develop procedures for decision-making most suited to the nature of the environment in which they are operating. Gilligan, Neale and Murray (1990) recommend, in broad terms:

'*Short-term operating and periodic control decisions should be made by junior and middle management who are involved in the day-to-day administration of the organisation, and not by the company's senior management. The task of senior management is to concentrate upon non-routine, non-recurring, strategic decisions in which there is a high degree of uncertainty regarding the outcome and for which, as a consequence, a far greater element of judgement and creativity is required. In those organisations in which senior management does become embroiled in the day-to-day, straightforward operating decisions, the effectiveness and motivation of lower levels of management is likely to suffer, whilst at the same time, because of the preoccupation with short-term decisions, less time is available for long-term issues, with the result that the managerial focus switches from long-range strategic development of the company to short-range control. Thus, insofar as it is possible to generalise, the primary concern of senior management should be with strategic decisions, whilst short-term operational decisions should be left in the hands of operating management. Middle management then acts as the meeting point between the two, taking as its focus the periodic control decisions.*'

Peter Drucker, in his book *The Practice of Management*, argues that a good deal of discussion about decision-making in business tends to focus on problem-solving, that is, on giving answers. He believes that this is the wrong focus because the most common source of mistakes stems from trying to find answers rather than seeking the right questions to ask. In simple routine decision-making the questions may be obvious, but for the decisions that really matter the skill lies in finding out what the situation is, and these are the specifically managerial decisions.

Ernest Archer (1988) studied more than 2000 managers, executives and supervisors, as well as the research of major writers on organisations. In his book *Decisions, Decisions*, he produced a framework which highlighted the decision-maker's need to monitor continually the environment in which decisions are made (see Figure 9.14). The model necessitates obtaining feedback on any deviations from expected, acceptable, pre-planned or normal states.

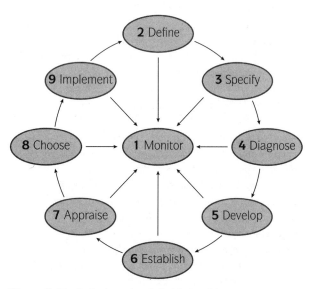

Figure 9.14 *Archer's modes of decision-making*

1. **Monitor**. First, it is essential that managers have a clear idea of how things 'ought to be'. The other eight stages involve the following tasks:
2. **Define** the decision or problem to be tackled and clearly state the boundaries.
3. **Specify** the objectives of the decision. What do you expect to achieve? What are the constraints?
4. **Diagnose** the problem or situation and analyse its cause.
5. **Develop** a range of alternative solutions and courses of action.
6. **Establish** criteria for weighing up alternatives.
7. **Appraise** the alternative solutions or courses of action.
8. **Choose** the best solution.
9. **Implement** the best solution or course of action.

An open-system decision model

Many of the decisions that need to be made by individuals within organisations involve uncertainty. In a complex, dynamic society change is ever-present. In such an environment it is helpful to develop an open-system approach to decision-making. (A closed-system approach assumes that organisations have clearly defined and unambiguous goals.)

An open-system approach dispenses with the notion that the effects of decisions can readily be computed and calculated, and works instead on the premise that at best information will be imperfect. An open-system model places emphasis on *feedback*, *learning* and *adaptation*, together with the effects of these upon ends and means. An open-system approach can be used to show how the decision-making process may be made more flexible. The system can then adjust to changing circumstances and to changing perceptions and understanding of available information. Figure 9.15 illustrates one way in which an open-system model might operate.

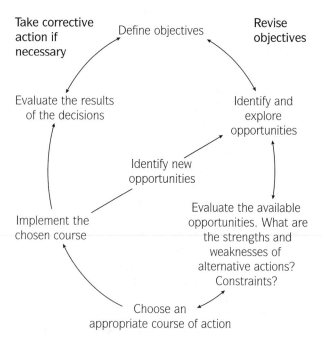

Figure 9.15 *The decision cycle*

Stage 1: Define objectives

Objectives are rarely clear-cut and this stage involves the identification of objectives to be pursued. These will be open to review. Setting objectives involves selecting courses of action that are appropriate to the organisation and establishing measures for assessing their attainment.

Stage 2: Identify and explore opportunities

The next stage is to identify as many opportunities for an organisation, division, department, operating unit, etc. as possible. Exploration involves identifying the potential impacts of these opportunities.

Stage 3: Evaluate opportunities and implications of taking a particular pathway/decision

Evaluation processes range from an inspired guess to a highly researched piece of analysis and assessment. Choosing a particular alternative in decision-making may be based on:

- *Previous experience*. Organisations and managers have a collective experience of handling similar decisions and activities. However, they may need to be careful when the decision is based on new considerations or a changed organisational environment.
- *Experimentation*. Various alternatives are tried to see which is likely to be the best (e.g. testing out alternative new products before deciding on the best choice).
- *Detailed research and analysis*. This is perhaps the best way approach. It requires a full understanding of the situation before a calculated decision is made.

At this point, the organisation should be considering whether making a particular decision will help it to meet its objectives.

Stage 4: Choose the action

Provided that the decision-maker can show a clear match between an action and objectives, he or she can then choose the most effective of the alternative courses of action. For example, if an organisation's objective is to achieve some measure of guaranteed success, it might choose a course of action that avoids risk. Alternatively, it might be prepared to take a risk if the objective is to achieve high returns.

If the chosen course of action does not look likely to meet the required objectives, the decision-maker should either reduce the target goal to manageable proportions or seek alternative courses of action to meet the original target.

Stage 5: Implement the chosen course

Once the groundwork has been covered and all aspects of potential decisions have been discussed, a decision can be made. The effects of the decision should then be closely monitored. Putting the decision into practice may quickly lead to the identification of new opportunities. For example, once the USA had implemented its space programme, researchers immediately became aware of fresh opportunities such as the Space Shuttle. These possibilities help organisations to meet their objectives in new and different ways.

Stage 6: Evaluate the results of the decision

The results of the decision need to be evaluated to improve the decision-making process. Corrective action can be taken if necessary. The decision-making cycle is an on-going process; the open-ended nature of the process means that the quality of decisions should increase with time.

The open systems approach highlights the importance of evaluation. Results need continually to be fed back to decision-makers so that they can reappraise decisions in the light of an increasing quantity and quality of information. A simple illustration of how this can have beneficial effects is in the training of cricketers using computer programs that simulate their bowling action. Programs have been developed which play back to the bowlers a picture of their action in bowling a cricket ball. The cricketers are thereby provided with feedback on current performance, enabling them to take corrective action, to appraise existing technique and to develop an understanding of new possibilities.

REFERENCES

Archer, Ernest, *Decisions*, Macmillan, 1988.

Burns, T. and Stalker, G., *The Management of Innovation*, Tavistock, 1961.

Drucker, Peter, *The Practice of Management*, Butterworth-Heinemann, 1994.

Gilligan, Neale and Murray, *Business Decision Making*, Philip Allen, 1990.

Greiner, L. E., *Evolution and Revolution as Organisations Grow*, Harvard Business Review, 1972.

Handy, Charles, *Understanding Organisations*, Penguin, 1993.

Huczynski, Andrzej and Buchanan, David, *Organisational Behaviour*, Prentice Hall, 1998.

Kanter, Rosabeth Moss, *The Change Masters*, Thomson Business Press, 1995.

Katz, D. and Kahn, R., *The Social Psychology of Organisations*, John Wiley, 1964.

Lawrence, P. R. and Lorsch, *Organisation and Environment*, Harvard University Press, 1976.

Mintzberg, Henry, *The Nature of Managerial Work*, Harper & Row, 1973.

Sadler, Philip, *Managerial Leadership in Post-Industrial Society*, Gower, 1998.

Simon, Herbert, *Models of Man*, Wiley, 1957

Taylor, F. W., *Scientific Management*, Harper & Row, 1947.

Walton, R. E. 'From control to commitment: transforming workforce management in the USA', in Clark, K., Hayes, R. H. & Lorenz, C. (eds), *The Uneasy Alliance: Managing the Productivity–Technology Dilemma*, Harvard Business School Press, 1985.

CHAPTER 10

Organisational Structure and Culture

This chapter investigates and evaluates how organisational structure and culture contribute to business success.

On completion of the chapter you should be able to:

- explain organisational culture
- identify and describe different organisational structures

- examine the relationship between an organisation's structure and culture, and the effects on business performance.

TYPES OF ORGANISATION AND ASSOCIATED STRUCTURES

There are many possible definitions of what makes an organisation. Here is a typical definition:

An organisation is a system, having an established structure and conscious planning, in which people work and deal with one another in a coordinated and cooperative manner for the accomplishment of recognised goals.

TASK

What do you see as being the key words in the suggested definition? Set out a list of the key words and explain what you think they mean.

In their highly acclaimed book *Organising and Organisation* (1993), Sims, Fineman and Gabriel argue that most definitions leave it unclear as to which human associations should be thought of as organisations. For example, it is easy to decide that armies and universities are organisations – but what about football crowds, tribes, theatre audiences etc? These authors therefore propose a set of criteria which they feel would be useful to define the 'general space' occupied by organisations. Their criteria are as follows:

- Organisations are associations of several people, who are aware of being members, and who are generally willing to cooperate.

- They are mainly long-term and survive changes of personnel.

- They profess some objectives which they pursue in a methodical, no-nonsense manner.

- They involve a certain division of labour, with different people assigned to different tasks. This may amount to a hierarchy, a matrix or some other structure.

- They may involve a certain degree of formality and impersonality.

TASK

Brainstorm a list of about twelve different associations of people. Which of these associations seem to fit the criteria outlined above for an organisation?

Organisational features

Most organisations have the following features:

- **A unique name**. This can range from the St John Ambulance Brigade to the Monster Raving Loony Party.
- **Objectives**. These identify the direction in which an organisation is seeking to move. By setting out a list of objectives, an organisation can check how successful it is in moving in the right direction.
- **Rules and regulations**. Some of these will be written down. Other, informal, codes of practice are not written down but are recognised and responded to. Some rules are imposed externally by laws; every college and university, for example, has a set of rules governing safety on the premises.
- **Patterns and structures**. Organisations, not surprisingly, are organised – they have set ways of doing things. In the army, for example, there is a clear structure comprising a hierarchy according to rank. Other organisations are more democratic, with many decision-makers with similar status.
- **Posts and offices**. People within an organisation have varied responsibilities. A football club, for example, may have a manager, a trainer, a coach, a ticket seller, ground staff, etc.
- **Chain of command**. In the majority of organisations there is a chain of command set out in official and unofficial codes. Organisational structures are discussed in detail later in this chapter.
- **Power**. Members of an organisation have varying levels of power vested in them. These powers may be set out in a written contract. For example, in a sports team the manager may select the team; the trainer may choose the training programme; the physiotherapist may set out a schedule for treating injuries; and so on.
- **Records**. Organisations need to have systematic and well-organised records.

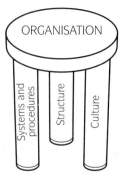

Figure 10.1 *The three-legged stool*

There are three principal components of an organisation. These are: (1) structure; (2) systems and procedures; and (3) cultures. BP have used the analogy of a three-legged stool (see Figure 10.1) – take any of the legs away and the whole thing collapses.

Organisational structure

The structure of an organisation can be defined in a number of ways. For example:

- Structure is 'those aspects of the pattern of behaviour in the organisation that are relatively stable and that change only slowly' (March and Simon, 1958).

- Structure is 'the relatively enduring allocation of work roles and administrative mechanisms that creates a pattern of interrelated work activities and allows the organisation to conduct, co-ordinate and control its work activities' (Child, 1984).

- 'Structure is a means for attaining the objectives and goals of an organisation' (Drucker, 1974).

Discussion point

What key differences do you see as being important in the above definitions of organisational structure?

Systems, procedures and processes

Sadler (1991) defines systems, procedures and processes as 'the relatively formal, prescribed and standardised ways of doing things that have been developed or adopted by the organisation. There will exist systems and procedures governing the core business processes, however these are defined.' For example, the car-maker Rover identified nine key processes as:

- product improvement
- new product introduction
- logistics
- sales/distribution/service
- manufacturing
- maintenance
- business planning
- corporate learning
- management of people.

Under each of these heading there is a whole range of systems and procedures. For example, under management of people there will be performance reviews and appraisal systems, remuneration systems, equal opportunity procedures, and so on.

Culture

Cultures of organisations are examined later in this chapter. They are difficult to define but generally relate to patterns of behaviours, based on shared values, common understandings, characteristic behaviours and symbols of various kinds.

Organisational architecture

The term **organisational architecture** refers to managers' more general views about their organisation and how it is structured. It focuses particularly on how traditional departments and more informal project teams can fit together, and on the role of work-teams.

Today a lot of emphasis is placed on work-teams. The idea is that a business can be seen as a series of projects carried out by small groups of people with complementary skills. This is a continuation of the movement away from the 'tall' or bureaucratic structure, which divides a business into clearly defined functions such as finance and marketing. In many organisations there has been a move towards flattening the organisational architecture. Gone are the days of the 'top-down' hierarchical company in which information flowed down through various layers; today organisations may be structured around groups of employees focusing on complete processes which are designed to meet the needs of consumers (see Figure 10.2).

In this new way of viewing an organisation, self-contained teams are responsible for a specific part of the business or a particular project. They work to targets set by central management. They take advice and assistance, as necessary,

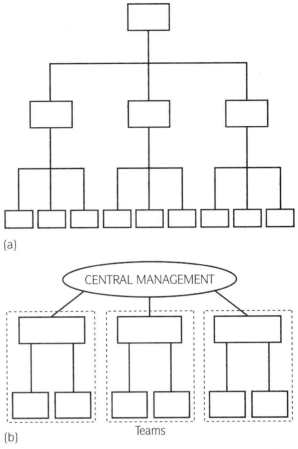

Figure 10.2 *Structures: (a) traditional hierarchical structure (the old way), and (b) the new way to view an organisation*

from specialist departments such as Research and Development, Finance, Personnel and Public Relations – although sometimes they have their own specialists. They also take goods and services from outside suppliers when these are judged to be more cost-effective. Occasionally, central management, or one of its teams, may decide to subcontract an entire project to an outside supplier.

Types of organisational structures

Modern companies are characterised by a broad array of organisational structures. These are described below.

Line organisation

Line organisation is the typical structure of a *hierarchy*. There are direct communication links between superiors and subordinates. Each member of the organisation has a clear understanding of the chain of command and to whom he or she is responsible. This type of structure can be very effective because of its clarity – there are set rules and procedures which can be referred to. Figure 10.3 illustrates the way in which communication flows downwards.

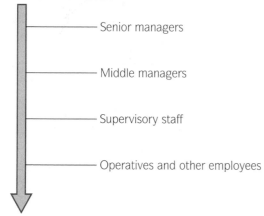

Figure 10.3 *The flow of communication in line organisation*

Line management is typically used to organise a firm's central activities such as the making and selling of products. In these areas there is a clear hierarchical framework. Larger organisations tend to have more rigid and bureaucratic structures than smaller ones. Although agreed and clear procedures are necessary, it is also important to have a degree of flexibility. Formal structures frequently undergo informal changes in the course of time as new situations arise.

Staff organisation

Staff organisation primarily serves the various line departments. Typical staff areas include personnel, corporate affairs, data processing, and office administration.

Staff departments typically cut across an organisation to provide a range of specialist services and consultancy skills. For example, any line department of a company might require specialist legal help from time to time, might want to have data processed or might need help with recruiting new staff. Figure 10.4 illustrates the way in which various staff areas can be made available to all line departments within an organisation.

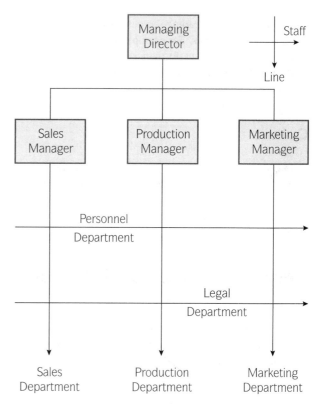

Figure 10.4 *Staff organisation*

A staff department might itself be organised as a hierarchy. For example, the personnel department could have several tiers below the personnel manager.

Combined line and staff organisation

Most medium and large businesses combine elements of line and staff organisation. There are a number of advantages to having this blend:

- The line departments are able to concentrate on their central roles of marketing, making, selling etc. while being complemented by specialist service departments.
- Line managers need to familiarise themselves only with information related to their core activities.
- Staff groupings can be called in to provide specialist information and advice in a number of key areas.

However, there are also a number of potential disadvantages of combining the two areas. One major disadvantage is that it can lead to confusion because there is less clarity over departmental responsibility and lines of authority. Unity of command is often thought to be the mark of an effective organisation. Where there is more than one centre of responsibility confusion can arise because one section can blame another for failure to carry out work effectively or for a breakdown in communication. Where department managers compete with one another to secure high-status work, or where they try to avoid less prestigious work, problems can occur.

Another potential disadvantage arises from the fact that line managers often rise to a particular position through many years of dedicated hard work (this is particularly true in production departments), whereas many staff managers are recruited with a university background. In this situation some line managers may resent a staff manager's rapid rise to managerial status. Equally, some staff managers may regard themselves as superior to those who have 'worked their way up'. These clashes can be detrimental to the smooth running of an organisation.

In addition, some line managers may resent having to listen to the opinions of staff managers with priorities that are different from their own. For example, a corporate affairs or personnel manager might try to push a company into employing more youth trainees in order to project a certain image within the community; whereas a production manager may be concerned with having a more experienced workforce.

In order to overcome these and other difficulties, it is essential for an organisation to devise a clear strategy to coordinate staff and line groupings. This strategy will involve setting out the goals of the company and then deciding on the responsibility of line and staff groupings. The responsibilities need to be set out in a clear statement of policy. Some large companies even have an 'organisation and methods' department with the responsibility for clarifying such issues.

Case Study

Clarifying objectives

In his groundbreaking book, *The Practice of Management*, Peter Drucker argues that:

'Objectives are needed in every area where performance and results directly and vitally affect the survival and prosperity of the business. These are the areas which are affected by every management decision and which therefore have to be considered in every management decision. They decide what it means concretely to manage the business. They spell out what results the business must aim at and what is needed effectively to work towards these targets.'

Questions

How can management by objectives enable a business to best create the right mix between line and service management/organisation?

Superstructure

The superstructure of an organisation is the way in which employees are grouped into various departments or sections.

Grouping by function

This is probably still the most common way of grouping employees. Functional organisation means that the organisation is divided into broad sectors, each with its own particular specialism or function (see Figure 10.5). There are a number of clear advantages to organising on a functional basis:

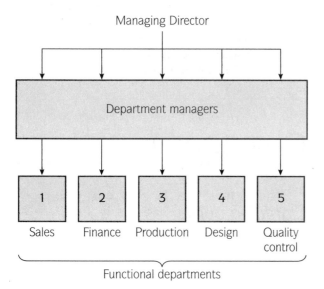

Figure 10.5 *Grouping by function*

- If groups of specialists are given control over specific work areas, this prevents wasteful duplication within an organisation. Invoices can be processed in one department, new orders won by another and payments collected by a third. Provided clear guidelines are laid down as to who does what, the organisation's members will be clear about their responsibilities.
- Specialists are able to work in a pool of like-minded people.
- Because each part of the organisation is pursuing its primary function, it will contribute to the overall well-being of the total system.

There are potential disadvantages:

- Narrow specialisation may restrict an individual's or department's ability to develop a global view of the whole organisation.
- Individuals cannot move easily between departments.
- Rivalry can develop between departments, which may then try to block one anothers' initiatives. Departments may pull in opposite directions – in some organisations you can hear complaints such as 'This company is run by a bunch of accountants!' and 'Not enough attention is being paid to selling!'
- As an organisation becomes larger, communication channels may become slower or distorted, particularly between upper and lower levels.

Grouping by product

When a large organisation produces a range of products, it may find it convenient to create a structure based on product lines. A firm in the publishing industry can have a newspaper division, a magazine and periodicals division and a books division. Each division then contains a mixture of all the specialist ingredients required to enable it to work independently. Pirelli, one of the world's leading tyre manufacturers, is divided into two divisions – for tyres and cables.

TASK

Identify three organisations which are based on product lines. What are its main product divisions?

A great advantage of the product structure is that divisions can concentrate on their own market area. It also becomes possible to assess the profitability and effectiveness of each sector. At the same time it is still possible to share expertise between divisions and to share services such as a combined transport fleet.

By isolating the various parts of a business organisation, it becomes possible to cut out loss-making divisions and to amalgamate divisions by merging them with similar divisions in other companies (see Figure 10.6). It also

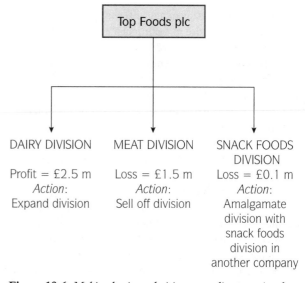

Figure 10.6 *Making business decisions according to regional profit*

becomes possible to generate competition within a company and to allow greater scope to create an internal promotion ladder.

Grouping by process

When the manufacture of a product requires a series of processes, separate departments can be set up to perform each process. To take the example of a publishing company, within each of the divisions there may be departments responsible for carrying out stages of production – editing the copy, page layout and design, printing, etc. (see Figure 10.7).

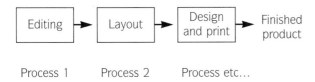

Figure 10.7 *Grouping by process in a publishing company*

Processes are key stages that take place in production, and can take place in any of the functions within an organisation but are typically associated with production. Key processes in the production of shoes might include cutting, shaping, forming, and completing the finished shoe. Key processes in marketing might include market research, advertising, promotions, etc.

In recent years it has been very fashionable to talk about **business process re-engineering** (BPR). In essence this means the identification of key processes which are required to meet customers' requirements, and then to focus on these processes to ensure that they are performed to the highest quality standards – where quality means conformance with customer requirements. By identifying the key processes and studying the links between these and the end consumer, it will be possible to create first-class integrated processes within the organisation.

For example, a well-known building society mapped out its key processes as shown in Figure 10.8. The emphasis is on the customer. The design and development of the organisation is built around the key links at the heart of the chain involved with developing customer relationships, and customer service, which are based on customer requirements. The management process is then designed to meet customer requirements. Profit is an important consideration, as shown by the balance sheet, but that will

be healthy only if the whole organisation is working towards meeting the customers' needs.

There are a number of clear advantages to organising on a process basis:

- It is possible to set up teams of like-minded specialists (e.g. designers).
- It becomes easy to identify points in the production process at which things are doing well or badly.
- It is easy to introduce new technology at a given stage of production and to familiarise the appropriate staff with new skills and working practices.

There are potential disadvantages:

- Process production works effectively only if there is a steady flow from one stage to another. If one process gets out of step by producing too much or too little, problems occur as stocks pile up or run out. This situation might arise if, say, one group of process workers goes on strike or has a high absenteeism level.
- Sections of employees may become too specialist and fail to communicate effectively with other sections.
- It may become difficult to transfer employees from one process to another if there are too rigid divisions between processes. Employees might prefer to stick with their existing work-group and continue to use the skills they have.

Grouping by geographical area

Large organisations tend to have branches spread throughout the country and sometimes overseas. Multiple retailing companies are a good example. Tesco has supermarkets in most major towns and cities in the United Kingdom, and it has expanded into eastern European countries like Hungary and Poland, as well as having supermarkets in western European countries like Germany, and a supermarket in Calais, France. In this case, groups of shops are organised into regional divisions which have local supervision for such things as training of staff and some aspects of distribution policy. Figure 10.9 illustrates another retailing organisation with five domestic divisions and three overseas divisions.

There are a number of clear advantages to organising on a geographical basis:

- Setting up distinct regional divisions makes it possible to respond quickly to local needs, issues and problems. The

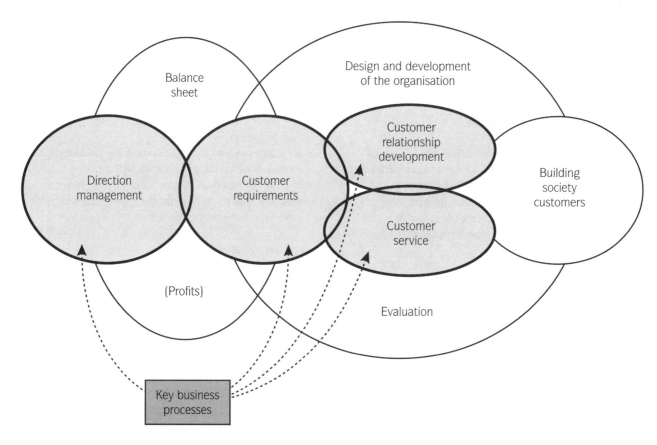

Figure 10.8 *Designing business processes around the customer*

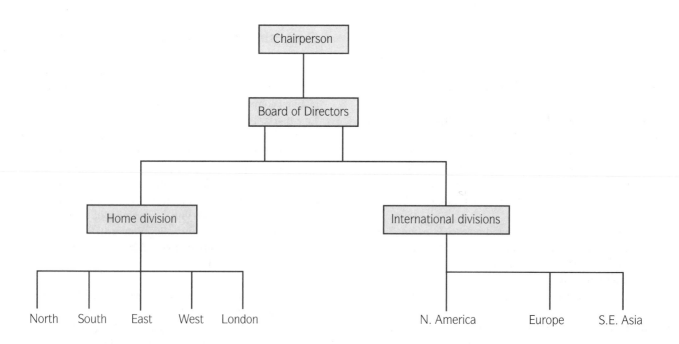

Figure 10.9 *Grouping by geographical area*

organisation thus becomes more sensitive to customers, employees and other groups. At the same time, it might be possible to cut through a lot of red tape if the regional groups are allowed to make their own decisions.

- Setting up national and regional divisions makes it possible to tailor the operations to local differences like language, laws and customs. Local knowledge is best gained by hiring local specialists.
- National governments often look more kindly on multinational divisions that have a local head office.

There are potential disadvantages:

- Having too many regional divisions can lead to wasteful duplication of facilities and roles. Too few divisions can lead to lack of coordination, gaps in communication and breakdowns.
- Having an extensive regional structure requires the creation of a series of management positions. It is not always easy to recruit personnel of the required calibre to fill these positions.
- Regional headquarters might take on a life of their own and start pulling in the opposite direction to central policy makers.
- Although the local divisions will frequently have the best understanding of the situation 'on the ground', they might find themselves at loggerheads with central officials many thousands of miles away.

Grouping by type of customer

Some organisations set up different structures to deal with groups of customers. In a department store, the restaurant operates in a different way and has different procedures from that of the department selling underwear. The furniture department needs to set out a process of documentation and to make arrangements for delivery to customers, which clearly contrasts with purchasing procedures for toys. Banks have a counter for foreign currency transactions and a department dealing with first-time accounts, as well as regular departments for dealing with private and business customers. Many businesses have different procedures for dealing with large and small customers. Separate departments may handle these accounts, using different types of paperwork, offering different rates of discount and treating customers in different ways.

The advantages of running an organisation in this way are:

- Different types of customer can be dealt with by separate departments.

- Customers will be more inclined to deal with a business that has departments concerned with their particular needs.
- It is easier to check on the performance of individual products.

There are potential disadvantages:

- Divisions may compete with one another for the use of company resources.
- The structure may be costly to set up and will be cost-effective only if there is sufficient demand.
- More administration and accounting services will be required.

Project forms of organisation

Today, project management is used widely in organisations. A project team is responsible for managing a particular project. Companies that make and sell goods employ product managers who pilot particular products from the initial development stage through to final production and sales. The product manager is there to plan, coordinate, initiate, persuade, and hurry things up.

The product manager seeks to synchronise and maximise effort across the various departments. An organisation that operates purely on functional lines can soon run into bottlenecks and confusion between the various departments, but a project manager can ensure that there is coordinated planning to bring resources and people together correctly. The project manager is there solely to coordinate the activities.

Case Study

Project planning at Northern Foods

This study outlines some of the steps involved in bringing out a new recipe dish – Minced Beef Hotpot – at Northern Foods.

The first stage was to allocate a project manager to be responsible for the development of the dish. Next, *concept development* started with the retailer (Marks & Spencer) drawing up a brief for the new product, which was passed to the manufacturer. At Northern Foods the development chefs then created the new recipe in a small kitchen. Samples were prepared by the chefs for trials.

Process development was the next step when both retailer and manufacturer were happy with the product. Food technologists were responsible for designing and implementing the process needed to recreate the original in the factory and to launch it into the marketplace. Making Minced Beef Hotpot for four people in a kitchen using a couple of saucepans and roasting dish in the oven is easy; but how do you make it in a factory on a large scale, maintaining strict standards of hygiene and retaining the home-cooked taste?

Factory layout had to be considered. The factory was divided into two sections which separated the raw and the cooked/processed foods. In the low-risk area, raw materials were to be stored and prepared, with raw ingredients loaded into cooking vessels at the barrier. In the high-risk area the cooked foods were to be packaged and prepared for despatch. Here, very strict safety and hygiene rules were to operate.

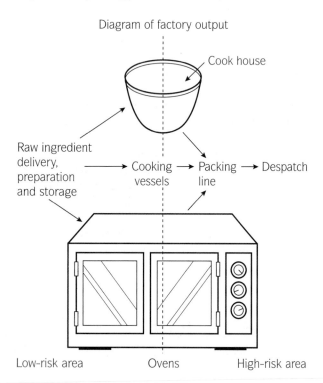

Diagram of factory output

Cook house

Raw ingredient delivery, preparation and storage → Cooking vessels → Packing line → Despatch

Low-risk area   Ovens   High-risk area

Next came *factory trials*. A specification was written for the new product which included the recipe, the suppliers of the ingredients, the processing and packing methods. The purpose of the first trial was to collect as much information as possible on the method, ease of processing, labour and time taken. Further trials were continued until the product was ready to launch.

However, before the product was finally ready for launch there were other key stages, including quality assurance checks, preparing the packaging, choosing the best heating instructions for consumers, etc.

At the *launch* the production process was monitored by development technologists. The retailer was present to observe the launch and approve the first packs off the line.

Questions

1. Why does the development of a new recipe dish require a project manager?

2. Who would have been involved in the project team?

3. Who was responsible for checking that the team worked to schedule, and hurried up working arrangements as and when required?

Strategic Business Units (SBUs)

The **strategic business unit** is an extension of the project management principle. An SBU is a distinct little business acting as part of a larger business unit. The SBU acts as though independent. This makes it possible for work-teams in an organisation to concentrate on ensuring that particular products are given priority. A large modern company may produce hundreds of different product lines; the only way to ensure that each is given priority is to give a group of people 'ownership' and responsibility for its development. The SBU must then meet given performance targets and is accountable to the senior management of the larger organisation.

Matrix structure

An organisation need not necessarily have a single pattern of organisation. Many large businesses combine two or more patterns in a **matrix structure** – for example, they might combine functional and geographical lines of command.

In a matrix structure any member of the organisation may belong to two or more groups (see Figure 10.10). In the illustration, groups of employees are organised into product development teams (e.g. Minced Beef Hotpot, Cannelloni, etc) as well as by functions (e.g. marketing or sales). In the example a particular group of workers, say production section A, will be accountable to both the project manager for Minced Beef Hotpot and the production manager. Each member of the organisation (below managerial level) is thus accountable to two or more managers. Marketing, sales and other key functional managers will have a global responsibility for their functions within the organisation, while divisional

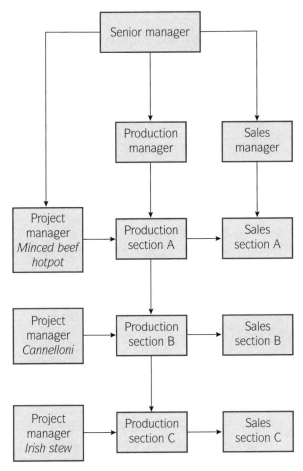

Figure 10.10 *Example of part of a mixed structure*

- The system makes it possible to draw groups from specific departments in the required numbers.
- There can be cross-fertilisation of ideas across departments rather than having departments working in isolation.

There are potential disadvantages:

- A complex matrix structure may be difficult to understand, and employees can lose sight of the major organisational aims.
- This system will often require extra administrative resources, costly in terms of time and money.
- Because a matrix establishes more than one chain of command, this can lead to power struggles, contradictory orders and general confusion.

Matrix and project organisation are becoming increasingly important because of the rapidly changing environment in which organisations operate. These structures support quick responses to changes. Also, with organisations setting clear targets and criteria to work towards, a project manager and team may be the best way to achieve the targets. The project manager can be given direct line authority over all the activities necessary to complete major end-results.

Deciding on an organisational structure

We have seen that each of the various approaches to running organisations has particular advantages and disadvantages. How can the best structure be chosen?

Obviously the size of the business is highly relevant – it is only worth having a project team if a project is large enough, it is only worth having a geographical structure if geographical markets are large enough, and so on.

The technology employed is important. Where different technologies are employed it is almost inevitable that there will be functional separation. Product divisions may be best if the technological differences apply to services.

The nature of the market is important. Where the market is differentiated it may be best to organise around different types of consumers. If the market is homogenous, other structures may be better.

The number and variety of skills is another factor. If only a limited number of skills are to be used, wide spans of

managers have responsibility for these functions on a divisional basis.

Each divisional manager will be responsible for a specific project. In order to carry out this project, he or she will be able to call on the full range of departments to collaborate in achieving project targets. Projects may be based on products, types of customer, geographical area, or any other specific criteria. Inevitably a matrix structure can be complicated and it needs to be clearly laid out.

There are a number of advantages to be gained from implementing a matrix structure:

- A matrix makes it possible to run an organisation so as to focus on a number of aims at the same time – for example, servicing different types of customers, servicing different regions, producing different types of products.
- A matrix gives an organisation extra flexibility to respond to new situations where there is an increase in demand for its resources.

control are possible and roles can be clearly defined. If many skills are required then it may be better to use team-working.

TASK

Choose an organisation that you are familiar with which is currently growing to operate on a larger scale. Suggest how the organisation can reorganise its structure in order to more effectively cope with its on-going growth.

Sadler (1991) sets out six major influences on decisions about an organisation. These are:

- *People's preferences*, particular those of top managers.
- *The strengths and weaknesses of key personnel*. The organisation is thus designed around the people rather than the people having to fit in with the organisational structure. (Interestingly a number of experts on football suggest that the best teams are built around the strengths of the playing staff.)
- *Situational factors* such as the nature of the task. For example, dangerous activities will require higher levels of control.
- *Influences depending on the scale and complexity of the organisation*. Large complex organisations will require more elaborate and highly sophisticated systems of organisation than smaller ones.
- *Theories about organisation design* which may be acquired by reading books, attending conferences, hiring consultants, etc.
- *Values, beliefs and attitudes*. Cultural factors can have a key influence on shaping the organisation.

TASK

The following ingredients have at certain times been suggested as being features of a successful organisation. Which of these factors do you think are important and which are not important?

a *Unity of purpose*. All parts of the organisation should work towards a common aim. If parts
work in different directions, this can be a source of confusion and is bad for the morale of employees.

b *Effective leadership*. Positions of authority and responsibility should be given only to those who are capable of being effective. Decisions can be implemented only if those in authority have the confidence and determination to see that they are carried out.

c *Flexibility*. An organisation should not be too rigid. It should be capable of altering course quickly if things do not go right, and adapt to changing circumstances.

d *Operational efficiency*. The operations must be studied and the results of this analysis used to ensure that things are done in the best possible way. At one level this involves looking closely at each operation to see that time is not wasted, that costs are kept down and that work is done accurately. In addition, the functioning of the whole organisation needs to be studied at a global level. It is important that the various parts of the organisation work together smoothly and in the same direction (this is called 'overall efficiency').

e *Good communication*. Each member of the organisation should understand clearly his or her rights and obligations. Lines of authority need to be clearly defined.

Organisations as socio-technical systems

Technology both influences and is influenced by an organisation's design. Changing the technology used will change the social system (i.e. people's roles and status). Technology consists of the processes of production and administration which involve a combination of equipment and machinery on the one hand, and a wide range of systems and procedures on the other. For example, production technology is made up of the machinery and the systems used in production control and the maintenance of equipment.

In recent years there has been considerable debate about the relationship between an organisation's size, the technology it uses, and its most appropriate structure. The size/structure issue is supposed to hinge on the tendency that, as organisations increase in size, they benefit from increasing specialisation and differentiation. This leads to an increasing number of subunits which are grouped into functional and other categories. As an organisation becomes more complex it requires more coordination and control, leading to structural changes, such as standardisation of rules and formal procedures. There is increased decentralisation, so that decisions can be made at lower levels, and more levels are created in the hierarchy. This leads to the growth of administrative, professional and clerical grades with the organisation. Personal supervision is replaced by more impersonal rules and regulations.

In the 1980s and 90s, large organisations tended to 'downsize', becoming leaner and fitter. The tendency was to strip out layers of administrative control to create more autonomous units. Clearly, there is a relationship between structure and size, but this is likely to vary considerably between industries and to be influenced by the technology employed. In the new organisations of the new millennium we are already beginning to see that successful organisations are reconfiguring around the most effective IT systems. Modern knowledge organisations are different in shape and structure from the old capital-intensive industries of the middle of the twentieth century.

The origin of the view that there is a close relationship between technology and structure is often taken to be **Joan Woodward's** study of manufacturing firms in south-east Essex between the 1950s and 60s. Woodward identified three different types of technical complexity in the firms she studied:

- *Unit or small-batch production* is for products that are made individually, for job production, for batches produced within a single week, etc.
- *Large-batch and mass production* is for batches requiring over a week to produce, and for assembly lines.
- *Process production* is for long or continuous standardised runs, repetitive procedures, for chemicals, gas, etc.

Woodward felt that technical complexity increases as one moves from unit towards process production. For instance,

in process production one is able to exert far more control and achieve far more predictable standardised results. Woodward drew out a number of relationships between technology and organisational structure:

- As technical complexity increases so too does the chief executive's **span of control** (the number of people he or she controls directly), the number of managers, the ratio of managers to employees, the proportion of administrative employees, etc.
- There is an inverse (U-shaped) relationship between technical complexity and the span of control of first-line supervisors and styles of management. In mass production the span of control is larger and employs formal mechanistic styles of management. At the two ends of the spectrum, unit production and process production, there is a smaller span of control and organic management styles.
- Within the three technology categories, the most successful firms are those in which there is the closest fit between organisation and technology (e.g. a mass production firm employing mechanistic formal styles).
- There is little or no relationship between size of the firm (numbers employed) and technical complexity and organisational characteristics.

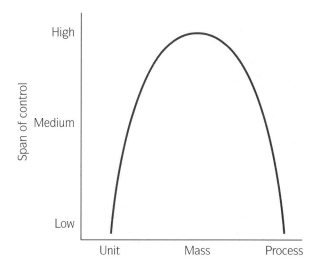

Figure 10.11 *Woodward's relationship between span of control and technology*

More recent work has thrown doubts on the validity of Woodward's findings. In particular, detailed research by the **Aston group** (which has been backed up by many other studies) set out to produce a more appropriate definition of technology. The Aston group focused on **'operations technology'** – that is, the equipping and sequencing of activities in the work flow. All organisations can be said to have an operations technology.

The Aston group identified a measure which they called **work-flow integration**. Clearly this is determined by the extent to which work-flow processes are interdependent, automated, measurable and adaptable for other purposes. Measures of work-flow integration can be applied to any organisation. Using this measure the Aston group found that technology is moderately related to the following basic dimensions of organisational structure:

• the structuring of activities
• the concentration of authority
• line control of work flow
• a supportive component.

More importantly they reported that factors other than technology were more influential in creating variations in structure. They therefore strongly downgraded the importance of technology in determining organisational structure.

The debate over the importance of technology in determining structure continues to sway back and forth, but the whole issue is clouded by the difficulty of defining 'technology' adequately. Indeed, it is often difficult to separate 'technology' from 'the organisation', particularly now that information and process technologies have come to dominate production.

There can be no doubt that today new technologies make it possible to change the ways in which organisations are structured. Project teams, for example, are able to share information and have instant access to data generated

thousands of miles away. Computers are able to simplify the administrative process so that many of the middle layers of an organisation can be stripped away. The net result is that organisations are able to contract. Smaller organisations can become more personal, particularly where the emphasis is on team-work.

Clearly, the types of technology that can be employed vary from industry to industry. However, many modern technologies such as 'number crunching' facilities and administrative procedures using IT, have a profound effect.

Centralisation and decentralisation

Centralisation means keeping major responsibilities within sections or units of the central headquarters or at the core of the organisation. **Decentralisation** describes a situation in which many specific responsibilities have been delegated to branches or away from the centre. Delegation is the process of assigning responsibilities and decentralisation is the end result (see Figure 10.12).

Organisations may choose to centralise certain key functions such as strategic planning and accounts, and purchasing in a retailing organisation. Other functions – such as recruitment – may be decentralised (i.e. left up to branches or departments).

While many firms are geographically centralised with major decisions being taken at the head office, others are organisationally centralised with decision-making being in the hands of a small group or section of management. When a centralised firm decides to push out new areas of decision-making to its middle or lower managers, or to its branches, then it is engaging in decentralisation.

Case Study

Centralisation/decentralisation at Shell UK

For any company, but particularly one with a wide geographical spread and a huge range of product types, decentralisation of

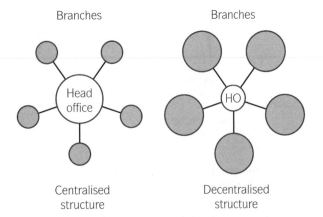

Figure 10.12 *The difference between centralisation and decentralisation*

one kind or another is essential. Most decisions, especially tactical ones, cannot be taken effectively at the centre, which may be miles or continents away, because they have to be taken quickly, on the spot, by people who know all the circumstances. There is often no time for a referral back to central office, even if it has a complete understanding of that particular problem.

One way of encouraging decentralisation that involves changing the structure of the company is to 'flatten' the organisational hierarchy by removing one or more of its layers, so that each divisional head reports directly to the Managing Director rather than to other directors who themselves report to the top person.

Another way is to create separate profit centres – sections of the overall business that are given the responsibility and resources (and guidance where necessary) to operate as if they were independent. For instance, Shell's bitumen business is now run by Shell Bitumen UK, a separate profit centre within Shell Oil UK. Emstar Ltd is responsible for Shell's energy management business in the UK, and Synthetic Chemicals Ltd, a subsidiary of Shell Chemicals UK, specialises in fine chemicals. Strategic decisions, with long-term implications for all parts of the company, are still taken centrally. Even so, many different people will be required to contribute to them, simply because the amount of input needed when a major decision has to be made can be immense.

Of course all decisions, at whatever level, are made in the context of the company's specific business objectives. These are determined by central management, but have to be in line with the general directions, capacities and culture of the company.

Questions

1. Why does Shell need to make some decisions centrally?

2. Why is it important for Shell to decentralise some of its decision-making?

3. How might Shell benefit from such decentralisation?

4. What criteria should be used to decide whether decisions must be made at the centre? Will these criteria change in the course of time?

Reasons for decentralisation

Not all situations can be understood in depth by the small number of people at the centre of an organisation. The information may be very complex, varied and specialised,

and it may be difficult to transfer information accurately from the edges to the top of an organisation.

Secondly, as in the Shell case study, decentralisation allows a swift response to local needs and conditions. Thirdly, decentralisation can encourage employee motivation. Giving local staff more responsibilities is likely to result in their feeling involved in the organisational decision-making process. Fourthly, an organisation that is strongly centralised needs to be highly regimented with little scope for individual initiative. This is what characterised eastern bloc centrally planned economies prior to *perestroika*. There is inflexibility and the need for constant supervision of subordinates.

Vertical and horizontal decentralisation

Vertical decentralisation exists when decision-making authority is pushed down through the layers of the organisation so that several layers of management and supervisory workers are allowed to make decisions. *Horizontal* decentralisation occurs when decision-making authority is pushed sideways across an organisation, perhaps by giving powers to the technocracy as well as to middle management.

Structural integration and business functions

There is no 'ideal' level of decentralisation for organisations. However, the goal should be to create the most efficient pattern of allocation of resources and to enable all problems to be given concentrated effort.

When dealing with complex and sophisticated tasks in a changing business environment it is often necessary to engage a range of experts in decision-making. This suggests a decentralised form of decision-making.

Tom Burns, in his book *Industrial Man: Selected Readings*, has described organic systems as those that are adapted to unstable conditions, when new and unfamiliar problems and requirements continually arise which cannot be broken down and distributed among specialist roles within a hierarchy. In this situation jobs lose much of their formal definition and the definitive and enduring demarcation of functions becomes impossible. Responsibilities and functions, and even methods and powers, have to be redefined constantly. Each individual has to do his or her job with a knowledge of the overall purpose and circumstances of the organisation. Interaction runs laterally as much as vertically, and communication between people of different ranks tends to resemble lateral rather than vertical command.

The trend today is towards flexible organisations, with teams of people coming together from various functional areas to work collaboratively on projects and in problem-solving activities. What is needed is a structure that allows the forming and reforming of expert groups, yet maintains the integrity of existing groups within the organisation. This structure will be more fluid than a matrix one.

AUTHORITY AND POWER

Creating an organisational structure is fundamentally concerned with the allocation of authority and power. Senior managers are authorised to make senior managerial decisions, and to do this effectively they will need to have appropriate power vested in them. In a hierarchical organisation greatest power and authority will be vested in offices at the top, and the command structure will be in a downward direction. In a modern flat organisation power is far more evenly distributed, although there will still be considerable differences in power and authority between different members of the organisation.

Today we talk about having 'trust' in our employees. Trust involves giving out more authority and power for individuals to make decisions. Accountability involves making them responsible for their actions. However, individuals can be made accountable only if they are given appropriate training and are rewarded in a way which is commensurate with their new levels of responsibility.

The traditional way of establishing formal patterns of authority is through the organisational chart, but we must be wary of assuming that such a chart is written in tablets of stone. In *The Folklore of Management*, in 1962, C. Randall wrote:

> *'Now, obviously, to know who is to do what and to establish authority and responsibility within an institution are the basic first principles of a good administration, but this is a far cry from handing down immutable tablets of stone from the mountain top. Not even the Ten Commandments undertook to do more than establish general guidelines of conduct. They contained no fine print and no explanatory notes. Even the Almighty expected us to use our own good judgement in carrying them out.'*

Organisational charts

In a very small organisation you are unlikely to find a formal structure. For example, in a one-person business the entrepreneur carries out most of the various business functions personally. Then, as a small firm grows a formal organisational structure starts to develop based on functional specialisms. The firm may then be divided up into hierarchical functional divisions.

Every organisational structure can be charted to show the departments, how they link together, and the principal lines of authority. This gives a snapshot view of how the organisation is made up. It shows lines of decision-making and levels of responsibility. Looking at a chart may expose any weaknesses in an organisation.

Organisational charts do have some potential drawbacks. For example, people lower down the chart may shirk their responsibilities by claiming that certain tasks belong to others. Secondly, such charts show only the formal structure of the organisation but miss out the highly significant informal links that usually exist, and which help to keep the organisation running efficiently.

Formal and informal structures

The formal structure of an organisation is based on employees' official roles. If you asked the head teacher of a school or a hospital administrator to draw an organisational chart, they would almost certainly set down the formal structure based on official definitions of what everyone should be doing. For example, the head teacher might present the chart shown in Figure 10.13.

However, concentration on formal structure may disguise what really happens. For example, in the school it may be that the head of the science faculty is frequently away, so that many of the managerial decisions in science are made by one or two of the heads of department. In the school there may be a number of teachers who regularly play golf together, and these teachers (whatever their ranks) could possibly be the major determinants of curriculum policy. In other words, decisions are made not only in staff meetings but also on the golf links. At the same time a number of teachers will be university graduates, and these may have a major say when it comes to making academic decisions about the curriculum (see Figure 10.14).

Managers, to be effective, should always be aware of these informal links. A lot of power may be vested in the

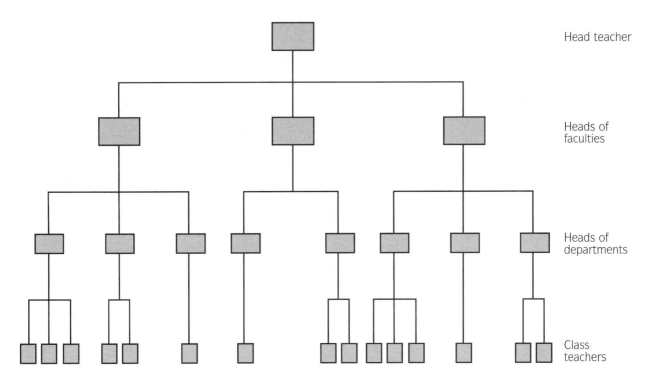

Figure 10.13 *The formal structure of a school*

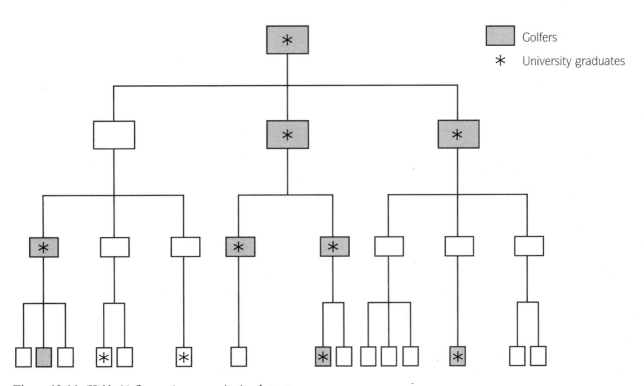

Golfers

* University graduates

Figure 10.14 *'Hidden' influences in an organisational structure*

informal, which is why people like secretaries and quite junior administrators can have a tremendous influence on organisational structure.

Case Study

The office mafia

At Midtown Secondary School the senior management team is made up of a head teacher, two deputy head teachers and three senior teachers. This group meets once a fortnight to discuss developments and policies. There is no set agenda – items to be discussed are usually decided by the head teacher and one of the deputies.

Other members of staff are consulted once a week at a 20-minute meeting before the school day starts on a Monday. The briefing involves the head teacher introducing policy issues and allowing staff to present feedback to the senior management team who group together to give out announcements.

A number of major decisions about the school are made by the school governors. The head teacher and senior deputy are part of the board of governors.

The head and deputies rely heavily on the secretarial staff for day-to-day administration. These office staff deal with all incoming phone calls as well as all routine correspondence. They also handle the day-to-day accounts of the school and are responsible for the disbursement of money for staff expenditures. Because the head and deputies do little teaching, they spend a lot of the day in the school office where they mix with office staff. This means that particularly close relationships have built up between senior teachers and secretarial staff.

Questions

1. Which groups within Midtown school are most likely to be involved in major decision-making processes about policy?

2. Is the informal structure of the school likely to be much different from the formal structure?

3. Which groups may feel that they are not playing an appropriate part in the decision-making process?

4. What suggestions do you have for improving the management of this school?

Levels within the organisation

When drawing up an organisational chart it is usual to distinguish levels of individuals or posts which have roughly equal amounts of responsibility. For example, at the top level there may be the managing director, under whom are the senior managers (e.g. those responsible for marketing and production). Beneath this there tends to be a range of middle managers each with specified levels of responsibility (e.g. departmental management). Supervisors are located beneath managers, and operatives are at the lowest levels (see Figure 10.15). The pattern outlined is the one we associate with a *hierarchical* organisation, rather than one which is based on an *empowerment* approach.

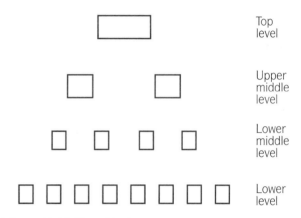

Figure 10.15 *Formal levels in an organisation*

Spans of control

The span of control of an individual is the number of people he or she manages or supervises directly. Figure 10.16 illustrates an organisation with a narrow span of control. No one member of this organisation is directly responsible for more than two subordinates.

There is a limit to the number of people who can be supervised effectively by one person, depending on the type of work involved. Choosing the best span of control means striking a balance between control and trust. A narrow span of control enables close supervision and fast communications. However, there can be disadvantages. For example, there may be too many levels of management, and because the organisation is 'tall' it may be costly to run. Also supervisors might tend to get too involved in their subordinates' detailed work.

Wider spans require much higher degrees of trust in subordinate staff, whilst needing fewer managers and

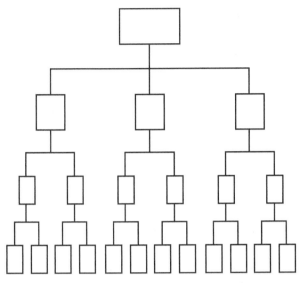

Figure 10.16 *A narrow span of control*

allowing a hierarchy with fewer levels. Typically, spans are widest where the work of subordinates is routine and repetitive, or where subordinates are experienced, competent and fully trained.

Case Study

Exodus 18: 17–25

When Moses' father-in-law noticed that he was spending too much time organising the Exodus of the Israelites, he gave the following advice:

'The thing thou doest is not good. Thou wilt surely wear away, both thou and this people that is with thee; for this thing is too heavy for thee; thou art not able to perform it thyself alone. Hearken now unto my voice, I will give thee counsel …Thou shalt provide out of the people able men … and place such over them, to be rulers of thousands, and rulers of hundreds, rulers of fifties, and rulers of tens. And let them judge the people at all seasons; and it shall be, that every great matter they shall bring unto thee, but every small matter they shall judge; so shall it be easier for thyself, and they shall bear the burden with thee. If thou shalt do this thing, and God commands thee so, then thou shalt be able to endure, and all this people shall also go to their place in peace.'

Questions

1. How sound do you think this advice was?

2. In what types of situation can this theory be applied?

3. Are there situations where this theory would be inappropriate.

It is very difficult to specify an exact figure for the most effective number of people to be within a span of control. Generally speaking, the higher up an organsiation an individual is the fewer people he or she should have in their direct span of control. The exact number will depend on factors that affect the time requirements of managing and the difficulty of management.

Harold Koontz has compiled a table which gives us some important considerations to bear in mind when deciding on the span of management (see Figure 10.17).

Configuration and reconfiguration

The configuration of an organisation is an important determinant of its success or failure. The configuration is the equivalent of a very detailed organisational chart.

- The *height* of the organisation is determined by the number of job levels from the chief executive to the most junior operative.
- The *width* is measured across the organisation (e.g. the number of people reporting to superiors at each level).

Cliff Bowman, in his book *Management in Practice*, identifies some of the major issues involved in the reconfiguration of organisations as they grow. In a relatively small organisation it may be easy to develop a simple top-down structure to deal with work tasks and problems as they arise. As the organisation grows, tasks become more complex and it is essential to avoid developing very messy structures for dealing with these problems. Problems often arise as to who is responsible for what, and who should make particular types of decision. Figure 10.18 depicts this diagrammatically. Structure 2 is clearly very messy and disorganised.

Clearly as organisations take on more work and expand into new areas they will require an upgraded level of

Narrow span	Wide spans
Great deal of time spent with subordinates because:	Little time spent with subordinates because:
• No or little training • Inadequate or unclear authority delegation • Unclear plans for non-repetitive operations • Non-verifiable objectives and standards • Fast changes in external and internal environments • Use of poor or inappropriate communication techniques, including vague instructions • Ineffective interaction between superior and subordinate • Ineffective meetings • Incompetent and untrained manager • Complex task • Greater number of specialists at lower and middle levels	• Thorough training • Clear delegation to undertake well-defined tasks • Well-defined plans for repetitive operations • Verifiable objectives used as standards • Slow changes in external and internal environments • Use of appropriate techniques such as proper organisation structure, written and oral communication • Effective action between superior and subordinate • Effective meetings • Competent and trained manager • Simple task • Number of specialists at upper levels (top managers concerned with external environment)

Figure 10.17 *Factors influencing the span of management*

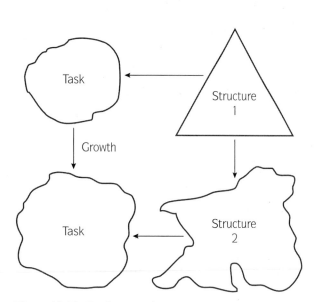

Figure 10.18 *Development of a messy structure*

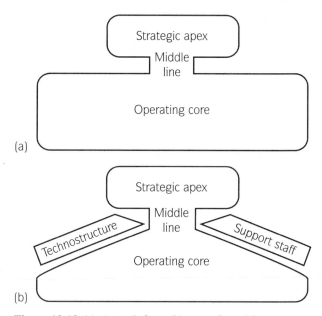

Figure 10.19 *(a) A simple form; (b) a reconfigured form*

organisation. This is particularly true today as organisations operate in a dynamic environment, with:

• unpredictable shifts in demand
• unexpected changes in sources of supply
• continual customer demands for creativity or novelty
• rapid technological changes.

The form of a very simple small organisation may be sketched as shown in Figure 10.19(a). The same organisation, as it becomes more complex, will increasingly become dependent on what **Henry Mintzberg** referred to as the **technostructure** – specialist staff who are responsible for quality standards and the ordering of materials. There will also be the need for new support staff who are concerned with providing a range of services like building maintenance, canteen facilities, public relations, and cleaning services. The organisation thus reconfigures to be more complex as depicted in Figure 10.19(b).

Developing an effective and efficient organisation depends on getting the right blend of roles. Clearly there is a lot of scope for tension. For example, middle-line managers may feel that the technostructure takes some decision-making powers away from them. Unless there is effective cooperation between these two areas there may be a great loss of potential. At the same time, support staff may feel that they are not really a part of the decision-making process at all, and this may lead to a lack of motivation. It is possible that support managers may begin to develop their own goals and objectives which contrast with the strategic goals. Clearly the well-managed organisation will be one in which decision-making is related closely to organisational objectives.

In recent times we have seen a new form of reconfiguration of organisations involving the stripping out of layers in order to create leaner and fitter structures which are more competitive. In particular, we have seen the hiving off of support staff into new self-managed companies which operate independently from the company they were previously part of. Canteen staff who might have worked for a major company in the 1980s often became part of the workforce of an independent contractor in the 1990s, and found themselves working for a number of organisations. Major corporations have increasingly **outsourced** a number of activities and operations which are not seen as being part of their core competency. Organisations today concentrate on the competence that give them competitive advantage and contract out non-core activities.

Symptoms of efficiency and deficiency

In judging whether an organisation is efficient or not, a number of contextual factors must be considered, including:

- the environment in which it operates (e.g. dynamic or static)
- the cultural background against which it is placed (e.g. different national and regional cultures)
- its internal culture (e.g. is it based on enterprise and

initiative or on routine procedures?)
- the technology it employs.

Kenyon Greene, in his book *The Adaptive Organisation*, has written that 'the concept of organisation and environment is one of the most critical to modern management'. Maintaining a fit between an organisation and its external and internal environments is crucial. Greene identifies the external environment as comprising:

- the natural
- the technological
- the human resources
- the political
- the social or socio-economic
- the market.

In the internal environment the most significant components are:

- productivity
- motivational dynamics (more job satisfaction)
- value and attitude change
- new organisational goals
- effects of new technologies
- uses and misuses of power.

Case Study

In search of excellence

In 1982, Peters and Waterman (in their book *In Search of Excellence*) set out eight characteristics of 'excellent' innovative US companies. These were:

a *A bias towards action*. These organisations have a 'can do' and 'let's try' approach. People within these firms are enterprising. Managers get out of their offices and keep in touch informally with what is happening throughout the organisation. At Hewlett Packard this is referred to as MBWA ('management by wandering about')

b *Keeping close to the customer*. These US companies have an obsession with the customer. They are market-led and are concerned to find out the real needs and wants of customers.

c *Automony and entrepreneurship*. Innovative companies foster many leaders and innovators at all levels of the organisation.

d *Productivity through people*. 'Excellent companies' treat the ordinary members of the organisation as the basic source of quality and productivity gains. Such organisations are opposed to an 'us and them' approach.

e *Hands-on, value driven*. Those at the top of such an organisation need to work hard to maintain the values of the company in a very public hands-on way. Senior managers are renowned for getting involved in the actual processes (design, selling etc.) thus publicly demonstrating their commitment to high standards.

f *'Stick to the knitting'*. These companies don't move into areas they know nothing about; they concentrate on what they can do best, and move on one manageable step at a time.

g *Simple form, lean staff*. 'Excellent' firms have a simple clear structure with only the necessary number of people being employed in each function.

h *Simultaneous loose–tight properties*. These companies are both centralised and decentralised. Independent decision-making tends to be pushed down to the divisions, to the product development team and to the shopfloor. However, some key aspects of the organisation are controlled from the centre; e.g. quality, reliability, action, regular communication and quick feedback.

Questions

1. Which of the above features of 'excellent' organisations are related to organisational structure?

2. Try to sum up in a brief statement of about 100 words Peters and Waterman's conclusions about aspects of 'excellent' companies.

3. In 1993, Peters and Waterman revealed that a number of the organisations that had shown excellence in 1982 had fallen behind. What environmental and internal factors may have contributed to this loss of excellence?

A number of business writers have pointed out that a major deficiency of many organisations is that they wait until a crisis descends upon them before responding. What organisations should do is anticipate changes and have pre-planned responses. They should:

- sense and measure the present state within the internal environment
- provide alternative future configurations of the organisation based on forecasting and judgement
- sense and measure the present state within the external environment.
- provide alternative future configurations which anticipate changes in the external environment
- provide an adaptable, dynamic model of on-going interrelationships between the organisation and the environment

- assess present and future goals, and ways of resolving conflicts between goals.
- provide clusters of flexible plans for change.
- provide and develop clusters of flexible actions which enable the organisation to move forward in a change environment.

The key is to develop self-organising/self-adaptive systems – literally 'the learning organisation'. Organisational structures need to be flexible and managers need to look to future changes. Unfortunately managers often place a low value on events, resources, people and situations that are at one remove in time and space, and place more value on the here-and-now. They also place too much reliance on things over which they have little control. Poor communication, disagreements and personality clashes can lead to low motivation and poor organisational performance.

Structures need to foster creative thinking and the ability to see possibilities that no-one has seen before. If managers expect people to be innovative, and give their permission for it, innovation is most likely to happen. However, this will occur only if the organisation is configured in such a way that decision-making is spread across the organisation, with informal structures and open communications. Managers need to trust employees and create reward systems linked to innovation and success. Importantly, employees should know that if they fail then they can learn from their mistakes. An entrepreneurial organisation will invest heavily in management development and training. There should also be a toleration of mavericks because they often make things work and come up with unexpected solutions.

It is not too difficult to spot the symptoms of an *inefficient organisation*. There will be a lack of clarity about who is to make the decisions and too many levels in the chain of command. There will be duplication of the same tasks in different segments of the organisation, and poor use of resources and time. There will also be an unwillingness to adapt to new circumstances or new problems.

Symptoms of inappropriate organisational structure

John Jackson and Cyril Morgan, in their book *Organisational Theory*, have identified the following symptoms of inadaptability in organisational structure:

- Organisational decision-makers may not be able to anticipate problems before they occur. There may be a tendency in the organisation to wait until problems occur and then react to them because the organisation simply does not have enough information to develop contingency plans.
- Decision-makers may err in trying to predict trends in their decision environment. Without proper coordination across divisions, the organisation may lose control over the relationship between its internal functioning and its environment.
- The organisation may not be able to get information for decision-making.
- The organisation, having identified a problem *vis-à-vis* its environment, may simply not be able to take corrective action quickly enough.

Symptoms of a poor fit between structure and environment may also reveal themselves in role conflicts and ambiguity. Clearly then there will be a need to tackle basic design issues for organisational structures. These symptoms are the kind of things managers should be aware of as indicators of dysfunctional organisational design.

THE HUMAN RESOURCE FUNCTION

In the last decade of the twentieth century there was a radical shift in many organisations towards an emphasis on **human resource management** (HRM). Here we provide an introduction to HRM. However, this perspective and function is dealt with in far greater detail in our companion volume *Human Resource Management for Higher Awards* (Dransfield, Howkins, Hudson & Davies, 1996).

The key to human resource management is that it is seen as a strategic concern for an organisation. Rather than being simply a specialised function (as personnel management used to be), it is a concern for all managers. No longer is 'people management' seen as being the preserve of a personnel department. Today, managers across the organisation are being given responsibilities for selecting, motivating, developing and evaluating employees. All managers therefore are taking on human resource responsibilities.

Perhaps more importantly, the emphasis has shifted from seeing employees as costs to seeing them as assets. There is an increasing recognition that employees are the most important resource in the organisation, particularly in creating a competitive edge.

In a well-received book on people at work, *Personnel Management* by Derek Torrington and Laura Hall, the authors set out to make a distinction between 'personnel' and 'human resource management'. In their early comments they suggest a number of reasons why some people have wanted to change to the term 'human resources':

- for a change or facelift for a new era of personal relationships
- because the terms 'manpower' and 'manpower planning' are sexist
- because personnel managers hope that adopting the new term may increase their status in the organisation.

They then follow this up by looking at some of the more substantive differences. They see 'personnel' as being a workforce-centred discipline. The importance here is that the people who work for the organisation are the starting point for personnel work. The human resource is in many ways a less flexible resource than money, materials and machines because it concerns people, who have thoughts and feelings and who are able to express their views. Personnel managers need to be able to understand the needs, wants, aspirations and views of the people in the organisation. So while personnel is a management function it is also concerned with the people at work. Personnel therefore is a mediating force between 'the management' and 'the employees'. Instead of personnel being seen as distinct, it provides this important mediating role (see Figure 10.20).

Because the personnel manager works at the interface between management and employees, he or she may spend more time working with ground-level workers than with

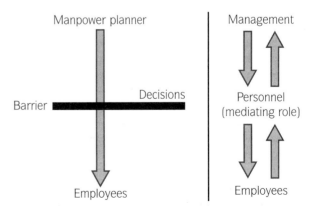

Figure 10.20 *The mediating role of personnel management*

Personnel management	Human resource management
• People have a right to proper treatment as human beings at work • People will only be effective if their job-related personal needs are met • Interventions are required by personnel to ensure that job-related personal needs are attended to • Because other line managers do not see themselves as people specialists they may neglect personnel work – necessitating the specialist personnel input	• Management of human resources is like any other form of resource management • Human resource management should be shared by people across the organisation rather than being split up artificially into work for specialists • People have a right to proper treatment as human beings at work • Efficient management with a focus on human needs is required across the organisation • Human resource managers are needed to support other managers in their human resource work and to make sure that the organisation is directed at a strategic level to human resource management • At the same time, human resource managers are concerned with making sure that there are enough people working in the right places, at the right time

Figure 10.21 *Contrasting personnel and human resource management*

senior managers. The personnel manager is therefore likely to take on board many of the cultural assumptions and values of ordinary people at work.

The distinction that Torrington and Hall make between personnel management and human resource management can be set out in a diagram as in Figure 10.21.

Some commentators argue that the difference between personnel management and human resource management is really just a matter of words. You could argue with equal force that a particular organisation has a personnel or a human resource focus. However, perhaps the important distinction is at a strategic level. Strategy is concerned with clearly identifying the core values of an organisation, and the direction in which the organisation wants to move.

The human resources approach is concerned that all managers should recognise the importance of the human resource rather than leaving it to the personnel manager. The emphasis should be that 'we are all human resource managers now' just as we are all 'marketers'. The business manager today needs to be a specialist in a field but also a competent generalist. A key part of this 'generalism' is concern for working relationships. Effective human resource strategies often lower costs of production, improve product development, and enhance marketing and other activities. Employees can create a competitive advantage for an organisation through innovation, creativity, flexibility, improved performance, superior customer care, etc. Importantly, people can provide a distinctive product or

service quality which cannot be matched even by the most sophisticated machines. People are more prepared to shop in department stores with friendly, knowledgeable staff, to eat in restaurants where they receive personal attention, and so on. The organisation needs to cherish and support the people who give it this distinctive edge. HRM therefore plays a key strategic role in the same way that marketing or finance does.

We can thus look at HRM as a strategic function. The tools and tactics of HRM are then concerned with particular activities such as recruitment, development, equal opportunities policy, etc. (see Figure 10.22).

Figure 10.22 *HRM as a strategic function*

Case Study

Change to an HRM perspective

In the early 1990s Central Bank – one of the UK's major high street banks – felt that it needed to change the way in which it treated its people. Increasingly banks were operating in a competitive environment driven by information technology. Gone were the days of the top-down hierarchical bank with the bank manager handling all key lending decisions from 'his' inner sanctum – the manager's office. Information technology made it possible to give responsibilities to junior members of the organisation who would be able to make key decisions supported by centrally created information systems. Information technology also made it possible to reduce staffing levels, and a number of branches were closed down in urban areas as telephone banking began to take off.

Up to the 1990s, the personnel department had played a key part in the bank, taking responsibility for recruitment and selection of staff, training, wages and salaries, etc. It was now felt that many of these tasks could be carried out at a branch level, supported by a central HRM department. Managing and looking after people was to become a branch rather than Head Office responsibility. For example, training courses and appraisal could be carried out largely within the branch. Key initiatives included empowerment of employees, the development of self-managing teams, quality circles, a greater harmonisation of terms and conditions of employment, team briefings, etc. In effect there was a whole raft of initiatives which were representative of the changed perspective. These changes were a key part of the organisation's strategic plan for the millennium and great emphasis was placed on HRM in the corporate mission statement and objectives.

Questions

1. What were the chief catalysts for the change in approach?

2. To what extent would you argue that Central Bank has moved from a personnel management approach to an HRM approach?

A stakeholder perspective

Organisations are made up of varying groups of stakeholders and their interests. Each group will have a different perspective as to what makes an effective organisation. For example, shareholders would regard an organisation to be effective if it delivered above-average profitability and growth leading to rising share prices; customers would emphasise things to do with value for money, quality and reliability of goods, courtesy of service and punctuality of delivery; suppliers would emphasise fair prices and prompt payment. Employees would emphasise the extent to which an organisation is a good employer – paying good wages, providing good working conditions, scope for satisfying work and security of employment, etc.

Modern HRM approaches should be based on ensuring an effective stakeholder approach. In particular, HRM should stress the importance of all employees as stakeholders in organisations. People work best if they feel that their employer values them and places a high priority on their contribution and worth to the organisation. The stakeholder perspective involves making sure that shareholders in an organisation are given value in terms of the dividends they receive, but it also places emphasis on ensuring that employees get a good value return on the contributions they put into the company – their efforts and commitment. By rewarding commitment you are most likely to get highly committed employees. The stakeholder perspective is thus a modern one which sees employees as having a strategic involvement in the company, rather than placing them at the bottom of the organisational pyramid.

Case Studies

Taking a stakeholder approach

Company X had building work going on during the summer of 1998. As a sweetener, they put water coolers in each of their offices. When the building work was finished, they took out the coolers. The response from employees was intense – people felt very resentful. They felt that their company didn't care about them.

Spedan Lewis, the son of the founder of the John Lewis Partnership, drew up a futuristic constitution which contained mission statements such as 'The Partnership's ultimate aim shall be the happiness in every way of its members' and 'The Partnership shall recognise that only fools put business too far before pleasure, especially health and happiness, and that there is almost infinite scope for imagination and energy in the promotion of happiness in the more important sense of that word'.

1. To what extent are each of the companies mentioned above using a stakeholder perspective that includes employees?

2. What organisations are you familiar with that operate a very strong stakeholder approach to HRM? Explain your answer.

Personnel management roles

It is not easy to identify with clarity the role of the personnel function within an organisation because it has such a wide variety of activities. Personnel work involves:

- a strategic and policy-making role, concerned with the development of the human resource mission
- a welfare role, concerned with looking after people and their needs
- a supporting role, concerned with helping line managers to develop their human resource work
- a bargaining and negotiating role, concerned with acting as an intermediary between different groups and interests
- an administrative role, concerned with the payment of wages, the supervision and implementation of health and safety codes and laws
- an educational and development role, concerned with education and training of employees and in supporting their career development.

These activities and many more demand considerable skills on the part of personnel specialists. The diverse strands pull a personnel manager in many different directions. Not least is the ambiguity between the personnel specialist's welfare role for employees, coupled with concern for the welfare of the organisation. This tension will be particularly obvious, for example, when the organisation needs to order redundancies or to restructure its operations.

In his book *The Management of Human Resources*, John Storey highlights different ways in which the personnel function contributed to management teams in 15 major employing organisations in the public and private sectors at the start of the 1990s. Storey collected evidence both from personnel managers and from line managers with whom they interacted; he identified four main types of practitioner in personnel work (see Figure 10.23).

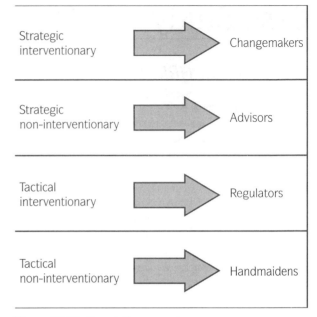

Figure 10.23 *Storey's four categories*

- *Handmaidens* are personnel managers who play a subservient role to line managers. Their role is relatively uncoordinated and lacking in clarity.
- *Regulators* play a more 'hands on' role which is based on setting out, putting into practice and monitoring the observance of 'employment rules' (which range from personnel procedure manuals to joint agreements with trade unions). Regulators can be seen as 'managers of discontent' concerned to develop temporary tactical truces with organised labour rather than creating an overall strategy for effective human relations.
- *Advisors* are personnel managers who are familiar with current development in their organisation but leave the running of day-to-day affairs to line and general manager colleagues. This involves a 'hands off' approach unless asked for help.
- *Changemakers* are concerned to place human relations management on a new footing. They try to create an effective working environment which fosters employee commitment. It is this group which sets out to create the human relations environment which fosters 'the new world of work' involving empowerment, team-work concern for the individual and the organisation.

Storey's research, published in 1992, indicates that line managers are taking increasing responsibility for HRM at ground level. He put forward the argument that, as organisations delayer, and particularly as they cut back headquarters staff, responsibilities become devolved to cost and profit centres at lower levels within the organisation. For example, in the 1980s Lucas Industries split up into 130 separate businesses, and managers in these business units took on increasing responsibility for the management of an array of resources. This meant that 'line managers have come to the fore ... not only as the crucial delivery mechanism for new approaches in human relations ... but more assertively, as themselves the designers and drivers of new ways'.

This research indicates that in a large proportion of major companies the development of an HRM approach in management is a reality. Line managers are taking on an increasing role in 'directly briefing employees, the whole raft of measures involving "managerial leadership"; the shift towards more individualised forms of pay; of more appraisal; of devolved management accountability; and of deproceduralising'.

However, it is important to bear in mind that such changes will be truly effective only when there is a commitment to HRM as a strategic mission of the organisation. At the same time it is clear that, in many if not most smaller companies, personnel continues to play a staff role in supporting line managers in recruiting, selection, etc. The place of the personnel function in an organisation will depend on a wide range of contextual factors, such as:

- whether the organisation is a traditional or relatively new one
- the personalities involved
- the type of organisation (people-intensive or capital-intensive)
- the availability of staff, and competition for people in the locality of the organisation.

Storey argues that senior management in many large companies now considers human resources at a strategic level. He quotes the example of an interview he had with the director of Ford of Europe, in which it was stated:

'Every month the Executive Committee of Ford of Europe moves, in the afternoon, from the boardroom to a more relaxed atmosphere to discuss the "people" issues of involvement, appraisal, employee relations, etc. ... In total it adds up to a very considerable proportion of the board's time.'

Traditionally, the personnel function is associated with the 'employment procession' of recruitment: selection – induction – training – transfers – termination of employment. However, in a modern business organisation personnel is also responsible for 'appraisal', which is a key part of monitoring and helping an employee to develop a clear career path and for the administration of disciplinary procedures; for workplace bargaining with unions; developing and supervising payments systems for employees; supervising

health and safety; equal opportunities; and many other areas related to employment.

Strategic goals for personnel

In *Personnel Management*, Torrington and Hall put forward the proposition that:

'Personnel management is a series of activities which, first, enables working people and their employing organisation to agree about the objectives and nature of their working relationships and, secondly, ensures the agreement is fulfilled.'

The important point being made is that at a strategic level it is essential to create a human resource strategy which is an integral part of corporate policy. It is then necessary to translate objectives into practical actions:

'Only by satisfying the needs of the individual employee will the employer obtain the commitment to organisational objectives that is needed for organisational success, and only by contributing or organisational success will employees be able to satisfy their personal employment needs.'

A number of specialists in the field argued that HRM exists only in practice when there is an integrated system of policies and practices for managing the human resource (e.g. for recruitment, selection, bargaining, employee development) which are at the same time integrated with the wider business strategy. This is the strategic view of human resource management. When we look at the implementation of HRM in practice, we can see that organisations use a variety of approaches. At one end of the continuum there are organisations that are genuinely working towards strategic HRM, where human resource considerations are a central part of organisational policy-making. At the other end of the continuum there are organisations that may use the term HRM but in reality operate a firefighting approach in which personnel activities respond to problems and difficulties in the workplace (see Figure 10.24).

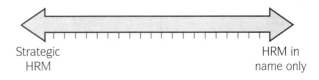

Strategic HRM   HRM in name only

Figure 10.24 *The HRM continuum*

At the strategic end of the continuum there are two varieties of HRM, the hard and the soft approaches. The *hard approach* recognises people as the key organisational resource but with an 'instrumental approach'; it is seen that if you treat people well they will provide better results for you. The mission of the organisation includes an important emphasis on the human resource but the overall intention is to maximise other organisational returns such as profits and sales. This is a business-oriented approach to strategic management.

A softer approach also recognises people as a key organisational resource, but the emphasis is on nurturing and developing people because they are people. The qualitative difference is that the softer approach emphasises humanity. Believers in the soft approach would also argue that this will lead to higher business returns.

The strategic approaches to human resource management enable positive and planned steps in the right direction. In a dynamic business environment, human resource managers need to stop focusing on short-term firefighting,

and to focus on long-term strategic planning. The reality, however, is that in many organisations personnel planning and policy-making plays second fiddle to other organisational planning. Personnel is frequently seen as a servicing function that responds to company objectives over which it has little influence. In the worst-case situation, a number of personnel managers respond to many and varied issues and problems as and when they arise. These four positions are illustrated in Figure 10.25.

Increasingly, though, organisations are seeking to develop a strategic approach which integrates HRM. This involves a shift from past practice. John Storey, in *Management of Human Resources*, identifies five types of managed change processes which can move the organisation towards HRM:

- *Type 1* is the top-down approach where management recognises the need for a strategic approach and sets out to impose HRM solutions. There is a clear vision from above, and a carefully planned approach to the management of change. However, if the vision is not communicated clearly, it may be ignored or rejected, so that at grass-roots there is no commitment to the new approach.
- *Type 2* is the top-down piecemeal approach. Rather than creating an integrated view of HRM, new initiatives are developed in the organisation in a piecemeal way. This may be the chosen way of operating for managers who take the view 'We'll try this first, see how it works, and then bring in the next bit!'. Unfortunately this creates contrasting practices within an organisation and may lead to a lack of commitment to change. Too many people will point out contradictions in policies and practices.
- *Type 3* is where various groups in an organisation will bargain over piecemeal changes. It has the advantage of greater participation, but it is riddled with the disadvantages of the piecemeal approach.
- *Type 4*, also called 'systemic-jointism', involves transforming the whole system to incorporate the HRM approach. It has the advantage of being a participative process based on shared understandings of change. This should lead to wholesale commitment to the new HRM approach. Unfortunately, in the real world this approach has rarely been used.
- *Type 5* is a mixture of the other four types.

Personnel policies

Effective human resource management will be based on plans and policies. These should reflect the organisational objectives. Clearly, organisations have different objectives depending on a range of factors such as: whether they are

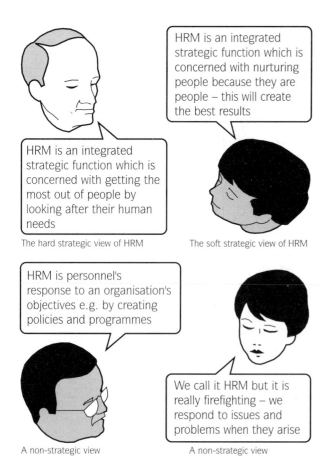

HRM is an integrated strategic function which is concerned with nurturing people because they are people – this will create the best results

HRM is an integrated strategic function which is concerned with getting the most out of people by looking after their human needs

The hard strategic view of HRM

The soft strategic view of HRM

HRM is personnel's response to an organisation's objectives e.g. by creating policies and programmes

We call it HRM but it is really firefighting – we respond to issues and problems when they arise

A non-strategic view

A non-strategic view

Figure 10.25 *The HRM continuum expanded*

in the public or private sector, whether they are public service or profit-making organisations, whether they are large or small, whether the organisational culture is entrepreneurial or conservative, and so on.

There are various ways of viewing the term 'policy'. It can be seen as an expression of broad intentions to achieve specific objectives. In this sense it refers to the theory which underpins the methods we use to arrive at objectives. For example, an organisation may have a policy to recruit the most able graduates available in the labour market; it is then a matter of putting this policy into practice.

The achievement of organisational objectives stems from the effective use of people. Long-range planning for the human resource is a complex process and will be successful only when the personnel team is regarded as an important part of the management team. In exploring human resource planning activities, it is useful to follow the line taken by Torrington and Hall in contrasting 'soft' and 'hard' approaches.

Soft approaches

'Soft' human resource planning involves:

- identifying where the organisation is at the moment
- setting out where the organisation wants to be in the future
- analysing environmental influences and trends
- establishing plans to take the organisation forward.

The vision of where the organisation wants to go should be derived from the mission statement, which should have a clear human resource element. For example, an organisation that emphasises the importance of innovation and flexibility will want to nurture flexible and imaginative people. The nurturing of these people will be based on care for individual training and development, on career and reward structures, and on many other factors.

Before identifying the direction an organisation wants to move in, it is essential to identify where it is coming from. This will highlight the changes that need to be introduced, the size of the changes, the resources required, the processes to be employed, and so on. An analysis of current resources is required in order to be able to forecast future needs.

Human resource specialists must work from the heart of an organisation in order to manage cultural change and to

help reshape the organisation. For example, if they wanted to create a 'virtual organisation' in which flexible teams were brought together for specific purposes, they could achieve this only by transforming interpersonal relationships in the workplace and by altering existing perceptions and attitudes. Human resource planning therefore involves careful collection of data about formal and informal systems and organisational cultures. This data needs to be analysed carefully and translated into plans covering organisation structure, recruitment, planning, etc.

Hard approaches

'Hard' human resource planning involves more traditional activities, such as looking at whether the organisation has enough people for the tasks to be done. Every organisation must know how many employees it will need to have in the short, medium and long term, the availability of appropriate people, and how they can be recruited. It must also assess their training and development needs. The staffing plan must match the objectives of the organisation which are established in its corporate plan (see Figure 10.26).

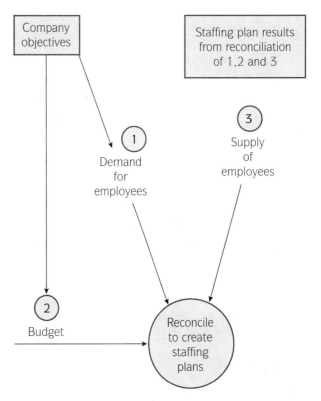

Figure 10.26 *Matching demand and supply at the right price*

Areas covered by human resource managers

Recruitment

The purpose of **recruitment** is to buy in and retain the best available human resources to meet the organisation's needs. It is therefore important to be clear about:

- what a job entails
- what qualities are required to do the job
- what incentives are required to attract and motivate the right employee.

A number of stages can be used to describe and set out the nature of particular jobs, including job analysis, job description, job specification and recruitment profiles.

Job analysis

This is the process of examining jobs in order to identify the key requirements of each. Job analysis can be conducted by direct observation of employees at work, by information obtained from interviewing job-holders, or by referring to documents such as training manuals. Information can be gleaned directly from the person carrying out a task and his or her supervisory staff. Three different stages of job analysis can be identified:

- *Task analysis* involves the study of a particular task which is aimed at achieving a particular objective or end-product. For example, a particular employee may have the task of ensuring that all the assemblers in an electronics factory are supplied with a steady flow of components.
- *Activity analysis* is the study of the elements involved in a given task. For example, one of the activities involved in circulating components in the electronics factory may be taking them down from the shelves in the stock room. Activities can be subdivided into physical (e.g. lifting, sorting) and mental (exercising judgement).
- *Skills analysis* is the study of the ability needed to carry out a given task effectively. A wide range of skills may be identified, such as the ability to work in groups, to work independently, to perform manual operations, to make calculations, to communicate, to follow written instructions, and many more.

Job description

This will set out how a particular employee is to fit into the organisation. It will therefore need to cover:

- the title of the job
- to whom the employee is responsible
- for whom the employee is responsible
- a simple description of the role and duties of the employee within the organisation.

Job specification

This goes beyond a mere description; in addition it highlights the mental and physical attributes required of the job-holder. For example, a job specification for a trainee manager's post in a retail store included the following:

> *'Managers at all levels are expected to show responsibility. The company is looking for people who are tough and talented. They should have a flair for business, know how to sell, and to work in a team.'*

Job analysis, description and specification can all provide useful information to a business in addition to serving as recruitment instruments. Another use is for staff appraisal, which is a means of monitoring staff performance and is a feature of promotion in modern companies. In some companies, employees and their immediate line managers discuss personal goals and targets for the coming time period (e.g. the next six months); the appraisal will then involve a review of employees' performance during the previous six months and the setting of new targets. Job details can serve as a useful basis for establishing dialogue and targets. Job descriptions can be used as reference points for arbitrating in disputes as to 'who does what' in a business. Job analysis can serve as a useful tool for establishing performance standards.

Recruitment profiles

The person responsible for interviewing and recruiting is not always the person with a specialist knowledge of the job in question. For example, the personnel department may be given the responsibility for recruiting staff for all of the functional areas within a company. Personnel will therefore ask for a **recruitment profile** giving the nature of the skills required, the type of person sought and a description of the job. The job requisition (recruitment profile) will therefore provide the specialist knowledge required to enable personnel to recruit the appropriate individuals. Recruitment profiles are also used to give advertising agencies and specialist recruitment companies more information.

Selection

Selection involves procedures to identify the most appropriate candidate to fill each post. An effective selection procedure will therefore take into consideration the following:

- keeping the costs of selection down
- making sure that the required skills and qualities have been specified, and developing a process for identifying them in candidates
- making sure that the candidate selected will want the job, and will stay with the organisation.

Keeping the costs of selection down will involve factors such as holding the interviews in a location that is accessible to the interviewing panel and to those being interviewed; ensuring that the interviewing panel has available to it all the necessary documentation, such as application forms, that should be studied before the interviews take place; and that a short-list is made up of suitable candidates, so that the interviews do not have to take place a second time, with new job advertisements being placed.

The skills required should have been identified through the process of job analysis, description and specification. It is important then to devise ways of testing whether candidates meet these requirements. One way of doing this is to study applicants' application forms and to interview the most suitable people. Some employers go further and give applicants aptitude tests, putting them through a number of 'real life' situations to see how they cope with given business situations.

To gauge whether applicants will stay with the organisation, it is important to ask them about their future intentions, and to familiarise them with the working environment into which they will be placed. There is no point in attracting a first-class candidate only to find that he or she does not like the working environment.

It is important to monitor the job selection process continually to see how effective it is. *Ratios* can be a useful method of appraising a selection process. These ratios may include:

Number of interviews to number of offers made.

The most effective ratios would involve the minimisation of interviews relative to offers made to fill the post as required:

Number starting work to number of suitable employees.

If a high number of workers who are offered employment prove to be unsuitable or turn down a job offer, there is clearly something wrong with the interviewing procedure.

Induction and training

These are another major area of personnel work. New workers in a firm are usually given an **induction programme** in which they meet other workers and are shown the skills they must learn. Generally the first few days at work will simply involve observation, with an experienced employee showing the 'new hand' the ropes. Many large firms have detailed training schemes which are conducted on an 'in-house' basis – this is particularly true of larger public companies such as banks and insurance companies. In conjunction with this, staff may be encouraged to attend college courses to learn new skills and get new qualifications. Training thus takes place both through:

- *on-the-job training* – learning through experience at work.
- *off-the-job training* – learning through attending courses.

Administration

The **administration** of benefits and compensation is another part of the HRM responsibility. Human resource managers play a key part in the creation of a strategy, plans, policies and procedures to ensure that the salary structure and benefits package is appropriate to attract, recruit and retain employees. Decisions made in this area will be crucial. Developing a competitive strategy involves attracting and keeping the best available people.

At an operational level the personnel department will be responsible for the payment of wages and salaries. Employees will contribute to a variety of benefit schemes, both those organised by the company and private ones. In many companies the administration of contributions (e.g. by deductions from wages and salaries) will be a routine administrative task. Personnel officers will be responsible for accounting for sickness, accident benefits and company pension schemes. Compensation will need to be awarded to organisation members who have suffered a loss through invalidity, work-related sickness, etc.

Appraisal

Appraisal is an essential part of human resource development. Appraisal schemes should be designed to provide a basis for regular discussions on objectives, achievements, development needs, and future career development. Appraisal should identify areas where the appraisee has performed well and areas in which improvements can be made. There may be discussion of the appraisee's readiness for promotion. A summary will be provided of any development needs and a record of any development provided during the year.

Promotion, transfer and termination

Developing procedures to move human resources to different positions of responsibility and to widen their experience through transfers, as well as termination of employment, will be an important area of human resource work.

Promotion within a firm depends on acquiring qualifications to do a more advanced job. In banking, for instance, staff are expected to pass banking examinations. At the same time a candidate for promotion must show a flair for the job. It is the responsibility of the training department within an organisation to make sure that staff with the right skills are coming up through the firm or being recruited from outside.

The personnel department has a responsibility for negotiating the smooth transfer of employees between departments. This may be necessary if employees are not able to 'get on', or if it is felt necessary to give an employee a 'change'.

Termination of employment may be the result of resignation, retirement, dismissal or redundancy. When employees retire after a long period of service to an organisation, they will appreciate some form of recognition for their service. Companies such as the John Lewis Partnership keep in contact with retired employees, and arrange regular reunions. At John Lewis, personnel staff will often attend the funerals of people who have worked for the company for many years, even though the funeral may be twenty or thirty years after the person retired.

The procedure for dismissal of employees must follow strict guidelines. On the other hand, redundancy occurs when a business or firm closes down, when part of a business closes down, or when particular types of workers are no longer required. It is the job that becomes redundant rather than the person.

Career development

One view of employee development is that it should focus on organisational needs. The purpose of development is to further the organisation. The alternative view is that individuals have a right to further their potential and the organisation should enable them to do so. When people see that the organisation is committed to their individual needs, then they in turn will be committed to the organisation. It is a two-way process.

The above outline of important activities which lie within the responsibility of personnel management make it obvious why it is important to have clear missions and objectives on which to base operational activities.

ORGANISATIONAL CULTURE

An organisation's culture is its personality. When you deal with an organisation and its people you will get a feel for its personality: Is it formal or informal? Is it highly professional or disorganised? Is it driven by a strong set of values? Is it welcoming? Of course an organisation may have more than one personality – the various parts may be driven by different cultures. Over time the culture of the organisation may change. The culture of an organisation exerts pressure on individuals working within it and so acts as a constraint on their behaviour.

Classification of organisational culture

Organisations are as unique as nations and societies. They have widely differing cultures and these are reflected in values, ideas and beliefs. The culture of an organisation influences the way in which it operates, so it is necessary to understand the culture before analysing how people might contribute to its success or failure. We need to examine broadly different types of culture before looking in greater depth at styles of management.

Rob Goffee and Gareth Jones, in their book *The Character of a Corporation*, (1998), introduce the notion of a **life cycle in a culture**. This generally starts with the communal, where a group is focused on performance, and often ends in the fragmented, where employees 'do their own thing'.

Four main types of culture are commonly recognised – power, role, task and person.

Power culture

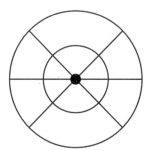

Figure 10.27 *The web structure of the power culture*

Centralisation of power is the key feature of this type of culture. It is frequently found in small entrepreneurial organisations where control rests with a single individual or a small group of individuals. The structure of power cultures can be illustrated as a web (see Figure 10.27). There is a central power source and rays of influence spread out from the centre. Decisions are made by high-status individuals rather than by the group. Decisions can be made quickly.

The weakness, however, is that people in the organisation may feel demotivated by the lack of challenge and suppressed by the individuals with power. Size is also a problem – the web can break if it has to support too many activities.

The old fashioned Ford organisation was often regarded to be the most representative of the power culture. One Ford manager made a comparison between the three organisations he had been part of – the Jesuits, the Navy and Ford: 'And of the three the Ford Motor Company was the most authoritarian, the most regimented and the most driven by fear.' The organisation's approach to management until the early 1980s was characterised by functional specialisation, hierarchy and tight control. The management style was confrontational. A 'Blue Book' defined the jobs and limits of authority of every employee.

Role culture

The **role culture** is typical of a bureaucratic organisation that is divided into layers of offices and officials. This type of organisation is divided by sets of functions that are determined by rules and procedures (see Figure 10.28). Such an organisation operates by using logic and reason.

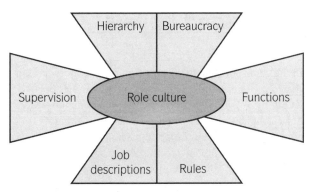

Figure 10.28 *Role culture*

The organisation could be arranged according to a set of functions – marketing, human relations, finance, etc. Its work is organised along these functionally distinct spheres of operation which focus on specific areas of competence.

In a role culture, power is hierarchical and is determined by an employee's position (e.g. field marshal, general,

colonel, major). The relationship between various roles is determined by job descriptions and set communication procedures. The system of supervision and the roles set out in a job description should make sure that job-holders carry out their allocated tasks – performance beyond this role is not required. Position is the main source of power, and rules and procedures are the main source of influence.

A major disadvantage of the role culture is that there is little scope for individual initiative. Job-holders can feel cramped by their position, as there is little scope for individual growth and development.

Task culture

A **task culture** is job- or project-oriented and emphasis is placed on completing a specific task. It is a *team culture*. The task determines the way in which the work is organised, rather than individuals or the rules of the organisation. A task culture can be illustrated by a net of which some strands are thicker and stronger than others (see Figure 10.29). Much of the power and influence lies at the interstices of the net.

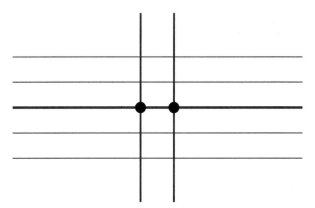

Figure 10.29 *The net structure of the task culture*

Bringing together a work-team for a particular project provides the basis for a task culture. The success of the team depends on the unifying power of the group to complete a specific task.

In task cultures employees may have considerable freedom, and this flexibility can make such organisations rewarding environments to work in. However, lack of formal authority and the considerable number of 'strands' can make management and control of a task culture difficult.

Today we see an increasing emphasis on task cultures in the creation of self-managing teams, and in the development of **quality circles**. Individuals will often be members of several project teams at the same time.

Person culture

In a person culture individuals are central – the organisation exists only to serve the interests of those within it. Not surprisingly, person cultures are more likely to be found in communities such as *kibbutzim* than in

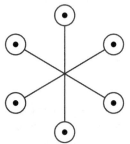

Figure 10.30 *The person culture*

profit-motivated enterprises. Other examples may include cooperatives, barristers' chambers and architects' partnerships, where there is a cluster of individuals or a galaxy of stars all operating at the same level (see Figure 10.30).

In a person culture, hierarchies are impossible except by mutual consent. Given a choice, many people would opt for this type of culture.

Cultural norms and symbols

Some writers use a short description to define culture – 'the way we do things around here'. However, when you scratch beneath the surface it is more complex than this. Some organisations have clear identities, but in many it is not obvious what they stand for and how they go about their business.

Culture is actually very difficult to define but it is an essential ingredient of a successful business. Goffee and Jones call their book *The Character of a Corporation: How Your Company's Culture Can Make or Break Your Business.* The writers identify four main types – fragmented, networked, mercenary and communal. The idea is not that any of these is right, just that one might be more appropriate; and of course many organisations have the characteristics of more than one type at any one time.

Norms

Norms – what is regarded as normal behaviour – can vary between organisations, even between those in the same

industry. Norms are usual patterns of behaviour within an organisation and there is a great deal of pressure on individuals to conform to these. They will manifest themselves in dress codes, attitudes to work, relationships between organisational members, patterns of doing business with other organisations, and a thousand and one other things. The pressure to conform will not always be obvious.

Symbols

Symbols are often a very good reflection of culture as well as helping to shape that culture. Symbols may appear in the form of logos, brand names, the language used within an organisation, corporate literature, advertising themes, and so on. For example, the name Rolls-Royce tells you something about the company and its association with quality and prestige – the literature produced by this organisation reflects the culture.

Organisations also tend to have their own language and jargon, such as terms they use to describe competitors, or even officials within the organisation such as 'the boss', 'the shrink', 'the egg head'. Parts of an organisation may attract particular names, such as 'the hot house'. New recruits adapt quickly to the language and become part of the culture, rather than being seen as novice outsiders. Even the building an organisation is housed in may be symbolic of its culture; it might be showy and magnificent, or grubby and hidden away.

Values and beliefs

In the course of time members of an organisation develop shared meanings and beliefs about the way things operate within the organisation and with the wider environment. For example, staff may come to share a belief that if management call an unexpected meeting then something is 'wrong'; if the company receives a new order then employees may believe their jobs are more secure; and so on. A general belief may arise among employees of the importance of its rules and procedures, so that those who fail to conform may be informally (or formally) given a dressing down by other employees.

In developing values and beliefs one of the first things a new employee learns is some of the organisation's legends – perhaps how the founder worked long hours and shunned formal education and training qualifications. Legends can stay with an organisation and become part of

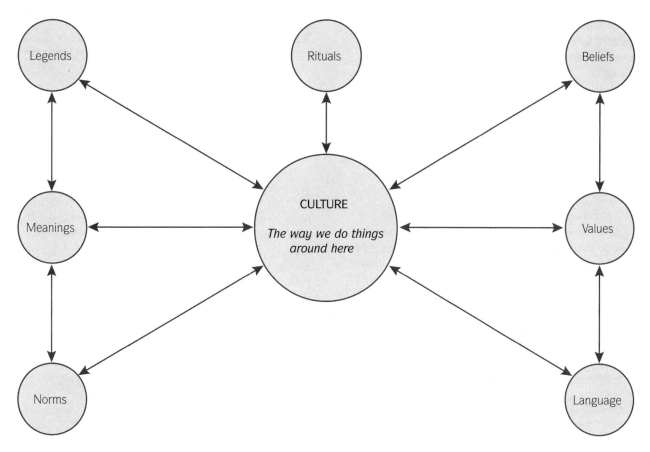

Figure 10.31 *Factors influencing organisational culture*

the established ways of doing things. Perhaps the founder's views about the importance of education and training will stay current; in the course of time there may be a 'culture shift' as new managers move into the organisation and change the old ways. However, a number of legends continue to be important determinants of 'the way we do things around here', even if it is only something as simple as following the founder's principle of leaving desks tidy at the end of the day (see Figure 10.31).

Development of the culture

Today a lot of emphasis is placed in organisations on creating the right culture. A key aspect of managing change, therefore, is concerned with moving towards a 'better' culture, a better framework for work. Increasing emphasis is placed on creating an appropriate mission, objectives and set of values for the organisation. A number of factors influence the culture and its development.

The history and ownership of the organisation

The history of an organisation has an important influence on its present culture. In the early days the organisation will take root, and a dominant culture will be put in place. In time this culture will alter as new people and new ideas enter the organisation, as new relationships are formed, and as the external environment changes. In studying cultures it is important to research their history by talking to people who have been involved at various stages of development and by looking through the paperwork and documents associated with each particular stage, such as advertisements, company policy documents, brochures and annual reports.

When we look at the early history of organisations and the way in which they operated during this time, we often find that they were heavily influenced by the values of their founders. Much of this vision may be deeply embedded in current culture.

When Anita Roddick set up Body Shop in 1976 she operated from a single shop in Brighton. She could never have dreamed of the ensuing success of the organisation. She says:

'The Body Shop style developed out of a Second World War mentality (shortages, utility goods, rationing) imposed by sheer necessity and the simple fact that I had no money. But I had a very clear image in my mind of the kind of style I wanted to create: I wanted it to look a bit like a country store in a spaghetti western.

'It is curious, looking back on it, how necessity accorded with philosophy. Even if I have had unlimited funds, for example, I would never have wasted money on expensive packaging – the garbage of conventional cosmetics. ... The cheapest containers I could find were the plastic bottles used by hospitals to collect urine samples, but I could not afford to buy enough. I thought I would get round the problem by offering to refill empty containers or to fill customers' own bottles. In this way we started recycling and reusing materials long before it became ecologically fashionable, but again it was born out of economic necessity rather than a concern for the environment.'

These early principles, imperatives and ideas have gone on to shape the predominant culture of Body Shop, which is identified today as an environmentally conscious company, with a deep-felt concern for important moral and ethical issues. It is likely that these values will continue to be a core ingredient of Body Shop values.

In the course of the history of an organisation, however, changes take place in culture. For example, Boots the chemist is now also a retailer of wines and spirits. It is inconceivable that the founder, Jesse Boot, who was a teetotaller, would have allowed such a development. Many of the early industrialists in this country came from Quaker families; e.g. Huntley and Palmer, and Rowntree. Originally, these companies placed a very strong emphasis on social values and paternalistic employment practices. Today, many of their organisations have become part of much larger groupings owned by shareholders, including major international financial institutions. This has often led to an increase in the emphasis on profits and a decline in the emphasis on social conscience.

Case Study

Changes in the retail cooperatives

Nowadays, some people think of the Co-op as just another supermarket chain. This is not the case. Co-ops place far greater emphasis on serving the community. The first Co-op was set up by a group of weavers in Toad Lane in Rochdale in 1844. At that time, these workers were being paid low wages partly made up of tokens, which could be exchanged only in the company shop where prices were high. Twenty-eight weavers, known as the Rochdale Pioneers, pooled money to buy foodstuffs at wholesale prices, which they then sold cheaply to members. Profits were shared among members in the form of a dividend depending on how much each had bought. Since then, Co-ops have spread and there are many retail outlets in Britain.

To become a shareholder in a Co-op you need only buy a £1 share and this entitles you to vote at meetings to choose the president and other officers of the local co-op society.

In the latter part of the nineteenth century the Co-ops flourished and societies sprang up all over Britain. It was the Co-ops that introduced the first supermarkets. However, the profit-oriented multiples like Tesco and Sainsbury's proved to be too competitive for the Co-ops, which were organised into too many small societies and did not really benefit from bulk buying. Many of the senior officials in Co-ops were people who had worked their way up through the ranks or who had won support in elections in their local areas, rather than professional managers. These inexperienced managers were generally not as efficient as those managing the new multiples, or as cut-throat. They also clung to their social conscience.

During the 1970s and 80s the Co-ops increasingly lost market share. They came to be associated with a rather dowdy image and downmarket products. The Co-ops have continued to suffer with the development of hypermarkets.

To fight back, small societies have merged together, closing hundreds of small shops and branches. During the 1980s the Co-op began to build its own Leo hypermarkets. It increasingly employed specialist managers with good qualifications and retailing experience. It began to develop a new, slicker image. Co-ops still continue to be located in many traditional working-class areas as well as having high street stores, which are often indistinguishable from those of other retailers. The Co-op has had to project a similar image to that of most other retailers – hi-tech checkouts, wide variety, clean and bright shops, and value for money. The Co-op continues to serve the local community, e.g. by sponsoring community projects and by offering customers a square deal. In the late 1990s the Co-op decided to get back to some of its first principles by focusing on ethical trading. Today it makes sure that all the products it purchases are produced and supplied under fair trading conditions which do not involve exploitation. In addition it makes sure that the products it sells are produced in such a way as to give maximum consideration to environmental values. The question is whether this emphasis on an ethical approach will convince enough extra customers to shop at the Co-op.

Questions

1. Compare and contrast your image of today's Co-op with the perceptions of your parents and grandparents. What are the major changes you can identify?

2. To what extent has the 'culture' of the Co-op been shaped by its history?

3. To what extent does the Co-op retain elements of its early culture?

4. Why has the culture of the Co-op changed over the years? Have these changes been inevitable?

The size of the organisation and its technology

The size of an organisation is likely to have a major effect on the culture. The larger an organisation becomes the more difficult it is to run it on informal, personal lines. Increasingly, the organisation will need to employ professional managers with a range of organisational theories. As organisations expand, new divisions and departments are created, leading to new structural forms. For example, a small school may have a single staffroom and a relatively small number of subject departments. As the school increases in size, it may develop a number of faculties made up of departments. Each faculty may then have its own staffroom and resource base. In the small school there may be a unifying culture, but as the school separates into faculties, faculty subcultures start to develop. The same type of development is common across a range of growing organisations; e.g. hospitals, businesses, and army regiments.

Because larger organisations are run by professional managers, they tend to try to put into practice the conventional wisdom of the day relating to organisational structure. For example, in the early 1900s managers in

manufacturing organisations and offices might have tried to create a functional bureaucracy, or an organisation based on scientific lines. More recently, managers have been trying to rearrange the organisational architecture, and new organisational forms have sprung up, such as the hollow organisation, the networked organisation, the learning organisation, the modular corporation, the virtual organisation, the horizontal organisation, and many more.

The technology of the organisation will also influence its culture. Often there will be a close relationship between technology and size. For example, as organisations expand, they are able to utilise economies of scale using highly mechanised and automated production systems. In organisations in which people spend most of their time working with large machines, they may have little contact with other employees. In contrast, in people-intensive organisations there will be much human contact.

Perhaps we can contrast a 'machine-centred culture' with a 'people-centred culture'. The nature of the work performed inevitably influences employees' perceptions of the work situations and values of the workplace.

Goals and objectives

In an effective organisation the culture will match with the objectives. A look at the aims and objectives of an organisation give us an initial feel for the formal culture of that organisation.

Different types of organisation will have different objectives. The objectives of charities, for example, will usually be quite different from those of profit-maximising organisations. These goals and objectives help to create the cultural frameworks which shape behaviours within the organisation. Petrock's *Non-Profit Making Strategies* has identified a number of major cultural frameworks of organisations (see Figure 10.32) which influence the ways in which staff are expected to function:

- *Bureaucratic frameworks* are conservative, traditional and hierarchical. Employees are expected to follow the rules and go through the 'right channels'. The organisation and individuals within it tend to follow 'risk-avoidance' strategies. Employees have the security of knowing how business will be conducted and do not have to take the responsibility for making unpredictable decisions. Clients will be confident that they will be treated consistently.
- *Entrepreneurial frameworks* allow employees to take risks and to be innovators. Empowerment and experimentation are key themes. However, the

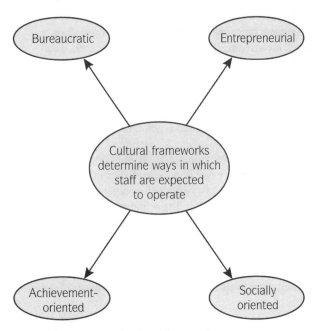

Figure 10.32 *Types of cultural framework*

For example, an organisation operating in an environment of rapidly changing technologies may feel that it needs to be at the cutting edge of technological development. By increasing the stakes in such development, it will make a contribution to perceptions within the industry that technology should be the driving force for competitiveness. The technological environment and the organisational culture of technology-driven development thus reinforce each other.

Similarly, organisations which have employees operating in overseas markets may find that these employees feed back into the organisation new cultural dimensions and styles. For example, the British manager who spends some time working for an American division may bring back new approaches, such as greater informality with subordinates and even a new style of dress. These new approaches may influence the traditions, norms and assumptions of the organisation. If a number of British managers start to bring in new ideas from abroad, this may lead to changes in business relationships in the UK.

organisation may become poorly focused, resulting in confusion.
- *Achievement-oriented frameworks* encourage employees to set high standards and to achieve these standards. This brings a lot of satisfaction when they are successful. However, the danger is that there may be an emphasis on setting unachievable goals, and employees may be pushed too hard so that a 'sweatshop culture' develops.
- *Socially oriented frameworks* emphasise the importance of relationships. Employees feel a strong sense of support and caring among themselves (e.g. in a school or hospital). However, if the organisation is poorly focused this can lead to confused and inappropriate decision-making and poor use of resources.

The external cultural environment

Organisational culture will develop also out of the organisation's relationship with its external environment. The relationship between culture and environment is a two-way process (see Figure 10.33).

Schein argues in *Organisational Culture and Leadership* that 'the environment initially influences the formation of the culture, but once culture is present in the sense of shared assumptions, those shared assumptions, in turn, influence what will be perceived and defined as the environment'.

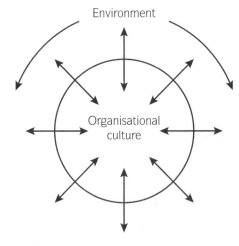

Figure 10.33 *Culture/environment interface*

Organisational ethics: product ethics, business practice and trading policies

The **ethics** of an organisation are important in determining 'the right way to do things around here'. For example, at the end of 1992 the Co-operative Bank announced its strategy of taking deposits only from, and offering financial services to, organisations that were not involved in controversial activities, including factory farming, blood sports, production of animal fur, the manufacture of tobacco and political repression. The bank believes it necessary to take up a stance in order to show the public that it is an ethical banker. It does not hide the fact that its ethical stance is likely to bring in new custom.

The ethics of an organisation will pervade all forms of organisational activity, such as whether 'white lies' are tolerated in business dealings, whether corners are cut in consumer safety, etc.

Making changes

The culture of an organisation can change owing to either unplanned or planned interventions in the range of factors that influence its culture. Changes in the external environment (e.g. an intensification in competition or a change in technology) will feed into changes in the internal culture. The personnel who make up an organisation also change. This will be particularly significant when the new people have the power to make influential changes.

Features of the culture itself are likely to determine the nature and extent of the change process. For example, some writers have contrasted change-oriented (morphogenetic) cultures with stability-oriented (homeostatic) cultures. In a morphogenetic culture, change will be regarded as a desirable process in its own right. In contrast, in homeostatic cultures change may be seen as a threat which needs to be avoided.

Significantly, there may be a deliberate decision to change the culture of an organisation. This will involve trying to shift the norms and assumptions in new directions. The process of change involves three steps (see Figure 10.34).

The model in the Figure 10.35 helps us to understand the considerations which determine whether change is worthwhile. Before making a change there has to be a genuine groundswell of opinion in favour. The individual/organisation has to decide whether it can cope with an appropriate new culture and whether it has the know-how and experience to put into effect a well-structured plan for change. Clearly, when these factors pull together there is a strong synergistic thrust towards change.

Barriers to change

In implementing change, however, an individual/organisation has to calculate the major barriers standing in the way, and to develop strategies for counteracting this

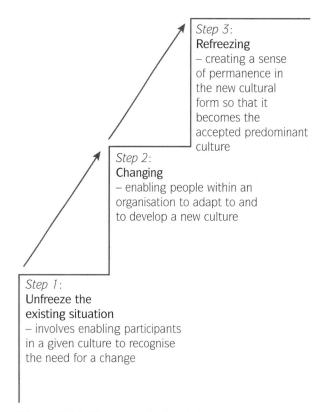

Figure 10.34 *The process of cultural change*

resistance. We can look at these barriers to change on an organisational and an individual basis.

Organisational barriers

- *Structural inertia*. The culture of an organisation will be frozen at a particular moment in time. The organisation will be organised in such a way as to maintain existing relationships and ways of going about things. It will take considerable force to break down these existing patterns. Change threatens the logic of the 'way things are currently done'. Clearly, the best chance of altering this logic is if there is considerable disquiet about existing patterns.
- *The existing power structure*. It is highly likely that organisational change will involve changing the balance of power. This will be resisted by those whose power is most threatened. In many cases, organisational change involves the removal or redeployment of people in senior positions in the organisation.
- *Resistance from work-groups*. Over time, the work-groups in an organisation become a powerful force based on formal and informal relationships between people. Work-groups develop **subcultures** and values. These can become very resistant structures which may be difficult to budge.
- *The failure of previous change initiatives*. If the organisation has previously experienced unsuccessful change

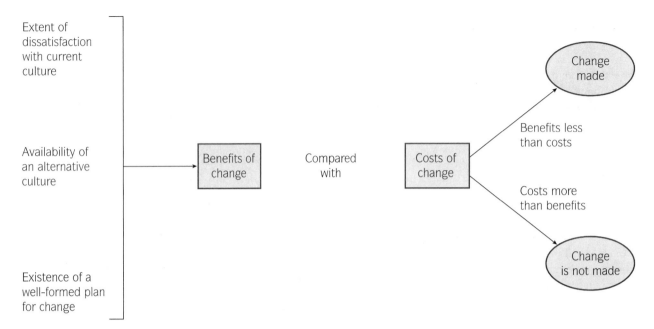

Figure 10.35 *Deciding whether it is worth changing the culture*

initiatives, then individual and groups may become resistant to change. They may treat the prospect of further change with disdain.

Individual barriers

In addition, there may be a number of important individual barriers to change. Individuals in the organisation may resist change for a number of reasons which are important to them – their reservations should not be treated lightly. They include:

- *Fears about the impact of the change on individuals and families.* For example, if the changes lead to restructuring and downsizing, then redundancy and unemployment will be inevitable. In addition, there will be the fear of downgrading and loss of status.
- *Fears about having to increase commitment to the organisation.* There may be a worry that extra hours and involvement will be required by the changes.
- *Fear of the unknown.* When people do not know what to expect, they may be reluctant to trade an old culture for a new one. Also, if they have a distorted view of what the change will entail (resulting, perhaps, from media reports about similar changes elsewhere) they will be resistant to change.
- *Tradition and set ways.* People who have been working in a particular way will often have the view: 'We like what we are doing around here'. They will thus be resistant to changing their ways.

- *Loyalty to existing relationships.* People within an organisation build up a loyalty to managers, to workmates, and the working team. They may not want to see them destroyed by new ways of working.
- *Failure to accept or recognise the need for change.* Often people will not see that there is a need for change. If things appear to be running smoothly, they will see little point in changing. However, the task of strategic management is to look beyond the 'here-and-now' and to anticipate needs in the near future.

Overcoming these barriers to change requires careful planning and attention to detail. Change needs to be introduced in a sensitive way.

Case Study

Highlighting a lack of shared values at British Cellophane

A shrinking market and growing competition prompted British Cellophane to review its culture. Cellophane manufacture is a complex chemical process, but up until the late 1980s the business had operated in a tradition-bound way. Up to this time British Cellophane had a conventional approach to management.

It was very much a top-down blame culture. In the early 1990s it recognised that it needed to change the way it went about its business.

The major problems stemmed not from marketing and distribution, but from inadequacies in its manufacturing. Management set out to improve teamwork by breaking down the mistrust between management and workers and creating a common approach to problem-solving. It created a training programme to tackle the problems under its business results scheme.

The training approach was geared to developing teamwork by concentrating on techniques to explore the effect of particular behaviour on working in teams. It also set out ways of tackling problems, planning ahead and seeing plans through.

The programme began with an initial diagnosis of the company's problems. Specific, measurable project aims were set. These were then translated into precise targets, down to individual shift level. A monitoring process was set up to log and measure progress.

The factory management identified the objective of reducing factory waste from 17.45 per cent to 15 per cent in March of the first year. This was translated into specific objectives at each level. The attempt was to create a permanent change in culture and attitudes, and in the way the organisation was run.

The market in which British Cellophane operated was a very tough one, declining at the rate of 12 per cent a year. There were a number of key producers, all competing for the remaining market. Research indicated that British Cellophane was suffering because there were no shared values and very little contact between sales staff and the shopfloor. A new step was taken to train people from various disciplines together. The shopfloor began to see that sales people were human and had problems, too. A major breakthrough came when people's behavioural patterns and attitudes started to change.

Changes were also made in the internal structure of the organisation. Training started at the top with the resetting of precise goals. The management structure was flattened. Previously, there had been eight or nine levels of management.

Management increasingly realised that productivity depended on sharing responsibility for production with the workforce: if it could not trust its workforce, it would be unlikely to succeed. Shared training helped to create shared methods.

A mark of the success of the project was the way in which a major programme of redundancy at the plant was handled. Only a year into the scheme, 40 per cent of the workforce had to be made redundant, yet production had to be pushed even higher. Efforts were made to do this as quickly as possible and without

disruption, and the company found alternative jobs for all who wanted them. At the same time, the drive to increase production was continued and output was raised by 30 per cent per employee per year. In the new atmosphere, people were seeking change instead of resisting it.

Questions

1. Why did British Cellophane need to change its culture?

2. How was the culture changed?

3. What was the effect of these changes?

4. Why and how might have employees resisted these changes?

5. Why do you think that employees were prepared to accept changes?

6. What lessons can be learnt from the case study about managing the change process?

Reactions to change

People within an organisation can respond to change in three main ways. They may **accept** the necessity of change and comply with the change process. Indeed, they may be quite thankful for the change. For example, people who have been labouring for a number of years in an oppressive organisation will welcome the 'new broom' approach that aims to introduce fesh, 'enlightened' ideas. Achieving acceptance for cultural change is perhaps the most important part of the process.

Resistance is a common reaction to change. This will take all sorts of subtle and unsubtle forms. For example, it may lead to personal antagonism (e.g. the cool atmosphere facing the new principal or senior management team). Employees may be slow in carrying out instructions or will deliberately misinterpret them in order to make new changes unworkable. Resistance may take the form of maintaining the old culture in an informal way in order to circumvent the new culture.

A more extreme form of resistance is **open conflict**. This may take the form of acrimonious flare-ups at staff meetings, deliberate sabotage and wilful destruction of the representations of the new culture. For example, a new organisational logo representing the 'new way of doing things around here' may be turned upside down, damaged or defaced. Those with power in the previous organisational structure may declare open warfare on the newcomers. Conflict is highly destructive and will begin to be resolved only when the usurpers gain the upper hand or when the old guard gains a decisive hold on its territory. Where cultural change brings open conflict, it is often tempting to draw comparisons with the behaviour of groups of apes and other primates, such as the staking out of territory and the ritual beating of chests.

Preparing for change

It is very important that the ground be prepared for the cultural change process. This involves carrying out an audit to find out whether the organisation is ready for change, identifying possible supporting forces for it, and estimating the strength of the resisting forces.

It is essential to identify clearly the supporting forces so that they can be maximised. Who is likely to be in favour of change, and what factors are most likely to encourage them to support it? How much power and influence do they have in the organisation? The key is to find ways of building on the strengths presented by supporting forces and on the potential of internal and external forces for change. In particular, the emphasis needs to be on winning the support of senior management and showing key stakeholders the benefits of change. At the same time, restraining forces and their powers need to be minimised.

The change process should be timed and planned to move the organisation towards an effective culture, as outlined in the progression shown in Figure 10.36. The movement towards the effective organisation culture is sometimes referred to as the **learning curve**. *Force-field analysis* is the term used to describe the process of identifying the constraining and supporting forces and their relative strengths.

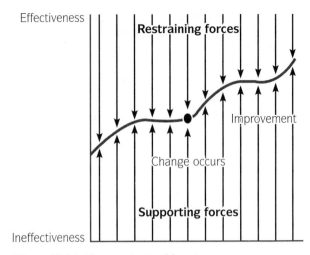

Figure 10.36 *The organisational learning curve*

Building the support for change

Building the support for change can only be successful if the groundwork is properly carried out. This includes:

- Identifying the main issues that concern people about proposed changes. Weaknesses in their reasons for opposing change can then be pointed out. The convert is often the best supporter of new ideas. If people know that their reservations are understood, they are most likely to respect the new views and ideas.
- Clarifying the reasons for and the need for change. The reasons should be set out in organisational terms rather than simply as someone's pet idea. If people perceive that the rationale for change is personal egotism or aggrandisement, then they are likely to oppose it. The reasons need to be stated in clear, impersonal terms.
- Avoiding, wherever possible, threatening existing group relationships (unless, of course, they represent the need for change). If change can be built on existing networks and relationships, then whole groups may agree to shift towards a new culture.
- Creating expectations that change will be for the better. The best way of doing this is by being able to identify tangible improvements. When expectations are translated into actual behaviours, then change is more likely to occur. People will not 'buy into' outlandish theories unless they can see the practical implications of change.
- Encouraging participation, which is a powerful influence on change. When members of an organisation share in the change process, they will be able to claim ownership of it. Change should not be forced upon people; they should be encouraged to implement the changes themselves.

- Making people within the organisation aware of how they will benefit personally. It is important to identify the rewards, incentives and long-term benefits of the change, and confirm that current benefits, such as pension schemes, are being protected.
- Maintaining effective communications, essential in building support for change. Everyone should be aware of the changes in advance. They need to know who will be affected and how they will be affected. Preparation for change may include awareness-raising training and development programmes.
- Involving the key stakeholders in the process. For example, Japanese companies starting up in the UK have appreciated the importance of involving unions in developing organisational cultures. It is important that organised groups of stakeholders be consulted and share joint responsibility for the change. Without this understanding, there is the potential for tension and conflict.

REFERENCES

Burns, Tom, *Industrial Man: Selected Readings*, Penguin, 1969.

Child, J., *Organisation: A Guide to Problems and Practice*, Harper & Row, 1984.

Dransfield, R., Howkins, S., Hudson, F. and Davies, W., *Human Resource Management for Higher Awards*, Heinemann Educational, 1996.

Drucker, Peter, 'New templates for today's organisations', *Harvard Business Review*, Jan/Feb 1974, p. 52.

Drucker, Peter, *The Practice of Management*, Butterworth-Heinemann, 1994.

Goffee, Rob and Jones, Gareth, *The Character of a Corporation: How Your Company's Culture Can Make or Break Your Business*, HarperCollins, 1998.

Greene, Kenyon, *The Adaptive Organisation*, Wiley, 1982.

Jackson, John and Morgan, Cyril, *Organisational Theory*, Prentice Hall, 1982.

March & Simon, *Organisations*, Blackwell, 1993.

Peters and Waterman, *In Search of Excellence*, 1982.

Petrock, John, *Non-Profit Making Strategies*, HarperCollins, 1990.

Randall, C., *The Folklore of Management*, Little, Brown, 1962.

Sadler, Philip, *Designing Organisations*, Kogan Page, 1991.

Schein, *Organisational Culture and Leadership*, Josey-Bass, 1992.

Sims, Fineman and Gabriel, *Organising and Organisation*, 1993.

Storey, John, *The Management of Human Resources*, 1992.

Torrington, Derek and Hall, Laura, *Personnel Management*, Prentice Hall, 1998.

Motivation Theories and Management Practices

A number of writers have argued that it is important to identify the traits necessary for leadership in particular areas of work. Management can turn on matters of process and experience, and many people in a profession can become good managers. Leadership requires very special personal qualities which fewer people in a profession have or are able to develop. However, it is possible to enable people to develop more of these qualities, although it is important to first pin down what they are and to set out how they can be developed. This chapter examines the broad relationship between motivation theories and management practices.

On completing the chapter you should be able to:

- discuss different leadership styles and the effectiveness of these leadership approaches

- explain the different motivation theories and their application within the workplace

- assess the relationship between motivation theory and the practice of management.

LEADERSHIP

Leadership in organisations

In the 1993 edition of Charles Handy's landmark book *Understanding Organisations*, the author wrote that 'leadership as a topic has rather a dated air about it'. He went on to suggest that in many modern organisations the emphasis has moved in the direction of self-management of groups and individuals. However, Handy then went on

to argue that leadership is still a vital skill, an ingredient in any organisation, and that we should not assume that people can automatically learn to lead without working hard at it and making a detailed study of the characteristics of good leadership. This chapter therefore starts out by examining some key aspects of research into leadership.

Leaders have a responsibility to achieve tasks set for them with the help of the groups that they lead. Hersey and Blanchard (1988) say that 'leadership occurs when one attempts to influence the behaviour of an individual or group'. Leaders have two *main roles* in the organisation:

- to make sure that a task or goal is achieved
- to maintain effective relationships within the organisation, including the relationship between the leader and other group members.

Effectiveness will be measured in terms of the way in which relationships enable tasks or goals to be achieved.

Halpin and Winer (1957) set out the following two dimensions of *leadership behaviour*:

- *initiating structure* – setting out the ways and means of accomplishing group goals, and coordinating activities of the group members
- *consideration* – motivating group members to accept group goals and to work together at achieving the group task while maintaining good relationships.

Hersey and Blanchard identify three *general skills* of leadership:

- *Diagnosing* – being able to understand the situation as it is now and knowing what can reasonably be expected in the future. The gap between what is and what can be expected, often referred to as the **performance gap**, is the problem to be solved. The effective leader will diagnose ways of closing this gap. Diagnosing is a **cognitive skill**.
- *Adapting* – changing one's behaviour and other resources in ways that help to close the performance gap. Adapting is a **behavioural skill**.
- *Communicating* – since diagnosis and adaptation are not sufficient unless one can get across what needs to be done and how it can be done. Communication is a **process skill**.

In performing the leadership role, a person will need to satisfy the following needs:

- *Task needs* – The task or purpose of the group must be carried out properly and efficiently. Group members will have confidence in a leader who is able to 'get things done'.
- *Group maintenance needs* – The leader has to 'hold the group together' while helping its members to work together efficiently, confidently and happily as a shared team.
- *Individual needs* – The leader also has to identify the individual needs of members and to create the right conditions and opportunities for these to be met.

These three types of needs are interdependent, and so successful leadership involves successfully meeting task, group and individual needs.

Organisational structures should be designed to enable leaders to lead. For example, an individual who is a good leader in a number of organisational settings may find it difficult to be effective in another setting because the structure (culture etc.) is unsuitable.

Managers and leaders

In their book *Leaders: The Strategies for Taking Charge*, Bennis and Nanus (1985) make an important distinction: 'Managers are people who do things right and leaders are people who do the right thing'. Their conclusion was based on a study of 90 leaders working in a range of organisations. In particular they noted that the leaders they interviewed were concerned with the purpose and direction of the organisations they headed, rather than the nuts and bolts. Today, we refer to this focus as 'mission'. Mission is concerned with giving an organisation and its members a clear direction to pull in.

Bennis and Nanus then went on to identify four necessary attributes for leaders:

- *Vision.* Being able to employ a vision helps the leader to win confidence. The successful leader will encourage other members of the organisation to share and believe in the vision.
- *Communication.* The effective leader will be able to communicate the vision clearly, not only through words and descriptions, but also by actively personifying the vision.
- *Trust.* This is all about consistency and integrity. The leader must convey the feeling that he or she can be relied on to deliver what they promise.
- *Self-knowledge.* The 90 leaders studied knew their own strengths and weaknesses. They built on their strengths.

Leadership is an important part of management. It is the process of motivating other people to act in particular ways to meet an organisation's objectives. The word 'leader' is derived from words meaning a path or road, the role of leader being one of giving direction to others and enabling them to follow the chosen path.

Philip Sadler, in his book *Managerial Leadership* (1988), argues that in complex organisations leaders need to be good managers. The goals of leadership must fit with the goals of an organisation, and the means adopted to achieve them must be the most economic compatible with achieving the aim. Effective leaders in organisations:

'...must be able to exercise managerial functions such as planning, budgeting, scheduling work and monitoring performance against targets. They must be able to function effectively within the inevitable constraints imposed by organisation structure and by the operating conditions derived from the organisation's environment. They must, in a word, be managerial leaders.'

Leadership traits

A **trait** is a characteristic feature or quality distinguishing a person. Many studies have been carried out that purport to identify certain traits that are found predominantly in good leaders or managers. Trait theories may be used, for example, to explain why certain individuals such as Richard Branson (Virgin) or Anita Roddick (Body Shop) have been particularly good 'leadership material'.

Discussion point

What traits do the people shown below have in common that make them good leaders?

Mo Mowlam

Rupert Murdoch

James Dyson

Christine Hancock

The trait approach is built on the assumption that certain individuals are born with or acquire outstanding qualities which enable them to be effective leaders. Desirable traits for strong leaders have traditionally been seen as self-assurance, dominance, intelligence, determination, decisiveness, and a desire to work hard to achieve targets. However, the traits which are appropriate for a modern organisation based on teamwork may be quite different, as suggested by Figure 11.1.

It is not too difficult, for example, to think of individuals who are intelligent, self-assured and decisive. However, these people may lack the sort of *sensitivity* and *interpersonal considerations* that are so essential in the modern workplace.

A number of writers have argued that it is important to identify the traits necessary for leadership in particular areas of work. Management can turn on matters of process and experience, and many people in a profession can become good managers. Leadership requires very special personal qualities which fewer people in a profession have or are able to develop. However, it is possible to enable people to develop more of these qualities, although it is important to first pin down what the qualities are and to set out how they can be developed.

It seems obvious that imagination, creativity and charisma are important characteristics of leadership. Passion and energy need to complement experience and ability. Leadership training becomes possible when the characteristics that are required by leaders in a particular type of organisation.

Strong leadership approach	Teamwork approach
Self-assurance	Self-assurance
Dominance	Sensitivity to others
Intelligence	Intelligence coupled with interpersonal skills
Determination	Perseverance
Decisiveness	Desire to work hard to create team goals, co-operation and team success.
Desire to work hard to achieve targets	

Figure 11.1 *Leadership traits for two forms of organisation*

Charles Handy is another writer who has identified and described a number of general characteristics which tend to be present in good leaders. This is how he describes them:

- Leaders should have above-average intelligence but not necessarily be geniuses. Often a down-to-earth sort of intelligence may be required if someone is going to work well with others.
- Leaders must take responsibility on themselves and show a certain amount of willingness to follow unexpected paths rather than wait for approval from others. They need to have that spark of creativity which will enable them to identify avenues for opportunity that others may see but not have the courage to pursue.
- Leaders need a good self-image which will give them the confidence to take others with them. However, leaders should also show respect for people with whom they work. It has been suggested that good leaders will adopt an 'I'm OK, you're OK' position when dealing with others, rather than a disdainful 'I'm OK, so that's OK'.

Handy also identified a 'helicopter factor' as being important for leaders. In other words, they need the ability to rise above a situation rather than being bogged down in minute details. In addition, good leaders need to be generalists: they should be able to build up an understanding of new situations quickly and apply broad-based experience of other fields and organisations.

Of course, trait approaches are not above criticism. You may be able to think of leaders who do not have the traits outlined. Also, the traits often identified by researchers tend to be rather vague. It can therefore be argued that the traits in themselves are not sufficient to describe the characteristics of effective leaders. Perhaps it would be more helpful to identify the leadership qualities that are useful in a *specific context* in order to identify the people who would be best able to lead in such a context.

Discussion point

Select five current leaders. To what extent do your chosen five appear to have the traits of leadership as outlined above? Perhaps you can focus on leaders with whom you work quite closely to consider their traits. To what extent does the leadership trait theory seem to be valid for them?

Case Study

Heroes defy the mould

In an article in the *Independent on Sunday* on 19 June 1994, Tom Peters discussed twelve of his heroes. He argued that they share, more or less, 13 traits that add up to a fair guide to success in general. The traits were described by Peters as follows:

(i) *Self-invented*. 'I am an American, Chicago-born,' begins Saul Bellow's novel *The Adventures of Augie March*, 'and go at things as I have taught myself, free-style, and will make the record in my own way.' All my Mount Rushmore nominees have chiselled their masterpieces from the granite of life in a distinct, unusual fashion. Standard career path? Forget it. One company, one job? Not even close.

(ii) *Ever changing*. I don't think any of my dandy dozen has a split personality in the clinical sense of the term; but surely all are chameleons, not bound by consistency they have tried a plethora of outfits while remaining desperately and passionately committed to whatever it is they are pursuing at the moment.

(iii) *Battered and bruised*. My heroes have screwed up things at least as often as they have gotten them right. Their collective motto could be: 'A road without potholes not a road worth travelling'. Failure does not seem to faze them. If anything, setbacks amuse them and motivate them.

(iv) *Inquisitive*. No question goes unasked for this squad of achievers. Sometimes I think there is literally nothing that does not interest them. They are determined to get to the bottom of any topic they touch – on or off the job. (Job? They are what they do. Job is not part of their vocabulary.)

(v) *Childlike*. This naive crew – who refuse to grow up – are not afraid to ask dumb (even very dumb) questions if they are not getting the message. Their appetite for knowledge and exploration is far greater than any fear they have of looking idiotic.

(vi) *Free from the past*. Gravity has no meaning for this group. They are not weighed down by history. In a flash they will thumb their noses at what only yesterday they were fervently espousing.

(vii) *Comfortable, even cocky*. My Hall of Famers are at ease with themselves, unperturbed by the idea of life as an elusive moving target – an adventure to be relished, mostly for its detours.

(viii) *Jolly*. These people laugh a lot. They marvel at human intrigues, and their appreciation of the absurd strokes their marvellous sense of humour. All of them have wrinkles – you know the kind .... those that can only be attributed to smiles and laughter.

(ix) *Audacious and a bit nuts*. They will try anything – from learning a language to starting a new career – with barely a moment's hesitation. Moreover, by the standards of the majority, they view the world through decidedly cockeyed glasses.

(x) *Iconoclastic*. Conventional wisdom, to my pilgrims, is like a red cape to a bull. I sometimes think they're only happy when they're on the 'wrong' side of an issue or truism.

(xi) *Multidimensional*. We're not dealing with saints. All members of this tribe have flaws, often as pronounced as their strengths. But, then, when was the last time you observed an insipid soul accomplishing much of anything?

(xii) *Honest*. It's not that they always tell the truth or are above pettiness. Hey, we're all human. It's just that this set is attuned to reality and especially to their own foibles. They are consummate and often quixotic truth-seekers, with little time for those who aren't as confused as they are.

(xiii) *Larger than life*. Our Gang of Twelve are all heroic. That is they paint the canvasses, large and small, with bold strokes. They are fearless in their own fashion. They embrace the circus of life, rather than shrink from it.

Questions

1. Do you think the traits outlined would 'add up to a fair guide to success'?

2. Is there anything you think should be removed from the list?

3. Is there anything you would like to add to the list?

4. Try to establish your own list of traits that you think would contribute to success based on your experience of working with 'leaders'.

5. Identify your own list of people who have some or all of these traits.

Management style

A person's management style is the pattern of behaviour he or she exhibits in carrying out a management role over a period of time. An assumption can be made that employees will work harder and perhaps better for managers who employ certain styles. The most common division of styles is between (a) tightly controlled management, (b) democratic management, and (c) loose or *laissez-faire* management. The differences can be summarised in a simple chart as in Figure 11.2.

Style of Management	Type of leadership	Features
Tightly controlled	Autocratic	Leader alone makes decisions Staff are told decisions and they carry out the tasks
Democratic	Persuasive	Leader makes decisions alone Others are persuaded by the leader that the decision is the right one
	Consultative	The leader consults before a decision is made The group will influence the decision, even though the leader has the final say
Laissez-faire	Loose	The leader does not force his opinions on the group There is no formal structure of decision-making

Figure 11.2 *Three management styles*

Case Study

Management with style?

A manager described his work for a major retail chain in the following way:

'Working in an environment that had enormous pressures from the City and shareholders, the style at Company X (a leading retailer) was set from the highest levels. A very autocratic style was in place in the branches, with the overall result being a "pass the buck" attitude. For example, if I failed to achieve a target, then as long as I had done everything by the book, and as I had been trained, then it was a case of it being "not my problem". the issue would then pass up the managerial ladder. The result of this was that there was very little ownership within the store, and people did not really care. This led to an "I'm alright Jack" attitude, in that as long as your section was running smoothly, then you were happy. Obviously the overall team spirit suffered. Indeed it was usually treated with amusement when it was a fellow manager being hauled over the coals, as it meant the store manager's attention was elsewhere. Very surprisingly, however, this morale-sapping attitude engendered a 'triumph through adversity' feeling amongst the layer of management I was a member of. It was this attitude that kept us going sometimes!'

Questions

1. How would you characterise the typical management style in the organisation described?

2. What do you see as being the strengths and weaknesses of such an approach in the retail environment?

3. What would you judge to be the most appropriate management style in retailing?

In his book *New Patterns of Management*, Rensis Likert (1961) outlined a model of styles which highlighted four types (see Figure 11.3).

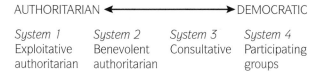

AUTHORITARIAN ←————————→ DEMOCRATIC

System 1	System 2	System 3	System 4
Exploitative authoritarian	Benevolent authoritarian	Consultative	Participating groups

Figure 11.3 *Likert's model of leadership styles*

- *System 1* – Under the exploitive authoritarian regime, threats and punishments are employed and communication and teamwork are poor.
- *System 2* – The benevolent authoritative regime is paternalistic and allows some opportunities for consultation and delegation.
- *System 3* – The consultative regime moves forwards to greater democracy and teamwork. Rewards are used instead of threats.
- *System 4* – The participative group regime is the ultimate democratic style, leading to commitment to organisational goals.

Tannenbaum and Schmidt (1968) outlined a continuum of management styles which fall between the authoritarian and the democratic (see Figure 11.4). In the diagram as we move further to the right (i.e. towards an increasingly democratic model) subordinates within the organisation are given increasingly more freedom to make decisions for themselves.

Charles Handy argued in favour of a supportive style of management because this is likely to foster:

- subordinate satisfaction
- lower staff turnover and grievance rates
- fewer intergroup conflicts.

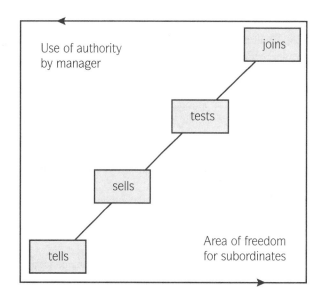

Figure 11.4 *Continuum of leadership styles*

Discussion point

Can you identify managers that lean most strongly to each of the styles outlined in Tannebaum and Schmidt's continuum? Give examples of decisions or behaviour which typify their approach.

Moreover this is usually the preferred style of subordinates. Handy argues that, although research findings indicate that style alone is not the only answer to effective management, a supportive style of management will lead to a higher degree of contentment and greater involvement by the working group.

Another aspect of management we need to look at is the contrast between **task-oriented** styles and **people-oriented** styles. A manager who is wrapped up in the task will be concerned mainly with output, work results and rigid standards. This may result in the leader trying to closely monitor each and every task that employees carry out. (Task orientation may thus be closely associated with scientific management and autocratic styles.) In contrast, a person-oriented style will show itself in a strong concern for employees. This manager may set out to boost morale and encourage employees to work together to get tasks completed.

The 'management grid' devised by Blake and Mouton is a matrix model of management which, instead of concentrating on autocratic versus democratic styles, looks at 'concern for people' and 'concern for production'. Again this is easier to understand by looking at a diagram (see Figure 11.5). Of the five styles of management shown in the grid, only [9:9] is the ideal style because it combines deep concern for people with clear concern for production – getting things done and keeping everyone happy. The compilers of the grid called this style 'Team'. Looking at the others:

- [1:9] is too concerned with people and gets very little done ('Country Club')
- [9:1] is too concerned with production and creates an atmosphere of low morale ('Task').
- [1:1] has no concern for people or output ('Impoverished').
- [5:5] shows some concern for people and some concern for production ('Middle-of-the-road').

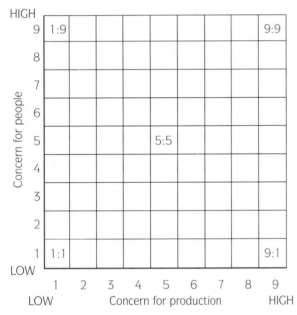

Figure 11.5 *A management grid*

The managerial grid enables managers to assess their own style and compare it with other possibilities.

Another dimension of style is the difference between a positive and a negative leader. A positive leader will emphasise rewards, which may be in the form of money, benefits, etc. or in the form of better working relationships. Negative leadership, in contrast, places more emphasis on punishments and sanctions. Negative leaders may stress their superiority and domination over others. These are bosses more than modern 'leaders'; they use power as a threat.

The contingency approach

Another approach to looking at management and leadership is based on **contingency theories**. These set out to account for the range of variables that may be relevant in a particular situation. The contingency model is very useful because of its recognition that management approaches can and do vary according to the situation, the types of decisions to be made, and who is involved in the decision-making process. Since management style is dependent on a range of contextual factors, tomorrow these factors may alter to require a different style of management. These variables include the task, the nature of the work-group, and the position of the leader in the group.

The contingency approach can produce valuable insights and clues about appropriate management and leadership in particular situations. For example, **Fred Fiedler** (1967) suggested that the appropriateness of using an authoritarian or democratic management style depends upon whether the situation facing management is 'favourable' or 'unfavourable'. A favourable situation would exist when:

- the leader is popular and trusted by members of the group
- the task is well-defined
- the power of the leader is high.

Fiedler felt that the first of these is the most significant. His findings led him to suggest that authoritarian approaches are most suitable in circumstances where (a) the task is well-defined and the leader is strong and highly respected; or (b) the task is ambiguous and the leader is not in a strong position relative to the group. In the first case, decision-making will be effective because subordinates will support a respected leader. In the second case, leadership must assert itself and clarify its aims for the organisation or go under. In contrast, where a task is ambiguous and the leader is well-respected, the leader can afford to draw in the whole expertise of the group while still retaining power and authority.

The '**best-fit approach**' can be used as an extension to Fiedler's work. It is based on the assumption that managers need to take account of four factors if they are to operate effectively: the leader, the subordinates, the task, and the environment. The *leader* will have a set of views about how things should be done and what is important. The *subordinates* will have a set of views about how they should be led and how things should be done. They will relate to tasks in different ways, and will have varying levels of commitment to group tasks. The *task* will vary in nature, complexity, time-scale and importance. Finally, the *environment* will vary according to the nature of the group, the position of the manager within the group, what the group or organisation is trying to achieve, and the structure and technology of the organisation.

The best fit approach argues that there is no single best style of leadership. Different styles are appropriate to different circumstances. The best style in a given group will be the style that most closely matches the requirements of leader, subordinate and task. The degree of fit can be measured on a scale running from 'tight' to 'flexible'. The three factors are then placed along the scale. In Figure 11.6(a) we have a situation in which the task is highly unstructured, but both leader and subordinates are comfortable in operating with a flexible approach – clearly there is a 'fit' between each of the key elements. However, in Figure 11.6(b) we have a leader whose preferred style is relatively authoritarian, working with a group whose members feel happier with a more flexible style, on a task

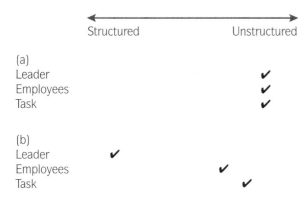

Figure 11.6 *(a) a good fit, and (b) a poor fit*

which is fairly ambiguous. Because of this lack of fit, problems and difficulties are likely to arise. In the real world it is possible that either the three elements will move some way towards each other, or the job will not get done.

Charles Handy argued that, confronted with lack of fit, in this way, leaders need to adjust factors towards a fit. In the short term it may be easiest to adjust managerial style. However, in the longer term the most benefit may be achieved by redesigning tasks.

Case Study

Qualities of leadership

In his book *Understanding Organisations*, Charles Handy wrote that individuals need to learn to do the following:

a develop and communicate a clear vision of the task, so that a sense of purpose develops in the group

b allow others to influence the vision, so that they are committed to it

c build up the trust and respect of their group so that they have the essential conditions to allow them to adapt their style to the contingency requirements

d remember that successful performance of their ambassadorial role is essential if they are to have freedom to behave as they think best within their group

e remember that they represent the organisation to their subordinates and should practice all the precepts enjoined on the senior managers.

Individuals and organisations should bear in mind that the individual who meets these requirements will tend to:

a have high tolerance for ambiguity and be good at handling open-ended problems

b be good at differentiating between people and situations

c have a clear self-concept which will tend to go with self-confidence

d have a high reservoir of energy

e be prepared to set moderately high standards for himself or herself and co-workers and to give and receive feedback on performance.

Questions

1. What form of management do you think Handy is advocating – autocratic, participative or free-rein?

2. To what extent does Handy advocate a 'contingent' approach to management.

3. What do you perceive to be the benefits of the approach outlined by Handy?

Philip Sadler, in a useful book *Managerial Leadership in the Post-Industrial Society* (1988), argues that the most productive approach to the study of management is to identify ways in which managerial work is changing. He describes four key shifts:

• *A shift from managing the production of tangible goods to the management of services.* In the post-industrial society the very large majority of managers (possibly up to 90 per cent) will be managing service-type activities. Until recently theories of management have largely been based on the manufacturing model. A lot therefore needs to be learnt from modern organisations that have a successful record of management in service industries.

- *Information technology.* The use of information technology is a key dimension for nearly all managers today. Enormous strides in information technology have made it possible to generate huge amounts of information very cheaply, to process this information very rapidly, to store it indefinitely in a very compact form, to retrieve it instantly, and to move it to any part of the globe. Now it is necessary to learn how to use this ability to improve our effectiveness in managing organisations.
- *Managing knowledge and talent.* Today knowledge is a hugely important asset of any organisation. What is needed, therefore, is a change in emphasis from managing labour- and/or capital-intensive organisations to managing knowledge-intensive organisations. The latter can be defined simply as the organisation which depends for its survival not upon an adequate supply of cheap labour, nor upon investment in modern plant and equipment, but on its ability to develop and market superior knowledge. However, the concept may need developing to 'talent-intensive' as well, to include industries and occupations such as films, television, the arts, popular music, advertising, public relations, investment analysts, bond dealers, dealers in futures markets, sports clubs – and any organisation that earns its income primarily by exploiting relatively rare human knowledge, talent, skill, aptitude, beauty etc.
- *Managing cultural change.* The transition from an industrial to a post-industrial society involves a cultural change for institutions. Organisations need to move and change away from being bureaucratic and based on top-down approaches to becoming more flexible and democratic with empowered workforces.

Leadership and organisational culture

Leadership plays an important part in shaping an organisation's culture. Bennis and Nanus (1985) argue that in order to provide an organisation with a sense of direction, a leader must develop a 'vision' which is a mental image of an achievable and desirable future state of the organisation. When an organisation is given a clear sense of its purpose and direction the individuals who belong to it are able to identify themselves both with their roles in the organisation and with the organisation's role in society. This has a powerful impact on their motivation to achieve. It generates enthusiasm, energy, pride, effort – a culture which can be felt very quickly when dealing with the organisation.

Edwin Baker (1980) lists ten techniques which leaders of organisations can use to influence corporate culture:

- *Role modelling.* The manager sets the example by behaving in ways consistent with the norms and values the organisation wishes to reinforce. For example, the chief executive of a Disneyland theme park picks up any litter he sees as he moves around.
- *Face-to-face communication.* The manager takes time to visit employees on-site and address them personally.
- *Written communication.* Company newsletters, posters, books, etc. are used liberally.
- *Positive reinforcement.* If you say you believe in developing people, then reward and give recognition where appropriate.
- *Recruitment policy.* Employ those people who fit the desired culture or who will be capable allies in achieving cultural change.
- *Promotion and transfer decisions.* Make sure that people who embody the desired culture are moved into key positions.
- *Training.* Ensure that all training, especially induction, covers company philosophy and is as concerned with attitudes and values as with methods and techniques.
- *Personnel policies.* Do not favour either single or marital status. Consider the abolition of time clocks and avoid lay-offs.
- *Physical factors.* Be aware of the importance of benefits of cleanliness, good housekeeping, use of colour, quality of employee facilities, open-plan offices, no executive car parking facilities, quality of customer reception facilities, etc.
- *Showmanship and symbolism.* Consider the benefits of 'roadshows', conventions, slogans, badges, supporting advertising campaigns, etc.

MOTIVATION THEORIES

Any person will be a better leader for understanding what motivates others, and what motivates himself or herself.

Motivation is the strength of commitment that individuals have to what they are doing. **Workplace motivation** is concerned with commitment to an organisation and its objectives and targets. In this section we set out to explore a range of factors influencing motivation at work, and approaches managers can use to motivate employees. The text draws heavily on research that has taken place in this field over the years.

Human needs and work

The American writer Studs Terkel suggested in his book *Working*:

> '[Work] *is about a search, too, for daily meaning as well as daily bread, for recognition as well as cash, for astonishment rather than torpor; in short, for a sort of life rather than a Monday-through-Friday sort of dying.*'

People have a wide range of attitudes towards work. Many see it simply as a means of earning money; others find that work is tremendously rewarding. Attitudes often depend on how much opportunity individuals are given to express their skill and talents. Some work is alienating because individuals are treated as part of the machinery; they are expected to do very boring and repetitive tasks without any responsibility. Some work is fulfilling because individuals are given a lot of freedom and the opportunity to be creative.

Conditions of work are important, too. Some modern workplaces are air-conditioned, brightly decorated and have a pleasant working atmosphere. Others are stifling in summer and freezing in winter; the premises are decrepit and personal relationships are discouraged. Pay can be used as an incentive to encourage people to work harder, but it cannot help them to enjoy their work.

Some of the things individuals might look for in a job include:

- a fair rate of pay, good opportunities for promotion and job security
- decent breaks and holidays
- prestige
- friendships with work colleagues

- opportunities to be creative and a degree of independence
- responsibility
- the opportunity to balance work and family life.

Generally, satisfaction will be greatest for those individuals who have the freedom to choose a job, and this will normally be those who have had the opportunity to acquire the most widely accepted range of qualifications and skills. Most jobs have some disadvantages, but workers will enjoy work if the disadvantages can be minimised.

We now consider the views of a number of leading researchers who have carried out detailed work looking at motivation in the workplace.

Needs theory: Maslow and Herzberg

Maslow

Abraham Maslow's theory of motivation has proved to be immensely popular since the mid-1950s. His theory is typical of a group of theories known as **needs (content) theories** which work on the supposition that unsatisfied needs create tensions which ought to be addressed. A **goal** is therefore identified which will address the unsatisfied need. A **behaviour pathway** is selected to achieve the goal.

Maslow (1954) suggested that, although it is difficult, if not impossible, to analyse individual needs, it is possible to develop a hierarchical picture of needs, split into five broad categories (see Figure 11.7).

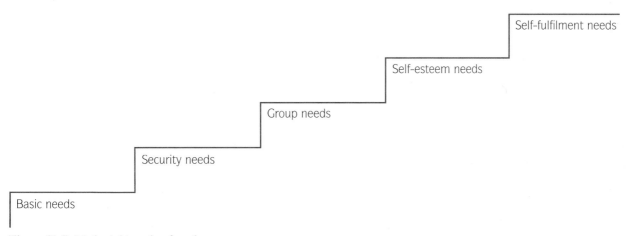

Figure 11.7 *Maslow's hierarchy of needs*

Basic needs are for reasonable standards of food, shelter, clothing and sex, and those other items that are considered the norm to meet the needs of the body and for physical survival. This base level will typically be met in modern industrial society by the exchange of labour for a wage packet or salary.

Security needs are also concerned with physical survival. In the context of the workplace, these needs could include physical safety, security of employment, adequate rest periods, pension and sick schemes, and protection from arbitrary actions.

Group needs are concerned with an individual's desire for love and affection. There will always be some people who are strong enough and happy to keep apart; however, the majority of people want to feel that they belong to a group. In small and medium-sized organisations (up to 200 people) it is relatively easy to give each member of the group a feeling of belonging. However, in larger organisations individuals can lose their group identity, becoming just another number, a face in the crowd. As we shall see later in this chapter, there are ways of dealing with this problem, for example by putting groups of workers into smaller work units with a common productive interest.

Self-esteem needs are based on an individual's desire for self-respect and the respect of others. Employees have a wish to be recognised as individuals of some importance, to receive praise for their work and to have their efforts noticed.

Maslow placed **self-fulfilment** at the top of his hierarchy. Self-fulfilment is concerned with full personal development and individual creativity. In order to meet this need, it is important for individuals to be able to use their talents and abilities fully.

Maslow argued that individuals first have to have their lower-level needs met; however, if they are not to experience frustration it is also important for their higher-level needs to be addressed. Frustrated employees are likely to develop a 'couldn't care less' approach or to become antagonistic to working life. Maslow felt that in modern industrial settings, if employees are to feel a greater commitment to work and to become more effective workers, it is necessary to meet these higher-level needs. Self-fulfilment at work creates the 'complete employee', the person who enjoys work and feels a direct involvement in it.

Higher-order needs for esteem and self-fulfilment provide the greatest drive to motivation and will grow in strength when they are satisfied.

Maslow's theory has been criticised for its apparent rigidity. It is questionable whether needs can always be ranked in a simple hierarchical form. Maslow himself questioned the validity of a rigid ordering of needs, because individuals are likely to have different priorities.

	Physiological	Safety and security	Love	Esteem	Self-actualisation
Being given the opportunity at work to use your full creative talents to the full in a safe, secure and rewarding environment					
Working part-time, for a pittance, with no job security or job satisfaction					
Doing monotonous, repetitive tasks, for a high rate of pay, in a well-organised and secure working environment					
Working very long hours in a risky job with high rewards, and an exciting work atmosphere					
Working in an atmosphere in which you are highly respected, but with little opportunity for promotion and with poor job prospects					

Herzberg

Another very influential piece of research work on motivation was carried out by Herzberg and his associates in the late 1950s as a result of an investigation into the sources of job satisfaction and dissatisfaction of accountants and engineers. Herzberg (1966) identified **dissatisfiers** associated with the context of the job, and **satisfiers** associated with the content of the job.

This in many ways complements the findings of Maslow. Herzberg argued that factors in the work situation act in different ways to motivate people to work well or badly. His original work looked at the good and bad working experiences of 200 engineers. He drew a distinction between what he called 'hygiene' factors (which potentially could act as dissatisfiers) and motivating factors or satisfiers.

The dissatisfiers relate to the *context* of jobs which may easily provide sources of dissatisfaction. Herzberg set out nine such dissatisfers:

- autocratic or arbitrary company policy and administration
- low pay
- poor working conditions
- antagonistic relationships between different levels in the hierarchy
- unfriendly relationships within the hierarchy
- unfair management and supervisory practices
- unfair treatment of employees
- feelings of inadequacy
- impossibility of growth and development.

Herzberg suggested that if these factors did not reach an acceptable standard, employee dissatisfaction might be expressed by absenteeism, poor levels of output, resistance to change, obstruction and/or other negative work practices.

In contrast, Herzberg pointed to five motivating factors, which relate to the *content* of jobs. These are factors which can increase the motivation to work better and harder.

- recognition of effort and performance
- the nature of the job itself – does it provide the employee with the appropriate degree of challenge?
- sense of achievement
- assumption of responsibility
- opportunities for promotion and responsibility.

On the basis of his research, Herzberg went on to suggest that jobs could be given more meaning if they incorporated elements of responsibility and a more creative use of abilities and opportunities, enabling employees to feel a sense of achievement.

However, Herzberg's thesis has since been criticised on a number of counts. The research methods he used were criticised because he did not try to measure the relationship between satisfaction and work performance. The size of the sample he used has also been criticised, and it has been suggested that his two-factor theory was an inevitable result of the questions asked and the way they were asked by the interviewers. Nevertheless, Herzberg's theory continues to be very popular and is one that appeals to practising managers.

Process theory: Vroom, Adams, and Porter and Lawler

Vroom

A number of motivation theorists has moved on from focusing simply on needs. They have developed what is known as **process theory** (also known as **cognitive theory** because of the way it focuses on people's perceptions of their environment and their interpretations and understanding of it). Process theory focuses on the psychological forces or processes that influence motivation.

Vroom's (1964) expectancy theory puts forward the notion that the key ingredients in motivation are:

- an individual's wants
- his or her estimation of the likelihood of meeting these wants.

This theory is also known as the 'path-goal' (P–G) concept.

An individual's wants at work may include promotion, a high salary, a particular job, a company car, and so on. Vroom used the measure *valency* to describe the level of a particular want, which can be placed on a scale from high to low. However, if high valency for a particular target is going to act as a motivator, the individual concerned must believe that the target is attainable, which is expressed as an *expectancy*. For example, an individual who wants to work up to the position in which he or she is entitled to run a company car, or manage a department at work, must believe that this goal can be met in the course of time. The implications of the theory are that working life should offer opportunities for the goals of employees to be met, and at the same time provide clear evidence that these targets are attainable.

Vroom set out a diagram (Figure 11.8) showing that valency and expectancy are the two key ingredients in motivation. The × sign indicates the multiplier effect created by the interaction of valency and expectancy.

Figure 11.8 *Vroom's dynamic of motivation*

Adams

Adams' work provides us with another insight into the terms of process theory. He developed what he called **equity theory** which is concerned with the perceptions that people have about how they are being treated when compared with others. To be treated equitably is to be treated in the same way as another similar group or individual. Equity is a comparative process involving feelings and perceptions. In simple terms, employees will feel motivated if they are treated equitably and demotivated if they feel they are being treated inequitably.

Adams (1965) identified two major types of equity. *Distributive equity* is concerned with the fairness with which people feel they are being rewarded in comparison with others. *Procedural equity* is concerned with the employees' views of fairness of the organisation's procedures (e.g. in relation to recruitment, selection, job progression).

Porter and Lawler

Porter and Lawler (1968) built on the work of Vroom and Adams to argue that managers are able to control employee behaviour by linking desired behaviour to rewards, in order to ensure such behaviour. They set out a detailed model identifying the ingredients of employee satisfaction. *Intrinsic rewards* stem from the job itself or the person carrying out the job, and include a sense of achievement, belief that you are valued in the workplace, recognition, etc. *Extrinsic rewards* stem from the actions of others (e.g. managers) and include factors such as pay, praise and promotion.

Successful management, then, involves providing meaningful and valued rewards to employees. Employees need to have the opportunity to engage in 'good performance', and expectations must be clearly communicated to employees. Rewards must be clearly and visibly linked to performance. The model is summarised in Figure 11.9.

Behavioural theory: Skinner

A brief word needs to be said here about the work of behavioural psychologists like B. F. Skinner, who play down the importance of internal psychological factors and instinct to focus on external factors that directly influence behaviour. They believe that learning takes place mainly through the process of reinforcement, both positive and negative. Actions can be rewarded or punished. Behaviourists believe that success in meeting goals should be met by positive reinforcement (incentives) and the process should be repeated on a regular basis. Thorndike's 'law of effect' (1911) is often cited as a basic principle for behaviour modification:

> *'Of several responses made to the same situation, those which are accompanied or closely followed by satisfaction (reinforcement) ... will be more likely to recur; those which are accompanied or closely followed by discomfort (punishment) ... will be less likely to occur.'*

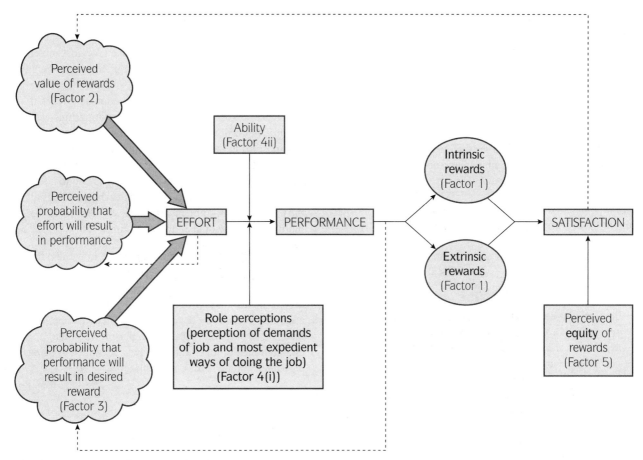

Figure 11.9 *Porter and Lawler's model of movtivation*

Other theories related to motivation

Schein

All theories related to motivation are based on assumptions about the underlying nature of human beings. Ed Schein (1978) has classified these under three main headings:

- *Socio-economic drives*. The assumption here is that people are driven by material urges alone. Satisfaction can be created by meeting these basic needs in the workplace.
- *Social drives*. His assumption is that people have a basic need to feel part of a group, and to be accepted.
- *Complex drives*. A much broader perspective of motivation is that people are driven by a host of factors which change over time and in different circumstances.

Schein's position, then, is that simplistic explanations of motivation should be avoided.

McGregor

Douglas McGregor's early distinction between **Theory X** and **Theory Y** approaches to management has proved to be extremely popular and one that many people can easily identify with. McGregor (1960) was able to define a management style based on providing workers with a degree of autonomy based on personal trust, and this has underpinned much recent thinking about changes in the workplace.

McGregor's Theory X managers believe that they are in charge of employees who need to be directed and controlled. His Theory Y managers believe more in involving workers, and creating opportunities for them to make positive contributions through motivating them.

The traditional theory of management as set out by **Fayol** is based on the assumption that the organisation is controlled and directed by management. Certain other basic assumptions are made in traditional theory, which McGregor characterises as Theory X. These are:

- The average person has an inherent dislike of work and will avoid it if possible. So management needs to emphasise productivity, incentive schemes and a fair day's work, and to denounce restrictions on output.
- Because people naturally dislike work, most people must be coerced, controlled, directed and/or threatened with punishment to get them to work towards business objectives.
- The average person likes to be directed, wishes to avoid responsibility, has little ambition and above all seeks security.

Against this view of human motivation and its implications for management of an organisation, McGregor proposed an alternative Theory Y. The underlying emphasis here is on 'integration' to replace direction and control. The assumptions about human motivation of Theory Y are:

- Physical and mental effort in work is as natural as play or rest. The ordinary person does not dislike work: it all depends on the conditions under which work takes place – it can be enjoyable or not.
- External control is not the only way to get people to work. If they are committed to objectives, then they will be motivated to work towards achieving them.
- The most significant reward that will motivate people to work is the satisfaction of an individual's self-actualisation needs. This can be the result of working towards an organisation's objectives.
- The average human being learns, when given the opportunity, to accept – and more importantly, to seek – responsibility.
- Many people can contribute to a business's objectives when given the chance.
- Currently the potentialities of the average person are not being fully used.

McGregor saw the potential to make organisations far more effective by unleashing the people that work for them. Organisations need to see themselves as interacting groups of people enjoying 'supportive relationships'. Ideally, members of an organisation will see its objectives as being personally significant to them.

McClelland

David McClelland (1961) argued that people have three basic needs driving needs, which he called nAch, nAff, NPow:

- for achievement (nAch)
- for affiliation (i.e. belonging) (nAff)
- for power (nPow).

He found that individuals with a high achievement factor display a number of characteristics. For example, they enjoy taking on responsibility, they like tasks that present a challenge and seek feedback on their performance. People with high affiliation or power factors will display other characteristics. People with high affiliation needs seek to establish and keep friendly and warm relationships with others. They will want to build effective and harmonious relationships in the workplace. People with a need for power will seek to control other people in the workplace. They will want to be responsible for others and to influence their behaviours. Although each person has all of the three needs in some measure, one of them tends to motivate an individual at any given time.

A business would therefore need to know how these three needs affect individual employees. McClelland's ideas have been used in the selection of managers, where tests are used to identify attributes associated with achievement, affiliation and power. If particular attributes can be matched to particular jobs, then a person with high affiliation needs, for example, may be identified as being particularly suitable for a particular job.

Lawler

E.H. Lawler (1986) sets out a model of **high-involvement management** which brings together some of the things we were saying earlier in this chapter about management approaches to involving and committing employees.

A high-involvement organisation's core values and principles must include the idea of employee involvement and responsibility for decision-making. Examples of assumptions are that:

- they can be trusted to make significant decisions about their work activities
- they can develop the knowledge to make decisions about the management of their work activities
- when people make decisions about the management of their work, the result is greater organisational effectiveness.

High-involvement management implies an organisational structure that has few levels of specialised management. The best way to ensure that decisions *are* made at lower levels is to have few levels of middle management. Modern information systems are the key to effective coordination and feedback in such organisations.

Leaders of high-involvement organisations are people who inspire loyalty, commitment and motivation through personal style and behaviour: leaders who energise people in ways that support self-motivations; leaders who help people move in positive directions, where questioning and debate are acceptable and part of the organisation's search for the best answer; leaders who help the organisation to know the right things to do rather than helping it to do things right.

Putting theory into practice

How have the theories of motivation introduced above been put into practice? To answer this, we can adopt a broadly historical approach, and Figure 11.10 illustrates the progression in the form of three major stages.

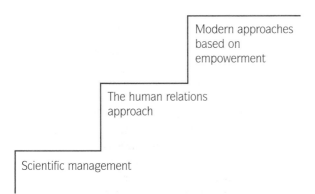

Modern approaches based on empowerment

The human relations approach

Scientific management

Figure 11.10 *The historical progression of theory-into-practice*

Scientific management

Scientific management is associated with Speedy Taylor and Fordism.

The aim of the scientific management approach was to increase efficiency by carefully planning workers' movements in efficient ways (see also page 193). The most famous exponent of scientific management was Frederick W. Taylor (nicknamed 'Speedy') who stated that:

> *'The principal object of management should be to secure the maximum prosperity for the employer coupled with the maximum prosperity for each employee.'*

Taylor set out to find ways of maximising the efficiency of labour using the stopwatch and 'time-and-motion' studies. He recorded the movements made by production line workers in order to reduce the movements and tasks

performed to the minimum for maximum efficiency. Labour tasks were thus reduced to machine-like efficiency. He felt that operatives would be prepared to work in this way to gain greater rewards in the form of higher pay. In his book *Scientific Management* (1947), Taylor outlined four principles of management:

- the development of a 'science of work' to replace the old rule-of-thumb methods by which working people operated (fulfilling optimum goals would earn higher wages; failure to do so would result in loss of earnings)
- scientific selection and progressive development of the worker, training each to be 'first class' at some task
- bringing together the science of work and the scientifically selected and trained workers for best results
- equal division of work and responsibility between workers and management, cooperating together in closer interdependence.

The car manufacturer Henry Ford was closely associated with this scientific management approach, and consequently the term **Fordism** came to be associated with mass manufacturing organisations producing high-volume output of standardised products with specialist machinery and extensive stocks of spare parts. Ford employed a very strict form of work discipline based on the Theory X approach we have described. Ford's workers were generally better paid than others, but working conditions were very strict and people had to toil. The term 'machine company' is associated with Fordism, because people were treated virtually as part of the machinery, and the organisation operated with machine-like efficiency. Taylor's and Ford's ideas were based heavily on the assumption that good wages are the key motivator.

Case Study

Henry Ford

Henry Ford was a farmer's son from Michigan. When he was 28 he decided to become a mechanic rather than a farmer. In 1898 he set up the Ford Motor Company with eleven associates. In 1908 the Model T, 'the car for the great multitude' was launched. By 1920 Ford had bought out his associates.

The way Ford managed his car plants was strongly influenced by a missionary zeal based on a belief that he could bring salvation and liberation to the world through machinery.

Unfortunately for Henry Ford, many of his assembly line workers did not tolerate repetitive physical labour of the kind offered at his Detroit factory. Working for Ford not only meant repetition, it meant committing yourself to a system of harsh discipline while at work and to a lifestyle outside of the factory gates 'free from any malicious practice derogatory to good physical manhood and moral character'. Ford was opposed to gambling, drinking alcohol, smoking and sex outside marriage. He set up a sociological department to monitor the behaviour of his employees.

As the company became more successful, Ford grew more and more sensitive to criticism. He appointed people to be his immediate subordinates who were authoritarian; for example Charles Sorensen became his Factory Superintendent.

Among line managers, office workers and shop personnel, Charles Sorensen quickly became the most feared man in the organisation. On the shopfloor he was known as 'Iron Charlie', master of the speed up. In 1921 on Ford's orders he ruthlessly doubled the speed of the assembly line, while simultaneously cutting the number of production workers by 30 per cent and cutting wages by 25 per cent.

Managers were also subject to ruthless control. Any manager who questioned Ford's authority was forced to resign or fired. At the height of the purges of management, the sociological department was abolished and replaced by the more ruthless service department. Ford controlled by fear. He believed that humanitarian and social considerations had no place in the work environment. Within his own organisation Ford regarded any signs of humanitarianism with contempt: 'There is altogether too much reliance on good feeling in our business organisation'.

Questions

1. What do you see as being the principal characteristics of Fordism?

2. Are there any situations in which Fordism is appropriate?

3. What do you see as being Ford's major achievements?

4. Is there room for Fordism today?

The human-relations approach

> *The human-relations approach identified by Elton Mayo's team showed that employees respond to interest taken in their work by others.*

Taylor's scientific management approach can be contrasted with the human relations school of thought. Elton Mayo and a team of researchers from the Harvard Business School carried out a series of experiments from 1927 to 1932 at the Hawthorne plant of Western Electric Company in Chicago. Initially Mayo had taken on board some of the assumptions of the scientific management school, believing that physical conditions in the working environment, the aptitudes of workers and financial incentives were the key ingredients in motivation.

To this end, Mayo had experimented with different levels of heating, lighting, lengths and frequencies of rest periods and other variables. However, the results of the experiments were inconclusive; for example, Mayo and his team were surprised to find that wide variations in the level of lighting had little or no effect on output.

During the course of the experiments, Mayo found that the productivity of the group studied kept climbing, irrespective of various changes. Mayo came to the conclusion that, as a result of the experiment, a great deal of attention had been given to the group and members of the group had come to feel much closer ties with each other. Mayo felt that this was the important factor, and his work led to an appreciation of the importance of the informal group in industry.

The **Hawthorne studies** moved the emphasis from the individual worker to the worker as a member of a social group. Mayo suggested that managers should establish and maintain a sense of group purpose in industry. A famous example of this is the Volvo car assembly plant, where the traditional assembly line has been scrapped and small teams of workers construct virtually the whole car. Not only do the workers build up a sense of group solidarity, they are able also to identify with the production process from start to finish.

These studies are also remembered for the 'Hawthorne effect': the very fact of being studied improved performance.

Modern approaches based on empowerment

> *Empowerment means the increased participation by employees in decision-making.*

Empowerment is regarded in management theory as a means of encouraging initiatives and entrepreneurialism in organisation members. In particular it may have an important part to play in helping women to rise above the 'invisible ceiling' that until recently kept them in low-status roles within an organisation.

Rosabeth Moss Kanter, in her widely acclaimed book *Men and Women of the Corporation*, argued that organisations needed to make fundamental changes to improve the quality of working life, and to create equal opportunities for all groups, as well as to enable all members of an organisation to use their talents to the benefit of the corporation. This would involve opening up management positions to individuals by promotion from a wide range of more junior positions, by changing systems such as appraisal and career development plans. Intermediate jobs might need to be created as a stepping stone to senior management. All this would involve developing empowerment strategies – such as autonomous work-groups, with decentralised authority and flatter hierarchies.

Empowering others in an organisation involves giving them the responsibility to use their talents and express themselves. Rosabeth Moss Kanter argues forcibly that:

> *'By empowering others, a leader does not decrease his power; instead, he may increase it – especially if the whole organisation performs better.'*

An organisation prospers when everyone in it believes that success depends on the excellence of his or her contribution. Short-term decisions made many times a day by individuals determine the quality of that day's work. Long-term decisions, again made by individuals, about their own career, training and ambitions, also affect the quality of their contributions.

The governing principle, whether recognised or not, is that everybody has a customer – either outside the organisation (the traditional 'customer') or inside. Both kinds of customer expect to be supplied with the product or service they need, on time and as specified. The principle holds good for everyone, whatever their level of skill and experience, whether their 'product' is answering a telephone in a helpful way or masterminding a major new project. It works to everyone's benefit. It gives the individual genuine responsibility and scope for initiative. And it virtually guarantees that the organisation's performance will be improved.

Some companies have organised themselves into empowered multi-skilled teams responsible for a whole product. Such teams can more easily focus on customer needs, and so direct and combine their specialist skills to meet those needs more effectively. They are also better at judging what effort and expenditure are needed to do that. Other important benefits follow from such an empowerment process. Individuals feel that their worth is valued. They can often make useful suggestions outside their specific area of expertise. They are no longer required simply to carry out orders, but to take responsibility for improving their own work and dovetailing it with the work of other specialists.

Organisations with a wide geographical spread usually benefit from decentralisation of one kind or another. Most decisions, especially tactical decisions, cannot be taken effectively at the centre, which may be miles or continents away. They have to be taken quickly, on the spot, by people who know all the circumstances. There is often no time for referral back to central office, even if central office had complete understanding of that particular problem. The IT revolution, by putting massive computer power into devices that can be carried around like notebooks and which can communicate instantly with other devices and their databases anywhere in the world, has made decentralisation even easier to handle and more dramatic in its effect.

Empowerment, then, is a way of thinking and working designed to enable everyone who has a good idea for improvement to carry the idea through, taking ownership of the idea themselves or in a team. In *The Pursuit of Wow!*, Tom Peters (1995) argues that:

> *'Hierarchies are going, going, gone. The average Mike or Mary is being asked to take on extraordinary responsibility. He or she may be on the payroll or, at least as likely, an independent contractor. In any event, the hyperfast-moving, wired-up, re-engineered, quality-obsessed organisation – virtual or not – will*

succeed or fail on the strength of the trust that the remaining, tiny cadre of managers places in the folks working on the front line.'

The above analysis has outlined some of the recent approaches based on empowerment. However, it is important to stress that it is often necessary to establish a set of boundaries to the empowerment process. Clear limits need to be established in giving employees autonomy. People can slip into irrational behaviours when given freedoms they cannot handle. In this sense true 'freedom' is not the absence of structure, but rather a clear structure which enables people to work with pre-set boundaries in an autonomous and creative way. It is important to establish the ground rules within which groups and individuals will be working so that they do not feel they are 'working in the dark'.

MOTIVATION AND PERFORMANCE MANAGEMENT

In their book *Managing Human Resources and Industrial Relations*, John Storey and Keith Sisson argue that **performance management** in its current sense implies:

> *'... an interlocking set of policies and practices which have as their focus the enhanced achievement of organisational objectives through a concentration on individual performance'.*

They say that the key elements are:

- the setting of clear objectives for individual employees, derived from the organisation's strategy and a series of departmental purpose analyses
- formal monitoring and review of progress towards meeting objectives
- use of the outcome of the review process to reinforce desired behaviour through differential rewards and/or to identify training and development needs.

In addition these three elements may be supported by improved communication processes and a sharing of vision within the organisation. In simple terms, therefore, the aim of performance management is to ensure that employees are motivated to perform in a way that best supports and dovetails with the focus and objectives of the wider organisation. One way of motivation is through incentives and rewards.

The concept of providing incentives and rewards for employees is based on a belief that they need some form of extrinsic motivators to encourage them to work. Indeed, many American companies still use the term 'compensation' implying that work is a negative experience for which employees have to be 'compensated' for doing. In the sections that follow we look at a range of incentives and rewards.

Incentives act as a carrot to induce employees to work harder (e.g. sales commission, bonuses, the prospect of promotion). Rewards, on the other hand, are used to provide benefits to those individuals who have already committed their efforts to an organisation. Employees who have worked hard should be rewarded for their efforts.

Incentives

The more motivated an employee, the better his or her performance is likely to be. Furthermore, the better the performance the more motivated the person is likely to become. The link is therefore in both directions.

However, we also need to take account of two further factors: (a) the ability of an individual to do the job, and (b) the effects of *too much* motivation. In particular, if someone does not have the ability they will not succeed, and motivation will evaporate. This more complex set of relationships is illustrated in Figure 11.11, where there is a positive correlation between ability, performance, motivation and job satisfaction.

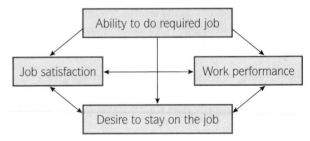

Figure 11.11 *Positive monitoring correlations*

We should also bear in mind that high performance rates have the potential to increase *stress*. If individuals are exposed to excessive pressures they will not be able to cope.

Sadler (1988) suggests that managers in service-focused organisations should take account of the following employee motivational factors if they want to create commitment. Employees need:

- to be reasonably satisfied (but not necessarily 'over the moon') about their own pay, status, working conditions, etc.
- to receive regular, frequent feedback from the customer as to the perceived quality of service provided
- to receive adequate recognition (financial and non-financial) from their own management when their performance justifies it
- to feel they are strongly supported in their front-line role by other personnel in the organisation at all levels
- to genuinely feel that their own top management puts the customer first – and that they are there to serve the customer and be served by the management
- to feel that service is a team operation, that they belong to the team and that it is a winning team
- to have the confidence that comes from having been properly trained for the job.

When these conditions are met, service employees give good service, customers are grateful, smile at them and thank them. This in turn reinforces motivation and a virtuous spiral is created.

Motivation models

In his book *Personnel Management Practice* (1996), Michael Armstrong identifies four models of motivation which he terms rational-man, human-relations, self-actualising, and complex.

The rational-man model

This model assumes that an employee responds to rewards and sanctions in the workplace as a means of improving performance (see Figure 11.12). Financial rewards encourage effort while punishments also push employees into working harder. However, such a model has only a limited appreciation of the complex nature of human needs.

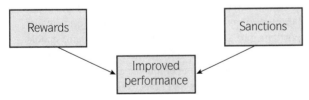

Figure 11.12 *The rational-man model*

The human-relations model

This approach argues that humans are complex creatures who require recognition, personal fulfilment and

satisfaction of social needs if they are to have the job satisfaction that will turn them into high performers (see Figure 11.13).

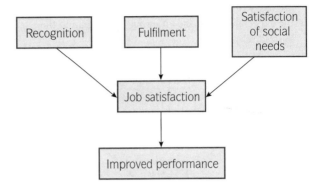

Figure 11.13 *The human-relations model*

The self-actualising model

This model draws on the work of Herzberg, Maslow and McGregor discussed earlier. The broad approach is that intrinsic motivating factors are more significant than extrinsic ones. If people are to be motivated in the long term they need to have their higher-level needs met (see Figure 11.14). Self-fulfilment is the key to real motivation, not just extrinsic factors such as rewards and sanctions.

Figure 11.14 *The self-actualising model*

The complex motivational model

Michael Armstrong argues that we need to develop a more complex understanding of motivation because human beings have a range of needs and expectations, because people work in widely differing situations, and because these situations are subject to continual change. He argues that there are two main factors determining the effort a person puts into a job (see Figure 11.15):

- the value of the rewards to the individual, insofar as they are likely to satisfy his or her needs
- the expectation that the effort put in will lead to the desired reward.

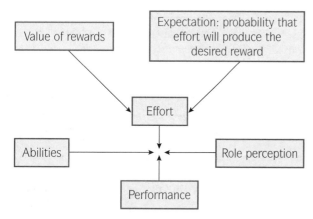

Figure 11.15 *The complex motivational model*

However, effort is not sufficient. As well as effort there are two other factors that influence motivation:

- ability – which depends on intelligence, manual skills, know-how, etc.
- role perception – the individual's feelings about his or her job.

If the individual has the same perception of the job as does the organisation, then this will reap maximum returns. However, if there is not a match between the individual's perception of the job and the organisation's perception, then this will lead to lower performance.

Motivation techniques

Michael Armstrong identified three basic approaches that have been adopted by motivation experts:

- *The carrot and stick approach.* This is the 'rewards' and 'sanctions' approach in which monetary rewards play a major part.
- *Motivation through the work itself.* Fulfilling work, as we have seen, can be motivation in itself for certain individuals.
- *The one-minute manager system.* This involves managers setting goals which subordinates can meet and giving

them positive feedback when they do something right and negative feedback when they do something wrong.

The range of motivational techniques includes:

a money as a reward or incentive
b clearly spelling out work requirements
c developing commitment from employees
d motivating through the work itself
e rewarding and recognising achievement
f exercising leadership
g building up teamwork
h training and developing people
i eliminating negative aspects of the work.

Rewards: monetary and non-monetary

Today, many organisations have moved on from policies and systems of 'salary entitlement' where pay increases where related to factors such as seniority and inflation. The new fashion for reward is 'paying for performance'. The current performance of employees in helping the organisation to meet its objectives is seen as the defining factor in determining pay.

Pay typically counts for 60–70 per cent of an organisation's costs (over 90 per cent in some cases). Organisations have therefore become acutely aware of the relationship between pay, individual performance, and organisational performance. To cover labour costs and other expenses, a company must earn sufficient revenue through the sale of its products or services. An employer's ability to pay is constrained by its ability to compete. Employees that best enable an organisation to compete are therefore most likely to receive higher rewards.

Performance-related pay schemes involve channelling larger portions of pay into incentive awards and smaller portions into fixed salaries. Variable pay systems enable organisations to concentrate far more effectively on cost control, and on directing employee activities to the organisational mission and objectives.

An organisation's reward scheme includes anything that an employee values and desires and that an employer is able and willing to offer in exchange for employee contributions. Financial rewards include direct payments (e.g. wages or salary) plus indirect payments in the form of employee benefits such as subsidised meals. Non-financial rewards include everything in a work environment that improves a worker's sense of self-respect and esteem by others (e.g. work environments that are physically, socially, and mentally healthy; opportunities for training and personal development; effective supervision, recognition, etc.).

The key objectives of pay and reward schemes are to:

- attract and keep staff of a suitable quality
- motivate good work performance
- control costs.

Key considerations and techniques employed are:

- to encourage achievement through performance related pay, financial incentive schemes, bonus payments, profit sharing, and merit rating
- to ensure fairness through job evaluation
- to monitor recruitment and retention of staff through annual reviews
- to control costs through salaries and wages surveys.

Traditional pay and reward schemes

Job evaluation

In organisations without formal pay scales, increments may be awarded by individual managers. Apart from budget constraints, there may be no overall strategy and no agreed criteria for awarding increments. Over the years, anomalies in pay develop. Within the same department, more demanding jobs may be paid less than easier jobs. Staff doing similar jobs, but in other departments, may be paid significantly different rates. The result is that there is no logic to the pay differentials.

This is usually concealed by a cloak of secrecy over pay-packets. Managers tell individuals not to reveal their pay and increments to other employees in case it upsets them. Payroll administration is unnecessarily complicated since there is a multitude of pay rates, some with insignificant differences between them. **Job evaluation** is a technique to design pay structures with logical differentials.

Job evaluation is the process of assessing, in an organisation, the value of one job in relation to another, *without* regard to the abilities or personality of the individuals currently holding the positions. It results in a pay range for each job. An individual's personal worth is recognised by awarding increments within the fixed range for that job.

Merit rating

Merit rating is a system whereby the individual employee is awarded increments or bonuses based on a systematic appraisal of his or her developed skill level and performance. Merit rating usually operates *within* a job-evaluated pay structure. Job evaluation sets the pay bands, while merit rating determines the position of the individual within the band. A typical pattern is:

Starter: degree of efficiency expected from a learner
Qualified: able to perform normal aspects of the job
Experienced: able to deal with all circumstances of the job
Superior: Ready for promotion, equivalent to starter of the next grade
Outstanding: Equivalent to qualified of the next grade.

The merit-rating scheme thus defines and weights the factors against which the manager assesses each employee, usually annually. Typical factors are volume and quality of output, initiative, adaptability, attendance and punctuality. Managers need to be trained to use the system.

Merit rating is not without its problems and critics. Such schemes are unpopular with unions which see merit rating as subjective and open to favouritism. From a management point of view, a weakness in most schemes is that an award once given is permanent, even if performance drops to a previous level.

Performance-related pay (PRP)

Automatic increases within fixed pay bands have largely disappeared from the private sector and are under pressure in the public sector. The trend is towards **performance-related pay** as the preferred method of deciding non-manual workers' progress through their salary bands. Merit-rating schemes, in the past, often relied on managers' subjective assessments of employees' personal characteristics. The increments, if awarded, were usually stepped and fixed. PRP schemes use performance and/or competence as the criteria for deciding the size of increments and therefore also the rate of progress through a salary band. The PRP approach is based on a management-by-objectives philosophy of agreeing:

- the key result areas of the job
- clear standards of performance and target levels of competence
- regular, objective reviews of performance and competence.

As a result of a PRP review the manager might, for example, assess an employee as outstanding, superior, standard or developing. The percentage pay increase awarded would then be influenced by:

- market forces in the labour market for that particular occupational group
- the financial state of the company
- the present position of the particular employee in the salary band.
- company policy on speed of progress through the salary band.

Guidance to managers might be expressed thus:

Review grade awarded:	Pay increase (per cent)
Outstanding	12
Superior	8
Standard	5
Learning	2

The scale of percentage increases might vary according to the employees' current position in the pay scale: larger for those at the bottom end of the scale, smaller for those nearer the top. The rewards for those already at the top of their salary band should be promotion. If that is not possible they might be awarded a lump sum (bonus) that, unlike other increments, is not consolidated into their salary.

Discussion points

1. What are the key characteristics of well-defined standards of performance?

2. What is meant by the term 'key result areas' and why is it an important concept?

3. What are the claimed advantages of the management-by-objectives approach?

Comments on performance-related pay

Like any other new or revived approach to management, PRP has its advocates and detractors. Here are some of the views that have been expressed:

- There is no clear evidence, either way, in the argument over whether or not the financial incentives offered in PRP increase motivation.
- For the majority of staff, the increments offered under PRP are too small to be significant. However, they communicate the importance management attaches to performance.
- There are important aspects of performance in some jobs that cannot be measured conveniently or satisfactorily. Advocates respond that *competencies* can be assessed instead.
- A narrow focus on annual targets can cause neglect of long-term results, quality and risk-taking innovation. The counter view is that there is no reason why these cannot be included in targets.
- Emphasis on individual review is divisive and harmful to teamwork.
- The need for control requires expensive bureaucracy.
- PRP is likely to fail if it does not fit the culture of the organisation. There needs to be acceptance of the view that important values can be quantified and assessed.

Financial incentive schemes

Most employees are paid a salary or an hourly or weekly wage that is fixed for the time being. Fixed rates are easily understood, cause few disputes and are simple and therefore cheap to administer. They are widely used for management, administrative and service jobs, where conditions may make it difficult to apply incentive payments even if the organisation wished to do so. The aim of financial incentive schemes is usually *to increase productivity*.

Incentive payments are given for reaching a standard of performance, which might be completing a unit of work within a given time. If the standard is set too high, the incentive is lost since it is impossible to earn a reasonable bonus. If it is set too low, the scheme becomes too expensive to the employer. Unless the workers have confidence in the way the standards are set, there are likely to be disputes. It is normal practice, therefore, for trained work study officers to set the standards, using work measurement techniques. The following are methods of incentive payments.

Payment by results (PBR)

For an individual the payment can be calculated on the number of acceptable units of work completed. This is called **piecework**. Alternatively it can be calculated on the time saved by working faster than the standard. For a group, a bonus can be calculated and then shared either equally or in proportion to their basic pay.

Measured day work

Work measurement is used to establish the number of staff needed to complete a given volume of work at standard performance. If the staff agree to work consistently at a higher pace of work – a bonus pace – they move on to a higher rate of pay, the **measured day-rate.**

Plant and enterprise schemes

Traditionally, payment by results has been applied to production work where performance can be measured accurately. Consequently some employees earn a bonus while others do not, which can cause dissatisfaction. In contrast, plant and enterprise schemes share the bonus benefit with all employees. There are various ways of calculating the bonus (e.g. the increase in the value of sales over the period, or the increase in the volume of production).

Profit-sharing

In this scheme of incentive payments, the bonus is a proportion of the profits earned by the company in the previous accounting period. The bonus may be divided between employees on various bases:

- in proportion to basic salary
- weighted by length of service
- gainsharing (sometimes known as 'value added').

Gainsharing has been adopted so that employees can be made more aware of the contribution that their efforts are making to the success of the organisation. The rewards they receive are calculated as a share of the value added in the production process. Such schemes will be successful only where there are strong working relationships between employees and managers and where value added is relatively easy to measure. Wages are an agreed proportion of the monetary sum derived by subtracting the cost of materials and other supplies from sales revenues.

Non-monetary methods of motivating

Pay, as we have seen, is only one means of motivating people at work. For example, if we look back at Maslow's hierarchy of human needs it immediately becomes clear that approaches such as providing opportunities for personal fulfilment in the workplace provide alternative avenues.The creation of empowered teams creates avenues to releasing individual creativity.

Reinforcement

The notion that positive experiences lead to motivation comes out of behavioural theory (see page 291). Positive reinforcement involves pleasant experiences while negative reinforcement involves unpleasant experiences. For example, when a new colleague joins a work-team and is praised for all his or her successes, however minor, this is likely to lead to group solidarity and increased motivation.

There are four main kinds of reinforcement:

- *Positive reinforcement.* This involves giving pleasurable rewards for desirable behaviour in the hope that it will be repeated.
- *Negative reinforcement.* This involves encouraging people to do things in the desired way in order to *avoid* criticism.
- *Extinction.* This involves withdrawing reinforcement which was previously employed to encourage certain behaviours. For example, if a supervisor regularly praised employees for good work and then withdrew this praise, the result might be a fall-off in the amount of 'good work' produced.
- *Punishment.* This involves sanctions and unpleasant consequences as a result of certain 'bad' actions.

Discussion point

Can your provide real examples of the four types of reinforcement outlined above in actual situations in which you were involved? How effective were these approaches?

Case Study

'KITA'

In an article in *Harvard Business Review* in 1968, Fred Herzberg contended that the traditional approach in America to get someone to do something was to kick him in the a*** – to give the employee 'KITA'. Herzberg identified a number of types of KITA:

- Negative physical KITA is literally just that and it was frequently used in the past. The impact of such actions, however, is not to create motivation; rather it leads to negative feedback and reaction.

- Negative psychological KITA, therefore, is the psychologist's solution where negative physical KITA is no longer acceptable. With psychological KITA the cruelty is not visible, and there is less risk of physical backlash. There are all sorts of opportunities to exert negative psychological KITA and these can be carried out through the organisation rather than by individuals.

However, negative KITA of any kind does not lead to motivation. As Herzberg says, the employee moves but is not motivated.

- Positive KITA involves giving rewards, incentives, more status, promotion etc. Many business people see this approach as likely to lead to increased motivation.

Herzberg draws a parallel here. He says that when he wants his dog to move he holds up a biscuit. However, it is the dog owner rather than the dog that is motivated: 'The dog wants the biscuit, but it is I who want it to move. Again, I am the one who is motivated, and the dog is the one who moves. In this instance all I did was apply KITA frontally; I exerted a pull instead of a push. When industry wishes to use such positive KITAs, it has available an incredible number and variety of dog biscuits (jelly beans for humans) to wave in front of the employee to get him to jump.'

Herzberg thus argues that KITA is not motivation because every time he wants his dog to move he has to kick it again. Similarly with humans, using KITA you can charge a man's battery, and then recharge it, and recharge it again. But 'it is only when he has his own generator that we can talk about motivation. He then needs no outside stimulation. He wants to do it.'

Questions

1. Can you give three examples of KITA from your own experience which illustrate the three types outlined by Herzberg.

2. In each case explain what the effect was on motivation.

Job enrichment

This involves giving employees an increase in responsibility and/or recognition. The aim is to make employees feel that their contribution has been upgraded so that it is more highly appreciated. Ways of doing this vary, from an employee being given a new title, to an extension of the perks associated with a particular job.

Job enrichment is also called the 'vertical loading' of work. Herzberg argues that job enrichment provides the opportunity for an employee's psychological growth. There are a number of principles associated with vertical job loading. Examples are given in Figure 11.16.

Principle	Motivators involved
• Removing some controls while retaining accountability	Responsibility and personal achievement
• Increasing the accountability of individuals for own work	Responsibility and recognition
• Giving a person a complete natural unit of work (module, division, area, etc.)	Responsibility, achievement and recognition
• Granting additional authority to an employee in his or her activity (job freedom)	Responsibility, achievement and recognition
• Making periodic reports directly available to the worker rather than to the supervisor	Internal recognition
• Introducing new and more difficult tasks not previously handled	Growth and learning
• Assigning individuals specific or specialised tasks, enabling them to become experts	Responsibility, growth and advancement

Figure 11.16 *Principles of vertical job loading*

Job enlargement

This involves giving an employee a greater range of responsibilities. A person who feels that a job is going 'stale', and as a result is losing interest in it, may be rejuvenated when asked to take on additional tasks. For example, an employee who has been used to handling routine mail and answering telephone calls may gain fresh motivation if asked to take on the additional responsibility of meeting clients and entertaining them as part of the public relations function.

Employee participation in decision-making

This can be a great motivator. The flattened organisational structure in which decisions can be made at all levels helps employees to feel important and valued for their contribution to the process. Effective employee participation goes beyond the factory floor suggestion-box.

Quality circles (QCs)

Quality circles are an important way of increasing participation in organisational activities. A quality circle is a study-group of volunteers (5–15 people) who meet regularly to work on a variety of operational and employee problems at work. The quality circle will be made up of ordinary working employees and their immediate supervisors and managers. One supervisor or manager will usually operate as the circle's leader.

Quality circles do not deal with theoretical problems. They are concerned with putting ideas into action. This involves in-depth analysis, proposals for action, and presentations to management on what could be or ought to be done. There are four main components of a quality circle framework (see Figure 11.17).

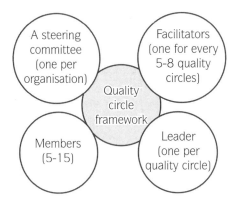

Figure 11.17 *Components of a quality circle framework*

The *steering committee*, staffed by senior managers, will make general policy and set up the framework and resources for the circles to operate. The *facilitator* is there to support the process in each of the circles as well as to provide an operational framework and guidance if required. The circles' *leaders* will often be the unit supervisors and they will stimulate discussion within their circle without dominating it. Leaders need to be familiar with problem-solving techniques and group dynamics.

The circles meet during company time, perhaps for one hour a week. Problem-solving techniques employed will include: brainstorming; graphs showing the frequency of problems; randomised sampling of product units produced; cause-and-effect diagrams.

CREATING A COMMITMENT STRATEGY

It is common sense that it is desirable for the management of an organisation to have a defined strategic goal and values, and that employees need to be committed to these goals and values. Armstrong (1996) identifies a range of steps which help to create this commitment. These are described below.

Communication programmes

In a large organisation in which different individuals and groups have different perceptions and interpretations, it is essential to persuade employees through constructive communications on a broad front. What is required is the delivery of the message using different and complementary channels of communication such as newsletters, briefing groups, videos, noticeboards, etc.

Education

Education is an important form of communication and should set out to increase knowledge and understanding, for example about total quality management. The aim will be to change attitudes over time.

Training

Training is designed to develop specific competencies such as more flexibility in the workplace. Commitment will be enhanced if managers can gain the support and respect of their teams. Management training can focus on giving managers the capability to create commitment.

Developing ownership

Commitment is most likely to occur when employees feel a sense of 'ownership of their work' (i.e. that they are working for themselves as well as for the organisation). This sense of ownership is most likely to occur where employees take on a responsibility for shaping their work and for bringing about any changes that take place in the organisation. Employees should be involved in the decision-making process so that they feel in no small way that they have made the decisions.

Developing a sense of excitement in the job

A sense of excitement can be created by concentrating on the intrinsic motivating factors such as responsibility, achievement and recognition, and using these principles to govern the way in which jobs are designed. Excitement in the job is also created by the quality of leadership.

Performance management

Performance management involves making a clear link between the objectives of individuals in the organisation and the overall objectives of the organisation. Individual objectives should be designed to fit in with organisational objectives.

Reward management

Rewards should be closely tied to the achievement of objectives which match the overall objectives of the organisation.

SUMMARY

In this chapter we have examined a variety of approaches to motivating people in the workplace. Today, the emphasis is very much on creating commitment, but that will be forthcoming only when employees feel a strong sense of ownership, and hence responsibility, for their work.

We have gone beyond the old approaches, such as KITA and scientific management, and moved towards an approach to organisational management which recognises the needs and aspirations of the individuals within the organisation. Of course, there are some situations in which people are more concerned with 'lower-level' needs satisfaction (e.g. when they need some money to pay off a debt or to put down a deposit on a mortgage). However, in the long term most people seek some form of deeper fulfilment. By studying different approaches to motivation you should have developed a clearer insight into the genuine approaches to helping individuals and organisations to actualise their 'higher needs'.

REFERENCES

Adams, J.S., 'Injustice in social exchange', in Berkowitz, L. (ed), *Advances in Experimental Psychology,* vol. 2, Academic Press, 1965.

Armstrong, Michael, *Personnel Management Practice,* Kogan Page, 1996.

Baker, Edwin, in *The McKinsey Quarterly,* autumn 1980.

Bennis, W. and Nanus, B., *Leaders: The Strategies for Taking Charge,* Harper & Row, 1985.

Blake, Robert, and Mouton, Jane, *The New Managerial Grid,* Houston, 1978.

Fielder, Fred, *Theory of Effective Leadership,* McGraw-Hill, 1967.

Halpin and Winer, *Factoral Study of the Leader Behaviour Description,* Ohio State University, 1957.

Handy, Charles, *Understanding Organisations,* Penguin, 1993.

Hersey, P. and Blanchard, K. H., *Management of Organisational Behaviour,* Prentice Hall, 1988.

Herzberg, F., *Work and the Nature of Man,* World Publishing, 1966.

Kanter, Rosabeth Moss, *Men and Women of the Corporation,* Basic Books, 1977.

Lawler, E.H. *High Involvement Management,* Josey Bass, 1986.

Likert, Rensis, *New Patterns of Management,* Harper & Row, 1961

Maslow, Abraham, *Motivation and Personality,* Harper, 1954.

McClelland, David, *The Achieving Society,* Free Press, 1961

McGregor, Douglas, *The Human Side of Enterprise,* McGraw-Hill, 1960.

Peters, Tom, *The Pursuit of Wow!,* Macmillan, 1995.

Porter, L.W. and Lawler, E.E., *Management Attitudes and Performance,* Irwin-Dorsey, 1968.

Sadler, Philip, *Managerial Leadership in Post-Industrial Society,* Gower, 1988.

Schein, E.H., *Career Dynamics,* Addison-Wesley, 1978.

Skinner, B.F., *About Behaviourism,* Knopf, 1974.

Storey, John and Sisson, Keith, *Managing Human Resources and Industrial Relations,* Open University Press, 1993.

Tannenbaum and Schmidt, *Control in Organisations,* McGraw-Hill, 1968.

Taylor, Frederick W., *Scientific Management,* Harper & Row, 1947.

Vroom, V.H., *Work and Motivation,* John Wiley, 1964.

The Behaviour of Individuals

This chapter sets out to identify the factors which influence the behaviour of individuals in organisations. It examines a range of psychological theories relating to the individual and personality types. Managers need to assess the implications of these issues for the effective management of people at work.

On completion of the chapter you should be able to:

- examine the factors which influence individual behaviour at work

- evaluate your own behaviour in a given organisational role.

DIAGNOSING BEHAVIOURAL PROBLEMS

Psychology is the study of human and animal behaviour. Organisations are interested in psychology because it offers them answers to two basic related questions about human behaviour at work:

- Why do people behave as they do?
- What can organisations do to get people to behave as organisations want them to?

Psychology can thus play an important problem-solving function for the organisation.

Concepts, principles and perspectives

Psychological research can offer insights into many work-related issues, such as:

- low or high levels of effort
- absenteeism

- aggressive behaviour
- errors
- design of workplace and equipment
- accidents
- stress
- resistance to change
- breaking rules
- learning skills slowly or quickly.

The choice of research method determines what aspects of behaviour are studied; it also determines the type of explanation produced. The main psychological perspectives include psychoanalysis, behaviourism, cognitive psychology, the phenomenological approach, and social psychology. We look below at the concepts and principles involved in each of these perspectives.

Psychoanalysis

Psychoanalysis (or the psychodynamic approach as it is sometimes called) was developed by Sigmund Freud (1856–1939). Most people today know a little bit about the work of Freud, particularly about the associations he drew between early sexual experiences and subsequent behaviour and neuroses.

Figure 12.1 *Sigmund Freud, one of the founding-fathers of psychoanalysis*

Freud believed that people are largely unconscious of the real forces that shape their behaviour. He compared the human mind to an iceberg; the smaller part above the water is termed 'conscious experience' while below it is the far greater mass termed the 'unconscious mind'. Strong drives and urges emerge from the depths of human nature. Many urges are repressed during the process of growing up, although they continue to be part of our character and may emerge in dreams, in neurotic and obsessive behaviour and sometimes in psychoses. The implication is that individuals do not fully understand their own behaviours and motivations. However, it is very important for work psychologists to understand the nature of what motivates and influences individuals in their behaviour patterns. Researchers can seek to find out as much as possible about motivations through interviewing, and other techniques such as word association, picture interpretation and sentence completion.

Freud separated the human psyche into three elements:

• The *ego,* which is the rational element, and which channels activities into socially acceptable behaviours
• The *id,* consisting of lusts and antisocial behaviours
• The *superego* (conscience) which is usually at odds with the id.

A theory of personality known as **transactional analysis** is in the same tradition as psychoanalysis, although it is concerned with everyday conversations rather than neurotic disorders. It shares the view that adult personality is subject to three sources of influences:

'The parent'

During our formative years our personal views are acquired from the family and other influential figures. These values are the basis of the many instant judgements we later make each day. They affect our relationships with others and act as a conscience for our own actions.

Such values, whilst necessary, may also be irrational, too sweeping or out of date, leading to inappropriate actions. We need, as part of our development, to expose and re-examine the hidden values which shape our attitudes.

When we are under the control of our parent component, our speech expresses approval or disapproval. We use words like 'should', 'ought', 'must', 'will', 'want you to'. The words, tone of voice, gestures and facial expression express prejudice, criticism, caring or nurturing.

'The child'

As human beings we are all subject to a range of feelings: anger, joy, affection, amusement, anxiety, curiosity and grief. Such feelings may be triggered by current events or by association with past events.

When our statements are under the control of our child component, we are likely to express towards others either stubborn or illogical behaviour, or playful, spontaneous acts and statements. It is not just the words that reflect this, but also the tone of voice and behaviour.

'The adult'

The adult component of personality is our rational, unemotional side. It is directed at objective gathering and processing of information. It tests both 'parent' and 'child' influences to see whether they are true and appropriate.

The theory suggests that we need all three of these components of our personality. Each, when predominant, gives a distinct tone to our statements and behaviour and produces a different response from those we are talking to. We use all three components in our conversations with others, but each of us has a tendency to use one of the three more frequently. A socially skilled person consciously chooses the mode suitable to the situation and to the person he or she is dealing with. Some organisations use transactional analysis as a method of improving employees' sensitivity and conversational skills in activities such as selling and management.

Critics of the psychoanalytical approach to human behaviour believe that it lacks scientific rigour. In their view, the concepts cannot be proved by scientific methods.

Behaviourism

Researchers dissatisfied with the intuitive approach of psychoanalysis thought that reliable advances in psychology would come only through the use of scientific methods. This means that the researchers study the available data on a problem. They form a hypothesis – a provisional explanation of cause and effect – and design experiments to test it. The design of an experiment must follow scientific rules, the purpose being to show that controlled changes in the independent variable (the cause) are responsible for the changes in the dependent variable (the effect). Other variables need to be held constant to rule out the possibility that one of them is responsible for the effect. This scientific discipline excludes conjecture about mental processes such as thoughts, beliefs and attitudes that cannot be isolated, observed and measured in this way.

The **behaviourist** approach to psychology suggest that the main influence on people's behaviour is their **environment**. Experience from infancy onwards shapes our behaviour. The events that provide the experience start with a stimulus and end with a response. For example, if subjects sit in front of equipment that puffs air into their eyes, they will blink. The stimulus is the puff of air; the blink is the response. The theory is that we can be conditioned to respond in particular ways to a stimulus by the rewards or punishments associated with that stimulus.

The early behavioural experiments used animals. For example, pigeons learned to operate controls with their beaks. The pigeons' random pecking was conditioned (shaped) by rewarding with food those peckings that approximated to the required movements. The required peckings at the controls were reinforced by the rewards.

Possible reinforcements to shape behaviour are:

• *Positive reinforcement*, where something pleasant follows the behaviour. Simple examples are praise given to someone learning a task, and money paid for extra output.
• *Negative reinforcement*, where the removal of something unpleasant follows the behaviour. An example is

rewarding diligence on a necessary but unpleasant task with a transfer to other tasks.
• *Punishment*, where something unpleasant follows the 'wrong' behaviour. Examples are disapproval, criticism, unpleasant assignments and reprimands.

Both negative and positive reinforcement *increase* the probability of the behaviour preceding them.

Punishment *suppresses* rather than extinguishes the behaviour it follows. It is effective only where it follows every incident immediately it occurs; otherwise the behaviour will re-emerge.

Later behaviourists suggested that learning takes place through imitation. We are conditioned through observing others' experiences and reinforcements as well as by our own direct personal experience. Social roles, (some would say stereotypes) such as mother, father, male and female, are learned in this way.

Case Study

B. F. Skinner

Skinner's name is most closely associated with behaviourism. In his book *Beyond Freedom and Dignity* (1973) he set out five simple rules for reinforcement to be positive:

a *Be specific*, but give as much information as possible. Speak of specific achievement, not all-round standards.
b *Be immediate*, giving the bonus or the pat-on-the-back today, not at the annual appraisal.
c *Make the targets achievable*, small, frequent wins being more reinforcing than one big one.
d *Remember the intangible*; the attention of one's superior may be more important than any bonus.
e *Keep it unpredictable*, because the unexpected bit of praise counts for more than the commendation that becomes routine.

Questions

1. How effective do you think are the suggestions outlined by Skinner?

2. Can you give practical examples of how they have been applied, misapplied, or not applied at all in a workplace you are familiar with?

Criticisms of behaviourism

- It limits the problems studied by psychologists because it concentrates on simple learning and leaves untouched perception, problem-solving, language and thinking.
- It implies a distorted or degraded view of human beings. A rat learning to run through a maze to find food, for example, is not a suitable model for explaining human behaviour.
- The concepts of stimulus, response and reinforcement become difficult to apply meaningfully away from a laboratory setting.
- Its rejection of reports by human beings of their experiences and feelings means that important areas of human behaviour are excluded.

The researcher John Barnes cites the example of an experiment carried out with a monkey in which the animal was rewarded with peanuts for completing a puzzle. The researchers expected that once the monkey had completed the puzzle enough times it would be full and would stop working on the puzzle. On the contrary, the monkey kept repeating the puzzle. It went on to fill its cheeks completely with nuts. Finally it started to throw the nuts round the laboratory while continuing with the puzzle. On another occasion the researchers rewarded a chimp by continually giving it new toys to play with to encourage it to work harder. Eventually the researcher looked through the keyhole of the door to see how the monkey was progressing – to be faced with the chimp's eyeball staring out at the researcher!

Cognitive psychology

Cognitive psychology is concerned with the mental processes which behaviourism excluded. Human behaviour is not a simple response to external stimuli. Human beings receive information (stimuli) through their senses. The processes of perception and interpretation of the messages coming into the brain through the nervous system are active and complex. The processes are affected by:

- the individual's personality, itself a product of genetic and social influences
- the individual's intelligence, memory and other mental skills.

Before responding to stimuli, the individual may make conscious choices related to his or her goals.

The study of cognitive processes and individual cognitive differences has practical implications for organisations. Intelligence, memory, verbal ability, numerical ability, spatial ability, perceptual speed, reaction times and motor coordination are relevant to job-design and personnel selection.

The phenomenological approach

The emphasis of the **phenomenological approach** is on human experience rather than behaviour. The argument is that behaviour is the outcome of an interaction between the environment and an individual's beliefs, attitudes, needs, expectations, perceptions and personal strategies. Behaviour is not simply the result of passive reaction to the environment.

Consider behaviour at a meeting of staff at a university (or in a business organisation you are familiar with). The meeting is discussing a proposed contentious change. The behaviour of the individuals may be affected by many factors:

- They will have different objectives and strategies in terms of serving personal interests, such as increasing the size of their budget, increasing the size of their department or getting promotion.
- They will have different relationships with the senior person and with others in the group; they will have alliances and enmities.
- They will interpret differently the motives of the other people present.
- They will have different values and attitudes to the topics under discussion. For example, they may have views about changes in learning methods and practices.

The phenomenological approach accepts **self-reporting** as a necessary part of studying human behaviour. The researcher can obtain limited information by asking the person who is the subject of the study.

Social psychology

The **social psychology** approach has been described by Gordon Allport as:

'an attempt to understand how the thoughts, feelings or behaviour of individuals are influenced by the actual, imaginary or implied presence of others.'

This is relevant at the various levels of grouping we have: society, class, family, organisation, working groups and pairs. Each of them has an impact on individual behaviour. We learn and apply patterns of behaviour for different social situations. We may not even recognise that we have been programmed by society to behave in certain ways. Smooth skilled interaction with other people in particular social situations requires that individuals know how to play their roles.

Potential embarrassment in a medical examination, for example, particularly when one person is male and the other is female, is managed by a series of social conventions or norms of behaviour. They include dressing and undressing behind a screen. Although the patient may be asked to expose intimate parts of the anatomy, the rest of the body may be covered. The language will be formal, rather than familiar, to maintain a professional distance. For a smooth interaction, both parties have to act the appropriate role. There are many regular patterns of behaviour for different situations which we act out on a daily basis.

Discussion point

Reflect on behaviour in a job-selection interview. What would be your chances as an applicant if you played the role of the interviewer rather than your assigned role as an applicant? Suppose you turned up in casual dress. After the introductions, you sat down uninvited in the more imposing chair. You dictated the pattern of the conversation. You started by asking what salary and holidays you would be allowed. How would you be viewed?

Since interactions between people are a significant feature in organisations, they have shown an interest in many of the applications of social psychology. The following are some examples:

- the influence of the immediate work-group or team on an individual's behaviour
- the effects of different leadership and management styles on team members' behaviour
- behaviour in negotiations in relation to its effect
- responses to conflict: passive, aggressive and assertive behaviours
- causes of stress and reactions to it
- the significance of non-verbal communication in face-to-face situations.

Methodology

Work psychologists use a range of techniques to carry out research on human behaviour, emotions and thought at work. A helpful distinction is that between research *methods* and research *designs*.

Research methods are the procedures employed to gather information. A **research design** is the overall strategy employed to carry out a piece of research. The design will depend on the perspective of the researcher and what is being studied. The following are typical research methods:

- *Interviews*. Interviews can be carried out with individuals or with work-groups. Data can be gathered using structured or unstructured questionnaires.
- *Observation*. The work psychologist may carry out personal observations, seeking as far as possible not to intervene or influence the work processes. *Participant observation* occurs when the researcher personally engages in the work tasks and environment to get first-hand experience. *Structured observation* involves creating a clear schedule of what to observe.
- *Diaries*. A diary may be kept by subjects to record key events, or to record feelings and thoughts.
- *Questionnaires and psychometric tests*. Questionnaires may be constructed to carry out detailed survey work. Psychometric tests may be used to assess aspects of personality, such as introversion/extroversion.
- *Psychophysiological assessment*. This approach involves measurement of a subject's neurological, biological, or physiological state as it relates to the individual's psychological functioning. For examples, level of stress can be recorded by measuring blood pressure, sugar level in the blood, etc.

• *Primary archives.* Primary research involves investigating existing records, such as previous records of absenteeism from work.

Case Study

Inspection and staff absence

A project carried out by Maurice Kogan and Margaret Maden investigated the impact of statutory inspections of 2000 English schools. The researchers employed a case study approach as well as interviewing a range of people involved in the schooling process.

One of the aspects of inspection identified was the level of stress it induces in schools. Increased stress was felt immediately before an inspection and was accentuated in the three months after. In some schools it was felt that inspections had resulted in retirements and resignations. The diagram below shows the impact of inspection on staff absence.

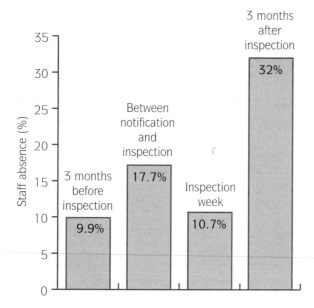

Questions

1. What does the diagram show? In particular, does it prove a relationship between stress and absences?

2. What methods would have been gathered to collect this information?

3. Could this information be used to improve approaches to school inspections?

Key aspects of research design

Experimental design

By carrying out experiments in work psychology it is possible to develop inferences about cause and effect. The researcher can examine the impact of a change in an independent variable on a dependent variable.

To take a classic example, the Hawthorne experiments conducted by Elton Mayo in 1927 (see page 278) included an experiment where six operators who assembled relays were isolated for intensive study in a special test room. These employees were subjected to various rest pauses, lengths of workday, and lengths of workweek, while their production was regularly measured. The researchers were unable to find a direct relationship between changes in physical working conditions and worker output. They went on to conclude that the new 'social setting' created in the test room accounted for increases in output.

When conducting experiments in work psychology it is standard practice to create a 'control group' alongside the 'experimental group'. Subjects in the control group should continue to operate in conditions as near to identical as possible to those in the experimental group; i.e. the work would be carried out by both groups in the same environment, with the same tasks. Subjects for the experimental and control groups should wherever possible be chosen at random.

Survey design

Surveys are a key ingredient of social science research. The strength of the survey is that it is possible to gather extensive amounts of quantitative data from a sizeable population, examining areas such as attitudes and events. Surveys can also be used to find out more about the relationship between two variables, such as the impact of school inspections on the stress levels of teachers.

Questionnaires do, however, need to be constructed carefully. Detailed thought needs to go into producing a questionnaire that will give valid and reliable evidence. It is important to consider the sample frame that will be chosen (e.g. random sample or selective sample). There is a detailed discussion of questionnaire design in Chapter 18.

Qualitative design

Qualitative research (in contrast to quantitative research) sets out to describe how individuals make sense of the situations they are in. It therefore involves in-depth research into individual cases, and places a strong emphasis on seeing the world through the eyes of the individual being studied. This is in tune with the phenomenological approach described previously. Detailed information is usually gathered over an extensive period using observation, often coupled with unstructured interviewing of a relatively small number of people.

Using this approach the work psychologist will often start with some loose ideas and then go on to develop a theory which is grounded in the findings which come to light as a result of the research (hence the term 'grounded theory'). The approach needs to be very systematic and rigorous and will involve collecting vast quantities of information which then needs to be sifted, sorted, analysed and evaluated to find meaningful interpretations.

Action research

This approach involves collaborative effort by researchers and the subjects of the research. Often a researcher will research their own practice in order to identify areas for change (e.g. when examining potential improvements in work performance and practice). Action research sets out to solve pressing problems for the people working with the researcher, and to create a more generalisable body of knowledge about the area being investigated.

SIGNIFICANCE AND NATURE OF INDIVIDUAL DIFFERENCES

Obviously, individuals differ in their work performance, how they mix with others, their willingness to take risks, and so on. Many of these differences are observable and measurable, although the validity and accuracy of these observations and measurements is open to question.

Physical differences

Individuals are tall or short, fat or thin, or just average! Sensory capacities (sight, hearing, touch and smell) may also be important in the work situation. Motor or mechanical skills may also be needed, such as hand/eye coordination on a moving production line and in many other lines of work. Physical aptitudes may be closely tied in with other abilities such as cognitive ones (related to thinking) and affective ones (related to the ability to form social relationships).

Differences in intelligence and aptitude

There is an on-going debate about the relative importance of 'nature' and 'nurture' in determining intelligence. That is, to what extent is intelligence determined genetically, and to what extent is it nurtured by environmental factors such as parental support, access to educational play facilities, travel, and quality of schooling? There seems to be evidence that supports both views.

Personality

Personality is widely regarded as a (possibly *the*) key factor in determining how successful an individual will be in working with others in an organisation. **Personality** can be defined as the sum total of all the behavioural and mental characteristics by means of which an individual is recognised as being unique. Personality gives individuals a distinctive social character.

In their book *Organisational Behaviour,* Huczynski and Buchanan (1998) argue that if the concept of personality is to be helpful in understanding human behaviour then it is necessary to accept two propositions:

- Human behaviour has stable and enduring characteristics. When we examine the way individuals behave over a period of time we are able to identify regularities in the 'ways we think and in what we do that can be identified and studied'.
- The distinctive properties of an individual's personality can be measured and compared with others.

Huczynski and Buchanan also remind us of the dangers of **stereotyping** in assessing personality. We are all informal personality theorists. However, research indicates that many are poor judges of other people's personalities. In social interactions we tend not to draw on all aspects of personality. We usually meet someone in a specific role relationship (e.g. student/lecturer, seller/buyer, doctor/patient). We tend to assess personality in terms of this role relationship. The tutor may appear to be confident and informed when working with a group of students, and the students may generalise that the tutor is 'always like that'. However, the students' initial view might be challenged if they were to encounter the teacher in other life-roles – wandering around lost in an airport terminal, or standing helplessly by the side of a motor vehicle after an engine failure. Generally speaking, however, we tend to meet people in organisations when they are performing specific roles. As a result we have only a limited insight into their personality.

As with intelligence, there is considerable debate as to whether your personality is inherited or determined by your environment.

Personality has an important impact on work behaviour and performance, as we shall see later in this chapter. Individual personality characteristics determine what type of jobs and work situations individuals are most comfortable in. A sociable extrovert may be comfortable contributing to working in teams in an open-plan office. An introvert, on the other hand, may be a lot more comfortable working on their own in front of a computer screen. Individuals with neurotic tendencies may find it difficult to work in stressful situations where they are not given a lot of on-going positive feedback and encouragement. Individuals who are 'perfectionists' with a strong achievement orientation may not like working with easy-going individuals who are happy in 'messy' work situations.

Self and self-image

Knowing oneself is an important part of an individual's psychological make-up. Individuals who know themselves *and like what they see* are far more likely to think kindly of others than individuals who have a poor **self-image**.

Self-image is something that builds up over many years through psychological and sociological influences. Individuals who receive good **feedback** about themselves and their performance develop the confidence and security to try out new things, and have a good sense of self-worth.

In the workplace it is important to give positive rewards and encouragement for good performance. We talk about giving 'positive strokes' to people to encourage them and to make them feel happy. Honest appraisal is the best way of helping individuals to know how they are doing. Of course, such appraisal needs to be carried out in an open and positive way rather than on the basis of apportioning 'blame'.

There are numerous exercises and techniques available for individuals to appraise their own strengths and

weaknesses. Clearly such techniques need to be more scientific than the type of hastily thrown together questionnaire published in popular magazines. The most effective techniques are designed to help people to examine their experiences systematically in the work setting and outside it, in order to arrive at an accurate assessment of their strengths and weaknesses. The importance of examining emotions as well as thoughts, and negative experiences as well as positive ones, is usually stressed.

Types of 'self'

- *The locus of control.* This approach is concerned with measuring the internal–external orientation of an individual, the extent to which the individual feels able to affect his or her own life. *Internals* are people who feel that they can control their own fate. *Externals* believe that much of what happens to them is beyond their own control. Internals attribute causes for events primarily to themselves – as a general rule internals tend to be more introverted, and concerned with their own actions and inner feelings, whereas externals are more extrovert and sociable.
- *Authoritarianism.* Authoritarianism is concerned with the extent to which individuals adhere strictly to patterns, rules and chains of command. The individual who has a leaning to authoritarianism wants to see everything played by 'the book'.
- *Self-monitoring.* This reflects the ability of an individual to adjust his or her behaviour to external or environmental factors. Some individuals are very sensitive to what is happening around them, whereas others are quite indifferent to their environment.
- *Machiavellianism.* This is drawn from the arch politician Count Niccolo Machiavelli, who in his book *The Prince* sets out how individuals can gain and use power. Machiavellianism is all about being able to use power and influence for your own interests. Psychologists have developed a series of instruments called **Mach scales** to measure a person's Machiavellian orientation.

Discussion point

How would you rank your own personality in terms of: (a) internal–external orientation; (b) authoritarianism; (c) ability to adjust according to your environment; (d) the Mach scale?

Towards the end of this chapter we return to look at the nature of the self in more detail.

Drives

Individuals have different **drives**, depending on their personality and the social and cultural environment in which they were brought up. David McClelland (*The Achieving Society*, 1960) carried out a number of studies of what drives people on and acts as a spur to motivation. He identified four main drives. People from similar backgrounds may share the same drives because of the way they have been socialised.

Achievement motivation

This is a drive that individuals may have to pursue and achieve specific goals that make it possible to climb the ladder of success. Accomplishment of these goals becomes important in its own right. Within an organisation, individuals with a strong achievement drive work hard and believe that they should and will receive personal credit for their efforts. As managers, people with this type of drive will expect employees to have the same achievement-oriented goals and values as themselves.

Some writers associate the Japanese idea of *kaizen* (continuous improvement) and the American work ethic with this achievement drive. Clearly this drive becomes difficult to accommodate in hard times – for example in periods of economic decline when opportunities become reduced.

Affiliation motivation

This drive is to associate with other people on a social basis. Affiliation-driven individuals respond best when they are complimented on their favourable attitudes and cooperation. It is sometimes argued that girls have a stronger affiliation drive than boys (i.e. being part of a friendship group and empathising with friends is an important female drive). Affiliation-motivated employees and managers seek to surround themselves with friends. However, managers with a strong affiliation drive may find it more difficult to make hard decisions.

Competence motivation

This is a drive to be good or competent at something. Performing a job or task well is seen as being a reward in its own right. Competence-motivated employees will seek to master tasks and skills, and strive for solutions to problems. Employees and managers with a competence motivation will generally perform their work duties well. It has been suggested that a simplistic comparison between a competence-motivated individual and an achievement-motivated one is that the former will ask 'How well can I perform the task?' whereas the latter will ask 'How much can I do?'

Power motivation

People with this motivation want to influence others and to change situations. They want to be in control of people and events. This may involve taking risks in order to achieve a position of power – and of course power can be used well or badly.

Power-motivated individuals often make effective managers but they may not always be popular. They are most likely to be successful if they seek power for the benefit of the organisation. When power is sought purely for personal reasons, they are unlikely to be successful because of the number of enemies they make.

PERCEPTION

Huczynski and Buchanan (see earlier) define **perception** as: 'the active psychological process in which stimuli are selected [by an individual] and organised into meaningful patterns'. Another definition is 'the process through which people receive, organise and interpret information from their environment'.

Person perception is very important in the workplace. In their book *Work Psychology*, Arnold, Cooper and Robertson (1998) define person perception as:

> '...how we perceive and interpret the behaviour and characteristics of other people, and the causes of events involving them'.

They consider person perception at three levels:

- perceiving the behaviour of other people
- perceiving the personality of other people
- perceiving the causes of events involving people.

Managers should be able to do these things well. They need to be wary of biases and distortions which affect their perception of people and events. Such impairments are likely to have two sources:

- *Information-processing inaccuracies.* Managers may seek to have a clear picture of people and events but may not have the cognitive facilities (or sufficient information) to weigh up what is going on.
- *Motivation or emotional inaccuracies.* Although managers may believe that they are trying to be accurate and impartial, they may really be working with emotional or motivational biases stemming, for example, from their desire to protect their own position or their own self-image.

Check your understanding

The variety of perception is often surprising. We make a gesture, such as a smile, which we think is unambiguous, but people perceive the smile in different ways. Some think we are being patronising, or cynical; others see the smile as being false; a further group may regard it as being lecherous. We go to watch a sports game in which our favourite player seems to have an incredible match and be the linchpin of the team. After the game we discuss the match with someone else who thought that our player was greedy and selfish and nearly threw the game away. Perception is thus a far more complex matter than it appears to be on the surface.

The three key ingredients of the perception process are the perceiver, the perceived and the setting (see Figure 12.2).

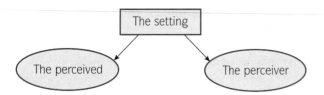

Figure 12.2 *The three key ingredients of perception*

The perceiver

The way in which the perceiver interprets the situation will depend on the person's needs or motives, their past experiences, their attitudes and values and their personality. It is clear that prejudices and stereotypes will be an ingredient of the perception process. Interviewers are said to form a substantial part of their view of the job applicant in the first few seconds of an interview. The motives of the perceiver are a crucial influence on perception. For example, if the perceiver has a strong need to get on with others, then they are likely to seek positive features of the person being perceived.

The perceived

Important factors here are contrast, intensity, size, motion and repetition or novelty. For example, imagine that you are interviewing five applicants for a job, four of whom are smartly turned out in conventional clothes and are fairly conformist in their attitudes and behaviours, while the fifth is unconventionally dressed with rings through her nose and lip, and is very vivacious in her approach and dynamic in an interviewing situation. The fifth person is likely to have a greater impact than the others. How you respond to this candidate will depend on the extent to which you see her contrast with the others as being important. You may view her distinctiveness in a positive way, or you may respond negatively. However, the chances are high that she would be the most memorable candidate in the interview situation.

Intensity can vary in terms of features such as brightness, colour and sound; for example, someone who talks in a very low voice will stand out from others who are easy to hear. People will be noticed on account of their physical proportions or size. Someone that is wearing a novel fashion accessory will stand out from the everyday.

The setting

The physical, social or organisational context of the perceptual setting is important in determining the perception process. For example, a lecturer might regard it as quite normal to have to queue behind students in the dining hall waiting for a meal. However, the same person would regard students as being rude if they expected him or her to wait for them to finish their conversations before starting a lecture.

Perceptual selection

Huczynski and Buchanan define **perceptual selection** as 'the process through which we filter or screen out information that we do not need'. We all screen out a considerable amount of what we see and hear because:

- we cannot take in everything
- we choose/select what we perceive.

The inevitable conclusion is that in this sense we do not always operate according to reality – what is out there – but what we make of what is out there. 'Reality' is thus a *social construction*. In interacting with someone or making sense of an event we:

- collect data
- fit the information into categories
- make predictions.

The creation of **categories** is one means by which we make sense of what we perceive. Unfortunately this often leads to the creation of stereotypes, and sweeping generalisations such as 'women can't take pressure', 'gay men are promiscuous', and 'fat people are lazy'. We often work through stereotypes because it then becomes easier to make assumptions about people.

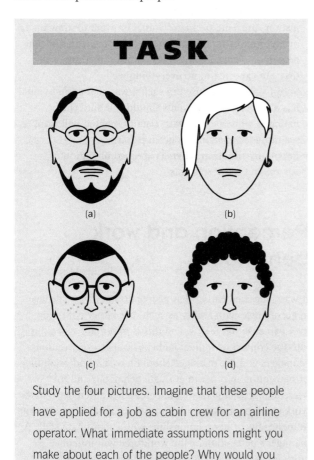

TASK

(a)   (b)

(c)   (d)

Study the four pictures. Imagine that these people have applied for a job as cabin crew for an airline operator. What immediate assumptions might you make about each of the people? Why would you make these assumptions?

In order to place someone in a category we first need to have information about them. Prior information comes through 'reputation' – what other people have said or written about the person. When we meet the person we begin to work with clues, such as their pattern of dress, their speech, actions and gestures. **Role signs** are particularly useful in creating an impression. So, when someone wears the dress of a particular occupation then we begin to make assumptions about them. For example, if we have a car accident and someone wearing a nurse's uniform comes to help an injured passenger we automatically assume that they are competent in medical matters (of course the nurse may be wearing the uniform for the first time on that day). Several house burglars have been able to dupe elderly people to let them into their house by pretending to work for an official organisation.

In his book *Understanding Organisations*, Charles Handy makes the point that we are very unscientific in collecting perceptual data. He gives four reasons for this:

- We collect very little. We form a stereotype from the first available perceptual information and regard that as adequate. Managers therefore need to learn to be 'smarter' and to look in greater detail and depth.
- We are prone to selection perception. We see and hear only what we want to see and hear, looking for data to support our initial assumptions and neglecting or not noticing contradictory evidence.
- The order in which the data are collected is important. Earlier perceptions tend to colour what comes after.
- Our own roles colour our perceptions. The same set of facts viewed from different angles will look different.

Case Study

Selective perception in the social services

In the middle of January 1999, a couple who disappeared with their two foster daughters after they were refused permission to adopt wrote an emotional letter pleading to be allowed to keep them. Jeff and Jennifer Bramley disappeared from their Cambridgeshire home in September 1998 with the two girls, aged five and three. In the letter the couple said:

'We Jeff, Jenny [and our two girls] *write this letter to tell the plight of a family that love each other and wishes to stay together.* [The girls] *were told about us and told we would be their forever Mummy and Daddy. After we had met the girls several times in their foster home, they came to live with us. They soon grew to love us as their Mummy and Daddy, as we grew to love them as our daughters. [They were both] looking forward to their new lives with us.'*

The Bramleys said they were good, honest, caring people who were willing to give up their home, friends and jobs to keep the girls 'with the parents they love and desperately want to share their lives with':

'We were approved to be [their] new Mummy and Daddy, they were placed with us for us to adopt. It is misleading to call us foster parents. Social services seemed pleased with us and told us everything was fine until one day they said we were too safety conscious by saying 'no' and 'don't' too often.'

Police were not able to track down the family for several months and there were few sightings. In early 1999 they were allegedly 'seen' by a retired clergyman on the North Yorkshire Moors Railway (subsequently it was proved to have been a false sighting, because the family was in Ireland at the time). He described the children as 'out of control' and said that the Bramleys, and particularly Jenny – looked depressed, worn-out and beaten.

Social services denied ever saying that the Bramleys were 'too strict', and totally dismissed rumours that they were considered too religious. There was also absolutely no suggestion of any kind of abuse. Quite simply, a spokesperson said, it was concluded 'after working with the couple for six months' that they seemed to lack the special parenting skills needed. When asked why the children had been placed with the Bramleys, the social service replied that placement 'is not a perfect science'.

Questions

1. What does the case study tell us about selective perception?

2. How in this case has selective perception led to difficulties?

3. What lessons can be learnt from the case by social service managers?

How do we organise perceptions?

A variety of schema help us to organise our perceptions. Schemas are cognitive frameworks that represent organised knowledge about a given concept or stimulus developed through experience. There are a number of types of schemas.

- **Self schemas** are used to organise perceptions about our own appearance, behaviour and personality.
- **Person schemas** are used by individuals to sort other people into categories such as types or groups, in terms of their perceived features: 'This person fits into that class or group, that one into another', etc. Unfortunately, this is often tied up with stereotyping. We know someone who we perceive in a certain way depending on our own interpretation and judgements about their behaviour. We then store this information away. Later on we meet someone who reminds us of the person we originally classified, and make an assumption that the new person fits into the same category. A male who has an unpleasant experience with a particular female may then treat another female in a way that is determined by prejudice about the earlier experience. In the workplace, managers may develop a concept of the 'good worker' and judge an employee on this basis. Psychologists use the term **halo effect** to describe the way in which we use just one attribute of an individual or event to draw up an overall impression about the total characteristics of that person or event. So, if someone does something well they are expected to do everything well.
- **Script schemas** are used in such a way that an individual has a view as to how events should roll out. The manager who operates with a script schema will want to see things happen in this given pattern.
- **Person-in-situation schemas** are a combination of person and script schemas.

Perception and work behaviour

It was suggested earlier that people do not always behave in accordance with reality as such, but rather with how they perceive that reality, and this is important when put into the context of individual behaviour in organisations. Managers and the managed should have an understanding of perception in order to evaluate behaviour and to overcome problems related to perceptual differences. In the work situation a manager's perceptions and selectivity can influence his or her relationships with subordinate staff. A manager's perception of the workforce will influence attitudes in dealing with people and the style of managerial behaviour adopted. Successful managers are those who have a good understanding of perceptual processes and how distortions such as stereotyping and misunderstandings come about.

Schermerhorn, Hunt and Osborn (1997) suggest the following outline of managerial skills that are appropriate to handling the perception process:

- Have a high level of self-awareness.
- Seek information from various sources to confirm or amend personal impressions of a given situation.
- Be empathetic; that is, be able to see a situation as it is perceived by other people.
- Avoid common perceptual distortions that bias your views of people and situations.
- Be aware of various kinds of schemas and their possible impact.
- Be aware of attribution theory and its consequences. (Attribution theory is the study of how people seek to (a) understand the cause of an event, (b) assess responsibility for the outcomes of the event, and (c) evaluate the personal qualities of the people involved in the event.)
- Avoid inappropriate actions.
- Influence the perceptions of other people in a constructive way.

Discussion point

Think of situations where differences in perception have caused problems in the workplace. How might a more detailed knowledge of perception have enabled these situations to be handled more effectively.

Attitude

There are many occasions at work when we are concerned about people's reactions. When we go for an appraisal interview we hope that the appraiser will be able to see our positive contributions and qualities in a favourable light. A manager explaining changes at work plans to get the cooperation of the staff. An employee asking for some concession hopes the boss' reaction will be favourable. In all of these situations, the outcome depends on the strength of the case and how well it is presented. It also depends on the **attitude** of the person receiving the information.

When the manager explains proposed changes at work, he or she presents the same information to all the employees addressed. However, each employee's understanding of the message will be different, since each perceives it differently. Their reactions will depend on their attitudes to the speaker and to the subject matter. Some will accept the truth of the manager's assurances that employment will be protected. Others may see the manager as untrustworthy and interpret the message to be scheming and concerned with downsizing of staff. Attitudes are the personal filters through which we interpret information (see Figure 12.3).

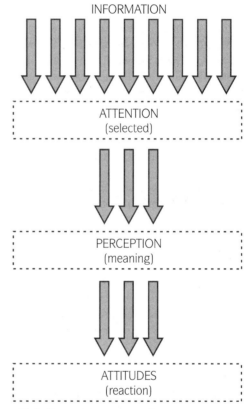

Figure 12.3 *Processing incoming information*

An attitude is a predisposition to act or react in a certain way to certain stimuli, people, situations and opinions. The reactions of people we know well are less likely to surprise us than are those of strangers. We know the attitudes of people close to us and we can therefore predict their reactions more closely. Job satisfaction is a specific attitude that indicates the degree to which individuals feel positively or negatively about their jobs. It is an emotional response to the tasks that have to be completed as well as the physical and social conditions in the workplace. Arnold, Cooper and Robertson (1998) suggest that 'feelings represent the *affective* component of an attitude, thoughts the *cognitive* component, and predisposition to act the *behavioural* component'. Attitudes are evaluative in that they reflect a person's tendency to feel, think or behave in a positive or negative manner towards the object of the attitude.

Functions of attitudes

Our attitudes help us in several ways to get through problems, avoid mistakes and take advantage of opportunities. For example, every day our senses are bombarded by a mass of stimuli – sights and sounds, words and behaviour. We need to process them mentally and react appropriately. We reduce the chaos of this mass of stimuli by two processes. First, our senses select only some of the stimuli for conscious attention. Second, our attitudes provide a basis for snap judgements on situations and people. We therefore do not need to think about our responses from first principles, and the stimuli are processed with a 'frame of reference'. In this way, too, attitudes give us a feeling of stability and continuity. In particular, attitudes shared with other people make it easier to relate to and communicate with them.

Negative attitudes may originate from past unpleasant experiences of people and situations. They reduce the chance of being involved again in the same or similar circumstances. Positive attitudes have the opposite effect.

Attitudes can also be a way of protecting self-image. People with deep feelings of inferiority may bolster their own self-image by negative attitudes towards some other group. Denigration of the other group allows the attitude holder to experience feelings of superiority.

Finally, attitudes are a way of expressing values that are important to us. For example, the attitude of a teenager, as exhibited by opinions, dress and speech, may be expressing a central value of independence from adults. Workers who respond better to requests rather than orders may be expressing, by their attitude, central values of autonomy and personal dignity.

Formation of attitudes

Does it bother you if you are late for an appointment? How do you feel if other people are late and keep you waiting? Would you stay off work with a bad cold or would you struggle to keep going? How do you feel when other members of your team take a day off because of a cold?

Irrespective of your attitudes to punctuality and absence, you can probably justify your views rationally in terms of

'not letting others down', 'spreading the infection' and 'getting better more quickly'. It is also possible that you are really responding with attitudes to punctuality and minor illness that you acquired from your family upbringing or from some later training.

We may have been taught values directly or we may have learned them through the example of influential others. Such attitudes may be internalised and resistant to change. Even when rationally we behave in contravention of the earlier attitudes, we may still experience guilt feelings. The person who has rationally stayed at home with a heavy cold may still feel guilty about his or her action.

Our attitudes are developed or shaped by subsequent life experiences. Joining an organisation is likely to mould our attitudes, but not necessarily uniformly for all members. In the book *Psychology in Business*, Eugene McKenna (1987) cites examples of attitudes common to chartered accountants (such as a reluctance to take risks unless the outcome can be predicted accurately, and an emphasis on caution) and attributed to their training and job experience.

Significant life events, such as unemployment, ill-health and death in the family, can cause changes in attitudes. However, two individuals undergoing the same experiences will not necessarily form the same attitudes. There is the question of how new attitudes fit the web of existing attitudes. There is the variable of the individual's personality. Some people are more resistant to attitude changes than others. For example, army training and discipline secures obedience; in a few cases it may be compliance rather than a true conversion of values.

In the aforementioned book *Psychology in Business*, Kelman suggests three possible reasons for attitude changes:

- *Compliance*. This occurs when a person adopts the attitudes of another for anticipated extrinsic rewards. The other person might be, for example, a boss or a client. The reward might be a sale, promotion or a pay increment. The attitude is supported by no genuine belief; it is held solely for instrumental reasons. For illustration of these attitudes, listen to the views expressed by subordinates in the presence of an opinionated, authoritarian boss; then listen to their views when the boss is not present.
- *Identification*. These are attitudes adopted to maintain a relationship, valued for its own sake rather than for extrinsic rewards. In a work context, people may have positive attitudes to their job to please a person they respect and admire.

- *Internalisation.* This occurs when an individual adopts an attitude because it fits his or her own personal set of values. A racist's attitudes to any new issues involving ethnic minorities are likely to fit the pattern of his or her other racist attitudes.

Discussion point

Think of a deeply held attitude you hold about a particular work practice. What were the roots of this attitude? Under what circumstances might your attitude change?

Attitudes are nearly always measured by self-report questionnaires. Their measurement thus depends on what subjects say about their feelings, beliefs and/or behaviours to particular objects/events or individuals.

Aptitude and ability

The term **aptitude** is used to describe the capability of an individual to learn something. Our experience tells us that we have aptitudes in some areas of learning and not in others. The term **ability** is used to describe the capacity of an individual to perform the various tasks needed for a particular job. Our abilities to carry out different jobs vary according to our natural aptitude, our experience, education, and training. Clearly intelligence is a component of natural aptitude. *Aptitudes are potential abilities, while abilities are the knowledge and skills that individuals already have.*

Organisations are interested in these concepts for all sorts of reasons, and a number of tests have been devised to measure mental and physical aptitudes and abilities. As well as IQ (intelligence) tests there are a range of other tests and devices for measuring ability. They include:

- verbal ability tests
- numerical ability tests
- diagrammatic ability tests
- spatial ability tests
- mechanical ability tests
- manual dexterity tests.

Other ways of testing aptitude and ability are:

- personality questionnaires – structured pen-and-paper tests
- work samples – producing a sample of work to show ability
- in-tray/in-basket exercises
- trainability – on-the-job testing of ability
- interviews
- handwriting tests – to show personality characteristics, etc.

There is always considerable controversy over which approaches are the most reliable. At the end of the day, organisations will tend to opt for those methods which provide the best results in terms of performance.

Clearly if attitudes are predispositions to respond to someone or something in one's environment, then an organisation will want to employ people who have positive attitudes to the organisation's goals and objectives. If we take this approach, then the objectives of the organisation will define what constitutes appropriate attitudes. Ability will then be measured in terms of an individual's talent to work in the right way and produce the desired results.

Intelligence

There is some debate as to whether intelligence is a facet of personality or whether it should be seen as a separate psychological characteristic in its own right.

Intelligence certainly has a number of ingredients. It is usually associated with the ability to solve mathematical and other logical problems, and correlates well with a person's aptitude to be successful in specified tasks. There are a number of ways of measuring intelligence and aptitude. Organisations may use tests which purport to measure intelligence and aptitude when they feel that these tests are helpful in selecting employees for posts requiring particular qualities. The variety of recognised mental abilities is illustrated by the list below:

- *Verbal comprehension.* Verbal reasoning tests may include rearranging sentences, fitting in missing words, etc. Such tests have traditionally been used for selection purposes.
- *Word fluency.* Tests in this category might include solving anagrams, identifying rhyming words, etc.
- *Number.* Tests usually include mental and written arithmetic calculations, to be completed within a time period.
- *Space.* Tests involve arranging shapes into sequences and identifying relationships between shapes.

The behaviour of individuals **303**

- *Associative memory*. This often involves memorising associated words by rote.
- *Perceptual speed*. Tests in this category involve rapid visualisation of similarities and differences in figures, shapes and text.
- *Induction or general reasoning*. This may be tested by working out a rule in a series of numbers, or other tests involving identifying patterns and rules.

Intelligence and aptitude inevitably influence the ways in which individuals tackle tasks. Gordon Pask, in his book *An Approach to Cybernetics*, has made an interesting point about the way individuals approach learning tasks – he distinguishes between 'holists' (those who tackle the whole problem) and 'serialists':

> *'An individual student may be good at "seeing things as parts of a whole" or, conversely, he may have a special aptitude for "stringing sub-problems into sequences", which (on resolution) lead to the solution of a large problem.'*

In other words, some students (and employees) like to take a broad look at a new area (of study), including information which they do not yet need, before they begin to see an overall picture. Others prefer to work steadily through a relatively narrow sequence and the broad picture emerges in the course of time. It can be quite irritating for a serialist to have to listen to a lecture given by a holist, and vice versa!

Another distinction that is often drawn is between convergent and divergent thinkers. **Convergent thinkers** prefer tasks where solutions are clear-cut – there may be one obvious best way of solving a problem. The convergent thinker hones in on the problem and works systematically towards its solution. In contrast, the **divergent thinker** sees many different ways of tackling a problem. Divergent thinkers thrive on uncertainty which encourages them to be creative; they can conjure up all sorts of alternatives and different views on going about something.

Several influential writers have also stressed the importance of **lateral thinking**. This is a way of solving problems by employing unorthodox and apparently illogical means. The lateral thinker is prepared to take risks and would be an invaluable member of a team which required creativity, flair and offbeat solutions to problems.

Different jobs have different requirements and it is important to be able to test an individual's ability to do a particular task. For example, secretaries may be tested on speed and accuracy, including spelling and use of grammar. Capability and competence are likely to develop with education,

training and experience. Today the divide between vocational and academic work is increasingly becoming blurred. The emphasis is perhaps moving away from learning a body of knowledge for its own sake towards learning what can be applied in practical contexts. NVQs, for example, are concerned with developing applicable work-based competences, while GNVQs are concerned with developing more broad-based general competences which effectively prepare individuals for the changing world of work.

INDIVIDUAL BEHAVIOUR AT WORK

In this section we examine a range of key issues relating to individual behaviour at work, particularly drawing on personality and trait theories.

Personality studies

Kagan and Havemann (*Psychology: An Introduction*, 1976) define personality as:

> *'...the total pattern of characteristic ways of thinking, feeling and behaving that constitute the individual's distinctive method of relating to the environment'.*

In everyday parlance we use the term 'personality' to identify those characteristics that make an individual 'different', although in doing so we often tend to generalise: they have a bubbly personality, or they have an outgoing personality, or they are shy and retiring, or they have a dreary personality; or in some cases they have 'no personality at all'. Personality is thus concerned with key characteristics of an individual.

We usually tend to focus on those elements of a person's character which are stable and distinctive. In other words we are mainly concerned with the individual 'acting in character', although from time to time we are also interested to explain why an individual behaves in an 'uncharacteristic way'.

- *Stable characteristics* are those which typify the individual over a period of time – always having a sunny, optimistic, sociable nature for example.
- *Distinctive characteristics* are those which set the individual apart. For example, a group of production line workers may all be reliable and efficient employees, but what makes Joe distinctive is her ability to take on a leadership role in a crisis.

Nomothetic and ideographic approaches to personality

Nomothetic studies

The **nomothetic** approach is concerned with the scientific collection of data about groups and individuals, as represented by the studies by the Eysencks outlined in this section. The nomothetic approach investigates large numbers to find out what is 'normal' or average in these groups and compares individuals with the norm. The terms 'norm' and 'average' are used in the statistical sense – so people who deviate from the norm are not to be thought of as abnormal or social outcasts!

The nomothetic approach is built on the assumption that personality is primarily inherited and that environmental factors and experience have a smaller impact. Although this concedes the difficulties that measuring personality brings, it maintains its claim that it is possible to measure and predict the ways in which personality types would behave in given circumstances.

Ideographic studies

The *ideographic* approach, in contrast – associated with researchers such as Carl Rogers – is concerned with understanding the uniqueness of individuals and the development of the self concept. This approach considers personality development to be a process which is open to change and is not static. It regards individuals as responding to the environment and people around them, and views the dynamics of these interactions as playing a key role in shaping personality.

Traits and types

H. J. and M. J. Eysenck (*Personality and Individual Differences*, 1985) developed an approach to personality based on scientific study and statistical work. The Eysencks set out to identify underlying personality traits that might be used to explain human behaviour in a range of different settings. The notion of traits fits quite closely with the everyday description of personality – shyness, extroversion, introversion etc.

Trait theorists employ **factor analysis** to outline the structure of human personality. The Eysencks and a number of other psychologists have carried out detailed work using personality questionnaires on a large number of people to find out how they feel and behave in various situations. The two key dimensions to emerge from factor analysis are **extroversion/introversion** and **neuroticism**. People who are extrovert are lively, sociable and excitable, while neurotics are characterised by anxiety and tension. Of course all individuals combine elements of extroversion and neuroticism but one aspect tends to dominate.

Extroverts prefer to work in a sociable environment, such as an open-plan office. They enjoy being given a variety of challenges where they are invited to come up with new ideas and to express these ideas in an open forum. They work readily with other people, although they may fail to fully take into consideration the needs of others who are more withdrawn. H. J. Eysenck believed that extroversion and introversion were both the products of nature and nurture. He believed that extroverts need higher levels of stimulation to attract and keep their attention. They therefore need to operate in work environments where there is a lot happening and where change frequently takes place; they can't concentrate on the mundane and the routine for too long. Managers therefore need to identify extroverts in the workplace and find appropriate situations and work patterns to bring the best out of these individuals.

In contrast, introverts are able to concentrate for longer periods on given tasks. Introverts need less stimulation to remain 'on task'. They can therefore be channelled into doing tasks which enable them to focus and concentrate for lengthy periods. However, they may need to work in situations where they will not be annoyed by what they see as being unnecessary distractions.

Of course, it is simplistic to assume that everyone fits neatly into a category – extrovert or introvert, and so on. The important thing is that managers recognise these tendencies and provide meaningful work situations which allow everyone to fulfil themselves and commit themselves to working patterns. In a similar way it is important to recognise neuroticism as a personality trait and to organise work so that it does not become too stressful for individuals who are likely to feel threatened by confusing and unstructured work situations.

The Eysencks' work also provides a theory of the origin and development of personality which is based on a combination of inherited, neurological differences and environmental influences (nature and nurture). The most widely used measuring instruments used by psychologists taking this approach are the following:

- The *Eysenck Personality Inventory* (EPI) is based on a questionnaire involving self-reporting by subjects. This measures extroversion and neuroticism.

- The *Eysenck Personality Questionnaire* (EPQ) measures extroversion and introversion, and psychotism. In 1991 this questionnaire was built into a new *Eysenck Personality Scale* (EPS).

Work carried out by the Eysencks and other trait theorists has claimed to identify the existence of five key major personality factors, termed 'the big five'. These factors are believed to represent the basic dimensions of personality. They are:

- extroversion-introversion
- neuroticism
- conscientiousness
- agreeableness
- openness to experience.

Conscientiousness is the person's orientation towards organisation, objectives and meeting targets. Openness relates to the individual's ability to be influenced by new experiences (rather than having a closed, conservative approach). Agreeableness is the extent to which an individual is good natured and eager to cooperate with others.

Understanding self and others

In his book *Mind, Self and Society* (1934), G. H. Mead suggested two components of the self:

- The 'I' comprises the unique, individual, conscious and impulsive aspects of the behaviour of the individual.
- The 'Me' encompasses the wider norms and values of society that each individual learns and internalises'.

Mead used the term 'generalised other' to refer to the set of expectations that an individual believes wider society has of that person. 'Me' is the part of self where these generalised attitudes are organised. The 'Me' is simply a mental process that helps us to reflect objectively on our own behaviour. In contrast, the 'I' is an impulsive component of the self. While we have external pressures on us to conform – it is also possible to be creative and to impose elements of the 'I' on the wider environment.

Carl Rogers (1947) later represented the two sides of the self as shown in Figure 12.4.

Personality is not stable because over the course of time we are exposed to new experiences and learning, which as a

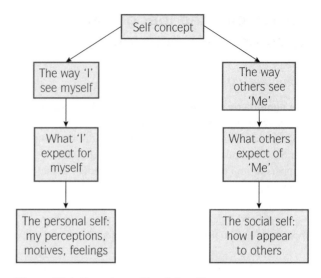

Figure 12.4 *Rogers' two sides of the self*

result of perceptions and motivations lead to behaviour changes. The concept of 'self' is thus changed over time. We use the expression **personality change** to describe this process. For example, as a result of losing a job, or going to prison, a person's self concept may be given a severe battering. Conversely, on being promoted in the workplace or as a result of job enrichment or enlargement an individual may develop a much more positive self concept. The process of empowerment in the workplace is designed to make individuals feel a lot better about themselves and about the organisation they work for.

Individuals can develop a self concept which matches reality, by developing perceptions which are conscious, organised and accepted. Well-adjusted individuals are flexible and can respond to change in a smooth way.

In contrast, 'maladjusted' individuals see as threatening those experiences and feelings which do not tally with their self-image. For example, they may feel threatened and belittled by experiences when they do not appear to be in control, or are made to feel 'stupid' by another person or in a given situation. They use defence mechanisms to deny their experience of the situation. They may blame someone else for causing the threat to their self-image. Psychological tension may build up in the individual – causing them to 'hit out' at others and to act in an unpredictable and hostile way in situations they are not comfortable with.

Carl Rogers believed that at the centre of human personality is a desire for full realisation of potential, which requires an appropriate and positive social environment. This environment will exist in the perfect form when the individual is treated with 'unconditional positive regard'. There are very real implications for the work environment because it involves an atmosphere in which you are valued, trusted, accepted and respected, even when you have certain negative characteristics. This is why human resource management and empowerment have been such important strands in the organisation of the modern workplace. In an ideal environment the individual will repay the organisation by being trusting, flexible and spontaneous.

SUMMARY

We have examined a range of psychological theories relating to the individual and personality types. Clearly, managers need to assess the implications of these individual differences for the effective management of people at work. Most importantly, it must be recognised that every individual is different and will need individual attention. Simply to treat everyone as if they are the same is inappropriate, although many organisations recruit people (and groups of people) to do certain types of work on the basis of personality assessments (batteries of tests to identify personalities which fit with given work situations).

Equally important, it also helps if individuals in the workplace have a good understanding of their own personality traits. If you are the sort of person who is very task-oriented and enjoys working on your own and dislikes the distraction of an endless succession of team meetings and group-working situations, then clearly it would be inappropriate for you to seek a position that exposes you continually to sitting in a 'touchy feely' circle with a group of work colleagues. Alternatively, if you are a team-playing extrovert then you will not want to work in an office mulling over figures or doing analytical research. Managers therefore need to think carefully about the psychology of the workplace in order to construct working environments which meet the needs of others and of themselves. Work will be enjoyed only if it is enjoyable, and will be enjoyable only if it corresponds/fits with the individuals' disposition to enjoy work.

REFERENCES

Arnold, J., Cooper, C. and Robertson, I., *Work Psychology,* 3rd edn, FT/Pitman, 1998.

Eysenck, H. J. and Eysenck, M. J., *Personality and Individual Differences: A Natural Science Approach,* Plenum, 1985.

Handy, Charles, *Understanding Organisations,* Penguin, 1997.

Havemann, E. and Kagan, J., *Psychology: An Introduction,* Harcourt Brace Jovanovich, 1976.

Huczynski, A. and Buchanan, D., *Organisational Behaviour,* Prentice Hall, 1998.

McClelland, David, *The Achieving Society,* Free Press, 1960.

McKenna, Eugene (ed), *Psychology in Business,* Laurence Erlbaum, 1987.

Mead, G. H., *Mind, Self and Society,* University of Chicago Press, 1934.

Pask, Gordon, *An Approach to Cybernetics,* Hutchinson, 1961.

Rogers, Carl R., 'Some observations on the organisation of personality', *American Psychologist,* vol. 2, 1947.

Schermerhorn, J., Hunt, J. and Osborn, R., *Managing Organisational Behaviour,* John Wiley, 1997.

Skinner, B.F., *Beyond Freedom and Dignity,* 1973.

Groups and Group Dynamics

This chapter focuses on enabling students to develop an ability to work with others based upon an understanding of groups and group dynamics.

On completion of the chapter you should be able to:

- describe the nature of groups and group behaviour

- investigate the factors that lead to effective teamwork and the influences that threaten success.

THE NATURE OF GROUPS

Groups and teams

In her book *The Change Masters* (1995), Rosabeth Moss Kanter argues that 'one way or another, the innovating organisation accomplishes a high proportion of its productive changes through participation'. This chapter examines approaches to enabling participation in the organisation through group and team work, and moves beyond a tongue-in-cheek definition coined by Rosabeth Moss Kanter that 'participation is something that the top orders the middle to do to the bottom'!

In his book *Understanding Organisations* (1993), Charles Handy defines a **group** as any collection of people who perceive themselves to be a group. Handy therefore uses the notion of the subjective feeling of *belonging* as defining the group. He cites the example that 'a dozen individuals in a pub by random chance are not a group, although they may be interacting (talking), have a common objective (drink and socialisation) and be aware of each other'. Handy goes on to say that given an emergency, say a fire in the pub, then that random group of individuals will rapidly develop a collective group

identity because they start to perceive themselves as a group, with another sort of objective and with needs for other sorts of interaction.

When people start to perceive themselves as a group they will begin to develop ways of creating shared bonds, such as a name for the group, a common way of dressing, or sharing of language and assumptions. However, unless people feel a need to develop 'groupness' they will continue to exist as random collections of individuals. Most people feel a need to belong to a group although this need will vary according to such factors as individual personality characteristics. For example, new students in a university setting typically join groups in the first few days of entering a new course. Some of these groupings are self-selected while others develop by chance (e.g. someone in the adjoining room in a hall of residence, or the person you sat next to in the first lecture). Students may hang on to these initial groupings well past the time when the need for the 'grouping' (e.g. security) has disappeared.

Team goes well beyond 'group'. An effective team will share a common sense of purpose and identity. Bonds and shared perceptions will be tight, so that the team members feel that they are supporting each other. We examine the nature of teams and team formation later in this chapter.

A number of important factors influence the effectiveness of a group, including its size, the flow of communication within the group and the style of management.

There are a number of reasons why it is easier to make decisions within small groups (i.e. five or six people) rather than larger groups. The more people are drawn into the decision-making process, the more difficult it is to involve everyone, the more difficult it is to get everyone to agree, and the higher the level of dissatisfaction with the way the group operates. Individuals find it more difficult to identify with the group, and subgroups start to form. In order to prevent this fragmentation, it is increasingly likely that a leader will need to take centralised control over decision-making as the size of the group grows.

Despite the disadvantages of large groups, there are also a number of advantages. A large group will be able to call upon a greater pool of skills, energy and resources. A further benefit is that, if a wide number of members of an organisation feel that they are involved in the decision-making process, they may be more willing to implement policies.

The way in which an organisation is managed will have a significant effect on how well its groups and teams operate.

Communication within the group

The main factors influencing the flow of communication within a group are its formal organisation, its informal organisation, and the means of communication employed.

Research carried out by Bavelas (1948) and Leavitt (1951) suggested that there are four main types of communication network, as depicted in Figure 13.1. The wheel and chain networks are typified by a **centralisation** of the flow of information. Effective decision-making here depends to a great extent on those in key central positions and on the quality of the communication channels to them. These centralised forms seem to exhibit the following characteristics:

- They are highly effective at making and carrying out straightforward, well structured predictable activities.
- Levels of satisfaction for group members are relatively low compared with those for members of less centralised groups.
- The centralised form helps to strengthen the leadership position in such groups.

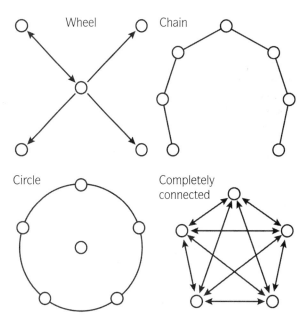

Figure 13.1 *Communication networks*

- A stable structure rapidly emerges in the group.
- The group becomes dependent on those with greatest access to relevant information.

Such a group structure lends itself to short-term operating control decisions. In contrast, the circle network and the completely connected network lend themselves to a more open, **decentralised** form of decision-making. Members of these groups are mutually interdependent, and share the decision-making process. The group is not so dependent on key individuals, and levels of satisfaction are usually greater. Disadvantages are that, because responsibility is shared, there may not be an effective mechanism for pushing decisions through. There may be a lot of talk about action without the mechanisms required to create action.

Task, action schedule and process

Whenever a group is required to work together there will be three strands involved in the group working or team process (see Figure 13.2).

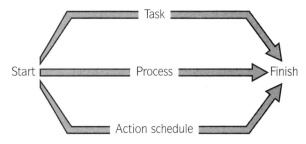

Figure 13.2 *Stages in group working at a specific activity*

The task

The **task** is the content of the work. For example, the task of a management meeting may be to decide on the location of a new factory; the task of an interview may be to select the best candidate to take up a particular post. Thus, the task is the conversion of information and opinions from group members into decisions or recommendations. In general terms this covers *what* has to be done by the team and *why*. Most groups give a lot of attention to the task.

Action schedule

The **action schedule** is concerned with how a group will be organised to do a given task. The schedule will cover such questions as who will fill the necessary roles, how progress will be checked and monitored, how it will be ensured that the group will keep to the time schedule. It will also deal with the procedures of decision-making – how to ensure that everyone gets a say, how conflict will be dealt with, etc. In general, the action schedule will cover the *where* and *how* of decision-making. Most groups will give some attention to their action schedule.

For example, an action schedule for a meeting might set down when the meeting will take place, who will attend, who will run the meeting, how decisions would be voted on, and other procedural matters.

Process

The **process** is the interaction that takes place between members of a group. It is about how people work together, their relationships and the feelings created by their behaviour within the group. It involves interpersonal skills such as listening to others and helping others to join in a discussion. It involves expressions of feelings and the giving and receiving of feedback. In general it covers *who does what and when*. Many groups pay little attention to process.

These three threads of group working are all important in group decision-making. A group that concentrates on its action schedules and its process entirely may have a wonderful time but is unlikely to achieve the task. It will not be long before morale suffers and the group disintegrates. In contrast, concentration purely on the task is likely to lead to arguments about how things should be organised, and inattention to group members' thoughts and feelings will lead to mishandled resources and to misunderstandings.

Case Study

Different approaches

A group of individuals were brought together as an experiment to work on a project. Half of the group had backgrounds of working for charities and social service organisations, the other half came from large business organisations. They were given four days to plan the delivery of a consignment of materials in Africa. The members of the group with commercial business experience immediately wanted to set targets, plan schedules and get the project organised. In contrast, the members with voluntary sector experience wanted to start off by carrying out activities designed to weld the group together into a bonded team.

Questions

1. Why do you think the two 'parts' of the group wanted to set about the project in different ways?

2. How did their approaches vary?

3. Which of the approaches do you feel would have been the most appropriate in the situation?

Case study comment. The reader may be interested to know that in this particular instance the section of the group working for the business organisations proved to be more effective, at least in the short run. Because of the urgency of getting the task done they were able to come up with solutions, whereas the other individuals spent so long getting to know each other that they failed to come up with practical proposals. This does not, however, prove that the task-oriented approach is better.

Formal groups and informal groups

Formal groups

A formal group is one created for a specific purpose; it might be a work-group, a project team, a committee, a board of a company, etc. In contrast, an informal group develops in a less structured way (e.g. the *ad hoc* meeting or discussion, the luncheon group). A formal group is recognised as 'official' and will normally be set up to perform a set task or group of tasks. Often in organisations such a group will set about transforming given inputs into outputs (e.g. raw materials and other resources into final end-products, or accounting information into a set of finished accounts).

Rensis Likert (1961) thought that a key role for a manager in an organisation was acting as a linchpin between a range of interlocking groups. Likert felt that managers create a network structure by simultaneously acting as superiors in some work-groups and as subordinates in higher-level work-groups. The networking of an array of work groups creates the 'total organisation'.

It is possible to identify a variety of work-groups depending on their level of permanence. Permanent work-groups are the type that frequently appear in organisational charts as departments, divisions or teams. They vary in size. The common feature is that they are created to perform an on-going work function. Eventually they may be closed down or reconfigured.

Temporary work-groups (or task groups) are set up simply to solve a problem or perform a defined task before being wrapped up. A good example of a temporary work-group is a 'task force'.

Groups may be enjoyed or hated by their members. For example, a student may like or dislike a particular lecture or tutorial group. An employee may be happy or unhappy with a grouping of work colleagues.

Formal groups have far more structure, and apparently clearer purposes, patterns and ways of going about things than an informal group. They have clearly defined rules and schedules. Formal groups are usually created specifically to work towards predetermined objectives, whereas informal groups just 'happen'.

Informal groups

Informal groups come into existence spontaneously within the organisation rather than being officially created. Most formal groups, in fact, contain more than one informal grouping. Friendship groups are a type of informal group that develop among people who naturally 'get on' with one another. For example, in a school staffroom or a works canteen you will generally find informal groupings of people that have developed over a number of years. Friendship may be extended outside the work environment or may just take place at work. Interest groups are made up of people with shared interests, which may be job-related or may be focused on interests outside work. For example, an informal interest group may be made up of people who play for the same football team or who share a common interest in the Internet.

Informal groups are very important and often support work objectives. They may help work to be done better and faster, and support commitment in the workplace. Shared interests and friendship help to solidify commitment to the organisation. Informal groupings help individuals to satisfy some of their higher level needs in the workplace – a sense of belonging, a sense of security and shared interest, shared goals and values, and so on.

Psychological groups

In *Organisational Psychology* (1970), Edgar Schein went one step further to identify the importance of **psychological groups** which meet four criteria. Members of a psychological group:

- Truly interact with one another
- Perceive themselves to be part of a group
- Share a common sense of group purpose
- Are psychologically aware of one another.

For groups to work effectively it is helpful if they operate as psychological groups. Most informal groups qualify but many formal ones do not. For a group to meet the final criterion, then group members need to understand what each other member needs from the group and what each is prepared to contribute.

Discussion points

1. Consider a formal work-group that you are a member of. To what extent does this group operate as a psychological group?

2. Can you think of examples of informal groups acting within a formal group?

The purpose of teams

A team is a small group of people working together to achieve a common purpose. The difference between a team and an ordinary work-group lies in the idea of *mutual responsibility*, *reciprocity* and *common commitment*. Any sports team manager will tell you that they are seeking to turn a collection of talented (or not so talented) individuals into a collective unit that builds on individual contributions to an overall shared responsibility for high-level performance.

Dumaine (1994) identifies five common types of team:

- *Management teams*. These are made up of managers representing various functions, such as production and sales. They coordinate the work of other teams.
- *Problem-solving teams*. These are groups of employees who work together as a team to solve a specific problem and then disband.
- *Work-teams*. These are an increasingly popular type of team, undertaking the daily work of the organisation. When they are empowered they are known as self-managed teams.
- *Quality circles*. These are groups of workers and supervisors meeting from time to time to discuss workplace problems and suggest solutions.
- *Virtual teams*. A characteristic of this new type of teamwork is that members talk and participate by computer.

Dumaine suggests that a common problem with the use of teams is that organisations do not think carefully enough about what type will be most effective for the job. In some cases teams may be over-used. Does the task in hand really require interaction in a team or would it be more effectively undertaken by an individual?

Schermerhorn, Hunt and Osborn (1997) distinguish between teams that recommend things, teams that make or do things, and teams that run things.

- Teams that recommend things are created to study specific problems and recommend solutions to them. Typically they work with a target completion date and are disbanded when the task is completed.
- Teams that make or do things perform ongoing tasks, such as marketing or finance, and operate on a permanent or semi-permanent basis as a general rule. Long-term working relationships are therefore important in this type of team.
- Teams that run things consist of individuals with major responsibilities in an organisation or organisational subunit. Such teams will need to identify organisational objectives, values and purposes and help others to fulfil these ends.

In recent years, downsizing in organisations has meant that many middle-management responsibilities have been shifted down on to teams of employees who have also taken on the authority to make decisions.

The emphasis on teamwork suggests that well-organised teams will outperform the same group of individuals operating in isolation. It is therefore important to identify the processes involved in team-working and some of the characteristics of an effective team.

TEAMS AND TEAM-BUILDING

Most organisations introduce **teamwork** because of the perceived benefits of motivation of personnel and reduced costs from more effective working practices or decisions. Team-work occurs when the members work together to improve performance through sharing core values, all of which promote the use of skills to accomplish common goals. Teamwork is most likely to be successful when it operates in a supportive environment. The atmosphere within the organisation therefore needs to support cooperation and trust.

There are a number of aspects of **team-building**, including:

- helping team members to identify shared objectives and purposes
- developing interpersonal skills within team members (e.g. listening skills, supporting skills, encouragement skills)
- developing team rewards for supportive behaviour
- developing collective problem-solving skills
- building up a store of personal goodwill to overcome problems
- developing team confidence and competence
- recognising personal strengths and weaknesses, technical and personal.

Today there are a variety of approaches to team-building. It may involve meetings to discuss insights into work-related issues, or alternatively might involve putting the team in a fresh context (e.g. an outdoor activities weekend based on team collaboration).

The development of teamworking skills may include exercises and sessions which seek to explore and develop relevant skills. Tasks may be devised for groups to help them develop consensus decision-making or listening skills. The typical *stages* of team-building are shown in Figure 13.3.

- A problem is identified in terms of existing team relationships or an opportunity to build a new team structure.
- Group members work together to gather data relating to the problem or opportunity.
- Group members collaboratively analyse the data and create a plan for improvement.
- Group members collaboratively create action plans for improvement.
- The action plan is implemented by the group.
- The group collaboratively evaluates the impact the new plans are having.
- The process is improved.

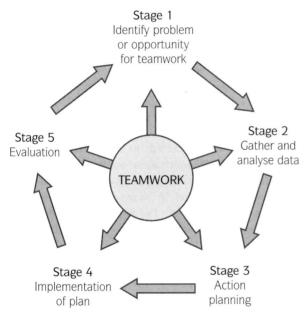

Figure 13.3 *The team-building cycle*

Case Study

A case for teamwork

Until recently the plant at Super Cement Ltd was operated using an old-fashioned relationship between managers and employees. Basically, the managers made the decisions which they then passed on to employees in a tightly written rulebook and lists of instructions. This worked well for a number of years. Employees were used to doing what they were told and their work was highly routine.

However, over the years the cement industry has changed and become a lot more competitive. As a result Super Cement has replaced much of its existing plant with new automated machines requiring a smaller workforce. The equipment is more reliant on computer control and other types of automation. This means that a lot more responsibility needs to be given to ground-level employees. In addition it is essential for employees to work in teams who pool skills and knowledge. These teams need to be highly 'bonded' to ensure maximum success.

Questions

1. Why would the old top-down approach be no longer appropriate?

2. What teamworking skills do you think the 'new type' of employee at Super Cement needs to learn?

3. How should Super Cement go about making sure that its employees develop these new skills?

Selecting team members

The process of **team selection** is quite different from the selection of individuals or groups. The process should involve identifying potential members with a specific contribution to make to the team, or with the ability to pull with the team.

Team selection therefore is rarely concerned with finding the individual with the highest intellect, the greatest information technology skills, the highest level of competence in a work-related task, etc. Rather, team selection will be concerned with identifying a range of personality traits, such as the ability to listen to others, to encourage others to share their ideas, to help the team to move forward, and to make a contribution to shared decision-making processes.

Training people in teamworking

There are two broad approaches to training people in teamworking: experiential learning and counselling.

Experiential learning is learning by carrying out real or simulated tasks. This may involve analysing case studies. More often it involves undertaking a number of brief tasks which can be completed successfully only if people use the necessary team skills. After each task the team, with the guidance of the trainer, analyses what lessons were learned from the exercise.

The success or failure of experiential learning depends on how seriously the team takes the tasks. In many programmes the outcome of each task has no real consequences for those taking part, so the tasks may not be taken seriously unless the trainer is skilled in motivating the team.

This is why many business schools now include some outdoor activities within their MBA courses. If a team indoors is asked to build a Lego tower to meet certain criteria, and it collapses, nobody worries too much. If they are asked to build a raft and float across a river, failure is more memorable and any lessons tend to be remembered. The consequences of failure are then real.

A **counselling approach** is usually more appropriate with senior management teams, in which the trainer is more a consultant and mentor and works both with the team and with its individual members.

Case Study

Core Solutions

Core Solutions is a national partnership of counselling and development organisations based in the Scottish Highlands. It uses consultancy counselling and outdoor activities to provide an individually tailored service to develop boards of directors. Building trust within the team is central to its activities. It argues that trust is the basis of open and collaborative relationships. It holds teams together and reduces resistance to change. Transferable team skills are now essential if one wants to get things done. Bonding people together into teams is no longer a luxury but a necessity.

Questions

1. Why do people who normally work in teams need to engage also in team-building activities?

2. What do you think the advantages are of developing experiential teamworking in outdoor activities as opposed to simulated games in indoor workshop sessions?

Team roles

When people work together in a team, they adopt particular roles. For example, one person may have the role of monitoring progress, checking the time-keeping or acting as leader. There is a tendency for one member to take on the task functions and for others to adopt the maintenance role.

Task functions are those which help the group to get tasks done as effectively and efficiently as possible, including:

- proposing objectives, clarifying goals
- seeking information and opinions
- keeping the group on track
- summarising ideas
- suggesting ways forward
- evaluating contributions.

Team members who take on the **maintenance role** offer support and encouragement to the group. This involves:

- supporting other group members
- ensuring all members of the group are included
- reconciling disagreements and reducing tension
- making suggestions for compromise
- monitoring the group.

The effectiveness of a team will, to some extent, depend upon the mix of roles which team members take on. Successful teams tend to have a range of appropriate personalities and qualities. In *Management Teams: Why They Succeed or Fail* (1981), Robert Belbin identified eight roles required within a well-functioning team:

- The *chairperson* coordinates the efforts of the team to ensure that it makes best use of its resources in achieving its goals.
- The *shaper* sets objectives and priorities and drives the team towards successful completion of the task.
- The *plant* comes up with new ideas and strategies.
- The *monitor evaluator* is able to analyse problems and evaluate progress.
- The *resource investigator* is outgoing and will explore and report on ideas and developments from outside the group.
- The *company worker* is an administrator rather than a leader and good at carrying out agreed plans.
- The *teamworker* supports the team, helps to keep it together and tries to improve communication between members.
- The *finisher* maintains momentum in the team and plays an important part in getting the task finished.

Belbin suggested that, although team members may tend towards one of these roles, most people would also be able to undertake a second role.

If people have particular attributes and ways of working which suggest that they will tend to take up particular roles, then it is obviously important that there is a balance of roles in order to produce an effective team.

Discussion point

Think about groups and teams of which you have been a member for work-related tasks (e.g. doing a combined class project, or a workplace project as part of a part-time job). Can you identify particular individuals who tended to play any of the roles outlined above? Which of the roles came most naturally to you?

Team-mapping

Research has shown that individuals like to organise their work in various ways. Management consultants have attempted to devise techniques for identifying people's work preferences in order to be able to decide which roles they could take on in a team situation. For example, the McCann Team Management Index can be used to discover information about people's work preferences, which are then used to place individuals on a Team Management Indicator as in Figure 13.4.

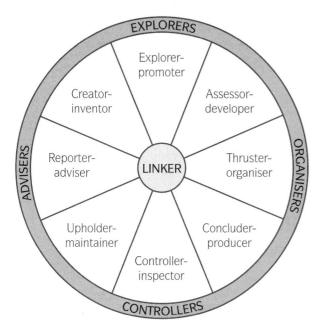

Figure 13.4 *The Team Management Indicator*

Margerison McCann describes nine key team roles, as follows.

- *Reporter–advisers* are good at generating information and gathering it together in such a way that it can be understood. Such people are usually patient, and prepared to delay making a decision until they know as much as they can about the work to be done. Some people feel that they procrastinate and put things off. However, for the reporter–adviser it is better to be accurate than to put forward advice which later might be seen to be in error. Such people are invaluable as 'support' members of the team, but they are not likely to be the ones who will get things organised. Indeed, their concern is to make sure that the job is done correctly.

- *Creator–innovators* are people who have a number of ideas which may well contradict and upset the existing way of doing things. Such people can be very independent and wish to experiment and pursue their ideas regardless of the present systems and methods. They need to be allowed to pursue their ideas without disrupting the present way of working until their new approaches have been proved. Many organisations therefore set up research and development units (often separated from the production units) to allow such people to develop their ideas and see if they come to fruition. On every team it is important to have people who are idea-oriented and to give them an opportunity to talk through their views, even though it may seem at the time to be disturbing the existing way of operating.

- *Explorer–promoters* are usually excellent at taking up an idea and making people enthusiastic about it. They will find out what is happening outside the organisation and compare new ideas with what is being done by other people. They are also good at bringing back contacts and information and resources which can help the innovation move forward. They may not necessarily be good at controlling details, but they are excellent at seeing the wide picture. They are very capable of pushing an idea forward, even if they are not always the best people to organise and control it.

- *Assessor–developers* look for ways and means in which an idea can work in a practical way. Their concern is to see if the market wants the innovation and they will therefore test it against some practical criteria. Very often they will produce a prototype or do a market research study. Their whole interest is in developing an innovation to the point where it can work. However, once they have done this, they will probably not be interested in producing it on a regular basis. Instead, they prefer to move off and look at another project which they can assess and develop.

- *Thruster–organisers* are the people who get things done. Once they have been convinced that the idea is of interest, they will set up procedures and systems and make the task into a work reality. They push people and systems to ensure the deadlines can be met. They can be extremely impatient but they get things done, even if it does mean that on the way certain 'feathers are ruffled'.
- *Concluder–producers* take great pride in producing a product or service to a standard. They will do this on a regular basis and feel that their work is fulfilled if their quotas and plans are met. Indeed, they like working to set procedures and doing things in a regular way. The fact that they produced something yesterday does not mean that they will be bored with producing it tomorrow. This is in contrast to the creator–innovators who dislike doing similar things day after day and want the variety and challenge of doing things differently. For the concluder–producer the important thing is to use existing skills rather than to continually change and learn new ways of doing things. They therefore enjoy reproducing things and achieving the plans that they set.
- *Controller–inspectors* are people who enjoy doing detailed work and making sure that the facts and figures are correct. They are careful and meticulous. Indeed, one of their great strengths is that they concentrate for long periods of time upon a particular task. This contrasts with the explorer–promoter who continually needs a wide variety of tasks. Controller–inspectors like to pursue something in depth and to make sure that the work is done according to plan in an accurate way. They are extremely valuable in financial and quality issues.
- *Upholder–maintainers* are very good at making sure the team has a sound basis for operations. They take pride in maintaining both the physical and social side of work. Such people can very well become the 'conscience' of the team and provide a lot of support and help to team members. They usually have strong views on the way the team should be run based on their convictions and beliefs. If these are upset, such people can become rather obstinate and difficult. However, when they believe in what the team is doing, they can become a tremendous source of strength and energy and often make excellent negotiators.

In the middle of all these work functions are the *linkers*. These are people who map close to the centre of the team and therefore have considerable coordinating abilities. All of the other roles that we have mentioned also involve some aspects of linking, but the people closer to the 'hub' of the team are more able to coordinate and integrate the work of others. Essentially, all managers should look towards developing linking skills, whatever other key

strengths they have. However, not all managers are good at linking, in which case they need to have someone on their team who can perform this role. On many occasions the manager needs to make a conscious effort, otherwise the team will begin to disintegrate.

Discussion points

1. If an organisation is aware of the preferences and strengths of individuals, it should be possible to select and develop more effective teams. Which of the above roles do you see as being most essential for a well-functioning team? Is it possible to rank them in any way? To what extent does the importance of each role depend on the situation?

2. The following have been identified as the qualities of a successful team worker: (a) a good listener; (b) good persuasive communication skills; (c) can express technical ideas lucidly to people from other disciplines; (d) receptive to new ideas; (e) not afraid to look foolish by airing new or unconventional ideas; (f) understands and is committed to the team's objectives; (g) can give and take constructive criticism; (h) trusts and is trusted by fellow team-members; (i) expresses feelings honestly and openly; (j) does not claim personal credit for a team success. Which of these characteristics do you honestly believe to represent most closely the way in which you operate in a team situation?

Stages in team development

In their book *The Wisdom of Teams* (1993), Jon Katzenbach and Doug Smith argue that there is a threshold that a group must cross before it become a team. Their definition of a team is:

'... a small number of people with complementary skills who are committed to a common purpose, performance goals and an approach for which they hold themselves accountable'.

Katzenbach and Smith make the point that managers need to be able to understand the ingredients of a team if they are to operate a successful organisation. They set out a simple framework for the development of teams, and show a team performance curve (see Figure 13.5).

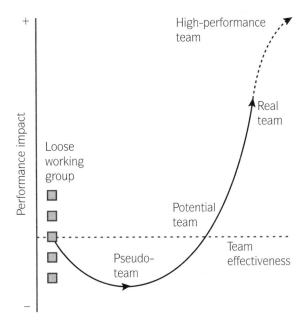

Figure 13.5 *A team performance curve*

- *The loose working group.* This is a collection of individuals for whom there is no real opportunity or need to become a team. Each work-group member produces something that helps the task to be completed without feeling a real part of the team. Being a part of the work-group places no more demand on an individual than if he or she were working independently.
- *The pseudo-team.* In this situation there is no joint benefit of being a part of the team. Indeed, each member's performance is worse than if working alone. This is because there is no focus, no common sense of purpose and no set of goals. The group members are confused as to what they should be doing or how they should be working together. At some stage in your life you are almost certain to work in a pseudo-team. It is very frustrating. Team members are 'feeling their way in the dark'. This may generate antagonism between members, and the team will quickly crumble.
- *The potential team.* This is a collection of individuals with a clear performance need. They are seriously seeking to improve their impact on the group. In other words, they

are aware that there is a need for something to be done in order to improve their performance and they want to do it. Unfortunately, however, they lack clarity about their aims as well as the discipline needed for a common working approach. Also, they will not have established the final criterion – mutual accountability. Many organisations are full of potential teams. This provides a real opportunity and a challenge for management.
- *The real team.* It is worth repeating that a real team is 'a small number of people with complementary skills who are committed to a common purpose, performance goals, and an approach for which they hold themselves mutually accountable'.
- *The high-performance team.* In addition to meeting the definition for a real team, this group will also be deeply committed – even beyond the team set-up – to the personal growth and success of its members. It will significantly outperform other teams.

Taking a different approach, Tuckman and Jensen (1997) identified four phases of team development: forming, storming, norming and performing.

- *Phase 1: Forming.* A number of individuals come together. They start to exchange ideas and gather information about the nature of the task; what needs to be done and when? They also explore how other members of the group operate and what behaviour is acceptable.
- *Phase 2: Storming.* The group begins to exchange ideas as they try to reach agreement on objectives and strategy. There is often conflict and disagreement.
- *Phase 3: Norming.* The group begins to share ideas. Group cohesion starts to develop and members start to act collaboratively.
- *Phase 4: Performing.* The group, now a team, is able to turn its attention to the task. A pattern of working is established. Members may assume particular roles or functions. Every member of the team is therefore able to make the best possible contribution.

Different groups or teams will obviously go through this cycle at different rates and may face different problems at each stage. The early stage of group formation, when there is no leader, may be dominated by particular individuals. At this point quieter members may not be heard. If a group is very task-focused then while in the short-term progress may be rapid, the group may face long-term difficulties. Social relationships in the group may be so poor that no team spirit is evident. On the other hand, an over-emphasis on team processes may mean that the task is never completed.

Teams may well go through these phases in a non-linear way, repeating earlier phases in the cycle. A change in

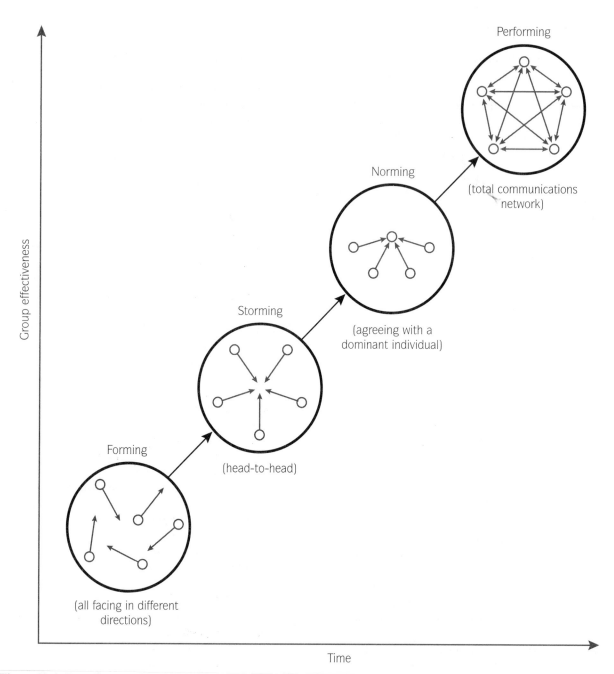

Figure 13.6 *From 'forming' to 'performing'*

membership, for example, may cause the group or team to revert to an earlier phase.

Team cohesiveness and identity

We use the term 'cohesiveness' to describe the degree to which members of a team are attracted to and motivated to remain a part of the team. Creating a **team identity** is thus an important part of creating such cohesiveness. In recent years we have become used to footballers lifting up the front of their shirt and kissing them after scoring a goal, to show their loyalty to a club and a team. It is argued that the most successful Premier League teams are the ones that have this sort of team identity. Teams have an identity when they are distinctive – when you are a team member you are proud of the fact. A number of organisation's have extensive 'tests', 'rituals' and 'initiation' ceremonies which people need to pass through. When they are successful they can wear the team insignia. To choose an extreme example, to become part of a Hell's Angels chapter you have to show absolute allegiance to the team – first of all by doing menial tasks for existing members, and then by carrying out a serious offence against the mores and laws of society in order to win your place in the Hell's Angels.

Case Study

Hartson joins 'The Crazy Gang'

The Wimbledon football team is famous for its initiation ceremonies in order to become a member of 'The Crazy Gang'. When John Hartson joined Wimbledon from West Ham in mid-January 1999 he was given a typical welcome. First his new team-mates hung his designer tracksuit out of the changing-room window at the club's training ground and set it ablaze. Next he was thrown into a puddle of water. It was not the sort of treatment most £7.5 million strikers would have expected, but Hartson took it in good heart. 'I am up for a laugh and maybe if a new player signs next week I will be getting involved,' he said.

Questions

1. What is the function of the initiation ceremony that John Hartson went through at Wimbledon?

2. What characteristics do you think a player would need to have to fit into the Wimbledon set up?

3. What might be the benefits of creating the sort of team identity that Wimbledon have?

4. Can you think of other organisations that have initiation rituals in order to build team identity?

Team cohesiveness tends to be high when:

- the team consists of members with similar attitudes, ages, backgrounds and needs
- the members respect each other's abilities
- they share common objectives
- team tasks require interdependent efforts
- team size is relatively small

- the team is physically isolated from other groups
- the team experiences and is able to share performance success.
- the team is able to cope successfully with temporary setbacks and failures.

Team cohesiveness can be further enhanced by:

- rewarding effective team performance
- improving the quality of interactions between team members
- creating competition and rivalry against other teams
- keeping the team together for fairly lengthy periods of time.

Loyalty

In a highly cohesive team, members value their place and are very loyal. The individual members conform to group norms. The level of cohesiveness and the extent to which members conform to team norms is a very good indicator of the likely success of the team. Of course, it is also true that when a team is not performing very well then some members will start to blame other individuals and team cohesiveness will decline. Successful organisations are likely to be based on the 'winning team' principle. They will have highly integrated teams of people who share the same values and aspirations. There will be a strong bond between team members, which leads to powerful group norms.

Research tends to indicate that the harder it is to get into a team, the more committed successful individuals will be. They will be prepared to make 'sacrifices' to get into the team (e.g. by training and hard work). Once they have achieved membership they will want all their efforts to be worthwhile, and will strive to maintain the success of the team. Their motivation will drive towards the successful achievement of team objectives.

Rivalry with other teams is also a strong driving force. When individuals can identify a common enemy, they will work closely together to defeat this 'threat'. For example, during both world wars all social classes in Britain worked together as never before. Everyone perceived themselves to be threatened by a common enemy so they were prepared to forget their divisions and cooperate. (Of course, once the threat disappears, the old rivalries and divisions may come to the surface again.)

The team spirit tends to increase the longer the team is together. Another important ingredient is the achievement of success, as in the adage 'nothing succeeds like success'. The winning team may continue as such for a long time because of cultural expectations that arise within the team. In cricket we talk about the great West Indian teams of the 1970s and 80s, and in football we recall the 'Busby Babes'. These teams were successful with a relatively small playing personnel over a number of years. Business can learn a lot from the 'winning team' approach.

Case Study

Brian Kidd at Blackburn Rovers

Jack Walker was the man who poured millions into Blackburn Rovers as Chairman to turn it into a top-flight European club, with big-name players such as Alan Shearer and Ashley Ward. Blackburn won the English Premiership in 1995.

However, the glory year turned out to be the beginning of a nightmare. First Kenny Dalglish left as manager. His successor and former partner Ray Harford followed him as relegation worries and player discontent replaced previous harmony. Roy Hodgson's arrival from Inter Milan in July 1997 was supposed to signal a new order. When he left, the team had hit rock bottom in the Premiership and players' confidence was also at basement level.

Skipper Tim Sherwood had become so disconsolate he seemed certain to be leaving, too, The feeling among the rest of the players was that Premiership survival may already be beyond them.

When Blackburn appointed Brian Kidd as manager in late 1998 they were taking a gamble. He had formerly been Alex Ferguson's 'number 2' at Manchester United. When he took the job there was as much doubt about his managerial abilities as surprise that he had left United. He found himself forced to answer suggestions that he may not have the personality to be his own boss. Yet within seven games (four wins and three draws) it appeared that Jack Walker had made the right decision.

With Kidd it quickly appeared that things were on the upturn. After watching Blackburn beat Leeds in early January 1999, Walker stated: 'On the evidence of what has been happening I think we have got it right. Brian has done a smashing job so far and what is plain is that there is a new spirit about the team and the whole place.' One of the players, the Republic of Ireland winger Damien Duff, said: 'Everybody is really bouncy again. We

are enjoying our football and enjoying our training. Brian Kidd has really shown he knows what management is all about.'

Questions

1. Why do you think players had lost their team spirit prior to Brian Kidd joining the club?

2. How was he able to win back 'team spirit' at the club.

3. Football is a notoriously fickle game. What has happened to Brian Kidd and Blackburn Rovers since this book was written?

The concept of **tribal features** has been applied by some business writers to the impact of organisational culture on groups and individuals. (A tribe is a social division of people based on common descent, territory and culture.) They argue that people will increasingly take on the shared values of a particular organisational culture. They will begin to develop the same assumptions and values. They may start to dress alike and to use the same sort of language. They will begin to think in similar patterns and feel more comfortable with someone from their own tribe. They may be quite hostile to the attitudes and values of people from other tribes.

Discussion point

What 'tribal features' can you identify in an organisation that you are familiar with?

Commitment to shared beliefs

A basic feature of teamwork is that each member's outcome depends not only on his or her own actions, but also on the actions of others in the team. This interdependence strongly encourages mutually beneficial behaviour. For example, for a bobsleigh team to win a gold medal at the winter Olympics every member must give 100 per cent to the team effort. This can come about only if the team has a set of shared beliefs.

Today it is widely recognised that one can generate shared beliefs in an organisation by placing a strong emphasis on employee involvement (EI). Terms such as 'empowerment' and 'participation', have become very fashionable, and **EI groups** have been created in many modern organisations. EI groups meet regularly, often outside their normal work units, for the purpose of jointly addressing important workplace issues. EI is closely tied up with 'total quality' and 'continuous improvement' concepts. Employee involvement and quality circle groups make important contributions in dealing with work related problems and issues. By involving employees in this way they feel that they have a shared ownership of the processes and practices of which they are a part, that they have a vested interest in the success of their teams and in the success of the whole organisation. Such approaches are particularly successful when employees also are given shares in the organisation so that they are owners as well as employees.

The notion of the **self-managing team** (SMT) is an extension of the employee involvement process. Self-managing teams are small groups of people empowered to manage themselves and the work they do on a day-to-day basis. A self managing team will be one in which the members:

- make decisions on who does what in the team
- decide on work schedules and patterns
- are multi-skilled to do more than one job
- train each other to do jobs performed by the team
- evaluate each other's performance and team performance
- are jointly held accountable for the team's performance.

In a self-managing team there is on-going discussion of work, and there will be rotation and sharing of jobs. Such a team will only be successful when the aims and objectives are clear from the start, and where team members have played a key role in defining those objectives.

Multi-disciplinary teams

In their book *Super Teams* (1986), Hastings, Bixby and Choudry-Lawton set out a good example of cross-departmental teamworking in the case of a company called Logicorp which manufactures and installs electronic surveillance equipment. The company had been growing very quickly over a ten-year period, through acquisition and opening overseas subsidiaries. It had reached 1000 employees and was set to double again in a two-year period. The company was determined to preserve some of the traditional strengths it had gained from operating as a smaller company while growing to a larger company. In particular it wanted individual employees to identify with the organisation's success, its informal inter-departmental networking, and

attitudes which encouraged creativity and innovation. The company therefore set up two types of teams:

- inter-departmental teams, working on operational problems spanning departments
- task forces, working on strategy – including policy and organisational issues.

Training in teamworking was provided. Teams worked through four stages of activity over a 3–6 month period:

- negotiating success criteria with project sponsors
- exploring the problem and arriving at solutions
- reporting to the board and winning approval
- setting up an implementation programme and in many instances managing the implementation process.

The types of issues tackled by these teams were:

- What new areas should the company enter in the future in the light of growth objectives?
- What structures would the company need to sustain innovation and motivation?
- How could the quality of customer service be improved?

TEAM DYNAMICS

In his book *Process Consultation* (1988), Edgar Schein points out that when new teams are formed, or when people join teams for the first time, they have concerns about a number of issues. These relate to:

- participation (will they be allowed to participate?)
- goals (do they share the same goals as other team members?)
- control (will they have any control and influence over the team?)
- relationships (how should they interact with other people?)
- processes (will they be able to cope with the processes?).

Schein believes that individuals behave in a way that reflects these concerns, which can lead to problems in working as a team. He identifies three types of situation where 'anxious' new members of a team may not contribute effectively (at least in the short term) because of their anxiety:

- The **tough battler** wants to make sure that they carve out a place in the team. They therefore take an aggressive stance which often means crossing other team members and may go against creating a cohesive team. The tough battler is a bit like a dog that cocks its leg up against every available tree to claim territory. You can probably identify such individuals in teams that you have worked in.

- The **friendly helpers** are seeking to be liked within the group – they are looking for love. They may go around trying to be friendly with everyone and may join cliques, and subgroups to win extra friendship. Rather than contributing their skills to the group they tend to waste team time by seeking friendship.
- The **objective thinkers** are uncertain in a new team situation because they are trying to think out the fit between the team aims and objectives and personal aims and objectives. Until they are sure that the team is pulling in a direction which fits with the requirements of the individual, they may contribute little.

It is not just in creating new teams that anxiety occurs. Anxiety is an on-going aspect of **group dynamics**. Within a team individuals play roles. (A role can be defined as a set of expectations for the behaviour of an individual playing a particular part, or holding a particular position in the team.) When the role of an individual is not clear this will cause anxiety and uncertainty and lead to failure of the team to perform optimally. When roles change over time, **role ambiguity** may crop up – team members are now not sure what they should be doing, or how their role has changed. Members of the team become unsure about what others expect of them. Role conflict will arise when team members are unable to respond appropriately to the expectations of others. **Role negotiation** is therefore an important dynamic of group interactions. Individuals within a team need to work out their roles in relation to each other and in terms of meeting team objectives.

Group norms

Some of the most important rules in an organisation are unwritten; these are **group norms**. Norms are generally agreed, informal rules which guide a group member's behaviour. Often group members may not realise the full impact of these norms because they become taken for granted. The norms may relate to such matters as working extra hard when a deadline needs to be met, contributing to the farewell presents of colleagues, keeping the office tidy, etc. Many of the norms of an organisation will contribute to its success. There are essentially two types:

- **Prescriptive norms** set out behaviour that should be carried out, such as being polite to customers, recycling envelopes within the organisation, etc.
- **Proscriptive norms** set out behaviour that should not be carried out, such as sitting in the head of department's chair, pinching someone's bottom, etc.

Working groups establish prescriptive and proscriptive norms which become deeply embedded in the organisation's culture. They can develop in various ways.

- Over a period of time, ways of doing things can become institutionalised within a particular organisation (e.g. calling a senior manager Mrs Smith, rather than Molly).
- Norms can carry over from previous practice and situations (e.g. when a doctor changes from one group practice to another, he or she will continue the professional conduct of allowing routine patients only 10 minutes of time).
- Explicit statements from other group members ('That's the way we do it around here!') can lead to norms.
- A critical event in the group's history can lead to a norm. A particular event determines the way things are handled in future (e.g. a member of a Premier League football team makes an off the cuff comment to the media which is widely misreported; the club's players agree that in future they will not talk to the media).

Normative pressures are very important in organisational life. In an entrepreneurial organisation there may be a strong emphasis on hard work and commitment. This value rubs off on all group members. By contrast, in a non-entrepreneurial organisation the norm may be that everyone goes home at 5 pm and does not think about the organisation until they arrive at work the next day.

Norms reflect both the formal culture of an organisation and informal relationships between people. The more formalised rules and codes of behaviour are an important part of the cultural framework. Many will have corresponding sanctions if they are not complied with. However, in some organisations norms are not clear-cut and there is considerable scope for interpretation.

Decision-making behaviour

It is generally accepted that the quality of decision-making by a group is likely to be enhanced because of the quantity and quality of input. It is also clear that the cost to organisations of teams instead of individuals undertaking tasks is high. It is important, therefore, that teams make quality decisions, and that their work is more effective than individual efforts. Vroom and Yetton (1973) identified three criteria for measuring the effectiveness of decision-making:

- the quality of the decision reached
- the time it takes to reach the decision
- the extent to which the decision is accepted by those it affects and who have to work with it.

One of the advantages of team decisions is that there should be a higher commitment to the decision and its implementation if people have shared in making it. Schein (1988) identifies the following six methods by which groups make decisions:

- *lack of response* – an action is chosen simply as a result of lack of interest or lack of discussion
- *authority rule* – one person dominates and establishes the course for action
- *minority rule* – a small group dominates and establishes the course for action
- *majority rule* – a vote is taken to choose from a range of alternatives
- *consensus* – there is some disagreement about the best course, but everyone agrees to try a particular option
- *unanimity* – everybody wants to follow the same course of action.

Some of these approaches will be far more effective than others, according to the circumstances. For example, if decisions are made by lack of response then a very haphazard approach is being adopted with no clear commitment to anything. In decision by authority, the decision can be made quickly but its effectiveness depends on the quality of the leaders thinking on the subject and their overall knowledge of the field. A similar criticism can be levelled at decision by minority. A common form of decision making is by majority rule. The problem with such an approach, however, is that there will be winners and losers. Some people may vote for an ally or to spike someone else's guns, rather than through the logic of the decision to be made. Decision by consensus is helpful in that it builds up a spirit of loyalty and trust within the organisation; individuals are prepared to try others ideas even though they may not be convinced that this is the best course. A unanimous decision is where everyone agrees on the best course of action after detailed debate. If such an approach is taken then everyone gets behind the decision, and feels a shared ownership for it.

Discussion point

Think of a group or team you are familiar with. Which of the above approaches to decision-making is most frequently used, and why? What is the effect on morale and motivation?

Schermerhorn, Hunt and Osborn (1997) suggest the following approach for achieving group consensus:

- Avoid blindly arguing your case. Present your position clearly and logically, but listen to others' reactions, considering them carefully before pressing your point.
- Do not change your mind just to reach agreement and avoid conflict. Yield to or support only those positions you believe have merit and sound foundations.
- Avoid using 'conflict-reducing' procedures, such as majority vote, tossing a coin, averaging or bargaining.
- Try to involve everyone. Seek out and respect differences of opinion. Allow disagreements to bring a wide range of information and opinions to the deliberations.
- Do not assume that someone must win and someone must lose when discussion reaches a stalemate. Keep pressing to find an alternative acceptable to all members.
- Discuss the assumptions underlying positions, listen carefully to one another, and encourage the participation of all members.

Dysfunctional teams

Dysfunctional teams are those that fail to pull in the desired direction. From the discussion throughout this chapter, it can be deduced that the main causes of dysfunctionality are:

- lack of clear aims and objectives
- confusion over whether the emphasis is on the task, the process, or the action schedule
- inability of team members to operate as a team
- personality clashes
- lack of effective processes for managing the team
- uncertainty in the environment.
- inability of the team to cope with change.

Clearly there are a range of solutions to these difficulties. Team-building can be used to try to reconstruct the team.

Team-building will involve helping individuals to work better together, to clarify aims and objectives, and to clarify processes.

A dysfunctional team is a major problem for any organisation because it leads to wasted resources, particularly to wasted time, and to the demotivation of individuals. It is not surprising that people want to leave or abandon dysfunctional teams. To avoid dysfunctional teams you should take into account all of the lessons suggested in the earlier parts of this chapter.

REFERENCES

Bavelas, A., *A Mathematical Model of Group Structure*, Applied Anthropology, vol. 7, 1948.

Belbin, Robert, *Management Teams: Why They Succeed or Fail*, Butterworth–Heinemann, 1981.

Brian, R., *The Trouble with Teams*, Fortune, 1994.

Dumaine, R., *Team Structures*, Penguin, 1994.

Handy, Charles, *Understanding Organisations*, Penguin, 1993.

Hastings, N., Bixby, C. and Choudry-Lawton, A., *Super Teams*, Gower, 1986

Kanter, Rosabeth Moss, *The Change Masters*, Thomson Business Press, 1995.

Katzenbach, Jon and Smith, Doug, *The Wisdom of Teams*, Harvard Business School Press, 1993.

Leavitt, H. J., *Some Effects of Certain Communication Patterns on Group Performance*, Journal of Abnormal and Social Psychology, 1951.

Likert, Rensis, *New Patterns of Management*, McGraw-Hill, 1961.

Schein, Edgar, *Process Consultation*, Addison-Wesley, 1988.

Schermerhorn, J., Hunt, J. and Osborn, R., *Managing Organisational Behaviour*, John Wiley, 1997.

Tuckman, B. and Jensen, N., *Stages in Small Group Development*, Group and Organisational Studies, vol. 2, 1997.

FURTHER READING

Arnold, J., Cooper, C. and Robertson, I, *Work Psychology*, 3rd edn, FT/Pitman, 1998.

Cole, G. *Personnel Management*, 4th edn, Letts, 1997.

Dransfield, R., Howkins, S., Hudson, F. and Davies, W., *Human Resource Management for Higher Awards*, Heinemann Educational, 1996.

Guirdham, M., *Interpersonal Skills at Work*, Prentice Hall, 1990.

Huczynski, A. and Buchanan, D., *Organisational Behaviour*, Prentice Hall, 1998.

Mullins, L. J., *Management and Organisational Behaviour*, 4th edn, Pitman, 1996.

Schermerhorn, J., Hunt, J., and Osborn, R., *Managing Organisational Behaviour*, John Wiley and Sons, 1997.

ASSIGNMENT

UNIT 3

Task 1

The supermarket chain Asda has set out to create a style of management which it calls 'The Asda Way of Working' (AWW). Senior management feels that the traditional style of management in supermarkets in the UK is based on a 'tell-and-do' top-down authoritarian approach. The tell-and-do approach has drawbacks; it:

- intimidates through power
- makes authoritarian decisions
- praises rarely
- is concerned only with results
- pressurises individuals who have to report directly to their line managers.

There tends to be a 'blame culture' in which subordinates are held responsible for faults and problems. In contrast the AWW is intended to:

- create commitment to top performance
- encourage self direction
- asks for direct reports (rather than telling)
- treat people as individuals
- be open to disagreements
- motivate with benefits
- provide useful feedback

Carry out an investigation of different approaches to management in two supermarket chains in your areas (possibly using Asda as one source). You will need to find out about the management approaches by directly interviewing managers and employees of the chosen organisation. If it is not practicable to focus on supermarket chains, then choose another form of retail organisation. Evaluate the strengths and weaknesses in the management approaches in the two organisations. Contrast the management theories you have identified with other well-known approaches to management. Set out your findings in a 1250 word report.

Task 2

1. Explain in abut 100 words what is meant by the term 'organisational culture'. Then describe the organisational culture of an organisation that you are familiar with in terms of (a) legends, (b) norms, (c) values, (d) practices, (e) language, (f) rituals, and (g) other aspects that you feel reflect the culture.

2. Describe the organisational structure of the organisation you have chosen. Use charts and diagrams to illustrate this structure.

3. What is the relationship between the structure and the culture of the organisation that you have chosen to study? How does this relationship impact on the performance of the organisation?

Task 3

1. Choose two leaders you have worked for who employed quite different styles of leadership. Describe the style of each person and show how the style employed impacted on the effectiveness of the leader.

2. Choose three different motivation theories as described in this chapter which are also in use in an organisation that you work for or have worked for in the past (or in which a friend or relative works). Describe each of the three theories and explain how they have been applied in the workplace.

3. Assess the relationship between the motivation theories you have described and the practice of management.

Task 4

1. Describe what you consider to be the key psychological explanation of individual behaviour at work in terms of: (a) personality, and (b) perception.

2. Evaluate your own behaviour in a given organisational role (e.g. your job role, or your role as a student) in terms of your personality, and the way you perceive relationships in the workplace.

Task 5

The Industrial Society carried out a survey into teamworking in 1997. It reported that 86 per cent of the 408 human resources managers questioned said their organisation had invested significantly more in team-building over the previous two years. Moreover, one in ten employers spent up to half of their training budget on team-related training. The growth in team-building training at the time was undoubtedly linked to *corporate restructuring*. With extensive delayering and the move to flatter organisations, there is much more teleworking, homeworking and hot-desking. As organisations altered their structures it was essential to build a strong sense of teamwork and team identity.

Modern organisations are changing their structures and looking at how to maintain a sense of being in a team when people are no longer so accessible to each other. Moreover, growing use is being made of project teams to handle one-off assignments. These are put together for the duration of a project and then dissolved. An individual may be a member of several project teams at once. In this instance people need to develop transferable teamworking skills which they can carry from one team to another. They have to understand better what being a team member means. They also have to accept personal responsibility. They have to move away from the idea that the leader is accountable for managing the work of the team to one in which individual team members are all accountable. As a result, individuals need to develop an understanding of collective effectiveness. One of the core building blocks is interpersonal skills – listening, questioning, giving feedback, being able to put your ideas across effectively, and managing conflict within the group. Another building block is having much more clarity about team objectives.

1. By examining teamworking you have been involved in as part of your Higher Awards course (or ones at work), identify the key factors that lead to effective teamwork and the influences that threaten the success of teamwork (draw on practical examples).

2. What is a group? What are the main characteristics of group behaviour that are distinct from individual behaviour?

Organisations, Competition and Environment

Objectives and Purposes of Organisations

There are many ways of classifying organisations. They can, for example, be large, medium or small; local, or national or international; primary, secondary or tertiary; etc. Whatever the type of organisation, it will have its **objectives** and **purposes**, and will have various **stakeholders**. This chapter examines all these facts, together with the **responsibilities** of organisations.

On completion of the chapter you should be able to:

- identify a range of objectives appropriate to an organisation

- identify three stakeholder objectives in an organisation and evaluate the extent to which they are achieved

- explain the responsibilities of an organisation and the strategies used to meet them.

THE ORGANISATION IN ITS ENVIRONMENT

An organisation has traditionally been defined as a group of people with a common purpose. According to this view, the organisation is a distinct entity separate from its environment. A boundary can thus be drawn between the organisation and its environment. The organisation thus has to maintain an adaptive equilibrium with its environment: the need for change occurs first outside the boundary and the organisation adapts accordingly. Of course, today organisational theory has moved on and now examines a much more direct interrelationship between organisations and the environment, in which organisations themselves create changes in the environment. For the time being, however, we will take a traditional view, in which an **organisation** can be identified as all or some of the following:

- a physical place – for example, a supermarket store such as Asda in Grantham
- a particular group of people – all the people who work for Asda
- a set of goals with systems – Asda as a profit-oriented organisation, which shares profits with employees, and with customers through lower prices, and with buying and selling systems designed to achieve certain goals
- structures, procedures, informal behaviours and cultures for achieving goals – at Asda, a system of rewarding employee loyalty, procedures for showing customers where goods are if they can't find them, and a general ambience of enthusiasm and customer care.

The **environment** in which an organisation operates is all or some of the following:

- a physical place – for example, the edge of Grantham's main shopping area where Asda is located
- a set of conditions – for example, a competitive retailing market involving organised buying and selling conditions and trading rules
- a collection of individuals and other groups – suppliers, customers, local council officials, VAT inspectors, competing organisations etc.

TYPES OF ORGANISATIONS

There are many ways of classifying organisations: large, medium or small; local, national or international; primary, secondary or tertiary; etc. However, for the purpose of examining the objectives and purposes of organisations perhaps the most useful classification is shown in Figure 14.1.

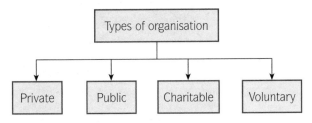

Figure 14.1 *One way of classifying organisations*

Private organisations

The classic division of organisations in this country is between the private and the public sectors (see Figure 14.2).

The UK has a thriving private sector made up of large and small organisations, both new and old. Some of these are very small, being owned by a sole trader. Many start-up businesses are like this: electricians, plumbers, painters and decorators, signwriters, graphic designers, etc. In the course of time the sole trader may take on a partner to bring more capital into the business or to share the workload. Partners are found in a range of relatively small business enterprises, such as doctors' and dentists' surgeries, groups of solicitors and accountants, as well as building firms, plumbers, central heating engineers, and so on.

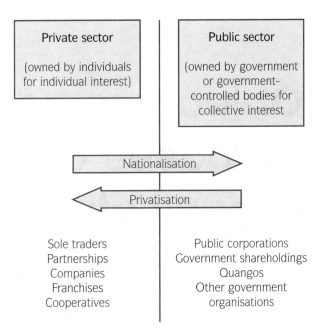

Figure 14.2 *The main sectors of the British economy*

One advantage of running such a small business is that the owners are able to retain control. The sole trader or partners are able to make all the decisions and share out the profits. However, sole traders and ordinary partnerships run the risk of not being able to meet their business debts and having to sell up private possessions to meet the debts of the business (see Chapter 23). It is therefore tempting to take on **company status**, usually first as a private company, by selling shares. Companies have to be registered but are granted legal protection known as **limited liability**. With limited liability the shareholders stand to lose at a maximum the value of their shareholding.

Once an organisation takes on company status it will have access to further and greater sources of capital. In particular, public companies are able to sell their shares through the stock exchange. Large quantities of shares can then be sold to a wider share-buying public.

However, once a company becomes public, the original owners can lose control as a result of actions by people who buy into the company. For example, the famous British company Rowntrees of York was bought up by the Swiss giant, Nestlé.

There is another important risk to becoming a public company. When a public company fails to provide satisfactory returns to shareholders in the form of dividends, then a number of existing shareholders will want to sell up their shares. Subsequently the share price falls, enabling a predatory buyer to buy up the company at a knock-down price. The buyer can then close down plant and offices and sell off the assets of the company, to earn quick financial rewards.

The pressure on organisations in the private sector, therefore, is very much on making profits. If you fail to make a healthy profit, it will be difficult to raise fresh capital from lenders, and you also stand to lose the confidence of existing shareholders. Creating **shareholder value** through high profits is a key objective of private sector businesses.

Case Study

British Land

In December 1998, John Ritblat, the chairman of British Land, declared his intention to carry on expanding Britain's largest and most successful property group despite fears of an impending property slump. He stated: 'Our long-term view remains positive, particularly in the City of London, where we are continuing to take advantage of good investment opportunities.' He said this at the time British Land had reported a slight fall in profits to £50.1 million.

This view was at odds with many commentators in the City who believed that British Land was vulnerable to a downturn. These worries had driven shares in the company down from their peak of 803p each in March 1998 to 475p in December.

The main concern was that Mr Ritblat splashed out heavily on two projects just before the stock market dived in August. First, British Land bought the building occupied by the European Bank for Reconstruction and Development for £206 million. It then signed a joint venture with Railtrack to develop a new 65 000 square metre building in Broadgate next to Liverpool Street station. The complex project involved British Land building a raft over the railway tracks before it could start building. These deals, and others around Broadgate, meant that British Land's exposure in the City of London's Square Mile accounted for almost half of its portfolio at a time when there was a lot of other land also available from competing land developers, for example at Canary Wharf. However, the underlying philosophy at British Land was that it was buying up land while it was available: 'You've got to grab things when you can.'

In December 1998, forecasts put British Land's net asset value for the year to 31 March 1999 at about 600p per share. This means that the group's shares are hardly overvalued.

Questions

1. Why does British Land need to yield a good return to its shareholders?

2. What are the dangers of investing too heavily in new land?

3. What are the potential gains?

4. What type of people are most likely to become shareholders in British Land?

5. Is the philosophy 'You've got to grab things when you can' a good one?

6. What do you see as being the objectives and purposes of British Land?

Public organisations

In business there are three major elements of public-sector involvement:

- direct state participation through public corporations, known as the nationalised industries, and other Crown corporations
- industries in which there is public-sector involvement together with private investment, (e.g. the government held a 39 per cent share in British Petroleum from the Second World War until the late 1980s, when shares were sold to the public)
- industries in which there is a public-sector involvement at local government level rather than at the level of national government.

Businesses that receive support from the government to establish new activities, such as research and development or product development in a particular field, make up a fourth group.

Public corporations

In the UK the government (or 'the state') still owns a number of industries and businesses on behalf of the people. Most of these take the form of **public corporations**.

A public corporation is set up by an Act of Parliament. Examples of public corporations are the Bank of England

and the British Broadcasting Corporation (BBC). Once a public corporation has been formed, the government appoints a chairperson to be responsible for its day-to-day running. There are a number of reasons for setting up public corporations. These underpin the 'objectives' of such organisations.

- *To avoid wasteful duplication.* Imagine the problems caused by having three electricity supply infrastructures operating in one town.
- *To set up and run services that might not be profitable* (e.g. a ferry service to some of the islands of Scotland, a postal service to remote villages). Clearly, there is a community interest objective in these cases.
- *To gain the benefits of large-scale production*; i.e. using the nation's resources in a rational way.
- *To protect employment, particularly in areas of high unemployment.* A government-run activity may continue where a private-sector one would move out.
- *To control industries that are important to the country* (e.g. central banking, and broadcasting.

When a public corporation is set up, an independent body is also formed to protect consumers' interests. Consumers can take their complaints to this body. The government keeps the power to make major decisions about how public corporations should run, such as whether to close down large sections of the railway network. However, the chairperson and managers of the public corporation decide the day-to-day issues, such as wages and, in the case of the BBC, programming. If the government tries to interfere in these areas, there is considerable public debate.

Whereas a limited company has to make an annual report to its shareholders, a public corporation must present its annual report to the appropriate government minister, who makes a verbal report to Parliament. At this time MPs have the opportunity to criticise or support the way in which the corporation is being run. A committee of MPs has the job of studying the running of each public corporation and of reporting on its operation. For example, there is a Select Committee acting as a watchdog for the BBC. Figure 14.3 highlights some of the aspects of decision-making and control in a public corporation.

In recent years there has been a sustained period of privatisation of government enterprises. **Privatisation** means the denationalisation of state-controlled industries. We are all familiar with privatisations such as the sale of the electricity boards, the water boards, British Telecom and British Gas. However, privatisation also includes the sale of council houses, the contracting-out of local-

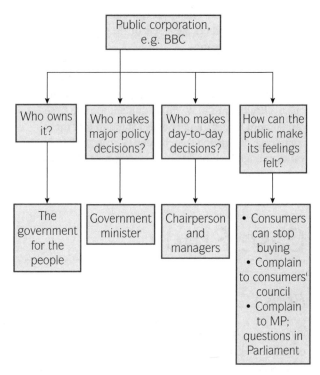

Figure 14.3 *Influences on decision-making in a public corporation*

authority controlled services, such as street cleaning, and the introduction of private prisons.

Other central government enterprises

Government also controls the activities of:

- government departments
- public companies in which the government has a shareholding.

When an activity is run by a government department, a minister is in overall charge. The department is staffed and run by civil servants (e.g. the Customs & Excise Department, which deals with the collection and supervision of some taxes). The major criticisms of such a form of organisation from the business point of view are:

- decisions are made slowly because there are many links in the chain of command, usually wrapped up in rules and regulations
- the organisation may appear to be inefficient because of lack of competition
- there is no external agency to protect the public's interest by checking on how the department is run. While in

many cases there will be a mechanism for making complaints, it may be so complex as to be inaccessible to the ordinary person.

Ministers hope the shake-up will improve the efficiency of the Post Office, which will be allowed to pay its workers more provided productivity improvements are made.

Case Study

The Post Office a half-way house to privatisation?

In December 1998 the government promised to free the Post Office from day-to-day state control and transform it into a 'world class' company. The Post Office had been pressing for change for quite a while. In an increasingly competitive marketplace in which new private carriers were taking an increasing share of the market, the Post Office wanted the commercial freedom to compete.

Announcing the decision, the Secretary of State for Trade and Industry said that customers would get a better service following his decision to create a 'Post Office Plc' which will remain in the public sector but with much greater commercial freedom than at present.

The proposals include a removal of the Post Office's monopoly in delivering letters costing up to £1 to send. However, the Secretary of State ruled out an immediate privatisation of the organisation, even though the sale of 49 per cent of the government's shareholding was favoured by the Treasury and could raise £2 billion. The minister said that privatisation would pose a threat to the survival of sub-post offices and create 'massive uncertainty' until legislation could be introduced in two or three years.

A new independent regulator will protect consumer interests by maintaining the present universal delivery service at the same price. The regulator will also relax the Post Office's monopoly on letters costing up to £1, which is expected to be cut to about 50p.

In return, the Post Office will be allowed to compete in a competitive market by investing an extra £1 billion over five years in new products and technology and to forge partnerships with other postal operators.

Although the Treasury will continue to cream off some of its profits, the payments will be reduced from an estimated £335 million in 1999 to £207 million. In future the government will take about 40 per cent of its profits, instead of the 80 per cent in recent years.

Questions

1. What do you see as being the principal objectives of a state-run postal service?

2. How might these objectives change after a partial or full privatisation process?

3. List the major advantages and drawbacks of the proposed changes in the running of the Post Office.

Local government enterprises

In the UK certain services in local areas are supervised by locally elected councils. These councils usually run some form of business organisation, such as municipal car parks, leisure centres, bus services and public toilets. However, since the late 1980s council activities too have been subject to the policy of privatisation. Today, many activities such as road cleaning and refuse disposal are contracted out to those firms that put in the lowest tender for a particular job. Council officials simply monitor the effectiveness with which the work is done and may refuse to continue a contract if work fails to meet the required standards.

Local councils receive money from two main sources: a grant given to them by central government, and a local tax. Local councils often subsidise loss-making activities, such as parks, which provide a benefit to the community.

For the year 1999–2000, the government determined that of the £50.6 billion required for local government spending in the UK, £11 billion would come from local council taxpayers. The remaining £39 billion would be channelled from central government sources to local government: £20 billion largely from income tax payers, £13 billion from business rates, and a further £6 billion from special grants.

Public sector objectives

The above remarks indicate some of the difficulties in establishing objectives for public-sector organisations.

Many public-sector activities involve only limited competition, so it is difficult to establish how efficient they are. How do we know if particular activities are taking too long and are wasting resources? What criteria are used for establishing targets when it is difficult to make comparisons (except with past performance)?

In 1948 the government set out the objective for nationalised industries. They were to meet the demand for their product at a reasonable price which would enable them to break even over a number of years. In the years that followed there was much criticism of the way in which the targets were set for public corporations. Under the break-even policy, for example, it was possible to charge some customers who could be supplied cheaply (such as gas users in cities) the same price as other customers who were far more expensive to supply (gas consumers in remote areas).

In 1961 the government set more precise financial targets for public corporations. Taking into account conditions in the **market**, the targets became the rate of return on the assets employed in a specific industry.

In 1967 even more stringent rules were set, whereby the cross-subsidisation of one group of consumers by another was to be avoided. New investment was expected to yield a rate of return similar to what the investment capital would earn in the private sector. It was recognised that some activities of public corporations (e.g. supplying to rural areas and engaging in activities which were not profitable) were of a social rather than a commercial nature (see Figure 14.4). These social contributions needed to be given a money value, and the government would provide a subsidy to meet these activities.

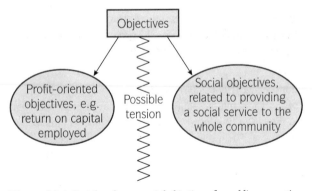

Figure 14.4 *Social and commercial objectives of a public corporation*

In 1979 the newly elected Conservative government embraced a policy of privatisation. The emphasis was on cutting out unprofitable operations in order to make these industries attractive to prospective shareholders. Over the years, this has meant cutting down loss-making operations

such as some steel works, coal mines and shipyards. A large number of nationalised industries were privatised during the 1980s, including electricity, telephones, British Gas, British Steel, British Aerospace, British Airways, British Shipbuilders, the National Bus Company, the British Airports Authority, the National Freight Corporation, British Rail and British Coal.

In the Acts that privatised these industries, the government set up regulatory bodies, such as OFTEL (for telecommunications) and OFWAT (for water), with the responsibility for checking that the privatised industries keep to established rules governing prices, competition and the quality of service offered. Today's remaining nationalised industries are expected to meet financial targets and to show a real rate of return on assets that indicates resources are being used as effectively as if the capital were employed by the private sector.

Public-sector organisations, meanwhile, such as the National Health Service and the BBC, have been broken down into a number of independent sections. Each section (e.g. a hospital or group of hospitals) is expected to manage its own budget and to use resources efficiently. In many ways the Labour government has continued to support the notion of competition but has found it difficult to privatise fresh industries because there is little commercial advantage in privatising what remains (except, for example, in the case of the Post Office).

Under the Labour government there has been a move away from privatisation in the case of GPs acting as independent fundholders. Increasingly, these funds will be taken back from the fundholder to be managed by centralised purchasing authorities. Small practices were finding it very difficult to manage the business side of their practice and carry out their medical duties at the same time.

Charitable organisations

A **charity** is an organisation set up to raise funds and support other people or a cause. The objectives of charities are to raise enough funds, or a surplus, to use for helping others. A surplus is a balance from the income of a charity after all costs have been paid. This contrasts with the profit-based objective of a private-sector organisation. The management of charity work is overseen by a group of trustees – volunteers with a reputation as responsible citizens. Many will have a variety of experience in both charity and business activities. Charities have to register as such and must produce annual accounts that are available for anyone to see.

Most charity organisations start out as good ideas – someone recognises the need for such an organisation and acts accordingly. For example, Shelter was set up in 1966 to help the many homeless people on the streets. The Toybox Charity was founded in 1991, by the Dyason family, who were horrified by a television documentary showing the plight of some of the 250 000 children orphaned by civil war in Guatemala. The charity has grown into a comprehensive rescue strategy for children who live on the streets of Guatemala City.

War Child was founded in 1993 by film-makers Bill Leeson and David Wilson as an emotional response to the plight of children caught up in the war in former Yugoslavia. Initially raising money through entertainment events and public appeals, War Child set out to bring immediate material help to children of all ages and ethnic backgrounds. With a few old trucks and the help of a handful of unpaid volunteers, War Child began delivering food, clothing and medical equipment to wherever it was needed most. It also supplied musical instruments and CDs to young people and radio stations, and initiated a diabetes programme supplying insulin and blood-testing equipment throughout Bosnia. In all, thanks to significant financial support from the general public and the music and entertainment industries, War Child provided millions of pounds worth of aid to the former Yugoslavia. War Child has grown from a two-man organisation working out of a sitting room in North London, into an international aid agency with offices in half a dozen countries. Now, the charity is also involved in development initiatives, such as the rehabilitation of war-traumatised children and 'education for peace' programmes. At the heart of War Child's philosophy is the realisation that the war-scarred younger generation is the key to a peaceful future.

Charities employ paid managers and workers (unlike voluntary organisations, which rely on the goodwill of their staff). Many large charities employ resources on a large scale in the same way as private business organisations. These resources need to be managed effectively and efficiently to ensure that they are used in the optimum way to meet the needs of various stakeholder groupings. Today, therefore, charities employ professional business managers who are accountable for using resources in the best possible way to meet the objectives of the charity.

Voluntary organisations

A **voluntary organisation** is another radical alternative to the 'for profit organisation'. It is a 'not-for-profit organisation'. It is set up, organised, staffed and run by people who are working purely on a voluntary basis, usually for a 'good cause'. However, just because an organisation is run as a voluntary activity does not mean that it should not operate in a professional way. Voluntary organisations like any other use scarce resources – these need to be used to optimal effect, or else money and time will be wasted. Examples of voluntary organisations are the Women's Royal Voluntary Service (WRVS) and Voluntary Service Overseas (VSO).

People who work for these organisations will receive no more than is required for living, travel and other forms of expenses. However, the voluntary organisation needs to establish clear objectives, and then create structures, policies and practices that best enable the organisation to meet these objectives.

AIMS OF ORGANISATIONS

Organisations need to have aims and objectives to be able to focus on the clear direction needed for success in the modern business world. The aim is the overarching goal for the organisation, which can then be broken down into a subset of objectives to achieve the aim. To take a military parallel, the aim may be 'to win the war' and the objectives will be the subset of major requirements which must be met in order to achieve that. Business organisations' aims usually relate to profit, market share, return on capital employed, sales, growth, levels of service and customer/user perceptions.

Establishing objectives may be done in a number of ways, such as by looking at what is 'normal' in the industry, or previous years' figures. A third element, which is a popular one, is growth in earnings per share. Clearly, shareholders are major stakeholders in the organisation and this is an objective they can relate to. Of course, a danger of focusing on earnings per share is that the company may begin to borrow more money in order to maintain earnings per share.

Once the organisation has established corporate objectives in financial terms, then these objectives need to be segmented into divisional objectives and profit-centre objectives. The expected rate of return from each division may well depend on the amount of risk taken and on market conditions.

Management by objectives

In his book *The Practice of Management* (originally published in 1954, latest edition 1995), Peter Drucker set out the concept of **management by objectives** (MbO), in which managers set specific objectives for each area of business performance, including the work and progress of subordinates, and set attainable targets at each level of the organisation, agreed by consultation. These objectives need to be coordinated with the strategic objectives of the whole organisation. MbO is now a widely used business practice which can be used to upgrade targets in the light of experience. Most managers use management by objectives either explicitly or implicitly in their actions. The MbO approach is closely associated with organisations which have detailed planning structures focused on a clear mission.

Peter Drucker wanted to find out how best to manage a business to make sure that profits are made and that the enterprise is successful over time. He felt that business objectives help management to explain, predict and control activities. The business should establish a number of objectives in a small number of general statements. These statements can then be tested in the light of business experience, and it becomes possible to predict performance. The soundness of decisions can be examined while they are being made, rather than by looking back on what has happened. Performance in the future can be improved in the light of previous and current experience.

Figure 14.5 shows that specific objectives can act as a standard to measure performance. If objectives are not met, they may need to be readjusted or processes and activities altered. Alternatively, if they are met, new and higher objectives can be set. Such objectives force the business to plan its aims in detail and to work out ways of achieving them. Management is the job of organising resources to achieve satisfactory performance.

Drucker listed eight areas in which performance objectives need to be set out:

- market standing
- innovation
- productivity
- physical and financial resources
- profitability
- manager performance and development
- worker performance and attitude
- public responsibility.

Managers need information which enables them to measure their own performance and the performance of their organisation. MbO provides an excellent link between aims and performance, and aims and measurement of performance.

Profit as an aim

Business organisations need to make **profits** if they are to move forward and grow. A company has responsibilities that extend well beyond its purely commercial ambitions. However, it should organise itself in such a way that it can meet all its responsibilities and still make a profit. According to Drucker:

> *'It is the first duty of a business to survive. The guiding principle of business economics, in other words, is not the maximisation of profits; it is the avoidance of loss. Business enterprise must produce the premium to cover the risks inevitably involved in its operation. And there is only one source for this risk premium: profits.'*

Unless a business makes a profit it cannot afford to modernise itself, install new technologies, or take commercial risks with, say, new product ranges. Nor can it continue to fulfil its social responsibilities. Nor can it justify the investment of its owners – private individuals or institutions such as pension funds and insurance companies – who need to seek the best possible long-term return on their resources.

In a free competitive market, and in all but the shortest term, profit is the measure of how good a business is, how

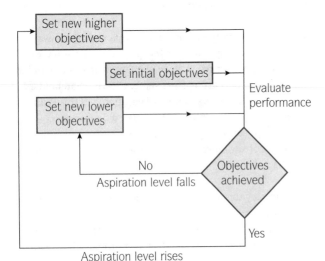

Figure 14.5 *Using objectives as a standard*

well-run and how effectively it meets its responsibilities to all its stakeholders. However, according to Drucker:

'Profit is not a cause. It is the result – the result of the performance of the business in marketing, innovation and productivity. It is at the same time the test of this performance – the only possible test, as the Communists in Russia soon found out when they tried to abolish it in the early twenties. Indeed, profit is a beautiful example of what today's scientist and engineers mean when they talk of the feedback that underlies all systems of automatic production: the self-regulation of a process by its own product.'

Note that there is a key difference between **profit maximisation** and **making a profit**. Profit maximisation is concerned with making as much profit as you can over a period. Profit maximisation occurs when there is the maximum difference between the total revenue coming into a business and the total cost being paid out. If we measured profit simply in money terms, then it would seem logical to assume that in the long term the rational business will seek to maximise the difference between its total revenue and its total cost. Accountants, for example, claim to be able to quickly weigh up the success of a business in terms of 'the bottom line'.

And, of course, profit is a major driving force. For example, at the end of the twentieth century many business writers recognised Coca-Cola as an object lesson in how to conduct a business well. Coca-Cola ploughs 60 per cent of its profits back into the business, into product development and opening up new markets. Coca-Cola is able to make high profits on a very high sales figure. It then puts these profits back into research and development, promotion and advertising, market research, opening up new distribution channels etc. It is thus able to out-compete all its rivals. Profits yield higher sales and still higher profits.

Setting profitability as the key aim for an organisation should then determine the way the organisation runs. In the past this often led to a very mechanistic approach in tightly controlled top-down organisations in which a strong emphasis was placed on driving down costs. Today, many business writers see the route to profit as creating priorities which are focused on enabling the organisation to develop its full potential – for example by identifying and meeting the needs of customers (a marketing orientation) and bringing the best out of staff (a human resource orientation).

In his book *Emotional Capital*, Kevin Thomson argues that very few companies know how to capitalise on the power of an asset they glibly describe as their 'most valuable'. He says that they instead seek to value and capture 'know-

how', or 'intellectual capital', as the measure that truly defines the effectiveness of a workforce in any company. However, Thomson argues that this is a fallacy.

'Harnessing and managing knowledge is one thing, but organisations need to manage the emotions, feelings and beliefs that motivate people to apply that knowledge constructively. Then, and only then, can a company's lifeblood – emotional capital – make an impact on financial performance.'

Organisations therefore not only need to clarify their aims (e.g. profitability), they also need to develop a clear picture of how best to achieve those aims.

'The business of business is business!' according to Milton Friedman (1994). Profitability is the chief spur to business activity. However, in a study carried out by Shipley in 1981 (*Journal of Industrial Economics*), the author concluded that only 15.9 per cent of a sample of 728 UK firms could be regarded as 'true' profit-maximisers. This conclusion was reached by cross-tabulating replies to two questions shown in Figure 14.6. Shipley considered as true maximisers only those firms that claimed both to maximise profits and to regard profits to be of overriding importance. Of course, there are a number of criticisms that can be levelled at any form of statistical analysis of motivations. However, there would appear to be a clear case for arguing that profit is only part of a set of business objectives.

		Percentage of all respondents
1. Does your firm try to achieve:		
	a maximum profits?	47.7
	b satisfactory profits?	52.3
2. Compared with your firm's leading objectives, is the achievement of a target profit regarded as being:		
	a of little importance	2.1
	b fairly important	12.9
	c very important	58.9
	d of overriding importance	26.1
Those responding both 1(a) and 2(d)?		15.9

Figure 14.6 *Responses from a sample of 728 firms*

TASK

Try out the questions outlined above on a group of managers to whom you have access.

Market share as an aim

Many firms seek to be **market leaders**, others to improve their **market share**. Those going for leadership may want to sell more products than all rival brands combined, or simply to sell more than the next-best-selling brand. The most reliable indicator of market share is relative to other brands – that is, the ratio of a company's market share to that of its largest competitor:

$$\text{Relative market share} = \frac{\text{Market share of the company}}{\text{Market share of the nearest competitor}}.$$

A well-known study by the Boston Consultancy Group argued, on the basis of statistical information, that a ratio of 2:1 would give a 20 per cent cost advantage (i.e. you would be able to operate with costs 20 per cent lower than your nearest rival). If you dominate the market you can produce on a larger scale than your rivals. You can therefore spread your costs over a larger output. You can then produce more cheaply than rivals. Profits can then be ploughed back into research, advertising and further expansion to maintain market leadership.

We can illustrate the relationship between market share and cost leadership by means of a simple diagram (see Figure 14.7). Whereas the market leader produces at point A, market followers are faced by higher costs at lower outputs – points B and C.

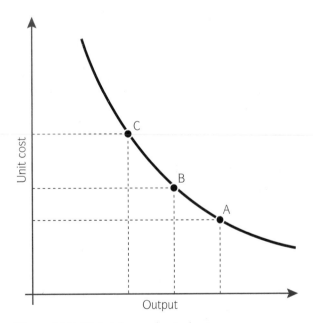

Figure 14.7 *Market share and cost advantage*

Case examples from the real world demonstrate clearly why firms seek market leadership. For example, for a number of years Tesco and Sainsbury have had roughly equal market share as supermarkets. Many of the products they sell are standard items, such as Andrex toilet paper, Heinz baked beans, Walkers crisps. If you have the largest market share then you are able to spread your costs over a larger output (for example the costs of distributing toilet paper, beans and crisps). Lose market share and your unit costs relative to those of rivals are likely to rise. Firms become progressively more or progressively less competitive over time. A deteriorating performance is likely to have an on-going effect, unless drastic actions are taken. Business people work to a simple maxim – gain the lion's share of the market and the profits will follow.

If an organisation has the aim of being the market leader this will impact on its objectives and the way it carries out its business. For example, the organisation may focus on providing extra value for money compared with rivals to win increasing market share. A supermarket will offer discounted petrol and 'loss leaders', more variety, better service, additional extras, stay open longer, etc., in order to win increasing market share. An organisation that strives for market share will often sacrifice short-term profits in order to win a bigger share of the market – as witnessed in the price war between national newspapers in the late 1990s.

Case Study

Taking advantage of market leadership

In a recent statement to shareholders, the chairperson of a company producing the leading name in branded nappies made the following points.

'Over the last few years we have sought to drive our advantage home. Our product is recognised as being the most reliable, convenient and useful on the market. We currently have three times the sales of our nearest rival producer, and this has enabled us to pass the advantage of scale production on to consumers. We firmly believe that the road to success is to "gain the lion's share of the market and then watch the profits flow in". We will continue to find out what our consumers require in an ever-changing marketplace in order to better meet their needs.'

Questions

1. How will the company benefit from making three times as many sales as the nearest rival?

2. How will consumers benefit?

3. Explain how gaining the lion's share of the market will lead to a flow of profits.

4. How can competitive advantage today, lead to further competitive advantage tomorrow?

Sales as an aim

In some companies the salaries earned by managers depend on the size of the business. Thus, their aim may be to make the business as large as possible. Controlling a large business concern might also give an individual satisfaction derived from the power at their command. Increased **sales** might also mean reduced sales for competitors, which in the long term can be seen as being consistent with a policy of profit maximisation.

In a college or school, a head teacher's or principal's salary will increase when the number of students goes over a certain threshold. This is of particular significance for senior managers who are relatively close to retirement age, as their pensions will be determined by their final few years' salary. Such managers have a big incentive to increase the number of students in their colleges. And, of course, they don't have to deal with the problems of over-expansion once they have retired!

Peter Drucker points out that a number of business people argue that 'we don't care what share of the market we have, as long as our sales go up'. Drucker says that this view sounds plausible enough but it does not stand up under analysis.

> 'By itself, volume of sales tells little about performance, results or the future of the business. A company's sales may go up – and the company may actually be headed for rapid collapse. A company's sales may go down – and the reason may not be that its marketing is poor, but that it is in a dying field and had better change fast.'

Absolute sales figures are meaningless on their own. They need to be projected against actual and potential market trends. It is also important to look at sales as a percentage of the market. A business that supplies less than a certain share of the market is a marginal supplier and may be squeezed out.

A big incentive to increase sales is that the cost of making additional sales will often fall as sales rise. As a general rule, therefore, companies will be happier with higher sales figures. Study any company report and you will immediately notice the high prominence given to **turnover** as a financial highlight. This may be because turnover is the figure which is most likely to show improvement year on year. Of course it is important to examine sales in relation to other figures which appear in the accounts.

ROCE as an aim

Return on capital employed is frequently used as an aim for a business (see Chapter 7). The idea behind ROCE is that the capital invested in a business could be invested in alternatives. The next-best alternative is termed the **opportunity cost** (i.e. the sacrifice, what is given up).

ROCE is a measure of an organisation's return on capital invested. In simple terms, if the XYZ company invests one million pounds on a particular project and gets a 10 per cent return, then this is the ROCE. When deciding whether to put £100 in the Better Building Society or the Not So Good Building Society, you will be influenced by the fact that Better Building Society offers you 10 per cent interest compared with NSGBS's 8 per cent.

In establishing the required ROCE for a particular organisation, a key consideration will be what the return would be on the capital invested in its next-best use. After all, shareholders will not be keen to keep their shareholding in a public limited company like Shell if they could make a better return on BP shares, or in oil industry shares if they could make a better return by investing in entertainment.

Setting an aim based on ROCE means that an organisation must create tight sets of objectives and operational standards to ensure that it meets the financial requirements. Clearly ROCE as an aim will help the organisation to focus on providing shareholder value. In recent years ROCE has also been used as an aim in public-sector organisations (e.g. to achieve a return on capital invested equivalent to what the investment could have earned in the private sector). In the newly privatised industries, regulators also often set targets for ROCE, although the intention here may be related to controlling profiteering and to stop the exploitation of consumers.

Growth as an aim

A firm that **grows** quickly may find it easier to attract investors and thus be able to produce on a larger scale. However, one of the biggest mistakes that business people make in the early days is that of overtrading. If that happens, there might not be enough cash to pay bills in the short term, managing a large staff can be difficult, and so on. It is surprising how many people fall into this trap. Often someone will set up a new business and, because of its early success, decide to expand, only to find it difficult to manage a larger business, or to bring in the extra customers that are needed. A fairly common pattern is for an entrepreneur to start with one business interest, expand to two or three interests, and then end up with no viable business interest.

Businesses that aim for growth are ones with a higher propensity to accept risks. Such organisations may be more willing to borrow, and to look to join or take over other existing concerns. An organisation with a growth focus will need fairly dynamic structures because people in the organisation have to learn to live with regular change.

One form of growth is to move into a number of markets. This makes it possible to spread risks. If one market fails, another may support the loss. However, opening into new markets also exposes a business to fresh risks.

Level of service

Customer service is a term to describe the overall activity of identifying and satisfying customer needs, and keeping them satisfied. The term 'service' is used in three distinct ways.

- *To contrast an intangible 'product' from tangible ones.* Services are intangible things like a train journey, a hair-cut, or advice on investment.
- *As an extra you get when you buy a product.* You buy a TV set and the shop will 'service' it for you – that is, it will make sure the TV will continue to work.
- *As an overall description of the desired relationship between a supplier and a customer.* 'Service' in this sense is based on the premise that every commercial transaction is a service.

For example, if an oil company assumed that the function of its retail network was simply to sell petrol and lubricants it would quickly lose business to competitors. Its real function is to supply a 'customer service' – in its case the service of enjoyable, trouble-free motoring. Petrol and lubricants are only part of that. The provision of somewhere to rest and refresh, to eat and drink, to buy gifts and groceries, to make a phone call and buy a newspaper, and all in a clean, friendly environment, is an equally important part.

In an age of competitiveness, it is not surprising that service is given a high priority in many organisations. In a range of surveys of the importance of elements in the marketing mix, service has come out as being the third most important ingredient behind product and price, but ahead of advertising, promotion and sales effort. More importantly, with each passing year customer service has been ranked higher as an important ingredient in the marketing mix. In their book *Relationship Marketing*, Christopher, Payne and Ballantyne, argue that customer service has become so important for two main reasons.

- *Changing customer expectations.* In almost every market the customer is now more demanding and more sophisticated than, say, thirty years ago. With changing customer expectations, competitors are seeing customer service as a competitive weapon with which to differentiate their sales.
- *The need for a relationship strategy.* To ensure that a customer service strategy which will create a value proposition for customers is formulated, implemented and controlled, it is necessary to establish it as having a central role and not one that is subsumed in various elements of the marketing mix.

Case Study

Service at John Lewis

The following relates to service at the John Lewis Partnership, as described by the organisation.

Here are some examples of the myriad services we offer:

- We install and balance long-case clocks
- We make rugs to most shapes, sizes or designs
- We make curtains, pelmets and blinds to measure, for any window, whether it be in a palace, a wendy house or your home
- We make club ties to order
- We have a full re-upholstery and loose-cover service for all traditional or modern suites, armchairs and sofas

- We sell extra-small baby clothes for premature babies
- We make pillows, pillowcases, sheets and quilts to any shape or size.

Our selling assistants are ready to offer help when you need it. All receive extensive training and most are full-time, permanent staff, so whoever you speak to will know what they are talking about. If they cannot answer your question themselves, they will do their best to find out. Examples of the high level of service on offer include the following:

- Our children's shoe-fitters are professionally trained in measuring children's feet
- We offer an expert bra-fitting service, our assistants being trained to fit junior and maternity bras, and bras for special needs like sport or mastectomy
- It isn't our policy to persuade you to buy something, we only help and advise.

Questions

1. What does the above tell you about the aim and objectives of the John Lewis Partnership?

2. Why do you think it focuses on these aims and objectives?

Customer/user perceptions

What do customers and users think and feel about the organisation? Most modern organisations want to be seen in a favourable light. It is **perception** that drives purchases and customer loyalty. If you think that 'You can be sure of Shell', then you may become a lifelong Shell user. If you believe that 'Coca-Cola is the real thing' then you will become a keen drinker.

Positive perceptions take a long time to build, and can be destroyed in just a few minutes. When Gerald Ratner told the world (through the media) at a business dinner that most of his jewellery was 'crap', his business folded within months. Today, organisations continually seek improvements in their product and service to make sure that they are thought of well: that they are 'the world's favourite airline', 'the team you can trust', 'the customer's first choice', and so on.

The best way to create customer belief in a product is to ensure total quality systems at every stage at which the

product, the brand and the company comes into contact with its many publics.

STAKEHOLDERS

The idea of stakeholders

In simple terms, **stakeholders** are individuals, groups and organisations who have some level of involvement in particular decisions or sets of decisions. The notion of stakeholders in organisations has been a popular one with business writers for at least twenty years, particularly for those who examined the nature of corporate strategy and the nature of ownership of the organisation. In recent years 'the stakeholder economy' has become a popular phrase. In political terms, it is used to emphasise the idea of a 'one-nation' society in which the views of all the relevant parties in a given situation are taken into account in decision-making.

This notion of stakeholding represents a radical perspective compared with the situation in most organisations in the past. Traditionally, this country was characterised by top-down, command and control organisations after the Second World War. Decisions were made above and passed down to those lower down in the organisation. Managers talked about having 'the right to manage'; i.e. the right to make most of the decisions in an organisation. Owners of organisations expected to have a major say because, after all, it was 'their organisation'.

Inevitably this led to a 'them and us' approach in organisations. On the one side were the managers and owners and on the other side the workers. This led to continual power struggles. Managers saw workers as being 'obstructive and bolshie', workers saw management as 'grasping and capitalistic'. In the 1970s the UK was notorious for its ineffective labour relations. Strikes were frequent and disputes were often unpleasant and based on mistrust. Today there has been a move to a new view of organisational theory which is based more on shared interests. This change has come about for a number of reasons.

First, the years of Conservative government between 1979 and 1997 were ones of considerable insecurity for employees in this country. Successive pieces of legislation weakened the powers of trade unions. At the same time employment was cut in many of the traditional industries which were bastions of trade unionism (e.g. coal mines, steel, automobile manufacture and printing industries). Confrontational approaches by unions tended to be self-defeating because they appeared to lead to increasing job losses.

Second, the Japanese economy flourished for much of this period. Japanese business practice was based far more on reducing the divisions between managers and employees, through shared workplace facilities, the use of quality circles, etc. Japanese industry was characterised by more of a consensual view of business practice. At the same time Japanese companies were building strong links between the various parts of the supply chain (e.g. between the supplier of components, the manufacturer and retailing outlets). This pointed the way towards partnership agreements in the supply process.

Third, the 1980s were a decade of market orientation. It was a time in which organisations recognised that business practice needed to be determined in far greater measure by the needs and wishes of consumers. Instead of running a production-oriented organisation in which new ideas and decisions were to be dictated by managers, a major new driving force would be the consumer.

Fourth, there was a growth of competition on a world-wide scale. Today we live in a complex integrated global economy. In such an environment business organisations will be successful only if they employ best practice. There is no scope for the dinosaur organisation that continues to use outdated practices. Increasingly it is being recognised that success is best generated by organisations based on creating values which are shared by all the stakeholders of the organisation.

Fifth, the power and influence of stakeholder groups has grown within and without the organisation. For example, community and pressure groups have increasingly forged ways of exerting real power and influence in organisational decision-making. They have developed new ways of building on their stakeholder rights to force organisations to take account of their wishes and desires.

Lastly, there has been the growing influence of the media. They are able to show an organisation in a 'good' or 'bad' light. This means that organisations need to view the media as an important stakeholder within the organisational environment. In addition, stakeholder groupings within an organisation are able to use media coverage to give their point of view a lot more sway and influence.

Who are the stakeholders in a business?

First let us examine the concept of a 'good business'. A good business has several distinguishing characteristics.

- It makes a profit by supplying products or services that people want to buy.
- It contributes to its own and the community's long-term prosperity by making the best possible use of resources.
- It minimises waste of every kind and where possible promotes its reuse or recycling.
- It respects the environment, locally, nationally and globally.
- It sets performance standards for its suppliers, and helps in their achievement.
- It offers its employees worthwhile career prospects, professional training, job satisfaction and a safe working environment.
- It expects the best from its employees and rewards them accordingly.
- It acts at all times as a good citizen, aware of its influence on the rest of society, including the local communities living near its factories and offices.

If a company is to remain a 'good business', all those characteristics are required. For instance, no business can continue to earn a profit if it fails significantly to make the best possible use of available resources. It would simply be overtaken by competitors who do. And in making the best possible use of resources – whether raw materials or human potential – it automatically contributes to the general prosperity.

Of course 'best possible use' implies more than simply best possible use in the short-term. Any company short-sighted enough to exploit resources simply for immediate gain, and at the expense of the environment or the customer's best long-term interests, would soon fail; public hostility, customer boycott and, possibly, prosecution would see to it. A good business is always a good citizen.

And since the most important resource available to any company is its people, they must be looked after, trained and generally enabled to fulfil their potential.

A good business will also remain aware of the 'knock-on' effects of its activities. Investment in a new factory may attract workers from outside the area and increase the local population significantly. It is not enough for the company simply to pay good wages and offer good conditions at work. It will also help to ensure that housing and other social facilities are in place – co-operating as necessary with the local authorities. Likewise, if a factory has to be closed, or a significant proportion of the staff made redundant either because of a business downturn or internal inefficiencies, the company will work with others to help the displaced staff find new employment.

The closing of a factory, or even down-sizing, can lead to the closure of a variety of companies supplying either the factory itself (with raw materials and services) or the workers and their families (with food, clothing, entertainment, etc.). A good business will therefore think long and hard before deciding to close and, where appropriate, will make every effort to encourage other companies to take over the site.

Thus it can be seen that a business has responsibilities to a range of interested parties, people who have a 'stake' in what the company does. A company's stakeholders so defined include its customers and owners, its workforce and suppliers (and their families), those living near its site, as well as special-interest groups, and of course society as a whole, including society in its role as steward of the environment. Balancing these responsibilities is difficult but far from impossible. In fact, companies now realise that there is a synergy between the disciplined, innovative approaches needed to satisfy a purely commercial responsibility and those needed to satisfy, say, a problem of worker safety. They help each other.

As we have seen, a company has responsibilities that extend well beyond its own purely commercial ambitions. However, it should organise itself in such a way that it can meet all its responsibilities and still make a profit. Unless it does, it cannot afford to modernise itself, install new technologies, or take commercial risks with, say, new product ranges. Nor can it continue to fulfil its social responsibilities.

Discussion point

How can each of the groups identified in the text influence organisational decision-making and threaten the survival of the organisation if they are not listened to?

The range of stakeholders will vary from organisation to organisation. A popular response to a question of who the *main* stakeholder in some organisations are might run as follows:

a premier division football club – the supporters
a school – the pupils/parents
a public company – shareholders
a church – the congregation.

For most organisations the consumers are key stakeholders, as are the owners. Examine a particular organisation in more detail and it quickly becomes obvious that there is a wide variety of stakeholders. Stakeholders in Manchester United Football Club, for example, include: the supporters, the shareholders, the playing staff, the management team, the suppliers of sporting equipment, building materials, electricity (e.g. for floodlights) and foodstuffs, the groundstaff, programme sellers, car-park attendants, financial institutions that have lent the club money, visiting supporters of competing teams, people who live near the football ground, and the media. So a football club has a wide range of stakeholders. Some of these will have interests that complement each other, while some have conflicting interests.

In the past it was far more commonplace for organisations to serve a narrow group of stakeholders rather than balance the interests of a range of stakeholders. For example, a football club might be dominated by a small number of shareholders who ran the club in their own interests and showed little respect for the views of the ordinary fans. While this continues to happen in some measure in a number of football clubs, the emphasis has increasingly moved towards taking into account the wishes of a much broader range of stakeholders.

Discussion point

Identify those groups of Manchester United stakeholders that have complementary interests and those that may have some conflicting interests. How may these interests differ?

The typical range of stakeholders for most business organisations can be summarised as in Figure 14.8.

Stakeholder objectives

Peter Drucker makes the point that to manage a business is to balance a variety of needs and goals, and he then goes on to write that 'objectives are needed in every area where performance and results directly and vitally affect the

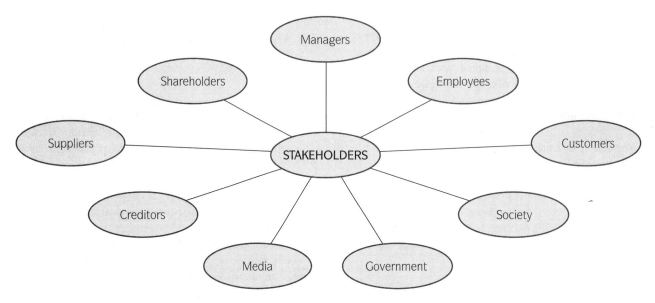

Figure 14.8 *The myriad of possible stakeholders*

survival and prosperity of the business'. Satisfying stakeholder objectives can be successfully achieved only by creating an agreed view about organisational objectives which considers each group of stakeholders.

The role of a stakeholder in an organisation should be to make a positive contribution to the success of that operation. Clearly this is most likely to happen in those organisations which empower their stakeholders to have a say in the decision-making process. Where stakeholders are excluded from this process they are likely to be antagonistic and to play a negative role, one which works against the values of the organisation.

Values

Stakeholders are groups of individuals whose **values** are likely to be different in some ways while being similar in other ways. It is important to understand the significance of this for an organisation. Our values affect the way in which we behave, and it is possible to alter our behaviour so that we behave contrary to our values. But that creates a tension and we tend, in due course, to revert back to our 'natural behaviour'. The most successful businesses are those where the staff share similar values and moral principles since these guide individual and corporate behaviour.

If the stakeholders in a business have very different values, tensions are likely to lead to arguments and poor performance. If, on the other hand, stakeholders share the key values there is greater chance of success.

For example, a group of innovative and creative employees may want to help an organisation to make decisions but be dominated by an autocratic and repressive manager. Another situation in which dissonance can occur is when employees have a 'public service' motivation – they want to serve the wider community – but are constrained in their actions by the organisation's drive to make all of its activities concerned with maximising profits. Also, imagine a situation in which there are a range of stakeholders with a deep concern for preserving the environment, faced by an organisation with poor waste management policies leading to pollution.

Balancing the interests of stakeholders

It is increasingly common these days for organisations to try to encapsulate the shared values of their staff and other stakeholders into a **values statement** which sets out their beliefs. These business values should help to determine the culture of the organisation.

Values and **behaviour** are closely linked. If employees share the values of the organisation, this will be reflected in individual behaviour and consequently in the organisation's behaviour. It is therefore important for the organisation to create a values statement and vision which clearly matches that of its stakeholders – a belief in serving the community, in working hard to create the best quality standards, in behaving in an ethical way, in considering the needs of individual customers, etc. John Collins and Henry Porras, in their book *Built to Last: Successful Habits of Visionary Companies*, argue that values create 'a sense of purpose beyond making money that guides and inspires people throughout the organisation'.

Many modern organisations create a values statement which they publicise widely to employees and other stakeholders. For example, a recent values statement for British Telecom was:

> We put our customers first
> We are professional
> We respect each other
> We work as a team
> We are committed to continuous improvement

It is essential that these values statements go well beyond simply being words on paper. They need to be represented in the reality of everything that an organisation does.

Accommodating pluralism

Organisational theory in the 1990s has recognised the importance of taking a **pluralistic approach**, which is contrasted with a **unitary** approach.

With a unitary frame of reference an organisation has a single value system, and seeks to create the mechanisms to best meet the needs of this system. Many modern theorists now recognise that organisations operate in an environment of internal and external *diversity*. An organisation is made up of many different people, frequently formed into common-interest groups. The organisation interacts with an environment similarly based on diversity. Even the most committed 'strong culture' companies need to attend to pluralism.

For pluralists, the challenge in maintaining order and in ensuring sensible and controlled development is not to ignore, suppress, gloss over or eliminate differences between people (actions which are likely at best to enjoy only a limited and temporary success). The need is to develop greater sensitivity towards multicultural differences, accepting and welcoming, and continually looking for ways of expressing, accommodating and reconciling them. Thus if management is to be successful, rather than cosmetic or deceptive, it will have to comprehend comparative values and belief systems. The starting point is for managers to understand themselves, first, and then go on to recognise the value of diversity.

Influence and power

There are four major types of **power** which stakeholders develop or acquire. These are personal power, legitimate power, expert power, and political power. We have already met these levels of power *within* the organisation.

Personal power

This is power possessed by certain individuals or collections of individuals. For example, a powerful stakeholder group in an organisation may consist of the major shareholders. Another good example of this form of power occurs where a company has one or a few major customers or suppliers; for example, Marks & Spencer is often the sole customer for a number of companies in the textile and food-processing industries. Personal power therefore lies in the hands of people or groups who make a major contribution to an organisation. If an individual were to sell a shareholding in Eurotunnel this would not cause the board to have sleepless nights; however, it would be quite different if a major international bank were to withdraw its support.

Personal power also exists when an individual or group is able to strongly exert pressure on an organisation through personality or charisma. For example, Henry Ford ran the Ford Motor Company with an iron hand – what he said went. In a similar way there are some highly charismatic leaders of pressure groups who are able to gain tremendous support for their views, for example on environmental issues.

Legitimate power

Legitimate power is created within an organisational structure through clearly set out codes, practices, and channels of communication. For example, in a hierarchical organisation most of the power is vested in those positions at the top of the organisation. In a more democratic organisation, perhaps based on a teamwork structure, teams and team members would expect to be able to take important decisions. Within organisations, clear conventions develop over time as to who can rightfully make particular decisions.

Expert power

Expert power is based on the specialised knowledge possessed by certain individuals and groupings. In the past this gave considerable power to managers in an organisation – because they usually had most access to information about what was going on. This is no longer the case. Today it has been increasingly recognised that 'ordinary' employees have considerable expertise and skills – that they can be given the power to make decisions about the areas in which they have expertise.

In addition, 'marketing' has given a considerable thrust to new forms of stakeholder expert power. For example, consumers have most access to knowledge and understanding of what gives them satisfaction. The consumers are thus the 'experts' about what should be produced, how and where and need to be listened to closely. In a similar way members of a local community are 'experts' about ways in which production should take place in their 'back-yard'. Organisations must create the right channels to listen to these views. Ignore your local experts and you may quickly be faced with strong opposition from vociferous, well-informed individuals.

Political power

Political power stems from being supported by key groupings within a particular setting. To gain political power an individual or group will need to be able to work with people and social systems to gain support and allegiance from them. Gaining political power involves having an understanding of those factors most likely to encourage others to support you, and how systems can be used in your favour. Politicians have to set out to appease various groups in order to maintain their power base. Political leadership also involves having access to sanctions and rewards. A number of tactics can be employed to obtain and retain political power.

Managing organisations today should be seen as a highly political exercise involving the creation of effective coalitions between stakeholders. It may not always be possible to gain the support of all stakeholders. However, the key to successful management often lies in maximising this support while at the same time minimising any sources of long-term opposition.

Conflicts between stakeholders

A stakeholder puts something into the organisation and gets something out. The power that goes with this stakeholding will depend on many factors, but generally speaking the most important will be the extent to which the organisation is dependent on the stakeholder.

Stakeholders can make organisations dependent on them in a number of ways, such as by supplying key resources or key skills. A supplier of a major component can exert a lot of pressure on an organisation, as can a key knowledge worker, and as can suppliers of finance. And, of course, all businesses are dependent on their customers.

Stakeholders can also exert power through their ability to make demands on the organisation (e.g. in the case of a powerful trade union, or a strong pressure group which has the ear of the media).

Although the objectives of organisations usually reflect a general agreement between stakeholders about values and aims, it frequently happens that policies adopted tend to favour some groups of stakeholders over others (see Figure 14.9).

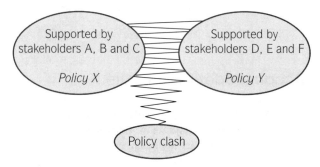

Figure 14.9 *Policy clashes within an organisation*

Examples of such **policy clashes** might include:

- how much of the company's profits should be distributed to shareholders
- whether employees should be given more of a say in decision-making
- whether an organisation should be allowed to expand its operations in an area of natural beauty, etc.

The following list describes further situations in which stakeholder conflicts may occur.

- *Interpretations of who the organisation should serve.* One of the strongest arguments put forward against building societies converting to public limited companies was that they would no longer serve their members' (e.g. savers' and borrowers') interests but instead would primarily serve the needs of shareholders. In a similar way, conflicts can arise over the interpretation of business objectives (e.g. where a new managing director introduces policies which seem to fly in the face of existing practice).

- *Deliberate misinterpretations of objectives.* At any time it is possible for stakeholders with the responsibility for making key decisions to deliberately misinterpret objectives, often to increase their own power and prestige. Individual managers may start to create their own policies and practices which further the interests of their own departments.
- *Changes in strategies and policies.* Dynamic organisations adjust their direction according to changes in circumstances. Unless these changes are communicated to and agreed by all key stakeholders, some people may continue working using old approaches while others adopt the new ones. This may result from deliberate sabotage or genuine lack of understanding.
- *Internal politics.* Segments of an organisation may be allied with particular stakeholders (e.g. employees) while other segments are allied to others (e.g. shareholders). This is likely to lead to clashes within the organisation and between the organisation and its external stakeholders.
- *Bad management.* Poor management allied with poor communication can create an atmosphere in which stakeholder conflicts arise.
- *Inevitable differences in objectives, policies and procedures.* There is a certain inevitability in the way conflict may arise in organisations through a lack of shared priorities. Organisations are made up of people rather than machine parts, so differing aspirations and understandings are almost certain to lead to conflict.

Coalitions between stakeholders

It makes sense to forge a **coalition** between stakeholders who share similar interests. The coalition may be developed over a long period or may be created to fight on a common front over a specific issue.

In terms of marketing, the most significant alliance is that forged with the end consumers. However, it is also possible to see all of your stakeholders as consumers – i.e. each and every stakeholder group is 'buying' from your organisation, so you must strive to win their loyalty and commitment.

Marketing orientation thus involves treating all stakeholders as customers and seeking to satisfy their aspirations and needs. This is most likely to occur by creating open communication channels, and using sophisticated research techniques to find out what exactly each and every stakeholder seeks from the organisation.

Achieving stakeholder satisfaction

Identification of aspirations

The starting point in achieving stakeholder satisfaction is to find out exactly what it is that the stakeholder aspires to. For example, do employees want to have more say and influence in decision-making? This can be found out by using techniques such as employee appraisal.

Do customers want products which are more environmentally friendly? This can be found out by market research. Do creditors want to be paid more quickly? This can be found out by creditor surveys. What do citizens who come into contact with the company want to see happening? This can be found out by holding open forums and public meetings. Each of the above examples highlights the importance of open communications.

Satisfaction and dissatisfaction cycles

Modern organisations use the expression 'growing more contented customers'. The implication is that you can create **satisfaction cycles** as an on-going process: a satisfied customer will want to build a stronger relationship with an organisation, a stronger relationship builds customer satisfaction, etc. This is a virtuous circle. In contrast, dissatisfied customers will want to loosen their relationships with an organisation, leading to a downward spiral.

The concept of a customer can be extended to include stakeholders and of course includes the 'internal customer' (stakeholders within the organisation). 'Internal customers' are people inside the company receiving products (usually unfinished) or services from their colleagues also in the company.

This extended concept is useful for several reasons. It enables people inside the company to realise the importance of what they are doing. It makes the point that the quality of the products and services sold to the external customer depends on the quality of products (perhaps only half-finished products) and services provided to colleagues within the company. Perhaps most usefully it helps people to realise their own significance – each person is an expert with something unique and essential to contribute.

Identifying powerful stakeholders

Managing organisations effectively involves a considerable amount of politics and alliance broking. It is important to have an idea of the relative strengths and influence of stakeholders within an organisation. Woe betide the company that misjudges the power of influential stakeholders such as the media!

Johnson and Scholes, in their widely read and influential book *Exploring Corporate Strategy*, have identified a number of **matrices** which serve as useful tools to those who seek to make changes in business policy and need to examine the implications of their actions for the various stakeholders within the organisation.

The power/dynamism matrix

This is a helpful way of assessing, in the early stages of developing a new strategy, where 'political effort' might be needed to influence key stakeholders (see Figure 14.10).

PREDICTABILITY

	High	Low
Low	A: Few problems	B: Unpredictable but manageable
POWER		
High	C: Powerful but predictable	D: Greatest danger or greatest opportunities

Figure 14.10 *The power/dynamism matrix*

The power/dynamism matrix focuses on the amount of power that groups of stakeholders have (high or low) and the predictability of their views in relation to a key change in business policy (high or low):

- Stakeholders in the A and B groups have low power. However, this does not mean that they are unimportant, because their views may be used to influence other stakeholders.
- Stakeholders in the C group have high power but their views are predictable. There should be no surprises.

- Stakeholders in the D group are the most difficult to influence or persuade and their views may also be the most difficult to predict. In managing change or in developing policy, therefore, it is important to pay considerable attention to this group in order to seek their support for change.

The power/interest matrix

This matrix examines stakeholders in relation to the power they hold and the degree of interest they show in the organisation (see Figure 14.11).

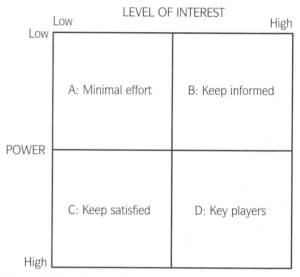

LEVEL OF INTEREST

	Low	High
Low	A: Minimal effort	B: Keep informed
POWER		
High	C: Keep satisfied	D: Key players

Figure 14.11 *The power/interest matrix*

Bargaining options

Successful management therefore involves a careful assessment of the aspirations of its stakeholders, an understanding of their sources of power, and the mapping of the levels of predictability, interest and power of these groupings.

There are a number of **bargaining options** available to managers in seeking to win the support of stakeholders. One option is to ignore a stakeholder's interest completely, but clearly this is a risky strategy as the stakeholder may be able to gain considerable support for their case. Frequently we come across stories in the press where individuals have been unfairly dismissed at work, where customer complaints have been ignored, or where a company has ridden roughshod over the local community. When these cases come to light they lead to the loss of goodwill by the company, and internal dissension.

Another negative option is to fight the stakeholder, perhaps by taking the stakeholder to court (e.g. where a company takes a libel action against someone who it feels to be defaming the name of the organisation). Again, this is a high-risk strategy because it brings the dispute out into the public arena.

A third option is to set out to appease the stakeholder, perhaps by making some concessions (e.g. by offering compensation to individuals and groups who suffer because of the company's actions).

A more positive approach is to try to win the stakeholder over by some form of persuasion. This involves opening up a dialogue with opposing stakeholders (e.g. by the use of newsletters or public meetings). When Shell UK was accused of being unfriendly to the environment in its intention to place derelict oil rigs at the bottom of the sea, it arranged a series of public meetings in an effort to convince detractors that this was the Best Possible Environmental Option (BPEO).

Another option is to form a coalition (a special relationship) with the stakeholder based on shared interests. Again this will involve the opening up of communication channels on a wide front.

The organisation can also take on board the stakeholder's feelings by offering pride of place in developing on-going strategy. This could take place if the stakeholder is able to put forward a convincing case.

Finally, the organisation might take the path of transforming itself into a new pattern which is determined by the stakeholder (e.g. when one company is taken over by another which previously had been the junior partner in the relationship). In a similar way a vocal group of shareholders might take over control of a company and refashion it in the way they see fit.

Informing and communicating

Today we live in an information age, so there are all sorts of ways of supplying information to stakeholders – newsletters, press releases, e-mail, the Internet, press and television advertising, etc. However, *effective* communication takes place only when the messages sent out are received clearly by the stakeholders to whom they are directed, and at the same time these stakeholders have the opportunity to communicate their aspirations and wishes to the organisation.

Good communication plays an important role *within an organisation*. It may help to coordinate the activities of various departments, transfer information or initiate some form of action. What is needed is a grapevine, an information system that allows the free flow of communication between interested parties.

External communication is concerned with how an organisation is viewed by outsiders. The 'listening' organisation will be well placed to create an effective relationship with its clients.

The concept of corporate mission

Corporate mission is now seen as being very important in helping an organisation to meet successfully the objectives of stakeholders. Cambell, Devine and Young, in their book *A Sense of Mission*, state that while mission for some organisations is simply a way of setting out the business goals, for others it is more a declaration of their beliefs and values. They argue that mission should appeal to the minds (strategy) and the hearts (values and beliefs) of stakeholders. Their model of an ideal mission comprises four elements.

- *Purpose* – what is the company for? Clearly, this will have a far broader stakeholder appeal if it goes beyond commercial goals. For example, George Merck, the son of the founder of Merck, one of the world's biggest pharmaceutical companies, said that: 'Medicine is for the patients. It is not for the profits'.
- *Strategy* – setting out how the purpose will be achieved.
- *Behaviour standards* – setting out the standards of performance and behaviour patterns involved in implementing the strategy. For example, when British Airways set out to become 'the world's favourite airline', its means to achieving this was through giving exceptional customer service by acquiring the staff, the planes, and the systems to deliver such service.
- *Values* – the underlying beliefs which provide the momentum to achieving the mission.

Creating a mission statement goes well beyond writing something down on a piece of paper. If the mission is to be effective, then it will be created through an extensive process of multi-directional communication involving all of the stakeholder groupings. Missions should not be created from above and imposed downwards and outwards; it is necessary to involve systematic communications and the sharing of ideas between all those involved with the organisation. Missions should represent stakeholder interests.

RESPONSIBILITIES OF ORGANISATIONS

Organisations have a range of responsibilities to their stakeholders. Key areas are described below, and are picked up in more detail in other parts of the book.

Physical performance

The **physical performance** of an organisation is concerned with output and productivity. Clearly physical performance is relatively easy to measure in manufacturing industry; it is a lot more difficult to assess in services where intangibles are produced.

Production can be seen as a response to market research. In meeting the needs of a market, businesses need to consider the 'Six O's' (see Figure 14.12).

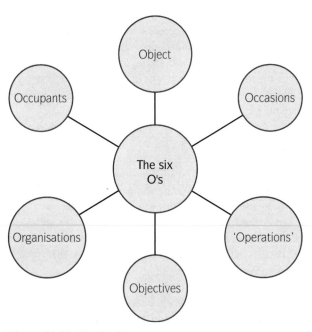

Figure 14.12 *The Six O's*

- **Occupants.** Which individuals make up (occupy) the market? For example, as an organisation are we concerned with a mass market, such as that household water and electricity? Or are we talking about a market made up of a narrower band of consumers, such as pigeon fanciers or social workers?
- **Object.** What do our consumers wish to buy? What benefits are they looking for?
- **Occasions.** When will consumers purchase our product? Will it be every week, every month, or once a year? What time of the day are they most likely to make a purchase? When we find the answers to these questions we will be able to provide goods at the right time for our consumers.
- **Organisations.** Who is involved in the decision to purchase? When selling goods we need to aim our sales pitch at the purchaser. For example, if selling a textbook to a college, one needs to target the lecturers who will make the purchasing decision.
- **Objectives.** Why do consumers buy particular goods or services? If we can find out why people make a purchasing decision, we will be better placed to provide a solution to their buying problem.
- **'Operations'.** How do consumers buy products and services? For example, do they pay cash, or use some form of credit? If we know their preferred method, we can make it easier for them to make a purchase. For example, if a car manufacturer knows that buyers are most likely to buy a car with hire-purchase instalments over three years, the right credit terms can be made available.

Operations are also, of course, those processes and methods by which an organisation uses its resources to produce something or to provide a service. For example, in a factory, operations are the processes used to turn raw materials and other inputs into finished products. In a restaurant, operations take place when food is prepared in the kitchens and served to customers at the tables. Banking operations are concerned with converting given inputs into desired financial outputs. Hospital operations are concerned with converting given inputs into desired medical outputs, and so on. Figure 14.13 shows one way of expressing this.

TASK

Identify another three types of organisation, and set out a table indicating the operations, and some of their main inputs and outputs.

Organisaton	Operational inputs	Outputs
Bank	Cashiers Management staff Computer hardware Premises Energy	Deposits Overdrafts Other financial services
Hospital	Medical staff Management staff Ancillary staff Equipment, beds, building etc. Medicines Energy	Healthier patients Care
Schools	Teachers Textbooks Classrooms Sports facilities	Educated and healthy students

Figure 14.13 *Some of the inputs and outputs of three types of organisation*

Organisations depend upon the skills of their operations managers (in manufacturing often referred to as production managers). They need to be able to organise operations to produce products that satisfy consumers. It is often said that production is at the 'sharp end' of business activity. What this means is that if production does not produce the right goods at the right time, then the organisation will fail. Targets have to be met and standards kept up. Failure to meet targets and standards can be disastrous.

Production management involves controlling and coordinating the organisation's resources such as finance, capital equipment, labour and other factors. Timetables and schedules are needed to show how these resources will be used in production.

Figure 14.14 shows how operations management involves successfully transforming inputs into desired goods and services. Note that we can make a distinction between *transforming* resources and **transformed** resources:

- managers, employees, machinery and equipment are a firm's transforming resources
- the transformed resources are the materials and information which they process.

The kind of operations an organisation carries out will, of course, depend on what is being processed. A useful distinction is between operations which focus mainly on processing either materials, information, or customers.

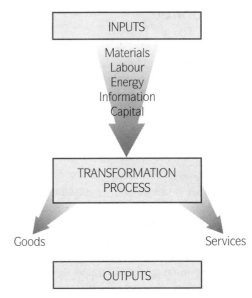

Figure 14.14 *Transformation of resources*

Figure 14.15 demonstrates how various organisations can be grouped under these three headings.

Mainly processing materials	Mainly processing information	Mainly processing customers
Manufacturing firm	Accountant	Hairdresser
Oil refinery	Market researcher	Leisure centre
Post Office	Statistical office	Hospital

Figure 14.15 *Grouping organisations according to what is processed*

Managing for quality

It is essential that an organisation's operations be carried out in an efficient way. Today organisations set out to ensure **efficiency** by engaging in a process of **managing quality**. This emphasis on quality is largely borrowed from the success of Japanese business practice in the 1980s.

Quality

We use the term 'quality' in the context of 'producing a good or service to customer requirements' (often referred to as 'fitness for purpose'). In UK industry we can identify three stages that have been involved in moving towards quality: quality control, quality assurance, and total quality management (TQM).

Quality control

Quality control is an old idea. It involves inspectors checking finished goods and detecting and cutting out components or final products which do not meet the required standard. It can involve considerable waste as substandard products have to be scrapped.

Quality assurance

Quality assurance is less wasteful than quality control. It occurs both before and during production, and seeks to stop faults happening in the first place. Quality assurance, like quality control, aims to make sure that products are produced to preset standards, but this is the responsibility of the workforce working in teams, rather than of traditional inspectors.

Total quality management (TQM)

TQM is the most complete form of operations management. It is concerned with encouraging everyone in the workplace to think about quality in everything they do. Every employee sets out to satisfy customers, placing them at the heart of the production process.

Quality procedures

To ensure that the quality systems do work, the organisation must have in place various **quality procedures**.

First, the organisation must define the responsibilities for all aspects of quality and allocate the necessary authority to act on any problems. All aspects of the quality assurance procedures should be documented, with accurate information, correctly transmitted and recorded. For example, in a manufacturing company the design department might accept a modification, requested by a customer, to the normal basic design. Unless the manufacturing instructions to departments are carefully controlled, some departments may use the standard design rather than the revised version.

If a fault is discovered in any output, it may be that the whole of that production batch is affected and should be recalled for examination. It is good practice, therefore, to mark production in such a way that faults can be traced to the date of manufacture, the production batch, and the particular machine or operator.

Certificates

Reliable quality is a prime concern when deciding which supplier of a good or service to use. Retail organisations like Marks & Spencer have, for many years, extended their own quality-control procedures into their suppliers' organisations to ensure reliability. A reputation for quality is important, but it can be established only over time. This presents problems for organisations tendering for orders from new customers. The **International Standard (IS) 9000** certificate indicates to potential customers that the quality procedures of the certificate holders are reliable, and by implication that they are capable of delivering consistently the promised quality product or service.

Efficiency and effectiveness

Today's modern organisations use many **performance indicators**, ranging from the traditional accounts, and productivity measures such as output per labour hour, to more modern indicators such as school and hospital league tables showing value added, and measures of teacher performance. However, in this context an important distinction must be made between an **efficient** and an **effective** organisation.

Efficiency

For some organisations it is imperative to be able to compete with others *on the basis of cost*, so the emphasis will be on cost minimisation. Costs are kept to a minimum when resources are used efficiently. The key question will be how well those resources have been used, regardless of the purpose for which they are used. An efficient organisation might adopt measures of efficiency such as profitability, or output per employee, or machines being used to full capacity, and so on.

Since all inputs used by an organisation are costly, they must be used in such a way that waste is kept to a minimum. When everything possible has been done to minimise costs, we can say that the firm is operating at its technically most efficient point.

A manager focusing on efficiency would argue that efficiency occurs:

- when for *labour* the percentage of time spent idle is minimised

- when for *materials* the percentage of waste or scrap is minimised
- when for *machinery*, output per machine-hour is maximised so that machines are used to their full potential.

Business efficiency will stem from the best possible mix of manpower, machines, materials, money and managers (see Figure 14.16).

In service industries, quality is a major source of customer satisfaction or dissatisfaction. In his book, *Managerial Leadership in the Post-Industrial Society*, Philip Sadler suggests that efficiency and cost control in service operations can be improved by 'industrialising' a service. There are three ways in which this can be done.

- By *automation* – using technology as a substitute for human involvement. Examples are automatic teller machines, luggage X-ray machines, automatic highway toll collectors, coin-operated car washers.
- By *rationalisation* – improving working methods in a systematic way. This covers a wide range of activities involving human service operations following carefully defined procedures which are simultaneously economic and provide customer satisfaction. (Frequently the speedier the service the lower the cost and the greater the customer satisfaction.) Examples range from cleaning a hotel room to completing the sale/purchase of a house.
- By *standardisation* – limiting the range of variability in the service. Examples are restricted menu restaurants as in a McDonald's, packaged tours, and unit trusts.

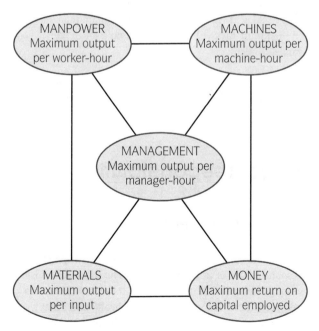

Figure 14.16 *Measures of efficiency*

Effectiveness

An effective organisation may be concerned to show that it is better than competitors, for example by developing and sustaining unique products. An organisation that stresses effectiveness may concentrate on quality rather than quantity. The effective organisation will seek to channel resources into those aspects of activities that emphasise its edge over competitors ('competitive advantage').

Organisations and their subsystems work towards the achievement of a multitude of objectives in a variety of different categories – long-range or short-range, strategic or operational, general or specific. Clearly, for an organisation to be effective it must be able to express its objectives in an easily understandable way.

Johnson and Scholes, in their book *Exploring Corporate Strategy*, argued that the effectiveness of an organisation can be critically influenced by the ability to get all parts of its value chain working in harmony. They suggested a number of measures of effectiveness.

- *Use of people.* People should be used in such a way as to meet the real objectives of the organisation.
- *Use of capital.* An organisation should use capital in such a way as to serve its real needs.
- *Use of marketing and distribution resources.* Marketing and distribution resources should be used to meet the best needs of the organisation.
- *Use of research knowledge.* Research knowledge should be used to meet the needs of the organisation most effectively.
- *Use of production systems.* This needs to be geared towards the basis on which the organisation competes.
- *Exploitation of intangible assets.* These include image, brand name, and market information.

The organisation that is both efficient and effective will use its resources efficiently to meet organisational objectives effectively. A useful question to ask is always: 'It is efficient, but is it also effective?' In other words, is it really helping us to meet our objectives and to develop a competitive advantage.

Equal opportunities

Equal opportunities exist in the workplace when individuals have identical rights and responsibilities regardless of gender, racial group, age, physical characteristics, sexual orientation or other features. All business organisations must seek, as a minimum, to meet equal opportunities legislation which is a statutory responsibility.

Sex and marital discrimination

The **Sex Discrimination Act 1975** aims to make sure that both sexes are treated equally in the workplace. It is illegal for employers to discriminate in the following key areas:

- selection procedures
- terms on which employment is offered
- opportunities for training and development
- fringe benefits
- choice of who will be made redundant.

Unlawful discrimination means giving less favourable treatment to someone because of their sex or because they are married or single.

Under the Act, discrimination can be either *direct* or *indirect*. Direct sex discrimination occurs when someone is treated less favourably than a person of the opposite sex would be in the same circumstances. For example, if only men are made managers, and sex is the criterion for appointment, this counts as direct discrimination.

Indirect sex discrimination is less easy to pinpoint. It means introducing a requirement which on the face of it applies equally to both men and women, but which in practice can be met by a much smaller proportion of one sex than the other – for example, when an organisation restricts certain grades of work to males.

Direct marriage discrimination means treating a married person less favourably than an unmarried person of the same sex. For example, a policy not to recruit married people for a job that involved being away from home would be classed as discrimination.

The **Sex Discrimination Act 1985** also covers victimisation. Victimisation means treating someone less favourably than others because, 'in good faith' they have made allegations about discrimination or unfair treatment.

Race discrimination

The **Race Relations Act 1976** aims to protect members of ethnic minorities from discrimination and unfair treatment.

Equal pay

The **Equal Pay Act 1970** states that employers must pay equal amounts to men and women if they are doing the same work, or work which rates as being equivalent, or if they are doing work of equal value. Under the Act, anyone making a claim for equal pay must be able to compare themselves with a person of the opposite sex doing the *same or equivalent work*.

Disabled workers

The **Disabled Persons (Employment) Acts 1944 and 1958** state that employers of more than 20 people must employ a quota of disabled people. The present quota is 3 per cent of the workforce. However, in practice few firms have been prosecuted for falling short of this target.

Managing diversity

Recently, a number of writers have suggested that organisations should take a 'managing-diversity' rather than an equal-opportunities approach. The latter are based on equality and the idea that when people are in the same situation they should be treated in the same way. In contrast, a managing-diversity approach sees gender and other forms of differentiation as *relevant*. Currently many organisations are still organised around the needs, values and approaches of a particular segment of the workforce – white males. If organisations are to maintain their success in the future, they will need to draw on a much wider range of talent.

The differences between an equal-opportunities and a managing-diversity approach are summarised in Figure 14.17.

Legal responsibilities

Health and safety

Health and safety at work is one of the most important responsibilities of any organisation. The organisation is responsible to all its employees and those who come into contact with it. The requirements of health and safety legislation are dealt with in detail in Chapter 24 which focuses on the legal framework.

Managing diversity	Equal opportunities
• Ensures all employees maximise their potential and their contribution to the organisation	• Concentrates on discrimination
• Embraces a broad range of people, no one is excluded	• Is perceived as an issue primarily for women, ethnic minorities and people with disabilities
• Concentrates on movement within an organisation, the culture of the organisation and the meeting of business objectives	• Concentrates on the numbers of groups employed
• Is the concern of all employees, especially managers	• Is seen as an issue to do with personnel and human resource practitioners
• Does not rely on positive action/affirmative action	• Relies on positive action

Figure 14.17 *Managing diversity and equal opportunities compared*

Consumer and employment law

Every good or service that is sold must meet certain standards. Some of these standards are laid down in law, some in voluntary codes of practice within an industry. Others are set by individual businesses. The legal and voluntary systems set out a fair framework for trading, and also to help to settle disputes that may arise.

Businesses must also meet their statutory requirements covering the protection of employees' rights in the workplace. The legal framework for employment protection is very detailed and has been built up over hundreds of years.

The responsibilities of employers to consumers and employees are set out in detail Chapters 22 and 24 which are concerned with the legal framework of business.

The outside world

So far in this section we have focused on the responsibilities of organisations towards customers, employees, health and safety requirements, equal opportunities etc. The organisation also has an important responsibility to the natural environment, and in terms of ethical practice.

The natural environment

Increasingly organisations state that they are committed to the notion of **sustainable development**. Critics doubt whether this is true. For example, some argue that if the major corporations were asked to show in their end-of-year accounts the cost of putting the environment back to the state it was in at the beginning of the year, then the cost would more than outweigh any profits the company had made. No major corporation using this approach would have made a real profit for at least fifty years, yet each year corporations are able to pay dividends to shareholders!

In recent years serious attempts have been made by economists to build environmental considerations into the market mechanism. But while it is barely controversial to state that a major policy objective should be to create sustainable development, nobody is clear exactly what it means. A useful starting definition was provided in 1987 by the World Commission on the Environment and Development:

> '... development that meets the needs of the present generation without compromising the ability of future generations to meet their own needs.'

Development is generally seen as something that is positive. It means being better off tomorrow than we are today. But what exactly is development? Measures such as GNP (gross national product) express the living standards of people measured in terms of quantities of goods that can be purchased, but there is a significant difference between the terms 'standard of living' and the 'quality of life'.

In *Blueprint for a Green Economy* (1989, 1993), David Pearce suggests that sustainable development involves enhancing both the standard of living and the quality of life. The value of the environment is an important part of this quality of life and we need to consider:

• the environment
• the future
• equity.

Pearce introduces the term 'futurity' to refer to the principle of taking a long-term view of things. If one generation leaves the next with less wealth than it inherited, then it has made the future worse off. We also need to think about the nature of this legacy. The history of recent development has often involved the conversion of 'natural wealth' such as reserves of ores, oil and timber into 'capital wealth' (factories, car parks, cinemas etc.).

Pearce suggests that it is not good enough simply to argue that growth is taking place because our stock of 'wealth' is increasing. Instead he argues that sustainable development involves leaving a legacy of capital wealth *and* natural wealth to future generations.

Pearce also suggests that we need to tackle the issue of fairness between one generation and another (intergenerational equity) and between people living on the planet at the same time (intragenerational equity). If we fail to tackle the issue of **equity** we will never get agreement about how to move forward.

Organisations need to develop sound strategies to contribute to sustaining and enhancing the national and international environment. To generate wealth, firms and other organisations engage in production and the consumption of resources. Needless to say an expanding economy is one that is likely to pollute more. If this is true for the UK it must also be true for all the countries in the world, with Brazil, India, Vietnam and others all aspiring to the living standards of the West.

Growth, though, comes with associated costs. Extra cars that bring freedom to travel have resulted in congested cities and health problems. The costs of growth appear in many aspects of modern life.

The responsibility of organisations towards the environment is a major issue. Today a company's environmental performance is increasingly central to its competitiveness and survival. The following illustrations give a very stark warning to businesses that fail to take action:

- One of the world's largest paper-producing companies committed a minor, technical environmental violation in the American state of Maine. In May 1992 the US government imposed a three-year ban on government paper purchases from the company.
- The German government's privatisation programme in the Bittefield region of the former East Germany ground to a halt when Western investors, concerned about environmental clean-up costs, were unwilling to buy shares in a single business.
- An American bank foreclosed on a $1 million building mortgage, thereby becoming the legal owner of the property. However, in doing so it inherited an environmental clean-up bill of $2 million.

If polluters take little or no account of their actions, but they have an effect on the rest of society with money and time being needed to clear up the problem, the conclusion must be that the output of these industries is less than optimal for society as a whole. Economists call the costs of pollution **externalities** because, although private costs and benefits determine what goods are made and purchased, these may come at a social or external cost to the community.

Discussion point

Does the solution lie in allowing the marketplace to solve the problem, so that well-informed consumers choose the products that do least harm to the environment? Or is there a need to take a more interventionist line that brings organisations face to face with the consequences of their actions?.

Environmental policy: making a start

All aspects of an organisation's operations, from accounting to production and distribution, have an impact on the environment, and the policy should recognise this fact.

In practice, companies and organisations are being encouraged to take a long hard look at all their activities. Government departments are producing information for distribution to companies, colleges and universities. This provides a framework to review current operations and to set objectives to review waste. The following headings are a guide to the comprehensive nature of this approach.

The mission statement

A commitment to the environment and other corporate responsibility issues implies a fresh look at the mission statement and a re-evaluation of corporate objectives and the needs of stakeholders. Creating a greener mission and objectives might include sustainable growth, obligations towards staff, and even a larger timeframe over which the company plans its activities.

Environmental audit

An **environmental audit** is an evaluation of a company's performance, carried out regularly, systematically and objectively. The procedure began in the USA as an assessment of a company's compliance with official regulations on the environment. Now its role has been extended. Today, environmental auditing is a management tool to improve practices as well as ensuring that the company's and the government's policies on the environment are fulfilled. The audit should be carried out by personnel who are expert in the technologies used at the sites to be inspected, and they should have the enthusiastic backing of top management.

A typical environmental audit in the oil industry consists of a visit by the audit team to the site – which could be a refinery, a factory, an offshore oil production platform, a laboratory, or a distribution depot. During the visit, the team interviews staff and inspects records, facilities, equipment and the immediate surroundings of the site according to a systematic testing procedure. As a result of the visit, the team prepares a detailed report. Following discussion an action plan is agreed. This in turn becomes a regular agenda item at management meetings to ensure that the action plan is effectively monitored. The audit is repeated at regular intervals.

The benefits of auditing include:

- more effective compliance with company environmental goals and official regulations
- increased employee awareness of environmental requirements
- improved environmental training
- reduction of waste
- better environmental reporting to government and public.

Structural change

This focuses on the organisational changes required to incorporate the issues raised in the mission and objectives and brought to light through auditing. It can include the identification of responsibility for these issues in the senior management team. Germany leads the way on this, with the majority of companies having a board member with explicit responsibility – perhaps a reaction to that country's stringent environmental legislation.

Supporting the mission on environmental approaches

It is easy to produce statements of the policy of the organisation and then assume that this is enough to satisfy various groups. As with any major initiative, it has to

receive the wholehearted support of senior managers. This will be best achieved when it is clear to them that an environmentally aware company can achieve improvements in environmental performance indicators at the same time as exploiting new opportunities in the marketplace.

Staff

The workforce generally is in support of the reduction in waste and the promotion of greener production processes. This is especially so amongst the younger recruits and female managers, with the implication being that a company that is seen as half-hearted or antagonistic in its approach to environmental issues will find it harder to recruit or retain people of the right calibre.

Systems

To make a success of becoming a greener organisation, new approaches will be required. The Department for Education and Employment (DfEE), for example, encourages colleges and universities to review their activities. They are dependent on paper to produce handouts for students, to circulate memoranda, to keep minutes of meeting and so on, and the question has been asked: Are there alternative ways to disseminate information of this type that are more environmentally friendly? A further example is that inner city colleges and universities have problems with the parking facilities for students and staff, with the traditional demand for more spaces to be created. In Liverpool, the John Moores University has a long-term objective of reducing car-parking spaces and cooperating on the development of public transport links, which will contribute to the creation of more opportunities to develop new buildings and reduce pollution in the city.

In essence the **green organisation** would wish to:

- measure and control overall performance
- provide and process the relevant information
- reinforce the strategies through appraisal and rewards
- develop new products and technology
- replace existing systems and activities with more efficient ones.

The move towards environmental excellence will require a step-by-step approach. This has been summarised by John Elkington in his book *The Green Capitalist* as follows.

- Develop and publish an environmental policy.
- Prepare an action programme.
- Arrange the organisation and staffing of the company, including board-level representation.
- Allocate adequate resources.
- Invest in environmental science and technology.
- Educate and train.
- Monitor, audit and report.
- Monitor the evaluation of the green agenda.
- Contribute to the environmental programmes.
- Help to build bridges between the various interested groups.

When organisations observe the growing European and UK legislation, the creation of various inspectorates to reinforce compliance, the more active involvement of pressure groups such as Friends of the Earth, and a more litigious approach to penalise companies and organisations who flout the law, they should consider it to be good management practice to start on the adaptive process before they find themselves the subject of a hefty fine and with the expense of rectifying problems they have created.

'Responsible' means 'Realistic'

Resources are not infinite. In environmental matters companies and countries can deal only in tradeoffs. If too many resources are spent reducing pollution in one area, that might leave inadequate resources for reducing pollution in another or for providing services that society considers essential. Sometimes the removal of one pollutant increases production of another. The dilemma can be summed up in the phrase 'best practical environmental option' (BPEO).

But what is 'best' and what is 'practical'? Technology is advancing rapidly. What was best only a few years ago is practical now. Also, since standards are rising, what was thought best only a few years ago might be thought unacceptable now, and improved technology allows a new 'best' to be achieved. There is still a choice to be made. The way to stop all pollution from motor transport is to ban all motor transport; this is not a sensible option at the present, so a balance has to be achieved and society as a whole must determine where that balance lies so that companies have targets to aim for and standards by which to be judged. Companies can then use their resources, experience and creativity to achieve the targets set for them – and of course, in so doing, suggest new and even higher targets.

Discussion point

1. Do you agree that industry should seek to work to the best practical environmental option, or is this too soft a target?

2. Give an example of a practice which is currently regarded to be the BPEO. Is the standard set high enough?

3. Can you think of a better alternative than the BPEO?

Ethical practice

Ethics are moral principles or rules of conduct which are generally accepted by most members of a society. They involve what individuals and groups believe to be right and what is considered to be wrong. An 'ethic' is therefore a guide as to what should be done or what should not be done.

From an early age, parents, schools, religious teaching and society in general provide us with moral guidelines to help us to learn and form our ethical beliefs. Many ethics are reinforced in our legal system and thus provide a constraint to business activities, while others are not. In areas covered by law, there may well be social pressure to conform to a particular standard. Pressure groups often set out to force individuals or organisations to operate in an 'acceptable' way.

Through the media we hear about questionable business activities – issues such as insider dealing, animal rights protesters involved in disputes with organisations producing cosmetic and pharmaceutical products, protests about tobacco sponsorship, and trading links with unfriendly or hostile nations. As a result, consumers have become more aware of the ethical and moral values underlying business decisions.

Today's consumer is more concerned than ever before about what an organisation stands for, who it trades with, what it does, whether it supports any political party, whether it is an equal opportunities employer and how it behaves in the community as a whole. When *Which?* carried out a survey, 63 per cent of those who responded were concerned about the activities of companies they might invest in.

Case Study

Responsibility for what?

The philosopher Robert Frederick poses some important questions about the responsibility of businesses to the community. He puts forward his arguments in the following manner.

• A number of people seem to think that it is obviously true that businesses have a responsibility to protect the environment. These responsibilities go beyond what is required by law and regulation. Businesses frequently have the knowledge and the resources to limit environmental damage from their activities. To refuse to take responsibility for these actions can be seen as irresponsible and a neglect of moral duty.

• A business person may reply that businesses have only a limited power to serve the economic needs of society and must operate within the bounds of law and regulations. However, a business has no moral obligation to try to solve other social problems which may be partly caused by its activities. Businesses have no moral duty to do more than meet the requirements imposed on them by law and regulation.

• A basic ethical principle is that you should 'do no harm', because creating harm violates the rights of another person not to be harmed. However, perhaps this should be limited to a statement that you should do no 'unwarranted' harm. For example, in a football game if one person is accidentally hurt in a tackle, then this is acceptable because the injured party must

have been aware that going into a fair tackle sometimes causes hurt. If a knowledgeable and competent investor loses money on the stock market, his or her rights have not been violated. The harm in both examples is an acknowledged risk of participating in the activity. If, on the other hand, the footballer were to have his watch stolen while he was on the floor, or if the investor were to be trampled underfoot in a rush by floor traders to sell on the announcement of bad news, then their rights would have been violated.

• The same principle can be applied to business life. If individuals or groups are harmed by business activity, and the harm is unrewarded in that it is not offset by a balancing benefit, or if the harm is unnecessary in that it is a preventable rather than an inevitable peril of ordinary life, then there has been a violation of the right not to be harmed.

Questions

1. What is your view on the nature of harm outlined by Robert Frederick?

2. How important is it to develop into a strategy a series of business principles related to the notion of harm?

3. Discuss a series of examples where 'harm' may have been caused by business activity?

4. What do you understand by business ethics? How high a priority should organisations give to business ethics?

Local and National Economy

All organisations operate within three economies: the local, the national and the international.
This chapter describes the mainstream economic systems and investigates the key features of
the local and national economy in which organisations operate.

On completion of this chapter you should be able to:

- explain the major features of an economic system

- analyse differing views of the role of the state, and their implications

- discuss the impact of two policies on an organisation

- investigate the significance of a regional or local development issue and the impact on an organisation

We can look at the effect of the economy on organisations at a number of levels. Organisations may be as directly affected by local changes as by national or international ones; for example, the closure of a major factory in a town may hit local people harder than any effects of a world recession.

Macroeconomics is the study of large-scale economic changes that tend to affect the whole of the nation's economy. Macroeconomics views the larger economy as a system. Major changes to the system will therefore impact on the components of the system. For example, a downturn in economic activity associated with the 'trade cycle' is likely to impact on all firms operating within the economy. Changes in macroeconomic variables, such as the base interest rate or the rate of inflation, will impact on all businesses (although to a greater or lesser extent, depending on the nature of the business).

Microeconomics is concerned with smaller parts of the overall system. For example, instead of looking at the overall market for consumer goods, we may focus on the market for a particular good (e.g. the market for new television sets). Rather than focusing on the general market for labour in the economy, microeconomics may focus on the market for electricians in Grantham, and so on.

TYPES OF ECONOMIC SYSTEM

Until the late 1980s it was common practice to classify world economies into:

- the first world – the richer, developed market-based economies including West Germany, the United States, Japan and the United Kingdom
- the second world – the socialist and communist states such as East Germany, the Soviet Union, North Korea and China
- the third world – developing countries such as Rwanda, Ethiopia and Bangladesh

In the late 1980s this classification was to become defunct as a number of communist regimes collapsed and as a number of former third-world countries experienced dramatic increases in growth rates.

Since 1989 the success of market economies has led some to assume that a certain type of free-market economic structure has become the basis for economic activity across the globe. However, it is relevant to ask whether the type of economic system we see in the UK and the USA is to be found in other economies in the European Union, Japan, China, Burma and in the remainder of the world's nation states. The organisation of economic activity differs remarkably across these economies, so there are important differences that will be of significance for companies and managers trading abroad.

All societies must develop a system for dealing with three interrelated issues.

- What will be produced?
- How will it be produced?
- For whom will it be produced?

We can illustrate the wide differences in possible systems by looking at two imaginary island communities which are dependent on fishing and farming. Call these two communities Sealand and Skyland.

In Sealand all decisions are made by a small group of chieftains. The chieftains decide who will do the fishing and who will do the farming. They decide how many hours are to be put into each activity and how the necessary equipment will be made (e.g. the fishing boats, agricultural implements). They have also decided that everyone will receive an equal share of the produce – except for the chieftains, who will have a double portion of everything.

In Skyland there is no organising group. Individuals are left to their own devices. They decide individually what to make and they trade or store their surpluses. They decide how to produce their equipment, and how long to spend at particular activities. They consume the bulk of their own produce, except for what they can exchange.

In the past, the basic economic problems were solved by custom and tradition; for example, the way crops were grown and shared out was decided by folk tradition. In many parts of the world traditional economies have given way to three major systems:

- the planned system
- the free-market system
- the mixed system.

Within these three basic models, there will be a wide range of variations and differences.

Any society must decide how to use the resources that are available to it. Choices have to be made which involve sacrifices. The challenge facing each country is how this should be done. Should it be left to individuals and organisations to bid for resources, on the basis that they can produce what people need as long as it is profitable for them? If they fail to produce what is required, then they cease to trade, and the resources that they were using can be purchased and used by others to produce profitable items. We know this as the **free-market solution**, which involves solving the problem of scarcity by providing a rationing mechanism based on price and profit.

A major challenge for the free-market approach is whether it can build a long-term future, with the requirement to undertake investment that may not be profitable for some considerable time. Will the market be able, for example, to provide for skills in the workforce that may be needed ten years (or further) into the future?

TASK

1. Make a list of eight strengths and eight weaknesses of each of the economic systems described.

2. Devise a third system which you would regard as preferable to those of Sealand and Skyland. In what ways do you think that your system is preferable?

3. Why might other people disagree with you? What would be the reasoning behind these objections?

Discussion point

One of the major problems facing the UK economy in the last half of the twentieth century was a *skills gap* between the nation and its major competitors. This skills gap existed in a wide range of occupational areas. Do you think that the free market is likely to lead to a solution to the skills gap in this country, or should the government intervene to provide the sort of educational and training opportunities that would close this gap?

What is true for education and training can also be the case for health, social security, policing and defence, which then introduces a high-profile role for government. This **mixed-economy** regime also incorporates anti-competitive measures to deal with the rise of monopolies and monopolistic practices that free markets have a tendency to create.

Likewise, the problem of externalities – such as air and land pollution – can create a role for government. It can try to measure the pollution costs borne by the general community, and reach a decision as to the most effective way to deal with this.

The **planned economie**s of eastern Europe and the old USSR took the role of government to be of paramount importance. Under the label of 'democratic socialism', the state owned the means of production in the name of the people, arguing that a market system exploited the masses, by building up profits that benefited the minority at the expense of the majority. A market solution was divisive and degrading for the population, so the state had to organise production and distribution, in order to resolve the problem of scarcity without the exploitation normally associated with capitalism.

These three broad-based classifications of the free market, mixed and planned, are useful devices for seeing the basic differences that exist between them in trying to resolve the problem of scarcity. A degree of caution is required when using this approach. It is clear that many countries do not conform to the classification allotted to them, so even under the old Soviet-style planned economies immense differences could be found between Hungary, East Germany and the USSR. Likewise, the mixed economies of France, Germany and the UK show clear preferences in respect to government intervention that goes some way to explaining their problems over European integration. Moving further afield, where would the Islamic countries of Iran, Iraq and Syria be placed?

Many approaches to internal business focus on the **degree of risk** associated with business opportunities in overseas countries. One aspect that has not been mentioned so far is the **degree of political and legal control** exerted by government and the regulatory agencies. From the brief description of the three economic systems, it is clear that legal and regulatory control in a planned economy would be high, with individuals given few opportunities to own property or to have ownership rights when it comes to natural resources or the assets of an enterprise. Free- and mixed-market approaches would create opportunities for individuals and groups to have ownership rights, as private companies provide a high proportion of the output that a society requires. Figure 15.1 is a method of rating the economic and political–legal systems based on the opportunities created or devised to set up private enterprises, own projects and promote individual freedom.

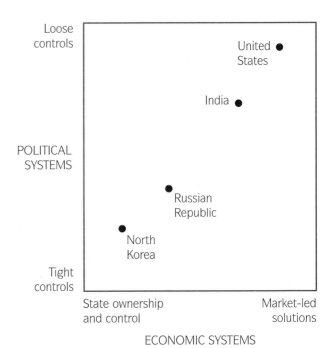

Figure 15.1 *The politico-economic field*

Planned systems

Planning involves some form of official coordination of activities. This can take place at either a local or a centralised level. Planning authorities will be responsible in some way for the creation of targets, systems and procedures. The process of organised planning is most commonly associated with countries in the former communist bloc.

It is worth examining some of the common features associated with centrally planned economies. However, it must be stressed that in recent years many communist countries have experienced substantial phases of economic reform, such as *perestroika* in Russia. Such changes have involved a relaxation of price controls and of production control from the centre and a greater freedom to set up private enterprises.

Countries with centrally planned economic systems (including Kampuchea, North Korea, Cuba and China) represent a large proportion of the world's population and industrial output. It is interesting to note that in recent times increasingly large parts of the Chinese and Cuban economies have been liberalised. However, central authorities still play a major role. We should not underestimate the importance of the Chinese economy which is expected to take over early in the twenty-first century as the world's major economic superpower.

Although there are wide differences in the economic organisation of centrally planned economies and their respective stages of development, there are also a number of important similarities.

- The means of production are publicly owned. This takes the form of state, collective or cooperative ownership. However, decisions about their use can be made in a variety of ways, ranging from collective decision-making to decision-making by a small committee of people.
- Planning is centralised and strategies to increase the quantity and/or quality of overall output are laid down by the planning authority.
- There is a market for consumer goods (although consumers will not necessarily have the freedom to spend money in the way they would wish) and a market for labour. Wages are paid, and a large proportion of consumer goods are exchanged in the market, in transactions using some form of money.
- Prices for all goods sold by the state are decided by planning authorities. They are not able to change spontaneously.
- Nearly all decisions relating to capital formation will be made and controlled by planning authorities. Capital formation is the production of those goods and equipment that go into further production, such as that of factory machinery.

The key feature of a planned, or **command**, economy is that it is planning committees who decide what will be produced, how it will be produced and how products will be distributed. Smaller groups such as factories and other business units submit their plans to a local committee, who decide which resources will be made available to each local area, which in turn will allocate resources to each factory, farm or other productive unit.

Productive units are often set production targets, and are then given a quantity of resources and a time constraint to meet the targets.

Advantages of a planned economy

1. Effective long-term strategies can be developed taking into account the needs of the total system.
2. Planning can be carried out according to the collective needs and wants of each of the individual parts of a system.
3. Duplication of resources can be eliminated.
4. Resources and products can be shared out more equitably according to the dominant value system prevailing in that society.
5. Planning decisions can be made in a consistent manner.
6. The system can be shaped in such a way as to reflect the social and political wishes of a group of people.

Disadvantages of a planned economy

1. Heavy-handed planning and control may stifle individual enterprise.
2. The process of planning itself uses up scarce resources for administration and supervision.
3. The absence of the profit motive removes the spur to individual effort and enterprise. It is argued by some that people are more inclined to work harder and to make personal sacrifices if they can profit from doing so.
4. The process of communication between consumers and producers can become distorted so that the goods that are produced fall far short of consumer requirements. If planning decisions are made well in advance of consumption decisions, then by the time goods appear in the marketplace tastes and fashions may have changed.
5. Where price controls are established, unofficial black markets may develop, leading to bribery and corruption.

Case Study

Changes in economic systems

In the period 1945 until the end of the 1980s it looked as if the world economic system would continue to be divided between two sets of economic ideologies and principles – state planning and the market economies. In the socialist economies decisions were made by central planners working to models of how resources should be utilised. At one stage, for example, planners in the Soviet Union had created a huge model of their system which they housed in an aircraft hangar. They used markers to represent flows of goods between industries. It was not surprising that while the model was effective in the confines of the hangar, it led to glaring inefficiencies in the real world. The third world of the developing countries, as they were called at the time, was a battleground between the two ideologies.

Then, suddenly at the end of the 1980s the whole house of cards came tumbling down, first with *perestroika* bringing an end to the Soviet Union and the Cold War, and other movements such as Solidarity in Poland. The reunification of Germany saw an end to the old Cold War frontier between the Western and Eastern powers.

Figure 15.2 *The dismantling of the Berlin Wall in 1989 led to the reunification of Germany*

At first there was a rush by countries like the Czech Republic, Hungary, East Germany and Poland to embrace market systems. However, these solutions have not always been successful, and it was not surprising that a few years later countries like Poland took a few steps back towards the protection of socialism. Poland is seeking to join the European Union early in the twenty-first century and recognises the importance of opening up freer markets if it is to be accepted. However, at times of extreme hardship, such as international recession and stagnation in the world economy, Poland has sought to create key aspects of social welfare protection while advancing some way towards capitalism. The free-market solution is not an easy option for economies that have been struggling to use their resources effectively for a number of years.

Questions

1. What do you see as being the five major points of difference between a centrally planned economy and a free-market one? Set out your answer in the form of a table.

2. Why do you think that at the end of the 1980s citizens of eastern European countries were so keen to embrace the market system?

3. Why was accommodating to the free market not an easy transition?

4. Why have some countries taken some steps back towards socialism?

The free-market system

In a free market, the production decisions about 'what?', 'how?' and 'for whom?' are made by consumers and producers; the government does not intervene. Consumers in effect 'vote' for a certain pattern of output by the way in which they distribute their spending between the alternatives on offer. How much they are prepared to pay is thus a reflection of the strength of consumer preferences. (Some people think that it does not always work quite like this; they think that producers often decide what they would like to make and then persuade consumers to follow their wishes through advertising.) The prices at which producers offer their goods for sale will depend on their production costs. The prices charged will thus reflect the relative scarcity of the various resources needed in order to produce that good for the market. If a product sells well firms will be inclined to produce it; if no one buys the product firms will stop making it, since under the market system firms seek to make profits from all the goods they sell. Producers are thus forced to pay attention to the wishes of consumers in order to survive.

The interests of consumers and producers conflict. Consumers want to pay low prices while producers would like to charge higher prices. The market serves to strike a balance, with profits settling at just those levels that match the strength of consumer preferences with the scarcity of resources. When prices change this acts as a signal for the pattern of production and consumption to alter. For example, when a new fashion style becomes popular, the producers are able to charge a higher price and to put more resources into producing more such garments, while for clothes that are no longer fashionable manufacturers may be forced to lower their price, put less resources into their production and eventually stop making them altogether.

Advantages of the free-market system

1. Production reflects the wishes of the consumer.

2. The system is flexible in the way it can respond to different conditions of demand and supply.
3. Individuals have greater freedom to make their own demand and supply decisions.
4. Scarce resources do not have to be wasted on administering and running (planning) the system.
5. It is argued that the free market will lead to larger, better-quality outputs at lower unit costs.

These arguments are succinct but extremely powerful. Their power is reflected in the way in which most economies in the world have moved towards freer market systems in recent years.

Disadvantages of the free-market system

1. The free-market system does not guarantee everyone what many would regard to be the minimum acceptable standard of living in a healthy society. The price mechanism, when it is freely operating, fails to provide a 'safety net' for citizens less able to compete, including the sick and elderly.
2. There are some goods which by their very nature include elements of what is known as 'non-excludability'. For example all ships using a particular seaway benefit from its lighthouse; all citizens (except perhaps for pacifists) could be seen to benefit from a national system of defence. If we take the example of bridges, it is immediately apparent why the price system could not always be effective as a means of provision. If people were made to stop and pay to go over all bridges the traffic system would rapidly snarl up. It is worth bearing in mind, however, that when new roads were being built and road traffic was less common, many toll bridges were used in this country. Today, we still have many examples of toll bridges and tunnels, but they usually have little impact on traffic flows because of the use of automated toll pay booths, and other devices designed for speed. However, it is easy to see that these work only when they are few and far between. Chaos would arise if London's bridges all operated on a toll payment system.
3. The free market can lead to great inequalities. Those with the means to purchase large quantities of goods can use their money to ensure that the goods and services they want are produced (hence taking away resources from other products). One way of looking at the **opportunity cost** to society of producing luxury goods (speedboats, expensive clothes) is to consider the inability of society to meet the needs of the less fortunate.

4. Resources may not be able to move as freely as a pure market theory would suggest. Regarding human resources (labour), people may be resistant to moving to new areas and away from their established roots. They may be reluctant to learn new skills which offer high pay packets if they feel that the job does not meet their needs for such factors as self-respect, pride in the job or the ability to work at one's own pace.
5. Many buying decisions are made by consumers with an imperfect knowledge of the market. Producers frequently change the details of their products, including price, shape, size and packaging. This makes it very difficult for consumers to weigh up alternative purchases, and many buying decisions may be based on impressions rather than hard evidence. For example, a recent survey conducted by the authors reveals that, out of a sample of 400 shoppers, fewer than 10 per cent of them could remember the prices of five randomly selected commonly used items in their shopping basket.
6. In a free market many resources can be wasted through the high failure rate of new businesses. A lot of time and money is spent on setting up a new business. When it closes down after a few months, many of its resources may end up as little more than scrap.

The mixed economy

In the real world no economy relies exclusively on the free market, nor can we find examples of purely planned economies. A mixed economy combines elements of both the free market and planned systems; some decisions are made solely through the private sector while others are made by the government.

The United Kingdom is a good example of a mixed economy. Some parts of industry are owned and operated by the government but large chunks of the business world remain in private hands. The **public sector** is that part of the economy that is government-owned; the **private sector** is that part of the economy that is owned by private citizens.

Throughout much of the twentieth century, government spending in the UK has made up a significant percentage of all spending. Then, during the 1980s and until 1997, steps were taken by Conservative administrations to reduce the relative size of government spending. A major aim of the Conservatives since coming into office in May 1979 was the restoration of **market forces** throughout the economy.

With the return of a Labour administration in 1997, the emphasis has moved towards the creation of a **social market** in which the government plays a role in helping the market to work more efficiently, making sure that large organisations do not take advantage of less powerful individual organisations, and ensuring a measure of social justice.

In a mixed economy, one of the central issues of debate will be about the nature of the mix between the private and public sectors.

A new economic order?

The following is based on an article by William Halal and Alexander Nitikin in *Business and the Contemporary World*, autumn 1993.

It is arguable that both capitalism and communism are poor ways of managing the use of resources. Communism over-controls, capitalism under-controls. Communism suffers from scarcity, capitalism from over-consumption. Even the outrageously priced black markets produced by planned economies have their counterparts in capitalism – perfectly legal 'white markets' for outrageously priced luxury items which are restricted to the wealthy because most people cannot afford the prices.

Rather than regard the crisis of communism as an inevitable capitulation to capitalism, we can view it as a similar process to the transition Americans experienced during the Great Depression of the 1930s. The Depression occurred because of a severe failure in the market system, but it was cured by a variety of social welfare programmes which succeeded in stabilising the American economy.

Russia lags behind the United States in its development by about fifty years, so it is now making a similar transition with many close parallels. Just as Franklin Roosevelt led Americans through a painful adjustment after the Great Depression, Mikhail Gorbachev provided – and Boris Yeltsin continues to provide – the same charismatic but troubled leadership as Russia struggles through a similar transition. And, just as America did not abandon capitalism but instead corrected its flaws by adopting some elements of socialism, Russia seems likely to develop an advanced form of democratic, market socialism.

Opinion polls taken in 1991 showed that most citizens in the former Soviet Union favoured some form of democratic market socialism. In Poland the Democratic Left Alliance bases its appeal on the best features of socialism and capitalism. In China, too, a survey found that two-thirds of the population favoured a form of 'democratic socialism'.

This concept of a socially guided market economy offers a logical solution to the current crisis of communism because it could provide the advantages of the free market while retaining some sense of orderly control. Over time, the private sector in eastern Europe and Russia should grow from its present size to about 50–70 per cent of the economy. But these are socialist societies, so they should also ensure employment, medical care, housing and pensions to buffer their citizens from the hardships of the market. It would also be best to maintain strategic control, perhaps through a regulation of state ownership over banking, utilities, transportation and other quasi-public industries. Perhaps the most crucial strategy would be to encourage some form of democratic economic governance in which workers, government, the public and managers share control of large organisations and key industries, offering a fresh application of socialist principles. Current examples of such practices include workers' councils, decision-making by democratically elected central bodies, employee share ownership plans, various types of privatisation, joint stock companies, self-managed teams and other aspects of 'new socialism'.

Of course, it is important to note that Russia today, as is the case with many other eastern European countries, runs on a political knife-edge. In the 1990s Boris Yeltsin was a major figure in moving Russia in the direction of market reforms. However, there continue to be strong undercurrents of nationalism and a belief by many that communism at least created jobs for everyone. In 1997, Yeltsin suffered serious ill-health, creating a feeling of uncertainty in the country. It remains to be seen which way Russia and other countries will turn. Whatever happens they will not tread an easy path and along the way there will be many hardships.

TASK

Outline the key features of (a) capitalism, (b) socialism, and (c) the 'new socialism'.

Discussion points

1. What have been the major obstacles facing eastern European economies that are moving towards a freer market system?

2. Why might the 'new socialism' be more appropriate for Russia and Poland than a free-market solution?

3. What features of the 'new socialism' outlined above are also features of the UK economic system?

4. Do you think that capitalism or socialism is the most appropriate path for a modern economy? Or is there an alternative way forward?

THE ROLE OF THE STATE

Much of the political debate in recent centuries, and particularly in the twentieth century, has concerned the role of the state in the life of the nation, in fashioning relationships between nations, and in the relationships between individuals and organisations.

The spectrum of political philosophy

The mainstream spectrum of political philosophy in relation to business in the economy runs from pure **communism** at one extreme to completely **free markets** at the other. Ideological battles have been waged in the twentieth century between the communists (adherents of Marx, Lenin, Trotsky and Stalin) and the followers of the free market (adherents of Adam Smith, Friedrich Hayek, Milton Friedman etc.).

The communists see the state as representing the interests of the community – and hence of individuals. Communists contrast this view with a philosophy of *individualism* based on self-interest. For example, in *The German Ideology*, (1939) Karl Marx and Friedrich Engels wrote:

'All history is the history of man's enslavement to an alien power, the world market. After the communist revolution, with the abolition of private property, this power will be dissolved. Then genuine spiritual riches will be available to each individual. He will be free of national and local limitations, be enabled to enjoy the "all-sided production of the whole earth". The natural co-operation of men hitherto forced by the rule of the market system, will arise spontaneously in the wake of the communist revolution.'

Communists therefore placed a strong emphasis on the role of the state and the planned economy as representing the people's interests. This view is in clear contrast with that of neo-liberal thinkers (supporters of the free market), one of whom summed up free-enterprise ideology with the phrase 'least government is best government'.

One of the most important contributions that economists can make is to shed some light on how the economy can best serve the interests of each and every person in a society. **Joseph Schumpeter**, the great Austrian economist, wrote the following in 1942:

'Queen Elizabeth [the First] *owned silk stockings. The capitalist achievement does not typically consist in providing more silk stockings for queens, but in bringing them within the reach of factory girls in return for steadily decreasing amounts of effort.'*

Schumpeter was arguing that the **'market'** serves to meet the needs of the consumer, while at the same time providing the **employment** that enables people to become consumers. Since Schumpeter's time, technological progress has continued to erode privilege. The Green Revolution has helped to bring to tens of millions in Asia and elsewhere the food security previously familiar only in wealthy nations. And, of course, the multimedia PCs currently being snapped up by many families in this country offer computing power comparable to that used only by rocket scientists three decades ago.

Schumpeter's vision describes how the long sweep of capitalist development reduces inequality – eventually. Yet when innovations first appear, they can make life worse for poorer people, sometimes for decades. Some three centuries ago, the development of high-yield crops to feed livestock paved the way for massive increases in agricultural output, and this led to the population boom that accompanied the Industrial Revolution. Ultimately, this led to an increase in living standards beyond anyone's dreams, but the short-term impact was misery as peasants could no longer graze their animals on common or fallow land. Naturally, such changes are bitterly resisted.

Adam Smith, the famous British economist, provided a strong case for capitalism. In his book, *The Wealth of Nations* (1776), he argued the case that producers of goods will supply to the market what consumers wanted in order to make profits. The driving force behind this process was personal greed – but the effect of this greed was the betterment of society.

Economic perspectives

Over the course of time various groups of economists have presented differing theories as to how the economy works.

The classical economists

The **classical economists** follow in the line of Adam Smith, arguing that the market is the best way of deciding how resources should be used in society (the allocation of resources). They argue that the market leads to the best solutions because the forces of demand reflect people's preferences for what goods and services should be supplied. Interfere with this market at your peril. Anyone who artificially tries to set prices at 'non-market rates' will create *inefficiency*, leading to waste and unemployment. We use the term **neo-classical economist** to denote a modern-day adherent of the principles of the free market.

Marxist economists

Marxist economists would argue that there is no such thing as a free market. The market is a 'smokescreen' for the exploitation of the proletariat (those who do not own capital) by the capitalist class. Once the proletariat fully realise the extent of this exploitation they will rise up and destroy the system to replace it with 'advanced communism'. Modern-day Marxists are described as **neo-Marxists**.

Keynesian economists

Keynesian economists (supporters of the ideas of the English economist John Maynard Keynes) provide another challenge to the classical school. They argue that the market provides no guarantee of efficiency. We can never be sure that the supply of goods in the economy (national output) will be purchased in its entirety by consumers. Should total demand fall short of total supply then producers will want to cut back on their level of output (rather than carry the cost of unsold stocks). Once output starts to decrease, then people will have less money in their pockets (as some of them start to lose their jobs). A fall in income leads to a fresh fall in spending and a downward spiral in the economy. Keynes provided a strong case for government interference in the economy to manage the level of demand in order to encourage producers to produce enough goods to guarantee full employment.

The ideas of Keynes gained popularity in the period from 1945, after the Second World War. Between 1945 and 1979 all the major political parties committed themselves to the creation of full employment.

The classical revival, 1979–97

In the late 1970s, classical economics became popular once again; indeed it became the new orthodoxy. In the 1950s and 60s, Keynesian policies had seemed to work and unemployment had been low. However, in the 1970s many economies experienced rising levels of unemployment coupled with rising inflation. Inflation was now seen as the evil that was more likely to destroy economies rather than unemployment.

The neo-classical economists argued that it was government interference (expenditure and resource waste) that had created an inefficient economy. The emphasis was then on reducing the role of the state (e.g. through the privatisation of industry) and on using the interest rate as a way of taking inflation out of the system. Higher interest rates encouraged saving and hence cut back on expenditures.

The UK's mixed economy

In the nineteenth century the UK government played only a small part in the control of the economy. Today, the proper role of the government is open to debate, but most people accept that it should at least try to influence economic activity. Why has this change in attitude taken place over time?

In some towns in the 1920s, over half of the potential labour force were unemployed. Many people felt, in the light of the terrible suffering and waste during this period, that the government should play a central role in creating and sustaining employment. Most of the politicians who made the key decisions in this country from the Second World War onwards had vivid memories of this period. Politicians of all parties were therefore prepared to give high priority to curing unemployment.

The 1970s was a period of rapid increases in prices. People felt the effects of inflation in different ways depending, amongst other things, on how much power they had to raise their own incomes to cope with price rises.

The general effect of price rises is to distort the working of the price system. Trading ideally needs to take place in settled conditions. If you expected to be paid £100 in three months' time you would be very disappointed if you found that when you received payment you could purchase only half of the goods you would have been able to obtain today.

If people become reluctant to trade, then fewer goods will be produced for sale. If fewer goods are made, fewer people are employed in production. Price disturbances can therefore cause the whole economy to stagnate.

After 1979, with the election of Margaret Thatcher's first administration, economic policy in this country changed dramatically. The emphasis was very much on resurrecting a liberal model of the economy based on competition and free enterprise. Many industries previously owned by the state, such as telecommunications, fuel and power, rail and air transport, were privatised (sold to shareholders). Services such as health and education were increasingly placed in a competitive environment in which individual units became self-managing and responsible for handling their own budgets. Of course, there is a strong emphasis on public accountability. Local managers need to be able to show how they are spending their funds. They need to manage their budgets wisely. Citizens have far more access to complaints and appeals procedures. In addition, privatised industries are subject to the controls of 'regulators' who are there to ensure fair competition and to ensure that the rights of all stakeholders are effectively maintained.

The 'Third Way'

In 1997, Britain elected a Labour government with alternative views about how the economy should be run. This they labelled the 'Third Way'. In particular, in the autumn of 1997 the Chancellor of the Exchequer, Gordon Brown, emphasised that the prime target for economic policy should be that of getting rid of unemployment.

However, many argue that the government has failed to articulate fully the nature of its 'Third Way'. What is clear is that Labour's emphasis on modernisation is based on a belief that the market must play a key part in macro- and microeconomic decision-making. Firms need to operate in a competitive environment in which the state does not grant unfair subsidies to 'lame duck' industries.

The Third Way seems to be concerned with unleashing enterprise and market forces in the economy while *at the same time* ensuring key social provision to support social policies, including the protection of weaker members of society. So, for example, Labour turned round the previous Conservative government's policy of 'Care in the Community' for the elderly and people with mental problems. Some individuals were to be given greater provision and care both to protect them and to protect society.

A new paradigm?

A further way of thinking about the economy has recently arisen in the United States. According to this view, recent developments in the world have created a situation in which both unemployment and inflation can be kept at low levels. This optimistic view is based on the belief that underlying productivity growth has been greatly boosted by the revolution in information technology and other spinoffs from the microchip. This, it is claimed, has greatly boosted the potential output of the services sector, but the official GDP statistics have not correctly accounted for this change. Hence policymakers have not fully appreciated just how much productivity has actually risen.

A second assertion is that wage inflation has been held down by the opening of a new global labour market, in which competition from the developing world has depressed the wages of unskilled workers in the West.

If these assertions prove correct then there is scope for optimism about economic growth. We might see the possibility of more and more goods becoming available to the ordinary person.

Government policy objectives

Macroeconomic policy objectives determine the environment within which businesses operate. To achieve a balance between them is a difficult task for any government. Inevitably the pressure to tilt the balance one way or another is affected by political conditions as well as economic, and these should be understood when reviewing a particular government's policy achievements. Governments have five broad objectives, which are:

- sustainable economic growth
- low inflation
- falling unemployment or full employment
- balance-of-payments equilibrium
- controlled government borrowing.

Before looking at each of these, it will be useful to examine how **demand** in an economy can be assessed and monitored.

Total demand in an economy comprises:

- *Consumer spending* (C) – what you and I and other consumers spend on consumable items such as bread, cheese, wine and cinema visits, and on consumer durables such as watches, washing machines, video recorders and cars.
- *Investment spending* (I) – what business organisations spend on goods which go into further production (e.g. on factory buildings, machinery, tools and equipment).
- *Government spending* (G) – what the government spends on consumable items (e.g. on petrol in a police car), and on investment items (e.g. buying a new police station).
- *Exports* (X) – British goods and services which are sold abroad in return for payments from foreigners.

Hence the total demand to be met by the economy would appear to be C + I + G + X. However, from this we need to take away *imports* (M) – of foreign goods and services which are bought in this country, for which payments leave the country to go to foreigners. The total demand (sometimes referred to as **aggregate monetary demand** or AMD) is thus represented in the following way:

$$AMD = C + I + G + X - M.$$

This aggregate demand and the changes that either increase or decrease it are of vital importance to the economy and the government.

The largest part of aggregate demand is made up of consumer spending (C). Whilst the other aspects of demand are important in their own ways, it is still the confidence of consumers that can provide strong growth prospects for the economy. For example, investment by businesses will be strongly influenced by C. If consumers are spending less then there will be little incentive to businesses to invest in new capacity. If consumption is likely to boom then it may pay to invest in new capacity.

Government approaches to spending and taxation can significantly influence the other elements of aggregate demand. Government control over its own spending and taxation is termed **fiscal policy**. The government also uses **monetary policy** to control the economy. Monetary policy is the control over the quantity and price of obtaining money. Of course, the price of borrowing money is the interest rate.

While one can blame the government of the day for mis-timing changes in its monetary and fiscal policies, it is by

no means easy to judge when these should take place. Figure 15.3 shows the **business cycle** that economies have traditionally been seen to move through. The obvious conclusion to draw would be to use forecasting methods to predict when a downturn (or even a recession) was due to occur and adjust policy accordingly. Likewise a boom, with its associated problem of inflation and production bottlenecks, could be headed off with appropriate changes.

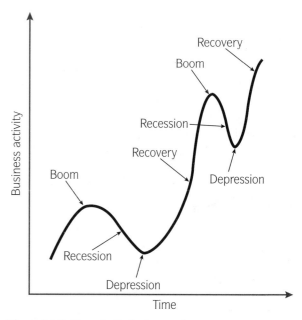

Figure 15.3 *Stages in the business cycle*

Despite the common criticism of government policy errors, a number of problems have to be faced by any administration. These can be seen as a series of **lags** when information is uncertain or unclear. For convenience these lags may be grouped under three headings: recognition, administration and operation.

Recognition lag

This is the time it takes to collect enough information so that a reasonable analysis can take place. Governments rely on **indicators** to provide them with a comprehensive analysis of the economy, and studies of the UK business cycle suggest that economic indicators fall into four broad groups:

- *longer leading indicators*, which point to likely turns in activity about a year in advance (e.g. the CBI's quarterly survey, and surveys of trends in business optimism)

- *shorter leading indicators*, which indicate turning points six months in advance (e.g. new car registrations)

- *coincident indicators*, which mark current turning points (e.g. retail sales)
- *lagging indicators*, which confirm turning points about a year after they have happened (e.g. unemployment, and investment in plant and machinery).

In theory these indicators should show where in the business cycle the economy stands. Four stages can be seen to repeat themselves.

- *Boom*
  - consumer spending rising quickly
  - output capacity reached; labour shortages occur
  - output can be increased only by new labour-saving investment
  - investment spending high
  - increase in demand stimulates price rises
  - business profits high
- *Recession*
  - consumption falls off
  - many investments suddenly become unprofitable and new investment falls
  - production falls
  - employment falls
  - profits fall; business failures increase
  - recession can turn into severe depression
- *Depression*
  - heavy unemployment
  - low consumer demand
  - over-capacity (unused capacity) in production
  - prices stabilise or even fall
  - business profits low (confidence low)
- *Recovery*
  - investment picks up
  - employment rises
  - consumer spending rises
  - profits recover
  - business confidence rises
  - prices stable or rise slowly.

Whilst the workings of the business cycle are complex and there are various schools of thought on what causes recession – and what are the most appropriate policies to stimulate a recovery – most economists accept the cycle as a useful model which can identify the main dynamics of the economy.

What appears to be possible from the use of indicators and the business-cycle model is that a government can use monetary and fiscal policies to 'fine-tune' the economy. Examples are moving interest rates higher to head off inflation and to cool the economy down, or using extra government expenditure to spur the economy forward

when growth threatens to slow. However, the recognition lag means that time has to elapse before a meaningful set of statistics can show that a problem has occurred. For example, an indicator showing one month's inflation up on the previous month would not be a justifiable foundation for action. Two, three, or even up to six months of rising inflation should spur the government to action.

Administration lag

Once a trend has been identified the choice of actions to control a problem is potentially large, but most administrations have clear economic preferences that determine the choice of **control instrument** they wish to use. In the 1970s and throughout a large part of the 1980s, the Labour and Conservative parties differed markedly in their economic philosophies. Labour preferred a more interventionist policy based on Keynesian **demand management**, while the Conservatives favoured a monetary policy and **supply-side improvements**. In the late 1980s and throughout the 1990s both parties' ideas converged, with a more pragmatic combination of supply-side and demand-management initiatives.

Whatever the constraints on choice, there is still an issue in choosing the most appropriate course to take.

Operation lag

Once a course of action has been chosen – say, increasing interest rates – it will take some time to impact on the economy, with perhaps a period of three to six months elapsing before the full impact of the change can be seen.

These three lags or delays may mean that it can be six months to a year before a turning point in the cycle has been identified, action taken and some effect is seen. Also, the influences of the international markets may force changes through that no government could ever envisage. A government's ability to choose its own policy direction may be severely curtailed.

Economic growth levels

Economic growth is a goal for all governments. However, it is not just that growth of any level is desirable, but that growth should be such that it generates enough demand to maintain existing jobs, create new jobs and increase the wealth of the nation. This normally means that growth of less than 2 per cent will cause problems for the economy, leading as it will to a loss in jobs as productivity gains will be greater than the change in demand. What, then, will be acceptable levels of growth, and how will this be measured?

Growth is measured as the change in the 'gross domestic product' (GDP) of the country over the year, after subtracting an amount due to the level of inflation to produce a figure for **real growth**. The long-term growth pattern of the UK economy is considered to be $2\frac{1}{2}$ per cent a year, although the business cycle means that this figure can fluctuate from year to year.

Growth, though, can produce its own problems, and this requires a closer look at its underlying factors. If growth is fuelled mainly by changes in consumer demand (the main component of aggregate demand), then this could cause problems with the balance of payments by sucking in imports. If growth is generated by changes in investment and more exports, then a so-called 'golden scenario' may be produced, which seem to provide for more **sustainable growth**. But even here there is a downside, with investment being paid for at the expense of consumption, leading to a loss of the important '**feel-good factor**' in the nation.

The contrast between the mid-1980 growth patterns and those of the mid-1990s shows the difference. In the 1980s, credit and loans were easy to obtain, house prices were rising quickly (providing a base against which lending could take place), and consumption was encouraged. The problems came when the housing market collapsed as inflation and interest rates peaked, imports soared and the economy experienced **negative growth** – that is, a period over which the economy actually shrank. Compare that with the economic growth a decade later and notable differences emerge. In the 1990s the housing market remained sluggish, with lenders (banks and building societies) and borrowers cautious over taking on more financial burdens. Industry, however, turned its attention to export markets and invested to compete overseas. The annual economic growth rate moved from negative growth to a more healthy 3 per cent plus, in the mid 1990s. Unfortunately in the late 1990s industry suffered from a rising pound which made a number of industries less competitive on international markets.

The make-up of growth is of great importance to business. As we have seen, it is possible for governments to play a role in setting the conditions for growth, either through lowering interest rates and/or increasing the amount of spending on capital projects or job-creation programmes. The first approach may be justified on the grounds that

inflation is low, but may be set at a level that encourages extra consumption based on credit creation (an issue we shall explore later in the section on inflation), thereby producing a consumer-led boom. The second approach has to be judged very carefully to take out the party political aspect. All parties use public spending to pursue economic and social objectives (we will ignore the political aims that may also be a part of government expenditure), so what is at issue here is how these can be paid for. If extra **government borrowing** is undertaken, it may **crowd out** private-sector borrowing, thereby leading to an increase in interest rates, putting pressure on private-sector investment. If this happens then the growth phase will be short-lived.

Businesses prefer a stable economic environment. The influence of the business cycle suggests that this is unlikely, creating a difficult set of decisions for government to be able to encourage conditions for growth, whilst at the same time having enough scope to invest in the nation's **infrastructure** and to provide social benefits to those who need them.

In recent times we have come to look at sustainable growth in a new way. Increasingly the impact of the economy on the **environment** is being accounted for in economic decision-making. The new notion of sustainability is one which considers the impact of economic actions on future generations, and across existing generations – the twin concepts of intergenerational (between-generations) equity and intragenerational (within-generations) equity. Since the Conference on Human Environment in Stockholm in 1972, the words 'sustainable development' have been at the centre of the environment and development debate. The term has become best known as one that links the ideas of environment and development, the social and the economic. The best-known definition is one that was presented by the report of the World Commission on Environment and Development, known as the Brundtland Report, and published in 1987 as *Our Common Future*:

'[Sustainable development] *meets the needs of the present generation without compromising the ability of future generations to meet their own needs.*'

Other definitions of sustainable development have included:

'... *living on the Earth's income rather than eroding its capital*' (British Government White Paper, *This Common Inheritance*, 1990)

'... *development which improves people's quality of life, within the carrying capacity of the Earth's life support systems* (United Nations Environmental Programme, 1995).

While governments continue to place strong emphasis on securing economic growth, increasing emphasis is placed on ensuring that this growth does not take place at the expense of uncontrollable environmental degradation.

Inflation

Control of **inflation** is given a high priority by the government, particularly as international comparisons have shown that the UK's level of inflation is too high compared with that of Japan, Germany and other advanced industrial countries.

The measurement of inflation can be undertaken in a number of ways. The most common method is by the **retail price index** (RPI), which expresses, on a monthly basis, changes in the price of goods and services purchased by the average family. The RPI is now more often referred to as the **headline measure** of inflation because it is the one that is frequently quoted in newspaper headlines. The preferred measure used by the government, excluding mortgage payments to make comparisons easier with other countries, is known as the **underlying rate** of inflation (or RPIX).

Both the headline and the underlying figures produce a picture of inflation as consumers experience it in the shops. However, there is a need to look at inflation as experienced by industry, particularly as this will provide – it is hoped – ample warning of inflationary pressures building up in the economy. Changes in the prices of imports and changes in factory-gate prices are monitored to see what trends are emerging in raw-material and wage costs that could feed through into retail prices, and hence to the RPI. The difficulty here is that factory-gate prices may not have a large impact on retail prices because pressure in the distribution chain may be to keep prices down in the face of consumer resistance.

Measuring inflation can provide the 'moving picture', but there is still the need to predict the problems that are likely to come with it. In particular:

- any economy experiencing inflation higher than its international competitors loses out on competitiveness
- when there is inflation, companies and trade unions have to try to set prices and wages in an unpredictable situation, causing problems for both sides of industry
- groups of people on fixed and low incomes which are not 'index-linked' (adjusted to allow for inflation) experience a loss in buying power, and these groups do not have the protection of a trade union or staff association to argue their case.

Inflation is a problem, so what are the factors that cause it? There are numerous theories concerning its causes and likely cure, and these can be summarised under two general headings: **supply-side** and **demand-led** pressures.

- *Supply-side theories of inflation*
  The emphasis here is on the pressure put on firms to raise their own prices by influences such as higher raw-material costs, wage increases, and other members of the supply chain who have power to raise their prices. The government can monitor and to a certain extent control the wage and other supply-side pressures, so it is not always the case that inflation will rise because of them. Demand may be weak in the economy, keeping profits down rather than allowing prices to rise. If this happens, firms will still wish to rebuild their profit margins by price rises when the conditions are favourable – a factor monitored by the CBI's quarterly survey of companies' price intentions.
- *Demand-led inflation*
  Demand here relates to government spending (and borrowing), credit availability and real disposable incomes. Here again, it is not a straightforward issue to look at changes in wages and disposable income (income measured after tax and other commitments have been deducted). Households may well experience an increase in both of these but, because the future is uncertain, they feel the need to rebuild their financial position by saving, and so do not come forward to spend their money. If, though, this situation is experienced for any length of time, the so-called 'feel-good' factor can come into operation and feed into the marketplace.

In practice a multitude of factors feed through into inflation, building up pressures that are difficult to resist. Through most of the 1980s the UK government took the view that monetary conditions – the level of the supply of money – were the main indicators and cause of inflation. Policy was aimed at adjusting interest rates to keep both inflation and monetary growth in check. In the late 1980s and into the next decade, a more comprehensive view was taken – a view shared across the political divide. This approach takes account of both demand-led and supply-side pressures, adjusting the policy according to the interpretation of the data available. This process is now made public by means of publicising the relevant discussions between the Chancellor of the Exchequer and Governor of the Bank of England – showing the conclusions they arrive at on the current situation and on the likely future course of inflation. These discussions can then feed through into action to tighten or relax monetary/and or fiscal policy. One of the first measures Gordon Brown took as the new Labour Chancellor was to give independence to the Bank of England to decide on appropriate interest rates for the economy.

The last decade of the twentieth century saw a dramatic dampening down in price increases in most developed countries. Today, low prices can best be described as a function of two separate forces.

- *Global competition.* The spread of free trade in the postwar period, and the likes of China entering into the Western capitalistic economy, has unleashed unprecedented levels of competition which has removed pricing power from almost everyone.
- *Technology.* The advent of the PC revolution and the dramatic fall in the price of computing power generally has provided almost limitless potential for productivity gains, eroding almost completely the pricing power of labour, itself a large part of the engine of inflation.

Case Study

Inflationary pressures in 1998

Consumer spending started to come under pressure in 1998 from high interest rates, a slowing economy, the absence of building society windfall profits, and a profound unease about the collapse of economies in South East Asia.

However, the axe did not fall equally on all types of spending or goods. People were still spending widely on cars, restaurants, financial ventures and exotic long-haul holidays, with trips to China, India, Australia and Thailand taking over a lot of business from traditional holiday destinations such as Spain, France, Italy and Greece.

Sales of cars, catering and other services far outpace the 4.5 per cent rise in consumer spending, while the trade gap in travel widened by 50 per cent in the years 1997 and 1998.

While the above was welcome, something had to give, and that something is the high-street and 'big ticket' items such as computers, furniture, carpets, clothing and footwear. Several companies in these sectors experienced considerable difficulties.

In 1998 the signs were not so ominous in 'small ticket' sales such as food and household products from the supermarkets and out-of-town superstores, which were competing more with the high streets on clothing, toiletries, banking, insurance, petrol, plants, newspapers and hardware.

Questions

1. What signs of recession do you find highlighted in the above article?

2. Why are the effects felt unequally?

3. What do you think would have been the impact on individual prices in various market sectors of the effects outlined above?

4. What do you see as being the likely impact on the RPI? How would this be calculated?

5. What is the current state of the RPI?

Unemployment

Background

For approximately 20 years prior to the Second World War, **unemployment** had averaged at least 10 per cent. The war effort fully employed all our resources, and in 1944 the government published a White Paper pledging the maintenance of full employment after the war. The will to provide this was matched by the means as stated in the White Paper.

> *'The government accepts as one of their primary aims and responsibilities the maintenance of a high and stable level of employment after the war ... total expenditure must be prevented from falling to a level where general unemployment appears.'*

For the next 25 years, unemployment averaged only 1.8 per cent. However, a major concern over the policy of maintaining full employment was that it was accompanied by inflation. When a Conservative government came to power in 1979 it placed a lot of emphasis on trying to cut back on price increases.

In recent years we have seen the resurgence of high unemployment, so that the first half of the 1990s was characterised by unemployment at well over two million people. In the late 1990s, however, the employment position improved somewhat, although there is considerable uncertainty about the situation in the first decade of the new millennium. However, it is clear that on-going unemployment is a problem confronting most industrialised countries, including former 'star' economies such as Germany and Japan.

When we look in detail at unemployment figures we are presented with some interesting findings. For example:

- unskilled and semi-skilled manufacturing workers are twice as likely to be unemployed as skilled manual workers
- manual workers on the whole are twice as likely as non-manual workers to be unemployed
- in the 50+ age group, twice as many have been unemployed for over a year than in the 18–25 age group.

There is always considerable disagreement over the exact number of unemployed people in the UK at any time, because unemployment figures are collected in a variety of ways. The figures should always be treated with caution for this reason.

UK unemployment 1960–97

The sale of goods and services is highest when the economy is growing strongly. Therefore, economic growth leads to a higher demand for labour to produce those goods and services and a lower rate of unemployment. The figures for unemployment and economic growth in the UK since the 1960s confirm that every time economic growth is negative, unemployment rises and does not fall back until the economy starts growing again.

However, after each recession in Europe, unemployment has not returned to pre-recession levels. For instance, as a result of the recession of 1974–75, in the UK, unemployment rose from 2.1 per cent to 5.2 per cent in 1977. When economic growth recovered, unemployment fell back only to a minimum of 4.6 per cent. More recently the UK has shown that this trend can be broken. Unemployment currently continues to fall even though today's rate of 6.6 per cent is lower than the lowest rate attained (7 per cent) during the most recent phase of rapid economic growth in the 1980s (see Figure 15.4).

Causes of unemployment

There are many explanations of how unemployment is caused. One cause may be a downswing in the trade cycle, a period of recession leading to general unemployment. In a period of recession, there is a downward multiplier effect in the economy. An initial fall in demand is multiplied into fresh falls in demand. For example, a building contractor

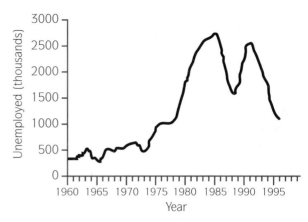

Figure 15.4 *UK unemployment 1960–97 (annual averages)*

lays off some employees. These employees lose their wages, which they are then not able to spend in local shops. The local shops lose sales, make lower profits and may lay off further labour. This fresh fall in spending leads to further contractions. With a downward multiplier, spending, income, output and employment will all fall. The term **cyclical** (or general) **unemployment** is used to describe unemployment resulting from downturns in the trade cycle.

Structural unemployment arises from longer-term changes in the economy, affecting specific industries, regions and occupations. For example, the coal industry in regions such as Central Scotland, South Yorkshire and the East Midlands has been in decline for a number of years because of the development of new substitute fuels such as gas, oil and electricity, and the importing of cheap coal from Australia, Nigeria, Russia and other places. The effects of structural unemployment could be reduced if people moved away from declining industries and areas and into new, expanding areas. However, these changes do not occur smoothly, so the economy suffers from 'structural problems'; hence structural unemployment is a major economic factor.

It has been argued that new technology is a cause of **technological unemployment**. The argument is that the introduction of new technology is destroying jobs and trade while at the same time imports from low-wage developing countries are undercutting goods produced in this country. However, a number of studies contradict this. For example, the OECD Job Study (June 1995) asserted that 'history has shown that when technological progress accelerates, so do growth, living standards and employment'. New technology generates *new* products, new services and therefore *new* jobs. Fewer workers may be required in some production processes where specific tasks are taken over, but rising production boosts incomes and the demand for new jobs in the economy as a whole.

The above arguments indicate that there are considerable differences in opinion about the causes of unemployment. However, it is apparent that the government has a major role to play in ensuring that unemployment does not rise above 'acceptable' levels. But what those levels are is a subject for debate.

Cures for unemployment

No single cure or aspect of government policy could cope with all the causes, so as with inflation it is convenient to group the initiatives together, under supply-side and demand-led headings.

The cures for unemployment can only be summarised here. All political parties will seek to combine these approaches to gain the maximum possible benefit. In recent years the economy has not been able to deliver full employment – the fall to 6 per cent in the 1980s was a short-lived success that soon petered out as inflation and then recession took their toll. The problem for the UK and many of the European Union countries is how to achieve an effective record of job creation whilst maintaining a grip on inflation. High rates of growth, low inflation and a successful record of helping the long-term unemployed would be required to approach the goal of 'full employment'.

Supply-side solutions

Here the emphasis is on improving the quality of the nation's workforce and other factors of production. The workforce can be improved by training as well as by encouraging people to think about setting up their own businesses. In addition, the unemployed can be given help in looking for work and improving their communication skills, so that they appeal to prospective employers. There are numerous organisations involved in this process, from the Training and Enterprise Councils (TECs) through to local authorities, who can all provide a valuable contribution.

In July 1997, the Labour government unveiled its rationale for a New Deal by emphasising a new approach to welfare reform in this country.

'In the new economy ... where capital, inventions, even raw materials are mobile, Britain has only one truly national resource: the talent and potential of its people. Yet in Britain today one in five of working-age households has no one earning a wage. In place of welfare there should be work ... It is time for the welfare state to put opportunity again in people's hands. First, everyone in need of work should have the opportunity to work. Second, we must ensure work pays. Third, everyone who seeks to advance through employment and education must be given the means to advance. So we will create a new ladder of opportunity that will allow the many, by their own efforts, to benefit from opportunities once open only to a few.'

The 1997 budget then (amongst other reforms) went on to announce preliminary ideas for the New Deal and these were expanded in the March 1998 budget.

TASKS

1. Research what was included in the New Deal for young people. A good source of information for this is the March 1998 budget, and a case study 'Making the labour market work better' (DfEE, *The Times 100*, 1998–99).

2. How effective has the New Deal been? Carry out a search of Internet sites using New Deal as your key words to explore various views.

Demand-led initiatives

This is a more contentious area than the supply-side initiatives outlined above. Keynesian economic theory focuses on aggregate demand (total demand) which can be affected by withdrawals or injections of money. For example, a rise in taxes would withdraw money demand from the system because consumers would have less money to spend. Other withdrawals result from households saving more money or spending more on imports rather than on UK-produced goods. Injections into the system arise when businesses decide to invest more, when the government increases its expenditure, or when we sell more exports to foreigners (see Figure 15.5).

One solution to a lack of demand in the economy is to inject extra public expenditure into the system, thereby boosting activity, which can lead to job creation. The difficulty with this is that the government has to borrow the funds, which may ultimately lead to higher interest

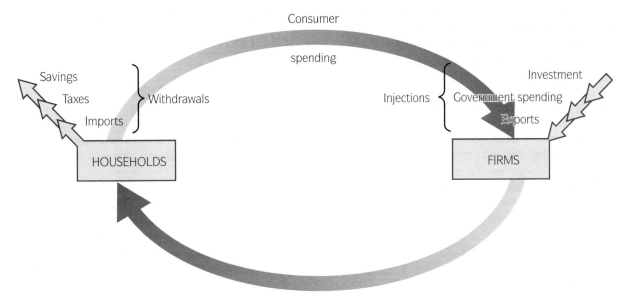

Savings
Taxes
Imports
Withdrawals

Consumer
spending

Injections

Investment
Government spending
Exports

HOUSEHOLDS

FIRMS

Incomes as a reward for contributing to production

Figure 15.5 *Injections and withdrawals from the economy's circular flow*

rates and the crowding out of private-sector investment, as noted earlier. A further criticism is that the boost to expenditure could, over time, lead to higher inflation, an effect that could set back economic progress.

Demand management is a difficult policy to implement, but despite the possible side-effects the policy should not be discarded as it offers a viable way forward.

The balance of payments

All countries trade internationally, with the UK being heavily dependent on this for about 30 per cent of its gross domestic product (GDP). While smaller economies, such as Switzerland and Norway, are heavily dependent on trade, it is unusual to find a large economy, such as the UK, with so much of its prosperity resting on this activity. Any difficulties experienced in the international trading position of the UK will have a severe impact on the well-being of the whole economy.

The **balance of payments** is a record of transactions between residents and non-residents of the UK. The difference between credits (exports) earned by residents and debits (imports) earned by non-residents produces either a favourable balance (a surplus) or an unfavourable balance (a deficit). The balance-of-payments account provides information on flows of goods, services and capital, but it is the movement of goods and services,

summarised in the **current account**, that provides a useful guide to the health of the economy.

Although the accounts always balance, as they would do for a business organisation, it is the deficits or surpluses on the current account that act as a guide. So, for example, a surplus on this account would suggest that the economy was experiencing favourable trading conditions. However, this line of reasoning should not be taken too far because a surplus is not the same as profit, a thing that is seen as a measure of success. One country's surplus is another country's deficit, so a large surplus is frowned on by international bodies such as the International Monetary Fund. This raises a question as to the acceptable size of a surplus – when is it acceptable or unacceptable to the international community?

The current account is broken into two sections – a **visible** account showing trade in tangible goods, and an **invisible** account showing trade in services. For a number of years the UK has tended to show a loss on visible trade and a surplus on invisible trade, thanks in large measure to financial services traded through the City of London.

A deficit is a situation that a country would clearly wish to amend. But here the same problem emerges – a large deficit builds up debts for the economy and should be dealt with, whilst a small deficit is easy to finance and may be tolerated if the reason for it is to bring in capital goods and raw materials from abroad.

A small deficit of, say, half to one per cent of GDP is manageable and can be financed; but a deficit that showed an increase to 4 per cent of GDP, as happened in the 1980s, was unsustainable. If this reasoning is transferred to surpluses, then the same conclusions can be drawn.

With large deficits the problems are related to the incapacity of the economy to meet demand, either because demand is rising too quickly or because there are structural problems with declining and uncompetitive industries. In addition, the exchange rate, if it is fixed, may be forcing exports out of the marketplace. Possible solutions would be to let the exchange rate find its right market level, and put the brakes on the economy by fiscal and monetary measures.

Large surpluses appear to be a mixed blessing, apart from attracting the criticism of other countries that such prosperity is at their expense. Here the problem will be increased pressure on the exchange rate, either allowing it to float upwards to new levels, or (if it is fixed) pressure to see it revalued – an outcome that exporters would not welcome. A long period of surpluses could even result in the threat of punitive action by countries or trading blocs, a threat that the UK would have to take very seriously. The solution could be a combination of relaxing fiscal and monetary policy, or seeing the currency move higher, a shift which would be possible only if other economic factors permitted such a move.

The aim is to see the current account in balance or, more practically, to see small deficits or surpluses that can be sustained over time.

Public (government) borrowing

Governments need to borrow money to finance their activities, particularly on a day-to-day basis when income is low. The demands of delivering public services require financing. The short-term financing arrangements are not particularly contentious, but long-term borrowing, leading to a high **public-sector borrowing requirement** (PSBR), has an impact on the economy that is seen as negative. It may crowd out private-sector investment by causing an increase in interest rates, and by the fact that the government is a better credit risk than companies.

The pressure on the government to borrow money becomes greater in times of slow growth and recession, particularly as revenue goes down in these periods.

Government social interventions

The need for cooperation

If societies work as groups of people cooperating together, they can seek equitable solutions to common problems. We can illustrate the need for cooperation in the following way.

Imagine that there are two cars heading for one another on a collision course. Each driver can veer to the left or to the right. If both veer to their right or both to their left, a collision is avoided. Therefore there needs to be some form of coordination of the decisions of the drivers if the worst is to be avoided. Cooperation can be made effective by establishing social institutions, in this case a convention about driving on the left or right side of the road. The Highway Code 'codifies' UK driving rules and regulations. The cooperation that results from all UK drivers obeying the Code leads to benefits for all.

If people concentrate on looking after just their own interests, this may be harmful to society as a whole. What is best for me alone might not be best for the whole community. Fisherfolk who consider no interests but their own may quickly deplete an essential national and internal resource by overfishing, so that fish stocks dwindle. Individuals who use aerosols to make their hair look nice may exacerbate the harmful effects on the ozone layer, and so on.

To achieve the benefits of cooperation it is essential to have a referee or umpire who makes sure that all parties in society keep to rules that are of benefit to the whole community.

Market failure

Markets working on their own are unlikely to maximise economic efficiency. There will be a tendency for too much of some goods to be produced and too little of others. In the extreme case of complete **market failure**, the market will fail to exist, so that certain goods will not be produced at all. The chief cause of market failure is the inability of individuals to work cooperatively, for a number of reasons.

- **Poor information.** Buyers and sellers are not clear about what goods are available in the marketplace and at what prices.

- **Externalities.** The act of producing some goods and services has knock-on harmful effects such as noise, waste, dereliction, etc. Externalities exist when the actions of consumers and producers also affect third parties. In a free market, how could we make people pay for the costs created by externalities?
- **Public goods.** Public goods are those for which, at any output, consumption by extra consumers does not reduce the quantity consumed by existing consumers. Examples of pure public goods include: the peace and security of a community, national defence, the law, air pollution control, fire protection, street lighting, weather forecasts and public television. If we take the example of peace and security, it would be very difficult to make people pay privately for a police service that everyone benefits from.
- **Imperfect competition.** Competition in the marketplace does not take place on equal terms between competitors. Some firms are much larger than others and are able to sell goods in bulk at lower prices. Because of their size they are able to 'see off' competitors. Once they are in a position of power, they could start to exploit consumers.
- **Uncertainty.** In the marketplace, consumers and producers may be unwilling to make products or to carry out transactions when they cannot see into the future.

There are therefore a number of possible roles for the government which combine economic and social functions.

An allocative role

Given the existence of market failure, the government has a role to play to enable the effective use of resources. For example, it can subsidise activities which are poorly provided for by the market. There are other resources which the government might want to ration. For example, if everyone wanted to visit Stonehenge at the summer solstice the monument might rapidly deteriorate from over-use. The government therefore limits access to the site on this day, and makes people pay a charge on other days, to restrict entry (as well as to raise revenue). Successive generations, therefore, will be able to benefit from the site. Everyone is better off in the long term. In this way, the government **allocates** some resources to maximise the benefits to the community.

A distributive role

The government helps to **redistribute** income and wealth in society by taking taxes from individuals and businesses and giving benefits to citizens. Clearly, there are many views as to what social justice means. Contrast the views of Karl Marx:

'From each according to his ability, to each according to his need'

and those of Margaret Thatcher:

'Let all our children grow taller, yet may some grow taller than others'.

The problem that faces society is to decide which particular distribution of incomes and welfare it prefers, and then to consider alternative measures which will take it from its existing distribution to its most preferred.

A stabilisation role

Economies periodically suffer from inflation, unemployment, lack of real growth, balance of payments problems, etc. The government will use economic policies to try to **stabilise** the economy; for example, it will try to cut down spending when prices are rising too quickly.

A regulatory role

The government administers a general system of law and justice which **regulates** the behaviour of individuals and organisations.

Case Study

State could pay grannies to mind the baby

Early in 1999 the Labour government was examining a scheme whereby parents of single mothers could be offered incentives to help their daughters to raise their children as part of a new attempt to tackle the growing problem of teenage pregnancies.

Prime Minister Tony Blair had made the issue of teenage mothers a key priority of his social exclusion unit, established to look into and suggest remedies for the problems caused by poverty and deprivation. The issue is particularly pressing not only because of the dramatic rise in the number of teenage pregnancies, but also because the resulting children are more likely to have health problems and even to die in infancy.

Labour ministers were studying proposals to encourage grandparents actively to help their young children to raise their offspring. This could be done either through financial incentives or through penalties. Other suggestions include establishing hostels, with training centres and crèches, for young mothers to help them off benefit and into work.

One problem with mobilising grandparents is that offering incentives would mean paying money to those who are already helping their daughters. Critics complain that these are the very people who raised their own children to become teenage mothers.

Ministers and officials had come to the view that teenage pregnancies and parenthood are a phenomenon of social exclusion. A number of government ministers believed that there are clear links to ill-education, poor social conditions and poverty. With little expectation or opportunity, young girls can regard becoming a mother as giving them status.

Questions

1. To what extent should the state be involved in such social decision-making?

2. What do you see as the strengths and the weaknesses of the scheme outlined?

3. How could a line be drawn between legitimate state social activity and that which should be beyond the province of the state?

GOVERNMENT POLICIES

To achieve macroeconomic goals, both monetary and fiscal policies will be used to move the economy towards the desired outcome. Further reflection might also reveal the fact that fiscal and monetary measures contain within them other attributes that the government of the day wishes to exploit.

For example, increasing the level of taxation to cope with a high public-sector borrowing requirement (PSBR) might well achieve its goal, but deciding which taxes will be raised or introduced is a major policy issue that has other

implications. Pursuing the tax example a little further would show that Conservative governments between 1979 and 1997 wanted to shift the tax burden away from direct taxation (such as income tax) towards indirect taxation (like VAT). Although the overall tax burden was not reduced, the shift was made to allow taxpayers to keep more of their earned income initially and then make choices about how to spend it (or save it). Increasing the VAT rate and bringing more items into the net allows market forces to operate as freely as possible. The Labour party has sought to continue to allow consumers this choice but has moved the emphasis back partly towards direct taxation, to enable it to pursue other government objectives.

The government needs to assess both the macroeconomic issues and the effects of its policies on the behaviour of industries, or on individual organisations and companies. Additionally, provision of government services involves consuming resources in order to supply them, and seeking to regulate business activity via health and safety legislation, employment law, and so on.

The importance of government – whatever the political rhetoric – is clear for all to see. The Conservative party sought to reduce the intervention of government, but the role of the state at the end of 18 years of Tory rule was still extensive. The Conservatives left the state's overall share of the economy virtually undiminished: 44 per cent of GDP in 1979 and 43 per cent in 1996. Since 1997 the Labour party has already increased the influence of government in a wide range of areas of decision-making and spending. Both parties are fully aware that, from the provision of goods and services through to the regulation of the economy, the party of government has a key role in helping the country maintain its success. It is necessary to look at policy instruments a little more closely.

Monetary policy

The essence of monetary policy is to control **interest rates** and/or the **supply of money**. The government of the day creates targets for money supply growth coupled with targets for public spending.

Interest rates are set in line with the prevailing economic conditions, and particularly with respect to forecasts for inflation. The point of focus here is not the economic rationale for the changes in rates, but the impact that increasing or falling rates will have on business activity. Today the base interest rate is determined by the Bank of England rather than by the government.

A falling base interest rate should encourage industry to borrow and invest in producing new goods, boosting future production. Similarly the benefit to the consumer is felt by reducing the mortgage burden, thereby boosting disposable income and leading to a higher rate of consumption. The effects of a falling interest rate may take time to come through, as mitigating circumstances play their part. For example, because of negative equity (the situation house-owners find themselves in where the current values of their properties are less than their mortgage loans), a fall in interest rate may not bring forward extra demand until such time as house prices rise.

Increasing the base interest rate produces the opposite effect, hitting consumption and investment, although here again there may be a time-lag. Using the mortgage market example again, mortgage repayments may be adjusted only after a delay, so an immediate interest rate increase may not raise monthly payments until some months have elapsed. Retired people who rely on an income from their savings will actually see their income increase.

Money supply changes are monitored carefully by the government for signs of inflationary pressures. Changes in M0 (mainly notes and coins in circulation) and M4 (M0 plus retail deposits in banks and building societies) can cause the Bank of England to put further pressure on monetary growth by various interventions in the financial markets, as well as by interest rate changes. This can result in restricting credit, with all that implies for consumption.

Fiscal policy

Fiscal policy is made up of two elements: **taxation** and **government expenditure**. In 1999–2000 the public expenditure plans were for £349 billion divided as follows:

	£bn
Social security	102
Health services	61
Defence	22
Education	41
Transport	9
Housing and environment	13
Law and order	19
Industry, agriculture and employment	15
Other spending	41
Debt/interest	26

These categories of expenditure were balanced by tax and other receipts of the following:

	£bn
Income tax	88
National Insurance contributions	56
Corporation tax	30
Value added tax	54
Excise duties	36
Council tax	13
Business rates	16
Other receipts	56

The planned expenditure represents a large proportion of GDP, so any decisions to cut public spending have a sizeable impact on the nation's economic prosperity. This emphasises that the scope for action enjoyed by the government is not as great as first imagined. A further limiting factor is that a large part of the expenditure plans are covered by legally binding commitments, such as those on social benefits and education that account for large areas of expenditure.

Taxation is not simply a means to gain revenue, it also allows the pursuit of further political objectives. We have already referred to a shifting of the burden to indirect taxes such as VAT, but published figures reveal how large a dependence is still placed on income tax. A government can pursue other goals; for example, the tax on cigarettes can be increased to help to deter smoking, and unleaded petrol can be taxed less heavily for environmental reasons, to provide a price advantage over leaded fuel.

If policy objectives can be pursued using taxation, then it is equally clear that expenditure can be used for the same purpose. Student recruitment has been encouraged, first in higher education and then in further education, by providing extra funding; export guarantee cover has been made cheaper; and so on. What this means for business is that opportunities to supply goods and services in the new spending areas can be created, or taken away as funds dry up.

Industrial policy

Despite the large share of GDP that is still accounted for by public expenditure, the privatisation of nationalised industries has reduced direct state intervention in industry. The main policy initiatives are summarised below.

Enterprise culture

There have been initiatives to help create small businesses and to reduce the tax burden on them. Additionally the enterprise culture has been used to introduce an internal market into the National Health Service, to bring in compulsory competitive tendering for local authority services, and to introduce students to the world of business early in their studies. Most recently (1999) we have seen the government give more freedom to the Post Office to operate in a competitive environment and in a more market-orientated fashion. The Labour government has followed its Conservative predecessor in emphasising the role of enterprise.

Reduction of subsidies

The aim of both Conservative and Labour governments has been, where possible, to reduce subsidies or phase them out altogether. Whether it be in steel production or shipbuilding, running the railways or the operation of the BBC, the market has been asked to work without the distortion of subsidies. However, the new Labour government has created some new subsidies, for example in creating employment under the new deal (see below).

Privatisation

Many things, from council houses to public utilities, were sold off from 1979 onwards. However, the Labour government has found it increasingly difficult to privatise further because nearly all of the enterprises that private investors see as being a worthwhile investment have already been sold.

Privatisation does not on its own create competition, so regulations and the gradual introduction of competition have been seen as the way to reduce the monopoly power of water, electricity, gas and other utilities.

In October 1998, Tony Blair tried to explain his 'Third Way' to senior civil servants by giving examples. These included his government's use of a public–private partnership, rather than outright privatisation, to modernise the London Underground; government cooperation with the Wellcome Foundation, a charity to invest in public research laboratories; and an invitation to private firms to help raise school standards in designated 'education action zones'.

Deregulation

Sometimes referred to as 'reducing red tape', the purpose of deregulation is to eradicate as many restrictions as possible. Progressively governments have sought to remove the 'dead hand' of unnecessary regulation while creating new regulatory powers where they are necessary to ensure fair competition in the marketplace.

Incorporation

From trust hospitals to further-education colleges, incorporation allows the organisation to make more decisions on its own, and crucially to be free of local authority control. Funding becomes more centrally controlled and the organisation is rewarded (or not) on its success in meeting nationally determined performance criteria.

Mergers and business practice

There are various regulating agencies that review mergers, monopoly power and unfair trading. New Labour has followed the line of maintaining a competitive industrial framework while at the same time providing funds to attract employment-creating initiatives in the UK.

Social welfare policy

Social welfare is a key aspect of government policy, and social security, health and education are three major components of government expenditure in this country. Indeed, it is difficult to disentangle the connections between economic and social and welfare policies. When Tony Blair stated that his government's priority policy was 'Education, Education, and Education', he was not only promising a basic entitlement for all citizens to have a high standard of education, he was also making a connection between a well-educated workforce and international competitiveness in a world in which the 'knowledge worker' is the greatest asset of the modern economy.

The earlier Conservative governments placed an emphasis on creating an enterprise culture in which people would have the incentive to go out to work – 'to get on their bikes to seek work', as Norman Tebbit (a Conservative minister) described it. The Conservatives sought to reduce the role of the 'nanny state', which not only protected those genuinely in need, but also enabled people to avoid work and social responsibilities. The Conservatives reduced income taxes and decreased some state benefits, which was intended to give people more of an incentive to work. Critics of the Conservatives pointed out that they failed to differentiate between the 'shirker' and the 'needy', and that they failed to introduce effective programmes to create real opportunities for job-seekers.

The Conservatives also sought, through the policy of 'Care in the Community', to reduce the number of elderly people, and those with physical or mental difficulties, taking up hospital beds and places in state accommodation. Many such people were placed back in the community, often in sheltered accommodation. However, this led to a series of difficult situations because of a failure to provide adequate care. (For example, a number of people with mental problems failed to carry on taking their medicines.) A number of highly publicised cases led to a rethink of this policy, which was partially reversed by the incoming Labour government.

Discussion points

During her time as prime minister, Margaret Thatcher stated:

'Too many people have been given to understand that if they have a problem it's the government's job to cope with it ... They're casting their problem onto society. And, you know, there is no such thing as society. There are individual men and women, and there are families. And no government can do anything except through people, and people must look to themselves first. It's our duty to look after ourselves and then, also, to look after our neighbour. People have got the entitlements too much in mind, without the obligations. There's no such thing as entitlement, unless someone has first met an obligation.'

1. What do you think Margaret Thatcher meant by this statement in relation to social welfare policy?

2. To what extent do you agree or disagree with the statement?

Labour's 'Third Way' involves differentiating between those economic policies which are best left to market forces, and key social policies involving the protection of individuals and the community which need to be steered by a paternalistic state. A major emphasis has been on creating new opportunities for people to make a go of things in society: 'Instead of welfare there should be work'. Labour believes that work provides dignity, and opportunity for individuals; they can stand on their own feet rather than feel that they are receiving handouts from the state, and so are less than complete citizens.

Labour's 'New Deal' for young people includes the options of a subsidised job with an employer, a subsidised job in voluntary-sector employment, a subsidised job with the Environmental Task Force, or a subsidised period of full-time education leading to a recognised qualification.

Labour's 'Welfare to Work' programme is not without its critics, particularly those who see the reduction of state benefits as a threat to the genuine needs of specific groups of people such as the disabled. Such critics argue that benefits should not be cut off from those who have no realistic opportunity to hold down a job. However, the government would contend that everyone should have the opportunity to have a decent job. This involves creating the opportunities and the belief that everyone can move from welfare to some type of work, paid or unpaid.

Examples of Labour's welfare-to-work policies include:

- a lone-parents initiative offering practical help in returning to work (specially trained personal advisers help participants to overcome barriers to employment and encourage them actively to seek work)
- the provision of childcare for pre-school and school-age children.

Labour has also introduced a national minimum wage to make sure that all employees receive a wage which prevents them from being exploited in the labour market.

Case Study

The Third Way

In an article entitled 'Goldilocks politics' (*The Economist*, 19 December 1998), the authors wrote that Margaret Thatcher's political and economic doctrine for Britain was fairly clear: 'a combination of privatisation, patriotism, hostility to trade unions, and above all a belief in people taking responsibility for themselves instead of expecting the state to look after them'. These ideas were imitated in a number of countries. In contrast, the Blairite notion of a Third Way, though proving popular in a number of countries, is less transparent: 'Trying to pin down an exact meaning in all this is like wrestling an inflatable man. If you get a grip on one limb, all the hot air rushes to another.' The *Economist* writers tried to get to grips with the notion, which had been picked up by Bill Clinton in the United States, and in Germany by the new Chancellor Gerhard Schroder:

'In Mr Clinton's vision of the Third Way, government does not just provide services; it is an "enabler and catalyst", a partner with the private sector and community groups. The president wants government to be fiscally disciplined and less bureaucratic. It should not try to solve all of people's problems, but to create the conditions in which people solve their own. For his part, Mr Blair says that the Old Left championed indiscriminate and often ineffective public spending, but that the Third Way concentrates on making sure that the spending produces the desired results. He also says .... that governments should be friendly to private enterprise. ... In short, these new politicians want to make government smaller and cleverer, fiscally sound, and friendly to business. And in Britain's case they mark a clear departure from the big, stupid, overspending, business-hostile Labour governments of the 1960s and 70s.'

Questions

1. In your own words, write a paragraph describing Labour's Third Way.

2. Write another paragraph setting out the changes from the former Conservative government's policy.

Policies for regional and local development

In the UK there is considerable disparity in the economic fortunes of the different regions. Increasingly output and employment have moved towards the South East and East Anglia at the expense of regions such as the South West, North West and North. Population and the existence of a large market has favoured the South East with its strong links to the Continent and well-established infrastructure.

Successive governments have had different strategies for dealing with **regional and local inequalities**. Prior to 1979 there was a strong emphasis on subsidising areas of high unemployment and declining job opportunities. However, from 1979 the emphasis was switched to market forces, allowing areas which were performing poorly to decline while dynamic areas were allowed to grow. Of course, these policies were tempered by employment subsidies to declining regions. In particular, the **European Union** provided regional structural funds to ease hardship in the hardest hit areas.

The current Labour government is committed to competitiveness and allowing the market to work effectively. However, the government recognises that long-term unemployment may be particularly acute in certain geographical areas and these have therefore been designated as **Employment Zones**. Participants in

employment schemes in these areas are able to engage in intermediate-labour-market activity or receive training or help with becoming self-employed. Employment Zones are being developed by local partnerships and should be characterised by innovation.

Regulatory bodies

Competition is an essential element in the efficient working of markets. It encourages enterprise and widens choice. It enables consumers to buy the goods they want at the best possible price. By encouraging efficiency in industry and competition in the domestic market – whether between domestic firms alone or between them and overseas firms – competition contributes to our national competitiveness.

In recent years we have seen the privatisation of certain industries that formerly enjoyed a virtual state monopoly. In creating these new privatised industries it has been necessary to instil an appropriate competitive environment which involves fair play between competitors, which ensures the rights of consumers, and which is in the national interest. We have therefore seen the creation of regulatory bodies in key industries: Ofgas in the gas industry, Oftel in telecommunications, Ofwat in water, etc. In plain terms the new privatised companies have to work within certain constraints which are established for them – i.e. **regulation**.

We can illustrate the process of regulation by taking the specific example of the water services industry, and show how the Director General of the Office of Water Services (Ofwat), the Department of the Environment, the Environment Agency, and the Drinking Water Inspectorate play a crucial role in regulating the industry.

We live in a society in which there is a pressing demand for rises in environmental standards, and specifically the supply of clean water and reduction in industrial effluents and discharges. These improvements come at a cost, and with this in mind water companies have been allowed to increase their charges. Limits (price caps) have been set on these price increases in order to protect consumers.

The price rise cap for most regulated utilities in the UK is of the form 'RPI minus X'. That is, prices for each utility are in most cases allowed to increase less quickly than prices generally (as measured by the retail price index) by a factor X, which reflects both future efficiency gains and the financial position of the company. However, for water the price rise cap is in the form 'RPI + K', known as the 'K

factor'. The *K* factor is itself made up of two elements: the $-X$ factor which applies to all utilities, and a $+Q$ factor for improvements in quality standards. This means that the water companies are allowed to raise prices by more than inflation to account for the improvements to efficiency that they have made. Clearly this varies from company to company.

The government wants to ensure the existence of a water services industry which serves the public interest. The Secretary of State for the Environment and the Secretary of State for Wales appoint companies to take responsibility for water and sewage, as well as appointing the Director General of Ofwat. In addition the government minister is responsible for creating the regulatory framework for the industry. What has happened in this country is that this framework has been built on the basis of three principal regulators who work closely together.

- *The Director General of Ofwat*, whose key role is to make sure that the water companies run their businesses in a financially viable way enabling them to meet all the expectations that the public has of them in terms of quality of service and other requirements. The Director General must also make sure that the interests of customers are being protected.
- *The Environment Agency*, whose main duty with regard to water resources is to make sure that sufficient water is provided for water companies to allow them to meet the needs of their customers. It has a secondary duty to ensure that the natural environment is protected from the effects of contaminated waste water.
- *The Drinking Water Inspectorate*, whose role is to make sure that water companies meet very strict and detailed quality and health standards.

Today, quality and environmental standards for the water and sewerage industry are determined mainly by a European Union framework binding on the industry in each of the 15 member states of the Union. The cost of making sure that such standards are met falls largely on customers through price increases.

The functions of the regulators of other industries are broadly in line with the processes described here for the water industry.

CONCLUSION

This chapter has outlined a variety of ways of managing an economic system, and has examined the various instruments and policies that have been utilised for economic management in recent times. In the new century the UK government and private enterprise will continue to play major roles in determining the environment in which business operates.

As economies mature, so too (hopefully) does our understanding of how best to manage these economies. Today, most people recognise that heavy-handed regulation of the economy is counterproductive, in that it leads to inefficiencies and poor resource use. Too much time and effort, for example, is wasted on bureaucratic procedures. Both Conservative and Labour governments in recent years have supported policies of privatisation in this country. The current Labour government has set out a series of policies under the heading 'In Place of Welfare', which suggests a move away from the notion of a 'nanny state' formerly associated with socialism in this country. However, the market cannot simply be left to look after itself. The state plays an important supporting role in ensuring that the market works in a fair and sensible way. The state needs to support those individuals who cannot even start to compete in a competitive environment, and it needs to make sure that the strong and the advantages are not taking unfair advantage of their privileged positions by stacking up the odds in their favour (for example by creating monopoly positions).

External Market Factors

This chapter investigates the main external market factors which may influence an organisation.

There is a broad division into **demand-side** and **supply-side** factors.

On completion of this chapter you should be able to:

- explain the different market structures

- use three different examples to illustrate the relationship between market forces

- explain the possible ways that an organisation may gain competitive advantage

MARKET TYPES

Most people now live in societies in which the buying and selling of goods takes place in the **marketplace**. Buyers purchase the goods which best meet their requirements with a given income. Sellers set out to meet these needs and wants in such a way that they are able to make profits.

The act of selling/buying is called a **transaction**, and every day billions of transactions are made in local, regional, national and global markets. Most are face-to-face transactions (e.g. when you purchase the daily paper in your local newsagent). However, selling and buying do not have to involve face-to-face transactions. For example, oil trading is nearly always done by telephone, with the traders accessing up-to-the-minute information from all over the world via their computer screens. So a market does not necessarily involve a physical trading place; it occurs whenever buyers and sellers engage in transacting business.

Discussion point

What examples can you think of from your own personal experience where selling and buying do not involve face-to-face trading?

Markets determine:

- the price at which goods are sold and bought
- the quantity supplied to the market by producers and sellers
- the quantity demanded from the market by buyers.

It is this interaction between demand and supply which creates the **market price**. The market is a very important part of our lives. If people want goods badly enough and are prepared to back up their wants with purchasing power, then they will create a great demand for a product.

This will encourage suppliers to satisfy the demand with goods and services which are sold to the market in order to make profits.

- *Buyers*
  - are driven by their wants and needs
  - are constrained by the size of their disposable income, and the demand placed on this income by the intensity of demand for alternative goods and services
- *Sellers*
  - are driven by their desire to supply goods and services at a profit
  - are constrained by their ability to produce goods, these constraints including the cost of production and the extent of technical know-how.

Competion is a major influence on business. The intensity of competition in the marketplace will be determined largely by the conditions of demand and supply, including such factors as the numbers of buyers and sellers, the ease of supply, the intensity of demand, etc. A firm's prices and many other policies will be influenced by the level of competition it faces.

It is common practice to classify markets according to the level of competition that exists within them. At one extreme we have *highly competitive markets*, at the other we have a monopoly in which there is only a *single supplier to the market* (see Figure 16.1).

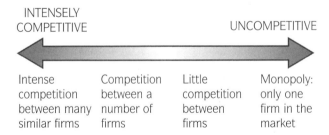

Figure 16.1 *The spectrum of competition in the marketplace*

Nevertheless, the fact that there are many firms in a market does not necessarily lead to intense competition (firms may tacitly collude in setting prices). In the real world, some of the most competitive situations occur when there is a relatively small number of firms, each of a similar size, each seeing the other as a competitor, and producing or selling a similar range of products or services to the same target audience.

The key features of a **market environment** are:

- the number of sellers and buyers operating within the market (the greater the number of each, the more likely the market is to be competitive)
- how easy it is for firms to enter the market (the greater the ease of entry, the more chance of competition)
- the influence which individual firms operating in the market have over prices (the greater the influence an individual firm has, the less competitive will be the market)
- whether there are substitutes for products being sold (the greater the number of substitutes and the closer the similarity between products, the greater will be the level of competition)
- any collusion between buyers/and or sellers (firms can restrict competition by working together)
- the level of knowledge in the market (the more knowledge that consumers have, say, of alternative prices and offers being made by different sellers, then the greater the intensity of competition; the same applies to sellers' knowledge of competitors and their actions).

TASK

Compare two product or service markets in your locality. How competitive are they? Weigh up the competitiveness of each market in terms of the factors listed above.

Market structures can be classified as monopoly, oligopoly, monopolistic (imperfect) competition or perfect competition (see Figure 16.2). At one extreme the monopoly market has a single supplier controlling the market and setting prices, while at the other extreme is the perfectly competitive market in which there are many firms, no barriers to entry of new firms, and with such a high degree of price competition that firms accept a price determined by market forces (supply and demand). Between these extremes lie oligopoly (competition between a few suppliers) and various states of monopolistic competition, where businesses operate in conditions which contain some element of monopoly restriction (e.g. where products are slightly differentiated, or where there are some barriers to market entry).

Figure 16.2 *Classification of market structures*

Perfect competition

The notion of **perfect competition** is one about which much has been written over the years. It does not apply to a real state in the world but to *an ideal*. It does not exist because: products are rarely, if ever, identical; it is unlikely that firms can freely enter and exit from markets; buyers and sellers do not have perfect knowledge of the market, etc. However, we should study the concept of perfect competition because it provides a justification of the importance of competition; i.e. that perfect competition leads to an efficient use of resources, and protects consumers from exploitation by suppliers.

In a state of perfect competition the supplier cannot charge more than the market price, because consumers can switch their purchases to rival suppliers. In the perfectly competitive market, producers will continue to supply additional units of output (marginal units) up to the point at which the cost of producing the marginal unit (marginal cost) is equal to the market price. This is a state of high efficiency because the price in the market reflects the marginal cost of producing units of output. Finally, no producer will charge *less* than the market price because the costs of production will not be covered (including a margin for profit which is just sufficient to keep the producer in the marketplace).

For perfect competition to exist within a market, a number of conditions would have to be met.

- There would have to be a large number of buyers and sellers so that no one person or organisation alone could affect the market.
- Freedom of entry to and exit from the market would have to exist for buyers and sellers.
- There would have to be homogeneity of products (i.e. all products must be identical).
- Buyers and sellers would need perfect knowledge of the market.

It is clear that a perfect market exists only in theory, although there are in fact some close approximations which are near-perfect, particularly in commodity markets.

There are some important lessons to be learnt from a study of 'perfect markets'.

- In perfect competition, organisations are 'price takers' as each has no influence over the price.
- Given the intensity of competition in the marketplace, consumers benefit from the efficient, low-cost nature of the good or service being provided as well as the plentiful choice of suppliers.
- Firms are free to enter or leave the market, rapidly eliminating the potential for profit or loss in the market.
- Perfect competition provides an ideal model against which real markets containing monopolistic components can be compared.
- Perfect competition provides a rationale and justification for competition, thereby supporting arguments for privatisation, monopoly and mergers legislation, etc.
- Perfect competition suggests a way in which societies can make best use of scarce resources.

Case Study

Why perfect competition cannot be the rule

In 1942, Professor Joan Robinson, one of the great British economists of the twentieth century, had the following to say about perfect competition in *An Essay on Marxian Economics*:

'The orthodox theory is based upon the assumption of perfect competition. Under perfect competition no individual producer can affect the price of his commodity by altering his rate of output. Each producer is conceived to maximise his profits by producing such a rate of output that marginal cost to him is equal to price – marginal cost being defined as the addition to total costs caused by a small unit increase in the rate of output. In the short period, with given capital equipment, marginal cost is equal to marginal prime cost – the addition to outlay on wages, raw materials, power and wear and tear entailed by a small unit addition to output. Thus price, at any moment, is equal to marginal prime cost, and the excess of receipts over total prime costs, which provides for overhead costs and net profits, is equal to marginal minus average prime cost, multiplied by output.

'Now, in the general run of manufacturing industry, prime cost begins to rise sharply, as output expands, only when the full capacity output of the plant is approached. It follows that, with perfect competition, any firm which is working at less than full capacity output must be losing the whole of its overhead costs, and can have no motive for continuing production. Thus, under perfect competition the rule must be: full capacity output or no output at all.

But, in reality, full capacity working is a rarity, even in times of average prosperity, while slump conditions normally lead to a reduction in the rate of output from all plant, rather than a complete cessation of production from some plants, side by side with full capacity working for the rest. It appears therefore that, in reality, perfect competition in selling commodities cannot be the rule, and that the excess of price over prime cost cannot be accounted for solely by the difference between marginal and average prime cost.'

Robinson then went on to show how because of this difficulty, economists proceeded to outline a theory of imperfect (monopolistic) competition which was more aligned to real world conditions. In imperfect competition it is assumed that the individual producer is not faced by a price for his commodity over which he has no influence; on the contrary, an increase in his output can be sold only if he lowers his price, or undertakes greater selling costs (for advertisements and the like).

Questions

1. Why can't perfect competition occur in the real world?

2. Why is imperfect (monopolistic) competition a more realistic model?

3. Why is it necessary to understand the nature and benefits of perfect competition as a model?

Monopoly

An organisation that does not have to face competition is said to have a **monopoly** in the market. It may have only limited outside pressure put on it to be competitive. We must be careful, however, not to assume that monopolies are necessarily inefficient or all bad. Monopolies can put a lot of money into product development and research in order to keep ahead of *potential* competitors.

In practice, single control over the supply of a product rarely exists and we tend to talk about *degrees of monopoly*. In the UK, the Monopolies and Mergers Commission (MMC) regards a monopoly as a situation where either one or a group of producers control at least 25 per cent of a market. There are a few state monopolies left – for example, the Bank of England has a monopoly in the production of bank notes (most state monopolies disappeared with the privatisation of industries like gas, water and electricity). In the private sector you are more likely to find local monopoly situations rather than national ones – for example, a petrol station may have a monopoly in the selling of petrol in a remote area of the country.

Monopolies are often in a position to erect **barriers** to stop others from entering the market. Given its strength and dominant position in the market, a monopoly can dictate market price and is a 'price-maker'. Since there may be few substitutes for monopoly products, the monopolist has considerable discretion in price-fixing, and price-raising, in order to maximise profits.

Monopoly power may mean that consumers are faced with restricted output at much higher prices than if more competition existed. For this reason, monopolies frequently have the power to abuse their position and make decisions which are against the public interest. From a government's point of view it is important to monitor the actions of monopolies to make sure that practices do not work unfairly against the interests of consumers.

A monopolist may wish to increase revenue and profit by means of price discrimination. This occurs when different prices are charged to consumers in different parts of the market for the same product. To discriminate like this it must be possible to divide the market into clear segments (see Chapter 2).

Imperfect (monopolistic) competition

Imperfect competition lies between pure perfect competition and pure monopoly. Firms operating in such markets sell products that are differentiated in some way from rivals' products. This differentiation may be very slight (e.g. in packaging or branding), or may be considerable. The firms in the market are able to point to differences between their products and those of rivals, which gives them some leeway in determining the price of the products rather than taking the market price.

In imperfect competition:

• goods and services are not homogenous
• there will be some forms of barrier to the free entry of new competitors to the market
• consumers and competitors will not have perfect knowledge of the market
• firms are able to point out areas of differentiation from competitors.

In an imperfect market firms are able to charge prices which are higher than the marginal cost of producing a product. Resources are therefore not used in the most efficient way.

Case Study

French Boules

The French boule has been given its own trading standard or 'Norme Française'. To be sold legally in France, boules must be constructed of thick, pure steel, have no blemishes or solder marks, and must be hollow.

The French market for boules (80 per cent of the world market) is dominated by two companies, Obut and Boules JB. They produce five million boules a year and remain overwhelmingly in control. A typical set of three boules costs anything from £20 to £100 when supplied by the two leading manufacturers.

However, recently French manufacturers have been worried by the flood of cheap imports from Asia, which are often stuffed with earth, sand, clay or mercury to bring them up to the throwing weight. Criticisms of the imported boules are that they fail, when striking other boules, to make the satisfying clunking sound which, according to some accounts, gives the game of pétanque its name. The imported boules are also reputed to have a tendency to explode on impact, showering players with shrapnel. Some 10 per cent of boules sold to ordinary weekend pétanque players now come from abroad.

Questions

1. How might Obut and Boules have been able to build up a dominant position in the boules industry?

2. What would be the likely impact of this monopolistic position on consumers?

3. Why have the French introduced a 'Norme Française'?

4. What will be the impact of this standard on the boules industry?

5. What will happen to competition in the longer term in the boules industry?

Oligopoly

Oligopoly is a very important form of imperfect competition and has been frequently studied because many business organisations in modern economies operate in oligopoly markets.

Oligopoly means competition between the few and exists where just a small number of firms dominate the market. The French boules industry with two firms dominating production, is a special type of oligopoly called a **duopoly**. A good example of a duopoly in this country is sugar, where Tate & Lyle produces mainly from sugar cane imported from countries like Mauritius, and the British Sugar Corporation produces 'Silver Spoon' mainly from sugar beet, much of which is grown in this country.

Oligopolies can be intensely competitive, or they may **collude** to operate as virtual monopolies. In this country the purpose of the Monopolies and Mergers Commission is to prevent monopolistic practices and so a keen eye is kept on oligopoly markets. For example, Tate & Lyle and the British Sugar Corporation have been in trouble for coordinating the prices they charge to supermarket chains.

Today, we have a classic example of an oligopoly situation in the provision of satellite television to households. BSkyB, which is part of the News International Corporation run by Rupert Murdoch, has sought to develop a dominant position in home broadcasting. Until 1998, BSkyB was very successful in dominating the satellite television market. Its principal selling technique was to gain a monopoly over broadcasting live sporting occasions such as Premier football matches, world championship boxing, and rugby tours by the British

Lions. To watch these events people had to subscribe to Sky.

However, with the advent of digital broadcasting in late 1998, households now had the potential to be able to receive over 200 channels in their homes. BSkyB therefore devised a marketing strategy which involved creating a package of entertainment channels including sports, news, the arts, entertainment, nature and a variety of other channels. Their biggest rival was OnDigital, which launched slightly after Sky. However, by 1999 Sky was well ahead of OnDigital, selling digital systems in the proportion of 4:1. In order to win market share BSkyB had to offer a very competitive rate to new and existing subscribers. Clearly, in such a competitive oligopoly environment consumers will benefit from the intense competition. However, it remains to be seen whether, if BSkyB gains a virtual monopoly in the market, it then starts to push prices upwards.

Oligopolies can therefore either operate in a highly competitive way, pulling down prices and offering more and more benefits to consumers; or, they may act in a restrictive and monopoly-like way. Government therefore plays a key role in the market to make sure that, where oligopolies exist, they operate in a competitive way.

Many commentators believe that oligopolists have a tendency to be competitive when they are seeking to gain a larger share of the market. However, once they have achieved the larger share of the market, they tend to act in a more monopolistic fashion. Of course, businesses need to take a long-term view and be competitive so that rivals are not tempted to enter the industry.

Industries in which large profits are to be made are likely to attract new firms to enter the market. These new entrants may be firms that are already successful in another field. For example, you only need to look at the history of Virgin to realise that Richard Branson is adept at spotting existing monopoly/oligopoly markets where opportunities exist because the monopolist in the market has not been exposed to strong competition. Branson moved into contraceptives because the existing monopoly producer, London Rubber, had faced virtually no competition for many years. He also moved into railways, an industry which had previously been dominated by the state-run British Rail. He moved into Virgin Air at a time when British Airways faced only limited competition.

There are many examples of oligopoly markets in the UK today, including national newspapers, breakfast cereals, banking services, soups, washing powders, pet foods, petrol, disposable nappies, confectionery, fast food, and supermarkets. A common feature of these markets is **product differentiation**, often through products with a strong brand identity.

Take the example of petrol. It is a product which appears to be highly homogenous but can actually be differentiated in many ways. Service stations compete over:

- range of petrols, diesel, and other fuels
- range of customer services (fast service, paper towels to wipe hands after filling up, toilets, a range of extra products such as cosmetics, newspapers, etc.)
- light, flexible hoses
- a place to check tyre pressure, vacuum the car, etc.

There are no set rules as to the degree of competition existing in oligopoly. Each producer will spend money on actions designed to foster brand loyalty – such as advertising and promotion – and will attempt to differentiate its products from others that are available.

However, there is always the danger that open warfare with regard to pricing and other elements of competition will be to the disadvantage of all producers and sellers. The ability to make profits, and to plough profits into promotion, research and product development, is viewed as being of crucial importance. Though such markets are typified by lulls and surges in the extent of competitive practices, prices are often stable for long periods. Prices tend to follow the price of the leading brand (the price-leader), though there is danger of collusion.

MARKET FORCES AND ORGANISATIONAL RESPONSES

The term **market forces** refers to the interaction of demand and supply. **Demand**, in economics, is the quantity of a good or service that purchasers will buy at a given price; while **supply** is the quantity that producers will provide for a price. An equilibrium or balance will be successfully achieved when the quantity customers are willing to buy at a certain price matches the quantity that producers are willing to sell at the same price.

The link between suppliers and demanders through the market is the **price**. The price helps to express what consumers want and are willing to pay for as well as what suppliers are willing to provide.

Power relations in the marketplace

The distinguishing feature of a **market economy** is that consumers can spend their money as they think fit. Consumers are free to choose one pair of jeans rather than another, Coke or Pepsi, margarine or butter. This freedom of choice is supposed by many people to support the argument that 'the consumer is king' in a market economy. The consumer effectively 'votes' (with his or her income) for resources to be channelled into certain goods or services rather than others. The clothes shop that fails to keep up with fashion trends will rapidly find out that sales fall off. But how much **power** does the consumer really have? Inevitably, there are a number of important restrictions to consumer power.

Firstly, individual consumers have only limited incomes. With the development of new market-based economies in eastern Europe in the early 1990s, it did not take consumers long to find out that without incomes they had very little power in the marketplace. This is true of any market economy – the possession of a sizeable income gives an individual far greater power to claim scarce resources for his or her own use.

Secondly, the power of consumers depends in part on the intensity of competition in the marketplace. If there are three petrol stations at the end of your street they are far more likely to respond to your wishes than if there is only one petrol station within 20 miles. When a new Asda supermarket store opened in Grantham in December 1998 offering consumers a wide range of choice, Safeways introduced a host of new features (e.g. a fish and butchery counter) in order to offer consumers a similar level of choice.

Thirdly, consumers have more power the greater the proportion of a commodity they purchase. For example, a wholesaler who buys half the output of a potato farm may be able to influence the size, type and quality of potatoes grown on the farm. The wholesaler may also be able to negotiate a bulk discount. A person who turns up at the farm gate to buy one bag of potatoes will have virtually no influence.

Fourthly, consumers have greater influence if they can organise themselves into buying groups. For example, if several retailers join together to purchase items they may be able to gain better discounts and other terms.

Fifthly, consumers have greater influence the more they know about a product. The greater the knowledge, the better the opportunity to make an informed purchase from a position of strength. An experienced buyer is unlikely to be taken in by woolly sales talk.

Finally, consumers are in a stronger position if they are supported by consumer-rights organisations and government legislation. Consumer and government bodies can help to spread information, and to insist on minimum standards in production and selling.

To summarise these points, we can say that consumers have more power in markets in which:

- they have considerable buying power
- competition exists
- individual consumers are responsible for significant proportions of all purchases
- they are organised into buying groups
- they are informed
- they are protected.

It follows that producers have more power when all or some of these considerations do not apply. For example, producers have considerable power when consumers have little information about what is available, there are few suppliers, or there are many consumers. At the end of the day, one of the key factors determining power relations is the *urgency* with which a purchase or a sale needs to be made.

Demand in the marketplace

Demand is the quantity of a product that consumers will be prepared to buy at a given price over a period of time. There are three important features in this definition.

- Individuals must be willing and able to purchase a product. For example, we may all want a better car, but only a few may have the ability to buy one.
- There is a direct link between demand and price.
- A time period is involved. Over a longer period of time, if prices change, demand will also change.

The best way to demonstrate the dynamics of demand is to use an example. If the price of a colour printer for a computer is £500, John will be prepared to buy one printer. If it is more than £500 he will not be willing to buy one. If the price, however, fell to £300 he might be prepared to buy two, one for his home and one for his office. We can set out John's demand for computer printers:

Price	Quantity
More than £500	0
£500	1
£300	2

Quite clearly, as the price of printers falls they become more affordable, and consumers may be prepared to purchase them instead of spending their money on alternatives. In this example, therefore, there is an inverse relationship between the quantity demanded and the price; i.e. as price goes down, quantity demanded goes up. (Note that this is not the case in all situations, as there are some examples such as luxury items or shares where demand may increase as price increases.) Equally, one printer will be very useful to John, as will two. However, if the price continues to fall there will come a point at which John has enough printers, and then further price falls will not entice fresh purchases by him at the same rate. We can see this, for example in the purchase of television sets. At one time most households had a single family television. However, as incomes have risen, and the price of televisions has fallen, we have moved on to a situation where some households have a television set in nearly every room.

In the example we concentrated on one individual's demand for a product. Some markets are made up of just a few consumers, but some are made up of a few hundred, whilst others are made up of thousands or even millions of consumers. We talk of a 'global market' where demand for a product is worldwide.

Demand schedules can be set out by adding together the individual demands of all consumers in a particular market. For example, the demand schedule below shows the possible national market for a particular type of printer in a six-month period; the figures could have been gathered through market research.

Price of printer (£)	Quantity demanded (per year)
1000	500
800	1 000
600	10 000
400	12 000
200	14 000

The information in the demand schedule can be illustrated in the form of a **demand curve** (see Figure 16.3).

For the moment it is convenient for us to think of demand as fitting a nicely drawn curve, but of course in the real world demand patterns are not so simple. The demand for products varies considerably with fresh price changes. Some price rises will have little effect on quantities bought, while other quite small price rises may be critical.

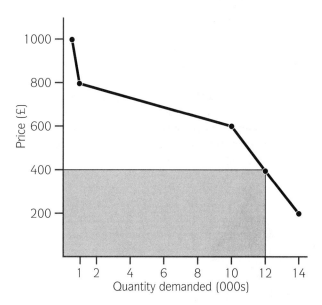

Figure 16.3 *A demand curve for a printer*

By taking a single point on the curve – for example, £400 – it is possible to read off the total expenditure on the product at that price (£400 with a demand of 12 000 product units would yield a total market expenditure of £4.8 million). This is an important concept for the organisation and is shown by the shaded rectangle in Figure 16.3.

Elasticity of demand

As and when prices change, this could affect consumers and suppliers as well as other competitors within the marketplace. It is important for all concerned to understand what will happen if prices change. The degree to which these parties may be affected by a price change is shown by the concept of 'elasticity'.

Elasticity of demand is a measure of how much the quantity demanded of a good responds to a price change.

- Demand is said to be **elastic** if the proportional change in quantity is greater than the proportional change in price. For example, if the price increases by 5 per cent and the quantity demanded falls by 6 per cent, demand is elastic.
- There is **unitary elasticity** of demand when the proportional change in quantity is equal to the proportional change in price – for example, if the price falls by 5 per cent and demand rises by 5 per cent.
- Demand is said to be **inelastic** if the proportional change in quantity is less than the proportional change

in price – for example, if the price falls by 5 per cent and demand increases by only 2 per cent.

For all normal goods, a rise in price will lead to a fall in demand and a fall in price will lead to a rise in demand.

The responsiveness of consumers to price changes is critical for producers. We can safely conclude that producers may consider price reductions if demand is elastic and they may consider price rises if demand is inelastic.

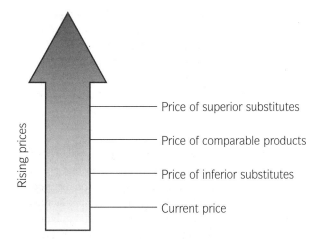

Figure 16.4 *Prices of soft drinks in the marketplace*

However, as we have seen, elasticity varies considerably as we alter the price. Figure 16.4 describes the implications for a soft drinks manufacturer of increasing price. If it does this, at first sales will not fall off by much because consumers will remain loyal to this cheaper brand which is better than slightly higher priced (but inferior) substitutes. At first, then, demand will be *inelastic* as the price rises. However, as price rises into the bracket of prices charged by comparable and superior products, then demand for this brand will become increasingly *elastic*. Sellers need to carry out extensive market research to find out what will be the likely effects of raising or lowering prices.

Measuring elasticity of demand

If quantity demanded is very responsive to price changes, then a small change in price will lead to a relatively large change in demand. In this case we would say that demand is elastic. For example, many popular fruits have an elastic demand at their existing market prices, so that if say the price of a type of apple rose by 2 or 3 pence then customers could easily switch to cheaper substitutes such as another type of apple, or to pears.

Where quantity demanded is relatively unresponsive to price change we say that demand is inelastic. An example of this would be the case of someone addicted to smoking 40 cigarettes a day. Even though the price of cigarettes goes up they still continue to smoke 39 or 40 because their demand is highly inelastic (i.e. responds little to a price change). Of course, there are limits to this – if the price of cigarettes doubled or trebled then the cigarette smoker might have to look for substitutes.

To be precise, *elasticity of demand can be defined as the relationship between the proportionate change in price and the proportionate change in quantity demanded*. This can be given a numerical value by using the formula:

$$\text{Elasticity of demand} = \frac{\text{Percentage change in quantity demanded}}{\text{Percentage change in price}}.$$

TASK

Calculate the elasticity of demand in the following examples.

1. A good falls in price by 50 per cent, from £1 to 50p. The quantity demanded increases by 100 per cent, from 1000 to 2000. What is the measure of elasticity of demand? (It should be expressed as a negative figure because price and quantity are moving in opposite directions.)

2. A good falls in price from £1 to 50p and the quantity demanded increases from 1000 to 1250. What is the measure of elasticity of demand?

A key aspect of elasticity of demand is the impact on sales revenue. Total revenue to a supplier is price multiplied by quantity demanded (sales). As price changes, sales also change, and therefore so does total revenue. The crucial question is: To what extent will total revenue change as a result of a change in price? It is possible to use measures of elasticity to show the effect of price variations and their influence on total revenue (see Figure 16.5).

Type of elasticity	Change in price	Effects on total revenue
Inelastic →	increase	increase
	decrease	decrease
Elastic →	increase	decrease
	decrease	increase

Figure 16.5 *Relationship between elasticity and total revenue*

Factors influencing elasticity of demand

Correct pricing is critical. If prices are judged by consumers to be too high then the lack of sales may ruin a business. If the prices are too low it may not be possible to recover costs. A number of factors influence price elasticity.

- *The price of competitive products.* In competitive markets sellers have little choice over what prices they charge. When competitors alter prices firms may have to alter their prices too, particularly when prices fall.
- *The proportion of income that households spend on a particular commodity.* Most households spend a lot on housing, clothes, fuel and food. When the prices of items in these categories rise, households may be forced to cut back spending. However, there are items that are bought rarely and cost relatively little – for example, salt, food seasoning, shoe laces and so on. When these items rise in price, quantities bought will not be greatly affected.
- *The price of the good or service.* We have already seen that the current price is critical. If it is already considered to be high, then a price rise may lead to a greater fall in demand than if the initial price is considered low.

- *The necessity of making a fresh purchase.* When your watch is old you can still use it provided it works well – you do not have to purchase a new one. This is not the case with soup – when you have finished one tin you will want to

buy another one if you like the soup. The demand for **consumer durables** may therefore be more elastic as a result of a price increase than the demand for **consumer disposables** such as foodstuffs.
- *Whether a good is a basic necessity or not.* Goods which are 'essentials' will have inelastic demands. We cannot easily do without items such as bread and milk, but we can do without many exotic and fancy foods that we buy only on special occasions. The same applies to many other commodities such as clothes and luxury models of cars.

Another very important factor influencing elasticity of demand is the time period in question. In the short term, consumers may feel that it is necessary to buy a particular good or service. Given more time, however, they may better appreciate the benefits of looking around and switching to alternatives. A product which at one time seemed indispensable may lose its sales as time moves on and new substitutes replace it.

Movements along the demand curve

For convenience we will now redraw the demand curve as a straight line in order to simplify the text (see Figure 16.6).

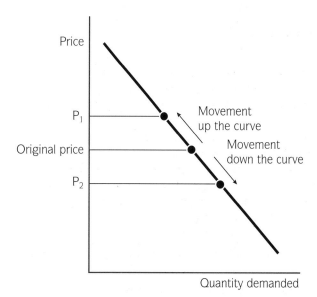

Figure 16.6 *A simplified demand curve drawn as a straight line*

- If the price of a good rises we can refer to 'a move up the demand curve'.
- If the price of a good falls we can refer to 'a move down the demand curve'.

The market-place is a dynamic concept, and price is not the only factor that alters demand. The behaviour of both producers and consumers may be affected by a number of other influences, including:

- changes in tastes
- changes in population
- changes in income
- changes in inherited wealth
- changes in the price of substitutes
- changes in the price of complements
- the weather.

Tastes

As time moves on, new products become more fashionable and popular while others go into decline. A classic example is in the home music industry. In the 1960s and 70s everyone was into 'vinyl' records, and then in the 1980s tapes became all the rage. However, in the mid-80s CDs took over. Today vinyl is very rare, tapes are losing shelf space, and CDs are everywhere. Of course this hasn't pushed the price of CDs up because the supply of CDs and the technology and scale of their production have improved enormously (see Figure 16.7).

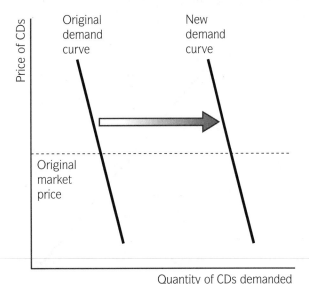

Figure 16.7 *An increase in demand for CDs*

A pronounced example of a rapid shift to the left in the demand curve for a product occurred in 1996 with the BSE scare that led to a dramatic fall in demand for beef products. In the same period the public developed a new demand for ostrich and venison steaks and burgers. More recently, the demand for beef has gone back almost to its previous level as people have become less worried – although demand may plummet if BSE deaths increase.

Population

Population statistics can be very helpful for forecasting changes in demand. Demographers (people who combine population statistics) frequently make predictions about future population trends based on existing statistics and trends. Predictions based on the size of the population in different age groups are particularly easy to chart because, once a child has been born, he or she will become steadily older.

Populations can be classified in a number of ways, including by age, sex, locality, race, background – or even by the newspaper they read.

Demand forecasters will often analyse population statistics according to clusters of relevant factors, for example females in the 25–35 year-old age group living in Essex.

An increase in the relevant population will tend to move the demand curve for a product to the right – for example if Essex girls are fond of the perfume 'Charley', and their numbers increase. A decrease in the relevant population will tend to move the demand curve to the left.

Income

The more money people have, the easier it is for them to buy products. The amount of money that people have to spend on goods is known as their **disposable income**, (i.e. their pay minus taxes and deductions).

Average incomes tend to rise over time and this will lead to a general increase in the level of demand for goods. The demand for individual items, however, will be related more to changes in the incomes of different groups, such as teenagers (for teenage magazines and fashions), pensioners (for retirement homes, winter sun holidays) and others.

The demand for most products will rise as a result of an increase in incomes for the relevant population; this will lead to a shift in the demand curve to the right. Rising incomes will tend to result from improved job opportunities, and increases in the demand for goods.

Some products may become less popular as incomes rise. These are goods that come to be regarded as inferior when people's spending power increases. The consumer who was once happy to rent a flat, wear second-hand clothes and drive a second-hand low-powered car may switch to buying a house, wearing designer labels and driving a status-symbol car when his or her income increases sufficiently.

We can thus state the relationship between income and demand in the following way:

For most products the demand curve will shift to the right when income increases, and to the left when income falls. In the case of inferior items, however, demand would shift to the left when income rises.

Inherited wealth

A number of studies have highlighted the level of inherited wealth now enjoyed by middle-aged households. The overall effect is that a sizeable number of middle-aged households inherit a considerable amount of wealth which is rapidly turned into spending power. An increase in inherited wealth in this way can have an important effect in raising the demand for products and thus shifts demand curves to the right.

The price of substitute products

The demand for products that have close substitutes will often be strongly influenced by the price of the substitutes. This is the case, for example, with different brands of tinned fruit and soups, or different brands of petrol, because there are many brands to choose from.

The demand curve for a product is likely to shift to the right if a substitute product rises in price (see Figure 16.8). The demand curve for a product is likely to shift to the left if a substitute product falls in price (assuming that other factors influencing demand do not alter at the same time).

The price of complementary products

Some products are used together so that the demand for one is linked to the price of another. An example of this might be a word processor and a floppy disc or CD-ROM. If a particular brand of word processor were to rise in price, then potential buyers might switch their purchases to an alternative brand. This would also reduce the demand for the floppy discs that are compatible with the original brand of word processor.

The weather

For some products the weather is another factor influencing demand. Not many people will be bothered to buy antifreeze for their car in warm seasons. Interestingly

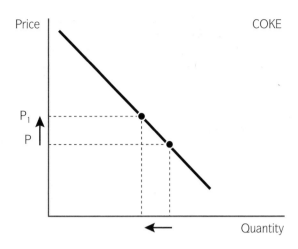

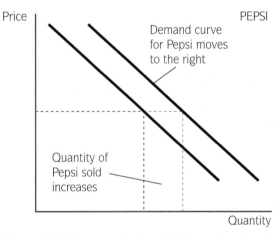

Figure 16.8 *Changes in the demand for Pepsi when the price of Coke increases*

enough, the motor industry has combated the seasonal demand for antifreeze – by calling it antifreeze in winter, and coolant in the summer.

Case Study

Changing patterns of demand for sports equipment

In 1998, Britons spent £3.5 billion on sports goods – £1.8 billion on clothing, £1 billion on footwear and £620 million on equipment – a 48 per cent rise in six years.

The growing fascination with fitness is highlighted by the fact that one in five adults took up a new sport in 1998, according to a report published by the market research organisation Mintel. Activities for fitness, rather than competition, were the most popular. Swimming was top, chosen by 19 per cent of the converts, followed by weight-training or other gym activities, attracting 18 per cent, and keep-fit picked by 14 per cent.

Half of those taking part in a sport regularly used a sports centre in 1998. A third of those surveyed had used a private club.

Football is by far the most popular team sport and is played regularly by 10 per cent of the people surveyed – compared with 2 per cent who played cricket and 2 per cent who chose rugby. Team sports players spent an average of £103 on clothing, compared with £45 for all sports enthusiasts.

Spending on soccer goods reached £360 million in 1998 with clothing accounting for £210 million – driven up from £60 million in 1992 by sales of replica kits.

The number of men playing golf went up from 12 per cent in 1992 to 14 per cent, with significant increases among those aged 15–24 and from middle-income groups. But the proportion of well-off males playing golf declined, and only 1 per cent of women play golf regularly.

Questions

1. Illustrate by means of a demand curve the increase in demand for football clothing.

2. What are the major influences on demand highlighted in the article? Explain how each of these has contributed to changes in demand in two sporting areas.

Supply in the marketplace

Supply is the quantity of a product suppliers are willing to make available and provide for a market at given prices over a period of time. There are two important features in this definition.

- It underlines the role of price in determining the quantity which suppliers are willing to provide for the market.
- As with demand, a time period is involved.

To simplify our supply analysis we will assume that companies seek to make profits. The profit from selling a good is the difference between the total revenue at the price at which it is sold and the total cost of producing and selling it. The quantities of the good that the company offers will therefore depend on the price it receives for each unit sold relative to the cost of producing each unit.

As price rises (other things remaining the same), the company will at first make a larger profit on each item it sells. This will encourage it to make and sell more. However, the company may face rising costs as it expands production beyond the limit that it had originally planned (for example, the cost of paying employees at overtime rates will increase). For these reasons we should expect that companies will offer more for sale at higher prices, and as they increase their output they will ask for higher prices.

This can be shown by developing a **supply schedule** which shows the supply side of a market, for example for printers. Assuming that price is the only variable and that other supply factors remain constant, as price falls the quantity supplied falls, and as price rises the quantity supplied rises:

Price of printer (£)	Quantity supplied (per year)
1 000	16 000
800	12 000
600	10 000
400	8 000
200	2 000

The information in the supply schedule can now be used to construct a **supply curve** (see Figure 16.9).

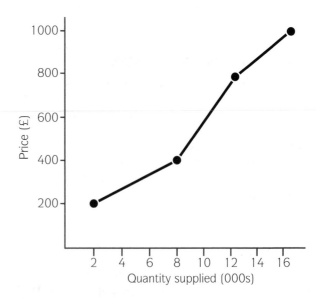

Figure 16.9 *Supply curve for a printer at various prices*

Elasticity of supply

Elasticity of supply measures the responsiveness of supply to changes in price. If producers can increase production substantially as price increases, their supply is said to be elastic. Conversely, if producers fail to respond to an increase in price, their product may be described as being inelastic in supply. Elasticity of supply can be calculated in the following way:

$$\text{Elasticity of supply} = \frac{\text{Percentage change in quantity supplied}}{\text{Percentage change in price}}.$$

Supply is said to be elastic when the quantity changes by a greater proportion than the price change. Inelastic supply is when the quantity changes by a smaller proportion than the price change.

Factors influencing elasticity of supply

Time has a great influence on elasticity of supply. We can identify three time periods.

- *The momentary period*. At a moment in time it is impossible to alter supply. In a shoe shop at 3.30 pm on a Saturday afternoon there may be only three pairs of size 7 Reebock trainers in stock. In business we define the momentary period as that in which it is impossible to alter both our fixed factors of production (such as the machinery or buildings in a processing plant) and our variable factors (such as labour and energy).
- *The short period*. Between 3.30 pm and 4.00 pm on a Saturday afternoon it may be possible to rush extra Reebock training shoes to the shop from a local warehouse. In business we define the short period as the period in which fixed factors remain fixed, but variable factors can vary.
- *The long period*. Because of a general increase in the demand for Reebock trainers, a factory producing them may expand its plant and equipment. In business we define the long period as the period in which all the factors of production can become variable. If the demand for Reebock trainers increases on a national scale, then the company may build new factories to meet the increased demand.

We can illustrate elasticity of supply in different time periods. Momentary supply is represented by a vertical line, short-period supply by a relatively inelastic supply line, and long-period supply by a relatively elastic supply line (see Figure 16.10).

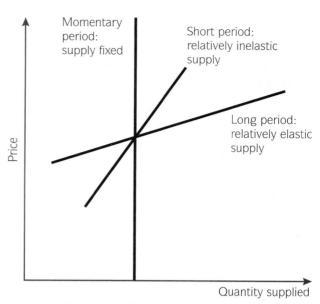

Figure 16.10 *Influence of the time factor on elasticity of supply*

What constitutes a short or long period varies from company to company and from industry to industry. For example, it takes a lot longer to increase fresh flower production than it does to expand artificial flower production. Some products have an extended long term (e.g. coffee and rubber production), while others have a shorter long term. If you have ever grown cress on your window sill you will known that it can be grown within days.

Discussion points

1. What products can you think of that have a very short long period?

2. What products can you think of that have a very long short period?

Elasticity of supply also varies according to how close to **capacity** a company or an industry is running. If a factory is using only half its machines, it could be relatively easy to expand production. However, if the factory is already working at full capacity, the company would have to invest in new plant in order to expand its supply.

Another factor influencing elasticity of supply is the availability of **components and raw materials**. In order to expand production it is necessary to increase inputs. If inputs are readily available, then supply will be far more elastic than if inputs are scarce. Another factor is the cost of producing additional outputs. If the extra cost of producing additional units is rising sharply, then producers will be reluctant to expand output in response to higher prices.

Changes in supply

In addition to price, there are a number of factors that influence the supply of a product. These include:

- prices of factors of production
- prices of other commodities
- changes in the level of technology
- producers' objectives
- the weather
- government policies.

If one of these factors alters, the conditions of supply are said to have changed. Changes in one or a combination of these factors may cause bodily shifts in the supply curve. The supply curve can shift in either a leftward or a rightward direction. In Figure 16.11, a shift to the left from SS to S_1S_1 indicates that smaller quantities will be supplied than before at a given price, while a shift to the right from SS to S_2S_2 indicates that larger quantities will be supplied than before at given prices.

Prices of factors of production are important because production is based on the combination of factor inputs in order to produce outputs. If the cost of a factor rises then it will be more expensive to produce outputs. As factor prices rise, fewer factors will be used in production, and hence the supply of a product will fall.

For example, let us assume that an agricultural crop requires three main inputs: land, labour and chemical fertiliser. If the cost of one or more of these inputs were to rise, then farmers might cut back on the acreage committed to this particular crop. Conversely, if the price of one or more factors of production were to fall, then supply conditions would move in favour of increased production and supply is likely to shift to the right.

By looking at the **prices of other commodities** in areas of production, it may be possible to switch from production of less profitable products to more profitable lines. For example, many arable farmers have a certain degree of flexibility over which crops to grow. A shipyard can choose to build tugs, oil rigs or bulk carriers. If a particular line becomes more profitable, then scarce resources such as equipment, time and materials can be switched into producing it and away from producing other products.

Changing levels of technology means that more output can be produced with fewer resources. The supply curve for a product may shift to the right. Modern technology based on use of computers and robotics has enabled a number of producers to produce larger outputs at lower unit costs – for example in car production, newspapers and the processing of cheques by banks.

Organisations have a range of both business and marketing **objectives** and, to a large extent, supply will be seen to follow such objectives. For example, expansion may be a goal in itself, so the firm might produce more to gain market share or to increase its profile.

The **weather** may be a major factor in the supply of many goods and services. A number of products respond to changes in the weather, not least the appearance of umbrella sellers at the entrances to underground stations in rainy weather! The supply of agricultural products depends very much on changing weather conditions.

Government policies may include further regulation of a market, or deregulation, or perhaps subsidies or taxation. Such policies may either encourage or discourage producers to provide products for the market and, at the time of introduction, may have a marked effect on the marketplace for a particular type of product.

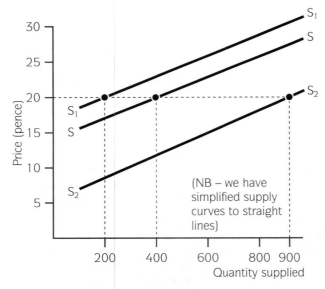

Figure 16.11 *Shifts in the supply curve*

Case Study

City centre cinema boom

In a spate of cinema building unprecedented since the war, in excess of 500 new screens are to be built in Britain by 2002 bringing the total to more than 2500, the highest since the mid-60s.

The Australian-based firm Hoyts plans 150 screens at 15 multiplex centres, including sites in London, Liverpool, and Dartford. Hoyts is opening these sites in Britain in the belief that there is a lot of potential in the UK market. The cost of opening cinemas in Britain is higher than elsewhere, so cinema providers need to be confident. The multiplex approach including cafés and restaurants is a very big attraction.

Odeon Cinemas, a division of Rank Leisure and the largest chain in Britain with 77 theatres, is also planning to open a number of new cinema complexes – 30 by the year 2003. Other companies, including Warner Village (a joint venture between Time Warner and Village Roadshow) and Virgin, are also likely to open new cinema complexes.

The revival of cinemas in Britain since the mid-80s is well known, but the speed at which the market continues to grow has surprised many people. Research indicates that, on average, each Briton visits the cinema either twice or three times a year. It is hoped that this figure will rise to the US figure of five visits a year. The table below shows the rise in cinema admissions since the mid-80s.

Year	Number of cinema screens	Total admissions (millions)
1946	4600	1640
1950	4583	1390
1960	3034	500
1965	1971	326
1970	1529	193
1984	1275	54
1997	2349	139
2002 (estimates)	2800	185

The revival of the cinema industry in Britain has been attributed to investment in the theatres, better marketing and the development of US-style multiplex sites, the first of which was opened in 1985. These sites now account for 50 per cent of all visits. Better seats, easier parking and more films have all helped to boost attendances from a record annual low of 54 million in 1984. The film industry has also helped itself. Blockbuster films have been a great success. Films like 'Titanic' and 'The Full Monty' have become essential viewing for nearly everybody, rather than luxuries.

Questions

1. Explain the changing pattern of supply in the cinema industry from 1946 onwards.

2. What has triggered off the increase in supply in recent years?

3. Which of the supply factors outlined have been most important in creating change?

Formation of a market price

In the marketplace the forces of demand and supply will interact to create a **market price**. In economics this is more usually called the 'equilibrium price' and is the price at which the quantity demanded equals the quantity supplied.

To illustrate this point, consider a fictional daily demand and supply schedule for fish at a small fishing village. When the price of fish is high, the owner of the only fishing boat will (we assume) spend more time fishing than when it is low. Conversely, consumers will want to purchase more fish at low than at high prices:

Price of fish (p)	Quantity demanded	Quantity supplied
60	300	600
55	400	550
50	500	500
45	600	450
40	700	400
35	800	350

This information can then be plotted on a graph (see Figure 16.12). If you study this graph, you can see that there is only one price – the equilibrium price – at which the wishes of consumers and the supplier coincide, i.e. 50p. At this price the quantity that will be bought and sold is 500.

The market provides a mechanism for bringing the decisions of consumers and producers into line automatically, even though the two groups have different motives (the producer will want to sell at the highest possible price, and the consumer will want to purchase at the lowest possible price).

The process of forming an equilibrium price can be appreciated by considering two *disequilibrium* situations

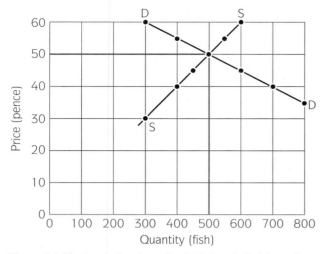

Figure 16.12 *Demand and supply of fish in a daily fish market*

(see Figure 16.13). If, for example, we consider the price of 60p, we will see that the owner of the fishing vessel would be prepared to work longer to supply 600 fish. However, at 60p consumers would only be prepared to buy 300 fish – thus leaving a surplus stock of 300 fish which would go unsold. In this situation the owner of the fishing boat would lower prices and resort to working fewer hours.

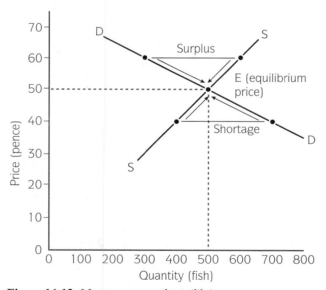

Figure 16.13 *Movements towards equilibrium*

Alternatively, if the price of fish was pitched at 40p, consumers would be prepared to buy 700 fish. However, the owner of the fishing vessel would be prepared only to work long enough to catch 400. There would now be a shortage of fish – stocks would rapidly sell out and customers would try to *bid up the price*. This would make it worthwhile for the owner of the fishing boat to work longer hours.

This example illustrates the working of market forces. At prices above 50p too much will be produced and so forces will interact to pull the price down to 50p. At prices below 50p too little will be produced, and so forces will interact to pull the price up to 50p. At 50p, prices are just right and so there is no tendency to change.

This analysis is, of course a simplification. In the real world markets rarely move in such a way towards equilibrium as consumers and producers frequently lack important market information which would help them to respond promptly to market changes.

Markets in motion

So far we have analysed the formation of an equilibrium price solely in terms of the relationship between price and demand and supply. This has been like taking a snapshot under the assumption that factors other than price do not alter, but it has provided us with an important insight into how markets operate.

Producers and consumers respond to **price signals**, and in this way their wishes and plans are coordinated by the market mechanism. These wishes and plans change regularly since, as we saw earlier, there are a number of factors influencing demand, and a number of factors influencing supply so that markets are constantly in motion.

Changes in the marketplace lead to adjustments by consumers and producers. Demand and supply curves change shape and position, and very quickly a new equilibrium position is established. However, this will be only a temporary equilibrium point because markets are characterised by change. Indeed one beauty of the marketplace is that it can accommodate changes.

Whenever a factor changes which affects demand or supply there are four basic changes which may take place (see Figure 16.4). These illustrate:

(i) a shift in the demand curve to the right, resulting in more being bought at a higher price
(ii) a shift in the demand curve to the left, resulting in a smaller quantity being bought at a lower price
(iii) a shift in the supply curve to the right, resulting in more being supplied at a lower price
(iv) a shift in the supply curve to the left, resulting in less being supplied at a higher price.

The best way to show how the market dynamics work in this process is through an example. Imagine that, for a

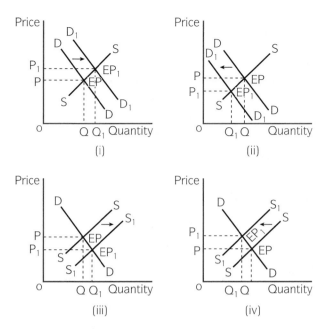

Figure 16.14 *Changes to the equilibrium price*

variety of reasons, fish suddenly becomes a more popular dish for consumers to have – tastes have changed in favour of fish. At present 0Q is produced at an equilibrium price of 0P. Following this change in tastes the demand curve shifts to the right, causing a new equilibrium of EP_1 where the new demand curve intersects the original supply curve. Equilibrium price therefore rises to $0P_1$ and the equilibrium quantity to $0Q_1$.

Now that this new market equilibrium has been formed, bad weather may affect the ability to put the fishing fleet to work. This is clearly a factor affecting supply which shifts the supply curve to the left. As we would expect, at the new equilibrium position of EP_1, the price of fish rises to 0P1 and the quantity of fish on the market falls to $0Q_1$.

Of course, in a truly dynamic market there is a range of supply and demand changes which all occur at the same time – technology is changing (a supply factor), incomes are changing (a demand factor), the incomes of consumers are changing (a demand factor), costs of factor inputs are changing (a supply factor), etc. The market is thus truly dynamic. However, static analysis taking one change at a time does help us to understand the nature and complexity of the marketplace.

Other elasticities

Another important measure is **income elasticity**. This simply expresses how demand responds to changes in income. Income is an important influence on both individual and whole-market demand. For many people the size of increase in income over a time period will affect their ability to buy products. The relationship between increases in income and the sale of luxury products tends to be significant, particularly when contrasted with the sale of inferior goods.

In most years the total income of the country rises (i.e. the national income, GNP, increases). As incomes rise so does the ability of consumers to buy new goods; people move into bigger houses, acquire better cars, buy a range of new gadgets, clothes and food. More expensive goods can replace inferior products.

Income elasticity can be measured by:

$$\text{Income elasticity} = \frac{\text{Percentage change in quantity demanded}}{\text{Percentage change in income}}.$$

Normal goods are those for which demand increases as income goes up. *Inferior goods* are those for which demand falls as income goes up.

Another important influence on the price of a good is the price of other products, particularly if these products are either substitutes or complements. **Cross-price elasticity of demand** refers to the relationship between the change in demand for one product against a change in the price of another product. It is measured by:

$$\frac{\text{Cross-price elasticity}}{\text{of demand}} = \frac{\text{Percentage change in demand for product X}}{\text{Percentage change in price of product Y}}.$$

For example, Pepsi-Cola is viewed as a substitute for Coca-Cola (and vice versa). If the price of Pepsi were reduced we would expect to see a fall in demand for Coke. In contrast, with complementary products such as bricks and mortar, if the prices of cement and sand – the ingredients of mortar – go up, then sales of bricks would go down as consumers buy less because of the change in the price of the complement.

ISSUES RELATING TO SUPPLY

In this section we shall be examining a number of key issues relating to the supply of goods to the marketplace including: the nature of cost structures; the economies of large-scale production; the growth of organisations; the importance of the labour market in determining supply; the impact of technology on organisations; the cultural environment; and the concept of competitive advantage.

A business organisation seeks to supply goods to the market in ways that best meet its corporate and business objectives. An understanding of supply conditions is an essential ingredient of understanding how firms supply to the market.

Cost structures

The cost of production is a key determinant of supply. A supplier to the market needs to be able to cover costs and a margin for profit (although the firm may be prepared to carry a short-term loss for a limited period).

In Chapter 7 we looked in detail at the accountant's view of costs. The accountant takes a pragmatic view which is the approach widely used in business. However, it is also helpful to look at cost structures from the point of view of the economist – because the economist is concerned with the way in which society rather than the individual business unit uses resources.

The economist sees that a business organisation has two types of costs, fixed and variable. **Fixed costs** do not vary with output. **Variable costs** vary with the level of output produced.

Fixed costs include the payment of rates and rents by an organisation, fixed salaries, interest payments on borrowings, etc. Variable costs (for a manufacturing company) include the raw materials that go into a product, energy use which is related to the quantity of products manufactured, labour costs which vary with the level of output, etc.

The *total fixed cost* for a firm (say £X) can be represented as a straight line on a diagram comparing costs with output (see Figure 16.15).

Figure 16.15 *The total fixed-cost 'curve'*

The *total variable cost*, in contrast, is likely to be a curve which starts at zero and then rises as output rises. However, the rate of increase will not be directly proportional to output (a straight line). Rather it will be a curve which changes in slope as output increases. This is because the efficiency with which goods can be produced varies as we increase output. If the firm produced a very small output then goods would not be produced very efficiently. For example, machinery and buildings would not be used at anything near their optimum capacity. (Imagine using your oven at home to cook a very small pie – what a waste!) However, as output starts to increase, then efficiency will also increase and so rising variable costs are spread over a larger output (putting more baking in the oven at the same time). However, there comes a point at which existing capacity is being used to produce too many outputs (you have put too much in the oven so that many of the pies aren't being baked efficiently – some are being undercooked while others are burnt at the edges).

We can therefore represent total variable cost in the following way (see Figure 16.16). At first the cost is rising steeply relative to output increases. Then total variable cost is rising slowly relative to output increases. Finally, total variable cost is rising quickly compared with gains in output.

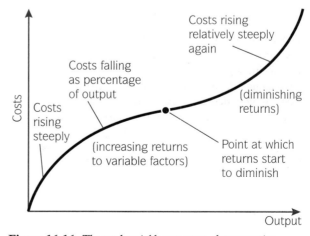

Figure 16.16 *The total variable-cost curve, demonstrating increasing and decreasing returns to variable factors*

If we now convert our pictures of total fixed and variable costs to *averages*, this will enable us to look at *costs per unit of output* (**unit costs**). We have assumed that the fixed cost of producing one unit is X (Figure 16.15), so the average cost of producing two units if $^1/_2X$ each, three units one-third X, four units one-quarter X and so on. In other words, **average fixed cost** (AFC) will keep on falling as output increases (see Figure 16.17). In simple terms we can see that a firm will benefit from expanding output *because it is able to spread its fixed cost over larger and larger outputs.*

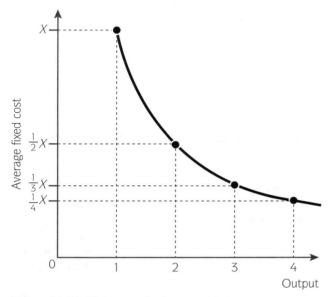

Figure 16.17 *The average fixed cost curve*

Average variable cost, in contrast, has a characteristic U shape (see Figure 16.18). At first average variable cost falls as the firm uses more and more variable factors (variable labour, raw materials, variable energy, etc.) with the

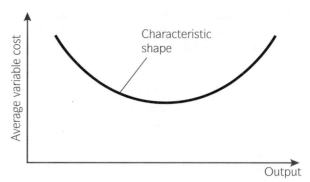

Figure 16.18 *The average variable cost curve*

existing stock of fixed factors (land, machinery, etc.). However, eventually there comes a point of diminishing returns to the variable factors, and average variable cost starts to rise again.

We have to add together the fixed and the variable costs (i.e. Figures 16.17 and 16.18) to produce a diagram for average total cost (see Figure 16.19). This looks very similar to the one for average variable cost (i.e. U-shaped). Of course, the *average total cost* (ATC) curve will start at a much higher point to include fixed costs. It will also reach its optimum (lowest point) at a slightly higher output than for average variable cost, because the spreading of average fixed costs over larger outputs will pull the curve down. (For a short period of increasing output the impact of falling average fixed costs will have a greater impact in pulling average total cost down than diminishing returns will have in pulling average total costs up.)

The average total cost curve now shows us the *unit cost* of producing different levels of output. For example, the unit cost of producing 1000 units of output is £5, of producing

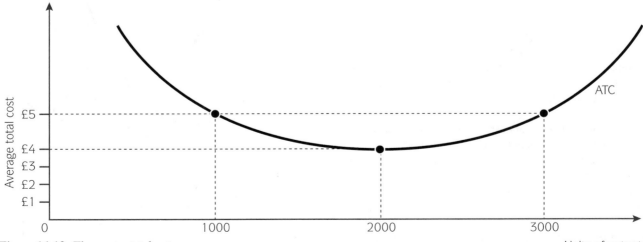

Figure 16.19 *The average total cost curve*

2000 units of output is £4, and 3000 units of output is £5 again. Alternatively, we can read off the total cost to a firm from producing different levels of output. For example:

1000 units: total cost is 1000 x £5 = £5000
2000 units: total cost is 2000 x £4 = £8000
3000 units: total cost is 3000 x £5 = £15000

The actual amount that the supplier decides to produce is determined not only by cost. The other side of the equation is *revenue* (which is determined by demand). The supplier therefore needs to take cost and revenue into account when deciding how much to produce.

According to the economist the decision about how much to produce will be determined by the relationship between marginal cost and marginal revenue. The **marginal cost of production** is the cost of producing one extra unit of output. The **marginal revenue** is the revenue received from producing one extra unit of output.

If the marginal revenue is greater than the marginal cost then it will pay the producer to produce that unit. The producer therefore keeps on producing extra units until the point at which marginal cost equals marginal revenue (see Figure 16.20). To the economist this fact is highly significant because in a hugely competitive market (perfect competition) the marginal revenue to the producer is the same thing as the price of the good. The consumer is therefore paying a price which is equivalent to the marginal cost of producing the good – i.e. the true cost or opportunity cost of the good. If perfect competition existed in every market then resources would be used in the most efficient way because people would be paying the true cost of producing units of output.

It is important not to be confused by the fact that economists view marginal cost in a different way from accountants. The accountant draws marginal cost as a straight line. The economist draws the marginal cost as a curve as a result of the economist's analysis of diminishing returns to variable factors.

The economists' view of costs is very important because it lies at the heart of the philosophy and ideology of competition. However, if you want to examine the way in which costs are analysed in a practical way by business people then you should examine the pragmatic business perspective in the accounts section of this book (Unit 5).

The economist shows that under perfect competition the firm has to go along with the market price. The average

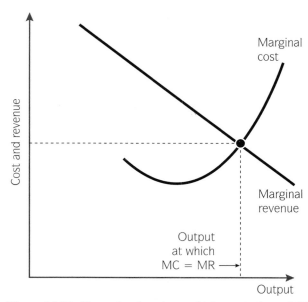

Figure 16.20 *Illustrating the point at which marginal cost (MC) is equal to marginal revenue (MR)*

revenue from each unit sold is therefore given by market price and will be the same as the marginal revenue (the revenue gained from selling one more unit).

Under perfect competition, therefore, the firm will produce where marginal cost is equal to marginal revenue, which is also the point at which marginal cost is equal to average revenue (price) (see Figure 16.21). A margin for the normal profit in the industry is included in the cost curves.

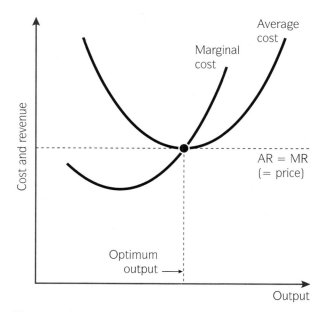

Figure 16.21 *Output under perfect competition*

In monopolistic (imperfect) markets, however, there is scope for profit. The supplier is able to charge a price which is higher than the marginal cost of producing the last unit produced. Profit is represented by the shaded area in Figure 16.22. This represents:

Total revenue – Total costs

which is the same as:

(Average revenue × Output) – Average cost × Output).

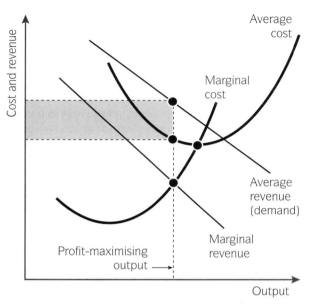

Figure 16.22 *Profit maximising in imperfect (monopolistic) markets*

The major criticism of monopolistic situations from the point of view of the economies' use of scarce resources is that the monopolist is able to make abnormal profits at the expense of consumers and is able to restrict output to less than the most efficient output.

Economies of scale

Economies of scale are quite simply 'the advantages of being big'. Large organisations have many advantages over small ones which enable them to develop a **competitive advantage**. There are two generic types of economy of scale.

- *Internal economies* are the advantages to the individual firm from being big.
- *External economies* are the advantages to firms in an industry or area resulting from the growth and development of that industry or area.

Internal economies of scale

Internal economies of scale accrue to a business from the growth process. As a firm becomes larger it is able to reap a number of economies, or advantages of size. Because of economies of scale the larger farmer, for example, is able to produce larger outputs at lower unit costs of production.

Economies of scale can be illustrated in the following way. Figure 16.23 shows how a firm is able to produce higher outputs at lower average costs from expansion over five time periods:

1980 – relatively small scale
1985 – increase in scale
1990 – further increase in scale
1995 – even further increase in scale
2000 – relatively larger scale.

Note that each average cost curve *starts* at a higher point (to benefit from economies of scale you usually incur higher fixed costs). However, each curve has a lower

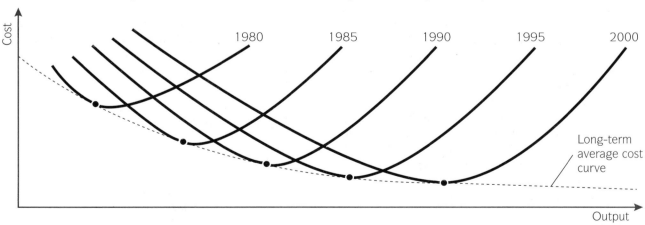

Figure 16.23 *How the long-term average cost curve is constructed*

optimum point. We can draw an *envelope curve* (the dashed line) running through the optimum points of each curve, to show long-run average costs. The latter curve illustrates 'increasing returns to scale' (i.e. economies of scale).

Economies of scale stem from a number of sources:

- *technical* economies of scale
- *managerial* economies of scale
- *financial* economies of scale
- *commercial* economies of scale
- *marketing* economies of scale
- *risk-spreading* economies of scale.

We can illustrate these by taking the example of a hotel business. Initially the organisation owns a single hotel, with a fairly small kitchen and only ten rooms. It then sells the small hotel and buys two larger ones. It then buys a chain of large luxury hotels. In the examples that follow we show how it can spread its costs over much larger outputs.

Technical economies

In the small hotel techniques of production are very basic. For example, all the booking of rooms is done through a manual handwritten process. In the kitchen dishes are washed by hand, and the laundering of sheets and pillowcases is done in an old and unreliable frontloading washing machine. Within the hotel the staircase takes up quite a bit of space as does the reception area.

In the larger hotels, however, it is possible to benefit from advanced techniques of production: a computerised booking system, purpose-built catering equipment in the kitchen, such as dishwashers. There is a centralised laundry. Another technical advantage in the larger hotels is that more rooms can be built into the building per square metre of hotel space, because there is a centralised staircase and reception area. These features are more lavish but don't use up such a high proportion of valuable space within the hotels. Another key technical advantage when the hotel chain expands is that it can employ specialist staff – cleaners, receptionists, porters, waiters etc. – each of whom is an expert in their own field. Specialists are more productive than generalists in meeting customer needs.

Managerial economies

In the same way that larger hotels are able to employ specialist labour, the chain is also able to employ specialist management. For example, most businesses need a financial specialist. One of the early problems of the Tesco organisation founded by Jack Cohen was that Cohen did not have a very firm grasp of financial affairs. This was quickly put right when he employed a highly skilful financial manager. A large hotel chain is able to employ a restaurant manager, a customer services manager, an entertainment manager, etc. These managers are able to help the hotels to produce larger outputs (more contented customers) at lower costs per unit.

Financial economies

Most businesses need to raise external finance (e.g. through loans and overdrafts). They may also raise finance through the issuing of shares. A small hotel may be able to borrow money, but it will probably have to do so at quite a high rate of interest. A hotel chain which borrows in bulk is likely to be a good client of a bank. Banks are therefore more likely to lend money to a hotel chain at a lower interest rate than to a small hotel. In addition a large chain will find it far more cost-effective when raising capital through shares than a company that wants to borrow only a relatively small amount.

Commercial economies

Commercial economies are concerned with buying and selling. A large hotel chain will be able to buy in supplies on much better terms than a small hotel. For example, the large hotel may need to purchase 2000 eggs per week compared with the small hotel's 100. The large business will be able to get a considerable discount from a local supplier such as a farmer who can supply regularly. The cost of transporting large quantities of purchases will also be much smaller per unit than the cost of transporting small quantities.

Marketing economies

The unit cost of marketing will also be much lower for a larger business. For example, the costs of market research, advertising and promotion can be spread over a much larger number of customers. Indeed, the cost of marketing may be so prohibitive for the small hotel that it might engage only in a limited amount of marketing at a high cost per hotel visitor.

Risk-spreading economies of scale

The hotel business is highly seasonal and subject to other fluctuations. The hotel chain will therefore probably diversity its interests to spread its risks. For example, it may put on banquets, and run a casino which tide it over slacker periods. In contrast the small hotel has fewer options, perhaps providing facilities for small conferences, and offering accommodation at cheap rates to students to bide itself over the slack times.

Internal diseconomies of scale

There are also *disadvantages* in getting too large and these are referred to as **internal diseconomies of scale**. It is clear how this can happen in the hotel business. If you expand the size of your business but the number of customers does not increase more than proportionately, your costs will not be spread over a larger output. Worse than this, scale often leads to inefficiencies such as bottlenecks and administrative problems. Organisations that grow too fast too quickly are notoriously difficult to manage. Technical and managerial diseconomies may abound.

> ## Discussion point
>
> What internal diseconomies are you aware of in large organisations you are familiar with?

External economies of scale

Concentration

If similar organisations develop in the same geographical area, a number of benefits arise. Examples are a skilled labour pool, a reputation for the area for the quality of its work, local college courses tailored to meet the needs of that particular industry, and better social amenities. If the infrastructure supporting the hotel industry develops in an area (e.g. the development of cleaner beaches, leisure and tourism courses at the local college), then all firms in the hotel industry will benefit.

Information

Larger industries have information services and employers' associations designed to benefit the members (e.g. the Hoteliers' Association).

Dis-integration

In areas where certain industries develop, component industries or service industries develop to help with maintenance and support services. There may be a strong taxi industry to ferry guests to hotels, a hotel laundry service, etc.

Growth of organisations

Organic growth

Organic growth (or 'scale expansion') of the existing organisation involves moving on from a smaller to a larger organisation financed through internal profits, by raising more capital from shareholders or by borrowing money in the form of loans and other means. Generating profit is a very important means of financing growth. However, when firms want to quickly change the scale of their operations they will seek fresh capital for the business, either by seeking extra funds from stakeholders or by going to banks and other financial institutions to borrow money. The process of raising finance is covered in Chapters 1 and 2.

The story of Marks & Spencer provides a good example of scale expansion of an existing organisation. Michael Marks came to this country as a Russian émigré. He initially set up as a travelling pedlar going from door to door. When he had generated some profit he decided to expand and took on a partner, Tom Spencer. Each contributed capital to the business. They moved on to market trading before setting up some small retail outlets. In later years Simon Marks (the son of Michael) wished to expand the business on a larger scale and so created first a private and then a public company, eventually raising large sums of capital to finance the expansion which has led to M&S's current high street infrastructure in the UK.

Mergers or takeovers

A quicker and more dynamic form of growth is possible through mergers or takeovers, which involve the integration of a number of business units under a single umbrella organisation. A **merger** is a situation in which two or more enterprises 'cease to be distinct'. A **takeover** is a kind of merger and occurs where one company buys a majority shareholding in another company.

It is possible to distinguish at a general level between full legal mergers and mergers involving only changes in the ownership of the companies concerned. A legal merger transfers the assets and liabilities of two or more companies to a single new or existing company. The companies whose assets are merged may all disappear into a new company (companies X and Y merge to form a new company Z), or one of the companies involved may absorb the other, (e.g. X takes over Y). In addition to enjoying the benefits of being larger, the new organisation will have a larger market share, will probably be more competitive in export markets and, depending on the type of merger, could be in a position to control raw material supplies or the sales of finished products. Sometimes the easiest way to achieve larger scale production is to merge; this brings financial and marketing economies of scale.

A **horizontal merger** takes place when two firms producing goods of a similar type at the same stage of production join together. A **vertical merger** takes place when two firms producing goods of a similar type at different stages of production join together. **Backward vertical integration** involves the takeover of a supplier, and **forward vertical integration** involves joining with a firm at a later stage of production.

It is common practice today for organisations in industries that are only loosely related to join together in order to maximise risk-bearing economies of scale. For example, a firm producing toothpaste may join with a soap manufacturer in order to benefit from similar channels of marketing and distribution (e.g. supermarkets and chemists). We describe this as **lateral integration**. Where a company moves into unrelated fields simply to diversity we refer to this as **conglomerate integration**.

Discussion point

What types of economies of scale will flow from: (a) horizontal integration, (b) vertical backward integration, (c) forward vertical integration, (d) lateral integration, and (e) conglomerate integration?

There have been many reasons for merger activity in the UK and Europe in recent years. The following are a few examples.

- There has been a spreading of the global activities of companies. For example, in the world soft drinks and confectionery market there is considerable pressure on a company like Cadbury Schweppes to seek a bigger share of the market. Market size usually leads to competitive advantage (see page 338). For an organisation like Cadbury Schweppes this involves taking on huge corporations like Coca-Cola and PepsiCo, Nestlé and Mars. On a European level the creation of the 'single market' opened the door to huge pan-European corporations.
- There is intense pressure put on organisations by shareholders to increase earnings per share. Shareholders, often in the form of giant financial institutions, are all too aware of the relative earnings on the different parts of their portfolio. They will switch finance towards successful organisations and divert finance away from those which are less successful.
- When the market undervalues the real value of a company and there are high real interest rates (such as in the UK in the 1980s and early 90s), this means that profits are heavily discounted. It therefore is cheaper to buy existing companies than to expand into new ones.
- Acquisitions allow established companies to change direction quickly and to reposition themselves (e.g. when Virgin acquired existing railway networks).
- Acquisitions help companies to plug a gap in their current portfolio of assets.
- Mergers can help to integrate organisations with converging technologies, such as those using continuous flow production methods, or new forms of information technology (e.g. telecommunications and media).
- Acquisitions help organisations to spread their sphere of influence (e.g. a French or American utility company buying into the UK utilities market).
- Mergers enable companies to acquire the benefits of synergy (synergy is usually explained through simple mathematics in the form of $2 + 2 = 5$). In other words the sum of the parts working together in an effective merger are greater than the individual components involved in the merger.

The labour market

The **labour market**, like any other market, involves buyers and sellers. In this case the buyers are employers and the sellers are those people who are prepared to sell their labour services. Of course the labour market is split up into a number of sub-markets – the market for teachers, for electrical engineers, for nurses, etc.

The labour market is so important in supply today because most of the successful major global businesses are knowledge organisations – in which knowledge and human intelligence are key assets.

The labour market is of crucial importance in supplying to organisations people with the right skills to meet the growth in demand in new areas of the economy. Today the employees in greatest demand are knowledge workers. The labour market will be effective only if it is supported by highly effective education and training to provide people with the right skills. This is why, for example, information technology (IT) teaching in schools has been given so much emphasis in the UK's curriculum in recent years.

It is also very important to have **mobility** in the labour market. In other words, the supply of labour must be capable of responding very quickly to changes in demand for labour.

- If demand for certain types of labour increases, then supply must quickly follow.
- If demand for certain types of labour falls, then supply must be reduced.

Unfortunately mobility is often restricted in the real world, so when demand for a particular type of labour increases then supply is slow in responding. This may be because of the length of time and commitment that is required to train employees to develop new skills.

Another restriction to mobility is the fact that employees are resistant to wage decreases when the demand for their particular type of work goes into decline. This leads to rising unemployment as labour prices itself out of a job.

The classical and neoclassical economists (see page 368) viewed immobility in the labour market as a major cause of business inefficiency. They argued, for instance, that in the 1920s and 30s a major cause of long-term unemployment was the trade unions preventing wages from falling when the demand for the products of certain industries went into decline. Between 1979 and 1997, Conservative governments set out to address this problem and to create 'flexible' labour markets (i.e. ones which enabled the smooth operation of the forces of demand and supply). Today the Labour government has taken on board the importance of flexibility, as have most governments in Western Europe. However, Labour sees that flexibility will be successful only if it is supported by high-class education and training programmes.

For a detailed analysis of changes in the world of work in recent years, you should read *Human Resource Management for Higher Awards* (1996), a companion volume in the Heinemann Higher Awards series.

The impact of technology on organisations

Technology is the result of using our knowledge to develop tools, products and processes for human purposes. We live in an age of dramatic technological developments in most areas of production. In particular the impact of information technology has had a profound effect in speeding communications and slashing costs of production of millions of goods and services. One of the major results of the IT revolution is that small companies can compete with large companies on far more equal terms. The so-called 'information revolution' has also led to massive changes in the way businesses are run. The following are a few examples.

- Company databases are no longer the exclusive property of head office. Everyone with a laptop or pocketbook computer can have access to them – and, via the Internet, to a world of information beyond.
- Computer-aided manufacturing has raised levels of quality and accuracy. Factory robots have taken over many routine, repetitive, noisy and dirty jobs, leaving people free to supervise.
- Sales specialists are able to offer customers a complete range of personalised options, with computers taking care of registering orders, requesting items from stock, scheduling delivery, etc.
- Global IT networks allow users to communicate instantly around the world. This is especially true of the financial markets, where currency transactions take place 24 hours a day.
- Routine accounts work can be done anywhere in the world.
- Even highly skilled work requiring close working contact with managers can be contracted-out to sites thousands of miles away. For instance, engineers in Aberdeen designing offshore oil platforms can work with qualified draughtsmen and women in India. The time difference enables the work to be carried out overnight.

In their book *Organisational Behaviour*, Huczynski and Buchanan identify three ways in which the word 'technology' can be used in terms of its impact on business.

- *Apparatus* – meaning machines and associated tools
- *Technique* – meaning skills and procedures
- *Organisation* – meaning the way in which social organisation is manipulated to foster production.

This broad definition suggests that we must always regard technology as encompassing both tangible elements (machines) and intangible elements (social relations), with new machines requiring new skills and even new work patterns for workers. This might appear to be a fairly banal observation, but far too often investment in machinery is wasted if the organisation is not altered to accommodate the change. To explain this further we can look more closely at two examples, computer-integrated manufacturing (CIM) and just-in-time (JIT) production.

Computer-integrated manufacturing covers the computer-aided design of products, the use of computers to assist in the production process by, for example, giving instructions to machines, and the (partial) automation of

administration by (amongst other things) computerising the customer order process. This allows the company to produce customised products in whatever number the customer requires.

World class manufacturing (WCM) firms or those aspiring to that status, also want to invest in CIM, but the organisational impact must be considered; many firms overlook this fact at their peril. For example, this type of manufacturing requires flexibility on the part of the workforce, a reduction in the levels of hierarchy, and multiskilling. These changes are not easy to introduce and may be resisted by those whose traditional role and status are threatened. It is asking a lot to keep the old ways of working running alongside the new system and expect to be successful.

Just-in-time production is a technique that focuses on the organisation of work flows to provide a quick, high-quality, flexible production approach that leads to minimum waste and stock levels. The Japanese car industry is often cited as an example, where the car is not built until the customer orders it, so that the suppliers and the car manufacturer are linked into a **demand-led system**. This is a radical departure from the traditional mass-production techniques that looked for economies in long production runs and capacity utilisation. JIT requires that production be as smooth and effortless as possible, because the customer will be unable to purchase from stock and is not going to be impressed if told that there has been some malfunction in production. If production is to be maintained, then the maintenance and production team will have to be able to deal with a machinery problem immediately it occurs, an approach that would have been impossible when strict divisions existed between the work of production and maintenance staff.

The links between firms and their suppliers become critical under JIT, and any disruption due, for example, to industrial action would be catastrophic.

Figure 16.24 summarises the types of production process seen in firms. For each approach it can be appreciated that the key elements to look for are the machines, skills and work organisation to be found in firms using it.

Likewise, the choice of approach would itself be related to the type of industry under consideration. The impact of JIT, for example, has been a popular focus for the media in the UK, and many industries have adapted it to their own requirements.

What is certain, though, is that the use of JIT is not as widespread as many suppose, especially where the type of product or the demand for it is such that this method is, at the moment, inappropriate.

Job production. This is the production of items in separate jobs, often used when a product is being made to order. In job production, work will not commence until an order has been received, and it is difficult to keep stocks in advance of the order. Workers are often highly skilled, with each job requiring individual planning and preparation.

Batch production. This occurs when a batch of items is produced in one go, where the items are not for any one specific customer, or when being made at regular intervals in specific quantities. This means that batch production requires work to be passed from one stage to another, with each group of workers carrying out a specific function, so that planning and the design of the system are given a high priority.

Flow production. This happens when a product is made on a continuous basis. Examples of this are paper and oil, where treatment of the item is undertaken via a continuous process (process production). Another example would be mass production of white goods. Here the standardisation of the method and equipment is high, with very specialised equipment being required to facilitate the process.

Although these three types of production are distinguishable, many manufacturers adopt more than one type. In car production, for example, the final assembly may be undertaken using the flow production approach, while certain components may have been produced using batch production. Whichever approach is used, the same issues apply – with tools, techniques and organisation being adapted to provide the best possible use of resources.

Figure 16.24 *A summary of types of production*

Service industries

The use of technology has been a key focus of interest in services as competition has increased and standards of service have been expected to improve.

As outlined in other sections of this book, services and goods are usually distinguished by the intangible elements of services compared with the tangible aspect of goods. In practice, however, services often have tangible elements. Technology is used to support the service, rather than to interfere with the important interaction that takes place between the service provider and the customer.

Many financial services, such as insurance and banking, now use telephone ordering to keep costs down and to provide an efficient service. Although this is popular with many customers, banks have been accused of reducing the all-important direct human link that traditional sales outlets provide – a fact noted by the banks as they seek to maintain a branch network alongside telephone banking.

Technology and work

New technologies require new skills and have the potential to reduce the amount of time spent on boring and repetitive tasks. They can also reduce skill and produce boring and repetitive jobs. Both trends can be seen throughout industry, and management faces the task of responding to this challenge.

For example, improved information systems allow senior managers to centralise decision-making based on the regular collection, interpretation and dissemination of information – a development that bypasses middle management and makes it redundant. The problem is to reorganise with a smaller middle-management group, with more responsibility passed down to teams and individuals. However, this is not an easy process, with redundancy costs, morale and motivation issues all contributing to a situation that can weaken the reorganisation effort.

Technology can also involve sub-contracting work to other organisations, over which the manager has no direct control. A further development is that, with the push to the creation of a communication highway, people can work from home without the need to meet together in offices – a move that can mean that some staff seek to become self-employed and work for several companies.

In his book *The Age of Unreason* Charles Handy suggests that a new form of organisation will emerge, which he describes as a 'shamrock', based around a core of essential executives and workers supported by outside contractors and part-time help. Although this form has been seen before, it has been confined to small companies and professional partnerships. What is new is that it is now being seen in large organisations and in the public sector. Handy suggested that by the end of the twentieth century only 50 per cent of all jobs would be traditional full-time ones, with a fairly clear career structure. The remainder would be self-employed and part-time.

Technology and changes in manufacturing processes and the way services are delivered will continue to influence work organisation. Clearly organisations will need to ride the wave of technological changes so as to make the most efficient use of costs – maximising the organisation's competitive position.

Technology and innovation

It is important to remind ourselves that innovation in business has become a strategic issue. Innovation can involve the creation of new products, improvements to existing ones, enhancing the quality of the production process to contribute to cost reduction, or simply responding more flexibly to customer requirements. Whatever the mixture, innovation along these lines can be found in firms and organisations throughout the private and public sectors, and the competitive drive to improve products, systems and procedures will mean a constant review of organisational structures.

The cultural environment

Societies, regions and areas often have different **cultures**, although a diversity of cultures is usually contained within modern societies. Some regions and areas are characterised by people with similar backgrounds, experiences, histories and tastes while other areas are genuinely multicultural. For example, London is a modern multicultural society with hundreds of ethnic, religious, racial and age groupings. In contrast, large parts of Poland are peopled by Poles who are of broadly the same ethnic, religious and racial group. The same is true in China where hundreds of millions of people are of the same racial group.

Business organisations need to have a good understanding of the cultural characteristics of people in the societies in which they operate. Having this understanding enables the business to avoid behaviour which may be offensive, and to avoid carrying out actions which cut across the norms of particular societies. Understanding the cultural environment makes it possible for organisations to supply products, to create working conditions, and to foster relationships which are sympathetic and sensitive to the needs and requirements of these societies. A key competitive advantage can be gained by organisations who develop joint ventures in markets which they are not familiar with, or by appointing managers and employees at senior levels from the societies and markets with which the country is trading.

Above all, the company that fosters genuine relationships based on mutual trust and understanding of other cultures will always beat the rival organisation which deals in stereotypes and patronises people from other societies.

The concept of competitive advantage

Organisations continually seek **competitive advantage** over rivals (i.e. approaches to out-competing the competition). In his book *Competitive Advantage*, the American business writer Michael Porter suggests that there are two major ways to be competitive.

Firstly, a business gains competitive advantage from becoming the producer that produces at the **lowest cost**. This can be done by producing goods in a very efficient way using the best technology. It can also be done by producing and selling very large quantities. Companies like Coca-Cola and the soap powder manufacturers are able to produce individual items at very little unit cost because they literally produce millions of units. Just imagine the economies of scale which Coca-Cola is able to pack into each bottle or can of Coke so that the unit cost of production is virtually zero. Each additional Mars bar that runs off the Mars production line at Slough must do so for a very low cost indeed.

In order to gain the advantages of being a low-cost producer the company needs to have a very big share of the market. One of Michael Porter's simple business lessons is that if you gain the lion's share of the market then the profits will follow. The bigger your share of the market, the more chance you have of driving your costs down relative to those of competitors.

Secondly, **differentiation** involves making your product 'better' than that of rivals whilst at the same time making sure that the product is bought by customers. A Rolls-Royce is different from other motor cars, it is also very expensive. It is a success because enough people are prepared to buy the product owing to its special quality. There are all sorts of ways of differentiating products – through customer service, through promotion, through advertising, through branding, etc. The key way to differentiate your product is to add value to it so that consumers perceive it as being better value than rival offerings.

To add to Porter's two ways of being competitive, we can add a third concept – that **of choosing a market to compete in**. Some products compete in a very broad market (e.g. supermarkets) but the organisation may choose to sell top-of-the-range items and low-price discount items. Other businesses compete in a much narrower market; for example, specialist food shops such as delicatessens sell a much narrower range of products to a more select group of customers.

So, as well as choosing whether to compete through low cost or differentiation, businesses must also choose whether to sell to a mass market, or to a narrow focused market. The alternatives for seeking competitive advantage are set out below:

- mass market, coupled with low costs: own-brand baked beans, bottom-of-the-range washing-up liquids, low cost-margarines, etc.

- mass market, coupled with differentiation: Heinz baked beans, Kit Kat, Kellogg's Corn Flakes, etc.

- narrow market, coupled with low cost: specialist discount bottom-of-the-market retailers, second-hand clothes and book shops, etc.

- narrow market, coupled with differentiation: Renault Twingo, exclusive tailors, etc.

Firms that focus on low costs will set out to have the lion's share of the market, enabling them to produce more cheaply than rivals. Firms that focus on differentiation compete through providing goods that meet consumers needs better than rival products.

Developing a competitive advantage is all about combining an understanding of market forces and the marketing mix. Choosing the most competitive marketing mix should help to stimulate demand, as well as creating a supply advantage for a firm.

Discussion point

What factors do you see as being the main contributors in giving the following organisations a competitive advantage?

- BMW
- Manchester United
- Halifax
- The Late Shop

- Marks & Spencer
- Poundstretcher
- Microsoft

CONCLUSIONS

This chapter has been concerned with ways in which organisations can gain a competitive advantage.

On the demand side, competitive advantage is concerned with creating an inelastic demand for your product so that consumers are prepared to pay a premium price. The demand curve can be made more inelastic by making your product more desirable in all sorts of ways – for example, making it more environmentally friendly, giving it more sex appeal, giving it additional extras or more attractive packaging, getting fashionable people to adopt it; and a thousand and one other ways of differentiation to enable you to gain monopolistic advantages.

On the supply side, you can force down your costs relative to those of rivals in order to exploit economies of scale from having a bigger market. Creating competitive advantage is therefore an on-going and crucial objective for the modern business organisation.

The European Dimension

This chapter sets out to explore the significance of the European dimension for UK-based organisations. The features and functions of the European Union are traced from its early beginnings as the European Coal and Steel Community up to the present day.

On completion of this chapter you should be able to:

- explain the features of the European Union

- identify two policies of the EU and analyse the impact on a UK-based organisation

- analyse the arguments for and against UK entry into the European Monetary Union

- analyse the challenges and opportunities for UK businesses of enlargement of EU member states

INTRODUCTION

This chapter explores one of the major influences on the United Kingdom economy in recent years. The development of ever-closer links with the European Union (EU) accelerated in the 1980s and 90s. There are two major threads to this union: greater economic ties, and greater political ties (see Figure 17.1).

The business world is concerned mainly with the economic ties. A number of large companies in the UK want to have even greater economic ties within the EU. In particular they would like to be part of European Monetary Union (EMU) because this, they claim, would mean greater simplicity and security in doing business with our European neighbours. For example, there would not be the uncertainty of changes in the value of currencies against each other. There would not be the costs incurred in

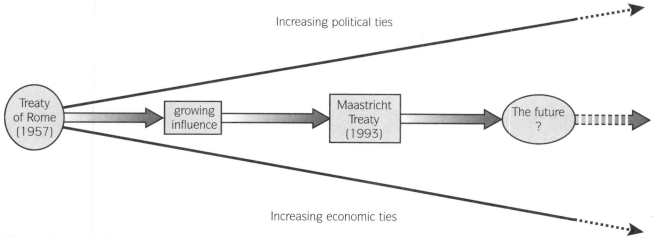

Figure 17.1 *A tale of two treaties*

changing money from one currency to another. Moreover, some businesses want to see enlargement of the EU to include more of the former eastern bloc countries – in particular the Czech Republic, Hungary and Poland which have fairly dynamic economies. More economies put together like this provide a bigger single market to sell into, which is always attractive to business.

However, there is no consensus about greater political ties. The main worry about greater political union relates to policies and rules being determined outside the UK. Rather than decisions being made by parliaments in the UK, increasingly decision-making is being carried out by EU institutions. There is the fear of losing autonomy and lack of regional focus.

There is also a fear of losing control over internal economic policy. When the UK government is in charge of controlling the UK economy it can take measures which are UK-focused – for example lowering interest rates to encourage spending in the economy when there is a recession. If decisions about interest rates were taken by the European Central Bank, then the Bank would be pursuing European-wide objectives which may exclude an immediate concern for what is happening in the UK. This could harm business. Instead of UK business people being able to lobby the government in Westminster for change, they would have to turn to Brussels and Strasbourg, far more remote centres of government.

A further problem is the potential for waste that is inherent in a very large 'superstate' like the European Union may become. In 1999, for example, there was widespread concern in the EU about corruption that had led to waste in a number of EU areas of administration, such as subsidies to farmers. The danger is that if you have such a large and bureaucratic system then it becomes very difficult to identify waste and inefficiency.

In this chapter, therefore, we set out to outline the nature of key European institutions and policies and to show how these impact on UK businesses.

BACKGROUND TO THE UNION

Throughout the course of history, attempts have been made to bring the European nations together into a single system – the Roman and Napoleonic Empires are examples of this.

Although the European Union is the only example of a democratic attempt to unite (politically and economically) the European nations, unity is not a new idea.

Origins of the EU

The 'rebirth' of the European idea was taken up by European and US leaders at the end of the Second World War in an attempt to bring lasting stability, security and prosperity. They aimed to achieve this by means of economic cooperation and integration. It was hoped that European economic integration would accomplish two political objectives.

- The founding fathers of the Union intended to make further wars amongst the European neighbours a practical impossibility. They set out to do this through increased cooperation and understanding between the nations, and by integrating their economies so closely together that war would become economic suicide.
- By the end of the Second World War, the balance of world power had shifted; the United States and the Soviet Union were the new superpowers. It was hoped that a strengthened bloc of economically united and democratic western European nations would halt the spread of communism from the east.

Main steps to unification

The European Coal and Steel Community

The first step towards European unification was the creation of the European Coal and Steel Community (**ECSC**) in 1951. The ECSC aimed to 'pool' German and French coal and steel resources. The French and Germans were to give up their sovereignty on policy issues relating to their respective coal and steel operations to an independent High Authority which would manage and coordinate policies in this field, thus linking two of their essential resources. Italy, Belgium, Luxembourg and the Netherlands also joined in the venture. The ECSC was hailed by its drafter Jean Monnet as:

'The first expression of the Europe that is being born'.

The European Economic Community

The next step towards unification came in 1956 when the six countries of the ECSC agreed plans to form a

European Economic Community (EEC). For a number of years after the Second World War, the countries of western Europe had debated the benefits of adopting a **Free Trade Area**; it was thought that this would promote trade, increase prosperity and help the countries' economies in the processes of reconstruction and redevelopment. However, the European countries were divided on how this was to be achieved.

The six members of the ECSC felt that a free trade area would not be sufficiently binding to deliver the security and economic benefits to which they aspired. They favoured a **supranational** model of organisation, in which countries would give up a portion of their decision-making powers to a higher authority (as in the ECSC). This was to be reinforced by the adoption of a **common customs union** and **tariffs barrier**.

Britain and another group of European countries (Denmark, Portugal, Switzerland, Norway, Austria and Sweden) preferred a free trade area based on **intergovernmental** cooperation. They objected to the idea of giving up a portion of their **sovereignty** – their ability as separate nations to control policy-making in every policy area.

In 1957, the ECSC six signed the **Treaty of Rome**. This effectively created both the EEC and **EURATOM** (the European Atomic Community). Together with the ECSC, these three organisations became known as the 'three communities' (see Figure 17.2). Because of the objections outlined above, the other western European countries declined to join the organisation, although most of them eventually became members.

Figure 17.2 *The 'three communities' in 1957*

The Single European Act

The **Single European Act** was eventually signed by twelve members of the EEC in 1986. Its aim was to kick-start the flagging process of European unification, and with this purpose in mind a deadline was set for the completion of a **'Single Market'** by 1992.

The Single Market

The Single European Act created a European **common market** protected by a customs union and an external tariffs barrier. A common market involves the free movement of goods, trade, labour, services and capital between a group of countries. For member countries the Single Market area now became their 'home market'. One problem was that although the Treaty and Act had removed the most obvious barriers to trade (customs duties and tariff barriers) the member states found other ways of protecting their true home markets against their 'internal' trading partners. Although they had promised to remove all barriers to trade, in practice they used **non-tariff barriers** to give their markets at home an unfair advantage. Examples of non-tariff barriers include state aid such as production subsidies, market-sharing cartels, use of different technical rules and standards (e.g. different specifications on packaging design or composition), a refusal to recognise other states' professional or educational qualifications, etc. Non-tariff barriers are generally hard to detect, and the EEC's practice of unanimous voting to make decisions meant that removing them was a slow process.

To summarize, the intention of the Single European Market Act was to create an internal European trading space, free from any national trading barriers. The aim of the Act was to remove the hidden, non-tariff barriers to trade which might otherwise prevent member states from trading with each other on an equal basis.

The **Cecchini Report** (1992) identified four main consequences of a well-organised Single Market which would be of benefit to business. These are linked as shown in Figure 17.3.

- *Cost reductions*. Because companies would produce on a larger scale in a new mass market, this should lead to falling costs for each unit of production.
- *Improved efficiency*. Industries would need to reorganise to serve mass markets. This reorganisation, coupled with competition, should increase efficiency.

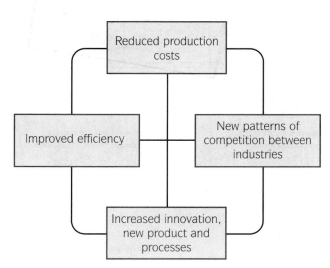

Figure 17.3 *Theoretical benefits of a Single Market*

- *New patterns of competition.* Those industries and areas with the most effective resources would make the biggest gains.
- *New innovations, processes and products.* These would flow from the larger, more competitive, market.

The Maastricht Treaty on European Union

Over the years, members of the EEC have massively increased the scope for action at European level. Whole new swathes of policies have been added to the original three areas summarized in Figure 17.2. Recent additions include a **common fisheries policy** limiting the size of catches, the types of nets that can be used, etc., and an **environmental policy** governing water quality standards, regulations relating to air pollution, etc.

Discussion point

Try to identify either (a) the impact of the EU common fisheries policy on UK fishing businesses, or (b) some of the impacts of EU environmental policy on a local business.

After much debate, the Maastricht Treaty was ratified in November 1993. The Treaty significantly alters the shape of the European Community. Many of the new policies have been placed within the existing EEC treaties. This means that they operate within the normal framework of Community decision-making. They are given a supranational character; i.e. the member states' governments no longer have direct control over what happens in those fields of policy.

However, in addition to revising the existing European Community treaties, the new treaty incorporates two new areas of policy cooperation – the **Common Foreign and Security Policy** (CFSP) and **Justice and Home Affairs**. The member states have promised to 'cooperate' on issues arising in these new areas, and decisions will be made on 'intergovernmental' rather than on 'supranational' lines. This means that normal community decision-making procedures will not apply in these two areas; the European Court of Justice will have no powers of jurisdiction, the European Commission and the European Parliament will have only limited roles to play, and the main sources of power will come from the Council and the European Council both of which are accountable to national parliaments (these institutions are described later in the chapter).

The Maastricht Treaty increased the part played by the European Parliament, allowing it to block laws in some areas and giving it the power to approve or reject the European budget. The Parliament also has the power to censure (and remove if necessary) European Commissioners. The Commission is now accountable to the Parliament.

Maastricht enables the European Court of Justice to take action against those who do not implement agreed EU rules. It also defines the scope for EU activity in such areas as education and training and health by setting out the sort of action the EU should take. Maastricht also enabled EU action in other areas, such as protecting the environment.

Because the scope of European cooperation has been extended to include policies made on intergovernmental as well as supranational lines, the new structure of the EU has been likened to a Greek temple. The overall 'building' (the EU) is now supported by three 'pillars' (see Figure 17.4):

- the revised EEC treaties (supranational)
- the Common Foreign and Security Policy (intergovernmental)
- Justice and Home Affairs (intergovernmental).

What else was new in the revised treaty?

- Any national of a member state of the EU is now an EU citizen and may live, reside and move freely anywhere in the EU.

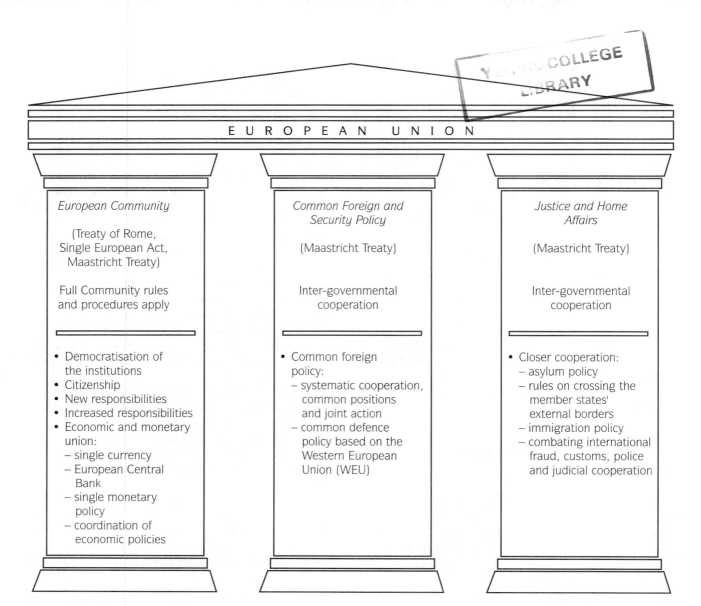

EUROPEAN UNION

European Community

(Treaty of Rome,
Single European Act,
Maastricht Treaty)

Full Community rules
and procedures apply

- Democratisation of
  the institutions
- Citizenship
- New responsibilities
- Increased responsibilities
- Economic and monetary
  union:
  – single currency
  – European Central
    Bank
  – single monetary
    policy
  – coordination of
    economic policies

*Common Foreign and
Security Policy*

(Maastricht Treaty)

Inter-governmental
cooperation

- Common foreign
  policy:
  – systematic cooperation,
    common positions
    and joint action
  – common defence
    policy based on the
    Western European
    Union (WEU)

*Justice and Home
Affairs*

(Maastricht Treaty)

Inter-governmental
cooperation

- Closer cooperation:
  – asylum policy
  – rules on crossing the
    member states'
    external borders
  – immigration policy
  – combating international
    fraud, customs, police
    and judicial cooperation

Figure 17.4 *The European Union 'temple'*

- The treaty includes new provisions in European monetary policy and set 1999 as the deadline for the final stage of monetary union: the replacement of existing currencies by a common European currency, the euro.
- The Social Chapter (see below) aims to give the Union a 'human face' and prevent unfair competition in the Single Market.

What does cooperation in justice and home affairs mean?

The member states will designate for joint action areas of common interest and concern, such as crime, law and order, and immigration. 'Joint action' means that the member states will decide upon common courses of action for the designated areas and will subsequently promise to respect the agreements and act together in those areas. Areas already designated for joint action include customs cooperation, international fraud, drug addiction, and Europol (an organisation set up to help cross-border police cooperation in the fight against international crimes such as terrorism, fraud or drug trafficking).

What does cooperation in common foreign and security policy (CFSP) mean?

The CFSP works on the same principle as Justice and Home Affairs, in that the member states designate areas of common concern for joint action. Alternatively, and depending upon the particular circumstances, they might choose to react to a particular event by adopting a 'common position' or by issuing a 'joint statement'. For example; the members of the EU might collectively issue a statement condemning country X for its poor record in human rights, or for its persecution of a particular section of its population. Under the CFSP, the member states have been able to deal with issues such as the Yugoslav war, the Middle East peace process and stability in central and eastern Europe. Action in the field of the CFSP does not yet include defence, although it does allow for the possibility of a common defence policy at some future point in time.

The Social Chapter

The **Social Chapter** was created with two main purposes in mind.

- *As part of an attempt to give the European Union a 'human face'*. Those involved in shaping the EU realised that it appeared bureaucratic and detached from ordinary people. They took account of the fact that European unification was not just an economic venture and that it needed the understanding and support of the people in order to succeed.
- *In order to guard against 'social dumping'*. As part of the attempt to run a fair Single Market, the member states wanted to prevent countries with poorer social standards from reaping benefits over those with more stringent standards. By maintaining differences in social standards – particularly with regard to employment (minimum pay, annual holiday entitlement, maternal leave, health and safety at work, etc.) – one country could maintain an advantage over the others in attracting employment opportunities created by foreign investment.

The 'Social Chapter', is not actually part of the Treaty on European Union; it is a protocol (an agreement) attached to the treaty. It was initially signed by eleven member states, not including Britain: France, Germany, Italy, Belgium, Netherlands, Luxembourg, Spain, Portugal, Greece, Ireland and Denmark.

The eleven signatories wanted to increase their joint cooperation in the field of social policy, using the aims set out in the **Social Charter** as their basis for doing so. The Social Charter is a non-binding agreement which was adopted at the Strasbourg summit in December 1989. It laid down certain social policy aims and objectives for the member states:

- freedom of movement
- employment and remuneration
- living and working conditions
- social protection
- freedom of association and collective bargaining
- vocational training
- equal opportunities
- information, consultation and participation for workers
- health and safety in the workplace
- protection for children, elderly and disabled persons.

All of the above have important implications for UK firms. In the 1990s, enlightened UK companies introduced the new requirements voluntarily in anticipation of being obliged to make the changes at a later date.

Originally the eleven wanted to incorporate the Chapter into the treaty. Britain, however, objected to this and consequently the eleven made a separate agreement on social policy – a protocol, which is attached to the treaty but not a part of it. Other social policy provisions that were included in the original EEC treaty and extended by the Single European Act still apply to Britain, but Britain was exempt from any decisions made under the Social Chapter protocol. This has changed now that Labour has signed up to this protocol (as have other new members of the union).

Even though the protocol is not part of the treaty and therefore not subject to normal Community decision-making processes, it allows the signatories to 'borrow' the use of the Community institutions in order to make decisions legally and communally binding.

Article 1 of the Social Chapter outlines the Community's main aims in implementing a social policy:

> *'The Community and the member states shall have as their objectives the promotion of employment, improved living and working conditions, proper social protection, dialogue between management and labour, the development of human resources with a view to lasting employment, and the combating of exclusion.'*

An example of regulations resulting from EU social policy are the Working Time Regulations (part of EU health and social requirements rather than a direct part of the Social Chapter). Under the previous Conservative government the UK had tried to avoid having to comply with the EU's working time directive which stemmed from the Social Chapter. The British government referred the matter to the European Court of Justice which, in the autumn of 1996, ruled that Britain should adopt the 48-hour week legislation.

Case Study

Working Time Regulations 1998

In November 1993, members of the Council of Ministers decided by majority vote to introduce a directive on working time under Health and Safety Article 118A. This enabled Council members to introduce a 48-hour maximum working week. This directive then was implemented in the **Working Time Regulations 1998**.

The Regulations give rise to wholly new rights and obligations relating to work and rest. The principal provisions are for:

- a limit on average weekly working time to 48 hours (though individuals can choose to work longer)
- a limit on night workers' average normal daily working time to 8 hours
- a requirement to offer health assessments to night workers
- minimum daily and weekly rest periods
- rest breaks at work
- paid annual leave.

The Regulations also implement provisions of the **Young Workers Directive** which relates to the working time of adolescents (those over the minimum school leaving age but under 18). Adolescents are given rights that differ from those of adult workers. These relate to health assessments for night work, minimum daily and weekly rest periods, and rest breaks at work.

The Regulations define a worker as someone to whom an employer has a duty to provide work, who controls when and how it is done, supplies the tools and other equipment and pays tax and National Insurance contributions. However, these are indicators rather than exhaustive or exclusive criteria. The majority of agency workers and freelancers are likely to be workers in the context of the Regulations.

The Regulations do not apply to certain classes of workers (apart from juveniles) in a number of sectors, including: air transport, rail, road transport, sea transport, inland waterways and lake transport, sea fishing, and 'other work at sea' (essentially offshore work in the oil and gas industries).

Some of the measures can be adapted through agreements between workers and employers, so as to allow flexibility to take account of the specific needs of local working arrangements.

Questions

1. From a business point of view, what do you consider to be the main arguments for and against the adoption of a 48-hour maximum working week?

2. From a social point of view, what do you consider to be the main arguments for and against the adoption of a 48-hour week?

3. Can you think of any organisational or procedural problems that might arise through the implementation of the 48-hour week ruling?

4. Which kinds of business organisations will benefit from the 48-hour week ruling, and which will not?

Subsidiarity

The concept of **subsidiarity** first emerged in the 1989 Social Chapter and was subsequently incorporated into the 1992 Treaty on European Union. The principle of subsidiarity is that action should be taken at Community level only when it is more effective and appropriate to do so than it would be at national level. The intention is to attempt to clarify the blurred line of policy responsibility between the Community and the member states, by adopting a general rule that decisions should be made at the lowest governmental level.

Discussion point

In practice, the concept of subsidiarity has been used as a means to justify fewer decisions being made at European level and to justify more decisions being made at European level. Can you think of a reasonable explanation for this apparent paradox?

The Labour government which came into power in 1997 was committed to signing the Social Chapter. Today UK industry is bound by the requirements of this Chapter, so that all organisations must now conform to the requirements.

Enlargement of the EU

Since its creation, the EEC has progressed and developed enormously. The Community has been enlarged five times and there are now **fifteen member states**. The original nations in 1957 were France, Germany, Italy, Belgium, the Netherlands and Luxembourg. They were joined in 1973 by Britain, Ireland and Denmark; in 1981 by Greece; in 1986 by Spain and Portugal; in 1990 by East Germany (owing to reunification with West Germany); and in 1995 by Sweden, Finland and Austria. The size of the EU has therefore grown progressively (see Figure 17.5). Today the market size is in the region of 350 million and is still growing:

Countries	Year	Population (millions)	Total population (millions)
Original six members	1960	180	180
UK, Ireland, Denmark	1973	64	244
Greece	1981	10	254
Spain, Portugal	1986	50	304
East Germany	1990	16	320
Austria, Finland, Sweden	1995	22	342
Czech Rep., Hungary, Poland, Slovakia	?	65	407

Figure 17.5 *European Union total population growth*

There are clearly many benefits which are likely to arise for UK-based companies stemming from an enlargement of the European Union. The Czech Republic and Hungary have already made large steps towards developing market economies. UK companies have set up a number of joint ventures and taken over business concerns in these markets. Many Polish, Czech and Hungarian consumers are already taking on board patterns of consumer spending and a taste for consumer goods at much higher levels than before. They have developed a taste for Western goods.

As these economies have been reconstructed they have sought to replace their existing capital goods industries with newer technologies and methods imported from the West. On the consumer good side, for example, we have seen Cadbury setting up chocolate and confectionery manufacturing plant in Poland, and in the capital goods industry Ready Mixed Concrete (RMS) and other building companies such as Costain have set up joint ventures in the former East Germany, Poland and elsewhere. Shell is building new pipelines for the transportation of gas and oil in some of these countries. We are able to benefit from purchasing raw materials, foodstuffs and some finished manufactured goods from these countries while selling them more sophisticated goods.

The overall impact of the expanding EU is to create a growing market which provides opportunities for economies of scale and all of the advantages associated with the expansion of production. Of course, UK companies have to meet the competition presented by these newly emerging economies, particularly where firms in these countries have created new partnerships with rival EU companies.

ORGANISATIONS

This section looks at the major European Union institutions which are having such an important impact on individuals and businesses in the UK. We first examine the overall nature and functions of these institutions.

In most democratic countries/states, governments are organised around a set of institutions which collectively combine to produce 'governance' (i.e. policies, decisions and the implementation of policy). These institutions usually perform the following functions:

- a *legislative function* (a body that decides which policies should be passed and which laws and regulations created)
- an *executive function* (a body that translates policies into action programmes)
- a *democratic function* (a democratically elected body such as a parliament, performing a watchdog type function: a democratic overseer of the executive and legislative bodies)
- a *judicial function* (a system of law courts that safeguards and interprets the country's constitution and enforces the country's laws).

Although the EU has no government as such, it has institutions (decision-making bodies) which collectively operate to provide the member states with 'governance'. There are five main institutions: the Commission, the Council, the Parliament, the European Court of Justice and the European Council. The tasks of governance are shared out between the institutions so that each performs a separate function. Collectively the functions interlock, so that the whole system works interdependently.

The EU is the product of a combination of different political approaches. These approaches are reflected in the make-up of the union's institutions. For example:

- The Council of Ministers and the European Council are organised along **intergovernmental** lines. That is to say, they work mainly on the basis of seeking cooperation, agreement and understanding between the representatives of the member states. Both these institutions are accountable to their national parliaments.
- The Commission and the Parliament have a more **supranational** and **federal** character, respectively. They are more representative of the collective interests of the member states and they are not accountable to national parliaments.

The European Commission

The **European Commission** has a president (who is chosen by the heads of the member states) and a 'college' of 20 **Commissioners**, who are similarly appointed by the member states. Each country appoints one Commissioner and the five larger countries appoint two (generally one from the ruling government party and one from the main opposition party). Each Commissioner is given a 'portfolio': 'environment', 'agriculture', 'competition', etc. Each has a 'Cabinet', a small team (usually about six) who generally help the Commissioner in his or her work, by giving advice, by keeping in contact with other Commissioners or interested parties, and by informing the Commissioner about what's happening in the Commission and the Community.

As an organisation the Commission employs another 2000 people as policy-makers and around another 10 000 in secretarial, interpreting and translating functions. The Commission is divided into 23 **Directorates-General** (with similar functions to the civil service) with each Commissioner being responsible for one or more. Some are powerful bodies in their own right (such as Directorate-General VI – Agriculture), while others have much less influence. There is a Director General for each Directorate.

In its **legislative role**, the Commission makes policy proposals which are sent to the Parliament and Council to be debated and decided upon. Although the Commission does not itself have a large legislative role, the ability to propose policies gives it some significant power in setting the Community's policy agenda, in helping to shape 'what gets done' at Community level. The Council also gives the Commission a role in making 'secondary' legislation. This means that the Commission can pass policies of a technical or administrative nature – these often help to smooth the path of the broader and more important policies that are passed by the Council.

In its **executive role**, the Commission ensures that the policies passed by the Council are acted upon by the member states. The Commission sends out regulations and directives which inform and direct the member states as to what (or what not) to do. The Commission depends on the member states' own civil services to help it in accomplishing this task, as the Commission itself has very few regulatory groups or officials actually enforcing Community regulations 'in the field'.

The Commission plays an important role in conducting the Community's external trade relations. It negotiates important agreements on behalf of the Community, such as the General Agreement on Tariffs and Trade (GATT).

The Commission also maintains diplomatic relations (small parties of permanent delegates, rather like embassies) with organisations and countries outside the Community.

Key functions of the Commission

The Commission's functions are sometimes listed under six main headings.

- *Conscience of the Community and Union*
  The Commission has a responsibility to promote the 'European Ideal'.
- *As guardian of the treaties*
  The Commission plays a key first-stop role in the process of ensuring the implementation of treaty requirements and Community law, although the European Court of Justice (discussed later) is the final arbiter in the latter case.
- *As the executive of the Community*
  The Commission forms the executive responsible for implementing the decisions reached by the Council. The Commission is further tasked to implement rules in the areas of competition and merger policy and to administer funds such as the Social and Development Funds.
- *As the coordinator of a range of policies*
  The coordinating function seeks to ensure that the left-hand of policy knows what the right hand is doing and that different strands of policy are working towards common objectives.
- *As an honest broker and diplomat*
  The Commission has to be able to persuade and try to bring together, various interest groups, concerns and preoccupations of the member states, pressure groups and the wider European public, while trying to promote Community interests.
- *As the initiator of Community law.*

The Council of Ministers

The **Council of Ministers** is the main legislative arm of Community decision-making. Organised on intergovernmental lines, it is the Council that decides (always with the advice of and sometimes in conjunction with the Parliament) which policy proposals become law and which do not.

The Council of Ministers is a generic name for an organisation which actually consists of several councils. Each council is responsible for a particular policy area and is attended by the appropriate national ministerial representatives; for example, the member states' environment ministers will meet in the Environment Council. The most important council is the General Council, where the member states' foreign affairs ministers meet. The General Council also deals with generally sensitive issues, or issues where the member states' representatives are likely to disagree. There are also Technical Councils for the whole range of policy areas: fisheries, the budget, transport, the environment, the internal market, etc. The regularity with which these councils meet reflects their workload, their status and the amount of interest that the Community has in their sector at any given moment.

The Council of Ministers has a presidency which rotates at six-monthly intervals between the member states. The president calls meetings, and works to promote agreement between the Council members and to ensure the smooth and effective operation of the Council.

The Council of Ministers reaches decisions on issues by voting. There are three voting mechanisms.

- *Unanimity*. The Council must here reach a decision by unanimous agreement. This is the most difficult agreement to gain and has been used by member states to stall agreements and to preserve their national interests at the expense of Community progress. In recent years, majority and qualified majority voting have been extended in order to speed up the decision-making process.
- *Qualified majority voting*. In this system each state is allocated a number of votes according to population; a winning majority constitutes 70 per cent of all votes cast. The allocation of votes is weighted so that the smaller states are protected from 'bullying' tactics (see below).
- *Majority voting*. In this system a simple majority is required; all states have one vote each.

The treaties stipulate which voting mechanism should be used for each policy area. In cases where qualified majority voting is applied the following weighting is used (1999 figures):

Austria	4	Italy	10
Belgium	5	Luxembourg	2
Denmark	3	Netherlands	5
Finland	3	Portugal	5
France	10	Spain	8
Germany	10	Sweden	4
Greece	5	UK	10
Ireland	3		

For a qualified majority decision, at least 62 votes are required out of the total of 87.

The Parliament

The **European Parliament** has 626 members and provides democratic representation and control at European level. The Parliament sits in Strasbourg, although it has committee meetings in Brussels and officials based in Luxembourg. Members of the Parliament (MEPs) were originally appointed by the member states, but direct elections to the Parliament began in 1979. MEPs receive the same salary as MPs and sit in cross-national political groups rather than nationally. The Parliament performs three basic functions:

- it has a role in Community decision-making
- it has certain powers over the budget
- it performs the task of a democratic watchdog over the other Community institutions.

Although traditionally the Parliament does not have a strong role in Community decision-making, its scope for influencing legislation has increased in recent years. Originally, the Council only had to consult Parliament before making a final decision as to whether to adopt or reject a policy proposed by the Commission. It did not have to act upon Parliament's advice. This was called the 'Consultation' or 'single-reading' process and is still used in certain policy fields (notably the Common Foreign and Security Policy and Justice and Home Affairs). The Single European Act 1986 increased parliamentary powers of decision-making by giving Parliament the right to a second reading of the proposed policy text; this was known as the 'Co-operation procedure'. This procedure effectively made it harder for the Council to ignore the Parliament's advice and increased the likelihood of some of the Parliament's suggestions being incorporated into the Council's final decision. The Treaty on European Union 1992 gave the Parliament a third reading ('Co-decision procedure') which effectively allows the Parliament equal decision-making power with the Council. If the Council cannot demonstrate that it has taken Parliament's advice sufficiently into account, Parliament can reject the policy. Occasions on which the Co-operation and Co-decision procedures may be used are specified in the treaties. In addition to these powers, the Community needs Parliament's approval for the accession of new members and for the conclusion of international agreements.

The European Parliament has the power to adopt or reject the Community's budget plan. This is very important because unless Parliament approves the budget, the Community cannot implement its planned annual policy programme. Consequently, the Commission, whose task it is to draw up plans for the budget, does so in consultation with the Parliament. This is done in order to ensure that Parliament will not reject the final draft.

The European Parliament has certain powers of approval over the investiture of the Commission President and the Commissioners. The Parliament also has the power to force the entire college of Commissioners to resign (as it did in 1999), although it cannot dismiss individual Commissioners. In addition to this, the Parliament has some supervisory powers; it examines monthly and annual reports, submitted to it by the Commission, and it can also set up committees of inquiry. Management of the EU budget, for example, is notorious for inefficiency, bureaucracy and corruption.

The European Court of Justice

The **European Court of Justice** consists of 15 judges each appointed by the member states for a six-year term (which is often renewed). The judges are assisted by nine Advocates-General, who do much of the preparatory work for the cases. The Court also employs about 650 staff, who perform administrative or language services tasks. In 1988, a Court of First Instance was created to rule on:

- disputes between the Community and its staff
- actions filed against the Commission under provisions included in the ECSC treaty (see page 417)
- aspects of competition rules.

The main Court is not like a European version of a British court (nor should it be confused with the **European Court of Human Rights**). It does not deal with criminal or family law. It is a *constitutional* court, more akin to the United States' Supreme Court, and is mainly confined to economic and commercial law – such as ruling on questions appertaining to the Single Market. The Court has two main functions: it interprets the Community's written constitution (in other words, the Community's treaties) and tries to ensure that the law is correctly upheld in the interpretation and application of the treaties; and it upholds, interprets and rules on laws made by the Community institutions.

The Court rules in disputes between:

- the member states
- the EU and the member states
- the institutions (e.g. between the Council and the Parliament – such disputes might touch on a violation of the correct procedure for making Community decisions, or of an infringement of one institution's rights and competences by another)
- individuals and the EU.

The Court also gives opinions on other international treaties and gives preliminary rulings. This happens when a dispute waiting to go before a national court is referred by the national court to the Court of Justice.

The member states and their citizens are legally bound by Community law, which applies in fields where national law is deemed insufficient. Community law overrules national law, except in circumstances where national law is tougher and is not seeking to protect a member state's home market at the expense of free trade rules in the Single Market (for example, environmental law).

The Court constitutes one of the most supranational elements of the Community. The member states do not simply cooperate with each other, they have agreed to accept common laws (in many policy areas) ruled upon and interpreted by an independent body. It is not the member states who interpret how and when to apply Community law, it is the Court; if it were left to the member states there probably wouldn't be effective common laws.

The Court of Auditors

The **Court of Auditors** is based in Luxembourg, and is made up of 15 members appointed by the Council of Ministers. It has substantial investigative powers and is responsible for the external auditing of all revenue and expenditure in the EU budget. This court recently uncovered £3 billion worth of errors and fraud in the administration of the Common Agricultural Policy.

The European Council

The **European Council** is the twice -yearly meeting of the heads of the member states. Although inter-state summits had previously been called, the Council was not formally put on a statutory basis until the 1974 Paris summit. The European Council was established at a time of 'Euro sclerosis' when the Community was flagging in dynamism. It was created to help, give direction to, and breathe new life into, the project of unification. It was also institutionalised as a way of promoting cooperation and coordination between the states and to promote understanding between the heads of government.

The Council is composed of the heads of state or of government. They are 'assisted' by the Ministers for Foreign Affairs and a member of the Commission. The presidency of the European Council is held concurrently with the presidency of the Council of Ministers. European Council meetings are held in the country of the Council's president and it is his or her task to organise and chair meetings and to seek agreement amongst the other members.

The European Council deals with new projects for unification (e.g. monetary union and the single currency). It discusses sensitive issues that the Council of Ministers has not been able to resolve, and it responds to developments/events which occur on the international scene.

The legislative process

The **legislative process** for the European Union is complex. After consultation and preparation, draft legislation is prepared by the relevant Commissioner(s) and is presented to colleagues, where it must be examined and adopted by majority vote before delivery to the Council of Ministers. After consideration, it is passed to the European Parliament. Agreement must be reached at all stages before the proposal can be adopted and published in the Official Journal of the Community before it becomes a Decision or a Regulation.

A **Regulation**, once adopted by the Council of Ministers, is binding in its entirety and applicable as it stands to all member states. A **Directive** is binding in its objectives, but the form and method of implementation to achieve the results are left to members. A **Decision** is similar to a regulation but may apply to only one or more states. The Commission can also adopt **Recommendations** and **Opinions**, which have no legal force and are only advice.

EUROPEAN MONETARY UNION (EMU)

EMU refers to that section of the Maastricht Treaty which provides for the creation of a **'monetary union'** between EU members. Individual currencies such as the pound, or the franc, the mark and the lira would, in effect, cease to exist and would be replaced by a single currency, known as the **euro**.

A single currency

For the *individual UK citizen* this would mean that they could spend the domestic currency, the euro, in any other country in the EMU. In principle, it would therefore mean that people would move their personal assets – bank balances or other financial assets – much more easily from any part of the EMU to any other part (as they are, at present, able to do in the UK). Were Britain to join, from the monetary point of view, transactions with citizens of other members of the EMU would be little different from transactions at present with other citizens of the UK. We do not think of transactions across the borders of England, Scotland, Wales or Northern Ireland as in any way problematic. This could soon be true of transactions with other European countries.

For *companies*, such a development could be even more significant. International trade does not consist of large numbers of 'one-off' transactions. By and large it consists of well-established trading relationships between companies and individuals who know each other well and who have a substantial track-record of mutually beneficial commercial transactions. Some of these take place between different sections of the same international organisation – Ford Motors in the UK trading with Ford Motors in Belgium, for instance. Very many of these relationships are enshrined in contracts which specify products, prices and conditions of supply months, and sometimes years, ahead. Such arrangements offer security of service and a guarantee of essential components some way into the future. The production process is planned some time in advance of intended delivery dates. Clearly it is advantageous to companies if prices are also negotiated in advance, in order to secure future supplies of components or finished goods at pre-determined prices.

Where the trade is conducted within a single country with a single currency, this presents little problem in principle. An agricultural cooperative in the Paris basin would not think twice about agreeing to purchase a Renault tractor from a local supplier, in three months' time at a fixed price. They may, however, have cause to ponder about importing a tractor from a supplier in the UK at a fixed price in three months' time. For instance, between late August and late November in 1996, the value of the franc fell by over 15 per cent against the pound sterling. If the price had been agreed in advance in sterling the French cooperative would have paid in November at least 15 per cent more francs in exchange for the sterling required to purchase their British-made vehicle than they expected when they signed the contract in August 1996.

In these circumstances, then, the exchange rate between currencies can play havoc with perfectly sound commercial calculations and can make international trading a hazardous business. Of course, companies try to build into their contracts safeguards against currency fluctuations, but no safeguard is foolproof or free of cost. Such fluctuations discourage medium- and long-term trading relationships and make longer-term commitments, such as major investment decisions across international boundaries, riskier than domestic investment. It is clear, therefore, that for individuals, firms and investors, currency fluctuations add uncertainty and cost to cross-border trade.

It is possible to reduce some of the uncertainty by establishing a **fixed-parity exchange level** between two or more currencies. In 1944, the **Bretton Woods Agreement** sought to establish a postwar system of fixed international rates of exchange in which currencies were permitted to float against each other only within narrow bands. The disadvantage of this scheme was that it could operate only if trade patterns were relatively stable and if international speculation in currencies was made extremely difficult. This was achieved by limiting capital transactions between currencies. In turn, this had the undesirable effect to restricting opportunities for real capital investment abroad.

The Community next attempted to create a similar system in the form of the ERM, the **Exchange Rate Mechanism**. This mechanism was designed to restrict currency fluctuations between European currencies by establishing large gold and foreign-currency reserves which the central banks of Europe could use collaboratively to stem a 'run' on any currency – in effect preventing speculators from causing large short-term swings in the value of any particular currency. However, the events leading to the departure of the pound sterling from the mechanism (when Chancellor Norman Lamont took the pound out of the ERM after failing to stem speculation by changing the bank rate several times in the course of one afternoon) make it clear that, even with substantial resources, substantial inter-Bank cooperation and the willingness to take drastic action, speculators will not be discouraged if they feel that they have a 'killing' to make by continuing to sell any particular currency.

The advantage of a common currency across Europe, as opposed simply to an exchange rate mechanism, is that if one currency prevails there is no opportunity for international speculation against those member states which share the same currency. This would produce as much medium- or long-term certainty regarding impending price fluctuations as would be true of domestic trade. Thus an important element of risk would be eliminated from cross-border trade. Moreover, costs of international financial transactions should be substantially reduced, since all would be conducted in a single currency, obviating exchange commission charges by banks.

However, *there are disadvantages to a single currency*, which are highlighted in the case study below.

Case Study

The manifesto of the (now defunct) Referendum Party

The following are edited extracts from the general election manifesto of the former Referendum Party, set up by the late Sir James Goldsmith, a prominent businessman with extensive European financial interests.

'Britain could be on the brink of surrendering all its powers to determine interest rates, the rate of inflation, levels of unemployment and the rate of growth. That is what will happen if the government of the day commits the country to monetary union. The **European Central Bank** [ECB] would take over these responsibilities in 1999.

'Sterling would be irrevocably fixed to the euro, and Europe's new synthetic currency would take over from national currencies. … The Treasury and the Bank of England will lose virtually all their powers over monetary policy. The Bank will be a sort of agent – an errand boy – for the ECB. … The ECB will control interest rates and credit throughout all participating countries. The same for all. It does not matter whether one country is suffering from a long slump and another is feeling the heat of incipient inflation; all and every one must be given the same medicine under the ECB.

'Monetary union is seen as the linchpin of this greater union centred around Germany. The concentration of monetary power spawns the concentration of budgetary and political power, and ultimately of security and foreign policy.'

Questions

1. What do you see as being the main points of criticism of the single currency by the Referendum Party?

2. How valid are these criticisms?

The birth of the euro

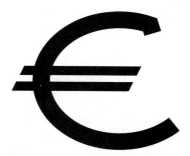

Figure 17.6 *The sign of the euro*

On 1 January 1999, eleven sovereign nations finally handed over control of their currencies to a committee of bankers. The meeting took less than 30 minutes. Five hundred blue balloons were released into the sky over Brussels. The euro, the world's newest, least visible and second most important currency was born (weighing in at slightly more than a dollar or just over 70 pence). Britain was the only EU member declining to join.

However, the currency (notes and coins) will not appear in public until 2002. Up to that time the franc, mark, lira and others will remain, nominally, in the pockets and wallets of the citizens of the eleven nations. The euro will be used only in the form of plastic money and cheques (and even then only if a shop or restaurant is willing to take it).

In real terms the ten old currencies died on 1 January 1999. They have ceased to exist as independent instruments of national pride or economic policy. They are now mere accounting units of the euro. Their exchange rates against the new currency were locked until the euro finally sweeps them away in July 2002. The eleven finance ministers of the 'euro nations' decided that a euro is worth 1.955583 deutschmarks, 6.55957 French francs, and so on. All decisions affecting the euro, on interest rates or monetary flows, will be taken by the European Central Bank in Frankfurt. Jacques Santer, the then European Commission President, stated:

> 'Europe can speak with a single voice. It is now up to us to proceed. We embark on the next stage leading to political unity, which I think is a direct consequence of economic unity, so Europe can play a leading role on the international stage, even including a common defence policy.'

This goes well beyond the introduction merely of the euro; it heralds a new departure for Europe. The creation of the single European currency will progressively demand more cooperation on the big economic and political decisions affecting everything from public spending to unemployment and, up to a point, taxes. In turn, this will demand more direct democratic control of decision-making in Brussels, which would itself be a federalising influence – another step towards some form of 'European government', however loosely drawn.

The EEC/EC/EU has always proceeded in this way. It sets ambitious but abstract economic targets – the common market, the single market, now the single currency. The often unseemly struggle to achieve these targets, and make them stick, forces member states to draw closer and closer together politically.

There are good economic arguments for the euro. It has already helped to shelter Europe from the worst of the Asian economic crisis of the late 1990s. The euro countries have minimal inflation and low interest rates. The Organisation for Economic Cooperation and Development (OECD) predicts that the EU will be the most dynamic region of the world in the early twenty-first century. But the euro was not invented for these reasons alone. It was also invented to answer the threat from German unity by forcing more European economic, and therefore political, unity. A single European currency will, from 2002, bring Europe alive to its citizens for the first time. There is potential in the euro for the creation of a truly European political consciousness.

A summary of the arguments for and against economic and monetary union are set out in Figure 17.7.

A week after the launch of the euro, two of the four EU 'outs', Denmark and Sweden, were sending clear signals of their desire to sign up to the single currency as soon as possible. Opinion polls in these countries were moving increasingly behind the need to be part of the system.

The reasons for Denmark's apparent conversion were the smooth debut of the single currency, after a few months during which the euro had shown its worth as a shield against global currency turbulence; and the growing fear that the country could not afford to sit on the sidelines. In Sweden, such arguments resonated even more strongly. The moment of truth came in the summer of 1998 as the Asian economic crisis, followed by the financial meltdown in Russia, threatened to turn Nordic financial markets inside out. In the event, Sweden (as well as Norway, which is not an EU member) took a buffeting; but not neighbouring Finland, despite its common border and long historical associations with the former Soviet Union. In both Scandinavian countries, industry is strongly in favour of the euro. Like Britain, both Denmark and Sweden easily meet the economic qualifications for membership. Unlike in Britain, however, fears over being marginalised in Europe now outweigh reluctance to make the surrender of national sovereignty implicit in the euro.

Arguments for	Arguments against
• A fixed exchange rate will end currency instability in Europe	• National governments will have less control over monetary policy
• Unstable markets have caused economic crises in the past, forcing governments to choose between high interest rates (leading to unemployment) and currency devaluation (leading to high inflation)	• Global economic shocks are likely to affect member states in different ways
• Low interest rates and a fixed exchange rate will encourage more progressive and long-term government domestic policies, and boost trade and investment	• Unemployment could increase, at least in the short term, if a government comes under pressure to cut public expenditure owing to restrictions relating to the requirement to limit its deficit
• No one member of the EU will be able to dictate monetary policy	• Critics fear that the German central bank (the Bundesbank) will dominate proceedings
• The euro should be strong enough to compete against the dollar and the yen on world markets	• The European Monetary Institute and European Central Bank might not look beyond the issue of price stability and might ignore the knock-on social and political effects of monetary policy

Figure 17.7 *Arguments for and against EMU*

Discussion point

1. Is the creation of the euro just one step in a larger process?

2. Should the UK get fully involved in making this process work?

3. What are the implications for UK business of a truly European 'space' and political and economic area?

THE EU BUDGET

The budget of the European Union is relatively small at around 88 billion ecus, which is only approximately 1.2 per cent of the members' GDP. The largest share of the budget goes on the Common Agricultural Policy (CAP), followed by Regional and Restructuring Policies. The Germans are the largest contributors to the budget of the EU (in recent years they have wanted to see this burden reduced).

The budget must, year on year, be substantially in balance. In 1985–86 the budget was in substantial deficit, which led to reform, particularly of the common Agricultural Policy which was limited to 75 per cent of the growth of the overall budget, and the setting of four-yearly targets with annual reviews.

In the mid-1980s Margaret Thatcher argued very aggressively the case for reducing the UK's contribution to the budget. It was argued that the UK contributed a disproportionate amount compared with, for example, France which, despite being an 'industrialised nation' was a net beneficiary of the CAP. This was the source of an on-going rebate won by the Conservatives. However, the rebate has been called into question.

Figures 17.8 and 17.9 show the contributions and receipts of EU nations in the budget in 1997, and the main programmes (policy areas).

Country	Contributions (per cent)	Receipts (per cent)	Ratio of receipts to contributions (per cent)
Austria	2.7	2.4	89
Belgium	3.8	2.0	53
Denmark	1.8	3.0	167
Finland	1.4	1.4	100
France	17.7	14.0	79
Germany	29.3	13.0	44
Greece	1.4	7.0	500
Ireland	1.1	4.0	364
Italy	11.4	17.0	149
Luxembourg	0.2	0.2	100
Netherlands	5.9	8.5	144
Portugal	1.5	4.0	267
Spain	6.3	14.0	222
Sweden	2.5	2.5	100
UK	13.1	7.0	53

Figure 17.8 *Contributions to, and receipts from, the EU budget*

1 Ecu ≈ £0.73	Ecus (billions)
European Agricultural Guidance and Guarantee Fund (guarantee section)	42.305
Structural operations (e.g. other agricultural regional, transport, fisheries)	31.279
Training, youth, culture and other social	0.748
Energy, EURATOM safeguards and environment	0.193
Consumer protection, industry and trans-European networks	0.880
Research and technological development	3.450
External action (overseas development aid)	5.807
Common foreign and security	0.050
Guarantees, reserves and compensation	0.541
Administrative expenditure	2.293
Total	87.996

Figure 17.9 *Expenditure by policy areas for 1997*

Check your understanding

It is important to realise that, because the European Union creates a dynamic economic space and trading area, the richer nations are going to be the prime beneficiaries of advances in trade and competition. Inevitably the poorer regions and nations will suffer. These nations and regions therefore should be net beneficiaries of the budget, to enable them (a) to maintain elements of traditional lifestyle, and (b) to restructure and develop more advanced new infrastructure.

The biggest difficulty over the budget is that it is a 'zero-sum' game: if one country pays less, another must pay more. Any attempt to increase the budget of the EU will therefore inevitably lead to increase bickering between nations.

Import duties and levies

The development of an economic community can be seen as involving a number of steps with each step leading to closer cooperation (see Figure 17.10).

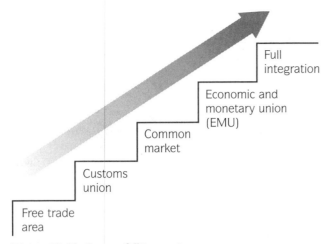

Figure 17.10 *Steps to full integration*

The early stages of creating the EEC (European Economic Community) were in large measure concerned with breaking down **import duties** and **levies**, which were concerned with cross-border trade within the EU, and the creation of a **common external tariff** between the EU and the rest of the world.

Free trade

Developing a free trade area involved getting rid of some of the barriers to free trade. In particular, it involved the removal of **quotas** and **tariffs** between members of the trading community.

Customs union

In 1986, the Community created a **customs union** with moves towards positive integration of economies. In addition to the free trade area, member states operated a common external tariff. This meant that an import from a non-member country (e.g. Canada) would carry the same tariff whether it entered France, Germany, Italy or any other member state. Within the customs union the member states developed common trading policies and moved towards equal conditions for individuals, firms and groupings operating within the union.

Common market

The creation of a **common market** took the integration process a step further. A common market involves the free

movement of factors of production (land, labour, capital and enterprise) and the free movement of goods. Over the years, we have seen a harmonisation of policies designed to create freedom of movement. The Single European Act 1986 highlighted what are known as the four freedoms (see Figure 17.11).

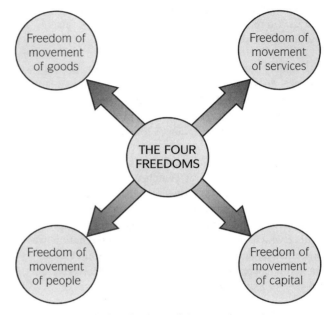

Figure 17.11 *The four freedoms of the common market*

Economic and monetary union

As we have seen earlier in this chapter, economic and monetary union is becoming a reality with the creation of a single European currency, and a central European Bank in Frankfurt. To create EMU the participating countries progressively brought their economies into line, reducing their inflation rates and interest rates below a given figure, limiting the size of central government budget deficits etc. Once these were in line (the theory ran) then the economies could be run more or less as a single entity through a central banking institution.

Full integration

Full integration still remains for the future and will depend on greater political cohesion. Economic policies on, for example, taxation and spending would be determined by EU institutions. We will see whether this will happen, but probably not for quite a long time.

Agricultural import levies

The Treaty of Rome and ensuing legislation and policies from the EU guaranteed incomes to farmers by setting **minimum prices** for agricultural products. These minimum prices set out to ensure that farmers earn enough to keep farming. The price that the Common Agricultural Policy (CAP) guarantees will normally be higher than the free market price (see Figure 17.12). The CAP is discussed further below.

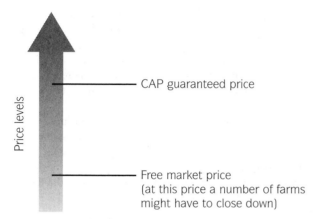

Figure 17.12 *The CAP price*

EU producers are also protected from cheaper imported foodstuffs from the non-EU countries (e.g. American cereals). Imported non-EU foodstuffs can be sold only at a threshold price (see Figure 17.13).

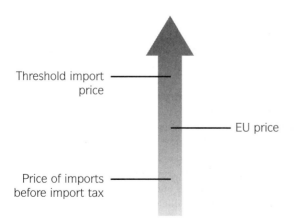

Figure 17.13 *Some EU foodstuffs can be given a competitive edge*

Import taxes are placed on these imports to bring them up to this threshold price. The effect of this important policy is to make EU foodstuffs more competitive within the internal market.

The result of guaranteeing farmers minimum prices is that more goods are provided than can be sold (as Chapter 16 showed in its analysis of demand and supply). This is a very wasteful policy as the surplus has to be stored, at an additional cost.

In recent years some of the worst excesses of these protectionist policies have been cut back, particularly as a result of greater cooperation in the world resulting from the creation of the **World Trade Organisation** which seeks to cut back on international restrictions on trade through cooperative actions between countries.

Value-added tax (VAT)

In order to come into line with the European Community, the UK had to abandon its former expenditure tax ('purchase tax') to introduce a system of **value-added tax**. VAT, as the name suggests, is levied on the value added in the production process by a firm. Typically a firm buys in inputs from another firm, adds value to these inputs, and then sells on its final products (either to another producer or an end consumer). For example, in a given month a jeans manufacturer may buy in £100 000 worth of material for processing into jeans. At the end of the month the firm may be able to sell the jeans on to retailers for £250 000. The firm has therefore added £150 000 of value, a sum that is taxed at the current rate. Today most products that consumers buy have a VAT element, although there are some exceptions such as children's clothes and other necessary items (strictly, they carry a VAT rate of zero per cent).

Tax harmonisation

In recent years increasing pressure has built up for the greater equality of tax systems within the European Union in order to create a level playing field for competition between firms, as well as helping to harmonise social policies. As long ago as July 1987 when the Single European Act was passed, reference was made to **tax harmonisation**. Five priorities were listed:

- to create a uniform VAT basis
- to bring excise rates closer together
- harmonisation of taxation which directly affects capital movements
- harmonisation of company taxation
- extending duty-free concessions throughout the EU (this has now been abolished).

In 1999, Oscar Lafontaine, the newly appointed German finance minister, thrust tax harmonisation to the top of the agenda, supported by the new German premier, Gerhard Schroeder. He called for the rapid harmonisation of tax rates throughout the EU. However, Lafontaine resigned his position later owing to differing opinions on policy.

The Common Agricultural policy (CAP)

The main purpose of the **Common Agricultural Policy** has been to guarantee future supplies of food in Europe. The experience of rural decay during the inter-war period, and food shortages during the Second World War (caused by the strategic interruption of food imports to Europe), prompted the European leaders in the postwar era to make plans for the revival and modernisation of the agricultural industry. The intention of the CAP was therefore to make Europe self-sufficient in the production of its own food and non-reliant on the importation of food from countries outside the EU. The CAP was adopted by the Community in the 1960s in order to realise those intentions.

The main objectives of the policy were thus:

- to keep people on the land to ensure a viable agricultural sector
- to prevent rural decay
- to ensure reasonable incomes for farmers
- to modernise the agricultural industry and make it more efficient.

To greatly simplify the explanation, the policy works basically on the two-fold principle of (a) subsidising farmers, and (b) protecting the price of their produce within the common market from directly competitive exposure to lower 'world prices', such as those maintained outside of the common market.

Protecting the farmers

The CAP enables farmers to keep the price of their produce in the Single Market artificially higher than the price outside (i.e. the flat price paid in the rest of the world – the 'world price'). This is achieved by placing an import tax on all cheaper foodstuffs entering the common market. This creates a 'threshold price' (see Figure 17.13) – the import tax effectively raises the price of cheaper imports up to the same level as that of the common market (and often higher).

Subsidising farmers

The farmers are subsidised by EU citizens/consumers who pay an artificially high price for their food products. They are also subsidised by the member states, who pay large sums of money to the Community budget so that the EU can guarantee a market for their produce. When farmers produce too many goods for the market, the EU buys up the surplus and stores it (hence the notorious 'wine lakes' and 'butter mountains'). This ensures a stable price for foodstuffs and a good income for farmers.

Many people feel that the CAP is ripe for reform. In 1999 it still took 50 per cent of all EU spending. The most likely reform is a shift from support through high guaranteed prices paid by consumers towards direct income subsidies to farmers paid by taxpayers. This is likely to increase rather than decrease the EU's budget in the short term.

In 1997, **Agenda 2000** was presented by the European Commission. This includes proposals for reforming the CAP, bearing in mind past experiences, international trends, enlargement of the EU and the budgetary controls affecting member states. Agenda 2000 is basically the farm and financial reforms needed to prepare for the EU's eastward enlargement.

Regional policy

Jacques Delors, who was a major figure as EU President until 1994, set out the **Delors proposals** covering the period 1987–97. These have since been extended by Jacques Santer to the year 2007.

The emphasis in these proposals was on moving the union towards economic and social cohesion. The Delors proposals recognised that the growth of free trade in the internal market of the union would not lead to benefits for all **regions**. Therefore it was essential to provide assistance and support for economically backward and declining regions. Economic and social cohesion policies set out to make sure that the less-favoured regions also benefit from the advantages of free trade among the member states. The Delors package therefore set out to double the money available for restructuring policies.

Between 1987 and 1992 the proportion of the EU budget allocated to structural funds increased from 17 per cent to 27 per cent, and today this is nearer 40 per cent. Europe certainly has plenty of poor regions, from the eastern Lander of Germany to southern Italy to the Scottish Highlands.

The EU is made up of an advantaged 'core' and a disadvantaged 'periphery'. The 'depressed south' is the most serious regional problem facing the EU at present. The European Commission identifies a number of types of 'disadvantaged' regions. These are as follows.

- *Lagging regions*. These have never really started to develop. There are a number of such regions in the Mediterranean zone with poor communications, low-output agriculture and very low incomes for many people.
- *Declining industrial regions*. These are areas in which industry was once important but has now gone into decline, such as the north-west of England and parts of South Wales.
- *Peripheral regions*. These are far from the centre of large markets (e.g. the Highlands and Islands of Scotland, Ireland and Sicily).
- *Border regions*. In the past a number of border regions were favoured because of the services they offered (e.g. warehousing for goods being traded between countries). With the lifting of border restrictions these areas now require assistance.
- *Urban problem areas*. The big cities of Europe, such as Paris, Lyon and London, have particular social problems associated with crime, congestion, drugs, pollution, etc.
- *Rural problem areas*. Some areas with poor climates for farming have particular problems. These areas have been adversely affected by reductions in subsidies to agriculture. The EU has a number of structural funds which provide help and support to these areas – for example, for projects in declining coal and steel communities, helping with assistance and training schemes to deal with long-term unemployed, the promotion of development schemes in rural and lagging areas, and increased employment help for young people.

Funds are channelled to the poorer nations of the Community – Ireland, Portugal, Greece and Spain – particularly for developing infrastructure such as transport and communications systems, and for training projects. The Delors proposals have been behind the on-going increase in the proportion of money spent on regional support.

CONCLUSION

This chapter has outlined the key changes which have taken place in the European Union in recent years. Change has been frequent and dramatic and this process will continue at an accelerated pace in the new century.

What is clear is that the economic fortunes of this country, its businesses and its people, are tied up with the fortunes of our neighbours in an unparalleled way. Today new directives and regulations are created by the legislative bodies of the EU and implemented by its executive functions. UK businesses have to comply in all sorts of ways, ranging from the standards of products (e.g. size and colour of certain types of fruits, and the labelling of foodstuffs), emission controls and standards for industrial processes, the employment conditions of staff, and a whole raft of other requirements. In the next few years our currency will almost certainly be replaced by the euro, and increasingly we will have to comply with EU taxation regimes. In the not so distant future it is possible that we will be governed from the centre of the European Union, although there will be considerable scope for subsidiarity. The challenge for UK businesses is to anticipate future changes and to make appropriate responses in terms of business policy and practice.

FURTHER READING

Brewster, D., Business *Economics: Decision-Making and the Firm*, Dryden Press, 1997.

Dawes, B. (ed.), *International Business, a European Perspective*, Stanley Thornes, 1995.

Dunnett, A., *The Macroeconomic Environment*, Longman, 1997.

Griffiths, A. and Wall, S., *Applied Economics*, Longman, 1997.

Hornby, W., Gammie, B. and Wall, S., *Business Economics*, Longman, 1997.

Hurl, Bryan, *Privatization and the Public Sector*, Heinemann Educational, 1997.

Needham, D. and Dransfield, R., *European Business Studies*, Stanley Thornes, 1994.

Sloman, J., *Economics*, Harvester Wheatsheaf/Prentice Hall, 1997.

JOURNALS

The Economist

ASSIGNMENT

Task 1

Choose an organisation for which it is relatively easy to access information through company reports, through writing to the organisation, and particularly through accessing web sites for that company. Suitable organisations would include Body Shop, Nestlé and Virgin. Alternatively choose an organisation to which you have direct access (e.g. one where you work).

Provide a company profile for potential shareholders who have little knowledge about the organisation and its affairs. The profile should identify the key objectives of the organisation. These objectives should be contrasted with two other organisations having different sets of objectives. The profile should be presented in an attractive way using a computer graphics and word-processing package.

Identify all the key stakeholders in the organisation and the objectives of three of these stakeholders. Show the extent to which the objectives of these latter stakeholders are met. One of the groups of stakeholders (assuming that you have chosen a private-sector organisation) must be the shareholders.

Set out all the responsibilities of your chosen organisation, and show in detail how three internal responsibilities are met (e.g. equal opportunities, health and safety requirements, consumer protection) and how one external responsibility is met (e.g. environmental practice).

Task 2

Imagine that you work for a major UK company in a sector of your choice. The company has recently set up a joint venture with an eastern European partner. Representatives from your partner company are to visit the UK and you have been given the responsibility for briefing them. In your briefing you will need to do the following:

a Set out the main points of difference between the UK mixed economy system, and conditions which previously prevailed in eastern bloc communist states.

b Contrast the differing views of the role of the state held by the current government in power in the UK and the previous government.

c Discuss the impact of two recent policies of the present government on business in the UK.

d Outline the significance of a regional or local development on an organisation in the economic sector that you have chosen.

Task 3

A number of companies operating in the UK have been able to win considerable market share. Gillette, the global market leader in shaving materials, is easily the dominant force in men's shaving. In Britain 15.9 million men are wet-shaving, and 9 million of them use a Gillette product. The nearest rivals are Wilkinson Sword with 2.8 million, and Bic with 2.6 million. Because of its competitive advantage and the profits that flow from this, Gillette is able to invest considerable sums in product research, development and improvement. For example, when Gillette launched its Mach 3 (triple-bladed razor) in the United States in late 1998 it was able to advertise 'the billion dollar blade' – a conservative estimate of how much it had cost over seven years to turn the protoype into the production-line model.

a Identify another company which is able to enjoy such dominance of a market in the UK. Show how the firm has been able to develop its monopoly-like position. Set out the benefits to consumers of having such a large firm dominating a market, and also outline some of the negative impacts.

b Contrast the monopoly-like structure you have outlined with a second market in which there is intense competition between many small producers and/or suppliers. Show how this competitive market has developed over time. Set out the advantages and disadvantages to consumers of having such a competitive structure.

Task 4

The following information appeared in the national press in January 1999:

> The cost of potatoes has more than doubled because of last year's wet weather. The British Potato Council said yesterday that the average farm-gate cost of a tonne of spuds had risen from £78 to £167 in 12 months. Much of last year's harvest was wrecked by heavy rainfall at crucial times of the year. This should lead to increases in the price of chips.
>
> A spokesperson for the British Potato Council stated that fish and chip shops like to use the Maris Pipers variety, which in 1998 cost anything from £35 to £90 a tonne as they left the farm. In 1999 a tonne costs anything between £80 and £230, depending on the quality.
>
> The yield of the potato harvest was 6.2 million tonnes in 1998, compared with 6.8 million tonnes in 1997.

a Use demand and supply diagrams to show why the price of chips was expected to rise in fish and chip shops (i.e. explain the effect of a rise in price of potatoes).

b Identify two other goods or services where there have been clear demand and supply changes in recent months. Illustrate these changes by using demand and supply diagrams. Explain what the impact of these changes will have been on relevant business organisations.

c Choose a popular product or business, such as a confectionery bar, a well-known travel agent, a leading hotel chain, a brand of bottled water, etc. Show how the firm or product has been able to gain a competitive advantage in its chosen marketplace.

Task 5

Imagine that you work for a well-known broadsheet newspaper. In the light of current interest in Britain's place in the European Union, you are asked to produce a two-page spread covering a range of issues. These are:

a An 'idiot's guide' setting out in easy-to-understand terms the key features of the EU.

b A feature focusing on a local UK business, showing the impact of two EU policies on the business.

c A discursive article setting out the arguments for and against UK entry into the European Monetary Union (EMU).

d An illustrated article showing the current members of the EU and the countries seeking to join. The article should analyse the likely impact on UK businesses of such an enlargement process.

Quantitative Techniques for Business

Statistical Techniques

This chapter introduces the nature of statistics and covers a variety of basic statistical techniques. It looks at the collection of statistics from primary and secondary data sources, and the graphical and diagrammatic representation of information and its analysis using representative values, cumulative frequency and measures of dispersion.

On completion of the chapter you should be able to use statistical techniques to collect and analyse data. To achieve this you must demonstrate the ability to:

- prepare and implement a plan for the collection of primary and secondary information for a given business problem

- classify and record data

- solve problems involving the analysis and calculation of statistical quantities from frequency distributions.

WHAT ARE STATISTICS?

Mention of the word 'statistics' ('stats') conjures up images of lists of numbers. In fact, this was the word's original meaning. State-istics were originally the collection of population and economic information vital for the state. Today, the study of statistics is much more than this. It has become a well-regarded scientific method of analysis, playing a central role as a basis for decision-making throughout all types of organisations.

Every organisation has to make decisions, and often such decisions are influenced by a host of both internal and external factors which can make decision-making very difficult. In an uncertain world, organisations require information upon which to base and often justify their decisions. Though statistics help to fulfil this role, care must be taken in their use or, as Gibson (1997) points out, there is always the danger that 'many people use statistics rather like a drunken man uses a lamp post: more for support than illumination'.

Much of the information that organisations have to deal with on a day-to-day basis involves figures and so is **quantitative** in nature. For example, how might a movement in an exchange rate or in interest rates affect the business organisation? What does a recent survey imply about the strength of demand for different product ranges? How do recently published accounting figures affect the business organisation? In answering these questions the key feature of the information available is that it is numerical. To understand the implications of figures at any level, clearly some basic knowledge of statistics is required in order to be able to extract and synthesise the body of information to provide a clearer picture of exactly what it means. Although decision-making calls, eventually, for common sense, problem-solving skills and an ability to communicate, these skills are enhanced by an ability to analyse numerical data.

DATA SOURCES

According to the *Oxford Dictionary* the word 'data' means 'facts or information used in deciding or discussing something'. In all organisations data arise in many different areas and as a result of many different activities. Statistical analysis involves making sense of data in a variety of different ways. This may include collecting data, summarising them, extracting information from them, analysing and interpreting them in the best possible way.

It has been said that in statistics, we do not deal with questions of what *is* but of what *could be*, what *might be*, or what *probably is*. For example, consider the following statements:

- Business organisations will gain as they enjoy the benefits of Economic and Monetary Union (EMU).
- Low prices do not always maximise revenue.
- To improve market share we need to target our new range of products at the 18–25-year-old age group.

It is difficult to be sure of the truth of these statements. With each there is a relationship between more than one variable (a variable is something that can be measured or observed). As a result, we need techniques for dealing with uncertainty so that better decisions can be made in an uncertain environment. It must be remembered that statistics are not meant to be a substitute for experience. They cannot replace the intuitive instinct of focused managers, who have intrapreneurial perceptions about how to develop their business units. They can, however, help such managers to fine tune their instincts and to sharpen their capabilities.

It is possible to explore data rather like an investigator. It may also be possible to use data to construct and test models or hypotheses as a basis for decisions. The use of computers has changed the ways in which data can be manipulated and handled, allowing data analysis to take into account assumptions, and to test inferences. The use of computers has also massively expanded the environment in which data are used, bringing about an explosion of information requiring some form of summary and analysis. As a result, it has become even more important to identify the right data and discard what is not required in order to produce succinct summaries which can be handled, interpreted and used as a base for good decision-making.

With so much data available, managers have to consider what data they require. Thorough and accurate information is clearly likely to affect the quality of

decision-making, whereas misleading information may result in poor decisions.

It is important to make distinctions about the sort of data collected. Whereas internal data consist of information extracted within an organisation, external data are found outside the organisation in the environment in which it operates (see Figure 18.2).

There is no point collecting information if it might not be required. There are many examples where money has been spent on information gathering, only for the data not to be used. Before gathering information several important questions need to be asked:

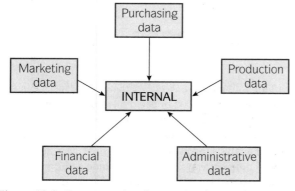

Figure 18.2 *Some examples of internal and external data*

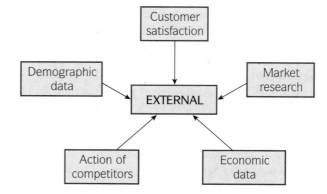

- What are the precise objectives of the exercise? It is important to consider the aims of the exercise to ensure that time is not spent upon collecting information that might not be needed.
- What is to be measured? Identifying the areas of interest or concern is central to the research process.
- What units of measurement are to be used? For example, should information be collected in pounds, euros or both?
- What degree of accuracy is required? To obtain a higher degree of accuracy more time and effort will have to be spent collecting the information.
- Is obtaining the information cost-effective? The whole point of the exercise – to collect information – must be worth the expenditure.

Primary and secondary sources

Primary data consist of figures collected by an organisation for its own purposes. These will not exist in any identifiable form and will have to be collected first-hand. The information is therefore 'straight from the horse's mouth' and is specifically commissioned by the host organisation.

Though organisations might prefer to collect primary data, as information collected for a specific purpose is likely to be more useful, the time it takes to collect, as well as the cost and circumstances mean that it is not always possible to do so. **Secondary data**, collected by others, may be used instead. The problems associated with collecting secondary data are that the information available might not present a complete picture; for example, it could be out of date, there may be little knowledge of how such data are collected, and the reason for collection may not be known.

Secondary data are numerous and wide ranging. All published statistics are a form of secondary data, and a set of reference sources is useful for all organisations. For example, useful information may be gathered simply by looking at:

- company reports
- business publications such as *Investors Chronicle*
- newspapers and magazines such as the *Financial Times* and *The Economist*
- trade periodicals and professional magazines
- published reports from research agencies.

Survey methodology

When collecting primary data, it is important from the outset to consider the purpose of the survey, as this will not only influence the questions asked but also determine the methods used for the survey. The starting point is always to consider precisely what you want to know. For example, do you need to know totals such as the market for a particular product, or do you require more precise information broken down into key areas for analysis? There is no point collecting too much data or data which is too detailed, if some of those data is unlikely to be used. Similarly, it is pointless collecting data if they are not going to provide the answers to the questions posed. A survey takes time and is a costly exercise. Therefore, in order to maximise the use of resources, it is also important to match the target dates and budget requirements to the nature and purposes of the research.

As surveys generate considerable data, it is important to think about what you are going to do with that data and how the results of the survey are to be analysed. Planning the analysis may provide the basis for the testing of a hypothesis or answering the questions related to the survey. It may also provide the basis for further and more detailed research.

The four main methods of collecting information are as follows:

1. **Face-to-face interviews.** These are probably the best way of obtaining accurate and up-to-date information. A good interviewer will draw the right information out of the respondents and encourage them to be honest. However, this form of interviewing can be time-consuming and expensive, particularly if the respondents need to be visited.

2. **Telephone interviews.** Though this method is cheaper, with a saving on travel costs, some respondents might find this sort of interviewing intrusive. They may also be less willing to provide certain answers over the phone. If the phone book is used for producing a sampling frame, this would not include people who were ex-directory.

3. **Postal questionnaires.** As these do not require trained interviewers, they are a relatively cheap method of collecting information. However, response rates are usually low and even 30 per cent would be considered high. Such a poor response might introduce bias into the sample where a large number of respondents with a particular view express their feelings through the

questionnaire. Others may find the questionnaire difficult to fill in, and therefore become under-represented.

4. **Direct observation.** This can be a useful and convenient way of collecting information. For example, it may be possible to count the number of customers entering a store. Remote monitoring is an extension of direct observation – details of viewer TV habits can be collected electronically.

Whichever method of data collection is used, there is a problem of non-response. In some cases a poor response rate may be simply because the respondent is busy. Where this happens follow-up interviews or postal reminders can prompt a response. As some people who do not answer the questionnaire might have different views from others, their response may be particularly valuable.

TASK

Which method of data collection would you use in each of the following instances?

1. A local authority wants to know if there are enough car-parking spaces for shoppers in town.

2. A local politician wants to estimate the support for his or her party.

3. A large consumer goods organisation is planning to launch a new food product into a competitive sector.

Sample frame

Surveys may either be carried out on people or upon observable events. For example, a survey may attempt to assess the purchasing habits of a group within the population. Alternatively, it may be used on a production line to assess quality.

In obtaining information, the ideal situation would be to interview every member of the target group or to monitor all performances. This is known as a **census**. However, in most instances, this would be impractical because of the sheer size of the task and the cost and time involved. By **sampling**, it is possible to obtain conclusions by putting questions to a group which is representative of a larger

number of respondents. There are two rules which must be followed when sampling:

1. *A sample must always be of at least a certain size*. In most instances, the larger the sample, the more reliance can be placed upon the results as truly representative of the targeted group.

2. *Each item should have an equal chance of being chosen*. This is known as random sampling. Provided a sample is chosen at random, then there is a good chance that a representative cross-section will be chosen.

It is claimed that any sample chosen on the basis of a subjective method will introduce some element of bias. In fact, most errors of bias occur because of the human element. For example, imagine trying to base a random sample upon the *Yellow Pages*. Bias may be introduced because:

- some traders do not appear in the directory
- the eye may be drawn to larger, more prominent advertisements
- anyone with a popular surname would stand out less
- the directory may be out of date.

The individual items chosen by a sampling technique are known as sample units; and a **sampling frame** is the list of all the units in a population as far as they can be ascertained (see Figure 18.3). In a random sample each item in the sampling frame has an equal chance of being chosen. If the sampling frame is incomplete or inaccurate, then so will be the sample that is drawn from it. The accuracy of the sample in estimating the attributes of the population will also depend upon:

- the size of the sample (the larger the sample, the greater the probability that it is representative of the population)
- the sampling method used
- the range of values in the population (the greater the

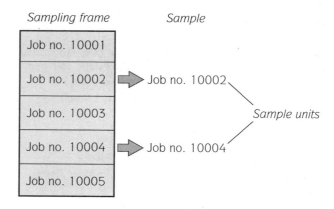

Figure 18.3 *Sampling frame*

variability of the population, the more difficult it will be to construct a representative sample).

Sampling methods

A number of sampling methods have been developed to address the problems of obtaining a representative sample in different circumstances. These include the following:

1. Simple random sampling. This is a straightforward approach and is the preferred method where the whole population can be included in the sampling frame. As its name implies, a data number is assigned to each sample unit and random numbers are generated to choose the sample. Each item has an equal chance of being selected for the sample.

Random numbers can be taken from random number tables (see Figure 18.4 for an example) or can be generated on a spreadsheet using the =RND() function (Microsoft Excel). Numbers are chosen from the random number table by reference to the highest data entity number.

2. Stratified sampling. One criticism of simple random sampling is that it may not accurately reflect the weighting of different groups within the population. Stratified sampling ensures that the different groups are properly represented and allows the random selection of items within each group.

Many manufacturers of complex engineering products monitor the cost of materials by constructing their own index of material costs. Materials used may fall into distinct groups whose costs are subject to different market conditions. Groups could be steel, wiring, mechanical components, electrical components, computer chips, paints and packaging materials. Once each group has been weighted according to the latest purchase value, individual items within each stock group can be selected using random numbers.

As stratified sampling is used for large populations where there are distinct groups of items, it can result in valuable information about each group in the population. For example, for a particular year, it may be found that packaging costs are up 20 per cent and the cost of computer chips is down 50 per cent.

3. Systematic sampling. Systematic sampling can be used where the sample must be a certain percentage of the population, even if the population size is unknown at the outset. It is often used for quality control checks, with items chosen at regular intervals having taken the first item on a random basis. For example, if it is decided that 1 per

23	46	69	49	07	79	04	30	57	04	92	47	80	45	76	15	09	57	54	82
19	98	14	02	08	61	84	80	06	40	38	83	55	04	14	87	38	83	06	23
90	27	57	32	87	03	95	63	75	46	09	57	31	98	62	38	20	13	08	24
10	24	54	22	56	15	68	68	69	74	44	97	60	54	70	75	17	99	64	88
67	04	59	25	62	13	37	81	68	75	23	57	65	92	83	09	48	39	69	32
39	27	73	36	12	87	05	51	25	39	96	33	38	31	58	19	25	47	28	28
31	96	70	20	33	52	23	24	59	13	55	92	18	20	10	82	55	97	05	21
19	02	98	36	30	04	80	99	70	37	70	18	97	35	49	48	74	40	68	82
04	72	58	53	59	40	15	59	62	91	43	48	17	10	52	27	14	25	02	44
60	07	25	77	59	26	54	98	19	62	83	20	75	32	35	60	93	49	69	90
33	15	32	32	47	26	44	60	03	89	46	40	98	43	46	43	55	39	73	44
13	87	96	57	90	84	38	28	44	78	03	61	11	80	63	80	04	60	91	66
10	03	55	86	02	20	23	66	59	26	82	58	69	28	12	34	60	03	24	07
11	94	39	62	06	12	58	92	61	59	63	09	28	84	47	01	47	26	28	74
12	12	04	56	29	45	56	21	61	65	71	63	24	96	50	99	94	97	01	14
48	61	95	93	82	87	24	08	82	93	59	91	59	30	90	26	29	62	60	76
23	82	44	31	83	81	16	85	00	68	05	69	20	56	86	38	18	37	70	26
19	93	28	02	10	77	01	13	81	87	15	02	04	90	66	82	38	48	80	29
06	11	25	65	13	53	08	06	89	02	31	35	94	70	38	62	37	97	78	98
97	57	86	64	84	02	02	76	91	14	06	45	16	82	23	07	31	44	71	05

Figure 18.4 *Random number table*

During a particular month there were 450 instances of workers recording 'idle time' on their time sheets. An investigation to find reasons for this unproductive labour cost is to be based on a sample of 50 labour bookings. Each of the 450 occurrences is assigned a number and a random number table (see Figure 18.4) is to be used to select the sample.

Starting at a random point in the table, it is possible to work along the rows or down the columns to select data entity numbers. Taking as a starting point the sixth column of four digits, the first numbers are as follows:

Table		Use	
92	47	924	7
38	83	388	3
09	57	095	7
44	97	449	7
23	57	235	7

The population of labour bookings has three digits (450) so taking the first three digits from 92 47 gives 924. This is too high a number, so is ignored. The next four bookings to be taken from the sampling frame have numbers 388, 95, 449 and 235. When the bottom of the column is reached it is necessary to start at the top of the table again using the next three unused digits. The procedure is continued until the 50 numbers have been obtained.

is taken at the same time every day, when in fact the quality of work may not be uniform throughout the day.

Although bias can be introduced into systematic sampling, for example if the sampling frame is not truly random and the sample interval is inappropriate, in its basic form it is a random method where individual items have an equal chance of selection. However, there may be circumstances where items should not be given equal weighting in the selection process.

To ensure material usage is being properly controlled, it has been decided to obtain a sample of 30 stock-issue notes to check authorisation signatures. The total number of stock issues during the period under review was 695 and each stock-issue note had been referenced from 1 to 695 accordingly. Using a random number table and starting from column 1, identify the 30 issue notes to be investigated.

4. Quota sampling. The sampling methods described so far have resulted in the random selection of items. In the case of quota sampling, items are not preselected but are chosen by the person collecting the data. The only stipulation is that there should be a fixed quota, either in total or for known groups in the population. For example, when investigating reasons for job cost overruns, it may be decided that ten jobs should be reviewed in each of three production departments. The method introduces bias in the sampling process as matters of convenience may decide the selection of specific jobs. Despite this, the method is widely used in practice because it is simple to carry out and it minimises the time spent on investigative exercises.

Sample error

A precise measure of a data set can only be achieved by undertaking a census of the whole population. Samples are inaccurate for what they leave out of the analysis, so it follows that the bigger the sample, the more accurate the analysis. Sampling error can occur where:

- the sampling frame is incomplete – for example records are excluded because it would be inconvenient and time-consuming to visit a distant location

cent of items are to be checked and the first item chosen was the 46th item, subsequent items would be the 146th, 246th, 346th and so on.

It is important that the interval between selections does not coincide with a regular pattern in the data set. For example, a quality check sample based on an interval of 100 may not be appropriate for a business that also produces 100 items a day. The result will be that the sample

- there is subjective choice in which items will be sampled
- the sample is not strictly adhered to – for example where records are missing
- the sample frame for systematic sampling is not randomly organised.

TASK

Diverse Engineering Ltd works as a sub-contractor for the manufacture of electrical components. The firm has experienced a wide range of gross margin percentages on individual jobs which the factory director suspects is due to poor price estimating on work passing through the machine shop. Over the past year, the business has completed 250 jobs with the following numbers for each factory department: 157 machining, 203 fabrication work, 98 assembly of supplied components. Analysis is to be based upon a sample of 40 jobs completed during the year.

1. Describe how each of the sampling methods could be used by Diverse Engineering.

2. Evaluate the advantages and disadvantages of each method for this particular exercise.

Despite these problems samples are widely used to estimate population characteristics such as mean and standard deviation. It is therefore important to recognise that even when you are using a sampling method that results in true random selection, there will always be the potential for error. The calculation of the sample mean will only be an approximation of the population mean.

Questionnaire design

The design of a questionnaire is fundamental to the success of any survey. A questionnaire is a systematic list of questions designed to elicit information from respondents about:

- specific events
- their attributes

- their values
- their beliefs.

Designing a good questionnaire is not easy. A badly constructed one can irritate the respondent and affect the quality of the data collected, maybe even leading to biased results. Another problem may arise if very few completed forms are returned, or if those returned are only partially completed. In addition, if the questionnaire is being administered by an interviewer, there is always the danger that the interviewer may misinterpret the question and introduce his or her own bias in a way that prompts certain answers from the respondents.

Before administering a questionnaire the best way to check it is to carry out a **pilot survey**. This will identify any potential problems with the questionnaire's design and will help to avoid the waste of time, money and effort that results from a defective survey.

The language used within a questionnaire is particularly important. It must be neutral and easy to understand and not be designed to influence the opinions of the respondent. Questions should be phrased as unambiguously as possible to avoid any misunderstandings. For example, it would be wrong to phrase a question, 'Do you make a habit of visiting restaurants?' as the question lacks precision. It is also important not to use pompous, technical or unusual words which might confuse the respondent.

A good questionnaire will:

- ask questions which relate directly to information needs
- not ask too many questions
- not ask leading or intimate questions
- fit questions into a logical sequence
- use the language of the target group
- not use ambiguous questions
- avoid questions relating to sexuality, politics and religion unless they are relevant to the survey
- not rely upon the memory of the respondent, particularly if it is an event of many years past
- include 'check questions', where you expect people to provide unreliable answers. For example, people often round off their ages to the lowest decade. A date of birth question could be inserted later in the form to double-check their first answer.

Sequencing the questions logically is very important. It may be useful to start with a few factual questions which are easy to respond to. These may be followed up by some form of multiple-choice questions before introducing questions that require the respondent to think about the issues to be researched. The questionnaire may be closed with 'filter questions' which help to locate the respondent in the sampling frame.

The questions in a questionnaire may be 'open' or 'closed'. **Open questions** allow the respondent to give an opinion and may encourage him or her to talk at length. **Closed questions** usually require answers picked from a range of options (which may be simply yes/no). Most questionnaires use closed questions (see the examples in Figure 18.5), so that they can be answered quickly and efficiently, and the answers are easier to analyse. The purpose of closed questions is to get respondents to commit themselves to a concrete answer. The problem with open questions is that they are difficult to analyse. Closed questions tie respondents down so that they have to make decisions within a limited range of choices.

Which of the following banks do you have an account with?
(Tick the relevant boxes)
Abbey National ☐
Barclays ☐
Lloyds TSB ☐
HSBC ☐
Nat Westminster ☐
Yorkshire ☐

Do you like the layout of our new shops?
Very good ☐ Good ☐ Satisfactory ☐ Poor ☐ Very poor ☐

Figure 18.5 *Some examples of closed questions*

To help interviewers operate a questionnaire, sometimes a **prompt card** is used. This means that, if several or all of the questions in the questionnaire have the same range or set of answers, these can be numbered and the respondents' answers can be recorded as numbers (see Figure 18.6).

Abbey National	01
Barclays	02
Lloyds TSB	03
HSBC	04
Nat West	05
Yorkshire	06

Figure 18.6 *An interviewer's prompt card*

Some questionnaires are designed so that respondents can concentrate on the questions that are relevant, and then skip over questions that do not relate to them.

Question 6 *Do you have a bank account with Barclays?*
Yes ☐
No ☐
If your answer is No proceed to question 20.

Figure 18.7 *Respondents can skip irrelevant questions*

Remember that once the questionnaire has been compiled it should be piloted. The pilot survey should be a small-scale replica of the actual survey and should endeavour to duplicate the same conditions.

Case Study

Consumer survey

Look at the extract from the survey in Figure 18.8 and work in small groups to answer the questions below.

PERSONAL INFORMATION

1. What is your occupation?

Clerical	☐	Shop assistant	☐
Director	☐	Skilled tradesperson	☐
Manager	☐	Student	☐
Manual	☐	Teacher	☐
Professional	☐	Unemployed	☐
Retired	☐	Other	☐
Self-employed	☐		

2. Do you work from home?
Yes ☐
No ☐

3. Do you run a business from your home address?
Yes ☐
No ☐

4. Are you considering setting up your own business?
Yes ☐
No ☐

5. Do you own a personal computer?
Yes ☐
No ☐

6. Are you connected to the Internet?
Yes ☐
No ☐

Continues

7. Would you consider running a franchise?

Already running one ☐   No ☐

Yes ☐

8. With training, would you consider selling any of the following products?

Financial services ☐   Cosmetics ☐
Home improvements ☐

9. Do you own a mobile phone?

Yes ☐

No ☐

10. Which income group are you in?

Up to £5000 ☐   £20 001–£30 000 ☐
£5000–£10 000 ☐   £30 001+–£40 000 ☐
£10 001–£15 000 ☐   £40 000+ ☐
£15 001–£20 000 ☐

11. How many children live in your household?

None ☐   Three ☐
One ☐   Four or more ☐
Two ☐

12. Please give the date of birth and sex of each child.

1 ☐D☐D☐M☐M☐Y☐Y   Boy ☐   Girl ☐
2 ☐D☐D☐M☐M☐Y☐Y   Boy ☐   Girl ☐
3 ☐D☐D☐M☐M☐Y☐Y   Boy ☐   Girl ☐

13. How many credit cards to you have?

One ☐   Three ☐
Two ☐   Four or more ☐

Figure 18.8 *Consumer survey*

Questions

1. Identify the probable purposes of at least one question in the survey. What sort of information might this question elicit?

2. Comment upon the presentation of the survey. What might be the potential problems for the respondent?

3. Give an example from the survey of what you would consider to be (a) a good question, and (b) a poor question.

4. If you were managing such a survey, how would you encourage consumers to fill it in?

INTERPRETATION OF CHARTS

How data are presented largely determines the effectiveness of the data handling exercise. The recipient of the information has to understand it before he or she can act upon it. The use of summary tables and graphical presentations can be a valuable part of the communications process.

Information can be displayed in the form of a frequency distribution or table, as a chart or as a graph. The nature of the data collected and the circumstances for which they are needed will determine the way in which data are presented.

Graphical and diagrammatic presentations

Charts are eye-catching and enable information to be presented in a form that can be readily understood. A chart or graphical presentation may make information more meaningful.

A **pictogram** is a diagrammatic form of display which uses pictures instead of numbers (see Figure 18 9). The symbols used in the pictogram must be simple, and items represented by a symbol must be shown in a key.

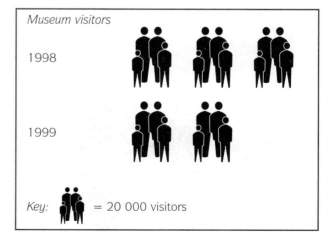

Figure 18.9 *Pictogram of the number of visitors to a museum, 1998–9*

In a **pie chart**, each slice represents a component's contribution to the total amount. The 360° of the circle is divided up in proportion to the figures obtained. The area of each segment of the pie is in proportion to the values or **frequencies** of each class of data.

Check your understanding

To prepare a pie chart to show batch sizes, first divide up the 360° of the pie according to the relative size of each variable in the data set.

Batch size	Frequency	Degrees
100	8	96
200	5	60
300	11	132
400	4	48
500	2	24
	30	360

The number of degrees to represent each batch size is calculated by comparing the frequency for each class with the total frequencies recorded:

$$\text{Degrees} = \frac{\text{Frequency of item}}{\text{Total number of frequencies}} \times 360 \text{ degrees}$$

For example, the degrees for batch size of 100:

$$= \frac{8}{30} \times 360 \text{ degrees} = 96 \text{ degrees}$$

Using a protractor, the pie chart can now be drawn (see Figure 18.10).

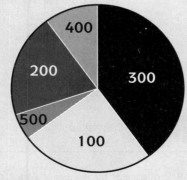

Figure 18.10 *Pie chart of batch sizes*

Bar charts are an easily understood medium that can be used to good effect in business. Bar charts are drawn against a horizontal axis describing the variables, and a vertical axis showing value. The height of each bar corresponds to the frequency for each variable. In general, bar charts are used with **qualitative** and discrete **quantitative** variables (described below). However, classes of **continuous data** (see below) can be presented, provided the labels make clear that the horizontal axis is not a continuous scale. For the discrete data example, in Figure 18.11, even if the batch sizes had increased by irregular amounts (say 100, 250 and 500 items), it would still have been acceptable to space the bars equally as the batch sizes are labels only. To show the discrete nature of the data, each bar is separated by a space.

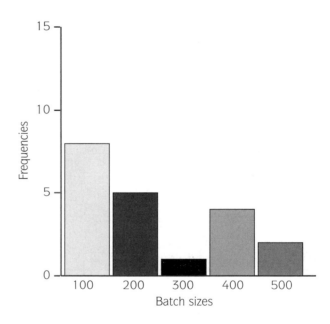

Figure 18.11 *Bar chart of batch sizes*

FREQUENCY DISTRIBUTIONS

A **variable** is a piece of data that has been measured or observed, for example the unit cost of products or labour wage rates. A **data set** is a list of the variables that have been collected. It may be the whole population of variables or a sample from that population.

A variable may be either **qualitative** in the sense that the label given to the variable is not numerically significant, for example cars categorised according to colour; or the variable may be **quantitative** that is it is expressed in numerical terms, such as production batches being grouped by their size (batches of 100, 200, 300, etc.).

Quantitative data can be further analysed into whether they are continuous or discrete. **Continuous data** are characterised by many possible values, where the incidence of any one value will be correspondingly low. For example, the amount of time taken to do a task can be measured down to minutes and seconds.

Discrete data have distinct values that are not subdivided with intermediate values, for example the number of tasks needed to complete a job or the number of doors on a car. Discrete data are often characterised by whole numbers but not necessarily so. For example, standard hourly rates of pay of £3.65, £4.50 and £5.80 are discrete items against which the numbers of workers can be recorded. In this example, it is not possible for workers to earn £3.80 per hour.

As data come in, the likelihood is that they will not be in any kind of order. By introducing order we can begin to understand something of the values and concentrations of the values being presented.

Generation from raw data

An **array** is a simple arrangement of figures into ascending or descending values. The number of days' credit for 20 customers varies as follows:

| 12 | 21 | 32 | 65 | 18 | 20 | 14 | 51 | 81 | 32 |
| 31 | 45 | 16 | 51 | 71 | 40 | 24 | 32 | 18 | 33 |

We can arrange this in ascending order:

| 12 | 14 | 16 | 18 | 18 | 20 | 21 | 24 | 31 | 32 |
| 32 | 32 | 33 | 40 | 45 | 51 | 51 | 65 | 71 | 81 |

Tally marks are a quick and useful method of counting totals by displaying them in the form of matchsticks. After every four marks, the fifth crosses through the previous four, so totals can be easily counted. The average age of a

company's employees could be presented in tabular form, as shown in Figure 18.12, to develop a frequency table.

Age range	Tally marks	Number of employees
Under 20	II	2
21–30	IIII IIII I	11
31–40	IIII IIII II	12
41–50	IIII III	8
51–60	IIII	5
Over 60	III	3
Total employees		41

Figure 18.12 *Using tally marks to construct a frequency table*

Check your understanding

Look at the following sample of factory batch sizes:

300 100 500 200 100 400 300 300 100 400

100 100 200 300 100 300 300 400 300 200

300 100 500 400 300 300 200 100 200 300

A frequency table is prepared after tallying the frequency of each batch size (see Figure 18.13).

Batch size	Frequency	Cumulative frequency
100	8	8
200	5	13
300	11	24
400	4	28
500	2	30
	30	

Figure 18.13 *Frequency table of batch sizes*

The **cumulative frequency** (running total of frequencies, see page 456) is useful to demonstrate the number of frequencies falling in a range of variables. For example, 80 per cent ($\frac{24}{30}$) batches do not exceed 300 items.

Grouping

Frequency tables can be developed where a variable occurs a number of times. They simply summarise the data by grouping together the same variables. The frequency table is suitable for qualitative and discrete quantitative data.

Where there are large number of variables, presentation may be improved if frequencies are grouped into classes. This technique is particularly appropriate for continuous quantitative data or where the number of discrete values is too great to provide a clear summary of the data. The resulting table is called a grouped frequency table.

Class boundaries

The following data describe the time taken to inspect a sample of 30 stock deliveries received by a factory:

Minutes

4.5	8.7	6.7	10.6	13.8	5.0	11.8	7.0	12.0	10.1
11.2	18	15.2	10.1	7.0	9.1	12.3	8.4	13.8	13.2
16.4	7.3	13.0	12.4	22.2	10	5.4	8.1	10.9	14.4

Figure 18.14 shows how a frequency table of the data would be constructed. The number and size of each class is a matter of judgement, but between five and 12 classes can show trends without losing the benefits of summarised data.

Inspection in minutes	*Frequency*	*Cumulative frequency*
5–7	7	7
8–10	7	14
11–13	9	23
14–16	5	28
17–19	1	29
20–22	1	30
	30	

Figure 18.14 *Frequency table of inspection times*

For further analysis it is essential to understand the boundaries of each class of data. Where there are continuous data, it is particularly important to define class boundaries clearly as the boundaries are often not the same as the specified class limits. For example, in the 8–10 minutes class in the frequency table in Figure 18.14, values ending in 0.5 of a minute are rounded up to the next class (see Figure 18.15).

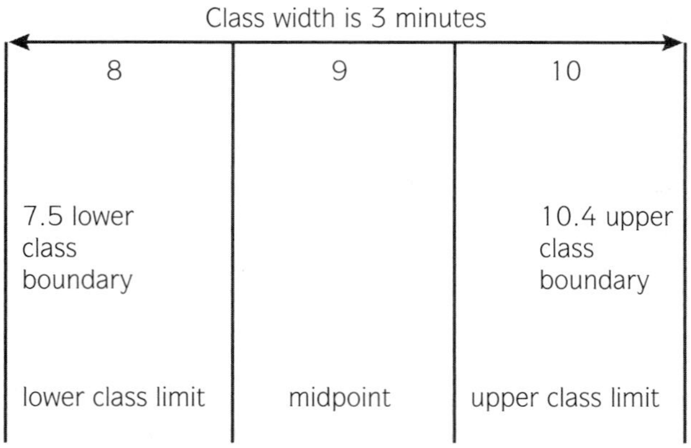

Figure 18.15 *Definition of class boundaries*

TASK

The following number of machine breakdowns has occurred each hour over a 40-hour week:

8	15	43	12	51	2	4	19
4	18	39	56	12	23	27	28
11	2	5	25	18	51	19	50
12	5	6	29	16	57	19	33
24	37	18	3	12	6	60	39

Construct a grouped frequency distribution from these data using: (a) six class intervals of equal width, (b) class intervals of ten.

Irregular intervals/histograms

A **histogram** is a variation of a bar chart in which it is the area, and not necessarily the height, of the bar that represents the frequency. Where the bars are of equal width, there are regular class intervals and the height of the bar is then proportional to the class frequency. However, there may be irregular intervals for ranges of data where few items are recorded. In these circumstances it may be appropriate to increase the class widths.

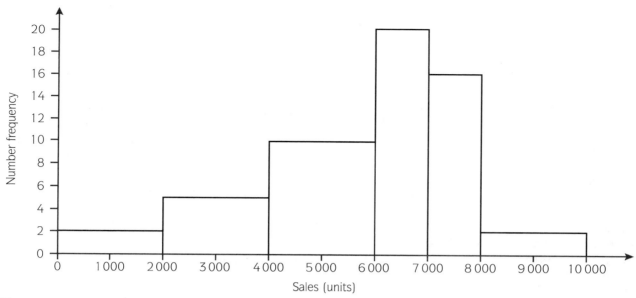

Figure 18.16 *Histogram of frequency of sales*

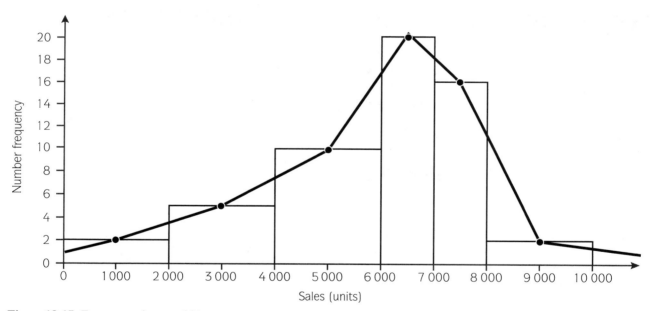

Figure 18.17 *Frequency polygon and histogram*

Look at the following data:

Sales per salesperson (units)	No. of salespersons
Up to 1 999	2
2 000–3 999	5
4 000–5 999	10
6 000–6 999	10
7 000–7 999	8
8 000–9 999	2

To construct a histogram, the first three bars will be the normal height; the fourth and fifth bars will need to be twice as high to compensate for £1000 being only half the standard class interval (see Figure 18.16).

Clearly, therefore, if the class intervals are different the height of each bar needs to be worked out. In many situations, however, it is more than likely that the class intervals will be the same and that this procedure will not be necessary, so that the histogram can be drawn straight from the frequency distribution.

Frequency polygons

Whereas bar charts and histograms are stepped graphs, it is sometimes desirable to show frequency distribution in the form of a single curve. Such a curve is known as a **frequency polygon**. It is drawn by constructing a histogram, marking off the mid-points of the top of each rectangle and then joining the mid points with straight lines (see Figure 18.17).

The curve of a frequency polygon is extended at both ends so that it cuts the axis at points half a class interval beyond the outside limits of the end classes. The area of the frequency polygon is exactly the same as that of a histogram, since the area lost as each rectangle is cut by the polygon has the same area as each triangle added. If the frequency polygon is smoothed out, it is known as a **frequency curve**.

REPRESENTATIVE VALUES

Having broken down the data into a manageable form, we need to be able to draw useful information from them. A measure of central tendency provides one method of doing this.

Mean, median and mode

Central tendency is a measure of middle values. When we talk about middle values, we normally think of an average. An average, as we know it, is an arithmetic mean, but two other measures of average or central tendency are the **median** and the **mode**. Each method of calculating the mean, median and mode will be demonstrated using the following data:

2   6   4   3   5   6   3   4   3   2

The median is the middle value in the data set. First it is necessary to sort the items by order of value:

2   2   3   3   3   4   4   5   6   6

As this is a data set with even numbers of items, there are two middle values, so it is necessary to take a simple average of the two values:

$$\text{Average} = \frac{3 + 4}{2} = 3.5.$$

The mode is the value that occurs most frequently. In this example the value 3 is the mode. Where there are two values that occur most frequently, then the distribution is said to be **bimodal**.

The median and mode are easy to calculate and both exclude extreme values in the distribution that may distort the identification of a typical value. The mean is calculated by adding all the values together and dividing by the number of items:

$$= \frac{2 + 6 + 4 + 3 + 5 + 6 + 3 + 4 + 3 + 2}{10} = 3.8.$$

Where the data is grouped the mean $= \dfrac{\Sigma fx}{\Sigma f}$

where f = frequencies, x = mid-point of each class.

Check your understanding

Look at the frequency table in Figure 18.18.

Inspections in minutes	Frequency	Mid-point	Frequency × mid-points
5–7	7	6.0	42.0
8–10	7	9.0	63.0
11–13	9	12.0	108.0
14–16	5	15.0	75.0
17–22	2	19.5	39.0
	30		327.0

Figure 18.18 *Frequency table of inspection times and mid-points*

To calculate the mean:

$$= \frac{327}{30} = 10.9 \text{ minutes.}$$

Unlike the median and mode, the mean considers all items in the data set to find a central point. This fact, however, also leads to the mean's disadvantage as it tends to be influenced by extreme values in the data set. Perhaps most importantly, however, the mean can be used with other mathematical techniques to interpret data further. The median and mode tend to have a limited application other than being averages that are simple to understand.

Calculation from raw data

A company's production levels over 50 days were as follows:

```
5   6   2   6   5   2   6   4   6   5
5   6   4   5   3   5   6   5   6   5
6   5   3   3   2   4   3   2   3   5
4   3   5   2   1   5   2   5   1   4
5   4   4   4   5   3   5   2   4   5
```

From these levels we can derive the frequency distribution as shown in Figure 18.19.

Daily production level (units)	Frequency	Level × frequency
1	2	2
2	7	14
3	7	21
4	10	40
5	16	80
6	8	48
	50	205

Figure 18.19 *Frequency distribution table of daily production*

As the mean is simply the total set of numbers divided by the number of items, to calculate this we could either:

1. add up all of the daily production levels and divide by 50 – this can be time-consuming and prone to error; or

2. use the frequency distribution table (see Figure 18.19) – by multiplying the value of daily production level by the frequency (f) with which it occurs, a similar total to 1 is achieved, which can then be divided by the number of days (50):

$$\text{Mean} = \frac{205}{50} = 4.1 \text{ units per day.}$$

The median is the middle number in a distribution or array of figures. In our distribution of 50 days' production levels we have an even number of figures. If we are calculating the median for a frequency distribution, it is usual to accept the middle value as $\frac{(n+1)}{2}$ if the total frequency (n) is an odd number, and as $\frac{n}{2}$ if the total frequency (n) is an even number. As we have 50 values, the median will be $\frac{50}{2}$ and therefore the 25th number. The 25th number reflects a daily production level of four units in ascending order.

If data are incomplete, the median can still be calculated. For example, if you do not have information about the amount of some lower or upper salaries but know how many employees you have, you can still determine the median item. Also, as the median uses only one value in a distribution, it is not changed or distorted by extremes.

Finding a mode in a grouped frequency distribution can be done only with approximate mathematical accuracy. The following figures relate to value and frequency:

Value	Frequency	
At least:	Less than:	
10	20	5
20	30	12
30	40	18
40	50	10
50	60	4

The mode is approximated by:

$$L + \left[\frac{(F - Fm - 1) \times c}{2F - Fm - 1 - Fm + 1} \right]$$

where

L	=	lower limit of modal class
$Fm-1$	=	frequency of class below modal class
F	=	frequency of modal class
$Fm+1$	=	frequency of class above modal class
c	=	class interval.

Our estimate of the mode would therefore be:

$$\text{Mode} = 30 + \left[\frac{(18 - 12) \times 10}{(2 \times 18) - 12 - 10} \right]$$

$$= 30 + \left[\frac{(6 \times 10)}{(36 - 22)} \right]$$

$$= 30 + 4.28$$

$$= 34.28.$$

Since when calculated this way the mode is only an estimated figure, its use is limited for further statistical processes.

Appropriate uses

Each average – whether mean, median or mode – possesses certain advantages and disadvantages in use. Some are more suitable than others, though this depends largely upon the kind of data to which they are applied. The benefit of using each of these forms of averages is that it is:

- easy to use
- easy to understand and interpret
- suitable for arithmetic interpretation.

The arithmetic mean is widely understood and its calculation is not complicated, though it may be lengthier than other averages. Though the value of every item is included in the distribution, and a few high or low values may distort the average, there is an arithmetic exactness about the figure. The arithmetic mean cannot be measured or checked by graphical methods and is not likely to correspond to any actual value in the distribution.

The mode is an actual value, representing the majority of cases, which is not made unrepresentative by extreme values. It is easy to understand and can be shown graphically. Where there are two or more modes (bimodal) with a widespread distribution, the mode loses its value as an average. The value of the mode can only be approximated over a grouped frequency distribution.

Extremely high or low values do not distort the median as a representative average. The median is an actual value which is readily obtained even if we do not know the values of all of the items. Though the median gives the value of only one (the middle) item, the surrounding items may have the same value. However, if the number of items are spread erratically above or below it, the median may lose its value as a representative figure.

TASK

Comment upon the use of the average for representing the information in Figure 18.20. In what other ways could the information be meaningfully analysed?

	April				
	1992	1993	1994	1995	1996
Male	306.1	317.2	325.0	338.2	352.9
Female	215.9	221.2	230.5	241.2	248.7

Figure 18.20 *Average gross weekly earnings (full time) (£), East Midlands, 1992–6*

CUMULATIVE FREQUENCY

Cumulative frequency involves the adding of successive additions as frequencies are recorded. As they are cumulative the frequencies build up. For example, look at the table of salaries in Figure 18.21. The *'cum' less* column at any one stage shows the total number of workers earning less than the upper limit of that particular class interval. For example, 404 workers earned less than £39 000. The *'cum' more* column shows at any stage the number of workers earning more than the lower limit of that class interval. For example, 96 workers earn more than £40 000. Cumulative frequency curves can then be drawn from the table using straight lines to join each of the points in the graphs (see Figure 18.22a and b). (These curves are often known as **ogives**, which is a term similarly used in architecture to describe an 'S' shape.)

Salary (£000)	No. of workers	'Cum' less	'Cum' more
10–19	50	50	500
20–29	234	284	450
30–39	120	404	216
40–49	80	484	96
50 and over	16	500	16
	500		

Figure 18.21 *Monthly salaries*

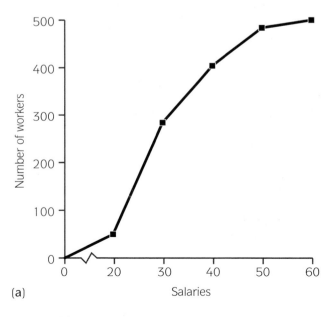

(a)

Figure 18.22a *Cumulative less than frequency curve*

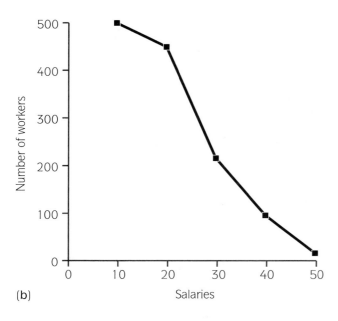

(b)

Salaries

Figure 18.22b *Cumulative more than frequency curve*

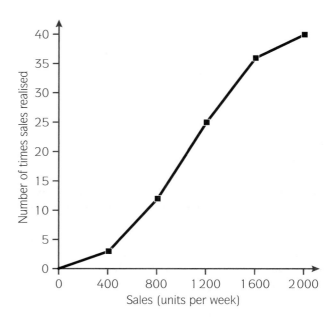

Sales (units per week)

Figure 18.24 *An ogive*

Tables and charts

Graphs show the relationship between two variables and can be presented in the form of either a straight line or a curve. Whereas frequency polygons show frequency distribution (see page 450), cumulative frequencies of a distribution are represented by an ogive in a graph. Figure 18.24 depicts a firm's sales totals over 40 weeks as shown in Figure 18.23. Any point on the graph will not relate sales achievements directly to output in the same way as an ordinary graph, but it will indicate how many times the number of sales units (or less than that number) was achieved.

Output (units)	No. of times sales realised (weeks)	Cumulative frequency
0– 400	3	3
401– 800	9	3 + 9 = 12
801–1 200	13	3 + 9 + 13 = 25
1 201–1 600	11	3 + 9 + 13 + 11 = 36
1 601–2 000	4	3 + 9 + 13 + 11 + 4 = 40
	40	

Figure 18.23 *Sales totals*

TASK

You work for a building society in Bristol and have been asked by your branch manager to present the following information in a graphical form as part of an exploration of your branch's activities:

Percentage of loans granted

House prices (£)	Buyers
Under 50 000	3
50 000–99 999	7
100 000–149 000	44
150 000–199 000	38
200 000–249 000	18
250 000–299 000	6

1. Draw a histogram and frequency polygon.

2. Construct a cumulative frequency table and use it to draw an ogive.

A **Lorenz curve** is a form of cumulative frequency curve which can be used to demonstrate the disparity between a range of actual distribution and a line of equal distribution, thereby highlighting the equality or inequality of any range of distribution.

Probably the most common application of the Lorenz curve is to highlight the distribution of wealth within a society. By glancing at a Lorenz curve (see Figure 18.25), it is possible to relate levels of equality or inequality. For example, if the distribution is completely even, this shows that wealth is spread evenly between members of society (there is no concentration of wealth). If the distribution is uneven (a feature of all societies), then this will appear as a difference between the line showing the actual distribution of wealth and a line of equal distribution. In Figure 18.25 we can quickly see that the distribution of wealth in country A is far more even than in country B.

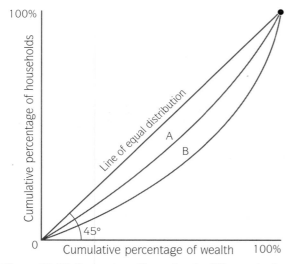

Figure 18.25 *Lorenz curve illustrating the differences in the distribution of wealth in two countries*

It is possible to draw a Lorenz curve to show the relationship between the size of an organisation and the output of the industry in which it operates. In Figure 18.26,

No. of employees	No. of firms	Output (tonnes)
Under 50	40	3 000
50–99	80	12 000
100–199	120	21 000
200–299	135	48 000
300 and over	25	36 000
	400	120 000

Figure 18.26 *Numbers of employees and output*

the size of the firm is measured by the number of employees. In order to construct a Lorenz curve, these figures need to be broken down further. Figure 18.27 includes a column that calculates each figure as a percentage of its column total, as well as a column that lists the cumulative total percentages; the cumulative total percentages are the figures required to construct the curve (see Figure 18.28). If all firms were of equal size, then 25 per cent of output would have been produced by 25 per cent of the firms and this would be represented by the line of equal distribution. The extent to which the Lorenz curve deviates away from the line of equal distribution reflects the degree of inequality.

No. of firms			Output (tonnes)		
No.	%	Cumulative %	No.	%	Cumulative %
40	10	10	3 000	2.5	2.5
80	20	30	12 000	10.0	12.5
120	30	60	21 000	17.5	30.0
135	34	94	48 000	40.0	70.0
25	6	100	36 000	30.0	100.0
400	100		120 000	100.0	

Figure 18.27 *Cumulative total percentages*

The Lorenz curve in Figure 18.28 shows that, as we would expect, large firms generate more output. By looking at the curve at its furthest point from the equal distribution line, we can see that 60 per cent of firms control 30 per cent of output, and so it is clearly not equally shared.

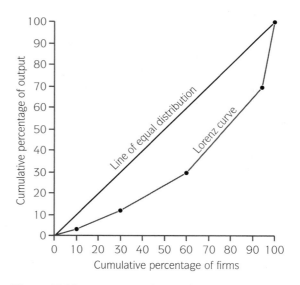

Figure 18.28 *Lorenz curve showing the distribution of production between firms*

TASK

A market research agency is undertaking a survey on behalf of a company concerned about falling sales in a town in Scotland. The company is particularly interested in changes in the distribution of wealth caused by recent factory closures and increasing unemployment levels. After an extensive survey involving a carefully worded questionnaire, the agency has extracted the figures shown in Figure 18.29 relating to the spread of wealth in the area.

Wealth (£ per adult)	No of people	Total wealth (£m)
Under 10 000	1 200	9.5
10 000–49 999	1 500	52.5
50 000–99 999	1 300	97.0
100 000–149 999	400	50.0
Over 150 000	100	20.0
	4 500	229.0

Figure 18.29 *Distribution of wealth*

1. Construct a Lorenz curve.

2. Comment upon the distribution shown by the graph.

Interquartile range (IQR) and percentiles

Although averages are important in providing us with information about the middle of a distribution, they do not tell us how other figures in the distribution are spread. Information might reveal the same mean, but the spread of some data might be tight while others might be well dispersed.

A **range** represents the difference between the highest and lowest values in a set of data. It is easy to find and provides information about a spread of figures:

Range = Highest value – Lowest value.

The problem with looking at a range is that it might be affected by one extreme value and it provides no indication of the spread between values. The range for 4, 4, 4, 4, 4 and 20 000 is 4 to 20 000. This is misleading in terms of both values and the spread between the extremes. This disadvantage can be overcome and extreme values can be ignored by slicing away the top and bottom quarters and then analysing what is left.

Whereas the median is the middle number of an array of figures and represents 50 per cent, a **quartile** represents one quarter or 25 per cent of a range. The lower or first quartile is the area below which 25 per cent of observations fall, and the upper or fourth quartile is the value above which 25 per cent of observations fall:

Interquartile range = Upper quartile – lower quartile.

From this, conclusions can be drawn about the middle 50 per cent of data analysed.

Check your understanding

We can extract the lower quartile, median, upper quartile and interquartile range from the following array of 20 numbers:

4	5	8	9	15	18	20	22	24	29
32	35	37	40	44	44	48	52	58	60

The lower quartile will be the value below which 25 per cent of the numbers will fall and therefore be 25 per cent of 20 and the fifth value of 15. Using $\frac{n}{2}$, the median will be $\frac{20}{2}$ giving the tenth value. This is 29.

The upper quartile will be the value above which 25 per cent of the numbers fall. As there are 20 values in the array, it will be 75 per cent of 20 and the fifteenth value is 44.

Whereas the range for this set of figures is 54 and extends from 4 to 60, the interquartile range will be the upper quartile of 44 less the lower quartile of 15 which is 29.

Although the interquartile range, or **quartile deviation**, is easy to understand and is unaffected by extreme values, it might not be precise enough for a large sample. In these instances it could be necessary to use **deciles** or **percentiles**. Deciles relate to the various tenths of a distribution. From our example, the first decile will be 10 per cent of 20 and the second value of 5; the second decile will be the fourth value of 9; and so on. Percentiles relate to hundredths of the way through a distribution. The 95th percentile of our values will be 95 per cent of the 20 values and so therefore will be the nineteenth value of 58.

MEASURES OF DISPERSION

As we have seen, while the average of a set of data gives a central value, additional measures are required to determine how values are spread around this central point.

Definition and use of the range

Consider the following distributions:

Group A:	15	16	18	20	21
Group B:	5	10	17	25	33

Both groups have a mean of 18, but the distribution in Group A is much less dispersed than in Group B. As we have seen, the range takes into account the difference between highest and lowest values by taking the difference between the highest and lowest values in the data set. So, for Group A the range is 6, and for Group B it is 28. Although simple in concept, the range does provide a measure of dispersion that is easily understood and is a valuable addition to the knowledge about the central value.

The disadvantage of the range is that it considers extreme values only and does not describe how the items are spread within the range. The two distributions in Figure 18.30 have the same range, but clearly the values in Machine Shop A are more concentrated around a central point than in Machine Shop B.

Machine shop A

Scale – minutes	11 12 13 14 15 16 17 18 19 20
Readings	⊙ ⊙⊙ ⊙⊙⊙⊙⊙⊙⊙ ⊙ ⊙⊙

Machine shop B

Scale – minutes	11 12 13 14 15 16 17 18 19 20
Readings	⊙⊙ ⊙ ⊙⊙⊙⊙⊙ ⊙⊙ ⊙⊙ ⊙ ⊙

Figure 18.30 *Machine shop readings*

IQR and standard deviation

As we saw earlier, the interquartile range (IQR) is the difference between the upper and lower quartiles and thus includes the middle half of the observations when they are put into an ascending order of magnitude. Unlike the range, it is not likely to be affected by a few extreme values and so is thus a more robust statistic, particularly useful for describing skew distributions.

One measure of dispersion that further analyses a group of values and makes use of all observations is the **mean deviation**. This measures the average of all values in a distribution from the mean. When it averages the differences between the actual values in a distribution and the mean, it ignores the negative signs of differences. For the figures of 5, 6, 13, 20 and 26, the arithmetic mean (x) is:

$$\frac{5 + 6 + 13 + 20 + 26}{5} = \frac{70}{5} = 14.$$

The differences from the arithmetic mean are:

$$5 - 14, 6 - 14, 13 - 14, 20 - 14, 26 - 14$$

and these are:

$$-9, -8, -1, 6, 12.$$

If we ignore the negative signs, we can find the mean deviation as follows:

$$\frac{9 + 8 + 1 + 6 + 12}{5} = \frac{36}{5} = 7.2.$$

The mean deviation or average differences from the mean is therefore 7.2, and the more usual way of expressing this is:

Mean deviation $= \dfrac{\Sigma(x - \bar{x})}{n}$

where $(x - \bar{x})$ means the difference between the mean and the actual value but ignoring the negative signs.

The major problem of all the methods of dispersion looked at so far is that they have limited uses in further analysing data. Having worked out a quartile or decile, you then know more about a distribution, but there are few further uses for this information. As the mean deviation ignores the plus and minus differences, it also has limited uses for statistical processing. This is not the case for the **variance** and **standard deviation**, which have widespread use in statistical analysis and are considered the most important measures of dispersion.

Instead of ignoring the minuses in differences from the mean, the variance and standard deviation square the differences, and this process instantly eliminates the negative signs. When the squared differences have been averaged, a variance is created and the square root of this variance provides the standard deviation. This can be seen more clearly from an example.

Check your understanding

If the output of a machine over five days was 4, 5, 5, 7 and 9 units, the arithmetic mean would be 6. The variance measures the extent of the dispersion around the mean by:

1. calculating the difference between the number of units produced each day and the arithmetic mean, shown as $x - \bar{x}$

2. squaring the difference $(x - \bar{x})^2$

3. finding the average of the total of these squared differences, shown as:

   $\left[\Sigma(x - \bar{x})^2\right]/n$, where n is the number of values (see Figure 18.31).

x	$x - \bar{x}$	$(x - \bar{x})^2$
4	−2	4
5	−1	1
5	−1	1
7	1	1
9	3	9
	$\overline{0}$	$\overline{16}$

Figure 18.31 *Output of a machine*

The variance would be:

$\dfrac{16}{5} = 3.2$ units.

The standard deviation is the square root of the variance. In our example this will be:

$\sqrt{3.2} = 1.79$ units.

Thus we have an arithmetic mean of 6 units, a variance of 3.2 and a standard deviation of 1.79 units. By taking into consideration frequency (f) and denoting standard deviation as s, we can show its formula as follows:

$$s = \sqrt{\frac{\Sigma f(x - \bar{x})^2}{n}} \quad \text{or} \quad \sqrt{\frac{\Sigma f(x - \bar{x})^2}{\Sigma f}}.$$

The example given in Figure 18.32 takes into consideration frequency and has an arithmetic mean ($\bar{x}$) of 6. The standard deviation will be $\sqrt{1.4} = 1.18$.

Value (x)	Frequency (f)	$x - \bar{x}$	$(x - \bar{x})^2$	$f(x - \bar{x})^2$
4	4	−2	4	16
5	6	−1	1	6
6	9	0	0	0
7	8	1	1	8
8	3	2	4	12
	$\overline{30}$			$\overline{42}$

Figure 18.32 *Calculating standard deviation*

Although it is sometimes difficult to understand the significance of standard deviation, it can be said that the greater the dispersion, the larger the standard deviation. As all values in the distribution are taken into account, it is a comprehensive measure of dispersion capable of being developed further.

Rentawash Ltd rents washing machines through its network of high street shops. As part of its rental agreement, the costs of all services and repairs not caused by improper use are suffered by the company. In previous years the mean cost of a call-out to a faulty washing machine has remained steady at around £35 for materials and labour. Costs of individual repairs have been distributed symmetrically around this mean with a standard deviation of £4.

The company's cost accountant is now concerned about the costs incurred in respect of a new model, the SF 102. An earlier investigation has satisfied the accountant that the actual number of call-outs in relation to the number of machines is not unusual.

The following sample of call-out costs relating to the SF 102 has been selected:

£32 £42 £39 £33 £57 £34 £35 £37 £32 £36

£39 £35 £38 £36 £37 £60 £36 £34 £33 £36

£36 £42 £40 £35 £33 £37 £35 £38 £51 £32

1. Construct a frequency table.

2. Calculate the mean, mode and median.

3. Draw a bar chart.

4. Calculate the variance and standard deviation.

5. Explain what your results show.

Case Study

Making the meaning of British Steel's results

The year ended 29 March 1997 proved to be a difficult one for British Steel due to weak prices in major markets and the strength of sterling. Despite these difficulties the business made a profit of £451m and earnings per share of 15.22p.

All UK businesses were affected by the pricing and currency situation, but Avesta Sheffield AB, British Steel's 51 per cent Swedish-owned stainless steel subsidiary, was particularly badly hit. Furthermore, it delayed commissioning and rationalisation costs so that its contribution to British Steel's results before tax for the year amounted to a loss of £7m compared with a profit the previous year of £228m.

Capital expenditure during the year amounted to £413m, the highest level since 1991. The largest project completed in the year was the new steelmaking and continuous casting plant and the upgrading of the hot steel mill in Alabama, USA.

During 1996/7 turnover, while 2 per cent higher than the previous year, included the full-year effect of the consolidation of Avesta Sheffield AB. For steel industry products, turnover of £6 327m and sales volume of 15.2 million tonnes (mt) were also affected by the consolidation effect. Setting this aside, there was a reduction in turnover of 6 per cent, an increase in sales volume of 2 per cent and average revenue per tonne down by 8 per cent.

In the UK, sales volume amounted to 7.5 mt, of which 6.6 mt were in British Steel's main finished products. UK demand for these products at 11.3 mt was 2 per cent below the level of the previous year, largely as a result of destocking.

Questions

1. What role do figures play in relaying information back to British Steel's stakeholders?

2. How might some of these stakeholders wish to analyse such data?

3. What other information might they require?

Use of spreadsheets

According to Laudon and Price Laudon (1991), 'Electronic spreadsheet software provides computerised versions of traditional financial modelling tools – the accountant's columnar pad, pencil and calculator'.

SALES OF POPULAR WINES							
BOTTLE	TOTAL JAN-JUN	TOTAL JUL-DEC	ANNUAL TOTAL	COST PRICE	STOCK VALUE	SELLING PRICE	PROFIT PER BOTTLE
CHABLIS	96	138		£5.30		13.25	
BEAUJOLAIS	120	138		£2.60		6.5	
BURGUNDY	150	156		£3.30		8.25	
CLARET	116	156		£3.30		8.25	
MERLOT	130	156		£1.90		4.75	
SHIRAZ CABERNET	155	156		£2.60		6.5	
RIOJA	143	156		£4.60		11.5	
SAUVIGNON	146	156		£2.60		6.5	
TOTAL							
AVERAGE							

Figure 18.33 *A computer spreadsheet*

A spreadsheet (see Figure 18.33) is organised in grids of columns and rows. Its greatest benefit for statistical analysis is that when one or more values are changed, all other related values on the spreadsheet are instantly computed. Spreadsheets are particularly valuable for applications where numerous calculations with pieces of data are related to each other, or for applications which require some form of 'modelling', as well as for considering the options from a decision through 'what-if' analysis, so that a number of alternatives can be quickly evaluated without the necessity of changing large amounts of data. Most spreadsheets include graphics functions which allow the user to present data in a variety of forms such as line graphs, bar graphs or pie charts.

Perhaps the most important aspect of spreadsheets is that you can define formulas within the spreadsheet, so that the computer will automatically undertake specific calculations. As a result, spreadsheets are used for many different purposes in which manipulating numbers in rows and columns can solve business problems.

Spreadsheets are not only helpful for generating information but also for communicating findings for other people. For example, using a spreadsheet it is possible to generate presentation graphics, so that results can be communicated professionally and graphically.

For numerical summaries, such as budgets and lists of expenses, spreadsheets can be used to compute totals, averages and other values. These applications allow totals and subtotals to be determined quickly and displayed. With a spreadsheet, by altering the variables, the user is effectively asking 'what if?' questions, which allows complex calculations and summaries to be determined. For example, a spreadsheet could be used to work out the rate of return on an investment over a 12-month period, with the user varying both the deposit and the rate of interest, to find out the various values.

Like any other tool, the spreadsheet can be misused. Before it became available, many decisions were based largely on instinct. Now spreadsheets not only provide financial facts but also the tool to manipulate figures from the desktop of any manager. However, spreadsheets rely on figures alone, and cannot take account of the many other variables and intangibles which make up the decision-making process.

Formalised Procedures

Francis Galton in his book *Natural Inheritance* points out that 'whenever a large sample of chaotic elements are taken in hand and marshalled in the order of their magnitude, an unsuspected and most beautiful form of regularity proves to have been latent all along'. In the disordered business world, it is important to make sense of information relating to the characteristics of each environment to understand more clearly the nature of its operations so that good decisions can be based upon developed predictions. It is never likely to be easy to make accurate predictions about all business activities and events. For example, it is possible to measure the speed of a satellite but not that of a snowflake in a blizzard!

The aim of this chapter is to develop your understanding of formalised forecasting procedures. It builds upon Chapter 18 by introducing a wider range of useful statistical techniques, including time series analysis, correlation, regression analysis and forecasting analysis.

On completion of the chapter you should be able to produce forecasts based on formalised procedures. To achieve this you must demonstrate the ability to:

- use formalised methods to forecast results

- assess the reliability of the forecasts made.

FORECASTING AND PLANNING FOR THE FUTURE

Uncertainty is a feature of all organisations, whether this is due to external factors or to the dynamic processes within a business. Though management planning is often an imprecise art, struggling to achieve clarity and purpose in a changeable and sometimes hostile environment, it has been said that the future belongs to those who plan for it best. Statistical analysis helps organisations to think about the future and provides a range of powerful and often very necessary tools to help with this planning process across a business organisation. For example, marketers often plan several years ahead and try to build flexibility within their plans to cater for changes as and when they occur. Financial planning is an integral part of an organisational strategy. The financial plan itself is a set of financial statements that predict the resource implications of making strategic decisions. No production planning can take place without predicting future production capacity, the raw materials, people and production costs required to meet the sales expected.

Predictions, which involve making sense of events at some future time, are called **forecasts**. One dictionary definition of the word forecast is 'to calculate, estimate, conjecture beforehand, to estimate the probable course or outcome of'. The process of arriving at forecasts is known as **forecasting**. There are a number of ways of forecasting the future based upon either economic variables or factors within a business organisation.

TIME SERIES ANALYSIS

Many aspects of business can be measured against time. For example, sales volumes, costs of resources used, staff absenteeism, sales and production figures. A **time series** is the name given to a series of figures or variables that have been recorded through time. The series consists of the successive values of a variable that changes over a period of time. Values may be affected by various factors over time and, for general analysis purposes, it is generally accepted that there are four components of a time series:

1. **Trend.** There is an underlying trend in individual values being recorded. For example, the long-term change in sales may be a gradual increase despite volatile movements up and down each month.

2. **Seasonal fluctuations.** Many organisations experience changes according to the seasons including sales of ice-cream, garden materials and seaside holidays. Less obvious situations may be confirmed with time series analysis, for example many fish and chip shops experience falls in demand during hot summer spells.

3. **Cyclical fluctuations.** Some businesses have variations in demand over periods of more than one year. Capital goods manufacturers and construction firms experience marked variations in their business activity depending upon the phase of the economic cycle. Their fortunes are often a magnification of conditions in the general economy as they benefit early and disproportionately from an upswing in the economy, but suffer from a dearth of sales as economic growth slows. There may be other cycles that affect particular types of businesses. A computer services company may have identified marked variations in demand corresponding to the periodic launch of new processing chips or the issue of new software releases. To measure the effect of cycles, it is often necessary to have data covering a considerable number of years.

4. **Irregular or random variables.** This component contains variations that cannot be explained by any of the other three components of the time series.

In order to forecast future values, a time series must be analysed for its component parts. A forecast value will be the sum of items 1–3, with a qualification based on the range of irregular variations experienced to date.

Derivation and use of moving averages

The first step to understanding a time series is to remove variations due to seasonal and cyclical factors. This is done by smoothing individual values by a technique called **moving averages**.

The principle of the moving average technique is to find an average value during a cycle. Therefore, to find the seasonal variation, values need to be averaged for a one year period on a moving basis. The same method applies to cyclical variations, except that the moving average will be based on the length of the cycle being considered.

Centred trend, seasonal variation and seasonally adjusted data

The best way to illustrate centred trends, seasonal variations and seasonally adjusted data is through a series of illustrations.

Example

The Weary Traveller Hotel is situated in the heart of England and caters mainly for business travellers, but also enjoys some tourist trade. Figure 19.1 shows the hotel's sales figures for the past four years, with the first quarter starting on 1 January each year.

Year	Quarter	Sales (£000)	Total for year (£000)	Moving average (£000)	Centred average (£000)
1	1	180			
	2	189			
			764	191.000	
	3	205			191.500
			768	192.000	
	4	190			192.500
2	1	184			193.875
			779	194.750	
	2	193			195.625
			786	196.500	
	3	212			196.750
			788	197.000	
	4	197			197.750
			794	198.500	
3	1	186			199.375
			801	200.250	
	2	199			200.500
			803	200.750	
	3	219			201.250
			807	201.750	
	4	199			202.625
			814	203.500	
4	1	190			204.125
			819	204.750	
	2	206			205.250
			823	205.750	
	3	224			
	4	203			

Figure 19.1 *The Weary Traveller Hotel: sales figures*

The method for developing the moving average and extracting the moving trend is as follows:

1. Add the values for the first 12 months of sales. The total is recorded on the line between the second and third quarters, as this is the middle point in the series.

2. Continue one quarter at a time down the series of values calculating the total for a moving 12-month period until the last quarter is reached. The second total will therefore include sales for quarters 2, 3, 4 and 5.

3. Calculate the quarterly moving average by taking the 12-month total and divide by 4.

4. It is necessary to identify the moving average figures against specific periods. Calculating a **centred moving average** does this. The centred moving average is not required where the moving average is calculated from an odd number of values, for example where the moving average is based on days in the week.

5. The next step is to estimate the **seasonal variation** for each quarter. There are two widely recognised methods of isolating the trend from seasonal and cyclical variations. These are often referred to as the **additive model** and the **proportional model**. The additive model uses an absolute value for each variation, whereas the proportional model relates the size of the variation to the underlying trend. For example, the current trend for umbrella sales indicates a weekly sales turnover of £1000. However, because it is now winter, the seasonal variation adds £500 to that figure giving a turnover of £1500 per week. The underlying trend for umbrella sales is forecast to be £1200 per week for next winter.

Using the additive model, the weekly sales forecast for the same time next year will be £1200 plus the seasonal variation of £500, giving a total of £1700.

The proportional model, however, requires the seasonal variation to be stated as a proportion of the trend and is therefore currently 50 per cent (£500/£1000). For next winter, sales will therefore be forecast as £1800 (£1200 + 50 per cent).

The proportional or multiplicative model is often considered the most appropriate for business applications and is the one illustrated further here. Unless there is a steep underlying trend, the results from each method will be similar.

If we continue with the example relating to the Weary Traveller, we can isolate the seasonal effect – see Figure 19.2. To do this, the method is as follows:

1. Divide each quarter's sales by the centred moving average to give a seasonal index. For example, the index for quarter 3 of year 1 is 1.0705 (205/191.50), which shows that this season has contributed more than average sales.

2. The seasonal variation is deemed to be explained by the average of the indices for the same quarter each year. Therefore, in this illustration the average seasonal index is the average of three figures (see below). If it is found that the total of the seasonal indices does not quite add to 4, the components are adjusted on a pro rata basis.

3. Applying the average seasonal index to each quarter's sales provides a deseasonalised sales figure. For example, quarter 3 sales of £205 000 are divided by 1.0790 to give deseasonalised sales of £189 991.

Year	Quarter	Period number	Sales (£000)	Centred moving average (£000)	Seasonal index (sales/centred moving average)	Average seasonal index	Deseasonal sales (£000)
1	1	1	180				191.94
	2	2	189				190.05
	3	3	205	191.500	1.0705	1.0790	189.99
	4	4	190	192.500	0.9870	0.9887	192.19
2	1	5	184	193.875	0.9491	0.9378	196.20
	2	6	193	195.625	0.9866	0.9945	194.07
	3	7	212	196.750	1.0775	1.0790	196.48
	4	8	197	197.750	0.9962	0.9887	199.27
3	1	9	186	199.375	0.9329	0.9378	198.34
	2	10	199	200.500	0.9925	0.9945	200.10
	3	11	219	201.250	1.0882	1.0790	202.97
	4	12	199	202.625	0.9821	0.9887	201.29
4	1	13	190	204.125	0.9308	0.9378	202.60
	2	14	206	205.250	1.0037	0.9945	207.14
	3	15	224				207.60
	4	16	203				205.34

Figure 19.2 *The Weary Traveller hotel: seasonal effect*

Quarter	Calculation of average seasonal index	Average seasonal index	Adjusted seasonal index
1.	$\dfrac{0.9491 + 0.9329 + 0.9308}{3}$	0.9376	0.9378
2.	$\dfrac{0.9866 + 1.9925 + 1.0037}{3}$	0.9943	1.9945
3.	$\dfrac{1.0705 + 1.0775 + 1.0882}{3}$	1.0787	1.0790
4.	$\dfrac{0.9870 + 0.9962 + 0.9821}{3}$	0.9884	0.9887
	TOTAL:	3.9990	4.0000

If the deseasonalised sales show a linear relationship to time, then the trend can be represented by a straight line that can be extrapolated for future periods. The line of best fit may be drawn by hand or more accurately by calculating a least-squares regression line. In this example, the period number and the deseasonalised sales figures correspond to a correlation coefficient of 0.9647.

Using the above data:

$$b = \frac{\Sigma xy - (\Sigma x^3 \Sigma y)/n}{\Sigma x^2 - (\Sigma x)^2/n}$$

$$= \frac{27393.15 - (136^3\, 3175.568)/16}{1496 - 18496/16} = 1.1789$$

$$a = \frac{\Sigma y - b\Sigma x}{n} = \frac{3175.568 - 136b}{16} = 188.45$$

The equation of the line is therefore Y = 188.45 + 1.1789X, where X represents the time period number, and Y represents the trend sales figure.

The trend line can be extrapolated to enable forecasts for future periods to be made, or alternatively, the line formula allows trend sales figures to be calculated. The trend forecast is then adjusted for seasonal variations by multiplying by the seasonal component.

To forecast sales for year 5 for the Weary Traveller Hotel, see Figure 19.3.

Forecasts obtained by this method will be accurate only to the extent that past conditions apply to future periods. The trend may be affected by a cyclical variation that has not yet been identified, and of course the seasonal variation may change. Of particular significance is the fact that irregular variations have not been accounted for. These can be quantified as they are the differences between the deseasonalised figures and the trend (centred moving average). Future forecasts can be qualified with an error range based on these past irregular variations.

Year	Quarter	Period number	Trend using line equation component	Seasonal sales	Forecast (£000)
5	1	17	Sales = 188.45 + (1.1789 × 17) = 208.49	0.9378	195.52
	2	18	Sales = 188.45 + (1.1789 × 18) = 209.67	0.9945	208.52
	3	19	Sales = 188.45 + (1.1789 × 19) = 210.85	1.0790	227.51
	4	20	Sales = 188.45 + (1.1789 × 20) = 212.03	0.9887	209.63
					841.18

Figure 19.3 *The Weary Traveller Hotel: forecast sales for year 5*

Case Study

Working in the clothing industry

Robert Cook is a clothes retailer with several distinctive boutiques in towns in the Thames Valley. Given the size of his recent investment in new shops, and the state of the industry, he is particularly concerned about the possibilities of changes in sales and market conditions over the next 12 months. Figure 19.4 shows Robert's sales figures for the past four years.

	Jan.–Mar. (£000)	Apr.–June (£000)	July–Sept. (£000)	Oct.–Dec. (£000)
1996	552	640	610	630
1997	540	635	580	615
1998	530	614	575	608
1999	522	611	565	601

Figure 19.4 *Sales figures*

Questions

1. Explain to Robert the importance of forecasting sales. How do external conditions affect his ability to make accurate forecasts?

2. Use moving averages to isolate the seasonal variation in the sales figures.

3. Calculate least-squares estimates for the line representing the underlying sales trend.

4. Forecast sales for the four quarters of the year 2000.

CORRELATION

When working for organisations and making observations in the business environment, business people frequently draw conclusions based upon what they perceive as the strength of the observed relationship between two variables. For example, they may observe a relationship between the price of a product and the demand for it. Similarly, they may identify a link between advertising and sales, or the qualifications of candidates and their ability to undertake a job role. According to Hanke Reitsch in *Fundamentals of Business Statistics* (1986), 'Correlation analysis focuses on the strength of the relationship between two variables and is used in exploratory work when a researcher or analyst attempts to determine which variables are important'.

Sometimes there is the need to measure the strength of the relationship between two variables. Where a change in one item takes place at the same time as another, there is said to be a **correlation** between the values of the two items. The variable that is being predicted is the dependent variable Y, and its change is correlated to an independent variable X. It is important to understand that correlation is about an association rather than 'cause' and 'effect'. There may be many different reasons why two variables vary together. For example:

- Changes in Y causes changes in X.
- Changes in X cause changes in Y.
- Changes in some other variables, such as Z, independently cause changes in X and Y.
- The relationship between X and Y is simply a coincidence, with no causal relationship.

	Jan.	Feb.	Mar.	Apr.	May	June	July	Aug.	Sept.	Oct.	Nov.	Dec.
Average temperature (°C)	3	5	8	11	13	18	21	22	18	11	6	4
Sales (£000)	12	13	12	16	18	30	45	50	28	14	8	9

Figure 19.5 *Monthly ice-cream sales*

Scatter graphs

A scatter graph can be prepared to provide an initial view as to whether variables are correlated. The independent variable X is plotted on the horizontal axis and the dependent variable on the Y axis.

The data shown in Figure 19.5 relate to sales made by an ice-cream manufacturer during the past year. A scatter graph is shown in Figure 19.6. It shows that there is some correlation between sales and average daily temperatures.

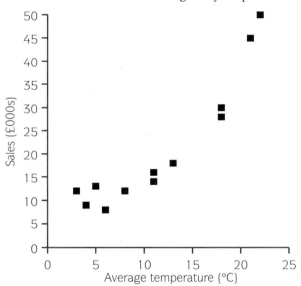

Figure 19.6 *Scatter graph of ice-cream sales*

Positive and negative correlation

Correlation (see Figure 19.7) is considered to be positive when the least-squares line (or line of best fit) has an upward slope. This occurs when the relationship between X and Y is such that small values of Y tend to go with small values of X and large values of Y tend to go with large values of X. Correlation is said to be negative when

the least-squares line has a downward slope. This occurs when large values of Y accompany small values of X and small values of Y tend to go with large values of X. Where the least-squares line is horizontal, there is no correlation.

Correlation coefficient

The **correlation coefficient** *r* is a measure of the linear relationship between two variables. It is calculated from *n* pairs of values of variables X and Y.

$$r = \frac{\dfrac{\Sigma xy - (\Sigma x \times \Sigma y)}{n}}{\sqrt{\Sigma x^2 - \dfrac{(\Sigma x)^2}{n}} \times \sqrt{\Sigma y^2 - \dfrac{(\Sigma y)^2}{n}}}$$

The coefficient is a value from −1 to 1. A value of zero indicates strong evidence of no linear relationship between the variables, whereas −1 shows a perfect negative linear relationship and +1 a perfect positive linear relationship. A positive coefficient indicates that as one variable increases or decreases in value, so does the other. A negative coefficient indicates that as one variable increases, the other decreases and vice versa. The coefficient will be at least 0.75 or −0.75 if there is a significant relationship between the variables. Such a result should be confirmed by research conducted on a new, larger sample.

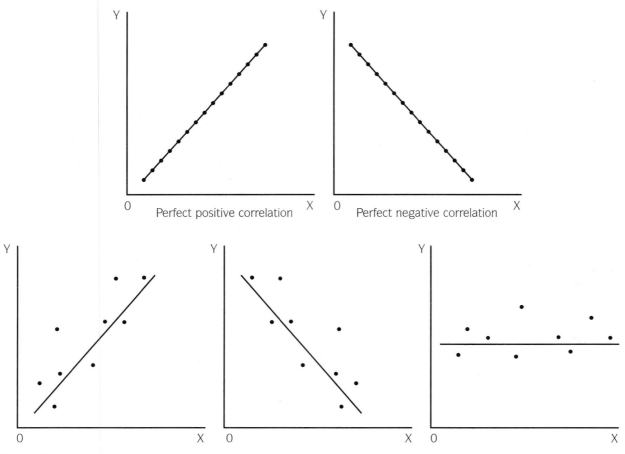

Figure 19.7 *Positive and negative correlations*

Check your understanding

ColorPress Ltd is a printing company specialising in wrappers for food products. The managing director believes there may be a relationship between the number of colours used on a print run and the resulting profitability of work done. For the last ten print runs the number of colours (X) has been recorded with the job's respective profit margin percentage (Y) (see Figure 19.8). Three further columns have been produced to calculate XY, X^2 and Y^2. Calculate the correlation coefficient of number of colours to profit margin percentage.

Number of colours (X)	Profit margin (%) (Y)	XY	X^2	Y^2
4	15	60	16	225
5	12	60	25	144
4	11	44	16	121
6	16	96	36	56
3	9	27	9	81
5	16	80	25	256
7	18	126	49	324
6	16	96	36	256
8	20	160	64	400
6	17	102	36	289
Σx	Σy	Σxy	Σx^2	Σy^2
54	150	851	312	2352

Figure 19.8 *ColorPress Ltd: number of colours used and profit margin*

$$n = 10$$

$$r = \frac{851 - (54^3\ 150/10)}{\sqrt{312 - 2\ 916/10^3} \times \sqrt{2\ 352 - 22\ 500/10}}$$

$$= \frac{851 - 810}{\sqrt{20.4} \times \sqrt{102}} = \frac{41}{45.61} = 0.8987$$

The coefficient of correlation shows a fairly strong relationship between the two variables.

TASK

Calculate the coefficient of correlation for the data given earlier on temperature and ice cream sales (see page 469).

The correlation coefficient can be calculated quickly and accurately using a computer *spreadsheet*. The data relating to X and Y above could be keyed into columns B and C of a spreadsheet. The numerical data keyed into rows 2–11 can then be referred to by the following function keyed into a vacant cell:

=correl(b2:b11,c2:c11)

This function is in the fomat =correl (1st data range, 2nd data range).

TASK

Cavetron UK Ltd manufactures on a batch production basis to customer orders. The following sales and profit figures relate to individual jobs completed in June:

Sales (£000) :
23 82 26 52 36 46 67 97 20 10 5 59

Profit (£000) :
4 22 5 11 7 11 15 29 3 1 0 14

The factory manager has noticed a possible relationship between the size of the job and the percentage profit earned.

1. Using a spreadsheet, calculate the correlation coefficient of profit margin percentage to sales.

2. Comment on the relationship.

Significance level

It is possible to get indications of a strong positive or negative correlation purely by chance. For example, suppose we had two coins and together we threw heads. In a business context we are looking at whether one variable has had a relationship with another. It is reasonable in this context to assume that there is no relationshp between the two coins. This is called a **null hypothesis**, i.e. our hypothesis is that there is no special effect working between the two coins.

If we continue and each throw another two heads, we may well start questioning the results. After all, what is the probability of us both throwing three heads in a row?

Probability of throwing 2 heads together
$= 0.5 \times 0.5 = 0.25$

Probability of throwing 2 heads together twice
$= 0.25 \times 0.25 = 0.0625$

Probability of throwing 2 heads together three times
$= 0.0625 \times 0.0625 = 0.00390625$

These results are starting to look rather improbable. Such a low level of probability is reached that we may want to reject the null hypothesis. This level of 'unbelievability' is the **significance level** at which we conclude that the results are *significantly different* from those which we expected. After the third throws of our coins we would say that the results are *significant*.

The choice of significance level is subjective and two people may have chosen to question the above results at different stages. If we choose a low probability as our significance level we reduce the risk of making premature assumptions about possible corrrelations. Usually a 5 per cent (or a probability of less than 0.05) significance level is chosen. This level is not the only one used; 1 per cent is also used, but of course it is harder to prove that results are significant. The above results would be significant using both 5 per cent and 1 per cent significance levels.

REGRESSION ANALYSIS

Where there is a strong correlation in a scatter graph, the dots arrange themselves in a narrow band, which may be curved or straight. If the band of dots is straight, the correlation is said to be linear. A straight line can represent the relationship between the two variables.

The techniques of regression analysis can be used to express the readings on a scatter graph in terms of a straight line. This may be useful once it has been established that there is a linear correlation between two variables as the line could then be extrapolated to aid forecasting.

Derivation of regression equation

The formula for a straight line is:

$$Y = a + bX$$

where a is the point at which the line intercepts the vertical axis and b represents the gradient of the line, i.e. the changes in Y relative to X.

If the values of a and b are known, then the line can be drawn by inserting values of X into the formula and calculating the corresponding value of Y. The values of X used should be within the range of values contained in the data set.

For a scatter graph it is possible to draw a 'line of best fit' by eye. The process requires a line to be drawn that is as near as possible to each of the points plotted. Where there is a cluster of points, the resulting line will tend to pass between them.

However, the values of a and b can be calculated where an accurate line is required for n pairs of observations. The

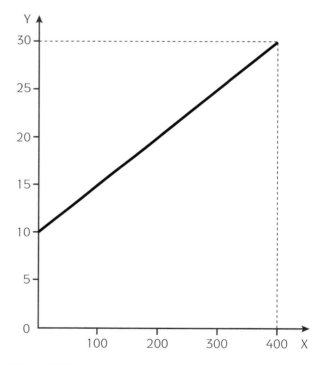

Figure 19.9 *A straight-line graph*

values calculated are **least-squares estimates** because the resulting line minimises the sum of the squared distances away from each point.

$$a = \frac{\Sigma y - b\Sigma x}{n}$$

$$b = \frac{\Sigma xy - (\Sigma x \times \Sigma y)/n}{\Sigma x^2 - (\Sigma x)^2/n}$$

Using the data from the example of ColorPress Ltd on page 470, the values of a and b can be calculated:

$$b = \frac{851 - (54^3\,150)/10}{312 - 54^2/10} = \frac{851 - 810}{20.4} = 2.01$$

$$a = \frac{150 - b54}{10} = 4.146$$

Using the values of a and b above, together with a value of say 8 for X, it is possible to find a corresponding value for Y using the general formula for a straight line (see above).

$$Y = 4.146 + (2.01 \times 8) = 20.2$$

The line drawn according to this formula is called a least-squares line. It will pass through the following two points: where ($Y = 4.146$, $X = 0$) and ($Y = 20.2$ and $X = 8$).

The formula can now be used to predict a future value of Y for any value of X between 3 and 8.

TASK

1. Calculate least-squares estimates for the data given earlier on temperature and ice-cream sales (see page 469).

2. Draw a line of best fit for advertising to sales using these estimates.

FORECASTING ANALYSIS

Forecasting involves explaining or predicting events that will occur at some future time. Although forecasting is concerned with the future, often the starting point for the forecasting process is to look at what has happened in the past to use that experience in planning for uncertainty in the future. In this way forecasting involves observing regular events and historical sequences with the underlying assumption that the future will probably follow the same degree of consistency, i.e. what has happened in the past will either to a greater or lesser extent continue to happen in the future.

Preparation of forecasts

On pages 466–467 we used time series to forecast sales for year 5 for the Weary Traveller Hotel. The rationale of using time series is that, having observed the regularity or movement of data through time, we can predict that what has happened in the past will, to some extent, continue to happen or will happen in the future. Thus the trend equation, which in that situation was $Y = 188.45 + 1.1789X$, was used to extrapolate from the data and extend the trend into the future so as to estimate a value which lies beyond the range of values used to derive the trend equation.

Example

The following trend equation has been calculated by the method of least squares from company sales data extending back over a period of years. It describes the long-term growth in sales of a manufacturer of bedroom furniture.

$$Y = 64.4 + 2.88X$$

The origin of the equation was 1999. Y = total annual sales in millions of pounds. The 1999 trend value is £64.4 million and the growth forces are estimated to be producing a £2.88 million increase in sales units each year. Substituting X = 4 (for a four-year trend) into this trend equation, we find that, based on the long-term growth forces alone, the 1993 expected total sales are:

$$Y = 64.4 + 2.88(4) = £75\,920\,000.$$

If the manufacturer's sales were uninfluenced by seasonal variations, we could estimate the 2003 monthly sales in exactly the same way. However, it is possible to use a seasonal index, calculated from recent historical data by the ratio to moving average method, to show variations in sales.

Modifying the trend equation for use with monthly data is done by dividing £64.4 by 12 and 2.88 by 144 (by 12 and then 12 again) and then, shifting the origin back to January, we get:

$$Y = 6.22 + 0.02.$$

By working backwards, £6.22 million is the trend value for January 2003. By substituting X = 1, 2, 3 through to 11 in this equation, we can derive the trend values for the other 11 months of 2003 to show the values in Figure 19.10. The pronounced seasonal variation arises from seasonal influences for bedroom furniture with sales low in November, December, January and February and high in April, May and June. The seasonal index is calculated from historical data using the moving average method with sales at 77 per cent in January and 140 per cent in May. By multiplying the trend value by the seasonal index for each of the 12 months, monthly sales can be predicted. Though trends and seasonal patterns have been taken into account, there may be cyclical and other irregular influences affecting these data.

Month	Trend value	Seasonal index	Predicted monthly sales for 2003
Jan.	6.22	0.77	4.79
Feb.	6.24	0.73	4.56
Mar.	6.26	1.02	6.39
Apr.	6.28	1.25	7.85
May.	6.30	1.40	8.82
Jun.	6.32	1.20	7.58
Jul.	6.34	1.00	6.34
Aug.	6.36	1.05	6.68
Sep.	6.38	0.98	6.25
Oct.	6.40	1.04	6.66
Nov.	6.42	0.81	5.20
Dec.	6.44	0.75	4.83

Figure 19.10 *Predicted monthly sales of bedroom furniture, 2003*

On pages 472–473 we saw how regression analysis could be used to predict values reflecting the way in which variation in an observed random variable changes with changing circumstances. The example of ColorPress Ltd showed how regression provides a useful way of estimating changes in one variable from another.

Although there are many problems in which one variable can be predicted accurately in terms of another, predictions should improve if additional relevant information is included. For example, it would be possible for an organisation to make better predictions about new staff if it considered not only their years of experience but also their education and personality. Similarly, it would also be possible to make better predictions about the performance of equipment if more factors related to the performance of that equipment were on hand. As a result, though mathematical formulas can be used to express relationships between more than two variables, they are commonly expressed as linear equations such as:

$$Y = b_0 + b_1 x_1 + b_2 x_2 + b_3 x_3 + \ldots b_k x_k.$$

In this example Y is the variable which is to be predicted while x_1, x_2, x_3 through to x_k are the known variables upon which predictions are to be based. The main problem in deriving a linear equation for more than two variables that best describes a given set of data is that of finding numerical values for each variable.

Reliability

The real problem with using a range of statistical techniques for forecasting and planning for the future is that there are too many variables which need to be taken into account. Though some are quantifiable and clearly predictable, some are not. The projection of past experience to an uncertain future is always likely to be speculative and hazardous, but there are always likely to be occasions when decisions have to be made upon estimates and incomplete knowledge.

Quantitative Techniques

In a modern and increasingly competitive business world it is important that the resources of people, materials, capital and equipment are deployed in a way which provides an organisation with the maximum competitive advantage. Over the past fifty years there has been a rapid growth in the use of mathematical techniques to solve organisational problems and aid the process of decision- making. This chapter introduces the quantitative techniques of inventory control, linear programming, networking and indexes.

On completion of the chapter you should be able to apply quantitative techniques business situations.
To achieve this you must demonstrate the ability to:

- use appropriate quantative techniques to address business problems
- justify decisions made as a result of using the techniques.

INVENTORY CONTROL

One key decision which almost every organisation has to take is how much stock to hold. Inventory control is the quantitative art of controlling the amount of stock held, in the various forms stock may take within an organisation, to meet the demands placed upon it. An organisation may thus store just a few items or many millions. Even organisations in the service or public sectors will need to maintain inventories in order to provide a service. For example, a school will need to maintain stocks of books, pencils and rulers, and a petrol station will need to maintain stocks of each different type of fuel to meet the demands of its users.

Hax and Candea (1984) emphasise the key ingredients necessary to maintain an efficient inventory system:

Production-inventory systems are concerned with the effective management of the total flow of goods, from the acquisition of raw materials to the delivery of finished products to the final customer. A production-inventory system is composed of a large number of elements which have to be managed effectively in order to deliver the final products in appropriate quantities, where they are required, at the desired time and quality, and at a reasonable cost.

Inventory systems are more usually classified into two groups:

- **Independent demand inventory** – these are final demand goods that will be used or consumed by customers as finished goods.
- **Dependent demand inventory** – these are items that are used in the manufacture of a finished product. For example, the manufacture of a car will usually comprise more than 2 0000 dependent items. The effective use of these items is determined by an operations management system.

Some items may be both independent and dependent. For example, spectacle frames will be independent demand for a manufacturer of such frames and dependent demand for a group of opticians. Another classification subdivides stocks held, in particular by a manufacturing business, into three categories: finished product stocks waiting to be despatched (independent demand); raw materials stocks held in stores and used to make up products (dependent demand); and a separate category between these two types called in-process stocks (work-in-progress) which occur naturally as part of the production process.

In an ideal world, if the precise demands upon an organisation were always known in advance and if suppliers always supplied on time, there would be little need to hold any form of inventory other than work-in-progress. The quantitative nature of the problem would be that of scheduling the stocks because all of the parameters of the problem would have been defined. In practice, as demand is not known in advance and trying to estimate it precisely might reduce the organisation's flexibility, it is important to keep stocks as a buffer between the vagaries of demand and supply. Stocks, therefore act:

- as an insurance against higher-than-average demand to ensure that the changing requirements of customers can be met
- as an insurance against uncertain supplier delivery times (lead times)
- as an opportunity to take advantage of price fluctuations – for example people who buy coal in the summer at lower prices, assume that the savings in material costs outweigh early investment and storage costs
- to take advantage of bulk discounts – such discounts may more than compensate for storage costs
- to minimise any production delays caused by shortages.

The aim for any inventory control system, therefore, is to maintain the quantities of stocks held by the organisation in a way which meets many of the above objectives but also optimises other management criteria, such as

minimising costs associated with holding stocks while at the same time maximising customer service.

Periodic review and reorder level

Organisations work with inventory policies. With a reorder policy, orders for replenishment are usually placed when stock in hand equals or falls below a fixed value M which is the reorder level. With a reorder-level policy, therefore, the amount of inventory is reviewed *continuously*. A replenishment order placed within a reorder-level policy is for a fixed quantity. The solid line in Figure 20.1 represents the actual inventory where a finite lead time exists. The lead time is the time delay between placing a replenishment order and its delivery. The broken line indicates the inventory that would be held if no lead time existed.

The reorder quantity control policy assumes that the stock level is known exactly at every point in time; this is the only way in which we can tell that the reorder level M is reached, when a replacement order for Q is made (M,Q). Zimmerman and Sovereign in *Quantitative Models for Production Management* (1974) call this 'perpetual inventory control system'.

It is possible to think of situations when reorder or continuous review systems are not a good choice. For example, if a supplier accepts orders once a week, there is

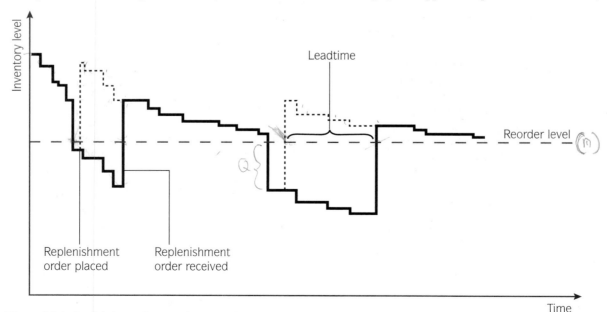

Figure 20.1 *Stock balances for a reorder-level policy*

no reason to review the stock of those items more often. Instead of using a continuous review system, it is possible to operate with periodic reviews with the stock status determined periodically. The time between the two reviews would be the review period spanning R periods of time.

When the review costs are small so that the costs of processing transactions are small compared with ordering costs, a continuous review system can lead to lower overall inventories than a periodic system. Using a MQ policy offers protection over the l-period replenishment lead time. Under a periodic review period, the situation is different because replenishment decisions are made R periods apart. If the current decision time is t, the next replenishment period will be $t + R$, and with delivery time this will be $t + R + l$. It thus follows that under a periodic review system the safety stock must be large enough to provide protection against the length of time $l + R$.

Therefore, under:

- **a reorder system**, an organisation will adopt an MQ policy: when the inventory reaches M units, Q is ordered.
- **a periodic review system**, if at a review time, the inventory is less or equal to M, an amount nQ is ordered ($n = 1, 2, 3, ...$); multiple n should ensure that after the order is placed the available inventory reaches a level in the interval of $MM + Q$. If the available inventory is greater than M, no order is placed.

Economic order quantity (EOQ)

F. W. Harris first proposed in 1913 the use of calculus to derive the first economic order quantity (EOQ) model; it was meant as an approach to inventory management and not simply another mathematical formula. The EOQ approach is therefore an application of mathematical modelling to inventory planning.

There are four steps to developing the EOQ approach to inventory management:

1. *Collect all relevant cost and unit demand information.* Cost information typically includes costs such as carrying costs, ordering costs, setup costs and shortage costs. The unit demand of the inventory item under consideration must also be forecast.

2. *Develop a total annual cost (TAC) function.* This defines total annual cost as a function of a single variable – order quantity – which may be denoted as Q:

$$TAC = f(Q)$$

Therefore, in this model we are stating that TAC is a function of Q. The objective is to find a Q that will minimise TAC.

3. *Use differential calculus to find the derivative of the TAC function.* The derivative of its function defines its slope.

4. *Set the derivative equal to zero and derive the EOQ formula.* The TAC function is usually a U-shaped cost curve like the one shown in Figure 20.2. TAC is a function of the order quantity Q. If we can find the **zero-slope value** (or the value of Q where the slope of $f(Q)$ equals zero), then we can determine the cost-minimising EOQ value of Q^* (the asterisk signifies that Q^* is the optimal Q of all possible Qs).

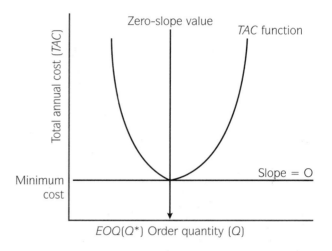

Figure 20.2 *Zero-slope value for a TAC function*

The basic EOQ model is based upon a number of assumptions. These are as follows:

1. Annual carrying costs per unit and costs per order are the only relevant costs and can be accurately estimated.

2. Annual demand can be estimated and is linearly consumed by customers.

3. Average inventory level is the order quantity Q divided by 2. However, if a safety stock is left over from a previous period, average inventory will be greater than Q divided by 2.

4. With demand linear and certain, there are no stockout costs. With this assumption there is no situation where stocking is out of inventory and therefore no costs.

5. There are no quantity discounts on large orders.

6. Lead time is known and fixed.

The basic *EOQ* model determines the value that is Q^*. It also determines an order point at *OP* in units to show when to place the next Q^* size order. Figure 20.3 shows that an order of Q^* arrives and is used linearly until it reaches the order point. A second inventory order of Q^* is then placed at the beginning of the LT lead time period. The same sequence of events repeats over time. An inventory manager therefore simply has to determine Q^* and *OP*, and the entire fixed-quantity inventory ordering system can be defined.

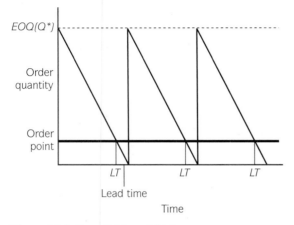

Figure 20.3 *Basic EOQ model behaviour*

There is a four-step approach to *EOQ* modelling:

1. *Collect cost data.* These types of data are relevant for this model: carrying costs and ordering costs. Carrying costs include insurance, handling, shrinkage, obsolescence and the cost of capital. Ordering costs include fixed charges to place an order. Together they create the *TAC* function as follows:

    TAC = Annual carrying costs + Annual ordering costs.

2. *Develop the TAC function.* To obtain annual carrying costs the following elements need to be defined:

    $$I = \frac{\text{Carrying costs per year}}{\text{Total of all costs of inventory per year.}}$$

    C = Cost of inventory item.

    Q = Order quantity (this is unknown at this point).

    $\dfrac{Q}{2}$ = Average inventory.

Multiplying I by C gives us the cost to carry one unit for one year of inventory. So the resulting expression to carry costs is the product of the year is the cost per unit of inventory and the average inventory held in stock:

$$\text{Annual carrying costs} = IC\left(\frac{Q}{2}\right).$$

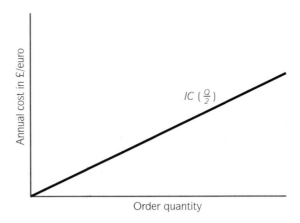

Figure 20.4 *Carrying cost curve*

Figure 20.4 shows a carrying cost curve. In order to obtain the ordering cost function we denote the following elements:

  S = The cost in pounds or euros to place one order (the average ordering costs per order).

  D = Annual demand in units of inventory.

If we divide D by Q, we obtain the number of orders placed per year. So the resulting expression for ordering costs is the product of the cost to place one order and the number of orders placed per year.

$$\text{Annual ordering costs} = S\left(\frac{D}{Q}\right).$$

Figure 20.5 shows an ordering cost curve. Adding the annual carrying costs to the annual ordering costs gives us the TAC curve.

$$TAC = \text{Annual carrying costs} + \text{Annual ordering costs.}$$

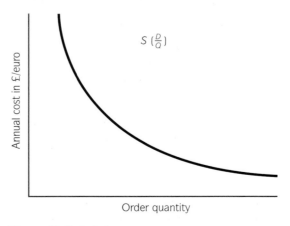

Figure 20.5 *Ordering cost curve*

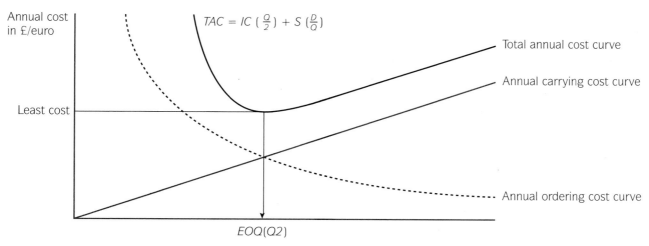

Figure 20.6 shows the combination of the two cost

Figure 20.6 *Total annual cost curve*

Therefore $TAC = IC \left(\dfrac{Q}{2}\right) + S \left(\dfrac{D}{Q}\right)$

Figure 20.6 shows the combination of the two cost functions resulting in a U-shaped *TAC* curve. The lowest point of the curve is the minimum cost value of Q^*. This is the economic order quantity. To find this *EOQ* point we must use the rules of differential calculus to find the slope of the *TAC* function.

3. *Use calculus to find the slope.* The *TAC* has only one variable, Q. Other values are constraints. The derivative of the *TAC* function denoted as $d(TAC)$ in respect to Q is:

$$\frac{d(TAC)}{d(Q)} = \left(\frac{IC}{2}\right) - [(SD)Q^{-2}]$$

4. *Set the derivative to zero and solve for Q.* By letting:

$\left(\dfrac{IC}{2}\right) - [(SD)Q^{-2}] = 0,$ and taking the square roots of both sides, we obtain:

$Q^* = \sqrt{\dfrac{2SD}{IC}}.$

If, therefore, an inventory situation fits the EOQ model's assumptions, this formula will generate a cost-minimised order quantity.

Demand reorder timing

Production planning involves meeting fluctuating demand requirements and involves making key decisions about production levels, work-force levels and inventories. Given the changing demand requirements, planning is geared towards the best use of these resources. The critical problem for many organisations is that the times and quantities imposed by demand requirements seldom coincide with the times and quantities which use the organisation's resources efficiently. Where changes in production are likely to occur, it is important to plan production in a way which enables effective resource allocation.

Before attempting to implement an effective inventory control system it is important to analyse the customer demand to which the system will be subjected. When analysing demand it is usual to measure the **demand per time** unit rather than just the size of actual orders. This is because all inventories are dependent upon the time factor, either in the form of review periods before reorder or because of leadtime variations. An estimate of the mean demand per time unit will provide an indication of what demand will be required over a typical time period. This mean value can only be predicted from past data. To use such a value to predict what will happen in the future implies that what has happened in the past will happen again.

It is the case that rarely what has happened in the past is likely to happen in the future. Standard deviation can be used to find out how the demand per unit time fluctuates above the mean value. The standard deviation helps the user to estimate the probability that the demand per unit time will exceed a specified value during a certain time period, so that the correct reorder decisions can be made.

There are many methods of forecasting the average value of demand for the future. One key factor would be whether demand data are from a stationary distribution where values tend to remain constant. The simplest form of an estimate for the mean value is the moving average, calculated by dividing the sum of the demand in the last n time periods by n (see pages 465–468).

Case Study

Cullimore Toys

In recent years Cullimore Toys has seen its business expand rapidly in an ever-changing business environment for toys. Julie Stanton, the Managing Director, is particularly concerned about not being able to meet orders, because of low stock levels.

Shortly after setting up the business Julie set up an inventory system and, debugged of computer misinformation, it greatly improved the operations and flexibility of the business.

However, recently there have been a number of complaints from customers who have had to wait an unexpectedly long time for their orders. Though the inventory manager increased inventories to act as a safety stock she is under constant pressure to keep stock levels low to reduce costs. The business environment fits the *EOQ*'s assumptions.

It is clear that Cullimore Toys requires a major overhaul of its inventory systems. So far Julie has resisted change and has even used taxi cabs to meet customer orders at short notice.

Questions

1. What are the disadvantages of low stock levels?

2. Describe the advantages of continuous reorder levels over periodic reviews.

3. Cullimore Toys is introducing a new item. The cost of the inventory is £1, the annual demand is 1380 units, the carrying cost is 10 per cent and the cost to place an order is £2. What is the optimal *EOQ* value?

4. How could Cullimore Toys attempt to predict demand?

LINEAR PROGRAMMING

Where competing activities make demands on limited resources, choices have to be made which optimise business objectives. Some situations place more than one **constraint** on the decision-maker. Where this happens, linear programming may be the appropriate technique to use.

Formulating the problem

For the technique to be used certain conditions must be present:

1. The problem requires an objective to be optimised. Typically, exercises in this area are about allocating resources to minimise cost or to find the product mix that maximises profit.

2. There must be a linear relationship between the resources used and the outcome aimed at. Fortunately, the usage of many resources is in proportion to output and, in many other cases, the simplification does not distort the outcome significantly. Examples include materials, labour hours and machine time.

3. There are a number of constraints affecting the stated objective. These may include limited amounts of physical resources, such as materials, labour and productive capacity. Other constraints include a limited market or inadequate finance to fund operations.

Graphical solution and constraints

Linear programming problems can be solved by either the **graphical approach** or the **simplex method**. The graphical approach is described here, although it is appropriate only where there are just two variables to choose between. The simplex method uses matrices and has no restrictions on the number of alternatives for which values are required. The objective and constraints of the decision-maker are best expressed in mathematical form.

Example

Suitcase Ltd produces and sells two types of cases: holdalls and cabin bags. The two materials used, leather and silk,

are in limited supply and so the company's management has to decide on the product mix that optimises profit from their usage.

	Leather	Silk (from a one-metre roll)
One holdall uses:	2 m²	20 cm
One cabin bag uses	1 m²	20 cm
Material available:	100 m²	1400 cm

Holdalls and cabin bags contribute £16 and £12 respectively to overheads and profits. A maximum of 50 cabin bags can be sold.

The objective is to maximise contribution. First calculate the total contribution from holdalls, which is £16 multiplied by the number of holdalls, and the total contribution from cabin bags, which is £12 multiplied by the number of bags. In mathematical terms the **objective function** is therefore:

Maximise £16H + £12C

where H is the number of holdalls and C is the number of cabin bags.

Each constraint is also expressed in mathematical terms. Leather usage is 2 m² for a holdall and 1 m² for a cabin bag, but usage cannot be more than 100 m² in total. The formula is therefore:

Leather constraint $2H + 1 C \leq 100$ m².

Similarly the silk constraint can be expressed as:

Silk constraint $20H + 20C \leq 1\,400$ cm.

In addition, the maximum number of cabin cases that can be sold is 50:

Sales constraint $C \leq 50$.

The objective function and constraints are shown as lines on a graph. The axes represent the variables for which values are required. In the example of Suitcase Ltd the vertical axis can represent the number of holdalls and the horizontal axis the number of cabin bags. To find a suitable scale for the axes, start by finding the maximum value possible for each variable from the constraint equations. This is done by giving a value of zero to the other variable. In the case of the leather constraint, no more than 50 holdalls could be produced if the total 100 m² is divided by 2 m². It is useful to tabulate the results:

Constraint	Maximum number of holdalls	Maximum number of cases
Leather constraint	50	100
Silk constraint	70	70
Sales constraint		50

The horizontal axis should be scaled to 70 for holdalls and the vertical axis to 100 for cabin bags.

The constraint lines can now be drawn using the points already identified in the table above. In drawing the leather constraint line, it is known that two extreme production possibilities exist: either 50 holdalls and no cabin bags or 100 cabin bags and no holdalls. The leather constraint can be drawn as a straight line between these two points, one on each axis. Taking any point along this line provides a product mix that uses all of the $100\,m^2$ of leather available. Any point below and to the left of this line is a feasible product mix, although it will not make full use of the leather available. All points above the line relate to product mixes that require more leather than is available. The other constraint lines can also be drawn (see Figure 20.7).

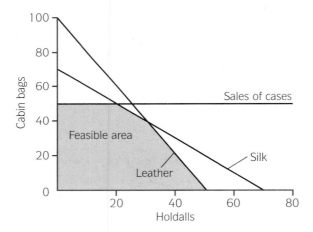

Figure 20.7 *Suitcase Ltd – constraints*

The shaded area in Figure 20.7 represents the **feasible area**. Any point taken within this area corresponds to a product mix that is possible, as it is below and to the left of all the constraint lines. A point on a constraint line will maximise the usage of that constraint. The point where the leather and silk constraint lines intersect identifies the product mix that consumes all of both materials. However, this is not necessarily the mix that satisfies the objective function.

The objective function when drawn as a line needs to reflect the relative profitability of each of the products.

The objective function will be maximised the further it can be drawn away from the origin, as that equates to more products being produced. The objective function is drawn so that any point along the line produces the same value (in this case contribution) even as product mix is changing.

It is necessary to find the number of each variable which, on its own, would achieve a given objective total.

Objective function:

Maximise £16H + £12C.

For a contribution of £480 for example:

Value on the horizontal axis where $C = 0$, £16H = £480, $H = 30$.

Value on the vertical axis where $H = 0$, £12C = £480, $C = 40$.

For a contribution of £1200 for example:

Value on the horizontal axis where $C = 0$, £16H = £1200, $H = 75$.

Value on the vertical axis where $H = 0$, £12C = £1200, $C = 100$.

Figure 20.8 shows the objective function for the above two different contribution levels. Notice that the gradient of each line is the same. It is this relationship between the profitability of one product and the other that needs to be incorporated into the solution of the problem. To produce one fewer of one of the products requires a fixed amount of the other product to make up the contribution otherwise lost.

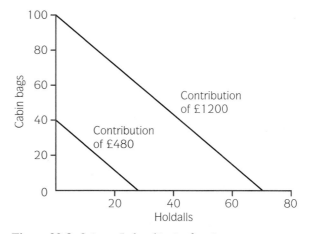

Figure 20.8 *Suitcase Ltd – objective function*

The point where the objective function is furthest from the origin but still on the boundary of the feasible area provides its maximum value. At this stage, it is not important where the objective function is drawn on the graph, provided the gradient is correct. Drawing an objective function equal to £1200 on the constraints graph produces an objective function that is outside the feasible area (see the dotted line in Figure 20.9). By moving this line towards the feasible area the optimal mix of variables is identified where the boundary of the feasible area is first hit.

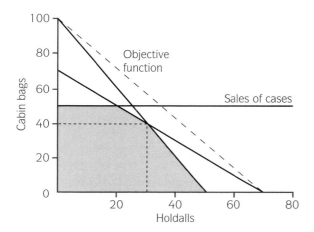

Figure 20.9 *Suitcase Ltd – solution*

In this case, the solution is where the leather and silk constraints also intersect, i.e. to produce 40 cabin bags and 30 holdalls. However, the optimal solution could have been at any of the points where the constraint lines intersect one another or intersect one of the axes. If the objective function had been steeper (i.e. holdalls were even more profitable, relative to cabin bags), the solution may have been to produce 50 holdalls and no cabin bags. If the objective function had been shallower (i.e. where cabin bags had been more profitable than holdalls), the solution may have been to produce 80 cabin bags and no holdalls, or to have produced 50 cabin bags and 20 holdalls.

The example of Suitcase Ltd involved maximising the objective function. The graphical approach can also be used to solve a minimisation problem. For example, the objective function may be to minimise cost by considering different mixes of factors of production. The same method is used as for maximising, except that the optimal point is furthest to the left of the feasible area.

The graphical approach to linear programming is simple in concept and provides an easily understandable representation of the problem. The effect of changes to underlying assumptions can easily be seen on the graph and other solutions can be evaluated for their distance from the optimal point. It is also easy to see and measure the amount of each resource that is underutilised, as this is represented by the distance between the optimal point and the appropriate constraint line.

The method has a number of disadvantages. It can be used only for two variables and the graph becomes cluttered and confusing if there are many constraints. It also assumes that units of production can be split, so it is important that only whole numbers are read from the diagram scales.

TASK

The Little Chip Choc Company is a small confectionery manufacturer. It is currently preparing for Easter and is having to decide on the mix of chocolate eggs and chocolate rabbits which maximises the contribution to overheads and profit. Unfortunately, due to a mistake in the purchase ordering, the chocolate and creme filling to be used are in limited supply.

	Chocolate	Creme filling
One egg uses:	50 g	50 g
One rabbit uses:	50 g	20 g
Material available:	800 kg	500 kg

Product contribution is 6p for a rabbit and 10p for an egg.

1. Find the product mix that maximises contribution.

2. Calculate the maximum contribution and analyse the use of the material available between the two products.

TASK

St Mary's is a private college specialising in accountancy and business and finance courses. The college has experienced three main constraints in providing courses. There are 40 hours per week available to run courses in the computer suite, and the time of accountancy staff available is limited to a maximum of 90 hours per week.

Each type of course requires the following use of limited resources:

	Computer suite hours/week	Accountancy staff hours/week
Accountancy course	5	10
Business and finance	2	6

There is demand for a maximum of three accountancy courses and 14 business and finance courses. Accountancy courses contribute £10 000 to overheads and profits, business and finance courses contribute half that amount.

1. Find the product mix that maximises contribution.

2. Calculate the maximum contribution.

3. Quantify resources that are underutilised.

NETWORKING

When coordinating a project, it is essential to map out the sequence of events that must be carried out. Activities need to be performed in a planned sequence, for example in building a house the walls are normally assembled before the roof is put on; the layers of a sponge cake are made before the icing is put on, etc. These events can be linked in diagrammatic form as in Figure 20.10, where before B can be started, A must be completed.

TASK

B&T Woodworkers Ltd manufactures and sells two products: pine beds and tables. Each product goes through three stages of production: cutting, turning and assembly. There is limited capacity at each stage. Production times are:

	Cutting hours	Turning hours	Assembly hours
One bed	3	4	4
One table	2.25	4	2
Total hours available each week	54	64	48

Contribution to overheads and profit amounts to £120 for a bed and £80 for a table.

1. Find the product mix that maximises contribution.

2. Calculate the maximum contribution.

3. Quantify resources that will be underutilised.

4. What type of decision-making problems is linear programming used for?

5. Problems that can be solved by linear programming must have certain characteristics. Describe two of them.

6. Explain the following terms: (a) objective function, (b) constraints, and (c) feasible area.

7. The graphical approach cannot solve all linear programming problems. What is the basic limitation of its use compared to the simplex method?

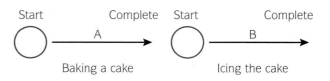

Figure 20.10 *Serial events in network analysis*

Some activities do not have to take place in sequence; they can be carried out simultaneously. For example, the icing could be prepared at the same time as the cake is being baked. This is illustrated in Figure 20.11, which shows that before you bake the cake and/or prepare the icing, you need to mix the ingredients for each, but the later stages of production can be carried out simultaneously.

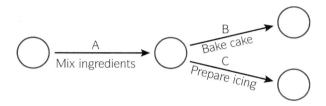

Figure 20.11 *Simultaneous activities in network analysis*

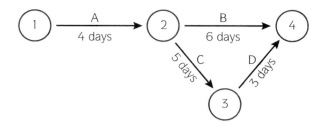

Figure 20.12 *Introducing time to a network analysis*

It now becomes easy to calculate the minimum time required to carry out a particular project. Those activities that take the longest to complete in moving from one state to the next in a project are described as 'critical' activities. The **critical path** of a project is the sequence that these activities follow. It is essential that the activities are done well and that they are given priority because delays to them will delay the completion of the project as a whole. This too can be illustrated by a simple diagram (see Figure 20.13). Activities A and B can be carried out simultaneously, as can C and D. However, activities A and C are the critical activities in that, if they fall behind in their execution, the whole project will suffer.

TASK

The organisation you work for is trying to design a network of activities for a new administrative procedure. You have been asked to map out programmes of activities in such a way as to create the most efficient process of planning. Set out a network diagram to indicate the performance of the following activities:

Activity	Relation to other activities
A	Must be done first
B	Can be started only when A is finished
C	Can be started only when A is finished
D	Requires completion of B
E	Requires completion of C and D
F	Completes project and must await completion of all other activities.

Network analysis can be used to map out programmes of activities in a way that creates the most effective planning. A further important ingredient in constructing a network is *time*, which is a crucial element in project planning. Time needs to be incorporated into the diagram (see Figure 20.12).

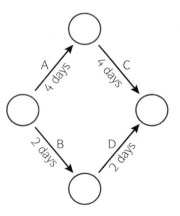

Figure 20.13 *Establishing priorities in a network analysis*

Critical path analysis

As we have already seen, the critical path is the sequence of key activities that determine the time needed to complete a project.

Think of any activity that you or your organisation has to carry out. Then answer the questions below. (You will need your answers to complete the next task on page 487.)

1. List all the tasks that need to be carried out, how long each will take and in what order they need to be done. (Are there some tasks that have to be finished before others can be begun, and if so which are they?)

2. Draw a network to show the links between each task, representing each with a circle, identifying it with a letter or number and connecting the circles using arrows pointing from left to right to show the order in which the tasks must take place. The circles are the **nodes**, i.e. points in time when one or more activities finishes or starts.

A 'network' is a series of activities and nodes showing the sequence of activities and the time-scale involved. We can break down each of the circles (nodes) into three components – the top half of the circle gives the number of the activity and the bottom half can be used to show the

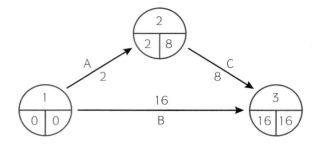

Figure 20.14 *An example of critical path analysis*

earliest and latest times for finishing the activity. For example, in the set of activities shown in Figure 20.14, the earliest time to complete activity C is 16 days. This is because activities A and C can be completed in ten days, it takes 16 days to complete activity B and so the earliest time to arrive at node 3 is 16 days. The latest time to finish an activity is calculated by working backwards from the end of a project.

Figure 20.15 shows the number of days required to finish a project with 12 nodes in it. Latest times are calculated by working backwards from right to left across the diagram. (Note that the two activities drawn in dotted lines are 'dummy activities', ones which do not use up time or resources.) The pathway that is the most urgent, i.e. the critical path – the one where, if tasks are held up, the whole project will be pushed behind schedule – can be highlighted using a thicker line or colour to indicate it. In Figure 20.15 the critical path is B to E to F to H to J to N to P. The critical path will be the one for which both the earliest and latest times are equal at each and all of the networked nodes. In other words, every activity will need to start and finish on time or delay will take place.

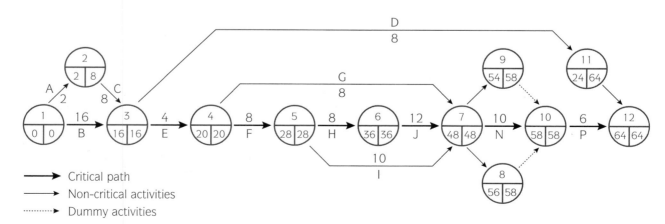

➤ Critical path
➤ Non-critical activities
┄┄➤ Dummy activities

Figure 20.15 *A 12-node critical path*

TASK

Look back at the task you completed on page 486 and produce a critical path analysis of the activity you chose. Highlight the critical pathway.

Planning and control involve putting the emphasis on activities along the critical path to ensure the success of a project. If performance of these activities falls below standards, then extra resources will need to be channelled into them immediately or new techniques and plans devised to put the process back on course.

Activities which do not lie on the critical path will not be so urgent (which is not the same as saying that they are not 'critical' in the ordinary sense). The term **total float** is applied to the period by which a non-critical activity can, if necessary, be extended without increasing the total project time. Clearly, an activity should not extend beyond its total float time.

Case Study

Program Evaluation and Review Techniques (PERT)

PERT was first developed by the US navy and was used successfully in the development of the Polaris Weapon System in the late 1950s. In the 1960s and 1970s it became particularly popular as a management technique. Today the principles of PERT are still widely used under different names (for example process re-engineering).

PERT uses time-event network analysis. For example, Figure 20.16 might represent the major milestones of progress in the developments and assembly of a passenger airline. Some of the steps might be as follows:

1. Take decision that project will go ahead.
2. Set out and procure engines for aircraft.
3. Complete plans and specification for the aircraft.
4. Complete drawings of main body of aircraft.
5. Award contract for tail section.
6. Award contract for construction of wings.
7. Finish manufacture of main body of plane, including internal fittings.
8. Complete assembly of engine.
9. Receive wings from subcontractor.
10. Receive tail from subcontractor.
11. Assemble various components of aircraft and deliver to airline.

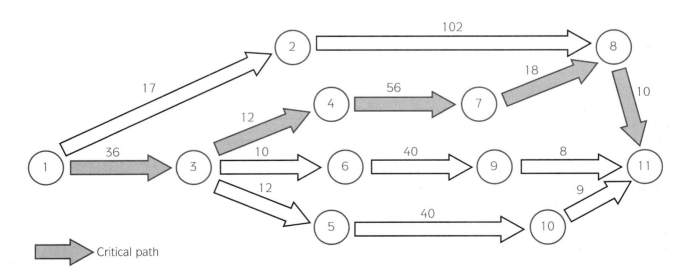

Figure 20.16 *Planning aircraft assembly*

In Figure 20.16, only one time is shown for each of the activities. In the original PERT programmes three separate times were shown:

- **The optimistic time** – the best-case scenario; the time that will be taken if everything goes to plan.

- **The most likely time** – the project engineer's 'realistic' estimate of what is most likely to happen.

- **The pessimistic time** – a worst-case scenario; the time that will be taken if each set of activities falls behind schedule.

Questions

1. What is process re-engineering?

2. How might it help project planning?

3. Who benefits from this process?

Slack time and crashing activities

Many projects are of such complexity that it is extremely difficult to predict the various outcomes, even though considerable planning has taken place beforehand. In today's world an organisation needs to plan for almost every eventuality. For example, when activities do not take place to schedule, then **slack time** for other resources might occur where they are waiting for other events or stages to be completed. Similarly, if planning does not run smoothly, more than one stage might require the use of the same resources and so activities may be **crashed.**

Network analysis is inappropriate when activities cannot be clearly identified and broken down into discrete sections. It is also inappropriate for routine mass production operations, though it could be used in the first instance to make plans for such operations. Its prime focus is upon time rather than upon costs. Costs, however, are an extremely important part of any planning process and an organisation ignores costs at its peril. For example, a weakness of central planning in the former Soviet Union was that resources were wasted in trying to meet time deadlines at any cost.

There are, however, a number of key benefits of network and critical path analysis:

- It forces managers to plan projects properly.
- Planning has to work down the line from managers to subordinates. Each person involved in the plan will need to take responsibility for part of the sequence.
- Emphasis is placed on the critical path.
- There can be forward-thinking control because time plans are made in advance of activities taking place. It is possible to measure performance against predetermined standards.
- Because the network of activities is broken down into discrete sections, it becomes possible for managers to target their reports and recommendations to the correct point in the organisation.

Gantt charts

Gantt charts are named after Henry Gantt, a management scientist who lived during the early years of the twentieth century. They are bar charts which compare actual progress with forecast progress. They can be used as a visual tool to indicate whether performances are on schedule. Figure 20.17 shows how information given in tabular form can be displayed as a Gantt chart.

Month	Forecast	Actual	Percentage
1	300	240	80
2	350	350	100
3	400	440	110

Figure 20.17 *A Gantt chart*

Using software in project management

One of the most important functions of management is to plan. For many the process of planning is not easy to undertake, particularly in a form which others can understand. Without a prescribed format, it is difficult to put a plan on paper so that it is intelligible to others. In the past, project planners simply used squared paper, a pencil and a good supply of erasers. Poor project planning might, for example, lead to a loss of production, business competitiveness or confidence in those who lead project teams.

Project management

Traditional organisations are structured with a pyramidal hierarchy. Relationships with departments then follow functional, product or geographical boundaries. Formal communication is directed down through a chain of command. These traditionally structured organisations work well in stable environments, but, because they are rigid they are often unsuitable for dynamic environments characterised by project situations.

A **project** is a non-routine set of activities culminating in a specific objective. It generally has a specific start date and finish date.

Project management is the process of ensuring that the project meets its objectives within the planned time-scale, and within the budgeted cost and resource budgets. Project management therefore involves a wide range of skills including:

- project planning
- client management
- quality management
- team leadership and communication skills.

Though planning software can only help with the first of these, the ability to produce clear and concise reports can assist the project manager in communicating.

A good project plan can:

- communicate to others in the organisation what is to be achieved
- demonstrate to the client how the project objectives will be achieved

- gain support from team members
- gain approval for the project
- demonstrate the requirement for additional resources or funding
- provide a baseline against which progress can be measured and controlled
- highlight cash flow requirements.

The project manager is the focal point for bringing together resources designed to meet project objectives. The project team is supported with a range of essential services. The project manager and team take responsibility for integrating people from various functions and then integrating them into the project.

Milestones help break projects into discrete segments to simplify the planning and control process. Times and costs can be assigned to each segment. By doing this, managers divide a complex project into a number of simpler parts to maintain control over each of the parts. Approval is then provided at the end of each stage to move on to the next stage. This is particularly useful in identifying whether a project is having problems, experiencing any form of slippage or beginning to go wrong so that key decisions such as investment can be made about its future.

Project management software

The breaking up of complex projects into stages for evaluation lends itself to the use of some form of computer project planning software which would enable managers to get rapid answers to questions. Project management software has been around for more than ten years, and many packages currently available have been through a number of evolutionary stages.

Modern software is very easy to use and offers a high-quality presentation on screen and when printed. However, a key element is not only that the software is easy to understand, but also that it can be closely related to the project.

All project management systems are essentially databases with the fields interrelated by predefined formulae. The various project views are simply graphical representations of the database data.

Project management software packages uses critical path method (CPM) as the scheduling method. The technique was developed by DuPont and Remington Rand in the 1950s to improve project scheduling methodology. CPM involves the calculation of the critical path, being the sequence of linked tasks forming the 'longest' route through the project. By determining which tasks are critical, it is therefore possible to shorten project duration by focusing resources on these tasks.

Critical path analysis (see above) is an important decision-making technique used in project planning. Once the critical path has been identified it becomes possible for project managers to keep a close eye on this sequence of activities to make sure that tasks are being completed on time. If problems arise it may be possible to plough extra resources into activities along this path.

MS Project, like many other project planning packages, uses Gantt charts to ensure the effective planning of activities, and compare actual progress with forecast progress. The Gantt chart uses the logical sequence of activities identified by critical path analysis and allows the project team to monitor its performance against the plan.

TASK

1. What is meant by project management?

2. Describe how project management software might assist with the completion of a project? In what areas are project planning tools unlikely to be useful? Explain why.

3. What are (a) critical path analysis, and (b) a Gantt chart? Explain how these tools help with the process of project planning. Why are they useful?

4. Explain how you would evaluate the success of a project. What criteria would you use?

INDICES

To provide a measure of how values change over time, it is sometimes necessary to construct an index. An index number is a measure, over time, designed to show average changes in the price, quantity or value of a group of items. The best-known index is the **Retail Price Index** (RPI). It measures general price inflation in the economy and is used by the government and other organisations as a basis on which wages and pensions might be altered (see page 493).

Simple index

How an index is constructed is particularly important as this will determine whether it accurately reflects the values it is measuring. The principle is to compare the value of items against a base value determined for a base period. It is a matter of convenience which base period should be used, providing accurate and comparable values can be obtained.

Example

An office cleaning company has decided to construct an index of hourly wage costs (see Figure 20.18). It uses 31 December 1996 as its base period. For each year the index is calculated, the current hourly rate is compared to the base value and multiplied by 100. So for 1999, $(£2.98/£2.72) \times 100 = 109.6$.

31 December of:	1996	1997	1998	1999	2000	2001
Hourly rate (£)	2.72	2.80	2.85	2.98	3.20	3.50
Wage cost index	100.0	102.9	104.8	109.6	117.6	128.7

Figure 20.18 *Index of hourly wage costs*

It is easy to interpret each value of the index in relation to the base period. Wages in 1997 were 2.9 per cent higher than in 1996 and wages in 2000 were 17.6 per cent higher. To determine the change between years other than the base year, take the change in the index and compare this with the earlier index number.

For example, to determine the wage increase in percentage terms during 2001:

$$= \frac{(128.7 - 117.6)}{117.6} \times 100\% = 9.4\%.$$

Aggregate index

The indices shown so far are price or relative indices. Many other types of index applying to many different areas are frequently used. As all are averages of one kind or another, they have the advantages and disadvantages common to many averages. In the same way that there are no perfect averages, so there is no perfect index.

A printing business wishes to construct an index of paper costs. The costs of a standard roll of paper over the past ten years has been:

	X0	X1	X2	X3	X4	X5	X6	X7	X8	X9
Cost	£123	£125	£127	£131	£135	£138	£142	£148	£153	£155

1. Construct the index for each year using X0 as the base period.

2. What has been the percentage increase in costs between X4 and X9?

The aggregate index takes into account weights. An index has to represent the relative importance of the different items it is monitoring. For example, for a house builder, the cost of bricks will be far more important than the cost of nails. It therefore becomes necessary to weight items according to their relative value.

The change in cost levels can either be due to a change in price or a change in the mix of items purchased. If the emphasis is on monitoring price changes, then it is important that the method isolates the change in total value caused by price movements from changes in quantities.

The **Laspeyre price index** weights all prices according to quantities used in the base period.

The index is calculated $= \dfrac{\Sigma p_n q_n}{\Sigma p_0 q_n}$

where p = price

q = quantity

n = in current period

o = in base period.

The **Paasche price index** weights prices according to current period of usage, and this requires all past values of the index to be recalculated. This method may be difficult to implement where current quantities are not yet available.

Case Study

Fabsteel Ltd

FabSteel Ltd, a steel fabricator, incurs only two direct costs; the cost of labour and the cost of sheet steel. All products require a similar mix of labour and materials and so for pricing purposes the management has decided that price lists can be updated more conveniently using an index based upon prime cost. Using 1996 as the base period, the relative weighting of the two input costs are to be decided by reference to the total quantities used in that year (see Figure 20.19).

31 December of:	1996 (£)	1997 (£)	1998 (£)	1999 (£)	2000 (£)	2001 (£)
Hourly rate	5.50	5.90	6.25	6.50	6.80	7.15
Steel sheet/ square metre	2.25	2.30	2.29	2.38	2.45	2.49
Total hours	85 000	87 000	88 000	91 000	92 000	91 000
Total steel square metres	122 000	135 000	145 000	163 000	181000	185 000

Figure 20.19 *FabSteel Ltd: direct costs, 1996–2001*

Each year's material and labour costs are weighted using 19X3 quantities (see Figure 20.20).

31 December of:	1996 (£)	1997 (£)	1998 (£)	1999 (£)	2000 (£)	2001 (£)
Hours in base period	85 000	85 000	85 000	85 000	85 000	85 000
Metres of steel in base period	122 000	122 000	122 000	122 000	122 000	122 000
Base quantities × period rate:						
Labour	467 500	501 500	531 250	552 500	578 000	607 750
Steel sheet	274 500	280 600	279 380	290 360	298 900	303 780
Cost of 19X3 resources used	742 000	782 100	810 630	842 860	876 900	911 530

Figure 20.20 *Weighted costs*

The total prime cost index can now be calculated with 19X3 equal to 100 (see Figure 20.21).

31 December of:	1996 (£)	1997 (£)	1998 (£)	1999 (£)	2000 (£)	2001 (£)
Prime cost index	100.0	105.4	109.2	113.6	118.2	122.8

Figure 20.21 *Total prime cost index*

Questions

1. Rework the index for FabSteel Ltd using the Paasche method for constructing a price index.

2. Evaluate the differences between the two indices.

Where an index represents a population of hundreds or possibly thousands of items, then by necessity the index will be based on a sample of items. To monitor the change to as large a proportion of costs as possible, there will be a need to bias sampling to large value items. For a price index of stock materials, this could be achieved by using a systematic sampling technique, or perhaps by simply choosing the 100 items with the highest annual purchase value.

However, for a materials price index it is important that the index reflects the nature of stock categories and the unique market conditions affecting individual categories. Consider the following items taken from the stock records of an engineering company involved in the manufacture of products containing mechanical and electronic components:

Components	Annual purchases (£)
Steel bar	200 000
Circuit board C34	40 000
Circuit board C35	40 000
Circuit board C36	40 000
Circuit board C37	40 000
Circuit board C38	40 000

If it were decided that all items with purchases of over £100 000 would comprise the materials cost index, then clearly the steel bar would be included and all of the circuit boards would be excluded. The problem is that taken together, the circuit boards have a combined purchases figure identical to the steel bar. Whole categories of stock that may have their own unique cost pressures

may be excluded because they are made up of a large number of different items.

The problem can be overcome by first identifying categories of items that should be represented by the index. The value of each category can then be given a weighting which will be represented by items taken from that category. In the example above, if the circuit board categories were represented by just one of the boards, it would carry the same weighting as the steel bar.

An index must remain relevant to current circumstances, just as the RPI is updated annually to reflect current spending patterns. This either requires the Paasche method to be used, or for the base period to be regularly reviewed in the case of the Laspeyre method.

TASK

A charity providing care in the community for elderly people charges its clients a standard hourly rate for services such as cleaning, shopping and gardening (see Figure 20.22). The charge is £2.20 per hour during 2002, up from £2.10 in 2001, irrespective of whether the work is undertaken by a volunteer or a paid worker. Unfortunately, 2002 sees the charity make a loss on care activities, having broken even in 2001 and despite having set the composite charge-out rate after agreeing wage rates for the year.

	1998	1999	2000	2001	2002
Volunteers' hours	5 200	6 300	7 350	7 580	6 950
Paid shopping					
Hours	800	900	1 000	950	1 000
Hourly rate	£2.00	£2.05	£2.10	£3.00	£3.10
Paid cleaning					
Hours	7 500	7 700	7 200	6 400	6 800
Hourly rate	£3.20	£3.30	£3.50	£4.00	£4.20
Gardening					
Hours	1 900	2 500	2 400	2 900	3 050
Hourly rate	£2.50	£2.60	£2.70	£3.10	£3.20

Figure 20.22 *Hours and hourly rates*

1. Calculate a composite wage rate index that could be used to monitor the charge-out rate in future. The base period for the index is to be 1998, and the weightings are to be based on the hours for 2002, including the unpaid volunteers' work.

2. Evaluate the data handled and advise the charity's management committee on the process it must go through when setting charge-out rates in future.

3. What implications does this have for maintaining a meaningful wage rate index?

Retail price index

The Retail Price Index is used as one method to measure inflation. It measures, on a monthly basis, the changes in the price of goods and services purchased by the average family, and is more often referred to as the headline measure of inflation. In the USA it is known as the US Bureau of Labor Statistics' Consumer Price Index where it is used as a measure of inflation which is used to adjust wages and prices so that measurements in constant dollars can be studied.

The RPI is an example of an official index. It was originally introduced to measure the cost of maintaining the standard of living of working-class households at a 1914 level. July 1914 was therefore fixed as a base, and a 'basket' of goods and services consumed by a typical working-class family of the time was selected with appropriate weightings allocated, which have been regularly updated.

There are a number of stages in constructing a price index. The first is to identify a list of commonly bought goods and services and a corresponding list of prices attached to such items. To take any individual as a purchasing unit would not really be satisfactory. As men, women and children tend to make different types of purchases, we would either require three lists or have to restrict the enquiry to one of these groups. Another question would have to be to analyse the type of household we are dealing with. Are they middle-income earners, do they have a small income or a large income? Finally, there is a time element. Every index number must have a starting point or a base year.

Using some, but not all, of the above criteria we can produce a simplified example for Country A where the four commodities included in its retail price index are bread, cheese, meat and vegetables:

Item	2000	2001
Bread	50p per loaf	55p per loaf
Cheese	130p per kg	125p per kg
Meat	160p per kg	180p per kg
Vegetables	40p per kg	50p per kg

Prices for bread, meat and vegetables have gone up but the price of cheese has fallen. We wish to produce a single index figure to reflect these changes but the table gives no indication of how important each item is to the cost of living and also tries to compare different units. This can be overcome by **weighting** each item in proportion to its relative importance. By selecting a weight the importance of each item and the units in which it appears are taken into consideration to produce a final figure which is directly comparable. The procedure for doing this is:

1. List all of the items with their prices.

2. Select appropriate weights.

3. Multiply prices by their weights.

4. Add the weighted prices together.

5. Produce an index by comparing the total weighted prices from the base year to the other year.

In our example we allocate a weight of 80 to bread, 50 to cheese, 30 to meat and 10 to vegetables. The weighted cost of living index is shown in Figure 20.24.

		2000		2001	
Item	Weight	Price (p)	Price × weight	Price (p)	Price × weight
Bread	80	50	4 000	55	4 400
Cheese	50	130	6 500	125	6 250
Meat	30	160	4 800	180	5 400
Vegetables	10	40	400	50	500
			15 700		16 550

Figure 20.24 *Weighted cost of living index*

By using 2000 as a base year and designating 100 to it we can see that:

$$\frac{16\,550}{15\,700} \times 100 = 105.41.$$

Prices over the year have risen by 5.41 per cent.

Deflation

We tend to make the assumption that the Retail Price Index is always likely to be rising, but there are situations where it could be falling when deflation occurs, particularly where items heavily weighted in the household budget are affected by falling prices. In these circumstances, though the base year will remain at 100, the subsequent yearly figures relating to the index will be less than 100.

FURTHER READING

Needham, D., and Dransfield, R., *Business Studies*, 2nd edition, Stanley Thornes, 1994.

Coles, M., *Financial Management for Higher Awards*, Heinemann, 1997.

Gibson, W., *Commercial and Industrial Statistics*, Hodder & Stoughton, 1997.

Daly, F., Hand, D.J., Jones, M.C., Lunn, A.D. and McConway, K.J., *Elements of Statistics*, Addison-Wesley, 1995.

Gregory, D., Ward, H. and Bradshaw, A., *Statistics for Business*, 4th edition, McGraw-Hill, 1993.

Chatfield, C., *Statistics for Technology*, 3rd Edition, Chapman and Hall, 1995.

Laudon, K.C. and Price Laudon, J., *Management Information Systems*: A Contemporary Perspective, 2nd Edition, Macmillan, 1991.

Carter, R., *Quantitative Methods for Business Students*, Heinemann, 1980.

Ostrom, C.W., *Time Series Analysis: Regression Techniques*, Sage, 1990.

Berenson, M.L. and Levine, D.M., *Basic Business Statistics: Concepts and Applications*, Prentice Hall, 1992.

Freund, J.E., Williams, F.J. and Perles, B.M. *Elementary Business Statistics: The Modern Approach*, Prentice Hall, 1993.

Lucey, T., *Quantitative Techniques*, DP Publications, 1992.

Payne, T.A., *Quantitative Techniques for Management: A Practical Approach*, Reston 1981.

Lee Sang, M. and Schniederjans, M.J, *Operations Management*, Houghton Mifflin, 1994.

Lewis, C.D., *Scientific Inventory Control*, Butterworth, 1981.

Hax, A.C. and Candea, D., *Production and Inventory Management*, Prentice Hall, 1984.

The Marketing Pocket Handbook, NTC Publications, published annually.

Reitsch, H., *Fundamentals of Business Statistics*, Charles Merrill, 1986.

ASSIGNMENT

It is not computers who take decisions, but people. Though numbers may isolate a problem or help to simplify complex alternatives, some factors can never be fully quantified. Decisions, therefore, usually depend not simply upon quantitative data but also upon qualitative considerations.

The purpose of this assignment is actively to involve you in examining a quantitative problem or issue within a small or medium-sized business. In solving this problem, it is important that you use at least one appropriate quantitative tool of analysis, supported by a full explanation describing how this enables the organisation to deal with the issue in question. In doing so you may refer to wider qualitative aspects of the problem.

The quantitative problem might be related to:

- planning, scheduling or coordinating
- accounting and costing
- stock systems and inventories
- measures of dispersion/spread
- market research data and its interpretation
- probability
- logistics
- forecasting methods
- operational research
- network and critical path analysis.

Your assignment should follow a rational process which uses a specified quantitative technique to engage with the planning process to identify alternatives and probabilities until the correct solution emerges.

Task

Focus upon an organisation. Meet and discuss this assignment with a member of the organisation. Emphasise the quantitative nature of the problem you are seeking to solve. You might find it helpful to discuss quantitative aspects of the business. Identify the nub of the problem from the discussion, remembering to discuss the different combination of key concepts and variables.

Think about whether you have met a similar problem before and the strategies you can use to unpick the problem. Decide upon the quantitative tools that you would like to use for solving the problem. If you are using a computer, decide what tools of analysis you are going to use as well as how you are going to use them. Construct the solution using quantitative tools. Analyse the data, taking into consideration wider qualitative considerations, and make a recommendation.

Legal and Regulatory Framework

Principles of Law

This chapter introduces you to the general principles of English law and how

they apply to the contractual process. It covers the formation of a valid commercial and

customer contract, the significance of its contents and the remedies available should it be breached.

On completion of the chapter you should be able to explain the general principles of the law of contract. To achieve this you must demonstrate the ability to:

- identify on what basis a contract can be made

- explain the significance of specialist terms contained in a specimen contract

- assess the validity of at least two contractual clauses contained in a specimen contract.

Introductory notes

Before reading this chapter you should note the distinction between two branches of law:

- **Common law** is law that has been developed through the courts and which is based on past decisions. With certain exceptions, the doctrine of **precedent** requires the courts to follow past decisions in cases with similar facts and covering the same points of law – although the doctrine of **equity** allows the courts in certain instances to ameliorate some of the harshness of the common law by looking at the essential fairness of the situation.
- **Statutory law** is created when parliament enacts new legislation through an **Act of Parliament** (or **statute**) which then becomes binding on the courts. Parliament's powers are limited to some extent by the European Communities Act 1972 which provides that an enactment of the UK parliament is subject to the direct applicability legislation of the European Union. Any Community legislation which is inconsistent with UK legislation must be given precedence.

Case references are included in the text to assist any further research you may want to undertake. An initial search through the catalogue system of either your own establishment's library or that of a large public library should assist you with the various abbreviations.

DEFINITION OF A CONTRACT

Any **contract** should indicate that there has been *'consensus ad idem'*, which means a meeting of minds between the two people or parties concerned. In theory, therefore, there should be no need for any legal intervention. In practice, some legal regulation of such promises is essential, not only from a moral standpoint but also from a commercial perspective in that the business world would come to a halt should broken promises be allowed to go unchecked. Legal theorists differ in their approach to this. One early school favours the doctrine of **freedom of contract** based on the assumption of equal bargaining power of the contracting parties; whatever is agreed between them, stands. Later theorists – and the courts – have chosen to modify this approach by examining the **reality** of the situation and by instituting a system of checks and balances where necessary. In this respect, the courts are assisted by:

- the volume of case law relating to contracts for the sale and supply of goods, and contracts of employment
- the establishing of certain essential elements that must be present before such contracts will be held to be valid.

ESSENTIALS OF A VALID CONTRACT

A landmark case in contract law is *Carlill v Carbolic Smoke Ball Co.* [1893] 1 QB256, in which a customer complained that a 'carbolic smoke ball' had not protected her from influenza despite the fact that the manufacturers of the product had advertised it together with a promise that they would pay £100 to anyone who had used the preparation three times daily for two weeks and who had then contracted influenza. To support their contention, they stated that they had deposited a sum of £1000 in a bank as a sign of their sincerity. When the case reached court, it almost unwittingly provided the perfect scenario for the court to restate the essential elements of a contract. These are:

- There must be an *offer*.
- There must be an *acceptance*.
- Some *consideration* must pass hands.
- There must be an *intention* to create legal relations.
- It must be in the *correct format*.
- The two parties must have the *capacity* to contract with each other.
- The contract must be for a legal *purpose*.
- There must be *reality of consent*.

The main argument used by the manufacturers was that the advertisement could not be regarded as a contract. It was an offer made to the whole world, not just one person, and could not therefore be enforced under the doctrine of **privity of contract**; i.e. that a contract must be between two people. This argument was rejected on the grounds that an offer *had been made to individuals* – those people who had bought the product in good faith believing the promises made. However, the manufacturers also maintained that:

- The offer was too *vague* since no time limit had been stipulated in which the user was to contract influenza
- there was no real *intention* to create legal relations, the advertisement being designed merely to raise interest.

These arguments, too, were rejected by the court. For further discussion on each one, see pages 501 and 503.

Offer and acceptance

Although in most cases it is quite clear when an offer has been made and accepted, on occasions there is a stage that precedes the offer – commonly known as 'the invitation to treat' or an expression of willingness to enter into negotiations. If, for instance, a prospective buyer walks into a supplier's salesroom, sees some furniture and asks to buy it, an offer will not have been made at that stage – only an invitation to the buyer to make a suitable offer. Further examples are:

- an announcement of the holding of an entrance scholarship examination to a particular school (an offer of a place had not been made to the candidates who passed the examination)
- a catalogue or newspaper advertising goods for sale at a certain price
- a price list
- a personal quotation of the price of goods
- a prospectus or advertisement for shares.

Note, however, that all the following have been held to be offers:

- an announcement that a train would run on time
- a display of deck-chairs for hire on the beach
- a 15-day temporary cover sent by an insurance company at the expiration of a policy.

Case Study

Read the following two cases and answer the questions below.

(i)   A council decided to allow its tenants to buy their council houses if they wished. One of them did so and completed the required application form which contained details of the sale price and mortgage arrangements. The council replied by sending details of the terms it 'may be prepared to sell at' and enclosing a form inviting applicants to purchase. The tenant completed the form and sent it back. In the meantime, however, the political control of the council changed and the practice of selling council houses was discontinued. The tenant sued the council for breach of contract. The council maintained that the documentation sent to the tenant was merely an invitation to treat and not an offer. Therefore there could be no acceptance.

(ii)   An intentionally simplified agreement for sale form was sent to a council house tenant who had enquired about the possibility of buying his house. The council at that time advised him that if he wished to go ahead with the sale he should sign the agreement and return it, when it would be countersigned.

The tenant did so. However, as in the previous case, before it was countersigned, the policy of selling council houses was changed and only those cases where the contracts had been exchanged were authorised to continue. The tenant sued.

Questions

1. Discuss what you think were the outcomes of each case – which did differ – giving reasons for your conclusion. Check your answer with the actual outcomes stated below.

2. Two cases with very similar facts but having two different outcomes is a clear example of a 'legal' rather than a 'logical' outcome – particularly if you happen to be the disappointed tenant. Indeed in the first case, Lord Denning maintained that there was an 'agreement in fact' which should be enforceable. Discuss the advantages and disadvantages of abandoning the concept of invitation to treat and allowing prospective buyers to be held to have made an offer when they first express a wish to purchase.

Counter offer

An offer must be **unequivocal**; i.e. absolute and without qualification. One of the arguments used by the manufacturers in the Carlill/Carbolic case was that the offer was too vague because no time limit had been specified. Although in that case the court decided that the product had been intended to protect its user throughout the course of its use, and that therefore the offer **was** sufficiently well defined, in other cases the vagueness of an offer has led to the conclusion that the contract is **inchoate**; i.e. incomplete. Even so the courts will try to assist the parties to a contract by ignoring as far as possible the vagueness of certain terms provided the rest of the contract seems satisfactory.

However, an offer must not introduce any new conditions, otherwise it becomes a **counter offer** which replaces the original offer. Interestingly, if an offeree does make a counter offer, he or she cannot change course and decide to accept the original offer. That has lapsed. If, however, the plaintiff has merely asked for further information the offer remains open.

TASK

For further information research the following cases:

- *Scammel v Ouston* [1941] AC 251
- *Hillas & Co. Ltd. v Arcos Ltd.* [1932] 1AER 494
- *Hyde v Wrench* [1840] 3 Beav 334
- *Stevenson v McLean* [1880] 5 QBD 346.

Revocation of an offer

A more difficult situation arises where someone makes an offer and then attempts to withdraw or **revoke** it. An offer can be revoked, but for this to be effective it must be communicated to the offeree **before** he or she has accepted the offer. When revocation is by letter the question arises as to whether it is effective when delivered or when read. The usual conclusion is that it is effective when the offeree has had a 'reasonable' time or opportunity to read it after delivery. (See page 502 for rules relating to communication of offer and acceptance.) An offer will be held to have **lapsed** in the following circumstances:

- if one of the parties has died
- if it is conditional and the condition is not satisfied
- by the passage of time.

> **Answer to case study above**
>
> In case (i) – *Gibson v Manchester City Council* [1979] 1 AER 972, the court decided that at no stage had a final offer been made to the tenant. The documentation merely illustrated the final arrangements the council **may** have been prepared to accept. In case (ii), *Storer v Manchester City Council* [1974] 3 AER 824 (CA), the sending of the agreement for sale constituted an offer. The form had been designed deliberately not to be too formal, and therefore a further exchange of documents was unnecessary. The contract was therefore completed when the tenant signed the agreement.

Acceptance

Once the offer has been made it has then to be **accepted** before the contract can proceed to the next stage. Although it is normally obvious that an acceptance has taken place, in some cases doubts can arise either because it is not clear that the acceptor is aware of the existence of the offer or, more likely, that the acceptance has not been absolute and unqualified.

An acceptance must not introduce any new terms into the contract, otherwise it again becomes a counter offer. Nor is it a final acceptance if, as is common business practice, the words 'subject to contract' are included in any written communications. Similarly an agreement to continue to negotiate until an agreement is reached is not enforceable – although a *negative* undertaking (even given orally) by a seller that he or she will not, for a given period, deal with anyone else once the purchaser has agreed to buy and is proceeding with the exchange of contracts *is* enforceable.

Communication of acceptance

An offer is valid only when it has reached the offeree. An acceptance, however, is valid immediately it has left the hands of the offeree. This principle was clearly established in *Household Fire Insurance Co. v Grant* ([1879] 4 Ex D 216) where it was held that an offer for shares was complete when the letter of allotment was posted, even though it was never received.

These basic principles, however, become slightly more complex when applied to more modern methods of communication such as e-mail, fax and the Internet.

Case Study

Read the following summary of an article in a legal journal:

Electronic communication enables messages to be sent and received outside working hours and it is therefore essential to determine the point of time at which such a communication should be treated as legally effective. In one case, *Mondial Shipping and Chartering BV v Astarte Shipping Ltd.* (Commercial Law Cases 1995), an agreement between the owners and charterers of a ship stated that the owners had the right to withdraw the vessel without any formality if the charterers were in default of hire. The agreement also contained an anti-technicality clause which obliged the owners to give the charterers 48 hours' notice, excluding Saturday, Sunday and holidays, before exercising their right to withdraw. Should the

charterer pay within 48 hours then the anti technicality clause obliged the owners not to withdraw their ship. However, the notice must not be premature.

When the hire charge for December was not received, the owners sent notice in an abbreviated form by telex at 11.41 pm on Friday 2 December. It was received instantaneously on the charterer's telex machine. When the hire charge was still not received, the owners withdrew their vessel on 7 December. The validity of the withdrawal depended on whether the notice fulfilled the requirements of the anti-technicality clause and whether or not it was premature. This in turn depended on when it was received.

Neither party disputed that the 'midnight rule' applied. Thus payment of the hire was not due until midnight on 2/3 December and notice given before then was premature. It was therefore necessary to determine when the notice was effective and this depended upon when it was regarded as having been *received*. The owner contended that it was effective when it was – or must be taken to have been – first read by a responsible member of the charterer's organisation, i.e. on Monday 5 December at 9 am or shortly afterwards. Thus it was not premature and consequently the notice was valid. The charterers, however, argued that the notice was received when it was printed out on their telex machine (11.41 pm on 2 December) and that therefore the notice was indeed premature.

The case was decided in favour of the owners. The court held that no universal rule can cover all such cases and that decisions should be reached by reference to sound business practice. Therefore the presumption that a communication sent out of business hours by telex, fax or e-mail is effective when business hours recommence on the next working day is in line with the common sense rule.

Source: Emily Haslam, *Contracting by electronic means*, New Law Journal, April 19 1996

Question

Discuss what dangers you think there may be in taking such an approach rather than relying upon a definitive ruling.

Consideration

Consideration is the third essential element of a contract, alongside offer and acceptance. In most cases it involves the promise of money in return for some goods or a service.

- **Executed** consideration exists where one party promises to do something in return for some form of action by the other. In other words, the owner of a lost dog promises to pay a reward to the person who finds it.
- **Executory** consideration exists where one party promises to do something in return for the promise of the other party to do the same. A potential purchaser promises to pay for a piece of equipment and the supplier of that equipment promises to deliver it.

However, not all consideration is valid.

Past consideration

Past consideration cannot be enforced i.e. the performance of an act in the hope that it will be rewarded. If, for example, a freelance market researcher carries out a series of marketing exercises for a manufacturer without first establishing that he or she is going to be paid for the work, a demand at a later date may not be legally enforceable (unless the court 'implies' a promise by the manufacturer that a reasonable sum of money should be paid for the work carried out). (See page 507 for further discussion on implied terms.)   \

Consideration must move from the promisee

Because the law places so much emphasis on a contract being between two parties alone, any consideration which

is provided by a third party – such as a friend or relative – is not normally permissible.

Real consideration

Consideration must be **real** to be enforceable. If, for instance, someone performs an act which he or she is already contractually obliged to do, then that act will not be regarded as consideration for any other contract.

Value or adequacy of consideration

However, provided *some* consideration passes hands, the courts will not normally be prepared to consider whether it is *adequate* consideration. Their usual stance is that the amount of payment is a managerial issue, not a legal one, although in certain circumstances they may regard inadequate consideration as evidence of duress, undue influence or mistake. (See pages 505 and 507 for further discussion.) Consequently, standard contracts in the world of the performing arts often contain a specific clause advising young performers in particular to consult a legal adviser before signing a potentially onerous contract. The employers may not be acting purely altruistically but merely trying to avoid adverse legal repercussions. One additional safeguard for some employees is the legislation enacted in the National Minimum Wage Act 1998 and Regulations 1999 which provide that a basic minimum wage rate be paid.

Intention to create legal relations

Although in the Carlill/Carbolic case the manufacturers contended that the advertisement was never intended to create legal relations, the court held that the depositing of the £1000 indicated it was more than merely an advertising gimmick and that therefore **intention** could be proved. In most cases, intention is clear, the only exceptions tending to be domestic arrangements which, for obvious reasons, are presumed not to intend to create legal relations. Even so, this can be rebutted if the family has split up or has been subject to an outside influence. Even commercial agreements may be rebutted where either party states clearly that the agreement is not intended to be legally enforceable.

Form of contract

Most contracts do not need to be in written form and an oral contract is just as binding (although far less easy to prove) than a written one. In *Mountstephen v Lakeman* [1871] LR 7QB 196, for instance, the chairperson of a local board of health was held personally liable to pay a building contractor whom he had verbally authorised to carry out some work, even though the board itself disclaimed responsibility on the grounds that (a) it had not authorised the chairperson to make the agreement, and (b) there was nothing in writing.

However, there are exceptions. These include some regulated agreements under the Consumer Credit Act 1974, contracts of marine insurance, and some contracts for the sale or other disposition of land. In addition, some contracts need not be in writing but must be **evidenced** in writing. The courts would not, for instance, enforce a guarantee in the absence of written evidence.

Capacity to contract

Not everyone is able to enter into a contract. For instance, people who are drunk or suffer from a mental disorder will not be able to enter a valid contract if it can be proved that they did not understand the nature of the contract and that the other party knew that to be the case.

Minors

Minors may enter into contracts but only under certain rather restrictive circumstances.

TASK

A solicitor is asked to advise a young client as to his rights. His client is 17 years old and on an impulse has started up a business to write computer software packages. He has rented some premises and furnished them extravagantly on the grounds that he wants to impress potential customers and cannot do so in dingy surroundings. He hires a van to transport all his materials and equipment. He also decides he needs some smart clothes as all he has at the moment are T-shirts, jeans and trainers – although, once having bought them, he now wants to get his money back as he feels the new clothes don't suit him. He doesn't think much of the premises he has leased and wonders if he can recover the rent he has paid.

He then decides that it's all been too much of an effort and that he'd rather backpack round Europe for a few months. He ignores the fact that he owes a number of people a substantial sum of money.

When he comes back he decides to try a modern apprenticeship. His employer spends a lot of money on him including sending him on a year-long part-time day-release course in advanced computer training at a local college. After a month he has another fit of inertia and leaves the company. The company tries to make him pay back the college fees. His other creditors are also pressing him for money.

1. Can the solicitor assure him that, because he is a minor, he is immune from all legal repercussions? Cases to assist you include:

Business organisations

In a business context, probably the most important application of the capacity to contract is the way in which it affects the contracting ability of business organisations. A sole trader has the capacity to contract as an individual. So, too, have a group of partners albeit that they may be both joint and severally liable for any contracts. (For further discussion on this point, see page 531.) An incorporated company is also regarded as a legal entity as the process of incorporation allows the company to separate its identity from that of its members – and consequently lessens the risk for its shareholders. Although the company will be held totally liable for its debts, the individual shareholders will have their liability limited to any amount outstanding to be paid on their shares (see *Salomon v Salomon Ltd.* [1897] AC 22). However, the concept of the 'veil of incorporation' does allow directors or other persons to be prosecuted if they appear to have acted fraudulently (for further discussion, see page 528).

Legal purpose

Illegal contracts

If two people enter into a contract for an illegal purpose, it will be unenforceable by either party.

Contracts contrary to public policy

What is probably a more relevant cause for dispute in this area, however, are contracts which, because they are contrary to public policy, are *prima facie* void (i.e. a contract with no legal force) even though not illegal. These include both contracts to remove a case from the jurisdiction of a court and contracts prejudicial to marriage. In addition, the Resale Prices Act 1976 makes it illegal for suppliers to agree to withhold supplies from suppliers who resell the goods in breach of any condition as to the price at which the goods may be resold.

Growing in significance are cases relating to contracts in **restraint of trade**. For example, employers are often concerned about employees who either have access to trade secrets and/or who possess high level transferable skills of benefit to a competitor. As a safeguard they often insert a restraint of trade clause into the contract, preventing particular employees from setting up in business on their own or transferring to a competitor, either for a specific period of time after leaving or within a certain geographical area. Because this type of clause is contrary to the principle of freedom of contract, it is *prima facie* contrary to public policy and therefore void.

However, albeit reluctantly, the courts are prepared to allow the insertion of such clauses provided they are not too restrictive. The restraint must be reasonable and designed to protect the business, not to stamp out competition. Nor must it form part of a contract which is considered by the courts to be onerous overall. In *Schroeder Music Publishing Co. Ltd. v Macaulay* [1974] 1 WLR 1308, for instance, the court held that a contract between a young musician and a music publisher was an unreasonable restraint of trade because it tied the musician to a very stringent set of terms and conditions, including allowing the publisher world copyright, the right to choose whether or not to publish, and the right to terminate the agreement at one month's notice.

Reality of consent

If the courts feel that the consent by one party to an agreement is not 'real' because of the presence of certain **vitiating factors** (i.e. factors affecting the validity of the contract), then the contract may be considered either void or voidable – a contract which the injured party has the choice of ending or continuing.

Mistakes

The old adage 'ignorance of the law is no excuse' applies to the law of contract in the same way as it does to other areas. Where, therefore, one of the parties to a contract claims there has been no real agreement because a **mistake** has been made, the courts will refuse to listen unless the mistake has been one of fact, not law.

Unilateral mistakes of fact are those made by one party. Consider the following examples.

- A person signs a contract in the mistaken belief that he or she is signing a completely different type of contract (*'non est factum'* – it is not my deed). This defence is rarely available to people of full capacity, who can see, read and write.
- Someone is mistaken as to some fundamental fact in the contract, and the other person *knows* that he or she is mistaken.
- Someone contracts with another person but is mistaken as to his or her identity, and that person *allows* the mistake to go uncorrected. In such cases, however, although not void for mistake, the contract is likely to be voidable for fraud.

Bilateral mistakes of fact arise where both parties are making false assumptions. 'Res extincta' describes the situation where there is a common mistake as to the existence of the subject matter of the contract. Another example of bilateral mistake is where two parties have reached agreement but have made an identical mistake as to the quality of the subject matter of the contract, if, for example, both believe a piece of furniture to be a genuine antique when in fact it is a modern reproduction. Occasionally there are cases of *mutual but non-identical bilateral mistake*, where, for instance, one person offers to sell one article – a car on a car lot – and the other person agrees but thinks he or she is buying the motor bike next to it.

Case Study

In *Lewis v Averay* [1971] 3 AER 907, the plaintiff (Lewis) agreed during a personal interview to sell his car to a man who said he was a well-known television actor and who gave him some evidence to confirm it. The man paid for the car with a cheque which was dishonoured a few days later. In the meantime, however, the car had been sold on to the defendant (Averay). When Lewis discovered the fraud he brought an action against Averay for the return of the car. The Court of Appeal

held in favour of Averay in that Lewis had effectively contracted to sell the car to the bogus television actor and therefore could not recover it from Averay or sue for damages. In his judgement, Lord Denning commented: 'this is another case where one of two innocent persons has to suffer for the fraud of a third'.

Questions

1. Why do you think the plaintiff decided to bring an action for mistake rather than fraud? Consider the difference between a void and a voidable contract and how that may have affected the decision.

2. An argument put forward on behalf of the plaintiff was that, although when the two parties meet face to face it is not usual to regard their identity as a vital term of the contract, a different conclusion should be reached if the seller has made it clear that the purchaser's identity is an essential part of the contract. What do you think are the merits and drawbacks of such an argument?

Misrepresentation

There can be no reality of consent if one of the parties to the contract makes a **misrepresentation** to the other, whether it be innocent, negligent or fraudulent. Misrepresentation arises in the following circumstances:

- If *there is a misleading statement*. Silence or non-disclosure is normally not misrepresentation except in certain limited situations.
- If the *statement made is a statement of fact*. Statements of law are excluded from this. So too are statements as to future conduct or intention, unless it is clear that the person who made the statement had no intention of complying with it. Statements of opinion are not normally actionable, although if the statement also involves a statement of fact, misrepresentation could be held to have occurred. A job reference, for instance, could contain a statement that the person concerned was highly recommended and also highly trustworthy. The first statement is difficult to contest, the second, if untrue, less so.
- If *it is not merely media hype* (although the manufacturers in the Carlill/Carbolic case may disagree). Even so, advertisers try to avoid being too definite. 'This is

probably the best product in the world' is definitely safer than 'This is the best product in the world'.
- If *the effect of the statement has been to induce the other party to act on it*. Obviously, if the person to whom the misrepresentation has been made knows that it is untrue, then he or she has no 'cause for action'.

See the Misrepresentation Act 1967 for the different remedies applying to each type of misrepresentation.

DURESS AND UNDUE INFLUENCE

No consent to a contract can be real if it has been obtained under **duress** by threats of violence to person or property. In addition to physical duress, however, there is economic duress, a more modern concept, which allows one party to claim that the inequality of the bargaining power between the two parties has affected the contract. If the courts agree, the contract then becomes voidable. Examples include:

- a contract between a shipowner and trade union for improved pay and conditions negotiated because the trade union had refused to make tugs available when the ship arrived in port to discharge her cargo
- a contract between two organisations where one of the parties who had agreed to erect stands for an exhibition to take place on a particular date, threatened to strike unless it received extra money

In addition the courts will sometimes hold that an 'unconscionable bargain' has been made between two parties, one of whom is at an obvious disadvantage because of old age, infirmity etc., and will therefore set that contract aside.

The courts might take a similar view if a contract has been negotiated which falls short of physical duress but which in some way places one party in a far weaker bargaining position than the other. The law recognises, for instance, that there are certain relationships which could lead to **undue influence**. These include parent or guardian and child, solicitor and client, trustee and beneficiary, religious adviser and acolyte – but no longer that of husband and wife. Nor is there deemed to be a special relationship between employer and employee, despite the demonstrably weaker bargaining position of some employees.

CLASSIFICATION OF TERMS IN CONTRACTS

Contracts can be expressed very informally, although generally the more money that is involved in the transaction, the more formal the written evidence of it tends to be. No matter how formal or informal, however, most contracts contain certain standard terms.

Express and implied terms

Express terms

These are the details of the contract, spelt out either orally or in writing, as a result of the negotiations between the two parties to a contract. Quantities, prices and schedules will be important amongst the express terms.

Implied terms

These are terms that form part of the contract *regardless* of the express agreement of the parties. Some are implied by statutes such as the Sale of Goods Act 1979 (see further page 515). Some are implied by custom (i.e. the normal dealings in a particular industry). Others are implied by common law, so that the courts are then able to 'read between the lines' of a contract to make it workable. In some circumstances a term is implied simply because, if asked whether or not it should be regarded as present, the 'average man' (or woman) would reply 'Of course it should'.

Conditions, warranties and innominate terms

Conditions

The conditions are the terms in a contract that are vital to the main purpose of the contract. *Conditions precedent* do not create a contractual obligation until the condition specified in the contract actually arises (e.g. if a sale of a house is dependent on someone being able to sell his or hers first). *Conditions subsequent* have the opposite effect; there is a contractual obligation on the occurrence of a specified event (e.g. a building contract that specifies a completion date).

Warranties

These are terms in a contract that are less vital (e.g. a term specifying delivery dates – provided the goods are not perishable or it has been specified that they are needed for some specific event or date).

Innominate terms

These are terms that may be described as either conditions or warranties, depending on the seriousness of the effect of any breach of the contract. If the breach has serious consequences then it will be a breach of a condition; if less serious, it will be a breach of warranty.

Distinction between the terms

The distinction between the foregoing terms is important. If the courts determine that a condition has been breached, the injured party will be able either to cancel the contract ('repudiate it') or claim damages. If a warranty has been breached, the contract will not be affected and the injured party will be able only to claim damages.

DISCHARGE OF A CONTRACT

Discharge by performance

Most contracts come to an end when they have been **performed** (i.e. when everything that was agreed to be done has been done). A major difficulty arises in this respect if part but not all of the contract has been performed. The common law rule is stringent and insists that unless there is complete performance, the other party to the contract is not obliged to carry out his or her part of the bargain. This stance has, however, been modified in certain circumstances:

- where the contract has been only partially performed, but that is acceptable to the injured party
- by the doctrine of 'quantum meruit' – an equitable **remedy** granting a payment for goods or services received in partial fulfilment of a contract – particularly where the contract has substantially been performed
- where it is clear that the parties intended one signed

contract – such as one for the delivery of a series of consignments of goods – to be a series of agreements (a **divisible** contract), then each agreement will be considered to be a separate contract.

Discharge by agreement

Obviously, if a contract is simply not working out and both parties recognise this, the contract can be ended by mutual agreement.

Discharge by breach

Where one party wants to end the agreement or fails to discharge his or her part of the bargain, a **breach of contract** occurs. Such a breach can arise

- through failure to perform the contract (e.g. non-delivery of goods, delivery of goods of the wrong quality, non-payment)
- by one party failing or refusing to perform his or her part of the contract
- through some action by one party which makes performance impossible.

Discussion point

Any breach which takes place before the time for performance has arrived is called an anticipatory breach. When this occurs the injured party has the option

a to sue at once for damages, or

b to wait for the time of performance to arrive to see whether the other party will be prepared at that time to carry out the contract.

If you were the injured party in such a case, what factors would influence you into taking either the first or the second course of action?

Discharge by frustration

A music hall burned down before the date it had been hired for a performance. The court held that the owner of the hall was not entitled to the hire payment as the contract was **frustrated**; i.e. incapable of being performed. This was not because of anything either party had done but because of an event outside their control. Consequently, the contract was treated as never having existed and the rights and duties of both parties were unenforceable. (See The Law Reform (Frustrated Contracts) Act 1943 for further discussion.)

Other examples of frustration include cases where:

- a professional singer fell ill and could not therefore appear in a production
- the outbreak of war prevented the completion of a contract for the delivery of goods
- the coronation of King Edward VII was postponed through his illness and thus prevented those who had booked accommodation at vantage points along the proposed route from watching the procession.

However, the courts have been much more reluctant to apply the doctrine of frustration if, for example:

- the agreement is impossible from the outset – in such circumstances the court would normally expect the parties to rely upon the doctrine of mistake (see page 505)
- the contract merely becomes too expensive to perform because circumstances have changed since the agreement was first negotiated
- the contract makes provision for frustration – if an event can be foreseen it is not beyond the powers of the parties to do something about it
- one party is responsible for the act that caused the frustration – as, for instance, where a shipowner agreed to transport some goods and then sold his ship before the transport took place
- the contract is for the sale of land and leases (although in more recent cases, doubt has been cast on this exemption).

SPECIALIST TERMS IN CONTRACTS

Some of the standard terms in a contract have already been discussed. However, many formal agreements tend to include additional and more specialist terms, sometimes relating to a particular industry, sometimes reflecting the importance of the contract itself.

Exclusion clauses

Although recognising the right of two parties to negotiate freely, UK law is suspicious of any attempts to circumvent the force of law by the introduction into the contract of **exclusion clauses** that limit liability for breach of contract. Consequently any exclusion clause is subject to fairly rigorous **interpretation** by the courts. When assessing its validity the courts will examine the following:

- How was the clause communicated to the other party? Communication must be made before the formation of the contract, otherwise the clause will be invalid.
- Is it contained in a signed or an unsigned document? If the document is signed, it is difficult for any party to disclaim liability. If it is not signed, then it will need to be proved that the document containing the clause was integral to the contract and could be expected to contain contractual terms.
- Can the clause be considered too onerous? If it can, it must be brought specifically to the attention of the other party. Indeed Lord Denning has made the point that the more unreasonable a clause is, the greater the notice that must be given of it (i.e. it should be printed in red ink with a red hand pointed to it!).
- Do any previous dealings of the parties indicate that it is normal for the particular clause to be included?

A second safeguard used by the courts to ensure that an exclusion clause is as **fair as possible** is to interpret its construction very strictly.

- They impose the **applicability rule** and will not extend the meaning of the clause to cover anything not mentioned. Consequently a clause in a contract exempting a firm of cycle hirers from contractual liability for any personal injury was not sufficient to exempt them from an action for negligence.
- They interpret any 'doubtful' clause against the person seeking to rely on it.
- They apply the **repugnancy rule** (i.e. the total non-performance rule). Where the clause purports to exclude liability for the actual performance of the contract, the court will dismiss it.
- They apply the rule of **absolute performance**, whereby the party will be able to rely on the exclusion clause only if he or she has performed his or her contractual obligations to the letter.

For discussion of the Unfair Contract Terms Act 1977 (supplemented by the Unfair Terms in Consumer Contract Regulations 1994), which offers further protection to the consumer in this area, see page 518.

see page 518.

Force majeure

A **force majeure** term is often inserted in commercial contracts to excuse performance under certain circumstances – Act of God, strikes, adverse weather conditions, etc.

Price variation

Most suppliers are reluctant to be bound by a fixed price in case they have miscalculated increases in the costs of raw materials, overheads, etc. What they therefore tend to do is to insert a term allowing a **price variation** in certain circumstances.

Retention of title

In most commercial contracts there is a **retention of title** clause outlining when, and in what circumstances, the property or 'title' of the goods will pass from the seller to the purchaser – normally when the goods have been paid for (S.19 of the Sale of Goods Act 1979). Should the buyer become bankrupt or go into liquidation, the seller will then be able to recover the goods as the title in the goods will not have passed to the buyer.

Liquidated damages

Many commercial contracts contain a clause stating the amount of **liquidated damages** to be paid as a result of a breach of that contract. This is permissible provided it is a genuine pre-estimate of the loss and not a penalty. For further discussion, see 'Calculation of damages' below.

REMEDIES FOR BREACH OF CONTRACT

Common law remedies

Obviously, in most cases where there has been a breach of contract, there will be a claim for some kind of recompense. Much depends on whether the problem is a breach of a condition (in which case the injured party has the choice of refusing to continue with the contract or of continuing with it but claiming damages), or breach of a warranty (in which case he or she may only claim damages).

Calculation of damages

The calculation of damages is based on the Latin maxim *'ubi jus ibi remedium'* – where a right exists, a **remedy** exists. The courts try, wherever possible, to remedy the situation by placing the injured party in the position he or she would have been in had the contract taken place. The damages awarded can be nominal, substantial or exemplary.

- **Nominal damages** are awarded when, although technically there has been a breach, no actual harm has been caused and the damages are therefore minimal.
- **Substantial damages** are awarded when the aim is to recompense the injured party for any adverse consequences of the breach of contract.
- **Exemplary damages** go beyond recompense. For some reason, normally as a social or moral response, the courts award the injured party damages greater that those arising from the loss. Such damages may be awarded, for instance, in cases where there has been a blatant breach of a contract of employment by the employer which has caused undue distress to the employee.

Damages can also be liquidated or unliquidated. As already mentioned, **liquidated** damages are allowed provided a court feels that they are a genuine pre-estimate of loss rather than intentionally punitive. If no such pre-estimate has been made, the damages payable are defined as **unliquidated** and it is left to the courts to determine the level of damages to be awarded. In doing so they will take into account:

- what loss has been suffered by the injured party
- the remoteness of the damage.

A major case in this area was *Hadley v Baxendale* [1854] 9 Exch 341, in which the plaintiff (Hadley) hired the defendant to transport a broken mill shaft to the manufacturer for repair. Baxendale promised to do so the following day but failed to carry out his promise. Hadley sued for damages for the loss of production that had occurred as a result. It was held by the court that he could not succeed in this claim because damages could be paid only for:

- losses arising naturally or in the normal course of events
- losses that may *reasonably* be supposed to have been in the minds of the parties at the time they made the contract and were the probable result of a breach of that contract.

In the Hadley case, the court felt that in the normal course of events Hadley could have been expected to have a spare mill shaft and to have informed the defendant in advance that the mill would have to close if the shaft was not repaired on time. Baxendale could not have been reasonably expected to have foreseen that.

Type of damage

Traditionally the courts were reluctant to award damages other than for financial loss, personal injuries and pain and suffering. More recently, however, they have awarded damages for inconvenience and discomfort, psychological suffering and psychiatric injury.

Mitigation of loss

Even if a breach of the contract has occurred, the injured party must show that he or she has tried to **mitigate** (reduce) the loss caused by the breach. He or she cannot recover for a loss that could reasonably have been avoided.

Case Study

In one case the plaintiff was the owner of a car which, although old, was in an excellent state of repair and had a market value then (in 1963) of £85. The car was damaged because of negligence by a third party and the cost of repairs was £192. The plaintiff claimed the £192 from the insurer plus the cost of hiring a car whilst the repairs were being carried out. The insurance company refused to pay. The case went to court where the plaintiff's case failed.

Questions

1. What might the plaintiff have done to mitigate his losses?

2. Do you think the duty to mitigate losses puts too heavy a burden on the plaintiff? Might it make the defendant less concerned about the effects of any breach of contract?

Equitable remedies

If the courts feel that the common law remedies already discussed are inappropriate, they have the discretion (but not the obligation) to consider certain so-called **equitable remedies**, as follows:

- **Rescission** – where, for instance, goods and/or money are returned to the original owners to restore both to the pre-contractual position. Obviously this remedy can occur only where rescission is possible (e.g. not where the goods have been transferred to a third party). Nor can it be applied if any benefit has already been enjoyed by the party requesting rescission.
- **Specific performance** – where the court orders the contract to be performed in cases, for example, where the seller is simply refusing to hand over some goods. Specific performance is rarely awarded in contracts of personal service because the courts feel that it would not lead to a satisfactory employer/employee relationship.
- **Injunction** – where the court orders a particular person not to break his or her contractual obligations. This

remedy should not, however, have the effect of indirectly enforcing the doctrine of specific performance. If, for instance, an employee is forbidden from working for anyone else in a specialist area such as the performing arts because he or she would be in breach of contract, the outcome may be that he or she has no option but to remain in the employment of the original employer.

Statutory remedies

Commercial contracts are considered of such importance because of the financial issues normally involved that additional safeguards are available should they be breached. Most of these are **statutory remedies** contained in a number of important Sale of Goods and Consumer Protection Acts discussed in Chapter 22, but Figure 21.1 summarises some of the main safeguards afforded by the Sale of Goods Act 1979 in relation to the transfer of property, risk, and title and delivery.

For example, once the goods or property have been transferred to the buyer, the buyer takes over the 'risk',

Section	Safeguards to title
S.17	Where there is a contract for the sale of goods, the property [title] in them is transferred to the buyer at such time as the parties intend it to be transferred
S.18(1)	Where there is an unconditional contract for the sale of specific goods, the property in the goods passes to the buyer when the contract is made and it is immaterial whether the time of payment and/or the time of delivery are postponed
S.18(2)	Where the goods are not in a deliverable state (i.e. goods which need altering), property does not pass until they are in such a state
S.18(3)	In the course of a conditional sale of specific goods, property does not pass until the condition is satisfied
S.18(4)	In the case of sales on approval or on sale or return, property passes when (a) the buyer signifies his or her acceptance to the seller, (b) the buyer retains the goods without giving notice of rejection

Figure 21.1 *Sections of the Sale of Goods Act 1979*

whether or not delivery has been made. However, where delivery has been delayed through the fault of either the buyer or the seller, the goods are at the 'risk' of the party at fault with regard to any loss that might not have occurred but for such fault.

Real and personal remedies

The breach of a contract for the sale of goods carries with it the same penalties as the breach of any other contract. However, the buyers and sellers of goods have additional remedies upon which they can rely.

Remedies of the seller

Real remedies 'against the goods'

Under S.39(1) of the Sale of Goods Act 1979, the unpaid seller has:

- a **lien** on the goods (i.e. the right to retain them if he or she is still in possession of them), even if property in them has passed to the buyer; this does not mean, however, that the seller can resell them at this stage
- the right to stop goods in transit in the case of the **insolvency** of the buyer
- a right of **resale** when the buyer repudiates the contract, when the contract expressly provides for resale if the buyer should default, or where the goods are of a perishable nature.

Personal remedies

In addition to the remedies against goods noted above, the seller can start a personal action against the buyer for payment of the price of the goods. Alternatively, the seller can claim **damages for non-acceptance**, the assessment criteria for which include:

- the presence or absence of an available market (i.e. whether or not the seller can readily dispose of the goods)
- the price at which the goods were eventually sold by the seller and whether it is more or less than the contract price
- whether or not there is any market for the goods given that they were manufactured or obtained specifically for the purposes of that contract.

Remedies of the buyer

The buyer has a number of options. He or she can:

- in some circumstances **repudiate** the contract and reject the goods
- claim damages for (i) non-delivery, (ii) breach of a condition or warranty, or (iii) wrongful interference
- demand specific performance of the contract.

TASK

Read the following extracts from a contract for the sale of goods.

6.1. The property in any goods delivered by the company to the buyer shall remain in the company until such time as the buyer has paid in full for those goods including any sums due by way of interest.

7. If the buyer commits a breach of any of the conditions in the contract or the financial standing of the buyer becomes unsatisfactory, the company may without prejudice to its other rights and remedies terminate this contract.

1. What is the significance in the passing of property (title) from seller to buyer?

2. Suppose the contract had been for sale of goods on approval. At what stage would property pass to the buyer?

3. What other remedies may the seller have against the buyer, other than the right to terminate the contract?

4. What remedies may the buyer have if the seller breaches the contract?

5. What factors will the courts take into account when assessing the measure of damages to either buyer or seller?

STANDARD CONTRACTS

Nowadays the vast majority of contracts for the sale and supply of goods are 'standard form' contracts which are pre-printed, pre-designed contractual forms containing standard clauses. Although these are useful in many ways, problems can arise over what is known as the 'battle of the forms' in which it is difficult to ascertain when an offer has been made and accepted. In *Butler Machine Tool Co. Ltd. v Ex-Cell-O Corporation Ltd.* [1979] 1 AER 965, for instance, the plaintiff (Mr Butler) sent the defendant a quotation for the supply of a machine, stating that delivery was to be made within 10 months of the order being placed. In the quotation was a clause stating that 'in case of costs increasing, the quoted cost would be increased'. The corporation ordered the machine using its own form which **varied the conditions** and which stipulated installation and delivery within 11 months. There was a tear-off slip at the bottom of the acceptance form asking Mr Butler to sign and return it and accepting the order 'on the terms and conditions stated therein'. The form was signed and returned. By the time the machine was delivered, costs had risen and Mr Butler tried to invoke the price variation clause. The corporation refused. The court held that the acceptance form from the corporation, signed and returned by Mr Butler, was a **counter-offer** that destroyed the original offer. With his signature on the form, Mr Butler had accepted the corporation's offer to purchase and therefore the contract was governed by the corporation's terms and conditions.

TASK

Larger companies are aware of the difficulties caused by standard contracts. Smaller organisations are less prepared.

1. What type of procedures do you think the larger organisations would have in place to prevent any 'battle of the forms' occurring?

2. What particular problems do you think would be experienced by smaller organisations and how would you suggest they be overcome?

Consumer Protection Legislation

HAPTER

This chapter introduces you to the way in which the law attempts to protect the consumer. It covers both common law and statutory law but concentrates in particular on the series of Acts and Regulations promulgated in recent years.

On completion of the chapter you should be able to identify key provisions contained in consumer protection legislation. To achieve this you must demonstrate the ability to:

• identify the source and content of the key statutory provisions relating to consumer protection

• assess the effectiveness of a provision found in the different Acts

• apply relevant legislation on consumer protection to a case study and present findings.

COMMON LAW RIGHTS OF THE CONSUMER

The law of **tort** (i.e. human behaviour which the law categorises as 'wrongful') does protect the consumer to some extent – in addition to any **contractual** rights and obligations he or she may have. A landmark case was *Donoghue v Stevenson* [1932] AC 562, in which the plaintiff (Donoghue) alleged that, because of the negligence of the defendant, a manufacturer of soft drinks, a bottle of ginger beer contained a snail, which appeared in a decomposed form when the plaintiff poured the contents into a glass. She suffered personal injury in the form of gastroenteritis and nervous shock. At that stage, she could not claim any contractual relationship with the manufacturer whose contract was with the supplier, and therefore she could not claim breach of contract. However, the House of Lords held that, despite the absence of any such relationship, a manufacturer owed a **duty of care** in tort to all people whom it could reasonably have been foreseen would be affected by his or her products.

If, therefore, a consumer feels that a product supplied is in some way harmful, he or she can use the tort of **negligence** to bring a claim against the negligent party. However, common law protects the consumer to only a limited extent. It is difficult, for instance, under common

Legal and regulatory framework

law for a consumer to claim that he or she has been misled as to the nature of a commercial agreement (unless an obvious misrepresentation has taken place), or that a term in it is unfair. Fortunately, statutory legislation has attempted to solve at least some of the problems, and it is the subject of the remainder of this chapter.

STATUTORY PROTECTION OF THE CONSUMER

Prior to 1893, customers or consumers had few **statutory rights** and the legal concept of 'caveat emptor' – **let the buyer beware** – was rarely challenged. However, there became a growing awareness that this concept allowed the balance of power to be tilted too much in the seller's favour and was difficult to sustain in the light of the increasing number of commercial transactions that were taking place at the end of the nineteenth century. Consequently, in 1893, Parliament passed the first Sale of Goods Act which was designed to codify the existing law. Since then it has been amended a number of times and consumer legislation has been introduced to cover:

- the sale of goods
- the supply of goods and services
- unfair contractual terms
- consumer credit agreements
- data protection.

In addition, many regulatory agencies have been established to monitor the implementation of the legislation.

The sale of goods

The major statutes in this area are currently the Sale of Goods Act 1979 (abbreviated to SOGA 79), the Sale of Goods (Amendment) Act 1994 (SGAA 94), and the Sale of Goods (Amendment) Act 1995 (SGAA 95).

The major provisions of the **Sale of Goods Act 1979** include the passing of property (or title) and remedies for breach of contract. These are discussed in Chapter 21. The Act also covers:

- terms that can be implied into a contract for the sale of goods (Sections 12–14)
- sale by a person other than the owner) Sections 21–23)

- the performance of the contract and the duties and rights of the seller and buyer (Sections 27–35).

Implied terms in a contract for the sale of goods

The following is an outline of the major provisions of SOGA 79 in this regard.

- *Section 12*
  There is an implied condition on the part of the seller that, in the case of a sale, he or she has the *right* to sell the goods. If the seller cannot pass rights of ownership to the buyer, he or she will be liable for a breach of a *condition*.
- *Section 12(2)*
  In addition there are two implied *warranties*: (a) that the goods are free from any third-party rights, and (b) that the buyer will enjoy 'quiet possession' of them.
- *Section 13*
  Where there is a contract for the sale of goods *by description* – if, for instance, they are ordered from a catalogue – there is an implied condition that the goods will correspond with the description.
- *Section 14*
  Where the seller operates a business, there is an *implied* term that the goods supplied are of *satisfactory* quality; i.e. that they meet the standard a 'reasonable' person would regard as satisfactory. This protection does not extend (a) to any defects that have been specifically drawn to the buyer's attention or to circumstances where the buyer has inspected the goods or the sample before making the contract (b) to situations where any special requirements of the buyer have not been made known to the seller before the contract has been agreed.

Case Study

In *Grant v Australian Knitting Mills Ltd.* [1936] AC 35, the court held that the plaintiff (Grant) was entitled to damages for having contracted dermatitis after wearing clothing purchased from the defendant that had been treated with certain chemicals. On the subject of the buyer's reliance on the skill and knowledge of the seller, one of the judges said that such reliance could be *inferred* from the fact that a buyer goes to a shop in confidence that the shopowner has selected the stock 'with skill and judgement'.

Questions

1. How can you tell that this decision is over 60 years old?

2. What do you think the main arguments would be today (based on SOGA 79)? Would it have made any difference if Mr Grant had had unusually sensitive skin?

3. The original stipulation in the Sale of Goods Act 1979 was that goods should be of **'merchantable'** quality. The Sale and Supply of Goods Act 1994 substituted the words of **'satisfactory'** quality. Discuss the possible reasons for the alteration.

Sale by a person other than the owner

Sections 21–23 of SOGA 79 provide that, where the goods are sold by a person who is not their owner, the buyer acquires no better a title to them than the seller had – unless the owner of the goods is by his or her conduct precluded from denying the seller's authority to them. The Latin maxim *'nemo dat quod non habet'* – no one can give what he does not have – applies here. Consequently, where a car was paid for by a dishonoured cheque and then sold on to a third party, the original seller was allowed to recover the car as good title had not been obtained by the third party.

Check your understanding

In what way does this differ from the outcome of Lewis v Averay as described in the case study on page 506?

Performance of the contract

Parties to a contract are, or course, allowed to make their own arrangements about delivery and payment. However, when the contract does not spell out the arrangements, SOGA 79 lays down certain rules to be followed, as follows.

- *Section 27*
  Payment and delivery are *concurrent conditions*; i.e. the seller must be ready and willing to give possession of the goods to the buyer in exchange for the price, and vice versa.

- *Section 30(1) (as amended by SSGA 94)*
  Where a transaction between two non-consumers (i.e. a business contract) is completed with a *slight* deviation in quantity – whether too much or too little – the buyer is not allowed to reject the whole consignment (although prior to SSGA 94 that was permissible). If the deviation is sufficiently great, however, rejection is still an option.

- *Section 31(1)*
  Unless otherwise agreed, a buyer will not be bound to accept *delivery by instalments*. Thus the seller cannot excuse short delivery by undertaking to deliver the balance in due course.

- *Section 31(2)*
  Where there is a contract of sale of goods to be delivered by stated instalments, which are to be separately paid for, and the seller makes defective deliveries in respect of one or more instalments, or the buyer neglects or refuses to take delivery of or pay for one or more instalments, it is a question in each case, whether the breach of contract is a *repudiation* of the whole contract or whether it is a *severable breach* giving rise to a claim for *compensation* but not a right to treat the whole contract as repudiated.

- *Section 34 (as amended by SSGA 94)*
  Unless otherwise agreed, the seller has to give the buyer a reasonable opportunity to examine the goods to see whether they conform with the contract.

- *Section 35 (as amended by SSGA 94)*
  In certain circumstances a buyer is deemed to have accepted the goods either through *actual intention* or by *conduct*, although the section goes into detail to indicate the circumstances under which a buyer will *not* be deemed to have accepted the goods unless he or she has had a reasonable opportunity to examine them. Consequently, people who, for instance, buy electrical goods and wish to try them out at home, will be able to do so and – within a reasonable time – be able to return them should they prove faulty.

Case Study

In *Regent OHG Aisenstadt v Francesco of Jermyn St* [1981] Com LR 78, the sellers contracted to sell 62 suits to the buyer. Delivery was in instalments at the seller's option. The sellers tendered the suits in five instalments. The parties then became involved in an unrelated dispute and the buyers refused to accept delivery of any of the suits. This was clearly a repudiation of the contract and the sellers would have been entitled to terminate it. They did not do so, however, and continued to try to deliver the suits. There were some problems over material, and on the fourth delivery the buyers were told that there was one suit short. The shortfall was not made up in the fifth delivery and the final result was a total delivery of only 61 suits. If the agreement had been for a single delivery of 62 suits, S.30(1) of SOGA 79 would have applied. However, obviously S.31 had also to be considered.

The court decided that, where there was a *conflict* between S.30(1) and S.31(2), the latter was to prevail and the buyer was not entitled to reject the goods.

Questions

1. To what extent do you think the court was influenced by legal reasons and to what extent by common sense?

2. Do you think a court is ever entitled to use a subjective rather than an objective approach towards a case and, if so, in what circumstances?

Supply of goods and services

Whereas the Sale of Goods Act 1979 concentrates in the main on the sale of goods, the **Supply of Goods and**

Services Act 1982 (Parts 1 and 2) (as amended by the Sale and Supply of Goods Act 1994) extends similar protection to other types of transaction and, in particular, to contracts for the supply of work, labour or services. The main provisions of SSGA 82 are as follows:

- *Section 12*
  A contract for the supply of services is one under which the supplier agrees to carry out a service. Note that it does not apply to contracts of service in employment or to apprenticeships (for further details on these, see page 538).
- *Section 13*
  Where the supplier is acting in the course of a business, there is an *implied* term that the supplier will carry out the service with *reasonable care and skill*.
- *Section 14*
  Where the supplier is acting in the course of a business, and the time for performance cannot be determined from the contract or ascertained by a course of dealings between the parties, there is an *implied* term that the supplier will carry out the service within a *reasonable* time.
- *Section 15*
  Where *consideration* cannot be determined by the contract, or from a course of dealings between the parties, the customer will be expected to pay a reasonable charge for the service.
- *Section 16*
  Sections 13–15 can be excluded by *express agreement*, provided the exclusion term complies with the *reasonableness test* under the Unfair Contract Terms Act 1977 (see further page 518).

TASKS

1. You work in a small company which employs a window cleaner. He is unreliable and not a particularly good worker. He has recently demanded an increase in payment. No written contract exists nor is there evidence of an oral one. Write a memo to your boss outlining what you think may be the legal arguments he or she can put forward in (a) refusing to increase his pay, and (b) in refusing to pay him at all!

2. Employees at a workplace are covered by a number of Employment Protection Acts.

Unfair contract terms

Common law traditionally protected customers from unfair or onerous *exemption or exclusion clauses* (see page 509). Further safeguards are now provided by the **Unfair Contract Terms Act 1977** (UCTA 77) (supplemented by the Unfair Terms in Consumer Contracts Regulations 1994 – UTCCR 94), although the Act protects only consumers, not business-to-business contracts. The Unfair Terms in Consumer Contracts Regulations 1995 – UTCCR 95) also offers some protection in this area.

The Unfair Contract Terms Act 1977

The following is an outline of some major provisions of UCTA 77.

- *Section 2(1)*
  There can be no restriction or exclusion of *liability* for death or personal injury resulting from *negligence*.
- *Section 2(2)*
  In the case of other loss or damage, there can be no restriction or exclusion of *liability* unless the term satisfies the requirement of *reasonableness*.
- *Section 6(1)*
  Certain *exclusion clauses* will be *void* under any circumstances in a consumer transaction (e.g. exclusion of Sections 12, 13,14, 15 of SOGA 79).
- *Section 5*
  In the case of *defective goods* supplied for private use or consumption, there can be no exclusion of liability either in the contract or in the guarantee.

Discussion point

Given that a large number of commercial transactions do take place between private buyers and sellers, why do you think the legislation excludes these deals?

Unfair Terms in Consumer Contracts Regulations 1994

These Regulations apply to any term in a contract between a seller or supplier who is acting for purposes relating to his and her business and a consumer. They hold to be unfair any term which is contrary to the requirement of **good faith**, and consequently creates an imbalance in the rights and obligations of the parties.

The strongest protection is given to persons who deal as consumers, although those dealing otherwise (e.g. where the goods are bought for use in a small business) are also covered. To be a consumer a person must be dealing, as a private buyer, with a person in business. Thus a contract between a private buyer and a private seller is not a consumer deal.

The following is a summary of the major provisions of UTCCR 94.

- *Schedule 2 sets out the criteria for reasonableness*
  - the strength of the *bargaining positions* of the parties
  - whether the consumer has had an *inducement* to agree to the term (e.g. where the goods were cheaper if the term were included)
  - whether the goods or services were sold or supplied to the *special order* of the consumer, in which case it might be fair to include a term relating to the possible unfitness of the goods for the intended purpose
  - the extent to which the seller or supplier has dealt *fairly* and *equitably* with the consumer
- *Schedule 3 gives a list of terms which **may** be regarded as unfair*
  - excluding or limiting the *liability* of a seller or supplier in the event of the *death* or personal *injury* of or to a consumer
  - requiring any consumer who fails to meet his or her obligations to pay a disproportionately high sum in *compensation* (e.g. a non-refundable deposit)
  - enabling the seller or supplier to alter the contract *unilaterally*
  - limiting the consumer's rights in the event of total or partial *non-performance* by the seller or supplier.

Unfair Terms in Consumer Contracts Regulations 1995

In more recent years the protection of the consumer has been extended by UTCCR 95. This gives consumers the right to **contest** a contract they consider to be unfair, through the courts of the Office of Fair Trading (for further discussion, see page 523).

The law also requires contracts to be written in 'plain intelligible language', with the wording clearly readable. To this end, the National Consumer Council (NCC) issued some guidelines to anyone who wishes to make a confusing document less confusing. They are listed in Figure 22.1.

- Decide what needs to be in the document and keep to essentials.
- Use a logical order, taking care not to hide away unusual or unexpected terms.
- Use familiar forms of address such as 'we' and 'you'.
- Avoid the third person.
- Leave out surplus words.
- Avoid legalisms.
- Split complicated sentences into several short sentences.
- Keep verbs active wherever possible.
- Use punctuation sensibly.
- Ensure that there is a clear layout and design (i.e. readable size print/suitable headings/bullet points, etc.).
- Use footnotes to explain certain obscure terms if they are essential to the meaning of the document.

Figure 22.1 *NCC guidelines*

TASK

Comment on the way in which the following paragraph has been constructed, bearing in mind the NCC's suggestions. Rewrite it in a simpler format.

It is suggested that monetary remedies are largely creatures of the common law courts whereas the majority of the non-monetary remedies in the English law of obligations have been formulated in the Court of Chancery. One 'summa divisio', accordingly, is that between common law and equitable remedies. However, this division has implications that go beyond the law of remedies in that a number of substantive areas of the law owe their existence to equitable remedies that have been able to exert influence directly or indirectly at common law, examples including mistake in contract, which developed around the equitable remedies of rescission and rectification or aspects of nuisance in tort associated with the remedy of an injunction.

Discussion point

'Not everything can be simplified. If a complicated issue is made to look simple by the wording used, surely there is a danger that the issue itself will not be treated as seriously as it ought to be – and that certain important points are therefore overlooked.' Discuss.

Consumer credit

Consumer **credit** is one of the most significant areas in which the law assumes the role of protector to the potentially weaker bargaining party. Consequently, the Consumer Credit Act 1974 (CCA 74) places controls upon organisations that provide credit facilities in the course of their business. All such organisations, with the exception of local authorities, must be **licensed** and the Act also lays down strict rules governing the form and content of credit agreements. The following are the major provisions of CCA 74.

- *Sections 44–47*
  If *advertisements* relate to the provision of credit or the hiring of goods of less than £15 000 in value, they must contain specific and accurate information.
- *Sections 48–54*
  It is an offence to sell from **door to door** at the homes of private individuals without their prior invitation in writing.
- *Sections 55–59*
  Credit agreements must be in a specified *format* giving the names and addresses of the parties concerned; the annual percentage rate of interest (APR); the cash price; the deposit and total amount of credit; the total amount repayable; the repayment dates and amount of each payment; the sums payable on default; and other rights.
- *Section 62*
  Copies of all signed agreements and contracts must be sent to the debtor within seven days of the agreement and must include details of *cancellation rights*. If the agreement is signed at home, then the prospective debtor must receive a copy of the agreement immediately. A further copy must be sent by post a week later and the buyer then has five further days in which to give the creditor written notice of cancellation.

- *Section 87*

  If the buyer *defaults* on the debt, the creditor must serve a formal default notice which gives details of the recovery action to be taken, and the action which can be taken to *remedy* the situation and the date by which this must be taken.

- *Sections 90–91*

  The creditor cannot *reclaim* goods sold under a *hire purchase agreement* once the buyer has paid one-third or more of the price, unless entitled to do so by court order.

- *Sections 94-97*

  No creditor can prevent a debtor from making an *early payment* to settle the debt and must respond to any request to give information as to how early payment may be made.

- *Section 99*

  If an agreement is cancelled, any sum paid by the debtor is *repayable* and the goods must be returned.

Data protection

The Data Protection Act 1984

Prior to 1984, a **computer database** was treated like a locked filing cabinet. Any information could be stored there provided it was not defamatory and it was available to be read by any person having the right key. The European courts, however, became concerned about the ways in which such databases could be misused, and so in 1981 the signatories to the Council of European Convention on Data Protection (including the UK) agreed to prohibit the transfer of personal data to countries that had not established a system of **data protection**. Partially to avoid economic isolation, the UK passed the **Data Protection Act 1984** which required:

- all organisations to register with the *Data Protection Registrar* if they wanted to store on a computer database any data relating to an identified person which includes an expression of opinion about that person but not an indication of the intentions of the data user in respect of that individual
- any data stored on the database to be
  – obtained and processed *fairly*

- held only for *lawful purposes*
- used or disclosed only in a manner compatible with *specified purposes*
- adequate, relevant and not excessive in relation to *purpose*
- *accurate* and kept up to date
- not kept longer than necessary for the specified *purpose*
- *protected* against unauthorised access and accidental loss
- *available* to the individual for inspection and, where appropriate, correction or erasure

Anyone who suffers damage as a result of data stored inaccurately is entitled to claim compensation; although two defences open to the data user are that reasonable care was taken to ensure that the data were accurate, or the data were obtained from the data subject and there is an indication that the data were received in that form by the data user.

The Data Protection Act 1998

One major drawback of the Data Protection Act 1984 is that it applies only to databases. Information stored in a filing cabinet is not covered by it – although the Access to Health Records Act 1990 allows employees to access any health records held by their employer whether in manual or computerised format.

Consequently, again as a result of EU concern, the **Data Protection Act 1998** was introduced which gives employees access to any paper files containing their personal details. As a result, once-confidential information in areas such as performance appraisal or disciplinary proceedings will now be open to inspection, and employers could well be subject to legal action for negligence or defamation should the information prove to be indiscreet. However, under **Article 13(g)** of the EU's Directive, there are circumstances where, for instance, the information relates to wage rates, redundancy negotiations or plans for promotion or demotion, and the employer is allowed to deny employees access to it.

TASK

Read the following extracts commenting on the Data Protection Act 1988.

a Where compliance with an employee's request for information or disclosure would result in disclosure of information relating to another individual – including information identifying that individual as the source of the information sought by the employee – the employer need not comply unless the third party consents, or it is reasonable in all the circumstances to dispense with his or her consent.

b Schedule 7 of the Data Protection Act 1998 sets out a number of exclusions from the right of access and information. In particular, there is an express exemption in the case of confidential references given by the employer for the purposes of education, training or employment, appointment to any office, or the provision by the employee of any service. It follows that employees will not be able to gain access to copies of personal references given by their current employer. The exemption relating to personal references does not cover references given by a third party (such as a former employer) that are held in an employee's current personnel file. In most cases, however, disclosure of the reference would necessarily entail disclosure of its author's identity. It could be argued, therefore, that the former employer's consent would be required before the reference could be disclosed to the employee, unless it is reasonable in all the circumstances to dispense with the consent.

1. Why should employees be denied access to references given by their existing employer?

2. Why should a former employer be concerned if an ex-employee reads a reference supplied by him or her, given that employers have a 'qualified privilege' in supplying references (i.e. they will normally be protected from a

Regulatory agencies

Given that the major rationale for most of the consumer protection legislation is to prevent one party taking advantage of another, it is important that mechanisms are in place to see that the law is enforced. A number of agencies have been established to act as 'consumer watchdogs'. The following are some significant examples.

National Consumer Council (NCC)

The NCC is an independent, publicly funded body which acts as a pressure group for consumer interests.

Consumers' Association (CA)

The results of the Consumers' Association's investigations are published in its monthly magazine *Which?* and supplements. These investigations are also often instrumental in introducing or promoting changes in consumer legislation. In addition there are a number of local consumer groups who carry out research into the quality of local services and publish the results to their members. Their central coordinating body is the **National Federation of Consumer Groups**.

Trade and professional associations

Many trade and professional associations have codes of practice to safeguard and promote the interests of consumers. The codes provide an alternative source of

consultation if a product or service proves unsatisfactory, together with procedures for **conciliation** and, in some cases, for **arbitration**. Interesting to note, however, is that the Consumer Arbitration Agreements Act 1988 specifies that any stipulation in an agreement with a consumer that future differences **must** be referred to arbitration cannot be enforced.

British Standards Institution (BSI)

The BSI is a voluntary organisation, one of whose functions is to lay down uniform specifications for certain products. In 1979, for instance, it introduced the British Standard 5750 (the so-called 'Quality Standard', now known as ISO 9000), under which if a company became registered as meeting the requirements of BS5750 then that company was recognised as being able to supply its goods or services to a stated level of quality.

Local authorities

The county councils and London boroughs employ **trading standards inspectors** who have extensive responsibilities in the enforcement of the Trades Descriptions, Consumer Credit and Fair Trading Acts. Many local authorities have also set up **Consumer Advice Centres** under the Local Government Act 1972 which give advice on purchases and on the making of complaints.

Ombudsmen

In some cases, the **ombudsmen** schemes assist the consumer. Examples include banking, broadcasting, building societies, estate agents, funeral directors, health services, insurance, investment, legal services, local government, pensions, and personal investment. However, the extent of the jurisdiction of a particular ombudsman depends on the scheme. For instance, the Corporate Estate Agents Ombudsman is concerned only with the large chains of estate agents owned by banks, building societies and insurance companies and cannot deal with complaints against independent estate agents.

Nevertheless, where jurisdiction does apply, the ombudsman can not only make an individual ruling and award compensation, he or she may also make a recommendation that certain business practices and procedures of the organisation in question be altered or improved.

Department of Trade and Industry (DTI)

The DTI has an Under Secretary of State for Industry and Consumer Affairs amongst whose duties it is to make regulations under the Consumer Credit Act and the Consumer Protection Act.

Office of Fair Trading (OFT)

The OFT was set up as a result of the Fair Trading Act 1973 and empowers the Director General of Fair Trading to

- keep under review the commercial supply of goods and services to consumers in the UK
- take action against individual traders who try to enter into unfair transactions with consumers
- provide information to the public
- encourage trade associations to prepare codes of practice for their members under S.124(3) of the Fair Trading Act 1973
- supervise and control the consumer credit industry as a result of the Consumer Credit Act 1974

Sadly, however, establishing these mechanisms for control has not necessarily meant that the protection of the consumer is now guaranteed.

Discussion point

'Nit picking rules and regulations harm consumers, not help them. Companies are so busy making sure that they do not fall foul of the law by paying dozens of clerks and lawyers to carry out basic monitoring duties, that they have less time to actually scan the horizon for new opportunities, look for new markets and generally keep their workforce in employment. Besides, customers aren't fools. They know whether or not they are getting a decent deal.' Discuss.

Case Study

Read the following edited summary from an article in a law journal.

The introduction of the Unfair Terms in Consumer Contract Regulations should have led to a rapid end for most exemption clauses and other oppressive clauses in standard-form consumer contracts. This European-directed legislation was not, at least initially, greeted with enthusiasm in official circles. The government's disdain was shown by the failure to bring it into force until six months after the expiry of the EEC-imposed deadline of 31 December 1995. The Office of Fair Trading, through its Director General, was given a monopoly over its enforcement, a task it has carried out so laxly as to make its effect virtually nugatory.

The regulations, for instance, can render invalid those terms that enable the businesses to unilaterally increase the price or require lengthy notice before the consumer can terminate an on-going contract. They can also enable the High Court to grant an injunction prohibiting the use of an unfair term after the Director General has referred it to them. However, some years after the legislation the Director General has yet to seek an injunction. Indeed it seems that the OFT has so little respect in the eyes of some industries that junior staff in many organisations are allowed openly to deprecate it and senior staff to put forward transparently ridiculous excuses for refusing to follow its directions.

The OFT is currently investigating 420 sets of allegedly unfair terms with a unit of eleven people employed to do so – a high ratio of staff to cases. At least 180 cases have been going on since March 1996. The OFT claims that around 200 businesses have changed their terms in response to demands. BSkyB has agreed to remove terms enabling it to unilaterally increase prices from its standard-form contracts, many local authority car-park operators no longer try to exclude liability for their own negligence, and some mobile phone companies have agreed to amend their terms, including reducing the previously standard 90-day notice period. Against this there are many companies OFT have not yet persuaded to amend their terms, possibly because they have identified OFT as a 'weak adversary'.

The OFT defends its approach because of the cost. It also argues that many businesses have difficulty in understanding the concept of the regulations and that it is 'time consuming' to try to convince traders that High Court litigation is seriously intended.

Source: Richard Colbey, *Unfair terms and the OFT*, New Law Journal, January 16 1998

1. Why do you think the government was apparently unwilling to introduce the regulations? How far do you think its 'disdain' for the legislation has affected the success of its implementation?

2. What is your opinion of the OFT's reasons for its possible lack of success?

3. This appears to be a case of legislation being passed which is not being implemented. What steps would you suggest should be taken to improve matters?

Formation, Management and Dissolution of Business Units

This chapter introduces you to the ways in which business units are formed, managed and dissolved. In particular, it covers the **sole trader**, the **partnership** and the **registered company**.

On completion of the chapter you should be able to understand and explain the legal provisions concerned with the formation, management and dissolution of all the above units. To achieve this you must demonstrate the ability to:

- identify the relevant legal principles which can influence the choice of a business unit

- explain the differences in the regulatory approach adopted for partnerships and registered companies with regard to their management

- describe the procedures for the dissolution of business units.

Modern lawmakers are anxious not to hinder the setting up of small businesses by the imposition of too many legal restrictions. Nor do they want to affect the economic viability of either a partnership or a company. What they do want to do, however, is to try to protect the public in the same way as they try to protect the consumer by curbing the power of irresponsible or unscrupulous businesses. Consequently they regulate the ways in which a business can be established, run and dissolved. The three main types of business units are the sole trader, the partnership, and the company.

NAMING A BUSINESS UNIT

Not all business names are acceptable, so before anyone sets about starting a business they should pay some attention to what the law allows in this area.

TASK

The following is a summary of the regulations relating to the choice of a business name.

The **Companies Act 1985** requires that the name of a company:

- must end in Ltd or Plc unless it is a private company limited by guarantee and is a charity or other organisation with non-commercial objectives
- will not be registered by the **Registrar of Companies** if the same name is already registered

- will not be registered if it is an offensive or criminal name or one implying the provision of sexual services.

The Business Names Act 1985 aims to prevent the use of a name for a company which suggests that it:

- is part of another company
- has the same name as another company
- is by 'royal' appointment
- is a society, institute or charity
- has some type of international connection
- is some type of financial organisation
- is connected to a government department.

It requires anyone trading under a business name to declare his or her real name and an address at which he or she can be contacted in the UK.

In addition, under sections 348 and 349 of the Companies Act 1985, a company must display its full name outside any place of business and outside its registered office. The required details must also be contained on the stationery. Failure to comply with the regulations is a criminal offence. An even greater penalty may be that non compliance may prevent a contract from being enforced even against someone who has defaulted on his or her obligations. In addition, the company or individual may be liable under the **tort of passing off** and in certain circumstances the directors of a company may be liable when, for instance, a contract is not signed with the full name of the company.

1. Research what is meant by the 'tort of passing off' and make a note of it for future reference.

2. Prepare a list of points you would make to a client who wishes to set up in business, explaining why it is important that the law is not broken in this area.

3. Add to that note the advantages that there are in not trading under his or her own name.

4. Discuss the relevance in modern society of the rules which forbid the use of certain names. What would you (a) delete from and (b) add to the list?

FORMATION OF A BUSINESS

The sole trader

Becoming a sole trader is relatively simple. All a prospective trader has to do after choosing an appropriate name is to find premises and register for value-added tax (if the annual turnover has reached a certain level).

Partnerships

Starting up a partnership is more regulated, partially because a partnership can be a very volatile relationship with frequent disputes and ultimate dissolution. The basic regulations include:

- Section 1 of the **Partnership Act 1890**, which defines partnership as 'the relation that subsists between persons carrying on a business in common with a view of profit'
- Section 45 of the same Act, which states that a business can be any trade, profession or occupation – although there are exceptions, such as barristers.

There are two types of partner.

- *Sleeping partners* take no active role in the management of the business but simply provide capital and draw profits.
- *General partners* (the most usual type) take an active part in the running of the business. Section 24(1) of the Partnership Act 1890 stipulates that all partners are entitled to share equally in the capital and profits in the business and must contribute equally towards the losses (although sleeping partners will generally have limited

liability for the debts of the firm under the **Limited Partnerships Act 1907**) (see further page 531).

A partnership, once formed, can start trading immediately – no formal agreement is required. Where a written **partnership agreement** does exist, the partners are free to decide the terms which specify the basis upon which each of them has agreed to work. However, the Partnership Act 1890 governs the relationships they may have with third parties (see page 530 for further discussion on this point).

Companies

Setting up a company is a more complicated process. **Corporations sole** (corporations such as Anglican bishoprics which enjoy perpetual succession) are of little importance in the commercial world. In contrast, **corporations aggregate** are of considerable importance. They include:

- **chartered** companies – those created by Royal Charter (e.g. the BBC)
- **statutory** companies – those created by Acts of Parliament (e.g. a nationalised industry)
- **registered** companies – those governed by the Companies Act 1985, as amended by the Companies Act 1989.

Registered companies

Under Section 1 of the Companies Act 1985, a company may be registered either as a public limited company or as a private limited company.

A **public limited company** must:

- end its business name with Plc (or plc or PLC)
- obtain a **certificate of incorporation** and a **certificate to trade** prior to trading
- have minimum initial capital of £50 000
- produce a set of audited accounts within seven months of the end of its own financial year
- register a **memorandum of association** that states it is a public limited company
- have at least two directors and two members
- have a qualified company secretary

A **private limited company** must:

- end its business name with Ltd (or ltd or LTD)
- obtain a certificate of incorporation prior to trading
- produce a set of audited accounts within 10 months of the end of its financial year.

The private limited company needs no minimum amount of capital – one member can start a private limited company with £1. It need have only two members and one director. (Single-member private companies limited by shares or guarantee are allowed by the Companies Single Members Private Limited Companies Regulations 1992). It may, depending on its size and turnover, be able to avoid certain of the regulations relating to the preparation and publication of accounts.

Public limited companies may sell shares and debentures to the public and institutions; private limited companies must not do so.

Limited liability

At first sight, **limited liability** would seem to be a great advantage to the owners of a business. In contrast to the situation with a partnership, the financial losses should the enterprise fail are limited to any amount outstanding to be paid on their shares. Private finances remain unaffected.

However, there are at least two circumstances where limited liability is not a significant advantage. The first is when there is little risk of substantial loss of personal capital (e.g. a business involving the giving of advice). The owner then expects to make profits by providing expertise in return for payment. Comparatively little is required in the way of capital expenditure, so the biggest potential loss (i.e. liability) is a claim for damages if bad advice is given. That could be covered by professional indemnity insurance. Secondly, limited liability is not helpful in a case where the owner risks everything he or she owns (e.g. if the owner's sole assets are what he or she has invested in the business). The owner will then lose everything when the business fails, whether it is limited or not.

Sometimes limited liability would be very desirable but cannot realistically be achieved because credit is needed but cannot be obtained without a personal guarantee. Many businesses rely on borrowed money, and a bank lending to a small company will often require a personal guarantee from the directors or shareholders. If the company cannot repay the loan the bank then has further security. This acts against the advantage of having limited liability.

Limited liability is most significant where there is substantial risk of loss of capital invested and the owner has private means not invested in the business. In such cases the requirement for limited liability will outweigh any other considerations.

Case Study

Read the following edited extract from an article in a legal journal.

The concept of the 'corporate veil' is based on the assumption that the company is an individual, whose component parts are obscured by a veil. It has its own contractual obligations (see *Saloman v A. Saloman & Co. Ltd*. [1897] AC 22). On each side of the veil there are individual persons who own, manage and work for the company. They, too, may have contractual obligations but their obligations must not be confused with those of the company.

However, the idea that people within a company cannot be held personally responsible for the company's actions – it is the company itself in its guise as an independent entity that assumes that responsibility – is not always regarded sympathetically by the courts. Typically the courts have justified their occasional intervention in cases where there has been a fraudulent use of a sham corporate structure (see *Gilford Motor Co. Ltd. v Horne* [1933] Ch 935 and *Jones v Lipman* [1962] 1 WLR 832).

Nevertheless, the principle survives because (a) it is simple and therefore allows consistent judgements, and (b) the idea of limited liability is at heart *economically efficient*.

Source: Bill Maughan and Stephen Copp, *Piercing the corporate veil*, New Law Journal, June 26 1998

Questions

1. Research the cases mentioned in the article and make a note of them for future reference.

2. Why is limited liability 'economically efficient'?

Discussion point

Even if limited liability is economically efficient, is it morally acceptable? If a business fails, someone has to be disadvantaged. Why should this not be the directors and shareholders, rather than the small businessman or woman who has supplied goods to the company on credit and risks losing all payment if the company collapses without any assets?

Discussion point

An entrepreneur will look for a high-risk enterprise with the possibility of large returns. A more cautious individual will look first of all for safety. How does that equate with the solicitor who goes into a partnership, and the future 'captain of industry' who sets up a company, when the latter's liability is likely to be limited and the former's is not?

Registration procedures

The rules for registration of a company are the same for both private limited and public limited companies. The basic documentation required is the Memorandum of Association and the Articles of Association.

The Memorandum of Association

This should contain details of:

- the name of the company

- the address of the registered office of the company
- the amount of the liability of the members
- the authorised capital
- the company objectives.

The final item can be more difficult than it looks. If, for instance, a company has stated in its objectives that it is going to manufacture motor cars, it may have problems in trying to expand its provision to include electrical goods and equipment. In legal terms such an action may be ruled **ultra vires** (i.e. beyond the limit of the company's powers and thus void at common law). However, Section 9(1) of the European Communities Act 1972 (later incorporated into Section 35 of the Companies Act 1985) offers some protection in that it allows a company to make a *general statement* as to its objectives (e.g. to trade as a commercial concern). Moreover, company objectives can be changed by virtue of a special resolution of the company concerned.

The Articles of Association

These should cover the internal administration of the company in areas such as the appointment of directors, the categories of shares and the meetings to be held. Where no such Articles exist, the model articles outlined in the Companies Act 1985 apply. What is important to note, however, is that the Articles constitute two distinct contracts.

- The Articles are a contract between the company and each member. In *Hickman v Kent or Romney Marsh Sheep Breeders' Association* [1915] 1 Ch 881, for instance, the Articles said that any dispute between a member and the company must be taken to arbitration. When a member tried to bypass arbitration and take his complaint direct to the High Court, he was held not entitled to do so.
- The Articles are also a contract between the members. Where, for instance, a member buys shares, he or she makes not only a contract with the company but also a collateral contract with the other members to observe the provisions of the Articles.

However, the Articles do *not* constitute a contract with outsiders. In *Eley v Positive Government Security Life Assurance Co.* [1876] 1 Ex D 88, the Articles stated that Mr Eley was to be employed for his lifetime as the company's solicitor. When the company ceased to employ him, he could not claim damages because the Articles did not constitute a contract between the company and him in his capacity as a solicitor.

Appointment of directors

Under Section 282 of the Companies Act 1985, a company must have a **board of directors**. Directors may be fee-paid supervisors acting as trustees for the shareholders, or senior executives who work as full-time directors of the company.

Discussion point

Section 319 of the Companies Act 1985 is designed to prevent directors entering into long-service contracts with a particular company. Both public and private companies may not incorporate into any agreement a term under which a director's employment with the company is to continue for a period of more than five years if, during that period, the company cannot terminate the contract by notice. Why do you think the legislators are so anxious to prevent company directors from negotiating long-term employment contracts?

Appointment of executive directors

Under Regulation 84 of the Companies Act 1985 the directors may appoint one or more of their number to an executive office, such as the company accountant or finance director. They may also decide on suitable payment.

Appointment of a chairperson

Companies are not required by law to appoint a chairperson. Since, however, in most cases they are bound to hold an annual general meeting of shareholders, there is an obvious need for a chairperson to control and manage the meeting. Regulation 91 of the Companies Act 1985 gives the board of directors specific power to appoint one of their number to be chairperson of the board and to remove him or her from that office at any time.

RUNNING AND MANAGING A BUSINESS UNIT

Running partnerships

Although sole traders have few statutory and common law obligations with which to comply (see page 539), members of a partnership are subject to much more extensive legal controls in the way they operate. The relationship between the partners is a **fiduciary** one, so each partner is in a position of trust *vis-à-vis* the other partners and is under a duty to disclose all information to them and act in their best interests. Even so, most partnerships have a written **Agreement** confirming the specific obligations of the partners, as specified in Sections 19–31 of the Partnership Act 1890. The following are the major provisions:

- to have an equal share of the profits and bear an equal share of the losses
- to be indemnified by the firm against any payment made and liability incurred in the course of the business
- to pay interest to a partner who makes a payment into the firm above his or her prescribed amount
- to have the opportunity to take part in the management of the business
- to have no entitlement to remuneration for his or her part in the business
- to agree to the introduction of a new member if the decision is unanimous
- to determine ordinary matters by a majority of the partners
- to keep the partnership books at the place of business to which all partners should have access.

Powers of partners

Any partnership is free to limit the activities of certain of the partners in, for instance, their ability to enter into contractual relationships on behalf of the firm. Such an agreement will merely be an *internal* one, even though breach of it would allow the partnership to be dissolved and the partner concerned excluded. Usually, however, Section 5 of the Partnership Act 1890 applies, which provides that where a partner is acting in the 'normal course of business' any contract that he or she makes will bind the firm.

The authority of a partner also depends on the type of business, although normally he or she would be expected to have authority to:

- sell any goods or property belonging to the firm
- purchase goods that would normally be used in the firm's business
- receive payments from third parties on behalf of the firm
- hire staff
- engage a solicitor to act for the firm
- to borrow money on behalf of the firm and to sanction payments in and out of the firm (in a commercial partnership).

Only where a partner is not acting in the normal course of business or has no authority to carry out that particular act – and the other party is aware of the lack of authority – will the firm not be bound. In both cases the **law of agency** applies, which defines the relationship between a *principal* and an *agent*. The function of the agent is to create a contract between the principal and a third party, and the agent may bind the principal to that contract by virtue of actual or apparent authority.

- *Actual authority* exists when the principal has expressly allowed the agent to carry out a certain act on his or her behalf.
- *Apparent authority* (or usual or ostensible authority) exists when the agent is given apparent authority to act on behalf of the principal.

was on the door and the licence continued in his name. Although Fenwick (the new owners) had forbidden him to buy cigars on credit, he did so and the plaintiff (Watteau) gave him credit personally since he was unaware of the existence of the defendants. When he did find out, he brought an action against the defendants for the price of the cigars.

It was held by the court that, as cigars were the type of articles normally sold in hotels and the manager was acting in 'apparent authority', the defendants were bound by the contract he had made.

Any action carried out must, however, be done in the 'normal type of business'. Anything the agent does outside what could reasonably be regarded as normal business will not bind the principal.

WATTEAU V. FENWICK HOTEL

Liability of partners

Section 10 of the Partnership Act 1890 makes all partners liable for any wrongful act or omission of one of the partners when it is carried out in the normal course of business or if the other partners agree to the act. Liability is **joint and several**.

A legal action by a creditor, for example, can be brought against one or all of the firm's partners; i.e. one or more can be isolated from the firm and sued individually. If, however, the creditor feels that one partner will have insufficient financial resources to cover the amount due, then the other partners can be sued jointly for the remaining debt.

However, it is possible for a partner to have limited liability under the **Limited Partnerships Act 1907** which provides that, with certain exceptions, such a partnership should not have more than 20 partners. The limited partner may be a corporate body or a sleeping partner. He or she cannot take any role in the management of the limited partnership. Nor does he or she have any power to bind the partnership or, generally, to call for its dissolution.

Running companies

Companies are normally managed by directors and shareholders. Regulation 70 of the Companies Act 1985 and Article 80 of the Companies Act 1948 give wide **powers** to the directors by allowing them to exercise 'all the powers of the company' unless company rules require otherwise (members may restrict the powers). With those powers come a range of **duties**.

Generally the duties of a director are more taxing than those of a sole trader or partner and are based on both common law and statutory law.

Fiduciary duties

A director owes duties to a company which are similar to those owed by a trustee to the beneficiaries under a trust. In particular, the director must account for any *personal* profit made in the course of dealings with the company. **Accountability** occurs when the personal profit is made and is not dependent on whether or not the company itself suffers a loss. However, the director is not accountable for the profits of a competing business he or she may be running, unless the Articles or contract of service stipulate otherwise, or unless he or she uses the company's property in that business, uses its trade secrets or induces the company's existing customers to deal with him or her. A director may not, either during or after service with the company, use confidential information entrusted by the company.

The other aspect of fiduciary duty is that the director must use his or her powers for the benefit of the company (i.e.

for the benefit of the shareholders as a whole) and not for the directors' own benefit.

Duty of skill and care

A director owes a **duty of care** to the company not to act negligently in managing its affairs. Nowadays directors are often experts in particular fields such as accounting or law, and therefore a high standard of care will be expected of them. In addition, executive directors employed by companies in a professional capacity have to comply with an objective standard of care, as do non-executive directors (those who do not take part in the day-to-day running of the business). However, in an early case, one judge made the point that directors:

- need not show a greater degree of skill than may reasonably be expected of a person with their knowledge and experience
- need not give continuous attention to the affairs of the company
- are not bound to attend all meetings of the board, although they ought to attend whenever they are reasonably able to do so
- may delegate duties to other officials in the company and trust them to be performed properly so long as there is no reason to doubt or mistrust them.

Discussion point

You are a new shareholder in a company and are given the above information on the duties of the company's directors.

1. Would any of them cause you concern? If so, which?

2. What alterations would you suggest to satisfy your concerns without placing too onerous a duty of care on the directors?

Duties to outsiders

Similarly, directors are under a duty not to act negligently so as to injure outsiders. In *Thomas Saunders Partnership v Harvey* [1989] 30 Con LR 103, the plaintiffs were architects, who were retained on a project to refit office premises. The defendant (Harvey) was a director of a subcontracting flooring company, who confirmed, wrongly, that the flooring the company offered conformed to the relevant specifications. The architects, having been sued by their client over this issue, sought a personal indemnity from the director as his company had by now gone into liquidation. Their claim for negligence succeeded even though the statement had been made on behalf of the company. The defendant was a specialist in the field and had assumed a duty of care when making the statement, and the court did not see why the 'veil of incorporation' should affect liability for individual negligence.

Similarly, a company director was held by a court to be personally liable for loss caused by the negligent misstatement of his or her company, even though the director dealt through the company and not directly with the person who suffered the loss.

Interestingly, there does not seem to be a duty owed to shareholders individually, and so there can be no claim by individual shareholders in respect of loss through the breach of fiduciary duty or negligence by a director. For further discussion on this point, see page 533.

Statutory duties

Under the Companies Act 1985, directors must

- notify the company of their interest in its shares or debentures or those of an associated company (Section 324)
- disclose any substantial non-cash transactions with the company (Sections 320–322)
- disclose personal interests in any contracts of the company (Section 317)
- have regard to the interests of the employees (Section 309) (see below for further discussion).

A director who is in breach of duty is jointly and severally liable with other directors to make good the loss. He or she must account for any secret profit made, and in such cases the company is usually able to avoid any contracts entered into with that director. However, a director may be protected from the effects of any breach if:

- the company waives the breach by ordinary resolution
- the company has indemnified and insured directors against liability for breach
- the court has granted relief under the powers available to it under Section 727 of the Companies Act 1985 where the director has acted honestly and reasonably and ought in all the circumstances to be excused.

Duties to employees

Since directors must exercise their powers for the benefit of the company, it could perhaps be assumed that they have therefore to take into account the interests of the employees of that company. However, although Section 309 of the Companies Act 1985 states that the matters to which directors must have regard should include the interests of the employees as well as the interests of its members, the section goes on to provide that the *duty* is owed by the directors to the company alone, and so the employees have no right of redress if they are in disagreement with the decisions of the board.

Duties to shareholders

Directors have the authority to manage the business of the company and to carry out all activities expressly or impliedly contained in its objectives clause. However, the law recognises that some checks on this power are necessary to ensure that ultimate control is vested in the 'owners' of the organisation, i.e. the shareholders.

Shareholders have the right in certain circumstances to take action on the company's behalf to prevent any harm occurring to it or carried out by it. They also have powers, exercisable in a general meeting, to:

- pass an ordinary resolution to remove a director before his or her term of office expires
- refrain from voting for the re-election of a director if the company's articles provide for retirement by rotation
- pass a special resolution to alter the Articles to lessen the powers of the directors
- pass a special resolution which gives the directors instructions on how they should act in relation to a particular matter.

However, although directors owe a duty to the shareholders as a single body, including both present and future shareholders, they do not owe a general duty to individual shareholders. For instance, no duty is owed to individual shareholders for any loss they have suffered through a fall in the value of their shares resulting from negligence, since the loss is that of the company (although under certain circumstances, minority shareholders may seek relief under Section 459 of the Companies Act 1985). Only occasionally will a fiduciary duty be owed to an individual shareholder, and that will depend on the facts of the case. One such example occurred where the minority shareholders in a small family firm sold their shares to the managing director after he had made misrepresentations to them. He was held to be in breach of his fiduciary duty.

In addition, although the directors control the day-to-day running of the company, the shareholders exercise the ultimate control though the annual general meeting and other 'extraordinary' general meetings. Decisions reached at such meetings are arrived at through the submission of resolutions which are then voted on. Since voting power is of considerable importance, the type of shares held by a shareholder assume significance as some carry full voting rights and others no voting rights at all.

In many instances, therefore, this gives rise to a group of **majority shareholders** and a group of **minority shareholders**, and it is the former who effectively run the company. Obviously the minority group then becomes marginalised and there is little the court can do to protect them – given that in *Foss v Harbottle* [1843] 2 Hare 461 it was laid down as a general principle that the courts will not interfere in the internal management of a company at the request of the minority shareholders. Even so, the courts will hear a claim brought by minority shareholders if:

- any proposed activities are *ultra vires* (see page 528)
- directors attempt to ratify, by an ordinary resolution, something requiring a special resolution which they did not obtain
- a wrong is inflicted on a member in his or her personal capacity through the action of the directors.

In addition, the Companies Act 1985 confers certain statutory rights on minority shareholders. These include Section 459 which gives a member the right to apply to the court for an order on the ground that the affairs of the company are being, or have been, conducted in a manner which is unfairly prejudicial to some members or that any actual or proposed act or omission of the company is or would be prejudicial.

Duties towards creditors

Where a company is **solvent**, directors do not owe any responsibility towards creditors. If, however, the company becomes insolvent, the interests of the creditors arise as they can control the assets of the company by means of insolvency procedures and, for all practical purposes, remove the control of the company from the shareholders. (For further discussion on insolvency, see page 536.)

Management of companies

Most companies have a formal meetings structure.

Annual general meeting (AGM)

This is a formal meeting to:

- receive the report and accounts as required by the Companies Act 1985
- declare a dividend (or none)
- elect and/or reappoint directors
- fix the remuneration of the auditors.

In accordance with Section 366 of the Companies Act 1985, every company (except certain private companies) must hold an AGM each calendar year and not more than 15 months may elapse between the date of one AGM and the next.

Extraordinary general meetings (EGMs)

EGMs may, subject to Articles, be convened at any time for the transaction of business which requires attention before the next AGM.

Class meetings

The holders of a class of a company's shares can meet in accordance with the Articles or conditions attaching to the shares whenever their rights are to be varied as a result of some action proposed to be taken by the company.

Board meetings

The **board of directors** meets to conduct the business of the company in the manner prescribed by the Articles of Association. Regulation 88 of the Companies Act 1985 gives the directors the authority to meet as they think fit. In private companies, meetings will be held when necessary. In public companies, meetings tend to be held more frequently and on stipulated dates. Where there are both executive and non-executive directors, meetings are normally held monthly, with intervening meetings of the executive directors only. Other organisations such as local authorities follow the same procedures and have regular fixed meetings for board members and more frequently held meetings of senior management teams.

DISSOLUTION OF BUSINESS UNITS

Cessation of trade by a sole trader

If a sole trader wishes to stop trading, he or she can do so simply by ceasing to trade. If the person is unable to pay debts, then a court may decide that he or she is **insolvent** and they may be declared bankrupt. However, some other options may be available:

- *Voluntary arrangement.* Under the **Deeds of Arrangement Act 1914**, a sole trader can come to an arrangement with his or her creditors to pay them a certain amount in the pound for each pound owed. Such an arrangement has the advantage that it can be made out of court, but it has the corresponding disadvantage that if a creditor is unhappy with the arrangement, he or she can petition the court to have the debtor made **bankrupt** (see page 535). In any case, a majority of creditors, who are owed a majority of the debt, must agree to the arrangement.
- *Use of a trustee.* A sole trader may put the running of the business into the hands of a **trustee** (normally an accountant) who will either manage or attempt to sell the business to pay off the creditors. Again the creditors must agree to the arrangement.

- *Grant of interim order.* An **interim order** may be granted to a sole trader upon application to a court, provided that he or she has not made an application in the preceding twelve months. The order will stop bankruptcy proceedings, normally for a period of 14 days, so any secured creditor will not be able to force the sale of a property upon which a charge has been made. Under an interim order a debtor must consult a Department of Trade and Industry registered insolvency practitioner (called a 'nominee') who will report back to the court on the viability of the debtor's proposal to resolve the matter. If the report is favourable then the court may extend the interim order to enable a meeting of the creditors to take place to determine the arrangement. If the arrangement is accepted by 75 per cent of the creditors (in value) then the order becomes binding upon all of them. The nominee will then supervise the arrangement and normally take possession of the debtor's property in order to comply with the arrangement.

Bankruptcy

If all else fails then bankruptcy proceedings will commence and the following steps will be taken.

- The sole trader's property will automatically pass into the hands of the **Official Receiver** except for any tools, equipment etc. necessary for the person to continue in his or her job. The person will also be able to retain basic necessary domestic items.
- Within 21 days he or she must furnish the court with a statement of affairs covering assets and liabilities, details of all known creditors and details of any securities held by the creditors. The Official Receiver normally becomes the **trustee in bankruptcy** (i.e. the person who is entrusted with the property of a bankrupt to sell and distribute the proceeds to the creditors in accordance with the provisions of the **Insolvency Act 1986**). He or she will try and recover any money owing to the sole trader, establish the claims of the creditors, sell off all the assets, and pay creditors in the order specified in the Insolvency Act 1986.

Creditors may be:

- *preferential* (payment to the Inland Revenue, VAT and car tax; payment of employees; payment of social security contributions)
- *unsecured* (e.g. trade creditors)
- *deferred* (e.g. someone linked to the bankrupt, normally by marriage, who will receive no payment until all other creditors have been paid in full).

Once a bankruptcy order is made, all debts owed by the sole trader will cease to be due, except those owed to the Crown such as payment of tax to the Inland Revenue. A first bankrupt is automatically discharged after three years. If he or she had owed less than £20 000 at the time of bankruptcy and the assets amounted to £2000 or more, then the period would be two years. If the person had been made bankrupt in the preceding 15 years he or she would have to wait five years before applying to be discharged.

During the period of bankruptcy, a person can continue in business but is prevented from obtaining credit of more than £250. If the credit limit is breached, a criminal offence is committed. During that period also, an undischarged bankrupt cannot become an MP, a councillor, a magistrate or a director of a company, or be concerned in the management of a company.

Dissolution of a partnership

When a partnership ends, there are a number of formalities to be observed which are set out in Sections 32–44 of the Partnership Act 1890. Subject to agreement between the partners, a partnership can be dissolved:

- at the end of a previously agreed fixed term
- at the end of what has previously been agreed to be a single undertaking
- by one partner giving notice to all the other partners that he or she wishes to dissolve the partnership.

In addition, a partnership can be dissolved in the following circumstances:

- by death, in a two-partner partnership (in other cases the partnership agreement will normally state the procedure to be followed upon the death of a partner)
- by bankruptcy of one of the partners – although the other partners can agree before the dissolution to continue without the bankrupt partner.
- through the occurrence of an event that makes it unlawful for the business of the firm to be carried on
- by order of the court – when a partner becomes in any way permanently incapable of performing his or her part of the partnership contract
- when one partner is guilty of committing an act that brings discredit or bad publicity to the firm
- where there are wilful or persistent breaches of the partnership agreement
- when the business can only be carried on at a loss
- where circumstances have arisen that, in the opinion of the court, make it just and equitable that the partnership be dissolved

- where a partner becomes so mentally ill as to be no longer capable of managing his or her affairs (Section 96 of the Mental Health Act 1983).

Once dissolution has been decided, Sections 37–44 of the Partnership Act 1890 set out the rules for the distribution of the assets.

Discussion point

Goodwill (i.e. the established reputation of the partnership) is an asset belonging to the partnership and is normally sold alongside the other assets. If you were a potential buyer, what information would you need to determine the value of the goodwill possessed by a particular partnership?

Dissolution of a company

There are several forms of company dissolution:

- *voluntary liquidation* because the members of a company no longer wish to carry on trading
- *compulsory liquidation* because the company cannot meet its debts
- *dissolution by the Attorney General* because the objectives of the company are offensive or illegal
- *dissolution by the Registrar of Companies* because the company has ceased to trade.

Voluntary winding-up

The winding-up of a company may be agreed at any time by its shareholders. A special resolution may be passed to effect the winding-up where the company is solvent, or by an extraordinary resolution where the company cannot meet its liabilities. Where a declaration of solvency is made the members of the company will be in control of the process. Where no such declaration is made, the company will be insolvent and the creditors will control the process. In a solvent winding-up the members will appoint a **liquidator** (i.e. a qualified insolvency practitioner) whose job it is to collect all money owed to the company, realise all other assets and pay off the creditors in accordance with the rules laid down in the

Companies Act 1985. In an insolvent winding-up, the creditors will make the appointment.

Once the resolution has been passed, the company does not cease to exist but it may not continue to trade other than for the purposes of enabling it to be wound up. The directors lose their powers upon the appointment of the liquidator, although they may be kept on by him or her to keep the business operating *pro tem* (for the time being). In an insolvent winding-up the employees will be dismissed, but again may be re-employed by the liquidator under a new contract.

Payment of creditors is based on very similar lines to that of creditors in a case of bankruptcy. After the preferential creditors have been paid, the liquidator will then pay off any creditors who have a floating charge over the assets of the company. The trade or unsecured creditors will then be paid, and finally the deferred creditors.

Compulsory winding-up

Section 123 of the Insolvency Act 1986 states that a company is unable to pay its debts when:

- a creditor who is owed £750 or more has served a demand for payment on the company which the company has failed to pay within three weeks
- **execution** has been issued – a warrant issued by the courts to enable bailiffs to seize goods belonging to the debtor – which has been returned unpaid
- it is proved that the company is unable to pay its debts
- the company's assets are proved to be less than its liabilities.

If the court grants a winding-up order, the Official Receiver again becomes the liquidator. As a consequence, staff are dismissed, all legal actions against the company are suspended and the transfer of any shares or property becomes void. When the liquidator has realised the assets of the company and paid off the creditors in the correct order, he or she reports to the DTI and may apply to the court for the company to be dissolved. The order of dissolution is sent to the Registrar of Companies who dissolves the company and advertises the fact in the *London Gazette*.

However, just as a sole trader and a partnership can make an arrangement with their creditors to avoid going bankrupt, so can a company make similar arrangements to avoid bankruptcy. It may enter into a voluntary arrangement whereby it agrees with creditors to either pay a composition (i.e. part payment of a debt in full settlement) or to rearrange the payment of its debts by, for example, negotiating a longer period of repayment. In order to do this it must appoint a nominee, who must be a qualified insolvency practitioner and who will present the proposal to both the court and the creditors.

Alternatively the company may go into **administration** – i.e. make an application to the court for an order of administration which may be granted if the court feels that it may enable the company to realise its assets more profitably than in a liquidation, allow the company to be sold as a going concern or enable approval of a voluntary arrangement. Such an application will freeze most of the company's actions so that any judgements made against it cannot be enforced and any other property in its possession cannot be recovered. The majority of legal actions concerning the company will also be suspended. If an order is granted it will no longer be possible for the company to be compulsorily wound up and the court will appoint an administrator who will be responsible for the management of the company. He or she is also bound to produce a proposal for the implementation of the goals outlined in the order. The proposal must be notified to the members and creditors and where accepted the order will normally be extended to allow the implementation of the report. Should it be rejected then the order is normally withdrawn by the court.

TASK

Either now or at an appropriate point in your studies, read the assignment at the end of Unit 6 (page 554) and complete the task relating to the dissolution of a business unit.

ROLE OF THE MAIN REGULATORY AGENCIES

One of the main objectives of the Companies Acts is to protect the general public and shareholders from being exploited by unregulated and potentially unscrupulous companies. As in the case of consumer protection legislation, therefore, a number of regulatory bodies have been established to ensure that the provisions of the Acts are in fact being implemented. The major agencies include the Registrar of Companies and the Department of Trade and Industry.

Registrar of Companies

The Articles of Association of a registered company must be supplied to the Registrar of Companies prior to incorporation. Like the Memorandum of Association, the contents will then be included in the company's file kept at Companies House in Cardiff. In addition, the Registrar must be supplied with a statutory declaration that all the requirements of the Companies Acts have been complied with. Having examined all the documents and ensured that they are in order, the Registrar then issues a certificate under official seal which certifies that the company is **incorporated**. The certificate is *conclusive* evidence that the company has complied with all the requirements of the Companies Acts and that it is authorised to be registered.

At the other end of the process, the Registrar may, under Section 652 of the Companies Act 1985, strike off the register a company that is defunct; i.e. one which is no longer carrying on a business. Consequently, would-be investors can at least assure themselves that the company in which they are interested in investing does exist and is subject to certain controls.

Department of Trade and Industry

The DTI has the power to order one of its inspectors to investigate the affairs of a company and Section 442(1) of the Companies Act 1985 provides that where there appears to be good reason to do so, the DTI may appoint inspectors to investigate and report on the membership of any company in order to determine the true identity of the persons financially interested in its success or failure or able to control or materially influence its policy.

If the DTI has investigated the affairs of a company and it appears to the Secretary of State that a **disqualification order** should be made because a person is unfit to manage or because public interest requires it, he or she may apply to the courts for such an order. The maximum disqualification period is 15 years.

Employment Protection Legislation

CHAPTER 24

This chapter introduces you to the way in which the law attempts to protect

employees both through the common law and by the introduction of statutory legislation.

On completion of the chapter you should be able to explain the key provisions relating to employment protection legislation. To achieve this you must demonstrate the ability to:

- identify the source and content of the key statutory provisions relating to employer protection

- describe limitations to their availability

- apply the relevant law on employment protection to a case study, and present findings.

All contracts, whether commercial or of employment, must contain certain essential elements. It could be argued, therefore, that once it is proved that a contract of employment contains these elements, no further action need be taken. However, the law is not so far removed from reality as to assume that the bargaining position between employer and employee is the same as that between the buyer and seller of goods. It recognises that in many instances the employee needs additional protection to prevent the balance of power from swinging too much in the employer's favour. Consequently both common law and statutory law afford the employee additional protection. In this context the word 'employee' is important, as self-employed workers or independent contractors are normally unable to take advantage of such protection.

Being an employee of an organisation or operating as an independent contractor is generally a matter of personal choice. In making that choice, the independent contractor should bear in mind that he or she will forgo the advantages of **employee status**:

- The employer is vicariously liable for employees. This

means that he or she will be liable to any other person who suffers harm or injury caused by the negligent act of an employee, if that employee is acting in the course of employment.
- Greater protection is afforded to employees by the sex discrimination, race relations, social security, and health and safety legislation.
- Greater protection is afforded by the Employment Rights Act 1996 (discussed on page 541).
- An employer owes certain implied duties and has certain implied rights when employing an employee rather than an independent contractor.

EMPLOYEE STATUS

In most cases it is clear whether a worker is an employee or is self-employed. Someone who is a personal assistant to a managing director is normally an employee. Someone employed to clean windows once a month is normally an independent contractor. However, on occasions the courts have had to deliberate on exactly who is an employee. Consequently several tests have been developed to assist them.

The control test

This was the original test used by courts to establish whether the employer could not only tell the person employed what to do, but also instruct him or her in the way the work should be done.

The organisation or integration test

With the advent of a more skilled workforce, the control test became difficult to apply in certain circumstances. Where, for instance, managers were in charge of professionally qualified people such as surgeons, accountants or computer programmers, they were unable to control totally what was done, simply because they did not know *what* should be done. Consequently, the organisation or integration test was introduced to determine whether the person in question was *fully integrated into the operation of the business*. Again, however, it became difficult to apply in all circumstances because the test was too wide.

The multiple test

Hence the multiple test was introduced. The courts now consider the contract *as a whole* in order to determine employee status. While the concept of control remains important, other criteria are considered. For an employee there is an obligation to work – the person concerned is not free to choose whether or not to work. In contrast, in an independent contractor/employer relationship it is recognised that there is 'mutuality of obligation' (i.e. a freedom to offer and a freedom to accept or reject the work in question). Also, for a self-employed person there is the freedom to work for other people at the same time. Other criteria are:

- the method of payment – whether it is a fixed sum paid at regular intervals, the payment of a fee, or the payment of a sum on completion of a job
- the liability for the payment of tax, National Insurance, sick pay or holiday pay
- eligibility for pension schemes or other fringe benefits
- the degree of the financial risk borne by the worker
- the freedom or otherwise for the worker to hire his or her own helpers.

TASK

You are asked to advise (a) a homeworker, (b) a casual worker, and (c) an agency worker about their employment status. What questions would you ask each of them to help you to give them the right advice? What advice would that be?

You may need to research the following cases to give you some important background information:

Nethermore (St Neots) Ltd. v Gardiner & Anor [1982] ICR 319

O'Kelly v Trusthouse Forte [1983] IRLR 369

McMeechan v Secretary of State for Employment [1997] IRLR 353.

COMMON LAW PROTECTION

Even prior to statutory legislation, the common law recognised that employers had certain **implied obligations** towards their employees. It counterbalanced those obligations by also giving them certain **implied rights**.

Major obligations of an employer

Pay

The employer has a duty to pay the employee an agreed remuneration for being ready and willing to work.

A limited duty to provide work

Only in exceptional cases is an employer compelled to provide an employee with work. The duty exists, for instance, where lack of work would mean a wage reduction or where the work is on commission or piecework. The duty also exists where lack of work may have a damaging effect on the employee's reputation. Two obvious examples would be actors or television presenters, but more recently the courts have shown some sympathy towards senior executives or employees with a high level of technical skill who need to work to maintain their skills at a particular level.

Expenses

There is the duty to indemnify the employee if he or she has necessarily incurred expenses in the course of employment.

The duty of mutual trust or confidence (or the duty to provide reasonable management)

The old legal terminology of 'master' and 'servant' has been replaced with 'employer' and 'employee'. This has signalled a change in the courts' view of the employment relationship and what could be considered to be reasonable behaviour by both parties. For examples of the breakdown of such a relationship, see page 545 for discussion of unfair dismissal.

Contractual rights

The employer has a duty to provide proper information to an employee about his or her rights under the contract. This is a relatively new area and has arisen from a House of Lords decision in *Scally v Southern Health & Social Services Board* [1991] ICR 771. New employees were not informed of their rights to enhance their years of pension entitlement, but the Lords held there to be an implied term that they *should* have been provided with this information.

The duty to ensure safety

Most of the legislation relating to the employer's responsibility for health and safety is now covered by the Health and Safety at Work Act and several EU Directives. However, the extent of the employer's responsibility in this respect can be illustrated by two cases reflecting modern attitudes towards health, and in particular towards stress at work and smoking at work.

In *Walker v Northumberland County Council* [1995] IRLR 35, a social work manager suffered a nervous breakdown and was off work for five months. On his return he was not given the support promised and his workload was

increased. He suffered a second nervous breakdown and was dismissed on the grounds of ill-health. The court found there to be no reason why psychiatric damages should be excluded from the scope of duty of care of the council provided it could have been foreseen that the employee was at risk. The first breakdown may not have been foreseen. The second should have been.

In *Waltons & Morse v Dorrington* [1997] IRLR 488, Ms Dorrington was a legal secretary and non-smoker who had worked for a firm since 1984. In 1992, she was moved to another office which was at the end of a corridor and close to the room occupied by three heavy-smoking solicitors. She complained. Although some modifications were made in the workplace that did not resolve the problem. As a result she left the firm and claimed constructive dismissal (for further discussion on this point see page 546). The Employment Appeal Tribunal upheld her claim on the grounds that:

> '*it is an implied term of every contract of employment that the employer will provide and monitor for employees, so far as is reasonably practicable, a working environment which is reasonably suitable for the performance by them of their contractual duties.*'

Major rights of an employer

An employer has the right to expect employees to act in **good faith**. They must be honest. In this case honesty means more than not stealing or defrauding the company. For instance, a betting shop manager habitually left IOUs in the till although he always repaid them. He continued to do so although he had been expressly forbidden. It was held that the employer was entitled to dismiss him. Similarly, in *Denco Ltd. v Joinson* [1991] ICR 172, the use of an unauthorised password to gain access to a computer was found to constitute gross misconduct because of dishonesty.

Employees also have a duty to disclose misdeeds. Although employees need not incriminate themselves, they have a duty not to mislead the employer. Indeed, in recent times there has been an increasing trend towards expecting senior managers to notify the employer of any serious breaches committed by fellow employees (for further discussion see page 542).

Employees must exercise reasonable skill and care. The degree of care expected may vary with the position held by the employee and the responsibility entrusted to him or her. The employee must also take care of the employer's property (although apparently there is no corresponding common law duty placed on the employer to safeguard the employee's property).

Other obligations of employees are:

- not to disclose confidential information of the company
- not to disclose information about inventions
- not to compete with the employer, and to account for secret profits
- to render **personal service** and be ready and willing to work
- to obey lawful orders.

TASK

You have been asked to outline to a new employee his rights and obligations under the common law. He asks you the following questions.

a 'What's the point of having an obligation to provide work even though it is a limited obligation? Surely no employer would be daft enough to go on paying an employee and not expect him to work.'

b 'I don't fancy the bit about telling tales on my mates. That's a recipe for disaster. It would cause more problems than it solved. Why look for trouble?'

c 'I don't understand the bit about personal service. What exactly does that mean?'

d 'Give me some examples about how I could disrupt a business so badly that I would be in breach of contract.'

Prepare a series of notes outlining your answers to him.

STATUTORY PROTECTION

The **Employment Rights Act 1996** (ERA 96) and its predecessors were introduced for the same reasons as were other forms of protective legislation. Although the common law does give the employee some protection, it is rarely able to develop sufficiently quickly to meet the needs of the modern business world. One of the major provisions of ERA 96 is the requirement that an employer should provide an employee with certain written terms and conditions of employment. This means that, for most employees, their rights and obligations are clearer because the law normally allows express terms in a contract to take precedence over implied terms.

Terms and conditions

A contract need not be in written form, but ERA 96 requires that certain **terms and conditions** must be in writing. They are:

- the names of the employer and employee
- the date when employment began
- whether the employment counts as a period of continuous employment with a previous employer, and the date of commencement of the previous employment where this is the case
- the scale or rate of pay and the method of calculating pay where the employee is paid by commission or bonus
- when payment is made (i.e. weekly or monthly), and the day or date of payment
- the hours to be worked, including any compulsory overtime
- holiday entitlement and holiday pay
- sick pay and injury arrangements
- entitlement to a pension scheme
- the length of notice of termination an employee must receive or give

- the job title
- the duration of temporary contracts
- the work location or locations
- any collective agreements affecting the job
- when the job requires work outside the UK for more than one month, the period of such work, the currency in which the employee will be paid and any other pay or benefits
- grievance procedures
- disciplinary procedures.

Certain of these particulars can be given by reference to a common document, such as a collective agreement or a staff handbook, but such information must be readily accessible to the employee at all times.

Other terms and conditions

In addition to the main terms in any written statement, employers may decide to include other express terms as they think fit. Some of the more common of these include:

- a 'dedication to enterprise' or 'whole time and attention' clause, which states the limitations under which an employee can undertake other work for a different employer either during or after working hours. (Sometimes the clause imposes a duty to inform on colleagues' misdeeds. Interestingly, the **Public Interest Disclosure Act 1998** has now become law. It protects 'whistleblowers' from being victimised or dismissed by the employer.)
- a variation clause, which is increasing in popularity and which allows an employer the unilateral power to alter the contract in certain circumstances
- a right to search employees
- a right to demand that employees undergo medical examinations
- a confidentiality clause which, although an implied term in a contract, is often used to emphasise the importance of confidentiality – particularly to junior staff who may not be under as great an implied duty at common law as their more senior colleagues
- an intellectual property clause, which details the ownership of copyright, designs and inventions made by the employee during the working relationship
- a restraint-of-trade clause, where an employee is prevented from working in a particular job or industry for a set time (look back to page 505 for further discussion on this point)
- a suspension clause, which gives the employer the right to suspend an employee with or without pay as part of a disciplinary procedure
- a lay-off and guarantee clause, which, in addition to any statutory rights the employees may have, allow them a specific rate of pay in respect of short-time working

- a dress code which sets out certain standards of dress and appearance.

TASK

Your boss is very keen that all employees in the organisation should look smart. She therefore produces a dress code. You, however, have some reservations because you think she might be in breach of certain sections of both the **Sex Discrimination Act 1975** (as updated) and the **Race Relations Act 1996**. Research the following cases and write a memo to her outlining as tactfully as possible the potential problems there may be in having too strict a dress code.

Schmidt v Austicks Bookshops Ltd. [1977] IRLR 360

Smith v Safeway Plc [1996] IRLR 496

Burrett v West Birmingham Health Authority [1994] IRLR 7

Kingston v Richmond Area Health Authority v Kaur [1981] ICR 631.

Additional statutory rights of employees

Not only are employees entitled to a written statement, they are also statutorily entitled to certain other rights.

Time off work

For public duties

Under certain circumstances, employees have a right to time off work, sometimes with pay. These include:

- trade union activities – both as a trade union member and as an official
- public duties – for work as a magistrate, member of an employment tribunal etc.

- a redundancy situation – to allow time off to look for another job or to make arrangements for training for future employment
- lay-off – to allow employees with four weeks or more of continuous service a guaranteed payment up to a maximum sum if they are not provided with work on a normal working day
- occupational pension schemes – for nominated trustees of occupational pension schemes
- antenatal care.

Holidays

Under the **Working Time Regulations 1998**, workers who have been employed for at least 13 weeks have a right to three weeks' paid annual leave. This right applies to both full-time and part-time workers and means that a part-timer working two days a week, for example, has a statutory right to six days' paid annual leave. Where a part-timer's working time is set in terms of hours, then the leave may also be expressed in terms of hours.

For sickness

Employers are required to provide **statutory sick pay** (SSP) on behalf of the government. SSP is currently paid by them for up to 28 weeks of incapacity for work during a three-year period. The first three days of sickness are 'waiting days' and no SSP is payable. However, during subsequent periods of sickness, if the employee has not been back at work following the first period of sickness for eight weeks or more, the periods are linked and there are no statutory waiting days. Under the SSP Percentage Threshold Order 1995, employers will recover on a percentage threshold scheme; i.e. the employers will take the National Insurance contribution (employer's and employee's) paid in any given tax month. They will then ascertain the SSP paid in the same month. If this is more than 13% of the NIC figure, they will recover the excess.

Payment details

Itemised pay statement

Before the introduction of employment protection legislation, there was no obligation upon employers to provide their employees with itemised pay statements. Provided payment was made, that was all the law required. However, ERA 96 now requires that employees must receive a statement before or at the time of receiving their pay, showing:

- gross pay and take-home pay together with the variable deductions which make up the difference between the two figures
- details of how it is to be paid.

Fixed deductions need not be itemised every pay day, provided the employer gives the employee a separate statement containing details of them every month.

Deductions from pay

Part II of the Employment Rights Act 1996 removed the right of employees to be paid in cash. Deductions from pay are unlawful unless (a) they are authorised by statute (in the case, for instance, of NI and tax deductions) or (b) they are included in a written contract of employment, or (c) the employee has put in writing beforehand his or her agreement to the deductions.

Discussion points

Rules relating to deductions from pay occur most frequently in the service industries, and normally arise through cash shortages or stock deficiencies. Deductions from workers' pay in the retail trades are limited to 10 per cent of the gross wages and may be made only within the period of 12 months from the date when the employee knew or ought to have known about them.

1. Why do you think the service industries are the most frequent user of the right to make deductions from employees' pay?

2. Why are more stringent limitations imposed upon employers in those industries?

Maternity rights under ERA 96

Basic rights

Basic leave for all pregnant women, irrespective of length of service, may commence at any time the woman wishes after the eleventh week before the expected week of childbirth. All women are entitled to a minimum of 14 weeks' maternity leave.

In order to exercise her right, the woman must notify her employer either not later than 21 days before the commencement date or as soon as is reasonably practicable. The notification must be in writing if the employer requests it, and the employer may also request a certificate from a registered medical practitioner or midwife.

Extended maternity leave

Women who have accumulated two years' continuous service by the beginning of the eleventh week before the expected week of childbirth have the right to return at any time before the end of 29 weeks beginning with the week in which the actual date of childbirth falls, provided they have notified their employer in writing at least 21 days in advance of the intended date of return. They may postpone their return by up to four weeks from the end of the 29 weeks provided they supply their employer with a doctor's certificate.

Restrictions on return to work

The ERA requires employers to suspend an employee on maternity grounds if there is a statutory requirement that they should do so (normally after consideration of the health of the mother and child). During the suspension the employee is entitled to be paid. In addition, the **Maternity (Compulsory Leave) Regulations 1994** prohibit any employee entitled to maternity leave from working, or being permitted by the employer to work, during a period of two weeks starting with the date of the childbirth.

Return to work

On her return to work an employee is entitled to be reinstated in the same kind of job she had before her absence. If this is no longer available, she must be offered another suitable job. She must also enjoy the same fringe benefits as she did before.

In the case of a company employing five people or fewer immediately before the end of a woman's absence on maternity leave, the woman does *not* have the statutory right to return to work if it is not reasonably practicable for the employer to permit her to return. It is up to the employer to prove that it is not reasonably practicable.

Many women want to work on a part-time basis following maternity leave, although this is inconsistent with the statutory right to return to the 'same job'. However, if an employer refuses to allow the woman to return on a part-time basis, she may bring a claim under the Sex Discrimination Act 1975 if she can show that she has suffered a detriment by the employer's refusal to agree to her return on a part-time basis.

Discussion points

1. Why is there a distinction made between large and small companies when the objectives of both are to make a profit and employ suitable staff to assist them to do so?

2. Why do you think the words 'immediately before the end of a woman's absence' are used?

3. In what circumstances do you think an employer could justify a decision that the job must be a full-time one?

Notice of termination

Prior to statutory legislation, the question of the length of notice of termination of employment was a contractual issue between the employer and employee. The ERA, however, now lays down certain minimum notice requirements. If a person has been continuously employed for at least one month, he or she must be given:

- not less than one week's notice if the period of continuous employment is less than two years
- not less than one week's notice for each year of continuous employment if the period of continuous employment is two years or more but less than 12 years.
- not less than 12 weeks' notice if the period of continuous employment is 12 years or more.

It is not necessary to give notice to any employee at the expiry of a fixed term as notice has been given at the start of the contract that it will end at a certain date. However, those employed on fixed-term contracts of one month or less and who have been continuously employed by the employer for at least three months have the same notice rights as other employees.

Employees must give their employers at least one week's notice if they have been continuously employed for one month or more. The period does not increase with longer service.

Working time

Recent legislation has concentrated on the hours employees can be expected to work. Of relevance here are the **Working Time Regulations 1998** (implementing the EU Working Time Directive 93/104/EC) and the **Young Worker's Directive** (EU Directive 93/33/EC). These working time regulations now provide that a person's average weekly working time (including overtime) should not have to exceed 48 hours, averaged over a reference period of 17 weeks. Individuals can agree to be excluded from the maximum working week requirement on a voluntary basis.

Night working should not have to exceed eight hours in each 24-hour period, over a reference period of 17 weeks. Provided compensatory rest is permitted or appropriate protection given, the rules on night working are excluded for 'special case' workers, and they can be modified or excluded for other workers by a collective or workplace agreement.

Adult workers must be permitted to take a rest period of not less than 11 consecutive hours in each 24-hour period, and a weekly rest period of not less than 24 hours in each seven-day period. Young workers are entitled to a daily rest period of 12 consecutive hours, except in unexpected and unpredictable occurrences where compensatory rest may be permitted within three weeks.

Adult workers whose daily working time exceeds six hours are entitled to a rest break in accordance with the terms of a collective or workplace agreement. Where there is no such agreement a minimum break of 20 minutes is laid down. Young workers are entitled to a rest break of at least 30 minutes after $4^{1}/_{2}$ hours' work.

Dismissal

If a contract of employment runs smoothly then its termination normally takes place on either the retirement or the resignation of the employee. Where, however, the relationship is troubled and is ended by the employer, the employee is entitled to claim legislative protection. Although, again, the major piece of statutory legislation is ERA 96, a White Paper published in June 1998, entitled *Fairness at Work*, most of which is now contained in the Employment Relations Bill 1999, has had some impact upon the rights of employees in cases of **unfair dismissal.**

The most highly publicised element of the White Paper was the reintroduction of compulsory recognition of a union having support from a majority of those voting on the issue and including at least 40 per cent of the workforce. Firms with 20 or fewer workers are exempt. It also proposed some 'family friendly' measures:

• Men and women with at least one year's service are given the right to three months' parental leave following the birth or adoption of a child. This is designed to bring the UK into line with the EU's Parental Leave Directive.

- Extended maternity leave is made available to women with one (rather than two) year's service, and basic maternity leave will be extended from 14 to 18 weeks.
- Workers are given the right to reasonable time off for family emergencies, regardless of length of service.

In addition, however, workers are now provided with additional unfair dismissal rights:

- The upper limit on unfair dismissal **compensation** is increased.
- Employees who are dismissed for taking part in lawfully organised official industrial action have the right to claim unfair dismissal.
- A ban is placed on unfair dismissal waivers in fixed-term contracts.

Actual dismissal

The first step a dismissed employee must take, if he or she does not accept the position, is to prove that dismissal has actually occurred. In most cases this is relatively simple, but there can be problems arising from the wording of the dismissal. If, for instance, there is an argument between a supervisor and employee and words such as 'get lost' or 'there's the door' are used, they could be construed as words of dismissal. Much depends on the circumstances. Is the working environment such that arguments of this sort occur frequently without any real intent to dismiss? Is there a marked difference in the status of both parties?

Constructive dismissal

Of equal importance is the concept of **constructive dismissal**. This is in some respects the reverse of actual dismissal, in that the employee leaves without having been dismissed because he or she feels that the employer has been in fundamental breach of contract and has forced its termination. Obviously this links closely with the employer's implied obligation to manage reasonably (look back to page 540 for further discussion). Examples include:

- unilaterally changing the terms of the contract to the employee's disadvantage (e.g. increasing the hours, reducing the pay)
- an unreasonable accusation of theft against an employee of good character and many years' standing
- an arbitrary refusal of a pay rise to one employee when everyone else receives one
- very abusive language on a number of occasions
- publicly criticising an employee, particularly in front of his or her own staff
- demotion.

Employer defences

Once the fact of dismissal has been established, the employer has a right of reply under Section 98 of the ERA. If the employer feels that the dismissal has indeed been fair, the action must be justified under one of a number of headings.

Lack of competency or qualifications

Until quite recently the claim that an employee was **incompetent** was normally accepted by the courts as a fair reason for dismissal, provided there was sufficient evidence. Nowadays, however, the courts tend to take the view that an incompetent employee should instead be offered assistance and training, and only when those avenues have been explored should a subsequent dismissal be held to be fair. Even so, employees have been judged to have been fairly dismissed if they have been too slow, too inflexible, unable to establish good working relationships and unable to meet targets. Similarly, an employee who had been expected to obtain a relevant qualification within a certain period after starting work, but failed to do so, was held to have been fairly dismissed

Misconduct

There are, of course, many types of **misconduct** which can result in fair dismissal. They include persistent absenteeism and lateness, the use of abusive language, disloyalty, disobedience, attitude, personal appearance, theft or dishonesty, violence or fighting. In addition many employers treat drink or drug abuse as a form of misconduct, although industrial relations specialists now tend to recommend that employees be counselled and treated for such disorders rather than disciplined, and some of the more liberal industrial tribunals agree with them.

It is unlikely that a single act of misconduct will be regarded as a good reason for dismissal (unless it is exceptionally grave). The courts will expect an official disciplinary procedure to have been followed, normally involving verbal and written warnings and even a suspension before a final dismissal. However, where the contract of employment contains an *express term* that a certain form of misconduct will result in instant dismissal, the courts will normally accept that a fair dismissal has occurred if an employee breaches that term.

Redundancy

Redundancy is potentially a fair reason for dismissal. It can, however, be unfair if selection for redundancy takes place in breach of a customary agreement or agreed procedure, or if it is based on union membership or activities.

Statutory ban

Dismissal is fair if the employee is not able to continue to work without contravening a statutory enactment. If, for instance, a person employed in the food preparation industry contracts a specified skin disease, the employer would be in statutory breach of a food hygiene regulation if the employee were allowed to continue working in that environment.

Some other substantial reason

SOSR is the legal term for 'miscellaneous'. If an employer feels he or she has a good defence to a claim for unfair dismissal, but that defence does not fall easily into any of the specified categories, he or she can use the defence of SOSR. If, for instance, an employer wishes to change the duties of an employee and the changes are regarded as reasonable, any refusal on the part of the employee may lead to fair dismissal.

Automatically unfair dismissal

In certain circumstances a dismissal will be regarded as **automatically unfair** (e.g. if it has been for a maternity or trade union reason). The employer will be able to offer no defence in such cases.

Overall test of reasonableness

It may sound like legalistic jargon to say that a dismissal may be fair but nevertheless still be regarded as unreasonable. However, there are occasions on which the courts may decide that, although a dismissal is *technically* fair, it is 'unfair in all the circumstances'.

- The employer must satisfy a tribunal that he or she complied with the pre-dismissal procedures which any reasonable employer could and should have applied in the circumstances of the case.

- Where there is a contractual appeal process, the employer must have carried it out and the employee must have been heard and allowed to put his or her case.
- Where conduct is the issue, the employer must show on a balance of probabilities that, at the time of the dismissal, he or she believed the employee was guilty of misconduct and that, in all the circumstances, it was reasonable for the employment to be terminated.

Redundancy

Fairness

An employee may be justifiably dismissed for reason of **redundancy** if his or her job function ceases to exist in the organisation. There can be little argument about this where an entire establishment shuts down. When that happens the usual 'remedy' for employees is the payment of redundancy sums which are based on age and length of service.

However, problems do sometimes occur where an establishment remains open but the need for a particular employee or group of employees diminishes. Dismissing such employees is potentially fair, but the way the situation is handled may make it unfair and lead to a claim for unfair dismissal compensation in addition to redundancy pay.

In order for employees in this situation to be able to claim unfair redundancy:

- they must have been employed in the same undertaking as continuing employees
- employees doing similar work must not have been made redundant.

Alternatively they must have been selected for redundancy for a trade union reason or in contravention of a customary arrangement or agreed procedure.

Even if redundancy is not unfair, it may be held to be *unreasonable* in some circumstances. For example, has the employer selected the employee unfairly? In the absence of an agreed procedure outlining and prioritising the basic criteria for redundancy, a tribunal will look at a number of factors to determine whether or not the selection has been fair.

Redundancy may be unreasonable if the employer has not made any reasonable effort to create alternative work for the employee, or has not consulted the employee nor given reasonable notice of impending redundancy.

In addition, in *Williams v Compair Maxam Ltd.* [1982] ICR 156, the Employment Appeal Tribunal added two further criteria for reasonableness:

- Where the employer recognises a union, the necessary consultations on redundancy should take place with that union. (See below for further discussion on this point.)
- When preparing the criteria for redundancy (whether or not with union agreement), the emphasis must be on those which are objective rather than subjective (e.g. on length of service, experience, efficiency).

Union consultation

The **Collective Redundancies & Transfer of Undertakings (Protection of Employees) (Amendment) Regulations 1995** (SI 1995/2587) impose an obligation upon employers to consult a recognised trade union where they are proposing to dismiss as redundant 20 or more employees at one establishment within a period of 90 days or less. They must also notify the Department of Trade and Industry at least 90 days before the first dismissals take place in the case of 100 or more redundancies, or at least 30 days in the case of 20 or more redundancies. Union consultation must cover:

- the reason for the redundancy proposals
- the numbers and descriptions of employees to be dismissed
- the method of selection for redundancy
- the procedure and timing of dismissals
- the method of calculating any non-statutory redundancy payments (i.e. payments in addition to the basic requirements).

It must also include a consideration of ways to avoid redundancies or reduce the number to be dismissed.

Discussion point

The concept of redundancy is a curious one. On the one hand it could be considered fair because the employer apparently has no option. On the other hand it could be considered unfair because the employee has done nothing wrong. Discuss in what ways you think the law has tried to deal with this apparent dichotomy.

Transfer of business

It used to be possible for an employer to transfer his or her business to another employer and in doing so deprive the existing employees of many of their employment rights, particularly those requiring a qualifying period of continuous employment. The **Transfer of Undertakings (Protection of Employees) Regulations** attempted to overcome this by stating that, when a transfer takes place, any employees who are currently employed immediately before the transfer automatically become the employees of the new employer – who takes over the employment protection liabilities.

These regulations (often abbreviated to TUPE 81) were updated in July 1998 by a new EU Directive which member states had three years to implement. The major provisions are as follows:

- There will be a *relevant transfer* where there is a transfer of an 'economic entity' which retains its identity. There will be *no relevant transfer* where there is merely an administrative reorganisation or a transfer of administrative functions of public administration authorities.

- Employees on fixed-term contracts or temporary employees cannot be excluded from the regulations on transfer.
- The transferor and transferee will, after the date of transfer, be jointly and severally liable for obligations arising before the date of the transfer from a contract of employment or employment relationship existing on the date of transfer.
- Collective agreements will transfer.
- Recognition agreements will transfer as long as the undertaking concerned preserves its autonomy.
- The transfer does not in itself constitute grounds for dismissal, although dismissal may still take place for economic, technical or organisational reasons entailing changes in the workforce.
- If the transfer involves a substantial change in working conditions to the detriment of an employee and the employment relationship is ended, the employer will be held responsible.

In the White Paper, *Fairness at Work*, the government made clear its intention to improve the operation of the law in this area. It proposed to prepare a new version of TUPE 81, and has not ruled out the possibility that the new regulations will be more favourable than the recent EU Directive.

TASK

A client asks your advice on the following items in his terms and conditions of employment:

- 'Where necessary, and for sound business reasons, the terms and conditions of this contract may be amended by the employer.'
- 'In the event of any gross misconduct, dismissal will be instantaneous. Otherwise the usual disciplinary procedures will be followed.'
- 'An employee may not work for any of the company's competitors after he or she leaves.'
- 'As a manager you will be expected to inform the managing director of any activities carried out in the workplace which may harm its efficiency and productivity.'
- 'You will be expected to work every second Sunday.'

Your client makes the following observations:

a Can my employer change my terms and conditions without my agreement? If so, do I have any remedy?

b Can you outline the 'usual disciplinary procedures'?

c I thought that when a contract ended, so did the rights and obligations on both sides. Surely my employer can't stop me from working for whom I please when I leave?

d I don't fancy being a whistleblower. Must I comply with that requirement?

e I'm a committed churchgoer. I don't want to agree to working on a Sunday. Can I object?

Research possible answers to his concerns and include them in a brief set of notes to be used when you next talk to him.

HEALTH AND SAFETY LEGISLATION

As already discussed in Chapter 22 on consumer protection, the supplier of goods has a common law duty of care towards the purchaser. The same principles apply to an employer in respect of his or her health and safety obligations towards an employee. However, although employers have an implied obligation to make sure that the workplace is safe, this obligation has been supplemented to a great extent by a series of Acts and regulations, many of them stemming from the EU.

The Health and Safety at Work Act 1974

The major Act remains the **Health and Safety at Work Act 1974** (HSWA 74). It does not have the drawback of its predecessors in being too detailed, and thus allowing the unscrupulous employer to comply with the letter but not the spirit of the law. Consequently it sets out the duties of employers in broad terms.

Section 2(1) outlines the general duty of the employer to ensure, 'so far as is reasonably practicable', the health, safety and welfare at work of all employees. Section 2(2) extends this duty to cover the maintenance of a safe system of work (including safe entrances and exits); arrangements for the safe use, handling, storage and transport of articles and substances; and the provision of information, training and supervision. It also makes the employer responsible for the provision and maintenance of a working environment that is safe, without risk to health and with adequate facilities and arrangements for employees' welfare.

Interesting to note, however, is that the Act followed common law to a certain extent and imposed *obligations on the employee* as well as on the employer with regard to responsibility for health and safety. Section 7(a) requires all employees to take reasonable care for their own health and safety at work *and* that of others who may be affected by their acts or omissions. Section 7(b) requires all employees to cooperate with their employer in the discharge of health and safety responsibilities. Section 8 requires all employees not to interfere intentionally or recklessly with, or misuse, anything provided in the interests of health, safety and welfare.

Discussion point

What is the difference between 'health', 'safety' and 'welfare'? Which do you think an employee might find the hardest to prove that an employer has breached, and for what reasons?

Regulatory requirements

A number of health and safety regulations have been brought in to comply with EU Directives. They are extremely detailed and therefore complement the HSWA in that the employee has the choice of relying on the broad-brush approach of the Act or, if relevant, of referring to the specific provisions contained in one of the regulations.

Workplace regulations

Amongst the most important regulations are the **Workplace (Health, Safety and Welfare) Regulations 1992** which cover the standards of care required in:

- the maintenance of the workplace and of equipment, devices and systems ventilation, temperature in indoor workplaces, and lighting
- cleanliness and the handling of waste materials
- room dimensions and space
- floors and organisation of traffic routes
- falls or falling objects
- windows and transparent doors, gates and walls
- ability to clean windows safely
- escalators and moving walkways
- sanitary conveniences
- drinking water
- accommodation for clothing and facilities for changing clothes
- facilities for rest and to eat meals.

Management regulations

Of equal importance are the **Management of Health and Safety at Work Regulations 1992**. These span a range of requirements relating to the management and organisation of health and safety at the workplace. For instance:

- A risk assessment must be carried out by every employer and self-employed person if the enterprise employs five or more people.
- The employer must ensure that employees are provided with health surveillance appropriate to the risks to their health and safety (as identified by risk assessment).
- One or more 'competent' persons must be employed as a safety officer.

- Existing emergency arrangements must be reappraised to take account of the conclusions of risk assessment.
- As under the HSWA, employees must be given information on all health and safety risks and mitigating measures adopted by the employer.
- Where two or more employers share a workplace, they must cooperate on health and safety matters.
- Employers (and the self-employed) must provide the employer of any person who may come to work on their premises with information about any risks and of the measures taken to deal with them.

Other EU Regulations

These include:

- Health and Safety (Display Screen Equipment) Regulations 1992
- Personal Protective Equipment at Work Regulations 1992
- Provision and Use of Work Equipment Regulations 1992
- Provision and Use of Work Equipment Regulations 1992
- Manual Handling Operations Regulations 1992
- Electricity at Work Regulations 1989
- Noise at Work Regulations 1989
- Reporting of Injuries, Diseases and Dangerous Occurrences Regulations 1993
- Control of Substances Hazardous to Health Regulations 1994.

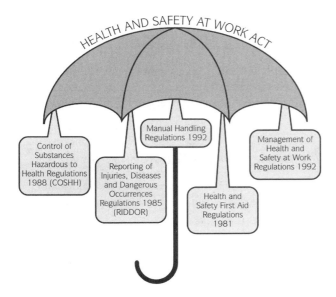

Figure 24.1 *The Health and Safety at Work Act is like an umbrella*

Monitoring of health and safety

Prior to the introduction of the Health and Safety at Work Act there were a small number of **factory inspectors** who were attempting to monitor compliance with health and safety legislation. Unfortunately their number did not increase in line with the increase in the legislation in this area, and it became increasingly apparent that irresponsible employers could ignore the law and take the chance that they would never receive a visit from an inspector. The HSWA and ensuing regulations therefore introduced **monitoring procedures** to try to ensure that internal as well as external inspections could take place which would be less easy for the employer to circumvent.

The safety adviser

Regulation 6 of the Management of Health and Safety at Work Regulations makes it clear that a safety officer or adviser should be appointed, but it gives no further details on his or her role. It is the employer's responsibility, therefore, to formulate a suitable job description for the needs of the establishment. In general the adviser will be expected to:

- be the company adviser on all health and safety matters
- give advance warning to senior management of any changes in health and safety legislation
- advise on health and safety training
- carry out safety inspections, investigate accidents and incidents, and ensure compliance with statutory reporting requirements
- liaise with external safety bodies
- maintain and update the company safety policy
- organise the safety committee (see below).

In many cases, too, the safety adviser may be expected to advise on and draft a **code of practice** for the company which the senior management team can then implement. The safety adviser should, of course, be aware of any industry-wide codes of practice.

The safety committee and safety representatives

Article 11 of the EC Framework Directive places emphasis on worker consultation and collaboration over health and safety. The **Safety Representatives and Safety Committees**

Regulations 1977 (SRSCR 77) and the **Health and Safety (Consultation with Employees) Regulations 1996** (HSCER 96) attempt to comply with this requirement by:

- allowing recognised trade unions to appoint safety representatives from among the employer's workforce (SRSCR)
- requiring employers to consult all employees not already represented by trade union safety representatives (HSCER).

The major functions of a **safety representative** are:

- to investigate potential hazards and dangerous occurrences at the workplace
- to examine the causes of accidents at the workplace
- to investigate employee complaints about health, safety or welfare
- to make representations to the employer about health, safety and welfare matters
- to carry out inspections
- to represent employees when consulting inspectors of the Health and Safety Executive (HSE)
- to attend meetings of the safety committee.

Safety committees must be given terms of reference. Usually they will include the following:

- to investigate and report on accidents or incidents
- to examine national health and safety reports and statistics
- to review health and safety audit reports
- to draw up works rules and instructions on safe systems of work
- to oversee health and safety training
- to promote and advise on relevant publicity campaigns
- to maintain links with external health and safety bodies
- to recommend updates to the company safety policy
- to consider and advise on impending legislation.

Check your understanding

From what you have already read in this chapter, what legal problems do you perceive may occur if the managing director of a company puts too much faith in the abilities of the safety adviser and committee?

Main regulatory agencies

Who inspects the inspectors? Internal monitoring mechanisms are normally the best way to make sure that health and safety legislation is being implemented, but external bodies act as a double safeguard. In addition they act in several other capacities. The main agencies are introduced below.

The Health and Safety Commission (HSC)

The **Health and Safety Commission** can make whatever arrangements it considers appropriate for the purposes of HSWA. It must ensure that adequate advice and information on health and safety is available, that research and training are undertaken when necessary, and that new regulations are prepared when needed. It will consult various parties and, with the permission of the Secretary of State, will conduct formal public enquiries into matters of public concern (such as factory explosions).

The Health and Safety Executive (HSE)

The **Health and Safety Executive** is the operational and enforcing arm of the Commission. Its main function is to make adequate arrangements for the enforcement of the relevant statutory provisions. It is also responsible for workings of the Health and Safety Inspectorate.

The Health and Safety Inspectorate (HSI)

The **Health and Safety Inspectorate** appoints inspectors who have the authority to visit premises, at any reasonable time, to carry out a number of searching inspections.

The Employment Medical Advisory Service

This is part of the HSE and gives advice and information on medical problems connected with employment.

Local government

Local authorities continue to enforce the remaining provisions of the Offices, Shops and Railway Premises Act 1963, as well as those of HSWA. The principal role is performed by district councils and usually by the department which has an environmental health function. In addition, enforcement in relation to activities such as petroleum licensing, certain explosives and the packaging and labelling of dangerous substances on consumer premises is normally carried out by **trading standards officers** or **fire authorities**.

FURTHER READING

Dobson, Paul, ed., *Charlesworth's Business Law*, 16th edition, Sweet and Maxwell, 1997.

Ellison, J., Bedingfield, J. and Harris, T. *Business Law*, 4th edition, Harrison Law Publishing, 1997.

Selwyn, N.M., *Selwyn's Law of Employment*, 10th edition, Butterworth, 1998.

ASSIGNMENT   UNIT 6

You and a group of former Business Studies students have set up a small business, in which you offer your services to companies to organise their conferences, exhibitions, seminars and other corporate events. Recently, however, you have experienced certain problems for which you have to find solutions.

Task 1

At the moment you are in a partnership. However, one of the other partners has caused the group a lot of problems and, even though he has now left, the rest of you want to explore the possibility of dissolving the partnership and setting up a limited company. The group asks you to carry out some research into how to do this and also what the advantages and disadvantages are of the proposed change. Prepare a memorandum to the rest of the group indicating what action should be taken and whether you recommend the change.

Task 2

A member of the office staff, who is one of your employees, has entered into an agreement for the purchase of some computer software. It has proved disastrous. It is very slow and is not capable of doing the work you want. The supplier refuses to take it back or to refund the money. You decide to talk to your member of staff to see whether there is any agreement in writing and, if not, what verbal agreement has been reached. Prepare the list of questions you would ask him or her to help you to determine what legal rights, if any, you may have against the supplier.

Task 3

Your business organised an important shareholders' meeting during which a number of things went wrong. The hotel facilities were not as good as you promised. The client's managing director has also complained that there were no seminar rooms available for individual discussions and, although you protest that she never mentioned that requirement, she contends that you should have realised that, by the very nature of the event, such facilities should have been made available. In addition the meetings documentation you prepared omitted a vital piece of information so that the shareholders were not able to vote

on a particular topic and a further meeting has had to be arranged. The managing director is refusing to pay your fee and is threatening to sue you for breach of contract. She also points out that in your promotional literature you claimed that 'no better service exists', which she says is a total fabrication.

You decide to hold an emergency meeting of your group. Prepare a list of points outlining (a) whether or not you feel the company is justified in refusing to pay the fee, (b) if there can be any comeback about your claim to be the best, and (c) what remedies the company may have if you are found to be in breach of contract. Include references to appropriate legislation and cases.

Task 4

One of your employees is causing you problems. He claimed that he was computer-literate but this is obviously not the case. He is also a poor timekeeper and on occasions you have heard him being rather abrupt with a potential client. One day you hear him criticising you to his colleagues. You lose your temper and give him a week's notice. A few days later a representative from ACAS, the arbitration and conciliation service, telephones you to say that your ex-employee wants to claim unfair dismissal. You are obviously concerned, not least because you are not sure what powers ACAS has. Consequently you decide to (a) research the role of ACAS in an industrial dispute, and (b) to check on whether you have been fair in dismissing the employee. Put your findings into a report to be discussed with your colleagues.

Task 5

A new employee is very health and safety conscious, and she sends you an e-mail with the following queries:

a 'I'm suffering a lot of eyestrain at the moment. I'm sure it's that new word processor.'

b 'I've hurt my back lifting all those heavy files.'

c 'It's too noisy and I've nowhere to eat my sandwiches at lunch.'

Research the relevant health and safety legislation and summarise your findings for your colleagues, together with some recommendations as to what improvements you ought to make to the existing working conditions.

Management Information Systems

Purpose and Scope

Although knowledge and experience help managers to make increasingly sophisticated

decisions, the increased pace of change in today's business environment, as well as the speed of

response brought about through the use of information and communication technologies, have generated a

constant demand by managers for better information. In order to make decisions, managers need the right

information to serve a wider range of needs. A systems approach to managing this demand can be met

through management information systems (MIS). It has been said that MIS are what the nervous system is to

the human body. This chapter introduces the role and function of management information systems in

business operations.

On completion of the chapter you should be able to explain the purpose and scope of MIS. To achieve this you must demonstrate the ability to:

- evaluate the need for and use of internal and external business information in organisations

- discuss the contribution and limitations of MIS as an aid to improving business performance

- evaluate the future impact of information technology on MIS and improvement in organisational performance.

DEFINITIONS OF MIS

We live in an information age, so called because many people, even if they do not realise it, work in information-intensive occupations. For example, accountants, teachers, lawyers, office workers and managers spend much of their working lives handling information. The original definitions of information were associated with knowledge, but now as a result of different ways of processing information, we find the word 'information' grafted into so many different walks of life that we live in constant danger of it being misunderstood. Now, instead of thinking about the information itself, knowing that we have got so much of it, we have to become much more aware of what we are going to do with it.

Definition of terms

One person may run a small business. That person may know the business inside out and may have no need for a formal system for dealing with information. But, as soon as the organisation grows, the management function is performed by people who are more specialised and may be removed from day-to-day activities. It is usually at this time that management information systems (MIS) are required.

MIS have become a field of study since the emergence of computer-related technologies. Like many other terms related to computers, MIS is not a static concept and is still evolving.

The emergence of MIS goes back go the 1950s. The first electronic computer developed for business purposes in 1951 must have posed many interesting questions as to what to do with it. In fact, early business applications centred on routine clerical and accounting operations such as payroll and billing. These were mainly **transaction applications**, named simply because they involved processing accounting transactions. The machines were prone to failure, difficult to operate and painstakingly slow.

Advances in disk technology made it possible to access data more quickly and in different ways. New programming systems helped to develop and refine **operating systems**. Each development contributed to the rise of MIS. As systems developed, though the transaction processing part of the system provided the operational data necessary to run an organisation more efficiently on a day-to-day basis, the management component became more important. Systems started to provide reports and information that enabled managers to make more effective decisions.

The increasing appearance of computer and communication technologies in offices during the 1970s and 1980s gave rise to links with MIS and created the potential for convergence, based upon the needs of users around each organisation. Some organisations used accounting information systems (AIS) and office information systems (OIS) for local information and decision-making needs of various departments and subsets of an organisation. In many instances such user-led developments led to disparate islands of technology within the organisation. In contrast, the aim today is for integration of such technologies across the organisation.

The more recent role for information technologies is to think about them as a strategic weapon. For example, information technology (IT) has the power to:

- change industry structures and alter the rules of competition
- create opportunities for competitive advantage with the provision of new ways to outperform rivals
- spawn new businesses and opportunities, often from within an organisation's existing operations.

Deconstructing the term MIS enables us to define each word in a business context:

- **Management** – being managed or people managing a business. Over recent years management has become more scientific and system-oriented.
- **Information** – knowledge made available to people within an organisation.

- **Systems** – sets of connected things or parts within an organisation which tie the planning and control by managers to the various operations.

There are a number of definitions of MIS, each with a slightly different emphasis or focus. Lucey (1995) emphasises the **decision focus** of his definition:

> *'a system to convert data from internal and external sources into information and to communicate that information, in an appropriate form, to managers at all levels in all functions to enable them to make timely and effective decisions for planning, directing and controlling the activities for which they are responsible.'*

He points out that MIS are different from data-processing systems because the key element is **management involvement**, so the emphasis is upon the use of information through user processes and not how it is provided through MIS processes (see Figure 25.1).

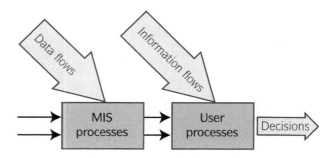

Figure 25.1 *Processes of a management information system*

Parker and Case (1993) consider:

> *'a management information system (MIS) to be any system that provides people with either data or information relating to an organisation's operations.'*

They then describe who the system is focused upon.

> *'Management information systems support the activities of employees, owners, customers, and other key people in the organisation's environment – either by efficiently processing data to assist with the transaction work load or by effectively supplying information to authorised people in a timely manner.'*

They also show that MIS include a number of subsystems (see Figure 25.2) such as the following.

1. **Transaction processing systems (TPS)** comprise routine day-to-day accounting operations.

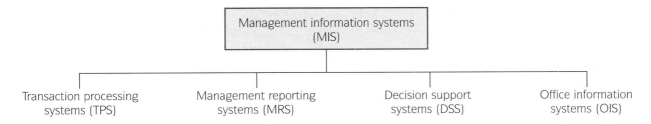

Management information systems
(MIS)

Transaction processing systems (TPS)	Management reporting systems (MRS)	Decision support systems (DSS)	Office information systems (OIS)

Figure 25.2 *MIS subsystems*

2. **Management reporting systems (MRS)** generate reports for decision-making processes.

3. **Decision support systems (DSS)** provide a set of easy-to-use modelling, retrieving and reporting requirements and are used by people making decisions.

4. **Office information systems (OIS)** involve the use of computer-based office technologies such as desktop software applications, including e-mail, teleconferencing and desktop publishing.

It could be argued that managers have always sought and utilised information, but in the past many were forced to rely upon haphazard sources. A modern management information system raises the process of managing from the level of guesswork and piecemeal information to the development of a system of information with sophisticated data process which enables managers to solve complex problems and make informed decisions.

As can be seen in Figure 25.3, MIS tie together the three components of management, information and systems. According to Murdick and Munson (1986), the management information system:

> *'not only provides information to assist managers in making decisions, but it may also be designed to provide decisions for repetitive classes of problems. The MIS, by providing a common set of data and information available to all managers, integrates the management of the company. Thus the company as a whole may be truly operated as a system, with all elements working towards common objectives.'*

Information extracted from a management information system might therefore be at a variety of levels for a range of users. For example:

1. **Strategic planning.** The strategic planning process uses both internal and external sources of information (see

page 561). In a dynamic and changing business environment information is geared towards helping an organisation to use strategic planning to adapt.

2. **Management control.** This is the process by which managers ensure that resources are obtained and used effectively and efficiently in the accomplishment of the organisation's objectives. Control involves planning. For example, are sales ahead of budget, does cost data support costing estimates, are policies in line with predictions? Most of the information for management control is generated internally.

3. **Operational control.** This ensures that tasks are carried out efficiently. At this level, tasks have been specified and methods determined. Information for operations involves providing those involved with the

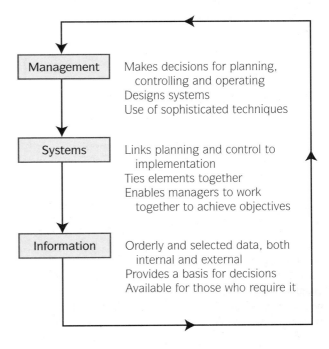

Management
Makes decisions for planning, controlling and operating
Designs systems
Use of sophisticated techniques

Systems
Links planning and control to implementation
Ties elements together
Enables managers to work together to achieve objectives

Information
Orderly and selected data, both internal and external
Provides a basis for decisions
Available for those who require it

Figure 25.3 *The links within MIS*

responsibility of executing tasks with the minimum of expenditure on resources.

As so many parts of an organisation's operations and information processes depend upon information, it is considered to be a key resource within every organisation. Skilfully handling information has become an important business objective. Though the terms data and information are used by some to mean the same thing, there are a number of differences. For example:

- data refer to stored facts – as data become filtered and disseminated, they take on meaning, and so become information
- data are inactive and just exist, whereas information is active and relevant and provides a basis for things to be done
- data are technology-based, whereas information is business-based and facilitates business decision-making
- though data may be gathered from various sources, it is the process of customising them for the needs of various users that transforms them into information (see Figure 25.4).

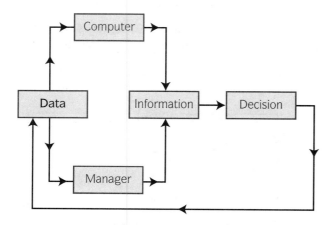

Figure 25.4 *Both computers and minds transform data into information*

As managers are frequently presented with statements containing information and data, they need to ascertain their quality. Information must be *pertinent*. This means that it must relate to the organisation and to matters of importance for the people dealing with that information to enable them to deal with an issue. Information must also be *timely* and available when required. Clearly, users do not want to be confused by misleading information, so it must also be *accurate*. Good information should therefore make a difference and *reduce uncertainty*.

Case Study

Comparing different systems

a Robin Jackman runs a small garden centre. His family have owned the business for more than 50 years. In this increasingly competitive area, they have remained competitive by offering personalised attention and service for customers. The garden centre is well regarded locally.

Robin holds a vast inventory of gardening and related implements. There is almost no item that he does not stock, including specialist plant and pool accessories. He has arranged the centre in such a way that there are items for almost every type of householder.

The key to his business success is his reputation and his ability to get people through the door. To increase this through traffic Robin produces a quarterly newsletter which is sent to more than 5000 households within a 5-mile radius of the centre and which provides practical hints and advice on garden maintenance. To produce this he uses a desktop publishing system (DTP). A typical issue of the newsletter contains articles on plant and bulbs stocks, fertilisers, organic gardening and gardening tools. It enables Robin to keep close contact with his customers.

The DTP is also used as a personal information system. It links in with spreadsheets and a database of customers. Robin is the only user.

b Reed Automotive leases cars to companies. In recent years Reed has been using stand-alone personal computers (PCs) to deal with its accounting, but with the opening of branches all over the north-east of England, a need arose for better access to on-line information. To meet this requirement the company purchased a large number of PCs and connected them to a wide area network (WAN). This provides data and information communication services between separated parts of the same organisation.

Though there were teething problems initially, the shared system improved access to information. For example, a number of employees could work on the system at the same time. When customers came to lease cars, credit checks could be carried out almost immediately with links between the system and a credit control bureau.

1. Compare and contrast both systems. Explain how they use information.

2. What other uses would you expect to be made of information from each organisation?

3. In what ways do such systems, albeit simple, enable each organisation to compete more effectively?

Internal and external sources of information for effective management

Different types of organisation require different types of systems which can regularly monitor data so that shifts or trends could be identified. For example, stockbrokers watch trends using computers monitoring shares and markets. Wherever a discernible shift takes place, clearly key decisions have to be made. Other business environments require less monitoring. For example, a local car showroom might want a system that monitors registrations both locally and nationally. Its approach is likely to be less structured.

There are many different sources of information for effective decision-making. Information sources exist from many different potential sources. A clear division can be made between internal and external data. **Internal data** are generated and made available within an organisation. Such data may come from a variety of sources such as cost accounting information. Other data may be more informal, for example word-of-mouth, facts, gossip and from personal observations.

External data are those extracted from the organisation's external environment. For example, it could include news of the launch of a new product by a competitor, changes in exchanges rates or new technological developments by other organisations in an industry. Informal external data would include personal contacts within the external environment. Given the broader nature of external data, they are particularly useful for making decisions about the direction of the organisation in the future such as those for strategic planning.

Examples of formal data might include:

Internal	External
Management reports	Information services
Management audits	Trade publications
Meetings	Industry consultants
Forecasts	Forums

Examples of informal data might include:

Internal	External
Conversations	Networking
Grapevine	Trade shows
Observation	Personal contacts

Internal and external data may also vary according to the nature and type of business (see Figure 25.5).

Type of business	External information	Internal information
Car manufacturer	Industry-wide innovations	Production figures
	Economic information	Quality tests
	Trade regulations	Waste figures
	Market share	Output per worker
	Political changes	Lead times
Supermarket chain	Market shares	Sales per employee
	Competitors' prices	Stock levels
	Demographic changes	Product lines
	Competitors' innovations	Number of stock-outs

Figure 25.5 *Relationship between management information and type of business*

Different MIS requirements for different types of organisation

At its simplest level, organisations adopt information systems in order to become more efficient, reduce costs and improve their competitive advantages. According to Lucey (1995), 'MIS exist in organisations in order to help them achieve objectives, to plan and control their processes and operations, to help deal with uncertainty and to help in adapting to change or, indeed, initiating change'. A key factor for any information system is its appropriateness for the type and nature of the organisation in which it is to be used. They must also be aligned with the requirements of the type of organisation in which they are to be used.

Organisations process and use information in order to produce outputs for their environment. They are, therefore, in part, information-processing entities. The people working for an organisation develop customary ways of working, with a series of relationships and arrangements about how work is undertaken. Large organisations may employ thousands of workers. Information needs for these organisations may include a large information system integrated with other divisions in different parts of the world. For example, the car manufacturer Ford as a global producer has to integrate its activities across the world into its headquarters in the US so that the information needs of the wider organisation can be met. On the other hand, small organisations such as sole traders may employ just a few people. Their information needs can be catered for using an integrated business software package, provided on a stand-alone PC.

USE OF INFORMATION

The way in which an organisation is structured is called its organisational structure, and often this will determine how information is used. For example, an organisation may be structured in the following ways:

- By function – departmentalising by work function such as marketing, operations or personnel might mean that organisations using this approach have a separate MIS department. One of the advantages of this is that all of the specialists are grouped together where they will have specific information needs and requirements.
- By product – where organisations such as Unilever or Procter & Gamble have diverse product ranges, they may structure along product lines. Organisations structuring in this way may have a separate MIS unit within each of the major divisions.
- By customer – publishers of books typically structure their divisions by customer type. For example, this book has been developed by an educational publisher based upon the needs of people in the institution you attend. As a result, this influences the company's information

requirements, both for the division and the organisation as a whole.
- By geography – where organisations are physically dispersed, the local operation will require an information system which not only integrates it into head office but also provides it with the flexibility it requires to be competitive.

Departmentalising along product, customer and geographic lines means, that when supported with a good management information system, organisations can respond to particular markets and segments. It provides them with the flexibility to react to market changes in order to remain competitive.

Within large organisations, a combination of structural approaches is usually found. For example, at corporate level strategic activities usually have a functional orientation such as marketing or group personnel. The next level of structuring may be by product group, area or customer group. The way an organisation is structured will have a significant effect upon how an organisation's information system evolves.

Integration, coordination and control via different levels of information

Traditional systems were centred upon different departmental functions and processes. As a result, data were treated as a separate component of functional analysis and process design. Traditional systems therefore replicated existing processes and applications to produce uncoordinated and incompatible files in each department or associated with each process (see Figure 25.6). The notion of integration mechanisms and systems had simply not been addressed.

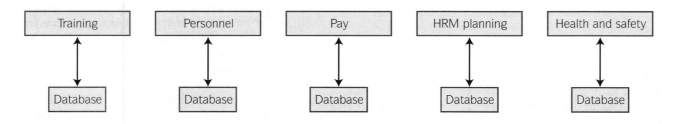

Figure 25.6 *Systems approach to human resource management (HRM)*

Integration of data processing involves rearranging systems development through organisation-wide planning of information requirements. The focus then shifts from a process or departmental application through to a data orientation. This new data-centred approach is often termed information engineering as it views data as the foundation for the design of an information system.

Where integration takes place MIS can be accessed and shared by multiple processes and users. The focus point of the stable data model is integrated information available across the organisation, with individual applications seen as peripheral. An example of an integrated data-centred approach is shown in Figure 25.7.

The **formal organisation** has a pattern of relationships defined by official rules, policies and systems. It is usually the one depicted on organisation charts with diagrams showing official relationships, departments and levels of management. Within the formal organisation there is:

- a unity of objectives and effort
- well-defined relationships, duties and responsibilities
- stability and predictability
- clear hierarchy of control and command.

The problem in terms of information is that there is more 'red tape' with formal and inflexible relationships. Information flows are inefficient with a lack of individual fulfilment for those working within a hierarchical and cumbersome system.

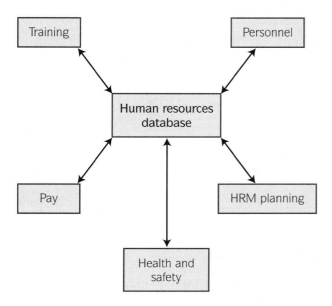

Figure 25.7 *Integrated data-centred approach to human resource management (HRM)*

Informal organisation focuses more upon people. Information arises from social relationships between teams of individuals who develop informal ways of getting things done. Informal organisation exists within every organisation to some extent. Social groups develop their own beliefs and ways of getting things done which are sometimes not the same as that of the formal organisation. For example, informal organisation may:

- use unofficial methods which are more efficient
- provide more satisfaction for employees
- coordinate activities more efficiently
- be more flexible and improve communication.

However, within informal organisation managerial authority may be undermined if a group runs counter to organisational objectives. Information may also be distorted through rumour.

According to Lucey (1995), 'Organisations choose structures which are thought to be most efficient for their particular circumstances and operating conditions'. This means that in order to be *flexible* they tend to combine the best features of functional, product and geographical organisational structures. Such organisations are often viewed as organic because they adapt to changing conditions and develop features such as network control structures, motivating management styles, flexible working practices and flatter organisational structures, all of which help to empower employees through the use of information and technologies.

One particular concept that has developed from high technology industries is that of the **matrix** structure. Within a matrix structure, project teams are combined with a conventional functional structure. The matrix is thus a combination of structures which enables employees to contribute to a number of activities or teams. In information terms it enables team members to use information to focus upon a number of aims at the same time, while also providing the flexibility to respond to new markets and opportunities as and when they arise.

The terms **centralised** and **decentralised** are important management concepts that are inextricably linked to the use and distribution of information. They are often used to describe the distribution of authority and decision-making within an organisation.

Centralised organisations are organisations with a clear-cut hierarchical structure in which decisions are made at the top of the hierarchy. Within such organisations there are likely to be different information requirements at the top of the hierarchy which are distinct from those further down. By contrast, within decentralised organisations decision-making is distributed as far down the management hierarchy as possible. This provides lower-level managers with considerable practice in making decisions and prepares them for moving up the hierarchy.

Issues of confidentiality

Though it is often said that no system can be 100 per cent secure, **confidentiality, security** and **privacy** are key issues when dealing with information. One of the main elements in developing an information system is to ensure that databases and systems are secure.

There are a number of reasons that these issues are of fundamental importance. For example, accidental, negligent or intentional disclosure of information to unauthorised people may enable them to use that information in a way that is neither intended nor legal. Similarly, information may be destroyed, modified or used incorrectly if it gets into the wrong hands.

Confidentiality refers to the limits on the use of information collected from individuals. This means that personal information should only be distributed to those who have a need to know and use that information, and should not be disseminated outside the organisation.

In order for information to be confidential it must be secure. Security is a technical condition for achieving privacy and confidentiality. It refers to the policies, procedures and technical measures used to prevent unauthorised theft, access or alteration to record systems. It can be promoted with a range of tools designed to protect access to software, hardware and communications networks.

Privacy is a broader term often used to encompass security and confidentiality. Three elements to privacy are:

- limits on the collection of information
- specific rights of individuals to access, review and challenge information kept about them
- management responsibility for record systems.

Data Protection Act

The Data Protection Act 1984 was passed to regulate the use of information for processing systems which relate to 'individuals and the provision of services in respect of such information'. The Act covers only the holding of computer records and not manual records.

The Act requires those using personal data to register with the Data Protection Register. Registered data users must then follow the eight principles of the Act.

1. Data must be obtained and processed fairly and lawfully.
2. Data must be held only for specific lawful purposes which are described in the entry into the register.
3. Data should not be used in any other way than those related to such purposes.
4. Data should be adequate, relevant and not excessive for those purposes.
5. Personal data should be accurate and kept up to date.
6. Data should be held no longer than is required.
7. Individuals should be entitled to access their data and, if necessary, have it corrected or erased.
8. Data must be protected with appropriate security against unauthorised access or alteration.

There are a number of exemptions to the Act, including information kept by government departments for reasons of national security, information the law requires to be made public, mailing lists (as long as the subjects are asked if they object to data being held for this purpose), payrolls and pensions information, clubs and personal data held by individuals in connection with recreational or family purposes. To ensure that data is held only for legitimate purposes, many organisations appoint a data protection officer.

Case Study

Code of Fair Information Practice

One way to protect data is to operate a code of practice governing the handling of information. The following code was conceived by a government advisory group in the US and constitutes the core of all of the country's privacy legislation and regulation.

1. **Openness.** There should be no secret systems.

2. **Individual access.** There should be a way for individuals to find out what information is kept on record about them, as well as how that information is used and for what purpose.

3. **Individual participation.** Individuals must be able to amend or correct data about themselves.

4. **Collection limitations.** There should be no limits on what kinds of information are collected and the manner in which they are collected.

5. **Limits on use.** Data collected for one purpose cannot be used for a different purpose without the subject's prior consent or knowledge.

6. **Disclosure limitations.** There must be legally enforceable confidentiality limits on the disclosure of personal data to outside parties.

7. **Information management.** Information-gathering organisations are responsible for the currency, accuracy and security of systems, as well as for compliance with privacy principles.

8. **Accountability.** Information-gathering organisations must be accountable for their personal record-keeping policies, practices and systems. Systems must be auditable so that the flow of information can be traced.

Questions

1. Comment upon the different elements of this code of practice.

2. Make comparisons between this code of practice and the Data Protection Act.

CASCADE OF INFORMATION

A management information system must be appropriate for the organisation for which it is designed and the persons within that organisation receiving that information. According to Lucey (1995), 'It must be tailored to suit organisational and personal needs otherwise it will be of little value'. For example, in a static external business environment an organisation will require a structured control system with a need for formal information. Whereas, in a fast-changing and adaptive environment, inputs and outputs need to be fluid and

cannot be rigidly defined. As a result, the information system must help the organisation to respond to opportunities as and when they arise.

Information needs at different levels

An organisation may simply have one or two levels of authority or many different levels. For example, in contrast to a small business, the British army has many different levels of authority. The number of levels influences the shape of the organisation and, in consequence, its information needs and requirements.

TASK

Working in groups, identify an organisation with a flat structure (see Figure 25.8) and an organisation with a tall structure (see Figure 25.9). Comment upon what you perceive to be the different information requirements for each type of organisation.

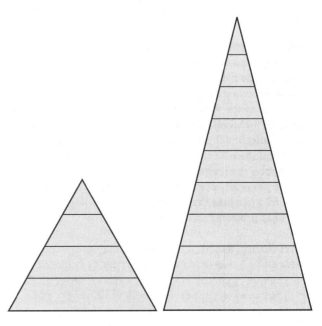

Figure 25.8 *Flat structure*   **Figure 25.9** *Tall structure*

Organisations with flat structures tend to be, though are not always, relatively small. They generally have few levels of authority and layers of management with a short chain of command. Where flat structures exist, particularly as organisations get larger, there is a broad span of control.

Tall structures are characteristic of much larger organisations with around eight or more levels of authority. Such organisations have a long chain of command with a narrow span of control. In these organisations there is more formality, specialisation and standardisation.

A number of factors determine the different information needs within an organisation. For example, the size of the organisation is likely to be a key factor relating to construction of MIS. The complexity and type of operations will also need to be considered. For example, in the further education sector, some large colleges may have more than 30 000 students on their roll. Bar codes may be used to identify each student and track and monitor their attendance, progress and successes. MIS systems for colleges are customised for these particular types of operations.

Technology is clearly a key factor determining how information needs can be met and by whom. As different technologies evolve, the ways in which information is dealt with may change.

Parker and Case (1993) point out that information systems are not simply products but socio-technical systems because they are composed of technology-related products and concepts that can only be fully understood within the context of the *people* and *organisations* which use them.

People are often overlooked as a component of MIS. Often where systems have failed, it is because the systems exceeded the mental and emotional capabilities of the people for whom the system was designed. Systems must be geared to the level of sophistication of the people using them. In addition, there are a number of physiological factors affecting the interaction of people and an information system. Though information systems might not involve the carrying of heavy objects, many MIS jobs can be physically demanding. Continuous attendance in front of a machine may cause eyestrain, headaches, neck and back problems and exhaustion.

Psychological factors also come into play as how people think and act may determine the success or failure of an information system. For example, as people perceive things in different ways, perhaps positively or negatively, steps may need to be taken to ensure that systems are viewed in the same way by all users. Some employees may be biased towards the proposed information system and are more likely to gain from its introduction. Other employees may be against the introduction of the system because they have preconceived, negative views of so-called 'technology pushers'.

Employees may have different feelings and attitudes towards work and their organisation, and this may affect how they respond to the introduction of the new system. No matter how hard they are encouraged to do so, some employees may be reluctant to change, or to interact with the information systems to make best use of the data available. There is evidence to show that senior managers are often unwilling to work with new systems because they feel that such work is beneath them, even if it helps to improve the quality of their decisions.

Though it is felt that moderate levels of stress might help to enhance the productivity of workers, an organisation's information system should not be viewed as a cause of stress, through increased anxiety or frustration. Other factors, within different levels of an organisation, affecting how people react to an information system may include information overload where users are flooded with data which reduces their ability to handle them, and a lack of flexibility created by the system through users not knowing what information they need and how to deal with it.

Though most have features in common no two organisations are exactly alike. There are many different factors which influence systems design and development within organisations. A key feature affecting the type of system will be the form of output produced by the organisation. The tangible form of output may be as goods or as services which disseminate information and provide advice, such as those required in the financial services sector. Given the diversity of organisational activities information systems may be tailored to industrial sectors, such as for colleges of further education, or even customised for each institution.

Paper-based and electronic systems

It is nearly 30 years since commentators started to speculate about the possibilities of a paperless working environment. Yet despite huge advances in office automation, the typical office has both paper-based and electronic systems.

A number of advances have made the paperless office possible today. Firstly, there have been major developments in computer technologies, with computers becoming smaller, cheaper and more reliable. There have also been considerable improvements in the field of telecommunications and other forms of office equipment with a convergence in technologies, and widespread use of systems such as e-mail and voice mail.

Case Study

Independent Insurance

In the insurance industry information technology has become a key element in providing organisations with a competitive advantage over their rivals. The industry has traditionally been associated with the generation of mountains of paper documentation such as policies, claims documents and quotations. As paper documents, key information was held in one part of the business where it was only accessible to a limited number of people at the same time. The documents required large areas of storage space, were difficult to access and took up a considerable amount of staff time.

Independent Insurance is an insurance group providing general and related services, operating principally in the UK. It recently made a decision to change the general maintenance and handling of information in a way which would provide better customer service by creating a paperless office. This involved revolutionising the way paper was handled by various work teams. As a result, all information such as post is scanned electronically and routed through the computer system to the person responsible for that work. Information in the form of electronic files is now accessible to various parts of the business, with all underwriting and claims automated.

Information is scanned centrally. Captured documents are held in electronic filing cabinets where they are accessible for workbaskets of individuals and groups within the business. The system has led to improved efficiency and productivity, while at the same time it has freed staff from mundane administrative tasks, allowing them to concentrate upon more interesting aspects of work.

Questions

1. What are the benefits of working in a paperless office environment?

2. How does such an environment affect the work roles of staff?

Horizontal and vertical levels of importance

It is possible to identify three levels of management within most organisations. These are:

- **strategic management** – includes the chief executive and board of directors
- **tactical management** – middle management includes departmental managers and functional managers
- **operational management** – includes lower-level managers such as supervisors.

There is a link between the nature and type of information flowing between the levels and how it is used for decision-making. The level and type of information as well as how it is presented will depend upon the **horizontal** and **vertical levels of importance** attached to each management role.

Over recent years there has been an erosion of the middle level of management which has a clear effect upon how information is distributed, as well as the nature and type of information provided. For example, strategic managers can now access information directly from operational levels. Many computer-based systems can make decisions such as stock replenishment which once were taken by managers. Some large organisations have broken down into semi-autonomous business units, for example the chemicals manufacturer ICI.

At the strategic level of management, managers are concerned about policies for the whole organisation. Information should relate to long-term planning and large-scale investment. It should therefore be wide and include external information as well as information within the business, so that forecasting can take place. From within the business managers will be concerned with aggregated figures.

Middle managers are concerned with monitoring of budgets and acquiring resources. The information they require enables them to develop operational policies. Operational managers need precise and detailed information related directly to their area of control. They have limited budget constraints and prescribed objectives enabling them to make routine day-to-day decisions.

Vertical communication often takes a top-down route. However, considerable gains can be made when senior managers listen to what other employees have to say. It is possible, however, that if there is too free a flow of communication up and down an organisation that this may lead to communication problems. Horizontal communication takes place across the organisation at similar levels and can lead to better decisions, encourage self-confidence and reduce stress. Communication at whatever level needs to be effectively channelled, otherwise it may lead to poor coordination and the creation of dysfunctional power relations.

Channels of communication

With any information system it is important that, given the appropriate span of control and area of activity, a manager should receive information appropriately focused upon helping him or her to carry out designated tasks and responsibilities. In order to do so a variety of different channels of communication may be used by organisations.

Face-to-face communications

- Informal meetings
- Formal meetings
- Talks and discussion groups
- Interviews

Visual communications

- Videos
- Charts
- Posters
- Logos

Oral communications

- Telephones
- Public address

Electronic communications

- E-mail and fax
- Data transmission networks
- Electronic Data Interchange (EDI)
- Pagers

Written communications

- Letters
- Memoranda
- Booklets and manuals
- In-house magazines/newsletters/circulars
- Notice-boards

INTERNAL AND EXTERNAL SOURCES

The growth of information systems has led to increasing value being placed upon data. Data are obtained in a variety of different ways. For example, reading, counting, observation or any other form of recording could obtain them. Day-to-day records within an organisation are called **raw data**. For example, details of transactions recorded on invoices or cheques would be raw data or output figures would represent raw data production figures.

As we saw earlier, data are derived from internal and external sources. Internal data are recorded using appropriate measuring and recording systems, while external data will be received in a variety of different forms such as bank statements, press releases or trade magazines. As the potential for collecting both internal and external data is almost limitless, organisations have to be selective in the data they collect. In order to do so, they should constantly monitor their data-gathering processes to ensure that the data obtained closely meet the organisation's specific requirements. The nature and type of data required will vary from business to business, depending upon the specific requirements of the type of organisation.

MIS data for planning and controlling the decision process

In order to identify the types of data an organisation requires, it must plan for the development of its data resources so that they can be used effectively in decision-making. James Martin, in *Strategic Data Planning Methodologies* (1982), suggests a data planning methodology that:

- defines the organisation's business environment
- builds an inventory of data
- defines the organisation's database environment
- supplies the framework for the development of applications, such as hardware and software.

This type of data planning makes the assumption that the data used by the organisation is likely to be relatively stable. For example, basic pieces of information such as customers, products and parts are not likely to change frequently.

In identifying data for planning and controlling the decision process the first step is to create a model of the organisation, showing the major areas of activity required to run the organisation. For example, this might include planning, finance, materials, production, marketing, sales, distribution, accounting and personnel. Each functional area would then have a number of processes. It would then be possible to analyse the processes related to that function, and extract the data classes that this would generate. This mapping process (see Figure 25.10) enables an organisation to identify the basic categories of information it might require and lays the foundations for database design.

Once the organisation and its databases have been modelled, data elements can be identified. This data-centred process to data planning is sometimes termed information engineering, as it views data as the foundation for the design of a system. The sequence of data planning

Functions	Processes	Data classes
Planning		Company
Finance		Contracts
Materials	Territory management	Orders
Production	Personal selling	Customers
Marketing	Sales administration	Budget/actual sales
Sales	Customer service	Prices
Distribution	Customer relations	Market research
Accounting	Sales plan management	Product groups
Personnel		Sales management

Figure 25.10 *Data classes for the sales function*

can also be used to relate the various stages of planning and control to database development (see Figure 25.11).

Within the business

Data are desirable commodities or resources. As data take on value they need to be kept and stored. Data represent a set of facts that describe a person, thing or transaction. They might include such things as date, size, quantity, description, amount, rate or place. Within an organisation

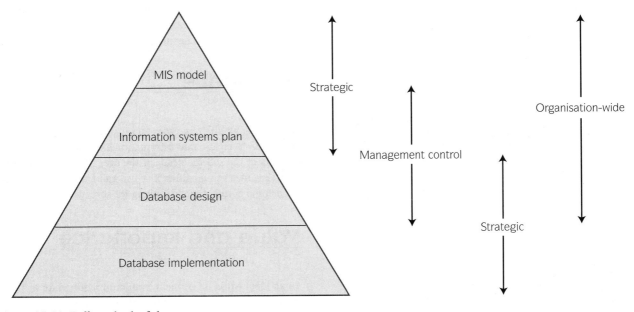

Figure 25.11 *Different levels of data*

data management systems are concerned with the capture, storage, retrieval and assembly of data in forms related to the requirements for that information.

As we saw on page 561, data within an organisation may take many different forms but are more usually divided into formal data and informal data. Formal data might include reports, forecasting systems, modelling and simulation, investigative reports, budgets, job descriptions, videos, organisation charts, Powerpoint presentations and any other data generated and prescribed by the processes and data classes required by the organisation. Informal data would include discussions, meetings, telephone conversations, personal records and correspondence.

In the marketplace

While managers must be familiar with data generated within the organisation, they must also be aware of data available outside the business. It is important that any data collected has the potential to improve managerial decision-making. There are many different influences in an organisation's operating environment, for example:

- the economic environment
- government influences
- legal influences
- environmental issues
- international and European influences
- social, cultural and demographic factors
- factors affecting specific markets
- competitive factors
- technology
- personnel and trade unions.

Formal sources of external information tend to include published reports, government statistics, scientific and technical reports, reports from trade associations and other published or broadcast media. Informal sources involve social contacts between members of organisations, correspondence and conferences.

EVALUATION OF INFORMATION

Good information should have value because it helps an organisation to focus upon and achieve its objectives. If, for example, a manager makes a bad decision because he or she has poor data, then the organisation has a clear problem. As a result, there is always likely to be concern about the quality of information as well as how that information is used.

Accuracy

If information is accurate, it can be relied upon for the purposes for which it is intended. Not all information, no matter how good it is, can be 100 per cent accurate, so there have to be ways of classifying information and its accuracy, for example to the nearest pound, or litre. At the strategic level, data might have to be rounded up to the nearest 1 000 or 10 000.

Within the organisation controls can check the accuracy of data. For example, when cheques are issued in payment for transactions, controls can ensure that the correct number of cheques are cut. Software can also be used to perform a number of checks to ensure the correctness of data.

Relevance

With so many different types and forms of information, it is important to ensure that information extracted from MIS is relevant to the specific needs of the user. When information is irrelevant it can be difficult to use and frustrating for those who come across it while looking for something else.

Value and importance

In an ideal world all of the information required for a decision would be available before that decision is made. This rarely, if ever, happens. What is required is information

TASK

Carry out an interview with a person working for a large organisation. Identify the sources of (a) internal data, and (b) external data, relevant to work he or she does. Find out how such data are used. How does the data differ from that available to others at different levels within the same organisation?

that relates closely to the various components of a problem, which can be applied in searching for a solution. It is important that there is confidence in the source of the information, and that this source is reliable. When information is used regularly it develops a value of its own.

Benefits of MIS

In an uncertain world in which we are faced with a barrage of information, some information is more useful than others. Information systems exist to generate good quality information which makes a difference for an organisation. To do this the information has to be timely and available when required. It also has to be pertinent and relate to the business in hand as well as to the matters that are important to the person requesting the information.

The decision-making process begins with the recognition that a problem of some kind exists. A problem is the difference between what the situation is now and what you want it to be. In making a good decision it is useful to have information not simply relating to the current situation but also about the desired situation. Making a decision involves making critical decisions about the problem and the current situation. Information systems:

- help to identify problems
- provide information about the current situation
- provide the basis for making decisions in order to reach a desired situation.

Information systems can also show exactly where an organisation or parts of it are at a point in time. By producing a series of reports an information system can provide useful performance data. This may link in with an organisation's objectives which show what is supposed to be happening. Some systems produce exception reports which list cases falling outside the standard or which are not meeting objectives.

Information systems also facilitate communication between groups of people with responsibility for decision-making. They may do this by providing a group of people with a common body of knowledge which needs to be considered. In addition, MIS may also be used as communication channels for decision-making, thus reducing the time spent in meetings.

MIS helps to reduce uncertainty, particularly where there is less than perfect knowledge. Such systems are particularly good at demystifying the unknown and creating a basis for better decision-making.

Information systems are also able to provide extensive historical records about performance, transactions and records of past decisions, each of which may be used for current decision-making.

Limitations of MIS

In recent years there has been considerable evidence that MIS have often failed to provide management with the information they have required. There are a number of reasons for this.

- Lack of management knowledge about IT and its applications has meant that many managers, though they have information readily available, have failed to see its potential and make the best use of it.
- In some circumstances top managers have failed to support the concept of MIS, which has meant that though the information may be there, avenues for using it have not been fully explored.
- Where managers have not been involved with the design of MIS, there has been a reluctance to use them. Often emphasis is upon the computer system and its traditional functions, rather than upon MIS and all that they can do.
- Many managers have not become information specialists and do not know what information they need, yet alone how to use it.
- Few MIS systems are perfect. It is possible that where MIS systems are developed without any form of consultation they can be haphazard and fail to meet organisational needs and requirements.

THE IMPACT OF THE IT REVOLUTION

It has been claimed that we have changed from an industrial society to an information society, with more information workers than in all of the other sectors combined. As a result:

- information and communications technologies have become a backbone of the National Curriculum, with the aim of computers in every classroom in every school
- there are a growing number of home personal computers, often connected to the Internet and accessible by the office through e-mail
- almost everybody has access to information sources never conceived of before

- computers have become good for calculations, storage, processing and retrieval of information
- the distinction between computer and human tasks is constantly changing. As organisations gain more skill in using computers, tasks previously involving managerial expertise are relinquished to the domain of the computer, for example credit scoring by banks.

The impact of IT developments

IT has not been developed simply as a technological imperative. A complex background of factors has influenced its development, many of which can be described as social factors and forces. If we think about how we live our lives now and then look towards the future, we might be able to identify how or whether we feel that changes in information technology:

- could affect us in the home as well as the workplace
- could be undesirable as well as desirable
- might even affect us morally and spiritually!

There are generally accepted to be two contrasting approaches about how IT might affect us in years to come. One is that of Utopia. Everything will be wonderful! IT will bring lots of benefits which will improve our life styles, create new wealth and bring new levels of perfection to the world we live in. In fact, it will go so far as to create social harmony, equality, better democracy, decentralisation and individual expression. On the other hand, there is the doom scenario. This sounds more like a game on the PC! Some think that it is technology that is perverting and irrevocably damaging society. It could lead to 'big brother' control of everything we do, create unemployment, introduce degradation into the workplace, cause a loss of skills and lead to a form of totalitarianism.

The more down-to-earth view is that certain elements of IT will turn out well, while others will turn out badly. The net result is likely to be complex and not simply good or bad, but with technology being dependent upon human interactions and arrangements.

Michael Marien, in his paper 'Some questions for the information society', *World Future Society Bulletin*, 1985, states that three types of preconceptions about technology should be avoided. These are:

No. 1 – *the uncritical, euphoric stance that is expressed by commercial interests, which invariably emphasise only the positive attributes of new technology.*

No. 2 – *the hypercritical, pessimistic stance that perceives all modern technology as a human disaster, or focuses solely on growing corporate or government control of information systems.*

No. 3 – *acknowledges both of these positions and concludes that there are opportunities for good and evil, centralisation and decentralisation, freedom and oppression, wealth and poverty.*

He believes that 'the reality, however, is likely to be complex and ambiguous, requiring many critical choices over time and incorporating elements of simultaneous euphoria and gloom that fluctuate in their balance'.

According to Sherry Turkle, in her 1984 paper 'Computers and the human spirit', 'I look at the computer not in terms of its nature as an "analytical engine", but in terms of its "second nature" as an evocative object that fascinates, disturbs equanimity, and precipitates thought.' The computer has become a decentralised 'self' with the authoritative support of science. Others argue that the computer is about reason. As it is linear, logical and self-governed it encourages this kind of thinking in us, and emphasises the importance of instrumental reason in our culture.

Human uniqueness is, however, based upon what computers cannot do. No matter what a computer can do, human thought can and will always be something else.

The future role of MIS

Making predictions about technology in the future is always likely to be risky. Organisations have always required technology-based products that cut costs, help to provide a better service, make people more productive and improve managerial decision-making in order to provide a competitive advantage. A number of issues and impacts are likely in future years.

- The connection of local area networks to wide area networks will continue as well as an increasing use of e-mail and the Internet, with more trading on the Internet.
- Electronic Data Interchange (EDT) should connect more organisations with suppliers and customers, and so facilitate more electronic trading and transactions.
- Imaging systems and document management systems should become common aspects of office technology, with further movement towards a paperless business environment.
- Technologies will continue to merge, with new ways designed to manage them.

- As systems become cheaper and easier to use, it is possible that they will do much of the work that was previously undertaken by computer professionals.
- There should be a further movement towards global communications tools, such as common standards for EDI.
- Many future programmes will contain elements of artificial intelligence (AI), which will enable computers to process at a near-human level of complexity.
- Software packages will become more friendly and easier to use.

As organisations become increasingly global, the multinational dimension will become an increasingly important element of MIS. Numerous changes will occur in such systems in the future, many of which will present new challenges, and will lead not only to different hardware and software, but also to a different way of working by managers and other end-users.

MIS as a Business Management Function

Managing information is about designing and implementing a management information system that turns raw data into something useful – information. Whereas data are facts that have been recorded and relate to the vast number of activities and transactions undertaken by the business, information is something useful to the person receiving it. In the business context information enables management to take action in the pursuit of business objectives.

On completion of the chapter you should be able to evaluate the use of management information systems (MIS) as a business management function. To achieve this you must demonstrate the ability to:

- compare and contrast MIS in two differing organisations

- propose an MIS solution and implementation process for a given organisation
- recommend training requirements to support MIS implementation in a given situation.

THE APPLICATION OF MIS

Small businesses have the advantage that the manager is involved in the day-to-day activities of the business. The manager knows about and is able to decipher information from the numerous daily events. But for management to function as the business grows and becomes more complex, formalised management information systems (MIS) are required that will provide information reliably and consistently.

The ideal MIS will convert data (from internal and external sources) into information that is relevant to the needs of individual managers. It will enable managers to make timely and effective decisions in the execution of their duties to plan and control business activities. With this aim in mind, information is increasingly being viewed as a strategic resource to achieve corporate objectives.

Management control and decision-making

The primary function of management is to *make decisions* to affect the future and achieve organisational objectives. Information, either historical or applying to the future, is a vital ingredient to help management fulfil their responsibilities. Both types of information are important.

- Information about the future enables managers to plan, co-ordinate, lead and motivate.
- Historical information enables managers to monitor performance against a benchmark as a basis for controlling future activities.

Decision-making functions are performed by a large number of employees at all levels of the organisational structure. Therefore managers need information that is appropriate to their responsibilities, and which must be:

- relevant
- timely
- reliable
- complete
- accurate enough for the task at hand.

Relevant information increases knowledge, reduces risk and enables management to take appropriate action. A particular piece of information may be more relevant to one manager than another because of the nature of the individual's work and his or her relative position in the organisational hierarchy.

Senior managers make strategic decisions concerning marketing, procurement of resources and the financing of the business. They need to take a holistic view of the business within its environment over a number of years. The issues they have to address tend to be unpredictable, are difficult to quantify and concern the future. Information needs are often satisfied using external sources of data that relate to evolving conditions.

TASK

Managing an airline is as much about filling seats as it is about flying planes. Describe what sort of information is vital in the airline business. Why is this information essential?

Middle managers have functional responsibilities and specialise in areas such as marketing, operations, human resource management and finance. Tasks are split between those that are routine and others that are irregular but are sufficiently structured to be solved by a clearly defined decision-making process. For middle managers, a major responsibility is the control of current operations. Information is needed to highlight variances to plan, so that time is concentrated on the management of exceptions rather than being wasted on the interpretation of large volumes of data. In addition, by contributing through the management of their functional area to the formal budgeting process, middle managers also have a planning horizon of between one and three years. Information for control purposes is derived from internal sources, but information for planning will require greater information from outside the business, depending on the responsibilities of the individual manager.

Junior managers supervise the day-to-day activities of the business. They work within the constraints of operational policy, so conditions tend to be relatively stable. Information needs are predetermined and this facilitates the use of standard forms and, for computer systems, the use of data input screens. Information is almost entirely historical, relates to individual transactions and, apart from sales orders, comes mainly from internal sources.

Case Study

The world of insurance

Insurance is about managing risk. For a motor insurer, the risk of a policy can be viewed in terms of claims history, age and occupation of the insured. A 40-year-old teacher who has never been caught speeding is a better bet than an 18-year-old student who crashed his father's car last month.

But, as all insurers have used the same formula, this has resulted in tighter margins and little room for error. The cleverer firms are now using more sophisticated methods of sourcing and analysing information. The ability to search vast banks of data to find a link between a policyholder's risk and some other variable can be just the head start they need. For example, it has been found that people who install smoke detectors in their homes tend to have fewer motor accidents.

One problem is getting hold of all this information without the applicant having to fill in a questionnaire running into reams of paper. Although this is not a perfect method, the smoke-detector question can be partly answered by looking at stored data sorted according to postcode. It may not be ideal, but knowing that the applicant lives in a house that has a 3 in 6 chance of having a smoke detector makes him or her a better risk than someone with a 1 in 6 chance.

Success in insurance is therefore about managing information effectively in order to provide the business with a competitive advantage.

Questions

1. How important is information for insurance companies?

2. What sort of information could improve their competitiveness?

In a commercial context, relevant information is information that can improve the profits and cash flow of an organisation.

The value of information
= Value of benefits – Costs of information.

The costs of providing information include:

- expenditure to investigate and design a system, including participation of users in the design stage
- cost of procuring or writing the software
- equipment purchases
- possible increase in staffing to operate the system
- expenditure on training
- disruption to work flow during system implementation.

The benefits of information cannot always be measured easily, but as an example, consider how important it is to have knowledge about business costs. Product costs enable important decisions to be made concerning pricing, product viability and make or buy situations. Process costs keep the focus on efficiency and its continual improvement as cost overruns can trigger management action for controlling future cost levels.

Information can also improve the utilisation of capital employed in the business. By forecasting levels of revenues and costs against the capital to be employed, financial resources can be allocated to the most rewarding projects. Information that facilitates good customer service and identifies problems promptly is clearly valuable. Products delivered to customers on time and to the desired quality, maximise the chance of repeat orders and minimise product returns and the cost of reworking.

For information to be appropriate, it also needs to be timely. Information is like a perishable good, it loses value over time. In fact, information that is superseded by events may become misinformation as managers react to yesterday's rather than today's problems. Information must also be received at the right frequency.

TASK

1. A customer requires a delivery of goods next week that will give profit of £2000. How valuable is that information if received (a) now, or (b) in 8 days' time?

2. A fault in a production process, which occurs on average once a week, costs £1000 in wasted resources every hour it remains undetected. What is the value of a management information system that reports within 15 minutes compared to one that provides feedback after two hours?

Managers should be initiating change in response to changes in circumstance, whether these are external influences such as technological change or internal conditions such as plant breakdown. An important indicator of management information systems' effectiveness is that appropriate action is being taken in response to the information provided. It shows that the information is not only relevant and timely, but that it is being received and understood correctly by management. Inaction could be due to:

- inappropriateness of message – not relevant, not timely, not accurate
- interference with or distortion of the message – incorrect mode of communication or incorrect format (for example user interfaces (see page 581) with a computer system, such as screen and printout formats, should be user friendly to help accurate data input and understanding of information output)
- problems with the receiver of information – lack of motivation or inability to act, perhaps because of insufficient training and skills
- information that is not being received by the right person.

It is vital that reports to managers are designed only after their precise information requirements have been established. In a system of **management by objectives**, individual managers at all levels are set objectives that support corporate objectives, but a failure to support managers with appropriate information will undermine their attainment of targets set. For example, a parcel courier may promise that 95 per cent of deliveries will be within the estimated drop-off time. If the distribution coordinator is unaware that major roadworks on a particular motorway are currently delaying 25 per cent of journeys made, then the business will fail to meet a crucial objective, and the eventual cost may be significant.

Management decision-making is a complex activity at both the individual and organisational level. The design of information systems must accommodate these realities to support managers in a way that takes into account a variety of styles, skills and knowledge.

Information systems should, therefore, facilitate individual decision-making to support managerial roles. Thus, it is important that MIS should be market- not product-oriented. They should be designed to satisfy the needs of internal customers, not to produce reports for which a circulation list is then designed. From the perspective of an information system, it is important that the system supports the requirements of each stage of decision-making. MIS should have general capabilities, be easy to use and flexible.

TASK

Consider the following needs for information and suggest possible levels of accuracy, timeliness and frequency that would be appropriate in each case.

a. A factory manager who has a £5000 budget for labour each month needs to know his actual wages spend.

b. A manager who leads a sales team that has a total sales target of £5 million per year requires historical sales performance figures.

c. The directors of an engineering company require financial projections to the end of the year to monitor their budget of £20 million sales and £2 million profit. Previous forecasts have been within 30 per cent of the actual outcome but to get nearer to 5 per cent steps would require more staff time at a cost of £10 000. It is considered that a forecasting error of 10 per cent either way will have to be tolerated however sophisticated the reporting system.

Human resource management

The human resource or personnel management area in most organisations is a function designed to support and impact upon other parts of the organisation. Today, most organisations have come to recognise their employees are a valuable, and expensive, resource. At the same time, the increasing volume of legislation, governing the management of human resources is more complex than it was in the past.

Typical activities carried out by human resource managers or personnel administrators include human resource planning, staffing (recruitment and selection), training and development, appraisal and termination. Human resource managers may also be responsible for the salary structure as well aspects of management such as equal opportunities. Figure 26.1 provides examples of the many different activities that may be supported by a human resource information system. As well as a wide range of software which can assist with these functions, there are also a number of on-line databases.

Computer-based human resource systems are also used for keeping employee records as well as in producing reports. These can help construct plans to estimate future staffing requirements and develop plans to support strategic staffing requirements.

Marketing

As well as the area of the organisation responsible for determining the identity of the actual goods or services offered to consumers, marketing is also responsible for pricing, promoting and distributing such goods or services. As marketing is one of the most crucial activities, with direct customer contact and involvement, it is important that there is a range of technologies to support any key decisions that might have to be made. For example, some retail organisations collect data daily for each of their outlets, so that performance can be constantly monitored.

Information for marketing decisions may come from a range of different sources (see Figure 26.2). Transactions processing data will provide direct, and often immediate, feedback from past marketing strategies. Market research data will largely comprise consumer-related data used to support marketing decisions. Market intelligence data may refer to information about the strategies of competitors.

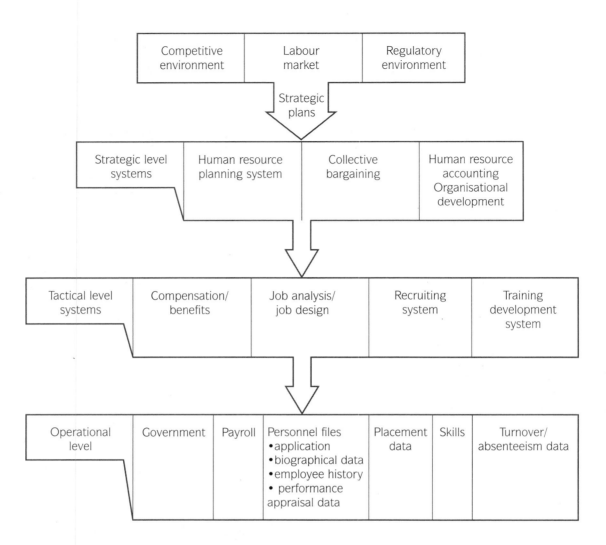

Figure 26.1 *A model of a human resource information system (HRIS)*

External environment data will enable marketers to monitor the external business environment.

Finance

As the financial area is the functional part of an organisation responsible for financial planning, it is one of the most important areas for management information. Though the ways in which an organisation carries out the finance functions might differ widely, in many organisations it is run by a financial controller whose responsibility is to oversee the transactions processing systems.

The three important decision-making activities in the financial area include forecasting, funds management and overall financial performance. The first two are oriented towards managerial planning, with financial performance, and auditing, geared towards managerial control.

A number of sources of information are needed to make financial decisions. They include the following.

- **Transactions processing data.** These data are some of the more useful data for audit and processing. They include revenues for the whole organisation as well as the expenses incurred for each of the functional areas.

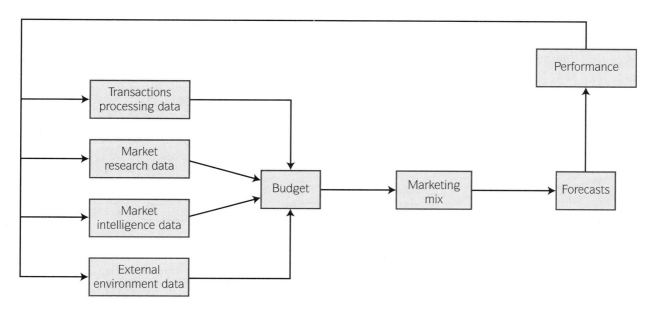

Figure 26.2 *Data flow within the marketing MIS area*

- **Internal forecast data.** During the planning process an organisation needs to estimate the expected revenues for each of the functional areas as well as make projections for revenues. These types of planning data are useful to determine how actual results differ from projected results.
- **Funding data.** These provide information upon specific sources of funds.
- **Portfolio data.** These show the current portfolio of securities held by an organisation as well as their prices in the marketplace.
- **Government regulations.** These are an important source of financial information.

Accounting information systems (AIS) are closely related to financial information systems. They have a variety of different components such as accounts receivable, payable, inventory processing and a control system. They also deal with the purchasing system, ledgers and payroll.

Production/operations/ manufacturing

This area within an organisation is responsible for producing goods or delivering a service. With shifting consumer tastes, shorter product life cycles, and global pressures, organisations today, more than ever, require responsive operations across a range of areas such as those shown in Figure 26.3.

The use of information and communication technologies starts with the design and technical specifications of the product, from which computer-aided design and computer-aided manufacturing are used to design a product before it goes into production. From then on, production will consist of production scheduling (deciding which goods will be produced in a given span of time), the physical act of producing the goods and the determination of stock levels.

Most computerised approaches model the production process as an integrated system. For example, one successful production model of an operations system is **manufacturing resources planning (MRPII)**. Within this system the sales forecast is used to identify the number of products that must be available for shipment at certain points in time. From this, a production schedule is prepared which establishes production goals to meet this projected demand. The schedule takes into account resources so that shopfloor, warehouse space and time capacities are not exceeded. The schedule highlights raw material requirements and then checks these against stock on hand to determine order requirements. Orders reflect mathematically determined optimal order requirements, which also minimise inventory-carrying costs. The MRPII system tracks the production process, checking the production schedule daily to determine daily requirements, allowing figures to be adjusted for new people assigned to jobs and new work-rates. The system also produces management reports on the current status of the production process.

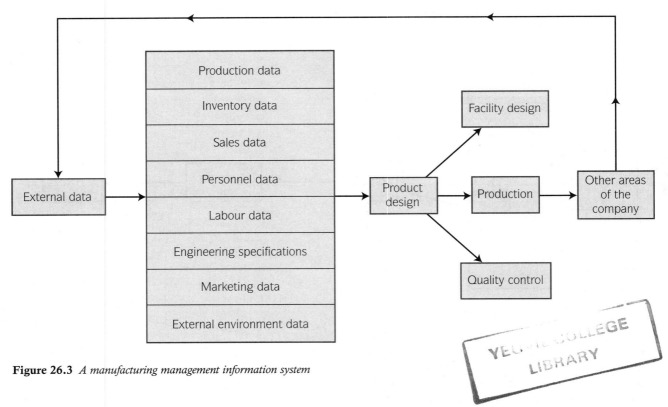

Figure 26.3 *A manufacturing management information system*

Computer-aided manufacturing (CAM) is an umbrella term used to describe the use of computers in manufacturing operations. It includes:

- **monitoring** – the use of computers to sequence operations such as the opening and shutting of valves in a chemical plant
- **numeric control** – the control of manufacturing processes by computers
- **robotics** – the use of computer-controlled machines to perform motor activities
- **optimisation** – finding the best or optimum way of allocating resources.

Distribution

Physical distribution includes all of the activities concerned with moving products, both inwards to manufacturer or outwards towards customers. Physical distribution management (PDM) describes the role of managers in developing, administering and operating systems to control the movement of raw materials and finished goods. Distribution helps an organisation to meet customer needs profitably and efficiently, enables manufacturers to provide goods for customers in the right

place at the right time and reduces the lead-time from when a customer first makes an order until the time that the order is delivered.

Technology is used across all of the areas of physical distribution, from the receipt and transmission of sales order information, through to order processing, inventory management of finished goods and logistics. It is used to support processes related to storage, handling and movement of goods or services. According to Philip Kotler and Gerry Armstrong in *Principles of Marketing* (1996), 'Logistics effectiveness will have a major impact on both customer satisfaction and company costs'.

THE DESIGN OF MIS

Management information systems consist of three parts: physical resources, human resources and the methods of bringing these resources together. Although computers are often used, MIS are more than just computer systems. The physical resources of MIS will also include such items as communication lines, manual records and manual filing systems.

The human resources used by a management information system will include all those involved from collecting data to those who actually use the information that is generated. Workers who record their activities on time-sheets and stores personnel who complete stores documentation are as much a part of the system as the computer operator who oversees the processing of data. Where a system requires human interaction between a human resource and a computer system, this is called a **user interface**.

It is how the physical and human resources are brought together as a working system that will determine the quality of information that is produced. The work of the **systems analyst** is to ensure the systems design meets the information needs of the business and makes efficient and effective use of the resources available. In a formalised management information system the three system elements will be documented and the roles of individual staff will be defined as part of their job descriptions.

MIS planning and systems development to support strategic objectives

Care needs to be taken in analysing the real information needs of management before a management information system is designed. The design of an information system is the overall plan or model for that system, which consists of all the specifications that provide the system with its unique form or structure. The design should show how the system will operate in order to meet strategic objectives.

The **conceptual design** lays out the components of the system and their relationship to each other as they would appear to users. It describes the inputs and outputs, functions to be performed and the flow of processing. The **physical design** is the process of translating the abstract conceptual model into the specific technical design for the system. It produces the actual specifications for the programs, hardware, telecommunications, security and backup. There are three basic design solutions for every systems problem.

1. Do nothing and leave the system unchanged.
2. Modify or enhance existing systems.
3. Develop a new system.

The **design process** describes all of the components of an information system as well as the ways in which they fit together to provide unified whole. The design components will consist of the following:

- **outputs** – what the system produces
- **inputs** – data fed into the system
- **database** – the format for storing either manual or automated information
- **procedures** – activities performed in the operation and use of the system
- **controls** – procedures that ensure the information system is performing as required.

A number of different factors shape the design of the system. These include:

- **the user information requirements** – for example, in what form and time-frame the system produces information
- **system requirements** – the demands upon the system
- **information processing technology** – the different technologies and how they are intend to be used
- **systems development methodologies** – the different approaches and methodologies for building information systems
- **organisational characteristics** – these include the tasks, people, structure and culture of the organisation.

The process of translating the design specifications of the system into software is a part of the **systems development cycle**. At this stage the strategic requirements for the system are translated into programmable code.

Day-to-day running, delivery and support

Managers should also be able to monitor and control performance. Where conditions are predictable and quantifiable, the actual outcome of a business activity can be compared with an expected or previous outcome. A **closed-loop control system** can then provide a feedback loop to control future operational activities. Because the system reports on conditions that do not conform to a predetermined standard, it permits 'management by exception'. Examples include quality failures, stock turnover and departmental expenses.

Systems that provide information concerning volumes of work passing through the business also require feedback mechanisms if they are to have any value. Volumes need to be reported in units of measure that are most meaningful to those involved in the operating process. For example, a car manufacturer may use the number of vehicles produced each day, and this measurement would be supported by other performance indicators concerning the utilisation of resources. Where throughput is inadequate, the feedback by management should be in the form of decisions that will correct the situation. The need for this type of system is essential in businesses with high fixed costs, such as an airline where utilisation of capacity is paramount for success.

Where a response to a situation can be predetermined, it may be possible to design an **automatic closed loop** that requires no additional action by management or staff. Some of the procedures used in controlling the credit afforded to customers are automatic closed loops. Depending on the age of overdue sales invoices, a computerised credit control system can automatically produce the appropriate standard letter without any action by a credit controller.

However, while many operational systems are best served with a control mechanism, automatic loops are not appropriate where conditions are predictable or relate to big issues. Consider the case of capital expenditure, for example. Although there may be a formal system that identifies company cars due for renewal, the actual purchase may require the authorisation of the managing director. This is because the expenditure is discretionary and would not be essential if the business currently had cash flow problems.

If no action is taken despite the information produced, or there is a failure in the communication of the desired action, there will be no control loop and the system will become an **open loop system**. For a financial reporting system this would imply that there is no budgetary control. The control of expenditure will depend on some influence outside the system.

The characteristics of MIS must suit the system's operating environment. Stable environments can have formal systems that are highly structured, but if conditions are likely to change, then the MIS must be flexible enough to adapt to new needs. Operating environments may alter due to changes in technology, politics, society, legislation, economic growth and relative competitive advantage.

During a systems review it is useful to adopt a pictorial view of MIS. This helps to identify the day-to-day data flows by considering information needs, data sources and possible system constraints. A **data flow diagram** (DFD) is good for establishing the system fundamentals without preconceived ideas about specific methods and physical resources. A DFD represents the problem in a logical and comprehensible manner, and the systems designer should not be afraid to include pictures of everyday office objects on the diagram if this facilitates understanding for all those concerned. An example of a DFD for a product costing system is shown in Figure 26.4.

A DFD becomes a basis for discussion between the analyst and user, allowing the user to participate in the system's design. During a systems review new ideas may develop and users may become more specific about their needs, as their understanding of what is possible also develops. This has the advantage of confirming the analyst's understanding of the system, thus minimising errors that may be costly to rectify later.

TASK

The following information is generated by a food retailer:

Purchasing	Central stores and retail outlet	Customer
About deliveries:	Stock orders	Reasons for shopping
Timeliness, accuracy	Operating costs	here and what new
and quality	Sales	products they would
Relative prices		like
of different		Customer complaints
suppliers		Product returns

Categorise the various systems that report the information into:

- automatic closed loop
- closed loop
- open loop.

Case Study

Preparing a data flow diagram

Wyminton College runs 400 courses with a total teaching staff of 150 lecturers. The college is experiencing problems

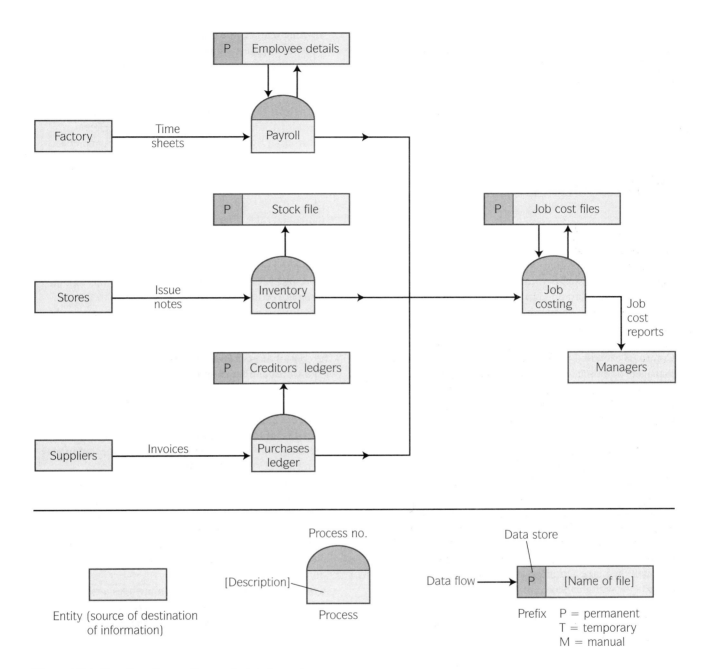

Figure 26.4 *Data flow diagram for a product costing system*

reconciling the names of students who attend classes with those who have actually registered and paid fees. The administration director has decided that student records should be computerised, which would help generate class registers preprinted with names of students who had registered and paid. However, an added complication is that some students are sponsored by employers who pay the college some time after the registration process. It has not been easy ensuring that all students' fees have subsequently been paid.

Questions

1. Describe the college's information needs.

2. Design a database to record student details.

3. Produce an outline design for a possible system making use of a data flow diagram.

Once information needs have been defined, specific requirements and constraints can be incorporated so that a more detailed system emerges. In particular, ideas should be forming on how data might be collected and the appropriate user interfaces for inputting data and receiving information. At this stage, when planning the day-to-day running of the system, a series of flow charts will show the systems logic in detail.

Evaluation of MIS

Control is a management process for ensuring that operations run to plan. In order to be successful an organisation must produce outputs in the form of goods or services that consistently meet organisational objectives. In order to do this, planning has to take place, alongside which there should be control systems which ensure that the plan takes place.

Control is exercised by the use of information. As most managers do not view operations at first-hand, it is essential that they have reliable and accurate information that allows them to exercise the control function, particularly for operational and tactical management.

Control is the activity which measures an organisation's deviations from planned performance to provide information allowing corrective action to be taken. This may either be to alter future performance in order to conform to the original plan or to modify the original plan. The control cycle will specify the expected performance against which it will compare the actual performance. The feedback of variations would come back to the manager who will then take actions to alter performance in accordance with the plan.

In order to facilitate control, safeguards may be put into the system through internal controls. These might include:

- **segregation of duties** – to prevent a single employee from manipulating the information system; for example where cash is received the system would require two people to open the post and list the cheques received, another person to record the receipt on the sales ledger, and a fourth person to make bank deposits
- **authorisation** – all transactions should be appropriately authorised according to an approval policy
- **supervision** – all staff should be supervised where control by documentation is difficult
- **organisation** – clear job boundaries and lines of reporting

- **arithmetical** – control totals and reconciliations should be built into the system, for example the regular reconciliation of the cash book to the bank statement and the nominal ledger to the personal ledgers.

Control tests require evidence that an internal system of control is working effectively, for example correct authorisation signatures on purchase invoices and effective passwords on computer systems. Where control tests are difficult to operate substantive testing may take place. This may include checking:

- individual sales transactions from sales orders and goods leaving the warehouse through to receipt of monies at the bank
- individual purchases from payments out of the bank, working back to the raising of purchase orders and the receiving of items into the stores
- the physical existence of assets that have been recorded in the accounts.

The control of performance helps to provide a wider view of the worth and functioning of MIS. Any review might include the following.

- **Periodic performance reports.** These may show how well the MIS have performed regarding planned spending and performance limits. This information may feed back directly to the elements of control.
- **User surveys.** Questionnaires and interviews help to determine how satisfied users are with the performance of MIS. For example, questions might relate to how users perceive the system to be working, the responsiveness of MIS to user needs and requirements, and what the systems are not doing but might be able to do.
- **System performance.** This often includes a range of objective and quantifiable measures relating to how well computer systems are performing. For example, how well are schedules met, is the response time for the system satisfactory and has the system error been at an acceptable rate?
- **Early warning signals.** Several early warning signals might act to alert users to problems in key areas of operations. For example, these may include any changes in the number of user complaints, increases in staff turnover and any changes in use or operation.
- **Effectiveness.** The key question is: has the system functioned as well as it was supposed to? If the MIS area is set up through a planning function, the success of the MIS may be evaluated by seeing how accurately planned operational performance of the system met with actual performance.

Case Study

Banking

Only a few years ago the clearing banks required an extensive network of grand buildings in prime locations. Today many of those buildings are being converted into pubs and restaurants as the high-street banks batten down the hatches in the face of new competition. They are not having an easy time in this age of information technology.

Large retailers such as Marks & Spencer have offered store credit cards for some years, but they are now offering financial products like unit trusts and pensions. Any organisation like Sainsbury's and Tesco with a large database of customers and plenty of processing power has the essential ingredients to turn itself into a bank. The overheads of running a back office with a telephone for a direct banking service are minimal compared to a branch network.

But, the retailers cannot afford to be complacent. If a pension can be bought down the telephone, why not a tin of baked beans?

Questions

1. Investigate and explain how managing information has replaced the role of branch management in the approval of bank lending.

2. Describe the information that you would consider necessary in the management of a bank branch.

3. Explain how you would evaluate the use of information for electronic banking.

Impact on organisational performance

A management information system will produce a range of both quantitative and qualitative information from internal and external sources. As organisations broaden their objectives beyond that of profit, distinct result areas of business organisation provide an opportunity for the impact of MIS and their performance to be assessed across the whole business. For example, these might include productivity, market position, employee attitudes, short-term and long-term goals, product leadership and staff development. These broad titles mask far more specific performance measures that might include:

- quality
- lead-times
- turnover
- direct labour productivity
- material costs
- overhead costs
- set-up times
- material yield
- deliveries on time
- inventory accuracy
- morale
- customer satisfaction.

Some organisations set broad targets designed to monitor and control performance across the business. For example, these might include:

- efficiency
- volume of output
- financial performance
- quality.

TYPES OF INFORMATION REQUIRED

Being a manager is largely about communicating information, whether passing instructions down the line of command or receiving feedback from below. But as a channel for information, managers can also be an obstacle to its flow, so organisational structure is an important determinant of a management information system's effectiveness.

Strategic, tactical and operational planning process

Management is often broken down into a variety of different levels of authority, which are usually summarised in some form of pyramid (see Figure 26.5).

Upper levels of management are involved with strategic decisions charting the whole business and its future, working towards long-term goals, objectives and plans. In order to meet such plans, particularly for large-scale businesses, managers require broad-based information

Figure 26.5 *The three levels of management*

about trends, both from within the organisation and from their external environment. Upper-level management is not always a precise business. Managers at this level have to have a vision of where they want the organisation to go and be able to move it towards that vision. Increasingly senior managers, having worked their way up the corporate ladder, are used to using technology to access the right sort of information to support their decision-making.

Senior managers will make decisions which have a wide effect upon the whole of the organisation. The information

they require will be less structured and summarised and include information from the external environment with a longer time horizon (see Figure 26.6). They will be asking questions such as:

• Are we in the right business areas?
• How are we structured to meet the challenges of our markets?
• Are resources allocated in the best way to meet the challenges the business faces?

These questions require long-term answers, with a vision often extending beyond five years.

The needs of middle managers are different to those of upper managers. Middle managers are involved with tactical decision-making, determining the best ways of getting things done as well as control of the organisation. They have to work out what to do to translate strategic financial, sales, marketing and other performance forecasts into results. As middle managers are caught between upper levels of management and lower levels of decision-makers, on the one hand they need to be seen to be achieving their targets while on the other they need to win the support of lower levels of decision-makers. They may be asking questions such as:

• What products should we be making?
• How do we invest capital in order to meet the strategic plan?
• What is the best way of pricing our plan?
• How do we make decisions about labour costs but also win the support of employees for what we are doing?
• What new methods of working are best to ensure that we meet the objectives of the plan?

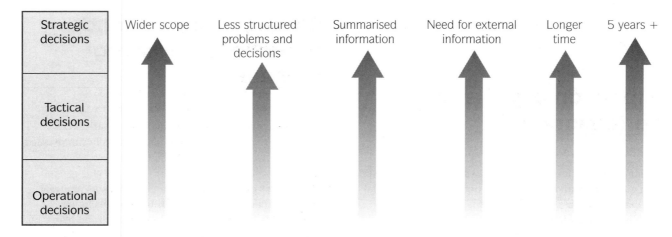

Figure 26.6 *Characteristics of different levels of decision-making*

The time-scale for tactical level decisions is likely to be between one and five years.

Lower levels of management are directly responsible for controlling operations so that higher-level targets are met. Such managers require detailed reports that describe what needs to be done by each part of the organisation in order to meet specified targets. Information is therefore highly structured and precise. Transactions data are useful for lower-level managers who may be dealing with decisions such as:

- How do we meet production and marketing objectives?
- What materials and resources do we require?
- What are the best ways of organising operations?
- What facilities do we require?
- How can we monitor what we do?

The time-scale for such decisions is less than 12 months.

Organisational structure is an important determinant of a management information system's effectiveness. In realising this, many organisations have undertaken rationalisation programmes, sometimes called **downsizing** or **delayering**, that have removed whole levels of management. Figure 26.7 illustrates the flow of information up and down a management hierarchy where the possibility of message distortion and information hold-up increase with the number of layers in a structure.

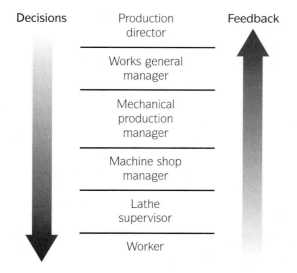

Figure 26.7 *Management information flows*

TASK

In recent years there has been a move away from highly structured, hierarchical organisations to flatter organisational structures, to promote greater flexibility in the face of environmental change. Suggest how MIS will have had to adapt to this change.

Different organisations and contexts

A management information system must be appropriate to the host organisation as well as the context within which individual managers have to make decisions. If it is not tailored to the organisation and the needs of individual managers, it will have little value.

Some organisations are very *formal* in the relationships and tasks they undertake. Such organisations will be governed by rules, policies and systems. Formal organisations will have relationships shown in organisation charts, which identify official relationships, levels of management control. In a formal organisation, there will be:

- a clear hierarchy of command and control
- well-defined relationships
- stability, with clear structures.

A formal organisation is more likely to be in a stable and unchanging environment, with a need for structured information in prescribed forms. The information system in this situation does not have to be adaptive.

Informal organisations allow employees either as individuals or in groups, to operate non-standard procedures and practices in order to get things done. To some extent, informal groups or individuals work within every organisation. Here social groups develop behavioural patterns, actions and objectives that sometimes challenge the formal organisation. Individuals may use untried and untested methods which are equally efficient. Such organisations are flexible and adaptive and may exist in a turbulent and volatile business environment where outputs are not rigidly defined. Information systems have to be able to adapt to meet such changing requirements.

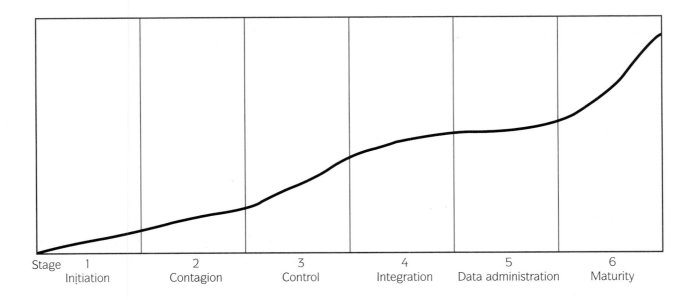

Figure 26.8 *The six stages of data-processing growth*

Time is especially useful for considering why decisions about information systems at one point may be inappropriate at another point. The stages of growth (SOG) curve is useful for understanding why different decisions have to be made during a systems maturation (see Figure 26.8).

There are six stages of growth.

1. **Initiation.** New technology is introduced to the organisation, with some users applying it and becoming comfortable with the technology.

2. **Contagion.** More users become familiar with the technology, and its use proliferates as demand for it increases. Enthusiasm grows for using the new technology.

3. **Control.** Management becomes increasingly concerned about the economics of the new technology. Its benefits and costs become key concerns. Users are made accountable for using the technology in a cost-effective way.

4. **Integration.** Systems continue to proliferate with new systems upgraded. Planning and control systems become formalised. The notion of integration within decision-making becomes more important.

5. **Data administration.** The value of data becomes increasingly important during this period. Data administration systems are set up to manage these data.

6. **Maturity.** Organisations that reach this stage are concerned that technology and management processes are integrated to become an effective functional entity.

THE EFFECTIVE USE AND SELECTION OF INFORMATION

For the conversion of data into information, data have to flow through certain processes. Unfortunately, the free flow of data is often obstructed because individual managers solve their own local information needs without taking a corporate perspective for MIS.

The free flow of information is more assured if all systems development work is coordinated by one senior manager. Standards can then be agreed for hardware, software and data-file structure that apply to the whole business. Very often the output from one system is manually keyed into another because of system incompatibility. The result is a delay in the flow of information, greater cost and the possibility of errors. Equally important is the need to break down the political barriers to data sharing. People may be reluctant to share data because information gives power, and the ignorant depend on those with knowledge for the effective performance of their duties.

The demands of data collection

Most of the information that flows through a business comes from the recording of financial transactions and the monitoring of business activities, although this may be augmented by data obtained from outside sources.

The methods adopted for the collection of data will depend upon the nature of the items being recorded and the relative costs of manual procedures and computer systems. They include the following:

- keyboard entries to a computer system
- manual recording, for example on to a time sheet or stores issue note, although this data may also be keyed into a computer system at a later stage
- Electronic Data Interchange (EDI), which enables data to be transferred from one computer system to another (problems of compatibility between systems have so far restricted the use of EDI, although it is widely used in the retail sector where large retailers can pass stock requirement details to suppliers)
- electronic input with transactions recorded by scanning equipment, including optical character recognition (used with utility bill counterfoils), magnetic ink recognition (used for clearance of bank cheques), optical mark readers (used for questionnaire boxes), electronic point of sale (bar codes used in retailing).

The processes of MIS maintain structured data stores that can be accessed to produce better management information. The production of information often requires data to be searched and sorted, and for calculations to be made. The principles are the same whether the system is manual or computerised. A manual system will maintain filing cabinets of paper records, whereas a computerised system will use electronic storage media to store files in digital form.

Where data are stored in a computer file, each record is usually structured into fields. A data field stores a certain type of information concerning each data subject, such as ages of employees and their addresses. Data records stored in this highly structured manner are known as **databases** and are a basis for sharing data between different applications.

A computer file containing details of jobs being worked in a factory, for example, would be called a **master file**, because it relates to permanent data concerning a subject. The record of individual cost items would be an example of a **transaction file**. The job number is the common field that will enable details from the master file and the transaction file to be combined for the production of a cost report.

Issues related to data overload and effective use

The management of an information system within a business should operate ideally as a working whole, without barriers to data flows caused by the operation of functional systems (see Figure 26.9). For example, data stored concerning a direct worker may include personal details, training undertaken, skills developed, wages paid, holidays taken, sick leave, hours worked and details of work done in that time. These data will have been input by different business functions, including production control, personnel department, the payroll section and the costing department. If all these data can be stored in one accessible place – a data warehouse – management information reports can be designed without a constraint on where the data are stored.

The desirability of using common data stores, of course, does not replace the need for specialised application software for the collection of data. Even in a coordinated system there will be distinct elements focused on particular business functions.

It should not be forgotten that informal information channels, often through personal contacts in the organisation, can make a valuable contribution to the information available for management. Some businesses with an open organisational culture and a relatively flat hierarchical structure encourage informal channels. Informal systems can also be useful for obtaining external information, and managers may be encouraged to participate in industry associations and local chambers of commerce where informal contacts can be built up.

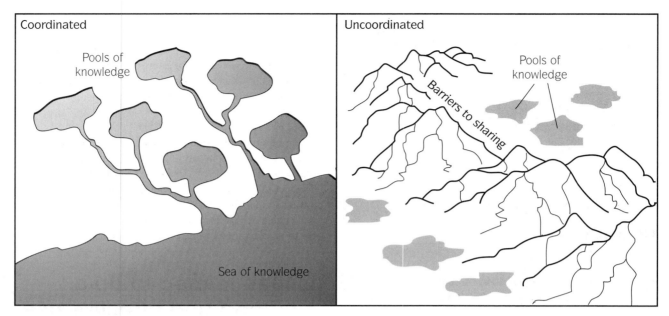

Figure 26.9 *Information flows*

There are a number of problems related to data overload and effective use. These may include the following.

- **Carelessness** – keying or inputting errors or computer operator error may cause considerable problems within a system. Operators may also damage a program during use or misplace a file.
- **Computer crime** – the use of computer resources for unauthorised or illegal acts. It is possible that a system may be sabotaged or is used for illegal purposes such as stealing money or products. Data 'diddling' refers to unauthorised modifications to data within a system, such as changing a person's qualifications on his or her academic record. There are a number of more specific problems caused by computer crime.
  - A *computer virus* is a logic bomb which acts as an illegal parasite, attaching itself to a host programme to reproduce and spreads chaos.
  - *Logic bombs* cause parts of the computer system to become inoperative or to malfunction as soon as a particular routine is executed. Logic bombs are more likely to be written by disgruntled programmers.
  - *Salami techniques* work under the assumption that if small amounts of money are shaved off from balances, they will not be closely checked. Accounts are particularly vulnerable to salami shavers.
  - *Leakage* results when data, programs or computer resources leave a site without authorisation, even when transported in a disk.
  - *Eavesdropping* allows a person to observe transmissions designated for someone else, for example looking at somebody else's e-mail.
  - *Wiretapping* involves setting up a special transmission path designed to divert the flow of data.
  - *Hacking* originally referred to computer professionals who solved or cracked problems. Today the term refers to where a person breaks into a computer system.
- **Natural disasters** – another problem related to storage of data is that of a disaster happening to a system. For example, an earthquake, fire, flood or other form of damage could cause the loss of key information, for which copies might not have been made.
- **Hardware and software failures** – power failures, damage caused by viruses and equipment failures may result in many problems for an organisation dependent upon the use of data.

Case Study

Glossy Printing Ltd

Glossy Printing Ltd operates a relatively old computerised financial accounts system on two networked personal computers. Unfortunately, not all of the software modules link automatically so, for example, although a sales invoice links with the sales ledger, it does not link with job costing. This has created hold-ups in the accounts office as staff wait for a computer to become free. Additionally, the directors have been complaining about the lack of historical information and that the reports they receive are not always in an appropriate format.

Because of the current problems the firm's accountant has chosen a new software package that requires computers with the latest processing chips and greater memory and disk space. A local hardware supplier can upgrade the existing machines at a lower cost than buying new machines.

The system will require some changes to office procedures, and the keying in of historical data would take an employee at least a week to complete. The accountant believes that other staff could be sent on training courses while the data were being transferred.

Questions

1. What might be the costs and benefits of the new system?

2. When would be the most convenient time to implement it?

3. What might the training requirements be?

4. What would be the main considerations in selecting software?

THE ROLE OF TRAINING

With so many people using computers in order to do their jobs more efficiently, the role of training in the use of information and information systems has become a top priority across many organisations. Training may be provided at a range of levels, including that for individuals and departments as well as across the organisation. Training may be directed at a specific application, such as how to interpret a particular database, or it might be aimed at increasing overall computer literacy of staff across the organisation.

Training needs at all levels of organisation

It has been said that 'there is no substitute for good training'. Training needs exist throughout each organisation at all levels. A common objective for training is to identify individuals who can provide support for others within all levels. These are usually enthusiastic and highly computer-literate people who take on the role of training. They are sometimes referred to as **power users**, because of their ability to help people in each of the functional and hierarchical levels by providing specialist advice and training support. Many organisations use power users, who become their experts within key activities and areas, and who provide support for other individuals.

Case Study

Roundhay Health Products Ltd

At Roundhay Health Products Ltd the management believes that well-trained users are important. As a result, the company will not allow staff access to the machines until they have been properly trained. With limited training resources and a mandate to run a lean three-person information systems department, proficiency is important. The company builds user confidence by offering training sessions that provide hands-on experience, videotapes and computer-based training. The information systems department also places standard user interfaces on most programs. It is felt at Roundhay that manuals are among the least desirable training tools, because users become intimidated by pages of notes.

To support day-to-day operations, each part of the organisation has a power user who provides the flexibility to meet training needs as and when they arise. Power users are also there to support senior managers as well as those involved in operations. The systems provided at Roundhay ensure that individuals across the organisation have access to training designed to meet all of their requirements, no matter what their level of operation.

Questions

1. Why is training so important for Roundhay?

2. Comment upon the different training methods used? Which would you prefer to be faced with?

3. How important is training across the whole organisation?

Trainees can be shown how to understand the decision-making environment related to their specialist areas, and how such decisions may be supported with the aid of information-processing tools. Training also helps users to become literate about a range of issues associated with computing. As senior managers understand more about their information needs and requirements, they also learn about IT systems and applications.

Training helps managers to understand the sort of criteria they need to use when purchasing IT systems, which they can relate to their own experiences. Training is also invaluable for communicating potential problems or issues such as data integrity and technological obsolescence as well as the knowledge of systems compatibility. Training also helps employees to pinpoint and solve their own problems, without the need for specialist IT support.

Benefits and limitations

Virtually everyone working in the area of IT must constantly retrain in order to understand the range of new technologies becoming available and their possible application to their working environment. Business systems are constantly being altered, and training has become an on-going requirement. Training helps senior managers to keep on top of change, to ensure that their organisation responds in the right ways to new initiatives. Information about change might come from exhibitions related to different trades, reading topical reports, periodicals and journals and through electronic media.

Some individuals may not be happy about having to rely upon sophisticated data information systems before

making decisions. Having made decisions in the past based upon good knowledge of the business, they may feel that using MIS simply adds to their role and overpowers them with data which confuses rather than aids decision-making. Such managers may have their own culture and series of priorities, viewing data management simply as an interference with their job role.

Another problem is that it is not always possible to find a pool of capable professionals able to cope with highly sophisticated MIS. Where this happens, employing such people may be a considerable expense, making the use of information a costly exercise. MIS professionals are especially required in developing parts of the world.

Conflicts may arise between computer professionals and users as well as between computer professionals and managers. For example, computer professionals may be perceived as being more concerned about the technology than the results of its use. In many organisations those involved in MIS have staff rather than line positions, so that those in line positions may have different views about systems and their use.

MIS convert data into information so that managers are better able to make informed decisions. It is important that at an early stage the information needs and requirements of the organisation are identified before considering how they could be satisfied. MIS harness the processing power of computers, although systems design should not be hampered by preconceived views of hardware and software resources. As with other management issues, managing information should be done on a contingency basis, with a corporate perspective of costs and benefits.

IT Systems and Applications

The word system is often used to discuss a series of connected things or parts as well as a scheme of action and a procedure. According to Philip Sadler in *Designing Organisations: The Foundation for Excellence* (1994), systems, procedures and processes in business are:

> *relatively formal, prescribed and standardised ways of doing things that have been developed or adopted by the organisation. There will exist systems and procedures governing the core business processes.*

It is therefore important for us to look at information technology (IT) business systems in order to appreciate how things are done, so that we can understand the components of IT, the components of the systems and the practical considerations in the workplace.

On completion of the chapter you should be able to identify and assess differing systems applications to store, retrieve and analyse data. To achieve this you must demonstrate the ability to:

- use integrated packages to produce management information data which synthesises text, spreadsheet and database information.

- identify and discuss the benefits and limitations of at least two different systems for improving business performance.

THE DEVELOPMENT OF IT

The US business author Peter Drucker saw the late twentieth century as the dawning of the age of the information-based organisation, the latest in the development of the modern business corporation.

At the beginning of the century management was separated from the ownership of a company, as shareholders handed over responsibility for its running to paid managers. This led to the growth of the command-and-control organisation made up of departments and divisions. Now we are entering a third period of change, with the development of information-based organisations of knowledge specialists.

In this third phase, members of staff are freed from day-to-day administrative tasks by computers. Computers bring a large proportion of employees closer to the work of management; departmental hierarchies are broken down, creating a much flatter organisational structure with the opportunity to develop more skills. Networking of computer systems gives people access to many disciplines. When a company uses a number of personal computers, it is possible that some of the information on one of these may be useful to another user. Then, rather than continually swapping data on floppy disks, it is possible to connect the machines together using a **local area network** (LAN). This consists of a mixture of hardware and software, which enables data to be transferred between the machines. Networking thus makes it possible for a range of experts to tap into each other's specialist skill areas while sitting at their own work-stations. Such employees no longer need to work in the same building, and may even be able to work quite easily from home. No longer is knowledge compartmentalised; instead, it has become part of a pool of mutually shared information.

We are still a long way from the widespread development of information-based organisations that are democratically structured. Rather than restructuring job design, many organisations have tended to automate the existing organisational structure. Dramatic contrasts can be made between companies that have combined information technology with a more effective decision-making structure and those that have simply borrowed the new technology and retained the existing structure. The point is illustrated by a TV report *Management in the Nineties*, which featured a comparison of two organisations in the pensions business, each of which was responsible for managing an investment portfolio of £15 million. It showed how a new-model business compared with an older style organisation. The traditionally run business is represented by a division of a bank, employing 108 professional staff and 36 support staff. The newcomer, Battery March, a Boston-based financial investment management firm, handles a comparable business, but with 18 professional staff and 17 support staff. From the outset, Battery March's founder operated on the principle that there was a better way of managing funds which would add value to the company's services. The operation was consciously organised to make best use of the creative contribution of analysts and professionals with a strong emphasis on teamwork. It was a vision that depended upon making the best use of information technology.

Buying and selling directly, computer to computer, takes care of some routine clerical work. Technology is also used extensively to monitor stock and fund changes, select the best options, and so on, to enable staff to concentrate more on the creative aspects of the business. As a result, Battery March enjoys lower costs and a record of highly effective performance.

It is not just younger companies like Battery March that are exploring the possibilities for innovative organisation. Rank Xerox, for example, has questioned the need for all white-collar workers to work in a central office. It is one of the trail-blazers in the use of networkers, i.e. home-based specialists and professional workers contracted to the company, but also working for other clients.

COMPONENTS

An information technology system is any system that provides information for activities carried out within an organisation. A management information system is one that provides such information for managers. However, it is increasingly common for a large number of people in organisations to have managerial responsibilities. Information technology solutions are therefore employed to provide effective communication systems serving all members of an organisation. Information comprises data that have been processed so that they are useful to the recipient.

An information system will be made up of the following:

- **Computer hardware** is the equipment, such as terminals and keyboards, that is used to gather, enter and store data and then to process data into usable information.
- **Computer software** provides the programmes that are used to operate the hardware and to produce information.
- **Data stored in databases** – the type of data stored will depend on the information needs of the organisation.
- **People** operate and use the information system.
- **Procedures** are the rules, instructions and methods for operating the information system.

Today, organisations increasingly seek recruits with IT capabilities or the willingness to develop these capabilities.

Before introducing computers to a communications and information system, it is necessary to carry out a **systems analysis** to investigate the ways in which the information system can be of use. Nowadays, the emphasis is usually on providing solutions that meet the needs of the organisation rather than buying commercially produced business packages.

Systems development is a procedure used to design and develop an information system. The systems analyst looks at an organisation as a coordinated whole and examines the ways in which the parts of the organisation fit together and support each other. He or she then attempts to integrate within the organisation and its needs a multilevel, cross-functional and timely flow of information. The resulting information system will then serve the needs of both the management subsystem and the operating subsystem.

An example of a modern computer-based information system is that operated by the commercial banks to handle customer information. A business or private customer may have several accounts with a bank: a current account, savings account, mortgage account and loan account. Using a customer information system, it is possible to cross-reference such accounts easily so that the bank can quickly call up statements of a customer's activities, even though the customer may be dealing with several departments of the bank. Such information makes it possible for a bank to develop a more detailed picture of its customers, to provide a better service, to supply up-to-date information and to market new services to existing customers.

Case Study

Waterside – the office of the future

At BA (British Airways) they don't like their new Waterside building to be described as the headquarters of the airline, as its sounds too hierarchical and elitist. The building has been described as Britain's most trend-setting office complex. The light in the building is natural and fresh. It is possible to sit within the building at a café beside a stream, shop at Waitrose's virtual supermarket or sit on a seat under a tree, reserved as a thinking area!

Waterside seems to combine informality with competence. It reflects new ways of working and a new business culture, with opportunities for flexibility and team building.

Technology provides the mechanism for such facilities. In the past people needed to be herded to particular places at set times in offices to remain in touch with each other. That was necessary in order to exchange letters, telephone calls and conversations. Waterside has 40 ever-ready video conferencing locations, an intelligent phone exchange which connects Digitally Enhanced Cordless Technology (DECT) phones so that a user does not have to remain in one place at any one time. The place is famous for 'hot desking'. There are lectern-style docking stations for visitors' laptop computers. The divisions that choose hot desking have a range of appointed areas, where individuals can either work quietly or in the company of others.

Those individuals with permanent desks work in an open-plan complex that allows a degree of privacy. Though the offices are not paper-free, there is very little. BA's new 'headquarters' is about changing the ways in which people operate. Though flexibility and computers deliver savings, good design has involved much social engineering, changing the nine to five culture to one of relationship management.

Questions

1. What types of communication does BA's type of office environment foster?

2. How does such a system change the ways in which employees operate?

3. Why is it important to allow free access to information using this system, rather than having top-down controls?

4. What are the benefits of such an office environment for BA's (a) staff and (b) customers?

5. How does technology support this changing office environment?

Capacity and capabilities of computers

The last three decades have shown a rapid increase in the pace of technological developments to support the notion of an IT revolution. At the centre of these developments are changes in the world of telecommunications and computing with the overlapping of stages of development and a convergence of such technologies. Information technology has thus become not just the fastest developing area of industrial and business activity but it also touches our lives in every area of activity.

- **In the home.** IT may be used through digital or satellite television, information database services such as teletext, the use of fax machines, e-mail, electronic shopping, banking through telephone-based services, energy control and other forms of entertainment and investigative learning.
- **Within government.** IT applications are used in defence, the collection and dissemination of information such as data required for benefits, the setting up and monitoring of technical standards, the enforcement of law and regulations, running the business of government economically and the making and executing of national economic and social policy.
- **In education and training.** Information technologies have major implications for education and training, with the applications of computer-based learning, the use of computers within schools for both learning and

investigation through the Internet, as well as e-mail and computer conferencing.

- **In banking, finance and retailing.** In recent years we have seen far-reaching changes in the world of banking, financial services and retailing, with an increasing number of applications such as loyalty cards, different methods of making payments and the changing nature of banking services such as home banking, as well as new opportunities to buy and sell securities.
- **In manufacturing and service industries.** Industries today are often said to be based upon shifting sand, with many sectors in areas of overcapacity and with increasingly competitive organisations determined to improve their market share. Methods of working are changing all the time to include optimised production technology scheduling production systems, robotics, computer-integrated manufacture linking all areas of manufacturing, the use of technology to improve supply chain management as well as Japanese practices facilitated by new methods of working and technologies.

Through all of the different areas listed above, the capabilities of computers have had a major influence upon many different areas in society. Microelectronic systems have affected the ways in which data are processed, stored and transmitted. As a result, given the massive capabilities of computers, important questions have been asked about the uses of information technology. For example, are rich or large commercial enterprises able to use technology to exploit their own power? Does IT increase the unequal balance of power between developed and developing countries? Could the use of information accessed through IT be a security threat to individuals? Will improved efficiency cause social problems and unrest?

Though we can accept that the capacity and capabilities of computers have increased immeasurably over recent years through a process that we have largely taken for granted, in almost every area of life from the workplace to the home, given the overwhelming process of change that has taken place, there are many further issues that need to be discussed in relation to this technology. The potential for massive interlinked databanks to be misused is enormous, particularly if information from such databanks is either out of date or inaccurate. For example, sometimes the sheer amount of information held in such databanks or on mailing lists has resulted in harassment from direct mail. Misused data could also lead to the denial of employment, credit or other rights.

Another issue associated with the increasing power of computers is that of surveillance and privacy. There is very little that we can do that is not in some way monitored, from walking through a public thoroughfare, to using a desktop machine in an office.

IT provides the opportunities for greater personal responsibility, improved access to information and democracy in a way that is cheap, reliable and effective. There are many new opportunities for the use of such technologies, in the home, the office and throughout the workplace. But, as we appreciate the power and capabilities of computers to perform new functions or activities, we have to balance these powers against socially negative consequences, particularly in people's homes and communities.

Servers and networks in cross-organisation communication processes

One of the key benefits for both organisations and individuals within those organisations is the ability to share information. The main feature of shared information systems is that they have more than a single user providing the opportunity to share:

- hardware
- programs and software
- data
- communications.

Shared systems allow multiple users to utilise a range of devices, for example a specialist high-resolution laser printer for architectural charting. No one application could justify the cost, but it is possible for a number of users to share the application.

Local area network

A LAN links together a number of computers, terminals, workstations, printers, scanners and other devices within either one building or a group of buildings. This is done by cables rather than by telephone systems, with the LAN acting as a 'highway' along which the data travel. Each device linked to a LAN is called a **node**. A network interface card has to be added to each microcomputer before it can be used on the LAN. A cable interface then links the computer to the LAN, and a **network operating system** is required to control its operation. A **gateway** can

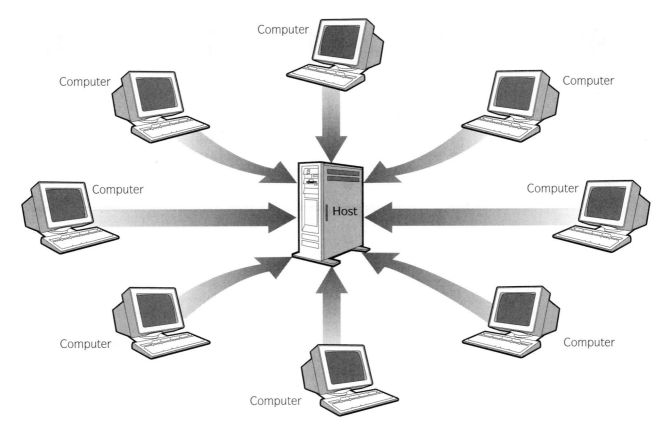

Figure 27.1 *A star network*

connect a LAN with a larger computer thus linking all of
the microcomputers with a central machine.

The physical layout of a LAN is called its topology. There are
three major types of topology. These include the following.

1. A **star network** links all of the machines in the LAN to
   a central computer. The computer then serves as the
   host or the **file server**. The file server controls the LAN
   as well as all of the messages through it.

2. A **ring network** connects all of the nodes in the LAN
   in a circular framework. With this type of network there
   is no host machine. Messages simply flow around the
   network until they reach their destination. This simply
   involves linking the microcomputers within an office.

3. A **bus configuration** is sometimes called a **broadcast
   network**. This uses a single cable known as a **bus**, and
   directs messages by identifying codes. With this system
   each computer carries out some management task. The
   failure of one node would not put the whole network
   out of operation.

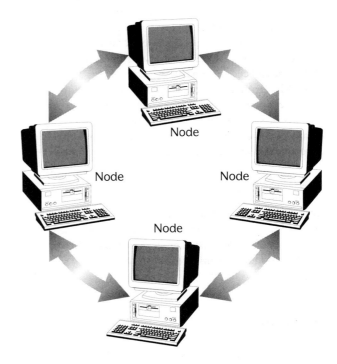

Figure 27.2 *A ring network*

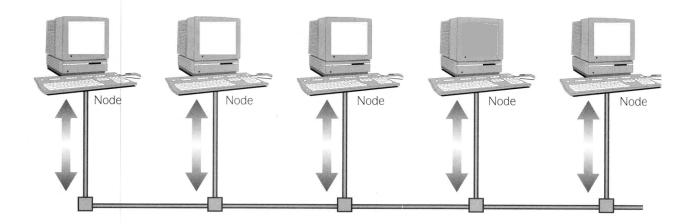

Figure 27.3 *A bus network*

Two commonly used types of system include the **Cambridge ring**, which uses a ring of cable to send a message to a device. If the ring is being used, a queue is formed. Another common system is the **Ethernet system**, which uses a single cable. A device examines the status of the network before sending a message. If it is already in use, it waits for a short time before trying again.

A key benefit of networks is that of sharing program costs. Less is charged for a single network version of a program than for many individual copies. For example, a single computer may store the programs used on all of the computers in the LAN. This also saves on storage space. Sometimes a licence fee has to be paid for every computer in a LAN carrying a particular program. Data sharing is a key benefit of LAN networks. Databases often represent the bulk of such systems, often storing accounting data, details of customers, sales support information and departmental-wide applications.

An increasing trend for shared applications within a large organisation is to provide an in-house Intranet. An Intranet comprises a range of pages covering a variety of applications such as internally advertised job vacancies, departmental performance figures or statements from key people within the organisation.

Wide area network

A wide area network (WAN) is a network that provides data communication services between companies or separated divisions of the same organisation. Telecommunication links are used to enable computers to communicate with each other regardless of their physical location. Star, ring or bus topologies may be used to connect LANs to WANs to provide an all-embracing system.

The key feature of a WAN system is that it provides a communications path to another network, wherever that might be. In doing so it creates the basis for worldwide communication. For example, a large organisation may have a mainframe with a star network of data-entry terminals. This is at the centre of a hierarchical network of departmental computers. LANs in bus and ring configuration may be interconnected from other parts of the organisation through a wider area network. The great advantage of the WAN is its flexibility. Once the start-up costs have been paid, the cost of a WAN is directly related to the actual services provided. There are, however, a number of problems with sharing data across international boundaries. These include:

- different time zones, working hours and holidays which vary according to different users
- language differences and their requirements upon different systems, reports and documentation
- the standardised use of equipment which may be different elsewhere
- rules and regulations regarding the transmission of certain types of data across international borders
- currency exchange regulations
- security, as a badly administered system may lead to abuse
- costs of training staff.

Case Study

The end of the lighthouse keeper

A tradition recently came to an end when North Foreland, Britain's last manned lighthouse went fully automatic. The immaculate green and white tower in genteel Broadstairs has been warning ships of the Goodwin Sands since the fifteenth century. The closure represents the end of an era, representing days when lighthouse keepers maintained lights and saved people who had fallen down cliffs.

Today, Eddystone, The Wolf, South Stack, Skerries, Lundy Island, Nash Point and many more still shine, but instead are controlled from Harwich via a bank of personal computers monitoring generators, burglar alarms, fire detection, radio beacons and satellite equipment. Where there were once over 300 lighthouse keepers, there are now two operators per Harwich shift. As an operation, it is smaller, cleaner, safer and more reliable. It is also cheaper.

It can be claimed that technological innovation has always been part of the history of lighthouses. The first automated lights appeared in 1915, when acetylene lights or gas lights were controlled by sun valves. More recently, ships have relied upon satellite navigation, the accuracy of which is enhanced by shore-based reference sites. Global positioning will soon render lights redundant.

Questions

1. Describe some of the technologies involved in the changing ways in which ships navigate.

2. Who benefits from such developments?

3. What are the social costs?

Electronic data interchange, electronic funds transfer and the Internet

Electronic data interchange (EDI) has the objective of simplifying business transactions between suppliers and their customers. It achieves this by allowing data, messages or documents to be transferred from one organisation's computer to another. The obvious benefits are savings on paperwork, time and the elimination of data rekeying. It follows that the more paperwork an organisation handles, the more apparent will be the potential benefits of introducing EDI. EDI allows a purchaser's computer to communicate directly with the supplier's machine over a telecommunication link so that goods can be ordered directly and payments can be made. An EDI standard such as EDIFACT (electronic data interchange for administration, commerce and transport) lays down a standard format for electronic documents so that any incompatibilities between different systems can be overcome.

Electronic Funds Transfer (EFT) is the electronic transfer of money into and out of and between bank accounts. For example, nearly all wages and salaries are paid by electronic means. The BACSTEL (Bankers Automated Clearing-house Telecommunications) system is used within the UK, while SWIFT (Society for Worldwide Interbank Financial Telecommunications) allows international transfers. The increased efficiency of electronic communications has also moved towards *electronic funds transfer at the point of sale* (EFTPOS), where the money required to complete a transaction is electronically transferred at the point of sale.

A key problem with any form of computer transfer is the establishment of some kind of audit trail, particularly where EDI is combined with some form of EFT.

The **Internet** has probably already surpassed expectations as a new way forward for exchanging and disseminating information, trading internationally, and for communicating and exchanging information with other organisations. It still has enormous potential for learning and investigation.

PRACTICAL USES

Before making decisions about the practical uses of different software applications, it is important to consider the design of the information system. **Systems design** is concerned with deciding how a system should be developed and involves the preparation and planning of an information system by drawings, sketches and plans. The form of design will depend on a number of factors including the following.

- **The resources available to an organisation.** The five basic resources of any organisation are machines, materials, money, methods and people. There would be no point in designing an expensive system for a company that had little money to spare.
- **The information requirements of users.** Systems design clearly needs to be coupled with an understanding of who needs what information, and in what form.
- **The user's ability to make use of the information provided.** The designer needs to make the system as user friendly as possible. This involves keeping jargon and technical language to a minimum. Other features that can be built into the system include speed of communication, to reduce waiting time.
- **The requirements for the system.** The designer needs to understand what is expected of the system, including:
  - cost
  - performance
  - reliability
  - flexibility
  - expected life-cycle.
- **The use to which data operations will be put.** A number of important operations can be carried out on data.
  - **Capturing data** involves recording data generated by an event or occurrence, for example from invoices, sales slips, meters, counters.
  - **Verifying the data** ensures that data have been recorded accurately, for example checking that an instrument is working correctly, or cross-checking recording procedures.
  - **Classifying data** entails putting different types of data into appropriate sections, for example the sales of a company could be classified according to the different departments that make the sales.
  - **Sorting data** involves placing data elements into a specified order, for example an inventory file could be sorted by money value, or by code number.
  - **Summarising data** can be used to aggregate data, for example by totalling various figures, such as sales, or by drawing up balancing figures for a balance sheet. Alternatively, it could be used to present data logically in a common form, for example by producing a list of all employees that were working the night shift on a particular date.
  - **Calculating by using data** involves computing various figures mathematically, for example adding, subtracting, dividing. Wages of employees can be calculated by multiplying hours worked by the wage rate and then subtracting necessary deductions.
  - **Storing data** involves transferring data to the appropriate medium, for example floppy disk,

microfilm, etc.
  - **Retrieving data** involves calling up information from the place of storage.
  - **Reproducing data** is the process of transferring the same data from one medium to another. At a simple level, this could involve photocopying material or commanding a computer to copy it, or calling up data from one screen to another, for example when dealing in stocks and shares.
  - **Communicating** enables the transfer of data from one place to another. This can take place at any stage of the data-processing cycle. The ultimate aim of information processing is to provide information for the final consumer.

Systems analysis reveals the order in which the above operations need to be carried out in particular activities. This information will be needed in systems design. The designer will then use a number of tools, such as flow charts and decision tables, to help produce the best possible design for the information system.

The systems designer will suggest alternative plans for implementation. Some of these will be set out as imperatives, i.e. features of design that must be adhered to, whatever the final system. The designer will also suggest a number of desirable features, which are optional.

It will then be necessary to find suppliers who are able to provide suitable equipment to meet the design needs. This might involve finding equipment that has the 'best fit' with the desired system in terms of cost, reliability and ease of maintenance. Other considerations will be the potential to extend a system in the event of future growth, and the overall level of support from the supplier, for example in the form of training. These and other factors will need to be weighed up before a final decision is made.

The practical uses of different software applications

All documents are composed of two major elements: **text** and **art**. Text comprises words, sentences and paragraphs. Art comprises everything else that could appear within a document, including lines, boxes, charts, drawings, clipart, scanned pictures, etc. Recently the boundaries between text and art have become blurred with many word processors either capable of generating art or of integrating art with text.

Word processing

Word processing has revolutionised the preparation of printed material, allowing many people such as managers to type their own memoranda and reports. Whether this is an effective use of time is debatable, but many users have become particularly effective using software word-processing packages such as Microsoft Word (see Figure 27.4) or Lotus Word Pro. Such packages eliminate the tedious labour associated with producing pages of good-looking text, allowing errors to be detected and corrected easily and quickly.

Figure 27.4 *Microsoft Word screen*

The basic function of a word processor is to manipulate text. Its great advantage is that it allows the user to make unlimited changes to text on screen before the final document is printed out. Word processors make life easier in the following ways:

- New text can be added to the beginning or middle of a document while the existing text moves to create space for it.
- Blocks of text can be moved around in the document that is being created.
- The text can be justified/unjustified or centred.
- A word or phrase can be searched for, and can be removed or replaced by another word or phrase. A spelling mistake which is repeated throughout a document can be corrected 'globally' in a single operation.
- Headers and footers consisting of specified text can be placed at the top or bottom of every page.
- Documents can be combined with a mail-merge facility allowing the same message to be sent to groups of people.

- Word processors offer the use of different printing styles and fonts, the ability to insert graphics, spreadsheets and output from other applications into the text, the use of the spell checker, thesaurus, word count and auto-correct functions and the insertion of borders, tables, bullets and numbers.

Word processing also allows users to separate the various tasks involved in producing documents so that they can do one or a few at a time. They do not have to think about phrasing, page layout and spelling at the time of inputting the text, but can go back later to focus upon the presentation of the text. Word processing has led to an enormous cost reduction, with fewer specialist typists and most individuals being responsible for producing their own documentation. As individuals use packages they become specialist in key functions, with a faster turnaround of work produced in a significantly better-quality format, that can be corrected and amended.

Desktop publishing (DTP) offers another method of producing documents and printed matter in a professional format. Using DTP it is possible to produce pages of combined text and graphics to a very high standard. Different graphics can be created, diagrams can be placed on pages with text flowing around them, and pictures can be introduced into the document and resized to fit the space available. DTP is used to produce a wide variety of printed items, including reports, newsletters, training materials and advertisements.

Spreadsheets

A spreadsheet is a table of numbers which can be organised and altered on a computer according to preset formulae (see Figure 27.5). Spreadsheets are particularly useful for forecasting and financial modelling, as they can show the effects of financial decisions without the need to repeat calculations manually.

Spreadsheets can be likened to a sheet of electronic analysis paper, organised into hundreds of columns and thousands of rows. They allow the user to manipulate and analyse both text and numerical data. Packages such as Microsoft Excel include sophisticated features that facilitate the construction of multidimensional spreadsheets where a value can be analysed in more than two dimensions. For example, an expenses budget may be analysed by type of expense, by department, by location and into 12 monthly periods. When constructing models, such as for budgets or project appraisal, the spreadsheet

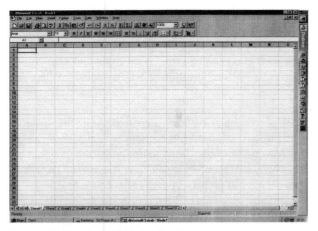

Figure 27.5 *Microsoft Excel spreadsheet screen*

automatically updates calculated cells each time numerical data is put in. Regularly performed procedures can be automated with a simple programming routine called a 'macro'.

For example, an organisation will make a forecast of all the money coming in and going out over a 12-month period. The spreadsheet can alter the inputs to calculate the effect of, say, lowering a heating bill by a certain amount each month. The computer will automatically recalculate the columns to change the heating figures, total cost figures and profits for each month.

In this way a manager, accountant, or any other user of a spreadsheet can quickly carry out business calculations such as introducing and finding out the effect of minor changes of variables. Spreadsheets not only provide support for simple data storage and retrieval they can also be used to communicate results, by offering powerful presentation graphics in the forms of charts and graphs, formed on the basis of the numerical information contained within highlighted cells.

Databases

A database is a store of information, or self-describing collection of integrated records, held on a computer. Examples may include anything from a list of customer accounts held by a bank or a building society to a record of members of a congregation and their addresses held by a parish priest or vicar. Another use might be to record tickets sold by a football club for various matches.

The essence of a database is that data can be accessed and analysed in a number of different ways, depending on the

needs of the user. For example, suppose that Amin Stores wishes to record the account details of all its customers. It would store the information in a number of **fields** – address, value of goods supplied, payments received and balance of the account. If a customer rings up asking for the state of his or her account, Mr Amin can simply order the computer to produce the appropriate information and display it on the screen.

A personal computer database allows the user to define the type, content and features of a database. Like a card index, data records can be accessed individually for enquiry purposes, but the computer's power is best applied to finding and sorting records according to specified criteria, for example a list of all those patients who receive meals on wheels and are vegetarian. Using the command language on some of the more sophisticated packages, the systems designer can automate procedures so that the user need have very little knowledge of the actual database functions.

The main benefit of a database is that data items can be stored and accessed from a variety of different routes, thus providing flexibility for handling information. A database is managed by a **database management system** (DBMS). This allows the user organisation to access information, so that more effort can be spent upon solving business problems. For example, a DBMS provides the user with three sets of tools.

1. It provides a means of defining the database itself, with a **data definition language** (DDL).

2. It provides a means of accessing, storing, retrieving and changing database data. This is done using **data manipulation language** (DML).

3. It provides easy-to-use tools to define the database and the database components, such as menus, reports and data-entry forms.

Case Study

Dataphobia

Some people feel that the prospect of managing data is intimidating and find databases particularly difficult to use. Each database will require input skills, flexibility of the user as well as querying and report capabilities. There are certain key ingredients of each database. These include the following.

- **Ease of use.** Menus have to be well organised, with data input, querying and reporting functions logically arranged.
- **Data input.** These programmes support text, number, date and logic fields. Variable-length memo fields allow the user to add notes to records.
- **Forms and views.** Having inputted data, it is useful to look at it. The **form view** looks like a paper form. It customises the view by rearranging fields and adding lines and boxes. A **table view** looks like a spreadsheet and lets the user access many records at once.
- **Queries and reports.** Querying is a method by which groups of records can be displayed. With **query by form** (QBF), a form pops up and users type in the values they require in the appropriate fields. **Query by example** (QBE) allows the user to deal with more complex instances to link files and add fields.

Questions

1. What might be the problems in interrogating databases?

2. Using your own organisation as an example, discuss how databases are used to support administration systems.

Financial packages

Financial packages are today an important element for nearly all types of organisations. The accounting function was the first department in most businesses to use computers extensively. The large volumes of similar transactions are well suited to being computerised. In addition to the efficiency of data handling, computerised systems have facilitated the use of the vast bank of data afforded for management reporting purposes.

For medium to large businesses accounting software may be bespoke or adapted to cater for the unique requirements of the business. Smaller businesses can utilise low-cost standardised packages written for personal computers, such as those offered by Sage or Pegasus.

Accounting databases (see Figure 27.6) are classified into two types of file:

- **master file** – information that identifies the data subject and is common for all transactions, for example name and address
- **transaction file** – information concerning each transaction, for example date, reference and amount paid.

Data subjects recorded on master files are referred to using a data key, such as an account number for ledger accounts and a payroll reference number in the case of an employee. Data keys greatly speed up the input of data but also allow ledger accounts to be logically structured for reporting purposes. To ensure all staff are coding transactions correctly and consistently, it is standard practice for the financial accountant to issue an account code list for nominal ledger purposes. This list provides the basic structure for the accounts system and is designed to suit business reporting needs, having regard to business activities and organisational structure. Typical features include income and expenditure codes that are common across the business, with function or location codes which enable transactions to be analysed by department (alternatively called profit centres or cost centres).

Case Study

Sage Accounting

Sage Accounting comprises accounting, payroll, time and billing, management and accounting software for all types of business organisations, in every sector, whatever their size.

The UK's best-selling accounting software is Sage 50. It is based upon an integrated approach to business which makes maximum use of accounting data. By making all of the facts and figures readily available, the organisation can benefit from the sharing of crucial information which enables all managers quickly to assess the current trading situation, and act to solve problems or seize business opportunities. For example, marketing managers could analyse trends more quickly. Sales can see who their best and worst customers are, and adjust their service levels. Sage 50 is a versatile accounting tool that deals with sales and purchases, stock control and order processing. It also generates invoices, statements, reports and sales letters.

Accounting packages simplify complex accounting tasks, eliminate repetitive routines and speed up procedures for delivering new levels of efficiency. For users, these packages

Accounting module	Master file details	Transactions	Output
Sales ledger accounting	Details of customers: • account number • name • address • bank details • credit limit	Sales invoices Cash received: • date • details • reference • value	Sales invoices Statements of account Sales journal Cash receipts list Analysis of sales by: • customer • sales area • product, etc. Age debtor analysis
Purchase ledger accounting	Details of suppliers: • account number • name • address • bank details	Purchase invoices Cheque payments • date • details • reference • value	Purchase journal Cheques and remittance advice Aged creditor analysis
Stock control	Details of stock: • reference no • description • supplier • unit of measure • control levels	Quantity and value: • receipts • issues • allocations	Stock movement enquiries Reorder lists Stock take lists
Payroll	Employee details: • payroll number • name • address • pay rates • tax code	Pay details: • hours worked • wages paid • tax and national insurance deducted	Payslip Bank transfer details Payroll summary, analysed by department End of year details P60 and P45
Nominal ledger	Account details: • account number • name • analysis code for reporting	Transactions from: • purchases • sales • payroll • stock movements • cash transactions	Account enquiries Trial balance Financial reports

Figure 27.6 *Computer modules for accounting*

enable them to develop a much tighter control over accounting procedures and practices.

Questions

1. Who are the users of accounting packages?

2. What are the benefits of using them?

3. How will such packages contribute to more efficient business operations around various parts of a business organisation?

Statistical packages

As well as using spreadsheets for presentation and interpretation of data, there are a number of statistical packages which lend themselves to the analysis of different sets of data, the most famous of which is SPSS. SPSS is a large company that delivers reporting, analysis and modelling software with a mission to drive forward the widespread use of statistics. Its primary markets are business intelligence and scientific research. SPSS packages can be used for survey analyses, quality control and forecasting, They allow business managers and researchers to use statistics for decision-making without having to be a mathematician.

Internal and external use of electronic communications

The purpose of **e-mail** (electronic mail) is to provide a means for creating, editing and distributing messages electronically. The mailbox is a computer terminal linked to a telephone network; it can put messages into the system and store messages that have been sent through the system. A message can be sent to several mailboxes at once, so that the system can be used also for internal memos in a company with several branches. The message will be stored in a terminal's memory until the mailbox is 'opened'.

The great benefit of e-mail is that it allows messages and data to be sent without generating paperwork. The sender simply types the message, and the system and the recipient do the rest. If he or she is out of the office, the machine can warn that person of the presence of the e-mail when the machine is switched on. An answer can be sent if appropriate. The message can, if necessary, be printed or, it can be saved in a folder for reference.

Some e-mail systems may only be local, allowing messages to be transmitted around one site using a LAN. Alternatively, an e-mail system may be connected to the telecommunications system so that it can reach other sites.

Another form of electronic communication is that of **voice mail**. Within a voice mail system, the user simples dials the system to record a message. The message can be reviewed or rerecorded daily, depending upon where the user is and what message he or she wishes to provide. The message is stored in the voice mailer's mailbox, and saved in audio form. The system then takes messages and calls. The user may access the system from his or her own phone, from any phone within the organisation or by dialling into the voice mail system from outside the host organisation.

The general term for a variety of systems that allow two or more people to communicate with each other orally and visually is that of **teleconferencing.** Telephone conferencing involves a number of individuals using hand-held phones. Loudspeaker phones allow a group of individuals to participate from one site in a hands-free conference. Videoconferencing uses cameras and screens, or the personal computer, to transmit video images. Where an organisation's staff might be many miles apart or located in different countries, this is a cheap way of saving on accommodation and time. However, one of the problems of teleconferencing is that some participants may not feel at ease with the equipment and be less willing to participate than they would otherwise do at a face-to-face meeting.

The **electronic conference** is a type of file sharing. Whereas with teleconferencing all of the participants participate at the same time, with electronic conferencing participants post messages on the agreed topic, in the same way as e-mail, except that all of the messages are shared by participants. Instead of sitting in the same room or responding at a set time, participants to the conference may read the messages over the next few days. Public electronic conference systems are called **bulletin boards**. To participate, individuals read the accumulated messages and then leave their own. Some bulletin boards provide conferencing systems called forums.

The Internet was created in 1969 as a defence network which linked the computers of a few thousand researchers and military personnel. Until recently, it was used by computer buffs or 'Netties' who wallowed in their own brand of computer jargon, but today it has become widely accessible to a growing group of users. The Internet now carries almost anything, from the late-night ramblings of a Star Trek fan, the plight of a third-world refugee and computer games software. No matter how obscure the information, it will probably exist on the Internet.

The business world has spotted the potential of the Internet with many organisations attempting to turn its potential into profit in areas such as electronic shopping, education, banking and entertainment.

The biggest spur to the development of the Internet, however, has been the realisation that it is a cheap way of communicating instantaneously with people on the other side of the world. For example, one recruitment agency in the UK has announced plans to place job adverts on the network; the main advantage being that the access offers employers the opportunity to select from a global pool of potential employees.

Different software applications

Computers and computerised databases can be used to assist in project planning. Computer programs allow projects to be broken down into a number of interrelated stages called activities. First the activities are defined and the time taken by each is estimated. Then the way in which the activities depend on each other is defined. The computer calculates the total time for the project and shows the activities which must be completed on time in order for the project not to be delayed.

For example, in the case of a project to build a new office, the activities and times might be as follows:

1. Prepare land and build foundations: 30 days.
2. Build walls: 30 days.
3. Build roof: 15 days.
4. Install equipment: 30 days.
5. Equip office: 20 days.

Activity 1 must be done first, then Activity 2, then Activity 3. However, Activities 4 and 5 – although they come after Activity 3 has finished – can be done at the same time. Therefore the total time for the project is 105 days (30 + 30 + 15 + 30), not 125 days. The computer output will also show that Activity 5 is not critical; that is, it can start late or take longer than planned without delaying the project. (See Figure 27.7.)

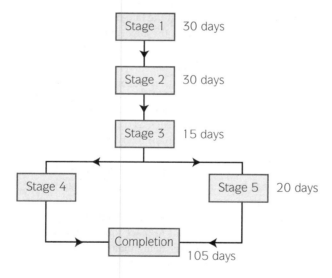

Figure 27.7 *Planning a new office*

Expert systems

Expert systems are growing in popularity. An expert system is a computer program consisting of a set of rules based upon the knowledge of experts. These rules can be used to form conclusions on information that the program is given. Imagine, for example, that all the rules that experts know about a particular subject such as geology are

inputted into a computer. Geologists could feed in all the information they have about the conditions in which particular minerals are found. The program could be used to support researchers looking for new mineral fields.

Expert systems are of particular use where a human expert is not available. One interesting use is in medicine where programs are currently being developed to aid diagnosis. The programs are designed to be used by the patient, not the doctor – the idea being that for personal and intimate problems a patient might obtain the answers to their questions more easily from a machine than from a person. It may also mean that minor problems can be diagnosed without taking up the doctor's time.

Presentation graphics

Presentation graphics, such as those produced by Harvard Graphics and Powerpoint, enable the user to produce the kinds of graphic images that are displayed during business presentations (see Figure 27.8). They comprise charts, lists of topics or key points. Though these types of programs were partly created to overcome the graphical limitations of spreadsheets, they have since developed into a valued application on their own. It is now possible to put a presentation on disk, and use this disk in another machine in conference room, lecture theatre or classroom, to provide the basis for a presentation.

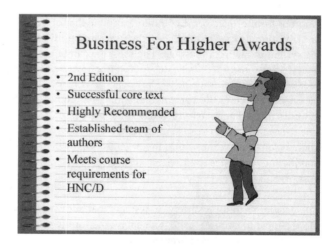

Figure 27.8 *Example of presentation graphics*

Paint and draw applications

Paint applications, such as Superpaint, specialise in allowing the user to develop or amend drawings using lines of various weights, thicknesses and textures. The user can fill in different parts of the drawing or manipulate pixels from either created or scanned pictures. Lettering can be added in various styles and fonts.

Draw applications, such as CorelDraw, specialise in producing line art, especially line drawings consisting of geometric shapes. Elements within a drawing can be enlarged or reduced and manipulated in a range of different ways. These programs are useful for logos, letterheads, etc.

TASK

Using draw, presentation or paint graphics, create a template for a presentation for other students within your teaching group, on an issue of your choice. The presentation should last ten minutes.

Many of the applications described in this chapter can be provided through an **integrated package**. For example, Microsoft Office comprises Microsoft's Access, Excel, Outlook, PhotoEditor, PowerPoint and Word.

Although information technology has great potential to liberate people from routine tasks and to provide them with new skills and powers, it can also have a number of dysfunctional effects. The computer in the workplace may limit employees' freedom of movement and stifle communication which formerly took place through conversation. For example, individuals within an office may use e-mail instead of discussing issues face to face.

Technology in itself is not a liberating force; it depends on the way in which the application of technology is managed. An employee placed in front of a computer screen carrying out routine operations may feel alienated and powerless.

K. Weick has identified the following five deficiencies of working with computers, which can lead to a chaotic understanding of the world.

1. **Action deficiencies.** The operator works with symbols on a screen, which are representations of the real world. The operator is thus divorced from real-world sights, sounds and actions.

2. **Comparison deficiencies.** The operator has to rely on one uncontradicted source of information – his or her computer terminal. Operators cannot move around, looking at things from different angles and perspectives.

3. **Affiliation deficiencies.** Working with a screen discourages the operator from sharing ideas and discussions with other people.

4. **Deliberation deficiencies.** On the screen it is hard to separate what is important from what is unimportant.

5. **Consolidation deficiencies.** Material on the screen does not look like work in progress. It presents a static picture rather than an on-going work-flow that needs to be built on and worked at.

These considerations are highly important. More and more people are engaged in activities involving the use of IT communications systems. These systems have tremendous potential to integrate work and to enhance fruitful independence in organisations. Increasingly, new systems are being developed which enable integration of software applications.

A major breakthrough in modern computing came with the development of graphical user interfaces (GUIs or 'gooies'). GUIs are designed to make technology easier to understand and use, and in so doing they have changed the face of computers. A GUI presents the user with a series of small pictures called icons which represent the various options available. A computer mouse is used to move an arrow around the screen and select the appropriate icon for the desired action. At the press of a key, the screen then redraws itself to show the next set of options. If the user has selected word processing, for example, the screen will change to provide a second series of options, and each option chosen will lead to a further set of options.

Window systems, such as Windows 98, go one stage further, giving the same type of graphical interface, but allowing the user to carry out several tasks simultaneously. For example, the user could be writing a document in the word-processing window while carrying out some other function at the same time in another window.

Today's book and laptop computers are light and easy to transport, and can easily be linked to vast communications networks. Hardware manufacturers, such as Apple, IBM and Motorola, have developed products that are compatible with all of the major software packages.

CONSIDERATIONS

There is no shortage of hardware and software designed to facilitate communication. However, the way in which an organisation is constructed may well determine their effectiveness. An organisation may have the best available resources, but unless it has an effective structure for its communications, its communication system may fail.

It is possible to identify a number of basic requirements for an effective communications network (see Figure 27.9). For example, it is important that:

• messages reach all of the individuals required
• both senders and recipients need to share an understanding of what is being communicated, and be able to act upon it
• channel sizes should be adequate. For example, a database which forms part of a management information system needs to be able to handle all of the enquiries made of it at any one time. If the channel size is not large enough, then organisations will need to introduce an organised queuing system. However, if communication channels are frequently overloaded, there is a strong case for the redesign of the system.

```
Hardware    ⎫
+           ⎪
Software    ⎪   Integrated effectively through
+           ⎬   organisation of communication
Databases   ⎪   = Effective system
+           ⎪   and information system to
People      ⎪   meet organisational needs
+           ⎪
Procedures  ⎭
```

Figure 27.9 *Construction of an organisation's communication system*

Costs

Costs and their feasibility come into the equation for an information system at an early stage where it has to be decided if the proposals are likely to provide a cost-effective solution to a problem. Costs will have a bearing on the design of the system as well as how it operates. At an early stage a feasibility study will help to justify spending substantial amounts, by showing whether the investment will create value for money.

The role of the systems analyst is central to the introduction of a new computer system, or for the updating of an existing one. The analyst has to determine through a project feasibility study whether the investment would be worthwhile, initially through an estimate of the likely costs against the benefits likely to be made. At the end of the process the analyst will produce a feasibility study which will make recommendations relating to the new proposals and the existing system.

Before any project gets underway, a full systems study is undertaken. This involves providing:

• a detailed examination of the area of business under review
• the recording of facts and information relating to the proposals
• an analysis of the strengths and weaknesses of the current system as well as the requirements for the new system
• a systems specification, identifying the costs and benefits of the new system.

Because of the high costs of running a management information system as well as the cost of salaries of those who would be managing and maintaining it, the introduction of a new system has to be meticulously planned. Following the completion of a project feasibility report, estimates have to be made for the effort required to develop the system as well as all of the other costs involved. As work is undertaken, progress should be monitored against these budget forecasts so that any discrepancies can be easily identified. As a project develops frequent meetings should monitor the project against target dates and installation costs, using control tools such as project planners, critical-path analysis and Gantt charts (see Chapter 20, pages 485–490).

Maintenance

Whenever a system is installed, it is likely to require further changes – **systems maintenance** – over time. Because a system's environment changes, it is important to manage this component as new data will have to be stored, retrieved in different ways, new computations have to be made and new reports generated. This maintenance could be done by staff involved with systems development or by technicians specialising in maintenance.

As each system is changed there is an increasing likelihood of errors. Systems have to be tested and retested to maintain their integrity. Testing through planned maintenance is called **staged maintenance**, which extends the life of systems by helping to ensure that errors do not creep in over time.

Virtually all facilities within an IT system require some form of maintenance programme. This is in order to:

- prevent failure
- ensure performance
- ensure reliability.

In order to optimise frequency maintenance, it is important to decide when and how a machine is to be maintained (see Figure 27.10). On the one hand, the cost of maintenance means that it is advisable to have infrequent maintenance checks, while on the other, the costs of failure in terms of loss of productive capacity, encourage frequent maintenance.

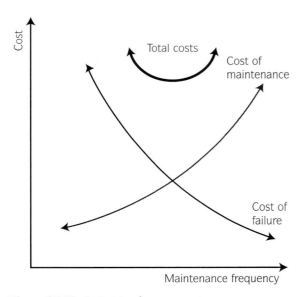

Figure 27.10 *Optimising frequency maintenance*

Training

In order to use all the hardware and software individuals require training. It is important that users understand how each application works, as well as how to use any system to achieve maximum benefits from it. Sometimes software is accompanied by guides and manuals which provide a reference source helping the user to use each package. Other software might come with either a tutorial program or some computer-based training. This can introduce the user to the basic features of the software.

Almost all of the popular software packages have become the subject matter of books. Bookshops and libraries are full of computer-based titles, and guides to different types of applications software.

Organisations, colleges and computer training agencies all provide a range of courses dealing in various software. Some organisations employ consultants to provide authoritative training and support for their employees.

FURTHER READING

Parker, C. and Case, T., *Management Information Systems*, 2nd edition, McGraw-Hill, 1993.

Lucey, T., *Management Information Systems*, 7th edition, DPP, 1995.

Murdick, R.G., with Munson, J.C., *MIS Concepts and Design*, 2nd edition, Prentice-Hall, 1986.

Kroenke, D. and Hatch, R., *Business Information Systems: An Introduction*, 5th edition, McGraw-Hill, 1993.

Harry, M., *Information Systems in Business*, Pitman, 1994.

Harrison, D., *Business Information Processing*, Pitman, 1986.

Laudon, K.C. and Price Laudon, J., *Management Information Systems: A Contemporary Perspective*, 2nd edition, Macmillan, 1991.

Knight, J., *Management Information Systems,* Pitman, 1996.

Robson, W., *Strategic Management and Information Systems*, Pitman, 1996.

Wilson, D., *Management Information*, Butterworth Heinemann, 1993.

Bloomfield, B., *Information Technology and Organisation: Strategies, Networks and Integration*, Oxford University Press, 1997.

Willocks, L.P., *Managing IT as a Strategic Resource*, McGraw-Hill, 1997.

Field, C., *New Strategies for Marketing Information Technology*, Chapman & Hall, 1996.

Bowers, D.S., *From Data to Database*, Chapman & Hall, 1992.

Wilkinson, C., *Information Technology on the Office,* 2nd edition, Macmillan, 1996.

Lester, G., *Business Information Systems,* Vol. 1, Pitman, 1992.

ASSIGNMENT

The purpose of this assignment is for you to find out how management information is used for planning activities within the organisation you attend, your place of work, or another organisation of your choice where you are able to conduct an investigation.

Task 1

Find out the information requirements of your chosen organisation.

Task 2

Find out the type of management information system used within your chosen organisation. Describe the different types of information (strategic/tactical/internal/external, paper-based/electronic, etc.) used. Explain how data are selected and the issues involved in the effective use of data.

Task 3

Find out the type of information available to different levels of managers. Using a case example, describe one situation which explains how that information is used on a daily basis.

Task 4

Explain how information is monitored for accuracy and relevance. Find out the limitations of the organisation's MIS. How could these limitations be overcome?

Task 5

Describe the role of training in supporting the IT needs of staff involved with the MIS.

Task 6

Identify one software package and describe how it is used to meet the needs of the clients of the organisation.

UNIT

8

Business
Strategy

Strategic Planning

This chapter examines the process of strategic planning. It explains the terminology used in strategic planning, considers why organisations need to undertake corporate planning and how such strategies are devised. The differing approaches to strategy and the planning process in small, medium and large organisations are also discussed.

On completion of the chapter you should be able to examine the process of strategic planning. To achieve this you must demonstrate the ability to:

- explain the role and setting up of objectives in the planning process

- discuss the strengths and weaknesses of the classical/rational, incremental and emergent approaches to strategy.

A STRATEGIC THINKER

Bernard Ladet is one of the most highly respected farmers in France (see Figure 28.1). His approach to farming his land represents the key aspects of corporate strategy which are outlined in this chapter. Bernard's land is located in the Cevennes region of France which is famous for its speciality *oignons doux* – sweet onions – which are a delicacy to eat and which don't make you cry when you peel them.

When Bernard Ladet first started to cultivate his land 35 years ago he took a long-term view. He recognised that agriculture is a cyclical business with good years and bad years. One year a crop does well, a few years later it may be in the doldrums. Bernard therefore decided to use his land to grow a range of popular items which would be dependable and would always have a ready market. He planted a variety of different types of fruit trees: cherries, apricots, plums, apples and pears; as well as strawberry and raspberry plants and vines for making wine. He also planted potatoes and *oignons doux*. In addition, he invested in hens to provide a ready supply of eggs, and planted pine trees to provide shelter for his land as well as a long-term investment.

Over the past 25 years his strategic overview, coupled with a continuous attention to detail has proved effective. Today, his trees are the finest in the region and bear a copious amount of fruit. His vines give a high-quality wine and every year he has an abundant crop of potatoes and his onions are eagerly awaited at the finest Paris restaurants. Above all, his pine trees are 25 metres high and provide a rich wood, which still provides a nest-egg for a rainy day.

From time to time, Bernard has altered the proportions of his land dedicated to different types of produce depending on medium-term conditions in the market. However, he has never had to take any panic measures. Everything has worked to the master plan which he set down 35 years ago. Bernard has ensured that his plan is a flexible one by continually developing it in the light of on-going evaluation procedures. Bernard Ladet typifies the visionary with a keen grasp of the master plan. His approach is an ideal representation of strategic thinking.

Figure 28.1 *Bernard Ladet – strategic visionary*

STRATEGIC CONTEXTS AND TERMINOLOGY

The role of strategy

Business strategy is concerned with developing a clear picture of the direction an organisation needs to go in, coupled with a well thought-out plan of how to steer the organisation in the chosen direction.

Two helpful definitions of business strategy are:

> *'Strategy is the determination of the basic long-term goals and objectives of an enterprise, and the adoption of courses of action and the allocation of resources necessary for carrying out those goals.'* (A. E. Chandler, *Strategy and Structure: Chapters in the History of the American Industrial Enterprise*, 1962)

> *'Strategy involves looking at the larger picture and developing major directions for an organisation to move in. It is concerned with the Generalship of business.'* (J. Kottler, *A Force for Change*, 1994)

These definitions help us to divide the strategic process into two distinct areas:

- **ends** – setting the longer-term goals as well as the shorter-term objectives.
- **means** – taking decisions and developing the ability to achieve the ends.

Many small businesses think of strategic or long-term planning as something that is only carried out by large businesses. However, the organisations that survive and prosper are those that meet their customers' needs by providing benefits to them at prices which cover the cost of providing them and produce both sufficient profit for reinvestment and also a share of the profit or a dividend which satisfies the owners or the shareholders. To do this effectively, the management writer Peter Drucker argues that organisations need to focus on the external environment in order to create a customer. Similarly, the Harvard academic Michael Porter argues that the way a business positions itself in the marketplace is of fundamental importance. Strategy involves matching effectively the business's competences (knowledge, expertise and experience) and resources with the opportunities and threats created by the marketplace. Strategy is therefore as essential to the small as to the larger organisation. According to Drucker, strategy is what converts plans into results. In Drucker's words, strategy 'converts what you want to do into accomplishment'.

Missions

Before an organisation can devise a strategy it must know where it is going – it needs to define the direction that the strategy will be devised to pursue. In other words, all organisations require to have an aim which they seek to work towards. Today it is common practice for organisations to set out their aim in a **mission** and/or a **vision** for the organisation.

J. Thompson (1990) defines mission as 'The essential purpose of the organisation ... the nature of the business(es) it is in and the customers it seeks to serve and satisfy'.

Figure 28.2 *Newcastle United's mission includes playing attractive football*

Aspect of mission	Supporting strategy
Play attractive football	Appoint a management team capable of delivering attractive football
Win trophies	Build the team and support structures that will ensure competitive success
Satisfy supporters	Success and value for money
Satisfy shareholders	Strategies that will keep crowds paying at turnstiles and for merchandise
Improve European position	Generate the success that will support a European strategy, e.g. purchase of world-class players

Figure 28.3 *The development of a strategy from a mission*

For example, Newcastle United Plc sets out its mission in the following way:

> *'The business of Newcastle United is football – our aim is to play attractive football, to win trophies, to satisfy our supporters and shareholders and to continually improve our position as a top European club.'*

Having established this mission (aim), it becomes possible to devise a strategy. Figure 28.3 illustrates how this might be achieved.

Corporate mission needs to be clearly defined and is usually set out in the form of a **mission statement**. This is a generalised form of objective, which outlines the overriding purpose of an organisation. For example, in 1962 the US President John Kennedy set out a mission for the country's space agency NASA to: 'Land a man on the moon and return him safely to earth'. Before the decade was over NASA had succeeded in both these objectives.

The mission statement of the motoring organisation the AA in the mid-1990s focused on people and service, to: 'Make AA membership truly irresistible and to be the UK's leading and most successful motoring and personal assistance organisation'. The AA has proved to be highly successful in achieving this mission so that many people think of the AA as being 'the fourth emergency service', after the fire, police and ambulance services.

Figure 28.4 *US President John Kennedy set a mission for NASA – he is shown here with astronaut John Glenn (centre) and his vice-president Lyndon Johnson (right) at Cape Canaveral*

A few years ago a Japanese motor-cycle manufacturer set itself the mission statement: 'We will crush, squash, slaughter Yamaha'. The Queens Medical Centre, in Nottingham, has this mission statement: 'To provide prompt, personal clinical care and promote the health of those served by the Queens Medical Centre. We will continue to advance as a centre of excellence in patient care, teaching and research, building on the unique features of the Queens Medical Centre'.

The mission for the organisation needs to be realistic given the organisation's existing resources and capabilities – and to provide a clear focus for organisational activity. Having a 'sense of mission' is not the same thing as having a 'mission statement'. It is possible for an organisation to have a mission statement but only a poor sense of mission. A mission statement may simply be propaganda or wishful thinking on the part of management.

The Ashridge Mission Model (created by the Ashridge Management School) sets out that mission should consist of four key elements (see Figure 28.5).

- purpose
- values
- strategy
- behaviour standards.

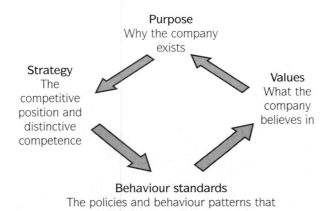

Purpose
Why the company exists

Strategy
The competitive position and distinctive competence

Values
What the company believes in

Behaviour standards
The policies and behaviour patterns that underpin the distinctive competence and the value system

Figure 28.5 *The Ashridge Mission Model*

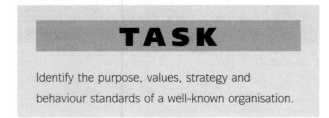

TASK

Identify the purpose, values, strategy and behaviour standards of a well-known organisation.

Visions

A vision is something more than a mission. The vision tends to be more futuristic and idealistic. The vision sets out what the organisation can become. You will often hear business and political leaders state 'I want to share my vision with you'. The vision therefore sets out an idealistic future for an organisation which hopefully can be grounded in reality.

Richard Koch (1997) defines vision as:

'An inspiring view of what a company could become, a dream about its future shape and success, a picture of a potential future for a firm, a glimpse into its Promised Land. A vision is a long-term aspiration of a leader for his or her firm, that can be described to colleagues and that will urge them on through the desert.'

Koch makes a useful distinction between mission and vision in the following way: 'Mission is why a firm exists, its role in life. Vision is a view of what the firm could become, imagining a desired future'.

Case Study

Starbucks

In the early 1970s two young Americans, Jerry Bald and Gordon Bowker, so enjoyed the coffee that they had at college in San Francisco that they wanted to turn it into a business proposition. Alfred Peet had an innovative way of roasting coffee beans that today is called 'dark roasted'. So, the two set up their own company – Starbucks – in Seattle selling coffee beans and grinding them for customers. People in Seattle were attracted to the new business, so that soon the entrepreneurs were able to buy their own roasting plant.

Howard Schultz, a sales representative for one of the equipment suppliers, first visited Seattle in early 1980 and liked the idea. Schultz was certain that if he worked with Bald and Bowker that he would be able to spread the business across the USA. In 1982 he became the company's marketing manager.

The vision

In 1983, on a visit to Milan, Schultz found that coffee bars in the city were an important meeting place. He was convinced that the idea could be translated to the US where coffee bars could become the 'Third Place' – an alternative gathering place, apart from work and home. Schultz believed that the coffee bar could replace the old-fashioned male oriented 'bar' in fulfilling this social function. However, Schultz was unable to get Bald and Bowker to share his vision. Starbucks now consisted of ten coffee bars – five in Seattle and five in San Francisco.

Schultz left the business to set up his own company in 1985 and by 1987 had three coffee shops, where people drank coffee, talked and ate cookies. Then Starbucks coffee shops in Seattle went on the market and Schultz snapped them up for $4 million, and at 34 became the president of the company.

The mission

Starbucks mission statement is as follows: 'To establish Starbucks as the premier purveyor of the finest coffee in the world while maintaining our uncompromising principles as we grow'. To support this mission the company has set a set of guiding principles, which are:

- to provide a great work environment and treat each other with respect and dignity
- to embrace diversity as essential to the way we do business
- to apply the highest standards of excellence to the purchasing, roasting and fresh delivery of our coffee
- to develop enthusiastically satisfied customers all of the time
- to contribute positively to our communities and our environment
- to recognise that profitability is essential to our future success.

These guiding principles stem from a **set of beliefs** about the way in which the company should run. They have evolved from Schultz's personal feelings about business. Schultz came from a poor family, and his approach to his new family of employees was strongly influenced by his own father's experience of employment. His father had broken a leg and received no pay while recovering. Schultz developed a strong belief that organisations should care for their workers. He also believed that if employees are going to be committed to their organisation and the products they sell they had to feel wanted, and that the company believed in them and cared for them.

Questions

1. What was Schultz's vision? When and how was he able to put this vision into action?

2. How is the vision in this case distinct from the mission?

3. How do the guiding principles support the mission?

An organisation's vision provides a key role in helping it to build a bridge between its past, present and future (see Figure 28.6). A vision therefore needs to be both inspirational and realistic. For example, Walt Disney's vision was simply 'to make people happy'.

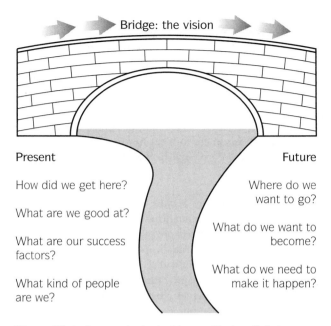

Figure 28.6 *An organisation's vision enables it to link the past, present and future*

Discussion point

If you were going to create a vision for an organisation that you are a member of, what would that vision be?

Strategic intent

Once an organisation knows where it wants to go (mission/vision), the emphasis should shift to getting there. How the organisation gets there depends on plans. These are called **strategies** and their purpose is to achieve the aim.

The strategy of an organisation needs to be in line with its **strategic intent** which is 'the overall medium- to long-term strategic objective of a company'. For example, Coca-Cola's objective of having its drink 'within arm's length of every consumer in the world', or Mercedes Benz's strategic intent – 'We wish everybody worldwide to own or aspire to own a Mercedes Benz'. Strategic intent should have a time-frame of at least ten years.

Hamel and Prahalad ('Strategic Intent', *Harvard Business Review*, 1989) argue that:

'companies that have risen to global leadership over the past 20 years invariably began with ambitions that were out of all proportion to their resources and capabilities. But they created an obsession with winning at all levels of the organisation and then sustained that obsession over the 10- to 20-year quest for global leadership. We term this obsession "strategic intent".'

Hamel and Prahalad give examples of strategic intent including Canon's intent to 'Beat Xerox', Honda striving to 'become a second Ford', and Komatsu to 'Encircle Caterpillar'.

Strategic intent, they say, is more than just an ambition, it also includes an active management process which focuses 'the organisation's attention on the essence of winning; motivating people by communicating the value of the target; leaving room for individual and team contributions; sustaining enthusiasm by providing new operational definitions as circumstances change; and using intent consistently to guide resource allocations'.

Goals and objectives

Mission, vision and strategic intent are all big concepts for an organisation. The organisation then needs to be able to focus these big ideas into practical steps. This is known as the **goals** and **objectives**. Traditionally, the term goal was used to describe the longer-term, open-ended aims of an organisation, whereas objectives were more focused on short-term, specific objectives. Today this is no longer the case. However, in many business books the terms goals and objectives are used interchangeably. To avoid confusion in your own writing decide how you are going to use these terms and remain consistent. It might be helpful here to make a distinction between:

- goals, as general objectives, and
- specific objectives.

John Thompson (1990) defines objectives as 'desired states or results, linked to particular time scales, and concerning such things as size or type of organisation, the nature and variety of the areas of interest, and levels of success'. He also makes a distinction between 'long-term objectives' which relate to the desired performance and results on an on-going basis; and 'short-term objectives' which are concerned with the near-term performance targets that the organisation desires to reach in progressing towards its long-term objectives.

The mission as a generalised aim for a whole organisation needs to be translated into practical objectives at each level within an organisation. Objectives therefore provide greater precision and clarity about strategic intent. The more specific these objectives can be the better.

Objectives are targets that must be achieved in order to realise the aims of the organisation so as to arrive at the chosen destination. An organisation sets objectives to break down the mission into component parts that can be identified, measured and achieved. Many objectives can be established in a clear and specific way so that they can guide the actions of the individuals that make up an organisation. Wherever possible, therefore, it is important to create specific objectives. Many of these objectives can be expressed in quantities, for example quantified objectives for responding to consumer complaints, quantified objectives for the reduction of waste, etc. However, you should bear in mind that some objectives are more easy to quantify than others, for example in running a school it may be possible to quantify objectives related to examination results, but it is not possible to establish quantifiable targets related to the spiritual or moral welfare of pupils, etc.

Objectives therefore need to have the following important characteristics:

- **They need to be made specific.** General objectives (goals) enable the organisation to break down the mission, vision, etc. into more manageable components. Specific objectives then help it to be even more precise. A specific objective is clear and precise. It gives direction, and it is then possible to check that the direction has been followed. For example, in a football match 'to get the ball forward' may not be a specific enough objective. To get the ball forward to the two target players is far more specific. In selling, to get Mars Bars into every confectionery retailing outlet in Britain is more specific than simply 'to get Mars products into more retail outlets'.
- **They need to be easily understood.** The managers who create objectives often play only a small part in the operationalisation of those objectives. Objectives need to be presented in clear and easy-to-understand language so that there is no ambiguity. For example, an objective 'to increase output' may lead to an increase in substandard products, when managers actually mean 'to increase the level of output of items which meet the required quality standards'.
- **They need to be widely communicated.** Today, organisational objectives frequently involve everyone in the organisation. Serious deficiencies will occur if key

objectives are not communicated widely to everyone concerned. For example, if the organisation places strong emphasis on objectives related to customer service, then these objectives need to be communicated to everyone in the organisation with an internal or external customer (i.e. every employee in the organisation). Communication of objectives needs to be closely tied up with training and development, and with communication channels in the organisation.

- **They need to be challenging** and should not be too easy to achieve. Objectives should stretch the organisation, its departments and people in a rewarding way. If objectives are set at too low a level, then they will not be taken seriously. Employees may take a minimalist approach to achieving these objectives. For example, in the 1970s the car manufacturer British Leyland had a reputation for creating low standards. Some night-shift employees were able to meet production targets quickly and then sleep or play cards for the remainder of the shift.

- **They need to be attainable.** At the same time, objectives should not be too demanding. When objectives are unattainable, this can lead to frustration and loss of commitment. People may feel that they are being given impossible demands, and thus become demotivated. Indeed, when they feel that the objectives set are 'a joke' they may deliberately set out to sabotage processes and activities.

- **They need to be measurable.** Objectives can provide a quantifiable measure of where the organisation is going. The quantified objectives should be far more precise than the broad aims which are set out in missions, visions and statements of strategic intent. By creating quantified objectives, it becomes possible to answer questions such as:
  - What do we need to do to meet the objectives?
  - How far have we come in meeting objectives?
  - Have we met the objectives?
  - What more needs to be done to meet the objectives?

Case Study

Aims (mission) and general objectives

British Waterways manages and cares for over 2000 miles of Britain's canals and rivers. It maintains canals for boating, angling and other uses. This involves:

- ensuring canals and rivers are safe places for people to enjoy
- looking after the whole environment, i.e. buildings and wildlife that are associated with canals and rivers
- endeavouring to ensure there is the right amount of water in canals and rivers
- earning income from a wide range of waterway-related businesses to reinvest in the future of the waterways.

The organisation's mission statement is:

'Our business is to manage the inland waterway system efficiently for the increasing benefit of the United Kingdom. We aim to provide a safe and high quality environment for our customers, staff and local communities. We take a commercial approach and strive for excellence in every aspect of our work. The heritage and environment of our waterways will be conserved, improved and made to work well for future generations.'

To work towards this aim, the general objectives are to:

- continue the successful growth of waterways for leisure use
- improve the waterways' environmental and heritage value
- create an adequate and secure financial base
- promote profitable use of the waterways and maximise third-party investment from private, public and voluntary sectors
- eliminate the backlog of maintenance
- increase productivity.

Questions

1. How closely do you think the general objectives fit with the mission?

2. Is there likely to be any confusion in working towards the general objectives?

3. Is there likely to be any conflict between different general objectives?

In creating the objectives for an organisation it is important to take a stakeholder perspective. Organisations consist of a range of stakeholders. The effective organisation will take its range of stakeholders into account when creating a set of objectives to support its mission. For example, the mission statement of the DIY chain Focus Do It All is: 'Focus Do It All will be the leading retailer in home enhancement, DIY, pets and craft products for families, providing quality, service and value.' The company's general objectives are then listed in terms of stakeholder requirements:

Customers: to deliver a pleasant and unique shopping experience in stores offering a combination of exclusive and innovative product lines, quality service and value for money.

Employees: to encourage a happy working environment, with the best training and internal communications programme in the industry and rewards that recognise outstanding performance.

Suppliers: to establish good working relations that rely on a mutual commitment, ensuring an efficient supply chain, where risks and rewards are shared.

City: to improve the profitability of the business by means of a successful management team and a differentiated offer, which attracts long-term relationships with investment analysts, institutional and private investors.

Specific objectives

Strategic objectives can be translated into more specific overall objectives, covering key result areas for the organisation. Peter Drucker in *The Practice of Management* (1994) identifies the following key result areas.

- Market standing.
- Innovation.
- Productivity.
- Physical and financial resources.
- Profitability.
- Manager performance and development.
- Employee performance and attitude.
- Public responsibility.

Specific objectives that could be drawn from some of the key result areas might include:

- to become the market leader (measured by market share) by next year (market standing)
- to increase output per head by 5 per cent within two years (productivity).

Specific objectives are often quantified objectives. As such they set out clearly what needs to be achieved to meet a required end result, for example to raise productivity by 3 per cent by the end of March, to achieve a turnover of £300 000 for the year, etc. It is through the creation of specific objectives that an organisation can measure its success in working towards its aims. Specific objectives are thus the milestones on the way to achieving organisational objectives and aims.

Case Study

3M's specific objectives

In one year 3M set itself the following set of specific objectives.

- Generate half its sales revenues outside the USA.
- Reduce the manufacturing cycle time by 50 per cent.
- Create US$5 billion sales from products developed within the last five years.
- Maintain research and development at high levels (running at 6.9 per cent of sales which was double the US average).
- Cut by one-third the time taken to get innovations to the market within four years.
- Reduce unit costs by 10 per cent in real terms within four years.

Questions

1. Why might these objectives have been helpful to the organisation?

2. What problems might they have caused?

3. Can you identify similar quantifiable objectives for a UK organisation?

4. Comment on the appropriateness of the objectives outlined.

There are three ways of establishing specific objectives:

- **By previous performance.** By looking at what has been achieved in the past, it becomes possible to establish appropriate specific objectives for the future. Of course, the improving organisation will want to improve on past performance.
- **By comparison with competitors.** Looking at what competitors are achieving is always a useful yardstick for establishing specific objectives.
- **Comparison against norms.** Specific objectives can be established as a result of detailed research into what is possible, taking advice from specialists and consultants, informed thinking, etc.

Although many people think that objectives should be measurable, so that their success, or otherwise can be identified, this is not always the case. Johnson and Scholes

(1998) state that 'open' statements of objectives can be just as helpful as 'closed' ones. They believe that open aims and objectives can play a crucial role in focusing strategy. They quote the example of open-ended mission statements. Statements such as 'to be a leader in technology' are not easily measurable, but they concentrate thinking within an organisation. However, Johnson and Scholes agree that closed objectives are essential in many planning situations and are particularly important where there is no scope for getting things wrong.

Specific objectives can be translated down to the lowest level of operational activity. For example, senior managers establish divisional objectives, and divisional managers then translate these into departmental and functional objectives.

Figure 28.7 *A hierarchy of objectives*

Core competences

Organisations need to do well those things that are important in their line of business. For example, Mars is a very successful producer of chocolate and petfoods. It has developed competences in producing these items. Organisations therefore need to identify the core competences and ensure that these are carried out in an excellent way. For example, Guinness has been particularly successful because it has shown exceptional competence in marketing and branding. In pharmaceuticals, research and development is a very important core competence. In

retailing, buying and merchandising are particularly important core competences.

An organisation's success therefore lies in:

- identifying its existing core competences
- identifying the core competences required by the market
- identifying the core competences required to be successful in production
- identifying the core competences of competitors
- building on its core competences so that they match the requirements of the market, and in production, and more than match those of competitors.

Mintzberg, Quinn and Ghoshal (1995) argue that: 'The distinctive competence of an organisation is more than what it can do; it is what it can do particularly well'. Mintzberg *et al.* write that it is important for organisation's to identify what they do well and then to build on this strength. Many organisations fail to do so. They provide an example to show the importance of building on core competence:

> *'Tacitly defining a typewriter as a replacement for a fountain pen as a writing instrument rather than as an input-output device for word processing is the explanation provided by hindsight for the failure of the old-line typewriter companies to develop before IBM did the electric typewriter and the computer-related input-output devices it made possible. The definition of product which would lead to identification of transferable skills must be expressed in terms of the market needs it may fill rather than the engineering specifications to which it conforms.'*

What organisations need to do therefore is to match market opportunity with their core competences.

An important ingredient of corporate strategy is to define the **scope** of an organisation's activities, i.e. the areas that it concentrates on. The scope usually relates to:

- a range of goods and services, for example confectionery and soft drinks
- not-for-profit activities, such as providing shelter for homeless people
- core markets, for example the UK, western Europe and Canada.

The scope of an organisation will both serve to define the core competencies of the organisation, and be defined by the core competencies of the organisation. 'You focus on what you do well, what you do well determines your focus'.

However, the ability to make a product well also depends on having high-quality people, equipment, marketing and other systems. Core competencies therefore relate both to products, to processes and to people and other resources.

A classic example of an organisation that has focused on its core competencies is Coca-Cola. Coca-Cola recognised that if it was going to win global market leadership, then it would need to stick to what it did best, i.e. making soft drinks. Coca-Cola concentrates on its most profitable lines, a process known in business as 'sticking to the knitting'. In 1984, 77 per cent of Coca-Cola's operating income came from soft drinks. Today, the figure is 97 per cent. By selling off businesses not sharing the same attractive financial fundamentals as the soft drinks business Coca-Cola now operates only in the high-return business.

Coca-Cola is successful because it has developed the right systems – relationships with suppliers, and buyers; because it has developed excellence in marketing; because it has a 'magic formula' for producing Coca-Cola; because it has mastered mass production techniques, etc. These represent some of the core competencies of the company. Coca-Cola focuses on its existing lines and processes because it knows that it does these things well. It would be foolhardy, for example, to branch out into making ball-point pens, running supermarket chains, or into the entertainment business.

Case Study

Heinz Europe-wide category management

Heinz is one of the most famous names in the food industry. Over time Heinz has developed a strong worldwide focus on eight global product categories in which it possesses unique competitive advantages and opportunities:

- foodservice
- infant feeding
- ketchup, sauces and condiments
- weight control
- seafood
- pet products
- frozen foods
- convenience meals.

In business it makes sense to concentrate on what you do best – your best lines. All organisations therefore need to build organisational structures which make it easy to:

- concentrate on best lines
- identify new opportunities arising in these areas
- channel resources and initiatives into best lines and particularly into new opportunities
- effectively manage best lines and opportunities
- encourage innovation and a 'can do' approach.

In the late 1990s Heinz introduced Project Millennia to enable the organisation to adapt and change in the way that would yield highest possible returns. As part of its worldwide reorganisation and growth initiative, Heinz unveiled plans to focus on Europe-wise category management of its core businesses. Products and markets which offer the greatest potential for future growth and return on investments benefit from this category management approach, while product development, manufacturing, sales and marketing are directed to exploit opportunities in the most cost-effective manner.

By using this new approach, Heinz is able to respond quickly to changing consumer patterns on a Europe-wide scale. If, for example, tomato-flavoured pizza bases prove to be popular with an individual country's customers, then Heinz has the operational systems and marketing strategies quickly to meet this area of growth at a pan-European level.

Heinz's forty operating units within Europe have recently been formed into five new business organisations.

1. European Grocery
   Main products: soups, beans and bean meals, pasta and pasta meals, ketchup, condiments, dressings, puddings, spreads and fillers.

2. European Foodservice
   Main products: bulk packs of soups, beans, ketchup, salad cream, dressings, tomato products and tuna, individual sachets/pots of ketchup, salad cream, dressings, sugar, salt, beverages, jams and other preserves.

3. European Retail Frozen and Chilled foods
   Main products: pizzas and related products, frozen ready meals, desserts, ice cream and bagel bites.

4. European Seafood
   Main products: canned tuna, salmon, mackerel, sardines and other seafood products.

5. European Infant Feeding
   Main products: canned and jarred babyfoods, infant formula

milks, dry cereal, babyfoods, rusks, baby juices, infant feeding accessories and adult nutritional products.

The decision to divide the business into these categories was a further staging post in the move to give greater pan-European focus to operating and marketing strategies. Sales, however, continue to have a 'country' focus.

One of the main reasons for changing the organisational structure has been that Heinz can now look at its categories on a pan-European basis making sure that resources are directed where the greatest prospects of growth and return lie.

One of the basic facts of business life which relates to large-scale production is that if an organisation can gain the greatest share of a market, it will be able to produce at lower unit costs than rival producers of similar products. It is not hard to see why. One of Project Millennia's aims for Heinz has been consolidation in order to become the lowest cost food producer in Europe.

Questions

1. What are Heinz's core competencies?

2. How has Heinz focused on developing these core competencies?

3. How will economies of scale help to ensure the success of Heinz?

Strategic architecture

The term strategic architecture refers to the process of building sets of interlinking competences that will enable an organisation to develop competitive advantage.

Organisations therefore need to identify the main sources of competitive advantage in the sector or market segment in which they are operating, for example having the fastest distribution links, the most rapid response to consumer requirements, the most reliable components, etc. They then need to design and build the core competences which enable them to win and maintain competitive advantage – the **strategic architecture**.

Richard Koch (1995) gives the example of Marks & Spencer as being an organisation that (up until the late 1990s) had developed excellent architecture. He showed

that Marks & Spencer ensured that its buying and merchandising functions remained absolutely first class; because in retailing nothing is as important as buying and merchandising. 'A retailer with excellent skills in finance, information technology, store management, credit management and marketing, but mediocre buying and merchandising, would be less successful than one with excellent buying and merchandising and mediocre competence in all the other functions.'

In other industries, the key to success has been in:

- skill at exploration (for example oil and gas)
- competence in recruitment and training (for example auditing and consulting)
- competence in site selection and judging the business cycle (for example property).

Quinn, Doorley and Paquette ('Technology in services: rethinking strategic focus', *Sloan Management Review*, 1990) argue that organisations today should structure around their core competences. They show how services have come to dominate the value chains of nearly all companies. This is because as manufacturing has become automated, the major value added to a product has increasingly moved away from the point where raw materials are converted into useful form and towards the styling features, perceived quality, subjective taste and marketing presentation, i.e. service activities.

Quinn *et al.* argue that management wastes a lot of time on issues which are not related to these essential service activities. Organisations are failing to focus and concentrate attention on the core competences which can generate strategic advantage. Quinn *et al.* recommend that managers should define each activity in the value-creation system as a service; carefully analyse each such service activity to determine whether the company can become the best in the world at it; and eliminate, outsource, or joint-venture the activity to achieve 'best in world' status when this is not possible internally. Organisations therefore should focus on those areas where they have genuine core competences which give competitive advantage. The successful organisation of the future would build its architecture around interlinking core competences which are the very best. These changes should lead to a more compact and focused organisation.

Hamel and Prahalad ('The core competence of the corporation', *Harvard Business Review*, 1990) believe that the following three tests can be applied to identify core competence in a company:

1. The core competence should provide potential access to a wide variety of markets.

2. The core competence should make a significant contribution to the perceived customer benefits of the end product.

3. The core competence should be difficult for competitors to imitate.

They state that few companies are likely to build world leadership in more than five or six fundamental competences.

Hamel and Prahalad use the term 'core products' to refer to the tangible link between identified core competences and end-products. 'Core products' are thus the physical embodiments of one or more core competences. Honda's engines, for example, are core products – lynchpins, better design and development skills – that ultimately lead to a variety of end-products.

Hamel and Prahalad say that 'senior management should spend a significant amount of its time developing a corporate-wide strategic architecture that establishes objectives for competence building'. They define strategic architecture as a 'road map of the future that identifies which core competencies to build and their constituent technologies'. They show that the strategic architecture would be different for every company but that it is helpful to think of a tree, 'of the corporation organised around core products and, ultimately core competences'. Developing strong roots depends on having a clear understanding of the core competences and, of course, these roots would need nurturing and protecting.

Strategic control

Control is always an important function of organisational design. Nowhere is this more important than in strategy. Control processes make it possible to check that objectives have been met, and to make adjustments to strategy as and when appropriate.

Peter Drucker in *The Practice of Management* states that to be able to control performance a manager needs to be clear about objectives and must be able to measure performance and results against these objectives. Therefore it should be seen as essential practice to supply managers with clear and common measurements in all key areas of a business. These measurements need not be rigidly quantitative, nor need they be exact. But they have to be clear, simple and rational. They have to be relevant and direct attention and efforts where they should go. They have to be reliable and understandable. Each manager should have the information he or she needs to measure performance and should receive it soon enough to make any changes necessary for the desired results. In addition, this information should go to the manager directly and not to his or her superior. It should be the means of self-control, not a tool of control from above.

The creation of objectives, and systematic appraisal of performance, and measurement of performance enables the general aims of the organisation to be translated into operational programmes and activities which can be controlled by individuals at all levels within the organisation (see Figure 28.8).

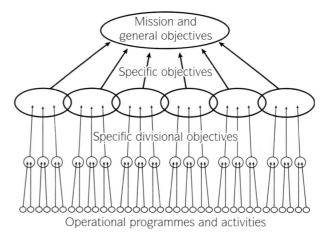

Figure 28.8 *Creating control mechanisms through objectives at every level within the organisation*

Johnson and Scholes (1998) show that control and information systems need to be used as a means of implementing strategy and for analysing strategic performance. Control needs to take place at three levels within the organisation:

- strategic level control
- management level control
- operational level control.

They give the example of a move into a new overseas market which would need controlling 'at a strategic level by an overall budget, at the management level by monitoring expenditures and motivating employees, and also at the operational level by ensuring that routine tasks are properly performed'.

To create effective control systems within an organisation, 'responsibility centres' will need to be created to take responsibility for specific aspects of strategy. The kinds of analysis that an organisation will need for control purposes are shown in Figure 28.9.

Types of analysis	Used to control
Financial analysis	
Ratio analysis	Aspects of profitability
Variance analysis	Costs or revenues
Cash budgeting	Cash flow
Capital budgeting	Investment
Market analysis	
Demand analysis	Competitive position
Market share analysis	Competitive position
Sales analysis	
Sales budgets	Effectiveness of selling
Human resource analysis	
Labour turnover	Workforce stability
Work/output measurement	Productivity
Physical resource analysis	
Product inspection	Quality

Figure 28.9 *Analysis for control purposes*

AN EVALUATION OF THE STRATEGY FRAMEWORK

The reason why and ways in which corporate planning and strategies are devised

Some organisations operate in a reactive way. In other words, they do not plan ahead; they simply respond to changes as and when they occur. This is a non-strategic approach. On page 613 we looked at the example of Bernard Ladet, a French farmer, who developed a long-term plan for his business from the outset.

Strategic planning is thus an important management tool to deal with the business environment by thinking your way to the organisation you want. It is an important management technique for leading from the top by mobilising all the component parts of an organisation and its resources behind an agreed corporate plan.

The strategic plan deals with the most important question for the organisation: 'Where are we going and how are we going to get there?'. Creating a strategic plan enables the organisation and its managers to shape the future. Strategic planning is holistic (i.e. dealing with the whole of the organisation). It is concerned with the fundamental issues involving the direction that the organisation takes.

Strategic planning is concerned with the big decisions that an organisation makes and primarily involves longer term planning, i.e. for four or five years. However, this does not mean that strategic planning needs to be made entirely at the centre or top of an organisation. As Michael Goold of the Ashridge Strategic Management Centre has said:

> 'In most large, multi-business companies, the trend today is towards decentralisation ... the essence of decentralisation is to locate primary responsibility for proposing strategy and achieving results with the general managers of individual profit centres or businesses, not with central management. The purpose is to ensure that strategies are based on detailed knowledge of specific product-markets, to increase business level 'ownership' of strategy and reduce the overload on the chief executive and his or her team ...'

In creating a strategic plan an organisation should start by seeking answers to four basic questions.

1. How did we get here? This involves reviewing the history and development of the organisation to identify what it currently does, and its current strengths and weaknesses.

2. Where do we want to go?

3. How will we get there?

4. How can we make our plans work?

The end purpose of strategic planning is to gain a competitive edge over rivals by strategically positioning the organisation in the right markets at the right time, securing rapid and profitable growth during good times, or survival in bad times.

Kerry Napuk (1996) has identified the characteristics of strategies as follows:

1. *They are rooted in the outside world which means you have to understand markets, opportunities, changes, trends and external threats.*
2. *Strategies are concerned with the product or service mix to be produced or offered and the markets in which the products or services will be sold.*
3. *Strategies often involve complex decisions that deal with a high degree of uncertainty.*
4. *Strategies must be flexible, requiring you to be sensitive and responsive to market changes.*
5. *Strategy is not about making a single document but rather it is a continual process of adapting to an ever-changing environment.*
6. *Strategies usually result in on-going improvements over time.*
7. *Strategy can also be defined as an action plan to deal with the commercial environment.*

It is helpful to make a distinction between strategic planning and strategic management. Strategic planning is the process of making strategic choices while strategic management is about producing the results from those choices. The end point of strategic action is to create the right combination of new products, markets and technologies that produce the right results. An organisation can create this combination by expanding successful existing products and businesses, adding new products or services, and by penetrating new markets, while dropping less successful products and markets.

The creation of the strategic vision

Creating a strategic vision is a very important step forward. It can only be done when the organisation has a clear understanding of itself ('who are we?'), and what it will be able to achieve in the medium to long term (mission). The vision sets out what the organisation would like to achieve. For example, Great North Eastern Railways (GNER) as a newly formed rail company in the late 1990s has the vision of 'creating the UK's ultimate travel experience' for the customer. This vision was created in conjunction with a set of core values and a mission statement as shown in Figure 28.10.

Who are we?	Core values		
	Customer focus	Distinctive	Innovation
	Safe and secure	Consistent	Aspirational
	Reliable	Teamwork	Valuing people
What we plan to achieve and how	Mission GNER is creating a golden era of rail travel by setting the highest standards of service, speed and quality in the UK.		
The essence of our promise	Vision Creating the UK's ultimate travel experience.		

Figure 28.10 *GNER's core values, mission and vision*

Organisational mission statements

The mission statement defines the fundamental, unique purpose that sets a business apart from other firms of its type and identifies the scope of the business operations in terms of products offered and market served. The concept of a corporate mission implies that throughout a corporation's many activities there should be a common thread that corporations are better able to direct and administer their many activities.

Today, it is fashionable for large organisations to place copies of their mission statement in prominent locations in the workplace so that employees are constantly reminded of it. Very often, part of the mission relates to creating quality working relationships.

US companies are fond of creating mission statements. Some mission statements are useful if they successfully answer the following question: 'What are we, the management, trying to do for whom?'.

Mission statements need to be readable. They must make immediate sense to the people who read them. They should also be brief. Unfortunately, many mission statements are not clear and are often confusing, and may be regarded with cynicism by those who read them.

Corporate planning and corporate objectives and the relationship with operational planning

A corporate plan is a plan for the whole organisation. It is concerned with the means by which the organisation will achieve its ends. For this to happen in practice the strategy needs to be operationalised. Figure 28.11 helps to illustrate how this can happen in a large organisation which is divided up into individual businesses, divisions and units.

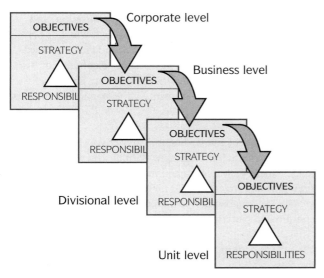

Figure 28.11 *Putting strategy into operation*

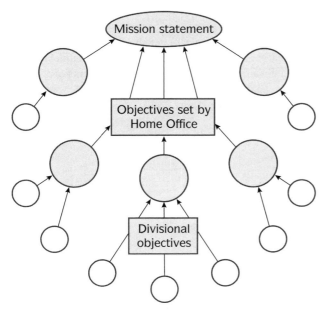

Figure 28.12 *Combining Home Office and divisional objectives*

Check your understanding

We can see how objectives, strategies and responsibilities work down an organisation by taking the example of the Nottinghamshire Police Force in the mid-1990s. Each year the Home Secretary sets National Key Objectives for the police force against which the performance of the force as a whole will be measured. The following were the five objectives set for the Nottinghamshire Force in 1995–6:

- to maintain and, if possible, increase the number of detections for violent crime

- to increase the number of detections for burglaries of people's homes

- to target and prevent crimes which are a particular local problem, including drug-related criminality, in partnership with the public and other local agencies

- to provide high visibility policing so as to reassure the public

- to respond promptly to emergency calls from the public.

Having acknowledged the key objectives set by the government, the Nottinghamshire Force agreed upon local priorities which for 1995–6 were as follows:

- to become more effective in crime detection

- to deal more effectively with telephone calls from members of the public

- to maximise the time available for officers to patrol.

These objectives were then broken down into smaller-scale objectives, for operating units and then for individual police officers within the force. The objectives were then used to produce divisional, unit and individual station plans within the force.

Objectives and target setting

Establishing objectives makes it possible to set targets within an organisation. For example, if an organisation has the objective of gaining a 20 per cent market share by 2001, then it becomes possible to establish specific targets for individuals, units, and divisions within the organisation. This could be done by creating weekly production targets for a section of a particular factory, sales targets for individual sales people, targets for the reduction of waste, etc. In the police force it is possible to set targets for the number of beat patrols that need to be carried out in a particular period of time, the minimum figure required for the detection of crimes, etc.

The targets that are set must be in line with the overall objective. They also need to be feasible and appropriate. This is why it is essential in the creation of objectives to involve a wide range of people in the decision-making process. There needs to be a free flow of communications and decision-making within the organisation. If a particular group of employees is expected to meet a target of 1000 units of output per week then they need to have the capacity and the resources to be able to meet this target. If they have been allowed a say in the establishing of the targets, then they will have been able to state whether the targets are feasible and appropriate (perhaps the target was set at too low a level).

Richard Pascale (*Managing on the Edge*, 1990) cites the example of a Ford senior manager who stated that: 'Management by objectives is not helpful. We do not want static objectives. We want a process that is obsessed with constantly improving things.' The implication here is that objectives and targets need to be more flexible.

Tom Peters (*Thriving on Chaos*, 1987) supports the need for flexibility, when he stated that:

> '*Performance evaluations, objective setting and job descriptions are three staples of management "control". All, though sound of purpose, typically become bureaucratic. They stamp in distinctions and rigidity rather than stamping them out. They impede fluidity.*'

DIFFERING APPROACHES TO STRATEGY

Classical/rational

The classical/rational view of management was based on the view that managers are able to manage the organisation in a scientific and organised way. The role of managers is to create the plans for the organisation, and the systems and control procedures through which these plans will be realised. This is a very confident view based on the assumption that managers have a clear view of changes in the external environment and are able to control the internal environment by the creation of systems and plans.

A simple view of management by objectives (MbO) fits in with the classical/rational view. Formal structures for management within an organisation are based on the setting of objectives. A clear hierarchy of objectives enables the organisation to channel its efforts in a coordinated pattern.

Chandler's definition of strategy (see page 614) fits in with the classical/rational approach. His view was based on the notion that an organisation establishes its goals and plans, and then sets out to achieve them in a linear way. There is a very clear assumption that the planner can plan for success.

Strategies can be formulated which are based on giving an organisation a clear direction. A widely used model for strategic planning is based on the three elements of strategic analysis, strategic choice and strategic implementation (see Figure 28.13).

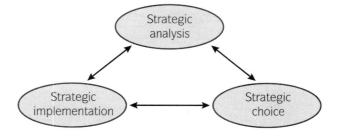

Figure 28.13 *A strategic planning model*

Strategic analysis is concerned with understanding the strategic position of an organisation, for example what sort of environment is it operating in? What is the scope of its operations? How can it match its activities to its environment? How can it match its activities to its resource capability? Does it have the systems, policies and activities that will enable it to meet its objectives? These questions are concerned with matching strategic intent and strategic reality.

Having carried out a detailed strategic analysis, then strategic planners will be faced with a number of potential choices – or alternative strategies. Having chosen a strategy, they can then put the strategy into practice – strategic implementation. It will then be necessary to monitor and evaluate the success of the chosen strategy.

This approach is based on the assumption that organisational planners are firmly in control. Of course, the reality in the modern world is that the planner seeks to manage and control, but often events move ahead, and strategies have to emerge to enable the organisation to manage change.

Case Study

Emergent strategy at ICI

Throughout the 1970s and 1980s one of the UK's biggest companies ICI had to struggle with a changing environment. The company focused on industrial chemicals which are very cyclical in nature (demand fluctuates with the trade cycle). ICI's strategy involved identifying new markets in the heavy chemicals industry and exploiting these markets. However, no sooner had it developed new products, for example new fertilisers, or gunpowder, than a foreign rival would copy the idea, so that any excess profits were short lived. Because of the nature of the product market ICI was operating in it was relatively easy to copy products.

In the 1990s therefore ICI decided to make a radical shift. It wanted to move out of heavy chemicals (which also gave the company a poor environmental record). It decided to move into high value-added consumer chemicals that involved a high research and development content that would be difficult to copy in the short to medium term. In particular, ICI decided to purchase a range of consumer chemicals from Unilever, including chemicals that go into eye-liners, lip glosses, etc. This was to be ICI's new core business. ICI therefore acquired the new

businesses. It intended to raise capital by selling off most of its heavy chemicals businesses to a USA buyer. Unfortunately, the US government blocked the US acquisition in order to prevent a monopoly situation arising in the United States.

ICI was faced with having to hold on to its old businesses (which were now heavily in loss) while seeking to expand its new businesses (with less cash than anticipated for product development). The strategy that emerged was thus one of having to pare down its older businesses while struggling to find cash for its new businesses.

Questions

1. What was ICI's intended strategy?

2. What was the strategy that emerged?

3. What problems resulted from the failures of the intended strategy?

4. What does this case study tell you about the ability of an organisation to plan strategy in a rational and organised way?

Incremental and emergent approaches to strategy

Over the course of time organisations adapt and change existing strategies and create new ones. H. Mintzberg, 1997 sets out an important distinction between realised strategy that is deliberate and realised strategy that emerges as a result of environmental changes (see Figure 28.14).

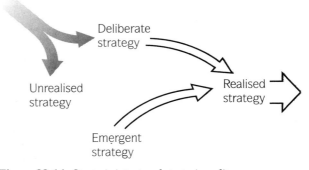

Intended strategy

Deliberate strategy

Unrealised strategy

Emergent strategy

Realised strategy

Figure 28.14 *Strategic intent and strategic reality*

When an organisation creates a strategy, for example to be the market leader in toothpaste and to have a minor share of the toothbrush market, it may find that environmental factors throw its strategy off course. Its strategy to be the toothpaste leader may be unrealised if a competitor comes up with a radically new offering that wins a large portion of the market. However, in the course of time the firm may find that it develops new forms of toothbrush technology, supported by a successful advertising campaign. This means that a strategy emerges for the firm to be a market leader in toothbrushes and a smaller player in the toothpaste market.

Johnson and Scholes (1998) argue that it is useful to think of strategic development as being part of a continuous process. They argue that 'there is a tendency towards momentum of strategy; once an organisation has adopted a particular strategy then it tends to develop from that strategy and within it rather than changing its direction'. Fundamental changes in strategy are relatively rare – although these major changes are very important.

Johnson and Scholes show that typically organisations change in an incremental way during which times strategies are formed gradually, or through piecemeal change during which some strategies are changed and others remain the same. Periods of continuity are ones in which the strategy remains the same. Periods of flux are ones in which strategies change but with no very clear direction.

However, times of major change should not be ignored. Global change to the organisation may need to come about where an organisation has lost touch with recent changes in its environment, or when the organisation identifies a major new opportunity requiring deep-seated change.

These alternative patterns of strategic change are illustrated in Figure 28.15.

J. B. Quinn (*Strategies for Change*, 1980) studied nine major multinationals to show that the central management process was one of logical incrementalism.

- Managers have a view of where the organisation should be in the future and try to move the organisation to this position in an evolutionary way. They do this by seeking to develop a strong 'core' business, but in addition try out 'side-bet' ventures.
- Effective managers recognise that they cannot fully predict what will happen in the organisation's changing

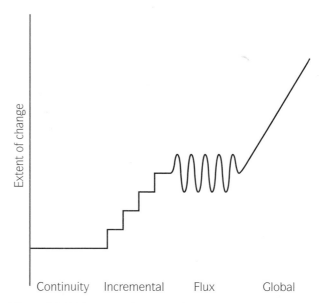

Figure 28.15 *Patterns of strategic change*

environment. However, they seek to be sensitive to signals in the environment by an on-going process of 'environmental scanning'.
- Effective managers encourage experimentation in the organisation, and they do not create objectives which are too rigid – thus allowing flexibility. Experimentation should also take place at several layers and within several organisational subsystems rather than just being the province of top management.
- Managers see such an approach as being effective. Gradual strategy implementation enables an improved quality of information for decision-making. Flexibility and creativity are also encouraged within the organisation.

The reality then is that corporate strategy is not based on a simple neat mechanical model. Rather it is a flexible process that allows strategy to change and emerge rather than to be fashioned in a simplistic rational way. Studies of organisations in practice reveal that this is indeed how strategy comes about and is developed. Strategy is thus an incremental process involving feedback from a range of sources and points within the organisation.

The incremental approach is based on the notion of strategy adapting in response to changes in the internal and particularly the external environments of the organisation.

Discussion point

Look at the strategy of an organisation with which you are familiar. Is it created and managed in a clearly defined rational way, or is it built up over time in an incremental way?

The interpretive approach to strategy

An alternative to classical/rational and incremental approaches is the interpretive strategy. This view sees the organisation as being closely related to its environment, but here the emphasis is on managers 'holding a cognitive map that provides a view of the world, helps interpret the changes the organisation faces, and provides appropriate responses' (Weick, 'Managerial thought in the context of action', in *The Executive Mind*, 1983). This approach places emphasis on the culture and values of the organisation in driving management views. Managers are motivated to believe and act in ways that are likely to produce favourable results for the organisation. The manager/leader in the organisation will seek to create the right sort of organisational culture to create positive results

THE PLANNING PROCESS

Approaches to planning and formulation of strategy and objectives in different types of organisations

Planning is concerned with looking ahead. This purpose was expressed forcefully by Henry Fayol, when he stated in 1949 that: 'The maxim "managing means looking ahead" gives some idea of the importance attached to planning in the business world, and it is true that if foresight is not the whole of management at least it is an essential part of it'.

Planning makes possible the coordination of decision making, so that there is a clear focus and direction for the organisation. Lack of coordination means that people are pulling in different directions. Planning also means preparing for the future so that the organisation is prepared and can take contingency measures if the future turns out to be different from what was originally anticipated. Planning also enables managers to take more control over future development.

Kerry Napuk (1996) has defined strategic planning as 'a total concept of the whole business involving a framework and a process that guides its future'. You can see from this definition that strategic planning involves considering g the organisation as a whole in order to come up with 'holistic' plans. These plans then are put into action. They are not plans that are filed away in company records – they are plans which provide an on-going direction to practical actions. The strategy needs to be shared among all members of the organisation so that they are all pulling in the same direction.

Who creates the strategic plans?

The ideal answer is that strategy should be created by a detailed, democratic consultation of all members of an organisation. In this ideal world the stakeholders would help to shape and thus own the strategy. At the end of the day the final creation of a strategy document and plan would be in the hands of a small group of senior directors with a good understanding of the issues involved. However, through the process of consultation of shareholders they would create a commitment to the strategy. This is a bottom-up approach to strategy.

The reality is that in many cases some important stakeholders will be consulted, but the major part of the strategy would be created at board level by the most powerful directors of an organisation. The strategic plan should be constantly reviewed and altered. Strategy is an on-going area for improvement.

The key questions in strategic planning and the processes that are associated with it are set out in Figure 28.16.

General questions	What the organisation must do
1. Where are we now?	Review past performance
2. Where do we want to be?	Establishes aims, purposes and targets for the organisation. Mission and vision statements
3. How will we get there?	Develop a strategic plan for the whole organisation
4. How can we make it work?	Establish operational or tactical plans
5. How will we know that we've arrived?	Evaluate performance, leading to an on-going review of performance

Figure 28.16 *Key questions and processes in strategic planning*

Small organisations

How relevant then is the strategic plan for the small organisation? Some people think that corporate strategy is just for companies/corporations. However, this is patent nonsense. Nearly every organisation operates in a dynamic environment and the organisation needs to keep in tune with this environment. Every organisation needs to ask key strategic questions.

- What is the scope of our activities?
- What are our core competencies?
- What are our key resources?
- How do we match our activities with our competencies and resources?
- How do we adjust to a changing environment?

Kerry Napuk (1996), an expert on strategic planning for small- and medium-sized companies, has devised a model for strategic planning which he terms a 'universal model', because it 'has been validated in several companies of various sizes at different stages of development across many different industries and in various countries'. He argues that it is possible to create such a model because the problems faced by organisations in developed countries are basically the same. Such problems deal with 'survival and growth'.

Medium organisations

Kerry Napuk argues that strategic planning is most suited for medium-sized companies because:

- they have enough resources to make an impact on the market(s) in which they compete (sufficient market presence)
- they are small enough to manage directly (direct management)
- they have management resources to create and implement plans.

Thus medium-sized companies are just the right size for a strategic management approach.

He defines medium-sized companies as ones with:

- 150–2000 employees
- sales between £10 million and £250 million.

Discussion point

Do you agree that medium-sized companies are the most appropriate for a strategic planning process? Support your arguments.

Napuk's model for strategic planning in small- and medium-sized companies is followed in this book and can be summarised as follows.

1. How did we get here?
   1.1. Successful factors

2. Where do we want to go?
   2.1 Vision
   2.2 Objectives
       (1) Internal evaluation: strengths and weaknesses
   2.3 Goals

3. How do we get there?
   3.1 Strategies
       (1) External evaluation: opportunities and threats

4. How do we make it work?
   4.1 Structure
   4.2 Implementation
       (1) Action programmes
   4.3 Review

Large organisations

The term corporate strategy is most readily associated with the major planning procedures of large organisations. Indeed, we tend to associate strategic thinking with top-level planning in such organisations. Large organisations often make plans which span several continents, a number of markets, and which affect the livelihoods of thousands of people. Clearly, such decisions need to be made by experts who have lots of information available to them, and the planning tools and systems to enable them to make the 'big decisions'. However, it is important to recognise that corporate strategy in a large organisation can only be carried out effectively by inputting ideas and information from a range of levels within the organisation. For example, lower-level supervisors and operatives within an organisation often have the best understanding of what is feasible and practical at an operational level. Too often the 'big planners' find that their plans have gone wide of the mark because of their inability to understand the contributions and systems which are 'running' the organisation at 'grass-roots' level.

Unit 8 of this book is largely concerned with corporate strategy in large organisations.

Richard Koch (1995) warns of the dangers of centralised strategy-making in the large corporation. He argues that the confidence of those that believe corporate strategists can come up with the right ways to lead a company to success is often unfounded. He believes that the corporate centre in large, or multi-business companies should wherever possible leave much of the strategic decision-making to individual business units within the company. He states that 'managers at the centre, however competent, are natural value destroyers'.

Koch's criticisms are as follows.

- Corporate centres are usually large and expensive to run. A lot of the profits made by operating businesses are swallowed up by the centre.
- Corporate centres don't add enough value to a business to justify their costs.
- Most corporate centres destroy more value than they add.

In *Corporate Level Strategy*, Goold, Campbell, and Alexander state that 'The conclusion we reach is that, while a few successful parents create value in multi-business companies, the large majority are value destroyers'. Value is destroyed by the centre making mistakes such as appointing the wrong chief executive, setting inappropriate targets and controls, making the wrong acquisitions, and most importantly by taking away responsibility from those running the individual businesses. The centre takes responsibility and hence motivation away from the constituent parts of an organisation.

The lesson to be learnt about corporate strategy in the large organisation, is that it needs to be based very much on the basis of empowerment, and allowing individual business units to take responsibility for their own strategic thinking, planning and actions.

The formal approach to planning compared to the ad hoc approach

Strategic planning is essentially about creating formal planning procedures which are extensive in scope. The organisation determines its future rather than muddling through and responding in a reactive way to change. The organisation that has planned strategically will be in charge of its future and will create a sense of confidence in its stakeholders.

Example: Flying by the seat of their pants

A TV documentary in January 1999 focused on the activities of a cut-price airline company in the UK. The company operates on a very tight budget offering discounted price flights to a range of destinations. The documentary exposed some of the weaknesses resulting from such an approach.

One of the company's planes was due to fly passengers to Nice in the south of France. However, when the plane approached Nice it was not able to land immediately because of a storm. The plane would have to queue for 45 minutes before landing. However, it was not carrying enough fuel to stay in the air for that length of time and had to divert to Lyon. Unfortunately, when the plane arrived at Lyon there was no arrangement for the company to purchase fuel from the petrol supplier (Elf) there. Elf was not prepared to supply unless it could be sure of payment. At one stage, it looked as if the pilot would have to buy the fuel using his own credit card! Eventually, an agreement was made with the airline's financial controller in England who had to be telephoned.

This is a good example of working out solutions without the support of clear planning and preparation. Organisations should not operate in this way – they need to have clear plans and procedures which enable them to deal with day-to-day eventualities. This operational effectiveness can only come about when the strategy is clearly planned and delineated at a corporate level within the organisation. For example, you would not expect a large organisation such as British Airways to encounter the problems described above.

Organisational change is a planned activity. It should take place through corporate planning. John Thompson (1990) writes that the most effective strategies of major organisations 'tend to emerge step by step from an iterative process in which the organisation probes the future, experiments and learns from a series of partial (incremental) commitments rather than through global formulations of total strategies'. He says that good managers are aware of the process and consciously intervene in it. He also states that effective strategy often results from 'a steam of decisions and information fed upwards from the lower management levels of the organisation'.

Strategy Formulation

Strategies are key planning processes for organisations through which they identify their futures.

This chapter looks at how strategies are formulated, which involves organisations considering the environment

in which they operate and their position in the market, analysing the strategic direction they might wish to take

and carrying out an internal audit, before finally formulating a strategy that matches resources with capability.

On completion of the chapter you should be able to analyse approaches to strategic planning. To achieve this you must demonstrate the ability to:

- conduct an environmental and internal audit of a given organisation

- develop an organisational strategy based on an audit.

EFFECTIVE STRATEGIES

An effective strategy will need to be based on each of the following characteristics:

- It should be sustainable – once established it should be able to run and be built on over time.
- It should be distinctive from competitors – the strategy should set out to help the organisation and its activities to be different from rivals.
- It should enable the organisation to gain a competitive advantage.
- It should exploit links with the business environment. Organisations need to change and adapt with the environment, and make effective links with the environment – for example by developing close links with customers.
- It should be based on a vision that enables the organisation to develop better links with the environment, for example, helping the organisation to move into bigger and better markets.

A strategy enables an organisation to build on its past, plan for the future and monitor its progress (see Figure 29.1). Creating an effective strategy is all about creating a match between the organisation's capabilities and the environmental conditions in which it operates. The organisation needs to carefully identify its key areas of competence, and the resources that are available to it. These capabilities then need to be matched to the environment and to the opportunities and risks that exist in the environment. Of course, the organisation will need to think of how it can extend its capabilities to best meet the challenges in its environment (see Figure 29.2).

ENVIRONMENT AUDITING

Organisations need to be in tune with their environment. In particular, they need to anticipate the sorts of changes that will take place in their environment and make appropriate plans for these. Environmental auditing enables the organisation to be proactive rather than

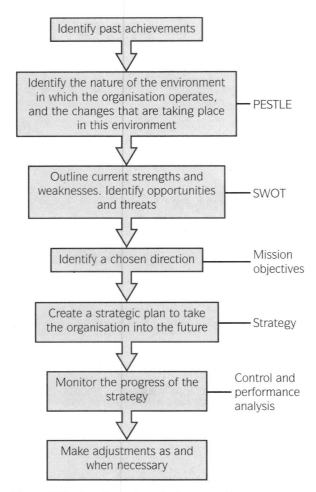

Figure 29.1 *Creating and monitoring strategies*

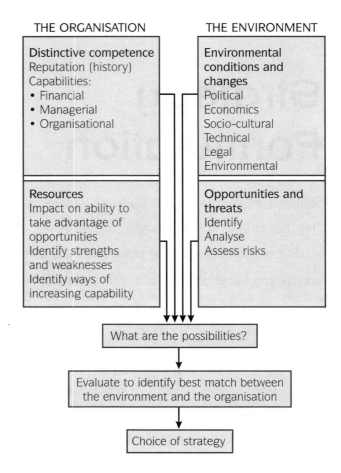

Figure 29.2 *Matching environment and organisation*

reactive. The effective organisation will put a lot of effort into the process of environmental auditing and scanning. The principal tools for carrying out this process are:

- PESTLE (Political, Economic, Socio-cultural, Technological, Legal and Environmental) analysis
- auditing the market – through competitor analysis
- SWOT analysis.

PESTLE analysis

Johnson and Scholes (1998) identify three key steps in analysing the environment in which the organisation operates (see Figure 29.3):

1. Auditing environmental influences involves identifying the environmental influences which have affected the organisation's development and performance in the past

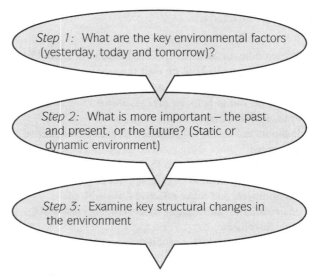

Figure 29.3 *Johnson and Scholes' (1998) three key steps in analysing an organisation's operating environment*

and trying to identify those that will be significant in the future.

2. Assess how uncertain the environment is in which the organisation is operating. If the environment is fairly static, then a historical and present analysis will be useful. However, if the environment is dynamic, then a more future-oriented analysis is required.

3. Carry out an explicit analysis of particular environmental influences. A **structural analysis** should identify the key forces at work.

A PESTLE analysis is concerned with auditing the external environment in which the organisation operates to identify the key influences on the organisation, and in particular to identify key changes that are taking place which will influence the organisation in the future. Examples of major changes in each of these categories in the external environment might include the following.

- **Political change.** The change from a Conservative government to a Labour one in 1997 meant that many organisations had to rethink their policies with regards to the relationship with the community. The Conservative government's philosophy had been very much based on individuals taking responsibility for themselves, whereas Labour places more of an emphasis on supporting the community. Businesses have therefore subtly changed their approach to community-related projects such as corporate sponsorship of 'good causes'.
- **Economic change.** The movement of the economy towards a slowdown, a factor which would have a negative effect on the sales of most businesses, would make an organisation reevaluate expansionary strategies.
- **Socio-cultural change.** The increasing trend of women going out to work has had a major impact on the way people eat. For some organisations this has created opportunities in the fast-food, ready meals, and restaurant sectors of the economy.
- **Technological change.** The change to digital television in Britain has forced organisations such as the BBC and the cable and satellite TV companies to alter radically the scope of their activities – moving resources from terrestrial to digital services and equipment.
- **Legal change.** Organisations need to anticipate and prepare themselves for changes in the law. For example, in recent years many organisations have been able to anticipate tighter legislation with regards to health and safety standards, enabling them to introduce the required changes well in advance of legal requirement.
- **Environmental change.** Increasingly organisations have had to develop environmental policies and practices. Today there are International and British Standards for environmental quality procedures. Organisations need to be in the forefront of making these changes.

Case Study

PEST analysis for Tesco

Figure 29.4 *Analysing Tesco*

A recent PEST (Political, Economic, Social, Technological) analysis for the supermarket chain Tesco by Howard Bacon (1998) revealed the following.

Political

Political decisions are out of the control of Tesco, but the company has to forecast changes and plan accordingly, rather than simply react. For example, the single European Market has both positive and negative outcomes for Tesco. It has allowed Tesco to move abroad, but foreign competitors have also provided fierce opposition to Tesco; the German company Aldi moved to the UK during the early 1990s recession and gained market share through low prices. The European Union's (EU) minimum wage legislation impacts on Tesco's costs as does other social protections under the EU's social chapter.

Economic

Tesco Chief Executive Terry Leahy (1998) predicts that there may be a recession, leading to reductions in consumer expenditure. Tesco may have to lower the prices of a range of its goods accordingly if this is the case. Tesco also intends to challenge fixed price and distribution costs, to reduce costs and offer cheaper prices to the consumer.

Social

Customer requirements for products and services are always changing. Tesco will continually need to monitor social attitudes, perceptions and aspirations in order to identify new ways of responding for example providing an Internet service, financial services, etc. Terry Leahy (1998) stated that 'customers want more one-stop shopping, and providing non-food products is becoming more important'. Tesco is even considering selling cars, as the company can see a gap in the market, by offering 30 per cent reductions.

Technological

Electronic Point of Sale (EPOS) and a range of other technological innovations have become important in the supermarket sector. EPOS is used for the management of stock, as each sale is catalogued automatically reducing the number of deliveries and cutting down on wastage. The net result is lower costs which can then be turned into cheaper products. Electronic Data Interchange (EDI) allows data to be transmitted between Tesco and its suppliers. Tesco has also developed a strategic network of warehouses designed to improve its delivery system.

Questions

Choose an organisation which it is easy to collect information about, for example a large local firm, a company which presents lots of information on the Internet, a company with a detailed annual report, etc.

1. Identify the following changes which are taking place in the environment in which the organisation operates:
   (a) three political changes, (b) five economic changes,
   (c) five social changes, (d) two technological changes,
   (e) two environmental changes and (f) two legal changes.

2. Decide which of these factors are so significant that together they constitute the **key structural changes** which are taking place in the environment in which the organisation operates.

Porter's 5-force analysis

Michael Porter, a Harvard academic, has argued that 'the key aspect of [an organisation's] environment is the industry or industries in which it competes'. He refers to five basic forces which he calls 'the structural determinants of the intensity of competition'. These, he believes, determine the profit potential of the industry. The five forces are:

- rivalry among existing competitors (competition)
- the bargaining power of buyers
- the bargaining power of suppliers
- the threat of new competitors entering the industry
- the threat of substitute products

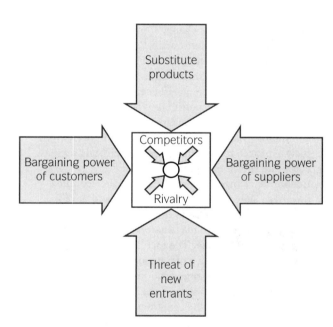

Figure 29.5 *Strategic forces and competitive strategy*

Porter argues that the strength of these five forces will determine not only the sort of competition a business has to face but also the profitability of the whole industry. Existing competition between competitors can be shown to be influenced by the other four factors (see Figure 29.5). Porter's model may be used to improve an organisation's analysis of the nature of competition by weighing up the relative strengths of the other four forces. Each of these forces is considered below.

The threat of new competitors

A new entrant to an industry poses a threat which influences the market share and profitability of others already in the marketplace. In some industries businesses may constantly enter or leave the marketplace, particularly in areas such as retailing. In other markets it may be difficult for newcomers to enter the market because of barriers to entry. These represent a series of influences which make it difficult for businesses to enter. Porter lists seven major barriers to entry.

- **Economies of scale.** If a newcomer is small and does not come into an industry with large-scale production, it will not benefit from economies of scale. It will therefore suffer from significant cost disadvantages. This fact alone may deter new entrants to the market who have not got the investment potential to use technologies and processes which enable them to compete on level terms with existing competitors.
- **Product differentiation.** Existing organisations in a marketplace may develop a brand heritage and loyalty with which customers can readily identify. This product differentiation may have taken many years to build up. Newcomers have to overcome such loyalties to get their brand accepted.
- **Capital requirements.** In some markets start-up costs and investment in research and production facilities to set up in some markets may be extremely large. These may provide a huge disincentive to newcomers.
- **Switching costs.** These are the one-off costs incurred when changing the use of resources to develop products for a different market. They may include the retraining of staff, use of a different computer system, product redesign or changing the uses of machinery.
- **Access to distribution channels.** This is a market barrier frequently overlooked. Where channels are long-established it may be difficult to get products through to dealer networks.
- **Cost disadvantages.** Newcomers to a marketplace, irrespective of their size, may incur some further cost disadvantages, such as locational costs and the higher cost of supplies.

- **Government policy.** Certain regulations may limit the numbers of competitors in an industry.

The bargaining power of buyers

Buyers will try to obtain the best possible deal for themselves. They will want better quality products at low prices and, if they succeed, they may force down the profitability of their suppliers. An organisation's profitability is therefore likely to be dependent on the bargaining strength of its customers. For example, imagine the differences between supplying a market where there are a few customers and a market where there are many. Whereas in the market with few buyers each buyer may dictate product quality, terms and price, in the market with many buyers this is unlikely to happen as individual buyers will exert less influence.

The bargaining power of suppliers

Suppliers may also influence profitability by exerting pressure for higher prices for their products. Their ability to do this depends on the number of suppliers to the industry, the relative importance of the supplier's product for the business, the nature of the product and the contractual nature of the relationship between the supplier and the buyer.

The threat of substitute products

Products and services produced by one industry may have substitutes that are produced by another industry. For example, coffee is a substitute for tea and vegetarian products may substitute for meat products.

According to Porter, where there are substitutes the returns of an industry may be limited by placing a ceiling on the prices an industry can charge: 'The more attractive the price-performance alternative offered by substitutes, the firmer the lid on industry profits'. According to this analysis, industries with fewer substitutes are more likely to be stable, and thus profitable, than those where products may be substituted readily.

TASK

Identify the barriers to entry in the markets for (a) beer manufacture, (b) petrol retailing, and (c) the manufacture of contraceptives.

TASK

What do you see as being the main 'structural determinants of the intensity of competition in the following industries/markets': (a) supermarkets, (b) digital television services, and (c) car manufacture.

CURRENT MARKET POSITION

As the previous section shows, a key element of the organisation's environment is its position in the market relative to competitors. Organisations need continually to appraise their market position in order to identify the most appropriate steps forward. An important measure of market power for the organisation will be its market share relative to that of competitors.

One way in which the organisation can gain a better understanding of its market position is to break down the market into its constituent segments and to examine market share within those segments. It may be possible to identify the extent of competition in each segment in a quantitative way by examining the market value of each segment and the relative market share of each competitor. An alternative qualitative approach is to identify the segments of the market which are important from a strategic point of view. Some segments will be important because they are growing, or because they involve less risk, or because they are very large.

Figure 29.6 shows how an organisation may analyse the market using a quantitative and a qualitative approach. Let us assume that the size of the market is worth £250 million and that there are three companies in the market: Leader, Follower, and Starter. There are two segments of the market – fashion, and non-fashion.

The relative market share of an organisation is usually measured by identifying the size of the market that a firm has in relation to its nearest competitor in a particular market segment. For example, in the UK wet-shaving market the leader Gillette makes three times as many sales as its nearest rival Wilkinson Sword. Gillette's market share then can be written as 3X or more simply as 3, whereas Wilkinson Sword's share would be written as 0.33X.

| | Market segments | | |
	Fashion (sales £m)	Non-fashion (sales £m)	Total (£m)
Leader	100	75	175
Follower	30	20	50
Starter	20	5	25

Figure 29.6a *Quantitative approach (sales value)*

Relative share should correlate with profitability over a period of time. If it does not then there may be one or more problems:

- The business segment has not been properly defined.
- The smaller competitor is operating in a much cleverer way than the larger one, for example by finding a better way of lowering costs or raising prices.
- The market leader is sacrificing short-term profit in order to make a longer-term gain in terms of competitive advantage.
- There may be overcapacity in the industry and the larger firm has a greater level of unused capacity.

Competitor analysis

There are two contrasting viewpoints in relation to the importance of analysing the competitive position of an organisation's competitors. One view is that an understanding of competitors, their actions and how to beat them is at the heart of competitive advantage. The other view is that an organisation should focus on its own business, identify its own core competences, concentrate on doing them really well, cut down its costs, identify and satisfy its customers, and forget about the competition.

The best way forward probably lies somewhere between these two viewpoints. There is no point in studying competitors simply because it seems the 'right' thing to do. In studying competitors, an organisation needs to have some fairly focused questions which are of use to its own development. Michael Porter argues that effective strategic management is the positioning of an organisation, relative to its competitors, in such a way that it outperforms them. Organisations therefore need to know something about the competitors that they wish to outperform.

Positioning maps are always helpful in contrasting an organisation's competitive strengths and weaknesses in comparison with the opposition.

| | Market segments | |
	Fashion	Non-fashion
Leader	Dominant	Dominant
Follower	Weak	Weak
Starter	Growing rapidly	Small but growing rapidly

Figure 29.6b *Qualitative approach (competitive position)*

Case Study

The position of Focus Do It All in late 1998

In 1998, Focus took over the do-it-yourself chain Do It All. At the time the public's perception of Do It All was that products were of above-average price but that the quality was not particularly high. As a result of the take-over the new management team at Focus Do It All was able to concentrate on changing the position of the company to a clear leadership position in the industry based on higher quality – see Figure 29.7 (produced by research into customer perceptions in 1998). The net result of the change was to transform the new organisation into a much higher profit position.

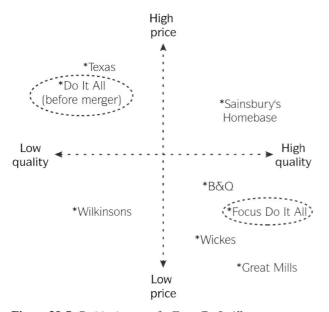

Figure 29.7 *Positioning map for Focus Do It All*

Questions

1. What do you see as being the main benefits of the repositioning exercise at Focus Do It All?

2. Can you identify any other opportunities in the market?

Prahalad and Hamel ('Competence of the corporation', *Harvard Business Review*, 1990) defined the successful organisation as the one that is able to exploit core competences and make growth possible. They stated that 'the critical task for management is to create an organisation capable of infusing products with irresistible functionality, or, better yet, creating products that customers need but have not yet even imagined'. They then went on to say that

> *'the diversified corporation is a large tree. The trunk and major limbs are core products, the smaller branches are business units; the leaves, flowers and fruit are end-products. The root system that provides the nourishment, sustenance and stability, is the core competence. You can miss the strength of competitors by looking only at their end-products, in the same way you miss the strength of a tree if you look only at its leaves.'*

Prahalad and Hamel defined core competences as 'the collective learning in the organisation, especially how to co-ordinate diverse production skills and integrate multiple steams of technologies'.

An organisation's competitive advantages, therefore, stem from its unique competencies which enable it to create market leadership by developing advantages which competitors are unable to provide at the moment.

By building effectively on its roots, the organisation is able to develop the trunk, branches, leaves and flowers which appear as visible advantages in the market place including:

- the firm's products, which are competitively priced
- the firm's markets
- the firm's technological orientation (i.e. technologically superior processes and products)
- product quality
- delivery
- flexibility of service, etc.

There are a number of observations to make about competitive advantages. Firstly, when these advantages are unique to the firm, they tend to be the strongest advantages. Secondly, when a firm does not possess a unique competitive advantage on which to build its strategy, it can create niches in the market. This is done by examining what the differences are between itself and its competitors which can be exploited in various ways, for example by developing

- new products
- new customer segments
- advantages in international markets.

Michael Porter suggests that there are three generic strategies which an organisation can pursue:

- overall cost leadership
- differentiation
- focus.

Operating in different markets, the firm can select different strategies or a combination of them for each market.

Cost-leadership strategy

A cost-leadership strategy is based on achieving low-cost production. This is normally associated with high-volume output, so that economies of scale, and experience and learning-curve factors, result in cost savings. Experience-curve economies come from the firm's increased expertise in managing the functional activities. The learning-curve economies are the result of employees becoming more efficient and effective as they learn from their mistakes over time, and so productivity increases.

Differentiation strategy

This involves differentiating the firm's products or services so that they will be perceived as being unique in quality, brand or some other feature. The firm is then in a position to market the products at a higher-than-average price, which consumers will be willing to pay. For example, the car manufacturer BMW holds a differentiated position in the car market in terms of quality and research and development.

Focus strategy

This involves concentrating on a small market, product or geographic segment. The organisation's efforts and resources are focused on serving a particular customer group and it does not compete on an industry-wide basis. For example, some computer software companies compete for certain customer segments such as the chemical industry or the financial services sector.

Porter's model is illustrated in Figure 29.8. Firms in the upper right-hand of the curve are profitable and successful because they have a larger market share resulting from lower prices and lower costs than their competitors, or because they have differentiated their product offerings and still capture a high market share. Firms in the upper left-hand corner of the curve are also successful because their focus strategy entails specialist products or markets which can command high prices. The firms having difficulties are

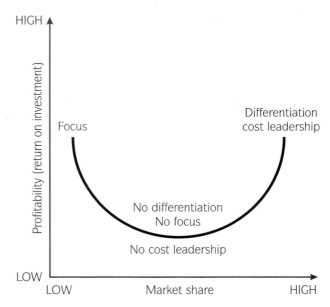

Figure 29.8 *Porter's general strategies model*

those situated in the middle portion of the curve, with fairly low market share and profits.

Porter's model also illustrates the trade-off between profits and market share. For example, a focus strategy would give the firm higher profits but at a cost, as it would have a smaller market share.

The Boston matrix

The Boston matrix is a widely used approach to assessing the competitive position of an organisation's products in the marketplace. It is used to evaluate the significance of each individual product or service produced by an organisation in relation to all the others, in order to establish future priorities and needs.

Bruce Henderson (1915–92), the founder of the Boston Consulting Group (BCG), invented what is now called the Growth/Share matrix. Henderson suggested that the profit margins earned by a product, and the cash generated by it, are a function of market share. The higher the market share is, relative to competitors, the greater is the earnings potential; high margins and market share are correlated. A second basic premise is that sales and revenue growth requires appropriate investment, i.e. sales will only grow if an organisation spends money wisely on advertising, distribution and development. The rate of market growth determines the required investment. High market share must be bought – by increased investment. Furthermore, no business can keep on growing forever. Therefore there will be times when products are not profitable because the sums of money being spent on developing them exceeds their earnings potential. In contrast, there are other times, mainly when the company has a high relative market share, when earnings exceed expenditure and products are profitable. Profitability is therefore influenced by market growth, market share and the stage in the product life cycle.

The intelligent organisation therefore needs to look at its portfolio of products to decide how to use this portfolio to maximum advantage. Successful mature products, where growth has slowed down and the required investment has decreased, tend to yield the highest returns. The profits from these products can then be channelled into new and exciting products that the company is seeking to develop. A review of a firm's portfolio of goods and or services (or markets) will identify which business activities should be maintained, reduced or eliminated.

A simplified version of the BCG portfolio matrix (for a detergent manufacturer) is shown in Figure 29.9. The aim of the matrix is to assist managers to determine the role of each business unit or product on the basis of:

- its market growth rate and market share relative to its competitors
- its cash flow potential.

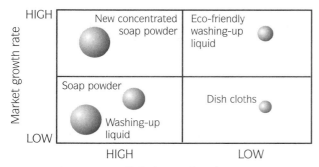

Figure 29.9 *Growth/share matrix for a detergent manufacturer*

Market share is shown on the horizontal axis relative to the firm's largest competitor, and market growth of the industry is shown on the vertical axis with *x* per cent of growth rate arbitrarily used to separate the markets into high and low growth. Each circle represents a product with sales equivalent to the area of the circle. In the example shown the organisation receives an on-going steady flow of profits from its traditional washing-up liquids and soap powders which are supported by a modest advertising spend. Its dish cloths are a poor selling item in a low growth market. Eco-friendly washing-up liquids are becoming more popular, but the firm has little presence in this market (perhaps it should change its thinking about this). It has a pleasing market share in the new concentrated soap powder market.

The four basic strategies that can be considered for a given product are as follows.

- For **cash cows** (products or businesses with a high market share in a mature market), maintain market share while at the same time generating large cash flows.
- For **star businesses** (products or businesses with a high market share in a growing market), build market share and thus improve their competitive position.
- For **question marks, (problem children)** (products or businesses in a growing market but without a high market share), increase market share using surpluses from cash cows.
- **Dogs** (products or businesses with low market share in static or declining markets) could be divested or harvested; if the latter, it is to generate short-term cash flows.

The four quadrants of the diagram (see Figure 29.9) can loosely be related to the product life cycle, with question marks representing the introduction stage, stars the growth stage, cash cows maturity and dogs saturation and decline.

The notion of portfolio analysis suggests the need to get the right balance across the organisation with areas which provide security and funds (cash cows) and others which provide for the future of the business (suitably handled question markets and stars).

Discussion point

Identify the cash cows, stars, question marks and dogs in the portfolio of an organisation that you are familiar with.

STRATEGIC DIRECTION

Having audited the environment (PESTLE) and the competitive position of the organisation (market positioning, Porter's generic strategies, Boston Matrix), the organisation needs to decide on a strategic direction that will best enable it to match this environment, given its existing resources. Possible strategies include:

- growth
- stability
- profitability
- efficiency
- market leadership
- survival
- mergers and acquisitions
- expansion into the global market place.

These strategies are best introduced through Ansoff's view of product/market expansion strategies.

The Ansoff matrix

Igor Ansoff is a Russian-American engineer, mathematician, military strategist and operations researcher. In *Corporate Strategy* (1965) Ansoff defined corporate strategy as 'The positioning and relating of the firm/organisation to its environment in a way which will assure its continued success and make it secure from surprises'.

In developing its portfolio strategy, an organisation can choose a number of alternatives to generate intensive growth. Figure 29.10 illustrates the possibilities open to the organisation – the grid is called Ansoff's product/market expansion grid.

	Current products	New products
Current markets	Product market penetration	Product market development
New markets	Market development	Diversification

Figure 29.10 *Ansoff's product/market expansion grid*

The four key strategies open to the firm are as follows.

Product market penetration

The firm tries to increase its product's share in the markets it currently services. It can achieve this in various ways.

- **Product-line stretching.** The firm adds new items to its existing product line in a market segment which it has already penetrated. The aim is to attract more customers from rivals and current non-users of the firm's products (i.e. to reach a broader market). For example, Coca-Cola has added new items to its basic product and now offers Diet Coke and Cherry Coke in some of its world markets. The Japanese car manufacturers first penetrated the European car market with medium-sized cars; this product line then stretched to small cars, and now they have extended their product lines to target the luxury segments of the car market.
- **Product proliferation.** This involves offering many different product types. For example, Seiko offers a variety of watches with different features, functions, etc.
- **Product improvement.** This involves updating and augmenting the existing product. It entails application of the latest technology to improve the product's capabilities, improving customer services, etc.

Market development

This strategy involves developing new markets for the firm's current product lines. Expansion of this type is most suitable:

- where minimal product modification is required
- where profit margins are diminishing because of intense price competition in the firm's existing markets
- if the product's lifecycle is similar in various markets.

Product market development

This strategy involves the firm maintaining its existing markets but developing new product markets within them. For example, a firm selling software to the industrial segment in market X might go after the consumer segment in the same market.

Diversification

Diversification strategies involve the firm entering new product markets outside its present business. The firm may wish to pursue this line of expansion in the following circumstances:

- when opportunities in the new product market are highly attractive
- when the firm wishes to reduce the impact of a negative environmental trend in its existing industry, for example to reduce the economic impact of a decline in cigarette smoking or the ageing of the UK population.

To diversify, a firm could engage in forward or backward integration whereby the outlets or sources of supplies are joined with the firm. This is prevalent in the semiconductor industries where manufacturers of microprocessors join forces with semiconductor producers to ensure a continuous supply.

Alternatively a firm may engage in conglomerate diversification strategy, which involves the firm expanding into businesses that have no relationship to its current product, markets or technology. For example, Coca-Cola purchased a movie company as a strategic move to counter a possible decline in the customer segment for its products, which is presently the youth group.

This overview of strategies has to be judged very carefully in order to ensure that the final choice fits best with circumstances found in the market and with the strengths of the company. In fact, there are all sorts of strategies that an organisation can engage in, depending on the sort of organisation, its resource capabilities and the nature of its environment. In 'Generic strategies', (see Mintzberg and Quinn, *The Strategy Process*, 1994), Henry Mintzberg outlined a range of families of strategies which he divided into five groupings. Managers seeking generic strategies for an organisation would be well advised to read this article, which first appeared in 1988. He illustrated each grouping with a simple diagram. These were as follows.

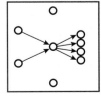

1. **Locating** the core business (i.e. identifying the real nature of what the core business is), which Mintzberg showed as a single node – one circle in a matrix of circles. Mintzberg shows that this is a complex process, in which organisations frequently seek to move on to new definitions of what their core business is in order to gain competitive advantage.

2. **Distinguishing** the core business, by looking inside that circle. This step involves identifying the characteristics that enable the organisation to achieve competitive advantage and so to survive in its own context.

3. **Elaborating** the core business – considering how the circle may be enlarged or developed in various ways.

4. **Extending** the core business – leading the circle to link up up with other circles (other businesses).

5. **Reconceiving** the core business(es) – in effect changing or combining the circles.

Let us examine a number of possible strategies which elaborate on the five groupings of families of strategies available to an organisation.

1. Growth

One of the most frequent strategies that organisations consider is growth. When an organisation considers growth it needs to think about the following.

- The external environment – for example, is there going to be enough growth in the market to warrant the purchase? Will the organisation be able to outcompete the competition?
- The internal environment – will the growth enable the organisation to build on and take advantage of its core competences? Does the organisation have a sufficient resource base to support the process of growth?

The Coca-Cola Corporation is an example of an organisation that has successfully engaged in a process of growth in recent years. It has ploughed back its profits into supporting its existing products in more and more markets, while at the same time developing new soft drinks, such as Diet Coke, Fruitopia. It has used the very large sums earned from its major cash cow to support the growth of the business.

Michael Porter ('How competitive forces shape strategy', *Harvard Business Review*, 1979) wrote that

> *'the key to growth – even survival – is to stake out a position that is less vulnerable to attack from head-to-head opponents, whether established or new, and less vulnerable to erosion from the direction of buyers, suppliers, and substitute goods. Establishing such a position can take many forms – solidifying relationships with favourable customers, differentiating the product either substantively or psychologically through marketing, integrating forward or backward, establishing technological leadership.'*

2. Stability

Stability is always an important strategy for an organisation. There are times when it will need to consolidate on its existing position. Stability makes sense when an organisation has experienced previous periods of rapid growth. The organisation then needs to establish clear systems and procedures that enable it to consolidate its position. For example, although the Virgin group is seen as a dynamic organisation which frequently moves into new areas, it also believes in consolidating new businesses once they are established. Virgin believes that once it has gone through a period of rapid expansion, for example moving into contraceptives, or into Virgin Cola, it needs to establish these lines before moving on to new things. This would involve ensuring that all systems within a new business venture are customer driven, and based on quality performance.

Many organisations will seek stability at times when the environment becomes a bit rocky. A useful analogy can be drawn with the piloting of an aeroplane. When the pilot hits a patch of bad weather, then all efforts will be focused on stabilising the aeroplane.

3. Profitability

Seeking profit is always an important ingredient of strategy, particularly in organisations in which shareholders are key stakeholders and where the stakeholders' perception of the organisation is influenced by the profit. Although organisations like to take a longer-term view on profits, where shareholders are influential (and where shareholders can switch their shareholding easily) organisations are also forced to consider the shorter

and medium term. As we have already seen, market share is often an important driver of profitability.

Charts showing relative market share in a number of industries illustrate this relationship between profits and market share. In Figure 29.11 the vertical axis shows the return on capital employed (ROCE) in the industry and the horizontal axis, the relative market share. You can see that Firm D with a relative market share of 2X its nearest rival has the highest return on capital employed.

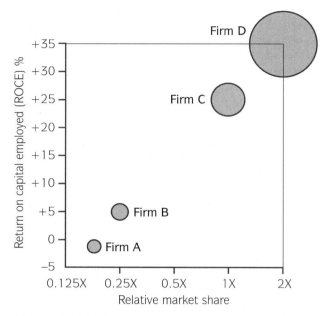

Figure 29.11 *ROCE and relative market share*

4. Efficiency

Johnson and Scholes (1998) identify efficiency as being an organisational strategy which is of critical importance 'for those organisations which either choose or are required to compete on the basis of cost competitiveness'. They cite the example of public services. Efficiency is concerned with how 'well' resources have been put to use, irrespective of the purpose for which they were deployed. There are all sorts of ways of assessing efficiency. For example, profitability is a broad measure of efficiency particularly in looking at profit in terms of the amount of capital utilised in the business (i.e. measures such as ROCE). Other measures of efficiency include labour productivity, yield, capacity fill, working capital utilisation and the efficiency of production systems.

5. Market leadership

Market leadership has already been discussed in some detail. Clear examples of organisations that have successfully won market leadership include Coca-Cola (in soft drinks), Gillette (in shaving products), Microsoft (in computer systems), etc. Market leadership is both a short-, medium- and long-term strategy. By winning market leadership, then an organisation's rivals will always be coming from a catch-up position and will be hampered by disadvantages, particularly in areas related to technology (economies of scale, research and development) and marketing (depth of consumer research, advertising spend, promotional activity, etc).

Case Study

Tesco wins market leadership from Sainsbury's

One of the biggest success stories in supermarket retailing in the 1990s in the UK was the establishment of Tesco as the number one spot market leader displacing its rival Sainsbury's from the number one spot, while at the same time beating off the competition of foreign discounters such as Aldi.

Over a two-year period, from February 1994 to February 1996, Tesco's sales increased by 38 per cent and Sainsbury's by only 14 per cent. Much of the Tesco gain occurred through increases in total square footage, with the opening of new stores and the purchase of William Low supermarkets. Over this period, therefore Tesco's gain was fairly evenly split between the relative increase in store space and the jump in sales per square foot. By April 1997 Tesco had 21 per cent of the UK retail market compared with Sainsbury's 20 per cent.

The increase in sales was achieved by an aggressive marketing effort which examined all possible aspects of winning customer loyalty. In particular, the introduction of a loyalty card in February 1995 was particularly successful in achieving:

- more sales per customer – customers usually divided their purchases across two or more stores; the loyalty card encouraged customers to increase their percentage of spend at Tesco

- an increase in the number of customers as a result of:
  - increased recruitment through the loyalty card,
  - increased retention, through loyalty.

In this period Tesco reviewed all of its existing operations and decided to focus on price, quality and service. New objectives were established, including the following.

1. *Product promotions*
   Objectives: to give customers a wide range of strong relevant promotions in all areas of the store.
   Example: Special Offer promotions throughout all stores every month.
2. *Product range*
   Objectives: to give customers what they want in one store.
   Examples: constant development of new and exciting food products; introduction of a wide range of clothing for all the family, CDs, videos, books, magazines, etc.
3. *Pricing*
   Objectives: to be competitive, especially on basic lines.
   Examples: Value lines and Unbeatable Value pricing, giving low prices on key brands and own-brand products.
4. *Customer service*
   Objectives: to provide customers with outstanding, naturally delivered personal service.
   Examples: Baby changing/feeding facilities; no-quibble money-back guarantee; 'one in front' queuing policy.

Questions

1. Why is it so important for Tesco to win market dominance in the supermarket industry?

2. What advantages flow from such dominance?

3. Why must Tesco's strategy be dynamic rather than static?

4. What influence are competitors' actions likely to have on Tesco's strategy? Give examples.

5. What is the relationship between Tesco's overall market leadership strategy, and its marketing strategies?

6. Survival

As noted in Chapter 14, Peter Drucker writes in *The Practice of Management* (1995) that

> *'It is the first duty of a business to survive. The guiding principle of business economics, in other words, is not the*

maximisation of profits; it is the avoidance of loss. Business enterprise must produce the premium to cover the risks inevitably involved in its operation. And there is only one source for this risk premium: profits.'

Drucker referred to the 'required minimum profit' as representing for the business enterprise 'at the very least the profit required to cover its own future risks, the profit required to enable it to stay in business and to maintain intact the wealth-producing capacity of its resources'. He sees businesses as being there fundamentally to serve customers and to innovate in order to progress and develop. The business will therefore be seeking a strategy which enables it to survive in the long term. Taking this view, the organisation will be seeking a safe path through a turbulent environment, powered by its resources and dynamic core competences, and steered by the intelligence of its strategists. We are all too aware of this survival imperative when we see the results of organisations which for a number of years have been tremendously successful, experience a downturn, run into difficulty, reshape and reposition, ride another wave, etc. Of course, some organisations go under, but the intent is there – the strategic intent to survive.

7. Mergers and acquisitions

Mergers and acquisitions are another key strategic route for the organisation. The organisation needs to look at its environment, its core competences and its resources, and match its strategy to these factors. Merging with another organisation often provides the best and most logical way to build on its core competences. There will often be clear synergies to be built in this way. The organisation will not only be able to build market share to drive competitive advantage but will also be able to build on its existing strengths or reduce existing weaknesses. Mergers and acquisitions fit with Mintzberg's notions of extending the core business, and reconceiving the core business. **Vertical integration** involves moving forward and/or backwards in the operating chain, and **horizontal integration** involves joining with parallel businesses.

Chain integration strategies involve organisations in extending their operating chains downstream or upstream, i.e. by integrating with activities which were previously carried out by suppliers or customers.

Diversification strategies refer to integrating with businesses not in the same chain of operation. A key reason for this would be to take advantage of common competence or to acquire a competence which is currently missing. Synergies are likely to result from such actions.

Strategies of entry or control relate to an organisation entering a new business by developing it itself or by buying an organisation already in that business. Virgin, for example, is famous for moving into new markets either by setting up new businesses from scratch, for example its own contraceptive business, or taking over an existing business, for example in the railway industry. Examples of strategies of entry and control include:

- full ownership and control
  - internal development
  - acquisition
- partial ownership and control
  - majority, minority shareholding
  - partnership, for example joint ventures
- partial control without ownership
  - licensing
  - franchising
  - long-term contracting.

Reconceiving the business can be carried out through a **business redefinition strategy**, for example in recent years ICI has redefined its main locus of business activities from being focused on heavy industrial chemicals to one based on high value-added consumer-oriented chemicals. It made this switch because of the weakness in its older market and the potential in its newer market. It was able to make the switch through selling off existing businesses and buying into newer ones. In 1998–9 Cadbury-Schweppes sold off its soft drinks businesses when it realised that it could not compete with the scale of operations at Coca-Cola and Pepsi.

8. Expansion into the global marketplace

The turn of the millennium will be recognised as a period in which large organisations reoriented the focus of their activities from national to global markets. It is in this period that we have really witnessed the birth of the transnational which sees its centre of operations and of its marketing activities as being the globe. These transnationals have global shareholders, global workforces, global markets, global suppliers and other global stakeholders. They are built on a set of competences that give them a distinctive competitive edge in this global arena.

Corporate strategy is all about identifying the strengths of the organisation and the opportunities which are ripe for exploiting in the global marketplace. Although the global marketplace comprises some common characteristics, it is also important to recognise diversity within it. For example, while Coca-Cola is able to sell Coke successfully throughout the globe, it recognises that opportunities are greater in hotter countries and in countries where the standard of living of large sections of the population enables them to pay the prices of soft drinks. Marketing campaigns need to take into account linguistic and cultural differences. Organisations like cigarette manufacturers recognise that while the sun may be setting for them in western economies where health legislation is catching up with them, there are huge opportunities in developing countries where people's incomes are rising to the extent where they prefer branded to unbranded products.

Creating global strategies requires detailed planning by corporate headquarters based on large quantities of information fed in from business centres which are spread throughout the tentacles of the organisation.

THE INTERNAL AUDIT

We have already looked in considerable depth at the external audit which the organisation carries out. This needs to be carried out hand in glove with the internal audit in order to get the best match between the organisation and its environment. The internal audit (see Figure 29.12) will be concerned with outlining the key resources of the organisation, the key competences, the capabilities of the organisation, its strengths and weaknesses in a range of areas including the product, organisational efficiency, distribution methods, operations, finance, policy and procedures. These are examined in the following section.

- What are our resources?
- What are our core competences?
- What are our strengths and weaknesses?
- What are our capabilities?

Figure 29.12 *The internal audit*

Benchmarking

Benchmarking is an excellent procedure for weighing up the existing performance of the organisation in comparison

with what 'can be achieved'. The process of benchmarking serves as a first-class internal auditing process which can be used to diagnose organisational weaknesses and identify ways of turning them into strengths.

Benchmarking is the process of identifying best practice in the areas of a business which are 'critical success factors' in terms of providing customer satisfaction. Benchmarking studies involve making comparisons with competitors' practices, the practices of businesses in other sectors, or with both.

The first western company to employ benchmarking was the Xerox Corporation which adopted the procedure from their Japanese subsidiary, Fuji-Xerox.

Philip Sadler (*Designing Organisations*, 1994) describes the process of benchmarking as involving a number of stages.

1. Decide which process to benchmark. This involves deciding what the critical success factors are that create and maintain customer satisfaction.
2. Develop accurate, objective descriptions of the existing processes affecting the critical success factors.
3. Decide what to measure and how to measure it.
4. Choose companies against which to benchmark.
5. Measure the 'competitive gap' – the measured difference between the current internal process's effectiveness and the effectiveness of the best practice identified elsewhere.
6. Implement the findings so as to close the gap.

Today many enterprising and ambitious companies set themselves the target of becoming the organisation that other organisations will want to compare themselves against, in other words they want to create the benchmark for their segment, or industry.

The use of McKinsey's 7S framework

Tom Peters and Robert Waterman's book, *In Search of Excellence* (1982), had a major impact on the way in which managers in organisations began to think about the strengths and weaknesses of their organisations. The work was based on a study by McKinsey of so-called 'excellent' US organisations. The authors concluded that the key to excellence lay in achieving a state of shared values among all employees in an organisation (see Figure 29.13).

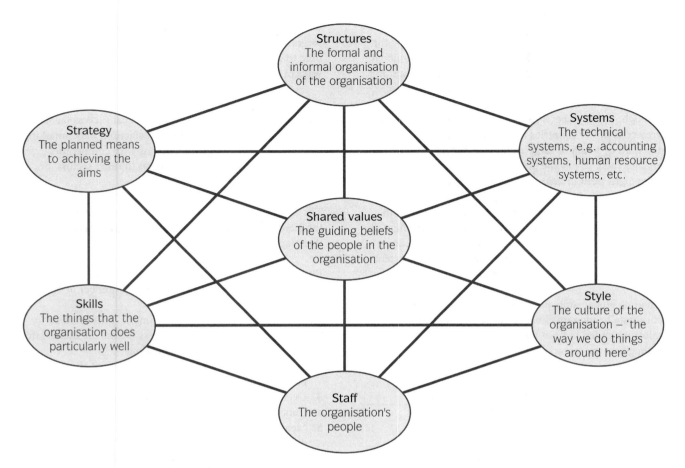

Figure 29.13 *McKinsey's 7S framework*

Peters and Waterman showed that management in the west had been placing too much emphasis on the 'hard' factors of strategic decision-making, i.e., structures, systems and strategy. They showed that excellent companies in the US and Japan placed just as much emphasis on the 'soft' factors of staff, style and skills and particular emphasis on 'shared values'.

In most of the 40 companies surveyed by McKinsey the role of one or more strategic leaders had proved to be very influential. Peters and Waterman concluded therefore that 'the real role of the chief executive is to manage the values of the organisation'. They argued that successful companies will get the basic fundamentals of working with their environment right, i.e. customer service, low-cost manufacturing, productivity improvement, innovation and risk-taking. In excellent organisations there is an emphasis

on simplicity – simple organisational structure, simple strategies, simple communications systems, etc.

Other characteristics that Peters and Waterman listed were:

- a bias for action
- closeness to the customer
- autonomy and entrepreneurship
- productivity through people (a human resource management approach)
- hands on, value driven (values are established through good communications; power and personality of the 'leader(s)' is crucial)
- stick to the knitting (successful companies know what they do well and concentrate on doing it well)
- simple form, lean staff (simple structures)
- simultaneous loose-tight properties (an effective combination of central direction and individual autonomy).

SWOT

One of the most useful tools in preparing the ground for organisational planning is SWOT (Strengths, Weaknesses, Opportunities and Threats) analysis. The organisation's resources (its strengths and weaknesses) are evaluated alongside the external environment (the source of opportunities and threats) before deciding on objectives and strategies (see Figure 29.14).

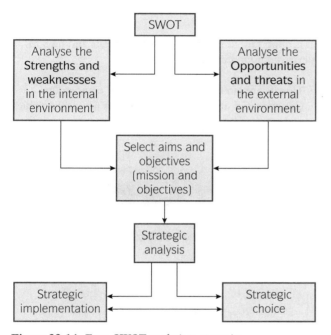

Figure 29.14 *From SWOT analysis to strategies*

Before the DIY group Focus took over the Do It All chain in 1998 it carried out a SWOT analysis to identify the prospects of the success of the take-over initiative in the dynamic DIY retailing environment. Focus took into consideration a range of possibilities for expansion, for example by building new premises, which would have been expensive, or by buying out an already established company. It decided on the latter.

The 'consolidation of both companies was seen to be an excellent fit, both geographically and strategically'. Focus saw the option of merging with the Do It All chain as a good opportunity as it had a number of qualities which would be good to incorporate into the new company such as the already established name, quality customer service, excellent product choice, with over 25 000 products, and an attractive store environment. Focus management saw that 'by joining forces we will become a larger, stronger chain

which is much better positioned to compete in the demanding DIY market'. The merger was seen to be a great opportunity to win increased market share. The aim was to build on the core competences of each organisation to make a bigger, stronger organisation making this more dominant in the marketplace but still offering the well-known names and services. A summary of the SWOT analysis for Focus prior to the take-over is shown in Figure 29.15.

Strengths	**Weaknesses**

Growing company
Well established
Well known in the north
Profit-making success
Differentiated goods:
  • DIY
  • Pet World
  • craft department
	Need to cover the
	  whole country
	Relatively small with only
	  72 stores

Opportunities	**Threats**

For expansion, i.e.
  purchase of Do it All
Growing market
Popularity of DIY
  TV programmes
Chance to reposition
  in the market
	Other DIY stores, e.g. B&Q
	Risk of a new business
	  venture
	Problems of integration

Figure 29.15 *SWOT analysis of Focus–Do It All merger*

Case Study

SWOT analysis for MidCity NH Facilities

NH Facilities is a trading agency of MidCity Healthcare NHS Trust appointed to maintain and ensure that the estate and facilities of MidCity Healthcare Trust and the clients it serves are safe, maintained and meet current government standards. It is a non-profit making organisation. MidCity Healthcare Trust employs approximately 2200 employees and has an annual income of £53 million. NH Facilities has a turnover of approximately £5.5 million.

NH Facilities set out the SWOT analysis shown in Figure 29.16.

Strengths	Weaknesses
Highly trained workforce Modern-thinking organisation with full technological resources Relatively large, well-established organisation	Lack of finance Not advertised outside the NHS Poor business/sales management to generate external income

Opportunities	Threats
To branch into the private sector, private hospitals/clinics and establishments	From private contractors able to offer more cost-effective service

Figure 29.16 *NH Facilities: SWOT analysis*

Questions

1. How might the SWOT analysis shown in Figure 29.16 have helped the organisation in creating the sorts of strategies designed for success?

2. How do you think that the organisation might have altered its current strategy in the light of the SWOT analysis?

John Thompson (1995) states that for an organisation to be managed well from the strategic point of view, it will need to have E-V-R congruence (see Figure 29.17).

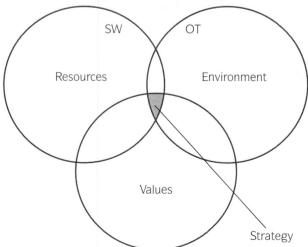

SWOT matches: Strengths/weaknesses (SW), Opportunities/threats (OT)

Figure 29.17 *E-V-R congruence*

- E – managers would need to understand fully the dynamics, opportunities and threats present in their competitive environment and to pay full regard to wider societal issues
- V – the values of the organisation would need to match the needs of the environment and the key success factors, and crucially, the values would need to be shared and followed throughout the organisation.
- R – the resources of the organisation (inputs) would need to be managed strategically, taking account of strengths, weaknesses and opportunities for the organisation.

It is important to recognise risks and threats and then to devise appropriate strategies to respond.

- Threats are often described in terms of competitors.
- Opportunities are usually thought of as new technologies and new markets.

TASK

Identify the threat and the opportunity in each of the following examples.

1. During the 1980s the oil and petrol producer Shell identified the 'top-up shopper' who pops into service stations looking for a variety of urgent goods from milk to newspapers, and from contraceptives to cheeseburgers. This provided the company with a potential new area for development bearing in mind that petrol sales were falling because out-of-town supermarkets were selling cut-price petrol as an incentive to attract shoppers.

2. During the 1980s a range of banks started offering 'hole-in-the-wall' facilities, for example cashpoint and other banking services which were all the more effective as a result of developments in computer-led banking. For each bank there was the fear that other banks would seize the competitive advantage.

3. In the 1980s the chocolate manufacturer Mars introduced the Mars ice-cream to take up the slack in chocolate demand in the summer months and particularly as a growing number of confectionery and chocolate producers were moving into the European market. They were able to do this as a result of a leap forward in production methods.

Quantification techniques can be very important in weighing up the opportunities that are available. Criteria such as the highest return, least risky and most feasible are helpful to put values on opportunities. Market research information provides a useful flow of information to support this process.

The internal audit of the organisation should clarify the nature of the following aspects of the organisation and its strategy:

- purpose
- scope of activities and markets
- product positions
- organisational efficiency
- distribution methods
- operations
- finance
- policy and procedures

Purpose

The purpose of the organisation is its overarching mission (general aim). We have already examined the mission of the organisation in the previous chapter. However, the organisation's mission should be subject to review on an on-going basis, as should the objectives of the organisation. In carrying out an internal audit of an organisation it is necessary to examine how appropriate the existing mission is given changes in the organisation's environment, and changes in the resource position, and changes in the core competences of the organisation over time.

A good example of an organisation which has had to review its purpose in recent times is the BBC which for many years had been the public face of British broadcasting in Britain. However, by the 1980s to many people the BBC had become too inward looking and had developed a culture of 'We know best; we are the best; we'll make it all ourselves; our size is our strength; what happens outside is their business'. By the late 1980s the BBC had become very bureaucratic and was overspending on its budget. But the world outside was changing, with dramatic impact as it moved into the digital revolution of the late 1990s that would introduce the potential for widespread competition in broadcasting with the advent of multi-channel television and radio services. In the early 1990s John Birt was brought into the BBC as its Director-General to help the organisation retain its licence to broadcast from the government. In order to win this right, wide-scale reforms needed to be introduced, including the creation of an internal market in the BBC and the division of the corporation into business units.

The BBC has been able to win the right to continue as the BBC and its charter entitles it to receive licence fees from television owners. In its Statement of Public Purposes (1998) the BBC has sought to build on its past while looking to the future. It aims:

- to nurture and cherish the rich diversity of the UK's heritage, identity and cultural life; bringing people together for moments of celebration, common experience and in times of crisis
- to enable all sides to join the debate on issues of national, regional and local significance through providing the most comprehensive news service, or range and depth, rooted in experience
- to reflect the nations, regions and communities of the UK to themselves and to the rest of the UK
- to help people broaden their horizons through learning, and by enriching their skills to provide something of particular value to all UK licence payers, exposing audiences to new ideas, to scientific discovery, to great art, music and writing, to the spiritual and uplifting
- to create programmes and services of real cultural value, offering the most gifted individuals in every area the opportunity to create fresh and pioneering television, radio and online services.

But the document also sets out that the BBC has new public purposes to reflect the changing environment:

- to ensure no one is excluded from access to new kinds of service made possible by new technology
- to use its ability to reach into every home to engage audiences in new experiences and to act as a trusted guide in a world of abundance.

Scope of activities and markets

A fundamental aspect of strategy is the clear identification of the scope of the activities and markets of the organisation. According to Mintzberg, scope is the extent of the market in which products and services are sold – 'scope is essentially a demand-driven concept, taking its lead from the market – what exists out there'. Johnson and Scholes (1998) point out that strategic decisions 'are likely to be concerned with the scope of an organisation's activities: does and should the organisation concentrate on one area of activity, or does it have many?'. For example, 20 years ago the scope of the activities of Manchester United Football Club was focused directly on footballing activities. Today the scope of activities is much broader so that in the annual report for 1998 the club gave details of not only the playing side of the club, but also of catering and conference revenues, sponsorship and royalty income, merchandising, the development of a 110-bedroom hotel, and the launch of MUTV with partners BSkyB and Granada.

Of course scope is not simply about defining the activities that the organisation engages in, it also concerns the strategies employed with regards to the segmentation of markets. Mintzberg identifies a range of segmentation strategies.

- **Unsegmentation strategy** – the 'one size fits all' approach of the model T Ford or salt. Today, however, most products are segmented.
- **Segmentation strategies** – producing products for particular market segments. Some organisations seek to be 'comprehensive' trying to serve all market segments, whereas others are 'selective', selling to a narrow range of segments.
- **Niche strategy** – focuses on a single segment.
- **Customising strategies** – pure customisation involves treating each individual customer as an individual market.

Product positions

A key aspect of strategy is to identify the positions of the organisation's existing goods and services in the market and the ideal positions for these goods and services. Often it becomes apparent that it is necessary to 'reposition', for example by moving a product up or down market. For example, in the mid-1990s the food manufacturer McVitie's repositioned its Hobnob biscuits to target them at a younger age group. The biscuits had originally been targeted at an older genteel audience. However, McVitie's found that the biscuits were most popular with younger males. They therefore refocused on this younger audience while seeking to retain their existing customer base.

Positioning is an important part of strategy because it enables the organisation to identify the most appropriate 'battlegrounds' for its products.

Organisational efficiency

It is essential that the various parts of the organisation are coordinated to create the maximum synergy between different products and strategic business units. Ansoff described synergy as the process whereby 2 + 2 = 5. Thompson sees strategy as taking place at three levels within the organisation.

- Corporate strategy is the responsibility of strategic leaders (the board) of the organisation.
- Competitive strategies are the responsibility of the various businesses within the organisation.
- Functional strategies are the responsibility of the various functions within the organisation – marketing, finance, production, etc.

Synergy is most likely to occur if all these strategies are linked in an effective organisational management system, which Drucker defined as 'doing the right things'. Each of the individual business units and functions must be "doing things right". Resources need to be managed to yield the highest possible return given the objectives of the organisation. Resources will be used effectively if they are being put to the most beneficial purposes. This synergy of strategies is illustrated in Figure 29.18.

Michael Porter (*Competitive Advantage: Creating and Sustaining Superior Performance*, 1985) sees the creation of a value chain as being of fundamental importance in organising the organisation and its relationship with other organisations. The value chain can be defined as an organisation's coordinated set of activities to satisfy the customer, beginning with relationships with suppliers and procurement, and going through production, selling and marketing and delivery to the customer. Each link in the value chain must seek competitive advantage, either by creating lower cost, or through differentiation.

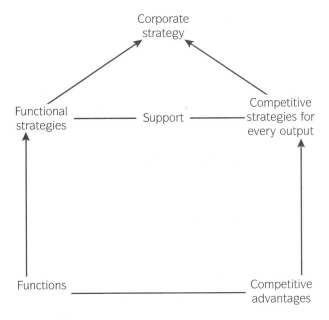

Figure 29.18 *Synergy between strategies*

1. inbound logistics, i.e. receiving, storing and distributing the inputs to the good

2. operations, i.e. transforming the various inputs into the final good

3. outbound logistics, i.e. collecting, storing and distributing the good to consumers

4. marketing and sales

5. service, i.e. the activities involved in enhancing the product, for example installation, repair, etc.

The four support activities are:

1. procurement, i.e. getting hold of the various resource inputs required for the primary activities

2. technology development

3. human resource management

4. management systems.

Distribution methods

Getting the products to the right place, at the right time and in the required state is an important part of strategy that is frequently overlooked. Sometimes organisations see distribution as being outside their control because they contract out this work. The intelligent organisation will see distribution as an important area to develop competitive advantage. Failure in this area can have serious consequences. For example, when the chocolate manufacturer Mars developed the Mars ice-cream it was unable to put the ice-cream into many small shops,

The value which consumers place on goods and services is determined by the way in which the activities required to design, produce, market, deliver and support the product are performed.

The organisation therefore needs to build a value chain with strong and effective linkages with suppliers and customers (see Figure 29.19).

Porter identified five main primary activities and four support activities which are key to the success of the value chain. The five primary activities are:

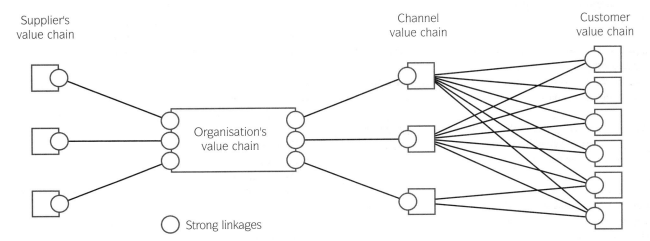

Figure 29.19 *Building a strong value chain*

newsagents and garages because the freezers in these shops were owned by Mars' rival Wall's.

Operations

Operations lie at the heart of the success of any organisation. It is only by organising operational activities in an efficient way that the rest of the organisation can flourish. In many ways it is the operations which will lie at the heart of the core competences of the organisation, i.e. what the organisation does particularly well, whether it be in drilling for oil (Shell), playing football (Manchester United), or producing crisps (Walkers). Manchester United as a business organisation is particularly successful because it is based on incisive strategic thinking, but it will only continue to be successful if its strategy supports at an operational level the playing of attractive, exciting and winning football.

The winning organisation therefore will continually audit and monitor its operations to make sure that they are of the highest standard. In a club like Manchester United this relates to a whole array of operational activities. A lapse in health and safety, floodlighting, or the sale of tickets could have a disastrous impact on the goodwill associated with the club.

Finance

Financial analysis is always helpful in strategy development because it enables an organisation to work out how well it is using its resources. Comparisons with other firms are particularly helpful in measuring how well the organisation is performing. Useful financial measures will include:

- return on capital employed (ROCE) – to measure overall performance
- profitability, gearing, liquidity – to make comparisons with other companies and risk assessment, etc.

These ratios are of use to the organisation for comparative purposes. When sensible comparisons are made these measures can be used to inform strategic thinking.

Financial analysis is also particularly helpful when it is related to the value activities which have been highlighted above (see Porter's value activities). For example, figures showing stock turnover will be of use in assessing delivery performance. Johnson and Scholes (1998) show that

because key value activities change over time, so too will the appropriate financial measure to monitor. For example, when a product is introduced a key factor to monitor will be sales volume. Once the product is established, profit/unit may become more significant, while during decline cash flow might be more significant to support the development of a new generation of products.

Policy and procedures

Policies are general statements which guide thinking and actions in decision-making. They are designed to guide the behaviour of managers in relation to the pursuit and achievement of strategies and objectives. They define an area within which a decision is made and ensure that the decision contributes to the meeting of an objective. For example, a large organisation will have policies on equal opportunities, the use of suppliers, health and safety at work, dealing with customers, etc. These policies will normally be set out in writing and need to be in tune with strategic objectives. Policies need to be updated to match changes in the environment in which the organisation operates (for example a change in government legislation on hours that employees may work) and changes in organisational objectives. Policies need to be audited on a regular basis to check that they are in line with organisational strategy.

Rules and procedures set out a required method of handling particular activities. For example, a rule about only dealing with suppliers who meet British and International Safety Standards or who comply with Codes of Practice on Ethical Business. Clearly, an organisation that creates strategies which are founded in ethical standards will want to see these principles carried through into policies, rules and procedures. By auditing policies, rules and procedures it becomes possible to check that strategy is translated into operational detail.

Koontz and O'Donnell (*Principles of Management*, 1968) suggest that the following principles determine the potential effectiveness of policies in relation to strategy.

- Policies should reflect objectives.
- Policies should be consistent.
- Policies should be flexible.
- The extent to which a policy is mandatory, as opposed to advisory, should be clear.
- Policies should be communicated, taught and understood.
- Policies should be controlled.

THE FORMULATION OF A STRATEGY

Creating a strategy for an organisation involves two stages – formulation of a strategy (covered in this chapter) and implementation of the strategy (covered in Chapter 30).

Kenneth Andrews (*The Concept of Corporate Strategy*, 1980) identifies the principal subactivities of strategy formulation as including identifying opportunities and threats and estimating the alternatives. Before a choice can be made, the company's strengths and weaknesses have to be appraised along with the resources.

Andrews calls the strategic alternative which results from matching opportunity and corporate capability at an acceptable level of risk – 'the economic strategy'. Of course, the choice of strategy also depends on the values of the organisation, and particularly of the influential stakeholders in the organisation. The choice of the appropriate strategy should also involve an ethical dimension.

Richard Rumelt (*Business Policy and Strategic Management*, 1980) makes a distinction between generic and competitive strategy. Generic strategy is concerned with identifying the mission and scope of the organisation in order to create a match with resources and environment. In contrast, competitive strategy is concerned with enabling an organisation to create a 'special competitive position or edge'. Of course, today strategy is seen as a vehicle for differentiating an organisation from others by identifying and developing core competences. Figure 29.20 identifies some of the differences that Rumelt drew between generic and competitive strategy.

Creating a competitive strategy involves exploiting the best opportunities and creating those advantages which are most difficult to copy. The major roots of competitive advantage are:

- superior resources
- superior competences
- superior position.

The first two of these have been covered already. Positional advantage is concerned with arranging an organisation's resources and competence to enhance their combined effectiveness, and thus to put the competition on the backfoot. This element of strategy has a lot in common with the notion of strategy as used in a game of chess, or

	Generic	Competitive
Measure of success	Sales growth	Market share
Return to the firm	Value added	Return on investment
Function	Provision of value to the customer	Maintaining or obtaining a defensible position
Basic strategic tasks	Adapting to change and innovation	Creating barriers and deterring rivals
Method of expressing strategy	Product/market terms, functional terms	Policies leading to defensible position
Basic approach to analysis	Study of group of businesses over time	Comparison across rivals at a given time

Figure 29.20 *The differences between generic and competitive strategy (Rumelt)*

in arranging armies into battle formations. It is all about outcompeting the opposition. Organisations therefore need to devise both generic and competitive strategies.

Strategy therefore consists of:

- defining the direction that the organisation will take in the long term, for example to be known as the global market leader in soft drinks provision
- defining the scope of an organisation's activities, for example to produce colas, fruit-flavoured soft drinks and cordials
- matching an organisation's activities to its environment, for example increasing market presence in all of the countries of the world, particularly in newly emerging markets where dynamic rates of growth are occurring
- matching the activities of an organisation to its available resources, for example ploughing back more profits into expansion, and buying back shares from shareholders in order to reduce the amount that the company has to pay out in dividends
- deciding how major resources will be used by the organisation, for example deciding to build new bottling plant in ten new countries per year over a five-year period
- setting out the goals and values of the organisation, for example to develop a customer-focused, ethical and environmentally conscious organisation
- deciding on the pattern of change that will take place in the organisation.

The realisation of resources to match strategic intent with strategic capability

It is helpful to look at strategy as resulting from a recipe which is identified from analysing opportunities and threats (stemming from environmental forces) and strengths and weaknesses (stemming from organisational capabilities) (see Figure 29.21).

Figure 29.21 *From recipe to strategy*

Of course the performance of the organisation will be determined by what happens in the environment as well as how the organisation uses its capabilities.

Having established the best opportunities to pursue, the organisation needs to ask two related questions.

1. What resources will be needed to convert these opportunities?
2. How can it obtain these resources?

When the organisation establishes its strategic intent, it needs to make sure that it has the resources required, i.e. its capability must match its intent. For example, when Focus wanted to take over Do It All it had to come up with the finance to make the acquisition possible. When Manchester United wanted to extend its ground capacity and to build a new training ground the club had to consider ways of acquiring the financial resources.

Organisations need to think long and hard about how they can build on their existing core competences and resources to achieve their strategic aims. They need to consider a whole range of resource-related questions.

- Do we have the existing financial resource base? If not, how can we acquire the necessary extra finance?
- Do we have the right products? If not, how can we make the right products ourselves, or do we need to join together with another organisation that will help us to create the right products?
- Do we have the right management? If not, what can we do to improve existing capabilities of management and to acquire managerial skills from outside?
- Do we have the right people? If not, what can we do to improve existing capabilities of our people and to acquire people with the necessary competence from outside?
- Do we have the right plant?, etc.
- Do we have the right systems and organisation?, etc.
- Do we have the right supply chain relationships?, etc.

The organisation needs to consider how it can bridge the gap between its strategic intent and its strategic capability (see Figure 29.22). Of course, for many ambitious organisations this involves a simple leap of imagination and a lot of hard work.

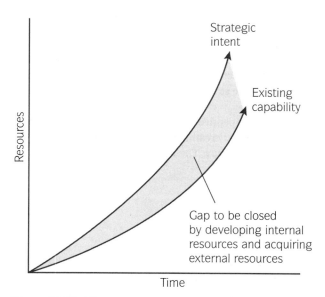

Figure 29.22 *The strategic intent–strategic capability gap*

Strategy Implementation

How then do organisations put their strategies into effect – what is the process of strategic implementation?

As we have seen in the previous chapter, organisational strategy is the process of positioning the organisation in its competitive environment and implementing actions to meet its aims and objectives and to compete successfully. The implementation of strategies should seek to maximise benefits and minimise risks. Successful strategic implementation should therefore involve the integration of strategy, organisational design (structure), people, systems and performance at every level in the organisation.

This chapter considers how organisations turn their strategic plans into operational reality. It looks at the way resources are allocated to implement the plans and the methods organisations use to evaluate whether corporate, operational and individual targets have been met.

On completion of the chapter you should be able to examine approaches to strategy implementation. To achieve this you must demonstrate the ability to:

- compare the roles and responsibilities for strategy implementation in two different organisations

- identify and evaluate resource requirements to implement a new strategy for a given organisation

- propose targets and time-scales for achievement in a given organisation to monitor a given strategy.

DEVELOPMENTS IN STRATEGIC THINKING

Traditional thinking about strategy (for example the writing of Alfred Chandler in the 1960s) saw the creation of strategy and structure and its being predominantly the responsibility of senior management. Today, increasing emphasis is placed on building winning strategies through a combination of senior management, management throughout the organisation, and teamwork building on the competence, and unique skills and abilities within the organisation.

Schermerhorn, Hunt and Osborn (*Managing Organisational Behaviour*, 1997) see the strategy process as a two-way street. Senior managers will select those 'systems goals they believe should define corporate success; form these goals into a vision; select a target position within the general and specific environments; and develop a design to accomplish the vision'. They will typically use generic strategies to guide their choices. At the same time the firm will develop specific administrative and technical competences over time. Schermerhorn *et al.* state, 'Middle- and lower-level managers institute minor modifications and adjustments to solve specific problems and capitalise on specific opportunities.' These adjustments will then be moved up the organisational ladder 'providing senior

Strategy implementation **659**

managers with the opportunity to adjust, modify, and build upon a generic strategy to develop a so-called competency strategy'. Of course, in a totally empowered organisation such inputs to on-going strategy will potentially stem from all of the people who work for the organisation. In a stakeholder organisation inputs to strategy can potentially be made by all stakeholders.

THE REALISATION OF STRATEGIC PLANS TO OPERATIONAL REALITY

Corporate or organisational strategies are made at the level of the whole organisation/company. They are then translated into a series of generic and competitive strategies for each business unit, and good/market. Functional strategies (if the organisation is organised on a functional basis) are designed to carry out the competitive strategies and these will be translated into a series of action plans. To complement this process the structure of the organisation is designed to break down the work and other tasks to be completed. The organisation will be structured into a series of divisions, business units or functions. The people that comprise these substructures will be working to objectives, targets, plans, programmes, policies and procedures which give them a direction for their activities. (See Figure 30.1.)

Of course, the translation of corporate strategy into individual action plans is not and should not be seen as a simple, static and one-way process. Rather it is a complex, dynamic and multi-directional process. As we have seen earlier, strategy formulation is an adaptive process responding to changes within and outside the organisation. Changes at lower levels within the organisation will lead to emergent functional, competitive and in turn corporate strategies. John Thompson (1990) argues that the behaviour of people within a structure leads to emergent strategies so that there is a continual circular process (see Figure 30.2).

John Purcell ('The impact of corporate strategy on human resource management', in J. Storey (ed.), *New Perspectives on Human Resource Management*, 1989) identifies strategic management as taking place at three levels in the organisation. At the top of the organisation 'first-order' strategies consist of decisions about the long-term goals and scope of activities: 'second-order' strategies lead to

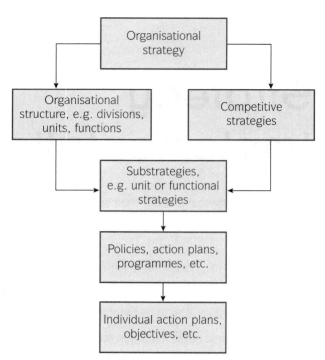

Figure 30.1 *The translation of corporate strategy into individual action plans*

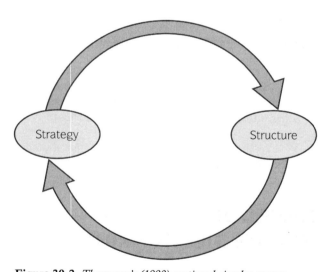

Figure 30.2 *Thompson's (1990) continual circular process*

decisions on the way the organisation is structured to achieve its goals; finally, 'third-order strategies' are concerned with all those mechanisms for 'making things happen' in an organisation.

Rosabeth Moss Kanter (*The Change Masters*, 1993) likens corporate change to architecture. She argues that the skill of corporate leaders, who she calls the ultimate change masters 'lies in their ability to envision a new reality and aid in its translation into concrete terms.' Of course, the plans must combine effectively with the everyday reality of building: 'Creative visions combine with the building up of events, floor by floor, from foundation to completed construction'. Moss Kanter provides a view of strategy in which the realisation of strategic plans can only come about when those involved with operational reality are able to make a contribution to decision-making and planning within the organisation: 'Effective organisations benefit from integrative structures and cultures that promote innovation below the top and learn from them'.

This kind of analysis of change provides a link between micro-level and macro-level innovation: the actions of numerous managerial entrepreneurs and problem-solving teams, on the one hand, and, on the other, the overall shift of a company's direction better to meet current challenges. The build-up of experiences from successful small-scale innovations – or even the breakthrough idea that an innovator's work produces, in the case of new products or new technological processes – can then be embraced by those guiding the organisation as part of an important new strategy. In short, action first, thought later: experience first, making a 'strategy' out of it second.

Of course, an organisation can effectively implement strategies only if they are appropriate to:

• the organisation
• the organisation's stakeholders
• the organisation's environment,
• the organisation's resources and competences.

All organisations need to know whether their strategies are worth putting into practice (can they be effectively implemented?). They, therefore, need to establish criteria to decide whether to go ahead with a plan or not. There are three important criteria for evaluating options: suitability, acceptability and feasibility.

Suitability is concerned with whether strategies fit the situation. For example, tools such as PESTLE, SWOT (see page 636), and other market and competitors' analyses provides a good view of the internal organisation and the external environment. The organisation then needs to look at whether its strategic options provide a suitable use of resources in a given environment, for example whether a strategy:

• fits with internal weaknesses or external threats facing an organisation
• builds on an organisation's existing strengths and environmental opportunities
• matches the organisation's stated objectives.

A key to success for most organisations is to create and modify as appropriate generic strategies that enable the organisation to build upon and refine its unique experience and competences. For example, the food manufacturer Heinz's Project Millennia strategy is concerned with building on its existing competences. Even though Heinz has a pre-eminent position in global food markets, it has reorganised its European operations based on product categories to be in the best position to create high-level returns.

Acceptability is concerned with whether a strategy will be acceptable to the organisation and to those with a significant interest in it. For example, is the level of risk acceptable and are shareholders and other stakeholders prepared to agree to the plans? They may have reservations based on what they consider to be ethical, fair and reasonable. For example, strategies involving high financial returns in a developing market may have to be shelved if influential stakeholders see the environmental costs as being too high a price to pay. In the late 1990s the oil and petroleum producer Shell UK realised that it would have to change its ethical and environmental policies because the company had lost touch in some measure with public perceptions of what constituted 'right' behaviour.

Feasibility is concerned with whether strategic plans can work in practice and, primarily, whether the organisation has adequate resources to carry out particular plans, for example whether:

• the funds are available
• the organisation will be able to sustain the required level of output
• the organisation will be able to deal with the competition that it generates
• the organisation will be able to meet the required market share.

All organisations constantly have to determine whether their strategic intentions are feasible. If Coca-Cola wants to dominate the world soft drinks market, then it needs to generate the capital and cash to expand and support its developing operations, etc.

Communication – selling the concepts

Communication is a two-way process. You are not communicating when you send a message which no one receives. Effective strategic implementation requires effective communication. Today it is widely recognised that effective communication in an organisation involves Employee Involvement (EI). EI can operate at a simple level, where managers listen to ideas coming from below. Alternatively, it can involve creating a role for employees in the decision-making process. When this is the case, the term empowerment or employee participation is used to describe the process. If employees are to be involved, there needs to be a framework for supporting them and formal channels of communication.

Case Study

Creating a key strategic change at Blue Circle Cement

Like many companies in the UK in the late 1980s Blue Circle Cement was desperately in need of change. Blue Circle is the UK's largest cement producer, supplying about half of the country's needs from ten cement works. In the mid-1980s it was decided to make a major investment in new highly automated, computer-controlled plant in a small number of cement works. It was decided that cement works which developed the new technology would also pioneer new modern work practices involving greater empowerment of employees.

The UK cement industry in the early 1980s was characterised by high manning levels of both salaried staff and hourly paid workers; relatively low wages and high overtime levels. A working week in excess of 60 hours was common. Restrictive working practices were the norm with strict demarcation between crafts and between process and craft workers. Productivity was very low and the amount of supervision was high. Morale was poor and conflict was common. Management and employee relationships were characterised by low levels of trust and an adversarial 'them and us', 'win/lose' culture. All change was regarded with extreme suspicion. Compounding the situation was the lack of international competitiveness, in particular in Europe. In the 1980s the UK cement market was in steep decline and under increasing threat from lower priced imports.

It was obvious that the organisation could not continue this way. Radical changes were needed to ways of working and to the culture of the organisation. A new vision was needed for the organisation as well as a radical change in working practice. Trade unions representing employees of Blue Circle agreed to support the change initiative, subject to negotiation with the view to creating a shared vision. The Advisory, Conciliation and Arbitration Services' (ACAS) Work Research Unit was also asked to assist in creating the vision.

First it was decided to identify best practice (i.e. the benchmarks) in other companies such as Pilkington Glass and Carreras Rothman. These visits were made by a joint group of management and shopfloor representatives to encourage growth of a new team spirit. The result of this research, fact finding, analysis and discussion was the creation of a new vision of how the business units could run. The shared vision for the future was to have a highly skilled and flexible workforce, working as an integrated team which, together with the new technology, would be able to compete with the best in the world.

Key elements of the new vision were:

- enhanced skills for individuals with a reduction in the number of job grades, leading to greater flexibility
- introduction of a simple pay structure with the elimination of paid overtime and bonuses and increased basic wage levels
- significantly reduced manning levels and a reduction in total labour costs
- new ways of working based on increasing team work and shared decision-making.

Team training was seen as being essential to build the new organisation. This involved everyone in the workplace and was given active support by shop stewards as well as the management team. The training programme included four main elements.

1. *A senior managers workshop*. This looked at all aspects of team building, leadership and teamwork. For example, it was concerned with procedures involved in building high-performance teams, and ways of ensuring that suitable resources were provided for team building. Management needed an indepth understanding of the training to be given to the rest of the workforce.

2. *Staff team training*. This was given to all middle managers and supervisors. Attendance at each session was organised so that all managers were accompanied by their supervisors. The focus was very much on putting teamwork into operation and ways of organising the team building workshops.

3. *Team leader briefings.* The role of the team leader was seen as crucial, so the purpose of the briefings was to prepare the leaders for the workshop session with their teams and to ensure as far as possible that they assumed a leadership role in team building.

4. *Team building workshops.* The workshop was the key element of the change process. During the workshop, an important part of the leader's job was to relax the team and ensure that its members became involved in the training experience. Because many employees were not used to the processes of teamwork it was necessary to encourage and develop participatory and co-operative approaches. Team members were asked to list all their concerns about the new ways of working. These were then displayed until the end of the workshop. The workshops included syndicate exercises, identification of roles within a team and leadership styles. Practice in working as a team was provided by problem-solving syndicates. The workshop concluded with an open forum with the manager in attendance responding to concerns and any unresolved matters.

It took Blue Circle two and a half years to research, negotiate, carry out training and implement new approaches to teamworking. The new equipment, technology and the new working practices dramatically improved the productivity and efficiency of the new model cement works. By the early 1990s these plant were the highest performers in the UK cement industry. Employees in these plant worked shorter hours and received higher pay.

When ACAS was asked to review attitudes of employees to the changes, the results were heartening with almost unanimous support for the changes. Employees found the increased variety and challenge in their jobs stimulating, and the development of teamworking increased employee involvement and sense of pride in the job, leading to improvements in commitment and morale. The new ways of working were subsequently introduced to all Blue Circle plants in the 1990s.

Questions

1. What do you see as being the key strategic changes which were taking place at Blue Circle in the late 1980s and early 1990s.

2. Why was effective communications required to ensure that this process was a success?

3. What were the main channels and processes of communication that are highlighted in the case study?

4. Why was greater employee involvement seen as being at the heart of the strategic changes?

The Blue Circle case study highlights the importance of involving and gaining the support of those people who will be affected by a strategy and strategic change. The implications of the new strategies and changes should be communicated widely, so that awareness and understanding is created and commitment and involvement sought. Incentive and reward systems will underpin the change. Philip Sadler (*Designing Organisations*, 1994) cites the example of how a company employing 300 people decided that it would express its mission as concisely as possible so that employees and customers could quickly grasp its meaning; and that all employees should develop a deeper understanding of the mission and a sense of ownership of the mission. A competition was organised in which employees were invited to enter phrases which they felt expressed the core mission. The prize for the winning entry was a flight for two on Concorde. The prize was sufficiently attractive to motivate virtually every employee to participate – and to involve their families, too, in many cases.

Kerry Napuk (1996) states that the guiding principle behind communication is simple: 'Clear communication of ideas helps people to see the need and logic for change. Understanding about the future also allows people to worry less about specific changes and helps them to think how they can contribute to the plan, not fight it'.

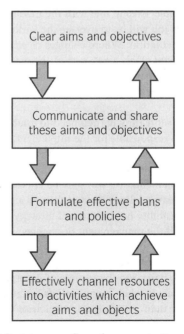

Figure 30.3 *A two-way flow of communication*

We can illustrate the important part played by communication in translating aims and objectives for an organisation (or part of an organisation) into the ground-level operational detail involved in implementing strategies. In Figure 30.3 this appears as a two-way flow showing how evaluation of the implementation of resource-related operations feeds back into the creation of aims and objectives.

Project teams

Strategic plans can most effectively be implemented through the mechanism of project teams. The modern organisation identifies a range of projects which can be handled by project teams. Some of these projects are short-lived, while others are on-going. Individual employees can and will often be members of several project teams at the same time. Project teams work towards achieving given objectives which are tied in to the overall strategy of the organisation. The work of these teams may lead to changes in the organisation's strategy over a period of time.

In terms of strategy implementation it is important to establish project teams with a responsibility for ensuring that different components or strategy are delivered. For example, at board level in a major organisation there will be a project team with overarching responsibility for strategic implementation. The team will need to work with clearly defined objectives in line with the mission of the organisation. Its job will be to oversee the various stages of strategy implementation. Where changes of strategic direction are taking place, a key part of the remit of the team will be the management of change and the development of new working practices in the organisation.

The central project team will then need to establish a range of project teams responsible for the implementation of strategy at other levels within the organisation, for example in specific business units, plants, etc. This cascade process for strategic implementation will only be effective if objectives are clearly delineated, and there is a clear sense of where responsibility lies in terms of strategy development and the management of change.

Rosabeth Moss Kanter sees what she calls 'segmentalism' as being a major barrier to the success of an organisation. Segmentalism occurs when organisations assign people to fragments rather than larger pieces; emphasise uncrossable boundaries between functions, between hierarchical levels, between central staff and field operations, and even

between kinds of people (for example racial and gender segmentation). The net effect is the creation of structural barriers to communications, to the exchange of ideas, to joint efforts to solve problems, and so on. People are confined to a particular category and thus the contribution that they can make to the organisation is limited. Segmentalism acts as a barrier at every stage of the problem-identification and solution-search process. The approach needs to be replaced by integration, based on an empowering commitment-based approach to work and problem-solving.

If people are to be committed to the organisation, its aims and strategies, then they must be involved. Employees at grass-roots level are likely to know the details of the business and what really happens better than their superiors and managers. If they are to be involved and encouraged to contribute their ideas for improvements, the result is likely to be both innovation and quality improvement. If managers and other employees are to make effective strategic contributions, it is important that they feel motivated.

Project teams are an important way of involving all employees in an organisation in making important positive contributions to the organisation and its strategies.

Case Study

Creating project teams at Equitable Life

The Equitable Life Assurance Company is the oldest mutual life assurance provider in the world. Founded in 1762, its values and principles remain as important today as they were in the days when its founders invented the principles of modern life assurance. Today the Society is a highly successful and innovative provider of both life assurance, pensions and other financial service products in the UK and in its international branches.

In recent years the environment in which the insurance industry operates has seen dramatic changes, with the development of new providers of insurance, greater international competition, and the introduction of Direct Services (over the telephone line). The most dramatic changes have involved the widespread use of information and communications technology.

Until recently, Equitable Life, like many other insurance companies, operated in a fragmented way. At its Aylesbury head office, each area dealing with a particular product was divided into departments dealing with a specific function, for example new business, renewal premiums, medical evidence, general servicing and claims payments. Processing across the organisational boundaries was common place as a customer often had queries about two different types of policy or two or more functions of an individual policy. In these circumstances, a letter would be photocopied and passed to the different departments. Alternatively, it would be answered in part by one area, then passed to colleagues in another department. This meant that the customer either received more than one letter in answer to a query, or after a considerable delay, a combined response.

However, in the mid-1990s all this was to change with the widespread use of information technology in the organisation and with the development of a new organisational vision – 'growing more contented customers'. The emphasis was now to be on customer service, i.e. building a personal relationship between the customer and the company, and more particularly between the customer and the people who represent the company to customers, for example the person you speak to when taking out a policy or making a claim.

Having decided on creating a strategy based on information technology, customer relations and new ways of working, Equitable Life had to put it into action – strategy implementation.

The result of the changes was that between mid-1992 and mid-1993 the Society took groups of staff through a radical change process. Their working environment and organisation altered completely from 'old style' to 'new style'. Customer servicing is now provided by a number of multi-skilled teams, each taking its share of all incoming written work across the entire range of individual products and processes. The work is randomly allocated by the system across all teams. A paper-in area handles all incoming paper, references it and scans the documents on to the image system for handling in the paperless servicing unit. Once the client's request has been dealt with, the resulting paper output is handled by a separate dispatch area called paper-out processing. This means that there is no need to handle clients' papers in the servicing area. A dedicated telephone call centre deals with all incoming telephone enquiries.

The removal of departmental barriers gives staff greater variety of work which they handle as a project team. The new approach focuses on the customer and not the task, and has removed the time-consuming, less interesting tasks which previously got in the way of providing good quality customer service.

Questions

1. What is the purpose of the project teams at Equitable Life?

2. How do the project teams help the organisation to achieve its strategy?

3. How might these teams help the organisation to adapt its strategy over time?

4. Why are the project teams likely to lead to organisational excellence?

The notion of the autonomous team has led to the creation of the 'self-managing work team'. Self-managing teams are typically small groups of people empowered to manage themselves and the work they do on a day-to-day basis.

The larger the team, the more difficult is the communication between members. In smaller teams, it is easier to make sure that everyone is involved in decision-making processes.

Japanisation

Many companies have set up Quality Circles – groups of employees who meet to make decisions about how their organisation can improve the way it does things. This idea was imported from Japan where it had been highly successful, and it is seen as a central part of that style of management known as Japanisation – the adoption of Japanese management thinking.

An interesting Japanese practice associated with project teamworking is *ringiseido*. When a solution is required to a work-related problem, one member of the project team writes down a suggested solution and passes it to another person in the team. Instead of judging the idea 'good' or 'bad', each person in the team adds his or her own ideas and developments to the original solution. By the time the original solution reaches the end of the chain the decision has been practically made by itself, and, of course all of the individuals involved in carrying out the decision will have been involved in the problem-solving exercise. They will know which areas are problematic and why.

In the Japanese model of decision-making the initial thrashing out of problems may take a long time, but once a decision has been made, it can be quite quickly implemented and its implications are widely understood.

Quality improvement ladder

One way in which a major strategic change can be put into effect involves developing a raft of mechanisms and procedures based around the building of teams with clear objectives in an organisation. An example of this is Blue Circle Cement which in the mid-1990s built a strategy focused on the principle of Total Quality as an on-going plan for continuous improvement in the organisation. The change-makers at Blue Circle designed a quality improvement ladder based on the empowerment of employees and the clear communication of changes. The ladder of improvement involved a number of steps (or rungs) as follows:

Step 1: Identifying barriers to involvement. It is important at the outset of the Total Quality process to identify any barriers to employee involvement. Clearly, if an organisation has a 'them and us' culture, then it will not be ready for successful change. What is required is a set of relationships in which employees and managers are prepared to envisage the desirability of a situation based on equal opportunities and mutual respect, and in which there is a strong motivation to do jobs well.

Step 2: Develop a common vision. Managers and employees need to share a vision. At Blue Circle this was based on building a highly skilled and flexible workforce.

Step 3: Develop the plan. This involves developing a plan based on the shared vision. At Blue Circle new working practices were introduced and there were changes in work relationships.

Step 4: Keeping people informed. This involves providing information to everyone in the workplace, for example informing employees what the effect of their work and actions is and will be.

Step 5: Developing the Total Quality concept. Having achieved a commitment to change, it is important to develop the Total Quality concept. This involves training and building up people's commitment to Total Quality so that all managers and employees share ownership of the concept.

Step 6: Build a supportive structure. In order to change to a culture of Total Quality it is essential for managers to alter their attitudes and approaches. This might also mean changing the management structure.

Step 7: Develop facilitators to help the process. To assist in the process of change it is necessary to gain the support of a cross-section of the workforce which has been trained to facilitate change. They should be able to offer unbiased support for the operational teams. This includes a full range of skills, including team composition, team dynamics, meeting skills, problem-solving skills as well as

being able to deal with a multitude of 'people' problems that arise in business.

Step 8: Empowerment flow. An empowered organisation results because the foundations are clearly in place to allow this empowerment to flourish.

Step 9: Improvement teams. At the centre of the process of continuous improvement are a number of improvement teams which are empowered to get things done using their own initiative.

Step 10: Customer focus. The organisation is now in a position to look after the needs of its customers with enhanced customer focus.

Step 11: Continuous improvement. The organisation has the mechanisms in place to ensure a process of continuous improvement.

Identification of team and individual roles

Answering the question 'who does what?' is an important part of strategy implementation. Napuk (1996) suggests that implementation of corporate strategy will be most effective where the organisation appoints teams to solve problems and implement the strategies:

> 'Every implementation team should have an identifiable leader. The importance of action teams cannot be ignored. The most effective way to get anything done in an organisation is to create a highly motivated team, provide a clear but tight brief, give the team authority and then monitor progress.'

Napuk believes that the creation of special implementation teams enables the organisation to achieve greater and faster results than any other single act during the implementation process. Team roles and individual roles need to be clearly identified if clashes and confusion are not to arise.

In the past corporate strategists often quoted the maxim that 'structure follows strategy', i.e. an organisation first devised its strategies related to products, markets, etc. and then designed its structure. Today we are not so sure. Tom Peters (*Liberation Management*, 1992) suggests top priority should be given to structure, followed by systems and people. Strategy, he argues should be set subsequently at strategic business-unit level. The role of 'top management' is to create a general business mission. Such an approach creates more dynamism within the organisation. It is the individual business units that are most likely to be dynamic and innovative – rather than being stifled by a corporate centre.

From an implementation point of view, whatever the organisation's preference with regards to strategy or structure there needs to be clarity as to the role of the team and the individual within the team. In a top-down type of organisation strategy will be created at the top and at lower levels individuals will be responsible simply for putting the strategy into practice – they are unlikely to feel greatly motivated in doing so. Moreover, individuals and units within the organisation may waste time seeking to shore up strategies which are patently unworkable or poorly oriented.

By contrast, in an empowered organisation part of the role of the team and the individual will be to generate new ideas and hence to generate change. In the empowered organisation teams and individuals are most likely to identify new and more demanding objectives which they feel can be attained as a result of changes which they fashion in working practices and arrangements. These changes can then feed back up the organisation to more ambitious strategies and plans at higher levels within the organisation.

Case Study

Missing the mark

A hospital worker wrote the following.

'The outpatient department in which I worked had its own answers to reducing waiting times, and I am sure this example is not isolated. Outpatient department waiting times are one of the worst problems the hospital faces. In the outpatient department of which I have experience, patients often waited at least two hours to be seen after their original appointment time. Superficially, the answer appears obvious, make fewer appointments in a day. This however increases the backlog of patients waiting for a first appointment. After original referral, the Patient's Charter requires a first appointment to be within 26 weeks of original referral with a target of 13 weeks. Patients were already waiting for up to six months for a first appointment. What is required is obvious, capital investment to expand the service, bigger buildings and more staff. This need was relayed back to Health Commissioners who were asked to invest in the service; they declined.

'Therefore, in order that an outpatient could receive an appointment within 26 weeks of referral, we placed the referral letter in a 'pending' file. In this way the patient did not appear in any of our audit figures until we were ready for it to, 26 weeks before the appointment time. We managed to reduce the two-hour wait after appointment time, but not by nearly enough to meet the 30-minute limit set by the Patient's Charter. However, by implementing this 'strategy', we were able to retain contracts with purchasers, and to meet the Patient's Charter requirements. The Secretary of State was also able to publish astounding results achieved by the Health Service in reducing waiting times.'

Questions

1. What was wrong with the process outlined above?

2. Why was there a lack of fit between the strategy and the way it was implemented?

3. How could the implementation process have been more effective?

4. How could improvements in the implementation process have enabled the strategy to be more achievable?

Responsibilities and targets

Within a team structure (or any other structure) it is essential to set out a clear definition of an individual's role. Performance can then be measured against agreed targets. In this way, individual and team targets can be set and progress monitored.

Within individual teams clear accountability needs to be set out in relation to assignments, i.e. who does what and who is responsible for what? Accountability is a key ingredient of management delegation and performance measurement.

We have already examined the way in which an organisation establishes objectives in order to pursue its general aim (mission). It is usually helpful to establish objectives at each level within an organisation so that individuals know what is expected of them. Responsibility for achieving these objectives will then rest with the relevant individual and with his or her supervisors in a hierarchical organisation. D. McGregor (*The Human Side of*

Enterprise, 1960) argues that people need objectives to direct their efforts, and if objectives are not provided by the organisation they will create their own.

Budgets are another approach used to translate strategic plans into concrete activities. Budgets can be planned for all sorts of organisational activities, for example to set production targets, sales forecasts, use of materials forecasts etc. Responsibility can be allocated to ensuring that budgets are met, and this can then be used as a measure of performance and to outline possibilities for improvement.

Milestones are very effective in establishing defined points to measure progress and hold team managers accountable. Each milestone must be defined clearly and be achievable. Milestones need to be tied to strategies to have meaning, and they have to be clearly communicated and accepted by the teams who are to reach them.

Temporary project teams can play an important part in helping to manage strategic change in an organisation. Peters and Waterman (*In Search of Excellence*, 1982) shows that such teams are often in evidence in the most successful large companies. Teams of managers are brought together from across the organisation to work on a particular project for a period of time before returning to their normal jobs. Because these teams may be short-lived, there needs to be particular clarity about roles and responsibilities in the team – the objectives of the team and individual objectives within the team. Temporary project teams are particularly effective in bringing about change, particularly where the managers concerned have developed experience of managing the change process.

H. E. Wrapp in the *Harvard Business Review* (1967) argues the case for imprecision in creating targets and objectives in organisations. He asks:

> '*Why does the good manager shy away from precise statement of his objectives for the organisation? The main reason is that he finds it impossible to set down specific objectives which will be relevant for any reasonable period into the future. Conditions in business change continually and rapidly, and corporate strategy must be revised to take the changes into account. The more explicit the statement of strategy, the more difficult it becomes to persuade the organisation to turn to different goals when needs and conditions shift.*'

Wrapp suggests that in creating responsibilities and targets in organisations it is healthy to rely on a certain degree of looseness. The tighter you wrap things up the less capable will individuals be of meeting challenges and responding to change. This provides a salutary lesson to those who see corporate strategy as a tight and scientific approach to achieving results.

Programmes of activities

A programme is a set of policies, procedures, rules and tasks which make up a particular course of action, for example a change programme within a particular organisation, or component of an organisation. On pages 664–665 we examined how the Equitable Life Assurance company introduced a programme of change to implement a new strategy in the late 1990s based on putting the customer at the forefront of the organisation and which involved developing self-managing teams using enhanced information technology facilities. Programmes need to be carefully designed so as to fit tightly with the strategic intent of the organisation.

Benchmarked targets at differing levels of the organisation

Creating benchmarked targets at differing levels of an organisation is a key step in creating and maintaining an excellent organisation. Benchmarked targets give employees something to aim for which is worth achieving and can be used to assess the organisation's performance. Benchmarking is an essential element of the diagnostic phase of performance improvement.

G. Milborrow (*Management Development to the Year 2000*, 1993) defines benchmarking as: 'the continuous process of measuring products, services and practices against the toughest competitors of those companies recognised as industry leaders.'

For organisations involved in international competition it is useful to benchmark against the best standards in the world. Benchmarking thus involves a comparative audit of your own and one or more organisations. The management consultants Coopers and Lybrand undertook a study of 105 board members drawn from *The Times 1000* in the mid-1990s which showed that:

- 67 per cent of the companies used bench marking
- 88 per cent of companies using bench marking did so regularly

- 82 per cent of benchmarked programmes were seen as successful.

The main areas regularly benchmarked were:

- customer service – 72 per cent
- manufacturing – 68 per cent
- human resources – 60 per cent
- information services – 35 per cent.

A good example of a UK-based organisation that widely uses benchmarking is the Great North Eastern Railway (GNER). Strategic planners, operational managers and employees regularly visit other companies and departments to collect ideas and to identify best practice. Best practice is then compared with existing practice at GNER. If GNER falls short of best practice in any way, then it sets in motion the procedures for closing the gap.

Benchmarks can be established at every level within the organisation (see Figure 30.4).

RESOURCE ALLOCATION

The resource allocation process is an important part of strategy implementation. Three major questions need to be considered when allocating resources:

1. What criteria should be used in the allocation of resources (for example rate of return, greatest immediate need, long term efficiency, etc.)?

2. How can resource needs be matched with resource availability? This is often a question of prioritising.

3. How can resource commitments be scheduled over a period of time?

Resources will need to be allocated to the best opportunities in the most efficient way. The best opportunities should be ranked by the organisation using the most appropriate criteria, including the relationship between risk and reward. Once strategic choices have been made it will be necessary to monitor closely the outcomes/results of strategic decisions in order to consider future resource allocation. The organisation will have decided the sorts of risks that it is prepared to take and the acceptable returns of capital employed and other measures.

Johnson and Scholes (1998) show that the two most important factors in determining the general approach to resource allocation are:

1. The degree of change required in the resource base for strategy to be implemented successfully – this may involve an overall change in the quantity of total resources required by the organisation, or it may involve a reallocation between different resource uses within the organisation.

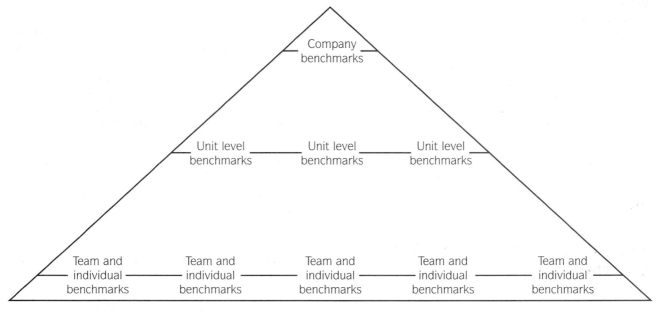

Figure 30.4 *Levels of benchmarking within an organisation*

2. The extent of central direction of the allocation process, i.e. to what extent the allocation process is determined by the centre of the organisation, or by the individual units within the organisation.

It is helpful to examine these key issues in relation to specific examples.

Example 1: Few resource changes

When there are few resource changes, then allocation tends to take place along historical lines, for example the English and Maths departments in a school each traditionally receive 15 per cent of the departmental budgets. Of course, this may be subject to change over time as new powerful, influential managers take over as heads of department in other areas, or if the numbers of pupils taking English or Maths rises or falls.

Example 2: A period of growth

During a period of growth it may be possible not to reduce the resource allocation to any of the units in the organisation, but simply to increase allocation selectively to those units most involved in the growth process. The centre of the organisation may act as an allocator of funds, with individual units having to compete for funds.

This sort of approach is used in national government budget allocation where individual ministers have to put forward the case for increases in funding. Clearly, the allocation process is driven both by politics as well as by need.

What is important is that the organisation pays careful attention to its general aims and ways in which these can be best achieved. As we saw earlier in the chapter, this will be most successful where there are clear patterns of open communication in the organisation.

A halfway house between open competition for resources and central allocation is termed constrained bidding. Individual units are able to compete for resources within a constraint or cap.

Example 3: Static or declining conditions

The allocation of resources is always difficult in a situation of decline because someone will always lose out. In the

worst cases this will result in closure of individual units. Resource allocation can either be carried out through central decision-making, or bidding by competing units. Once again, the compromise situation is constrained bidding.

At an operational level it is necessary to identify the resources that will be needed to implement chosen strategies. A particular danger in many organisations is that operational planners often take a backward-facing rather than a forward-looking view. In other words, they look at how resources have been allocated in the past rather than clearly identifying the ways in which resources will be required to meet new strategies.

Discussion point

From your own experience of the resource allocation process in an organisation that you are familiar with, do resource planners tend to take a backward-facing or a forward-looking view? What problems have resulted when planners have taken the historical view?

Johnson and Scholes (1998) feel that the central questions which need to be addressed in operational resource planning are:

1. Exactly what resources will a strategy require for its implementation? (Resource identification)
2. To what extent do these required resources build on or are a change from existing resources? (Fit with existing resources)
3. Can the required resources be integrated with each other? (Fit between the required resources)

Preparing a resource plan for an organisation involves a number of key considerations.

- **Defining the key tasks.** These are the key tasks around which the strategic change is fundamentally dependent for its success. They need to be identified so that resources can be focused on them.
- **Prioritising.** This involves deciding the order in which things should be done. Get your priorities right! Focus on what needs doing first, and then concentrate on what follows.

The identification of key tasks and priorities enables the organisation to allocate responsibilities, i.e. for attending to key tasks. Coordination and integration may need to be planned between key tasks.

- **Preparing an action plan.** In creating an action plan it is useful to start with the major area that is being changed and work from there. The action plan will set out a sequence of actions, timings and responsibilities. It will then be possible to monitor actions that are carried out against the actions in the plan. Budgeting is a useful component of action planning.
- **Identifying and testing key assumptions.** In creating a plan a number of assumptions will be made, for example about the amount of resources required for a particular activity, the time that will be required for a particular stage in the plan, the relative importance of the various activities, etc. It is important to identify and test out whether the particular assumptions that are being made are valid or not. Perhaps some of them are inaccurate or miss the mark. This needs to be checked before the plan is put into action.

The key resources in the allocation process are finance, human resources, materials and time.

Finance

Finance is always one of the key resources required for the implementation of any strategic plan. A budget sets out the financial requirements for the plan. The overall financial operating budget is often called the **profit plan**. Budgets are expressed in numbers, for example units of money, units of product, labour hours, machine hours, etc.

Budgeting is often a contentious issue. Those with most to lose will generally look to the past and ask why change is necessary. Those with most to gain will point to the vision for the future.

Capital budgeting will normally be an important part of a change process where the organisation is investing heavily in changes in its plant and equipment. **Divisional and departmental budgets** will be important when parts of an organisation are fighting for a greater share of organisational resources. **Revenue budgets** are important where the organisation (or parts of it) are concerned about having finance readily available for short-term financial management of new areas of development.

Individual programmes, plans and policies within the organisation will all carry financial implications. Careful

financial planning is therefore essential to make sure that strategies can be effectively implemented in practice.

The emphasis on finance found in most organisations stems from the profit objective. Some writers still argue that the profit objective is the primary objective of all organisations, except those that operate as charities and similar concerns. An organisation that concentrates on primary profit targets is able to establish a clear pattern of objectives, all directed towards the bottom line. For example, Figure 30.5 shows that at every level in the organisation the primary objective is profit. This is a simple model which gives clear direction. However, this model is frequently criticised. People who are finance-oriented, such as accountants, generally see things in terms of the bottom line. It is argued that they fail to take account of those strategies and processes that actually create the profits, for example marketing and human resource management. The implication is that the profit objective on its own is not sufficient. Policy making should involve as many decision-makers as possible from across the organisation.

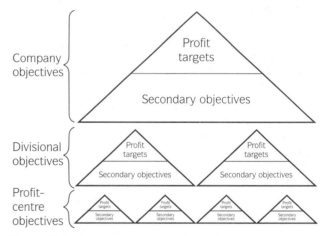

Figure 30.5 *Company objectives and unit objectives*

Human resources

Planning for human resources is one of the most important resourcing areas. Human resource planning can only be effective if personnel are regarded as a key factor by management. The human resource director should also play a central role in top-level corporate planning, and human resource managers should have a key input to business unit and operational plans.

Case Study

Prioritising people at Bass Breweries

The mission statement of the brewing arm of Bass Breweries reads:

1. Our primary objective is to establish an increasingly pre-eminent position in the UK beer market. We also intend to attain a leading position in overseas markets where opportunities to add value have been identified.
2. We will achieve these objectives by the following means:

- We will own an unrivalled range of brands.
- We will provide our customers with quality, value and service second to none.
- We will be highly cost competitive.
- **We will attract, develop and motivate a team of people of outstanding quality who will share in the success they generate.**
- We will create an entrepreneurial culture in a company which anticipates, responds to and shapes changes in the market.

3. In pursuing these objectives we will achieve superior financial performance and attractive returns for shareholders.

Questions

1. Why do you think that an organisation like Bass Brewers places emphasis on human resource development?

2. How do you think that the statements about human resource development at Bass will be translated into specific objectives and actions in its 'people at work' area?

From the organisation's point of view the purpose of human resource planning is to identify and meet future labour and staff requirements. This involves employing the right people, at the right time, with the right skills and commitment.

Creating a resource plan involves:

- forecasting likely future demand for labour and the future supply of labour in order to estimate and then fill the gap (if one exists) between demand and supply
- analysing and improving the present use of the existing resource. A human resource management approach recognises people as the most vital resource and tries to create genuine job satisfaction and commitment in the workplace. Managers need to integrate all aspects of their sub-plans so that they pull in the same direction. For example, one of the objectives of training to improve the organisation's responsiveness to customers might be to upgrade interpersonal and telephone skills. However, training will also impact on other aspects of human resource policy, such as recruitment and redeployment. It is essential to look at each aspects of policy as part of an integrated approach to resources.

Human resource planning needs to be considered in the same way as investment in products, i.e. strategically.

One of the key parts of planning for human resources is to create a working organisational structure. In designing a structure it is necessary to differentiate tasks into work packages and jobs linked to supervisory and management control.

Management and staff planning is necessary to identify the types of structures and relationships in the organisation as well as, for example, numbers of employees. Human resource planning needs, therefore, to be based on statistics and forecasts. Staff planning needs to be based around corporate planning, for example if old products are to be phased out and new ones introduced, then it may be necessary to develop plans for training, retraining, redundancies, recruitment, selection, etc.

Materials

At an operational level organisations always need a regular throughput of materials, and this will be an important function of logistics. Materials management certainly is a difficult issue for an organisation, but like all resource issues it is crucial. In recent years we have learnt a great deal from the Japanese about Just-In-Time (JIT) approaches to stock control and inventory levels.

Johnson and Scholes (1998) alert us to the importance of effectively managing each of the key ingredients of the value chain and the links in this chain. Three of Porter's primary activities in the value chain – inbound logistics, operations and outbound logistics – are all directly concerned with the handling and processing of materials. If the organisation is going to meet customer requirements in the marketplace, then it is necessary to make sure that all materials conform with requirements (the quality hallmark). An appreciation of the importance of resources such as materials reinforces the understanding that strategy is as dependent on effective operations as operations are on effective strategy – what is required is a top-to-bottom integrated emphasis on total quality standards within the organisation.

Time

In making decisions about resource utilisation to future strategies managers often neglect the importance of time. Yet time is of the essence in strategic implementation. Peter Drucker (*The Practice of Management*) writes that 'management always has to consider both the present and the long-range future. A management problem is not solved if immediate profits are purchased by endangering the long-range profitability, perhaps even the survival of the company.'

Time, like any other resource, needs to be allocated in a well-organised way. Time management experts often point out that successful managers are able to handle numerous and different activities by devoting themselves to one activity at a time. This means that they will focus on particular activities in a determined and persistent way rather than dividing their time over a range of activities. Deciding what to concentrate on requires the establishment of priorities.

One way of allocating time to make sure that tasks are completed within their deadlines is 'ABC analysis' (see Figure 30.6) which is a value analysis on the use of time.

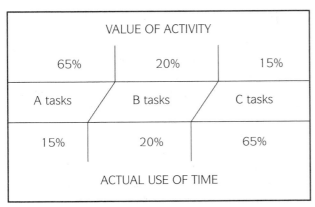

Figure 30.6 *ABC value analysis of the use of time*

- **A activities** are those that are ranked as being very important. They can be effectively carried out only by the person involved or by a team working with that person. They cannot be delegated.
- **B activities** are important, but can be delegated.
- **C activities** are less important, but usually represent the lion's share of the work (routine tasks, paperwork, telephone calls, etc).

Managers who are determined to meet deadlines will focus their efforts on the most important A tasks. They will seek to complete one or two A tasks per day, earmark a further two to three B tasks, and set aside some time for C tasks. ABC analysis is thus a form of critical path analysis (see page 485) which can be used to make sure that time is allocated within the organisation to meet strategic objectives in the most logical way.

REVIEW AND EVALUATION

An evaluation of the benchmarked outcomes in a given time period of corporate, operational and individual targets.

Richard Rumelt ('Evaluating business strategy', in W. Glueck (ed.), *Management and Business Policy*, 1980), suggests that business strategy evaluation is concerned with answering three major questions.

1. Are the objectives of the business appropriate?

2. Are the major policies and plans appropriate?

3. Do the results obtained to date confirm or refute critical assumptions on which the strategy rests?

Rumelt then shows how this process is extremely complex. The evaluation will require an extensive situation-based knowledge of the organisation, its objectives and its performance. Difficulties arise because:

- each business strategy is unique, and therefore depends on a situational logic
- for most managers in an organisation it is much easier to set and try to achieve objectives than to evaluate them
- formal strategic systems of strategic review can often create explosive conflict situations.

Having shown how difficult it is to evaluate strategies effectively, Rumelt then suggests the following tests of effectiveness which may prove helpful.

- **Consistency** – the strategy must not present mutually inconsistent goals and policies.
- **Consonance** – the strategy must represent an adaptive response to the external environment and to the critical changes occurring within it.
- **Advantage** – the strategy must provide for the creation and/or maintenance of a competitive advantage in the selected area of activity.
- **Feasibility** – the strategy must neither overtax available resources nor create unsolvable subproblems.

An essential component enabling the evaluation of outcomes is the management information system which can be used to measure progress accurately.

Gap analysis is a useful evaluative tool. It is used to determine the gap between what a company/unit/team/ individual's performance is and what it could be. We can illustrate gap analysis with reference to the 'profit gap', which outlines the gap between what a company's profits might be and what they are likely to be if it carries on operating as it is at the current time. The benchmark can be both the organisation's potential and the industry's current performance.

The gap provides a useful warning: 'If we don't do something to change the way we are working, we will start going backwards!' The starting point is to set out the desired profit target on a graph (see Figure 30.7 for simplicity this is represented by a straight line). The profit target is set out over the next few years. The second stage is to draw a profit forecast based on the assumption that the organisation makes no changes in its range of operations. There are three main ways of making the projections for this line:

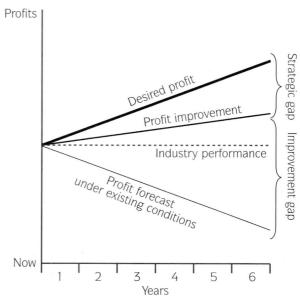

Figure 30.7 *Gap analysis*

1. The sum of the profit targets for individual operating divisions (probably the simplest method).

2. A model of the organisation's profits given certain assumptions.

3. Total up the results of the operating plans of all managers.

Whichever method is chosen, a line can be drawn showing the expected profit. Very often this line will move down, simply because by standing still in a competitive environment profits are likely to fall – divisional and line managers know this only too well.

Two more lines can be drawn on the graph.

- The **industry performance line** shows the return on an equivalent investment made within the industry in which the organisation is operating, for example by looking at figures for other companies. This will be easiest if there is a similar organisation operating in the same industry.
- The **profit improvement line** shows the improvements that could be made to profits by altering strategies in the existing sectors of the company.

The improvement gap identifies the scope for improvement by altering strategies in the existing sectors of the company. The strategic gap shows the scope for improvement by invigorating the organisation, by implementing new strategies, including movement into new sectors and activities.

Gap analysis identifies the importance of continued transformation of an organisation in dynamic markets. It is often complicated and time consuming to prepare and requires detailed forecasts and information. It may require more than just financial information.

Gap analysis is also used in the public sector in a slightly different way – to assess whether likely future demands for a public service will lead to a gap in its provision, and to anticipate the size of this gap, for example in the provision of hospital beds. The profit target line might then represent a forecast of desired use of service. The profit forecast line would represent projected provision of service under existing planning conditions.

CONCLUSION

This unit has examined the important role played by corporate strategy in the organisation. It should now be apparent that the appropriate strategy for an organisation is context driven. Organisations can learn a lot from studying how other organisations develop their strategies, but in the end each organisation needs to form its own strategies based on a clear understanding of situational factors. It is very important to understand the various frameworks and tools that support the development of corporate strategy – missions and vision, objectives and action plans, SWOT and PESTLE analysis, etc. but it must be remembered that a successful organisation rarely starts with strategy, rather strategy should be crafted from what the organisation does well (its competences), its relationship with the environment and its access to resources. Of course the best strategies will emerge from the wisdom of the strategists, and this wisdom will be most complete when it draws on all of the intelligence that lies within the organisation (supported by external advice and an understanding of the environment). This means that the organisation which is best able to think strategically will be the one that provides the channels for the wisdom that lies in every member of the organisation to be utilised for the purposes of ongoing improvement through well-crafted strategy.

All organisations need to utilise crafted strategy if they are to survive. One of the most successful businessmen of the twentieth century was Jack Cohen who founded the supermarket chain Tesco which in 1998 sold 17 per cent of the nation's food. Cohen survived on instinct. If he had a strategy it was the now famous 'pile it high, sell it cheap' philosophy. Cohen could spot a bargain and knew how to sell, once buying a hundred cases of out-of-date canned evaporated milk from a salvaged ship and selling them all at a profit with the slogan 'extra thick, extra value'. He successfully realised the external environment by providing bargains for the hard-up people of the East End of London.

However, Cohen was not a long-term strategist. In his biography of Jack Cohen and the Tesco company, David Powell (1996), wrote of Cohen: 'The only thing of which he was certain was that he was trading at a profit. What more did he need to know' and his 'ideas were unformulated, a rag-bag vision without definition'. For many years, Cohen's accounts were often worked out on the back of envelopes. As late as the 1950s he would compute the Tesco profit and loss account in his head.

Fortunately, Cohen brought in around him a team of people with more of a strategic view. In recent years Tesco has used corporate strategy with telling effect, having a good understanding of the environment in which it operates and how to build capacity to meet changing market conditions. For example, in the late 80s and 1990s, as people's living standards rose, Tesco's directors moved the organisation into the area of better-quality food while continuing to offer discounted and own-brand lines. Today Tesco is in the van of strategic thinking and planning. In an interview for *The Times* Sir Ian McLauren, a recent chairman of Tesco, explained the absolute importance of corporate strategy.

> 'There are no absolutes in the game of strategic planning, but as Tesco has learned, this does not diminish its importance. In fact, without the capacity to interpret the shifts that are taking place in the world around us, all the internal changes we have made (the development of new stores, the selection and training of new staff, the application of advanced systems, the creation of a new identity) would have been placed in jeopardy.'

Corporate strategy thus enables organisations to survive and hopefully to prosper. Strategy takes over where instinct is not sufficient on its own. In the turbulent world of modern business instinct is only a short-term recipe for success, in the long-term an organisation needs more than that ... it needs strategy!

FURTHER READING

Johnson, G. and Scholes, K., *Exploring Corporate Strategy*, Prentice Hall, 1998.

Kanter, R., *The Change Masters*, Thomson Business Press, 1996.

Koch, R., *The Financial Times Guide to Strategy*, FT/Pitman Publishing, 1995.

Mintzberg, H., Quinn, J. and Ghosal, S., *The Strategy Process*, European Edition, 1997.

Napuk, K., *The Strategy Led Business: Step-by-Step Strategic Planning for Small and Medium Sized Companies*, McGraw-Hill, 1996.

Thompson, J., *Strategic Management*, Chapman and Hall, 1990.

ASSIGNMENT

The assignment needs to focus on a real organisation that has engaged in a process of strategic planning, so that you have information to draw on. We have been using this assignment on the Business and Technology degree at The Nottingham and Trent University. At first glance it may appear difficult to collect information, because some organisations may want to guard their corporate strategies closely. However, in many organisations it is policy to include as many people as possible in the strategy formulation process, so information is made open for reasons of transparency of communication and shared ownership.

Students can choose to examine the strategy of:

- an organisation where they work and are able to interview managers
- an organisation that publishes a lot of information about strategy, e.g. The Body Shop, Tesco, Manchester United Football Club – this information can be found in company documents and on the Internet
- the organisation where the students are carrying out their studies – a university or college, or students' union of that institution
- an organisation that is undergoing strategic change, where the student is able to gain access to one of the individuals playing a key role in the change process, e.g. a local hospital, school, or police force.

Task 1 Examine the process of strategic planning

Identify the mission and objectives of an organisation you have chosen to study. Why does the organisation have a mission? What is the purpose of its objectives? How appropriate are the objectives?

Explain the strengths and weaknesses of the classical/rational, incremental and emergent approaches to strategy. Is the strategy of the organisation you are examining rational, incremental or emergent? Explain.

Task 2 Analyse approaches to strategic planning

Carry out a PESTLE analysis for the organisation you are studying. Identify the key structural ingredients of the environment in which it operates.

Carry out a SWOT analysis for the organisation you are studying, examining the strengths and weaknesses of the organisation, and the opportunities and threats in its environment over the next three years.

Outline an organisational strategy for the organisation, which provides an appropriate way forward given the environment, the organisation's resources and its core competences.

Task 3 Examine approaches to strategy implementation

Who is going to be involved in creating and implementing the strategy in the organisation you have chosen to study? What will be the roles and responsibilities of different individuals and groups in implementing this strategy? How does this compare with roles and responsibilities for strategic implementation in one other organisation you are familiar with?

What are the main resource requirements for the implementation of strategy in the organisation you have chosen to study?

Outline a set of targets and timescales for the achievement of strategy in the organisation you have chosen to focus on.

Name index

AUTHORS

Woodward, J. 231
Wrapp, H. 668

INDIVIDUALS AND COMPANIES

Subject index